IBM

International Technical Support Organization

The IBM TotalStorage DS8000 Series: Copy Services with IBM eserver zSeries

February 2006

SG24-6787-01

Note: Before using this information and the product it supports, read the information in "Notices" on page xxiii.

Second Edition (February 2006)

The examples and panels in this edition are derived from the levels of microcode, GUI, and DS CLI available in the field for the DS8000 as of February, 2006.

Contents

Figures

Notices

This information was developed for products and services offered in the U.S.A.

IBM may not offer the products, services, or features discussed in this document in other countries. Consult your local IBM representative for information on the products and services currently available in your area. Any reference to an IBM product, program, or service is not intended to state or imply that only that IBM product, program, or service may be used. Any functionally equivalent product, program, or service that does not infringe any IBM intellectual property right may be used instead. However, it is the user's responsibility to evaluate and verify the operation of any non-IBM product, program, or service.

IBM may have patents or pending patent applications covering subject matter described in this document. The furnishing of this document does not give you any license to these patents. You can send license inquiries, in writing, to:
IBM Director of Licensing, IBM Corporation, North Castle Drive Armonk, NY 10504-1785 U.S.A.

The following paragraph does not apply to the United Kingdom or any other country where such provisions are inconsistent with local law: INTERNATIONAL BUSINESS MACHINES CORPORATION PROVIDES THIS PUBLICATION "AS IS" WITHOUT WARRANTY OF ANY KIND, EITHER EXPRESS OR IMPLIED, INCLUDING, BUT NOT LIMITED TO, THE IMPLIED WARRANTIES OF NON-INFRINGEMENT, MERCHANTABILITY OR FITNESS FOR A PARTICULAR PURPOSE. Some states do not allow disclaimer of express or implied warranties in certain transactions, therefore, this statement may not apply to you.

This information could include technical inaccuracies or typographical errors. Changes are periodically made to the information herein; these changes will be incorporated in new editions of the publication. IBM may make improvements and/or changes in the product(s) and/or the program(s) described in this publication at any time without notice.

Any references in this information to non-IBM Web sites are provided for convenience only and do not in any manner serve as an endorsement of those Web sites. The materials at those Web sites are not part of the materials for this IBM product and use of those Web sites is at your own risk.

IBM may use or distribute any of the information you supply in any way it believes appropriate without incurring any obligation to you.

Information concerning non-IBM products was obtained from the suppliers of those products, their published announcements or other publicly available sources. IBM has not tested those products and cannot confirm the accuracy of performance, compatibility or any other claims related to non-IBM products. Questions on the capabilities of non-IBM products should be addressed to the suppliers of those products.

This information contains examples of data and reports used in daily business operations. To illustrate them as completely as possible, the examples include the names of individuals, companies, brands, and products. All of these names are fictitious and any similarity to the names and addresses used by an actual business enterprise is entirely coincidental.

COPYRIGHT LICENSE:
This information contains sample application programs in source language, which illustrates programming techniques on various operating platforms. You may copy, modify, and distribute these sample programs in any form without payment to IBM, for the purposes of developing, using, marketing or distributing application programs conforming to the application programming interface for the operating platform for which the sample programs are written. These examples have not been thoroughly tested under all conditions. IBM, therefore, cannot guarantee or imply reliability, serviceability, or function of these programs. You may copy, modify, and distribute these sample programs in any form without payment to IBM for the purposes of developing, using, marketing, or distributing application programs conforming to IBM's application programming interfaces.

Trademarks

The following terms are trademarks of the International Business Machines Corporation in the United States, other countries, or both:

AIX 5L™
AIX®
CICS®
DB2®
DFSMS/MVS®
DFSMSdfp™
DFSMSdss™
DFSMShsm™
DFSMSrmm™
Enterprise Storage Server®
ESCON®
@server®
@server®
eServer®
FlashCopy®
FICON®
Geographically Dispersed Parallel Sysplex™
GDPS®
HyperSwap™
HACMP™
IBM®
IMS™
iSeries™
MVS™
MVS/ESA™
NetView®
OS/390®
Parallel Sysplex®
pSeries®
Redbooks™
Redbooks (logo) ™
RACF®
RMF™
RS/6000®
S/390®
Sysplex Timer®
System/390®
SAA®
SANergy®
Tivoli®
TotalStorage®
VM/ESA®
VSE/ESA™
WebSphere®
xSeries®
z/OS®
zSeries®
z/VM®
z/VSE™

The following terms are trademarks of other companies:

Java, Solaris, Sun, and all Java-based trademarks are trademarks of Sun Microsystems, Inc. in the United States, other countries, or both.

Excel, Microsoft, Windows server, Windows, and the Windows logo are trademarks of Microsoft Corporation in the United States, other countries, or both.

Intel, Intel logo, Intel Inside logo, and Intel Centrino logo are trademarks or registered trademarks of Intel Corporation or its subsidiaries in the United States, other countries, or both.

UNIX is a registered trademark of The Open Group in the United States and other countries.

Linux is a trademark of Linus Torvalds in the United States, other countries, or both.

Other company, product, and service names may be trademarks or service marks of others.

Preface

This IBM® Redbook introduces you to the many benefits that can be obtained from using Copy Services with IBM @server® zSeries in the IBM TotalStorage DS8000 Series environment.

This redbook will help you install, tailor, and configure Copy Services for z/OS® on the IBM TotalStorage® DS8000 storage server series. It should be read in conjunction with the *IBM TotalStorage D8000 Series: Concepts and Architecture,* SG24-6452.

This redbook gives the details necessary to configure each of the Copy Services functions in a z/OS environment. There is a companion redbook that supports the configuration of the Copy Services functions in an open systems environment, *IBM TotalStorage DS8000 Series: Copy Services in Open* SG24-6788.

This redbook will help you design/create a new Copy Services installation, or to migrate from an existing installation; as well as addressing design functions and changes in terminology from other IBM Copy Services products. We include hints and tips to maximize the effective installation.

The team that wrote this redbook

This redbook was produced by a team of specialists from around the world working for the International Technical Support Organization, San Jose Center in IBM Mainz, Germany.

Cathy Warrick is a project leader and Certified IT Specialist in the IBM International Technical Support Organization. She has over 25 years of experience in IBM with large systems, open systems, and storage, including education on products internally and for the field. Prior to joining the ITSO three years ago, she developed the Technical Leadership education program for the IBM and IBM Business Partner's technical field force and was the program manager for the Storage Top Gun classes.

Bert Dufrasne is a Certified Consulting IT Specialist and Project Leader for IBM TotalStorage products at the International Technical Support Organization, San Jose Center. He has worked at IBM in various IT areas. Before joining the ITSO, he worked for IBM Global Services as an Application Architect. He holds a degree in Electrical Engineering.

Peter Kimmel joined IBM Storage in 1999. As an IT Specialist within ATS and the Mainz Storage Competence Center, he has worked with SSA, VSS, the various ESS generations, and the DS8000/DS6000 products, including Early Shipment Programs/early installs of new products and the Copy Services rollouts. As his main area of interest he specializes in performance of disk storage subsystems. Peter holds a physics Diploma (MSc) degree of the University of Kaiserslautern.

Peter Klee is working as an IT Specialist in ATS EMEA, located in Mainz, Germany. He has 10 years of experience in data centers since he has worked for the largest bank in Germany. He was responsible for the architecture and implementation of the data backup with Tivoli Storage Manager and finally the disk storage environment which was implemented with EMC Symmetrix, HDS Lightning, and ESS Model 800. He joined IBM in 2003 working for Strategic Outsourcing. Since June 2004 he has been working on the ATS EMEA performance team in Mainz. His main focus is Copy Services in the open systems environment for DS8000 and DS6000, especially Global Mirror.

Jukka Myyrylainen is an Advisory IT Specialist with IBM Global Services, Finland. He has several years of experience with storage product implementations on both zSeries and open systems platforms. He provides consultancy, technical support, and implementation services to customers for IBM's strategic storage hardware and software products. He has contributed to several storage related redbooks in the past.

Lu Nguyen is a software engineer at the IBM Open Systems Lab in San Jose, CA. He has been working with IBM Storage for the past six years, with experience in a wide variety of storage technologies including the Enterprise Storage System (ESS), DS8000, DS6000, DS4000, SAN Volume Controller, tape, and storage software. Prior to joining IBM Storage, he worked in IBM Software, responsible for Tivoli Storage Manager performance.

Gero Schmidt is an IT Specialist in the IBM ATS technical sales support organization in Germany. He joined IBM in 2001 working at the European Storage Competence Center (ESCC) in Mainz, providing technical support for a broad range of IBM storage products (SSA, ESS, DS4000, DS6000, DS8000) in open systems environments with a primary focus on storage subsystem performance. During his four years of experience with IBM storage products he participated in various beta test programs for ESS 800 and especially in the product rollout and beta test program for the DS6000/DS8000 series. He holds a degree in physics (Dipl.-Phys.) from the Technical University of Braunschweig, Germany.

Shin Takata is a certified IT specialist working for AP Advanced Technical Support in Japan. He has 22 years of experience in storage software and hardware in open systems and the S/390® environment. His current areas of expertise are disaster recovery solutions in open systems environments and other Copy Services solutions, such as HyperSwap.

Anthony Vandewerdt is an Accredited IT Specialist who has worked for IBM Australia for 16 years. He has worked on a wide variety of IBM products and for the last five years has specialized in storage systems problem determination. He has extensive experience on: ESS 2105; DS6800; DS8000; IBM SAN switches; 2145 SAN Volume Controller; IBM 3494 VTS and Nortel wave division multiplexors. He is a founding member of the Australian Storage Central team, responsible for screening and managing all storage-related service calls for IBM Australia/New Zealand. Anthony was a member of the original team that wrote the Concepts and Architecture Redbooks™ for DS6000 and DS8000.

Bjoern Wesselbaum holds a degree in Electrical Engineering from the University of Applied Science Luebeck/Germany. After the university in 1998 Bjoern joined IBM Germany in Mainz. Until 2002 he was working as Product Field Engineer for the 7133 SSA Drawer and in the Advanced Technical Support Team. Since 2002 Bjoern is working in Product Field Engineering for the 2105 and DS8000 Enterprise Storage Systems. His areas of expertise include AIX and other UNIX-like operating system storage attachments and Copy Services Solutions for open systems.

Stephen West is a Certified IT Specialist in the United States. He has 33 years of experience in Information Technology. He has extensive experience in storage software and hardware, and with S/390® and z/OS®. He has been a member of the Americas Storage Advance Technical Support (ATS) since 2001. His areas of expertise include disaster recovery solutions, with significant experience in sizing solutions and in problem determination. Recently he has worked as a member of the ATS team that delivered the DS CLI hands-on training to the field technical team members.

Front row - Cathy, Peter Klee, Jukka, Gero, Lu, Shin; Back row - Bert, Peter Kimmel, Bjoern, Anthony, Steve

Special thanks to:

Many thanks to the authors of the 1st edition of this redbook:

Cathy Warrick	Alexis Giral	Ferdinand Mendros
Bernd Albrecht	Ricardo Gozzi	Tim Starr
Werner Bauer	Juergen Hauser	Pierre Zone
Maria Brunet	John Lymer	

We want to thank Mathis Landzettel, Peter Klee, and Peter Kimmel for hosting us at the European Storage Competency Center in Mainz, Germany. They were able to supply us with the needed hardware, conference room, and all of the many things needed to run a successful residency.

Special thanks to Guenter Schmitt and Uwe Schweikhard, along with their colleagues of the Mainz TotalStorage Interoperability Center lab, for their help in reserving and setting up the hardware we used.

We also would like to thank:

Werner Bauer, Hans-Paul Drumm, Wilhelm Gardt, Gerhard Pieper, Torsten Rothenwaldt, Edgar Strubel, Juergen Wahrhusen, Jens Wissenbach
IBM Germany

Gitit Bar-El, Irit Dolev, Aya Kimelman
IBM Haifa

John Staubi
IBM Poughkeepsie

Thomas Fiege, Jack Flynn, Ed Hickman, Victoria Perris
IBM San Jose

Bob Bartfai, Lisa Gundy, Joe Hyde, Paul Jennas, Lee La Frese, Alan McClure, Rachel Mikolajewski, David Shackelford, Gail Spear, David V Valverde, Sonny Williams
IBM Tucson

Nick Clayton
IBM UK

Become a published author

Join us for a two- to six-week residency program! Help write an IBM Redbook dealing with specific products or solutions, while getting hands-on experience with leading-edge technologies. You'll team with IBM technical professionals, Business Partners and/or customers.

Your efforts will help increase product acceptance and customer satisfaction. As a bonus, you'll develop a network of contacts in IBM development labs, and increase your productivity and marketability.

Find out more about the residency program, browse the residency index, and apply online at:

ibm.com/redbooks/residencies.html

Comments welcome

Your comments are important to us!

We want our Redbooks™ to be as helpful as possible. Send us your comments about this or other Redbooks in one of the following ways:

- Use the online **Contact us** review redbook form found at:

  ibm.com/redbooks

- Send your comments in an email to:

  redbook@us.ibm.com

- Mail your comments to:

  IBM Corporation, International Technical Support Organization
  Dept. QXXE Building 80-E2
  650 Harry Road
  San Jose, California 95120-6099

Summary of changes

This section describes the technical changes made in this edition of the book and in previous editions. This edition may also include minor corrections and editorial changes that are not identified.

Summary of Changes
for SG24-6787-01
for The IBM TotalStorage DS8000 Series: Copy Services with IBM eServer zSeries
as created or updated on February 28, 2006.

February 2006, Second Edition

This revision reflects the addition, deletion, or modification of new and changed information described below.

New information

- Interoperability with DS6000 and ESS
- FlashCopy performance information

Changed information

- Improved interfaces details
- Updated Copy Services information
- Additional Copy Services example and scenarios
- Updated Copy Services and CLI migration appendix

Part 1

Overview

In Part 1 we describe the various Advanced Copy Services offerings for the DS8000 series and how they relate to previous Copy Services offerings available on the Enterprise Storage Server® (ESS).

This part also shows how the existing Copy Services functions from the ESS can coexist with the DS8000 series Copy Services. Similarly we discuss their use with the DS6000 series Copy Services.

With the announcement of the DS8000 series and of *Advanced Copy Services for z/OS* on the DS8000 series, we introduced some new terminology. We also introduced these terms for *Advanced Copy Services Version 2* for the ESS. These terms are detailed in the following document, *IBM TotalStorage D8000 Series: Concepts and Architecture,* SG24-6452, and are summarized in Table 1.

Table 1 Reference chart for DS Copy Services on DS8000.

DS8000 Function	ESS800 Version 2 Function	Formerly known as
FlashCopy	FlashCopy	FlashCopy
Global Mirror	Global Mirror	Asynchronous PPRC
Metro Mirror	Metro Mirror	Synchronous PPRC
Global Copy	Global Copy	PPRC Extended Distance
z/OS Global Mirror	z/OS Global Mirror	Extended Remote Copy (XRC)
Metro/Global Mirror for zSeries	z/OS Metro/Global Mirror	3-site solution using Sync PPRC and XRC
Metro/Global Copy	Metro/Global Copy	2 or 3 site Asynchronous Cascading PPRC

The Copy Services configuration is done using either the *IBM TotalStorage DS Storage Command-Line Interface,* DS CLI or the *IBM TotalStorage DS Storage Manager Copy Services Graphical User Interface*, DS GUI.

The following requirements and considerations should be noted:

- All DS8000 installations require at least an Operating Equipment License (OEL) key to operate. However, Copy Services functions can only be used where the appropriate License Key is installed.
- The key Copy Services license types are: OEL (Operating Equipment License), RMC (Remote Mirror and Copy or PPRC), and PTC (Point-in-Time Copy or FlashCopy). For DS8000 there is also RMZ (Remote mirror for z/OS).
- The DS CLI replaces both the ESS CLI and the ESS Copy Services CLI.
- The DS CLI can also be used for ESS 800 Copy Services, but not ESS configuration. For ESS configuration you need to continue to use the ESS Web Specialist or ESS CLI.
- The DS CLI can invoke Remote Mirror relationships with ESS 800, if the ESS 800 is at code level LIC 2.4.3.65 or above.
- The DS CLI can be used in reusable scripts, and provides a consistent interface for current and planned IBM TotalStorage products.
- The DS CLI now invokes a Copy Services function directly rather than invoking a saved task.
- The DS GUI can only be used for one-time execution of a Copy Services operation; it cannot save tasks.

Introduction

This chapter introduces the business drivers for Copy Services and provides a brief summary of the various Copy Services functions available on the DS8000 series. These services are very similar to the existing Copy Services for the IBM Enterprise Storage Server, and some models of the ESS are interoperable with the DS8000 as well as the DS6000.

1.1 Business requirements

The business environment with necessary management controls and requirements for data security and disaster recovery capabilities requires sophisticated tools and products. The Advanced Copy Services and their integration into the business environment is addressed in this chapter, as well as where they fit into today's business management processes.

1.1.1 Business continuity

In today's highly competitive and real time environment, the ability to manage all IT needs on a 24x7 basis makes the considerations for creation of copies and backups a core requirement for any IT deployment. Furthermore, many clients believe there is a real need to provide more pro-actively for Disaster Recovery and the Copy Services functions together with the IBM DS8000 can form part of these strategies.

The Copy Services functions can provide immediate copies of data, taking in effect a snapshot of the data stored at any point-in-time, known as FlashCopy. Copy Services can also facilitate local and/or remote copies for data retention and/or disaster recovery purposes. These functions are now known as FlashCopy, Metro Mirror, Global Copy, Metro/Global Copy, and Global Mirror. The z/OS environment supports a further variant, z/OS Global Mirror.

Once copies are created they can be maintained incrementally to be kept current, and most likely be utilized as part of the client's Information Lifecycle Management process.

1.1.2 Information Lifecycle Management

Information Lifecycle Management (ILM) is the process of managing information from creation to the time it is no longer required, and performed in a manner that aligns costs with the changing value during the cycle. The creation of large amounts of data on a day-to-day basis in the connected world of e-Business, and the proliferation of real-time multi-media applications brings a dimension to storage management that requires careful consideration. This is to ensure that it is both cost-effective and efficient for the business, and still delivers the required performance for the end-users. IBM offers hardware and software products, plus services that can form part of this provision.

Government legislation on data confidentiality and the time that personal records may be retained adds yet a further dimension to the requirements of any lifecycle management system.

The desire therefore is to keep only the required data in the most cost-effective way, with the required levels of security. Data access requirements have several levels, immediate, almost immediate, soon and possibly sometime in the near future. Over time the availability needed may, in fact, most likely, will change. Yet another factor is the data may be small or large in size. The ability to manage this requires sophisticated management tools, in real time assessing the hierarchical position of information elements and moving them as appropriate. Copy Services are an important factor in this process.

1.1.3 Infrastructure simplification

Now that many businesses have multiple IT systems with differing system needs and probably have different technologies and suppliers providing the equipment, the opportunity arises to consolidate some, or maybe most of these, into a more easily managed and secure environment.

An example could be replacing many mail servers with a single larger one using a redundant architecture, saving in administration time and effort. Similarly, with this example, the storage needs could be consolidated and centrally managed using a storage subsystem that can be connected to and used by many systems and applications concurrently. This allows the allocation of storage to the using applications dynamically, removing the need for spare capacity on many systems with the attendant overheads.

A similar logical view can be taken of both LAN and SAN environments, allowing the benefits of a professionally managed infrastructure that is designed as a core of the business, instead of an ad hoc assembly of components added as the immediate needs have grown.

Copy Services is a collection of functions that provide disaster recovery, data migration, and data duplication functions. With the Copy Services functions, for example, you can create backup data with little or no disruption to your application, and you can back up your application data to the remote site for disaster recovery.

Copy Services run on the DS8000 Storage Unit and support open systems and zSeries environments. These functions are supported also on the previous generation of storage systems called the IBM TotalStorage Enterprise Storage Server (ESS).

Many design characteristics of the DS8000 and the data copying and mirroring capabilities of the Copy Services features contribute to the protection of your data, 24 hours a day and 7 days a week (24x7). The licensed features included in Copy Services are as follows:

- FlashCopy, which is a Point-in-Time Copy function
- Remote Mirror and Copy functions, previously known as Peer-to-Peer Remote Copy or PPRC, which include:
  - IBM TotalStorage Metro Mirror, previously known as Synchronous PPRC
  - IBM TotalStorage Global Copy, previously known as PPRC Extended Distance
  - IBM TotalStorage Global Mirror, previously known as Asynchronous PPRC
- z/OS Global Mirror, previously known as Extended Remote Copy (XRC)
- z/OS Metro/Global Mirror

We explain these functions in more detail in the next section.

You can manage the Copy Services functions through a command-line interface (DS CLI) and a new Web-based interface (DS Storage Manager). You also can manage the Copy Services functions through the open application programming interface (DS Open API). When you manage the Copy Services through these interfaces, these interfaces invoke Copy Services functions via the Ethernet network. In zSeries environments, you can invoke the Copy Service functions by TSO commands, ICKDSF, the DFSMSdss™ utility, and so on.

We explain these interfaces in Part 2, “Interfaces” on page 19.

1.2 Introduction to Copy Services

We briefly describe each function of the Copy Services in this section. There are two primary types of Copy Services functions: *Point-in-Time Copy* and *Remote Mirror and Copy*. Generally, the Point-in-Time Copy function is used for data duplication and the Remote Mirror and Copy function is used for data migration and disaster recovery.

1.2.1 Point-in-Time Copy (FlashCopy)

The Point-in-Time Copy feature, which includes FlashCopy, enables you to create full volume copies of data in a Storage Unit. To use it, you must purchase the Point-in-Time Copy 2244 function authorization model, which is 2244 Model PTC.

When you set up a FlashCopy operation, a relationship is established between the source and target volumes, and a bitmap of the source volume is created. Once this relationship and bitmap are created, the target volume can be accessed as though all the data had been physically copied. While a relationship between the source and target volume exists, optionally, a background process copies the tracks from the source to the target volume.

Note: In this chapter, *track* means a piece of data in the DS8000; the DS8000 uses the logical tracks to manage the Copy Services functions.

See Figure 1-1 for an illustration of FlashCopy concepts.

Figure 1-1 FlashCopy concepts

When a FlashCopy operation is invoked, it takes only a few seconds to complete the process of establishing the FlashCopy pair and creating the necessary control bitmaps. Thereafter, you have access to a point-in-time copy of the source volume. As soon as the pair has been established, you can read and write to both the source and target volumes.

After creating the bitmap, a background process begins to copy the real-data from the source to the target volumes. If you access the source or the target volumes during the background copy, FlashCopy manages these I/O requests, and facilitates both reading from and writing to both the source and target copies. When all the data has been copied to the target the FlashCopy relationship is ended. There are several ways to configure PTC or FlashCopy, selected by optional parameters in the setup process.

1.2.2 Remote Mirror and Copy RMC (formerly Peer-to-Peer Remote Copy)

The new Remote Mirror and Copy license authorization enables several Copy Services functions dependent on the configuration and settings used.

The Remote Mirror and Copy feature or RMC (formerly called Peer-to-Peer Remote Copy, or PPRC) is a flexible data mirroring technology that allows replication between volumes on two or more disk storage systems. You can also use this feature for data backup and disaster recovery. Remote Mirror and Copy is an optional function. To use it, you must purchase the Remote Mirror and Copy 2244 function authorization model, which is 2244 Model RMC.

DS8000 storage units can participate in Remote Mirror and Copy solutions with the ESS Model 750, ESS Model 800, and DS6000 storage units. To establish an RMC (formerly PPRC) relationship between the DS8000 and the ESS, the ESS needs to have licensed internal code (LIC) Version 2.4.2 or later.

The Remote Mirror and Copy feature can operate in the following modes:

Metro Mirror (formerly Synchronous PPRC)

Metro Mirror provides real-time mirroring of logical volumes between two systems that can be located up to 300 km from each other. It is a synchronous copy solution where write operations are completed on both copies (local and remote site) before they are considered to be complete.

Global Copy (formerly PPRC-XD)

Global Copy copies data non-synchronously and over longer distances than is possible with Metro Mirror. When operating in Global Copy mode, the source volume sends a periodic, incremental copy of updated tracks to the target volume, instead of sending a constant stream of updates. This causes less impact to application writes for source volumes and less demand for bandwidth resources, while allowing a more flexible use of the available bandwidth.

Global Copy does not keep the sequence of write operations. Therefore, the copy is normally fuzzy, but you can make a consistent copy through synchronization (called a go-to-sync operation). After the synchronization, you can issue FlashCopy at the secondary site to make the backup copy with data consistency. After the establishment of the FlashCopy, you can change the PPRC mode back to the non-synchronous mode.

Note: When you change PPRC mode from synchronous to non-synchronous mode, you change the PPRC mode from synchronous to suspend mode at first, and then you change PPRC mode from suspend to non-synchronous mode.

If you want make a consistent copy with FlashCopy, you must purchase a Point-in-Time Copy function authorization (2244 Model PTC) for the secondary Storage Unit.

Global Mirror (Asynchronous PPRC)

Global Mirror provides a long-distance remote copy feature across two sites using asynchronous technology. This solution is based on the existing Global Copy and FlashCopy. With Global Mirror, the data that the host writes to the Storage Unit at the local site is asynchronously shadowed to the Storage Unit at the remote site. A consistent copy of the data is automatically maintained on the Storage Unit at the remote site.

Global Mirror operations provide the benefit of supporting operations over virtually unlimited distances between the local and remote sites, restricted only by the capabilities of the network and the channel extension technology. It can also provide a consistent and restartable copy of the data at the remote site, created with minimal impact to applications at the local site.

The ability to maintain an efficient synchronization of the local and remote sites with support for failover and failback modes, helps to reduce the time that is required to switch back to the local site after a planned or unplanned outage.

1.3 Copy Services functions unique to z/OS

The following functions are only available for z/OS environments, and are included here for reference and information.

z/OS Global Mirror RMZ (formerly XRC)

DS8000 Storage Complexes support z/OS Global Mirror only on zSeries hosts. The z/OS Global Mirror function mirrors data on the Storage Unit to a remote location for disaster recovery. It protects data consistency across all volumes that you have defined for mirroring. The volumes can reside on several different storage units. The z/OS Global Mirror function can mirror the volumes over several thousand kilometers from the source site to the target recovery site.

With z/OS Global Mirror, you can suspend or resume service during an outage. You do not have to terminate your current data-copy session. You can suspend the session, then restart it. Only data that changed during the outage needs to be re-synchronized between the copies. The z/OS Global Mirror function is an optional function. To use it, you must purchase the Remote Mirror for z/OS 2244 function authorization model, which is 2244 Model RMZ.

z/OS Global Mirror and Metro Mirror across three sites

This mirroring capability uses z/OS Global Mirror to mirror primary site data to a location that is a long distance away and also uses Metro Mirror to mirror primary site data to a location within the metropolitan area. This enables a z/OS 3-site high availability and disaster recovery solution for even greater protection from unplanned outages. To use it, you must purchase both of the following functions:

- Remote Mirror for z/OS (2244 Model RMZ) for the primary Storage Unit.
- Remote Mirror and Copy function (2244 Model RMC) for the primary Storage Unit and for the secondary Storage Unit at the alternate metropolitan site.

1.4 Advanced functions unique to z/OS

The following function is only available for z/OS environments, and is included here for reference and information.

Parallel Access Volumes (PAV)

This function is only available for z/OS environments:

- Parallel Access Volumes (PAV) is a performance enhancer for the z/OS operating system that was introduced with the ESS. It is available on the DS8000 in the z/OS environment with the purchase of the PAV 2244 function authorization model, which is 2244 Model PAV. This allows the creation of multiple UCBs for each volume to reduce I/O queueing. Along with the Workload Manager application, effective management of PAVs can be made locally and/or over members of a Sysplex.

2

The new Copy Services architecture

In this chapter, we introduce an overview of the structure of the Copy Services communication architecture in either an open or zSeries environment.

We cover these topics:

- Introduction to the new structure
- How does the new structure of Copy Services work?
- zSeries communication path for Copy Services

2.1 Introduction to the new structure

The Copy Services architecture for the IBM ESS 800 used a construct called a *Copy Services Domain* to manage Copy Services. The communications architecture for DS6000 and DS8000 is noticeably different. Instead of a Copy Services Domain, we now use the concept of Storage Complexes.

You can perform Copy Services operations both within or between Storage Complexes. An ESS 800 Copy Services Domain (at the correct firmware level), can for management purposes, appear to a DS6000 or DS8000 as an independent Storage Complex.

Now within a Storage Complex you will find management consoles, Storage Units, and in the case of DS8000, Storage Facility Images. First, we will define what each of these constructs are.

2.1.1 What is a management console?

A management console is a PC that is used to manage the devices within a Storage Complex. In the case of the DS6000, it is a PC with a Windows operating system, onto which the user has installed the DS Storage Manager Console software. This is usually referred to as a Storage Management Console or SMC. In the case of the DS8000, it is a dedicated PC that comes with a pre-installed Linux based operating system and pre-installed management software. The DS8000 console is called a Hardware Management Console or HMC.

In either case, the end-user interacts with the management console using either the Web browser based DS GUI, or the DS CLI (Command-Line Interface). It is possible using the DS GUI, to manage Copy Services operations on multiple Storage Complexes.

2.1.2 What is a Storage Unit?

A Storage Unit is the physical storage device (including expansion enclosures) that you see when you walk into the computer room. If you open a rack door and look at a DS6000 system enclosure (a 1750-511) and all its attached expansion enclosures (1750-EX1s), then you are looking at a single DS6000 Storage Unit. If you then look at a DS8000 sitting on the floor (with any attached expansion racks), then you are looking at a DS8000 Storage Unit. An example would be a 2107-922 with an attached 2107-9E2. Another example would be a 2107-9A2 with an attached 2107-9AE. In each example you would have a single DS8000 Storage Unit.

2.1.3 What is a Storage Facility Image (SFI)?

The Storage Facility Image construct is different for the DS6000 and DS8000.

DS6000 SFI

For the DS6000, the SFI concept does not really apply. You could say that each DS6000 Storage Unit contains one SFI. However, in general a DS6000 is always referred to as simply a Storage Unit. When using the DS CLI, there are separate commands to display a DS6000 Storage Unit or a DS6000 SFI. However, both will refer to the same device. Using the DS GUI, you only work with the DS6000 Storage Unit. The GUI will not offer an option to select a DS6000 SFI. In Example 2-1 we connect to a DS6000 Management Console using the DS CLI. We issue the `lssu` command to display the DS6000 Storage Unit and the `lssi` command to display the DS6000 Storage Facility Image. In each case we see the same serial number and the same WWNN (World Wide Node name). The Storage Unit and the SFI are the same.

Example 2-1 Difference between a DS6000 Storage Unit and DS6000 SFI

```
dscli> lssu
Date/Time: 13 November 2005 19:21:17 IBM DSCLI Version: 5.1.0.204
Name     ID                Model WWNN             pw state
=========================================================
13-00247 IBM.1750-1300247 511   500507630EFFFE16 On
dscli> lssi
Date/Time: 13 November 2005 19:21:44 IBM DSCLI Version: 5.1.0.204
Name ID               Storage Unit     Model WWNN             State  ESSNet
============================================================================
-    IBM.1750-1300247 IBM.1750-1300247 511   500507630EFFFE16 Online Enabled
```

DS8000 SFI

For the DS8000, the SFI concept is necessary because a DS8000 can be ordered as a model 9A2. In this model all resources in the DS8000 are divided between two separate machine images. This means that to all attached hosts, a single DS8000 Storage Unit effectively contains two DS8000s. It is like having two separate machines in one physical box.

This means that when using the DS GUI or the DS CLI, you have to be very clear whether you are working with the SFI or with the Storage Unit. For most operations you always work with an SFI. You can tell the difference very easily. The serial number of the Storage Unit always ends in zero. The serial number of the first SFI always ends in 1. If you have ordered a model 2107-9A2, then you will also have a second SFI. The Serial number of the second SFI always ends in 2.

DS8000 Model 921 and 922 SFI example

In Example 2-2 we connect to a DS8000 Management Console using the DS CLI. We issue the **lssu** command to display the DS8000 Storage Unit of a 2107-922. We then issue the **lssi** command to display the DS8000 Storage Image on that Storage Unit. The Storage Unit serial number is 7520780. The SFI serial number is 7520781. Note how the Storage Unit and the SFI have different WWNNs.

Example 2-2 Difference between a DS8000 Storage Unit and DS8000 SFI - Model 922

```
dscli> lssu
Date/Time: 13 November 2005 19:21:01 IBM DSCLI Version: 5.1.0.204
Name         ID                Model WWNN             pw state
=============================================================
2107-7520780 IBM.2107-7520780 922   5005076303FFF9A5 On
dscli> lssi
Date/Time: 13 November 2005 19:21:21 IBM DSCLI Version: 5.1.0.204
Name       ID               Storage Unit     Model WWNN             State  ESSNet
==================================================================================
ATS_3_EXP IBM.2107-7520781 IBM.2107-7520780 922   5005076303FFC1A5 Online Enabled
```

DS8000 Model 9A2 SFI example

In Example 2-3 we connect to a DS8000 Management Console using the DS CLI. We issue the **lssu** command to display the DS8000 Storage Unit of a 2107-9A2. We then issue the **lssi** command to display the DS8000 Storage Images on that Storage Unit. The Storage Unit serial number is 7520780. The SFI serial numbers are 7520781 and 7520782. The Storage Unit and the SFIs all have different WWNNs.

Example 2-3 Difference between a DS8000 Storage Unit and DS8000 SFI - Model 9A2

```
dscli> lssu
Date/Time: 13 November 2005 19:25:25 IBM DSCLI Version: 5.1.0.204
Name             ID                Model WWNN             pw state
==============================================================
2107_75ABTV1/V2 IBM.2107-75ABTV0 9A2    5005076303FFFE63 On
dscli> lssi
Date/Time: 13 November 2005 19:25:34 IBM DSCLI Version: 5.1.0.204
Name ID               Storage Unit     Model WWNN             State  ESSNet
============================================================================
-    IBM.2107-75ABTV1 IBM.2107-75ABTV0 9A2   5005076303FFC663 Online Enabled
-    IBM.2107-75ABTV2 IBM.2107-75ABTV0 9A2   5005076303FFCE63 Online Enabled
```

2.1.4 What is a Storage Complex?

A Storage Complex can be one or two DS8000 Storage Units managed by one or two DS Hardware Management Consoles (HMCs). A Storage Complex could also be one or two DS6000 Storage Units, managed by one or two DS Storage Management Consoles (SMCs). In Figure 2-1, you see a logical view of two Storage Complexes, each with one DS8000 Storage Unit. They are running Remote Mirror and Copy. Now because the two DS HMCs are linked via Ethernet, you could connect using the DS GUI to either DS HMC and manage Copy Services on both DS8000s.

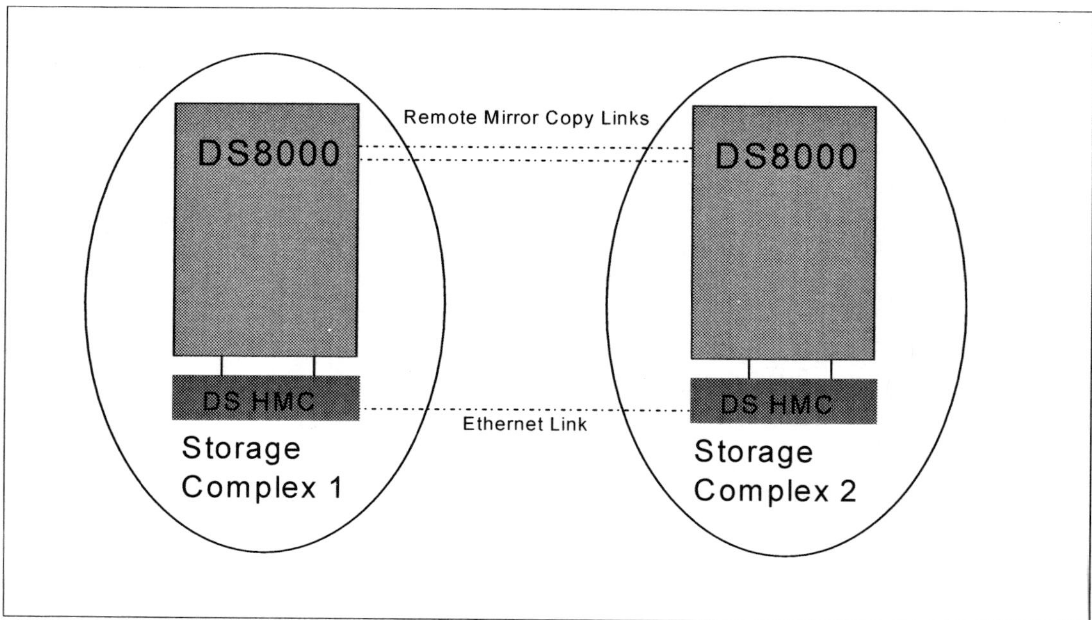

Figure 2-1 Logical view of a Storage Complex

Currently for the DS8000 and DS6000, we can manage two Storage Units in one Storage Complex. For ESS 800, we can manage up to eight ESS 800s in a single ESS Copy Services domain.

> **Note:** Only machines of the same type, like 2107, can be in the same Storage Complex. However, Storage Complexes with different machine types can be joined together. For example, a DS8000 Storage Complex and a DS6000 Storage Complex can be inter-connected.

2.2 How does the new structure of Copy Services work?

With the exception of zSeries commands (see "zSeries communication path for Copy Services" on page 17), communication to a DS6000 or DS8000 needs an available DS SMC or DS HMC. See Figure 2-2.

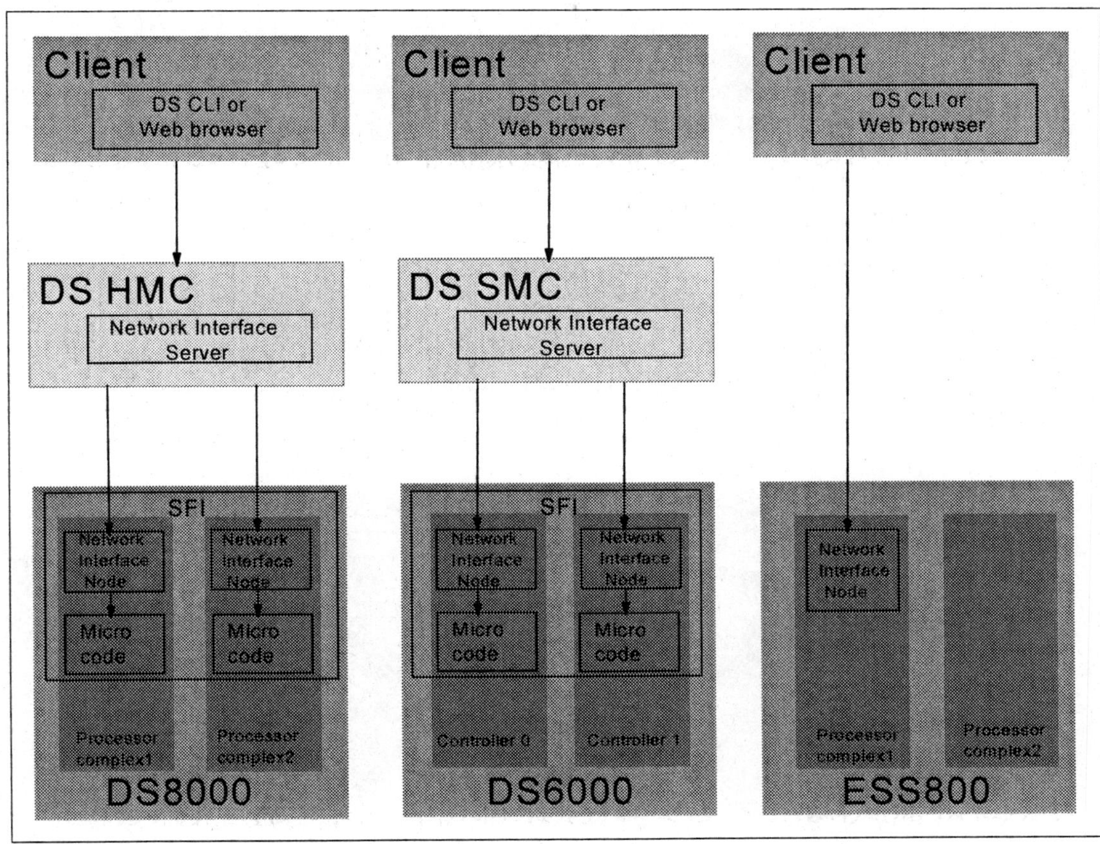

Figure 2-2 Network Interface communication structure

DS8000 management structure

Using Figure 2-2 we can see that:

- The client uses either the DS CLI or a Web browser GUI to issue commands to the Network Interface Server running on the DS HMC.
- The Network Interface Server software that resides on the HMC will communicate with the Client.
- The Network Interface Server software will communicate with the Network Interface Node, which resides on each server of a Storage Facility Image. From this point, the Network Interface will then talk to the microcode, which operates the DS8000.

1750 DS6000 management structure

Using Figure 2-2 we can see that:

- The client uses either the DS CLI or a Web browser GUI to issue commands to the Network Interface Server running on the DS SMC.
- The DS Network Interface Server software will reside on the DS SMC. This is what the client will communicate with.

- The Network Interface Server software will communicate with the Network Interface Node, which resides on each controller of the DS6000. From this point the Network Interface will then interact with the microcode which operates the controllers.

2105 ESS 800 management structure

Using Figure 2-2 we can see that:

- The client uses either DS CLI or a ESS Copy Services Web browser GUI to issue commands to the ESS 800 Copy Services Server running on an ESS 800 cluster. The client could also use the DS GUI to issue commands to the ESS 800 Copy Services Server if a DS6000 SMC or DS8000 HMC is available to route them through (not shown in the diagram).
- The ESS 800 Copy Services Server will then interact with the microcode which operates the ESS 800.

2.2.1 Remote Mirror and Copy between Storage Complexes

It is possible to use Remote Mirror and Copy between Storage Complexes as depicted in Figure 2-3. In this scenario we have three Storage Complexes. The complexes are interconnected at the top of the chart by Storage Area Network (SAN) connections (solid lines), and at the bottom of the chart by an Ethernet LAN (dashed lines).

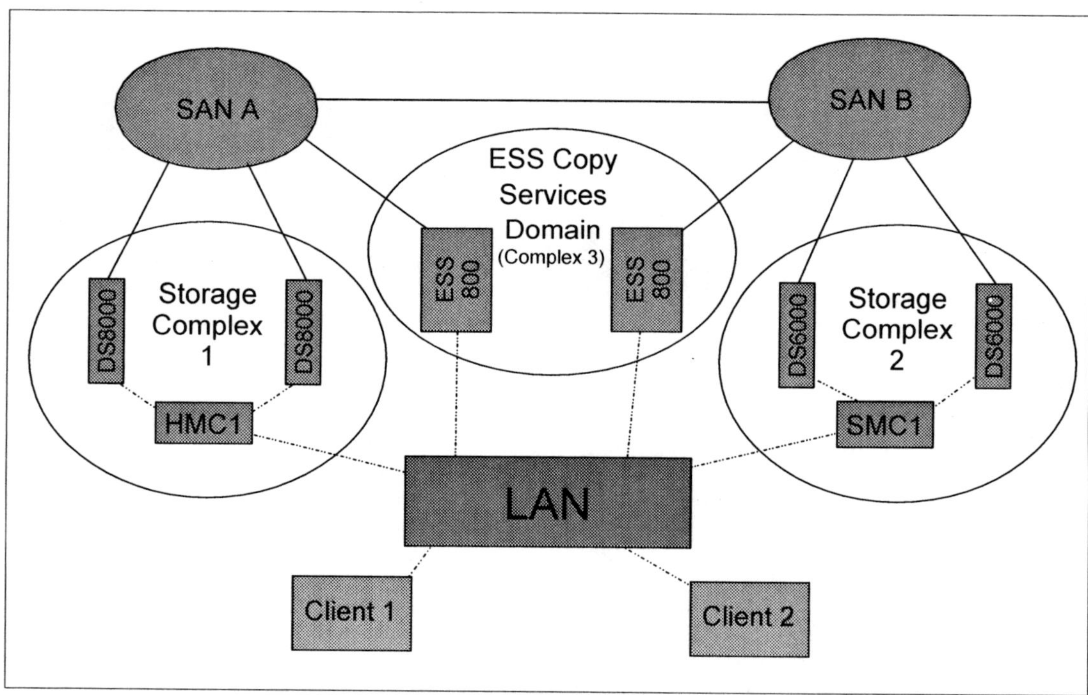

Figure 2-3 Remote Mirror and Copy between Storage Complexes

2.2.2 Differences between the DS CLI and the DS GUI

The DS CLI is not capable of managing several domains in a single session. However, if a single DS CLI client machine has network access to all Storage Complexes, then that client could issue concurrent DS CLI commands to each complex. Each complex would be managed by a separate DS CLI session. The DS CLI can be script driven, and of course scripts can be saved. So by using DS CLI, you can achieve automation.

The DS GUI is accessed via a Web browser. The DS GUI is not able to save tasks as we do on the ESS. Thus you cannot use the DS GUI to initiate a series of saved tasks. To do this we need to use the DS CLI. If you wish to use a single GUI to manage multiple Storage Complexes, then you need to define in the GUI all of the Storage Complexes. This will allow you to manage FlashCopy or Remote Mirror and Copy on, or between, every Storage Unit in every defined and accessible Storage Complex.

When you look at the structure in Figure 2-2, you can see that you need a working DS SMC or DS HMC in every Storage Complex, to communicate with that complex's DS6000 or DS8000. For an inter-Storage Complex Remote Mirror and Copy, the DS GUI will establish sessions to the source and target Storage Complexes to show all paths and LUNS. If no DS HMC or DS SMC is available at the remote Storage Complex, you cannot select this Storage Complex as a target.

It is possible to have two SMCs or two HMCs in a Storage Complex for the purpose of redundancy.

2.3 zSeries communication path for Copy Services

For the purposes of Copy Services, zSeries operating systems are able to issue Copy Services commands to the DS6000 and DS8000 via inband communication. This is done by sending commands via a FICON (or ESCON in the case of DS8000) host link to a conduit CKD volume. From there it gets passed to the microcode for execution. This is exactly the same as what is done with an ESS 800. Depending on the operating system, various software packages are available to issue commands, examples include TSO or ICKDSF.

The ability to send inband commands does not necessarily mean that the DS CLI or DS GUI do not have a role to play. To be able to issue a command to a DS6000 or DS8000, a zSeries operating system needs to be able to communicate with the relevant Storage Unit. We may have a remote Storage Unit which is not connected via FICON (or ESCON in the case of a DS8000) to an active zSeries operating system. This means we would not be able to access a conduit CKD volume on the remote Storage Unit. Now provided we have TCP/IP connectivity and an appropriate management station (such as a Windows host with a Web browser or DS CLI installed), we could use the DS CLI or the DS GUI to manage the remote Storage Unit. We could then use inband commands to manage the local Storage Unit. If the remote and local storage units were connected by RMC links, then we can also send some commands inband via the RMC links, such as commands to establish FlashCopies of the remote RMC target volumes.

Part 2

Interfaces

In this part of the book, we describe the interfaces available to manage Copy Services features of the DS8000. After presenting an overview of the interfaces, we discuss the options available, describe the various configuration considerations, and give you some examples of the use of the interfaces.

3

DS Storage Manager

This chapter provides an introduction to the DS Storage Manager, which can be used to configure and administer the DS storage system. The IBM TotalStorage DS Storage Manager is an interface that is used to perform logical configuration and Copy Services management.

We cover these topics:

- IBM TotalStorage DS Storage Manager Web-based Interface
- Connecting to the DS8000 DS GUI
- Managing the Storage Complex
- Creating a DS Storage Management Console PC
- Accessing the Information Center

3.1 IBM TotalStorage DS Storage Manager Web-based Interface

IBM TotalStorage DS Storage Manager is a Web-based management interface. It is used for managing the logical configuration of the DS8000 and for invoking Copy Services functions. The DS Storage Manager has an online mode and an offline mode; only the online mode is supported for Copy Services.

The DS Storage Manager can be used for almost all functions for Copy Services. The following function cannot be issued from the DS Storage Manager in the current implementation:

- Inband commands over a remote mirror link.

3.1.1 Advantages of using the DS GUI over the DS CLI or TSO

The DS Storage Manager GUI has the following advantages for managing Remote Mirror and Copy functions:

- It requires less specialized skills for effective use.
- It is a real time graphical interface to the DS8000 subsystem, which may present information more easily to some users.
- You do not need to install anything on your PC in order to manage Copy Services — a simple Web browser pointed to the DS HMC is enough.

3.1.2 Disadvantages of using the DS GUI over the DS CLI or TSO

The DS Storage Manager GUI has the following disadvantages for managing Remote Mirror and Copy functions:

- You cannot perform all supported functions from this interface.
- You cannot use this interface for automated actions.
- You cannot save your actions and reuse them later.

You still need to understand the implications of the actions you are performing (for example, you need to understand that a FlashCopy will overwrite the target LUN or volume).

3.2 Connecting to the DS8000 DS GUI

To connect to the DS8000 DS GUI through a Web browser, enter the Web site (URL) of Hardware Management Console 1 (HMC1), or if present, HMC2. The Web site consists of a TCP/IP address as shown in Figure 3-1, or a fully qualified name that the DNS server can resolve, with the correct port number. If, for instance, your HMC IP address is 10.0.0.1 and you connect to *http://10.0.0.1*, you will not get a successful connection. This is because the DS Storage Manager is accessible by connecting to either:

```
http://10.0.0.1:8451/DS8000
```

or

```
https://10.0.0.1:8452/DS8000
```

Clearly you should change the IP address to match the one used by your HMC.

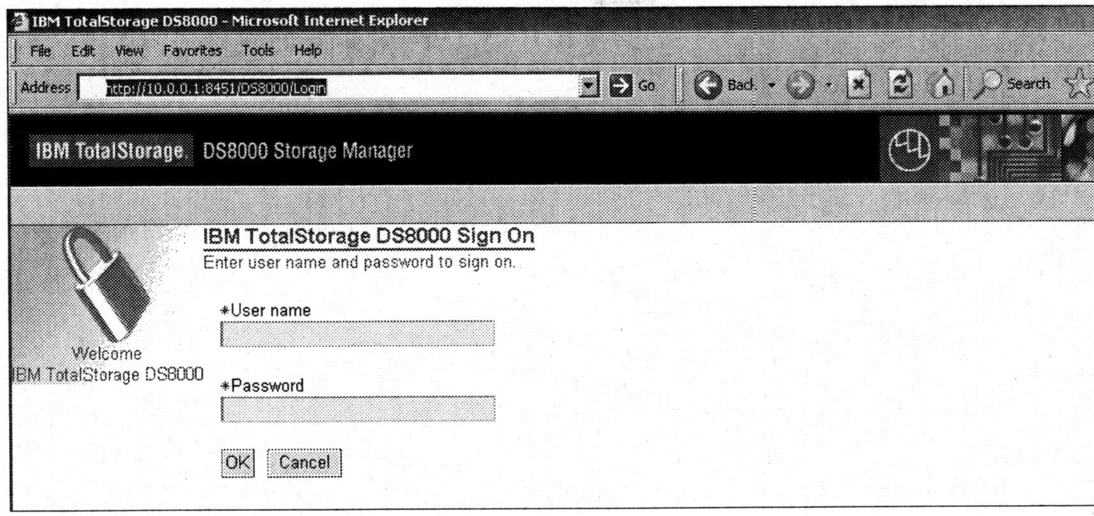

Figure 3-1 Connecting to a DS8000 with a Web browser

Logging in to the DS Storage Manager requires that you provide your user name and password. This function is generally administered through your system administrator and by your company policies. The preconfigured user ID and password are as follows:

User ID = `admin`
Password = `admin`

When you log on to the DS GUI for the first time using the *admin* user ID, you will be forced to change the password from *admin* to something more secure.

Accessing the Storage Manager when logged onto the HMC

When logged onto the DS8000 HMC directly, you can also access the DS Storage Manager.

Log on to the HMC with:

User ID: customer
Password: cust0mer

Then right-click on the HMC desktop and select Net → Browser → DS Storage Manager. This will start the Opera Web Browser. You will not be able to go to any other Web Sites from here.

Note: The ability to use the HMC to access the DS GUI means you do not need a separate PC to configure or manage the DS8000, unless you wish to use DS CLI. The DS CLI is not installed on the HMC, so it must be installed on an ethernet attached server or PC.

3.3 Managing the Storage Complex

A DS8000 is managed by either one or two HMCs. These HMCs and the Storage Units they manage, represent a Storage Complex. In Figure 3-2 we have connected to the Storage Complex managed by the HMC at the 10.0.0.1 IP address. This complex consists of one Storage Unit, as indicated by the arrow.

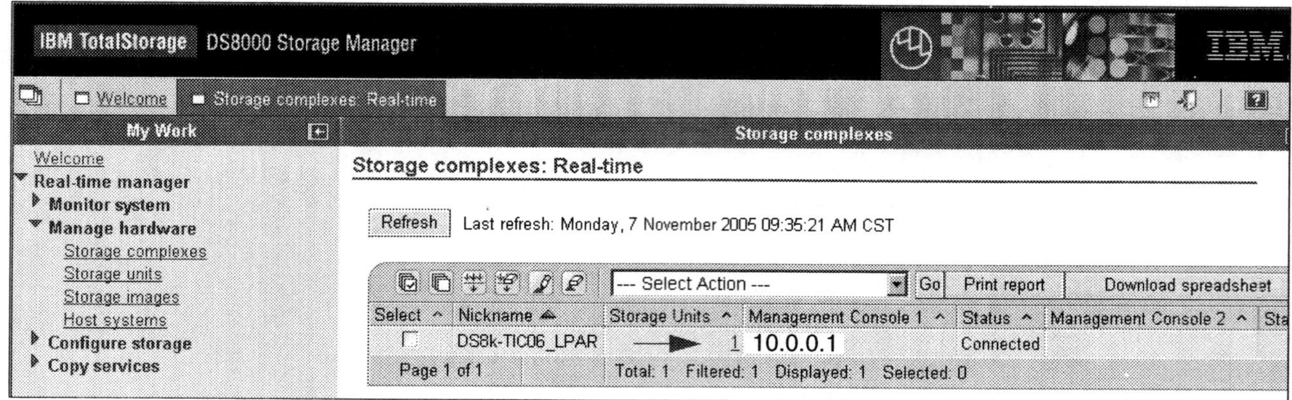

Figure 3-2 A single Storage Complex with a single Storage Unit

A simple scenario may be that we have two sites. At the production site we have a single DS8000 managed by its own HMC. Then at a remote site we have a second DS8000 managed by its own HMC. There is ethernet connectivity between the two HMCs. Because each HMC manages only the DS8000 at its own site, this means we have two Storage Complexes. If we wish to use a single GUI to manage Copy Services at either site, then we have to add these Storage Complexes to each other. Once we have done this, we can use the DS GUI connected to one HMC to manage Copy Services on either Storage Unit at either site, plus set up Copy Services relations between the two sites.

3.3.1 Procedure to add a Storage Complex

Note: To use the DS GUI supplied by the HMC in one Storage Complex to manage the Storage Units of the other Storage Complex, you have to do this operation once in each direction. This means you have to add Complex1 to Complex2 and then you add Complex2 to Complex1.

Important: Make sure the user ID you use to log on to the DS8000 DS GUI also exists on the other DS8000 Storage Complex and that it has the same password. If not, the operation to add the Storage Complex will fail. You will need to always use this same user ID for multi-complex management.

1. Connect to the DS8000 HMC using the DS GUI.
2. Click **Real-time manager**.
3. Click **Manage hardware**.
4. Click **Storage complexes**.
5. Select **Add** and click **Go**. Figure 3-3 shows the Add Storage Complex panel.

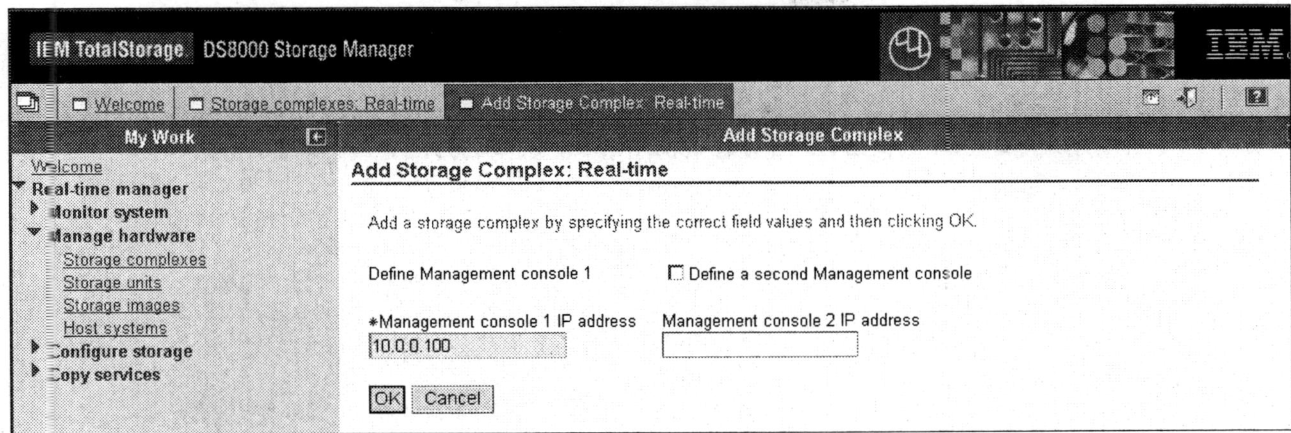

Figure 3-3 Add Storage Complex panel

6. Enter the IP address of the other Storage Complex's HMC into the *Management console 1 IP address* box. If the other Storage Complex has a second HMC, select the **Define a second Management console** box and enter the second HMC address into the *Management console 2 IP address* box. Now select **OK**.
7. When the add Storage Complex operation completes, the Storage Complex screen will now show the DS8000 HMC as an additional Storage Complex. In Figure 3-4 we can see the successful result. We have added a second Storage Complex that manages one Storage Unit.

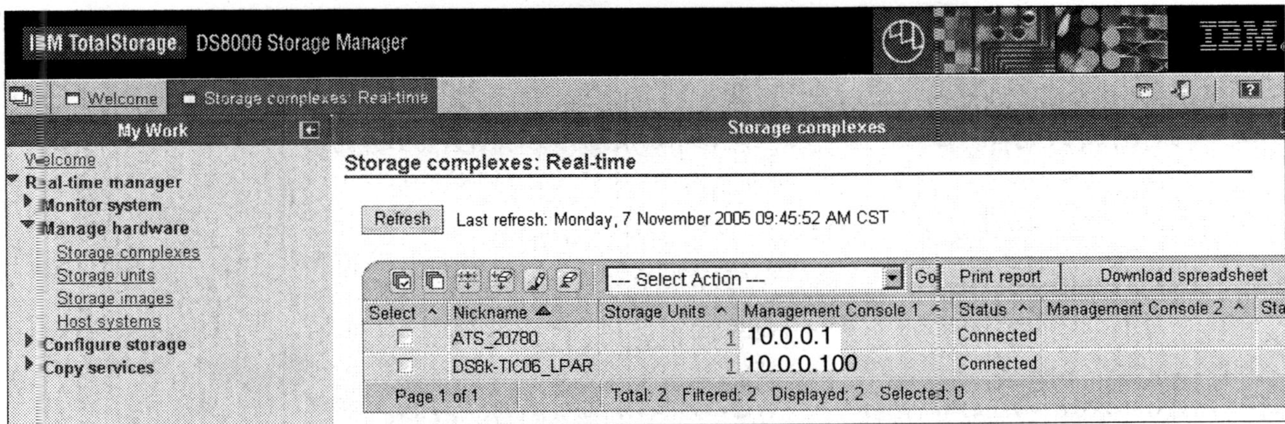

Figure 3-4 Successful addition of a Storage Complex

8. Having added one DS8000 Storage Complex to another, you are now able to use the DS8000 DS GUI to create paths and Remote Mirror and Copy pairs between either of the Storage Units. You can also use the DS8000 DS GUI to manage FlashCopy pairs on either DS8000. This is assuming all of the relevant licenses are present.

Note: The steps to add one DS8000 Storage Complex to another DS8000 Storage Complex cannot be performed using the DS CLI.

3.4 Creating a DS Storage Management Console PC

With a DS6000, it is necessary to install the DS Storage Management console software onto a separate PC in order to manager the DS6000. With the DS8000, however, this software is effectively pre-installed onto the DS8000 HMC. This means that there is no requirement to purchase a separate PC to manage the DS8000. However, there remains the option to actually install the DS Storage Manager software onto a separate PC. The main reason to do this, is that it will allow you to run a Simulated Manager for the purposes of creating offline storage configurations. These configurations can be applied at a later time. However, for the purposes of Copy Services, there is no benefit to having a separate DS Storage Management PC. Consequently it will not be discussed in this section. Note that a separate PC or server is still needed if you wish to use the DS CLI.

3.5 Accessing the Information Center

The Software Information Center displays product or application information. The system provides a graphical user interface for browsing and searching online documentation. The broad range of topics covered includes accessibility, Copy Services, device storage, host system attachments, concurrent code loads, input/output configuration programs, and volume storage.

Accessing the Information Center using a Web browser

You can connect to the Information Center using a Web browser. If your HMC IP address is 10.0.0.1 then you can access the Information Center running on that HMC at:

```
http://10.0.0.1:8455
```

If you wish to access the public version of the DS8000 Information Center, it can be located at:

```
http://publib.boulder.ibm.com/infocenter/ds8000ic/index.jsp
```

Accessing the Information Center from the DS GUI

The help panels are accessed by selecting the **?** symbol on the upper-right side of the screen, as indicated by the arrow in Figure 3-5.

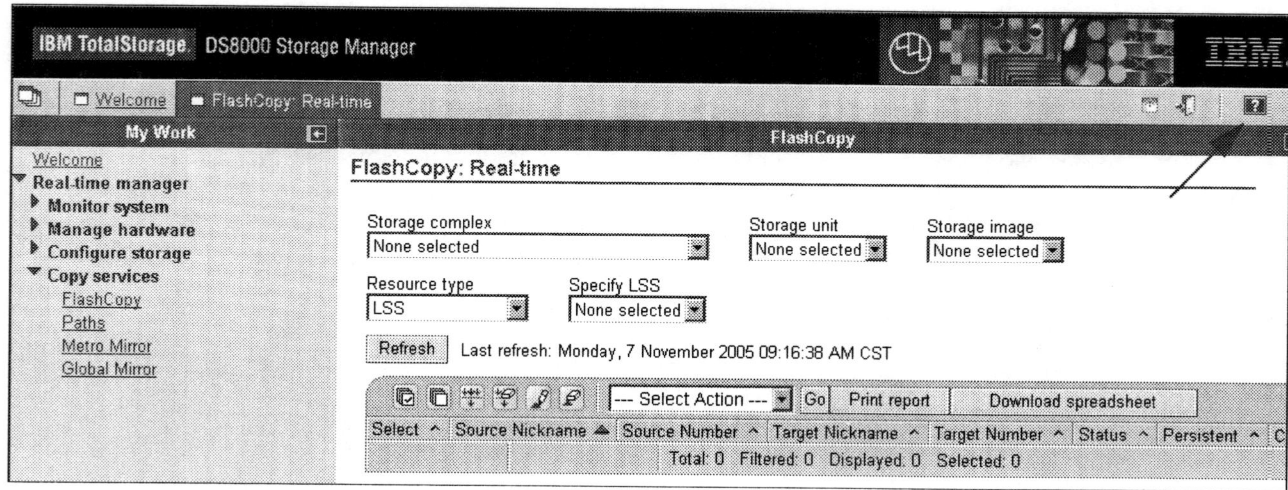

Figure 3-5 Help option location

The help panel is opened automatically on the current subject of the configuration screen as shown in Figure 3-6. In this example the FlashCopy main page was open when help was called, so the FlashCopy help main page was opened.

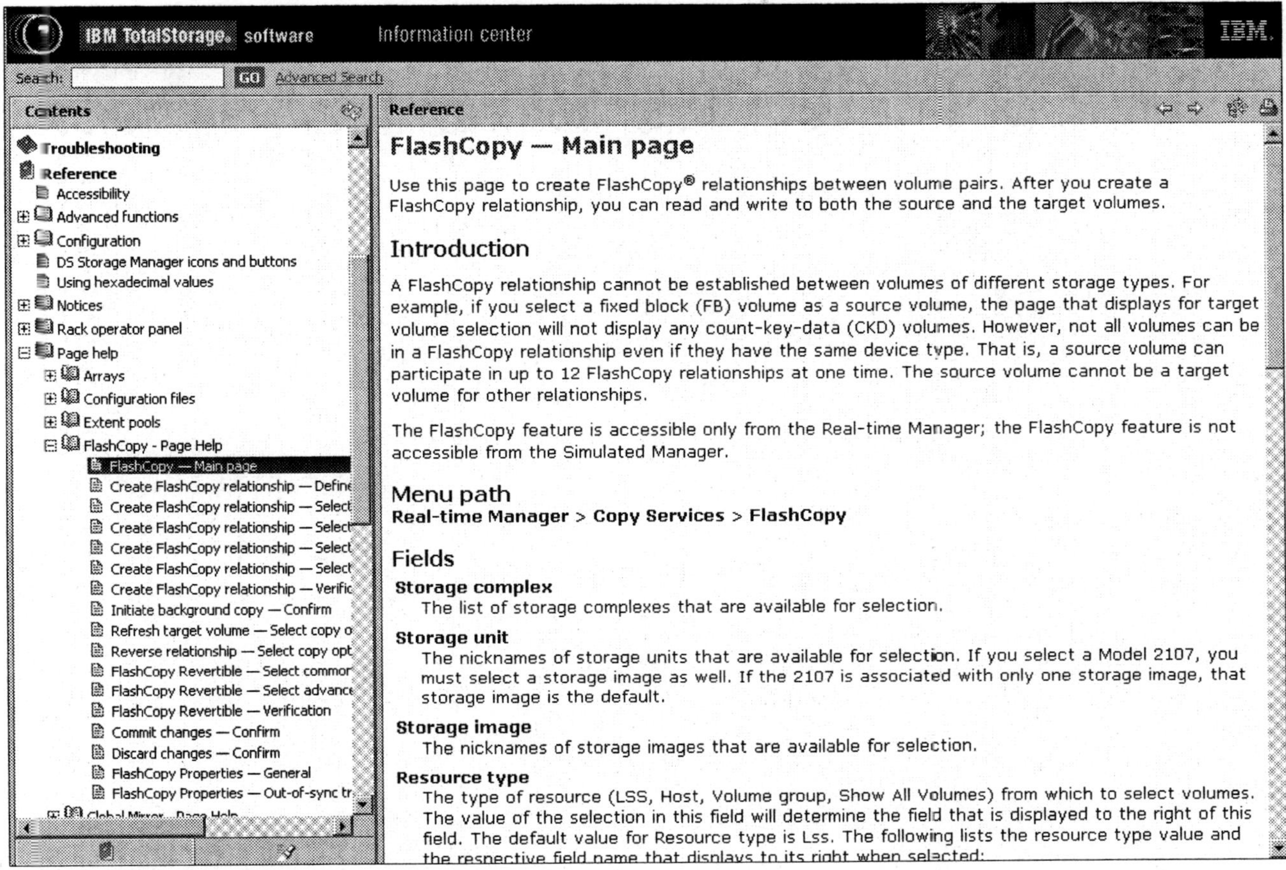

Figure 3-6 FlashCopy help Main page

DS Command-Line Interface

This chapter provides an introduction to the DS Command-Line Interface (DS CLI), which can be used to configure and administer the DS8000 storage systems. We describe how the DS CLI can be used to manage Copy Services relationships.

We cover these topics:

- System requirements
- Command modes
- List of the commands
- User assistance
- Return codes

4.1 Introduction and functionality

The IBM TotalStorage DS Command-Line Interface (DS CLI) enables open systems hosts to invoke and manage FlashCopy and Remote Mirror and Copy functions through batch processes and scripts.

While there is no support for z/OS as a server for the DS CLI, you can use the DS CLI from a supported server to control and manage Copy Services functions on z/OS volumes.

Note: Most z/OS environments choose to use one of the z/OS interfaces to manage their volumes. You may choose to use the DS CLI if you are also managing open systems volumes and want to use a single interface. However, with recent changes to TSO commands to enable control of open systems Copy Services functions, you may choose to use the TSO commands to manage both z/OS and open systems volumes.

The DS CLI provides a full-function command set that allows you to check your Storage Unit configuration and perform specific applications functions when necessary.

Before you can use the DS CLI commands, you must meet the following requirements:

- Your Storage Unit must be configured.
- You must activate your license activation codes before you can use the CLI commands associated with Copy Services functions.

The following list highlights a few of the specific types of functions that you can perform with the DS CLI:

- Create userids that can be used with the GUI and the DS CLI.
- Manage userid passwords.
- Install activation keys for licensed features.
- Manage Storage Complexes and units.
- Create and delete RAID Arrays, Ranks and Extent Pools.
- Manage host access to volumes (for open systems).
- Check the current Copy Services configuration settings.

4.2 Supported operating systems for the DS CLI

The DS CLI can be installed on these operating systems:

- AIX 5.1, 5.2, 5.3
- HP-UX 11i v1, v2
- HP-True64 5.1, 5.1A
- OpenVMS 7.3-1, 7.3-2
- Novell Netware 6.5
- Sun Solaris 7, 8, 9
- Windows 2000, Windows Datacenter, Windows 2003, Windows XP

Note: The DS CLI cannot be installed on a Windows 64-bit operating system.

The DS CLI is supplied and installed via a CD that ships with the machine. The installation does not require a reboot of the open systems host. The DS CLI requires Java™ 1.4.1 or higher. Java 1.4.2 for Windows, AIX and Linux is supplied on the CD. Many hosts may already have a suitable level of Java installed. The installation program checks for this requirement during the installation process and does not install DS CLI if you do not have the correct version of Java.

The installation process can be performed via a shell, such as the bash or korn shell, or the Windows command prompt, or via a GUI interface. If performed via a shell, it can be performed silently using a profile file. The installation process also installs software that allows the DS CLI to be completely de-installed should it no longer be required.

If you need any assistance to install the DS CLI, you can refer to the *IBM TotalStorage DS8000 Command-Line Interface User's Guide*, SC26-7625.

4.3 User accounts

The admin account is set up automatically at the time of installation. It is accessed using the user name **admin** and the default password **admin**. This password is temporary and you must change the password before you can use any of the other functions. There are seven groups the administrator can assign to a user. The groups and the associated functions allowed by the assignment are as follows:

- **admin:** Allow access to all storage management console server service methods and all storage image resources.
- **op_volume:** Allow access to service methods and resources that relate to logical volumes, hosts, host ports, logical subsystems, and Volume Groups, excluding security methods.
- **op_storage:** Allow access to physical configuration service methods and resources, including Storage Complex, Storage Image, Rank, Array, and Extent Pool objects.
- **op_copy_services:** Allow access to all Copy Services service methods and resources, excluding security methods.
- **service:** Monitor authority, plus access to all management console server service methods and resources, such as performing code loads and retrieving problem logs.
- **monitor:** Allow access to list and show commands. It provides access to all read-only, non-security management console server service methods and resources.
- **no access:** Does not allow access to any service method or Storage Image resources. By default, this user group is associated to any user account in the security repository that is not associated with any other user group.

Note: A user can be assigned to more than one user group.

Important: When a new user is created, the password that was initially set will be automatically expired and must be changed when the user first logs on.

4.4 DS CLI profile

You can create default settings for the DS CLI by defining one or more profiles on the system. For example, you can specify the HMC for the session, specify the output format for list commands, specify the number of rows per page in the DS CLI output, and specify that a banner is included with the DS CLI output.

If a user enters a value with a command that is different from a value in the profile, the command overrides the profile.

You have several options for using profile files:

- You can modify the default profile. The default profile, dscli.profile, is installed in the profile directory with the software. For example, c:\Program Files\IBM\DSCLI\profile\dscli.profile for the Windows platform.
- You can make a personal default profile by making a copy of the system default profile as <user_home>/dscli/profile/dscli.profile. The home directory, <user_home> is designated as follows:
  - Windows system: C:\Documents and settings\<user_name>
- You can create a profile for the Storage Unit operations. Save the profile in the user profile directory. For example:
  - c:\Program Files\IBM\DSCLI\profile\operation_name1
  - c:\Program Files\IBM\DSCLI\profile\operation_name2

> **Attention:** The default profile file created when you install the DS CLI will potentially be replaced every time you install a new version of the DS CLI. It is a better practice to open the default profile and then save it as a new file. You can then create multiple profiles and reference the relevant profile file using the `-cfg` parameter.

These profile files can be specified using the DS CLI command parameter **`-cfg <profile_name>`**. If the -cfg file is not specified, the user's default profile is used. If a user's profile does not exist, the system default profile is used.

> **Note:** A password file, generated using the `managepwfile` command is located at the following directory: <user_home>/dscli/security/security.dat.

The available variables and detailed description and information about how to handle them can be found in *IBM TotalStorage DS8000 Command-Line Interface User's Guide*, SC26-7625.

4.5 Command structure

This is a description of the components and structure of a Command-Line Interface command.

A Command-Line Interface command consists of one to four types of components, arranged in the following order:

1. **Command name:** Specifies the task that the Command-Line Interface is to perform.
2. **Flags:** Modify the command. They provide additional information that directs the Command-Line Interface to perform the command task in a specific way.
3. **Flags parameter:** Provides information that is required to implement the command modification that is specified by a flag.
4. **Command parameter:** Provides basic information that is necessary to perform the command task. When a command parameter is required, it is always the last component of the command, and it is not preceded by a flag.

4.6 Copy Services commands

We can classify the commands available with the DS CLI as follows:

1. `ls` commands: Give you brief information on the Copy Services state. See Table 4-1.
2. `show` commands: Give you detailed information on the Copy Services state. See Table 4-2.
3. `mk` commands: Used to create relationships. See Table 4-3.
4. `rm` commands: Used to remove relationships. See Table 4-4.
5. `options` commands: Used to modify some options in relationships that were previously created. See Table 4-5.

Table 4-1 List commands

Command	Description
lsflash	Lists of FlashCopy relationships.
lsremoteflash	Lists of Remote FlashCopy relationships (inband).
lspprc	Lists of Remote Mirror and Copy volumes relationships.
lspprcpath	Lists of existing Remote Mirror and Copy path definition.
lsavailpprcport	Lists available ports that can be defined as Remote Mirror and Copy.
lssession	Displays a list of Global Mirror sessions for a LSS.

Table 4-2 List detailed commands

Command	Description
showgmir	Displays detailed properties and performance metrics for Global Mirror.
showgmircg	Displays consistency group status for a Global Mirror session.
showgmiroos	Displays the number of unsynchronized (out of sync) tracks for a Global Mirror session.

Table 4-3 Creation commands

Command	Description
mkflash	Initiates a point-in-time copy from a source to a target volume.
mkremoteflash	Initiates a remote copy through a Remote Mirror and Copy relationship.
mkgmir	Starts Global Mirror for a session.
mkpprc	Establishes a Remote Mirror and Copy relationship.
mkpprcpath	Establishes or replaces a Remote Mirror and Copy path over a Fibre Channel.
mkesconpprcpath	Creates a Remote Mirror and Copy path over an ESCON connection.
mksession	Opens a Global Mirror for a session.

Table 4-4 Deletion commands

Command	Description
rmflash	Removes a relationship between FlashCopy pairs.
rmremoteflash	Removes a relationship between remote FlashCopy pairs.

Command	Description
rmgmir	Removes Global Mirror for the specified session.
rmpprc	Removes a Remote Mirror and Copy relationship.
rmpprcpath	Removes a Remote Mirror and Copy path.
rmsession	Closes an existing Global Mirror session.

Table 4-5 Options commands

Command	Description
commitflash	Commits data to a target volume to form a consistency between the source and target.
resyncflash	Incremental FlashCopy process.
reverseflash	Reverse the direction of a FlashCopy pair.
revertflash	Overwrites new data with data saved at the last consistency formation.
setflashrevertible	Modifies a remote FlashCopy pair that is part of a Global Mirror to revertible.
commitremoteflash	Commit data to a target volume to form a consistency (inband).
resyncremoteflash	Incremental FlashCopy process (inband).
revertremoteflash	Overwrites new data with data saved at the last consistency formation (inband).
setremoteflashrevertible	Modifies a remote FlashCopy pair that is part of a Global Mirror to revertible (inband).
unfreezeflash	Resets a FlashCopy Consistency Group.
failoverpprc	Changes a secondary device into a primary suspended and keep the primary in current.
failbackpprc	Usually used after a failoverpprc to reverse the direction of the synchronization.
freezepprc	Creates a new Remote Mirror and Copy Consistency Group.
pausepprc	Pauses an existing Remote Mirror and Copy volume pair relationship.
resumepprc	Resumes a Remote Mirror and Copy relationship for a volume pair.
unfreezepprc	Thaws an existing Remote Mirror and Copy Consistency Group.
pausegmir	Pauses a Global Mirror processing for a session.
resumegmir	Resumes a Global Mirror processing for a session.
chsession	Allows to modify a Global Mirror session.

Important: The Remote Mirror and Copy commands are asynchronous. This means that the command is issued to the DS CLI server and is accepted successfully, and you receive a successful completion code, however, background activity may still be occurring.

For example, a Metro Mirror pair will take some time to establish, as the tracks need to be copied across from the primary to secondary device. In this example you should check the state of the volumes using the **lspprc** command until the pairs have reached the Duplex state.

Note: The **mkflash** and **mkpprc** commands offer the **-wait** flag, which delays command response until copy complete status is achieved. You may choose to use this flag if you wish to be sure of successful completion.

4.7 Using the DS CLI application

You have to log into the DS CLI application to use the command modes. There are three command modes for DS CLI:

- Single-shot mode
- Interactive mode
- Script mode

4.7.1 Single-shot mode

Use the DS CLI single-shot command mode if you want to issue an occasional command but do not want to keep a history of the commands that you have issued.

You must supply the login information and the command that you want to process at the same time. Use the following example to use the single-shot mode:

1. Enter **dscli -hmc1 <hostname or ip address> -user <user name> -passwd <pwd> <command>**
2. Wait for the command to process and display the end results.

Example 4-1 shows the use of the single-shot command mode.

Example 4-1 Single-shot command mode

```
C:\Program Files\ibm\dscli>dscli -hmc1 10.10.10.1 -user admin -passwd adminpwd
lsuser
Date/Time: 24 de Maio de 2005 14h38min20s BRT IBM DSCLI Version: X.X.X.X
Name     Group State
=====================
admin    admin locked
admin    admin active
exit status of dscli = 0
```

Note: When logging in to the DS CLI, you can use the hostname or the IP address of the DS HMC.

4.7.2 Script command mode

Use the DS CLI script command mode if you want to use a sequence of DS CLI commands. Administrators can use this mode to create automated processes, for example, establishing Remote Mirror and Copy relationships for volume pairs.

You can issue the DS CLI script from the command prompt at the same time that you provide your login information:

1. Enter **dscli -hmc1 <hostname or ip address> -user <user name> -passwd <pwd> -script <full path of script file>**
2. Wait for the script to process and provide a report regarding the success or failure of the process.

Example 4-2 shows the use of the script command mode.

Example 4-2 Script command mode

```
C:\Program Files\ibm\dscli>dscli -hmc1 10.10.10.1 -user admin -passwd adminpwd
 -script c:\test.cli
Date/Time: 24 de Maio de 2005 14h40min22s BRT IBM DSCLI Version: X.X.X.X DS: IBM
IBM.1750-1367890
ID    WWPN             State  Type             topo     portgrp
===============================================================
I0000 500507630E01FC00 Online Fibre Channel-LW SCSI-FCP 0
I0001 500507630E03FC00 Online Fibre Channel-LW -        0
I0002 500507630E05FC00 Online Fibre Channel-LW SCSI-FCP 0
I0003 500507630E07FC00 Online Fibre Channel-LW -        0
I0100 500507630E81FC00 Online Fibre Channel-LW SCSI-FCP 0
I0101 500507630E83FC00 Online Fibre Channel-LW -        0
I0102 500507630E85FC00 Online Fibre Channel-LW SCSI-FCP 0
I0103 500507630E87FC00 Online Fibre Channel-LW -        0
Date/Time: 24 de Maio de 2005 14h40min36s BRT IBM DSCLI Version: X.X.X.X
Name ID               Storage Unit     Model WWNN             State  ESSNet
============================================================================
-    IBM.1750-1312345 IBM.1750-1312345 511   500507630EFFFC6F Online Enabled
exit status of dscli = 0
```

Attention: The DS CLI script can contain only DS CLI commands. Use of shell commands results in process failure. You can add comments to the scripts prefixed by the number sign (#).

Note: When logging in to the DS CLI, you can use the hostname or the IP address of the DS HMC.

4.7.3 Interactive mode

Use the DS CLI interactive command mode when you have multiple transactions to process that cannot be incorporated into a script. The interactive command mode provides a history function that makes repeating or checking prior command usage easy to do:

1. Log on to the DS CLI application at the directory where it is installed.
2. Provide the information that is requested by the information prompts. The information prompts might not appear if you have provided this information in your profile file. The command prompt switches to a **dscli** command prompt.
3. Begin using the DS CLI commands and parameters. You are not required to begin each command with dscli because this prefix is provided by the **dscli** command prompt.

Example 4-3 shows the use of interactive command mode.

Example 4-3 Interactive command mode

```
C:\Program Files\ibm\dscli>dscli
Enter your username: admin
Enter your password:
Date/Time: 24 de Maio de 2005 14h42min17s BRT IBM DSCLI Version: X.X.X.X  DS:
IBM.1750-1312345
.
dscli> lsarraysite
Date/Time: 24 de Maio de 2005 15h8min57s BRT IBM DSCLI Version: X.X.X.X DS: IBM.
1750-1312345
```

```
arsite DA Pair dkcap (Decimal GB) State    Array
================================================
S1     0                   146.0 Assigned A0
S2     0                   146.0 Assigned A0
S3     0                   146.0 Assigned A1
S4     0                   146.0 Assigned A1
.
dscli> lssi
Date/Time: 24 de Maio de 2005 14h42min59s BRT IBM DSCLI Version: X.X.X.X
Name ID               Storage Unit     Model WWNN             State  ESSNet
============================================================================
-    IBM.1750-1312345 IBM.1750-1312345 511   500507630EFFFC6F Online Enabled
dscli> quit

exit status of dscli = 0
```

Note: When logging in to the DS CLI, you can use the hostname or the IP address of the DS HMC.

4.8 Return codes

When the DS CLI is exited, the exit status code is provided. This is effectively a return code. If DS CLI commands are issued as separate commands (rather than using script mode) then a return code will be presented for every command. If a DS CLI command fails (for instance due to a syntax error or the use of an incorrect password), then a failure reason and a return code will be presented. Standard techniques to collect and analyze return codes can be used.

The return codes used by the DS CLI are shown in Table 4-6.

Table 4-6 Return code table

Return code	Category	Description
0	Success	The command was successful.
2	Syntax error	There is a syntax error in the command.
3	Connection error	There was a connection problem to the server.
4	Server error	The DS CLI server had an error.
5	Authentication error	Password or userid details are incorrect.
6	Application error	The DS CLI application had an error.

4.9 User assistance

The DS CLI is designed to include several forms of user assistance. The main form of user assistance is via the **help** command. Examples of usage include:

- **help** Lists all available DS CLI commands.
- **help -s** Lists all DS CLI commands with brief description of each.
- **help -l** Lists all DS CLI commands with syntax information.

If the user is interested in more details about a specific DS CLI command, they can use **-l** (long) or **-s** (short) against a specific command. In Example 4-4, the **-s** parameter is used to get a short description of the **mkflash** command's purpose.

Example 4-4 Use of the help -s command

```
dscli> help -s mkflash
mkflash The mkflash command initiates a point-in-time copy from source volumes to target
volumes.
```

In Example 4-5, the **-l** parameter is used to get a list of all parameters that can be used with the **mkflash** command.

Example 4-5 Use of the help -l command.

```
dscli> help -l mkflash
mkflash [ { -help|-h|-? } ] [-dev storage_image_ID] [-tgtpprc] [-tgtoffline] [-t
gtinhibit] [-freeze] [-record] [-persist] [-nocp] [-wait] [-seqnum Flash_Sequenc
e_Num] SourceVolumeID:TargetVolumeID ... | -
```

Man pages

A ***man page*** is available for every DS CLI command. Man pages are most commonly seen in UNIX®-based operating systems to give information about command capabilities. This information can be displayed by issuing the relevant command followed by **-h**, **-help**, or **-?**, for example:

dscli> **mkflash -help**

or

dscli> **help mkflash**

4.10 Usage examples

It is not the intent of this section to list every DS CLI command and its syntax. If you need to see a list of all the available commands, or require assistance using DS CLI commands, you are better served by reading the *IBM TotalStorage DS8000 Command-Line Interface User's Guide,* SC26-7625, or you can use the online help.

Example 4-6 shows some of the common commands used on a DS6000, which is very similar as on the DS8000.

Example 4-6 Examples of DS CLI commands

```
# The following command establishes flashcopy pairs
dscli> mkflash -dev IBM.1750-1300861 0100-0102:0300-0302
Date/Time: April 25, 2005 5:59:56 PM IST IBM DSCLI Version: 0.0.0.0 DS: IBM.1750-1300861
CMUC00137I mkflash: FlashCopy pair 0100:0300 successfully created.
CMUC00137I mkflash: FlashCopy pair 0101:0301 successfully created.
CMUC00137I mkflash: FlashCopy pair 0102:0302 successfully created.

# The following command establishes Remote Mirror and copy paths
dscli> mkpprcpath -dev IBM.1750-1300861 -remotedev IBM.1750-1300861 -remotewwnn
5005076303FFC03D -srclss 00 -tgtlss 02 I0030:I0031 I0100:I0101
Date/Time: 18:33:22 IST April 25, 2005 IBM DSCLI Version: 0.0.0.0 DS: IBM.1750-1300861
CMUC00149I mkpprcpath: Remote Mirror and Copy path 00:02 successfully established.

# The following command establishes Remote Mirror and copy pairs
dscli> mkpprc -dev IBM.1750-1300861 -remotedev IBM.1750-1300866 -type gcp 0006:0206
Date/Time: 18:43:31 IST April 25, 2005 IBM DSCLI Version: 0.0.0.0 DS: IBM.1750-1300861
CMUC00153I mkpprc: Remote Mirror and Copy volume pair relationship 0006:0206 successfully
created.
```

5

zSeries interfaces

This chapter discusses the zSeries interfaces available to manage DS8000 Copy Services functions.

We cover these topics:

- zSeries interfaces
- TSO
- ICKDSF
- DFSMSdss
- The ANTRQST macro
- z/TPF commands

5.1 zSeries interfaces

In addition to using the DS GUI or the DS CLI, there are several possible interfaces available for zSeries users to manage DS6000 or DS8000 Copy Services relationships. These are:

- TSO
- ICKDSF
- DFSMSdss
- The ANTRQST macro
- Native TPF commands (for z/TPF only)

All of these interfaces have the advantage that they do not need to issue their commands to the DS8000 HMC or DS6000 SMC. They can instead directly send commands inband over a FICON channel connection between the DS6000 or DS8000 and the zSeries operating system. DS8000 can also use ESCON connections. Sending inband commands allows for a very quick command transfer that does not depend on any additional software stacks.

5.1.1 Operating system alternatives

From an operating system point of view, the alternatives to the DS GUI and DS CLI break out as follows:

z/OS and OS/390

- TSO commands
- ICKDSF
- DFSMSdss
- ANTRQST application programming interface (API)

z/VM®:

- ICKDSF

z/VSE

- ICKDSF

z/TPF

- ICKDSF
- z/TPF itself

5.2 TSO

TSO commands are commonly used in z/OS environments to manage all kinds of operations. TSO commands may be generated by REXX or CLIST procedures. They may also be generated out of other software tools.

You can issue the TSO commands from procedures that are similar to the scripting approach in open systems environments.

Note that TSO requires a z/OS system at the recovery site when you recover a z/OS Global Mirror environment at the remote site.

Generally a TSO command has to specify a valid online z/OS device number. For path and pair establishment commands, this is regardless of which device, LSS, or storage server will actually perform the Copy Services function. Note that this approach is not yet implemented for the new Global Mirror TSO command support. The new Global Mirror TSO commands require an online VOLSER as a parameter.

For a detailed description of TSO commands to manage Copy Services, refer to the IBM publication, *z/OS DFSMS Advanced Copy Services,* SC35-0428.

5.3 ICKDSF

The zSeries ICKDSF utility offers a means of control for Copy Services functions. ICKDSF is the only direct interface for z/VM and z/VSE environments.

ICKDSF typically runs as a batch program, and so can be automatically run from batch scheduling products (for example, Tivoli Workload Scheduler).

More information on ICKDSF can be found in the *Device Support Facilities User's Guide and Reference*, GC35-0033.

5.4 DFSMSdss

The DFSMSdss commands can be used to manage Copy Services relationships. Detailed information can be found in the IBM publication, *z/OS DFSMSdss Storage Administration Reference*, SC35-0424.

5.5 The ANTRQST macro

The ANTRQST macro provides an application program call to the z/OS system data mover's (SDM) application programming interface (API). This macro allows you to call Metro Mirror, z/OS Global Mirror and FlashCopy functions.

For detailed information, see the IBM publication, *z/OS DFSMS Advanced Copy Services*, SC35-0428.

5.6 z/TPF commands

It is also possible to issue Copy Services commands using native z/TPF commands. An example would be the use of the **ZXCPY** command to initiate a FlashCopy on a z/TPF device.

Information about using z/TPF to control Copy Services can be found at the following Web Information Centre:

```
http://publib.boulder.ibm.com/infocenter/tpfhelp/current/index.jsp
```

Part 3

FlashCopy

In this part of the book, we introduce the IBM TotalStorage FlashCopy for DS8000 for a z/OS environment. We present an overview of the main features and describe the options to set up FlashCopy. We also show which interfaces can be used to establish FlashCopy relationships, and which important aspects should be considered when establishing a FlashCopy relationship.

We conclude this part with some examples, showing how FlashCopy is used in the daily business to support the various environments that need copies of production data.

6

FlashCopy overview

The IBM TotalStorage FlashCopy creates a copy of a logical volume at a specific point-in-time, which we also refer to as a Point-in-Time copy, instantaneous copy, or t0 copy (time-zero copy).

This chapter presents an overview of the IBM TotalStorage FlashCopy for a DS8000 in a z/OS environment. We describe these topics:

- FlashCopy operational areas
- FlashCopy basic concepts
- FlashCopy in an LPAR environment
- FlashCopy in combination with other Copy Services
- Data set level FlashCopy

6.1 FlashCopy operational areas

It takes only a few seconds to establish the FlashCopy relationships for tens to hundreds or more volume pairs. In a 24x7 environment, the quickness of the FlashCopy operation allows us to use FlashCopy in very large environments and to take multiple FlashCopies of the same volume for use with different applications.

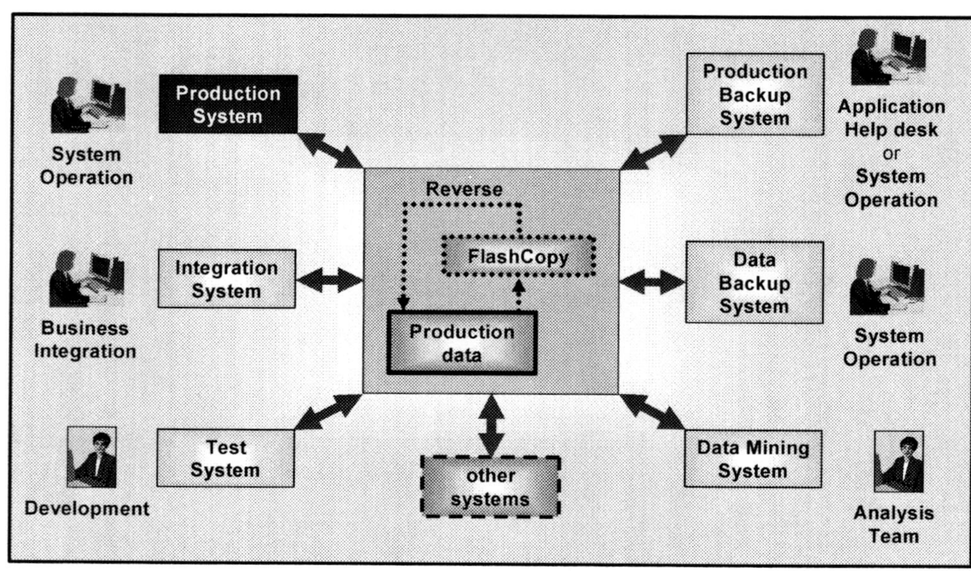

Figure 6-1 IBM TotalStorage FlashCopy and how it is used

We assume that FlashCopy can mainly be found in the following operational environments (see Figure 6-1):

- **Production backup system:**

  A FlashCopy of the production data allows data recovery from an older level of data. This might be necessary due to a user error or a logical application error. Let's assume that a user deleted accidentally a customer record. The production backup system could work with a FlashCopy of the data. The necessary part of the customer data can be exported and then be imported into the production environment. Thus, the production continues, and while a specific problem is being fixed, the majority of the users can work with the application without recognizing any problems.

  The FlashCopy of the data could also be used by system operations to re-establish production in case of any server errors.

- **Data backup system:**

  A FlashCopy of the production data allows the client to create backups with the shortest possible application outage. The main reason for data backup is to provide protection in case of source data loss due to disaster, hardware failure, software failure, or user errors.

- **Data mining system:**

  A FlashCopy of the data can be used for data analysis, thus avoiding performance impacts for the production system due to long running data mining tasks.

- **Test system:**

  Test environments created by FlashCopy can be used by the development team to test new application functions with real production data, thus speeding up the test setup process.

- **Integration system:**

  New application releases (for example, SAP releases) are likely to be tested prior to putting them onto a production server. By using FlashCopy, a copy of the production data can be established and used for integration tests.

With the opportunity to reverse a FlashCopy, a previously created FlashCopy can be used within seconds to bring production back to the level of data it had at the time when the FlashCopy was taken.

6.1.1 FlashCopy in a DS8000 LPAR environment

With the DS8000, IBM supports the LPAR technology for storage subsystems. A FlashCopy can always be established between volumes or datasets belonging to the *same* Storage LPAR or *Storage Image*. FlashCopy is not supported to go from a source volume in one LPAR to a potential target volume that belongs to another LPAR (Figure 6-2).

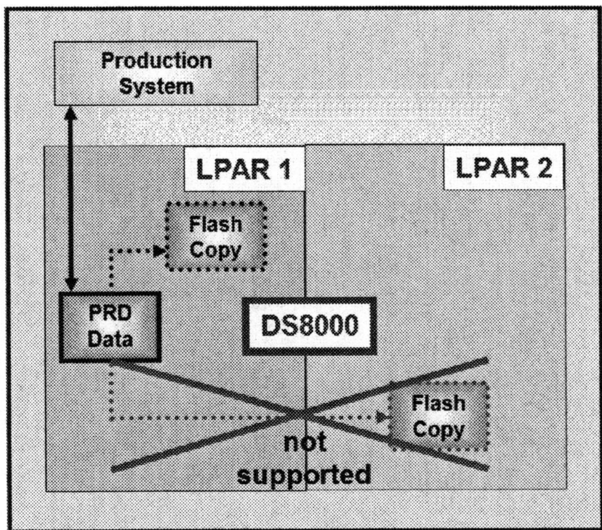

Figure 6-2 FlashCopy in a DS8000 LPAR environment

6.2 FlashCopy basic concepts

For the z/OS environment, FlashCopy can be used at the volume level and at the dataset level. Whenever source or target is used in this chapter without further specifying it, it refers to both a volume or a dataset.

By doing a FlashCopy, a relationship is established between a source and a target. Both are considered to form a FlashCopy pair.

As result of the FlashCopy, all physical blocks (full copy) are copied or only those parts, which are changing in the production data after the FlashCopy has been established (using the *nocopy* option).

Currently, the target volume needs to be the same size or bigger than the source volume whenever FlashCopy is used to flash a whole volume. FlashCopy also offers consistency groups, which allows multiple volumes to be FlashCopied at exactly the same instance. Typically, large applications such as databases have their data spread across several volumes and their volumes should all be FlashCopied at exactly the same point-in-time.

- **Establish FlashCopy relationship:**

  When the FlashCopy is started, the relationship between source and target will be established within seconds. This is done by creating a pointer table including a bitmap for the target.

  Let's assume that all bits for the bitmap of the target are set to their initial values. This represents the fact that no data block has been copied so far. The data in the target will not be touched during setup of the bitmaps. At this first step the bitmap and the data will look the way they are demonstrated graphically in Figure 6-3.

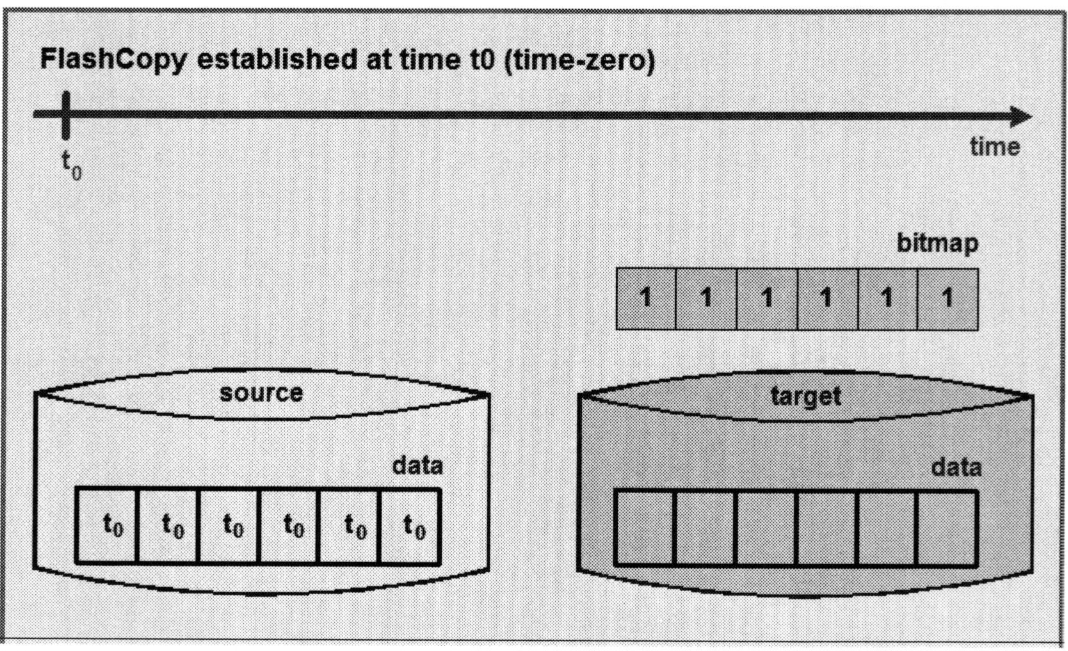

Figure 6-3 FlashCopy at time t0

Once the relationship has been established, it is possible to perform read and write I/Os on both the source and the target. Assuming that the target is used for reads only while production is ongoing, this could give us the picture shown in Figure 6-4.

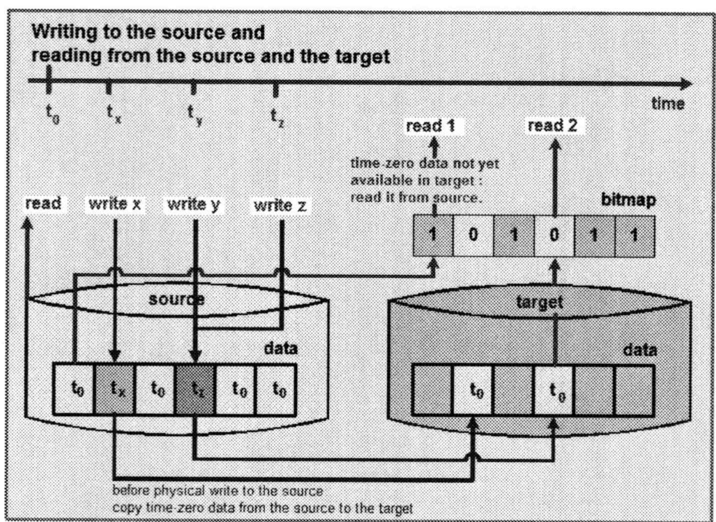

Figure 6-4 Reads from source and target volume and writes to source volume

- **Reading from the source:**

  The data could be read immediately (see Figure 6-4).

- **Writing to the source:**

  Whenever data is written to the source volume while the FlashCopy relationship exists, the storage subsystem makes sure that the time-zero-data is copied to the target volume prior to overwriting it in the source volume.

  To identify if the data of the physical block on the source volume needs to be copied to the target volume, the bitmap is analyzed. If it identifies that the time-zero data is not available on the target volume, then the data will be copied from source to target. If it states that the time-zero data has already been copied to the target volume, no further action is done (see Figure 6-4).

  It is possible to use the target volume immediately to work with the data. This can be done by just reading the data, but it is also possible to write data on it.

- **Reading from the target::**

  Whenever a read-request goes to the target while the FlashCopy relationship exists, the bitmap is used to identify if the data has to be retrieved from the source or from the target. If the bitmap states that the time-zero data hasn't yet been copied to the target, then the physical read is directed to the source. If the time-zero data has already been copied to the target, the read will be performed immediately against the target (see Figure 6-4 on page 48).

- **Writing to the target:**

  Whenever data is written to the target volume while the FlashCopy relationship exists, the storage subsystem makes sure that the bitmap is maintained. This way the time-zero data from the source volume never overwrites updates done directly to the target volume (see Figure 6-5).

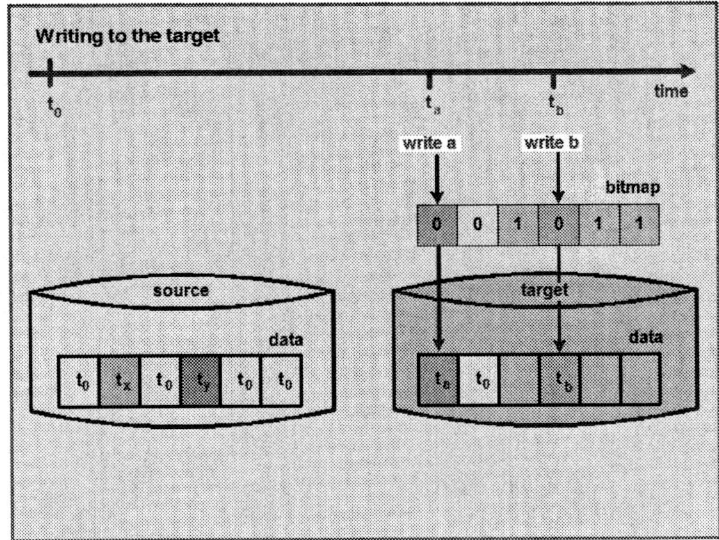

Figure 6-5 Writes to target volume

- **Terminating the FlashCopy relationship:**

  The FlashCopy relationship is *automatically ended* when all tracks have been copied from the source volume to the target volume. The relationship can also be *explicitly withdrawn* by issuing the corresponding commands in the supported user interfaces. If the persistent FlashCopy option was specified, the FlashCopy relationship must be withdrawn explicitly.

6.2.1 FlashCopy with full volume copy

When the *copy* option is invoked and the establish process completes, a background process is started that copies all data from the source to the target. Once this process is finished and if no updates on the target took place, this would give us a picture similar to the one in Figure 6-6. If not explicitly defined as persistent, the FlashCopy relationship ends as soon as all data is copied.

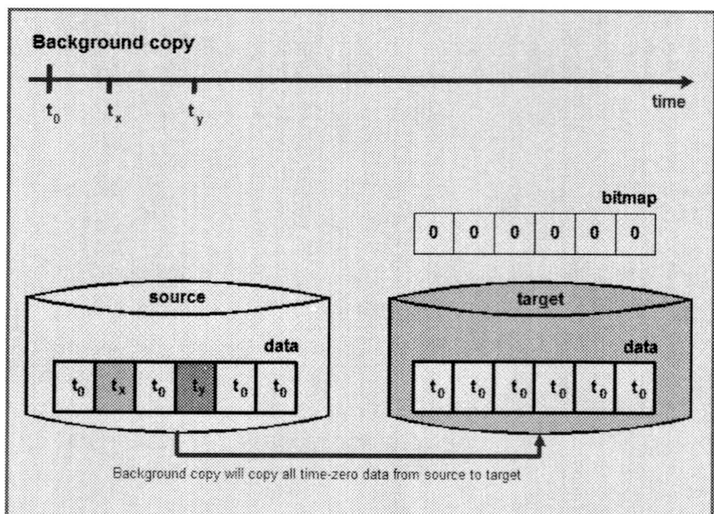

Figure 6-6 Target volume after full volume FlashCopy relationship finished

If writes took place for the target, this would give us a picture similar to the one in Figure 6-7.

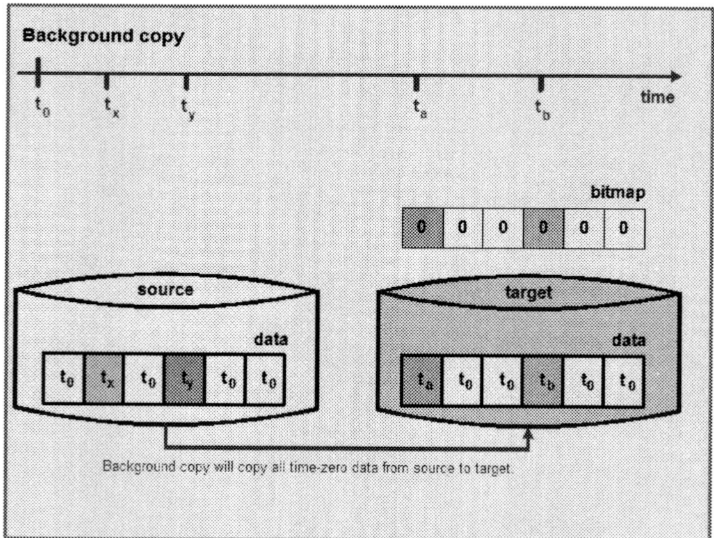

Figure 6-7 FlashCopy after updates to the target volume

6.2.2 FlashCopy with nocopy option

If FlashCopy is established using the *nocopy* option, then the result of the FlashCopy will be as graphically shown in Figure 6-4 on page 48 and Figure 6-5 on page 49. The relationship will last until it is explicitly withdrawn or all data in the source volume has been modified.

If the persistent FlashCopy option was specified, the FlashCopy relationship must be withdrawn explicitly.

6.3 FlashCopy in combination with other Copy Services

Volume based FlashCopy can be used in various combinations with other Copy Services, and it depends on the client's environment and requirements, which combination fits best. FlashCopy for datasets is not supported in any of the following scenarios.

6.3.1 Limitations with multiple FlashCopies

The following restrictions apply for FlashCopy:

- A FlashCopy source volume can have up to 12 FlashCopy target volumes.
- For each source volume, only one FlashCopy relationship can be reversed (the one having the *change recording* attribute).
- A FlashCopy target volume can have only one FlashCopy source volume.
- A FlashCopy target volume cannot be a FlashCopy source volume at the same time.

Note: At a specific point-in-time, a volume, a LUN, or a dataset can be only a source or a target.

Figure 6-8 Multiple FlashCopies

6.3.2 FlashCopy and Metro Mirror

As graphically shown in Figure 6-9, the following relationships are supported. For the primary system of the Metro Mirror, this means:

- A FlashCopy *source volume* can become a Metro Mirror *primary volume* and vice versa. The order of creation is optional.
- A FlashCopy *target volume* can become a Metro Mirror *primary volume* and vice versa. If you wish to use a FlashCopy target volume as a Metro Mirror primary, be aware of the following considerations:
  - The recommended order is to first establish the Metro Mirror, and then create a FlashCopy to that Metro Mirror primary using the *-tgtpprc* parameter (DS CLI) or TGTPPRIM(YES) (TSO) or PPRCPRIM(YES) (ICKDSF) or FCTOPPRCPrimary (DFSMSdss).
    - The Metro Mirror secondary will not be in a fully consistent state until the Metro Mirror enters the full duplex state.
  - If you create the FlashCopy first, and then establish a Metro Mirror of the FlashCopy target, you must monitor the progress of the FlashCopy background copy.
    - The Metro Mirror secondary will not be in a fully consistent state until the FlashCopy background copy process is complete.
    - Use the *copy* option to ensure that the entire FlashCopy source volume data is copied to the Metro Mirror secondary.

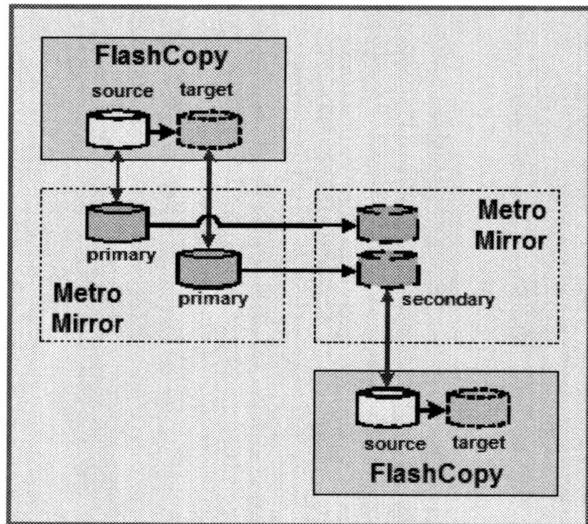

Figure 6-9 FlashCopy and Metro Mirror

On the target system of the Metro Mirror, the following feature is supported:

- A FlashCopy *source volume* can be based on the *secondary volume* for the Metro Mirror and vice versa. There are no dependencies on which relationship should be defined first.

6.3.3 FlashCopy and Global Copy

Similar to Metro Mirror, the following relationships are supported in combining FlashCopy and Global Copy (see Figure 6-10). For the primary system of the Metro Mirror, this means:

- A FlashCopy *source volume* can become a Global Copy *primary volume* and vice versa. The order of creation is optional.

- A FlashCopy *target volume* can become a Global Copy *primary volume* and vice versa. If you wish to use a FlashCopy target volume as a Global Copy primary, be aware of the following considerations:
  - The recommended order is to first establish the Global Copy, and then create a FlashCopy to that Global Copy primary using the *-tgtpprc* parameter (DS CLI) or TGTPPRIM(YES) (TSO) or PPRCPRIM(YES) (ICKDSF) or FCTOPPRCPrimary (DFSMSdss).
  - The Global Copy secondary will not be in a fully consistent state until the Global Copy is forced to the full duplex state.
  - If you create the FlashCopy first, and then establish a Global Copy of the FlashCopy target, you must monitor the progress of the FlashCopy background copy.
    - The Global Copy secondary will not be in a fully consistent state until the FlashCopy background copy process is complete and the Global Copy is forced to the full duplex state.
    - Use the *copy* option to ensure that the entire FlashCopy source volume data is copied to the Global Copy secondary.

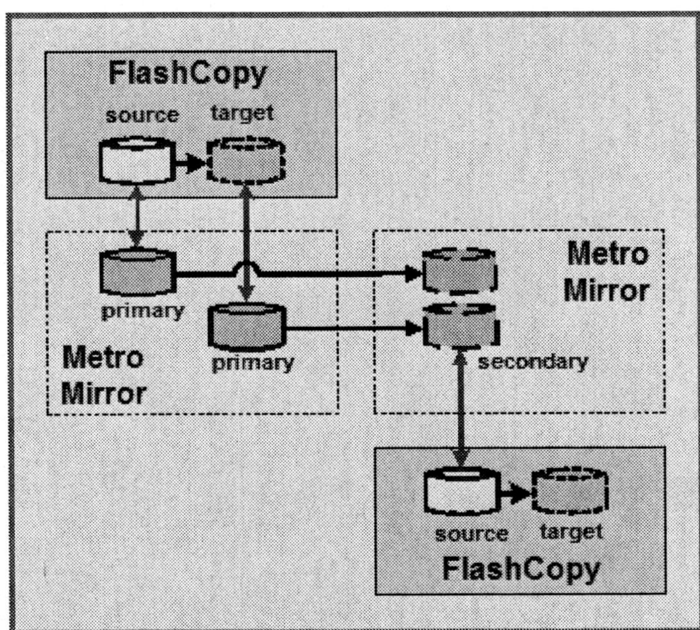

Figure 6-10 FlashCopy and Global Copy

On the target system of the Global Copy, the following feature is supported as well:

- A FlashCopy *source volume* can be based on the *secondary volume* for the Global Copy and vice versa. Definitions can be done in any sequence.

6.3.4 FlashCopy and z/OS Global Mirror

FlashCopy in combination with z/OS Global Mirror supports only one relationship at the primary site of the Global Mirror (see Figure 6-11).

- A FlashCopy source volume can become a z/OS Global Mirror source volume and vice versa. The relationships can be established in any time sequence.

> **Note:** A FlashCopy target volume cannot become a Global Mirror primary volume.

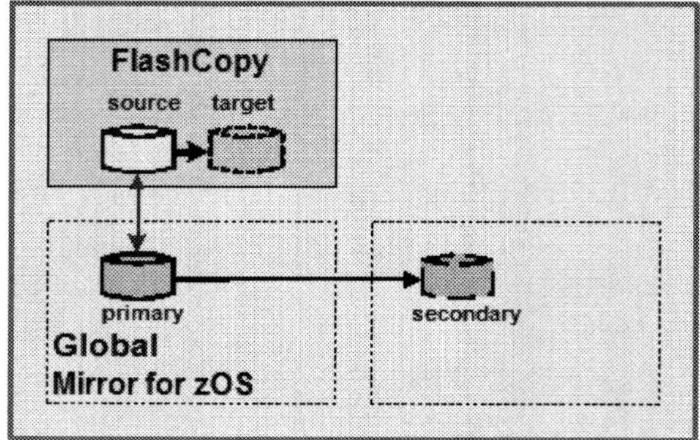

Figure 6-11 FlashCopy and z/OS Global Mirror

On the target system of the z/OS Global Mirror, the following FlashCopy relationship is allowed:

- A FlashCopy source volume can become a z/OS Global Mirror source volume and vice versa. The relationships can be established in any time sequence.

6.4 FlashCopy for z/OS data sets

The following characteristics apply for z/OS data sets that can be copied using the FlashCopy hardware function of the DS8000 (see Figure 6-12):

- All types of z/OS data sets are supported (sequential, partitioned, and VSAM datasets).
- The source data set and the target data set can reside in the same volume.

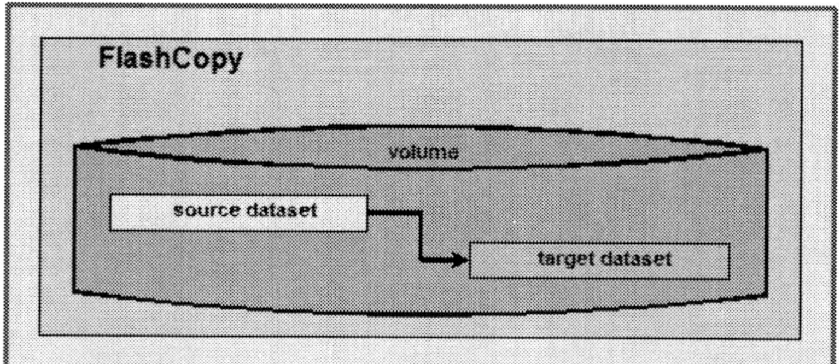

Figure 6-12 Source dataset and target dataset can reside in the same volume

- Source data set and target data set can reside on different volumes and in different locations within the volumes to which they belong.

7

FlashCopy options

This chapter presents an overview of the options for FlashCopy when working with DS8000 and a z/OS environment. Available options for FlashCopy are:

- Multiple relationship FlashCopy
- Consistency Group FlashCopy
- FlashCopy on existing Metro Mirror or Global Copy source
- Incremental FlashCopy
- Remote FlashCopy
- Persistent FlashCopy
- Data set FlashCopy
- Reverse restore and fast reverse restore

7.1 Options and interfaces

The setup of a DS8000 FlashCopy for a z/OS environment can be done using different environments. It is important to know, right from the beginning, for which purpose the target volume should be used afterwards. Knowing this, the options to be used with the FlashCopy can be identified and the environment can be selected that supports the selected options.

Supported environments are:

- DS8000 front ends:
  - DS CLI
  - DS SM
- z/OS host environment:
  - TSO
  - System Utilities (DFSMSdss, ICKDSF) or Macros (ANTRQST)

Supported options within the environments are those identified in Figure 7-1.

Interface / Function	DS front ends		zOS front ends			
	DS SM	DS CLI	DFSMSdss	TSO	ANTRQST	ICKDSF
Multiple relationship FlashCopy	✓	✓	✓	✓	✓	✓
Consistency Group FlashCopy	✗	✓	✗	✓	✓	✓
Target on existing Metro Mirror or Global Copy primary	✓	✓	✓	✓	✓	✓
Incremental FlashCopy	✓	✓	✗	✓	✓	✓
Remote FlashCopy	✗	✓	✗	✓	✓	✓
Persistent Flashcopy	✓	✓	✗	✓ (2)	✓ (2)	✗
Dataset FlashCopy	✗	✗	✓	✓ (1)	✓ (1)	✗
Reverse restore, fast reverse restore	✓	✓	✗	✓	✓	✓

(1) Extents can be specified, but the VTOC and the catalogs are not updated

(2) Persistent, full volume relationships are available via Incremental support

Figure 7-1 FlashCopy interfaces and functions

7.2 Multiple relationship FlashCopy

It is possible to establish up to 12 FlashCopy relationships using the same source. In other words, a source volume can have up to 12 target volumes. However, a target volume can still only have one source. Furthermore, cascading FlashCopy is not allowed (that is, a volume cannot be both a source and a target volume). No extra steps or parameters are required to take advantage of this feature.

Multiple relationship FlashCopy is also supported at the data set level, though not all interfaces that support the multiple relationship FlashCopy will support multiple relationships at the data set level. In Figure 7-1 we see that neither the DS Storage Manager or the DS CLI can support multiple relationships at the data set level. Also see Note 1 in Figure 7-1. This note points out that though TSO and the ANTRQST API support data set level FlashCopy, the VTOC and catalogs are not updated as they are with DFSMSdss.

Valid and invalid volume level combinations are shown in Figure 7-2.

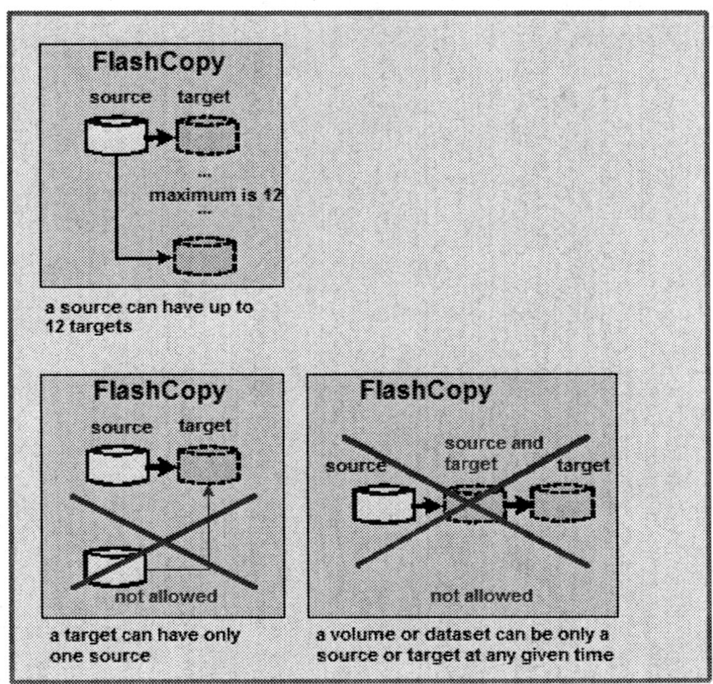

Figure 7-2 Combinations allowed with Multiple Relationship FlashCopy

7.3 Consistency Group FlashCopy

It is possible to establish a Consistency Group, by using those interfaces that support this function (see Figure 7-1 on page 56) by using the *freeze* functionality and identifying all FlashCopy pairs belonging to the Consistency Group.

Applications might have their data spread over multiple volumes. If FlashCopy should be used for multiple volumes, they all have to be at a consistent level, then the FlashCopy *freeze* functionality should be used when the FlashCopy is defined.

With the Freeze FlashCopy Consistency Group option, the DS8000 will hold off I/O activity to a volume for a time period by putting the source volume in extended long busy state. Thus, a time slot can be created during which the dependent write updates will not occur, and FlashCopy will use that time slot to obtain a consistent Point-in-Time Copy of the related volumes. I/O activity resumes when all FlashCopies are established, and the *run* functionality is invoked, or when the extended long busy (ELB) time slot expires (the ELB window is 2 minutes by default).

Consistency groups can be used to help create a consistent Point-in-Time copy across multiple volumes, and even across multiple DS8000, thus managing the consistency of dependent writes.

Note: Consistency Group FlashCopy for volumes residing in a mixed environment DS6000, DS8000, and/or ESS 800 is currently not supported.

7.4 FlashCopy target and Metro Mirror or Global Copy source

With this option the FlashCopy target volume can also be a primary volume for a Metro Mirror or Global Copy relationship (see Figure 7-3). The FlashCopy relationship can be established before the Metro Mirror relationship or the reverse order could be used.

Note: To properly interpret Figure 7-3, realize that the FlashCopy target volume is the same volume as the Metro Mirror source volume (the double headed red arrow implies they are the same volume).

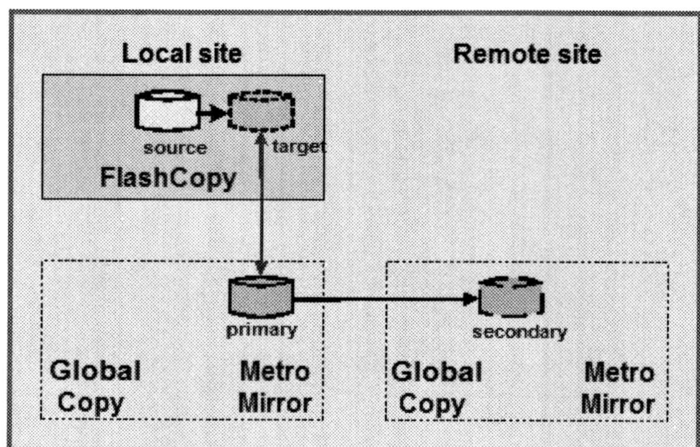

Figure 7-3 FlashCopy on existing Metro Mirror or Global Copy primary

7.5 Incremental FlashCopy (Refresh target volume)

Incremental FlashCopy provides the capability to *refresh* a FlashCopy relationship.

Attention: A refresh of the target volume will always overwrite any writes previously done to the target volume.

In order for an Incremental FlashCopy to be performed, the FlashCopy relationship must first be established with the *Start Change Recording* and *Persistent FlashCopy* options enabled. If *Incremental* FlashCopy is invoked via the ANTRQST API or TSO command, the default is to set the *Write Inhibit* bit and to not allow writes to the *Increment* FlashCopy target volumes.

With Incremental FlashCopy, the initial FlashCopy *copy* or *nocopy* relationship between a source and target volume is maintained.

Note: Incremental FlashCopy is supported at a volume level. It is not available for Data Set FlashCopy.

- **FlashCopy with nocopy option:**

  If the original FlashCopy was established with the *nocopy* option, then the bitmap for the target volume will be reset, and of course, the updates on the target volumes are overwritten. However, using the incremental option will automatically convert this relationship to a COPY relationship, and the background copy will begin.

- **FlashCopy with copy option:**

  If the original FlashCopy was established with the *copy* option (full volume copy), then the updates that took place on the source volume since the last FlashCopy will be copied to the target volume. Also, the updates done on the target volume will be overwritten with the contents of the source volume (Figure 7-4).

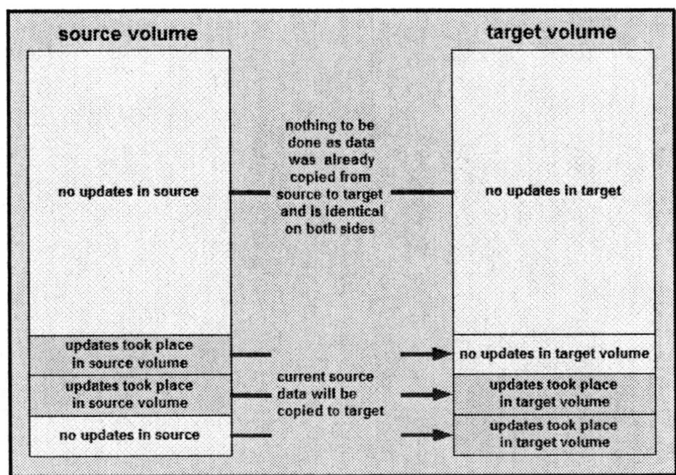

Figure 7-4 Updates to the target volume caused by a refresh target FlashCopy

When initializing a FlashCopy with the Start Change Recording activated, a second and third bitmap will be used to identify writes done to the source or the target volume (see Figure 7-5). All three bitmaps are necessary for incremental FlashCopy:

- Target bitmap: This bitmap keeps track of which tracks have not yet been copied from source to target.
- Source Change Recording bitmap: This bitmap keeps track of changes to the source.
- Target Change Recording bitmap: This bitmap keeps track of changes to the target.

These bitmaps allow subsequent FlashCopies to propagate data for those blocks for which updates occurred on either the source volume or the target volume. Every write operation to the source or target volume will be reflected in this bitmap by setting the corresponding bit to *0*.

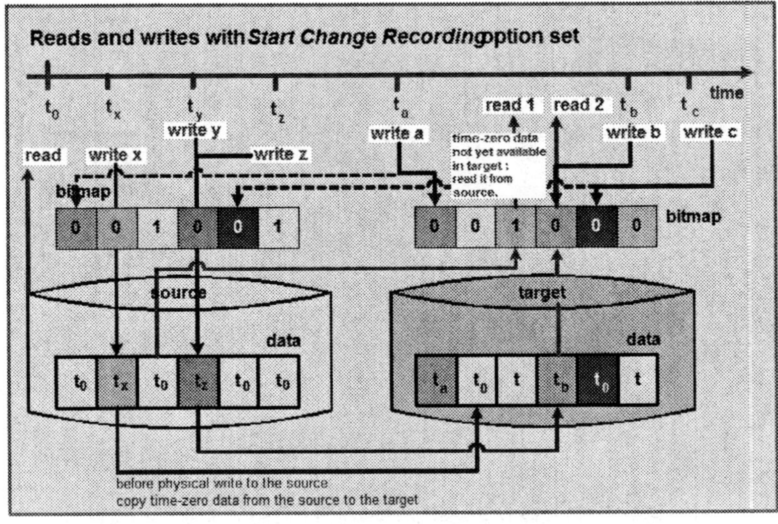

Figure 7-5 FlashCopy with Start Change Recording set

When the *Refresh* takes place, the bitmap used for *change recording* is used to analyze which blocks need to be copied from the source volume to the target volume (see Figure 7-6).

After the *Refresh*, which takes place only on the bitmap level, the new FlashCopy based on time-0' is active. The copy of the time-0'-level of data to the target is done in the background.

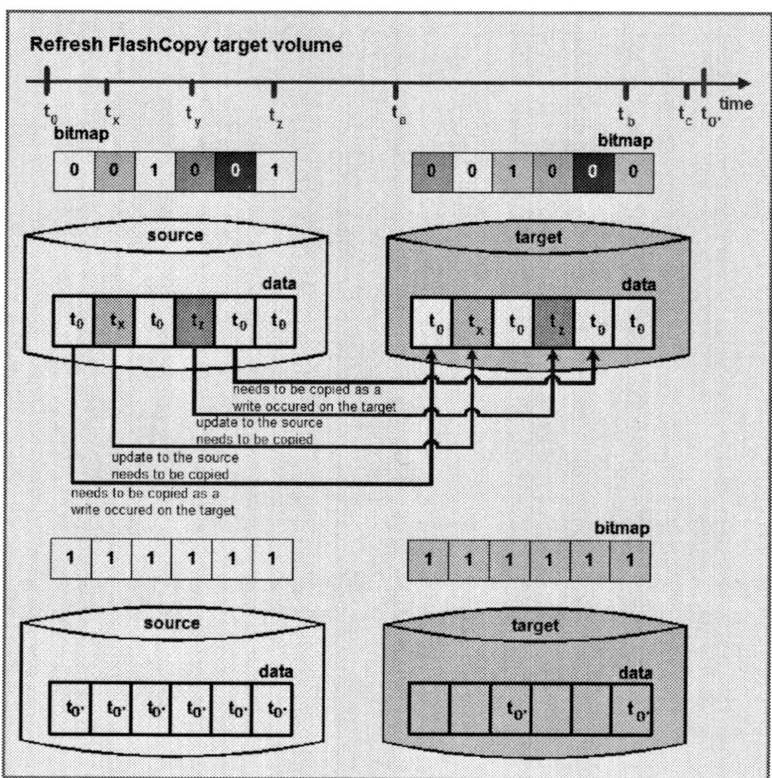

Figure 7-6 Refresh of the FlashCopy target volume

7.6 Remote FlashCopy

There are command interfaces (see Figure 7-1 on page 56) which are able to manage a FlashCopy relationship at a remote site. The commands can be issued from the local site and they are then transmitted over the Metro Mirror or Global Copy links. This eliminates the need for a network connection to the remote site solely for the management of FlashCopy.

The source volume selected for the FlashCopy at the remote site must be the secondary volume of the Metro Mirror or Global Copy pair. The secondary volume becomes the source volume in a FlashCopy pair. See Figure 7-7.

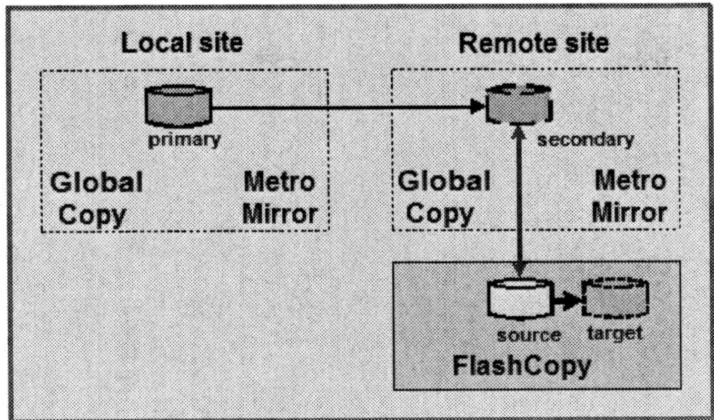

Figure 7-7 Remote FlashCopy

7.7 Persistent FlashCopy

The FlashCopy relationship will continue to exist until explicitly removed by an interface method. If this option is not selected, the FlashCopy relationship will exist until all data has been copied from the source volume to the target.

7.8 Data set FlashCopy

Data set FlashCopy is supported for volumes belonging to the z/OS and OS/390® environments only. This option is supported by the interfaces shown in Figure 7-1 on page 56. These are some characteristics of the Data set FlashCopy:

- The source and target volumes, to which the data set belongs, do not need to be the same size.
- The location within the target volume does not need to match the location within the source volume.
- Data sets can be copied onto the same source volume.
- Multiple relationship FlashCopy is supported with Data set FlashCopy.
- If a Data set FlashCopy relationship, established with DFSMSdss and with the *nocopy* parameter, is deleted, DADSM (the Direct Access Device Space Management component of z/OS) will start a background copy prior to deleting the data set. When all data is copied successfully, the FlashCopy relationship will end and the data set will finally be deleted.

7.9 Reverse restore

With this option the FlashCopy relationship can be reversed by copying over modified tracks from the target volume to the source volume. The background copy process must complete before you can reverse the order of the FlashCopy relationship to its original source and target relationship. Change recording is a pre-requisite for reverse restore.

Based on Figure 7-5, “FlashCopy with Start Change Recording set” on page 59, the bitmaps from source and target are exchanged and then handled as described with Incremental FlashCopy.

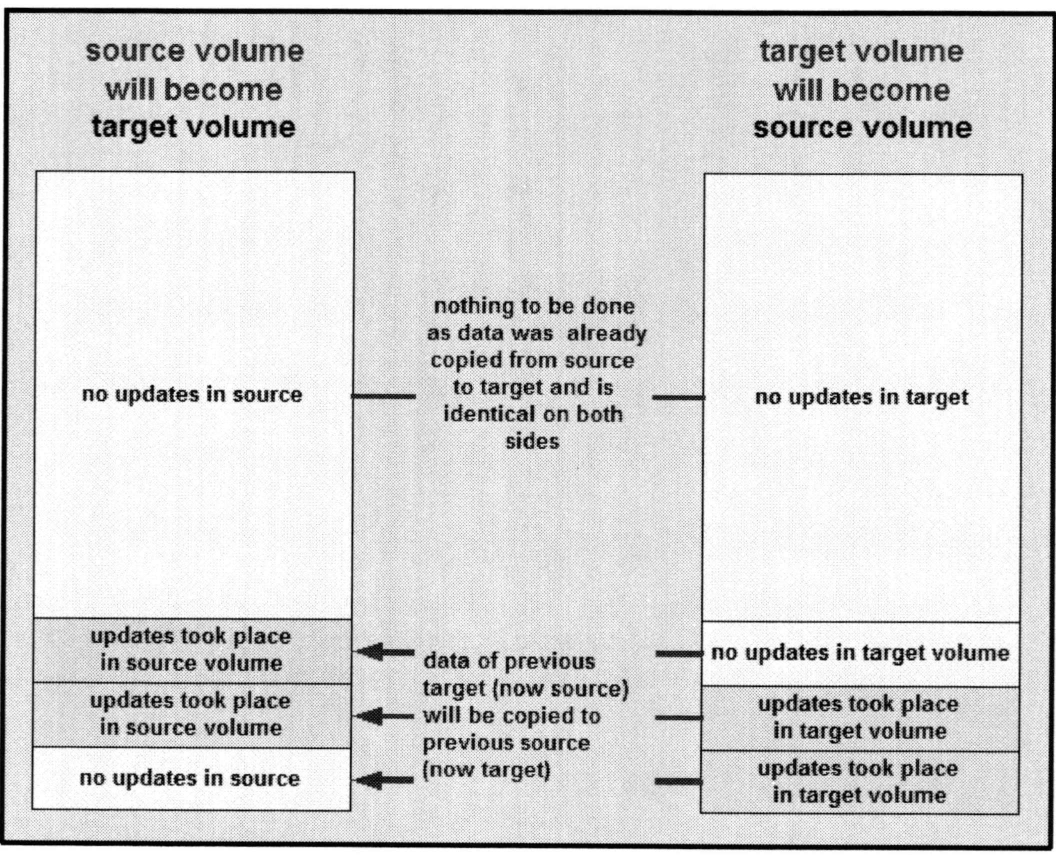

Figure 7-8 Reverse restore

7.10 Fast reverse restore

This option is used with Global Mirror. If you specify this option, you can reverse the FlashCopy relationship without waiting for the completion of the background copy of the previous FlashCopy.

FlashCopy configuration

In this chapter we handle configuration aspects for FlashCopy. These include:

- Planning for FlashCopy
- Activating FlashCopy

8.1 Planning for FlashCopy

FlashCopy is an optional feature of the DS8000 and can be ordered together with the DS8000. You may see that this feature is also called Point-In-Time Copy (PTC).

Once a DS8000 is running in production, it is possible to place an additional order to increase the capacity that can be FlashCopied. This will result in a new feature activation code that needs to be applied.

Note: Applying a new feature activation code that upgrades installed features or capacity is non-disruptive. The deactivation of an activated licensed function, or a lateral change or reduction in the license scope, is a disruptive activity and requires a machine IML (Model 921 and Model 922) or reboot of the affected Storage System LPAR (Model 9A2). A lateral change is defined as changing the license scope from FB to CKD or from CKD to FB. A reduction is defined as changing the license scope from ALL to FB or from ALL to CKD.

During planning of the DS8000 configuration, the capacity ordered for FlashCopy should be reviewed, and after activation of the features, it should be checked to see that it matches the capacity assigned in the DS8000 for FlashCopy.

The capacity to be handled influences the price of the FlashCopy option and can be any combination of the following features; see Table 8-1 and Example 8-1.

Table 8-1 FlashCopy features

Feature	Description
7200	Inactive
7201	PTC - 1 TB
7202	PTC - 5 TB
7203	PTC - 10 TB
7204	PTC - 25 TB
7205	PTC - 50 TB
7210	PTC - 100 TB

Example 8-1 FlashCopy example

```
A DS8000 has a total physical capacity of 15 TB and that capacity will be configured as:
     10 TB open systems (FB)
     5 TB zSeries (CKD)
Then, here's the required licenses:
Operating environment ==> 15 TB (equal to total machine capacity)
Parallel access volumes ==> 5 TB (equal to CKD-configured capacity)
Remote mirror for z/OS ==> 5TB (equal to CKD-configured capacity)

FlashCopy must either be:
     10TB if you want to use FlashCopy only with open systems (FB) data (equal to
FB-configured capacity)
     5TB if you want to use FlashCopy only with zSeries (CKD) data (equal to CKD-configured
capacity)
     15TB if you want to use FlashCopy with both open systems (FB) and zSeries (CKD) data
(equal to total machine capacity)
```

Again, FlashCopy is a separate feature code that can be ordered with the DS8000. The DS8000 does not automatically come with FlashCopy. If you do not order the feature code, you will not be able to use FlashCopy.

8.2 Activating FlashCopy

To prepare the activation of the license key for FlashCopy, an Internet page exists:

```
https://www.ibm.com/storage/dsfa/index.jsp
```

This page can be used to download keyfiles, which then need to be applied to the DS8000. The following information is needed for the download of the keyfile and should be prepared during planning:

- Model:

  The model of the DS8000 can be taken from the order.

- Serial number of the DS8000:

  The serial number of the DS8000 can be taken from the front of the base frame (lower right corner); especially if several machines have been delivered, this is the only way to obtain the serial number of a machine located in a specific point in the computer center.

- Machine signature:

  The machine signature can only be obtained using the DS SM or the DS CLI after installation of the DS8000. In a Web browser enter the URL of the DS HMC, for example:

  ```
  http://10.10.10.10:8452/DS8000
  ```

  On the following window, select on the left side, **Real-time manager** → **Manage hardware** → **Storage units**. In the resulting window, select the Storage Unit you are interested in from the list boxes and click **Select Action** → **Properties** (and **Go**). This displays the properties of the selected DS8000 including the machine signature.

- Order confirmation code:

  The order confirmation code is printed on the DS8000 series order confirmation code document, which is sent to the client's contact person together with the delivery of the machine or prior to delivery.

FlashCopy interfaces

The setup of a DS8000 FlashCopy for a z/OS environment can be done using different environments. It is important to know, right from the beginning, for which purpose the target volume should be used afterwards. Knowing this, the options to be used with the FlashCopy can be identified and the environment can be selected that supports the selected options.

Supported interface environments are:

- DS8000 front ends:
  - DS CLI
  - DS SM
  - DS Open API
- z/OS environment:
  - DFSMSdss
  - TSO
  - ICKDSF
  - ANTRQST

9.1 FlashCopy flow

The interfaces to support FlashCopy for the DS8000 in an z/OS environment are as follows:

- DS8000 interfaces:
  - DS SM: This is a graphical front end running in a Web browser and communicating with the DS Hardware Management Console (HMC).
  - DS CLI: The Command-Line Interface provides various commands that are executed on a supported workstation and communicate with the DS HMC.
  - DS Open API: A set of Application Programming Interfaces are available to be integrated in programs. The communication again takes place with the DS HMC.
- z/OS Interfaces:

  The following z/OS environment and utilities are available:
  - DFSMSdss: This is a z/OS utility that supports Storage Administrators.
  - TSO: This is an interactive environment to perform z/OS specific tasks.
  - ICKDSF: This is a utility.
  - ANTRQST: This is an application programming interface (API).

The FlashCopy flow adheres to the following sequence:

- FlashCopy is initiated by an interface.

  The initialization process of a FlashCopy takes only some seconds. At the end of this process FlashCopy is established based on the given parameters. This means that all the necessary meta structures have been established. No data has yet been copied.
- FlashCopy runs in the background.

  The parameters given at point of initialization identify how FlashCopy will work in the background, once it has been established. They will also identify which subsequent activities can be performed to work with this one FlashCopy.
- FlashCopy terminates.

  FlashCopy either terminates automatically if all tracks have been copied, or needs to be terminated explicitly if it has been defined as persistent.

9.2 Overview of FlashCopy Commands in the DS front ends

This section provides a brief overview of the commands used to manage FlashCopy. FlashCopy commands in the DS CLI are available to support local FlashCopy and remote FlashCopy. The DS SM front end and the DS Open API do not support remote FlashCopy.

9.2.1 Local FlashCopy

The commands or select options used in the DS8000 front ends to work with FlashCopy are listed in Table 9-1.

Table 9-1 Local FlashCopy using DS CLI and DS SM

Command Description	Command with DS CLI	Select option with DS SM
Create a FlashCopy:		
Create a local FlashCopy	mkflash	Create
Work with an existing FlashCopy:		
Display a list of FlashCopy relationships	lsflash	Main panel
Modify a FlashCopy pair that is part of a Global Mirror relationship to revertible	setflashrevertible	Restorable, Record Changes wizard
Commit data to the target volume	commitflash	Commit changes
Increment an existing FlashCopy pair	resyncflash (pre-requisites: -record and -persist)	Resynch target
Change the source-target-relationship A->B to B->A	reverseflash	Reverse relationship
Reestablish contents of target B by contents of source A as it was during last consistency formation	revertflash	Consistency groups currently not supported
Reset a FlashCopy Consistency Group	unfreezeflash	Consistency groups currently not supported
Run new background copy for persistent FlashCopy	rmflash -cp	Background copy
Terminate FlashCopy:		
Remove local FlashCopy	rmflash	Delete
	Is automatically removed as soon as all data is copied and FlashCopy pair wasn't established using the -persist parameter	

9.2.2 Remote FlashCopy

The commands to use FlashCopy remotely using the DS CLI are shown in Table 9-2. Remote FlashCopy is currently not supported with the DS SM or DS Open API front ends.

Table 9-2 Remote FlashCopy using DS CLI commands

Options	Command with DS CLI
Create a FlashCopy:	
Create a remote FlashCopy	mkremoteflash
Work with an existing FlashCopy:	
Display a list of FlashCopy relationships	lsremoteflash
Modify a FlashCopy pair that is part of a Global Mirror relationship to revertible	setremoteflashrevertible
Commit data to the target volume	commitremoteflash
Increment an existing FlashCopy pair	resyncremoteflash (pre-requisites: -record and -persist)
Change the source-target- relationship A->B to B->A	reverseremoteflash
Reestablish contents of target B by contents of source A as it was during last consistency formation	revertremoteflash
Reset a FlashCopy Consistency Group	Not available as remote command
Run new background copy for persistent FlashCopy	rmremoteflash -cp
Terminate FlashCopy:	
Remove local FlashCopy	rmremoteflash
	Is automatically removed as soon as all data is copied and FlashCopy pair wasn't established using the -persist parameter

9.3 Overview of FlashCopy commands in z/OS environment

FlashCopy commands in the z/OS environment are shown in Table 9-3.

Table 9-3 Local FlashCopy using DFSMSdss, TSO, and ICKDSF commands

Options	Command with DFSMSdss	Command with TSO	Command with ICKDSF
Create a FlashCopy:			
Create a volume FlashCopy	COPY FULL	FCESTABL	FLASHCPY ESTABLISH
Create a dataset FlashCopy	COPY DATASET		
Work with an existing FlashCopy:			
Display a list of FlashCopy relationships		FCQUERY	FLASHCPY QUERY RELATION
Relocate dataset extents on a DASD volume	DEFRAG	-	
Provide information why DFSMSdss couldn't use FlashCopy	DEBUG	-	
Terminate FlashCopy:			
Remove local FlashCopy	DUMP with FCWITHDRAW parameter	FCWITHDR	FLASHCPY WITHDRAW
	Is automatically removed as soon as all data is copied and FlashCopy pair wasn't established using the -persist parameter		

9.4 Local FlashCopies using the DS CLI front end

The DS CLI can be downloaded from the IBM Web site and then be installed on a workstation. It communicates with the DS HMC. For a detailed information about the DS CLI, refer to the IBM document, *IBM TotalStorage DS8000 Command-Line Interface User's Guide*, SC26-7625.

9.4.1 Parameters used in local FlashCopy commands

Similar parameters are used in the FlashCopy commands, and are discussed in the following sections. Refer to Figure 9-1 and Table 9-4.

Parameters	DS CLI Commands								
	mkflash	lsflash	setflash revertible	commit flash	resync flash	reverse flash	revert flash	unfreeze flash	rmflash
Source									
freeze	x				x				
Target									
tgtpprc	x				x	x			
tgtoffline	x		x		x	x			
tgtinhibit	x				x	x			
tgtonly									x
Flashcopy pair									
dev	x	x	x	x	x	x	x	x	x
record	x	x			x	x			
persist	x	x			x	x			
nocp	x								
seqnum	x	x	x	x	x	x	x		x
source:target	x	x			x				x
fast						x			
source				x			x		
cp		x							x
source LSS								x	
l		x							
s		x							
activecp		x							
revertible		x							
Command									
wait	x								
quiet									x

Figure 9-1 Overview of parameters used in DS CLI FlashCopy commands

- freeze: Consistency Group FlashCopy.

  With the DS CLI, it is possible to establish a Consistency Group by using the -freeze parameter and identifying all FlashCopy pairs and target volumes belonging to it.

- tgtpprc: Establish target on existing Metro Mirror source.

  When this option is selected, the target volume can be or become a source volume for a Metro Mirror or Global Copy relationship.

- tgtoffline: Permit FlashCopy to occur if target volume is not online for host access.

  When setting up the relationship, it is checked if the target volume is online or not.

Table 9-4 Combinations of volume offline or online and parameter permit target to be online

Status of target volume in z/OS	Permit FlashCopy to occur if target volume is online	Remarks
Volume is online	Not selected	FlashCopy definition is not possible
Volume is online	Selected	FlashCopy definition is queued until target volume goes offline
Volume is offline	Selected or not selected	FlashCopy will be started immediately

- tgtinhibit: Inhibit writes to target volume.

  If FlashCopy is active, writes to the target volume are not allowed (inhibited).

- record: Change recording.

  Activating the option *change recording* during setup of a FlashCopy enables subsequent refreshes to the target volume. To do so a second bitmap is created for the source volume, which keeps track of all writes to the source. This bitmap can later be used to refresh the target by only copying the updates from the source to the target.

- persist: Persistent FlashCopy.

  The FlashCopy relationship will continue to exist until explicitly removed by an interface method. If this option is not selected, the FlashCopy relationship will exist until all data has been copied from the source volume to the target.
- nocp: Full volume background copy.

  With the parameter nocp it is possible to identify if the data of the source volume should be copied to the target volume in the background or not. If -nocp isn't used a copy of all data from source to target takes place in the background. With -nocp selected only updates to the source volume will cause writes to the target volume to save the time-zero data there.
- seqnum: Sequence number for FlashCopy pairs.

  A number that identifies the FlashCopy relationship. Once used with the initial **mkflash** command, it could be used within subsequent commands to refer to multiple FlashCopy relationships.
- source:target: Identification of source volume and target volume.
- fast: Reverse FlashCopy before background copy finished.

  Allows you to issue the **reverseflash** command before the background copy finished.
- cp: Restrict command to FlashCopy relationships with background copy.
- sourceLSS: Reset Consistency Group for source logical subsystems.
- s: Display of FlashCopy pairs with **lsflash** command.

  The shortened output of the **lsflash** command is returned. Only the FlashCopy pair IDs are displayed.
- l: Display additional FlashCopy information.

  The standard output of the **lsflash** command is enhanced. The values for the copy indicator, out of synch tracks, date created, and date synchronized are additionally displayed.
- activecp: Selection of FlashCopy pairs with active background copy.
- revertible: Selection of FlashCopy pairs with revertible attribute.

9.4.2 Local FlashCopy commands

The following commands are supported with DS CLI.

Initiate FlashCopy using mkflash

With **mkflash**, a local FlashCopy can be established. Five coding examples for **mkflash** are shown in Example 9-1. Their meaning is as follows:

- **Example 1: 0001 → 0101**

  The FlashCopy between volume 0001 and volume 0101 is established with the following properties enabled: *BackgroundCopy (default if not specified differently using the -nocp parameter)*. All other properties are disabled. The background copy takes place immediately and once everything has been copied, the FlashCopy relationship will be automatically removed.
- **Example 2: 0003 → 0103**

  The FlashCopy between volume 0003 and volume 0103 is established and the following properties are enabled by default: *BackgroundCopy*, *Recording*, and *Persistent*.

Note: The parameter *-persist* is assumed and added whenever the parameter *-record* is used.

The background copy takes place immediately and the relationship will stay as a persistent relationship. Using other DS CLI commands it could be reversed and/or resynchronized.

- **Example 3: 0004 → 0104**

  The FlashCopy between volume 0004 and volume 0104 is established and the following properties are enabled: *BackgroundCopy* and *Persistent*. All other properties are disabled. The background copy takes place immediately. Once the background copy has finished the FlashCopy relationship will stay due to the persistent flag.

- **Example 4: 0005 → 0105**

  The FlashCopy between volume 0005 and volume 0105 is established and all properties of the FlashCopy relationship will be disabled. Due to the -nocp parameter, no full background copy will be done. Only the data changed in the source will be copied to the target prior to changing it. Over the time this could result in the situation that all data has been copied to the target. Then the FlashCopy relationship would end. It would also end once a background copy is initiated using the DS SM. This way, the relationship is temporarily persistent even though the property *Persistent* is not activated.

Example 9-1 mkflash commands

```
Script
mkflash -dev IBM.2107-7506571         -seqnum 01 0001:0101
Date/Time: July 11, 2005 6:29:51 PM CEST IBM DSCLI Version: 5.0.3.134 DS: IBM.2107-7506571
CMUC00137I mkflash: FlashCopy pair 0001:0101 successfully created.

mkflash -dev IBM.2107-7506571 -record  -seqnum 03 0003:0103
Date/Time: July 11, 2005 6:29:58 PM CEST IBM DSCLI Version: 5.0.3.134 DS: IBM.2107-7506571
CMUC00137I mkflash: FlashCopy pair 0003:0103 successfully created.

mkflash -dev IBM.2107-7506571 -persist -seqnum 04 0004:0104
Date/Time: July 11, 2005 6:30:02 PM CEST IBM DSCLI Version: 5.0.3.134 DS: IBM.2107-7506571
CMUC00137I mkflash: FlashCopy pair 0004:0104 successfully created.

mkflash -dev IBM.2107-7506571 -nocp    -seqnum 05 0005:0105
Date/Time: July 11, 2005 6:30:05 PM CEST IBM DSCLI Version: 5.0.3.134 DS: IBM.2107-7506571
CMUC00137I mkflash: FlashCopy pair 0005:0105 successfully created.

Listing of the properties of the FlashCopies
lsflash -dev IBM.2107-7506571 0000-0005
Date/Time: July 11, 2005 6:30:09 PM CEST IBM DSCLI Version: 5.0.3.134 DS: IBM.2107-7506571
ID        SrcLSS SequenceNum Timeout ActiveCopy Recording Persistent Revertible SourceWriteEnabled TargetWriteEnabled BackgroundCopy
==============================================================================================================================
0001:0101 00     1           300     Disabled   Disabled  Disabled   Disabled   Disabled           Disabled           Enabled
0002:0102 00     2           300     Disabled   Disabled  Disabled   Disabled   Disabled           Disabled           Enabled
0003:0103 00     3           300     Disabled   Enabled   Enabled    Disabled   Disabled           Disabled           Enabled
0004:0104 00     4           300     Disabled   Disabled  Enabled    Disabled   Disabled           Disabled           Enabled
0005:0105 00     5           300     Disabled   Disabled  Disabled   Disabled   Disabled           Disabled           Disabled
```

Display existing FlashCopies using lsflash

The command **lsflash** can be used to display a FlashCopy relationship and its properties. Parameters can be used to identify the subset of relationships to be displayed. Example 9-2 shows a script with several **lsflash** commands and the output of the script. This script is logically based on the example for **mkflash**. Here are the meanings of the various examples:

- Example 1: List all FlashCopies for volume 0004.

This command will display all FlashCopy relationships for volume 0004 using the standard properties to be displayed.

- Example 2: List all FlashCopies for identified volume range.

  This command will display all FlashCopy relationships for volumes 0001 to 0005 using the standard properties to be displayed.

- Example 3: List all FlashCopies for identified volume range, adding properties.

  Using the parameter -l the default output of the **lsflash** command is changed. It contains the additional properties: OutOfSyncTracks, DateCreated, and DateSynced.

- Example 4: List ids of all FlashCopies for identified volume range using -s.

  Using the parameter -s displays only the FlashCopy source and target volume for the range of volumes selected.

- Example 5: List all FlashCopies with background copy running.

  When using the parameter -activecp only those FlashCopy relationships in the range of selected volumes will be displayed for which a background copy is actively running. The output format is the default output.

- Example 6: List all FlashCopies with recording being enabled.

  When using the parameter -activecp only those FlashCopy relationships in the range of selected volumes will be displayed for which a background copy is actively running. The output format is the default output.

- Example 7: List all persistent FlashCopies.

  When using the parameter -persist only those FlashCopy relationships in the range of selected volumes will be displayed for which the property *Persistent* is enabled.

- Example 8: List all FlashCopies that are revertible.

  When using the parameter -revertible only those FlashCopy relationships in the range of selected volumes will be displayed for which the property *Revertible* is enabled.

- Example 9: List all FlashCopies with property BackgroundCopy enabled.

  When using the parameter -cp only those FlashCopy relationships in the range of selected volumes will be displayed for which the property *BackgroundCopy* is enabled.

Example 9-2 lsflash command

```
#--- Example 1
lsflash -dev IBM.2107-7506571 0004
Date/Time: July 11, 2005 6:40:12 PM CEST IBM DSCLI Version: 5.0.3.134 DS: IBM.2107-7506571
ID        SrcLSS SequenceNum Timeout ActiveCopy Recording Persistent Revertible SourceWriteEnabled TargetWriteEnabled BackgroundCopy
==============================================================================================================================
0004 0104 00     4           300     Disabled   Disabled  Enabled    Disabled   Disabled           Disabled           Enabled

#--- Example 2
lsflash -dev IBM.2107-7506571 0001-0005
Date/Time: July 11, 2005 6:40:29 PM CEST IBM DSCLI Version: 5.0.3.134 DS: IBM.2107-7506571
ID        SrcLSS SequenceNum Timeout ActiveCopy Recording Persistent Revertible SourceWriteEnabled TargetWriteEnabled BackgroundCopy
==============================================================================================================================
0003 0103 00     3           300     Disabled   Enabled   Enabled    Disabled   Disabled           Disabled           Enabled
0004 0104 00     4           300     Disabled   Disabled  Enabled    Disabled   Disabled           Disabled           Enabled
0005 0105 00     5           300     Disabled   Disabled  Disabled   Disabled   Disabled           Disabled           Disabled

#--- Example 3
lsflash -dev IBM.2107-7506571 -l 0001-0005
Date/Time: July 11, 2005 6:40:52 PM CEST IBM DSCLI Version: 5.0.3.134 DS: IBM.2107-7506571
ID        SrcLSS SequenceNum Timeout ActiveCopy Recording Persistent Revertible SourceWriteEnabled TargetWriteEnabled
BackgroundCopy OutOfSyncTracks DateCreated                  DateSynced
==================================================================================================================
==========================================================================
```

```
0003:0103 00      3            300      Disabled    Enabled    Enabled     Disabled    Disabled          Disabled
Enabled         0                Mon Jul 11 19:30:06 CEST 2005 Mon Jul 11 19:30:06 CEST 2005
0004:0104 00      4            300      Disabled    Disabled   Enabled     Disabled    Disabled          Disabled
Enabled         0                Mon Jul 11 19:30:10 CEST 2005 Mon Jul 11 19:30:10 CEST 2005
0005:0105 00      5            300      Disabled    Disabled   Disabled    Disabled    Disabled          Disabled
Disabled        50085            Mon Jul 11 19:30:13 CEST 2005 Mon Jul 11 19:30:13 CEST 2005

#--- Example 4
lsflash -dev IBM.2107-7506571 -s 0001-0005
Date/Time: July 11, 2005 6:40:59 PM CEST IBM DSCLI Version: 5.0.3.134 DS: IBM.2107-7506571
ID
=========
0003:0103
0004:0104
0005:0105

#--- Example 5
lsflash -dev IBM.2107-7506571 -activecp 0001-0004
Date/Time: July 11, 2005 6:41:02 PM CEST IBM DSCLI Version: 5.0.3.134 DS: IBM.2107-7506571

#--- Example 6
lsflash -dev IBM.2107-7506571 -record 0001-0004
Date/Time: July 11, 2005 6:41:08 PM CEST IBM DSCLI Version: 5.0.3.134 DS: IBM.2107-7506571
ID        SrcLSS SequenceNum Timeout ActiveCopy Recording Persistent Revertible SourceWriteEnabled TargetWriteEnabled BackgroundCopy
=================================================================================================================================
0003:0103 00     3           300     Disabled   Enabled   Enabled    Disabled   Disabled           Disabled           Enabled

#--- Example 7
lsflash -dev IBM.2107-7506571 -persist 0001-0004
Date/Time: July 11, 2005 6:41:15 PM CEST IBM DSCLI Version: 5.0.3.134 DS: IBM.2107-7506571
ID        SrcLSS SequenceNum Timeout ActiveCopy Recording Persistent Revertible SourceWriteEnabled TargetWriteEnabled BackgroundCopy
=================================================================================================================================
0003:0103 00     3           300     Disabled   Enabled   Enabled    Disabled   Disabled           Disabled           Enabled
0004:0104 00     4           300     Disabled   Disabled  Enabled    Disabled   Disabled           Disabled           Enabled

#--- Example 8
lsflash -dev IBM.2107-7506571 -revertible 0001-0004
Date/Time: July 11, 2005 6:41:22 PM CEST IBM DSCLI Version: 5.0.3.134 DS: IBM.2107-7506571

#--- Example 9
lsflash -dev IBM.2107-7506571 -cp 0001-0004
Date/Time: July 11, 2005 6:41:32 PM CEST IBM DSCLI Version: 5.0.3.134 DS: IBM.2107-7506571
ID        SrcLSS SequenceNum Timeout ActiveCopy Recording Persistent Revertible SourceWriteEnabled TargetWriteEnabled BackgroundCopy
=================================================================================================================================
0003:0103 00     3           300     Disabled   Enabled   Enabled    Disabled   Disabled           Disabled           Enabled
0004:0104 00     4           300     Disabled   Disabled  Enabled    Disabled   Disabled           Disabled           Enabled
```

Set an existing FlashCopy to revertible using setflashrevertible

The command **setflashrevertible** can be used to modify the *revertible* property of the FlashCopy relationship that is part of a Global Mirror relationship. The properties *Recording* and *Persistent* FlashCopy must be enabled to set a FlashCopy relationship to revertible using this command. This command needs to be executed prior to running a **commitflash** or **revertflash**. The following examples refer to those displayed for **mkflash** and **lsflash;** see Example 9-2 and Example 9-3 for the coding.

- Example 1: Set the FlashCopy relationship to revertible.

  This command will set the FlashCopy existing for source volume 0002 and target volume 0102 to revertible. Once the property *Revertible* is enabled, any subsequent commands will result in an error message similar to the one displayed in example 2.

- Example 2: Error occurs when trying to set FlashCopy relationship to revertible.

  When trying to set a FlashCopy relationship to revertible for which the property *Recording* is disabled, an error will result. The script will end after this command with return code 2 and any other commands following the one that causes the error will not be executed.

Example 9-3 setflashrevertible commands

```
#---------------------------------------------------------------
#--- script to set FlashCopy property Revertible to value enabled and display values afterwards
#---------------------------------------------------------------
#--- Example 1
setflashrevertible -dev IBM.2107-7506571 0002:0102
Date/Time: July 11, 2005 9:34:21 PM CEST IBM DSCLI Version: 5.0.3.134 DS: IBM.2107-7506571
CMUC00167I setflashrevertible: FlashCopy volume pair 0002:0102 successfully made revertible.
lsflash -dev IBM.2107-7506571 0000-0004
Date/Time: July 11, 2005 9:34:25 PM CEST IBM DSCLI Version: 5.0.3.134 DS: IBM.2107-7506571
ID        SrcLSS SequenceNum Timeout ActiveCopy Recording Persistent Revertible SourceWriteEnabled TargetWriteEnabled BackgroundCopy
==============================================================================================================================
0002:0102 00     0           300     Disabled   Enabled   Enabled    Enabled    Enabled            Disabled           Enabled

#--- Example 2
setflashrevertible -dev IBM.2107-7506571 0003:0103
Date/Time: July 11, 2005 9:53:07 PM CEST IBM DSCLI Version: 5.0.3.134 DS: IBM.2107-7506571
CMUN03027E setflashrevertible: 0003:0103: FlashCopy operation failure: action prohibited by current FlashCopy state
```

Commit data to target using commitflash

The command **commitflash** can be used to commit data to a target volume to form a consistency between source and target. It is intended to be used in asynchronous remote copy environments, such as Global Mirror. Therefore, its usage is discussed in greater detail in Part 6, "Global Mirror" on page 233. This section only discusses the basic usage of the command. Before the FlashCopy relationship can be committed, it needs to be made revertible. Typically, this is done automatically by an application such as Global Mirror. However, it can also be set manually. See Example 9-4.

- Example 1: Commit the FlashCopy relationship.

  This example shows the properties of the two FlashCopy relationships 0001:0101 and 0005:0105 using the lsflash command prior and after using the **setflashrevertible** command. After the **commitflash** command is executed the properties of the two FlashCopy relationships are listed again.

- Example 2: Error occurs when trying to commit FlashCopy relationship.

  When trying to commit a FlashCopy relationship that isn't revertible (property *Revertible* is disabled) an error will be the result. The script will end after this command with return code 2 and any other commands following the one that causes the error will not be executed.

Example 9-4 commit commands

```
#--- Example 1
lsflash -dev IBM.2107-7506571 0000-0005
Date/Time: July 11, 2005 10:29:29 PM CEST IBM DSCLI Version: 5.0.3.134 DS: IBM.2107-7506571
ID        SrcLSS SequenceNum Timeout ActiveCopy Recording Persistent Revertible SourceWriteEnabled TargetWriteEnabled BackgroundCopy
==============================================================================================================================
0001:0101 00     1           300     Disabled   Enabled   Enabled    Disabled   Disabled           Disabled           Enabled
0005:0105 00     1           300     Disabled   Enabled   Enabled    Disabled   Disabled           Disabled           Enabled
setflashrevertible -dev IBM.2107-7506571 -seqnum 01 0001:0101 0005:0105
Date/Time: July 11, 2005 10:29:35 PM CEST IBM DSCLI Version: 5.0.3.134 DS: IBM.2107-7506571
CMUC00167I setflashrevertible: FlashCopy volume pair 0001:0101 successfully made revertible.
CMUC00167I setflashrevertible: FlashCopy volume pair 0005:0105 successfully made revertible.
lsflash -dev IBM.2107-7506571 0000-0005
Date/Time: July 11, 2005 10:29:39 PM CEST IBM DSCLI Version: 5.0.3.134 DS: IBM.2107-7506571
ID        SrcLSS SequenceNum Timeout ActiveCopy Recording Persistent Revertible SourceWriteEnabled TargetWriteEnabled BackgroundCopy
==============================================================================================================================
0001:0101 00     1           300     Disabled   Enabled   Enabled    Enabled    Enabled            Disabled           Enabled
0005:0105 00     1           300     Disabled   Enabled   Enabled    Enabled    Enabled            Disabled           Enabled
commitflash -dev IBM.2107-7506571 0001-0005
Date/Time: July 11, 2005 10:29:45 PM CEST IBM DSCLI Version: 5.0.3.134 DS: IBM.2107-7506571
CMUC00170I commitflash: FlashCopy volume pair 0001:0001 successfully committed.
CMUC00170I commitflash: FlashCopy volume pair 0005:0005 successfully committed.
lsflash -dev IBM.2107-7506571 -l 0000-0005
Date/Time: July 11, 2005 10:36:19 PM CEST IBM DSCLI Version: 5.0.3.134 DS: IBM.2107-7506571
ID        SrcLSS SequenceNum Timeout ActiveCopy Recording Persistent Revertible SourceWriteEnabled TargetWriteEnabled BackgroundCopy
==============================================================================================================================
0001:0101 00     1           300     Disabled   Enabled   Enabled    Disabled   Disabled           Enabled            Disabled
0005:0105 00     1           300     Disabled   Enabled   Enabled    Disabled   Disabled           Enabled            Disabled
```

```
#--- Example 2
commitflash -dev IBM.2107-7506571 0003:0103
CMUN03027E commitflash: 0003:0003: FlashCopy operation failure: action prohibited by current FlashCopy state
```

Incremental FlashCopy using resyncflash

With the command **resyncflash**, an existing FlashCopy relationship can be incremented. To run this command, the FlashCopy relationship must have the properties *Recording* and *Persistent* enabled. To make sure an existing FlashCopy relationship can be incremented multiple times, it is necessary to repeat the *-record* and *-persist* parameters with the **resyncflash** command; see Example 9-5.

- Example 1: Increment a FlashCopy relationship.

  In this example, three FlashCopy relationships are created with the *-record* and *-persist* parameters. The **resyncflash** commands are executed using a different sequence number, which overwrites the one of the current FlashCopy relationship. The sequence number only changes if the **resyncflash** finishes successfully. The **resyncflash** for the 0001:01001 and 0005:0105 relationships take place using the *-record* and *-persist* parameter. Because the two parameters are omitted for the 0003:0103 FlashCopy relationship the two properties *Recording* and *Persistent* change to disabled for this FlashCopy relationship. As soon the background copy for this 0003:0103 FlashCopy relationship finishes the FlashCopy relationship will terminate.

- Example 2: Error occurs when trying to increment FlashCopy relationship.

  When trying to increment a FlashCopy relationship for which the properties *Recording* and *Persistent* are disabled an error will be the result. The script will end after this command with return code 2 and any other commands following the one that caused the error will not be executed.

Example 9-5 resyncflash commands

```
#--- Example 1
mkflash -dev IBM.2107-7506571 -record -persist -seqnum 01 0001:0101 0005:0105
Date/Time: July 11, 2005 10:47:34 PM CEST IBM DSCLI Version: 5.0.3.134 DS: IBM.2107-7506571
CMUC00137I mkflash: FlashCopy pair 0001:0101 successfully created.
CMUC00137I mkflash: FlashCopy pair 0005:0105 successfully created.
mkflash -dev IBM.2107-7506571 -record -seqnum 03 0003:0103
Date/Time: July 11, 2005 10:47:37 PM CEST IBM DSCLI Version: 5.0.3.134 DS: IBM.2107-7506571
CMUC00137I mkflash: FlashCopy pair 0003:0103 successfully created.
lsflash -dev IBM.2107-7506571 0000-0005
Date/Time: July 11, 2005 10:47:41 PM CEST IBM DSCLI Version: 5.0.3.134 DS: IBM.2107-7506571
ID        SrcLSS SequenceNum Timeout ActiveCopy Recording Persistent Revertible SourceWriteEnabled TargetWriteEnabled BackgroundCopy
=================================================================================================================================
0001:0101 00     1           300     Disabled   Enabled   Enabled    Disabled   Disabled           Disabled           Enabled
0003:0103 00     3           300     Disabled   Enabled   Enabled    Disabled   Disabled           Disabled           Enabled
0005:0105 00     1           300     Disabled   Enabled   Enabled    Disabled   Disabled           Disabled           Enabled
resyncflash -dev IBM.2107-7506571 -record -persist -seqnum 11 0001:0101 0005:0105
Date/Time: July 11, 2005 10:47:55 PM CEST IBM DSCLI Version: 5.0.3.134 DS: IBM.2107-7506571
CMUC00168I resyncflash: FlashCopy volume pair 0001:0101 successfully resynchronized.
CMUC00168I resyncflash: FlashCopy volume pair 0005:0105 successfully resynchronized.
resyncflash -dev IBM.2107-7506571 seqnum 13 0003:0103
Date/Time: July 11, 2005 10:48:00 PM CEST IBM DSCLI Version: 5.0.3.134 DS: IBM.2107-7506571
CMUC00168I resyncflash: FlashCopy volume pair 0003:0103 successfully resynchronized.
lsflash -dev IBM.2107-7506571 0000-0005
Date/Time: July 11, 2005 10:48:04 PM CEST IBM DSCLI Version: 5.0.3.134 DS: IBM.2107-7506571
ID        SrcLSS SequenceNum Timeout ActiveCopy Recording Persistent Revertible SourceWriteEnabled TargetWriteEnabled BackgroundCopy
=================================================================================================================================
0001:0101 00     11          300     Disabled   Enabled   Enabled    Disabled   Disabled           Disabled           Enabled
0003:0103 00     13          300     Disabled   Disabled  Disabled   Disabled   Disabled           Disabled           Enabled
0005:0105 00     11          300     Disabled   Enabled   Enabled    Disabled   Disabled           Disabled           Enabled

#--- Example 2
mkflash -dev IBM.2107-7506571 -nocp -seqnum 03 0004:0104
Date/Time: July 11, 2005 11:01:41 PM CEST IBM DSCLI Version: 5.0.3.134 DS: IBM.2107-7506571
CMUC00137I mkflash: FlashCopy pair 0004:0104 successfully created.
lsflash -dev IBM.2107-7506571 0004
Date/Time: July 11, 2005 11:01:45 PM CEST IBM DSCLI Version: 5.0.3.134 DS: IBM.2107-7506571
ID        SrcLSS SequenceNum Timeout ActiveCopy Recording Persistent Revertible SourceWriteEnabled TargetWriteEnabled BackgroundCopy
=================================================================================================================================
```

```
0004:0104 00     3          300      Disabled   Disabled  Disabled   Disabled   Disabled          Disabled          Disabled
resyncflash -dev IBM.2107-7506571 -record -persist -seqnum 14 0004:0104
Date/Time: July 11, 2005 11:01:58 PM CEST IBM DSCLI Version: 5.0.3.134 DS: IBM.2107-7506571
CMUN03027E resyncflash: 0004:0104: FlashCopy operation failure: action prohibited by current FlashCopy state
```

Reverse source-target relationship using reverseflash

The command **reverseflash** can be used to change the direction of the FlashCopy relationship. The former source becomes target and the former target becomes source. The data is copied from the target to the source; see Example 9-6.

- Example 1: Reverse a FlashCopy relationship.

  In this example, three FlashCopy relationships are created with the *-record* and *-persist* parameters. The **reverseflash** commands are executed using a different sequence number, which overwrites the one of the current FlashCopy relationship. The **reverseflash** for the 0001:0101 and 0005:0105 relationships take place using the *-record* and *-persist* parameter. Because the two parameters are omitted for the 0003:0103 FlashCopy relationship the two properties *Recording* and *Persistent* change to disabled for this FlashCopy relationship. This will terminate the 0003:0103 FlashCopy relationship as soon it is successfully reversed.

- Example 2: Reverse a FlashCopy relationship multiple times.

  It is possible to reverse a FlashCopy relationship multiple times, thus recopying the contents of the original FlashCopy target volume multiple times back to the original source volume. In this example the 0002:0102 was reversed once as part of example 1. Then changes are done to data residing on volume 0002. A subsequent **reverseflash** for 0002:0102 eliminates the changes done to 0002 and brings back the data from volume 0102 to volume 0002 as it was during the initial FlashCopy.

- Example 3: Reestablish original FlashCopy direction, reversing again.

  It is possible to reverse a FlashCopy relationship back again. In example 3 this is shown for the reversed FlashCopy relationship 0102:0002. Reversing it a second time and referring to it as FlashCopy pair 0102:0002 is similar to establishing a new FlashCopy for the volume pair 0002:0102. In this case a sequence number provided with the **reverseflash** is used to identify a new FlashCopy relationship.

Example 9-6 reverseflash commands

```
#--- Example 1
lsflash -dev IBM.2107-7506571 0000-0005
Date/Time: July 11, 2005 11:28:33 PM CEST IBM DSCLI Version: 5.0.3.134 DS: IBM.2107-7506571
ID        SrcLSS SequenceNum Timeout ActiveCopy Recording Persistent Revertible SourceWriteEnabled TargetWriteEnabled BackgroundCopy
===================================================================================================================================
0001 0101 00     1           300     Disabled   Enabled   Enabled    Disabled   Disabled           Disabled           Enabled
0002 0102 00     2           300     Disabled   Enabled   Enabled    Disabled   Disabled           Disabled           Enabled
0003 0103 00     3           300     Disabled   Enabled   Enabled    Disabled   Disabled           Disabled           Enabled
0005 0105 00     1           300     Disabled   Enabled   Enabled    Disabled   Disabled           Disabled           Enabled
reverseflash -dev IBM.2107-7506571 -record -persist 0001:0101 0005:0105
Date/Time: July 11, 2005 11:33:21 PM CEST IBM DSCLI Version: 5.0.3.134 DS: IBM.2107-7506571
CMUC00169I reverseflash: FlashCopy volume pair 0001:0101 successfully reversed.
CMUC00169I reverseflash: FlashCopy volume pair 0005:0105 successfully reversed.
reverseflash -dev IBM.2107-7506571 -record 0002:0102
Date/Time: July 11, 2005 11:33:27 PM CEST IBM DSCLI Version: 5.0.3.134 DS: IBM.2107-7506571
CMUC00169I reverseflash: FlashCopy volume pair 0002:0102 successfully reversed.
reverseflash -dev IBM.2107-7506571 0003:0103
Date/Time: July 11, 2005 11:33:33 PM CEST IBM DSCLI Version: 5.0.3.134 DS: IBM.2107-7506571
CMUC00169I reverseflash: FlashCopy volume pair 0003:0103 successfully reversed.
lsflash -dev IBM.2107-7506571 0000-0005
Date/Time: July 11, 2005 11:33:37 PM CEST IBM DSCLI Version: 5.0.3.134 DS: IBM.2107-7506571
ID        SrcLSS SequenceNum Timeout ActiveCopy Recording Persistent Revertible SourceWriteEnabled TargetWriteEnabled BackgroundCopy
===================================================================================================================================
0101 0001 01     1           300     Disabled   Enabled   Enabled    Disabled   Disabled           Disabled           Enabled
0102 0002 01     2           300     Disabled   Enabled   Enabled    Disabled   Disabled           Disabled           Enabled
0103 0003 01     3           300     Disabled   Disabled  Disabled   Disabled   Disabled           Disabled           Enabled
0105 0005 01     1           300     Disabled   Enabled   Enabled    Disabled   Disabled           Disabled           Enabled

#--- Example 2
```

```
reverseflash -dev IBM.2107-7506571 -record 0002:0102
Date/Time: July 11, 2005 11:42:17 PM CEST IBM DSCLI Version: 5.0.3.134 DS: IBM.2107-7506571
CMUC00169I reverseflash: FlashCopy volume pair 0002:0102 successfully reversed.
lsflash -dev IBM.2107-7506571 0002
Date/Time: July 11, 2005 11:42:30 PM CEST IBM DSCLI Version: 5.0.3.134 DS: IBM.2107-7506571
ID        SrcLSS SequenceNum Timeout ActiveCopy Recording Persistent Revertible SourceWriteEnabled TargetWriteEnabled BackgroundCopy
=================================================================================================================================
0102:0002 01     2           300     Disabled   Enabled   Enabled    Disabled   Disabled           Disabled           Enabled

#--- Example 3
reverseflash -dev IBM.2107-7506571 -seqnum 12 -record 0102:0002
Date/Time: July 11, 2005 11:46:34 PM CEST IBM DSCLI Version: 5.0.3.134 DS: IBM.2107-7506571
CMUC00169I reverseflash: FlashCopy volume pair 0102:0002 successfully reversed.
lsflash -dev IBM.2107-7506571 0002
Date/Time: July 11, 2005 11:46:39 PM CEST IBM DSCLI Version: 5.0.3.134 DS: IBM.2107-7506571
ID        SrcLSS SequenceNum Timeout ActiveCopy Recording Persistent Revertible SourceWriteEnabled TargetWriteEnabled BackgroundCopy
=================================================================================================================================
0002:0102 00     12          300     Disabled   Enabled   Enabled    Disabled   Disabled           Disabled           Enabled
```

Reset target to contents of last consistency point using revertflash

The command **revertflash** can be used to reset the target volume to the contents of the last consistency point. Like the **commitflash** command, this command is intended to be used in asynchronous environments like Global Mirror environments. Before this command can be issued, the relationship must be made revertible, either automatically as with Global Mirror, or manually using the **setrevertible** command. See Example 9-7.

- Example 1: Revert a FlashCopy relationship.

  In this example, three FlashCopy relationships are created for one source volume: 0001:0101, 0001:0104 and 0105. The **revertflash** command is executed for source 0001 and as the FlashCopy relationship 0001:0101 has the Recording and Persistent property enabled this command refers to this FlashCopy relationship 0001:0101. Any updates done to volume 0101 will be overwritten.

Example 9-7 revertflash commands

```
#--- Example 1
mkflash -dev IBM.2107-7506571 -record -persist  -seqnum 01 0001:0101
Date/Time: July 12, 2005 12:12:20 AM CEST IBM DSCLI Version: 5.0.3.134 DS: IBM.2107-7506571
CMUC00137I mkflash: FlashCopy pair 0001:0101 successfully created.
mkflash -dev IBM.2107-7506571 -nocp -seqnum 04 0001:0104 0001:0105
Date/Time: July 12, 2005 12:12:23 AM CEST IBM DSCLI Version: 5.0.3.134 DS: IBM.2107-7506571
CMUC00137I mkflash: FlashCopy pair 0001:0104 successfully created.
CMUC00137I mkflash: FlashCopy pair 0001:0105 successfully created.
lsflash -dev IBM.2107-7506571 0000-0005
Date/Time: July 12, 2005 12:12:27 AM CEST IBM DSCLI Version: 5.0.3.134 DS: IBM.2107-7506571
ID        SrcLSS SequenceNum Timeout ActiveCopy Recording Persistent Revertible SourceWriteEnabled TargetWriteEnabled BackgroundCopy
=================================================================================================================================
0001:0101 00     1           300     Disabled   Enabled   Enabled    Disabled   Disabled           Disabled           Enabled
0001:0104 00     4           300     Disabled   Disabled  Disabled   Disabled   Disabled           Disabled           Disabled
0001:0105 00     4           300     Disabled   Disabled  Disabled   Disabled   Disabled           Disabled           Disabled
setflashrevertible -dev IBM.2107-7506571 0001:0101
Date/Time: July 12, 2005 12:12:34 AM CEST IBM DSCLI Version: 5.0.3.134 DS: IBM.2107-7506571
CMUC00167I setflashrevertible: FlashCopy volume pair 0001:0101 successfully made revertible.
revertflash -dev IBM.2107-7506571 0001
Date/Time: July 12, 2005 12:12:44 AM CEST IBM DSCLI Version: 5.0.3.134 DS: IBM.2107-7506571
CMUC00171I revertflash: FlashCopy volume pair 0001:0001 successfully reverted.
```

Run new background copy for persistent FlashCopy using rmflash

Additional background copies for persistent FlashCopy relationships can be created using the **rmflash** command in combination with its *-cp* parameter; see Example 9-8.

- Example 1: Create new background copy of a persistent FlashCopy relationship.

  In this example the existing FlashCopy relationship 0001:0101 is used to create a new background copy.

Example 9-8 rmflash commands to create new background copy

```
#--- Example 1
rmflash -dev IBM.2107-7506571 -quiet -cp 0001:0101
Date/Time: July 12, 2005 12:19:29 AM CEST IBM DSCLI Version: 5.0.3.134 DS: IBM.2107-7506571
CMUC00143I rmflash: Background copy process for FlashCopy pair 0001:0101 successfully started. The
persistent relationship will not be
removed.
```

Remove local FlashCopy using rmflash

The command **rmflash** can be used to remove a FlashCopy relationship. Differently to most other commands, it doesn't return an error if the request runs for a FlashCopy relationship that doesn't exist. In scripts it should always be used with the *-quiet* parameter to avoid the confirmation prompt; see Example 9-9.

- Example 1: Remove a FlashCopy relationship

  In this example the existing FlashCopy relationship 0001:0101 is removed.

Example 9-9 revertflash commands

```
#--- Example 1
rmflash -dev IBM.2107-7506571 -quiet 0001:0101
Date/Time: July 12, 2005 12:22:06 AM CEST IBM DSCLI Version: 5.0.3.134 DS: IBM.2107-7506571
CMUC00140I rmflash: FlashCopy pair 0001:0101 successfully
removed.
```

9.4.3 FlashCopy Consistency Groups

Typically, large applications such as databases have their data spread across several volumes. In order to create a consistent copy or backup, the volumes should all be FlashCopied at exactly the same point-in-time. FlashCopy Consistency Groups are designed to achieve this exact purpose.

Create FlashCopy Consistency Groups using mkflash

Use the **mkflash** command with the *-freeze* parameter in order to create a FlashCopy Consistency Group. This command causes the DS8000 to briefly prevent I/O to the volumes in the Consistency Group. During this time, any I/O that comes from the host will be returned with a SCSI queue full error, which the host bus adapter will automatically retry. However, if the I/O is frozen for an extended period of time, there will be application errors on the host. For this reason, the Consistency Group should be unfrozen as quickly as possible.

Example 9-10 illustrates the creation of a FlashCopy Consistency Group that contains two FlashCopy pairs.

Example 9-10 Creating FlashCopy Consistency Groups

```
dscl > mkflash -dev IBM.2107-7506571 -freeze 1500-1501:1502-1503
Date Time: October 24, 2005 3:37:49 AM PDT IBM DSCLI Version: 5.0.5.6 DS: IBM.2107-7506571
CMUC00137I mkflash: FlashCopy pair 1500:1502 successfully created.
CMUC00137I mkflash: FlashCopy pair 1501:1503 successfully created.
```

Reset FlashCopy Consistency Group using unfreezeflash

The command **unfreezeflash** can be used to remove a Consistency Group for multiple volumes, for which FlashCopy relations were established using the *-freeze* parameter. This command removes the queue full condition and allows I/Os to continue on the source volumes. The **unfreezeflash** command is issued to the entire logical subsystem (LSS). See Example 9-11.

Example 9-11 unfreezeflash command

```
#--- Example 1
unfreezeflash -dev IBM.2107-7506571/00
Date/Time: July 12, 2005 12:27:06 AM CEST IBM DSCLI Version: 5.0.3.134 DS: IBM.2107-7506571
CMUC00172I unfreezeflash: FlashCopy consistency group for logical subsystem 00: successfully reset.
```

9.5 Remote FlashCopies using the DS CLI front end

The structure of the remote FlashCopy commands is similar to the ones for a local FlashCopy. The remote commands can be issued whenever a DS8000 mirroring takes place from one DS8000 to another DS8000. Then the FC links between two DS8000 that are used for mirroring purposes are used to run the FlashCopy commands on the remote DS8000. For detailed information about the DS CLI, refer to the IBM publication, *IBM TotalStorage DS8000 Command-Line Interface User's Guide*, SC26-7625.

9.5.1 Parameters used in remote FlashCopy commands

Most of the parameters for remote FlashCopy commands are similar to those for local FlashCopy commands. Two major exceptions between local FlashCopy and remote FlashCopy commands exist:

- Each remote command has the parameter *conduit* to identify the link to pass the command to the secondary DS8000.
- The local FlashCopy command **unfreezeflash** has no remote equivalent.

The description of the parameters that are the same for local FlashCopy and Remote FlashCopy can be found in 9.4.1, "Parameters used in local FlashCopy commands" on page 71. See Figure 9-2.

Parameters	DS CLI Commands							
	mkremote flash	lsremote flash	setremote flash revertible	commit remote flash	resync remote flash	reverse remote flash	revert remote flash	rmflash
Source								
freeze	x				x			
Target								
tgtpprc	x				x	x		
tgtoffline	x		x		x	x		
tgtinhibit	x				x	x		
tgtonly								x
Flashcopy pair								
dev	x	x	x	x	x	x	x	x
record	x	x			x	x		
persist	x	x			x	x		
nocp	x							
seqnum	x	x	x	x	x	x	x	x
source:target	x	x			x			x
fast						x		
source				x			x	
cp		x						x
source LSS								
l		x						
s		x						
activecp		x						
revertible		x						
Command								
conduit	x	x	x	x	x	x	x	x
quiet								x

Figure 9-2 Overview of parameters used in DS CLI FlashCopy commands

- conduit: Path to be used to transmit the remote command:

  In a remote mirror environment, FlashCopy commands are sent across mirror paths without the need for a network connection to the remote site solely for the management of FlashCopy. The conduit identifies the path to be used as the carrying path for the commands to the remote site.

9.5.2 Remote FlashCopy commands

The syntax of the remote FlashCopy commands is similar to the one for the local FlashCopy commands. Comparing the names of the commands gives us the results in Table 9-5.

Table 9-5 Command names for local and remote FlashCopy

Local Command	Remote Command	Remarks
mkflash	mkremoteflash	Establish FlashCopy
lsflash	lsremoteflash	List FlashCopy
setflashrevertible	setremoteflashrevertible	Set FlashCopy to revertible
commitflash	commitremoteflash	Commit FlashCopy on target
resyncflash	resyncremoteflash	Increment FlashCopy
reverseflash	reverseremoteflash	Switch source-target
revertflash	revertremoteflash	Reset to last consistency point
unfreezeflash	-	Reset Consistency Group
rmflash	rmremoteflash	Remove FlashCopy

9.6 Local FlashCopies using the DS SM front end

To use the DS SM front end GUI, a supported Web Browser needs to be installed on the workstation. The DS SM communicates with the DS HMC to support administrative tasks to be performed.

To use the DS SM, enter the DS HMC IP address in your Web browser as shown in Example 9-12. The password is set up by the administrator and needs to be changed during the first use of the DS SM.

Example 9-12 Starting DS SM

```
https://<ip-address>:8452/DS8000
```

9.6.1 Initiate FlashCopy using Create

After you login to the DS SM, select **Real-time manager** on the left, then **FlashCopy**. Identify the DS8000 for which you would like to initiate a FlashCopy. From the **Select Action** box, select **Create** and click **Go** to continue. See Figure 9-3.

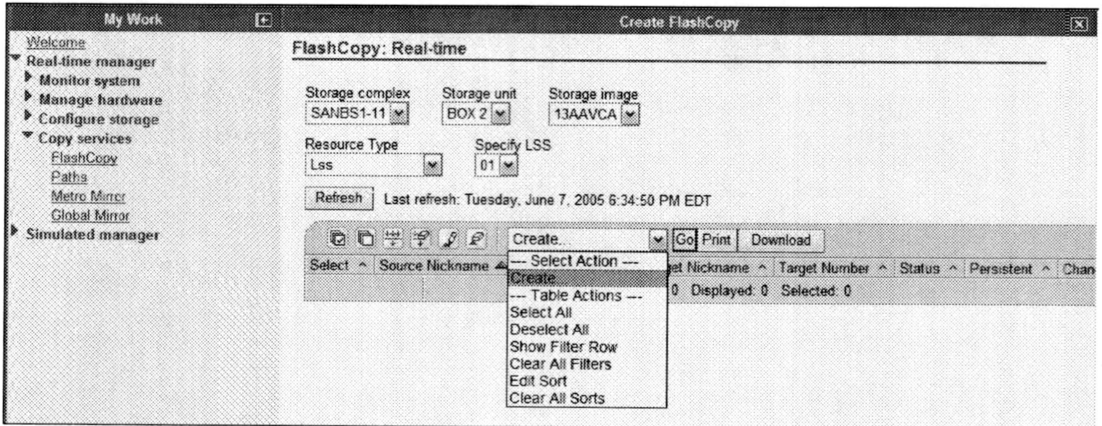

Figure 9-3 FlashCopy Create with DS SM

This selection will give you several windows, one after the other, to define the attributes going along with the FlashCopy.

- Define relationship type.

  Select **A single source with a single target,** or **A single source with multiple targets** (if you want to allow Multiple Relationship FlashCopy).

- Select source volumes.

  Select one or multiple source volumes by choosing the check box left of the volume identification. For each of the source volumes, you will afterwards be presented with a window to select one or more targets.

- Select target volumes.

  Select the target volumes (it is not allowed to have more than 12 target volumes).

- Select common options:

  As graphically shown in the window presented in Figure 9-4, the following options can be chosen. The data provided in this window will be used for all defined FlashCopy pairs. See more detailed information about the meaning of each of these parameters in 9.6.2, "Display properties of existing FlashCopy using the DS SM" on page 87.

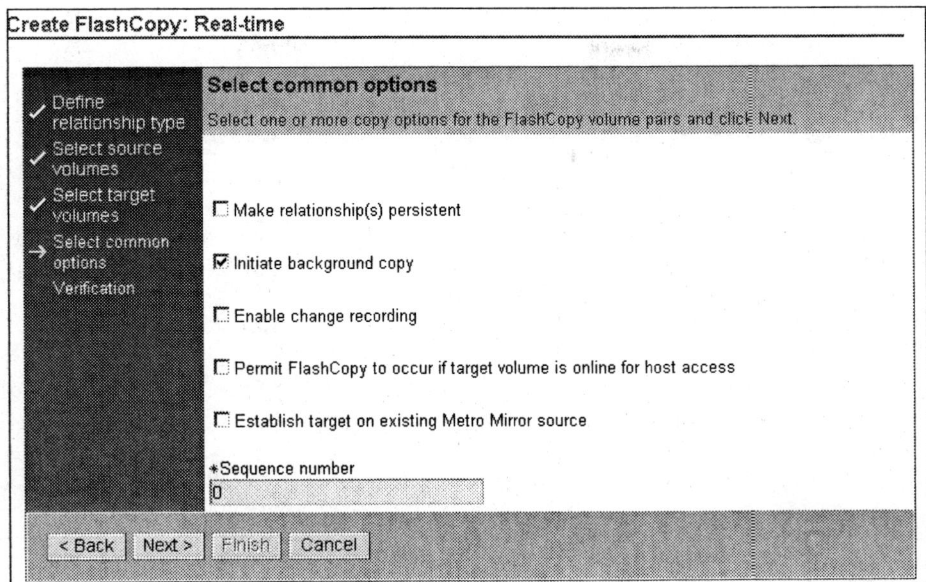

Figure 9-4 Common option window for FlashCopy

- Verification.

  In the following verification window, all information regarding the FlashCopy definition is displayed. If it isn't possible to establish the FlashCopy relationship (if, for example, a volume was requested to be offline, but isn't offline) then an information message is displayed on this window.

Comparing parameters for initial FlashCopy using DS SM and DS CLI

A FlashCopy can be defined by using the DS SM front end within a browser (selecting the **Create** for FlashCopy) or by using the DS CLI (using the `mkflash` command) on one of the supported workstations.

Using the DS SM, it is possible to define FlashCopies that will be generated immediately. It is currently not possible to store any FlashCopy tasks using the DS SM.

In Table 9-6 the parameters are shown that support the FlashCopy options when using the DS CLI command `mkflash` or the DS SM graphical front end using **FlashCopy create**.

Table 9-6 Comparison of options and parameters: FlashCopy in DS CLI and DS SM front end

Options	Parameter with DS CLI command *mkflash*	Parameter with DS SM *FlashCopy create*	Remarks
Options for the source volume:			
Multiple relationship FlashCopy	list of source:target volumes	multiple target volumes can be selected during *create*	
Consistency Groups for FlashCopy	freeze	-	Currently not supported with DS SM front end
Options for the target volume			
FlashCopy target can be Metro Mirror or Global Copy primary	tgtpprc	establish target on existing Metro Mirror source	
Permit target volume to be online in z/OS environment	tgtoffline	permit FlashCopy to occur if target is online for host access	this option exists only for CKD volumes (z/OS)
Inhibit writes to target volume	tgtinhibit	-	Resync target for z/OS
Options for FlashCopy pair:			
Identification of FlashCopy pair	dev or source:target	selected in windows	
Change Recording	record	enable change recording	
Persistent FlashCopy	persist	make relationship persistent	
Full volume background FlashCopy	nocp	initiate background copy	
Sequence number	seqnum	sequence number for this relationship	

9.6.2 Display properties of existing FlashCopy using the DS SM

On the DS SM front end window, select **Real-time manager** on the left, then **FlashCopy**. Identify the DS8000 (Storage Unit and LSS for example) for which you would like to display a FlashCopy. This will give you a list of all active FlashCopy relationships (see Figure 9-5).

By selecting the check box left of the FlashCopy of interest, the Select Actions for this FlashCopy relationship are changed, based on the attributes of the FlashCopy relationship and the possible actions to be performed on it. Use the **Select Action** → **Properties** and then select → **Go**, all attributes of the selected FlashCopy will be displayed.

Note: In case you are selecting multiple FlashCopy relationships, the **Select Action** → **Properties** *will not* be presented. Select only one FlashCopy relationship to view its properties.

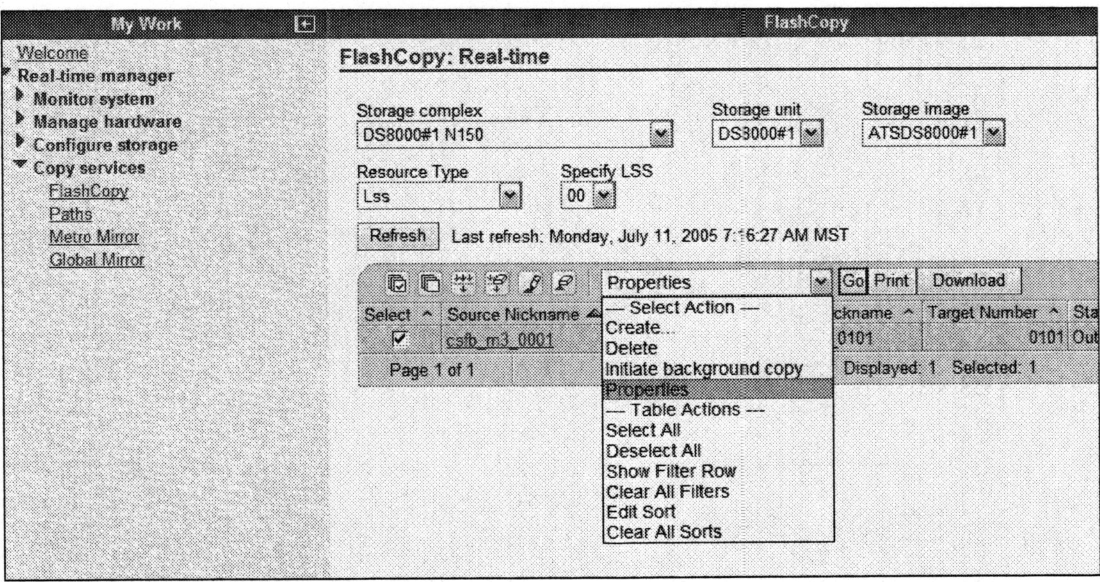

Figure 9-5 FlashCopy display properties

This selection will give you a window, with two folders:

- General:

  In this folder all properties of the selected FlashCopy are presented; see Figure 9-6.

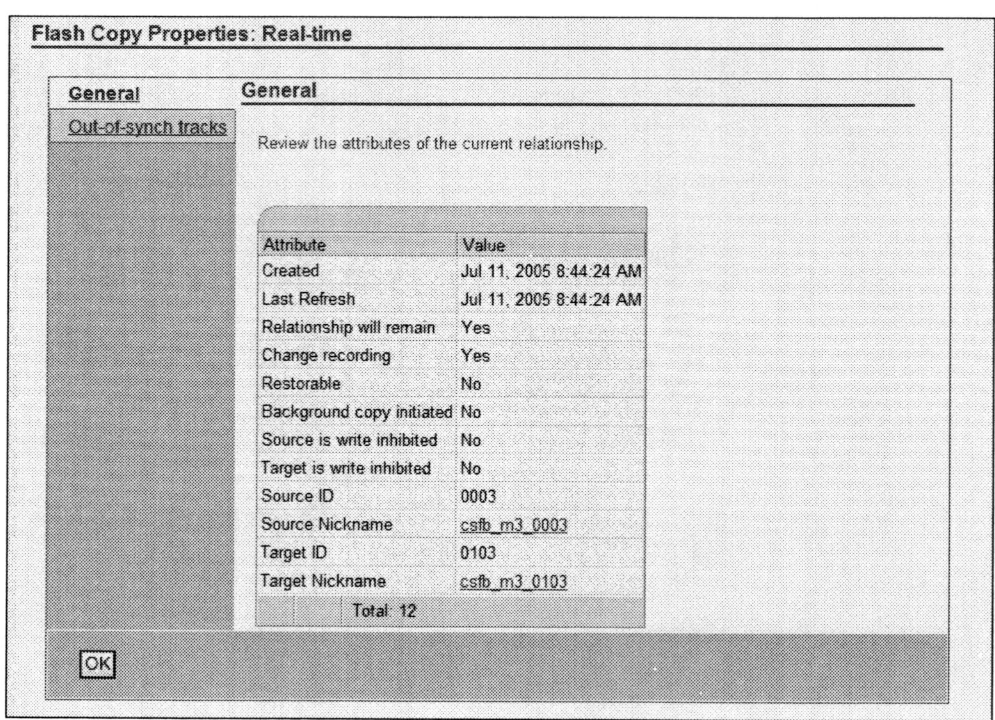

Figure 9-6 Out of synch tracks of FlashCopy relationship

- Out-of-synch tracks:

  The window displaying the out-of-synch tracks can be used to monitor how the FlashCopy performs in the background. A refresh interval can be set to refresh the display after a preselected period of time. For details, see Figure 9-7.

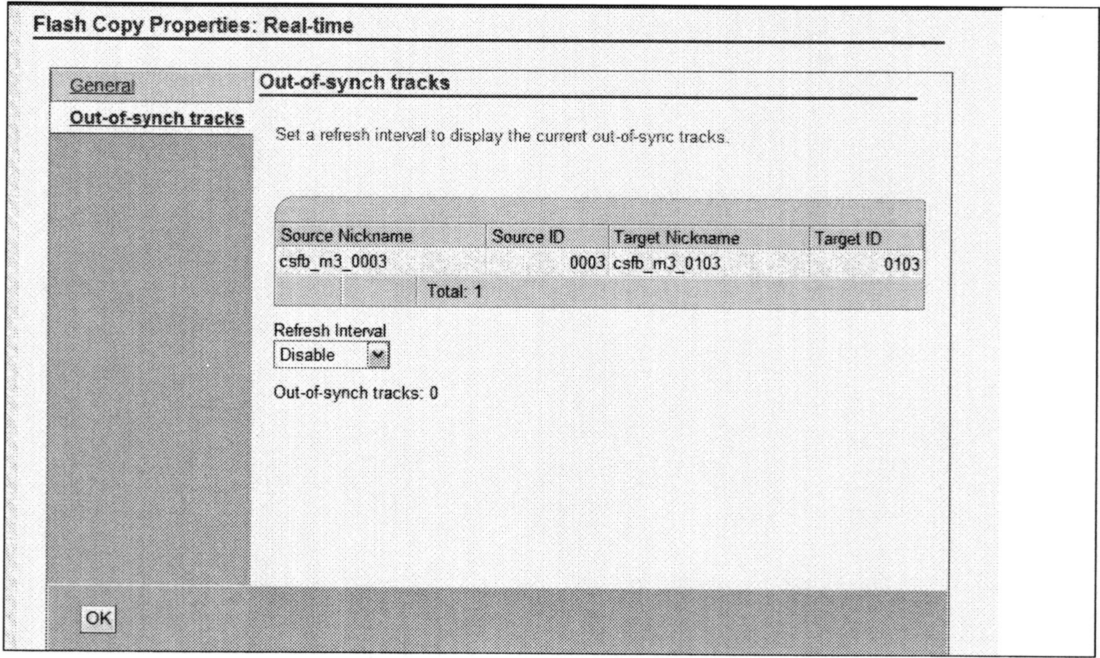

Figure 9-7 Display of out of synch tracks

Comparison of display properties from DS CLI and DS SM

Table 9-7 shows an overview of properties for an existing FlashCopy as presented when a **lsflash** command is executed in the DS CLI or an existing FlashCopy relationship was selected for display in the DS SM front end.

Table 9-7 Comparison of properties displayed for FlashCopy in DS CLI and DS SM front end

Properties with DS CLI command *lsflash*		**Properties with DS SM** *FlashCopy property*	
Property	**Contents**	**Property**	**Contents**
Source LSS			
SrcLSS	#	Source LSS in selection window	From selection list
Sequence Number the FlashCopy belongs to. Can also be used for consistency groups.			
SequenceNum	###	Sequence number from overview window	###
Shows if a Background Copy is currently running. If the DS CLI returns ActiveCopy=disabled this could be similar to out-of-sync tracks>0 or copy complete on the DS SM.			
ActiveCopy	Enabled or disabled	Status in overview window	Copy complete or out-of-sync tracks>0 or background copy running
Shows if recording was selected for both source and target volume to allow for later usage of resync.			
Recording	Enabled or disabled	Change recording	Yes or no
Shows if the FlashCopy is a persistent one.			
Persistent	Enabled or disabled	Relationship will remain	Yes or no
Identifies if the FlashCopy relationship can be changed by copying the contents of the target volume to the source volume			
Revertible	Enabled or disabled	Restorable	Yes or no
Identifies if the source can be used to write on it			
SourceWriteEnabled	Enabled or disabled	Source is write inhibited	Yes or no
Identifies it the target can be used by another server to write on it in parallel to the FlashCopy taking place			
TargetWriteEnabled	Enabled or disabled	Target is write inhibited	Yes or no
Identifies if a background copy was already done			
BackgroundCopy	Enabled or disabled	Background copy initiated	Yes or no
Using -l parameter with DS CLI:			
OutOfSyncTracks	A number	Out-of-sync tracks	A number
DateCreated	Date	Created	Date
DateSynced	Date	Last refresh	Date

9.6.3 Reverse existing FlashCopy using the DS SM

Display the list of active FlashCopies as described in 9.6.2, "Display properties of existing FlashCopy using the DS SM" on page 87. By selecting the check box left of the FlashCopy of interest, the available Select Actions for this FlashCopy relationship will be shown. If the existing FlashCopy relationship can be reversed, it is possible to choose the Select Action → **Reverse relationship** and then select → **Go**.

The next window displayed is shown in Figure 9-8. It displays those properties of the existing FlashCopy that might be changed during the reverse process. Their meaning is described in "Comparing parameters for initial FlashCopy using DS SM and DS CLI" on page 86. Changing the values of the parameters and then selecting → **OK** will start the reverse process for the FlashCopy.

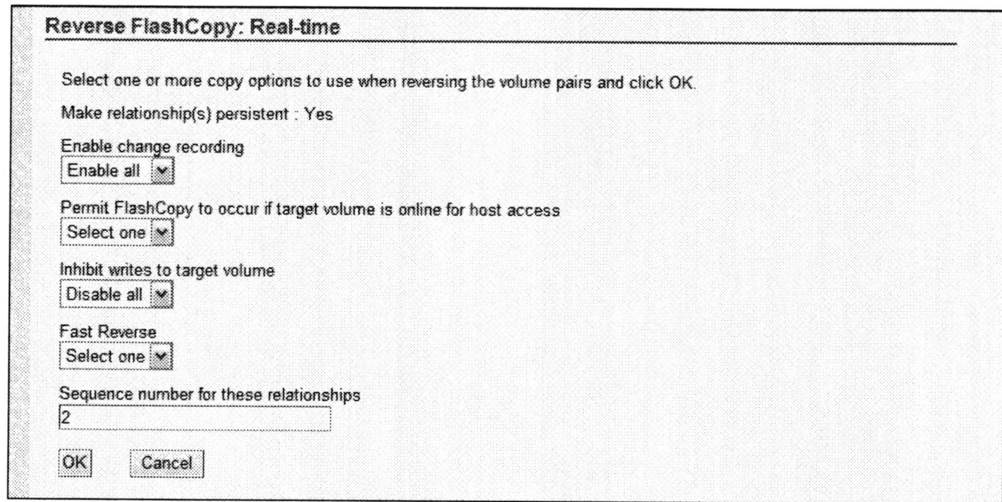

Figure 9-8 Parameters going along with reverse action

9.6.4 Initiate background copy for persistent FlashCopy relationship

On the DS SM front end window, select → **Real Time Manage**r on the left, then → **FlashCopy**. Identify the DS8000 (Storage Unit and LSS for example) for which you would like to increment a FlashCopy. This will give you a list of all active FlashCopy relationships (similar to Figure 9-9).

By selecting the check box left of the FlashCopy of interest, the available Select Actions for this FlashCopy relationship will be shown. It is possible to choose the Select Action → **Initiate background cop**y and then select → **Go**.

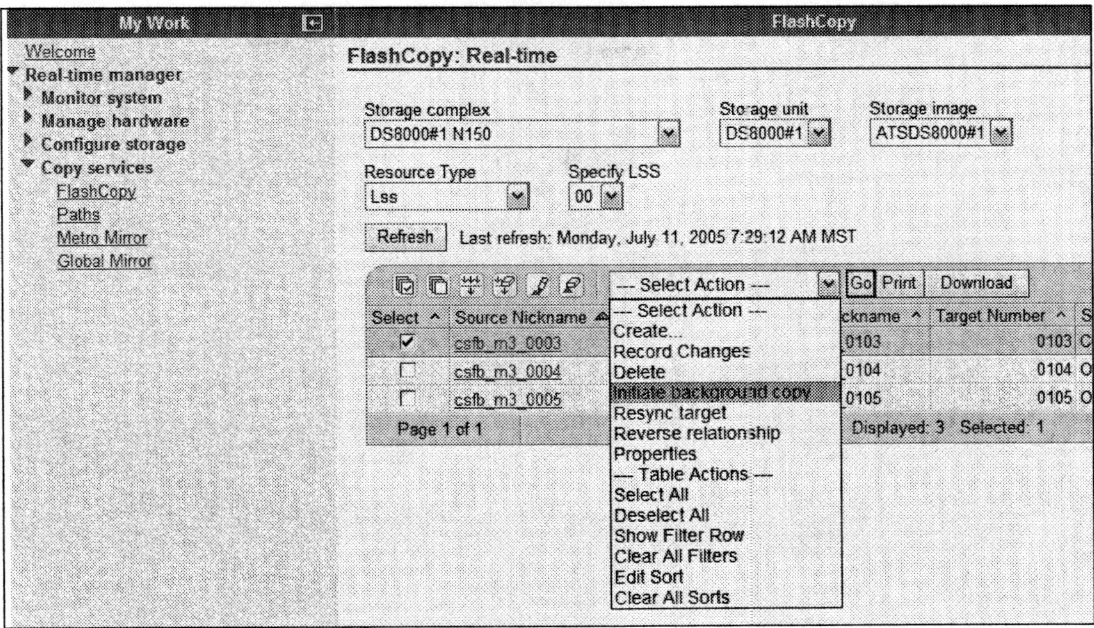

Figure 9-9 Initiate background copy

The next window displayed is shown in Figure 9-10. It prompts for the FlashCopy pairs for which the FlashCopy should run.

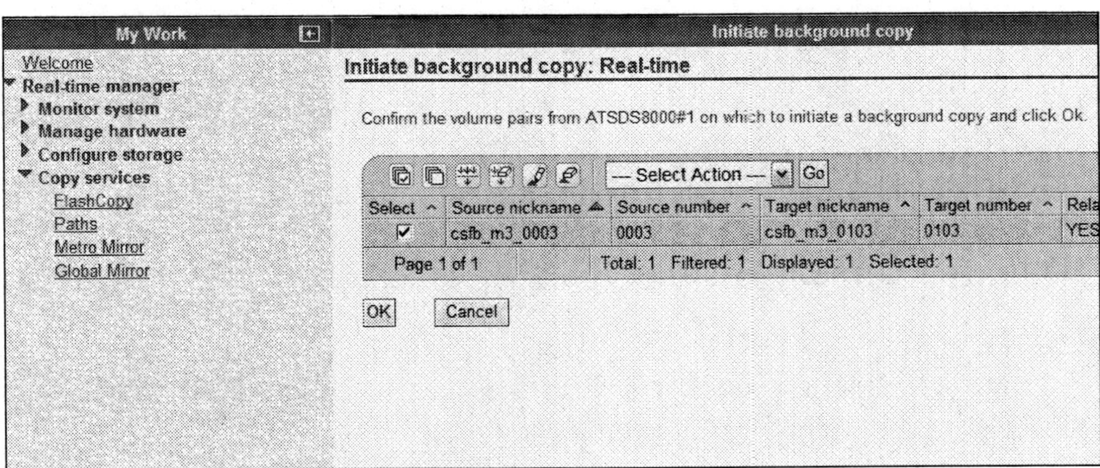

Figure 9-10 Prompt window for background copy

9.6.5 Resynchronize target using the DS SM

Display the list of active FlashCopies as described in Figure 9-11. By selecting the check box left of the FlashCopy of interest, the available Select Actions for this FlashCopy relationship will be shown. It is possible to choose the Select Action → **Resync target** and then select → **Go**.

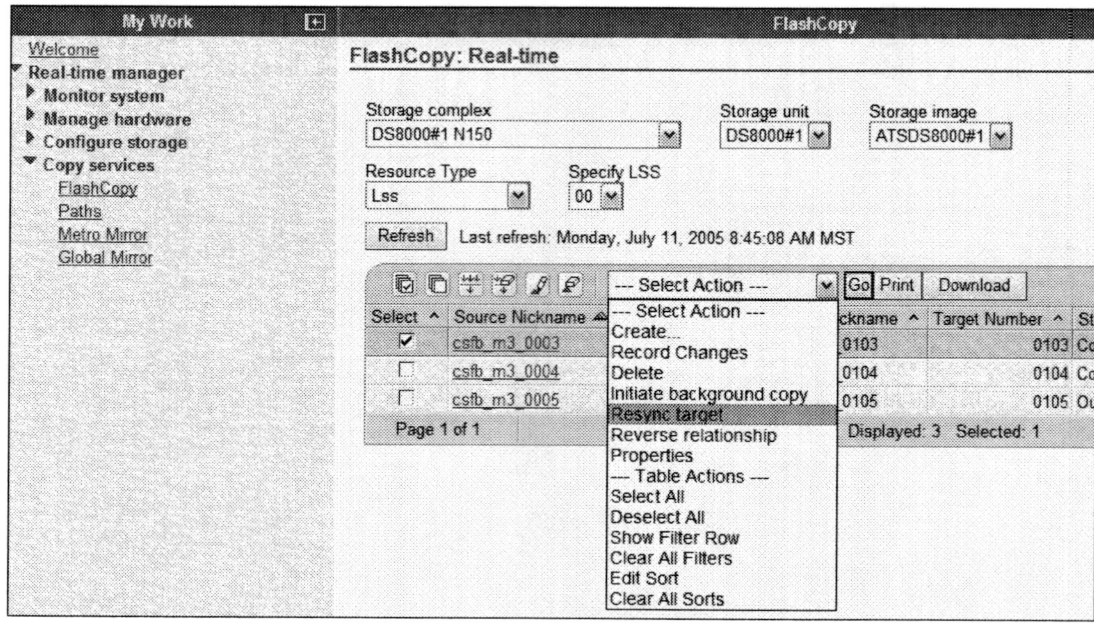

Figure 9-11 Resync target select option to resynchronize FlashCopy relationship

The following prompt window asks for more details for the resync request (see Figure 9-12).

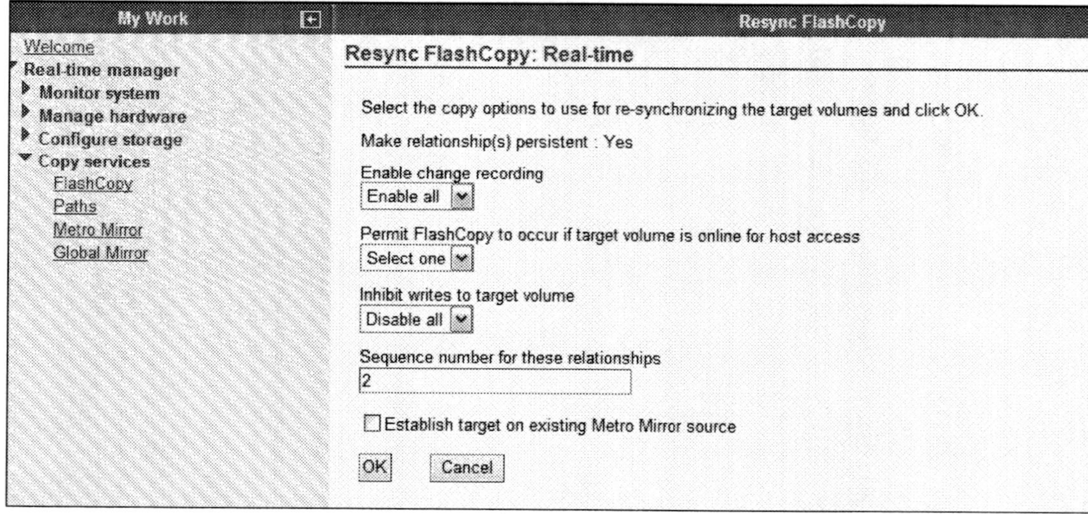

Figure 9-12 Prompt window to detail resync request for FlashCopy relationship

9.6.6 Delete existing FlashCopy relationship using the DS SM

Display the list of active FlashCopies as described in Figure 9-13. By selecting the check box left of the FlashCopy of interest, the available Select Actions for this FlashCopy relationship will be shown. It is possible to choose the Select Action → **Delete** and then select → **Go**. The next window is a prompt asking you to confirm the delete request (see Figure 9-14).

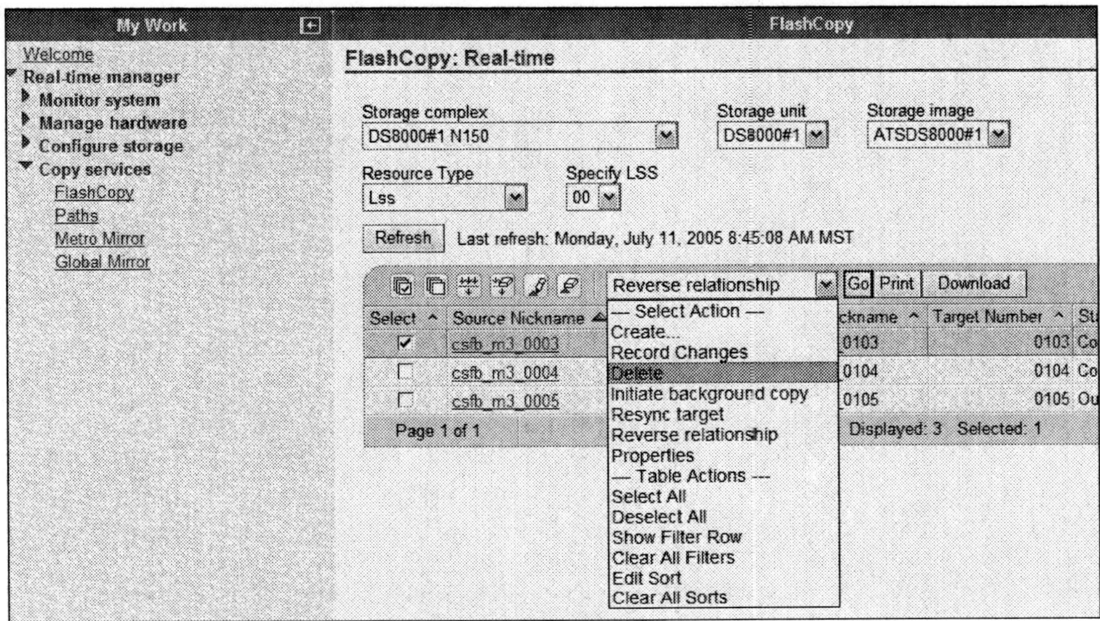

Figure 9-13 Delete select option to delete FlashCopy relationship

Figure 9-14 Prompt window to confirm delete request for FlashCopy relationship

9.7 z/OS interfaces for local FlashCopies

The following interfaces are supported to initiate a FlashCopy.

For z/OS and OS/390, a FlashCopy relationship can be established using:

- DFSMSdss utility
- TSO
- ANTRQST macro´
- ICKDSF

9.7.1 Initiate FlashCopy using DFSMSdss

The DFSMSdss Command COPY uses FlashCopy for volume copies and dataset copies. Detailed information can be found in the IBM publication *z/OS DFSMSdss Storage Administration Reference* SC35-0424.

For the best performance during COPY operations, specify any of the parameters in Table 9-8.

Table 9-8 Possible performance improvements adding additional parameters

Parameter for performance improvement with DFSMSdss command COPY	Performance improvements
ADMINISTRATOR	Allow a DFSMSdss-authorized administrator to bypass access checking to datasets and catalogs
ALLDATA(*)	Copy all allocated space (for organization type PS, PSU, PO, POU or null.
ALLEXCP	Copy all allocated space (for organization type PS, PSU, PO, POU or null, even if data sets are empty.
PURGE	Unexpired data sets on the target volume can be overlaid for a full or track copy operation

Full volume FlashCopy

DFSMSdss could implicitly use the hardware function of the DS8000 to perform the FlashCopy if the following requirements are met in conjunction with the COPY FULL command.

- The source and target devices must have the same track format.
- The source volumes and target volumes are in the same DS8000.
- The source and target volumes must be online.
- No other FlashCopy is active for the same source volume. If so, the copy will be done by DFSMSdss software based.
- The FASTREPLICATION(NONE) keyword must *not* be specified.

Not all tracks on the volume are copied when DFSMSdss invokes FlashCopy for a full volume copy - DFSMSdss requests FlashCopy for allocated extents only.

In order to balance between excluding free space and saving the number of FlashCopy relationships, up to 255 relations will be created for each full volume copy. If there are more than 255 extents on the volume, extents will be merged (to reduce the number of extents) resulting in some free space being copied.

In Table 9-6 on page 86, the parameters are shown that support the FlashCopy options when using the DS CLI command `mkflash` or the DS SM graphical front end using *FlashCopy create*. Table 9-9 below shows the options and parameters for DFSMSdss COPY FULL.

Table 9-9 Options and parameters used for FlashCopy with DFSMSdss COPY FULL

Options	Parameter with DFSMSdss COPY FULL	Remarks
Options for the source volume:		
Multiple relationship FlashCopy	Selected pairs	
Consistency Groups for FlashCopy	Not supported with DFSMSdss	
Options for the target volume:		

Options	Parameter with DFSMSdss COPY FULL	Remarks
FlashCopy target can be Metro Mirror or Global Copy primary	FCTOPPRCPrimary	
Permit target volume to be online in z/OS environment	No specific command	Volume online / offline will be handled by DFSMSdss as required
Inhibit writes to target volume	-	Not supported
Options for FlashCopy pair:		
Identification of FlashCopy pair		In commands
Change Recording	-	Not supported
Persistent FlashCopy		Not supported
Full volume background FlashCopy	FCNOCOPY	Also used: FCNC
Sequence number		Not supported
Options for DFSMSdss to force selection of FlashCopy:		
FlashCopy as preferred copy method for DFSMSdss	FASTREPLICATION	

The options supported during initial definition are as follows:

- Multiple relationship FlashCopy:

  It is possible to establish up to 12 FlashCopy relationships using the same source. When setting up a FlashCopy, it is necessary to identify if the source volume might be used in other FlashCopy relationships as well. Once a source volume is used in a FlashCopy without identifying it as a multiple relationship source volume, it is not possible to define other FlashCopies using this volume as source volume. Once established using the DS SM, this attribute can not be changed for an existing FlashCopy relationship.

- Consistency Group FlashCopy:

  With the DS CLI it is possible to establish a Consistency Group by using the *-freeze* parameter and identifying all FlashCopy pairs and target volumes belonging to it.

- Establish target on existing Metro Mirror source:

  When this option is selected, the target volume can be or become a source volume for a Metro Mirror or Global Copy relationship. When DS8000 FlashCopy is not used by the DFSMSdss utility then the *FCTOPPRCPrimary* is ignored.

  When *FCTOPPRCPrimary* is not specified or if the capability is not supported by the DS8000, then a Metro Mirror or Global Copy primary volume is not eligible to become a FlashCopy target volume.

Attention: A Metro Mirror or Global Copy pair currently in full duplex state will go into a duplex pending state when the FlashCopy relationship is established. When Metro Mirror or Global Copy complete the copy operation, the Metro Mirror or Global Copy pair will go to full duplex state.

- Permit FlashCopy to occur if target volume is online for host access.

  When setting up the relationship, it is checked if the target volume is online or not. See Table 9-10 for valid combinations of offline and online for volumes.

Table 9-10 Combinations of volume offline or online and parameter permit target to be online

Status of target volume in z/OS	Permit FlashCopy to occur if target volume is online	
Volume is online	Not selected	DS SM: error message, FlashCopy definition is not possible. DS CLI: ... in work ...???
Volume is online	Selected	DS SM: FlashCopy definition is queued until target volume goes offline DS CLI: ...in work....
Volume is offline	Selected or not selected	FlashCopy will be started immediately

- Inhibit writes to target volume:

  While FlashCopy hasn't finished, writes to the target shouldn't be possible.

- Change recording:

  Activating the option *change recording* during setup of a FlashCopy enables subsequent refreshes to the target volume. To do so, a second bitmap is created for the source volume that keeps track of all writes to the source. This bitmap can later be used to refresh the target by only copying the updates from the source to the target.

- Persistent FlashCopy:

  The FlashCopy relationship will continue to exist until explicitly removed by an Interface method. If this option is not selected, the FlashCopy relationship will exist until all data has been copied from the source volume to the target.

- Full volume background copy:

  It is possible to identify if the data of the source volume should be copied to the target volume in the background or not. If DFSMSdss uses the DS8000 FlashCopy, then the parameter FCNOCOPY is analyzed to identify if a copy should take place or not. If FCNOCOPY is specified, then the FlashCopy relationship stays persistent and only updates to the source are reflected in the target. If this parameter is omitted, then a physical copy of the data is done in the background and the FlashCopy relationship is ended after all data has been copied.

- FlashCopy as preferred copy method for DFSMSdss:

  The parameter FASTREPLICATION can be used to identify if the DS8000 FlashCopy should be used or not. Three types of the FASTREPLICATION parameter exist; see Table 9-11.

Table 9-11 Combinations of volume offline or online and parameter permit target to be online

Parameter	
FASTREPLICATION(PREFERRED)	(This is the default.) For DFSMSdss the DS8000 FlashCopy is the preferred method to move data. If FlashCopy can not be used the parameter CONCURRENT is used to identify if Concurrent Copy should be used. If CONCURRENT wasn't used or the Concurrent Copy fails traditional data movement methods will be used.
FASTREPLICATION(REQUIRED)	For DFSMSdss the DS8000 FlashCopy is the required method to copy the volume. If FlashCopy can not be used DFSMSdss fails the operation with error message ADR938E.
FASTREPLICATION(NONE)	DFSMSdss will not try to use the DS8000 FlashCopy.

Dataset FlashCopy

The DFSMSdss could implicitly use the hardware function of the DS8000 to perform the FlashCopy if the following requirements are met in conjunction with the COPY DATASET command:

- The source and target types are the same.
- The source devices and target devices are in the same DS8000.
- The source and target volumes must be online.

Note: Do not use the parameter *FASTREPLICATION(NONE)*, as it would not use FlashCopy.

The COPY DATASET could use the parameters as listed in Table 9-12 to support FlashCopy.

Table 9-12 Parameters with COPY DATASET

Parameters with *COPY DATASET*	Performance improvements
NOPACKING	If COPY DATASET is used for a partitioned dataset the nopacking option specifies that the data set is not to be compressed during copy. This allows DFSMSdss to invoke FLASHCOPY for the copy operation.
FCNOCOPY	Copy all allocated space (for organization type PS, PSU, PO, POU or null).
ALLEXCP	Copy all allocated space (for organization type PS, PSU, PO, POU or null), even if data sets are empty.
PURGE	Unexpired data sets on the target volume can be overlaid for a full or track copy operation

Depending on the type of dataset, however, the DFSMSdss command COPY DATASET does not always invoke the hardware function FLASHCOPY to perform the copy. Table 9-13 shows which functions are invoked by DFSMSdss depending on the type of dataset.

Table 9-13 Data mover for data set copy (to device of same geometry)

Data set type	Data mover	Notes
Sequential	DFSMSdss	
Partitioned (not PDSE)	DFSMSdss / IEBCOPY	All partitioned data sets that are not load modules are compressed during a copy. Specify NOPACKING if FlashCopy is to be used.

Data set type	Data mover	Notes
Partitioned (not PDSE) load modules	DFSMSdss / IEBCOPY	If copying partitioned load modules with REBLOCK, DFSMSdss calls IEBCOPY to copy the data set to a like device.
Partitioned data set extended (PDSE)	DFSMSdss / IGWFAMS	DFSMSdss calls the IGWFAMS utility when you are converting a PDS to a PDSE.
Direct nonrelative block address mode	DFSMSdss	
Direct relative block address mode	DFSMSdss	Specify the DFSMSdss RELBLOCKADDRESS parameter.
Indexed sequential to same track. Target volume uses VTOC index. Target space available.	DFSMSdss	
Indexed sequential (all other cases)	IEBISAM	
ESDS	DFSMSdss / IDCAMS	DFSMSdss calls IDCAMS if the target CISIZE, CASIZE, physical record size, or physical block size of the target is different from that of the source.
RRDS	DFSMSdss / IDCAMS	DFSMSdss calls IDCAMS if the target CISIZE, CASIZE, physical record size, or physical block size of the target is different from that of the source.
LDS	DFSMSdss/IDCAMS	DFSMSdss calls IDCAMS if the target CISIZE, CASIZE, physical record size, or physical block size of the target is different from that of the source.
KSDS or VRRDS	DFSMSdss / IDCAMS	DFSMSdss calls IDCAMS if any of the following is true: ► The CISIZE, CASIZE, physical record size, physical block size, imbed, or span attributes of the target are different from that of the source. ► The target data set is SMS and has an imbedded index or has key ranges, and the target volume count is greater than one. ► The target data set is non-SMS, the source component or components span multiple volumes, and there is not enough space on one target volume to contain the entire data set.
Key range data set	DFSMSdss / IDCAMS	DFSMSdss calls IDCAMS if the source and target CASIZE, physical record size, or physical block size are different; if the components span multiple volumes; for a KSDS with IMBED and either the source HURBA=HARBA or it has extended indexes.
Extended-format VSAM	DFSMSdss / IDCAMS	DFSMSdss calls IDCAMS if the target CISIZE, CASIZE, physical record size, or physical block size of the target is different from that of the source.
Integrated catalog facility user catalogs	IDCAMS (EXPORT/IMPORT)	
Undefined DSORG	DFSMSdss	

FlashCopy performance

This chapter discusses *best practices* when configuring FlashCopy for specific environments or scenarios.

We cover these topics:

- FlashCopy performance overview
- FlashCopy establish performance
- Background copy performance
- FlashCopy impact to applications
- FlashCopy options
- FlashCopy scenarios

10.1 FlashCopy performance overview

Many different parameters can affect the performance of your FlashCopy operations. One of the most important is the placement of your source and target volumes. There are also different FlashCopy performance modes, for example, COPY or NOCOPY, and scenarios, for example, short term or long term FlashCopy relationships. Another key option available with performance implications is to use incremental FlashCopy, that is, to periodically only copy changed data.

It is important to review the requirements for FlashCopy and to select the proper FlashCopy configuration per the requirements. In this chapter we examine when to use COPY versus NOCOPY and where to place the FlashCopy target volumes/LUNs relative to where the FlashCopy source volumes/LUNs are placed. We also discuss when and how to use *incremental* FlashCopy. This chapter focuses on performance issues, but there are many other business requirements that must be weighed when using FlashCopy. The designer should carefully consider all aspects of the implementation for each specific solution and should definitely evaluate the use of *incremental* FlashCopy for all FlashCopy applications.

Note: This chapter is equally valid for zSeries (volumes) and Open Systems (LUNs). Though both terms were included in the above paragraph, from this point forward only the term volume or volumes will be used, but the text would be equally valid if the terms LUN and LUNs were used, *unless otherwise noted.*

In general, you can achieve the best performance by distributing the load across all of the resources of the DS8000. In other words, you should carefully plan your usage so that the load is:

- Spread evenly across disk subsystems
- Within each disk subsystem, spread evenly across clusters
- Within each cluster, spread evenly across device adapters
- Within each device adapter, spread evenly across ranks

Additionally, it is always best to locate the FlashCopy target volume in a location that is on the same DS8000 cluster as the FlashCopy source volume. It is also good practice to locate the FlashCopy target volume on a different device adapter than the source volume, but there are some cases where this is really a *don't care* decision. Another choice available to the designer is whether to place the FlashCopy target volumes on the same ranks as the FlashCopy source volumes. In general it is best to not place these two volumes in the same rank. See Table 10-1 for a summary of the placement rules.

Tip: If the FlashCopy target volume is on the same rank as the FlashCopy source volume the user runs the risk of a rank failure causing the lost of both the source and the target volumes.

In the DS8000 it is much more meaningful to discuss volume location in terms of ranks and not in terms of logical subsystem (LSS) or logical control unit (LCU). On the ESS 800 and earlier IBM disk subsystems, the physical location of the volumes were typically described in terms of the logical subsystem LSS/LCU. If there existed more than a single rank in the LSS/LCU, then each of the ranks would have a range of volumes from that specific LSS/LCU. The LSSs/LCUs in a DS8000 disk subsystem are logical constructs that are no longer tied to predetermined ranks. Within the DS8000 the LSS/LCU can be configured to span one or more ranks but is not limited to specific ranks. There can be individual ranks that contain volumes for more than a single LSS/LCU, which was not possible before the introduction of the DS8000.

Table 10-1 Relative location: FlashCopy source versus FlashCopy target

	Cluster	Device Adapter	Rank
FlashCopy establish performance	Same cluster	Don't care	Different ranks
Background copy performance	Same cluster	Different device adapter	Different ranks
FlashCopy impact to applications	Same cluster	Don't care	Different ranks

Finally, you can achieve a small performance improvement by using identical rank geometries for both the source and target volumes. In other words, if the source volumes are located on a rank with a 7+p RAID-5 configuration, then the target volumes should also be located on a rank configured as 7+p RAID-5.

Note: Here is a brief review of some of the terms used:

Server: Also known as a cluster. A DS8000 partition capable of performing all DS8000 functions. Each DS8000 has two servers, also known as Server0 and Server1. You can issue the **`lsserver`** command to see the available servers.

Device Adapter (DA): A physical component of the DS8000 that provides communications between the *clusters* and the storage devices. The **`lsda`** command lists the available device adapters.

Rank: An Array Site made into an Array which is then made into a Rank. For the DS8000 a rank is a collection of 8 disk drive modules (DDMs). The **`lsrank`** command displays detailed information about the ranks.

Tip: To find the relative location of your volumes, you can use the following procedure.

1. Use the **`lsfbvol`** command to find out which Extent Pool contains the relevant volumes.
2. Issue the **`lsrank`** command. This command displays both the device adapter and the rank for each Extent Pool.
3. To determine which server cluster contains your volumes, look at the Extent Pool name. Even numbered Extent Pools are always from Server 0, while odd numbered Extent Pools are always from Server1.

The FlashCopy of a volume has two distinct periods of operation:

- Logical FlashCopy (also called *establish*)
- Physical FlashCopy (also called *background copy*)

The following subsections provide more guidance on the performance aspects of the following topics:

- FlashCopy establish performance
- Background copy performance
- FlashCopy impact to applications
- FlashCopy scenarios and discussion topics

10.2 FlashCopy establish performance

The FlashCopy establish phase, or logical FlashCopy, is the period of time when the microcode is preparing all things necessary, such as the bitmaps, to create the FlashCopy relationship so the microcode can properly process subsequent reads and writes to these volumes. During this logical FlashCopy period, no writes are allowed to these volumes. After the logical relationship has been established, normal I/O activity is allowed to both source and target volumes according to the options selected.

Refer to Figure 10-1 for the recommended placement of source versus target volumes for best FlashCopy establish performance.

When there are a large number of volumes to be FlashCopied, the method used to invoke the FlashCopy commands can influence the time to complete the logical FlashCopy for all FlashCopy pairs. For z/OS, an in-band invocation will source the commands to the microcode faster than an out-of-band method in most cases. An in-band establish is one that uses the CCW commands directly.

The fastest out-of-band method is the DS CLI. However, in some circumstances, such as if there are limited resources available on z/OS or there is a lot of parallelism, the DS CLI may be the faster method. The method to control or invoke FlashCopy should be selected based upon total solution requirements, not strictly on *logical* FlashCopy performance unless this is a critical performance issue for your application of FlashCopy. For open systems, the DS CLI is the fastest invocation method.

Additionally, there is a modest performance impact to logical FlashCopy performance when using incremental FlashCopy. In the case of incremental FlashCopy, the DS8000 must create three change recording bitmaps instead of one. However, the impact is negligible in most cases.

10.3 Background copy performance

The background copy phase, or physical FlashCopy, is the actual movement of the data from the source volume to the target volume. If the FlashCopy relationship is NOCOPY, then only write updates to the source volume will force a copy from the source to the target. This forced copy is also called a *collision*.

> **Note:** The term *collision* describes a forced copy from the source to the target because a write to the source has occurred. This occurs on the *first* write to a track after a FlashCopy only. Note that since the DS8000 writes to non-volatile cache, there is typically no direct response time delay on host writes. The forced copy only occurs when the write is destaged onto disk.

If the COPY option is selected, then upon completion of the logical FlashCopy establish phase, the source will be copied to the target.

> **Tip:** If there are many volumes being FlashCopied, then do not expect to see all pairs actively copying data as soon as their logical FlashCopy relationship is completed. The microcode has algorithms that will limit the number of active pairs copying data. This algorithm will try to balance active copy pairs across the DS8000 device adapter resources. Additionally, the algorithm will limit the number of active pairs such that there remains bandwidth for host or server I/Os.

Tip: The DS8000 gives higher priority to application performance than background copy performance. This means that the DS8000 will throttle the background copy if necessary, so that applications are not unduly impacted.

If the FlashCopy command is invoked with the COPY option, the source volume will be fully copied to the FlashCopy target volume in an expedient fashion. See the *physical* FlashCopy discussion and *Tip:* in 10.2, "FlashCopy establish performance" on page 102.

The recommended placement of FlashCopy source and target volumes for *physical* FlashCopy was described in Table 10-1 on page 101. For the best background copy performance, the implementation should always place the source and target volumes in different ranks. There are additional criteria to consider if the FlashCopy is a *full box copy* that involves all Ranks.

Note: The term *full box copy* has the implication that all rank resources are involved in the copy process. Either all or nearly all ranks have both source and target volumes, or half the ranks have source volumes and half the ranks have target volumes.

For full box copies, you should still place the source and target volumes in different ranks. When all ranks are participating in the FlashCopy, it is still possible to accomplish this by FlashCopying volumes on rank R0 onto rank R1, and volumes on rank R1 onto rank R0 (for example). Additionally, if there is heavy *application* activity in the source rank, performance would be less affected if the background copy target was in some other random rank that could be expected to have lighter *application* activity.

If background copy performance is of high importance in your environment, you should use incremental FlashCopy as much as possible. *Incremental* FlashCopy will greatly reduce the amount of data that needs to be copied, and therefore greatly reduces the background copy time.

10.4 FlashCopy impact to applications

The most important consideration when implementing FlashCopy is to achieve an implementation that has minimal impact to the application performance.

Attention: Again, these recommendations consider only the performance aspects. FlashCopy performance is only one aspect of an intelligent system design. You must consider all business requirements when designing a total solution. These additional requirements will help you to choose between COPY and NOCOPY and incremental FlashCopy.

The relative placement of the source and target volumes has a large impact on application performance, and this has been discussed in 10.2, "FlashCopy establish performance" on page 102.

In addition to the relative placement of volumes, the selection of COPY or NOCOPY is also an important consideration. Typically, the choice of COPY or NOCOPY depends primarily on how the FlashCopy will be used and for what interval of time the FlashCopy relationship exists. From a purely performance point of view, the choice of whether to use COPY or NOCOPY depends a great deal on the type of workload. The general answer is to use NOCOPY, but this is not always the best choice. For most workloads, including online transaction processing (OLTP) workloads, NOCOPY typically is the preferred option.

However, some workloads that contain a large number of random writes and are not cache friendly might benefit from using the COPY option, which is typically the preferred option.

Another critical determination is whether to use *incremental* FlashCopy or not to use *incremental* FlashCopy. Under the correct circumstances, incremental FlashCopy would have no impact to the critical online write updates and would significantly shorten the period of time to complete the periodic background copy.

> **Note:** The incremental FlashCopy **resyncflash** command does not have a NOCOPY option. Using **resyncflash** will automatically use the COPY option, regardless of whether the original FlashCopy was COPY or NOCOPY.

10.5 FlashCopy options

Incremental FlashCopy is only supported at the volume level. That is, *incremental* FlashCopy does not support z/OS data set level FlashCopy. Though incremental may be used with FlashCopy relationships established with either the COPY or the NOCOPY option, there are some differences in how the COPY and NOCOPY relationships affect the application write updates.

The COPY approach causes an initial copy of all source volumes, but then will only copy changed tracks when the incremental resync command is invoked. The NOCOPY approach does not perform an initial copy of the source volumes when the incremental resync command is invoked, but does copy on all first updates to source tracks since the preceding FlashCopy. Again, this copy only occurs when that track is destaged, so in many cases there is no impact to application performance.

The designer needs to consider the consequences of bursts of background copy, initially and following each resync (COPY option), which might impact the application — versus continuous impact, when there are collisions that require a source to target copy before the write update can complete (NOCOPY option).

If running incremental FlashCopy for an extended period of time, the COPY option could very well be the proper choice.

10.6 FlashCopy scenarios

This subsection will describe four scenarios. These scenario discussions assume the primary concern is to minimize the FlashCopy impact to the application performance.

10.6.1 Scenario #1: Backup to disk

In environments where Recovery Time Objective (that is, how quickly you can return to production after a failure) is of utmost importance, a FlashCopy backup to disk can help to achieve an extremely fast restore time. As soon as the logical FlashCopy is complete, it is possible to perform a reverse FlashCopy and restore your production data in seconds, instead of the several hours it would normally take to retrieve the data from tape.

When backing up to disk, it is important to take the necessary steps to protect your data. Remember that, until the background copy is complete, you still only have one physical copy of the data, and that copy is vulnerable. Therefore, it is important to always establish the FlashCopy with the COPY option. Otherwise, in the unlikely event you have a failure of your production volumes, you will also lose your backup.

One method for protecting against failure is to use multiple FlashCopy targets. FlashCopy supports up to 12 targets per source volume. With this feature, it is possible to keep up to 12 versions of your production data (for example, a FlashCopy backup every two hours for one day). Another method is to use incremental FlashCopy. Incremental FlashCopy copies only the data that has changed since the last FlashCopy, so the background copy completes much faster.

10.6.2 Scenario #2: Backup to tape

If the customer wishes to create a copy of the data only to back up that copy to tape, FlashCopy with the NOCOPY option has been the preferred approach, but we do also have some implementations where the COPY option is employed. The backup to tape is normally done shortly after the *logical* FlashCopy relationships have been established for all the volumes to be backed up to tape.

If using the NOCOPY option, the data being backed up to tape will be mostly from the FlashCopy *source* volumes. If this is the case, then the location of the target volumes is less critical and might be decided by considerations other than performance.

If using the COPY option, the data being backed up would come from the target volumes, assuming that the backup to tape does not start until the background copy completes. If the backup starts sooner, the data could come from a mixture of the source volumes and the target volumes. As the backup continues, more and more of the data will come from the target volumes as the background copy moves more and more of the data to the target volumes.

To achieve the least impact to the application and to achieve the fastest backup to tape, we recommend that the backup source volumes be evenly spread across the available disk subsystems and the disk subsystems resources. Once the backup to tape is complete, be sure to withdraw the FlashCopy relationship.

> **Tip:** Issue a withdraw command to each FlashCopy pair as soon as the pair has been completely backed up to tape. This eliminates any additional copying from the source volume, whether due to COPY or collisions.

These recommendations would be equally valid for a COPY or NOCOPY environment.

10.6.3 Scenario #3: FlashCopy during peak application activity

The best solution would be to fully explore alternatives that would move the FlashCopy activity outside of any high performance sensitive activity period. If it is decided to implement FlashCopy such that it does overlap such a performance sensitive period, then examine some of these options:

Again, the choice of whether to use COPY or NOCOPY depends mostly on business requirements, but with regards to performance, it also depends a great deal on the type of workload. This topic is discussed in 10.4, “FlashCopy impact to applications” on page 103. In general, NOCOPY is the preferred method, but you should also consider these points when choosing COPY or NOCOPY:

- Using NOCOPY. The argument here is that the *COPY* degradation of all I/Os to the box is a more severe impact to the application than the *NOCOPY* degradation to a subset of the write I/Os that result in collisions. Again, since the background copy only occurs when the writes are destaged from non-volatile cache, there is typically negligible impact to response time. If the workload is cache friendly, then potentially all of the responses will be served from cache, and there will be no impact from collisions at all.
- Using COPY. The goal of using COPY is to quickly complete the background copy so that application performance returns to normal. If COPY is used, then *all* I/Os will experience some degradation as they compete for box resources with the background copy activity. However, this impact may be somewhat less than the impact to the individual writes that cause a collision. If FlashCopy NOCOPY is active during a high application activity period, there could be a high rate of collisions, that is, destages being delayed so that the track image can be read and then written to the FlashCopy target track to preserve the point in time copy. The destage delay could cause degradation of the performance for all writes that occur during the delay destage periods. Note that it is only the first write to a track that would cause a collision, and only when that write gets destaged. The reads do not suffer the *collision degradation.*
- If using the COPY option, consider these tips: Examine the application environment for the highest activity volumes and the most performance sensitive volumes. Consider arranging the FlashCopy order such that the highest activity and most performance sensitive volumes are copied early and the least active and least performance sensitive volumes are copied last. The intent here is minimize the potential for collisions.

Note: One approach to achieve a specified FlashCopy order would be to partition the volumes into priority groups. Issue the appropriate FlashCopy commands for all volumes, but use COPY on only the highest priority group and NOCOPY on all other groups. After a specified period of time or after some observable event, issue FlashCopy commands to the next highest priority group from NOCOPY to COPY. Continue in this manner until all volumes are fully copied.

If a background copy is the desired end result and FlashCopy is to be started just before or during a high activity period, consider the possibility of starting with NOCOPY and converting to COPY after the high activity period has completed.

One might also want to examine the use of incremental FlashCopy in a high performance sensitive activity period. Incremental FlashCopy automatically uses the COPY option, so if the NOCOPY option was previously selected, using incremental FlashCopy may impact performance by causing a full background copy.

If the incremental FlashCopy approach is chosen, it might be best to create a FlashCopy COPY relationship during a quiet time. To minimize the amount of data to be copied when taking the desired point in time copy, schedule an incremental refresh sufficiently in advance of the point in time refresh to complete the copy of the changed data. Finally, take the required point in time copy with the incremental refresh at the required point in time.

10.6.4 Scenario #4: Ranks reserved for FlashCopy

Another configuration that should be considered is to split the ranks such that half of the ranks (capacity) are all source volumes and the remaining 50% of the ranks (capacity) are all target volumes.

Such an approach does have pros and cons. The disadvantage is the loss of 50% of the ranks for normal application processing. The advantage is that FlashCopy writes to target volumes will not compete with applications writing to the target volumes. This allows the background copy to complete faster, and thus reduces the interference with application I/Os. This is a trade-off that is must be made by the designer:

- Use all ranks for your application:
  - Maximize normal application performance.
  - FlashCopy performance is reduced.
- Use only half of the ranks for your applications:
  - Maximize FlashCopy performance.
  - Normal performance is reduced.

Note: If designing a FlashCopy implementation at the disaster recovery (DR) site, the designer has two separate environments to consider:

- DR mirroring performance with and without FlashCopy active.
- Application performance if DR failover occurs.

The solution should provide acceptable performance for both environments.

This configuration, that is 50% of the ranks (capacity) for FlashCopy source volumes and the FlashCopy target volumes on the remaining 50% of the ranks (capacity), has been suggested for the z/OS Global Mirror secondary configuration. In such a configuration, the z/OS Global Mirror journal volumes are placed on the FlashCopy target volume ranks. The FlashCopy target volumes for these journal volumes are placed on the z/OS Global Mirror secondary volume ranks.

Since all of the update data is first written to the journal volumes and then written to the secondary volumes, such an arrangement does split the non-FlashCopy secondary workload in half and can be implemented so as to utilize all ranks. During FlashCopy, the copy of the journal volumes from source to target is less stressful since there are relatively few journal volumes relative to the very large number of z/OS Global Mirror secondary volumes.

FlashCopy examples

This chapter shows some scenarios demonstrating how FlashCopy could support:

- Fast setup of test systems or integration systems
- Fast creation of volume copies for backup purposes

11.1 Create test system or integration system

Test systems or integration systems are needed to perform application tests or system integration tests.

As it is assumed that with test systems or integration systems, many write operations will occur over the time involved, we recommend doing a copy in the background environment.

11.1.1 One-time test system

Assume that an application is using one volume and a test system needs to be created to allow application tests or integration tests based on the contents of the production data. A FlashCopy is set up to copy the data once. The application typically needs to be quiesced or briefly suspended before executing the FlashCopy. Also, some applications cache their data, so this data may need to be flushed to disk, using application methods, prior to running the FlashCopy. This is not shown here. See Example 11-1.

Example 11-1 Create a one-time test system

```
#-----------------------------------------------------------
#--- remove existing FlashCopy relationships for volume 6100
#-----------------------------------------------------------
rmflash -dev IBM.2107-7506551 -quiet 6100:6300

#-----------------------------------------------------------
#--- establish FlashCopy relationships for source volume 6100
#-----------------------------------------------------------
#
mkflash -dev IBM.2107-7506551 -seqnum 01 6100:6300

#-----------------------------------------------------------
#--- list FlashCopy relationships for volume 6100
#-----------------------------------------------------------
lsflash -dev IBM.2107-7506551 -l 6100
```

11.1.2 Multiple setup of a test system with the same contents

Assume that an application test is needed multiple times with the same setup of data. The production volume is 6100, the test volume is 6300. Volume 6101 is chosen as an intermediate volume that gets its data once copying it from the production volume using FlashCopy. Then it is used as base for refresh of the test volume 6300.

Running Part 1 and Part 2 as one script would not work. The script would fail, as volume 6101 could not be the target for one FlashCopy relationship and the source for another FlashCopy relationship at the same time. Wait until the background copy for 6100:6101 finishes successfully before starting Part 2. Alternatively, you can also issue the **rmflash** command with the -cp and -wait parameters. These parameters cause the command to wait until the background copy is complete before continuing with the next step.

Whenever the test environment needs to be reset to the original data, just run Part 2 of the scripts or use the DS SM front end to perform a FlashCopy. See Example 11-2.

Example 11-2 Create a one time test system

```
Part 1
   #===========================================================
   #=== Part 1: establish FlashCopy relationship
```

```
#============================================================
#--- remove, establish, list FlashCopy relationships
#------------------------------------------------------------
rmflash -dev IBM.2107-7506551 -quiet 6100:6101
rmflash -dev IBM.2107-7506551 -quiet 6101:6300

mkflash -dev IBM.2107-7506551 -seqnum 01 6100:6101
lsflash -dev IBM.2107-7506551 -l 6100-6400
```

Part 2

```
#============================================================
#=== Part 2: establish FlashCopy 2 relationship
#=== 6100 -> 6300
#============================================================
#--- after the full volume copy of 6100 -> 6101 finished
#--- establish relationship from 6101:6300
#------------------------------------------------------------
mkflash -dev IBM.2107-7506551 -seqnum 02 6101:6300
lsflash -dev IBM.2107-7506551 -l 6100-6300
```

11.2 Create backup

Using a FlashCopy for backup can be done in various variations.

11.2.1 Creating a FlashCopy for backup purposes without volume copy

Volumes that are the result of a FlashCopy can be used by a backup server to backup the data to tape. As the backup process merely reads the data, one option could be to perform a FlashCopy without physically copying all data to the target. As soon as the backup of the data has finished, the FlashCopy relationship could be removed explicitly.

Doing backup based on the target volume allows you to use a target multiple times; see Example 11-3.

- Part 1: Establish FlashCopy volume A -> volume B with nocopy option
- Run backup
- Part 2: Remove FlashCopy relationship once volume backup has completed

Example 11-3 Create a backup copy

Part 1

```
#============================================================
#=== Part 1: establish FlashCopy relationship
#============================================================
#--- remove existing FlashCopy relationships for volume 6100
#------------------------------------------------------------
rmflash -dev IBM.2107-7506551 -quiet 6100:6300

#------------------------------------------------------------
#--- establish FlashCopy relationships for source volume 6100
#------------------------------------------------------------
mkflash -dev IBM.2107-7506551 -nocp -seqnum 01 6100:6300

#------------------------------------------------------------
#--- list FlashCopy relationships for volume 6100
#------------------------------------------------------------
lsflash -dev IBM.2107-7506551 -l 6100
```

After the backup has been taken, remove the FlashCopy relationship if you don't intend to use it for other purposes. Thus, unnecessary writes can be avoided. See Example 11-4.

Example 11-4 Create a backup copy

```
Part 2
   #============================================================
   #=== Part 2: remove FlashCopy relationships
   #============================================================
   rmflash -dev IBM.2107-7506551 -quiet 6100:6300
```

In complex application environments (for example, SAP), FlashCopy is often used as part of backup solutions. A good example of such solutions might be the Tivoli Data Protection modules in combination with Tivoli TSM.

11.2.2 Using an incremental FlashCopy for backup purposes

To have the safety of a real physical copy without always copying the full volume is something that could be achieved using the incremental FlashCopy. An initial full volume FlashCopy is followed by subsequent incremental FlashCopies, which only copy the updates that took place on the source volume. The target volume could be write inhibited. See Figure 11-5.

Example 11-5 Create an initial FlashCopy ready for subsequent incremental FlashCopies

```
Part 1
   #============================================================
   #=== Part 1: establish FlashCopy relationship
   #============================================================
   #--- remove existing FlashCopy relationships for volume 6100
   #------------------------------------------------------------
   rmflash -dev IBM.2107-7506551 -quiet 6100:6300

   #------------------------------------------------------------
   #--- establish FlashCopy relationships
   #------------------------------------------------------------
   mkflash -dev IBM.2107-7506551 -record -persist -seqnum 01 6100:6300

   #------------------------------------------------------------
   #--- list FlashCopy relationships for volume 6100
   #------------------------------------------------------------
   lsflash -dev IBM.2107-7506551 -l 6100
```

After the initial full volume copy, the following script supports the incremental copy of the FlashCopy relationship; see Example 11-6.

Example 11-6 Create an incremental FlashCopy

```
Part 2
   #============================================================
   #=== Part 2: resynch FlashCopy relationship
   #============================================================
   resyncflash -dev IBM.2107-7506551 -record -persist -seqnum 01 6100:6300
   lsflash -dev IBM.2107-7506551 -l 6100
```

11.2.3 Using a target volume to restore its contents back to the source

For each source volume one FlashCopy can exist with the *-record* and *-persist* attributes set. This volume can be used to refresh the source volume.

Logs may need to be applied to the target and then the target volume is reversed to the source volume.

To reverse the relationship the data must have been copied completely to the target before reversing it back to the source. To avoid a situation where the full volume needs to be copied with each FlashCopy, the Incremental FlashCopy should be used. As logs may need to be applied to the target volume prior to reversing it, the target volume should be write enabled. This example consists of the following steps (see Example 11-7):

- Part 1: Establish initial FlashCopy
- Part 2: Establish Incremental FlashCopy
- Part 3: Reverse the relationship

Applying application or DB logs needs to be carefully considered as well.

Example 11-7 Run initial FlashCopy to support refresh of source volume

```
Part 1
   #============================================================
   #=== Part 1: establish Incremental FlashCopy
   #============================================================
   #--- remove, establish, list FlashCopy relationships
   #------------------------------------------------------------
   rmflash -dev IBM.2107-7506551 -quiet 6100:6101
   mkflash -dev IBM.2107-7506551 -persist -record -tgtinhibit -seqnum 01 6100:6101
   lsflash -dev IBM.2107-7506551 -l 6100
```

After the initial FlashCopy, the Incremental Flashcopies can be used; see Example 11-8.

Example 11-8 Create an Incremental FlashCopy

```
Part 2
   #============================================================
   #=== Part 2: resynch FlashCopy relationship
   #============================================================
   resyncflash -dev IBM.2107-7506551 -record -persist -tgtinhibit -seqnum 01 6100:6101
   lsflash -dev IBM.2107-7506551 -l 6100
```

The reverse of the FlashCopy is done using the **reverseflash** command; see Example 11-9.

Example 11-9 Reverse the volumes

```
Part 3
   #============================================================
   #=== Part 3: reverse FlashCopy relationship
   #============================================================
   reverseflash -dev IBM.2107-7506551 -persist -record -tgtinhibit -seqnum 01 6100:6101
   lsflash -dev IBM.2107-7506551 -l 6100
```

Part 4

Metro Mirror

In this part of the book, we describe the characteristics and operation of DS8000 Metro Mirror. We also discuss considerations that you may find useful when planning the implementation of Metro Mirror.

Metro Mirror overview

In this chapter, we provide an overview of Metro Mirror on the DS8000 disk subsystem.

12.1 Metro Mirror overview

Metro Mirror (previously known as synchronous Peer-to-Peer Remote Copy, or PPRC) provides real-time mirroring of logical volumes between two DS8000s that can be located up to 300 km from each other. It is a synchronous copy solution where write operations are completed on both copies (local and remote site) before they are considered to be complete.

It is typically used for applications that cannot suffer any data loss in the event of a failure.

As data is synchronously transferred, the distance between primary and secondary disk subsystems will determine the effect on application response time. Figure 12-1 illustrates the sequence of a write update with Metro Mirror.

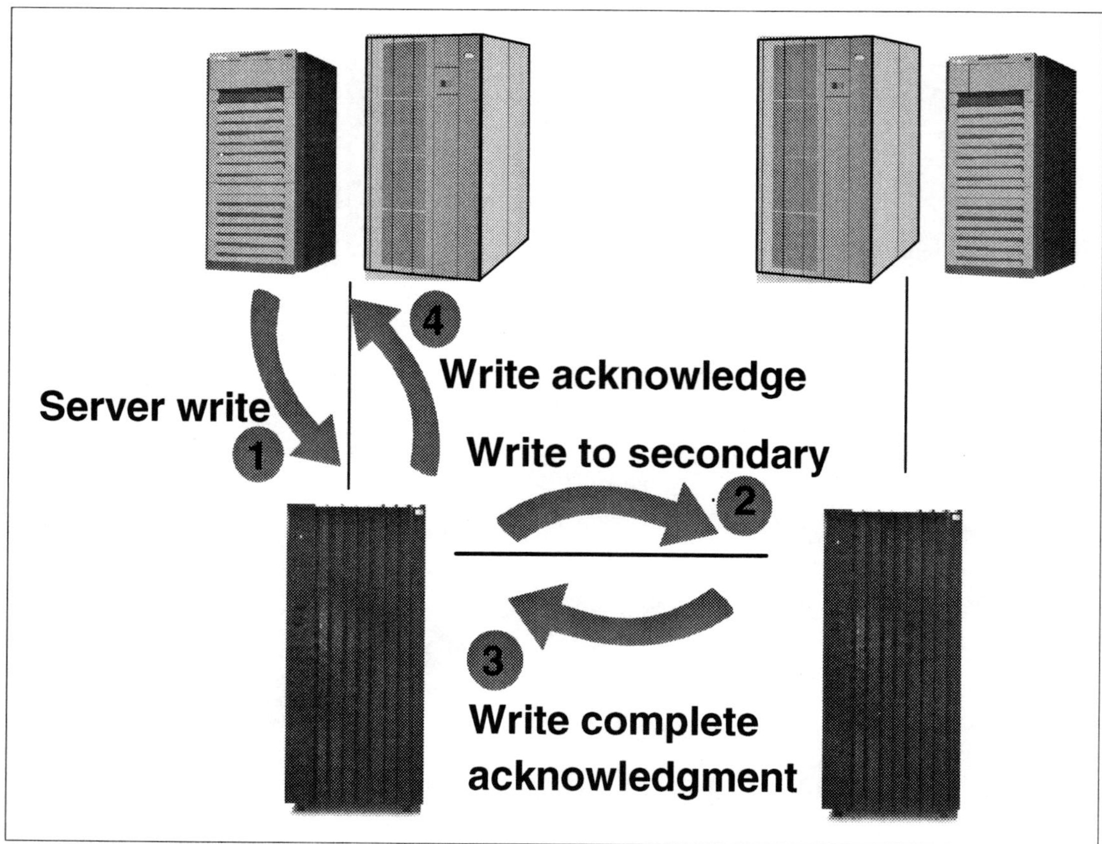

Figure 12-1 Metro Mirror

When the application performs a write update operation to a primary volume, this is what happens:

1. Write to primary volume (DS8000 cache and NVS).
2. Write to secondary (DS8000 cache and NVS).
3. Signal write complete on the secondary DS8000.
4. Post I/O complete to host server.

The Fibre Channel connection between primary and secondary subsystems can be direct, through a switch, or through other supported distance solutions (for example, Dense Wave Division Multiplexor or DWDM).

12.2 Data consistency

The redbook *IBM TotalStorage DS8000: Concepts and Architecture,* SG24-6452 introduces the concept of data consistency, and Consistency Groups. For Metro Mirror, consistency requirements are managed through use of the *Consistency Group* option when defining Metro Mirror paths between pairs of LSSs. Volumes or LUNs that are paired between two LSSs whose paths are defined with the Consistency Group option can be considered part of a Consistency Group.

Consistency is provided by means of the *extended long busy* (for z/OS) or *queue full* (for open systems) conditions. These are triggered when the DS8000 detects a condition where it cannot update the Metro Mirror secondary volume. The volume pair that first detects the error will go into the extended long busy or queue full condition, such that it will not do any writes. For z/OS a system message will be issued (IEA494I state change message); for open systems an SNMP trap message will be issued. These messages can be used as a trigger for automation purposes - to provide data consistency by use of the Freeze/Run (or Unfreeze) commands. For further discussion of these, refer to Chapter 13., "Metro Mirror options and configuration considerations" on page 121.

Important: The data on disk at the secondary site is an exact mirror of that at the primary site, during normal Metro Mirror processing (whether it will be during or after an error situation depends on the options specified for the pair and the path). Remember that any data still in buffers or processor memory is not yet on disk and so will not be mirrored to the secondary site. A disaster will then appear to be a similar situation to a power failure in the primary site.

12.2.1 Rolling disaster

In disaster situations, it is unlikely that the entire complex will fail at the same moment. Failures tend to be intermittent and gradual, and a disaster can occur over many seconds, even minutes. Because some data may have been processed and other data lost in this transition, data integrity on the secondary volumes is exposed. This situation is called a rolling disaster. The mirrored data at the recovery site must be managed so that cross-volume or LSS data consistency is preserved during the intermittent or gradual failure.

Metro Mirror of itself does not offer a means of *controlling* this scenario — it offers the *Consistency Group* and *Critical attributes*, which along with appropriate automation solutions can manage data consistency and integrity at the remote site. The Metro Mirror volume pairs are always consistent, due to the synchronous nature of Metro Mirror; however, cross-volume or LSS data consistency must have an external management method. IBM offers the GDPS® and eRCMF service offerings to deliver solutions in this area — refer to Appendix F., "Service offerings" on page 659 for more information.

12.3 Automation and management

Metro Mirror is a hardware mirroring solution. A volume (or LUN) is paired with a volume (or LUN) in the remote disk subsystem through a command, issued to the disk subsystem, through one of the interfaces. As the size of the environment grows, so does the complexity of managing it — you need a means of managing the pairs, ensuring they are in duplex status, adding volume pairs as required, monitoring for error conditions, and more importantly, for managing data consistency across LSS and across disk subsystems.

However you choose to do this, you need to consider the implications for:

- Design of the automation solution
- Maintenance
- Testing
- Support

All of these need to be thought about — you do not want to be in the situation where you are relying on your automation processes for consistent data in a disaster situation, only to find that it has not worked, or perhaps worse, you do not know that you do not have consistent data.

IBM offers services and solutions for the automation and management of the Metro Mirror environment. These include GDPS for high-end zSeries environments, eRCMF for open systems, and so on. Refer to Appendix F., “Service offerings” on page 659 for more information.

Metro Mirror options and configuration considerations

In this chapter, we discuss some of the options available when using Metro Mirror on the DS8000 disk subsystem.

We also discuss the configuration guidelines that should be considered when planning the Metro Mirror environment.

The DS8000 supports Fibre Channel (FC) Metro Mirror links only.

13.1 Initial disk synchronization

You may choose to do the initial disk synchronization in the Global Copy mode (review Chapter 12., "Metro Mirror overview" on page 117 and Chapter 17., "Global Copy overview" on page 187), then switch to Metro Mirror mode. This will allow you to bring all volumes to Duplex Pending XD state, which has little or no application impact, then switch to Full Duplex state. You can do this through TSO commands, DS CLI, or one of the other interfaces.

13.2 Clustering

Since the disk attached to the server is being mirrored using Metro Mirror, this offers some improved opportunities for high availability solutions.

IBM offers several solutions in this area, including GDS for Windows® environments, and HACMP™ for AIX. For more information refer to Part 9, "Solutions" on page 527.

13.2.1 GDPS HyperSwap Manager

The GDPS/PPRC services offering includes the GDPS HyperSwap function. This function can be used to mask some primary Metro Mirror disk subsystem problems or planned disk subsystem maintenance activities, by allowing the primary DASD to be swapped transparently from one site to another without requiring an application or system outage.

For more information, refer to Chapter 37., "GDPS overview and positioning" on page 529.

13.3 Freeze and run commands

Metro Mirror freeze and run commands are used by automation processes to ensure data consistency. We discuss their usage in this section.

13.3.1 Freeze command

Messages and environmental triggers related to Metro Mirror problems can be detected by your automation software. You can then use the TSO command CGROUP with the FREEZE parameter (or equivalent command through the other interfaces) to suspend all required secondary Metro Mirror operations.

The FREEZE option removes the Metro Mirror paths, and suspends the volume pairs for a given LSS pairing. If used in combination with the CGROUP(Y) option of the CESTPATH command, then an Extended Long Busy (for z/OS) or Queue Full (for open systems) condition will be forced on all the LSSs where the FREEZE is issued, and thus, all the I/Os to the respective primary volumes will be queued while in the extended long busy window. Once your automation process detects that the updates can be resumed, it can issue the CGROUP command with the RUN parameter. This command releases all I/O to the primary devices, but still leaves the secondary devices suspended at a point-in-time (with the FREEZE the associated paths are removed).

The default 2-minute timer of the extended long busy state gives the automation enough time to issue a CGROUP FREEZE command to the necessary LSSs. I/O resumes after the default 2 minutes if a CGROUP RUN command is not received.

The ICKDSF PPRCOPY FREEZE and PPRCCOPY RUN commands provide the same functionality as the TSO CGROUP FREEZE and CGROUP RUN commands.

If you are using the DS Command-Line Interface (DS CLI), you can use the `freezepprc` and `unfreezepprc` commands to provide the same functionality as the TSO CGROUP FREEZE and CGROUP RUN commands.

It is not possible to issue Consistency Group (freeze/unfreeze) type commands from the DS Storage Manager Graphical User Interface.

Note: To resynchronize your Metro Mirror environment once the problem has been resolved, you will need to redefine your Metro Mirror paths (they are removed as part of the CGROUP FREEZE command). You can then issue CESTPAIR commands with MODE(RESYNC) (or equivalent commands in the other interfaces).

Tip: We recommend the use of FlashCopy against your secondary volumes prior to a resynchronization. This is because you do not have data consistency until all volumes have reached the Duplex state.

13.3.2 Critical attribute

The critical attribute determines what will happen after a failed I/O to a secondary volume occurs. What happens will depend on how this attribute was set when the pair was established, and how the DS8000 was configured.

The critical attribute is set when establishing the volume pair. If using TSO commands, the CRIT parameter of the CESTPAIR command is used for this. If you are using the DS CLI, the critical attribute is set using the `mkpprc -critmode` parameter. If using ICKDSF, specify the CRIT(YES) parameter of the PPRCOPY ESTPAIR command. If using the DS Storage Manager GUI, select the **Enable critical volume mode** option in the Select copy options page when defining volume pairs.

If CRIT(NO) was specified in the CESTPAIR command (or equivalent options through the other interfaces) when the pairs were established, then following an I/O error completion to the secondary volume, Metro Mirror will suspend the volume and allow subsequent write requests to the Metro Mirror primary volume. The pair is suspended, the secondary volume does not receive any more updates, and the primary DS8000 will perform change recording, thus keeping track of the primary updates for subsequent re-synchronization.

If CRIT(YES) was specified with the CESTPAIR command (or equivalent options through the other interfaces), and if an I/O error to the secondary volume occurs, Metro Mirror will either allow or disallow subsequent writes to the primary, depending on how the DS8000 was configured. For z/OS the IEA491E message will present the reason SUSPENDED, CRITICAL-STATE, ALL WRITES FAILED. The Metro Mirror pair then remains in a suspended state until the problem is corrected and a CESTPAIR RESYNC or CDELPAIR command is later issued.

Whether subsequent writes to the primary volumes are allowed or not will depend on how the DS8000 LCU is configured:

- `chlcu -critmode enable`

  Or, DS Storage Manager GUI **Copy Services** → **Paths** → Select **LSS Copy Options** from the pull down list → **Go** → Accept or modify the selected LSSs from the **Select LSS** pull down list → Select the **Critical Mode** option to enable the setting → **OK**.

  – The volume pair is suspended and further writes to the source volume are not accepted if data cannot be sent to the target volume.

13.3.3 Consistency Group and critical mode combination

Table 13-1 shows what happens when the CRIT parameter of the CESTPAIR command, and the CGROUP parameter of CESTPATH command are combined. These options can also be set using the DS CLI, or with the DS Storage Manager GUI.

Table 13-1 Interaction of CRIT and CGROUP parameters

	CRIT(Y)	CRIT(N)
CGROUP(Y)	IEA494I with long busy state SNMP trap for open systems	IEA494I with long busy state SNMP trap for open systems
	Pair in error suspended	Pair in error suspended
	Unit check on primary device	No unit check on primary device
	IEA494I when suspended	IEA494I when suspended
CGROUP(N)	No long busy state	No long busy state
	Pair in error suspended	Pair in error suspended
	Unit check on primary device	No unit check on primary device
	IEA494I when suspended	IEA494I when suspended

The IEA494I message with SUSPENDED status is issued for the in-error pair to all z/OS images that have the primary volume online. An IEA491E message is returned to the issuing system of the next I/O that is attempted to the volume that is suspended. For open systems, an SNMP trap will be issued to the address specified when the DS8000 SNMP service was configured.

For further discussion on the CGROUP and the CRIT parameters, the following publication can be referenced: *z/OS DFSMS Advanced Copy Services*, SC35-0428.

13.4 Failover and failback

The Metro Mirror Failover and Failback modes are designed to help reduce the time required to synchronize Metro Mirror volumes after switching between the application and the recovery sites.

In a typical Metro Mirror environment, processing will temporarily failover to the Metro Mirror secondary site upon an outage at the primary site. When the primary site is capable of resuming production, processing will failback from the secondary site to the primary site.

With the Metro Mirror Failover Mode capability, when it is used during the failover to the secondary site, change recording is performed while processing is done on Metro Mirror volumes at the secondary site. When the Metro Mirror Failback Mode is used during the failback to the primary site, only changed data will be sent to the primary site to synchronize the Metro Mirror volumes, thereby helping to reduce the time required to complete the failback.

The Metro Mirror Failover and Failback modes can be invoked from the DS Storage Manager GUI, the DS Command-Line Interface (CLI), TSO commands, or by use of the ICKDSF utility.

We give an example of the use of Failover and Failback in 16.1.2, "Failover Failback using TSO" on page 173.

13.5 Metro Mirror links

Metro Mirror pairs are set up between volumes in LSSs, usually in different disk subsystems, and these are normally in separate locations. To facilitate ease of testing, the DS8000 does support Metro Mirror source and target on the same DS8000.

To establish a Metro Mirror pair, there needs to be a Metro Mirror path between the LSSs that the volumes reside in. These paths are bi-directional and can be shared by any Metro Mirror pairs in the same LSS to the secondary LSS in the same direction. For bandwidth and redundancy, more than one path can be created between the same LSSs, Metro Mirror will balance the workload across the available paths between the primary and secondary.

Note: Remember that the LSS is not a physical construct in the DS8000. Volumes in an LSS can come from multiple disk arrays.

Metro Mirror pairs can only be established between storage control units of the same (or similar) type and features. For example, a DS8000 can have a Metro Mirror pair with another DS8000, a DS6000, an ESS 800, or an ESS 750. It cannot have a Metro Mirror pair with an RVA or an ESS F20. Note that all disk subsystems must have the appropriate Metro Mirror feature installed (for DS8000 the Remote Mirror and Copy 2244 function authorization model, which is 2244 Model RMC). If your DS8000 is being mirrored to an ESS disk subsystem, the ESS must have PPRC Version 2 (which supports Fibre Channel PPRC links).

A path (or group of paths) needs to be established from each primary or source LSS to each secondary LSS with related secondary volume (or LUN). These logical paths are transported over physical links between the disk subsystems. The physical link includes the host adapter in the primary DS8000, the cabling, switches or directors, any wideband or long distance transport devices (DWDM, channel extenders, WAN) and the host adapters in the secondary disk subsystem. Physical links can carry multiple logical Metro Mirror paths, as shown in Figure 13-1.

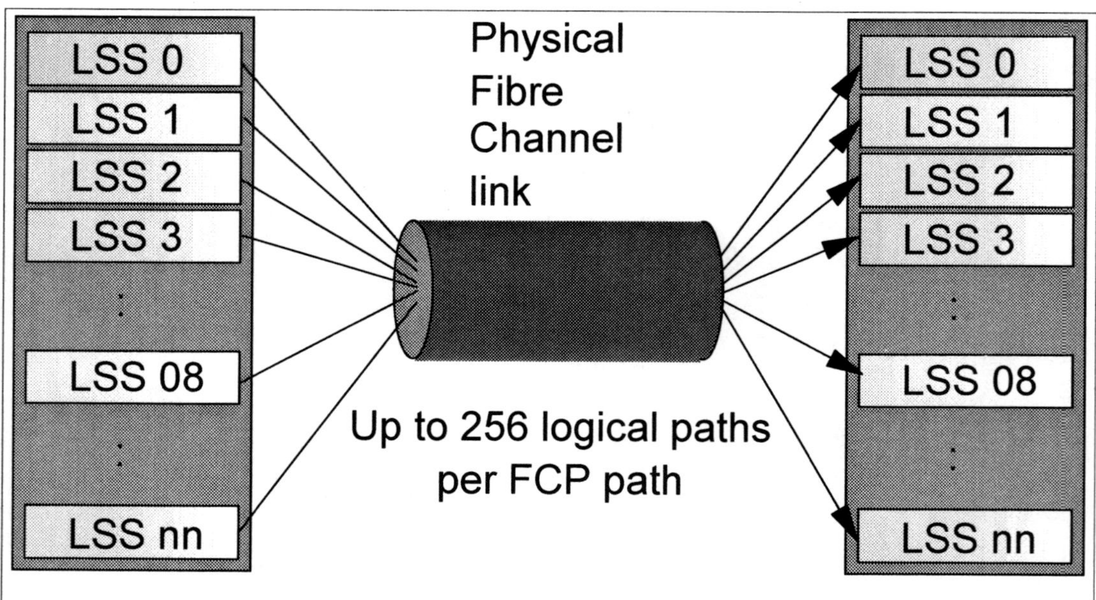

Figure 13-1 Logical paths

> **Note:** In general, when establishing a Metro Mirror pair we check that a Metro Mirror path exists. In some specific commands (like Metro Mirror Failover) we allow the establish even when the path does not exist.

13.5.1 Metro Mirror Fibre Channel links

A DS8000 Fibre Channel port can simultaneously be:

- Sender for Metro Mirror primary
- Receiver for a Metro Mirror secondary
- Target for Fibre Channel Protocol (FCP) hosts I/O from open systems and Linux® on zSeries

Although one FCP link would have sufficient bandwidth for most Metro Mirror environments, for redundancy reasons we recommend configuring two Fibre Channel links between each primary and secondary disk subsystem.

Metro Mirror FCP links can be direct connected, or connected by up to two switches.

Dedicating Fibre Channel ports for Metro Mirror use guarantees no interference from host I/O activity. This is recommended with Metro Mirror, which is time critical and should not be impacted by host I/O activity. The Metro Mirror ports used provide connectivity for all LSSs within the DS8000 and can carry multiple logical Metro Mirror paths.

13.5.2 Logical paths

A Metro Mirror logical path is a logical connection between the sending LSS and the receiving LSS. An FCP link can accommodate multiple Metro Mirror logical paths.

Figure 13-2 shows an example where we have a 1:1 mapping of source to target LSSs, and where the three logical paths are accommodated in one Metro Mirror link:

- LSS1 in DS8000 1 to LSS1 in DS8000 2
- LSS2 in DS8000 1 to LSS2 in DS8000 2
- LSS3 in DS8000 1 to LSS3 in DS8000 2

Alternatively, if the volumes in each of the LSSs of DS8000 1 map to volumes in all three secondary LSSs in DS8000 2, there will be nine logical paths over the Metro Mirror link (not fully illustrated in Figure 13-2). Note that we recommend a 1:1 LSS mapping.

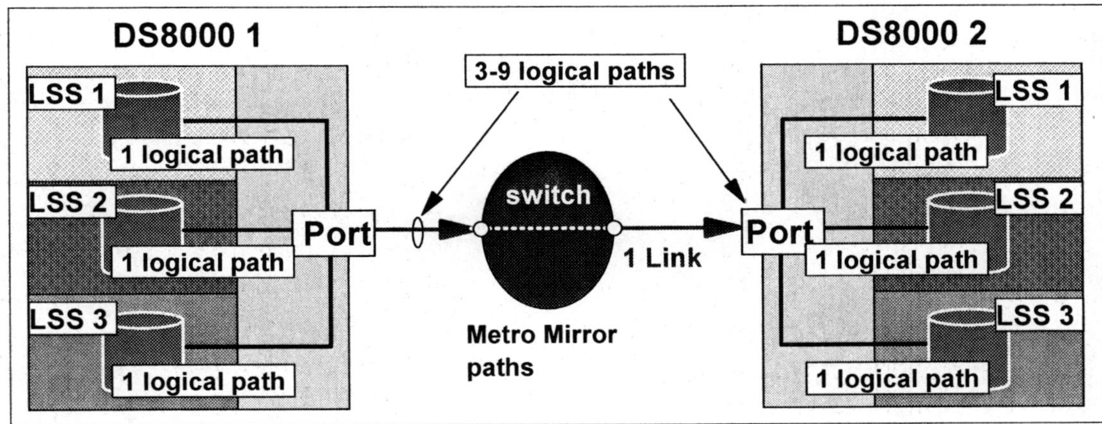

Figure 13-2 Logical paths for Metro Mirror

Metro Mirror links have certain architectural limits, as follows:

- A primary LSS can maintain paths to a maximum of four secondary LSSs. Each secondary LSS can reside in a separate DS8000.
- Up to eight logical paths per LSS-LSS relationship can be defined. Identical logical paths do require different physical paths.
- An FCP port can host up to 2048 logical paths. These are the logical and directional paths that are made from LSS to LSS.
- An FCP path (the physical path from one port to another port) can host up to 256 logical paths (Metro Mirror paths).
- An FCP port can accommodate up to 126 different physical paths (DS8000 port to DS8000 port through the SAN).

13.6 Bandwidth

Prior to establishing your Metro Mirror solution, you should establish what your peak bandwidth requirement will be. This will help to ensure that you have enough Metro Mirror links in place to support that requirement.

To avoid any response time issues you should establish the peak write rate for your systems and ensure you have adequate bandwidth to cope with this load — and allow for growth. Remember that only writes are mirrored across to the secondary volumes.

Tools to assist with this data collection include RMF™ in the z/OS environment.

More information on bandwidth and available connection options can be found in the redbook, *IBM TotalStorage Business Continuity Solutions Guide*, SG24-6547.

13.7 LSS design

Since the DS8000 has made the LSS a topological construct, which is not tied to a physical array as in the ESS, the design of your LSS layout can be simplified. It is now possible to assign LSSs to applications, for example, without concern regarding under-allocation or over-allocation of physical disk subsystem resources. This can also simplify the Metro Mirror environment, as it is possible to reduce the number of commands that are required for data consistency (see 13.3, “Freeze and run commands” on page 122 for more information).

13.8 Distance

The distance between your primary and secondary DS8000 subsystems will have an effect on the response time overhead of the Metro Mirror implementation. Your IBM Field Technical Sales Specialist (FTSS) can be contacted to assist you in assessing your configuration and the distance implications.

The maximum supported distance for Metro Mirror is 300 km.

13.9 Symmetrical configuration

As an aid to planning and management of your Metro Mirror environment, we recommend that you maintain a symmetrical configuration — in terms of both physical and logical elements. This will have the following benefits:

- Simplify management: It is easy to see where volumes will be mirrored, and processes can be automated.
- Reduce administrator overhead: Due to automation, and the simpler nature of the solution, overhead can be reduced.
- Ease the addition of new capacity into the environment: New arrays can be added in a modular fashion.
- Ease problem diagnosis: The simple structure of the solution will aid in identifying where any problems may exist.

Figure 13-3 shows this idea in a graphical form. DS8000 #1 has Metro Mirror paths defined to DS8000 # 2, which is in a remote location. On DS8000 #1, volumes defined in LSS 00 are mirrored to volumes in LSS 00 on DS8000 #2 (volume P1 is paired with volume S1, P2 with S2, P3 with S3, and so on). Volumes in LSS 01 on DS8000 #1 are mirrored to volumes in LSS 01 on DS8000 #2, and so on. Requirements for additional capacity can be added in a symmetrical way also — by addition of volumes into existing LSSs, and by addition of new LSSs when needed (for example, addition of two volumes in LSS 03 and 05, and one volume to LSS 04 will bring them to the same number of volumes as the other LSS). Additional volumes could then be distributed evenly across all LSSs, or additional LSSs added.

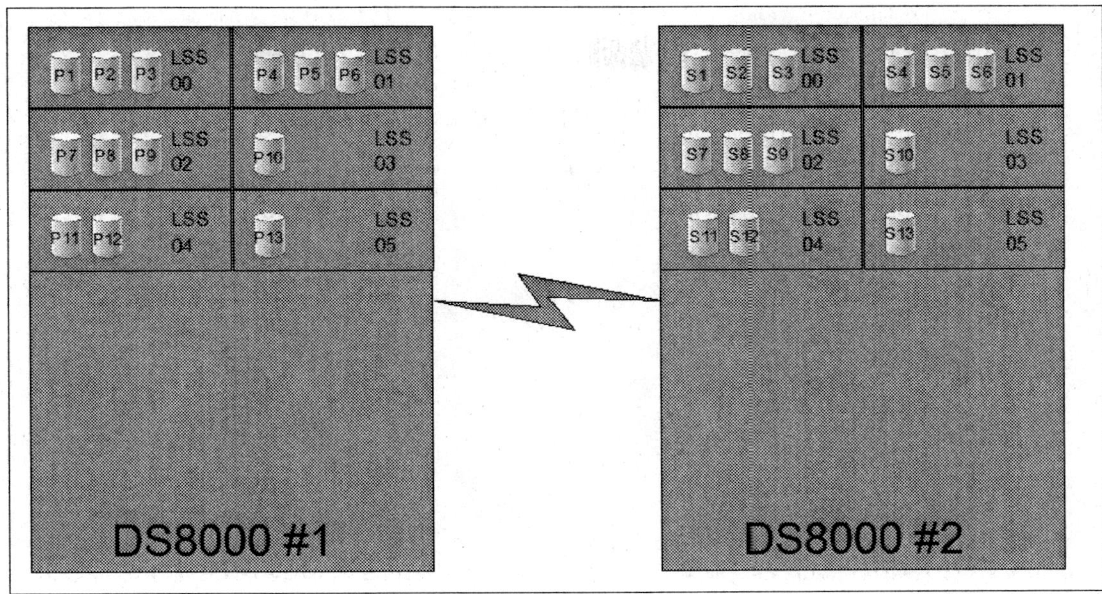

Figure 13-3 Symmetrical Metro Mirror configuration

As well as making the maintenance of the Metro Mirror configuration easier, this has the added benefit of helping to balance the workload across the DS8000. Figure 13-3 shows a logical configuration — this idea applies equally to the physical aspects of the DS8000. You should attempt to balance workload and apply symmetrical concepts to other aspects of your DS8000 (for example, the Extent Pools).

13.10 Volumes

You will need to consider which volumes should be mirrored to the secondary site. One option is to mirror all volumes. This is advantageous for the following reasons:

- You will not need to consider whether any required data has been missed.
- Users will not need to remember which logical pool of volumes is mirrored and which is not.
- You will not require a potentially complex volume pooling scheme (DFSMS Storage Groups).
- Addition of volumes to the environment is simplified — you will not have to have two processes for addition of disk (one for mirrored volumes, and another for non-mirrored volumes).
- You will be able to move data around your disk environment easily without a concern over whether the target volume is a mirrored volume or not.

You may choose not to mirror all volumes. In this case you will need careful control over what data is placed on the mirrored volumes (to avoid any capacity issues) and what is placed on the non-mirrored volumes (to avoid missing any required data). One method of doing this could be to place all mirrored volumes in a particular set of LSSs, in which all volumes have Metro Mirror enabled, and direct all data requiring mirroring to these volumes. On z/OS this could be accomplished using DFSMS Storage Groups and DFSMS Automatic Class Selection routines. Figure 13-4 shows a graphical view of this concept.

Though not mirroring all volumes might be the simplest solution to manage, it could also require significantly more network bandwidth. Since network bandwidth is a cost to the solution, minimizing this bandwidth may well be worth the added management complexity.

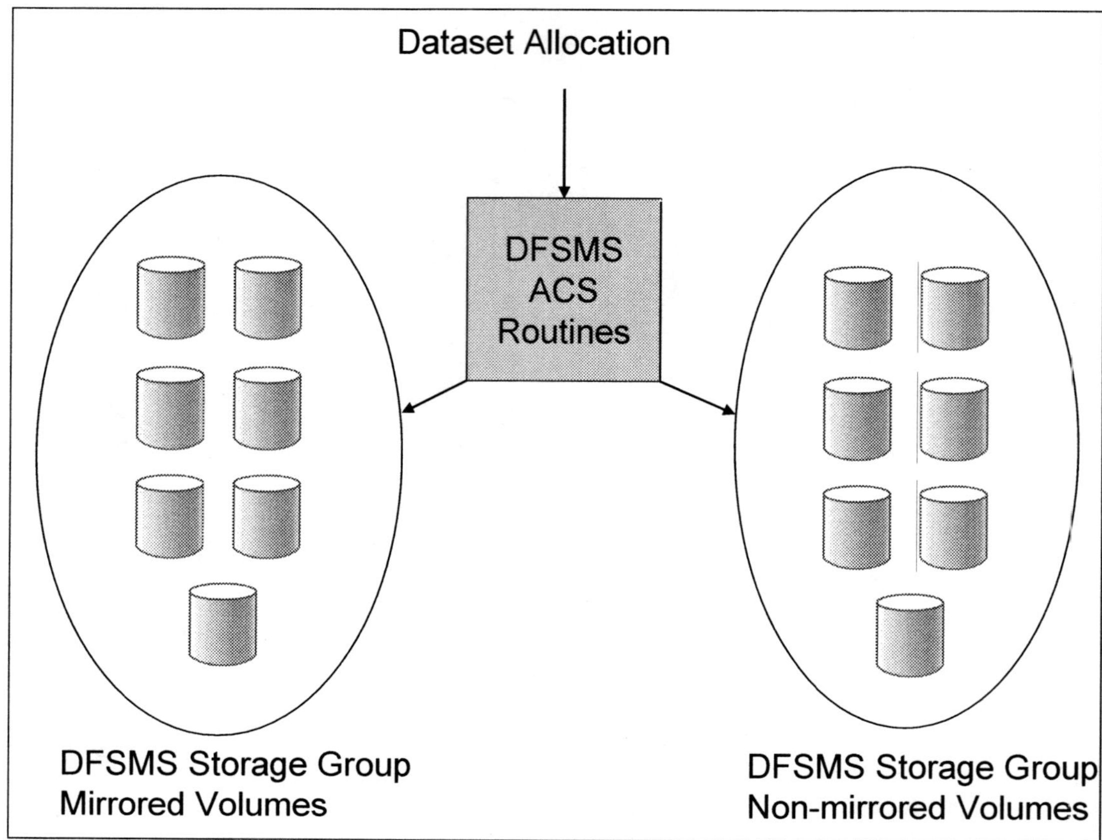

Figure 13-4 DFSMS Storage Group separation

Metro Mirror interfaces

In this chapter, we introduce the various interfaces available for the setup and management of Metro Mirror on the DS8000 disk subsystem.

14.1 Interfaces

In this section, we describe the various interfaces available for the configuration and control of DS8000 Metro Mirror for zSeries. In summary, these are the available interfaces:

- For z/OS and OS/390, the following interfaces can be used:
  - TSO commands
  - DS Storage Manager Graphical User Interface (DS Storage Manager GUI)
  - ICKDSF utility
  - ANTRQST application programming interface (API)
- For z/VM®:
  - DS Storage Manager GUI
  - ICKDSF utility
- For VSE:
  - DS Storage Manager GUI
  - ICKDSF utility
- For TPF:
  - DS Storage Manager GUI
  - ICKDSF utility
  - TPF itself
  - Other attached servers that support control of Metro Mirror

In addition, the DS Command-Line Interface (DS CLI) can be used to invoke Metro Mirror commands from a server that supports the DS CLI (for example, a Windows XP server), if that server has appropriate connectivity to the DS8000.

Figure 14-1 compares Metro Mirror commands in the various interfaces.

Table 14-1 Comparison of interfaces

Command	TSO	ICKDSF	DS CLI	DS Storage Manager
Establish path	CESTPATH	PPRCOPY ESTPATH	mkpprcpath	Copy services □ Paths □ Create
Establish pair	CESTPAIR	PPRCOPY ESTPAIR	mkpprc	Copy services □ Metro Mirror □ Create
Freeze Consistency Group	CGROUP FREEZE	PPRCOPY FREEZE	freezepprc	Not available
Thaw Consistency Group	CGROUP RUN	PPRCOPY RUN	unfreezepprc	Not available
Suspend pair	CSUSPEND	PPRCOPY SUSPEND	pausepprc	Copy services □ Metro Mirror □ Suspend
Query pair	CQUERY	PPRCOPY QUERY	lspprc	Copy services □ Metro Mirror
Query path	CQUERY PATH	PPRCOPY QUERY PATHS	lspprcpath	Copy services □ Paths

Command	TSO	ICKDSF	DS CLI	DS Storage Manager
Recover secondary	CRECOVER	PPRCOPY RECOVER	rmpprc -at src	Copy services □ Metro Mirror
Resume suspended pair	CESTPAIR MODE (RESYNC)	PPRCOPY ESTPAIR MODE (RESYNC)	resumepprc	Copy services □ Metro Mirror □ Resume
Delete pair	CDELPAIR	PPRCOPY DELPAIR	rmpprc	Copy services □ Metro Mirror □ Delete
Delete path	CDELPATH	PPRCOPY DELPATH	rmpprcpath	Copy services □ Paths □ Delete
Failover	CESTPAIR ACTION (FAILOVER)	PPRCOPY ESTPAIR FAILOVER	failoverpprc	Copy services □ Metro Mirror □ Recovery Action
Failback	CESTPAIR ACTION (FAILBACK)	PPRCOPY ESTPAIR FAILBACK	failbackpprc	Copy services □ Metro Mirror □ Recovery Failback

14.2 TSO

For z/OS, the TSO Metro Mirror commands offer a powerful and flexible interface to control your Metro Mirror environment. They can also be used for control of open systems volumes through the recent addition of support.

The TSO commands communicate with the DS8000 through use of a device number specified on the command. IP connectivity is not required.

TSO commands can be integrated into REXX programs for automation purposes.

Tip: If you are controlling open systems volumes through TSO commands, you need to have a z/OS volume in the same server to direct your command to. For example, for an open systems LUN in LSS 16, a z/OS volume in LSS 00 can be used for the device address. If you had a LUN in LSS 15, you can use a z/OS volume in LSS 01.

14.2.1 Command overview

A brief discussion of each command and some options are discussed below. Most TSO commands require the subsystem identifier (SSID) of the LSS to be specified; some require the channel connection address (CCA) of the volume also, and so we describe these first.

Channel connection address

Some Metro Mirror TSO commands require the use of the channel connection address (CCA) of the device in question. The CCA on a DS8000 is always relative to the LSS, and is always between 00 and FF. If the device numbers on the DS8000 have been generated as a contiguous group of 256 addresses, where each group belongs to an LSS (logical control unit), then the CCAs that are going to be used for the Metro Mirror commands are the last two digits of the device number.

For example, for device numbers AA00 - AAFF, the corresponding CCAs are 00 - FF. If you did not define the device addresses contiguously, you can get the CCA for a device by using the TSO CQUERY command, or the DEVSERV system command.

Subsystem identifier

During the installation and configuration process, each logical control unit (that is each LSS) is assigned a unique four-digit subsystem identifier (SSID). This setting is required to identify the control unit for the host for error reporting reasons and also for functions like Metro Mirror.

Each LSS must have a different SSID. It is recommended to assign consecutive SSID numbers to each LSS within an DS8000 box. This will simplify the configuration procedure and make it easier for the subsequent identification of the LSSs. LSSs attached to the same operating system image must have different SSIDs: *SSIDs must be unique*. z/OS checks during the IPL to insure that there are no duplicate SSIDs.

When establishing Metro Mirror paths, the SSIDs are used in the Metro Mirror TSO commands to identify the primary and secondary LSSs that will be paired.

When issuing commands to open systems volumes from TSO commands, you use a special SSID value. You can either use x'FFFF', if you are unsure what the value should be, or check the value using a CQUERY command.

CESTPAIR

This command is used to establish the Metro Mirror primary to secondary relationship. The primary and secondary volumes must have the same number of tracks on each cylinder, and the same number of bytes on each track. The secondary device must have the same number, or a greater number of cylinders, than the primary device. If it will ever be needed to swap the Metro Mirror direction, as in a failover/failback, then the volumes must be the same size.

This command has parameters that allow it to indicate whether the operation is an initial establish of volumes that were in the simplex state, whether it is a re-synchronization of a suspended pair of volumes, whether it is a Metro Mirror or Global Copy pair, or whether Failover or Failback processing is being requested.

Example 14-1 shows the command necessary to establish an initial Metro Mirror pair.

Example 14-1 Metro Mirror establish pair

```
CESTPAIR DEVN(X'2028') -
   PRIM(X'1710' 06571 X'28' X'00')      -
   SEC(X'1711' 06571 X'28' X'01') -
   OPTION(SYNC) MODE(COPY) ONLINSEC(NO) MSGREQ(YES)
```

In Example 14-1, the primary volume resides on LSS x'00' of the application site ESS. The SSID of the LSS is x'**1710**', the serial number of the DS8000 is **06571**, its CCA is x'**28**', and the LSS is x'**00**'. The secondary volume resides in LSS x'00' of the recovery site ESS. Its CCA is x'28'. This matching between the last two digits of the device number address and the CCAs of the primary and the secondary volumes is not mandatory, however, it is useful for working with the configuration. CCA is discussed in "CESTPATH" on page 135.

The MSGREQ(YES) parameter specifies that Metro Mirror wait until the initial full volume copy operation is complete before issuing the completion message ANTP0001I. If you are using automation, use this message as a trigger for other operations.

CESTPATH

When establishing a path between DS8000 for Metro Mirror, use the CESTPATH command. There must be a physical Fibre Channel connection between the two DS8000 subsystems. You need to know the SSID, World Wide Node Name (WWNN), and LSS number for the primary and secondary DS8000s. These can be displayed with the CQUERY command.

Example 14-2 shows an example of a CESTPATH command to establish Metro mirror paths.

Example 14-2 CESTPATH command

```
CESTPATH DEVN(X'2028') -
   PRIM(X'1710' 5005076303AAAAAA X'00') -
   SEC(X'1711' 5005076303AAAAAA X'01')      -
   LINK(X'00300200')            CGROUP(NO)
```

The example shown in Example 14-2 is establishing a loopback path to the same DS8000. The SSID of the primary volume is x'1710', the WWNN is 5005076303AAAAAA, and the LSS is x'00'.

The Link address specifies the DS8000 host adapter ports for the Metro Mirror path. The format of each Fibre Channel path address has the hex digit form of 00300200 where:

0030 Specifies the Fibre Channel adapter used for the path in the primary subsystem.

0200 Specifies the Fibre Channel adapter used for the path in the secondary subsystem.

CDELPAIR

The CDELPAIR command is used to specify the primary and secondary volumes to be removed from a Metro Mirror pairing. This command should be directed to the primary device; see Example 14-3.

Example 14-3 CDELPAIR command

```
CDELPAIR DEVN(X'2028') -
   PRIM(X'1710' 06571 X'28' X'00')      -
   SEC(X'1711' 06571 X'28' X'01')
```

Before issuing a CDELPAIR command, it should be verified that there are some active paths between the respective primary and secondary LSSs. If all of the paths that were established between both LSSs have been disabled, the CDELPAIR command will fail. After the failing CDELPAIR command times out, the state of the primary volume is simplex. The secondary volume remains in its previous state (duplex, pending, or suspended). You then need to issue a CRECOVER command to return the secondary volume to the simplex state.

In Example 14-3, the primary volume has SSID x'1710', the serial number is 06571, the CCA is x'28', and the LSS is x'00'.

CDELPATH

The CDELPATH command is used to delete established Metro mirror paths between a primary LSS and the corresponding secondary LSS; see Example 14-4. Only the paths to the specified secondary LSS are affected — all other paths to other LSSs are not affected.

Before issuing a CDELPATH command, a CDELPAIR command to all Metro Mirror volume pairs should be issued. The CDELPATH command may cause an ANTP0121I message if this sequence is not followed.

Example 14-4 CDELPATH command

```
CDELPATH DEVN(X'E12B') -
   PRIM(X'1071' 5005076300BBBBBB X'01') -
   SEC(X'1710' 5005076303AAAAAA X'00')
```

In Example 14-4 on page 136, the primary device has SSID x'1071', WWNN 5005076300BBBBBB and LSS x'01'.

CGROUP

The CGROUP command is used to control operations for multiple Metro Mirror volume pairs on a given LSS:

- **CGROUP FREEZE**

  Suspends Metro Mirror operations for all Metro Mirror volumes on the specified LSS pair. With the FREEZE parameter, Metro Mirror volume pairs are suspended and Metro Mirror paths are deleted for the specified LSS pair. If the Metro Mirror paths for the LSS pair were defined with Consistency Group enabled (CGROUP parameter of the CESTPATH command), then an Extended Long Busy (ELB) condition is initiated when CGROUP FREEZE is issued for the LSS. During the ELB window, update activity cannot proceed in the LSS where the freeze was done.

- **CGROUP RUN**

  Resumes all operations for the Metro Mirror volumes on the specified LSS. The CGROUP RUN command is used in order to reset the ELB condition and release application I/O to the primary volumes.

Tip: The CGROUP FREEZE command deletes the paths between the specified LSS pair. To restart normal Metro Mirror operation back again, the paths will have to be re-established and the pairs will have to be re-synchronized.

Example 14-5 illustrates the CGROUP command.

Example 14-5 CGROUP example

```
CGROUP DEVN(X'202A') PRIM(X'1710' 06571 X'00') SEC(X'1071' 24663 X'01') FREEZE
CGROUP DEVN(X'202A') PRIM(X'1710' 06571 X'00') SEC(X'1071' 24663 X'01') RUN
```

The parameters for the CGROUP command follow the usual pattern of SSID, serial number, and LSS.

Note: A single LSS can be paired with up to four other LSSs. Therefore, you may have to issue up to four CGROUP commands to suspend all pairs on a single primary LSS.

CQUERY

The CQUERY command is used to query the status of one volume of a Metro Mirror volume pair or all paths that are associated with the LSS for the device number that is specified. The CQUERY command can be issued to either a primary or secondary Metro Mirror volume. A host system that is attached only to a primary volume cannot obtain the status of the secondary volume for that pair. In the same way, a host attached only to the secondary volume cannot obtain the status of the primary volume.

Example 14-6 shows a CQUERY command for device number 2028.

Example 14-6 CQUERY command

```
CQUERY DEVN(2028)
```

The output of the CQUERY command (shown in Example 14-7) provides volume related information, such as SSID, CCA, LSS number, DS8000 serial number and WWNN.

Example 14-7 CQUERY output

```
ANTP8802I CQUERY DEVN(2028)
ANTP0090I CQUERY FORMATTED LVL 3 314
VOLUME REPORT
************** PPRC REMOTE COPY CQUERY - VOLUME *******************
*                                         (PRIMARY)    (SECONDARY) *
*                                        SSID CCA LSS SSID CCA LSS*
*DEVICE   LEVEL      STATE      PATH STATUS  SERIAL#      SERIAL#    *
*------ ---------  ----------  ----------- ---------    ---------  *
* 2028  PRIMARY..  SUSPEND(3)   ACTIVE..   1710 28 00   1711 28 01 *
*       CRIT(NO).......       CGRPLB(NO). 000000006571 000000006571*
* PATHS PFCA SFCA STATUS: DESCRIPTION                               *
* ----- --------- ------  -------------------                       *
*   1   0030 0200   13    PATH ESTABLISHED...                       *
*       ---- ----   00    NO PATH...........                        *
*       ---- ----   00    NO PATH...........                        *
*       ---- ----   00    NO PATH...........                        *
* IF STATE = PENDING/SUSPEND:     TRACKS OUT OF SYNC =   23813      *
*                                 TRACKS ON VOLUME   =   50085      *
*                               PERCENT OF COPY COMPLETE =  53%     *
*  SUBSYSTEM          WWNN                    LIC LEVEL             *
* -----------  ----------------             -----------            *
* PRIMARY....  5005076303AAAAAA             5.0.03.0196            *
* SECONDARY.1  5005076303AAAAAA                                     *
* SECONDARY.2  5005076300BBBBBB                                     *
* SECONDARY.3  5005076300BBBBBB                                     *
********************************************************************
ANTP0001I CQUERY COMMAND COMPLETED FOR DEVICE 2028. COMPLETION CODE: 00
```

Also, from the output information, you can check the number of primary updated tracks, which at that moment were not reflected on the secondary volume (TRACKS OUT OF SYNC). In addition, you can see the Metro Mirror volume state of the device and how many Metro Mirror paths are established.

The example shown in Example 14-8 shows a CQUERY for an open systems volume.

Example 14-8 CQUERY for open systems volume

```
CQUERY DEVN(6030) ODEVN(AAGXA X'00' X'16') VOLUME
```

In Example 14-9 we show an example of the output from a CQUERY for an open systems volume. Notice the SSID value (FF16).

Example 14-9 CQUERY output for open systems volume

```
ANTP8802I CQUERY DEVN(6030) ODEVN(AAGXA X'00' X'16') VOLUME
ANTP0090I CQUERY FORMATTED LVL 3 478
VOLUME REPORT
************** PPRC REMOTE COPY CQUERY - VOLUME *******************
*                                         (PRIMARY)    (SECONDARY) *
```

```
*                                          SSID LUN LSS SSID LUN LSS*
*DEVICE   LEVEL      STATE      PATH STATUS  SERIAL#      SERIAL#    *
*------ --------- ---------- ----------- ---------     ---------    *
* 6030  PRIMARY..  PENDING...   ACTIVE..   FF16 00 16    FF16 00 16 *
*       CRIT(NO).......       CGRPLB(NO). 0000000AAGXA 0000000AAVCA*
* PATHS PFCA SFCA STATUS: DESCRIPTION                                *
* ----- --------- ------ -------------------                        *
*   2   0000 0000   13    PATH ESTABLISHED...                        *
*       0100 0100   13    PATH ESTABLISHED...                        *
*       ---- ----   00    NO PATH............                        *
*       ---- ----   00    NO PATH............                        *
* IF STATE = PENDING/SUSPEND:     TRACKS OUT OF SYNC =    40523      *
*                                 TRACKS ON VOLUME   =    81920      *
*                               PERCENT OF COPY COMPLETE =  51%      *
*  SUBSYSTEM          WWNN                     LIC LEVEL            *
* -----------  ----------------             -----------             *
* PRIMARY....  500507630EFFFC6F              5.0.00.0000             *
* SECONDARY.1  500507630EFFFCA0                                      *
* SECONDARY.2  500507630EFFFCA0                                      *
*********************************************************************
ANTP0001I CQUERY COMMAND COMPLETED FOR DEVICE 6030. COMPLETION CODE: 00
```

CRECOVER

The CRECOVER command is used to allow the recovery system to gain control of the volumes. This command is issued from the recovery system (see Example 14-10). It signals the recovery DS8000 to force the secondary volume into simplex state, thus allowing the recovery system to gain control of the volume.

During this procedure the volume serial number can be verified and also it can be relabeled. The volume can be varied online after this command is complete.

Example 14-10 CRECOVER command

```
CRECOVER DEVN(X'2242') -
PRIM('X6060' 62019 X'42' X'00') -
SEC(X'8061' 68006 X'42' X'00') -
ID(VOL002 VOL001) -
MSGREQ(YES)
```

In Example 14-10, the CRECOVER command brings device x'2242' (on the recovery DS8000) to simplex state. It also changes the volume label from VOL002 to VOL001.

CSUSPEND

This command is used to suspend Metro Mirror operations between a volume pair. Metro Mirror stops mirroring data to the secondary volume and starts keeping record of the primary volume tracks that are updated. The information of which tracks were updated while the pair was suspended will be used later when the pair is re-established, to copy just the updated tracks.

In Example 14-11 a CSUSPEND command is issued for Metro Mirror primary volume 2028.

Example 14-11 CSUSPEND command

```
CSUSPEND DEVN(X'2028') -
   PRIM(X'1710' 06571 X'28' X'00') -
   SEC(X'1711' 06571 X'28' X'01')
```

Batch execution of Metro Mirror TSO commands

Batch procedures can be automated to manage Metro Mirror activities. JCL can be used to issue Metro Mirror commands in batch jobs, and automation procedures can be set to watch for their completion. Automation could analyze the results from previous job executions or Metro Mirror messages, and then schedule other jobs to be executed. Example 14-12 illustrates a batch job for executing a Metro Mirror TSO command.

Example 14-12 Batch job for executing Metro Mirror commands

```
//IKJEFT01 JOB MSGLEVEL=(1,1),MSGCLASS=A,NOTIFY=user id
//STEP1 EXEC PGM=IKJEFT01
//SYSTSPRT DD SYSOUT=*
//SYSTSIN DD *
CDELPATH DEVN(X'E12B') -
   PRIM(X'1071' 5005076300BBBBBB X'01') -
   SEC(X'1710' 5005076303AAAAAA X'00')
```

14.3 ICKDSF

The zSeries ICKDSF utility offers a means of control for Metro Mirror functions. ICKDSF typically runs as a batch program, and so can be automatically run from batch scheduling products (for example, Tivoli Workload Scheduler). It also supports VM and VSE systems.

More information on ICKDSF can be found in *Device Support Facilities User's Guide and Reference*, GC35-0033.

14.3.1 Setup of Metro Mirror with ICKDSF

Table 14-2 lists the Metro Mirror commands available with ICKDSF.

Table 14-2 ICKDSF Metro Mirror commands

Command	Description
PPRCOPY ESTPATH	Establishes Metro Mirror paths between a primary and secondary LSS.
PPRCOPY ESTPAIR	Establishes Metro Mirror volume pairs.
PPRCOPY DELPATH	Deletes Metro Mirror paths between a primary and secondary LSS.
PPRCOPY RECOVER	Allows a system to regain control of a volume on the secondary DS8000.
PPRCOPY SUSPEND	Puts a Metro Mirror pair in the suspended state.
PPRCOPY FREEZE	Suspends all Metro Mirror operations at the LSS level.
PPRCOPY RUN	Resumes I/O operations after a freeze with Extended Long Busy.
PPRCOPY QUERY	Queries the status of Metro Mirror volume pair and path status.

14.3.2 General ICKDSF job usage

All of the commands have to be addressed to a device, that is either online or offline to the system the job is submitted from. For offline volumes, the ICKDSF job has to address the volumes directly by specifying UNITADDRESS; see Example 14-13.

Example 14-13 Addressing offline volumes

```
//DELPTHRV JOB (ACCT),'DEL REVRSE PPRC PATH',
// CLASS=A,MSGCLASS=H
//STEP01 EXEC PGM=ICKDSF
//SYSPRINT DD SYSOUT=*
//SYSIN DD *
PPRCOPY DELPATH -
UNITADDR(3000) -
..................
```

Online volumes cannot be addressed directly and DD statements with the volume serial number have to be used. This assures the access to the volume serial number of the volume, regardless of what real address this volume resides on; see Example 14-14.

Example 14-14 Addressing online volumes

```
//DELPAIR1 JOB (ACCT),'ICKDSF DELPAIR',
//         MSGCLASS=X,NOTIFY=&SYSUID,MSGLEVEL=(1,1)
//*************************************
//STEP01    EXEC PGM=ICKDSF
//SYSPRINT DD SYSOUT=*
//VOL1      DD UNIT=3390,VOL=SER=DS6400,DISP=SHR
//SYSIN     DD *
 PPRCOPY DELPAIR DDNAME(VOL1) PRI(X'0002',AAVCA,X'00') -
  SEC(X'0003',AAVCA,X'00') LSS(X'00',X'01')
```

Display the Fibre Channel Connection Information Table

The ANALYZE command allows the user to specify the WWNN of the secondary Metro Mirror volume connected via Fibre Channel links. The Analyze pathing reports will include the Fibre Channel Connection Information Table. This information indicates the potential connectivity of the Fibre Channel ports in the DS8000 where the I/O is issued to each system adapter port in the DS8000 specified by the secondary WWNN.

For example, consider the following command, shown in Example 14-15:

Example 14-15 ANALYZE NODRIVE NOSCAN command

```
//IKJEFT01 JOB MSGLEVEL=(1,1),MSGCLASS=A,NOTIFY=user id
//STEP01    EXEC PGM=ICKDSF
//SYSPRINT DD SYSOUT=*
//VOL1      DD UNIT=3390,VOL=SER=DS6030,DISP=SHR
//SYSIN     DD *
 ANALYZE DDNAME(VOL1) NODRIVE NOSCAN SECWWNN(500507630EFFFCA0)
```

> **Note:** This command was issued against a DS6000 - similar output will be presented by a DS8000.

This would generate the following table seen in Example 14-16, showing that volume DS6030 with WWNN='500507630EFFFC6F' can potentially connect to a device with WWNN='500507630EFFFCA0' from:

- PRI SAID 0000 through secondary SAID 0000 and 0100.
- PRI SAID 0100 through secondary SAID 0000 and 0100.

Example 14-16 ANALYZE NODRIVE NOSCAN command output

```
FIBRE CHANNEL CONNECTION INFORMATION TABLE
PRIMARY WWNN = 500507630EFFFC6F, SECONDARY WWNN = 500507630EFFFCA0
```

```
+------+-------------------------------------------------------------------+
| PRIM |                                                                   |
| SAID |                    AVAILABLE SECONDARY SAIDS                      |
+------+-------------------------------------------------------------------+
| 0002 | ----                                                              |
+------+-------------------------------------------------------------------+
| 0102 | ----                                                              |
+------+-------------------------------------------------------------------+
| 0000 | 0000(0000) 0100(0000)                                             |
+------+-------------------------------------------------------------------+
| 0100 | 0000(0000) 0100(0000)                                             |
+------+-------------------------------------------------------------------+
       WHERE THE NUMBER IN PARENTHESIS IS THE RETURN CODE FOR THE SAID, AS FOLLOWS
         0000=POTENTIAL CONNECTION
         0001=NO POTENTIAL CONNECTION
         0002=PRIMARY ADAPTER OFFLINE
ICKDSF - MVS/ESA    DEVICE SUPPORT FACILITIES 17.0              TIME: 13:55:57
         0003=LINK FAILURE
         0004=INVALID TOPOLOGY
         0005=ERRORS DETECTED
         0006=SECONDARY WWNN INVALID
         0007=TIMEOUT DETECTED
```

PPRCOPY DELPAIR

The DELPAIR command is used to specify a Metro Mirror pair that will be removed from a Metro Mirror relationship returning the devices to a simplex state. An example of the JCL is shown in Example 14-17.

Example 14-17 ICKDSF DELPAIR example

```
//IKJEFT01 JOB MSGLEVEL=(1,1),MSGCLASS=A,NOTIFY=user id
//STEP01    EXEC PGM=ICKDSF
//SYSPRINT DD SYSOUT=*
//VOL1      DD UNIT=3390,VOL=SER=DS6400,DISP=SHR
//SYSIN     DD *
 PPRCOPY DELPAIR DDNAME(VOL1) PRI(X'0002',AAVCA,X'00') -
  SEC(X'0003',AAVCA,X'00') LSS(X'00',X'01')
```

PPRCOPY DELPATH

The DELPATH command is used to delete the defined Metro Mirror paths between a primary LSS and a secondary LSS. Only active paths to the specified recovery site LSS are affected; all other paths to other LSSs are unaffected. Refer to the PPRCOPY ESTPATH command for a description of the link or WWNN parameter.

Example 14-18 shows how to specify the PPRCOPY DELPATH command to delete a Metro Mirror path.

Example 14-18 ICKDSF DELPATH example

```
//IKJEFT01 JOB MSGLEVEL=(1,1),MSGCLASS=A,NOTIFY=user id
//STEP01    EXEC PGM=ICKDSF
//SYSPRINT DD SYSOUT=*
//VOL1      DD UNIT=3390,VOL=SER=DS6400,DISP=SHR
//SYSIN     DD *
 PPRCOPY DELPATH DDNAME(VOL1) -
  PRI(X'0002',AAVCA) -
  SEC(X'0003',AAVCA) WWNN(500507630EFFFCA0,500507630EFFFCA0) -
  LSS(X'00',X'01')
```

PPRCOPY ESTPATH

This command is used to establish paths between the primary and the secondary LSSs. Each ESTPATH command can establish up to eight paths from one application site LSS to a single recovery site LSS (Example 14-19).

Example 14-19 ICKDSF ESTPATH

```
//IKJEFT01 JOB MSGLEVEL=(1,1),MSGCLASS=A,NOTIFY=user id
//STEP01    EXEC PGM=ICKDSF
//SYSPRINT DD SYSOUT=*
//VOL1      DD UNIT=3390,VOL=SER=DS6400,DISP=SHR
//SYSIN     DD *
 PPRCOPY ESTPATH DDNAME(VOL1) -
  FCPP(X'00000100') PRI(X'0002',AAVCA) -
  SEC(X'0003',AAVCA) WWNN(500507630EFFFCA0,500507630EFFFCA0) -
  CGROUP(NO) LSS(X'00',X'01')
```

In Example 14-19 the FCPP parameter specifies up to 8 paths where each path is an 8-digit hexadecimal address in the form X'aaaabbbb', where:

'aaaa' is the primary system adapter ID (SAID).

'bbbb' is the secondary system adapter ID (SAID).

WWNN(X'pwwnn',X'swwnn')

This specifies the World Wide Node Name of the primary and secondary DS8000. Each WWNN is an 8-byte hexadecimal value X'wwwwwwwwwwwwwwww' where X'pwwnn' represents the primary WWNN and X'swwnn' represents the secondary WWNN.

PPRCOPY ESTPAIR

The ESTPAIR command is used to establish a Metro Mirror relationship between a primary and a secondary volume.

Example 14-20 shows the PPRCOPY ESTPAIR command.

Example 14-20 ICKDSF ESTPAIR example

```
//IKJEFT01 JOB MSGLEVEL=(1,1),MSGCLASS=A,NOTIFY=user id
//STEP01    EXEC PGM=ICKDSF
//SYSPRINT DD SYSOUT=*
//VOL1      DD UNIT=3390,VOL=SER=DS6400,DISP=SHR
//SYSIN     DD *
 PPRCOPY ESTPAIR DDNAME(VOL1) PRI(X'0002',AAVCA,X'00') -
  SEC(X'0003',AAVCA,X'00') MODE(COPY) MSGREQ(NO) OPTION(SYNC) -
  CRIT(NO) LSS(X'00',X'01')
```

FAILOVER and FAILBACK are optional parameters of the PPRCOPY ESTPAIR command. A sample failover and failback procedure is discussed in 16.1.2, "Failover Failback using TSO" on page 173.

PPRCOPY FREEZE

The PPRCOPY FREEZE command suspends operations for the Metro Mirror volumes on a given LSS pair. It is issued to control operations for multiple Metro Mirror volume pairs on the specified LSS pair. With the FREEZE command, Metro Mirror volume pairs are suspended and Metro Mirror paths are deleted.

Example 14-21 shows an example of a PPRCOPY FREEZE command.

Example 14-21 PPRCOPY FREEZE example

```
//IKJEFT01 JOB MSGLEVEL=(1,1),MSGCLASS=A,NOTIFY=user id
//STEP01    EXEC PGM=ICKDSF,TIME=30 ,PARM='NOREPLYU'
//SYSPRINT DD SYSOUT=*
//VOL1      DD UNIT=3390,VOL=SER=DS6400,DISP=SHR
//SYSIN     DD *
 PPRCOPY FREEZE DDNAME(VOL1) PRI(X'0002',AAVCA) SEC(X'0003',AAVCA) -
  LSS(X'00',X'01')
```

Attention: When a Metro Mirror path has been established with the CGROUP(YES) parameter, issuing PPRCOPY FREEZE will put devices for that LSS pairing into Extended Long Busy until a PPRCOPY RUN command is issued, or the timeout window (default two minutes) expires.

PPRCOPY QUERY

The QUERY command is used to query the Metro Mirror status of a volume and the associated Metro Mirror paths. A query can be issued to either a primary or secondary Metro Mirror volume.

A host system that is attached only to a primary volume cannot obtain the status of the secondary volume for that pair. In the same way, a host that is attached only to the secondary volume cannot obtain the status of the primary volume.

Example 14-22 shows a typical PPRCOPY QUERY command.

Example 14-22 ICKDSF QUERY command

```
//IKJEFT01 JOB MSGLEVEL=(1,1),MSGCLASS=A,NOTIFY=user id
//STEP01    EXEC PGM=ICKDSF,TIME=30 ,PARM='NOREPLYU'
//SYSPRINT DD SYSOUT=*
//VOL1      DD UNIT=3390,VOL=SER=DS6400,DISP=SHR
//SYSIN     DD *
 PPRCOPY QUERY DDNAME(VOL1)
 PPRCOPY QUERY DDNAME(VOL1) PATHS
```

Example 14-23 shows the output from PPRCOPY QUERY command.

Example 14-23 PPRCOPY QUERY output

```
1ICKDSF - MVS/ESA    DEVICE SUPPORT FACILITIES 17.0              TIME: 11:40:33
06/04/05      PAGE   1
0
0 PPRCOPY QUERY DDNAME(VOL1)                                         00070000
-ICK00700I DEVICE INFORMATION FOR 2028 IS CURRENTLY AS FOLLOWS:
-           PHYSICAL DEVICE = 3390
-           STORAGE CONTROLLER = 2107
-           STORAGE CONTROL DESCRIPTOR = E8
-           DEVICE DESCRIPTOR = 0A
-           ADDITIONAL DEVICE INFORMATION = 4A00003C
-           TRKS/CYL = 15, # PRIMARY CYLS = 3339
0ICK04029I DEVICE IS IN SUSPENDED PPRC STATE
0
0                    QUERY REMOTE COPY - VOLUME
0
                                                (PRIMARY)    (SECONDARY)
                                                SSID    CCA  SSID    CCA
 DEVICE  LEVEL     STATE            PATH STATUS  SER #   LSS  SER #   LSS
0------ --------- -------------- ----------- ----------- -----------
```

```
 2028    PRIMARY    SUSPEND(3)      ACTIVE       1710    28   1711    28
                                                 06571   00   06571   01
0
 PATHS  SAID/DEST               STATUS  DESCRIPTION
 -----  ---------               ------  ----------------
 1      0030 0200               13      ESTABLISHED FIBRE CHANNEL PATH
 2      0030 0084               13      ESTABLISHED FIBRE CHANNEL PATH
        0200 0024               13      ESTABLISHED FIBRE CHANNEL PATH
 2      0030 0084               13      ESTABLISHED FIBRE CHANNEL PATH
        0200 0024               13      ESTABLISHED FIBRE CHANNEL PATH
0
1ICKDSF - MVS/ESA    DEVICE SUPPORT FACILITIES 17.0                TIME: 11:40:33
06/04/05      PAGE   2
0IF PENDING/SUSPEND: COUNT OF TRACKS REMAINING TO BE COPIED = 23813
0
-ICK02206I PPRCOPY QUERY FUNCTION COMPLETED SUCCESSFULLY
-ICK00001I FUNCTION COMPLETED, HIGHEST CONDITION CODE WAS 0
0          11:40:33    06/04/05
0
0 PPRCOPY QUERY DDNAME(VOL1) PATHS                                         00071000
-ICK00700I DEVICE INFORMATION FOR 2028 IS CURRENTLY AS FOLLOWS:
-          PHYSICAL DEVICE = 3390
-          STORAGE CONTROLLER = 2107
-          STORAGE CONTROL DESCRIPTOR = E8
-          DEVICE DESCRIPTOR = 0A
-          ADDITIONAL DEVICE INFORMATION = 4A00003C
-          TRKS/CYL = 15, # PRIMARY CYLS = 3339
0ICK04029I DEVICE IS IN SUSPENDED PPRC STATE
0
0                            QUERY REMOTE COPY - PATHS
0
0       PRIMARY CONTROL UNIT INFORMATION
0
0            SERIAL                 WORLD WIDE
1ICKDSF - MVS/ESA    DEVICE SUPPORT FACILITIES 17.0                TIME: 11:40:33
06/04/05      PAGE   3
0            NUMBER   SSID  LSS     NODE NAME
0            -------  ----  ---  ----------------
             06571    1710  00   5005076303AAAAAA
0
0
0       SECONDARY CONTROL UNIT INFORMATION
0
0            SERIAL                 WORLD WIDE
0            NUMBER   SSID  LSS     NODE NAME
0            -------  ----  ---  ----------------
0            06571    1711  01
0
0
0       PATHS:
0            SERIAL                 WORLD WIDE
0            NUMBER   SSID  LSS     NODE NAME      PATH  SAID  DEST  S*
0            -------  ----  ---  ----------------  ----  ----  ----  --
        1ST: 06571    1711  01   5005076303AAAAAA    1   0030  0200  13
        2ND: 24663    1070  01   5005076300BBBBBB  .1.   0030  0084  13
                                                     2   0200  0024  13
        3RD: 24663    1071  01   5005076300BBBBBB  .1.   0030  0084  13
                                                     2   0200  0024  13
        4TH: .......  ....  ...  ................  ....  ....  ....  00
0
```

```
0        S*=PATH STATUS
0          00=NO PATH
0          01=ESTABLISHED
0          02=INIT FAILED
0          03=TIME OUT
1ICKDSF - MVS/ESA     DEVICE SUPPORT FACILITIES 17.0               TIME: 11:40:33
06/04/05       PAGE   4
0          04=NO RESOURCES AT PRI
0          05=NO RESOURCES AT SEC
0          06=SERIAL# MISMATCH
0          07=SCU SSID MISMATCH
0          08=ESCON LINK IS OFFLINE
0          09=ESTABLISH FAILED BUT WILL RETRY AGAIN WHEN CONDITIONS CHANGE
0          0A=SYSTEM ADAPTER HAS A HOST PATH ALREADY ESTABLISHED
0          0B=PATH CANNOT BE CONNECTED IN THE SAME CLUSTER
0          10=CONFIGURATION ERROR
0          11=CANNOT ESTABLISH PATH BETWEEN CKD AND FBA
0          12=LSS AND LINKADDRESS MISCOMPARE
0          13=ESTABLISHED FIBRE CHANNEL PATH
0          14=FIBRE CHANNEL PATH LINK DOWN
0          15=FIBRE CHANNEL PATH RETRY EXCEEDED
0          16=FIBRE CHANNEL PATH SECONDARY ADAPTER NOT PPRC CAPABLE
0          17=FIBRE CHANNEL PATH SECONDARY ADAPTER NOT AVAILABLE
0          18=FIBRE CHANNEL PATH PRIMARY LOGIN EXCEEDED
0          19=FIBRE CHANNEL PATH SECONDARY LOGIN EXCEEDED
0
-ICK02206I PPRCOPY QUERY FUNCTION COMPLETED SUCCESSFULLY
-ICK00001I FUNCTION COMPLETED, HIGHEST CONDITION CODE WAS 0
```

PPRCOPY RECOVER

The RECOVER command is used to allow the recovery system to regain control of a DASD volume. This command is issued from the recovery system. It signals the recovery site DS8000 to remove the volume from the Metro Mirror relationship (the volume becomes simplex), and thus gives the volume control back to the recovery system. During this process the volser can be verified, and also the volume can be relabeled.

PPRCOPY SUSPEND

The SUSPEND command is used to suspend Metro Mirror mirroring between a primary and the corresponding secondary volume. When the SUSPEND command is directed to the primary or secondary device of a Metro Mirror volume pair, the pair is suspended, and data is no longer mirrored onto the secondary volume. At the same time Metro Mirror starts tracking the primary volume tracks that are updated while the pair is suspended. This way, when the pair is re-established with the PPRCOPY ESTPAIR command, the option MODE(RESYNC) can be used to copy just the updated tracks to synchronize the volumes again. An example of the JCL is shown in Figure 14-24.

Example 14-24 PPRCOPY SUSPEND command

```
//IKJEFT01 JOB MSGLEVEL=(1,1),MSGCLASS=A,NOTIFY=user id
//STEP01   EXEC PGM=ICKDSF
//SYSPRINT DD SYSOUT=*
//VOL1     DD UNIT=3390,VOL=SER=DS6400,DISP=SHR
//SYSIN    DD *
 PPRCOPY SUSPEND DDNAME(VOL1) PRI(X'0002',AAVCA,X'00') -
  SEC(X'0003',AAVCA,X'00') LSS(X'00',X'01')
```

PPRCOPY RUN

The PPRCOPY RUN command resumes operations for the Metro Mirror volumes on a given LSS pair. If an extended long busy (ELB) condition was triggered by a previous FREEZE command, then the PPRCOPY RUN command can be used to reset the ELB condition and resume the I/O updates on the primary LSS volumes.

Refreshing the VTOC

If the secondary volume has more cylinders than the primary, the VTOC must be rebuilt in order to reflect the size of the volume before starting to use it. Example 14-25 illustrates an example of an ICKDSF batch job used for this purpose.

Example 14-25 ICKDSF VTOC Refresh

```
//IKJEFT01 JOB MSGLEVEL=(1,1),MSGCLASS=A,NOTIFY=user id
//STEP1 EXEC PGM=ICKDSF
//SYSPRINT DD SYSOUT=*
//DD1 DD DISP=SHR,UNIT=3390,VOL=SER=VOL001
//SYSIN DD *
REFORMAT DDNAME(DD1) VERIFY(VOL001) REFVTOC
/*
```

Note: To run the job to refresh the secondary volume's VTOC, the Metro Mirror volume pair must first be deleted.

14.4 DS Command-Line Interface

While the DS CLI will not run on the zSeries platform, it can still be used to perform operations on zSeries disk from a supported environment (for example, Windows XP). The DS CLI can be used to create scripts for set up and control of DS8000 functions. It is a flexible and powerful interface. The DS CLI commands are documented in *IBM TotalStorage DS8000 Command-Line Interface User's Guide,* SC26-7625.

14.4.1 DS CLI supported environments

The DS CLI is supported on the operating systems listed below, at the time of writing:

- ► AIX
- ► HP-UX
- ► HP Tru64
- ► Linux
- ► Novell Netware
- ► OpenVMS
- ► OS/400, i5/OS
- ► Sun™ Solaris™
- ► Windows

14.4.2 DS CLI command examples

In the following section we cover some of the more widely used DS CLI commands and give some examples of their usage. For most of these commands, you will need to know some (or all) of the following information:

- ► The serial number and device type of the source and target DS8000, identified by the **`-dev`** and **`-remotedev`** parameters.

- One way to get the serial number and device type is to use the **lssi** command.
- The serial number and device type will have the format IBM.2107-7506571, for example.

- The WWNN of the remote DS8000, identified by the **-remotewwnn** parameter.
  - The WWNN is also available using the **lssi** command.
- The LSS numbers of the source and target volumes.
  - The **lslss** command displays all of the LSSs on the system.
  - For a particular volume, the first two digits of the volume number represents the LSS. For example, volume D000 is located in LSS D0.
  - LSS numbers are two-digit hexadecimal numbers.
- The port IDs for source and target. Up to eight port pair IDs can be specified.
  - The **lsioport** lists the ports on the system.
  - A port ID will have the format I0102, for example.

Note: In many of the examples below, we are able to omit the **-dev** and **-remotedev** parameters because we specify them in the DS CLI profile. Using the profile can save a significant amount of typing.

Setting up a Metro Mirror environment

This section describes the commands you would use to set up a Metro Mirror environment. This includes the commands to set up the PPRC paths as well as the commands to create Metro Mirror relationships.

lsavailpprcport

The **lsavailpprcport** command lists the physical paths between your storage subsystems. Before creating the PPRC paths, you will want to use this command to show which ports you should use for the paths. Example 14-26 gives an example of an **lsavailpprcport** command with one path being specified.

Example 14-26 lsavailpprcport command

```
dscli> lsavailpprcport -l -remotedev IBM.2107-75ABTV1 -remotewwnn 5005076303FFC663 10:20
Date/Time: October 25, 2005 9:59:28 PM JST IBM DSCLI Version: 5.1.0.204 DS: IBM.2107-7520781
Local Port Attached Port Type Switch ID Switch Port
===================================================
I0143      I0010         FCP  NA        NA
I0213      I0140         FCP  NA        NA
```

mkpprcpath

The **mkpprcpath** command is used to establish Metro Mirror paths between LSS pairs on DS8000 subsystems. You can also use this command to replace existing paths.

This command is also used to create Consistency Groups using the **-consistgrp** parameter. For further discussion on Consistency Groups, refer to the following publication: *z/OS DFSMS Advanced Copy Services*, SC35-0428.

Example 14-27 gives an example of a **mkpprcpath** command with one path being specified.

Example 14-27 mkpprcpath command

```
dscli> mkpprcpath -remotedev IBM.2107-75ABTV1 -remotedev IBM.2107-7520781 -remotewwnn 5005076303FFC663
-srclss 10 -tgtlss 20 i0030:i0200
```

```
Date/Time: October 25, 2005 10:26:56 PM JST IBM DSCLI Version: 5.1.0.204 DS: IBM.2107-7520781
CMUC00149I mkpprcpath: Remote Mirror and Copy path 10:20 successfully established.
```

In this example, the following parameters are specified:

-dev The source DS8000, specifies the source Storage Image ID, which includes manufacturer, type, and serial number.

-remotedev The target DS8000, specifies the target Storage Image ID, which includes manufacturer, type, and serial number.

-remotewwnn Specifies the WWNN of the target device.

-srclss Specifies the LSS number of the source.

-tgtlss Specifies the LSS number of the target.

i0030:i0200 Specifies the source and target port ID pair.

mkpprc

The **mkpprc** command establishes either a Metro Mirror volume pair or a Global Copy volume pair. The **-mmir** parameter indicates a Metro Mirror pair. Some of the commands that can be specified are as follows:

-mode Selects a full copy or no copy. By default, Metro Mirror will perform a full copy from primary to secondary. If you are certain that the primary and secondary volumes are already in sync, you can specify the **-mode nocp** option and the Metro Mirror relationship will be in the full duplex state immediately.

-cascade Creates a cascading remote mirror and copy relationship. If you wish to cascade your remote mirror and copy (that is, make your Metro Mirror secondary a Global Copy primary), create the Metro Mirror first, and then specify this parameter when creating the Global Copy relationship.

-tgtonline Creates the Metro Mirror even if the target volume is online to host systems.

-critmode Specifies whether critical mode should be used. Critical mode prevents writes to source volumes if the PPRC paths have failed. For further discussion on the critmode parameter, the following publication can be referenced: *z/OS DFSMS Advanced Copy Services*, SC35-0428.

-suspend Suspends the relationship once the data has been copied. This parameter is not valid with the **-mode nocp** option.

-wait The command will not return until the copy is complete (that is, the state of the relationship is no longer Copy Pending).

Example 14-28 gives an example of its use. Additional examples are available in Chapter 16., “Metro Mirror examples” on page 171.

Example 14-28 mkpprc command

```
dscli> mkpprc -remotedev IBM.2107-75ABTV1 -type mmir -mode full 1000-1001:2000-2001
1100-1101:2100-2101
Date/Time: October 25, 2005 11:19:06 PM JST IBM DSCLI Version: 5.1.0.204 DS: IBM.2107-7520781
CMUC00153I mkpprc: Remote Mirror and Copy volume pair relationship 1000:2000 successfully created.
CMUC00153I mkpprc: Remote Mirror and Copy volume pair relationship 1001:2001 successfully created.
CMUC00153I mkpprc: Remote Mirror and Copy volume pair relationship 1100:2100 successfully created.
CMUC00153I mkpprc: Remote Mirror and Copy volume pair relationship 1101:2101 successfully created.
```

We have specified the **-type mmir** and **-mode full** parameters in this example, in order to establish a Metro Mirror pair, and to do a full copy of the volume. Notice that the volume pair is specified at the end of the command.

Removing a Metro Mirror environment

This section describes the commands you would use to remove a Metro Mirror environment. This includes the commands to set up the PPRC paths as well as the commands to create Metro Mirror relationships.

rmpprc

The **rmpprc** command is used to delete a Metro Mirror volume pair. Example 14-29 shows an example of its use. Note that we are required to confirm that we wish to delete this volume pair. We can use the **-quiet** parameter to suppress this confirmation message.

Example 14-29 rmpprc command

```
dscli> rmpprc -remotedev IBM.2107-75ABTV1 1000-1001:2000-2001 1100-1101:2100-2101
Date/Time: October 26, 2005 5:36:49 PM JST IBM DSCLI Version: 5.1.0.204 DS: IBM.2107-7520781
CMUC00160W rmpprc: Are you sure you want to delete the Remote Mirror and Copy volume pair relationship
1000-1001:2000-2001:? [y/n]:y
CMUC00155I rmpprc: Remote Mirror and Copy volume pair 1000:2000 relationship successfully withdrawn.
CMUC00155I rmpprc: Remote Mirror and Copy volume pair 1001:2001 relationship successfully withdrawn.
CMUC00160W rmpprc: Are you sure you want to delete the Remote Mirror and Copy volume pair relationship
1100-1101:2100-2101:? [y/n]:y
CMUC00155I rmpprc: Remote Mirror and Copy volume pair 1100:2100 relationship successfully withdrawn.
CMUC00155I rmpprc: Remote Mirror and Copy volume pair 1101:2101 relationship successfully withdrawn.
```

rmpprcpath

The **rmpprcpath** command is used to remove (delete) Metro Mirror paths. Again, we can use the **-quiet** parameter to suppress the confirmation message. An example of its use is shown in Example 14-30.

Example 14-30 rmpprcpath command

```
dscli> rmpprcpath -remotedev IBM.2107-75ABTV1 10:20 11:21
Date/Time: October 26, 2005 6:37:08 PM JST IBM DSCLI Version: 5.1.0.204 DS:
IBM.2107-7520781
CMUC00152W rmpprcpath: Are you sure you want to remove the Remote Mirror and Copy path
10:20:? [y/n]:y
CMUC00150I rmpprcpath: Remote Mirror and Copy path 10:20 successfully removed.
CMUC00152W rmpprcpath: Are you sure you want to remove the Remote Mirror and Copy path
11:21:? [y/n]:y
CMUC00150I rmpprcpath: Remote Mirror and Copy path 11:21 successfully removed.
```

> **Important:** The **rmpprcpath** command removes all Metro Mirror paths between the pair of LSS specified. It is not possible to delete a path from a group of paths with this command. To remove only certain paths, you can use the **mkpprcpath** to redefine the paths and omit the paths you wish to remove.

Managing a Metro Mirror environment

This section describes the commands you would use to manage a Metro Mirror environment. This includes the commands to manage Metro Mirror relationships and Consistency Groups, as well as commands to display information about Metro Mirror relationships and paths.

freezepprc

The **freezepprc** command is used to remove Metro Mirror paths and suspend volume pairs between a pair of LSSs, and is usually used to provide data consistency. The volumes will enter the Extended Long Busy state when this command is issued. Example 14-31 shows an example of the command. Notice that the LSS pair is specified at the end of the command.

Example 14-31 freezepprc command

```
dscli> freezepprc -remotedev IBM.2107-75ABTV1 10:20 11:21
Date/Time: October 29, 2005 12:30:08 AM JST IBM DSCLI Version: 5.1.0.204 DS:
IBM.2107-7520781
CMUC00161W freezepprc: Remote Mirror and Copy consistency group 10:20 successfully created.
CMUC00161W freezepprc: Remote Mirror and Copy consistency group 11:21 successfully created.
dscli>
```

unfreezepprc

The **unfreezepprc** command is used to take an LSS out of the Extended Long Busy condition after a **freezepprc** command has been issued. Example 14-32 shows an example of its usage.

Example 14-32 unfreezepprc command

```
dscli> unfreezepprc -remotedev IBM.2107-75ABTV1 10:20 11:21
Date/Time: October 29, 2005 12:30:53 AM JST IBM DSCLI Version: 5.1.0.204 DS:
IBM.2107-7520781
CMUC00198I unfreezepprc: Remote Mirror and Copy pair 10:20 successfully thawed.
CMUC00198I unfreezepprc: Remote Mirror and Copy pair 11:21 successfully thawed.
```

pausepprc

The **pausepprc** command is used to pause (or suspend) a Metro Mirror volume pair. Any updates to the source volume are tracked so the pair can be resumed at a later time, with only modified tracks having to be sent across to the secondary volume. Example 14-33 shows an example of the command.

Example 14-33 pausepprc command

```
dscli> pausepprc -remotedev IBM.2107-75ABTV1 1000-1001:2000-2001
Date/Time: October 26, 2005 11:00:21 PM JST IBM DSCLI Version: 5.1.0.204 DS: IBM.2107-7520781
CMUC00157I pausepprc: Remote Mirror and Copy volume pair 1000:2000 relationship successfully paused.
CMUC00157I pausepprc: Remote Mirror and Copy volume pair 1001:2001 relationship successfully paused.
dscli>
```

resumepprc

The **resumepprc** command is used to resume a paused (suspended) Metro Mirror volume pair. Example 14-34 shows an example of its usage.

Example 14-34 resumepprc command

```
dscli> resumepprc -remotedev IBM.2107-75ABTV1 -type mmir 1000-1001:2000-2001
Date/Time: October 26, 2005 11:05:28 PM JST IBM DSCLI Version: 5.1.0.204 DS: IBM.2107-7520781
CMUC00158I resumepprc: Remote Mirror and Copy volume pair 1000:2000 relationship successfully resumed.
This message is being returned before the copy completes.
CMUC00158I resumepprc: Remote Mirror and Copy volume pair 1001:2001 relationship successfully resumed.
This message is being returned before the copy completes.
dscli>
```

failoverpprc

The **failoverpprc** command is used to start a failover operation — it changes a secondary device into a primary suspended device while leaving the primary device in its current state. This command succeeds even if the paths are down and the volume at the production site is unavailable or nonexistent. You must then issue a failback command to completely reverse the direction of the Metro Mirror. Example 14-35 shows its usage for multiple volume pairs.

Example 14-35 failoverpprc command

```
dscli> failoverpprc -remotedev IBM.2107-7520781 -type mmir 2000-2001:1000-1001
2100-2101:1100-1101
Date/Time: October 27, 2005 8:05:42 PM JST IBM DSCLI Version: 5.1.0.204 DS:
IBM.2107-75ABTV1
CMUC00196I failoverpprc: Remote Mirror and Copy pair 2000:1000 successfully reversed.
CMUC00196I failoverpprc: Remote Mirror and Copy pair 2001:1001 successfully reversed.
CMUC00196I failoverpprc: Remote Mirror and Copy pair 2100:1100 successfully reversed.
CMUC00196I failoverpprc: Remote Mirror and Copy pair 2101:1101 successfully reversed.
dscli>
```

failbackpprc

The **failbackpprc** command can be issued against any remote mirror and copy volume that is in a primary suspended state. The command copies the required data from the source volume to the target volume in order to resume mirroring. The command is usually used after a **failoverpprc** command has been issued to restart mirroring either in the reverse direction (recovery site to production site) or original direction (production site to recovery site). However, this command also works if the target volume has been made simplex or is a secondary volume. The command performs a full or partial copy as required. Example 14-36 shows an example of the command.

Example 14-36 failbackpprc command

```
dscli> failbackpprc -remotedev IBM.2107-7520781 -type mmir 2000-2001:1000-1001
2100-2101:1100-1101
Date/Time: October 28, 2005 12:23:01 AM JST IBM DSCLI Version: 5.1.0.204 DS:
IBM.2107-75ABTV1
CMUC00197I failbackpprc: Remote Mirror and Copy pair 2000:1000 successfully failed back.
CMUC00197I failbackpprc: Remote Mirror and Copy pair 2001:1001 successfully failed back.
CMUC00197I failbackpprc: Remote Mirror and Copy pair 2100:1100 successfully failed back.
CMUC00197I failbackpprc: Remote Mirror and Copy pair 2101:1101 successfully failed back.
dscli>
```

lspprc

The **lspprc** command is used to list the status of a Metro Mirror pair. Example 14-37 shows an example of the command.

Example 14-37 lspprc command

```
dscli> lspprc  2000-2001 2100-2101
Date/Time: October 28, 2005 12:23:05 AM JST IBM DSCLI Version: 5.1.0.204 DS: IBM.2107-75ABTV1
ID        State        Reason Type         SourceLSS Timeout (secs) Critical Mode First Pass Status
=====================================================================================================
2000:1000 Copy Pending -      Metro Mirror 20        unknown        Disabled      Invalid
2001:1001 Copy Pending -      Metro Mirror 20        unknown        Disabled      Invalid
2100:1100 Copy Pending -      Metro Mirror 21        unknown        Disabled      Invalid
2101:1101 Copy Pending -      Metro Mirror 21        unknown        Disabled      Invalid
```

lspprcpath

The **lspprcpath** command is used to display the status of a Metro Mirror path. Example 14-38 shows an example of its use.

Example 14-38 lspprcpath command

```
dscli> lspprcpath 10-11
Date/Time: October 25, 2005 10:29:23 PM JST IBM DSCLI Version: 5.1.0.204 DS:
IBM.2107-7520781
Src Tgt State   SS   Port  Attached Port Tgt WWNN
```

```
==========================================================
10  20  Success FF20 I0143 I0010         5005076303FFC663
10  20  Success FF20 I0213 I0140         5005076303FFC663
11  21  Success FF21 I0143 I0010         5005076303FFC663
11  21  Success FF21 I0213 I0140         5005076303FFC663
```

14.5 DS Storage Manager GUI

The DS Storage Manager Graphical User Interface can be used to set up and control DS8000 Metro Mirror functions. It is user friendly, however, you cannot use it for automation activities, and certain Remote Mirror and Copy functions are not supported from this interface.

14.5.1 DS Storage Manager usage

The DS Storage Manager interface can be used by people who are less skilled or confident with the other interfaces. It is reasonably simple to use, however, it is usually slower than the other interfaces, and you cannot save actions for later use. In this section we give some examples of common tasks and process flow.

Establishing Metro Mirror paths

To establish Metro Mirror paths from the GUI, you can follow the process below. Figure 14-1 shows the Copy services Paths panel. You can see that there are already some paths defined. We will be defining two paths from LSS A0 of the current or Metro Mirror primary DS8300 to LSS 43 of the Metro Mirror secondary DS8300. We first go to the Select Action pull-down and click **Create**, then click **Go**.

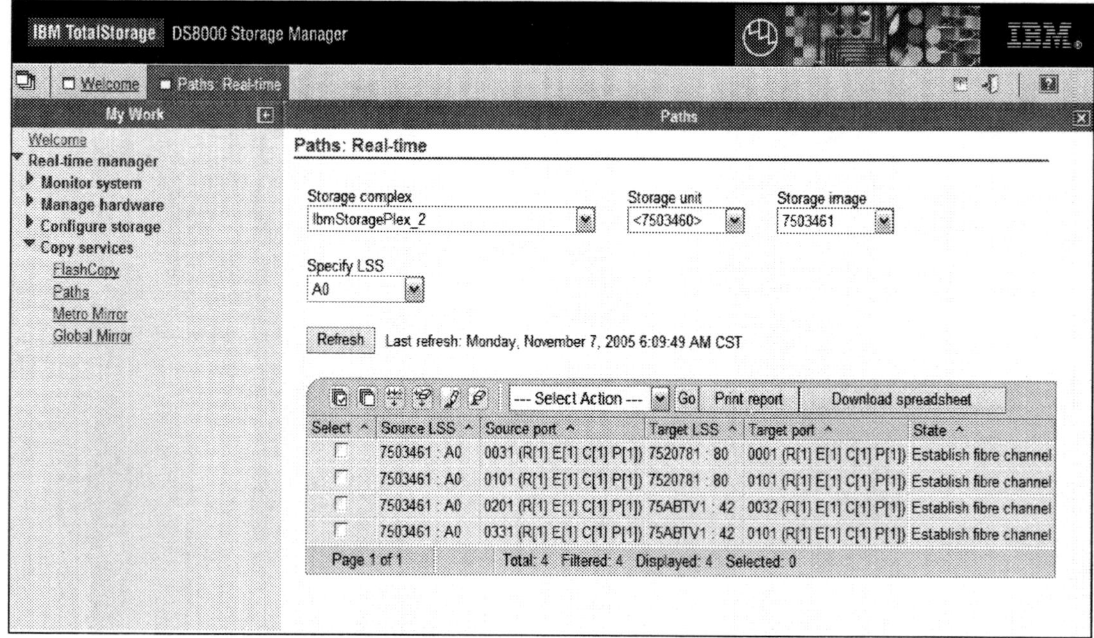

Figure 14-1 Copy services Paths panel

We are then taken to the next panel, shown in Figure 14-2, where we select the source LSS. We select LSS A0 from the pull-down list and then click **Next**.

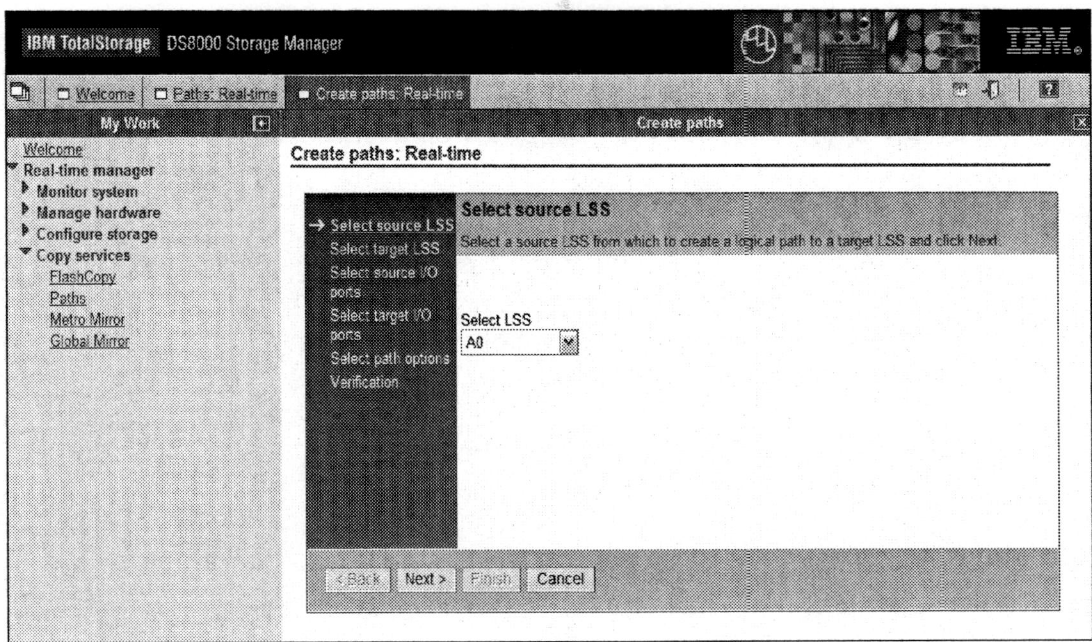

Figure 14-2 Select source LSS panel

We then need to select the target LSS, using the panel shown in Figure 14-3. Using the pull-downs we select the target Storage complex, Storage unit, Storage image and LSS. In this example we make the choices shown in Figure 14-4. We then click **Next** to proceed.

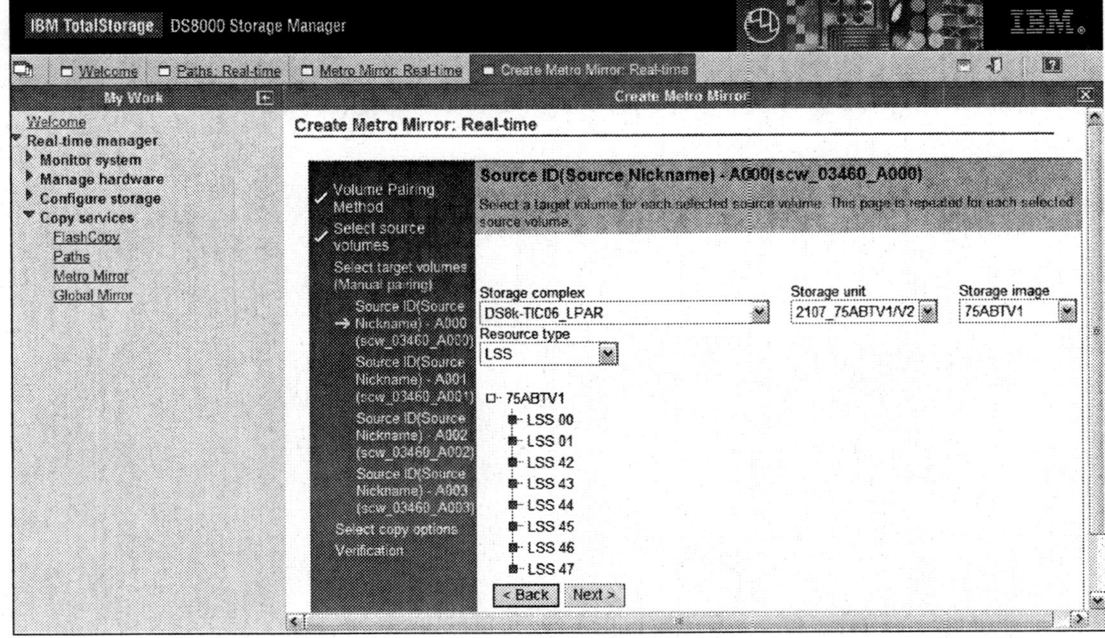

Figure 14-3 Select target LSS panel

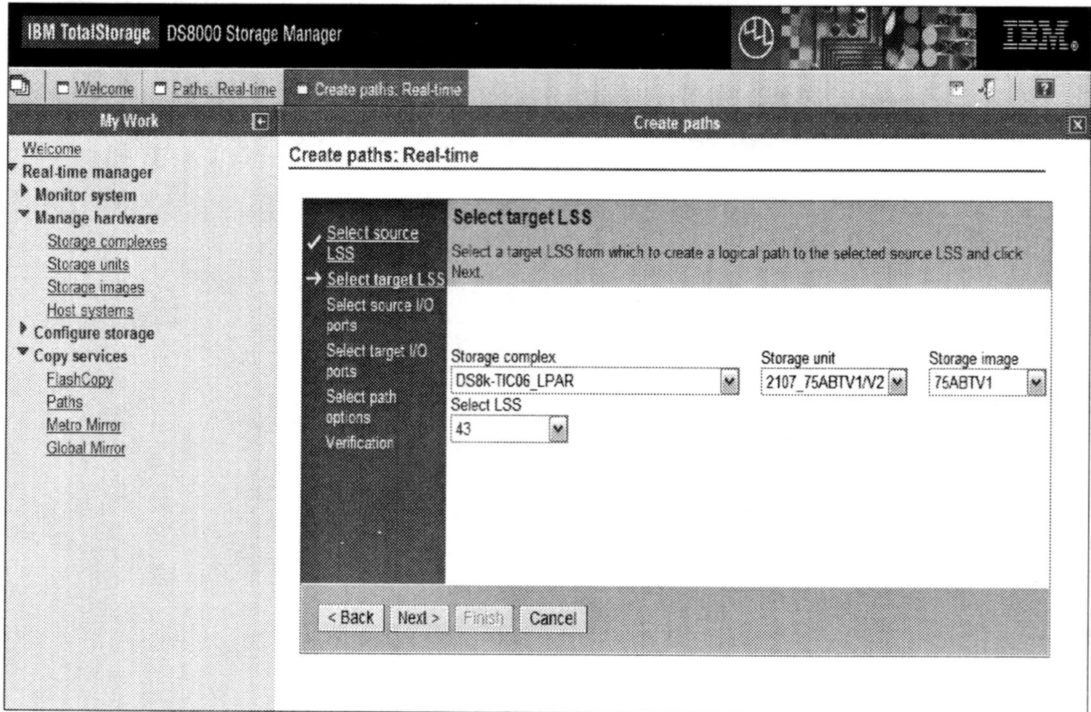

Figure 14-4 Select target LSS panel after selections

We now need to select the source I/O port, using the panel shown in Figure 14-5. We will select both ports shown to use for our Metro Mirror paths we are establishing. We can do this by checking (clicking) both boxes or by using the pull-down and selecting *Select All*. We then click **Next** to proceed.

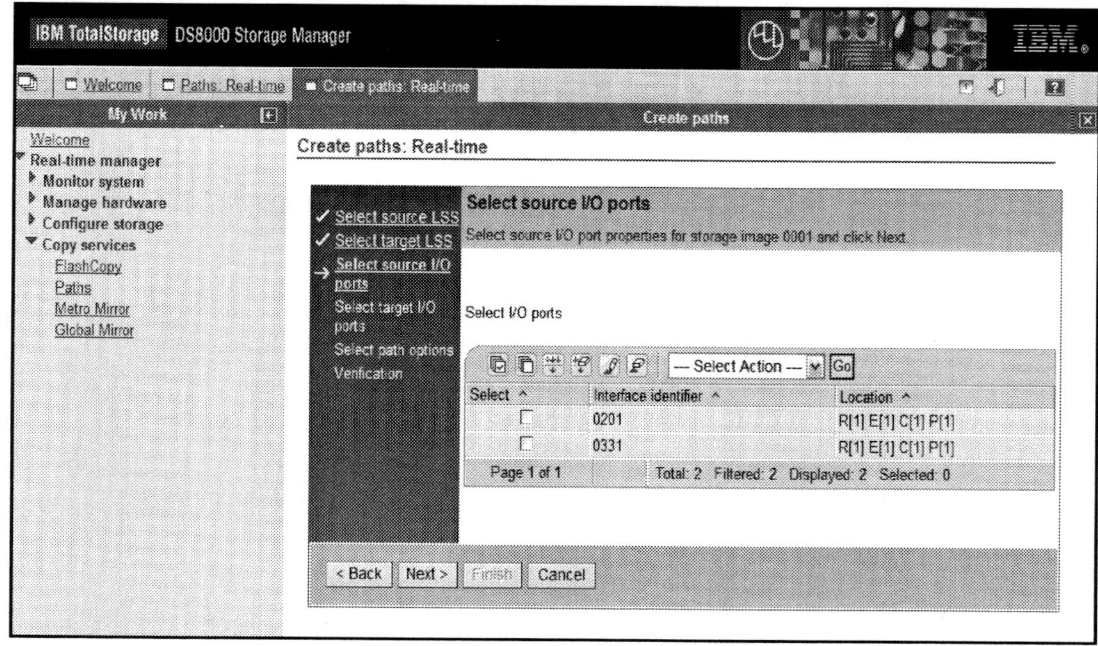

Figure 14-5 Select source I/O ports

We now need to define a target I/O port for each source port. In our example we have only a single target I/O port for each source I/O port, as shown in Figure 14-6. Another possible scenario is that there might be multiple choices for each source I/O port. Such an example is shown in Figure 14-7. Click **Next** to proceed.

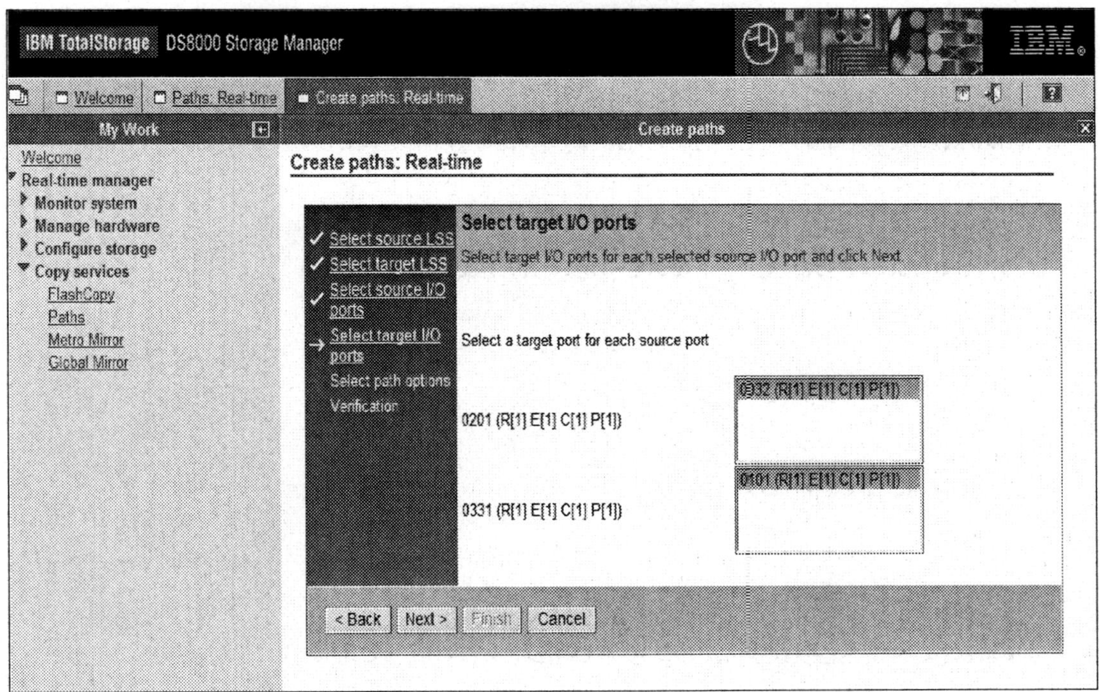

Figure 14-6 Select target I/O ports panel

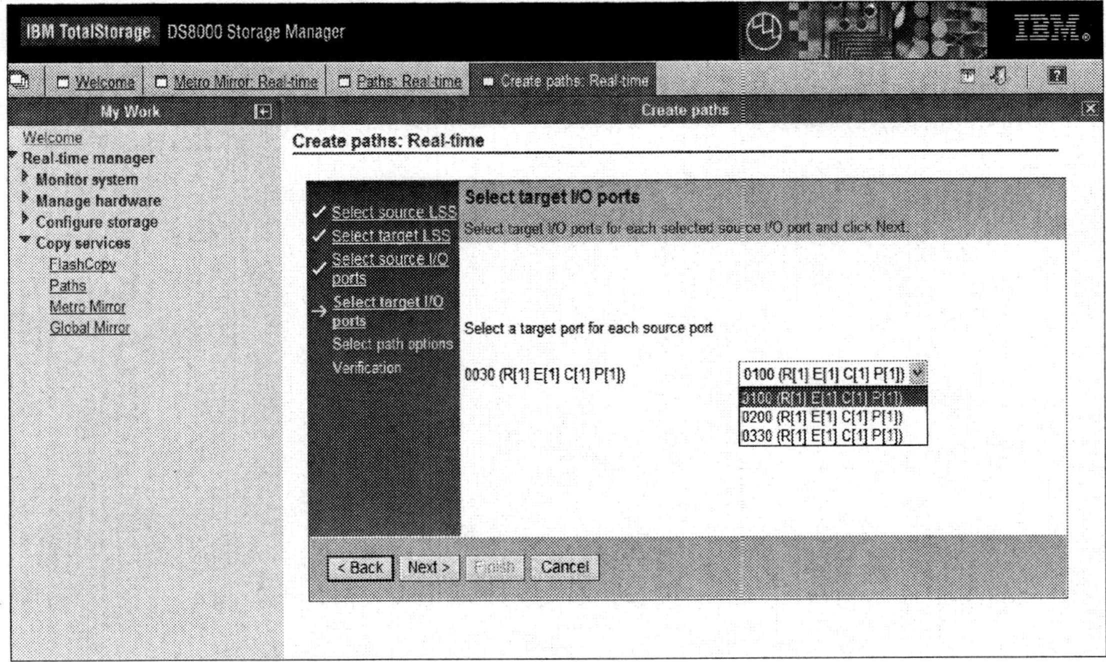

Figure 14-7 Select target I/O ports panel example alternative

We now see the panel shown in Figure 14-8, where we can select whether the paths will be a consistency group path or not, using the check box. We will select *Define as consistency group* and then click **Next** to proceed.

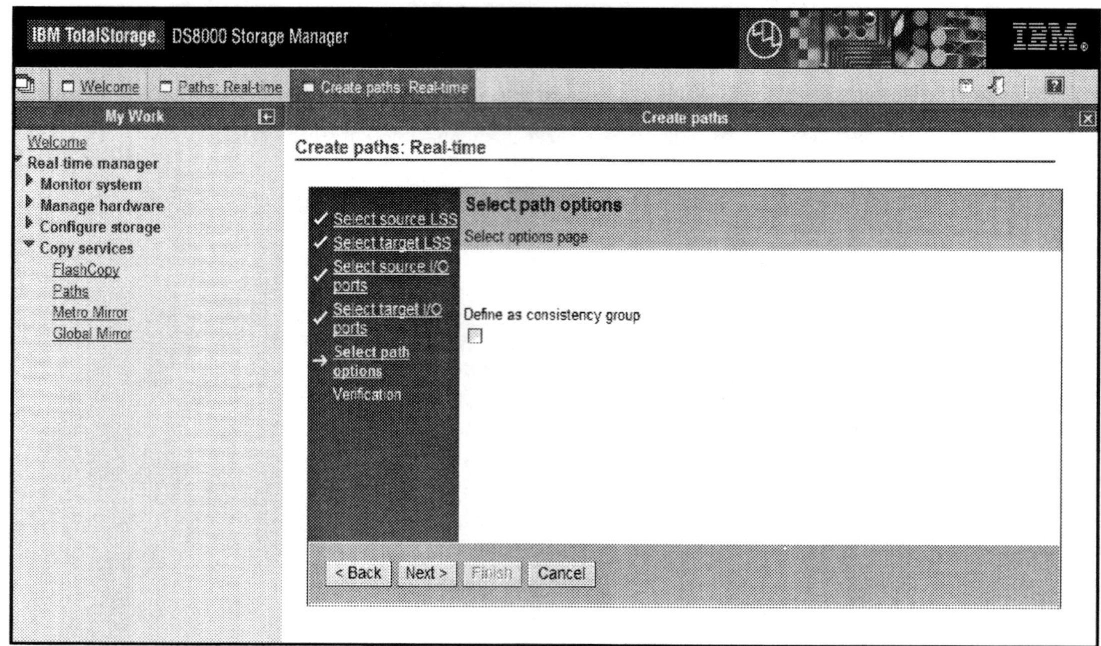

Figure 14-8 Select path options panel

We now see the verification panel, as shown in Figure 14-9, where we can check that everything has been selected correctly. If so, we can click **Finish**. If not, we can click **Back** or **Cancel** as appropriate.

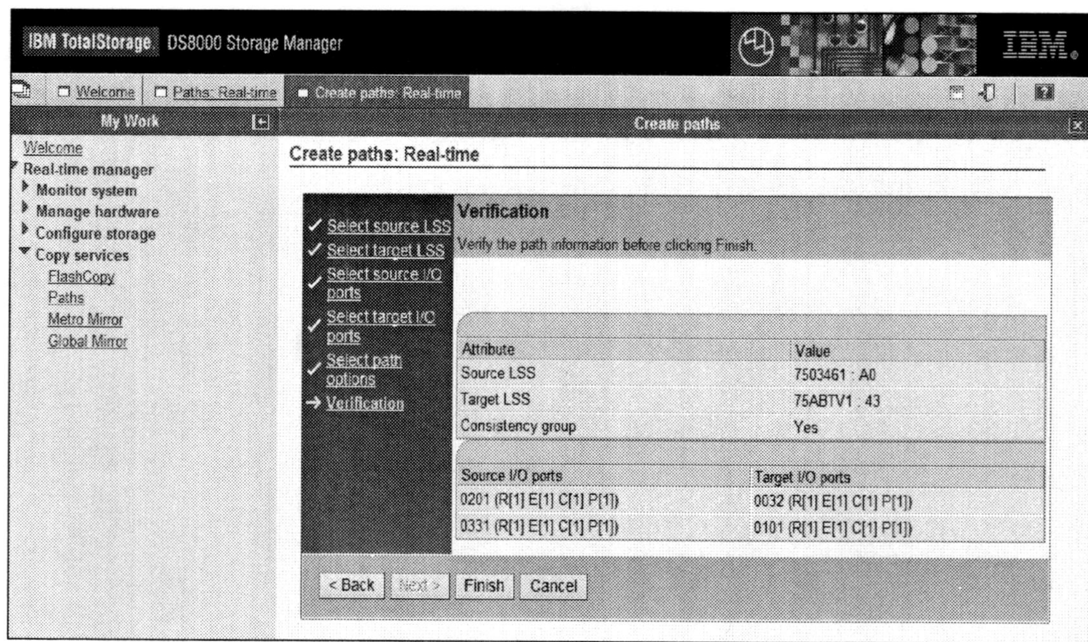

Figure 14-9 Create paths verification panel

After we click **Next** we are returned to a modified *Paths panel* which was our original starting point (see Figure 14-1), the *Copy services Paths panel.* This Copy services Paths panel has been modified and now appears as shown in Figure 14-10.

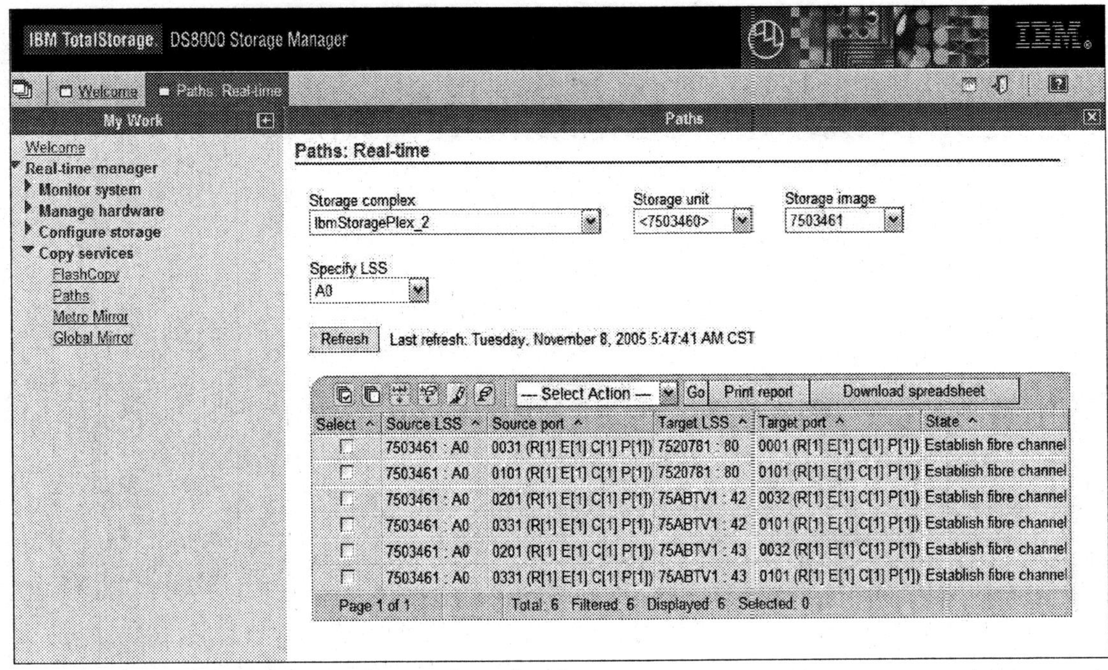

Figure 14-10 Copy services Paths panel - updated

Establishing Metro Mirror pairs

To establish a Metro Mirror pair from the GUI, you can follow the process below. Figure 14-11 shows the Metro Mirror panel once we have selected the Metro Mirror source Storage complex, Storage unit, Storage image, the Resource type (LSS), and the volume LSS. We have already selected the **Create** pull-down from the **Select Action** area.

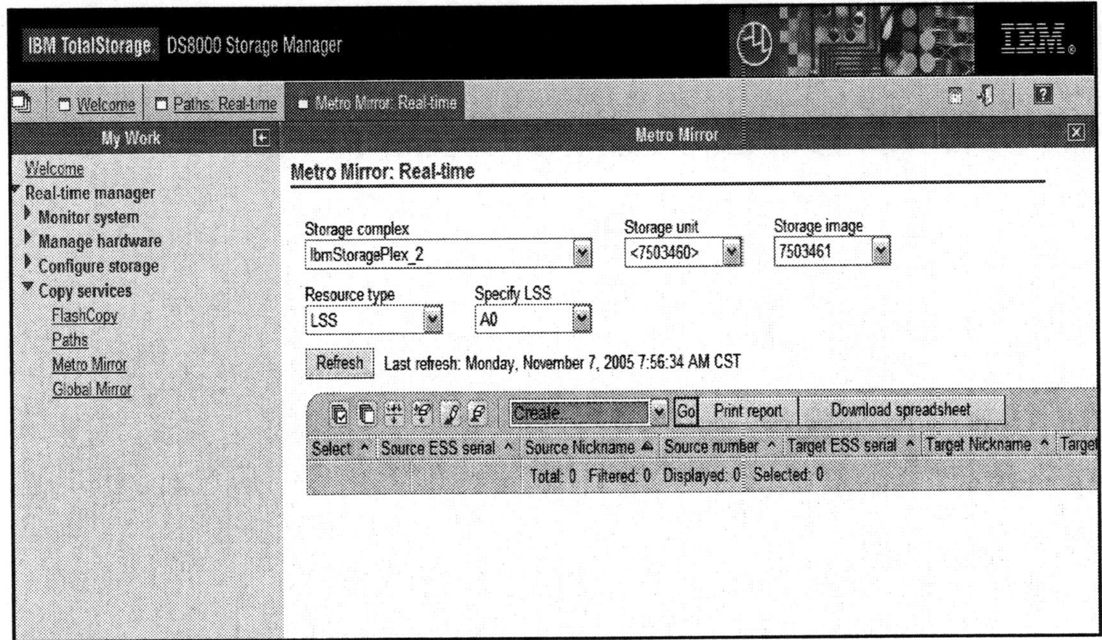

Figure 14-11 Initial Metro Mirror panel, Create pull-down selected

Once you have clicked **Go**, the panel as seen in Figure 14-12 is displayed. We now need to select either automated or manual volume pairing, and click **Next**. We will select manual selection.

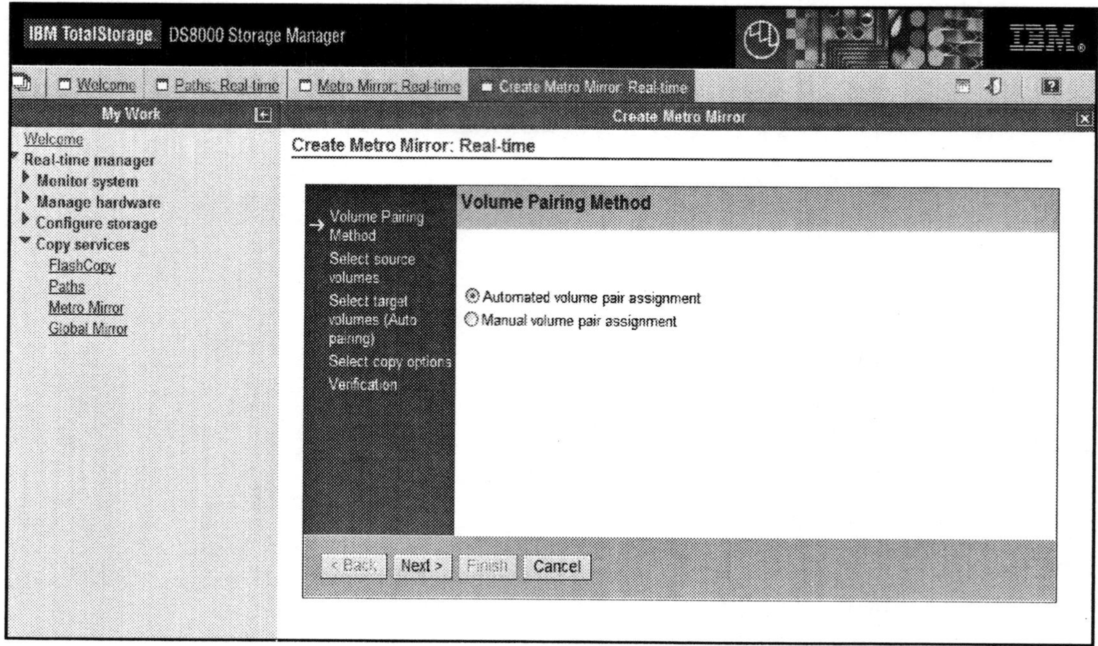

Figure 14-12 Select volume pairing method

We selected *Manual volume pair assignment*, and so we see the panel in Figure 14-13. We then need to page through the list of volumes presented, and find the ones for which we wish to establish the Metro Mirror volume pair.

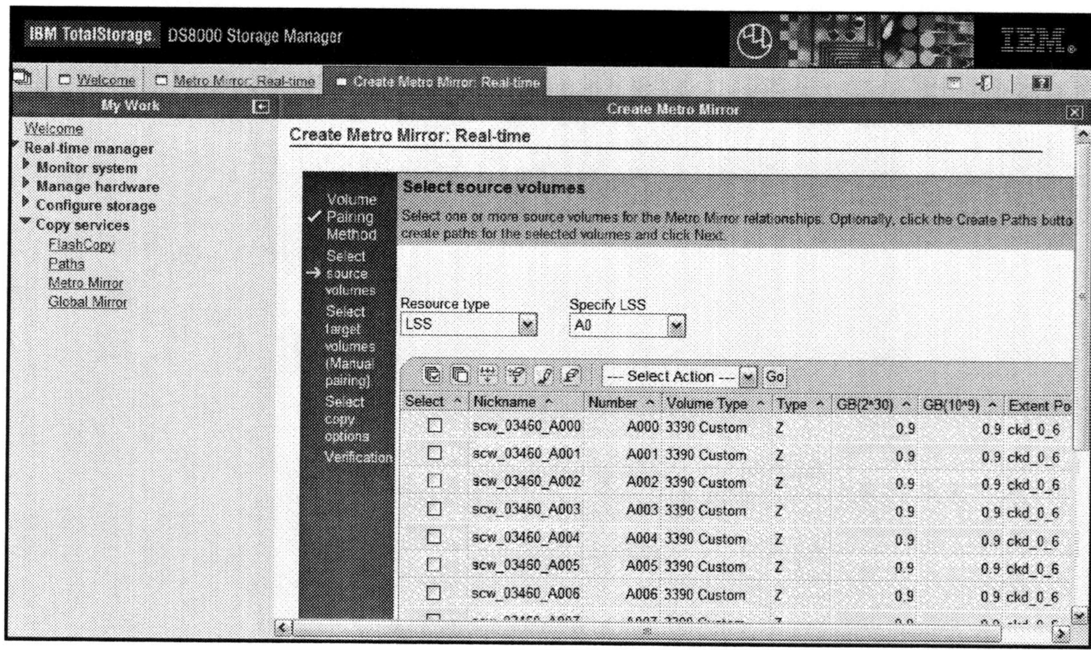

Figure 14-13 Manual volume assignment volume selection panel

To choose volume numbers A000-A003, we would select the check box for these volumes and click **Next** (use the scroll bars to locate the **Next** button at the bottom of the screen). We would then see the panel in Figure 14-14. Since we have selected four source volumes, we will be required to repeat the following source to target assignment four times, once for each of the selected volumes. The arrow identifies which source volume is to be assigned. We now need to select a target volume. We expand the target *Storage image* by clicking the small box in the circled area next to the target Storage image serial number (75ABTV1).

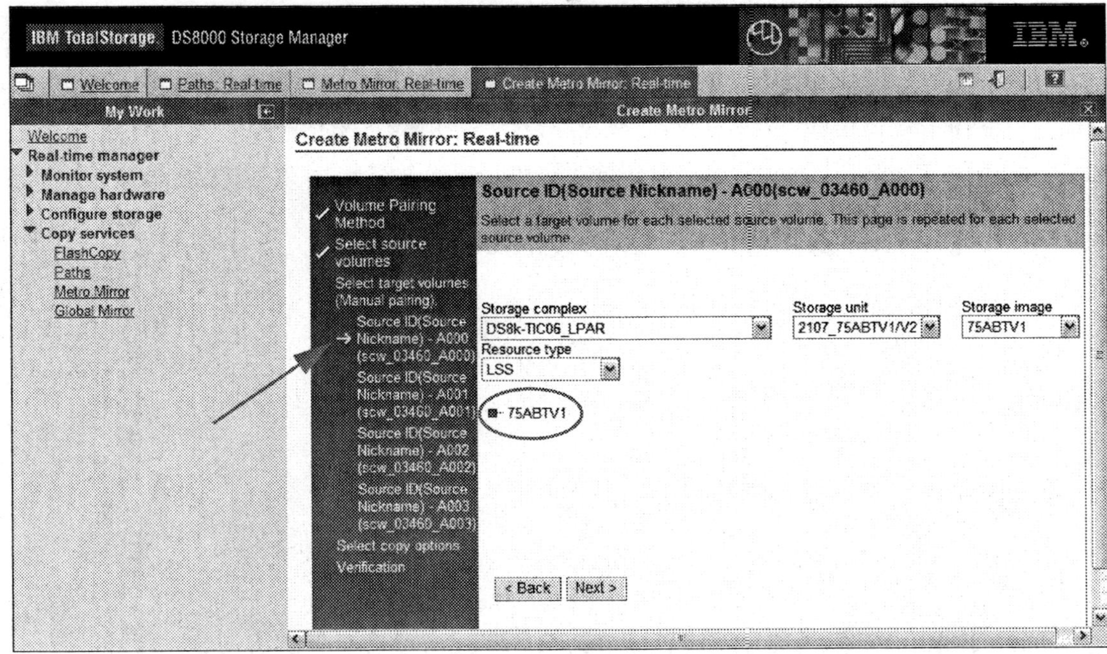

Figure 14-14 Select target Storage Unit

The panel will now display the available target LSSs for the Metro Mirror target Storage Image, as in Figure 14-15. We now select LSS 43.

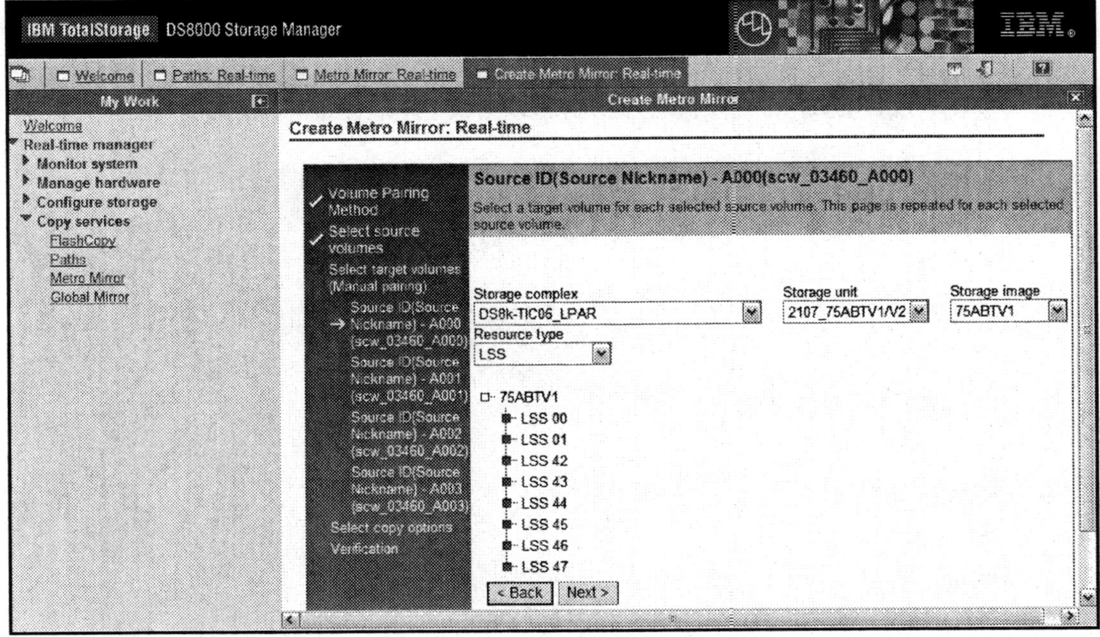

Figure 14-15 Select target LSS

The volumes available in LSS 43 will then be displayed, as in Figure 14-16. Note that device 4300 has been checked. We then click **Next**. Since there are more volumes to be paired, we are returned to the panel shown in Figure 14-14 with the single difference that the next source volume in the list is now the active source volume to be paired to a target volume. We will repeat the steps for each of the source volumes and sequentially select devices 4301, 4302, and 4303.

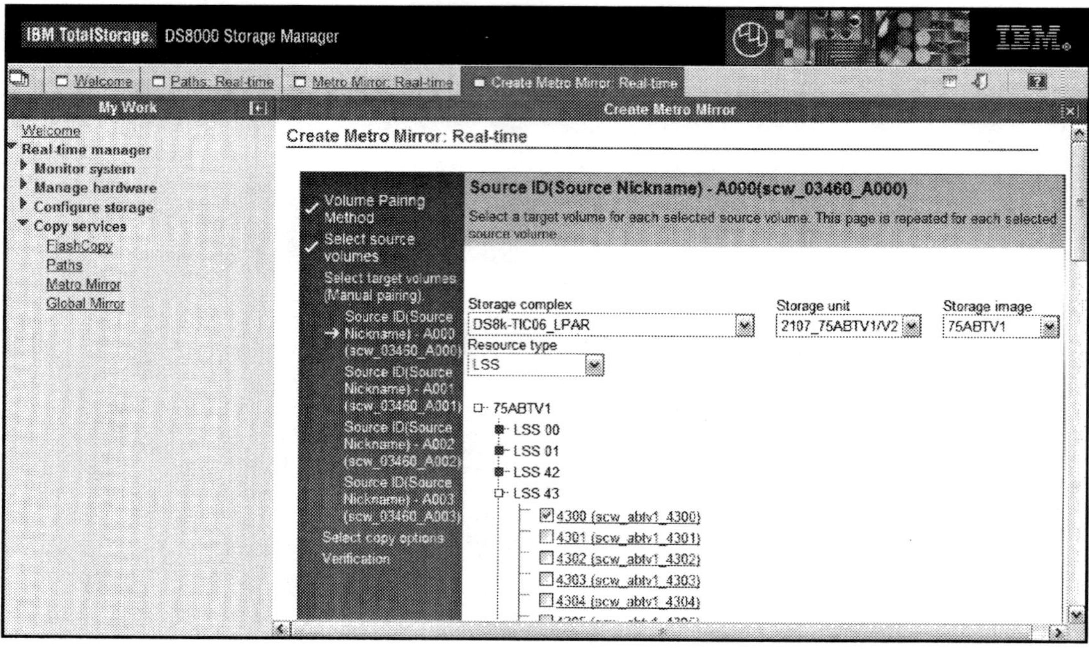

Figure 14-16 Target volume selection

When we click **Next** on the panel shown in Figure 14-16, after creating the last volume pair (A003 to 4303), the *Select copy options* panel will be displayed as shown in Figure 14-17. We can select the options we want for the Metro Mirror pair. Note that we have been focused upon Metro Mirror, but it is on this panel where we decide whether this is a Metro Mirror or Global Copy implementation. We have selected the radio button for **Metro Mirror**, and the check box for **Perform initial copy**. We now click **Next**.

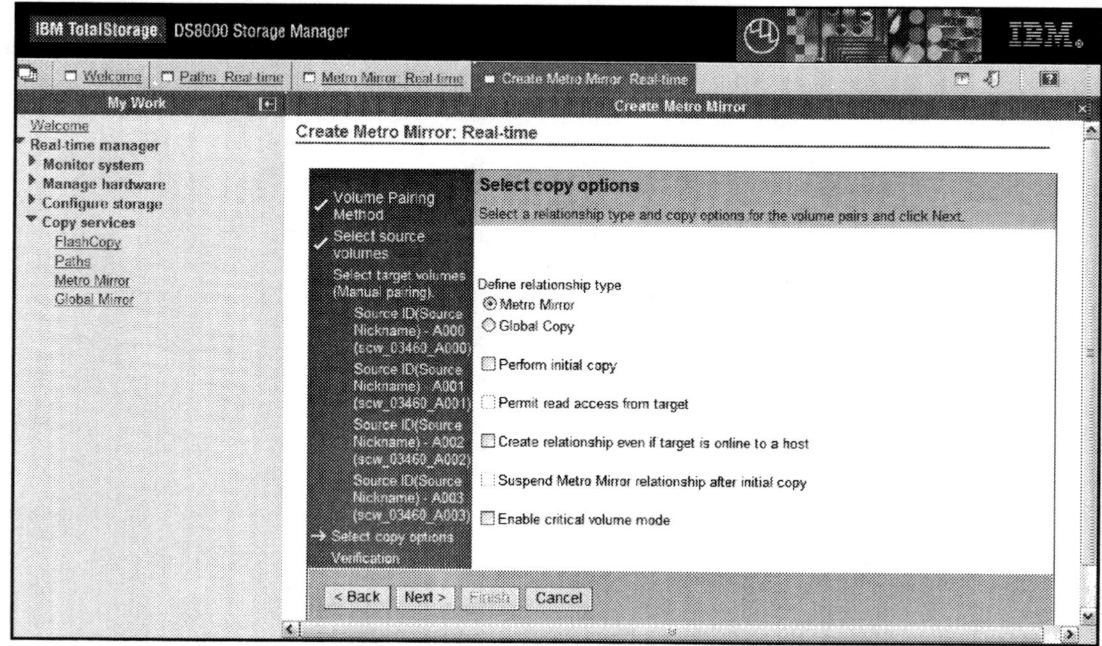

Figure 14-17 Metro Mirror options

The Verification panel is now displayed, as in Figure 14-18, where we can check our selections. If all is correct, we can click **Finish**. Use the bottom scroll bar to view all data that is not shown on the existing display. The right-most column indicates if there is any size inconsistency, and other non-visible columns show the target volume details.

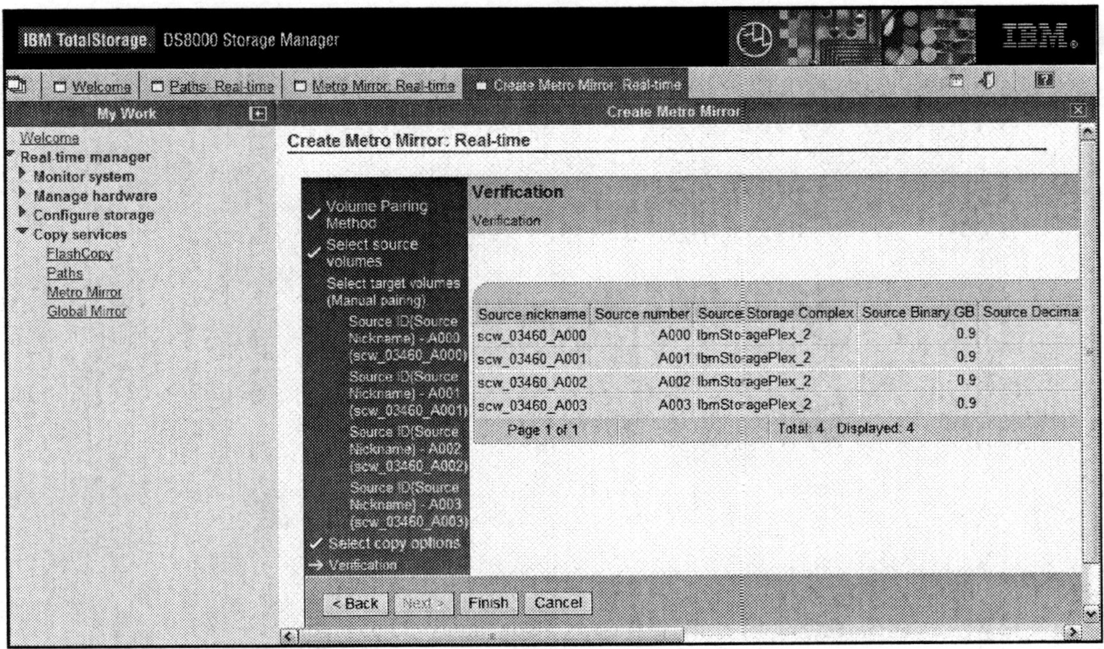

Figure 14-18 Verification panel

We now see the Metro Mirror panel indicating the successful creation of the Metro Mirror pair, as seen in Figure 14-19. If you scroll immediately to the far right you will likely observe that the volumes are in *Copy pending state*. In a short period of time all of the volumes should be in *Full duplex state*. Also to the far right is the Type column, where it will indicate either *Metro Mirror* or *Global Copy*. Figure 14-19 shows the panel after we have waited for a few minutes, then done a refresh. The pair is in full duplex state.

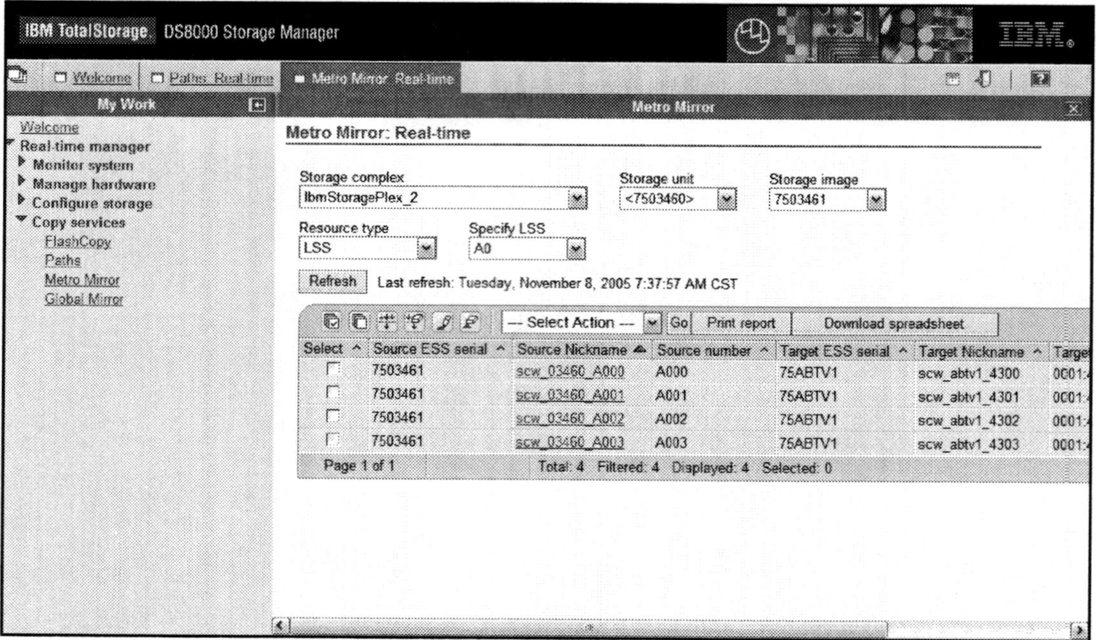

Figure 14-19 Metro Mirror pair established, full duplex state

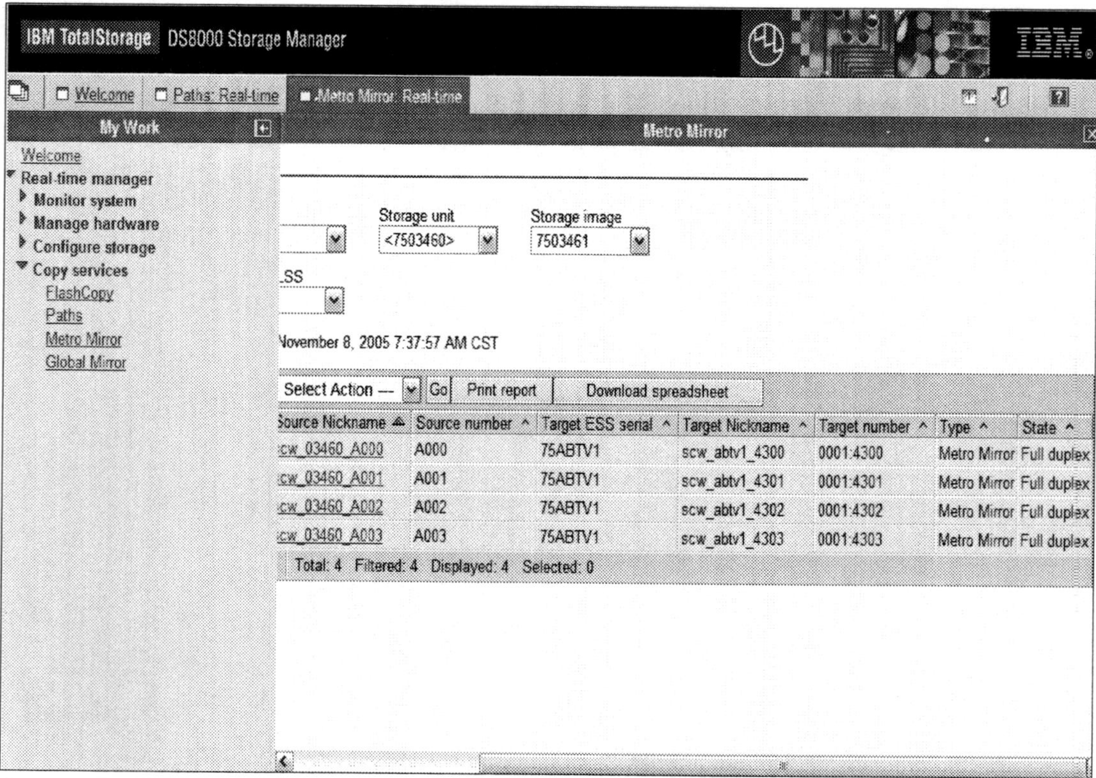

Figure 14-20 Metro Mirror established panel, view scrolled to the right

Suspend and resume suspended pair

To perform additional action on these synchronously mirrored volumes, select the volume or volumes of interest and click the *Select Action* pull-down. The result is shown in Figure 14-21. All four volumes have been selected and we select *Suspend...* and click **Go**.

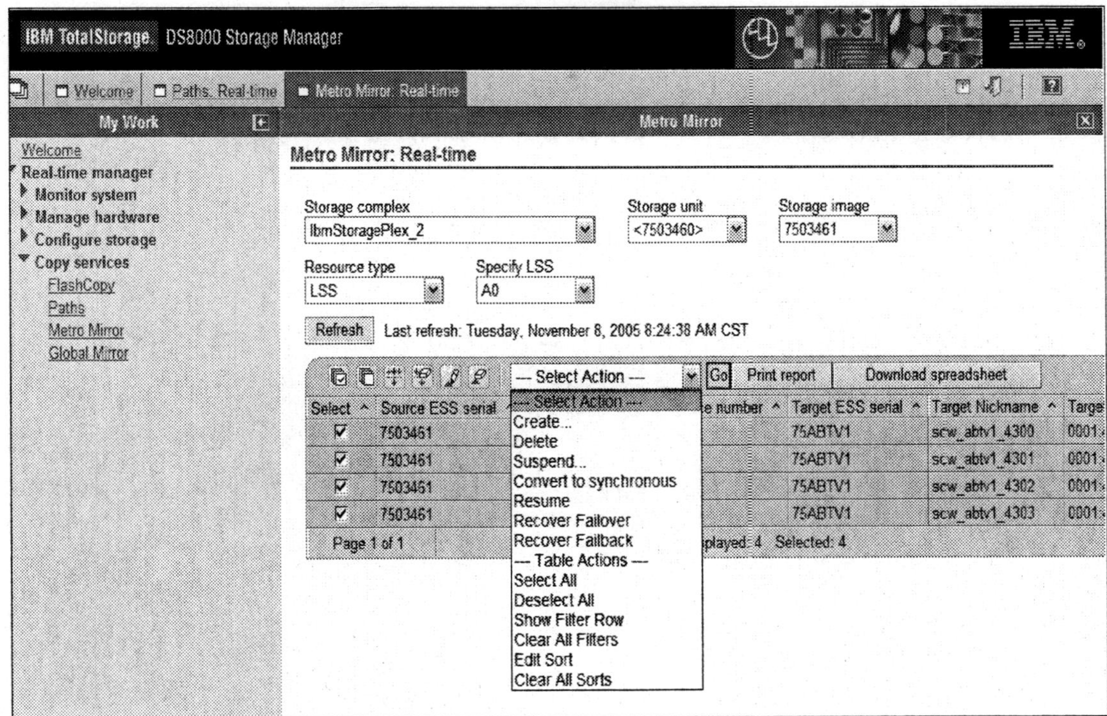

Figure 14-21 Select volume and action to perform

The next panel, shown in Figure 14-22, is where the choice to suspend at source or target can be made. We will select *Suspend at source* and click **OK**.

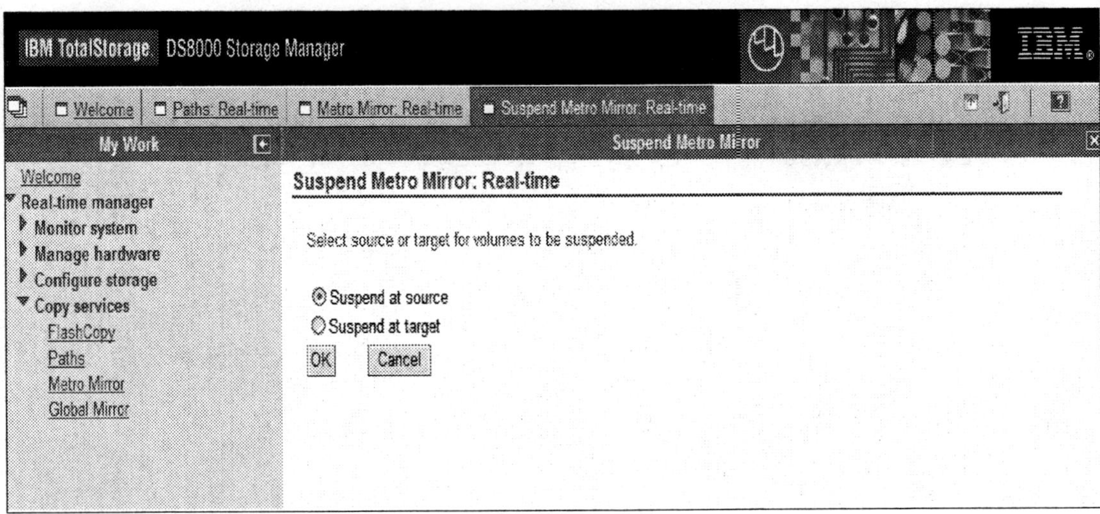

Figure 14-22 Suspend location selection panel

The next panel shown is in Figure 14-19 and Figure 14-20, but the state will have changed from *Full Duplex* to *Suspended* as shown in Figure 14-23.

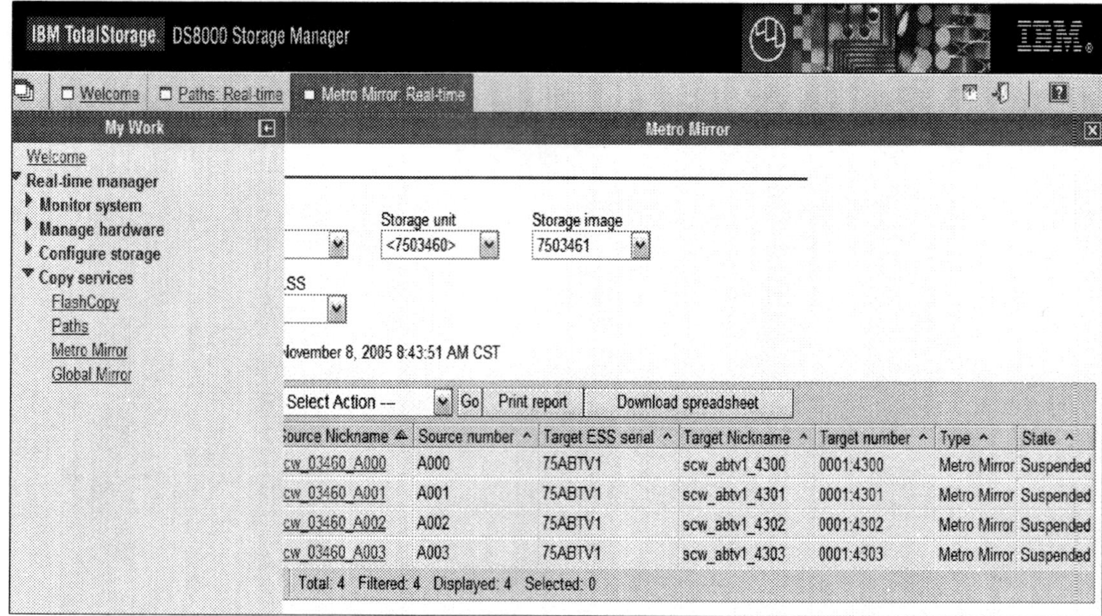

Figure 14-23 Metro Mirror volumes suspended displayed

To resume the suspended pairs, you can repeat the suspend process by selecting all four of the suspended volumes, select the *Resume* option, and click **Go**. You are then taken to the panel shown in Figure 14-24, where you confirm that you wish to resume the volumes in question. If everything is correct, click **OK**.

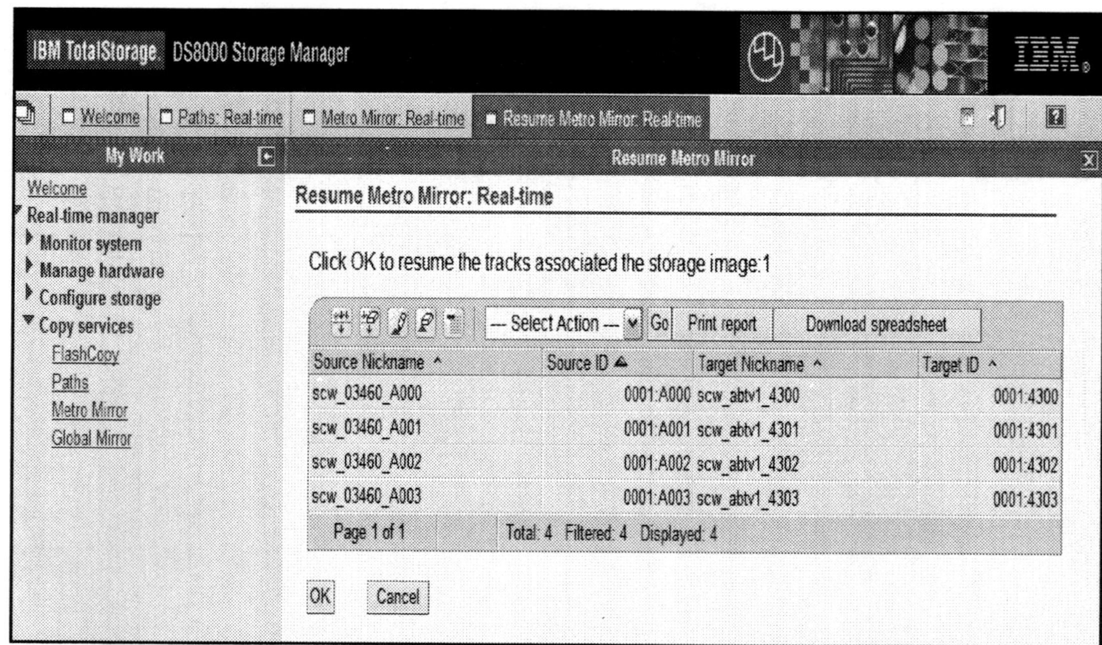

Figure 14-24 Confirm volume resume

You will then return to the Metro Mirror primary panel, Figure 14-19, and the volumes will either be in *Copy pending state* or *Full duplex state.*

14.6 ANTRQST API

The ANTRQST macro provides an application program call to the z/OS system data mover's (SDM) application programming interface (API). This macro allows you to call Metro Mirror, z/OS Global Mirror, and FlashCopy functions.

For detailed information, see the IBM publication *z/OS DFSMSdfp Advanced Copy Services*, SC35-0428.

15

Metro Mirror performance and scalability

In this chapter, we discuss some of the performance and scalability attributes of Metro Mirror on DS8000.

15.1 Performance

As Metro Mirror is a synchronous mirroring technology, it will introduce a performance overhead (for write operations) over a similar environment which has no remote mirroring. As part of the planning process for Metro Mirror you should understand this.

Bandwidth analysis and capacity planning for your Metro Mirror links should help to define how many links you need, and when you need to add more, to ensure best possible performance.

As part of your implementation project you may be able to identify and then distribute hot spots across your configuration, or take other actions to manage and balance performance.

Note that there will be no processor resources (CPU and memory) consumed by your Metro Mirror volume pairs (your management solution excluded), as this is managed by your DS8000 subsystem.

15.1.1 Peak bandwidth requirements

When you are researching your Metro Mirror link bandwidth requirements, you need to find the *peak sustained write rate* — remember that only writes will be mirrored across to the secondary volumes. For a typical z/OS system this peak is usually during batch processing, when many updates are occurring. It could be higher still during month-end or year-end processing.

You need to make allowances for this peak period when doing your bandwidth calculations.

15.1.2 RMF

Resource Management Facility (RMF) has the ability to collect and report on Metro Mirror link performance statistics for DS8000 subsystems, and used for capacity planning and trending reports. You will be able to track the utilization of the Metro Mirror links over time and introduce new links in a planned manner.

You can also produce reports on Extent Pool and Rank performance statistics using the RMF Post Processor, if you have enabled the collection of this data through the RMF PARMLIB member.

15.1.3 Disk Magic

Your IBM representative can arrange for a Disk Magic analysis of a proposed configuration. Disk Magic is an IBM-only tool which can assist with choosing a configuration which will meet your requirements.

15.1.4 Initial synchronization

When doing the initial synchronization of your Metro Mirror pairs, the DS8000 will use a throttling algorithm to prevent the Metro Mirror process using too many primary site resources. This may prolong the synchronization process if your DS8000 is busy at the time. You may choose to stagger your synchronization tasks, or to run them at a time of low utilization, to make this process more efficient.

15.2 Scalability

The DS8000 Metro Mirror environment can be scaled up or down as required. If new volumes are added to the DS8000 that require mirroring, they can be dynamically added. If additional Metro Mirror paths are required, they also can be dynamically added.

15.2.1 Addition of capacity

As we have previously mentioned, the logical nature of the LSS has made a Metro Mirror implementation on the DS8000 easier to plan, implement, and manage. However, if you need to add more LSSs to your Metro Mirror environment, your management and automation solutions should be set up to handle this.

The GDPS and eRCMF service offerings are designed to provide this functionality. Refer to Appendix F., “Service offerings” on page 659 for more information.

Adding capacity to same DS8000

If you are adding capacity into an existing DS8000, providing your Metro Mirror link bandwidth is not close to or over capacity, you may only need to add volume pairs into your configuration. If you are adding more LSSs, then you will need to define Metro Mirror paths before adding volume pairs.

Adding capacity in new DS8000s

If you are adding new DS8000s into your configuration, you will need to add physical Metro Mirror links prior to defining your Metro Mirror paths and volume pairs. A minimum of two Metro Mirror paths per DS8000 pair is recommended for redundancy reasons. Your bandwidth analysis will indicate if you require more than two paths.

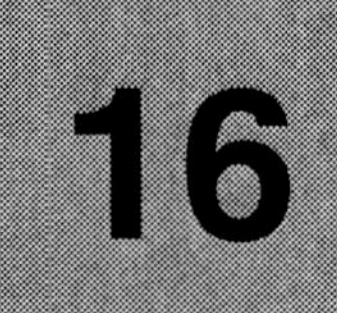

Metro Mirror examples

In this chapter we show some Metro Mirror scenarios where we use the various interfaces to control Metro Mirror. This is by no means a complete list of situations that may occur, it is intended as a sample.

16.1 TSO commands

In this section we give some example scenarios for the control of Metro Mirror functions using TSO commands.

16.1.1 Resynchronizing a suspended volume

To resynchronize a volume that is in a suspended state, we would need to obtain the necessary information for our environment (serial numbers, WWNNs, CCA and LSS numbers, and so on). We can do this using CQUERY commands. We can then reestablish our Metro Mirror pairs. We use CQUERY to check the status as we perform these actions.

Obtain information

To obtain the necessary information for our setup, we can use the CQUERY command, as shown in Example 16-1.

Example 16-1 CQUERY command to obtain information

```
ANTP8802I CQUERY DEVN(2028)
ANTP0090I CQUERY FORMATTED LVL 3 314
VOLUME REPORT
************** PPRC REMOTE COPY CQUERY - VOLUME ********************
*                                           (PRIMARY)   (SECONDARY) *
*                                          SSID CCA LSS SSID CCA LSS*
*DEVICE   LEVEL      STATE     PATH STATUS  SERIAL#     SERIAL#    *
*------ --------- ----------  ----------- ---------    ---------  *
* 2028  PRIMARY..  SUSPEND(3)   ACTIVE..   1710 28 00   1711 28 01 *
*       CRIT(NO).......       CGRPLB(NO). 000000006571 000000006571*
* PATHS PFCA SFCA STATUS: DESCRIPTION                              *
* ----- --------- ------  -------------------                      *
*   1   0030 0200   13    PATH ESTABLISHED...                      *
*       ---- ----   00    NO PATH...........                       *
*       ---- ----   00    NO PATH...........                       *
*       ---- ----   00    NO PATH...........                       *
* IF STATE = PENDING/SUSPEND:    TRACKS OUT OF SYNC =   23813      *
*                                TRACKS ON VOLUME   =   50085      *
*                              PERCENT OF COPY COMPLETE =  53%     *
*  SUBSYSTEM         WWNN                  LIC LEVEL               *
* -----------   ----------------          -----------              *
* PRIMARY....   5005076303AAAAAA          5.0.03.0196              *
* SECONDARY.1   5005076303AAAAAA                                   *
* SECONDARY.2   5005076300BBBBBB                                   *
* SECONDARY.3   5005076300BBBBBB                                   *
********************************************************************
ANTP0001I CQUERY COMMAND COMPLETED FOR DEVICE 2028. COMPLETION CODE: 00
```

We can see from the output that the device number 2028 is currently a primary volume, and is in Suspend state. The SSID, CCA, LSS and serial number information can be seen on the right side of the display for both primary (1710, 28, 00, and 06571 respectively) and secondary device (1711, 28, 01 and 06571). The path information is also shown (one path from primary Fibre Channel adapter 0030 to secondary Fibre Channel adapter 0200).

We can see that this volume is mirrored to the same DS8000 via a loopback path (as the serial number for primary and secondary DS8000 are the same).

We can record the information required for our Metro Mirror commands.

Resynchronize pair

To establish a Metro Mirror pair from TSO, you use the CESTPAIR command. We already have a pair established in the scenario above, however, it is suspended. We need to resynchronize it so the pair is in Duplex state again. The example shown in Example 16-2 is using the CESTPAIR command with the MODE(RESYNC) parameter to accomplish this.

Example 16-2 Resume suspended Metro Mirror pair from TSO

```
ANTP8802I CESTPAIR DEVN(X'2028') PRIM(X'1710' 06571 X'28' X'00')
   SEC(X'1711' 06571 X'28' X'01')            OPTION(SYN
ANTP8802I (CONT) C) MODE(RESYNC)
ANTP0001I CESTPAIR COMMAND COMPLETED FOR DEVICE 2028. COMPLETION CODE:
00
IEA494I 2028,PR2028,PPRC PAIR PENDING,SSID=1710,CCA=28
IEA494I 2028,PR2028,PPRC PAIR FULL DUPLEX,SSID=1710,CCA=28
```

> **Tip:** You may wish to do a FlashCopy of your recovery site prior to running the resynchronization, as the resynchronization process does not apply the updated tracks in the order they were updated, and so you will not have data consistency until the last volume pair is again in Duplex state.

16.1.2 Failover Failback using TSO

In this example we perform a failover and a failback using TSO commands. These options can be used in both planned and unplanned scenarios. We simulate a planned outage.

In these discussions, the volumes at the primary site are referred to as the A volumes, and the volumes at the recovery site are referred to as the B volumes. FlashCopy volumes are referred to as C volumes.

High level failover process

The high level process to do the failover in a planned scenario is as follows:

1. Quiesce applications at the primary site.
2. Issue the Metro Mirror CESTPAIR command to the secondary (B) volume as the DEVN, specifying the FAILOVER ACTION and reversing the original PRIMARY and SECONDARY parameters. This establishes the B volumes as suspended primaries, activates change recording on the B volumes, and releases write inhibit on the B volumes.
3. If desired, FlashCopy the B volume suspended primaries to C volumes to provide safe copies for interim disaster recovery protection.
4. Restart applications at the recovery site. This includes bringing the B volumes online.

Next we give some sample TSO commands to accomplish these actions.

CESTPAIR with FAILOVER

We use the CESTPAIR command with the FAILOVER ACTION to the B volume to reverse the original Metro Mirror direction and start change recording. The example is shown in Example 16-3. Notice that we have reversed the original PRIM and SEC parameters.

Example 16-3 Establish Metro Mirror pair using TSO

```
ANTP8802I CESTPAIR DEVN(X'2128') SEC(X'1710' 06571 X'28' X'00')
   PRIM(X'1711' 06571 X'28' X'01') ACTION(FAILOVER)
ANTP0001I CESTPAIR COMMAND COMPLETED FOR DEVICE 2128. COMPLETION CODE:
00
```

Syslog messages

In Example 16-4 we show the syslog messages from a failover operation. Notice that these devices are on DS6000 subsystems; however, the messages issued will be the same for a DS8000 pair. We are doing a failover from device 6030 to device 6430. In this example both primary and secondary devices are available to this LPAR, this may not be the case in all Metro Mirror environments. If both devices are not available from one LPAR you would have to issue commands on the system where the device is located.

Example 16-4 Syslog for failover operation

```
ANTP8802I CQUERY DEVN(6030)
ANTP0090I CQUERY FORMATTED LVL 3 227
VOLUME REPORT
************** PPRC REMOTE COPY CQUERY - VOLUME ********************
*                                          (PRIMARY)   (SECONDARY) *
*                                         SSID CCA LSS SSID CCA LSS*
*DEVICE   LEVEL      STATE     PATH STATUS  SERIAL#      SERIAL#    *
*------ --------- ---------- ----------- ---------    ---------  *
* 6030  PRIMARY..  DUPLEX....   ACTIVE..   2060 30 00   0002 30 00 *
*       CRIT(NO).......       CGRPLB(NO). 0000000AAGXA 0000000AAVCA*
* PATHS PFCA SFCA STATUS: DESCRIPTION                              *
* ----- --------- ------  -------------------                      *
*   1   0000 0000   13    PATH ESTABLISHED...                      *
*       ---- ----   00    NO PATH...........                       *
*       ---- ----   00    NO PATH...........                       *
*       ---- ----   00    NO PATH...........                       *
*  SUBSYSTEM         WWNN                     LIC LEVEL            *
* -----------  ----------------           -----------              *
* PRIMARY....  500507630EFFFC6F           5.0.00.0000              *
* SECONDARY.1  500507630EFFFCA0                                    *
*******************************************************************
ANTP0001I CQUERY COMMAND COMPLETED FOR DEVICE 6030. COMPLETION CODE: 00
ANTP8802I CQUERY DEVN(6430)
ANTP0090I CQUERY FORMATTED LVL 3 230
VOLUME REPORT
************** PPRC REMOTE COPY CQUERY - VOLUME ********************
*                                          (PRIMARY)   (SECONDARY) *
*                                         SSID CCA LSS SSID CCA LSS*
*DEVICE   LEVEL      STATE     PATH STATUS  SERIAL#      SERIAL#    *
*------ --------- ---------- ----------- ---------    ---------  *
* 6430  SECONDARY  DUPLEX....   ACTIVE..   2060 30 00   0002 30 00 *
*       ...............       ........... 0000000AAGXA 0000000AAVCA*
* PATHS PFCA SFCA STATUS: DESCRIPTION                              *
* ----- --------- ------  -------------------                      *
*   1   0000 0100   13    PATH ESTABLISHED...                      *
*       ---- ----   00    NO PATH...........                       *
*       ---- ----   00    NO PATH...........                       *
*       ---- ----   00    NO PATH...........                       *
*  SUBSYSTEM         WWNN                     LIC LEVEL            *
* -----------  ----------------           -----------              *
* PRIMARY....  500507630EFFFC6F           5.0.00.0000              *
* SECONDARY.1  500507630EFFFCA0                                    *
*******************************************************************
ANTP0001I CQUERY COMMAND COMPLETED FOR DEVICE 6430. COMPLETION CODE: 00
IEA494I 6030,DS6030,PPRC PAIR SUSPENDED,SSID=2060,CCA=30
ANTP8802I CESTPAIR DEVN(X'6430') PRIM(X'0002' AAVCA X'30' X'00')
   SEC(X'2060' AAGXA X'30' X'00')          ACTION(FAI
ANTP8802I (CONT) LOVER)
ANTP0001I CESTPAIR COMMAND COMPLETED FOR DEVICE 6430. COMPLETION CODE:
00
```

```
ANTP8802I CQUERY DEVN(6030)
ANTP0090I CQUERY FORMATTED LVL 3 239
VOLUME REPORT
************** PPRC REMOTE COPY CQUERY - VOLUME ********************
*                                          (PRIMARY)   (SECONDARY) *
*                                         SSID CCA LSS SSID CCA LSS*
*DEVICE   LEVEL      STATE      PATH STATUS  SERIAL#     SERIAL#    *
*------ --------- ---------- ----------- ---------    ---------  *
* 6030  PRIMARY..  SUSPEND(3)   ACTIVE..   2060 30 00   0002 30 00 *
*        CRIT(NO).......       CGRPLB(NO). 0000000AAGXA 0000000AAVCA*
* PATHS PFCA SFCA STATUS: DESCRIPTION                               *
* ----- --------- ------  ------------------                        *
*   1   0000 0000   13    PATH ESTABLISHED...                       *
*       ---- ----   00    NO PATH............                       *
*       ---- ----   00    NO PATH............                       *
*       ---- ----   00    NO PATH............                       *
*  SUBSYSTEM          WWNN                    LIC LEVEL             *
* -----------   ----------------            -----------             *
* PRIMARY....   500507630EFFFC6F            5.0.00.0000             *
* SECONDARY.1   500507630EFFFCA0                                    *
********************************************************************
ANTP0001I CQUERY COMMAND COMPLETED FOR DEVICE 6030. COMPLETION CODE: 00
ANTP8802I CQUERY DEVN(6430)
ANTP0090I CQUERY FORMATTED LVL 3 242
VOLUME REPORT
************** PPRC REMOTE COPY CQUERY - VOLUME ********************
*                                          (PRIMARY)   (SECONDARY) *
*                                         SSID CCA LSS SSID CCA LSS*
*DEVICE   LEVEL      STATE      PATH STATUS  SERIAL#     SERIAL#    *
*------ --------- ---------- ----------- ---------    ---------  *
* 6430  PRIMARY..  SUSPEND(3)   ACTIVE..   0002 30 00   2060 30 00 *
*        CRIT(NO).......       CGRPLB(NO). 0000000AAVCA 0000000AAGXA*
* PATHS PFCA SFCA STATUS: DESCRIPTION                               *
* ----- --------- ------  ------------------                        *
*   1   0100 0100   13    PATH ESTABLISHED...                       *
*       ---- ----   00    NO PATH............                       *
*       ---- ----   00    NO PATH............                       *
*       ---- ----   00    NO PATH............                       *
*  SUBSYSTEM          WWNN                    LIC LEVEL             *
* -----------   ----------------            -----------             *
* PRIMARY....   500507630EFFFCA0            5.0.00.0000             *
* SECONDARY.1   500507630EFFFCA0                                    *
* SECONDARY.2   500507630EFFFC6F                                    *
********************************************************************
ANTP0001I CQUERY COMMAND COMPLETED FOR DEVICE 6430. COMPLETION CODE: 00
```

Both devices are in Suspend state. Notice that for device 6430 the direction of the Metro Mirror pairing has been reversed. Since the volume is in Suspend state, changes will be recorded by the DS8000. At this stage you could start running your application in the secondary site.

High level failback process

The high level failback process in a planned scenario is as follows:

1. Quiesce the applications at the recovery site.
2. Use Metro Mirror establish path commands to create paths from recovery site to primary site (remember that paths are required for all LSS pairs).

3. Issue Metro Mirror establish pair commands to the B volume specifying the Failback action and reversing the original Primary and Secondary parameters. This will copy any changes recorded on the B volumes back to the A volumes. You will need to vary the A volumes offline if they are online at the primary site.
4. If you established a FlashCopy relationship (to C volumes) you can now withdraw it.
5. Check that Metro Mirror paths exist between A and B volumes. Reestablish if necessary.
6. Allow Metro Mirror pairs to reach Full Duplex state (use CQUERY command or check syslog for IEA494I messages).
7. Issue Metro Mirror Establish pair commands to A volumes specifying the Failover action with the original Primary and Secondary parameters. This will reestablish the A volumes as suspended primaries and will begin change recording on the A volumes. It will also release write inhibit on the A volumes. You can vary the A volumes online again at this point.
8. You can now restart your applications at the primary site.
9. Now issue the Metro Mirror Establish pair command to the A volumes, specifying the Failback action with the original Primary and Secondary parameters. This will resynchronize the A and B volumes in the recovery configuration and restore the pairs to Duplex state.

CESTPAIR with FAILBACK action (step 3, 9)

The command in Example 16-5 will reestablish the Metro Mirror pair and copy any changes across to the original primary volume (remember to keep the original Primary and Secondary parameters reversed).

Example 16-5 CESTPAIR with Failback - B to A (step 3)

```
CESTPAIR DEVN(X'6430') PRIM(X'0002' AAVCA X'30' X'00') -
         SEC(X'2060' AAGXA X'30' X'00') -
         ACTION(FAILBACK)
```

A similar command will be issued in step 10, however, with the original Metro Mirror direction, as shown in Example 16-6.

Example 16-6 CESTPAIR with Failback - A to B (step 10)

```
CESTPAIR DEVN(X'6430') SEC(X'0002' AAVCA X'30' X'00') -
         PRIM(X'2060' AAGXA X'30' X'00') -
         ACTION(FAILBACK)
```

Syslog messages for failback process

In Example 16-7 we see the syslog messages issued for the complete failback process. Notice that we had access to both devices from one LPAR and so could perform all operations from there. You may need to split operations if you don't have access to both devices. We are issuing CQUERY commands between each step of the process to check the status of our volumes. You can see the status changes and the direction of mirroring change as we progress through the process.

Example 16-7 Syslog messages for failback process

```
ANTP8802I CQUERY DEVN(6030)
ANTP0090I CQUERY FORMATTED LVL 3 257
VOLUME REPORT
************** PPRC REMOTE COPY CQUERY - VOLUME ********************
*                                          (PRIMARY)   (SECONDARY) *
*                                         SSID CCA LSS SSID CCA LSS*
```

```
*DEVICE   LEVEL      STATE     PATH STATUS  SERIAL#     SERIAL#    *
*------ ---------  ----------  ----------- ---------     ---------  *
* 6030  PRIMARY..  SUSPEND(3)   ACTIVE..   2060 30 00   0002 30 00 *
*       CRIT(NO).......       CGRPLB(NO). 0000000AAGXA 0000000AAVCA*
* PATHS PFCA SFCA STATUS: DESCRIPTION                              *
* ----- --------- ------  -------------------                      *
*   1   0000 0000   13    PATH ESTABLISHED...                      *
*       ---- ----   00    NO PATH...........                       *
*       ---- ----   00    NO PATH...........                       *
*       ---- ----   00    NO PATH...........                       *
*  SUBSYSTEM         WWNN                     LIC LEVEL            *
* -----------  ----------------            -----------             *
* PRIMARY....  500507630EFFFC6F            5.0.00.0000             *
* SECONDARY.1  500507630EFFFCA0                                    *
********************************************************************
ANTP0001I CQUERY COMMAND COMPLETED FOR DEVICE 6030. COMPLETION CODE: 00
ANTP8802I CQUERY DEVN(6430)
ANTP0090I CQUERY FORMATTED LVL 3 260
VOLUME REPORT
************** PPRC REMOTE COPY CQUERY - VOLUME ********************
*                                           (PRIMARY)   (SECONDARY) *
*                                         SSID CCA LSS SSID CCA LSS*
*DEVICE   LEVEL      STATE     PATH STATUS  SERIAL#     SERIAL#    *
*------ ---------  ----------  ----------- ---------     ---------  *
* 6430  PRIMARY..  SUSPEND(3)   ACTIVE..   0002 30 00   2060 30 00 *
*       CRIT(NO).......       CGRPLB(NO). 0000000AAVCA 0000000AAGXA*
* PATHS PFCA SFCA STATUS: DESCRIPTION                              *
* ----- --------- ------  -------------------                      *
*   1   0100 0100   13    PATH ESTABLISHED...                      *
*       ---- ----   00    NO PATH...........                       *
*       ---- ----   00    NO PATH...........                       *
*       ---- ----   00    NO PATH...........                       *
*  SUBSYSTEM         WWNN                     LIC LEVEL            *
* -----------  ----------------            -----------             *
* PRIMARY....  500507630EFFFCA0            5.0.00.0000             *
* SECONDARY.1  500507630EFFFCA0                                    *
* SECONDARY.2  500507630EFFFC6F                                    *
********************************************************************
ANTP0001I CQUERY COMMAND COMPLETED FOR DEVICE 6430. COMPLETION CODE: 00
ANTP8802I CESTPAIR DEVN(X'6430') PRIM(X'0002' AAVCA X'30' X'00')
   SEC(X'2060' AAGXA X'30' X'00')          ACTION(FAI
ANTP8802I (CONT) LBACK)
ANTP0001I CESTPAIR COMMAND COMPLETED FOR DEVICE 6430. COMPLETION CODE:
00
ANTP8802I CQUERY DEVN(X'6030')
ANTP0090I CQUERY FORMATTED LVL 3 266
VOLUME REPORT
************** PPRC REMOTE COPY CQUERY - VOLUME ********************
*                                           (PRIMARY)   (SECONDARY) *
*                                         SSID CCA LSS SSID CCA LSS*
*DEVICE   LEVEL      STATE     PATH STATUS  SERIAL#     SERIAL#    *
*------ ---------  ----------  ----------- ---------     ---------  *
* 6030  SECONDARY  DUPLEX....   ACTIVE..   0002 30 00   2060 30 00 *
*       ...............       ........... 0000000AAVCA 0000000AAGXA*
* PATHS PFCA SFCA STATUS: DESCRIPTION                              *
* ----- --------- ------  -------------------                      *
*   1   0000 0000   13    PATH ESTABLISHED...                      *
*       ---- ----   00    NO PATH...........                       *
*       ---- ----   00    NO PATH...........                       *
*       ---- ----   00    NO PATH...........                       *
```

```
*  SUBSYSTEM         WWNN                    LIC LEVEL              *
* -----------  ----------------           -----------               *
* PRIMARY....  500507630EFFFCA0           5.0.00.0000               *
* SECONDARY.1  500507630EFFFC6F                                     *
*********************************************************************
ANTP0001I CQUERY COMMAND COMPLETED FOR DEVICE 6030. COMPLETION CODE: 00
ANTP8802I CQUERY DEVN(X'6430')
ANTP0090I CQUERY FORMATTED LVL 3 269
VOLUME REPORT
************** PPRC REMOTE COPY CQUERY - VOLUME ********************
*                                          (PRIMARY)   (SECONDARY) *
*                                         SSID CCA LSS SSID CCA LSS*
*DEVICE   LEVEL      STATE     PATH STATUS  SERIAL#     SERIAL#    *
*------ ---------  ----------  ----------- ---------   ---------  *
* 6430  PRIMARY..  DUPLEX....   ACTIVE..   0002 30 00   2060 30 00 *
*       CRIT(NO).......       CGRPLB(NO). 0000000AAVCA 0000000AAGXA*
* PATHS PFCA SFCA STATUS: DESCRIPTION                              *
* ----- --------- ------  -------------------                      *
*   1   0100 0100   13    PATH ESTABLISHED...                      *
*       ---- ----   00    NO PATH............                      *
*       ---- ----   00    NO PATH............                      *
*       ---- ----   00    NO PATH............                      *
*  SUBSYSTEM         WWNN                    LIC LEVEL             *
* -----------  ----------------           -----------              *
* PRIMARY....  500507630EFFFCA0           5.0.00.0000              *
* SECONDARY.1  500507630EFFFCA0                                    *
* SECONDARY.2  500507630EFFFC6F                                    *
********************************************************************
ANTP0001I CQUERY COMMAND COMPLETED FOR DEVICE 6430. COMPLETION CODE: 00
ANTP8802I CQUERY DEVN(6030)
ANTP0090I CQUERY FORMATTED LVL 3 272
VOLUME REPORT
************** PPRC REMOTE COPY CQUERY - VOLUME ********************
*                                          (PRIMARY)   (SECONDARY) *
*                                         SSID CCA LSS SSID CCA LSS*
*DEVICE   LEVEL      STATE     PATH STATUS  SERIAL#     SERIAL#    *
*------ ---------  ----------  ----------- ---------   ---------  *
* 6030  SECONDARY  DUPLEX....   ACTIVE..   0002 30 00   2060 30 00 *
*       ...............       ........... 0000000AAVCA 0000000AAGXA*
* PATHS PFCA SFCA STATUS: DESCRIPTION                              *
* ----- --------- ------  -------------------                      *
*   1   0000 0000   13    PATH ESTABLISHED...                      *
*       ---- ----   00    NO PATH............                      *
*       ---- ----   00    NO PATH............                      *
*       ---- ----   00    NO PATH............                      *
*  SUBSYSTEM         WWNN                    LIC LEVEL             *
* -----------  ----------------           -----------              *
* PRIMARY....  500507630EFFFCA0           5.0.00.0000              *
* SECONDARY.1  500507630EFFFC6F                                    *
********************************************************************
ANTP0001I CQUERY COMMAND COMPLETED FOR DEVICE 6030. COMPLETION CODE: 00
ANTP8802I CQUERY DEVN(6430)
ANTP0090I CQUERY FORMATTED LVL 3 275
VOLUME REPORT
************** PPRC REMOTE COPY CQUERY - VOLUME ********************
*                                          (PRIMARY)   (SECONDARY) *
*                                         SSID CCA LSS SSID CCA LSS*
*DEVICE   LEVEL      STATE     PATH STATUS  SERIAL#     SERIAL#    *
*------ ---------  ----------  ----------- ---------   ---------  *
* 6430  PRIMARY..  DUPLEX....   ACTIVE..   0002 30 00   2060 30 00 *
```

```
*       CRIT(NO).......       CGRPLB(NO). 0000000AAVCA 0000000AAGXA*
* PATHS PFCA SFCA STATUS: DESCRIPTION                               *
* ----- --------- ------  -------------------                       *
*   1   0100 0100   13    PATH ESTABLISHED...                       *
*       ---- ----   00    NO PATH............                       *
*       ---- ----   00    NO PATH............                       *
*       ---- ----   00    NO PATH............                       *
*  SUBSYSTEM          WWNN                   LIC LEVEL              *
* -----------   ----------------           -----------              *
* PRIMARY....   500507630EFFFCA0           5.0.00.0000              *
* SECONDARY.1   500507630EFFFCA0                                    *
* SECONDARY.2   500507630EFFFC6F                                    *
*********************************************************************
ANTP0001I CQUERY COMMAND COMPLETED FOR DEVICE 6430. COMPLETION CODE: 00
ANTP8802I CESTPAIR DEVN(X'6030') PRIM(X'2060' AAGXA X'30' X'00')
   SEC(X'0002' AAVCA X'30' X'00')          ACTION(FAI
ANTP8802I (CONT) LOVER)
ANTP0001I CESTPAIR COMMAND COMPLETED FOR DEVICE 6030. COMPLETION CODE:
00
ANTP8802I CQUERY DEVN(6030)
ANTP0090I CQUERY FORMATTED LVL 3 283
VOLUME REPORT
************** PPRC REMOTE COPY CQUERY - VOLUME ********************
*                                           (PRIMARY)   (SECONDARY) *
*                                          SSID CCA LSS SSID CCA LSS*
*DEVICE   LEVEL      STATE      PATH STATUS  SERIAL#     SERIAL#    *
*------ ---------  ----------  ----------- ---------    ---------  *
* 6030  PRIMARY..  SUSPEND(3)   ACTIVE..   2060 30 00   0002 30 00 *
*       CRIT(NO).......       CGRPLB(NO). 0000000AAGXA 0000000AAVCA*
* PATHS PFCA SFCA STATUS: DESCRIPTION                               *
* ----- --------- ------  -------------------                       *
*   1   0000 0000   13    PATH ESTABLISHED...                       *
*       ---- ----   00    NO PATH............                       *
*       ---- ----   00    NO PATH............                       *
*       ---- ----   00    NO PATH............                       *
*  SUBSYSTEM          WWNN                   LIC LEVEL              *
* -----------   ----------------           -----------              *
* PRIMARY....   500507630EFFFC6F           5.0.00.0000              *
* SECONDARY.1   500507630EFFFCA0                                    *
*********************************************************************
ANTP0001I CQUERY COMMAND COMPLETED FOR DEVICE 6030. COMPLETION CODE: 00
ANTP8802I CQUERY DEVN(6430)
ANTP0090I CQUERY FORMATTED LVL 3 286
VOLUME REPORT
************** PPRC REMOTE COPY CQUERY - VOLUME ********************
*                                           (PRIMARY)   (SECONDARY) *
*                                          SSID CCA LSS SSID CCA LSS*
*DEVICE   LEVEL      STATE      PATH STATUS  SERIAL#     SERIAL#    *
*------ ---------  ----------  ----------- ---------    ---------  *
* 6430  PRIMARY..  SUSPEND(3)   ACTIVE..   0002 30 00   2060 30 00 *
*       CRIT(NO).......       CGRPLB(NO). 0000000AAVCA 0000000AAGXA*
* PATHS PFCA SFCA STATUS: DESCRIPTION                               *
* ----- --------- ------  -------------------                       *
*   1   0100 0100   13    PATH ESTABLISHED...                       *
*       ---- ----   00    NO PATH............                       *
*       ---- ----   00    NO PATH............                       *
*       ---- ----   00    NO PATH............                       *
*  SUBSYSTEM          WWNN                   LIC LEVEL              *
* -----------   ----------------           -----------              *
* PRIMARY....   500507630EFFFCA0           5.0.00.0000              *
```

```
* SECONDARY.1  500507630EFFFCA0                                     *
* SECONDARY.2  500507630EFFFC6F                                     *
*********************************************************************
ANTP0001I CQUERY COMMAND COMPLETED FOR DEVICE 6430. COMPLETION CODE: 00
ANTP8802I CESTPAIR DEVN(X'6030') PRIM(X'2060' AAGXA X'30' X'00')
   SEC(X'0002' AAVCA X'30' X'00')           ACTION(FAI
ANTP8802I (CONT) LBACK)
ANTP0001I CESTPAIR COMMAND COMPLETED FOR DEVICE 6030. COMPLETION CODE:
00
ANTP8802I CQUERY DEVN(6030)
ANTP0090I CQUERY FORMATTED LVL 3 292
VOLUME REPORT
************** PPRC REMOTE COPY CQUERY - VOLUME ********************
*                                          (PRIMARY)   (SECONDARY) *
*                                        SSID CCA LSS SSID CCA LSS*
*DEVICE   LEVEL      STATE     PATH STATUS  SERIAL#     SERIAL#    *
*------ ---------  ----------  ----------- ---------    ---------  *
* 6030  PRIMARY..  PENDING...   ACTIVE..   2060 30 00   0002 30 00 *
*       CRIT(NO).......       CGRPLB(NO). 0000000AAGXA 0000000AAVCA*
* PATHS PFCA SFCA STATUS: DESCRIPTION                               *
* ----- --------- ------  -------------------                       *
*   1   0000 0000   13    PATH ESTABLISHED...                       *
*       ---- ----   00    NO PATH...........                        *
*       ---- ----   00    NO PATH...........                        *
*       ---- ----   00    NO PATH...........                        *
*  SUBSYSTEM         WWNN                     LIC LEVEL             *
* -----------   ----------------            -----------             *
* PRIMARY....   500507630EFFFC6F            5.0.00.0000             *
* SECONDARY.1   500507630EFFFCA0                                    *
*********************************************************************
ANTP0001I CQUERY COMMAND COMPLETED FOR DEVICE 6030. COMPLETION CODE: 00
ANTP8802I CQUERY DEVN(6430)
ANTP0090I CQUERY FORMATTED LVL 3 295
VOLUME REPORT
************** PPRC REMOTE COPY CQUERY - VOLUME ********************
*                                          (PRIMARY)   (SECONDARY) *
*                                        SSID CCA LSS SSID CCA LSS*
*DEVICE   LEVEL      STATE     PATH STATUS  SERIAL#     SERIAL#    *
*------ ---------  ----------  ----------- ---------    ---------  *
* 6430  SECONDARY  PENDING...   ACTIVE..   2060 30 00   0002 30 00 *
*       ...............       ........... 0000000AAGXA 0000000AAVCA*
* PATHS PFCA SFCA STATUS: DESCRIPTION                               *
* ----- --------- ------  -------------------                       *
*   1   0000 0100   13    PATH ESTABLISHED...                       *
*       ---- ----   00    NO PATH...........                        *
*       ---- ----   00    NO PATH...........                        *
*       ---- ----   00    NO PATH...........                        *
*  SUBSYSTEM         WWNN                     LIC LEVEL             *
* -----------   ----------------            -----------             *
* PRIMARY....   500507630EFFFC6F            5.0.00.0000             *
* SECONDARY.1   500507630EFFFCA0                                    *
*********************************************************************
ANTP0001I CQUERY COMMAND COMPLETED FOR DEVICE 6430. COMPLETION CODE: 00
```

16.1.3 Management of open systems volumes with TSO commands

It is possible to manage Metro Mirror, Global Copy and FlashCopy of open systems devices through the TSO interface. We show an example of this in the following sections.

Establishing a pair

Similar to zSeries volumes, we first have to collect the information required. In this example we already have a path defined to the secondary subsystem. We issue a CQUERY command with the ODEVN parameter to check the status of the volume, as seen in Example 16-8. Notice that we need to direct the command (via the DEVN parameter) to a z/OS device with the same server affinity as the open systems volume (so in this example, we direct it to a volume in LSS 00, which has the same server affinity as LSS 16).

Example 16-8 CQUERY for open systems device

```
CQUERY DEVN(6030) ODEVN(AAGXA X'00' X'16') VOLUME
```

The serial number of the DS subsystem is supplied, along with the LUN number (x'00') and the LSS number (x'16'). The output will appear similar to Example 16-9.

Example 16-9 CQUERY for open systems device output

```
ANTP8802I CQUERY DEVN(6030) ODEVN(AAGXA X'00' X'16') VOLUME
ANTP0090I CQUERY FORMATTED LVL 3 472
VOLUME REPORT
************** PPRC REMOTE COPY CQUERY - VOLUME ********************
*                                    (PRIMARY)   (SECONDARY) *
*                                   SSID LUN LSS SSID LUN LSS*
*DEVICE   LEVEL      STATE      PATH STATUS  SERIAL#     SERIAL#    *
*------ --------- ---------- ----------- ---------    --------- *
* 6030  .........  SIMPLEX...   INACTIVE   FF16 00 16   .......... *
*       ...............       ........... 0000000AAGXA ............*
* PATHS SAID DEST STATUS: DESCRIPTION                              *
* ----- --------- ------  -------------------                      *
*   0    ---- ----   00    NO PATH...........                      *
*        ---- ----   00    NO PATH...........                      *
*        ---- ----   00    NO PATH...........                      *
*        ---- ----   00    NO PATH...........                      *
*  SUBSYSTEM         WWNN                   LIC LEVEL              *
* -----------  ----------------          -----------               *
* PRIMARY....  500507630EFFFC6F          5.0.00.0000               *
* SECONDARY.1  500507630EFFFCA0                                    *
* SECONDARY.2  500507630EFFFCA0                                    *
*******************************************************************
ANTP0001I CQUERY COMMAND COMPLETED FOR DEVICE 6030. COMPLETION CODE: 00
```

We can see that the device is in Simplex state. Note the SSID reports with special value FF16 — which is the open systems LSS number preceded with FF.

We wish to establish a pair with the secondary device on LSS 16, LUN number 00. The command format is as shown in Example 16-10.

Example 16-10 CESTPAIR command for open systems LUN

```
CESTPAIR DEVN(X'6030') PRIM(X'FF16' AAGXA X'00' X'16') -
         SEC(X'FF16' AAVCA X'00' X'16') OPENDVCS(YES) -
         OPTION(SYNC) MODE(COPY)
```

We use the OPENDVCS parameter and the special SSID value FF16 to identify that this is an open systems device, on LSS 16, and we wish to direct the command to the open systems LSS. The LUN number is supplied where we would normally supply the CCA, and the LSS number is supplied in the normal position. The output from this command and a subsequent CQUERY is shown in Example 16-11.

Example 16-11 CESTPAIR and CQUERY output

```
ANTP8802I CESTPAIR DEVN(X'6030') PRIM(X'FF16' AAGXA X'00' X'16')
   SEC(X'FF16' AAVCA X'00' X'16') OPENDVCS(YES)
ANTP8802I (CONT)     OPTION(SYNC) MODE(COPY)
ANTP0001I CESTPAIR COMMAND COMPLETED FOR DEVICE 6030. COMPLETION CODE:
00
ANTP8802I CQUERY DEVN(6030) ODEVN(AAGXA X'00' X'16') VOLUME
ANTP0090I CQUERY FORMATTED LVL 3 478
VOLUME REPORT
************** PPRC REMOTE COPY CQUERY - VOLUME ********************
*                                          (PRIMARY)   (SECONDARY) *
*                                          SSID LUN LSS SSID LUN LSS*
*DEVICE   LEVEL      STATE     PATH STATUS  SERIAL#      SERIAL#    *
*------ ---------  ----------  ----------- ---------    ---------  *
* 6030  PRIMARY..  PENDING...   ACTIVE..   FF16 00 16   FF16 00 16 *
*       CRIT(NO).......       CGRPLB(NO). 0000000AAGXA 0000000AAVCA*
* PATHS PFCA SFCA STATUS: DESCRIPTION                              *
* ----- --------- ------  -------------------                      *
*   2   0000 0000   13    PATH ESTABLISHED...                      *
*       0100 0100   13    PATH ESTABLISHED...                      *
*       ---- ----   00    NO PATH............                      *
*       ---- ----   00    NO PATH............                      *
* IF STATE = PENDING/SUSPEND:    TRACKS OUT OF SYNC =   40523      *
*                                TRACKS ON VOLUME   =   81920      *
*                              PERCENT OF COPY COMPLETE =  51%     *
*  SUBSYSTEM         WWNN                    LIC LEVEL             *
* -----------   ----------------            -----------            *
* PRIMARY....   500507630EFFFC6F            5.0.00.0000            *
* SECONDARY.1   500507630EFFFCA0                                   *
* SECONDARY.2   500507630EFFFCA0                                   *
*******************************************************************
ANTP0001I CQUERY COMMAND COMPLETED FOR DEVICE 6030. COMPLETION CODE: 00
```

We can see the Metro Mirror pair has established and the volume is in Pending state, with 51% of tracks copied so far.

16.2 ICKDSF

In this section we give some example scenarios for the control of Metro Mirror functions using ICKDSF.

16.2.1 Changing a path to Consistency Group

In this example we change a Metro Mirror path to a Consistency Group path. We might choose to do this if we were implementing a disaster recovery solution and we were now ready to implement our automation to detect Metro Mirror error messages and trigger data consistency actions from them.

Example JCL for ICKDSF

In Example 16-12 we show an example of an ICKDSF job that is defining a Metro Mirror path with the Consistency Group option. Notice that the PPRCOPY ESTPATH command replaces any path definitions that currently exist.

Example 16-12 ICKDSF PPRCOPY ESTPATH example

```
//ICKDSFJE JOB (ACCT),'ICKDSF ESTPATH',
//         MSGCLASS=X,NOTIFY=&SYSUID,MSGLEVEL=(1,1)
//*************************************
//STEP01    EXEC PGM=ICKDSF
//SYSPRINT DD SYSOUT=*
//VOL1      DD UNIT=3390,VOL=SER=DS643F,DISP=SHR
//SYSIN     DD *
 PPRCOPY ESTPATH DDNAME(VOL1) -
  FCPP(X'00000100') PRI(X'0002',AAVCA) -
  SEC(X'0003',AAVCA) WWNN(500507630EFFFCA0,500507630EFFFCA0) -
  CGROUP(YES) LSS(X'00',X'01')
```

In Example 16-13 we show output from a CQUERY command for device 643F, which shows that CGROUPLB(YES) is set. This indicates a Consistency Group path.

Example 16-13 CQUERY output

```
ANTP8802I CQUERY DEVN(643F)
ANTP0090I CQUERY FORMATTED LVL 3 621
VOLUME REPORT
************** PPRC REMOTE COPY CQUERY - VOLUME ********************
*                                          (PRIMARY)   (SECONDARY) *
*                                         SSID CCA LSS SSID CCA LSS*
*DEVICE   LEVEL      STATE     PATH STATUS  SERIAL#     SERIAL#    *
*------ ---------  ----------  ----------- ---------    ---------  *
* 643F  PRIMARY..  DUPLEX....    ACTIVE..   0002 3F 00   0003 3F 01 *
*       CRIT(NO).......       CGRPLB(YES) 0000000AAVCA 0000000AAVCA*
* PATHS PFCA SFCA STATUS: DESCRIPTION                              *
* ----- --------- ------  -------------------                      *
*   1   0000 0100   13    PATH ESTABLISHED...                      *
*       ---- ----   00    NO PATH...........                       *
*       ---- ----   00    NO PATH...........                       *
*       ---- ----   00    NO PATH...........                       *
*  SUBSYSTEM         WWNN                   LIC LEVEL              *
* -----------  ----------------            -----------             *
* PRIMARY....  500507630EFFFCA0            5.0.00.0000             *
* SECONDARY.1  500507630EFFFCA0                                    *
* SECONDARY.2  500507630EFFFC6F                                    *
********************************************************************
ANTP0001I CQUERY COMMAND COMPLETED FOR DEVICE 643F. COMPLETION CODE: 00
```

16.3 DS CLI

In this section we give some example scenarios for the control of Metro Mirror functions using DS CLI.

16.3.1 DS CLI freezepprc command

When you want to suspend all Metro Mirror pairs (and remove paths) between a pair of LSSs you use the **freezepprc** command (or its equivalent in the other interfaces). It is used for data consistency purposes to give a recovery point at your secondary site.

When the path is defined as a Consistency Group path, issuing a **freezepprc** command will cause an Extended Long Busy condition for all Metro Mirror pairs on the LSS pairing. Once you have issued **freezepprc** commands for all LSS pairs, you can then issue an **unfreezepprc** command (or equivalent in the other interfaces) to remove the Extended Long Busy.

freezepprc and unfreezepprc

To freeze Metro Mirror with the CLI you use the **freezepprc** command. An example of its usage is shown in Example 16-14, as well as an example of the **unfreezepprc** command.

Example 16-14 freezepprc DS CLI command

```
dscli> freezepprc -dev ibm.2107-7506571 -remotedev ibm.2105-24663 00:01
Date/Time: 4 June 2005 01:24:42 PM IBM DSCLI Version: 5.0.3.134 DS: IBM.2107-7506571
CMUC00161W freezepprc: Remote Mirror and Copy consistency group 00:01 successfully created.
dscli>
dscli> unfreezepprc -dev ibm.2107-7506571 -remotedev ibm.2105-24663 00:01
Date/Time: 4 June 2005 01:27:38 PM IBM DSCLI Version: 5.0.3.134 DS: IBM.2107-7506571
CMUC00198I unfreezepprc: Remote Mirror and Copy pair 00:01 successfully thawed.
dscli>
```

These commands can be issued by your automation routine to give you data consistency at the first error message (to prevent a *rolling disaster* situation). The **freezepprc** command would be issued to all LSS pairs as quickly as possible, followed by **unfreezepprc** commands when they had completed.

Part 5

Global Copy

In this part of the book, we describe the Global Copy feature of the DS8000. After presenting an overview of Global Copy, we discuss the options available, the interfaces to the feature, and some configuration considerations. We also provide some examples of the use of Global Copy.

17 Global Copy overview

In this chapter we describe the characteristics and operation of IBM TotalStorage Global Copy, previously known as PPRC-XD (Peer-to-Peer Remote Copy Extended Distance). Also discussed are the considerations for its implementation on the IBM TotalStorage DS8000.

17.1 Global Copy overview

IBM TotalStorage Global Copy (PPRC Extended Distance, PPRC-XD) is an asynchronous remote copy function for z/OS and open systems for longer distances than are possible with Metro Mirror. With Global Copy, write operations complete on the primary storage system before they are received by the secondary storage system. This capability is designed to prevent the primary system's performance from being affected by wait time from writes on the secondary system. Therefore, the primary and secondary copies can be separated by any distance. This function is appropriate for remote data migration, off-site backups, and transmission of inactive database logs at virtually unlimited distances.

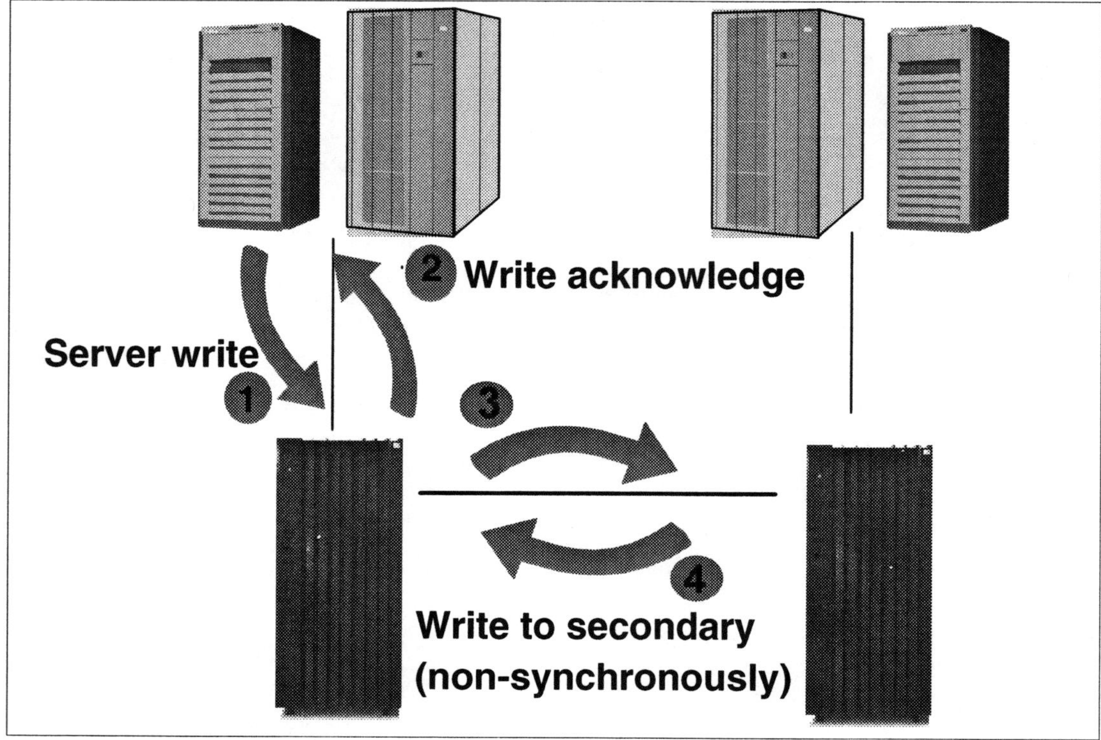

Figure 17-1 Global Copy

1. The host server requests a write I/O to the primary DS8000. The write is staged through cache and non-volatile storage (NVS).
2. The write returns to the host server's application.
3. At some moments later, that is, in a non-synchronous manner, the primary DS8000 will send the necessary data so that the updates are reflected on the secondary volumes. The updates are grouped in batches for efficient transmission.
4. The secondary DS8000 returns write completed to the primary DS8000 when the updates are secured in the secondary DS8000 cache and NVS. The primary DS8000 then resets its change recording information.

Note: The efficient extended distance mirroring technique of Global Copy is achieved using sophisticated algorithms. For example, if changed data is in the cache, then PPRC sends only the changed sectors. There are also sophisticated queueing algorithms to schedule each volume for processing of their updated tracks; and then the setting of the batches of updates to be transmitted.

17.2 Global Copy state change logic

Figure 17-2 Illustrates the Global Copy and Mirror state change logic. There are four different volume states:

- **Simplex**: The volume is not in a Global Copy relationship.
- **Suspended**: In this state the writes to the primary volume are not mirrored onto the secondary volume. The secondary volume becomes out-of-sync. During this time, Global Copy keeps a bitmap record of the changed tracks in the primary volume. Later, the volume pair can be re-started, and then only the tracks that were updated will be copied.
- **Full duplex**: Updates on the primary volumes are synchronously mirrored to the secondary volume. A Global Copy volume pair never reaches full duplex status. Even when no tracks are out-of-sync, the pair remains in copy pending status.
- **Copy Pending**: Updates on the primary volume are asynchronously mirrored to the secondary volume.

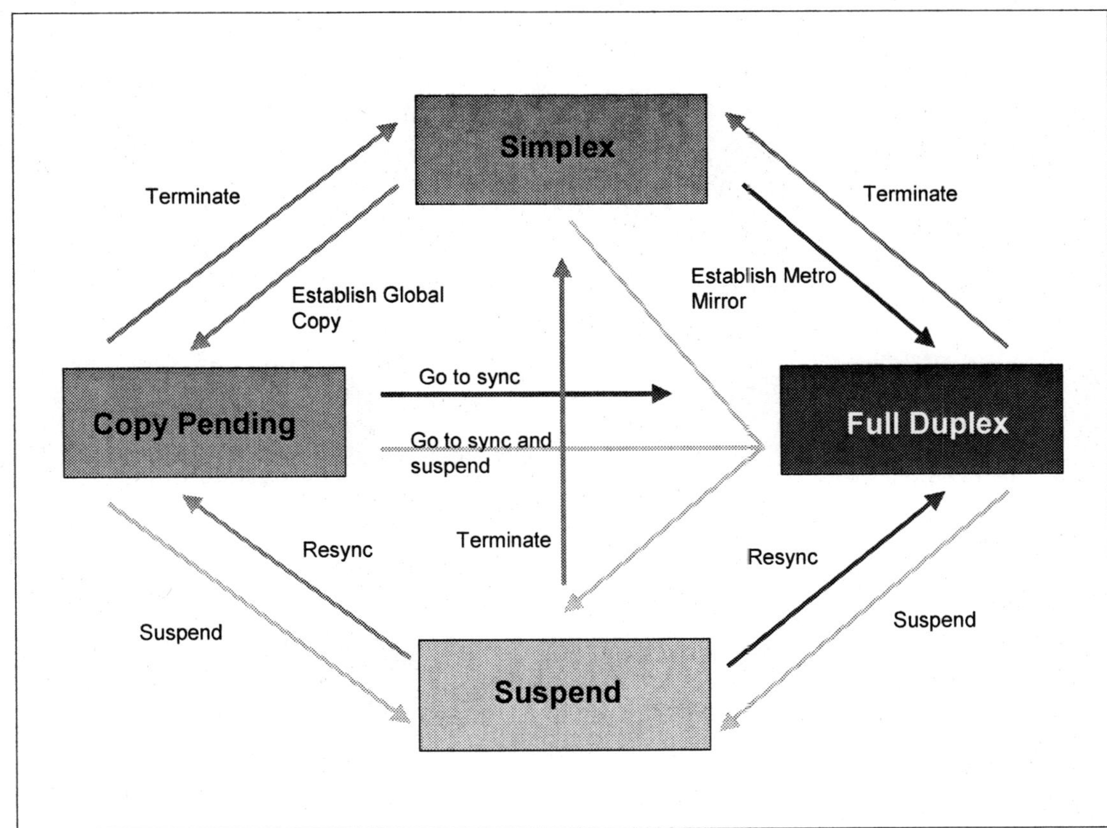

Figure 17-2 Global Copy and Mirror state change logic

- When you initially establish a mirror relationship from a volume in Simplex state, you have the option to request that it become a Global Copy pair (establish Global Copy arrow in Figure 17-2), or a Metro Mirror pair (establish Metro Mirror arrow in Figure 17-2).
- Pairs can change from the Copy Pending state, to Full Duplex state when a go-to-SYNC is commanded (go-to-SYNC arrow in Figure 17-2).
- You can also request that a pair be suspended as soon as it reaches the full-duplex state (go-to-SYNC and Suspended in Figure 17-2).
- Pairs cannot change directly from Full Duplex state to Copy Pending state. They need to go through an intermediate Suspended state.

- You can go from suspended state to Global Copy state doing an incremental copy (copying out-of-sync tracks only). This is a similar process as for the traditional transition from suspended state to SYNC state (RESYNC/copy out-of-sync arrow in Figure 17-2).

17.3 Global Copy positioning

The main points of Global Copy are listed in Figure 17-3.

Global Copy is a recommended solution for remote data copy, data migration and offsite backup - over continental distances without impacting application performance.

It can be used for application recovery implementations if application I/O activity can be quiesced and non-zero data loss RPO is admissible.

- It can be used over continental distances with excellent application performance
  - The distances only limited by the network and channel extenders capabilities
- Application write operations do not have synchronous-like overheads
- Fuzzy copy of data at the recovery site (sequence of dependent writes may not be respected at the recovery site)
- Recovery data can become a consistent point-in-time copy of the primary data, if appropiate application checkpoints are set to do global catch-ups
  - Pairs are synchronized with application group consistency
- Synchronizations can be done more frequently, because of short catch-ups
  - RPO still not zero, but improves substantially

Figure 17-3 Global Copy positioning

As summarized in Figure 17-3, Global Copy is a recommended solution for remote data copy, data migration, off-site backup, and transmission of inactive database logs, without impacting application performance, which is particularly relevant when implemented over continental distances. Global Copy can also be used for application recovery solutions based on periodic point-in-time copies of the data. This requires short quiescings of the application's I/O activity.

18

Global Copy options

In this chapter, we discuss some of the options available when using Global Copy on the DS8000 disk subsystem.

18.1 Establish a Global Copy pair

During establishment of a Global Copy pair for zSeries volumes, you have the following options to select; see Figure 18-1.

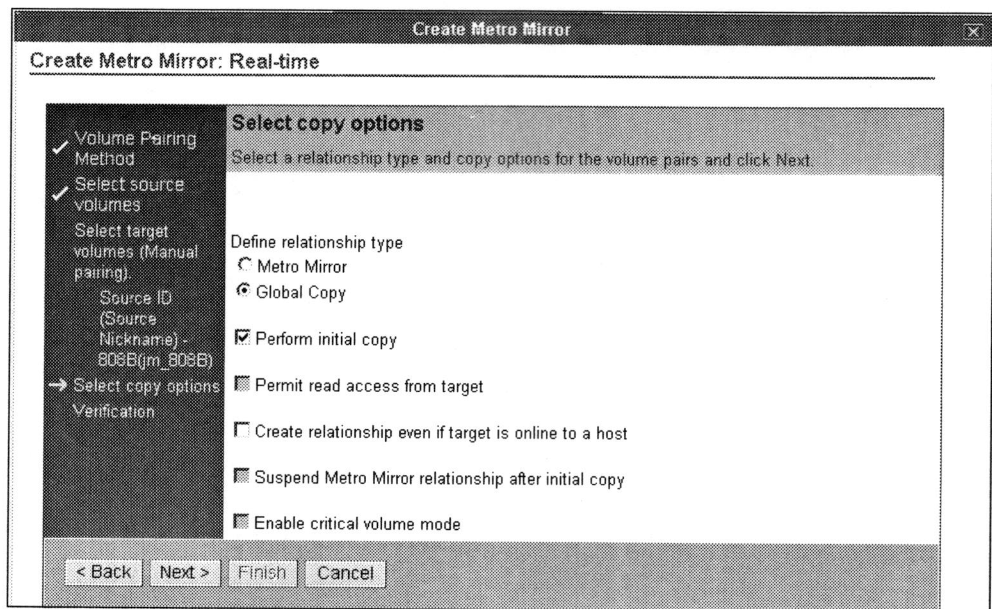

Figure 18-1 Global Copy options for CKD volumes

- **Perform initial copy**: This copies all tracks from the primary volume to the secondary, overwriting the whole secondary volume.
- **Create relationship even if target is online to host**: This allows a Global Copy volume relationship to be created even if the target volume is online to host systems.

> **Note:** The option *Permit read access from target* is valid only for open systems volumes. The option *Suspend Metro Mirror relationship after initial copy* does not apply to Global Copy. The *Enable critical volume mode* option is disabled, if *Perform initial copy* is selected for a Global Copy pair.

18.2 Catch-up transition

Copy Pending *catch-up* is the name of the transition for a Global Copy pair from its normal out-of-sync condition to a fully synchronous Metro Mirror pair. The pair goes from the *pending* state to the *duplex* state. At the end of this transition, primary and secondary volumes are fully synchronized, with all their respective tracks identical.

As a result of the catch-up, the Global Copy pair becomes a Metro Mirror pair. This will have an impact on application response times because write I/Os in a Metro Mirror pair are written to both primary and secondary volumes before the host application is acknowledged. For this reason, a Global Copy pair is normally synchronized only for short periods of time, typically to make a FlashCopy, and host application updates are quiesced for the duration. Refer to "Creating a consistent point-in-time copy" on page 195 for a more detailed discussion on the topic.

18.2.1 Go-to-sync using TSO

You can initiate a catch-up operation by commanding Global Copy to go-to-SYNC using the TSO command CESTPAIR. For the go-to-SYNC, the CESTPAIR command must be used with the OPTION(SYNC) and MODE(RESYNC) parameters (see Table 18-1).

Table 18-1 CESTPAIR parameter values for the go-to-SYNC transition

Operation	Volume pair state		CESTPAIR parameter values	
	From:	**To:**	**OPTION**	**MODE**
Go-to-SYNC catch-up	Duplex pending XD	Duplex	SYNC	RESYNC

Example 18-1 shows the TSO CESTPAIR command to change a Global Copy pair to synchronous mode.

Example 18-1 TSO initiated go-to-sync transition

```
CESTPAIR DEVN(X'400A') OPTION(SYNC) MODE(RESYNC) -
PRIM(X'4000' ABTV1 X'0A' X'00') -
SEC(X'8000' 20781 X'8A' X'80')
```

Note: The CESTPAIR command does not support the go-to-sync and suspend operation as ICKDSF and the DS CLI do. When using the TSO interface, in order to suspend as soon as the duplex state is reached, you have to automate it by triggering on the state change messages that the system issues.

18.2.2 Go-to-SYNC using ICKDSF

You can initiate a catch-up operation by commanding Global Copy to go-to-SYNC using the ICKDSF PPRCOPY CESTPAIR command. For the go-to-SYNC, the CESTPAIR command must be used with the OPTION(SYNC) and MODE(RESYNC) parameters

Example 18-2 shows the PPRCOPY ESTPAIR command to go from PPRC-XD mode to synchronous mode.

Example 18-2 ICKDSF initiated go-to-sync transition

```
//STEP    EXEC PGM=ICKDSF
//SYSPRINT DD SYSOUT=*
//SYSIN    DD *
 PPRC ESTPAIR UNIT(400A) OPTION(SYNC) -
 LSS(X'00',X'80') -
 PRI(X'4000',ABTV1,X'0A') -
 SEC(X'8000',20781,X'8A')
```

18.2.3 Go-to-sync using the DS Storage Manager

In the Metro Mirror panel you can display the Metro Mirror or Global Copy pairs and perform specific actions on them, see Figure 18-2.

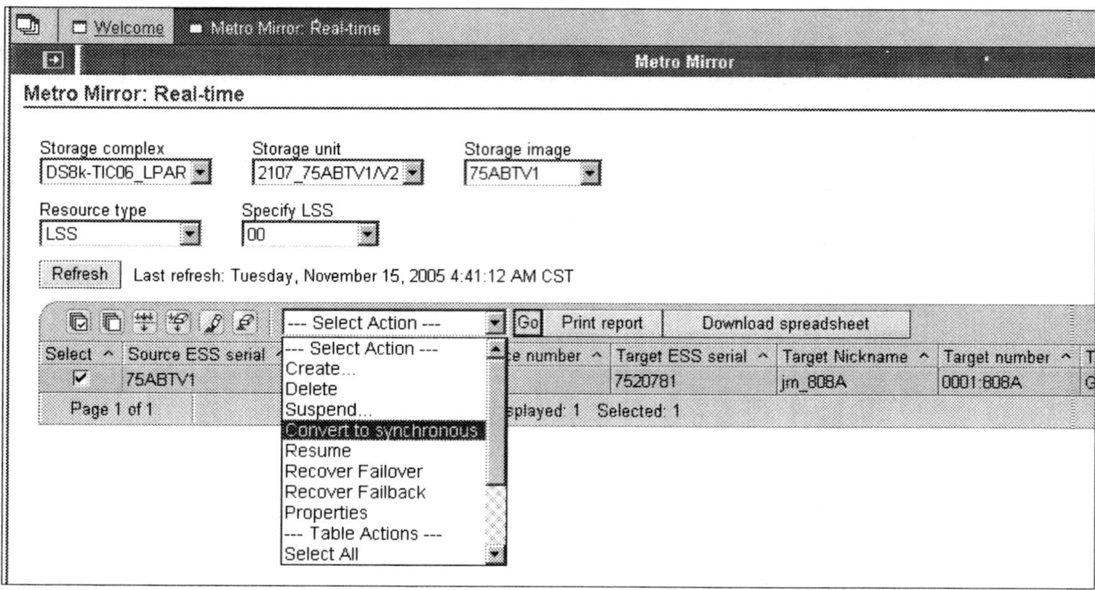

Figure 18-2 Convert to synchronous using GUI

To convert a Global Copy pair to a Metro Mirror pair, you can select the Global Copy pair and then choose **Convert to synchronous** from the Select Actions menu.

18.2.4 Go-to-sync using the DS CLI

You can also use the DS CLI command **mkpprc** with the option -mmir to synchronize a Global Copy pair, see Example 18-3.

Example 18-3 mkpprc command

```
dscli> mkpprc -dev ibm.2107-75abtv1 -remotedev ibm.2107-7520781 -type mmir  000A:808A
Date/Time: November 15, 2005 12:36:32 PM EET IBM DSCLI Version: 5.1.0.204 DS:
IBM.2107-75ABTV1
CMUC00153I mkpprc: Remote Mirror and Copy volume pair relationship 000A:808A successfully
created.
```

18.2.5 Display out-of-sync tracks

After a Global Copy pair is established, the volumes get the status Copy Pending. The Copy Pending status remains also if no tracks are out-of-sync. You can display the number of out-of-sync tracks with the DS CLI or with the DS Storage Manager. With the DS CLI you can use the **lspprc** command, see Example 18-4.

Example 18-4 lspprc command

```
dscli> lspprc -dev ibm.2107-75abtv1 -remotedev ibm.2107-7520781 -l 000A
Date/Time: November 15, 2005 12:34:06 PM EET IBM DSCLI Version: 5.1.0.204 DS:
IBM.2107-75ABTV1
ID        State        Reason Type        Out Of Sync Tracks Tgt Read Src Cascade Tgt Casca
===========================================================================================
000A:808A Copy Pending -      Global Copy 71030              Disabled Disabled    invalid
```

On the DS Storage Manager you can display the out-of-sync tracks in the Metro Mirror properties window, see Figure 18-3.

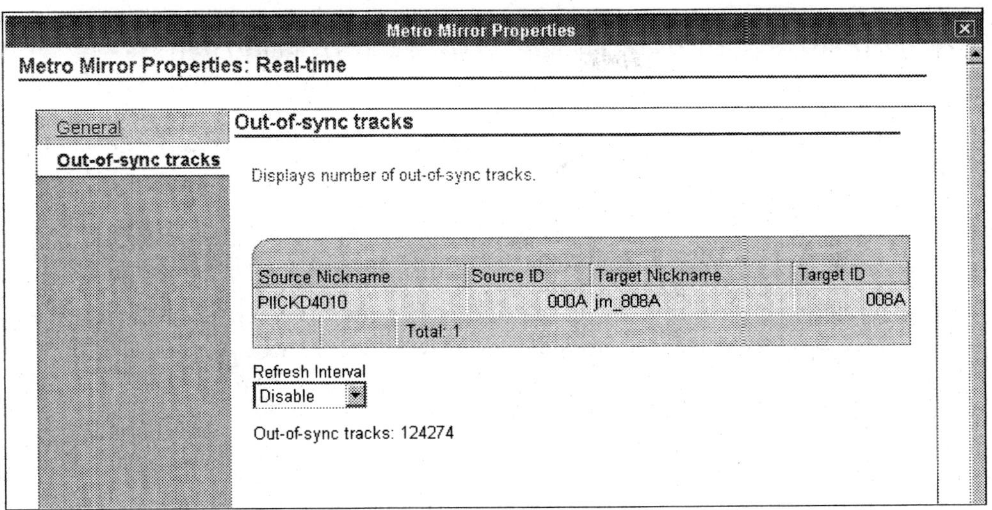

Figure 18-3 Out-of-sync tracks

18.3 Creating a consistent point-in-time copy

While the copy pair volumes are in the Copy Pending state, the secondary volumes maintain a *fuzzy copy* of the data:

- Because of the non-synchronous data transfer characteristics, at any time there will be a certain amount of updated data that is not reflected at the secondary volume. This data corresponds to the sectors that were updated since the last volume bitmap scan was done. These are the out-of-sync sectors.
- Because of the bitmap scan method, writes are not ensured to be applied on to the secondary volume in the same sequence as they are written to the primary volume.

When terminating the Global Copy relationship to establish host access to secondary volumes, the first issue may cause loss of transactions. Since a file system's or database's consistency depends on the correct ordering of write sequences, the second issue may cause inconsistent volumes. Therefore, to use secondary volumes by the host systems, you need to make them *point-in-time consistent*:

- The application needs to be quiesced and the volume pairs temporarily suspended. This is necessary to ensure consistency not only at the volume level, but also at the application level.
- The secondary volumes have to *catch up* to their primary counterparts. Global Copy catch-up is the name of the transition that occurs to a Global Copy pair when it goes from its normal out-of-sync condition until it reaches a full sync condition. At the end of this transition, the primary and secondary volumes become fully synchronized.
- A FlashCopy of the secondary volumes onto the tertiary volumes should now be performed, followed by resuming of the Global Copy pairs.

These tertiary volumes are then a consistent point-in-time copy of the primary volumes. Figure 18-4 summarizes this procedure, which provides a consistent point-in-time copy of the data:

1. Quiesce the application updates.
2. Synchronize the volume pairs by one of these methods:

– Perform the catch-up by issuing a *go-to-sync* operation. This can be done as described in 18.2, “Catch-up transition” on page 192. Now the volume pair leaves the Copy Pending state and will reach the Full Duplex state. From this moment, primary write updates would be synchronously transmitted to the recovery site, if the application updates were not quiesced.

– Perform the catch-up by waiting until all application updates are transferred to the secondary site.

You can monitor the number of out-of-sync tracks with the DS Storage Manager or with the DS CLI as shown in 18.2.5, “Display out-of-sync tracks” on page 194.

3. Suspend the Global Copy pairs after they reach the full duplex state. If you use PPRC Consistency Groups, issue a **Freeze** operation.

   At this point, we have a set of consistent secondary volumes.

4. You can resume the application. Updates will not be transferred to the secondary volumes because the pairs are suspended. The secondary volumes will remain consistent, and the application will not experience any response time impact.
5. Perform a FlashCopy on the secondary volumes.
6. Resume Global Copy mode for the copy pair.

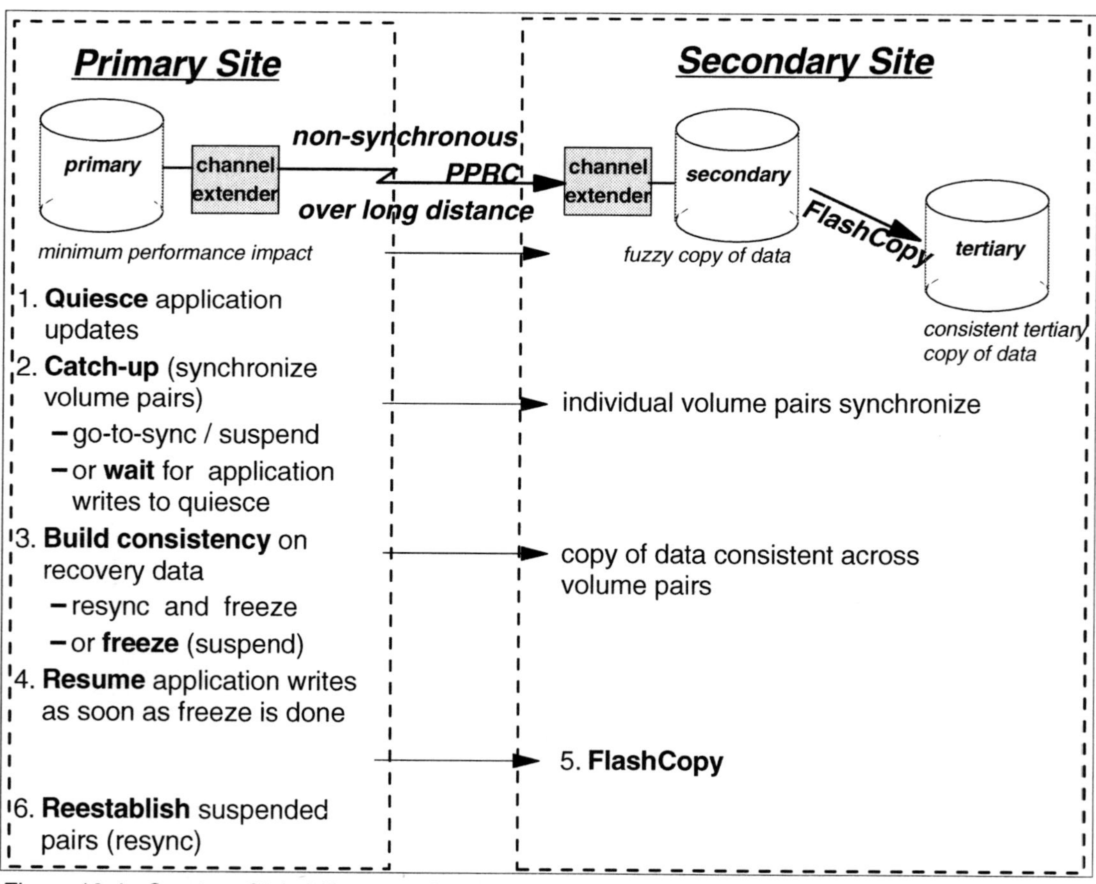

Figure 18-4 Create a Global Copy consistent copy

For application recovery based on point-in-time copies, you have to plan for appropriate checkpoints to briefly quiesce the application and synchronize the volumes pairs. When the recovery of the application is done, you must remember that, while in an active Global Copy relationship, the secondary volumes always have a current fuzzy copy of the primary volumes, so you have to keep the tertiary volumes where you *FlashCopied* the last globally consistent catch-up. As you can realize, this tertiary copy will not be reflective of the current update, but rather, any updates up until the last global catch-up operation.

18.4 Cascading

Asynchronous Cascading PPRC is a function of the Enterprise Storage Server (ESS), where the secondary volume of a Global Copy or Metro Mirror volume pair becomes the primary volume of another Global Copy or Metro Mirror relationship. Cascading allows you to set a remote copy relationship from a source volume through an intermediate volume to a target volume.

The two volume pairs in a cascaded relationship may be either Global Copy or Metro Mirror pairs with one exception: the first pair (source to intermediate) cannot be Global Copy if the second pair (intermediate to target) is Metro Mirror. The two pairs can be established in any order: first and second here do not refer to the order of establishment.

Refer to *IBM TotalStorage Enterprise Storage Server: Implementing ESS Copy Services with IBM eServer zSeries*, SG24-5680, for more information on cascading.

Cascading can be useful when migrating data from an ESS to the DS8000. If the volumes to be migrated are mirrored between two ESSs using Metro Mirror, you can set up a cascaded Global Copy from the secondary ESS to the DS8000. This way you can migrate the volumes without having to delete the existing volume pairs.

Cascading can also be used if you need to migrate data from an ESS model F20 to a DS8000. This cannot be done directly with Global Copy because the ESS F20 only supports ESCON remote copy links while the DS8000 only supports FCP links. The migration can be done using an ESS 800 (or ESS 750) as an intermediate unit, because the ESS 800 supports, with PPRC Version 2, both ESCON and FCP links. In this setup, the source volumes on the ESS F20 would be copied to intermediate volumes on the ESS 800 using Global Copy (or Metro Mirror), and they in turn would be copied to the target volumes on the DS8000 using cascading Global Copy. The intermediate ESS has to be at LIC level 2.4.3.65 or later in order to support Global Copy with the DS8000.

A cascaded relationship is established with the second volume pair (intermediate to target). In TSO, this is done by specifying parameter `CASCADE(YES)` on the **CESTPAIR** command, as in Example 18-5. In the example, device 400A is the intermediate volume.

Example 18-5 Cascading with TSO

```
CESTPAIR DEVN(X'400A') OPTION(XD) MODE(COPY) CASCADE(YES) -
PRIM(X'4000' ABTV1 X'0A' X'00') -
SEC(X'8000' 20781 X'8A' X'80')
```

The respective parameter for ICKDSF **ESTPAIR** command is `CASCADE` (Example 18-6).

Example 18-6 Cascading with ICKDSF

```
PPRC ESTPAIR UNIT(400A) OPTION(XD) MODE(COPY) CASCADE -
LSS(X'00',X'80') -
PRI(X'4000',ABTV1,X'0A') -
SEC(X'8000',20781,X'8A')
```

In DS CLI, a cascading relationship is established by specifying parameter `-cascade` on the **mkpprc** command, as in Example 18-7.

Example 18-7 Cascading with CLI

```
mkpprc -dev ibm.2105-22399 -remotedev ibm.2107-7503461 -type gcp -mode full -cascade
050a:031a
Date/Time: November 21, 2005 11:08:41 AM EET IBM DSCLI Version: 5.1.0.204 DS:
IBM.2105-22399
CMUC00153I mkpprc: Remote Mirror and Copy volume pair relationship 050A:031A successfully
created.

lspprc -dev ibm.2105-22399 050a
Date/Time: November 21, 2005 11:28:15 AM EET IBM DSCLI Version: 5.1.0.204 DS:
IBM.2105-22399
ID        State               Reason Type        SourceLSS Timeout (secs) Critical Mode
==========================================================================================
011A:050A Target Copy Pending -      Global Copy 01        unknown        Disabled
050A:031A Copy Pending        -      Global Copy 05        unknown        Disabled
```

In the example, 011A is the source volume, 050A is the intermediate volume, and 031A is the target volume. The **lspprc** command shows the status of both volume pairs where the intermediate volume 050A belongs. 011A:050A is the first pair where 050A is the secondary, and 050A:031A is the second pair where 050A is the cascading primary.

Notice that ESS F20 does not support DS CLI. The Global Copy relationships between the ESS F20 and the ESS 800 can be managed using TSO, for example, while the relationships between the ESS 800 and the DS8000 can also be managed using the DS CLI.

Global Copy interfaces

In this chapter we explain the interfaces used to manage Global Copy in a z/OS environment.

19.1 Comparison

Table 19-1 gives you an overview and comparison between the DS CLI commands and the appropriate DS Storage Manager actions.

Table 19-1 Comparison of commands

Task	TSO	ICKDSF	Command with DS CLI	Select option with DS SM
Global Copy paths commands:				
List available I/O ports that can be used to establish Global Copy paths.			lsavailpprcport	This information is shown during the process when a path is established.
List established Global Copy paths.	CQUERY PATH	PPRCOPY QUERY PATHS	lspprcpath	Copy Services □ Paths
Establish path	CESTPATH	PPRCOPY ESTPATH	mkpprcpath	Copy Services □ Paths □ Create
Delete path	CDELPATH	PPRCOPY DELPATH	rmpprcpath	Copy Services □ Paths □ Delete
Global Copy pairs commands:				
Failback	CESTPAIR ACTION(FAILBACK)	PPRCOPY ESTPAIR FAILBACK	failbackpprc	Copy Services □ Global Copy □ Recover Failback
Failover	CESTPAIR ACTION(FAILOVER)	PPRCOPY ESTPAIR FAILOVER	failoverpprc	Copy Services □ Global Copy □ Recover Failover
List Global Copy volume pairs	CQUERY	PPRCOPY QUERY	lspprc	Copy Services □ Global Copy
Establish pair	CESTPAIR	PPRCOPY ESTPAIR	mkpprc	Copy Service □ Global Copy □ Create
Suspend pair	CSUSPEND	PPRCOPY SUSPEND	pausepprc	Copy Services □ Global Copy □ Suspend
Resume pair	CESTPAIR MODE(RESYNC)	PPRCOPY ESTPAIR MODE(RESYNC)	resumepprc	Copy Services □ Global Copy □ Resume
Delete pair	CDELPAIR	PPRCOPY DELPAIR	rmpprc	Copy Services □ Global Copy □ Delete

Task	TSO	ICKDSF	Command with DS CLI	Select option with DS SM
Freeze Consistency Group	CGROUP FREEZE	PPRCOPY FREEZE	freezepprc	
Thaw Consistency Group	CGROUP RUN	PPRCOPY RUN	unfreezepprc	

In the following sections we explain the DS CLI commands and the DS Storage Manager tasks in more detail.

19.2 TSO commands for Global Copy

In z/OS systems, Global Copy can be managed using TSO commands. In this section we discuss the Global Copy commands that TSO provides.

For a detailed description of these commands, the following IBM publication can be referenced: *z/OS DFSMS Advanced Copy Services,* SC35-0428.

Command overview

An overview of these commands is presented in Table 19-2.

Table 19-2 TSO Commands

Command	Description
`CESTPAIR`	Establishing Global Copy volume pairs
`CESTPATH`	Establish Global Copy path
`CDELPAIR`	Deleting volume pairs
`CDELPATH`	Deleting paths
`CGROUP`	Controlling volume groups with FREEZE and RUN
`CQUERY`	Querying of the status of volumes and paths
`CRECOVER`	Recovering data on the recovery system
`CSUSPEND`	Suspending Global Copy volume pairs

CESTPAIR

This command has the optional parameter OPTION, which has two mutually exclusive values: SYNC or XD. You specify SYNC if you want to establish Metro Mirror (synchronous) pair. You specify XD if you want to establish a Global Copy pair.

For the pair to become a Global Copy pair (in addition to specifying the XD value for the OPTION parameter) you will also specify whether this pair comes from the simplex or from the suspended state. That is to say, whether this is an initial copy of a newly established pair, or if it is a re-synchronization of a suspended pair. To indicate this, you use the MODE parameter, specifying either COPY or RESYNC, respectively.

Example 19-1 shows the CESTPAIR command with the OPTION parameter value XD and MODE parameter value of COPY. This example illustrates a transition from a simplex volume state to a *Copy pending* volume state.

Example 19-1 Establish a Global Copy pair

```
CESTPAIR DEVN(X'400A') OPTION(XD) MODE(COPY) -
PRIM(X'4000' ABTV1 X'0A' X'00') -
SEC(X'8000' 20781 X'8A' X'80')
```

Table 19-3 summarizes the values of the CESTPAIR command parameters that you will be using when working with Global Copy pairs. Refer also to Table 19-3 for the parameter values when doing a go-to-sync transition.

Table 19-3 CESTPAIR parameter

Operation	Volume pair state		CESTPAIR parameter values	
	from	**to**	**OPTION**	**MODE**
Establish initial copy pair	*simplex*	*copy pending*	XD	COPY
Reestablish suspended pair	*suspended*	*copy pending*	XD	RESYNC

CESTPATH

Use the CESTPATH command to establish paths for Global Copy between two logical subsystems. There must be a physical link between the two Storage Images. You need to know the World Wide Node Name (WWNN) of the primary and secondary Storage Images, and the Subsystem Identifier (SSID) and LSS number for the primary and secondary LSS. These can be displayed with the CQUERY command.

Example 19-2 shows the CESTPATH command to establish two remote copy paths.

Example 19-2 CESTPATH command

```
CESTPATH DEVN(X'400A') CGROUP(NO) -
PRIM(X'4000' 5005076303FFC663 X'00') -
SEC(X'8000' 5005076303FFC1A5 X'80') -
LINK(X'00100143' X'00310102')
```

CDELPAIR

The CDELPAIR command is used to delete a Global Copy volume pair. This command should be directed to the primary device; see Example 19-3.

Example 19-3 CDELPAIR command

```
CDELPAIR DEVN(X'400A') -
PRIM(X'4000' ABTV1 X'0A' X'00') -
SEC(X'8000' 20781 X'8A' X'80')
```

Before issuing a CDELPAIR command, you should verify that there are some active paths between the respective primary and secondary LSSs. If all of the paths that were established between both LSSs have been disabled, the CDELPAIR command will fail. After the failing CDELPAIR command times out, the state of the primary volume is simplex. The secondary volume remains in its previous state (duplex, pending, or suspended). You then need to issue a CRECOVER command to return the secondary volume to the simplex state.

CDELPATH

The CDELPATH command is used to delete established Global Copy paths between a primary LSS and the corresponding secondary LSS; see Example 19-4. Only the paths to the specified secondary LSS are affected — paths to other LSSs are not affected.

Before issuing a CDELPATH command, a CDELPAIR command to all Global Mirror and Copy volume pairs should be issued. The CDELPATH command may cause an `ANTP0121I` message if this sequence is not followed.

Example 19-4 CDELPATH command

```
CDELPATH DEVN(X'400A') -
PRIM(X'4000' 5005076303FFC663 X'00') -
SEC(X'8000' 5005076303FFC1A5 X'80')
```

CGROUP

The CGROUP command is used to control operations for multiple Global Copy volume pairs on a given LSS:

- **`CGROUP FREEZE:`** Stops all host application I/O to the primary volumes on the specified LSS pair. With the FREEZE parameter, remote mirror and copy volume pairs are suspended and paths for the specified LSS pair are deleted.

  If the Global Copy paths for the LSS pair were defined with Consistency Group enabled (CGROUP parameter of the CESTPATH command), then an Extended Long Busy (ELB) condition is initiated when CGROUP FREEZE is issued for the LSS. All host application I/O to the primary is held off with a long busy condition for two minutes, or until a CGROUP command is issued with the RUN option. During the ELB window, update activity cannot proceed in the LSS where the freeze was done.

- **`CGROUP RUN:`** Resumes host application I/O for primary volumes on pairs whose primary volumes are on the primary LSS and secondary volumes are on the secondary LSS of the LSS pair identified in the CGROUP command which have been halted due to an earlier CGROUP FREEZE command. The CGROUP RUN command is used in order to reset the ELB condition set by CGROUP FREEZE and release application I/O to the primary volumes. The status of the volumes does not change; the primary volumes remain suspended.

> **Tip:** The CGROUP FREEZE command deletes the paths between the specified LSS pair. To restart normal Global Copy operation back again, the paths will have to be re-established and — if the I/O activity on the primary volumes was not interrupted during the freeze — the pairs will have to be re-synchronized.

Example 19-5 illustrates the CGROUP command.

Example 19-5 CGROUP command

```
CGROUP DEVN(X'400A') PRIM(X'4000' ABTV1 X'00') SEC(X'8000' 2C781 X'80') FREEZE
CGROUP DEVN(X'400A') PRIM(X'4000' ABTV1 X'00') SEC(X'8000' 2C781 X'80') RUN
```

> **Note:** A single LSS can be paired with up to four other LSSs. Therefore, you may have to issue up to four CGROUP commands to suspend all pairs on a single primary LSS.

CQUERY

The CQUERY command is used to query the status of one volume of a Global Copy volume pair or all paths that are associated with the LSS for the device number that is specified. The CQUERY command can be issued to either a primary or secondary Global Copy volume. A host system that is attached only to a primary volume cannot obtain the status of the secondary volume for that pair. In the same way, a host attached only to the secondary volume cannot obtain the status of the primary volume.

In Example 19-6, a CQUERY VOLUME command for volume 400A is issued. Parameter VOLUME is the default so it does not have to be specified.

Example 19-6 CQUERY VOLUME command

```
CQUERY DEVN(X'400A')
```

The output of the CQUERY command (shown in Example 19-7) provides volume related information, such as SSID, CCA, LSS number, and serial number. The TSO CQUERY command output for an XD pair returns the *duplex-pending* state and the number of out-of-sync tracks.

The number of out-of-sync tracks, tracks on volume, and percent of copy complete are not displayed if all tracks are in sync.

Path information is displayed only when the CQUERY VOLUME command is issued to the primary volume.

Example 19-7 CQUERY VOLUME command output

```
ANTP8802I CQUERY DEVN(X'400A')
ANTP0090I CQUERY FORMATTED LVL 3  881
VOLUME REPORT
************** PPRC REMOTE COPY CQUERY - VOLUME ********************
*                                          (PRIMARY)   (SECONDARY) *
*                                          SSID CCA LSS SSID CCA LSS*
*DEVICE   LEVEL      STATE      PATH STATUS  SERIAL#     SERIAL#    *
*------ ---------  ----------  ----------- ---------    ---------  *
* 400A  PRIMARY..  PENDING.XD   ACTIVE..   4000 0A 00   8000 8A 80 *
*       CRIT(NO).......       CGRPLB(NO). 0000000ABTV1 000000020781*
* PATHS PFCA SFCA STATUS: DESCRIPTION                               *
* ----- --------- ------  -------------------                       *
*   2   0010 0143   13    PATH ESTABLISHED...                       *
*       0031 0102   13    PATH ESTABLISHED...                       *
*       ---- ----   00    NO PATH............                       *
*       ---- ----   00    NO PATH............                       *
* IF STATE = PENDING/SUSPEND:     TRACKS OUT OF SYNC =  119475      *
*                                 TRACKS ON VOLUME   =  150255      *
*                               PERCENT OF COPY COMPLETE =  21%     *
*  SUBSYSTEM         WWNN                      LIC LEVEL            *
* -----------   ----------------             -----------            *
* PRIMARY....   5005076303FFC663             5.1.00.0212            *
* SECONDARY.1   5005076303FFC1A5                                    *
********************************************************************
ANTP0001I CQUERY COMMAND COMPLETED FOR DEVICE 400B. COMPLETION CODE: 00
```

Example 19-8 shows the output of the CQUERY PATHS command.

Example 19-8 CQUERY PATHS command output

```
ANTP8802I CQUERY DEVN(X'400A') PATHS
ANTP0095I CQUERY FORMATTED LVL 3  188
PATHS REPORT
*************** PPRC REMOTE COPY CQUERY - PATHS ********************
* PRIMARY UNIT: SERIALÄ= 0000000ABTV1 SSID= 4000 SS= 2107 LSS= 00  *
*              FIRST          SECOND         THIRD         FOURTH    *
*            SECONDARY     SECONDARY     SECONDARY     SECONDARY    *
*SERIAL NO: 000000020781  ............  ............  ............ *
* SSID LSS:    8000 80        .......       .......       .......     *
*    PATHS:        2             0             0             0       *
*            PFCA SFCA S*  SAID DEST S*  SAID DEST S*  SAID DEST S* *
*            --------- --  --------- --  --------- --  --------- -- *
*         1: 0010 0143 13  ---- ---- 00  ---- ---- 00  ---- ---- 00 *
*         2: 0031 0102 13  ---- ---- 00  ---- ---- 00  ---- ---- 00 *
*         3: ---- ---- 00  ---- ---- 00  ---- ---- 00  ---- ---- 00 *
*         4: ---- ---- 00  ---- ---- 00  ---- ---- 00  ---- ---- 00 *
*  SUBSYSTEM          WWNN                      LIC LEVEL           *
* -----------  ----------------           -----------               *
* PRIMARY....  5005076303FFC663           5.1.00.0212               *
* SECONDARY.1  5005076303FFC1A5                                     *
*                                                                   *
* S* = PATH STATUS:                                                 *
* 00=NO PATH           01=ESTABLISHED ESCON   02=INIT FAILED        *
* 03=TIME OUT          04=NO RESOURCES AT PRI 05=NO RESOURCES AT SEC*
* 06=SERIALÄ MISMATCH 07=SEC SSID MISMATCH   08=ESCON LINK OFFLINE *
* 09=ESTABLISH RETRY   0A=PATH ACTIVE TO HOST 0B=PATH TO SAME CLUSTR*
* 10=CONFIG ERROR      FF=UNABLE TO DETERMINE                       *
* 13=ESTABL FIBRE PTH 14=FIBRE PATH DOWN     15=FIBRE RETRY EXCEED *
* 16=SEC ADPTR INCPBL 17=SEC ADPTR UNAVAIL   18=FIBRE LOGIN EXCEED *
*********************************************************************
```

CRECOVER

The CRECOVER command is used to allow the recovery system to gain control of the volumes. This command is issued from the recovery system to the secondary volume. It signals the recovery Storage Image to force the secondary volume into simplex state, thus allowing the recovery system to gain control of the volume.

During this procedure the volume serial number can be verified and optionally relabeled. The volume can be varied online after this command is complete.

The CRECOVER command in Example 19-9 brings device x'308A' (on the secondary LSS) to simplex state. It also changes the volume label from RS400A to RS308A.

Example 19-9 CRECOVER command

```
CRECOVER DEVN(X'308A') ID(RS400A RS308A) -
PRIM(X'4000' ABTV1 X'0A' X'00') -
SEC(X'8000' 20781 X'8A' X'80')
```

CSUSPEND

This command is used to suspend Global Copy operations between a volume pair. Global Copy stops mirroring data to the secondary volume and starts keeping record of the primary volume tracks that are updated. The information of which tracks were updated while the pair was suspended will be used later when the pair is re-established, to copy just the updated tracks. In Example 19-10, a CSUSPEND command is issued for Global Copy primary volume 400A.

Example 19-10 CSUSPEND command

```
CSUSPEND DEVN(X'400A') -
PRIM(X'4000' ABTV1 X'0A' X'00') -
SEC(X'8000' 20781 X'8A' X'80')
```

Batch execution of Global Copy TSO commands

Batch procedures can be automated to manage Global Copy activities. JCL can be used to issue Global Copy commands in batch jobs, and automation procedures can be set to watch for their completion. Automation could analyze the results from previous job executions or Global Copy messages, and then schedule other jobs to be executed. Example 19-11 illustrates a batch job for executing a Global Copy TSO command.

Example 19-11 Batch job for executing Global Copy commands

```
//IKJEFT01 JOB MSGLEVEL=(1,1),MSGCLASS=A,NOTIFY=user id
//STEP1 EXEC PGM=IKJEFT01
//SYSTSPRT DD SYSOUT=*
//SYSTSIN DD *
CDELPATH DEVN(X'400A') -
PRIM(X'4000' 5005076303FFC663 X'00') -
SEC(X'8000' 5005076303FFC1A5 X'80')
```

19.3 Using ICKDSF to control Global Copy

Table 19-4 gives an overview of the ICKDSF commands that you can use to manage your Global Copy environment.

Table 19-4 ICKDSF commands for the Global Copy environment

Command	Description
PPRCOPY ESTPATH	Establishes Global Copy paths between primary and secondary LSSs.
PPRCOPY DELPATH	Deletes Global Copy paths between primary and secondary LSSs.
PPRCOPY ESTPAIR	Establishes a Global Copy primary to secondary volume relationship.
PPRCOPY DELPAIR	Deletes a volume pair.
PPRCOPY RECOVER	Allows a system to regain control of a volume on the secondary DS system.
PPRCOPY SUSPEND	Puts a Global Copy volume pair in suspended state.
PPRCOPY FREEZE	Suspends all Global Copy operations at the LSS level.
PPRCOPY RUN	Resumes I/O operations after a freeze with extended long busy.
PPRCOPY QUERY	Queries the status of a Global Copy volume pair and the status of paths.

For a detailed description of the ICKDSF commands, refer to the *Device Support Facilities User's Guide and Reference*, GC35-0033.

19.4 DS CLI (Command-Line Interface)

In this section we show an overview of the available DS CLI commands you can use for Global Copy. For detailed information, refer to the *IBM TotalStorage DS8000 Command-Line Interface User's Guide,* SC26-7625.

19.4.1 Global Copy path commands

You can use the following commands to establish and manage Global Copy paths.

lsavailpprcport

The **lsavailpprcport** command displays the Fibre Channel ports that can be used to establish Global Copy paths; see Example 19-12.

Example 19-12 lsavailpprcport command

```
dscli> lsavailpprcport -l -dev ibm.2107-75abtv1 -remotedev ibm.2107-7520781 -remotewwnn
5005076303FFC1A5 00:80

Date/Time: November 15, 2005 5:40:09 PM EET IBM DSCLI Version: 5.1.0.204 DS:
IBM.2107-75ABTV1
Local Port Attached Port Type Switch ID Switch Port
===================================================
I0010      I0143         FCP  NA        NA
I0031      I0102         FCP  NA        NA
I0140      I0213         FCP  NA        NA
```

lspprcpath

The **lspprcpath** command shows you the established paths from a LSS. In Example 19-13 we list the paths from LSS 00.

Example 19-13 lspprcpath command

```
dscli> lspprcpath -dev ibm.2107-75abtv1 00

Date/Time: November 15, 2005 5:40:56 PM EET IBM DSCLI Version: 5.1.0.204 DS:
IBM.2107-75ABTV1
Src Tgt State   SS   Port  Attached Port Tgt WWNN
=========================================================
00  80  Success 8000 I0010 I0143         5005076303FFC1A5
00  80  Success 8000 I0031 I0102         5005076303FFC1A5
```

mkpprcpath

With the **mkpprcpath** command you can establish remote mirror and copy paths between two LSSs. In the Example 19-14 we establish a path from 2107-75ABTV1 LSS 00 to 2107-7520781 LSS 80.

Example 19-14 mkpprcpath command

```
dscli> mkpprcpath -dev ibm.2107-75abtv1 -remotedev ibm.2107-7520781 -remotewwnn
5005076303FFC1A5 -srclss 00 -tgtlss 80 I0010:I0143 I0031:I0102

Date/Time: November 15, 2005 5:52:34 PM EET IBM DSCLI Version: 5.1.0.204 DS:
IBM.2107-75ABTV1
CMUC00149I mkpprcpath: Remote Mirror and Copy path 00:80 successfully established.
```

rmpprcpath

The **rmpprcpath** command removes all paths between two LSSs; see Example 19-15.

Example 19-15 rmpprcpath command

```
dscli> rmpprcpath -dev ibm.2107-75abtvl -remotedev ibm.2107-7520781  00:80

Date/Time: November 15, 2005 5:51:11 PM EET IBM DSCLI Version: 5.1.0.204 DS:
IBM.2107-75ABTV1
CMUC00152W rmpprcpath: Are you sure you want to remove the Remote Mirror and Copy path
00:80:? [y/n]:y
CMUC00150I rmpprcpath: Remote Mirror and Copy path 00:80 successfully removed.
```

You can suppress confirmation message CMUC00152W by adding parameter `-quiet` in the command.

19.4.2 Global Copy pair commands

You can use the following commands to establish and manage Global Copy pairs.

failbackpprc

You can issue the **failbackpprc** command against any remote mirror and copy volume that is in a primary suspended state. The command copies the required data from the source volume to the target volume in order to resume mirroring. The command is usually used after a **failoverpprc** command has been issued to restart mirroring either in the reverse direction (recovery site to production site) or original direction (production site to recovery site).

The command in Example 19-16 is issued to a former target volume 808A that was changed to suspended primary state by a preceding **failoverpprc** command. After the command completes, 808A becomes the source volume and 000A the target volume. Note that because the command reverses the copy direction, you first have to establish PPRC paths in that direction.

Example 19-16 failbackpprc command

```
dscli> failbackpprc -dev ibm.2107-7520781 -remotedev ibm.2107-75abtvl -type gcp 808a:000a

Date/Time: November 16, 2005 10:23:04 AM EET IBM DSCLI Version: 5.1.0.204 DS:
IBM.2107-7520781
CMUC00197I failbackpprc: Remote Mirror and Copy pair 808A:000A successfully failed back.
```

failoverpprc

You can use the **failoverpprc** command to change a secondary device into primary suspended state while leaving the primary device in its current state; see Example 19-17.

Example 19-17 failoverpprc command

```
dscli> failoverpprc -dev ibm.2107-7520781 -remotedev ibm.2107-75abtvl -type gcp 808a:000a

Date/Time: November 16, 2005 9:33:01 AM EET IBM DSCLI Version: 5.1.0.204 DS:
IBM.2107-7520781
CMUC00196I failoverpprc: Remote Mirror and Copy pair 808A:000A successfully reversed.
```

The command must be issued to the secondary device of a volume pair. The volume must be in full duplex, suspended, or pending-XD state, or a Cascading PPRC volume whose secondary state is full duplex, duplex pending, or suspended.

lspprc

The **lspprc** command shows you which volumes are in a Remote Mirror and Copy relationship; see Example 19-18.

Example 19-18 lspprc command

```
dscli> lspprc -remotedev ibm.2107-7520781 -l 000a-000b
Date/Time: November 16, 2005 11:09:37 AM EET IBM DSCLI Version: 5.1.0.204 DS:
IBM.2107-75ABTV1
ID        State        Reason      Type        Out Of Sync Tracks Tgt Read Src Cascade
==========================================================================================
000A:808A Suspended    Host Source Global Copy 0                  Disabled Disabled
000B:808B Copy Pending -           Global Copy 0                  Disabled Disabled
```

mkpprc

With the **mkpprc** command you can create a remote mirror and copy pair. To create a Global Copy pair, specify parameter `-type gcp`. See Example 19-19.

Example 19-19 mkpprc command

```
dscli> mkpprc -dev ibm.2107-75abtv1 -remotedev ibm.2107-7520781 -type gcp -mode full
000a:808a

Date/Time: November 16, 2005 11:02:55 AM EET IBM DSCLI Version: 5.1.0.204 DS:
IBM.2107-75ABTV1
CMUC00153I mkpprc: Remote Mirror and Copy volume pair relationship 000A:808A successfully
created.
```

freezepprc

With the **freezepprc** command you can stop the write activity on all remote mirror and copy primary and secondary volumes of a given source LSS and target LSS pair. The command creates a new remote mirror and copy Consistency Group. It places the source logical subsystem (LSS) in the long busy state so that no I/Os can be directed to it. It sets the primary volumes on the source LSS in suspended state. Secondary volumes are left in their current state. The command also removes remote mirror and copy paths between the source LSS and target LSS and sets the queue full condition for the primary volume. This causes the host to queue writes to the primary volume until the queue full condition is reset (with the **unfreezepprc** command). During the queue full condition, the primary volume reports long busy status.

The command in Example 19-20 freezes all I/O to volume pairs whose primary volume is on LSS 00 of IBM.2107-75ABTV1 and secondary on LSS 80 of IBM.2107-7520781.

Example 19-20 freezepprc command

```
dscli> freezepprc -dev ibm.2107-75abtv1 -remotedev ibm.2107-7520781 00:80

Date/Time: November 16, 2005 11:26:10 AM EET IBM DSCLI Version: 5.1.0.204 DS:
IBM.2107-75ABTV1
CMUC00161W freezepprc: Remote Mirror and Copy consistency group 00:80 successfully created.
```

pausepprc

The **pausepprc** command suspends a remote mirror and copy pair; see Example 19-21.

Example 19-21 pausepprc command

```
dscli> pausepprc -dev ibm.2107-75abtvl -remotedev ibm.2107-7520781 000a:808a

Date/Time: November 16, 2005 11:08:14 AM EET IBM DSCLI Version: 5.1.0.204 DS:
IBM.2107-75ABTV1
CMUC00157I pausepprc: Remote Mirror and Copy volume pair 000A:808A relationship
successfully paused.
```

resumepprc

With the **resumepprc** command you can bring a pair from suspended in Copy Pending mode as shown in Example 19-22.

Example 19-22 resumepprc command

```
dscli> resumepprc -dev ibm.2107-75abtvl -remotedev ibm.2107-7520781 -type gcp 000a:808a

Date/Time: November 16, 2005 11:14:43 AM EET IBM DSCLI Version: 5.1.0.204 DS:
IBM.2107-75ABTV1
CMUC00158I resumepprc: Remote Mirror and Copy volume pair 000A:808A relationship
successfully resumed. This message is being returned before the copy completes.
```

rmpprc

The **rmpprc** command removes the remote mirror and copy relationship from a volume pair and sets the volumes in simplex status; see Example 19-23.

Example 19-23 rmpprc command

```
dscli> rmpprc -dev ibm.2107-75abtvl -remotedev ibm.2107-7520781 000a:808a

Date/Time: November 15, 2005 5:45:48 PM EET IBM DSCLI Version: 5.1.0.204 DS:
IBM.2107-75ABTV1
CMUC00160W rmpprc: Are you sure you want to delete the Remote Mirror and Copy volume pair
relationship 000A:808A:? [y/n]:y
CMUC00155I rmpprc: Remote Mirror and Copy volume pair 000A:808A relationship successfully
withdrawn.
```

You can suppress confirmation message CMUC00160W by adding parameter `-quiet` in the command.

unfreezepprc

With the **unfreezepprc** command (see Example 19-24) you can thaw an existing remote mirror and copy Consistency Group. It resumes host application I/O activity for primary volumes on the Consistency Group that was created by an earlier **freezepprc** command. The **unfreezepprc** command is used to resets the queue full condition for the primary volume and release application I/O to the primary volumes. All queued writes to the source volume are written. The status of the volumes does not change; the primary volumes remain in the suspended state as set by the **freezepprc** command.

Example 19-24 unfreezepprc command8

```
dscli> unfreezepprc -dev ibm.2107-75abtvl -remotedev ibm.2107-7520781 00:80

Date/Time: November 16, 2005 1:11:30 PM EET IBM DSCLI Version: 5.1.0.204 DS:
IBM.2107-75ABTV1
CMUC00198I unfreezepprc: Remote Mirror and Copy pair 00:80 successfully thawed.
```

Note: Because the **freezepprc** command deletes the paths between the specified LSS pair, you have to re-establish them to resume normal Global Copy operation.

19.5 DS Storage Manager

The DS Storage Manager provides a graphical user interface to manage paths and Global Copy pairs. We show examples using the DS Storage Manager in the following sections.

19.5.1 Path panel

The Path panel is the central point in the DS Storage Manager to establish new paths and manage existing paths. You can get to the path panel as follows:

- Select **Real-time manager**.
- Select **Copy Services**.
- Click **Paths**.

Figure 19-1 shows the Path panel.

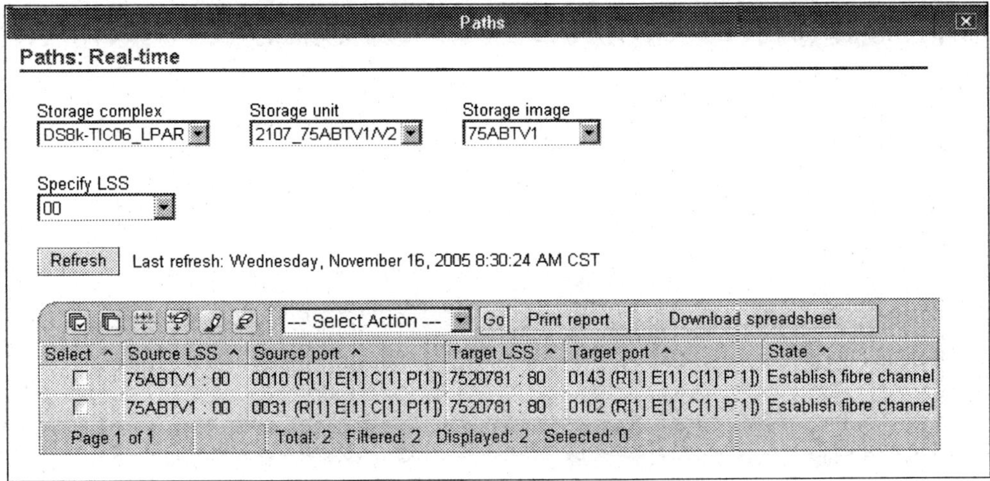

Figure 19-1 Paths panel

To display established paths, select in the Paths panel the Storage unit and the source LSS for which you want to display the paths:

- To create a new path, select from the **Select Actions** pull-down menu **Create** and click **Go**. A process will then guide you to establish a path.

When you have selected one or more paths, the pull-down menu gives you the following additional actions:

- From the **Select Actions** pull-down menu, you can choose **Delete** to delete the paths you have selected before.
- From the **Select Actions** pull-down menu, you can choose **LSS copy options** to modify the copy options for an LSS; see Figure 19-2.

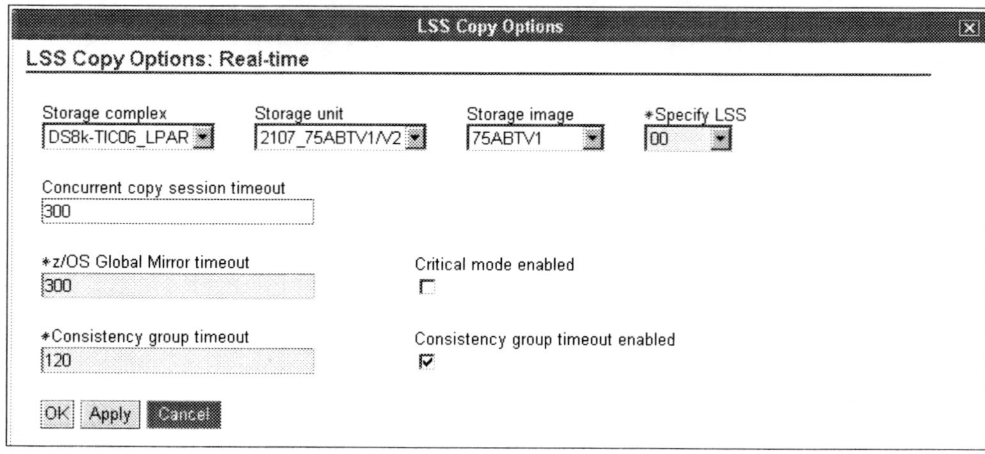

Figure 19-2 LSS Copy Options

19.5.2 Metro Mirror panel

The Metro Mirror panel is the central point in the DS Storage Manager to establish new pairs and manage existing pairs. You can get to the Global Copy panel as follows:

- Select **Real-time manager**.
- Select Copy services.
- Click **Metro Mirror**.

Figure 19-3 shows the Metro Mirror panel.

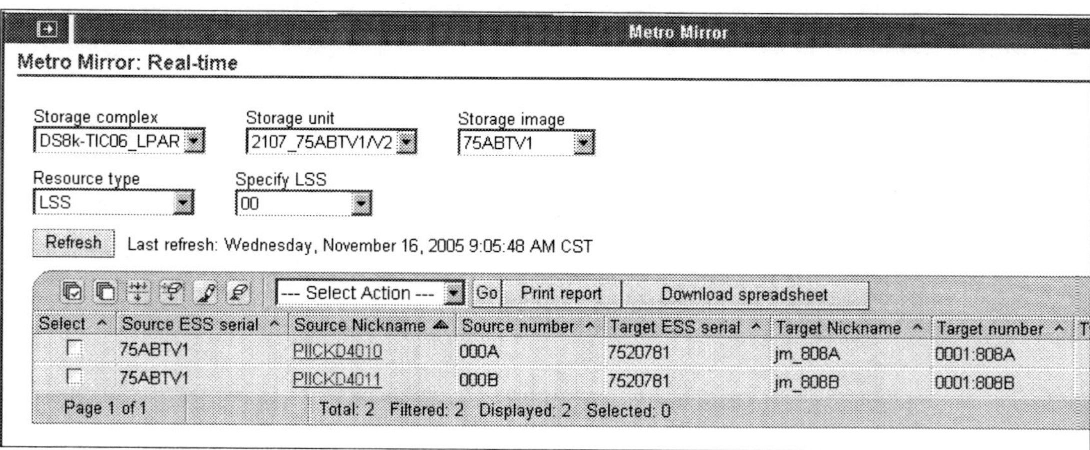

Figure 19-3 Metro Mirror panel

To create a new **Global Copy** pair, choose from the **Select Action** pull-down menu **Create** and click **Go**. The DS Storage Manager will guide you through the process to create a new pair.

When you select a Global Copy pair, the **Select Action** pull-down menu shows you additional actions you can perform to manage this pair; see Figure 19-4.

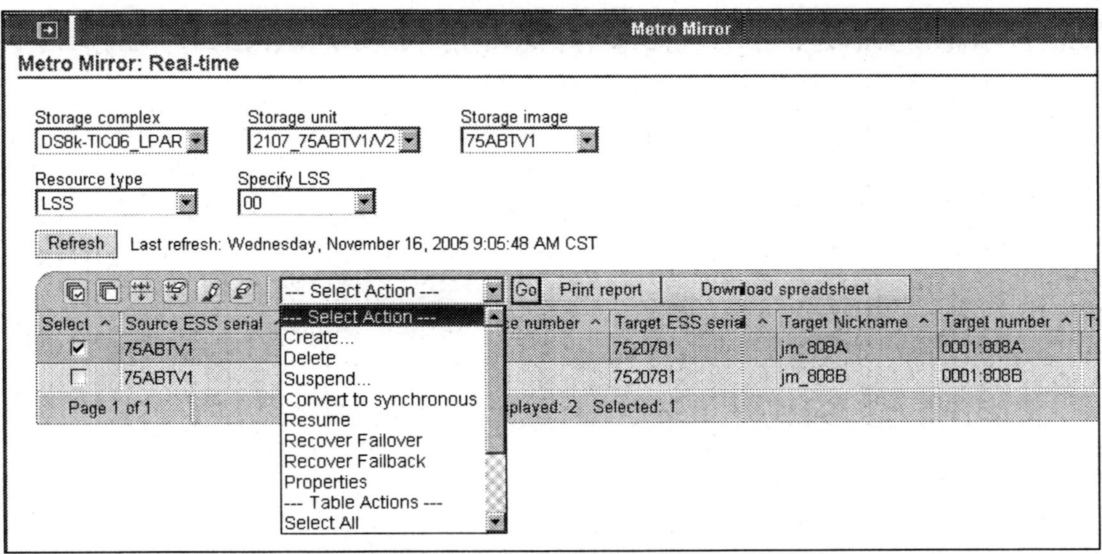

Figure 19-4 Metro Mirror panel

- **Delete**: You can use this action to delete a Global Copy pair.
- **Suspend**: You can use this action to suspend a Global Copy pair.
- **Convert to synchronous**: You can use this action to convert a Global Copy pair into a synchronous Metro Mirror pair.
- **Resume**: You can use this option to resume suspended Global Copy pair.
- **Recover Failover**: You can use this action to change a secondary device into a primary suspended device while leaving the primary device in its current state.
- **Recover Failback**: You can use this action to switch back to the primary site after a failover.
- **Properties**: You can use this action to view the remote mirror and copy volume pair properties, including the number of out-of-sync tracks.

Global Copy configuration considerations

In this chapter we discuss the configuration guidelines that you should consider when planning the Global Copy environment.

20.1 Hardware requirements

The DS8000 can interoperate with the Enterprise Storage Server (ESS) Model 750, and 800, and DS6000 Series systems in a Global Copy environment. Refer to the DS8000 Interoperability Matrix for more information:

`http://www-1.ibm.com/servers/storage/disk/ds8000/interop.html`

In order to use the Global Copy function, you have to purchase the Remote Mirror and Copy feature for the primary and secondary DS8000 systems. The Feature Code you have to purchase depends on the capacity you want to use for Global Copy, as shown in Table 20-1.

Table 20-1 Remote Mirror and Copy feature codes

Feature Code	Description	Models
7400	RMC - Inactive	921, 922, 9A2
7401	RMC - 1TB Unit	921, 922, 9A2
7402	RMC - 5 TB Unit	921, 922, 9A2
7403	RMC - 10 TB Unit	921, 922, 9A2
7404	RMC - 25 TB Unit	921, 922, 9A2
7405	RMC - 50 TB Unit	921, 922, 9A2
7410	RMC - 100 TB Unit	921, 922, 9A2

20.2 DS8000 I/O ports

The DS8100 can have a maximum number of 16 host adapters. Each host adapter has four ports that can be configured to support Fibre Channel or FICON®. The DS8300 can have a maximum number of 32 host adapters.

For Global Copy paths you need at least one Fibre Channel connection between the two DS8000 subsystems you want to set up a Global Copy path. For higher availability we recommend you use at least two Fibre Channel connections between the two subsystems on different host adapter cards on the DS8000.

The Fibre Channel ports used for Global Copy can be used as dedicated ports, that means they will only be used for the Global Copy paths or they can be shared between Global Copy and Fibre Channel data traffic, in this case you also need Fibre Channel switches for connectivity.

For supported SAN switches you can refer to the DS8000 Interoperability Matrix.

20.3 Global Copy connectivity

When implementing a Global Copy configuration, one requirement is the definition of the paths that Global Copy is going use to communicate between the primary and secondary DS8000. These logical paths are defined upon existing Fibre Channel links. Over one physical Fibre Channel link you can define up to 256 logical paths. The Fibre Channel links are bidirectional, that means you can setup on a existing Fibre Channel link, paths in both directions. The paths are defined between two LSSs. Figure 20-1 shows this setup.

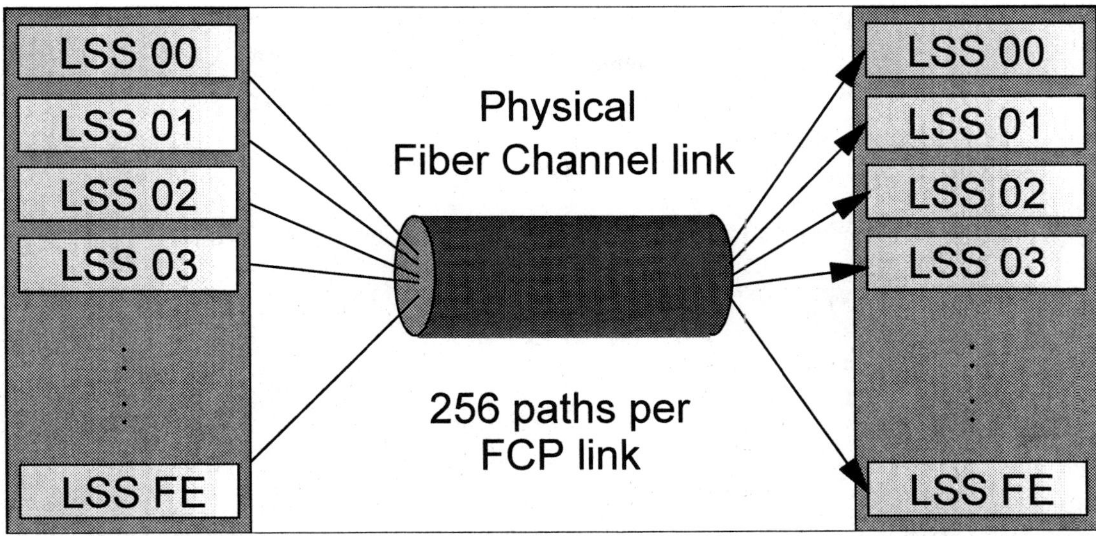

Figure 20-1 Logical paths

20.3.1 Distance considerations

The maximum distance for a direct Fibre Channel connection is 10 km. If you want to use Global Copy over longer distances, the following connectivity technologies can be used to extend this distance:

- Fibre Channel switches
- Channel Extenders over Wide Area Network (WAN) lines
- Dense Wave Division Multiplexors (DWDM) on dark fibre

Global Copy channel extender support

Channel extender vendors connect DS8000 systems via a variety of Wide Area Network (WAN) connections, including Fibre Channel, Ethernet/IP, ATM-OC3 and T1/T3.

When using channel extender products with Global Copy, the channel extender vendor will determine the maximum distance supported — between the primary and secondary DS8000. The channel extender vendor should be contacted for their distance capability, line quality requirements, and WAN attachment capabilities.

A complete and current list of Global Copy supported environments, configurations, networks, and products is available in the DS8000 Interoperability Matrix.

The channel extender vendor should be contacted regarding hardware and software prerequisites — when using their products in an DS8000 Global Copy configuration. Evaluation, qualification, approval and support of Global Copy configurations using channel extender products is the sole responsibility of the channel extender vendor.

Global Copy Dense Wave Division Multiplexor (DWDM) support

Wave Division Multiplexing (WDM) and Dense Wave Division Multiplexing (DWDM) is the basic technology of fiber optical networking. It is a technique for carrying many separate and independent optical channels on a single dark fiber.

A simple way to envision DWDM is to consider that at the primary end, multiple fibre optic input channels — such as ESCON®, Fibre Channel, FICON, or Gbit Ethernet — are combined by the DWDM into a single fibre optic cable. Each channel is encoded as light of a different wavelength. You might think of each individual channel as an individual color: The DWDM system is transmitting a rainbow. At the receiving end, the DWDM fans out the different optical channels. DWDM — by the very nature of its operation — provides the full bandwidth capability of the individual channel. As the wavelength of light is — from a practical perspective — infinitely divisible, DWDM technology is only limited by the sensitivity of its receptors, as the total aggregate bandwidth possible.

A complete and current list of Global Copy supported environments, configurations, networks, and products is available in the DS8000 Interoperability Matrix.

The DWDM vendor should be contacted regarding hardware and software prerequisites — when using their products in an DS8000 Global Copy configuration.

20.4 Other planning considerations

When planning to use Global Copy for point-in-time backup solutions, as shown in Figure 20-2, you must also consider the following requirements:

- If you are going to have tertiary copies, then within the target Storage Image you should have an available set of volumes ready to become the FlashCopy target.
- If your next step is to dump the tertiary volumes onto tapes, then you must ensure that the tape resources are capable of handling these dump operations in between the point-in-time checkpoints — unless you have additional sets of volumes ready to become alternate FlashCopy targets within the secondary Storage Image.

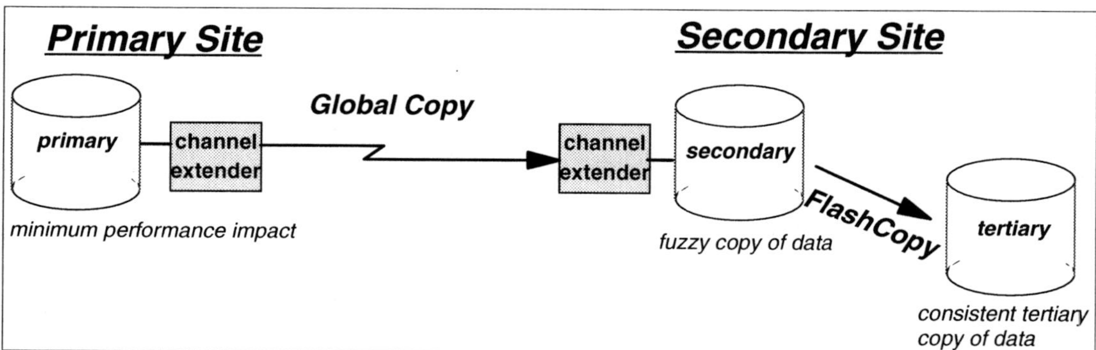

Figure 20-2 Global Copy environment

Global Copy performance and scalability

In this chapter, we discuss some of the performance and scalability attributes of Global Copy on DS8000.

21.1 Performance

As the distance between DS8000s increases, Metro Mirror response time is proportionally affected — and this negatively impacts the application performance. When implementations over extended distances are needed, Global Copy becomes an excellent trade-off solution.

You can estimate Global Copy application impact, as that of the application when working with Metro Mirror suspended volumes. For the DS8000, there is some more work to do with the Global Copy volumes — as compared to the suspended volumes — because with Global Copy, the changes have to be sent to the remote DS8000. But this is a negligible overhead for the application, as compared with the typical synchronous overhead.

Note that there will be no processor resources (CPU and memory) consumed by your Global Copy volume pairs (your management solution excluded), as this is managed by your DS8000 subsystem.

21.1.1 Peak bandwidth requirements

When you are researching your Global Copy link bandwidth requirements, you need to find the *peak sustained write rate* - remember that only writes will be mirrored across to the secondary volumes. For a typical z/OS system this peak is usually during batch processing, when many updates are occurring. It could be higher still during month-end or year-end processing.

You need to make allowances for this peak period when doing your bandwidth calculations.

21.1.2 Disk Magic

Your IBM representative can arrange for a Disk Magic analysis of a proposed configuration. Disk Magic is an IBM-only tool that can assist with choosing a configuration that will meet your requirements.

21.2 Scalability

The DS8000 Global Copy environment can be scaled up or down as required. If new volumes are added to the DS8000 that require mirroring, they can be dynamically added. If additional Global Copy paths are required, they also can be dynamically added.

21.2.1 Addition of capacity

As we have previously mentioned, the logical nature of the LSS has made a Global Copy implementation on the DS8000 easier to plan, implement and manage. However, if you need to add more LSSs to your Global Copy environment, your management and automation solutions should be set up to handle this.

The GDPS and eRCMF service offerings are designed to provide this functionality. Refer to Appendix F., "Service offerings" on page 659for more information.

Adding capacity to the same DS8000

If you are adding capacity into an existing DS8000, providing that your Metro Mirror link bandwidth is not close to or over capacity, you may only need to add volume pairs into your configuration. If you are adding more LSSs, then you will need to define Metro Mirror paths before adding volume pairs.

Adding capacity in new DS8000s

If you are adding new DS8000s into your configuration, you will need to add physical Global Copy links prior to defining your Global Copy paths and volume pairs. A minimum of two Metro Mirror paths per DS8000 pair is recommended for redundancy reasons. Your bandwidth analysis will indicate if you require more than two paths.

Global Copy examples

In this chapter we show a simple example of how you can establish Global Copy volume pairs and make FlashCopies with TSO. We also show how to use the DS CLI to migrate volumes from an ESS 800 to a DS8000 using Global Copy.

22.1 TSO example

In this example we show how to establish a Global Copy pair, then go-to-sync, make a FlashCopy of the secondary volume, and finally resume Global Copy using TSO commands.

In the example, the primary volume is 000A on LSS 00 of Storage Image IBM.2107-75ABTV1 (Image 1 of a 2107-9A2 LPAR machine). Its device number in the IODF is 400A. The secondary volume is 808A on LSS 80 of Storage Image IBM.2107-7520781 (a 2107-922). Its device number in the IODF is 308A. The FlashCopy target volume is 808B.

1. First, we establish two paths from LSS 00 to LSS 80 using CESTPATH command in Example 22-1. Use the CQUERY PATHS command to find out the SSID and WWNN of the primary and secondary LSSs.

Example 22-1 Establish paths

```
CESTPATH DEVN(X'400A') CGROUP(NO) -
PRIM(X'4000' 5005076303FFC663 X'00') -
SEC(X'8000' 5005076303FFC1A5 X'80') -
LINK(X'00100143' X'00310102')
```

2. Next, we verify with the CQUERY command that the paths have been established. The command output is shown in Example 22-2.

Example 22-2 Verify path status

```
ANTP8802I CQUERY DEVN(X'400A') PATHS
ANTP0095I CQUERY FORMATTED LVL 3  817
PATHS REPORT
*************** PPRC REMOTE COPY CQUERY - PATHS ********************
* PRIMARY UNIT: SERIAL#= 0000000ABTV1 SSID= 4000 SS= 2107 LSS= 00  *
*              FIRST        SECOND        THIRD        FOURTH      *
*            SECONDARY    SECONDARY    SECONDARY    SECONDARY      *
*SERIAL NO: 000000020781 ............ ............ ............  *
* SSID LSS:   8000 80       .......      .......      .......      *
*    PATHS:      2            0            0            0          *
*           PFCA SFCA S*  SAID DEST S*  SAID DEST S*  SAID DEST S* *
*           --------- --  --------- --  --------- --  --------- -- *
*        1: 0010 0143 13  ---- ---- 00  ---- ---- 00  ---- ---- 00 *
*        2: 0031 0102 13  ---- ---- 00  ---- ---- 00  ---- ---- 00 *
*        3: ---- ---- 00  ---- ---- 00  ---- ---- 00  ---- ---- 00 *
*        4: ---- ---- 00  ---- ---- 00  ---- ---- 00  ---- ---- 00 *
*  SUBSYSTEM         WWNN                      LIC LEVEL           *
* -----------   ----------------             -----------           *
* PRIMARY....   5005076303FFC663             5.1.00.0212           *
* SECONDARY.1   5005076303FFC1A5                                   *
*                                                                  *
* S* = PATH STATUS:                                                *
* 00=NO PATH           01=ESTABLISHED ESCON   02=INIT FAILED       *
* 03=TIME OUT          04=NO RESOURCES AT PRI 05=NO RESOURCES AT SEC*
* 06=SERIAL# MISMATCH 07=SEC SSID MISMATCH   08=ESCON LINK OFFLINE *
* 09=ESTABLISH RETRY  0A=PATH ACTIVE TO HOST 0B=PATH TO SAME CLUSTR*
* 10=CONFIG ERROR      FF=UNABLE TO DETERMINE                      *
* 13=ESTABL FIBRE PTH 14=FIBRE PATH DOWN      15=FIBRE RETRY EXCEED *
* 16=SEC ADPTR INCPBL 17=SEC ADPTR UNAVAIL    18=FIBRE LOGIN EXCEED *
********************************************************************
```

3. We then establish a Global Copy pair using the CESTPAIR command with the OPTION(XD) parameter shown in Example 22-3.

Example 22-3 Establish Global Copy pairs

```
CESTPAIR DEVN(X'400A') OPTION(XD) MODE(COPY) -
PRIM(X'4000' ABTV1 X'0A' X'00') -
SEC(X'8000' 20781 X'8A' X'80')
```

4. With the CQUERY command we verify that the pair has been established, as indicated by state `PENDING.XD` in the STATE column of the command output (Example 22-4). Since the command output does not show the number of tracks out of sync, there are none.

Example 22-4 Verify primary volume status

```
CQUERY DEVN(X'400A')
ANTP0090I CQUERY FORMATTED LVL 3  927
VOLUME REPORT
************** PPRC REMOTE COPY CQUERY - VOLUME ********************
*                                        (PRIMARY)   (SECONDARY) *
*                                       SSID CCA LSS SSID CCA LSS*
*DEVICE   LEVEL      STATE      PATH STATUS  SERIALÄ      SERIALÄ     *
*------ --------- ---------- ----------- ---------    ---------  *
* 400A  PRIMARY..  PENDING.XD   ACTIVE..   4000 0A 00    8000 8A 80 *
*       CRIT(NO).......      CGRPLB(NO). 0000000ABTV1 000000020781*
* PATHS PFCA SFCA STATUS: DESCRIPTION                             *
* ----- --------- ------  -------------------                     *
*   2   0010 0143   13    PATH ESTABLISHED...                     *
*       0031 0102   13    PATH ESTABLISHED...                     *
*       ---- ----   00    NO PATH...........                      *
*       ---- ----   00    NO PATH...........                      *
*  SUBSYSTEM         WWNN                    LIC LEVEL            *
* -----------  ----------------           -----------             *
* PRIMARY....  5005076303FFC663           5.1.00.0212             *
* SECONDARY.1  5005076303FFC1A5                                   *
*******************************************************************
```

Example 22-5 shows the output of CQUERY command issued for the secondary device. Note that the command output does not show any path information. If the output showed path information, it would relate to some other LSS pair where LSS 80 is the primary.

Example 22-5 Verify secondary volume status

```
ANTP8802I CQUERY DEVN(X'308A')
ANTP0090I CQUERY FORMATTED LVL 3  943
VOLUME REPORT
************** PPRC REMOTE COPY CQUERY - VOLUME ********************
*                                        (PRIMARY)   (SECONDARY) *
*                                       SSID CCA LSS SSID CCA LSS*
*DEVICE   LEVEL      STATE      PATH STATUS  SERIALÄ      SERIALÄ     *
*------ --------- ---------- ----------- ---------    ---------  *
* 308A  SECONDARY  PENDING.XD   ACTIVE..   4000 0A 00    8000 8A 80 *
*       ...............      ........... 0000000ABTV1 000000020781*
* PATHS SAID DEST STATUS: DESCRIPTION                             *
* ----- --------- ------  -------------------                     *
*   0   ---- ----   00    NO PATH...........                      *
*       ---- ----   00    NO PATH...........                      *
*       ---- ----   00    NO PATH...........                      *
*       ---- ----   00    NO PATH...........                      *
*  SUBSYSTEM         WWNN                    LIC LEVEL            *
* -----------  ----------------           -----------             *
* PRIMARY....  5005076303FFC663           5.1.00.0212             *
* SECONDARY.1  5005076303FFC1A5                                   *
*******************************************************************
```

5. Next, we synchronize the pair using the CESTPAIR command with the SYNC option shown in Example 22-6. Before doing this, host application updates should be quiesced because the volume pair now becomes a synchronous Metro Mirror pair and this will have an impact on application response times. By quiescing the updates, and by flushing the application write buffers to disk, we also achieve data consistency on the disks. Data consistency is required for the FlashCopy that follows.

Example 22-6 Go-to-sync

```
CESTPAIR DEVN(X'400A') OPTION(SYNC) MODE(RESYNC) -
PRIM(X'4000' ABTV1 X'0A' X'00') -
SEC(X'8000' 20781 X'8A' X'80')
```

6. With the CQUERY command, we can verify that the pair is now in full duplex state (Example 22-7).

Example 22-7 Verify full duplex status

```
ANTP8802I CQUERY DEVN(X'400A')
ANTP0090I CQUERY FORMATTED LVL 3  107
VOLUME REPORT
************** PPRC REMOTE COPY CQUERY - VOLUME ********************
*                                            (PRIMARY)   (SECONDARY) *
*                                            SSID CCA LSS SSID CCA LSS*
*DEVICE   LEVEL      STATE     PATH STATUS  SERIALÄ      SERIALÄ    *
*------ ---------  ----------  ----------- ---------    ---------  *
* 400A  PRIMARY..  DUPLEX....   ACTIVE..   4000 0A 00   8000 8A 80 *
*       CRIT(NO).......       CGRPLB(NO). 0000000ABTV1 000000020781*
* PATHS PFCA SFCA STATUS: DESCRIPTION                              *
* ----- --------- ------  -------------------                      *
*   2   0010 0143   13    PATH ESTABLISHED...                      *
*       0031 0102   13    PATH ESTABLISHED...                      *
*       ---- ----   00    NO PATH...........                       *
*       ---- ----   00    NO PATH...........                       *
*  SUBSYSTEM         WWNN                  LIC LEVEL               *
* -----------  ----------------          -----------               *
* PRIMARY....  5005076303FFC663          5.1.00.0212               *
* SECONDARY.1  5005076303FFC1A5                                    *
*******************************************************************
```

7. When the volume pair has reached full duplex state, the secondary volumes are consistent. We can now suspend the pair with the CSUSPEND command (Example 22-8).

Example 22-8 Suspend pair

```
CSUSPEND DEVN(X'400A') -
PRIM(X'4000' ABTV1 X'0A' X'00') -
SEC(X'8000' 20781 X'8A' X'80')
```

8. Next, we verify with the CQUERY command that the pair is suspended (Example 22-9). State SUSPEND(3) means that the Global Copy volume pair was suspended by a host command to the primary site storage control.

Example 22-9 Verify suspended status

```
ANTP8802I CQUERY DEVN(X'400A')
ANTP0090I CQUERY FORMATTED LVL 3  238
VOLUME REPORT
************** PPRC REMOTE COPY CQUERY - VOLUME ********************
*                                            (PRIMARY)   (SECONDARY) *
*                                            SSID CCA LSS SSID CCA LSS*
```

```
*DEVICE   LEVEL       STATE      PATH STATUS  SERIALÄ      SERIALÄ     *
*------ ---------  ----------   ----------- ---------     ---------    *
* 400A  PRIMARY..  SUSPEND(3)    ACTIVE..    4000 0A 00    8000 8A 80 *
*       CRIT(NO).......        CGRPLB(NO). 0000000ABTV1 000000020781*
* PATHS PFCA SFCA STATUS: DESCRIPTION                                  *
* ----- --------- ------  -------------------                          *
*   2   0010 0143   13     PATH ESTABLISHED...                         *
*       0031 0102   13     PATH ESTABLISHED...                         *
*       ---- ----   00     NO PATH............                         *
*       ---- ----   00     NO PATH............                         *
*  SUBSYSTEM          WWNN                     LIC LEVEL               *
* -----------  ----------------               -----------              *
* PRIMARY....  5005076303FFC663               5.1.00.0212              *
* SECONDARY.1  5005076303FFC1A5                                        *
************************************************************************
```

At this point, host application updates can be resumed because the updates will not be written to the secondary volume, so secondary volume consistency is preserved and application response time is not impacted.

9. Now we make an inband FlashCopy of the PPRC secondary volume using the FCESTABL command in Example 22-10. Inband FlashCopy is requested with parameter REMOTE(YES). The DEVN parameter specifies the address of the Global Copy primary volume. The SOURCE and TARGET parameters specify the FlashCopy source and target volumes. SSID is the Subsystem Identifier of the FlashCopy source volume. This must be the same value as that specified for SSID of the secondary device on the PPRC CESTPAIR command.

Example 22-10 Make FlashCopy

```
FCESTABL DEVN(400A) SOURCE(20781 30 8A) TARGET(20781 30 8B) REMOTE(YES) -
SSID(8000) MODE(COPY)
```

10. The final task is to re-establish Global Copy for the volume pair (Example 22-11).

Example 22-11 Restart Global Copy

```
CESTPAIR DEVN(X'400A') OPTION(XD) MODE(RESYNC) -
PRIM(X'4000' ABTV1 X'0A' X'00') -
SEC(X'8000' 20781 X'8A' X'80')
```

22.2 CLI example

In this example we show how to use CLI commands and scripts to migrate volumes from an ESS 800 to a DS8000 using Global Copy. In the example we have only two volumes. In reality, you would perform the steps for a larger number of volumes. In that case CLI scripts are particularly usefull as the command can be written in advance and modified if necessary. The example also shows the strength of the DS CLI in the management of CKD copy operations.

In the example, the source volumes are 050A and 050B on LSS 05 of the ESS 800 IBM.2105-22399. The target volumes are 031A and 031B on LSS 03 of the DS8000 IBM.2107-7503461.

The ESS Control Switch *WEB Copy Services commands for S/390 volumes* has to be enabled on the ESS 800, otherwise the DS CLI cannot be used to establish CKD volume pairs. If the control switch is disabled, the following message is issued: *CMUN03013E mkpprc: CKD management is disabled.* Contact your IBM service representative to enable the control switch. Follow the control switch change by a restart of the ESS Copy Services server.

1. We first check the WWNN of the target DS8000 system. We use the DS CLI in one-shot mode to issue the **lssi** command (Example 22-12). Profile ds8-03461.prf contains the necessary logon information for the DS8000 target system.

Example 22-12 Check target WWNN

```
C:\IBM\DSCLI>dscli -cfg ds8-03461.prf lssi
Date/Time: November 22, 2005 7:56:21 AM EET IBM DSCLI Version: 5.1.0.204
Name ID               Storage Unit     Model WWNN             State  ESSNet
============================================================================
-    IBM.2107-7503461 IBM.2107-7503460 922   5005076303FFC08F Online Enabled
```

2. Next we check what FCP ports are available for establishing paths between LSS 05 on the ESS 800 and LSS 03 on the DS8000. We use DS CLI in one-shot mode to issue the **availpprcport** command (Example 22-13). Profile ess-22399.prf contains the necessary logon information for the ESS 800 source system.

Example 22-13 Check ports

```
C:\IBM\DSCLI>dscli -cfg ess-22399.prf lsavailpprcport -dev ibm.2105-22399 -remotedev
ibm.2107-7503461 -remotewwnn 5005076303ffc08f 05:03
Date/Time: November 22, 2005 8:06:34 AM EET IBM DSCLI Version: 5.1.0.204 DS: IBM.2105-22399
Local Port Attached Port Type
=============================
I0084      I0003         FCP
I0088      I0002         FCP
I00A4      I0241         FCP
```

3. The next step is to establish PPRC paths from LSS 05 to LSS 03. The CLI script file to do this is shown in Example 22-14.

Example 22-14 Script estpath.cli

```
# Script to establish PPRC paths
mkpprcpath -dev ibm.2105-22399 -remotedev ibm.2107-7503461 -srclss 05 -tgtlss 03
-remotewwnn 5005076303ffc08f I0084:I0003 I0088:I0002
```

We execute script file estpath.cli using CLI script mode and check path status using CLI one-shot mode (Example 22-15).

Example 22-15 Establish paths

```
C:\IBM\DSCLI>dscli -cfg ess-22399.prf -script estpath.cli
Date/Time: November 22, 2005 8:31:12 AM EET IBM DSCLI Version: 5.1.0.204 DS: IBM.2105-22399
CMUC00149I mkpprcpath: Remote Mirror and Copy path 05:03 successfully established.

C:\IBM\DSCLI>dscli -cfg ess-22399.prf lspprcpath -dev ibm.2105-22399 05
Date/Time: November 22, 2005 8:32:00 AM EET IBM DSCLI Version: 5.1.0.204 DS: IBM.2105-22399
Src Tgt State   SS   Port  Attached Port Tgt WWNN
=====================================================
05  03  Success 7B00 I0084 I0003         5005076303FFC08F
05  03  Success 7B00 I0088 I0002         5005076303FFC08F
05  08  Success 8000 I0088 I0002         5005076303FFC08F
05  06  Success 6000 I000C I0103         500507630EFFFE16
```

Note that the **lspprcpath** command output also shows other paths besides the ones we are using.

4. We can now establish the Global Copy pairs. We first create the CLI script file (Example 22-16).

Example 22-16 Script estpair.cli

```
# Script to establish Global Copy pairs
mkpprc -dev ibm.2105-22399 -remotedev ibm.2107-7503461 -type gcp -mode full 050a:031a
mkpprc -dev ibm.2105-22399 -remotedev ibm.2107-7503461 -type gcp -mode full 050b:031b
```

We execute the estpair.cli script and then check pair status (Example 22-17).

Example 22-17 Establish pairs

```
C:\IBM\DSCLI>dscli -cfg ess-22399.prf -script estpair.cli
Date/Time: November 22, 2005 8:47:32 AM EET IBM DSCLI Version: 5.1.0.204 DS: IBM.2105-22399
CMUC00153I mkpprc: Remote Mirror and Copy volume pair relationship 050A:031A successfully
created.
Date/Time: November 22, 2005 8:47:54 AM EET IBM DSCLI Version: 5.1.0.204 DS: IBM.2105-22399
CMUC00153I mkpprc: Remote Mirror and Copy volume pair relationship 050B:031B successfully
created.

C:\IBM\DSCLI>dscli -cfg ess-22399.prf lspprc -dev ibm.2105-22399 -l 050a-050b
Date/Time: November 22, 2005 8:49:09 AM EET IBM DSCLI Version: 5.1.0.204 DS: IBM.2105-22399
ID        State        Reason Type        Out Of Sync Tracks Tgt Read Src Cascade Tgt Casca
===========================================================================================
050A:031A Copy Pending -      Global Copy 0                  Disabled Unknown     Unknown
050B:031B Copy Pending -      Global Copy 0                  Disabled Unknown     Unknown
```

5. The next step is to synchronize the Global Copy pairs so that the target volume will be consistent. This should not be done until the number of out of sync tracks for most of the volumes is close to zero. Before performing the step, the hosts using the volumes that are migrated should be shut down, because the pairs become synchronous Global Mirror pairs, which would have an impact on application write response times. The script to synchronize the pairs is shown in Example 22-18.

Example 22-18 Script syncpair.cli

```
# Script to synchronize pairs
mkpprc -dev ibm.2105-22399 -remotedev ibm.2107-7503461 -type mmir 050a:031a
mkpprc -dev ibm.2105-22399 -remotedev ibm.2107-7503461 -type mmir 050b:031b
```

We execute the script syncpair.cli and then check that all pairs are in full duplex status (Example 22-19).

Example 22-19 Synchronize pairs

```
C:\IBM\DSCLI>dscli -cfg ess-22399.prf -script syncpair.cli
Date/Time: November 22, 2005 9:06:28 AM EET IBM DSCLI Version: 5.1.0.204 DS: IBM.2105-22399
CMUC00153I mkpprc: Remote Mirror and Copy volume pair relationship 050A:031A successfully
created.
Date/Time: November 22, 2005 9:06:43 AM EET IBM DSCLI Version: 5.1.0.204 DS: IBM.2105-22399
CMUC00153I mkpprc: Remote Mirror and Copy volume pair relationship 050B:031B successfully
created.

C:\IBM\DSCLI>dscli -cfg ess-22399.prf lspprc -dev ibm.2105-22399 050a-050b
Date/Time: November 22, 2005 9:07:03 AM EET IBM DSCLI Version: 5.1.0.204 DS: IBM.2105-22399
ID        State        Reason Type        SourceLSS Timeout (secs) Critical Mode First Pass
===========================================================================================
```

```
050A:031A Full Duplex -      Metro Mirror 05       unknown        Disabled       Invalid
050B:031B Full Duplex -      Metro Mirror 05       unknown        Disabled       Invalid
```

6. We are now ready to stop mirroring and return the target volumes to simplex status. The script to do this is shown in Example 22-20.

Example 22-20 Script delpair.cli

```
# Script to delete volume pairs
rmpprc -dev ibm.2105-22399 -remotedev ibm.2107-7503461 -quiet 050a:031a
rmpprc -dev ibm.2105-22399 -remotedev ibm.2107-7503461 -quiet 050b:031b
```

We then execute the script and check that the volume pairs have been removed (Example 22-21). Before deleting the pairs, make sure that all pairs are in full duplex status.

Example 22-21 Delete volume pairs

```
C:\IBM\DSCLI>dscli -cfg ess-22399.prf -script delpair.cli
Date/Time: November 22, 2005 9:16:18 AM EET IBM DSCLI Version: 5.1.0.204 DS: IBM.2105-22399
CMUC00155I rmpprc: Remote Mirror and Copy volume pair 050A:031A relationship successfully
withdrawn.
Date/Time: November 22, 2005 9:16:40 AM EET IBM DSCLI Version: 5.1.0.204 DS: IBM.2105-22399
CMUC00155I rmpprc: Remote Mirror and Copy volume pair 050B:031B relationship successfully
withdrawn.

C:\IBM\DSCLI>dscli -cfg ess-22399.prf lspprc -dev ibm.2105-22399 050a-050b
Date/Time: November 22, 2005 9:16:54 AM EET IBM DSCLI Version: 5.1.0.204 DS: IBM.2105-22399
CMUC00234I lspprc: No Remote Mirror and Copy found.
```

After the volume pairs have been deleted, the host systems can be IPLed from the target volumes on the DS8000 and the applications started. In order to avoid duplicate volser messages and the related operator replies during IPL, you can physically disconnect the ESS 800 source system from the host, or change ESCON/FICON director configurations as relevant.

7. As a final clean-up step, we remove the paths between the ESS 800 and the DS8000. We do this by using CLI in one-shot mode (Example 22-22).

Example 22-22 Script delpath.cli

```
C:\IBM\DSCLI>dscli -cfg ess-22399.prf rmpprcpath -dev ibm.2105-22399 -remotedev
ibm.2107-7503461 -quiet 05:03
Date/Time: November 22, 2005 9:21:27 AM EET IBM DSCLI Version: 5.1.0.204 DS: IBM.2105-22399
CMUC00150I rmpprcpath: Remote Mirror and Copy path 05:03 successfully removed.

C:\IBM\DSCLI>dscli -cfg ess-22399.prf lspprcpath -dev ibm.2105-22399 05
Date/Time: November 22, 2005 9:22:06 AM EET IBM DSCLI Version: 5.1.0.204 DS: IBM.2105-22399
Src Tgt State   SS   Port  Attached Port Tgt WWNN
=========================================================
05  08  Success 8000 I0088 I0002         5005076303FFC08F
05  06  Success 6000 I000C I0103         500507630EFFFE16
```

Although the above example was carried out with CKD volumes, the procedure applies equally well to open systems volumes, because the same DS CLI commands are used for both CKD and open systems.

22.2.1 Cascading alternative

The example above assumes that the source volumes on the ESS 800 are simplex. However, they could also be secondary volumes of existing Global Copy or Metro Mirror pairs. In that case we could set up a cascaded Global Copy relationship by specifying the `-cascade` parameter on the **mkpprc** command in step 4 above as shown in Example 22-23.

Example 22-23 Establish cascaded pairs

```
C:\IBM\DSCLI>dscli -cfg ess-22399.prf mkpprc -dev ibm.2105-22399 -remotedev
ibm.2107-7503461 -type gcp -mode full -cascade 050a:031a
Date/Time: November 21, 2005 11:08:41 AM EET IBM DSCLI Version: 5.1.0.204 DS:
IBM.2105-22399
CMUC00153I mkpprc: Remote Mirror and Copy volume pair relationship 050A:031A successfully
created.

C:\IBM\DSCLI>dscli -cfg ess-22399.prf lspprc -dev ibm.2105-22399 050a
Date/Time: November 21, 2005 11:28:15 AM EET IBM DSCLI Version: 5.1.0.204 DS:
IBM.2105-22399
ID        State               Reason Type        SourceLSS Timeout (secs) Critical Mode
==========================================================================================
011A:050A Target Copy Pending -      Global Copy 01        unknown        Disabled
050A:031A Copy Pending        -      Global Copy 05        unknown        Disabled
```

Here, 011A is the source volume, 050A is the intermediate volume, and 031A is the target volume. The **lspprc** command shows the status of both volume pairs where the intermediate volume 050A belongs. 011A:050A is the first pair, where 050A is the secondary; and 050A:031A is the second pair, where 050A is the cascading primary.

Part 6

Global Mirror

In this part of the book, we describe IBM TotalStorage Global Mirror, which was previously called Asynchronous PPRC. The chapters in this part outline and discuss the following topics:

- Global Mirror overview:

  After presenting an overview of Global Mirror, we also provide an overview of data consistency and show how data consistency is provided through Global Mirror.

- Options for Global Mirror:

  We show how to use Global Mirror and explain the various configuration options for it.

- Interfaces to manage Global Mirror configurations:

  Besides the GUI and DS CLI, this also includes the new TSO command support for Global Mirror configurations. Also new here is the ANTRQST macro support for Global Mirror.

  ICKDSF has supported Global Mirror since Global Mirror has been available. This started with the ESS 800 and from ESS microcode level 2.4.0 on upwards.

  Global Mirror is going to be generally available on the DS6000 and DS8000 later in the year 2005. Global Mirror can be made available earlier through a RPQ process.

- Performance and scalability with Global Mirror:

  We discuss performance matters and configuration considerations for scalability.

- Examples for Global Mirror:

  Global Mirror examples provide more insight on how to use DS CLI, TSO commands, and ICKDSF, besides the DS Storage Manager or GUI to manage Global Mirror environments.

  For command details, refer to the latest suffix of the standard manual for Copy Services in zSeries environments: *z/OS DFSMS Advanced Copy Services*, SC35-0428.

Global Mirror overview

In this chapter we provide an overview of what Global Mirror is. We also discuss the need for data consistency at a distant site when synchronous data replication such as Metro Mirror is not possible.

An important section follows to emphasize that Global Mirror works similarly to a distributed application with a server and client relationship. This section also contains a step-by-step process to establish a Global Mirror environment.

Refer to the following books for further details and command descriptions:

- *z/OS DFSMS Advanced Copy Services*, SC35-0428
- *The IBM TotalStorage DS8000 Series: Concepts and Architecture*, SG24-6452
- *IBM TotalStorage DS8000 Command-Line Interface User's Guide*, SC26-7625

23.1 Replicating data over a distance

Replicating data over large distances, which usually go beyond 300 km, requires an asynchronous approach to replicate data. This in turn creates the need to provide additional means to ensure data consistency at the remote location. It even requires a solution that guarantees data consistency not only within a single disk storage server pair but also across multiple disk storage server pairs.

Within a disk storage server pair, a time stamp approach leads to consistent data at the remote storage server. The write I/Os can then be applied at the remote disk storage server in the same sequence as they arrived at the local disk storage server by sorting the I/Os by their time stamps.

But this time stamp concept is not sufficient when more than one disk storage server is involved at the local site to replicate data and provide data consistency at the remote site. This additionally requires a Consistency Group concept, which then allows you to spread data volumes over multiple storage servers at the local site and to provide data consistency concerning dependent writes at the remote site. z/OS Global Mirror, formerly known as XRC, is an example of such a solution and utilizes the concept of Consistency Groups combined with time stamped write I/Os for all involved primary volumes within a Consistency Group or session. See Part 6, "Global Mirror" on page 233 for more information regarding z/OS Global Mirror.

As with a synchronous data replication method, you may have to recover files at the remote site after a local or primary site failure instead of just restarting without the need to recover any files. This is briefly discussed in the next topic.

23.1.1 Synchronous data replication and dependent writes

The nature of synchronous data replication preserves data consistency for dependent writes (Figure 23-1).

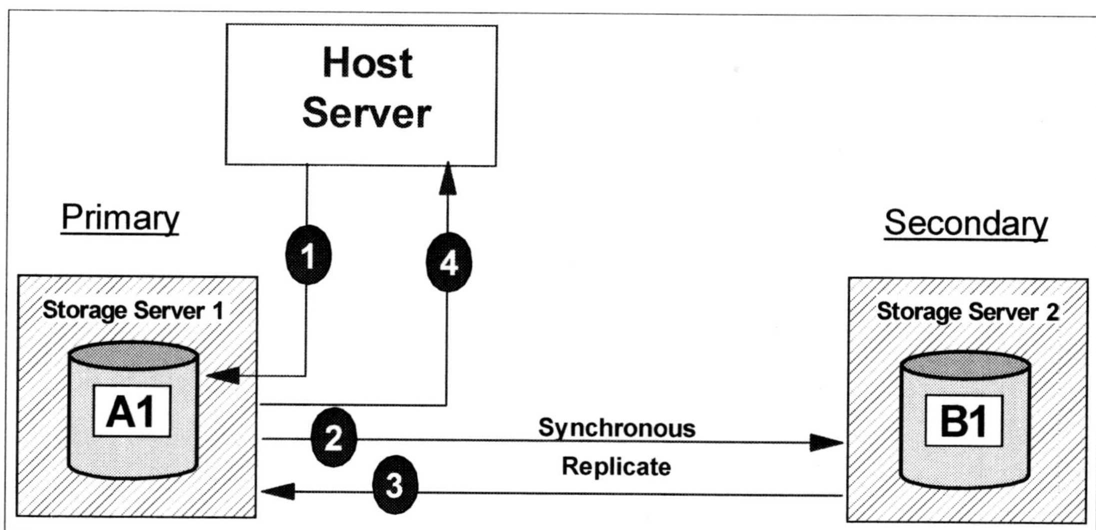

Figure 23-1 Synchronous data replication

For synchronous data replication such as Metro Mirror, an application write always goes through the following four steps:

1. Write the data to the primary storage server cache and present channel end to the server to free up the channel for further I/O. Note this does not end the I/O and does not present an I/O complete to the application.
2. Replicate the data from the primary storage server cache to the secondary storage server cache.
3. Acknowledge to the primary storage server that data successfully arrived at the secondary storage server.
4. Present device end to acknowledge successful I/O completion to the server, which is presented to the application and concludes this I/O.

Now the next I/O that depends on the successful completion of the previous I/O can be issued.

Synchronous data replication with dependent writes across multiple storage servers cannot guarantee to restart applications at the secondary site without data recovery after a failure at the primary site.

Consider a database environment that spreads across multiple storage servers at the local or primary site. Further assume that the remote copy volume pairs are defined with CRIT(HEAVY), which used to be CRIT(YES), and PPRC paths, which are not defined with the CGROUP parameter. Figure 23-2 demonstrates the process that occurs during a disaster in the absence of any automation software in place to handle I/O exceptions.

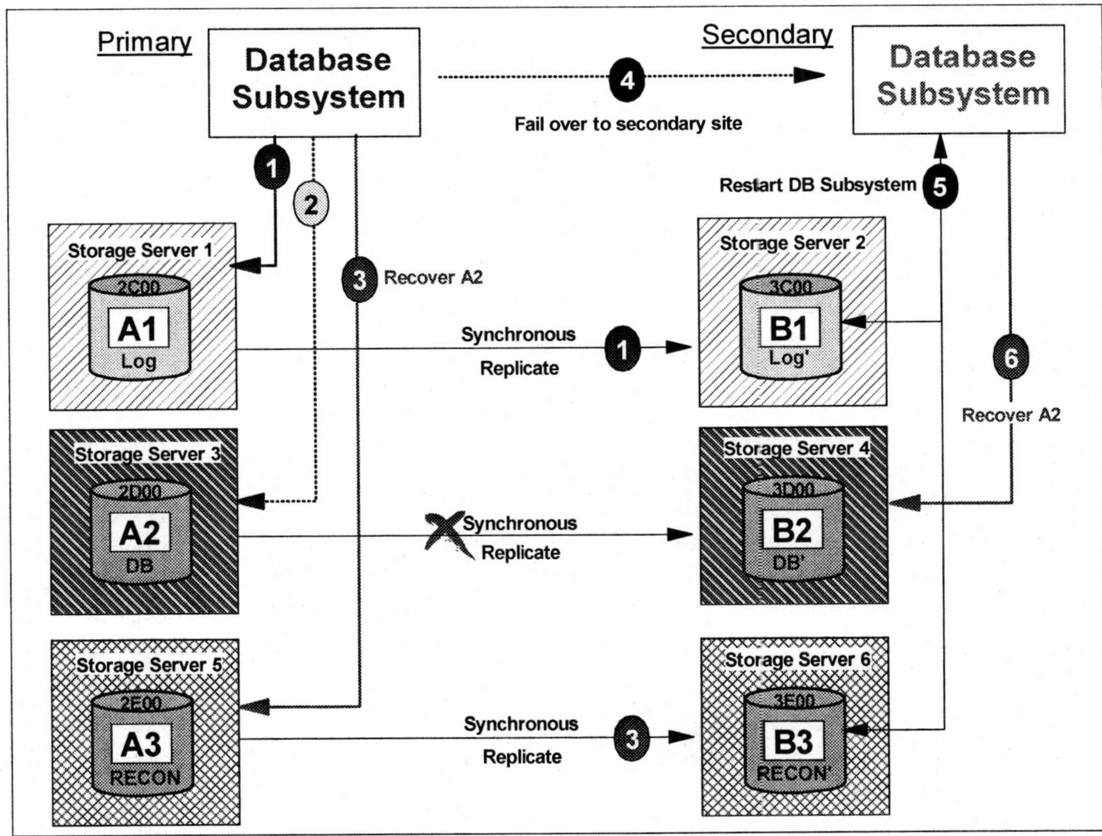

Figure 23-2 Synchronous data replication and unnecessary recovery after primary site failure

A database update usually involves three dependent write I/Os to ensure data consistency even in the event of a failure during this process.

1. Update intent to the logging files. Logging may happen to two logging files, which is dual logging, but this is not important for the example here.
2. Update the data.
3. Indicate update complete to the logging files.

This sequence of I/Os is also called a two phase commit process.

As shown in Figure 23-2 on page 237, the following sequence occurs:

1. Write update intent to logging volume A1.
2. Update data to database on volume A2 eventually fails due to a replication problem from the primary site to the secondary site and volume pairs are defined with CRIT(HEAVY). This may also be a severe primary storage failure and the beginning of a rolling disaster.
3. The database subsystems recognize the failed write I/O and indicates in a configuration file on volume A3 that one or more databases on A2 has to be recovered due to an I/O error. This gets replicated to the secondary site because the PPRC links between this storage server pair is still working or this particular primary storage server did not fail yet.
4. The primary failure eventually progressed and failed the primary site. The database subsystem is restarted at the secondary site after failing over to the secondary site.
5. At startup the database subsystem discovers in its configuration file that the database on A2/B2 has to be recovered as indicated before. This is actually not necessary because the data is synchronously replicated and both concerned volumes, volume A2 and volume B2 are identical and at the very same level of data currency. But the database subsystem will recover all concerned databases that are marked for recovery in the configuration files on A3, those on B3.
6. This recovery is actually not necessary because the data are perfectly in sync due to the synchronous replication approach. Nonetheless the recovery will take place because there was no automation window in place to freeze the PPRC configuration, which does remove all PPRC paths between primary site and secondary site before further I/Os continue to take place.

This does not happen with an automated solution such as GDPS, based on the freeze capabilities of the recent IBM disk storage servers. After failing over to the secondary site, the database subsystem would just restart without the necessity for a lengthy database recovery as before.

Figure 23-3 takes you through a rolling disaster scenario with automation software that takes advantage of the freeze capability of the DS8000. The sequence of events is indicated by corresponding numbers from 1 to 8.

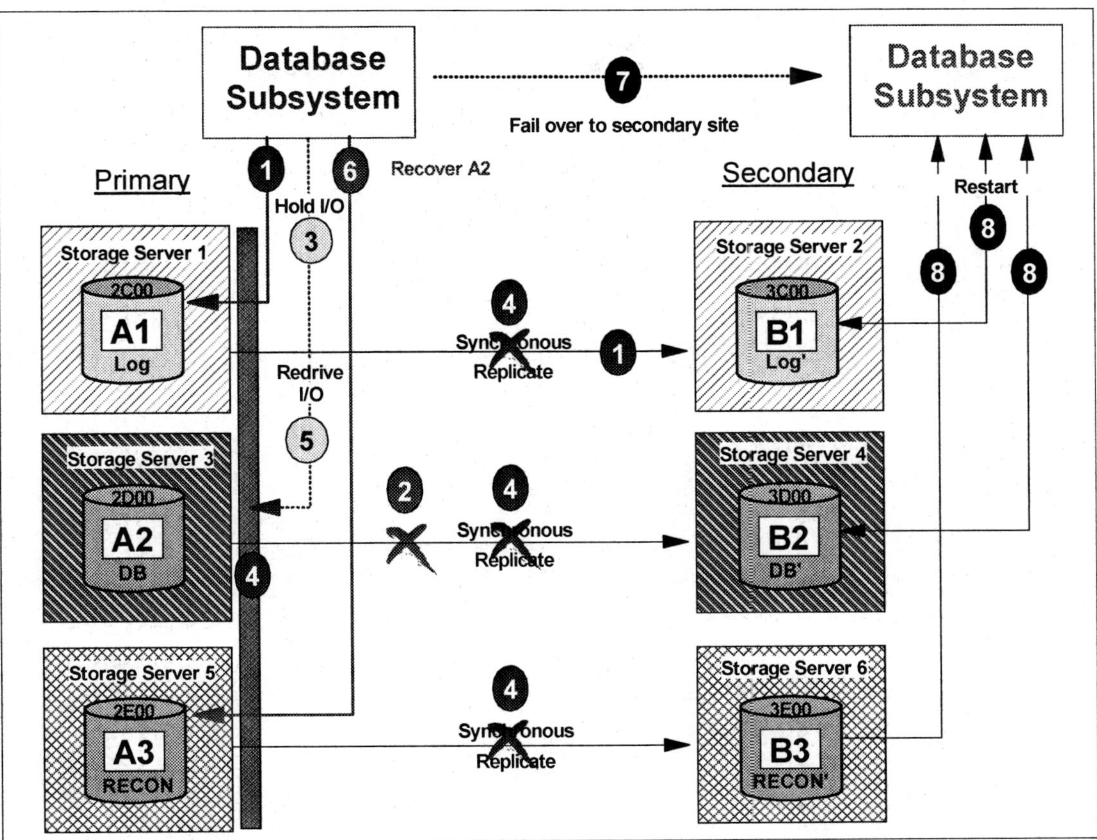

Figure 23-3 Synchronous data replication, freeze, and restart without recovery required

This is the sequence of events:

1. Update intent to logging file.
2. Link between A2 - B2 becomes unavailable or the storage server with A2 fails and a rolling disaster develops.
3. The first attempt to write to the database volume will return a unit check. The host re-drives the I/O. When only the links fail, the subsystem triggers an extended long busy (ELB). This is also called an automation window.
4. Within this automation window or ELB window, a freeze operation removes all related PPRC paths between both sites. From now on, no data is replicated any longer between both sites.
5. After the ELB expires or a RUN command is issued to end the freeze period, the I/O is re-driven, which may successfully complete when the pair is suspended or may fail when CRIT(HEAVY) is specified or the storage server 3 is not available any longer.
6. When the I/O fails, then a *recovery required* is written to the database configuration file on A3. Note volume A3 is no longer replicated due to the previous freeze. Note also that volume A2 and B2 are perfectly in sync due to the synchronous data replication between both sites.
7. The primary site eventually becomes unavailable and a failover to the secondary site is carried out.
8. Database subsystem restart discovers *no recovery required* indication because all related data is consistent and the database subsystems continues immediately after the restart phase is finished.

23.1.2 Attributes of synchronous data replication

In summary, this section describes the main characteristics that are required for a synchronous data replication such as Metro Mirror. For further information on synchronous data replication or synchronous PPRC, refer to Part 4, "Metro Mirror" on page 115.

The following attributes characterize synchronous data replication:

- Application write I/O response time is impacted. This response time degradation can be modeled and predicted.
- Local and remote copies of data are committed to both storage servers before host write I/O is complete.
- Data consistency is always maintained at the remote site as long as no failures occur. If a rolling disaster occurs, freeze/run is needed to maintain consistency.
- Bandwidth between both sites has to scale with the peak write I/O rate.
- Data at the remote site is always current.
- No extra means, such as additional journal volumes or tertiary copy, are required.
- There is no data loss, and a Tier 7 solution is achieved with automation software such as GDPS in a disaster recovery situation at the primary site.

This is different with an asynchronous data replication approach. We still require data consistency at a distant site in order to just restart at the distant site when the local site becomes unavailable.

23.1.3 Asynchronous data replication and dependent writes

Next, we outline the attributes that characterize a real asynchronous remote copy solution. An asynchronous remote copy approach is usually required when the distance between the primary site and the secondary site is beyond the supported distance for a synchronous remote solution. IBM's Metro Mirror supports a synchronous approach up to 300 km when utilizing PPRC Fibre Channel links.

Figure 23-4 provides an overview of the steps that an application I/O goes through when the data is asynchronously replicated.

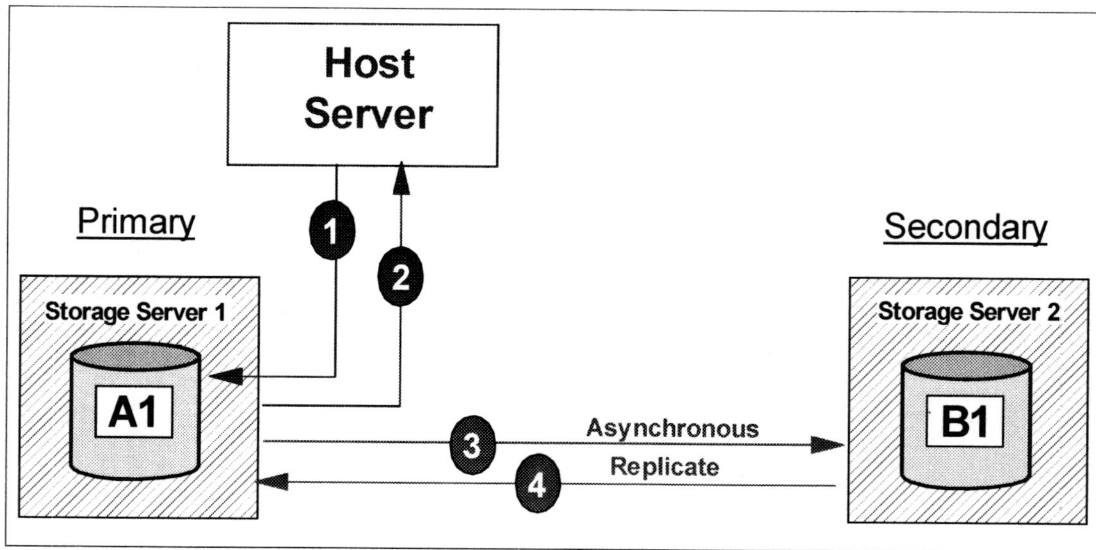

Figure 23-4 Asynchronous data replication

For an asynchronous data replication such as Global Copy, an application write I/O goes through the following steps:

1. Write application data to the primary storage server cache.
2. Present channel end and device end to the server and acknowledge to the application successful I/O completion. The application can then immediately schedule the next I/O.
3. Replicate the data from the primary storage server cache to the secondary storage server cache.
4. Acknowledge to the primary storage server that data successfully arrived at the secondary storage server.

Note the separation of data transmission between both sites from the I/O complete signal to the host server. This results in virtually no host application I/O impact or at most to a minimal degree only.

On the other side, there is no guarantee that the sequence of the arriving application write I/Os is preserved at the secondary site when replicating the data asynchronously from the primary site to the secondary site, as Figure 23-5 shows. Or in other words, the order of dependent writes is not preserved at the secondary site. Notice that the meaning of asynchronous data replication does not imply anything else but just replicating data entities from primary to secondary, as Figure 23-5 shows.

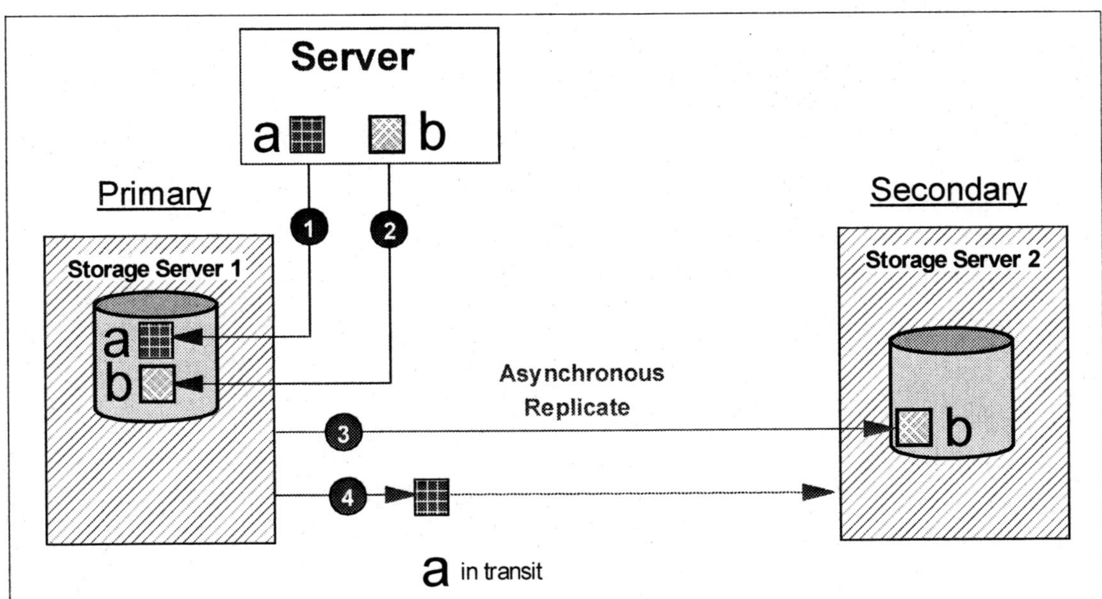

Figure 23-5 Global Copy: Sequence of data arrival not preserved at secondary site

Global Copy by itself as an asynchronous data replication method does not provide data consistency at the secondary site.

In Figure 23-5 the sequence of data arrival at the primary site is record **b** after record **a**. Due to the way Global Copy cycles through its out-of-sync bit map, it may replicate record **a** to the secondary site after record **b**. This assumes that, for example, record **a** is written to a disk location that the Global Copy replication cycle just passed before. Global Copy may approach another disk location that experienced just before an update with record **b**. Then record **b** gets replicated to the secondary site before the replication cycle starts from the beginning to fetch record **a** and then replicate record **a** to the secondary site. This sequence of events is indicated by the numbers in Figure 23-5.

This situation may get even worse when involving multiple storage servers at the primary site (Figure 23-6).

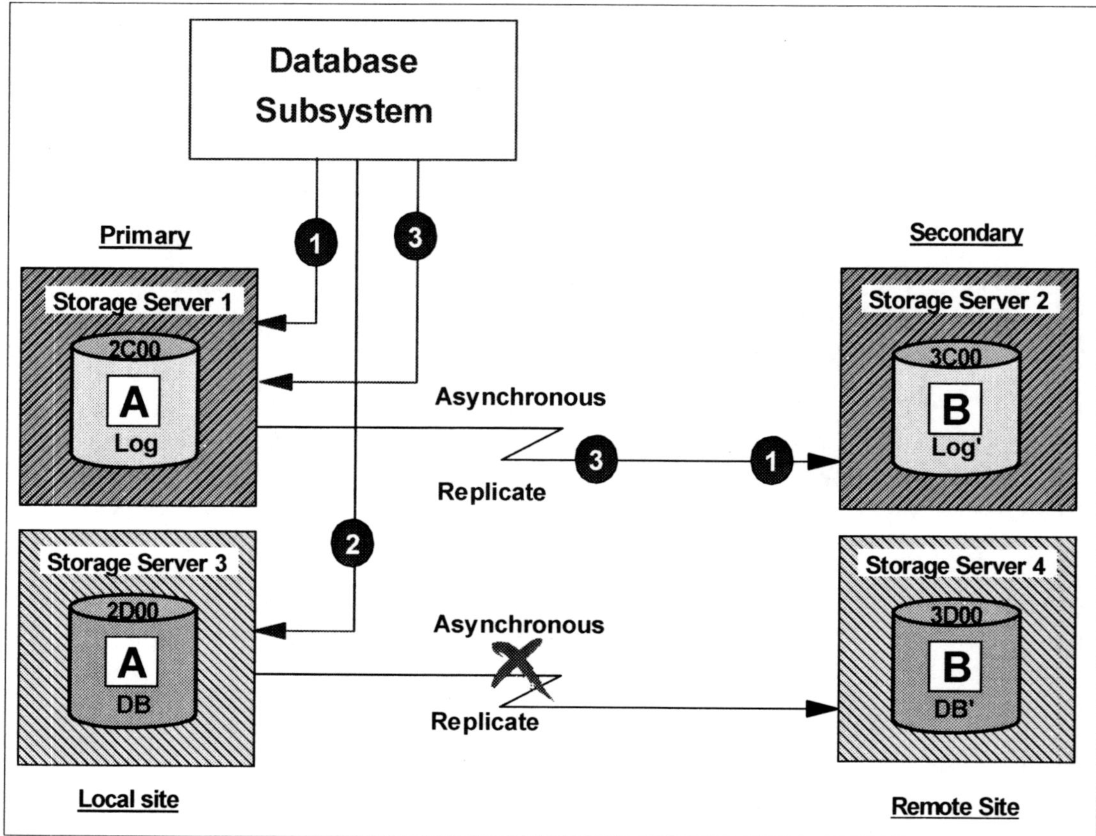

Figure 23-6 Asynchronous data replication involving multiple storage servers

As Figure 23-6 shows, dependent writes are not preserved when a failure occurs. So besides the arrival sequence within a storage server pair that is not guaranteed to be the same in both storage servers, there is another issue with data consistency and dependent writes across multiple storage servers at the local site.

Notice that the numbers in Figure 23-6 indicate the transfer of data as well as the sequence of its corresponding write I/Os. It may replicate record 3 first to storage server 2 before record 1 arrives in storage server 2. Record 2 may never make it to storage server 4 due to the connectivity problem between storage server 3 and storage server 4, which in turn may be the beginning of a rolling disaster. So consistent data cannot be guaranteed at the remote site without any additional measures, functions, and procedures.

The challenge is to provide data consistency at the distant site at any time and independent of the number of physical disk storage servers involved.

Metro Mirror by its own definition in conjunction with FREEZE/RUN automation window provides data consistency within a disk storage server pair or multiple disk storage server pairs. This is different for an asynchronous remote copy solution, such as, for example, Global Mirror.

An approach to improve this situation, as Figure 23-6 shows, is to combine Global Copy with FlashCopy and create a three-copy solution. But this requires a series of additional steps that have to be organized and carried out:

1. First, pause the application write I/Os at the local site to all involved A volumes. Note the challenge to manage *all* A volumes involved.
2. Then make sure all data is completely replicated from the local site to the remote site. This may be achieved to change the remote copy relationship from Global Copy to Metro Mirror. DUPLEX state for all volume pairs will then indicate that all data is replicated from the primary to the secondary site. Again note the challenge to identify all volumes.
3. Once this is achieved create a point-in-time (PiT) copy from all involved B volumes at the remote site. This may be a FlashCopy copy from all B volumes as FlashCopy source volumes in the remote site.
4. The FlashCopy target volumes then contain the status of the data that represents the A volumes when the application was paused or stopped.
5. Then restart or resume the application write I/O to the A volumes.

This sequence of events may be implemented to some extent into storage server internal code and into some interface support to manage such a system. All this is addressed in the Global Mirror solution. In order to minimize the application write I/O impact, Global Mirror introduced a smart bitmap approach in the primary storage servers. This allows you to resume the application I/O immediately after a very brief serialization period for all involved primary storage servers at the very beginning of a sequence of events as outlined above. The next section summarizes the necessary attributes of a consistent asynchronous data replication method.

23.1.4 Attributes of a consistent asynchronous remote copy solution

This section summarizes the attributes that characterize an asynchronous remote copy solution.

A consistent asynchronous solution for data replication has the following attributes:

- No impact, or at least only minimal impact, to application write I/O response time.
- Data replicated to remote site independent from application write I/O to local site.
- Data consistency and dependent writes are always maintained at the remote site.
- Data currency at remote site lags behind the local site. This is due to the potentially long distance between both sites and also due to network latency or bandwidth limitations.
- Bandwidth requirement between both sites does not have to be configured for peak write workload.
- The remote site is always less current than the local site. In peak write workloads this difference is going to increase. This does not necessarily apply to XRC, which tries to throttle host write activity to maintain a more constant data currency with potentially blocking the primary volumes for a brief period for host write I/Os. Global Mirror as another asynchronous remote copy approach does not throttle host write I/Os.
- Link bandwidth utilization is improved over synchronous solutions. Synchronous solutions require bandwidth to be configured for peak write workload. The bandwidth requires a capacity that may handle the average workload over 24 hours a day.
- Tertiary copy required to preserve data consistency.
- Data loss in disaster recovery situations is limited to data in transit and to data that still may be in the queue at the local site waiting to be replicated to the secondary site.

All these attributes are addressed by Global Mirror.

23.1.5 Basic concepts of Global Mirror

It is important to understand that Global Mirror works like a distributed application. A distributed application is usually built on a server to client relationship. The server functions as a supervisor and instructs the client. The client is able to do some work in an autonomic fashion but relies on the coordination efforts from the server (Figure 23-7).

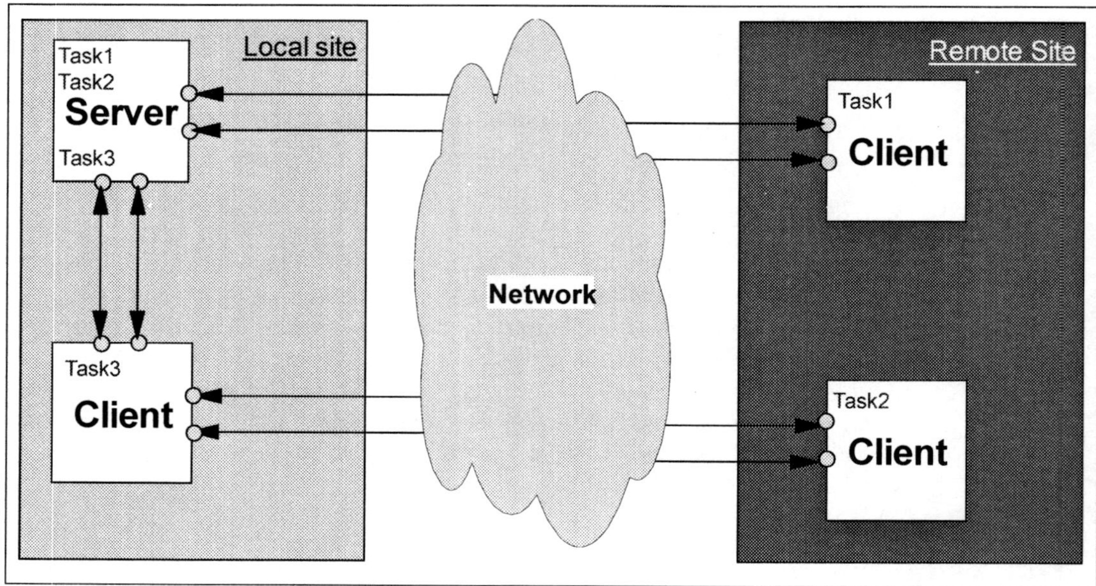

Figure 23-7 Distributed application

The server distributes the work to its clients. The server also coordinates all individual feedback from the clients and decides based on this feedback further actions.

It is very obvious in Figure 23-7 that the communication paths between the server and all its clients are key. Without communication paths between these four components the functions will eventually come to a complete stop. Matters get more complicated when the communication fails unexpectedly in the middle of information exchange between the server and his clients or to some of his clients.

Usually a two-phase commit process helps to provide a consistent state of certain functions and whether they have successfully completed at the client site. Once a function is successfully completed and is acknowledged to the server, the server progresses to the next function task. At the same time the server tries to do as much as possible in parallel to minimize the hit on throughput due to serialization and checkpoints.

When certain activities are dependent on each other it is required that the server coordinate these activities to ensure a proper sequence.

The server and client can be replaced by terms such as Master and Subordinate. These terms are used later in the following sections on Global Mirror (Figure 23-8).

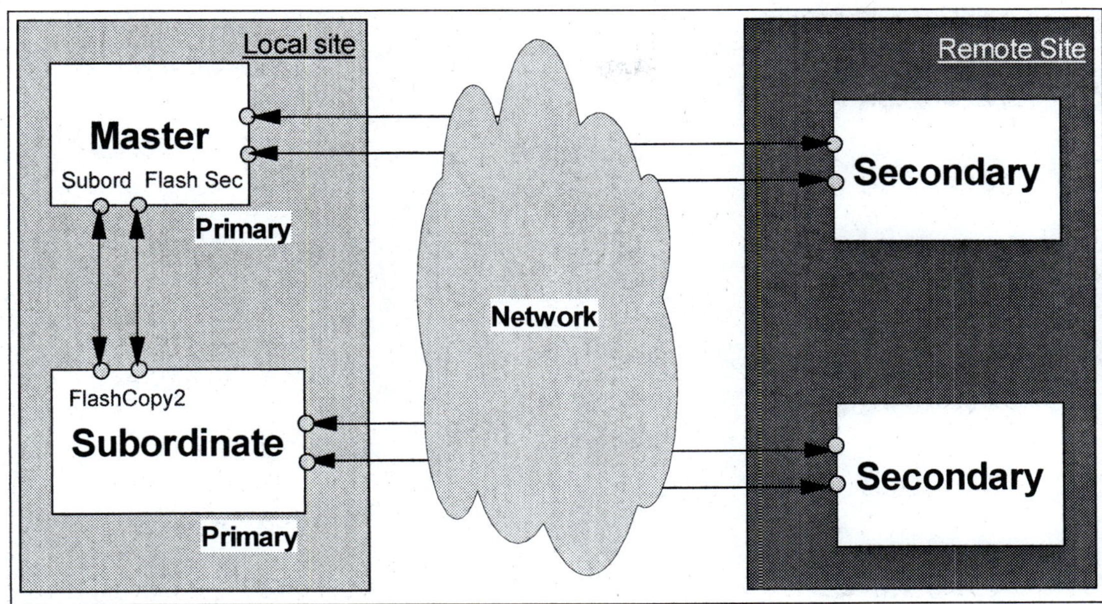

Figure 23-8 Global Mirror as a distributed application

Figure 23-8 shows the principal Global Mirror structure. A Master coordinates all efforts within a Global Mirror environment. Once the Master is started and manages a Global Mirror environment, the Master issues all concerned commands over inband communication to its attached subordinates at the local site. This may include a subordinate within the Master itself. This communication between the Master and an internal subordinate is transparent and does not need any extra attention from the user. The subordinates communicate via inband communication to all concerned secondary storage servers at the remote site that are involved. The Master also receives all acknowledgements from his Subordinates and their secondaries and coordinates and serializes all involved actions in the session.

The Master and Subordinate may be in a single storage server. Then the Subordinate is internally managed by the Master. With two or more storage servers at the local site, which participate in a Global Mirror session, the Subordinate is external and needs separate attention when creating and managing a Global Mirror session or environment.

The following sections explain how Global Mirror works and how Global Mirror guarantees consistent data at any time at the remote site. First we go through the process of how to create a Global Mirror environment. This, then, gives us a first insight on how Global Mirror works.

23.2 Build up a Global Mirror session

Global Mirror as a long distance remote copy solution across two sites is based on Global Copy and FlashCopy. It is the microcode that provides an independent mechanism to intelligently utilize Global Copy in conjunction with certain FlashCopy operations to provide consistent data at the remote site.

In order to understand how Global Mirror works, we explain how a Global Mirror environment or Global Mirror session is created and started.

This is a step-by-step approach and helps to understand further the Global Mirror operational aspects.

23.2.1 Simple configuration to start

In order to understand each step and to show the principles, a single application volume is shown (Figure 23-9).

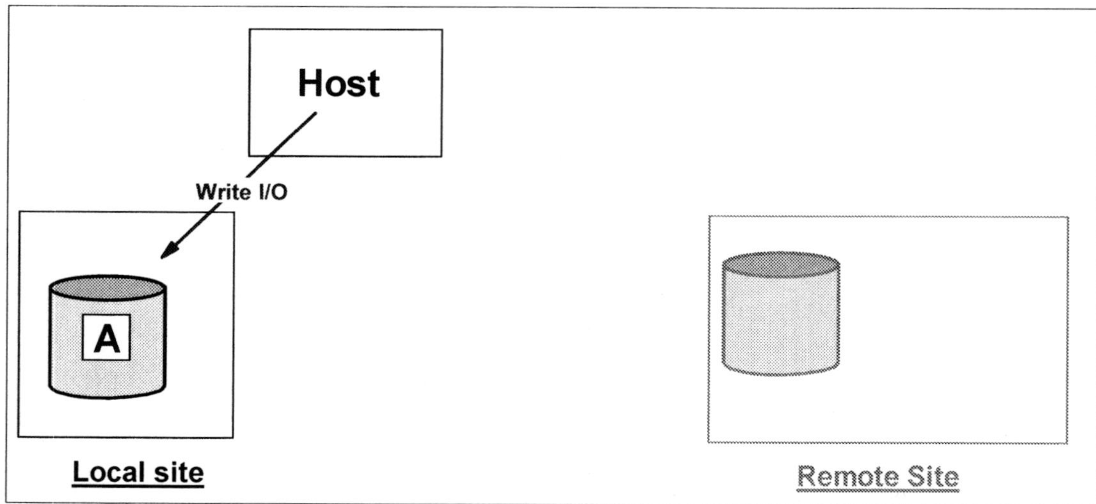

Figure 23-9 Start with simple application environment

We start with a simple application environment with a server that issues write I/Os to an application volume.

23.2.2 Establish connectivity to remote site

The next step assumes a distant site with a storage server. We want to interconnect both sites (Figure 23-10).

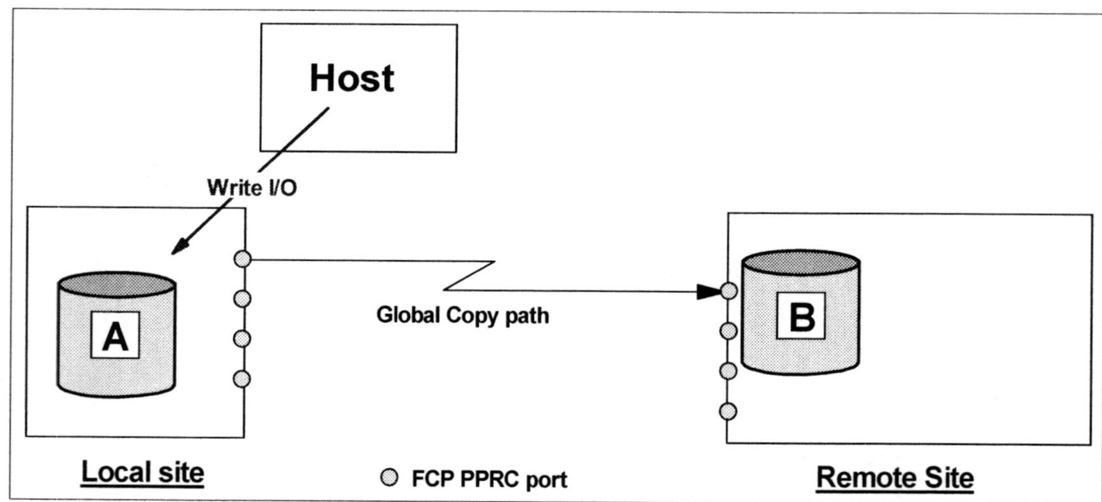

Figure 23-10 Establish Global Copy connectivity between both sites

Note that in Figure 23-10, we just establish Global Copy paths over an existing network. This network may be based on a fiber transport technology or on an IP based network.

The Global Copy paths are logical entities that are mapped onto a physical link or connection between both sites. Note that all PPRC related paths are based on FCP. The term Global Copy path just indicates that this PPRC path is intended for Global Copy volume pairs. Of course, such a path can be utilized by any other remote copy function as well.

23.2.3 Create Global Copy relationship between local and remote volume

Next, we create a Global Copy relationship between the local, or primary, volume and the remote, or secondary, volume. See Figure 23-11.

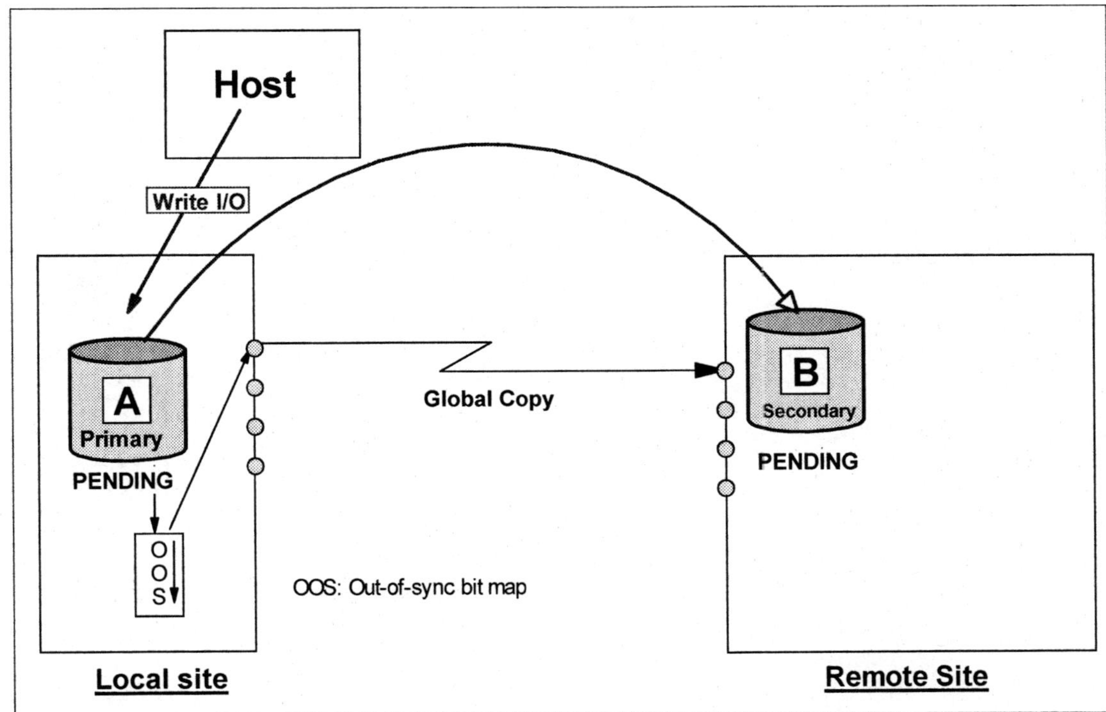

Figure 23-11 Establish Global Copy volume pair

Note that this step creates a Global Copy relationship between the primary volume and the secondary volume. It also changes the remote copy volume state from SIMPLEX to COPY PENDING. This COPY PENDING state applies to both volumes, PRIMARY PENDING and SECONDARY PENDING. This also immediately starts to copy the data from the primary volume to the secondary volume. After a first complete pass through the entire A volume Global Copy will constantly scan through the out-of-sync bit map. This bitmap indicates changed data as it arrives in the primary storage server. Global Copy replicates the data from the A volume to the B volume as indicated in this out-of-sync bit map.

In the following paragraphs we refer to the primary volume as the A volume and to the secondary volume as the B volume for simplicity.

Again, what is important to understand here is that Global Copy does not immediately copy the data as it arrives at the A volume to the B volume. Instead, this is an asynchronous process. As soon as a track is changed by an application write I/O it is reflected in this out-of-sync bitmap where all changed tracks are indicated. There are various numbers of concurrent replication processes that work through this bitmap to utilize the high bandwidth PPRC Fibre Channels to their maximum capacity.

This replication process keeps running until the Global Copy volume pair A - B is explicitly or implicitly suspended or terminated. Note already that a Global Mirror session command, for example, to pause or to terminate a Global Mirror session does not affect the Global Copy operation between both concerned volumes.

At this point data consistency does not yet exist at the remote site.

23.2.4 Introduce FlashCopy

FlashCopy is an integral part of Global Mirror and follows here as the next step in the course of establishing a Global Mirror session. See Figure 23-12.

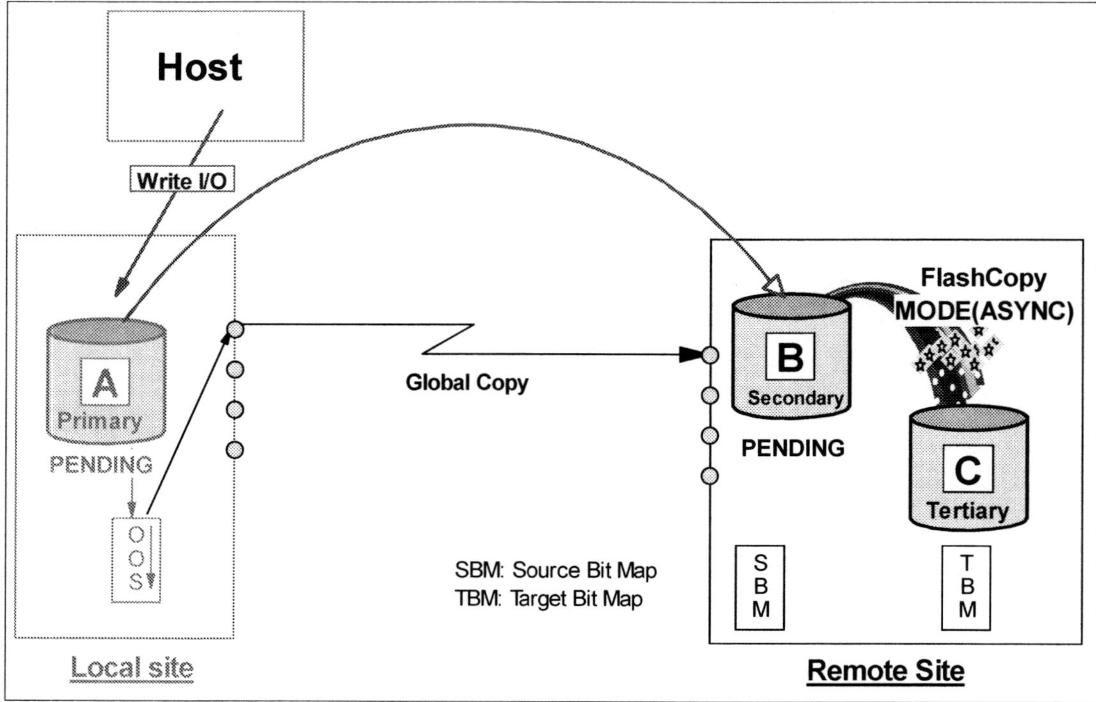

Figure 23-12 Introduce FlashCopy

The focus is now on the remote site. Figure 23-12 indicates a FlashCopy relationship with a Global Copy secondary volume as the FlashCopy source volume. Volume B is now both at the same time, a Global Copy secondary volume and a FlashCopy source volume. Within the same storage server is the corresponding FlashCopy target volume.

Note that this FlashCopy relationship has certain attributes that are typical and required when creating a Global Mirror session. These attributes are:

- **Inhibit target write:** Protect the FlashCopy target volume from being modified other than from Global Mirror related actions.
- **Start change recording:** Apply changes only from the source volume to the target volume bitmap, which occurred to the source volume between FlashCopy establish operations - except the first time when FlashCopy is established.
- **Persist:** Keep the FlashCopy relationship until explicitly or implicitly terminated. This parameter is automatic due to the NOCOPY parameter.
- **NOCOPY:** Note that NOCOPY does not start a background copy operation from source volume to target volume. It only maintains a set of FlashCopy bitmaps for the source volume and the target volume. These bitmaps are established at the first time when a FlashCopy relationship is created with NOCOPY. Before a source track is modified between Consistency Group creations the track is copied to the target volume to preserve the previous point-in-time copy. This includes updates to corresponding bitmaps to reflect the new location of the track that belongs to the point-in-time copy. Note that each Global Copy write to its secondary volume within the window of two adjacent Consistency Groups may cause FlashCopy I/O operations.

Some interfaces to trigger this particular FlashCopy relationship combine these attributes into a single parameter such as MODE(ASYNC) with the TSO command for z/OS.

23.2.5 Define Global Mirror session

To create a Global Mirror session does not involve any volume within the local site nor on the remote site. But the focus is back onto the local site, as Figure 23-13 indicates.

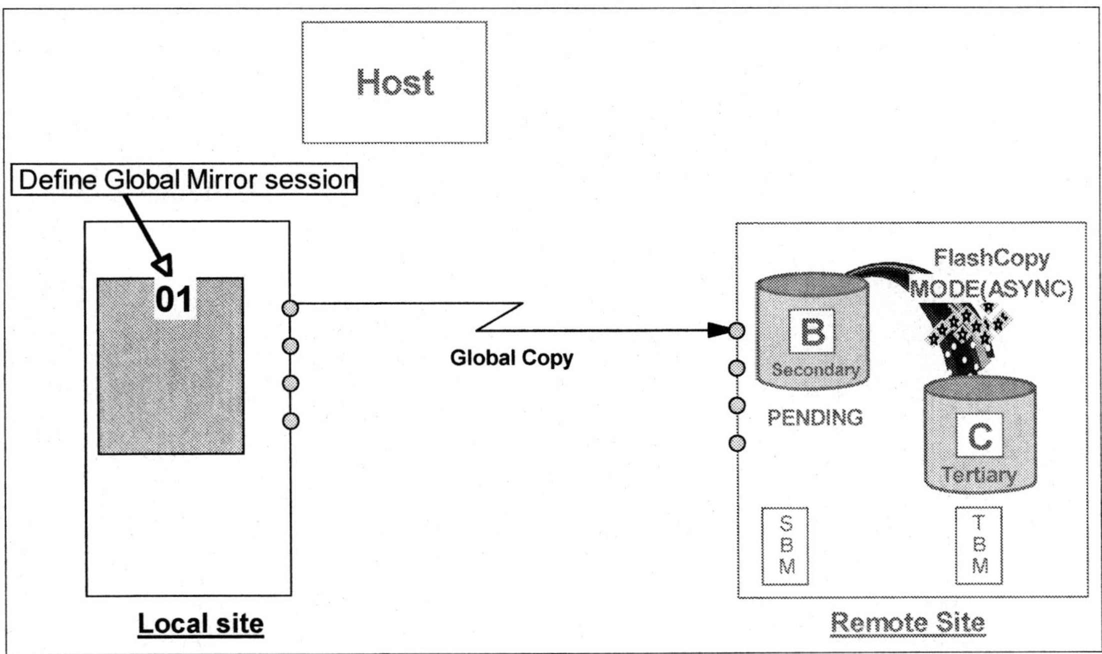

Figure 23-13 Define Global Mirror session

When you define a Global Mirror session, it creates a kind of token, which is a number between 1 and 255. This number represents a Global Mirror session, but nothing else more at this stage.

This session number is defined on a LSS level. Each LSS that potentially has volumes which have to go into this session needs a corresponding define session command. Currently only a single session is allowed per storage server. The architecture allows for more than one session and will be exploited in the future.

23.2.6 Populate Global Mirror session with volumes

The next logical step defines volumes into the Global Mirror session. The focus is still on the local site, as Figure 23-14 shows.

Note that only Global Copy primary volumes are meaningful candidates to become a member of a Global Mirror session.

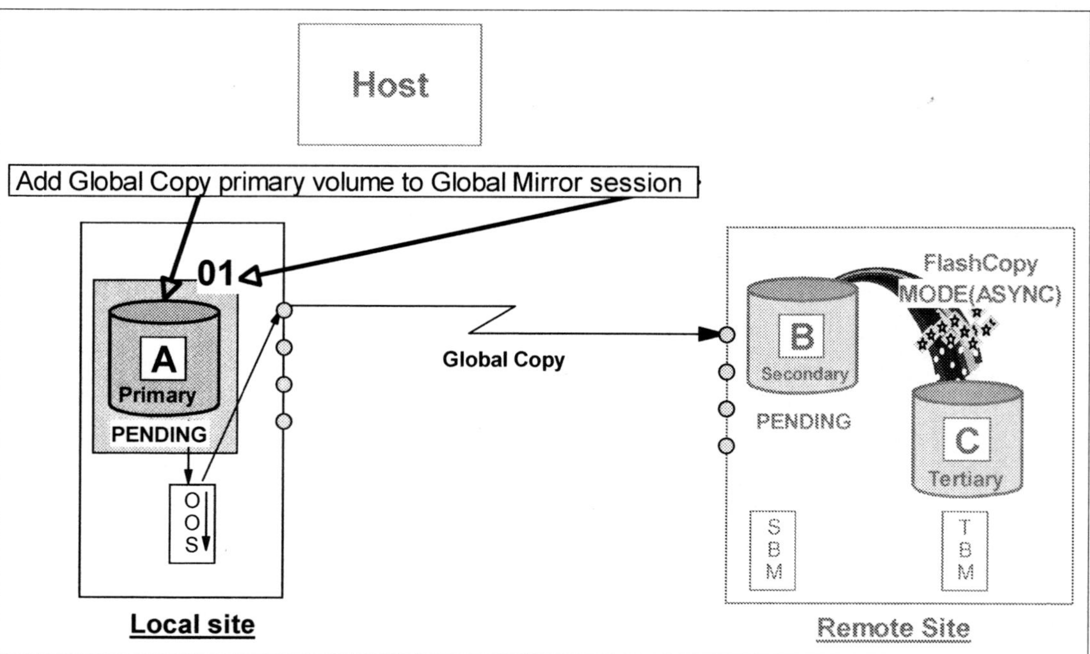

Figure 23-14 Add Global Copy primary volume to Global Mirror session

This process adds primary volumes to a list of volumes in the Global Mirror session. But at this stage it does still not perform consistency group formation.

Note that Global Copy continues to replicate the data as it arrives at the local site to the Global Copy primary volumes over to the corresponding Global Copy secondary volumes. Initially the Global Copy primary volumes are placed in a *join pending* status. Once a Consistency Group is formed, the Global Copy primary volume will then be added to the session and will be placed in an *in session* status.

Nothing else happens to the C volume after its original establishment in an Global Mirror session.

23.2.7 Start Global Mirror session

This is the last step and starts the Global Mirror session to form Consistency Groups at the remote site. As Figure 23-15 indicates, the focus here is on the local site with the start command issued to an LSS within a primary storage server. Through this start command you decide for the Master storage server and for the Master LSS. From now on, session related commands have to go through this Master LSS.

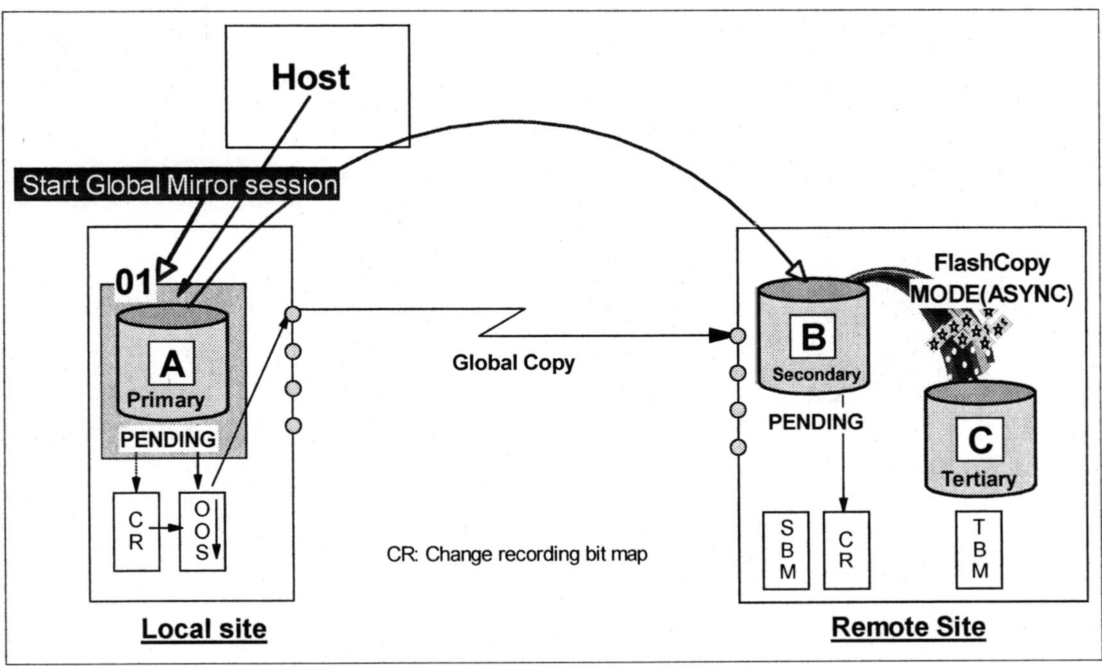

Figure 23-15 Start Global Mirror

This start command triggers events that involve all concerned volumes within the session and its corresponding volumes at the remote site. This includes a very fast bitmap management at the local disk storage server, issuing inband FlashCopy commands from the local site to the remote site, and verify that corresponding FlashCopy operations successfully finished. This all happens fully transparently and in an autonomic fashion inside the microcode of all involved disk storage servers.

All C volumes that belong to the Global Mirror session comprise the Consistency Group. Next, we form Consistency Groups at the remote site.

23.3 Form Consistency Group

To achieve the goal of creating a set of volumes at a remote site that contains consistent data, asynchronous data replication is not enough. Either a kind of journal or a third copy of the data volume is required to achieve this goal of consistent data at a distant site. With Global Mirror this third copy is naturally created through FlashCopy.

The microcode automatically triggers a sequence of events to create a set of consistent data volumes at the distant site. We call this set of consistent data volumes a Consistency Group. These events are managed by the microcode in an autonomically fashion.

The next sections describe the sequence of events that create a Consistency Group.

23.3.1 Consistency Group formation

To create a Consistency Group requires three steps that are internally processed and controlled through the microcode. These steps are fully transparent outside of the Licensed Internal Code (LIC) and do not require any other external code. The sequence of events is indicated by the numbers in Figure 23-16 and provides only a high level view that is sufficient to understand how consistency is achieved with Global Mirror.

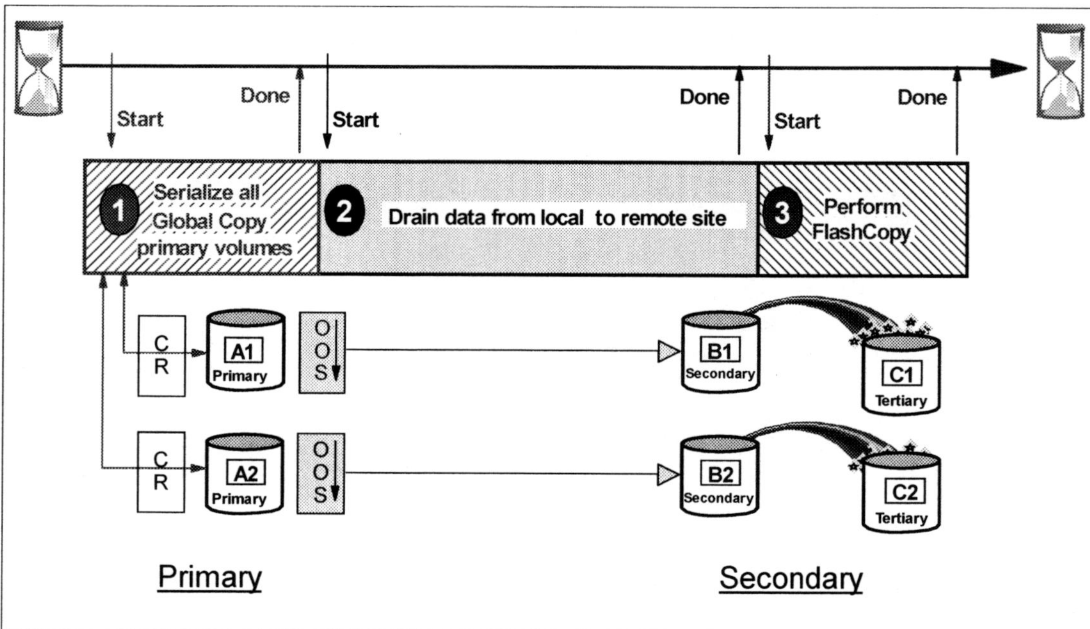

Figure 23-16 Form consistent set of volumes at the secondary site

Note that before step 1 and after step 3, Global Copy constantly scans through the out-of-sync bitmaps and replicates data from A volumes to B volumes as described in "Create Global Copy relationship between local and remote volume" on page 247.

With the trigger event to create a Consistency Group, the following steps occur in a serial fashion:

1. Serialize on all Global Copy primary volumes. This imposes a brief hold on all incoming write I/Os to all involved Global Copy primary volumes. Once all primary volumes are serialized, the pause on the incoming write I/O is released and all further write I/Os are now noted in the change recording bitmap. They are not replicated until step 3 is done, but application write I/Os can immediately continue.
2. Drain includes the process to replicate all remaining data that is indicated in the out-of-sync bitmap and still not replicated yet. Once all concerned out-of-sync bitmaps are *empty* - note that "empty" here does not mean in a literal sense — step 3 is triggered by the microcode from the primary site.
3. Now the B volumes contain all data as a quasi point-in-time copy and are consistent due to the serialization process in step 1 and the completed replication or drain process in step 2. Step 3 is now a FlashCopy that is triggered by the primary system's microcode as an inband FlashCopy command to volume B as FlashCopy source and volume C as FlashCopy target volume. Note that this FlashCopy is a two phase process to first issue the FlashCopy command to all involved FlashCopy pairs in the Global Mirror session. Then the Master is collecting the feedback and all incoming FlashCopy completed messages. When all FlashCopies are successfully completed, then the Master concludes that a new Consistency Group is successfully created.

FlashCopy applies here only to changed data since the last FlashCopy operation. This is due to the *start change recording* when the FlashCopy relationship was established. The FlashCopy relationship does not end due to the NOCOPY option, which is also assigned at FlashCopy establish time - see “Introduce FlashCopy” on page 248. Note that NOCOPY also does not require to do a physical background copy operation of any tracks. Only bitmaps are maintained and updated.

Once step 3 is complete, we have created a consistent set of volumes at the distant or secondary site. This set of C volumes represents a set of data consistent volumes or the Consistency Group. At this very moment B volumes and C volumes are a set of data consistent volumes, but only for this brief moment are both sets equal in their content.

Immediately after the FlashCopy process is logically complete, the primary systems's microcode is notified to continue with the Global Copy process. As you know Global Copy works on the out-of-sync bitmap. In order to replicate the data that arrived at the A volumes during step 1 to step 3 from the A volumes to the B volumes, the change recording bitmap is mapped over the empty out-of-sync bitmap and from now on all arriving write I/Os will end up again in the out-of-sync bitmap. From now on the conventional Global Copy process as outlined in“Create Global Copy relationship between local and remote volume” on page 247 continues until the next Consistency Group creation process is started.

23.3.2 Consistency Group parameters

In the previous paragraph we called the first step a serialization step. In Global Mirror terms this step not only serializes all related Global Mirror primary volumes but also coordinates with other disk storage servers when the Consistency Group spans over more than one primary disk storage server (Figure 23-17).

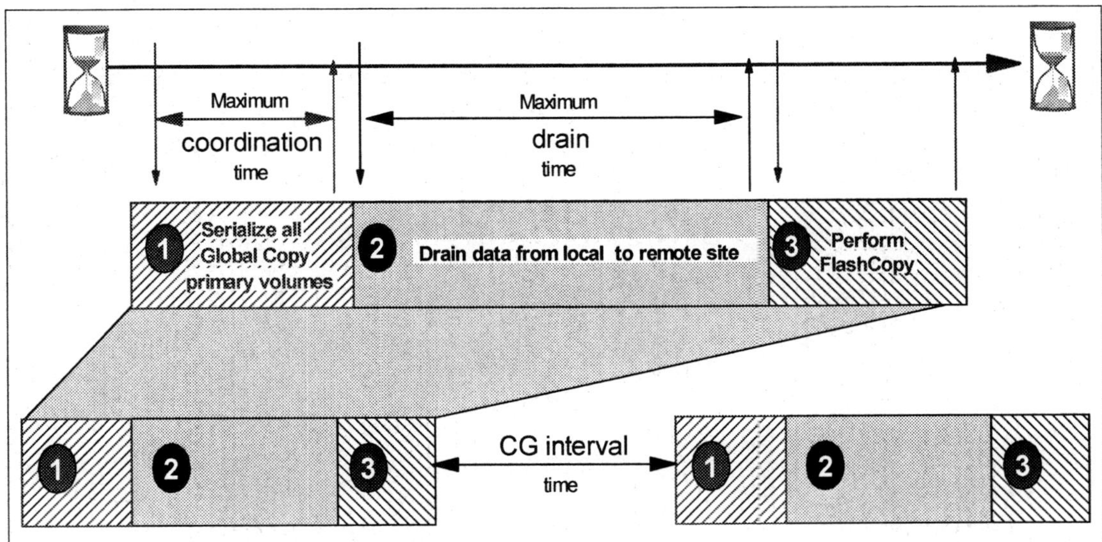

Figure 23-17 Consistency Group tuning parameters

There are three externalized parameters, and their default values can be overridden:

- Maximum coordination time dictates how long a host write I/O may be impacted during this coordination and serialization efforts for the Global Copy primary volumes that belong to this Consistency Group. The scope of this time limit is in terms of milli-seconds (ms). The default is 50 ms.
- Maximum drain time is the maximum time allowed to drain the out-of-sync bitmap once the process to form a Consistency Group is started and step 1 successfully completed. The maximum train time is specified in units of seconds. The default is 30 seconds.
  If the maximum drain time is exceeded, Global Mirror will fail to form the Consistency Group and will evaluate the current throughput of the environment.

  If this indicates that another drain failure is likely, Global Mirror will stay in Global Copy mode while regularly re-evaluating the situation to determine when to start to form the next Consistency Group. If this persists for a significant period of time, then eventually Global Mirror will force the formation of a new Consistency Group. In this way Global Mirror ensures that during periods when insufficient bandwidth is available, production performance is protected and data is transmitted to the secondary site in the most efficient manner possible. When the peak activity has passed, consistency group formation will resume in a timely fashion.
- Once a Consistency Group has been created, the Consistency Group interval time determines how long to wait before starting with the formation of the next Consistency Group. This is specified in seconds, and the default is zero (0) seconds. Zero seconds means that Consistency Group formation happens constantly. As soon as a Consistency Group is successfully created, the process to create a new Consistency Group starts again immediately.

There is no external parameter to limit the time for the FlashCopy operation. This is due to its very fast bitmap manipulation process.

But do remember that Global Mirror utilizes a distributed approach as well as a two-phase commit technique for activities between the Master and its Subordinate LSS. The communication between the local and the remote site is organized through the Subordinate LSS. The Subordinates function here partly as a transient component for the Global Mirror activities, which are all triggered and coordinated by the Master. This distributed concept allows always to provide a set of data consistent volumes at the remote site independent of the number of involved storage servers at the primary and/or at the secondary site.

24

Global Mirror options and configuration

In this chapter we provide a detailed description of Global Mirror options, including how to create a Global Mirror environment and how remove a Global Mirror environment. We discuss how to change Global Mirror tuning parameters and how to modify an active Global Mirror session. We also go through the details of a failover scenario in case of a primary site failure. In addition to these topics, we discuss configuration matters for Global Mirror environments.

For command details and syntax, refer to the corresponding manuals:

- *z/OS DFSMS Advanced Copy Services*, SC35-0428
- *IBM TotalStorage DS8000 Command-Line Interface User's Guide*, SC26-7625
- *Device Support Facility User's Guide and Reference Release 17*, SC35-0033

24.1 Terminology used in Global Mirror environments

First, we would like to define some terms that are used in context with Global Mirror. See Chapter 27., "Global Mirror examples" on page 341 for examples based on real commands in a test environment.

Global Mirror is intended for long distance data replication and, therefore, relies on the network structure and components used between two distant sites. This chapter does not cover network related topics between two distant Global Mirror sites. For more information on those topics, refer to the redbook, *IBM TotalStorage Business Continuity Solutions Guide*, SG24-6547, and in particular, Part III, Chapter 13, "Network transport options".

With Global Mirror, data consistency at the secondary site is guaranteed and does not impact application write I/Os. Global Copy, on the other hand, requires you to periodically quiesce the applications to create a consistent set of volumes at the remote site.

The following terms are used in the following sections and are briefly defined here.

Dependent writes

If the start of one write operation is dependent upon the completion of a previous write, the writes are dependent. Application examples for dependent writes are databases with their associated logging files. Also updates to catalogs, VTOCs as well as VSAM indexes and VSAM data components rely on dependent writes. For instance, the database logging file will be updated after a new entry has been successfully written to a table space.

The chronological order of dependent writes to primary volumes is the basis to provide consistent data at the secondary site through remote copy operations.

Consistency

The consistency of data is ensured if the order of dependent writes to disks or disk groups is maintained. With Copy Services solutions the data consistency at the secondary site is important for the usability of the data at the remote site. Consistent data for instance provides the ability to perform a data base restart rather than a data base recovery that could take hours or even days.

Data consistency across all secondary volumes spread across multiple disk storage servers is essential for logical data integrity.

Data currency

This term describes the difference of time since the last data was written at the primary site, versus the time the same data was written to the secondary site. It determines the amount of data you have to recover at the remote site after a disaster. This is also called *recovery point objective* or RPO. Only synchronous copy solutions such as Metro Mirror have a currency of zero or RPO = Zero. All asynchronous copy solutions have a data currency greater than zero.

With Global Mirror a data currency of a few seconds can be achieved, while data consistency is maintained by the Consistency Group process within Global Mirror.

For asynchronous replication, this means that the data is not replicated at the same time as the local I/O happens, but the data is replicated with a time difference to the remote site. Examples of non-synchronous or asynchronous replication methods are:

- Global Copy is a non-synchronous method that does not guarantee consistent data at the remote site.
- z/OS Global Mirror (formerly XRC) is an asynchronous replication method that guarantees consistent data at the remote site.

- Global Mirror is also an asynchronous replication method that provides consistent data at the remote site.

Session

A Global Mirror session is a collection of volumes that are managed together when creating consistent copies of data volumes. This set of volumes can reside in one or more LSSs and one or more disk storage servers at the primary site. Open systems volumes and z/OS volumes can both be members of the same session.

When you start or resume a session, the creation of Consistency Groups is performed and the Master disk storage server controls the session by communicating with the Subordinate disk storage servers.

There is also a session concept at the scope and granularity of an LSS. But all LSS sessions are combined and grouped together within a Global Mirror session.

Master

The Master is a term for a function inside a primary disk storage server that, by communicating with Subordinates in other disk storage servers, controls the creation of Consistency Groups and manages the Global Mirror session. The Master is defined when the start command for a session is issued to any LSS in a primary disk storage server. This determines who becomes the Master disk storage server.

The Master needs PPRC Fibre Channel communication paths to any one of the LSSs in each Subordinate disk storage servers.

Subordinate

The Subordinate is a term for a function inside the primary disk storage server that communicates with the Master and is controlled by the Master. At least one of the LSSs of each Subordinate primary disk storage servers needs PPRC Fibre Channel communication paths to the Master. It is used to enable the Master to communicate with the Subordinate disk storage server. This is required to create Consistency Groups of volumes in more than one disk storage server.

If all the volumes of a Global Mirror Session reside in one primary disk storage server no Subordinate is required, because the Master can communicate to all LSSs inside the primary disk storage server.

Consistency Group

This is a group of volumes in one or more secondary disk storage servers whose data must be kept consistent at the remote site.

Note: With Global Mirror this is done periodically and automatically, without disruption to the host I/O, and in a very short time.

Local Site

This is the site that contains the production servers. This and other publications use this term interchangeably with the terms primary, production, or source site.

Remote Site

This is the site that contains the backup servers of a disaster recovery solution. This and other publications use this term interchangeably with the terms secondary, backup, standby, or target site.

24.2 Create a Global Mirror environment

The following section recommends a certain sequence of steps to establish a Global Mirror environment. This is independent of the interface used to create a Global Mirror environment. Note that for illustration purposes, parameters and keywords are used in this section that apply to TSO commands or to the ANTRQST macro interface. ICKDSF does use different keywords that are described in 25.5, "ICKDSF support for Global Mirror" on page 312.

We are using a basic Global Mirror setup, as Figure 24-1 shows.

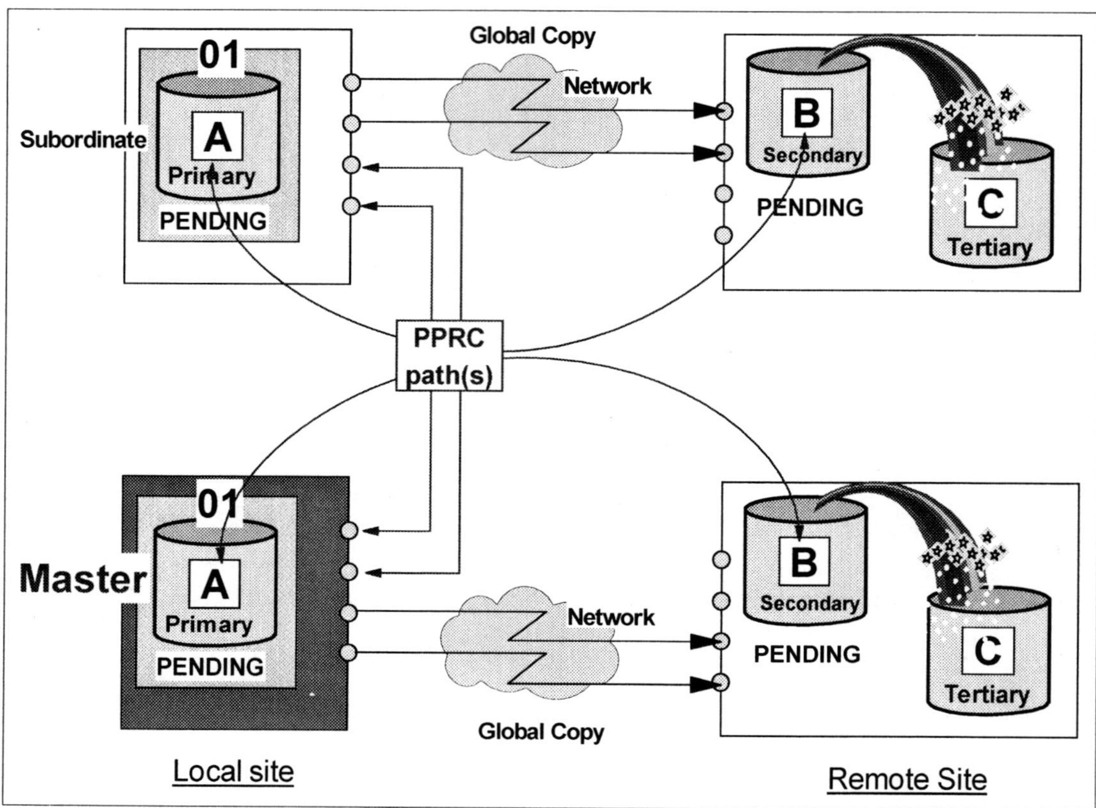

Figure 24-1 Global Mirror basic configuration with Master and Subordinate storage servers

The order of commands to create a Global Mirror environment is not completely fixed and allows for some variation. In order to be consistent with other sources and to not confuse the user with a different sequence of commands, we recommend a meaningful order and suggest the following steps to create a Global Mirror environment:

1. Establish the PPRC paths between the local site and the remote site. In Figure 24-1, these are the PPRC paths between corresponding LSSs at the primary site and the remote site utilizing the PPRC links that are configured through the network. Global Copy primary LSSs are represented by the A volumes in Figure 24-1 and their corresponding Global Copy secondary LSSs by B volumes.

   You may also establish PPRC paths here between the Master and any Subordinate storage server that will be part of a Global Mirror session. Note that these PPRC path(s) are established between local or primary storage servers at the local site. With only a single primary storage server, you do not need to define PPRC paths to connect internal LSSs within the primary storage server. The communication within a single primary storage server between the Master and the Subordinates within this storage server is transparent and internally performed.

2. Once the PPRC paths are established, start the Global Copy (PPRC-XD) pairs that are planned to be part of a Global Mirror session. Global Copy has to be established with the parameter MODE(COPY) and OPTION(XD) when you use CESTPAIR TSO commands. When you use ICKDSF use PPRCOPY ESTPAIR, which has also a parameter MODE(COPY) and OPTION(XD). It is recommended to wait until the first initial copy is complete before you continue to the next step. This avoids unnecessary FlashCopy background I/Os in the following step.
3. The next step is to establish FlashCopy relationships between the B and C volumes. The TSO FCESTABL command introduces a new parameter, MODE(ASYNC), which combines and implies the particular FlashCopy attributes that are required for this FlashCopy relationship. See 23.2.4, "Introduce FlashCopy" on page 248. ICKDSF explicitly requires the keywords CHRCD(YES) NOTGTWT(YES) and MODE(NOCOPY) in the corresponding FC ESTABLISH commands.
4. With external Subordinates, especially with more than one involved server at the local site, you need PPRC paths between the Master LSS and any potential Subordinate storage server at the local site. If you did not establish these paths in the very first step, then this is the time to create these PPRC paths before you continue with the next step.
5. Define a token that identifies a Global Mirror session. This is a session ID with a number between 1 and 255. Define this session number to the Master storage server and also to all potentially involved primary LSSs that are going to be part of this Global Mirror session and contain Global Copy primary volumes that belong to the Global Mirror session. All primary LSSs include all LSSs in potential Subordinate storage servers that are going to be part of the Global Mirror session.
6. The next logical step populates the session with the Global Copy primary volumes. You should put these Global Copy primary volumes into the session after they complete their first pass for initial copy.
7. Start the session. This command actually defines the Master LSS. All further session commands have to go through this LSS. You may specify with the start command the Global Mirror tuning parameters such as maximum drain time, maximum coordination time, and Consistency Group interval time.

You go through this recommended sequence independent of the interface used.

24.3 Modify a Global Mirror session

Once a session is active and running, you may alter the Global Mirror environment to add or remove volumes. You also may add newly arrived storage servers to a Global Mirror session or you may change the interval between the formation of each Consistency Group.

24.3.1 Add volumes to or remove volumes from a Global Mirror session

Volumes can be added to the session at any time after the session number is defined to the LSS where the volumes reside. Once the session is started, volumes can be added to the session or can be removed from the session also at any time.

Note: You only add Global Copy primary volumes to a Global Mirror session.

Volumes may be added to a session in any state, for example, SIMPLEX or PENDING. Volumes that have not completed their initial copy phase stay in a *join pending* state until the first initial copy is complete. If a volume in a session is SUSPENDED, it will cause Consistency Group formation to fail.

We recommend that you add only Global Copy primary volumes that have completed their initial copy or first pass, although the microcode will stop volumes joining the Global Mirror session until the first pass is complete. However, we recommend that you wait until the first initial copy is complete before you establish the FlashCopy relationship between the B and the C volume.

Note: You cannot add a Metro Mirror (formerly Synchronous PPRC) primary volume to a Global Mirror session. Global Mirror supports only Global Copy, or PPRC-XD, pairs. When Global Mirror detects a volume which, for example, is converted from Global Copy to Metro Mirror, the following formation of a Consistency Group will fail.

When you add a rather large number of volumes at once to an existing Global Mirror session, then the available resources for Global Copy within the affected Ranks may be utilized by the initial copy pass. To minimize the impact to the production servers when adding many new volumes, you may consider adding the new volumes to an existing Global Mirror session in stages. If possible and as a rough rule of thumb, add only a few volumes within a Rank during application peak I/O periods. Once the first initial copy is completed, add the next volume. Again, as a rule of thumb, plan for one or two volumes within a Rank during peak I/O load on the concerned Ranks for the first initial copy pass. Eventually this will be enhanced and controlled by the microcode in a future release, which then is going to pace the initial full copy during the first Global Copy establish.

Suspending a Global Copy pair that belongs to an active Global Mirror session will impact the formation of Consistency Groups. When you intend to remove Global Copy volumes from an active Global Mirror session, first remove the concerned volumes from the Global Mirror session. Example 24-2 on page 262 gives a TSO command showing how to remove Global Copy volumes from a Global Mirror session. Then withdraw the FlashCopy relationship between the B and C volumes, and finally, terminate the Global Copy pair to bring volume A and volume B into SIMPLEX mode.

Note: When you remove A volumes without pausing Global Mirror, you might see an error condition that the Consistency Group formation failed. However, this failure does not mean you have lost a consistent copy at the remote site because Global Mirror does not take the FlashCopy (B to C) for the failed Consistency Group data. This message indicates that just one Consistency Group formation has failed, and Global Mirror will retry the sequence.

24.3.2 Add or remove storage servers or LSSs

When you plan to add a new Subordinate storage server to an active session, you have to stop the session first. Then add the new Subordinate storage server and start the session again (with the updated RSESSION command when you use TSO commands). The session start command then contains also the new Subordinate storage server. This applies also to any other utilized interface to manage a Global Mirror environment. The same procedure applies when you remove a storage server from a Global Mirror session, which can be a Subordinate storage server only. In other words, you cannot remove the Master storage server.

When you add a new LSS to an active session and this LSS belongs to a storage server that already has another LSS which belongs to this Global Mirror session, you may add the new LSS to the session without stopping and starting the session again. This is true for either the Master storage server or for a Subordinate storage server.

24.3.3 Modify Global Mirror session parameters

The tuning parameters of a Global Mirror session may be modified by pausing the session and then resuming the session with new tuning parameter values. The parameters that you may modify are:

- Consistency Group interval time
- Maximum coordination interval time
- Maximum Consistency drain time

When you issue a start command after a pause command, as opposed to a resume, any value for the Consistency Group interval time, maximum coordination interval time, or maximum Consistency Group drain time in the start command is ignored. If these parameters have to be altered, you have to issue a resume command to the paused session with the parameters specified. When you resume a paused session without specifying these parameters, they will be set to their default values. See 23.3.2, "Consistency Group parameters" on page 253. When you require customized parameters to be used, you have to specify these values when you resume the session.

Important: When tuning with these parameters, be sure to check for errors in Consistency Group formation and in draining the out-of-sync bitmaps. A few errors are not significant and do not jeopardize the consistency of your Global Mirror. However, if failures repeatedly continue (no more consistency groups are formed), the percentage of successful Consistency Groups is unacceptable (many failures occur), or the frequency of Consistency Groups is not meeting your requirements (Recovery Point Objective-RPO), then the failures are a problem and need to be addressed.

24.3.4 Global Mirror and changed topology

The topology of a Global Mirror session, for example, the Master SSID, Subordinate SSIDs, and Subordinate serial numbers, cannot be altered through a pause and resume command sequence. When you resume the session after a pause and the Global Mirror topology is not the same as it was at the pause, the start of the session will fail.

If you need to change the topology of your Global Mirror session, you have to stop the session and start the session again with the new topology structure information in the start command.

Topology also refers to the list of storage servers that are Subordinates. You must establish PPRC paths between the Master and each Subordinate LSS. Just one LSS per Subordinate is sufficient. When you define the PPRC path you identify the primary as the Master LSS and its corresponding Subsystem ID or SSID. The secondary LSS in the PPRC path establish command points to a corresponding Subordinate that is identified by its SSID. These SSIDs are going to go into the topology specification, which defines the communication paths between Master and Subordinate storage servers. This topology is specified in the SBINFO parameter and is required for the following Global Mirror operations:

- Start a Global Mirror session.
- Stop a Global Mirror session.
- Pause a Global Mirror session.
- Resume a Global Mirror session.

Example 24-1 indicates the context between establishing the PPRC paths between Master and Subordinate to the Global Mirror topology information.

Example 24-1 Context between establish path and Global Mirror topology

```
CESTPATH    DEVN (X'6000')                          +
             PRIM (X'6000' 500507630EFFFC6F  X'00') +
             SEC  (X'6400' 500507630EFFFCA0  X'00') +
             LINK (X'00000000' X'01000100') CGROUP(NO)

  RSESSION   SNBR(01) VOLSER(AA601F)          +
             ACTION(START)                    +
             LSSTYPE(CKD) LSSNBR(00)          +
             MSSERIAL (AAGXA) MASTER(YES)     +
             SBINFO(6000,6400,AAVCA)
```

In Example 24-1, the sending Master SSID is 6000 and the receiving SSID in the Subordinate is SSID 6400. These are the SSIDs as they are defined in the establish path command. In the establish path command there is also a link between the SSID and its corresponding LSS number, which in both cases is x'00'.

The RSESSION example contains the topology information for the Subordinate and also the communication or control paths specification. SBINFO contains positional parameters in the following order:

- SSID of the sending Master LSS
- SSID of the receiving LSS in the Subordinate storage server
- Serial number of the Subordinate storage server

When the topology changes and needs to be reflected in an existing Global Mirror environment, you need to stop the session with the SBINFO specification, as it was at the previous start of the Global Mirror session. Then you adjust the SBINFO that it reflects the changed topology and start the session again, now with the new SBINFO specifications. See also “Add or remove storage servers or LSSs” on page 260.

24.3.5 Remove FlashCopy relationship

When you withdraw a FlashCopy relationship within a Global Mirror session, then the Consistency Group process is impacted. If a withdraw is required, then first remove the Global Copy primary volume from the session. Example 24-2 shows a TSO command that removes a volume from LSS 0C and two volumes from LSS 0D.

Example 24-2 Remove volumes from Global Mirror session

```
RVOLUME     SNBR(01) VOLSER(XX2C00)          +
              ACTION(REMOVE)                   +
              LSSTYPE(CKD) LSSNBR(0C)          +
              ESSSERIAL(27131)                 +
              VOLLIST  (00)

  RVOLUME     SNBR(01) VOLSER(XX2D00)          +
              ACTION(REMOVE)                   +
              LSSTYPE(CKD) LSSNBR(0D)          +
              ESSSERIAL(27131)                 +
              VOLRANGE (00:01)
```

Once the volumes are removed from the session, you may explicitly remove the corresponding FlashCopy relationship that was tied to this primary volume (Example 24-3).

Example 24-3 Remove FlashCopy relationship

```
FCWITHDR  SDEVN(X'3C00')  TDEVN(X'3E00')


   FCWITHDR  DEVN(X'2C00') SOURCE(73081 00 0C)  +
                           TARGET(73081 00 0E)  +
                           REMOTE(YES) SSID(3C00)
```

Example 24-3 shows the TSO FlashCopy command to remove a FlashCopy relationship. The first FlashCopy command assumes a host channel connectivity to the remote storage server. Then you may issue a simple FCWITHDR command with source and target volumes addressed by their z/OS device numbers. When there is no host connectivity established to the remote storage server, then you may use an inband FlashCopy command through the local Global Copy primary volume. Note that despite the removal of the volumes from the Global Mirror session, Global Copy keeps running and replicates newly arrived write I/Os over the PPRC links to the remote storage server. The second FCWITHDR command also propagates the FlashCopy command over the PPRC link to the remote storage server. SOURCE and TARGET parameters address the source and target volumes in the remote storage server. SSID addresses additionally the LSS 0C that contains the source volume.

Such a process may be needed when you want to change the FlashCopy targets within a Global Mirror configuration and choose, for example, another LSS for the FlashCopy targets. This may be needed because you want to replace the FlashCopy targets due to a skew in the load pattern in the remote storage server.

You may pause the session before such an activity and then resume the session again once the removal of the FlashCopy relationships is completed.

Note: A pause command will complete a Consistency Group formation in progress before it pauses to build further Consistency Groups. A stop will immediately end the formation of Consistency Groups.

24.3.6 Remove a Global Mirror environment

To remove a Global Mirror environment and remove all traces of Global Mirror we recommend the following order of steps to complete:

1. Terminate the Global Mirror session.
2. Remove all Global Copy primary volumes from the Global Mirror session.
3. Close the Global Mirror session.
4. Withdraw all FlashCopy relationships between the B and C volumes.
5. Terminate all Global Copy pairs.
6. Remove the PPRC paths between the local site to the remote site.
7. Remove the PPRC paths between the Master LSS and all concerned Subordinate LSSs.

24.4 Global Mirror and multiple disk storage servers

When you create a Global Mirror environment that spans multiple storage servers at the local site and probably also at the remote site, then you need to establish communication paths between the local storage servers (Figure 24-2).

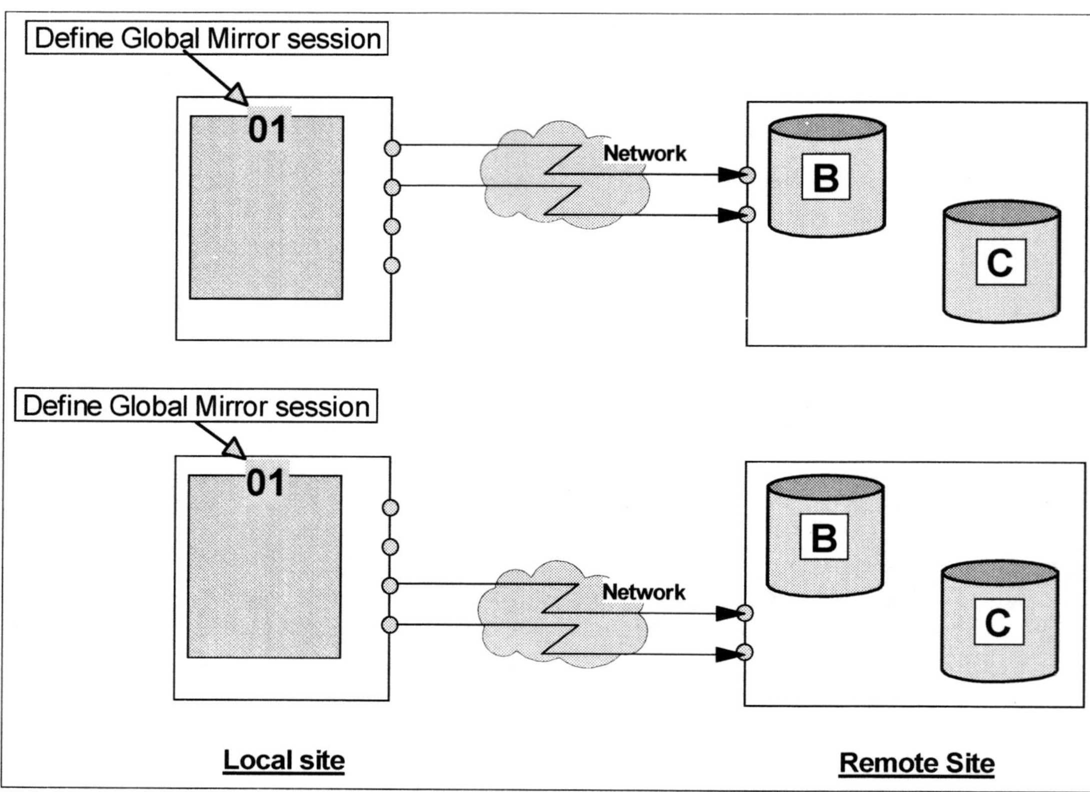

Figure 24-2 Define Global Mirror session to all potentially involved storage servers

Figure 24-2 shows a symmetrical configuration with a one-to-one mapping. You have to define the corresponding session with its number to all potentially involved LSSs at the local site. As implied here, there is still no connection between both local storage servers.

Therefore you have to establish corresponding Global Mirror control or PPRC paths, as shown in Figure 24-3.

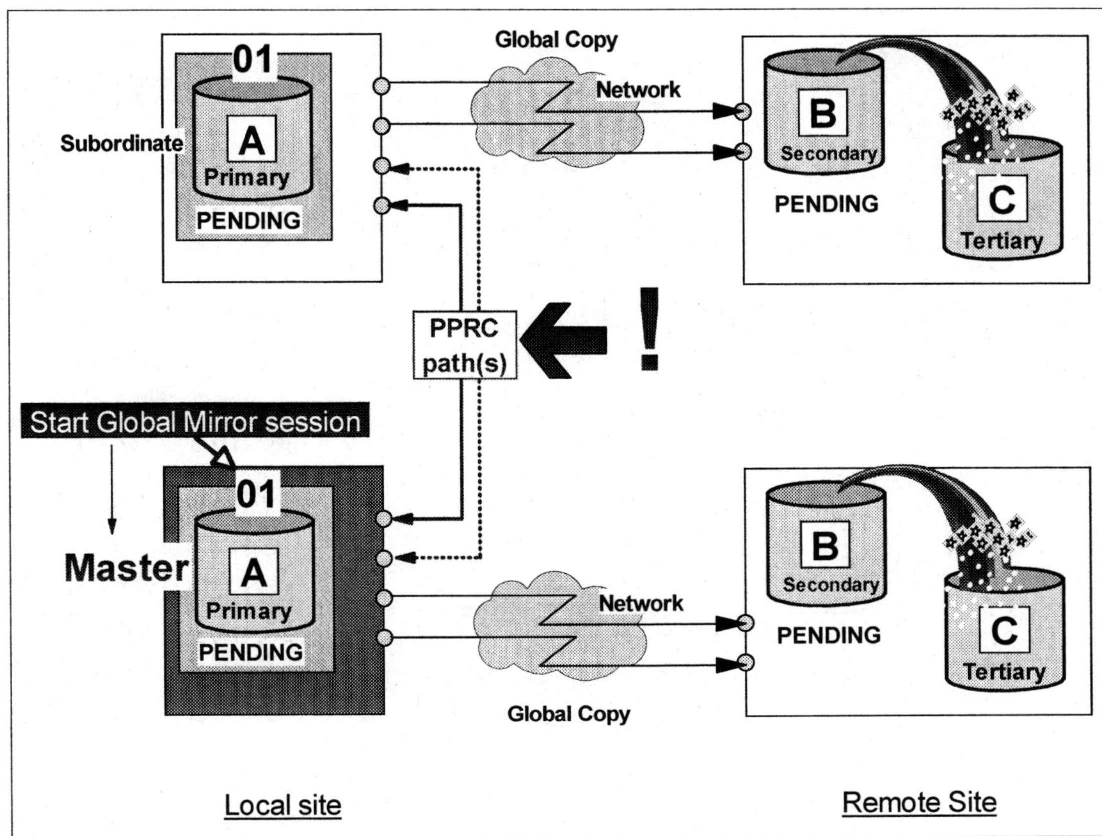

Figure 24-3 Decide for Master storage server and start Global Mirror session

Through the start command, you decide which LSS becomes the Master LSS and consequently which local storage server turns into the Master Global Mirror storage server. This Master acts indeed like a server in a client/server environment.

The required communication between the Master storage server and potential Subordinate storage servers is inband over PPRC paths between the Master and Subordinates. This communication is highly optimized and allows you to minimize the potential application write I/O impact during the coordination phase to about a few milliseconds. For details see 23.3, "Form Consistency Group" on page 251.

Note that this communication is performed over PPRC FCP links. There is at least one PPRC FCP link required between Master storage server and any potential Subordinate storage server. Figure 24-4 uses dashed lines to show the Global Mirror links or PPRC paths between the Master storage server and its associated Subordinate storage servers. These ports are dedicated for Global Mirror to communicate between Master and Subordinates.

Also shown is a shared port on the Master storage server and dedicated ports at the Subordinates. From a communication and traffic viewpoint, a link would be quite enough for the traffic between the Master and its Subordinates.

For redundancy, we suggest configuring two PPRC links or Global Mirror links. From a communication traffic viewpoint, two links are never stressed in any respect but are needed for high availability for such a configuration (Figure 24-4).

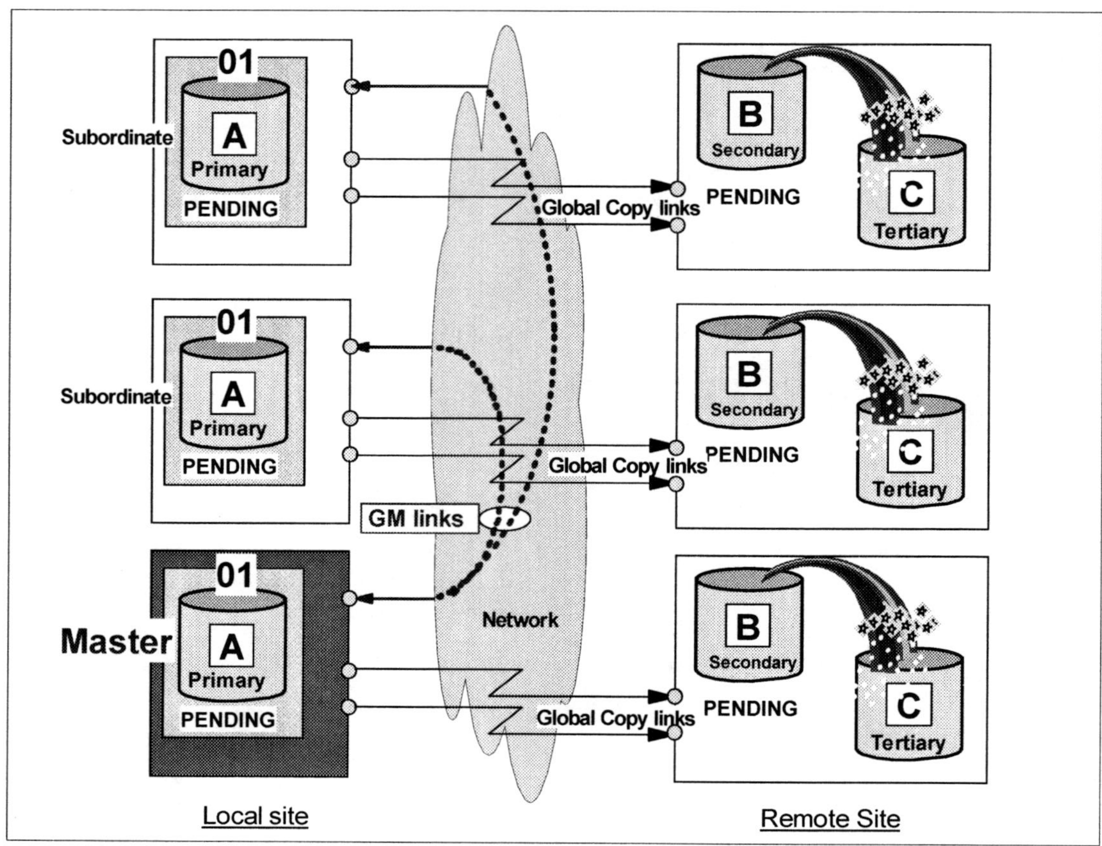

Figure 24-4 Global Mirror links or PPRC paths between primary storage servers

Note that when you create PPRC links over a SAN network, then the same storage server FCP ports may be used for these Global Mirror session links as well as for PPRC Global Copy links and host connectivity. However, for performance reasons, and to prevent host errors from disrupting your Global Mirror environment, it is often a good idea to use separate FCP ports.

In the example in Figure 24-5, an FCP port in the Master storage server is shared between a Global Mirror link to the other two Subordinate storage servers as well as a Global Copy port link to the corresponding secondary storage server. The corresponding ports at the Subordinate storage servers are shared also between the Global session link and Global Mirror link.

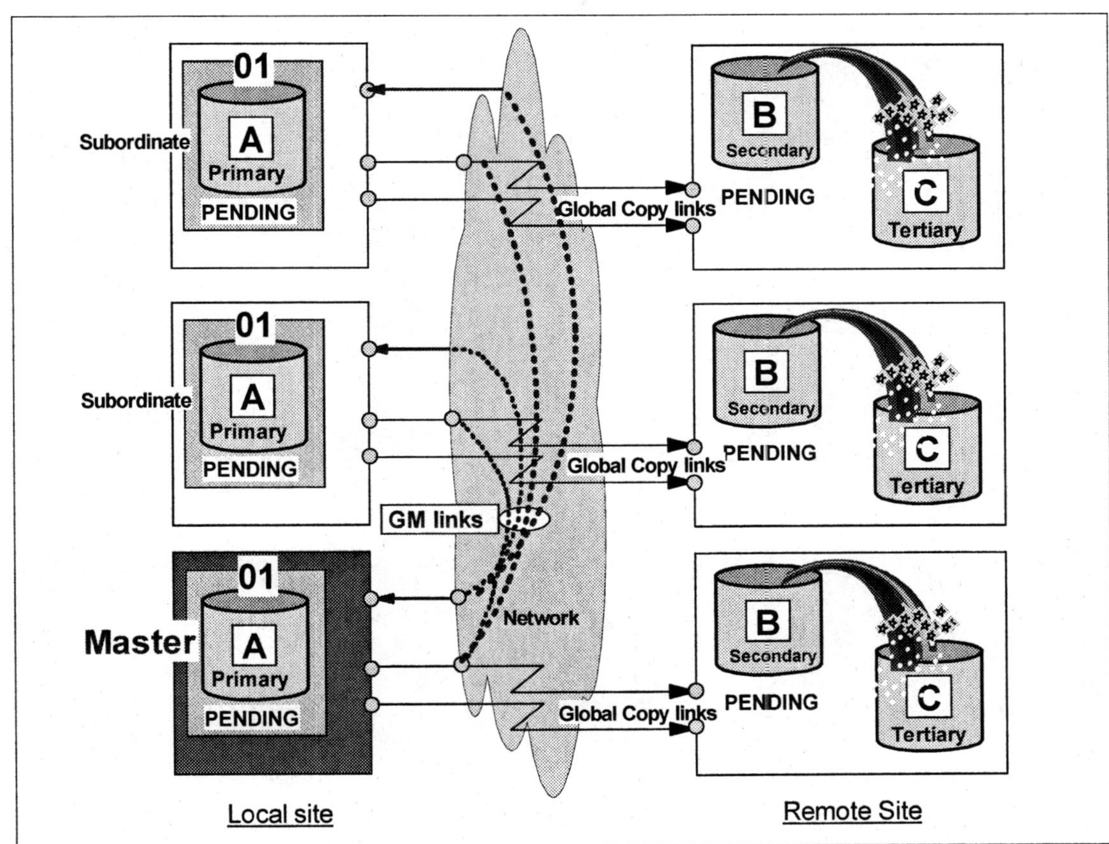

Figure 24-5 Dedicated and shared Global Mirror links

The configuration example in Figure 24-5 shows a mixed usage of certain ports whereas other ports are dedicated.

If possible, the ideal configuration would be the one shown in Figure 24-6. Again, from a performance and throughput viewpoint you would not need two Global Mirror links between the Master and its Subordinate storage servers. Dedicated ports for Global Mirror control communication between Master and Subordinate storage servers provides a maximum of responsiveness.

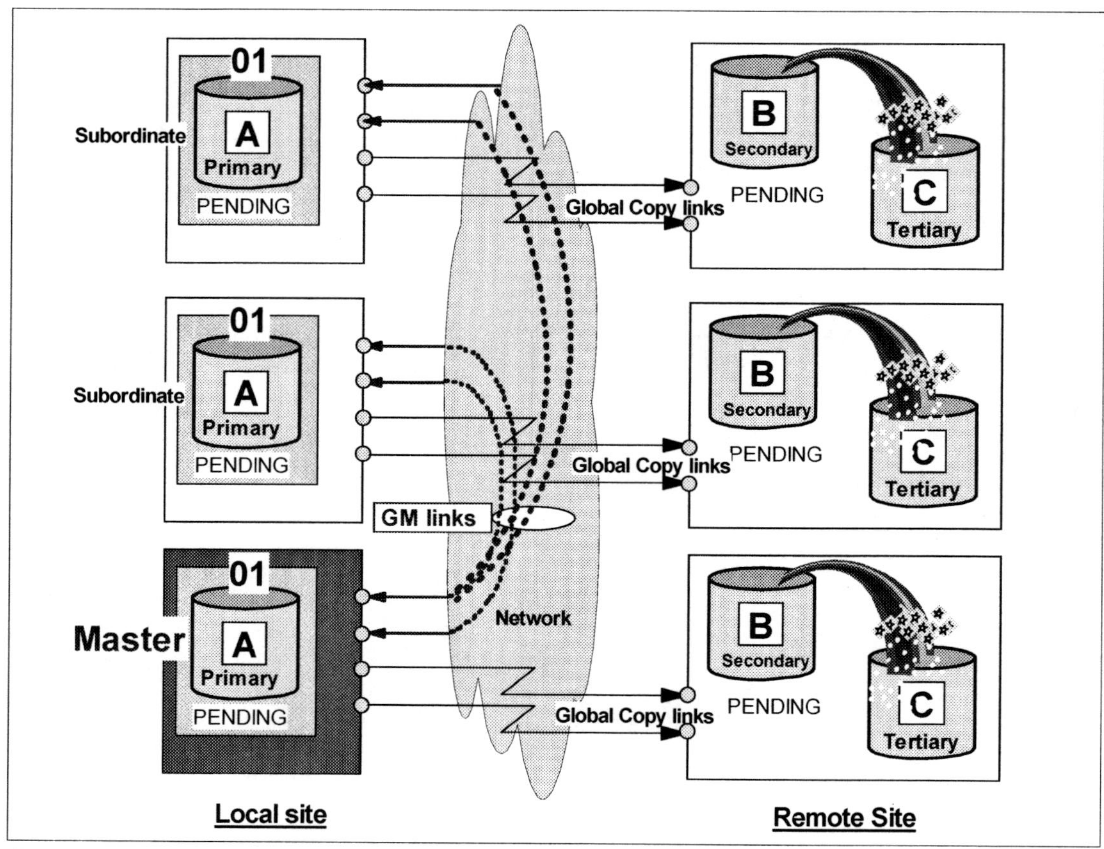

Figure 24-6 Dedicated Global Mirror links and dedicated Global Copy links

24.5 Connectivity between local and remote site

The choice of which interface to choose for Global Mirror management may depend on how a 2-site configuration is designed. A multi-host configuration allows you to configure and manage the remote site by the host systems at the remote site and vice versa for the local site. This does not require the use of inband commands. Alternatively, single site host configuration may allow you to even access the remote site by the local host, when the distance does not exceed standard FICON distance.

24.5.1 Multi-site host connectivity

Figure 24-7 shows a configuration with hosts connected to their local storage servers. Neither site has a host connection to the storage servers at the other site. This may be the case when the distance exceeds standard FICON capabilities. Global Mirror is a long-distance 2-site solution and allows you to put both sites apart at any distance. Figure 24-7 may be the basic configuration idea and the PPRC FCP links may be extended over either DWDM or Gbit Ethernet. Neither host can connect to the storage servers at the other site.

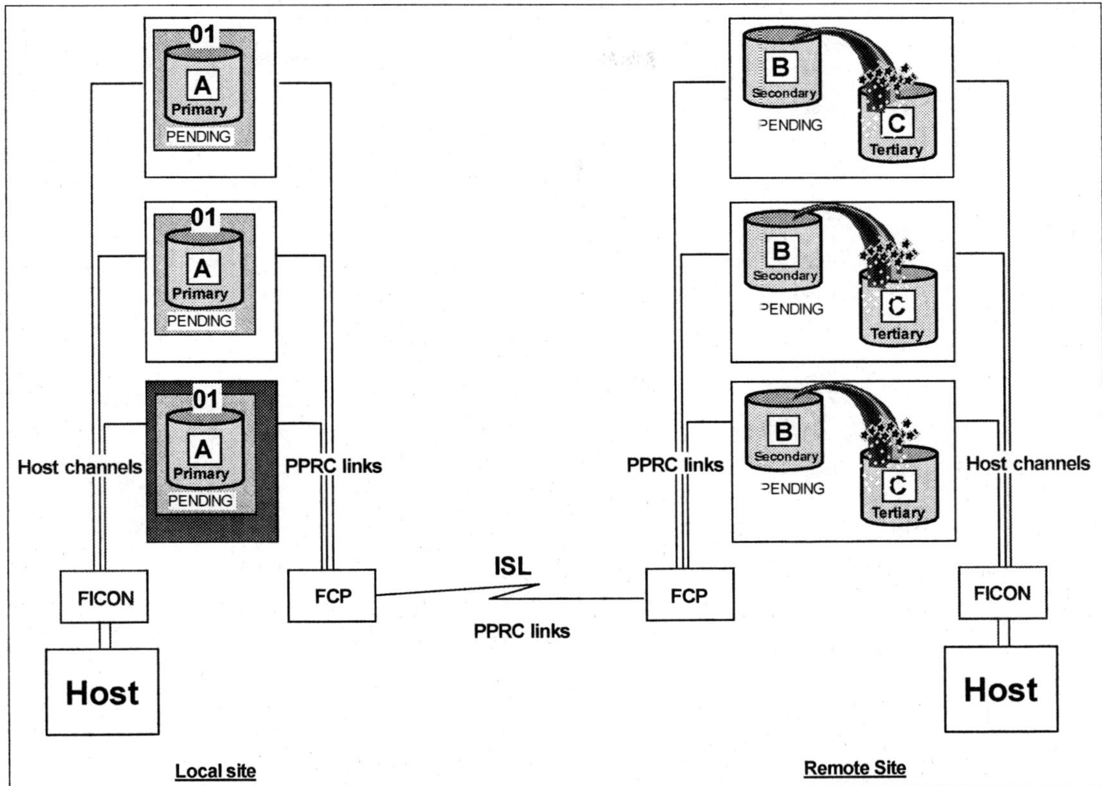

Figure 24-7 Host connectivity at both sites

In case of a failure at the local site the host at the remote site may recover from the Global Mirror configuration as discussed in "Recovery scenario after primary site failure" on page 271. Note that the host at the remote site requires a disk environment that is independent from the Global Mirror environment.

All Global Mirror related management commands may be issued at the concerned site. The local host may issue all commands that address the primary volumes. All commands targeted to the secondary or tertiary volumes may be issued from the remote host. From a management viewpoint this may not be the most desired solution approach to manage a Global Mirror environment. Figure 24-7 shows a typical 2-site disaster recovery solution with the application host at the local site. The host at the remote site may be a stand-by host or a system that hosts non-critical applications and may be expanded through CBU once a site failover happens from the local to the remote site.

24.5.2 Single site host connectivity

Figure 24-8 shows a single host configuration. This is again a 2-site disaster recovery solution although there is only a host in one site. Disaster recovery capability is provided on the storage server level.

Depending on how far apart both sites are from each other, there are two basic approaches:

1. Both sites are in FICON distance.

   This allows you to connect the host to both sites and manage either site from the host via conventional Global Mirror inband commands. Such a configuration may use cascaded FICON directors configurations to interconnect both sites by FICON channels. In case of a primary site failure, only on the scope of the storage servers, the failover may be managed from the local host. See "Recovery scenario after primary site failure" on page 271.

Attention: In this situation, you should seriously consider using a synchronous solution, especially Metro Mirror. Metro Mirror provides excellent disaster recovery protection with almost no impact to host I/O at short distances. Additionally, Metro Mirror environments tend to be significantly less complex than Global Mirror environments.

2. Both sites are not interconnected over FICON due to extended distances or the required network technology for FICON is not available.

   Global Mirror management concerning the remote storage servers may be issued through inband commands from the local site. This is limited to FlashCopy operations only. Besides the TSO and ICKDSF inband FlashCopy commands, you may consider to use DS CLI commands that provide also corresponding inband commands, which you issue at the local site and target to the remote site.

   Recovery operations as described in "Recovery scenario after primary site failure" on page 271 require host connectivity at the remote site when utilizing TSO or ICKDSF based Global Mirror commands. This may lead to a short term host installation at the remote site. To quickly recover the remote site you may consider using DS CLI commands, which do not require any host connectivity.

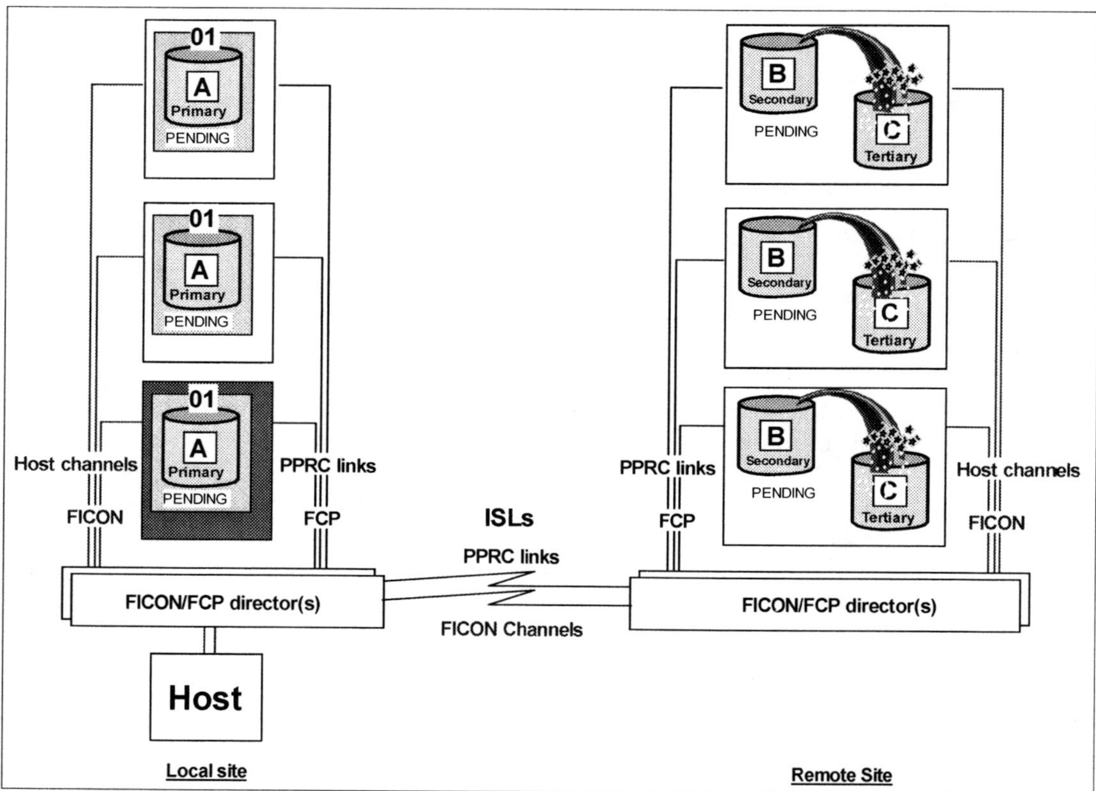

Figure 24-8 Single site host connectivity - with or without FICON connectivity between sites

Figure 24-8 indicates more than a single FICON/FCP director at both sites for availability reasons. Note that the Master and Subordinate PPRC paths are covered in a local SAN fabric represented in Figure 24-8 as FICON/FCP directors. Such a single host configuration suggests to physically separate host servers from storage servers.

24.6 Recovery scenario after primary site failure

This section covers the steps that you need to follow when a primary site failure requires you to recover at the secondary site when utilizing Global Mirror. This scenario does not discuss whether this is single site host connectivity or multi-site host connectivity, as discussed in 24.5, "Connectivity between local and remote site" on page 268.

24.6.1 Normal Global Mirror operation

Figure 24-9 shows a simple configuration with Global Mirror active and running.

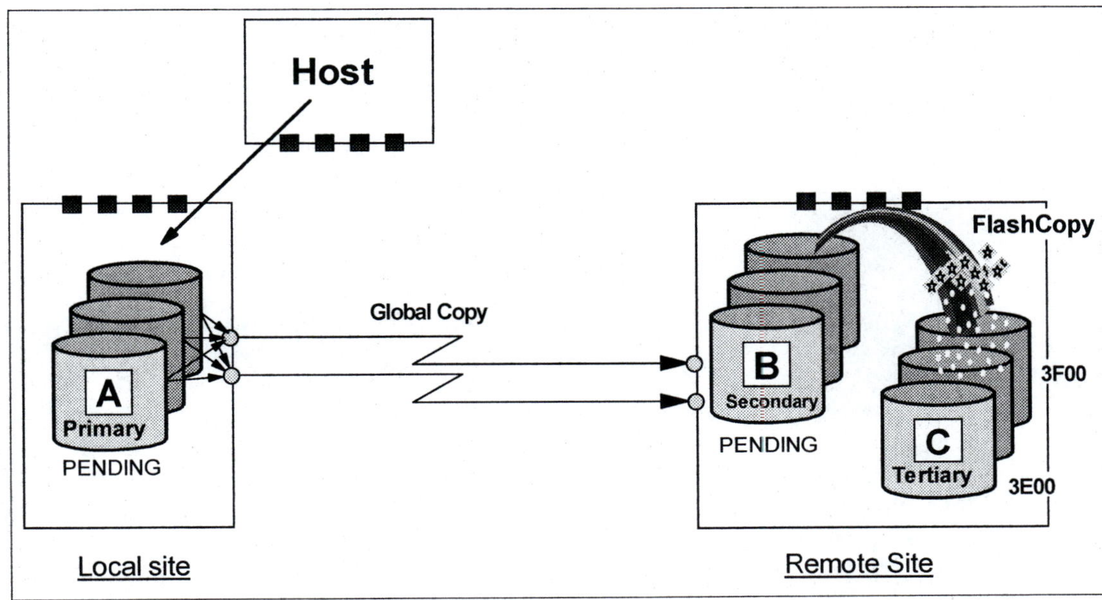

Figure 24-9 Normal Global Mirror operation

Host writes are replicated through Global Copy and Consistency Groups are created as tertiary copies. The B volume is a Global Copy secondary volume and FlashCopy source volume. The C volume is the FlashCopy target volume. The FlashCopy relationship is a particular relationship. See Chapter 6., "FlashCopy overview" on page 45.

24.6.2 Primary site failure

A failure at the local or primary site stops all I/O to and from the local storage servers. This may have some impact on the formation of Consistency Groups because the entire process is managed and controlled by the Master storage server that is the primary storage server. And this storage server just failed and cannot communicate any longer with its partners at the remote site.

The goal is to swap to the remote site and restart the applications. This requires, first, to make the set of consistent volumes at the remote site available before the application can restart at the remote site.

Once the local site is back and operational again, return to the local site. Before returning to the local site, apply changes from the remote site to the local site that may have happened when the application continued at the remote site. Then swap quickly back to the local site and restart the application where it used to run (see Figure 24-10).

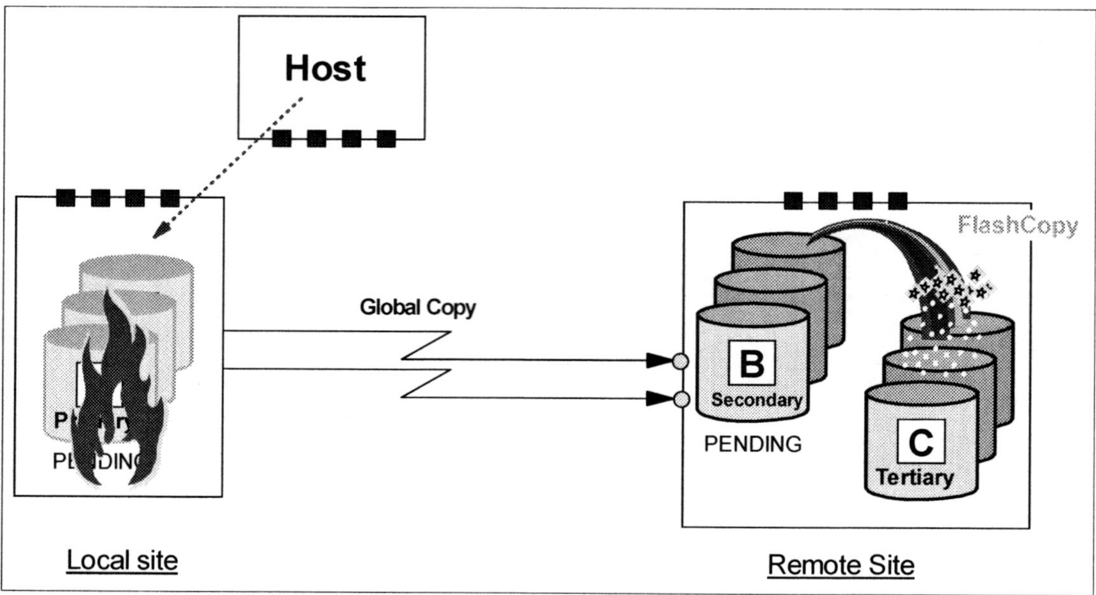

Figure 24-10 Primary site fails

When the local Global Mirror storage server fails, then Global Mirror can no longer form Consistency Groups.

Depending on the state of the local Global Mirror storage server, you may be able to terminate the Global Mirror session. Usually this is not possible because the storage server may not respond any more. Host application I/O may have failed and the application ended. This goes usually along with messages or SNMP alerts that indicate the problem. A proper automation may pick these messages up and start to react. A prominent example is a complete disaster recovery solution like Geographically Dispersed Parallel Sysplex™ (GDPS) or eRCMF.

If the formation of a Consistency Group was in progress, the FlashCopy state between the B volumes and the C volumes in the remote storage server may not be the same at this point-in-time for all relationships. Some FlashCopy pairs may have completed the FlashCopy phase to form a new Consistency Group and committed the changes already. Others may not have completed yet and are in the middle of forming their consistent copy and remain in a revertible state. And there is no Master any longer that controls and coordinates what may still go on for a brief period at the remote site. This requires a closer look at these FlashCopy relationships at the remote site before you continue to work with these volumes. There will be more discussion of this in the following sections. First, however, we just bring the B volumes into a usable state using the failover command.

24.6.3 Failover from B to A

Because the primary storage server may no longer be accessible, the following processing occurs from the remote site with a corresponding host connected to the remote storage servers. You may use either TSO commands or ICKDSF to issue corresponding commands to the remote storage servers.

When there is no host connected to the remote storage server, you may still manage the remote storage server through the Web based GUI interface or through DS CLI commands. This will allow you to perform all of the following steps also. We assume a host connection to the remote storage server that issues the Global Mirror commands to recover at the remote site and resume the application at the remote site (see Figure 24-11).

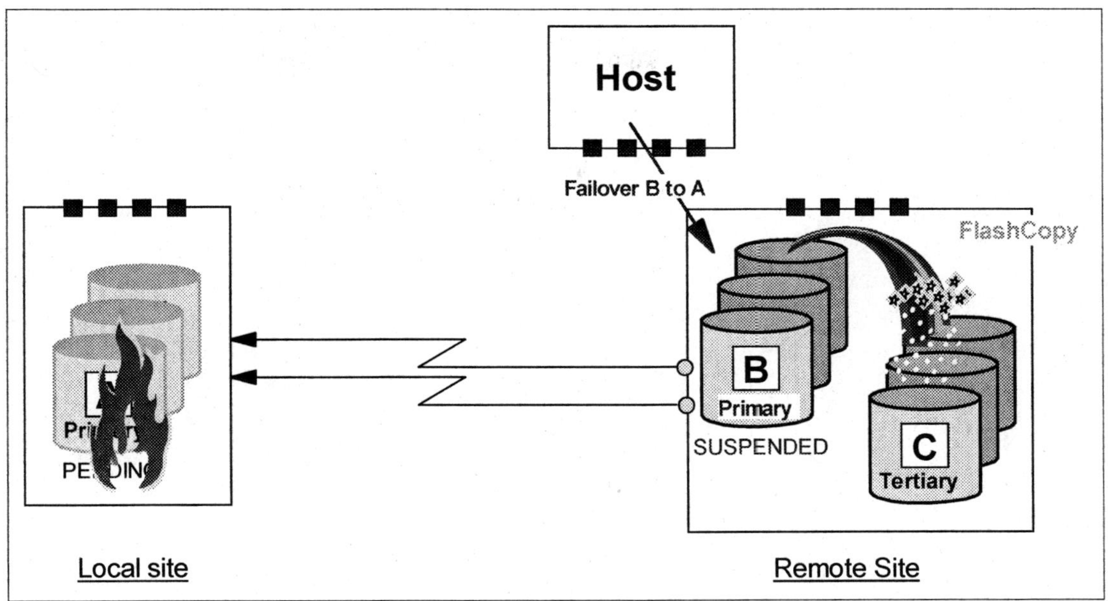

Figure 24-11 Failover from B to A

A FAILOVER to the Global Copy secondary volume turns the secondary volumes into primary volumes and suspends these volumes immediately. This sets the stage for change recording when application updates change the B volumes. Change recording in turn allows you to just re-synchronize the changes later from the B to the A volumes before returning to the local site and resume the application again in the local site. But at this stage the B volume does not contain consistent data and is still useless. We just changed its PPRC state from secondary to PRIMARY_SUSPENDED. Volume A remains PRIMARY_FULLDUPLEX unless a host writes to it.

The key with this establish PPRC command is the FAILOVER option. Understand also that the B volume is the primary volume and the A volume is the secondary when you issue the establish pair command, even though A may not be available in the case of a storage server failure, and the state of A remains PRIMARY_FULLDUPLEX. See Example 24-4.

Example 24-4 ESTPAIR command with FAILOVER action

```
//* ---------------------------- TSO --------- FAILOVER (3) ------ ***
//* ESTABLISH PPRC-XD PAIR(S) FAILOVER PRIM(B) -> SEC(A)           ***
//*                                                                ***
//*   NOTE: ACTION IS NOT VALID WITH MODE(COPY)                    ***
//* -------------------------------------------------------------- ***
//EPAIRFO EXEC PGM=IKJEFT01
//SYSPRINT  DD SYSOUT=*
//SYSTSPRT  DD SYSOUT=*
//SYSTSIN   DD DDNAME=SYSIN

 CESTPAIR  DEVN (X'3C00')                   +
           PRIM (X'3C00' 73081 X'00' X'0C')  +
           SEC  (X'2C00' 27131 X'00' X'0C')  +
           ACTION(FAILOVER)                 +
           ONLINSEC(NO)  MSGREQ(NO)  CRIT(NO) +
           OPTION(XD)                CASCADE(NO)
```

Note that this command just changes the PPRC state of the secondary volumes from SECONDARY_PENDING to PRIMARY_SUSPENDED. This command does not communicate to the other storage server at all, even though it is specified in the SEC parameter of the command. Once all FAILOVER commands succeed successfully, move on to the next step.

24.6.4 Verify for valid Consistency Group state

You have to investigate whether all FlashCopy relationships are in a consistent state. This means you have to query all FlashCopy relationships between B and C, which are part of the Consistency Group, to determine the state of the FlashCopy relationship at the time of the local site failure. Global Mirror might have been in the middle of forming a Consistency Group and FlashCopy may have not been completed to create a complete set of consistent C volumes (see Figure 24-12).

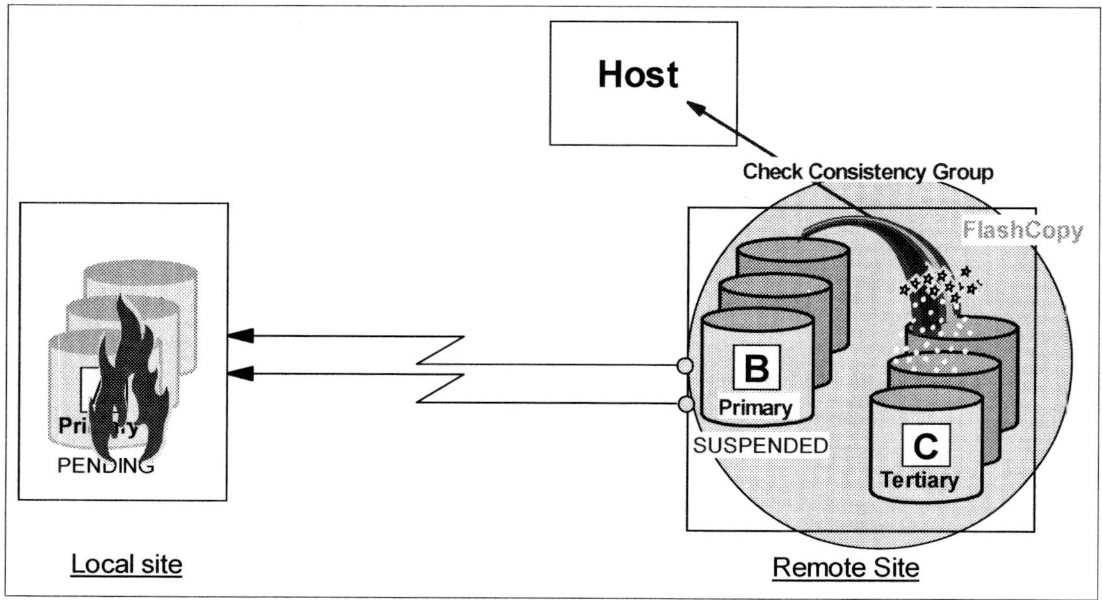

Figure 24-12 Check Consistency Group state

Each FlashCopy pair needs a FlashCopy query to identify its state.

If the local site is still accessible and even the primary storage server, you may consider using the RQUERY command to investigate on an LSS level first (Example 24-5).

Example 24-5 Query FlashCopy status via RQUERY on LSS level

```
RQUERY     SNBR(01) VOLSER(XX2C00) ACTION(GMPSTAT)
 RQUERY Output Volser(XX2C00) Action(GMPSTAT) Version(001)
 SNbr LSS GMPStatus  RvrtStatus FCSeqNbr TotVol OOSVol OOSTrks
 --   --  ---------- ---------- -------- ------ ------ --------
 01   0C  CGInPrgrs  AllNRv&Eq  428E2727      1      1 00007862
 READY
   RQUERY     SNBR(01) VOLSER(XX2D00) ACTION(GMPSTAT)
 RQUERY Output Volser(XX2D00) Action(GMPSTAT) Version(001)
 SNbr LSS GMPStatus  RvrtStatus FCSeqNbr TotVol OOSVol OOSTrks
 --   --  ---------- ---------- -------- ------ ------ --------
 01   0D  CGInPrgrs  AllNRv&Eq  428E2727      2      2 0000812C
 READY
```

Example 24-5 shows two pieces of information that are key to determine whether the C volume set is consistent or needs intervention to correct some states.

RvrtStatus or revertible status in Example 24-5 is indicated as *AllNRv&Eq* or all non-revertible and equal. This means that all FlashCopy operations for Global Mirror for volumes within this concerned LSS completed successfully and all changes are committed. This is a good state and does not require any further corrective actions. The query command shows the same for the second LSS within this Global Mirror session. An additional indication in Example 24-5 is the *FCSeqNbr* or FlashCopy sequence number that is equal for both involved LSSs.

Most likely the primary storage server does not respond any longer. Then you have to target the query commands to the FlashCopy source volumes. Example 24-6 shows FlashCopy query commands of four FlashCopy source volumes or B volumes.

Example 24-6 FlashCopy query of four FlashCopy relationships

```
TIME-09:36:44 AM. CPU-00:00:00 SERVICE-68 SESSION-00:00:00 JUNE 15,2005
READY
FCQUERY   DEVN (X'6400')
FCQUERY Formatted -2
DEVN SSID LSS CCA  CU      SERIAL       ACT    MAX XC PC CC RV  SEQNUM
6400 0002  00  00 1750 0000000AAVCA       1  50099  N  S  N  N 42B03957
FCQUERY COMMAND COMPLETED FOR DEVICE 6400. COMPLETION CODE: 00

FCQUERY   DEVN (X'6401')
FCQUERY Formatted -2
DEVN SSID LSS CCA  CU      SERIAL       ACT    MAX XC PC CC RV  SEQNUM
6401 0002  00  01 1750 0000000AAVCA       1  50099  N  S  N  N 42B03957
FCQUERY COMMAND COMPLETED FOR DEVICE 6401. COMPLETION CODE: 00

FCQUERY   DEVN (X'6402')
FCQUERY Formatted -2
DEVN SSID LSS CCA  CU      SERIAL       ACT    MAX XC PC CC RV  SEQNUM
6402 0002  00  02 1750 0000000AAVCA       1  50099  N  S  N  N 42B03957
FCQUERY COMMAND COMPLETED FOR DEVICE 6402. COMPLETION CODE: 00

FCQUERY   DEVN (X'6403')
FCQUERY Formatted -2
DEVN SSID LSS CCA  CU      SERIAL       ACT    MAX XC PC CC RV  SEQNUM
6403 0002  00  03 1750 0000000AAVCA       1  50099  N  S  N  N 42B03957
FCQUERY COMMAND COMPLETED FOR DEVICE 6403. COMPLETION CODE: 00
```

Example 24-6 shows for each single FlashCopy relationship a column headed *RV*, which stands for *revertible*. An *N* indicates that this FlashCopy relationship is not revertible and all changes are committed. All volumes show the same information for *RV*. The other column that you have to check is the *SEQNUM* or FlashCopy sequence number. This number is also identical for all four volumes in Example 24-6, which is good information. This leads you to conclude that:

- All FlashCopy pairs are non-revertible.
- All FlashCopy sequence numbers are equal.

No further action is necessary and the set of C volumes is consistent and a good copy.

Figure 24-13 shows the consistency group creation process. The action required depends on the state of the consistency group creation process when the failure occurred.

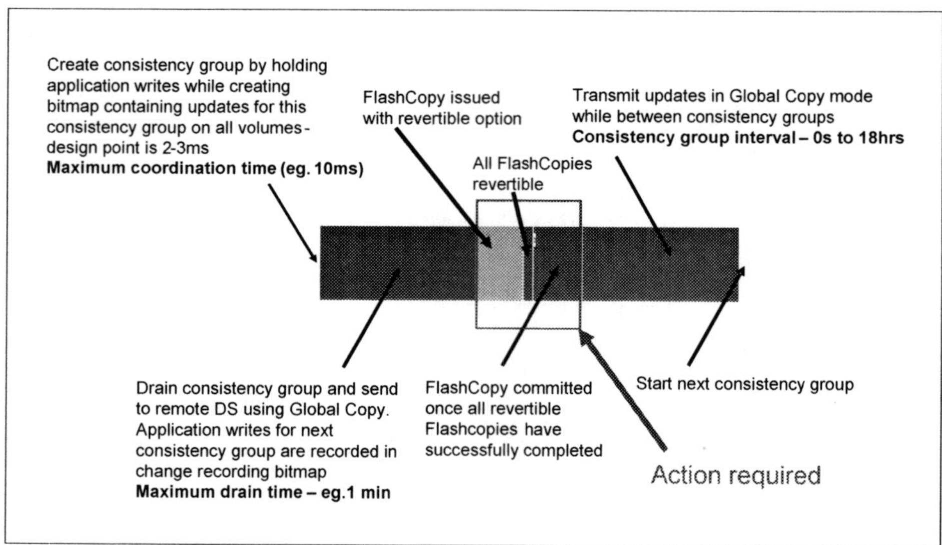

Figure 24-13 FlashCopy consistency group creation process

Depending on when the failure occurs, there are some combinations of revertible states and FlashCopy sequence numbers that need different corrective actions. Use Table 24-1. This is a decision table and reads in the following way: When column 2 AND column 3 are true, then take the action in column 4. Column 5 contains additional comments. Do this for each of the four cases. The cases are described in chronological order, starting from the left.

Table 24-1 Consistency Group and FlashCopy validation decision table

	Are all FC relationships are revertible?	Are all FC sequence numbers are equal?	Action to take	Comments
Case 1	NO.	YES.	No action needed. All C volumes are consistent.	CG formation ended.
Case 2	SOME - Some FlashCopy pairs are revertible and others are not revertible.	Revertible FlashCopy pairs' sequence numbers are equal. And non-revertible FlashCopy pairs sequence numbers are equal, but do not match the revertible FlashCopies sequence number.	*revert* FC relations.	Some FlashCopy pairs are running in a Consistency Group process and some have not yet started their incremental process.
Case 3	YES.	YES.	*revert* to all FC relations.	All FlashCopy pairs are in a new Consistency Group process and none have finished their incremental process.

	Are all FC relationships are revertible?	Are all FC sequence numbers are equal?	Action to take	Comments
Case 4	SOME - Some FlashCopy pairs are revertible and others are not revertible.	YES.	*commit* FC relations.	Some FlashCopy pairs are running in a Consistency Group process and some have already finished their incremental process.

If you see a situation other than the above four situations, then the Global Mirror Mechanism has been corrupted.

Case 1: FlashCopies still committed

This indicates the situation where all FlashCopy operations have completed their task (and the next FlashCopy operations have not been started). In this situation, we don't need any action to correct the FlashCopy status because we have consistent data in all C volumes. This state is also reached after the FlashCopies are complete, and Global Mirror is waiting to create the next Consistency Group.

Case 2: FlashCopies partially issued

The next step is to issue a FlashCopy command to all relevant volumes. When the FlashCopy is issued, its sequence number is incremented. This process is very fast, but if a failure were to occur at this exact moment, so the FlashCopy commands will have been issued and some will not.

In this case, there is a group of FlashCopy pairs that are all *revertible* and another group of FlashCopy pairs that are all *non-revertible*. Consistency can be restored if these two criteria are true:

- The FlashCopy sequence number for all revertible pairs is equal.
- The FlashCopy sequence number for all non-revertible pairs is equal too.

Then issue the FlashCopy withdraw command with the REVERT action to restore the FlashCopy relations to their prior state. You may run this command against all volumes. As stated before, it would not do anything to the non-revertible FlashCopy pairs but return an error message.

Case 3: FlashCopies all revertible

In the case where all of the pairs are revertible and all FlashCopy sequence numbers are equal, this indicates that all FlashCopy operations were running and none completed their task for the Consistency Group formation. This is indicated by the fact that all relationships are still in a revertible state and nothing was finished and committed. And all were involved in the very same Consistency Group set with identical FlashCopy sequence numbers. This suggests to return to the previous Consistency Group.

Example 24-7 shows a TSO command to withdraw a FlashCopy relationship between B and C volumes using the REVERT action parameter.

Example 24-7 Withdraw Global Mirror FlashCopy relationship with ACTION(REVERT)

```
//* -------------------------------------------------------------- ***
//FCWITHDR EXEC PGM=IKJEFT01
//SYSPRINT  DD SYSOUT=*
//SYSTSPRT  DD SYSOUT=*
```

```
//SYSTSIN   DD DDNAME=SYSIN

 FCWITHDR  SDEVN(X'6400' TDEVN(X'6500') ACTION(REVERT)
```

Example 24-7 restores the Consistency Group level between the source and target volume to the prior state before the current FlashCopy ran and resets the revertible state to NO. Then the FlashCopy relationship will be terminated.

When the FlashCopy relationship is not in a revertible state, the withdraw operation is not executed, as Example 24-8 proves.

Example 24-8 FlashCopy withdraw attempt with REVERT to a non-revertible state

```
READY
 FCWITHDR  SDEVN(X'6400') TDEVN(X'6500') ACTION(REVERT)
FLASHCOPY WITHDRAW DEVICE NOT IN A REVERTIBLE STATE
FCWITHDR COMMAND UNSUCCESSFUL FOR DEVICE 6400. COMPLETION CODE: 08
READY
```

Case 4: FlashCopies partially committed

When at the failure point, some of the FlashCopy operations completed their task to create a consistent copy and committed this process, they are no longer revertible. Other FlashCopy relationships may have not completed their task to contribute to a new Consistency Group formation. They are still in a revertible state. But all have the same FlashCopy sequence number. So all were involved in the very same Consistency Group. This allows you to commit the revertible FlashCopy relationships. To make the task easier, you may run a corresponding COMMIT to all FlashCopy pairs. Non-revertible FlashCopy relations would just return an error message.

Example 24-9 shows a FlashCopy withdraw with ACTION(COMMIT). This commits the FlashCopy relationship to its current state and resets the revertible state to NO. Note again, when you issue this command to FlashCopy pairs that are not revertible any longer, you are going to see only an error message and no action is performed.

Example 24-9 Withdraw Global Mirror FlashCopy relationship with ACTION(COMMIT)

```
//* ---------------------------------------------------------- ***
//FCWITHDR EXEC PGM=IKJEFT01
//SYSPRINT  DD SYSOUT=*
//SYSTSPRT  DD SYSOUT=*
//SYSTSIN   DD DDNAME=SYSIN

FCWITHDR  SDEVN(X'6400' TDEVN(X'6500') ACTION(COMMIT)
```

24.6.5 Establish consistent data on B volumes

At this point only the C volumes comprise a set of consistent data volumes. The B volumes per definition do not provide consistent data volumes, because Global Copy does not provide data consistency.

The involvement of both remaining volumes at the secondary site is required to create two identical volume sets. A second identical copy is necessary because you do not want to destroy your only good copy. Then an application restart may be repeated when something went wrong the first time, which is not unlikely after a disaster failover from the local site to the remote site. When you discover after the restart that something went wrong, you just FlashCopy again from the good copy and start again and you did not lose the state of your data that was good after the site swap. The aim is to have a consistent set of volumes to work with at the remote site and still have a copy of the data from before. The next step is then to create the same consistency on the B volumes what you have on the C volumes. This can be achieved with a new FlashCopy parameter ACTION(FRR) in the FlashCopy establish command. FRR stands for *fast reverse restore* (Figure 24-14). There are corresponding DS CLI commands.

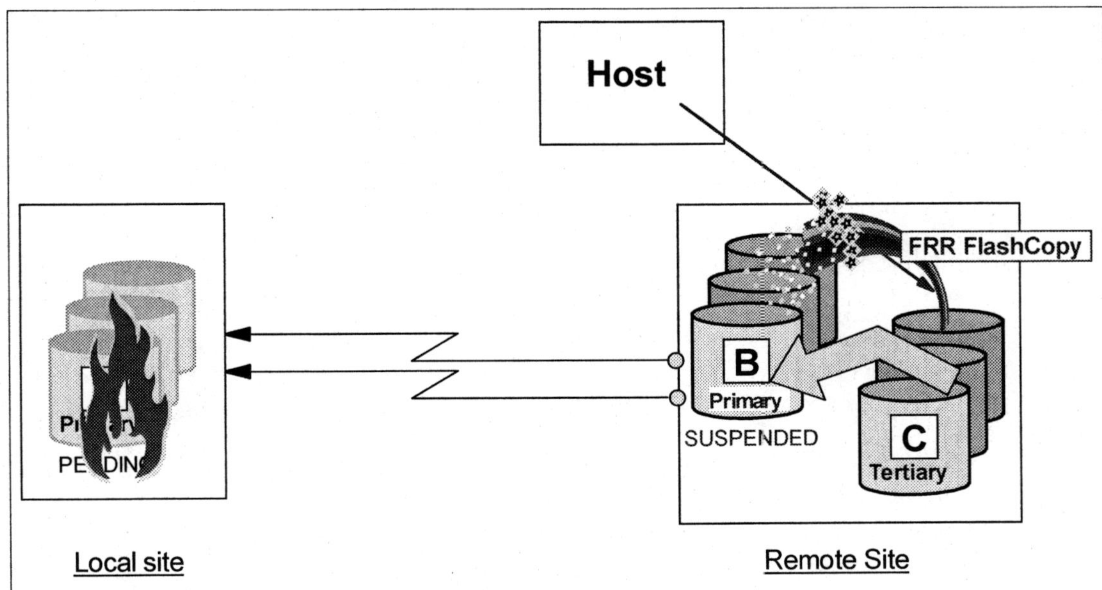

Figure 24-14 Establish consistent set of B volumes with C volumes as source

The command with fast reverse restore (FRR) is aimed to the FlashCopy target volume (C) as the new FlashCopy source, as Figure 24-14 shows. FRR is the parameter as implemented in the TSO FlashCopy command. The DS CLI uses a new FlashCopy command, **`reverseflash`**, for this particular FlashCopy operation with the parameter **`-fast`**.

FRR in the TSO FCESTABL command implies the following FlashCopy attributes:

- Start background copy from C to B.
- No change recording.
- Target volume may be a PPRC primary volume, which here is the suspended Global Copy primary volume. This is needed because the previous FAILOVER command changed the Global Copy secondary PENDING volume state to primary SUSPENDED state.
- Not persistent, which ends this FlashCopy relationship once the background copy completes. This allows you to check that all FRR operations completed before moving on to the next step.

FRR replicates all data from C to B and provides a physical copy on B from C — with some exceptions. Note that the previous NOCOPY relationship between B and C caused some I/Os from B to C. Changed tracks between two Consistency Group creation points will be preserved on the C volume after being copied over from the B volumes before they change there.

These tracks arrive at the C volume between Consistency Group formation and do not contribute to a consistent state because not all required data is physically on the C volume. So after the FRR triggered background copy completed from C to B the C volume is actually not usable. You need to establish as a next step another FlashCopy from B to C to make both volumes really identical. This FlashCopy may be the one you used to create a Global Mirror environment and is going to position the Global Mirror session for a following restart.

But first we perform the FRR from C to B and provide the corresponding TSO command in Example 24-10.

Example 24-10 Create consistent set of B volumes

```
//* ---------------------------- TSO ------------- FAILOVER (4) -- ***
//* FLASHCOPY C -> B FAST REVERSE RESTORE (BACKGROUND COPY C -> B) ***
//*        3E00 -> 3C00                                            ***
//*                                                                ***
//* NOTE: WAIT TILL ALL BACKGROUND COPIES COMPLETED BEFORE CONT.   ***
//* NOTE: FRR DOES NOT ALLOW REMOTE(YES)                           ***
//* -------------------------------------------------------------- ***
//FCFRR   EXEC PGM=IKJEFT01
//SYSPRINT  DD SYSOUT=*
//SYSTSPRT  DD SYSOUT=*
//SYSTSIN   DD DDNAME=SYSIN

 FCESTABL  SDEVN(X'3E00')  TDEVN(X'3C00') ACTION(FRR)
```

Note that the FlashCopy source volume for this command is the former FlashCopy target volume and vice versa. ACTION(FRR) combines all particular FlashCopy attributes into this single parameter.

You have to wait until all FRR operations complete successfully, before you proceed with the next step. Note that when the background copy completes, the FlashCopy relation will end. This is what you may query to determine when all FRR operations are complete.

24.6.6 Reestablish the FlashCopy relationship between B and C volumes

Here you may establish the former FlashCopy relationship between the B and the C volume, which was established before for Global Mirror (Example 24-11). This step is in preparation for eventually returning to the production environment at the local site, and setting up Global Mirror again. This is exactly the same FlashCopy command you may have used to establish FlashCopy when you created the Global Mirror environment in the first place. See 23.2.4, “Introduce FlashCopy” on page 248.

Example 24-11 Reestablish FlashCopy between B and C volume with MODE(ASYNC)

```
//* ---------------------------- TSO ------------ CREATE (3) ----- ***
//* FLASHCOPY B -> C START CHANGE RECORDING NOCOPY ETC. THROUGH    ***
//*                   MODE(ASYNC) OPTION (GET READY FOR GM)        ***
//* -------------------------------------------------------------- ***
//* SOURCE AND TARGET REQUIRED                                     ***
//* -------------------------------------------------------------- ***
//FCESTBL EXEC PGM=IKJEFT01
//SYSPRINT  DD SYSOUT=*
//SYSTSPRT  DD SYSOUT=*
//SYSTSIN   DD DDNAME=SYSIN

 FCESTABL  SDEVN(X'3C00') TDEVN(X'3E00') MODE(ASYNC)
```

Now you may restart the applications at the remote site using the B volumes. Note the B volumes are Global Copy primary volumes in SUSPENDED state, which implies that change recording takes place. Later this allows you to just RESYNC from B to A before returning to the local site.

Eventually you may also decide here to create another copy of this consistent set of volumes and create D volumes or preserve this set of consistent volumes onto tape. When you create the D volumes, this is just a plain FlashCopy command. Example 24-12 provides an example with the B volume as FlashCopy source volume and a new D volume as FlashCopy target.

Example 24-12 Create another set of consistent data volumes

```
//* ---------------------------- TSO ------------ CREATE (5) ----- ***
//* FLASHCOPY B -> D TO CREATE COPY TO WORK (TEST) WITH            ***
//* -------------------------------------------------------------- ***
//FCESTBL EXEC PGM=IKJEFT01
//SYSPRINT  DD SYSOUT=*
//SYSTSPRT  DD SYSOUT=*
//SYSTSIN   DD DDNAME=SYSIN

   FCESTABL  SDEVN(X'3C00')  TDEVN(X'3E02')
```

Note that this is a full volume FlashCopy. Because we re-established the Global Mirror related FlashCopy between B and C before, which includes the *start change recording* attribute, you can only use the same source volume for full volume FlashCopy. Since this is the first time we are creating the B to D relationship, an incremental FlashCopy is not possible. Also, only a single incremental relationship is allowed per source volume,

In a real disaster you might use the MODE(COPY) for the FlashCopy from B to C to remove the FlashCopy I/O overhead of MODE(ASYNC), which implies *start change recording* or incremental FlashCopy.

24.6.7 Restart application at remote site

At this stage you may restart the application at the remote site and work with the consistent set of B volumes (Figure 24-15).

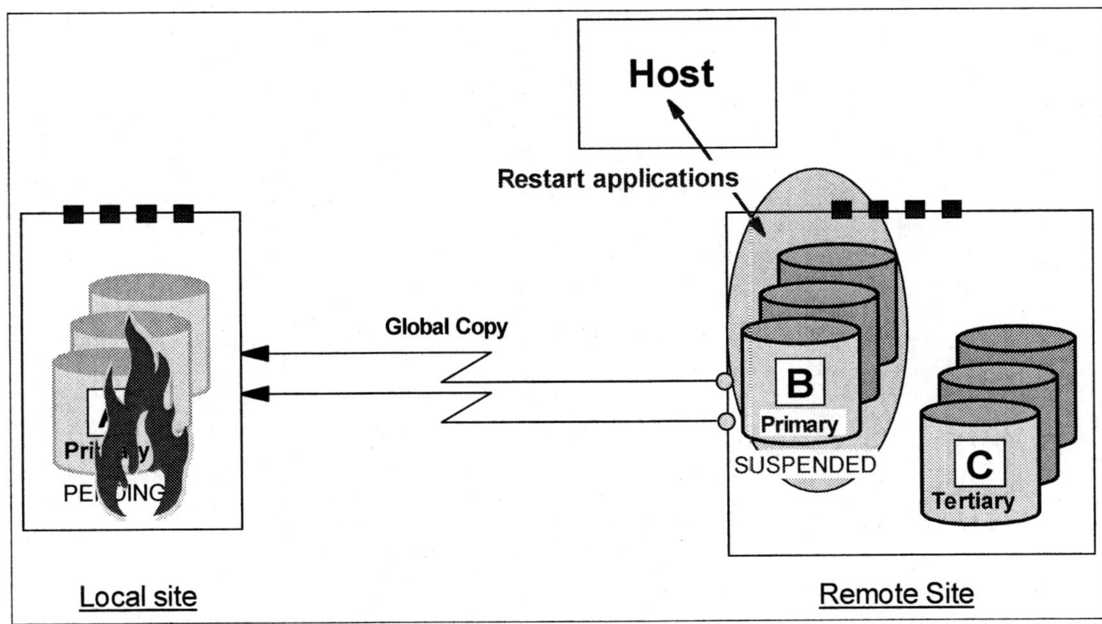

Figure 24-15 Restart applications at remote site

Note the primary SUSPENDED state of the B volumes, which implies change recording and indicates the changed tracks on the B volumes.

When the local site is about to become ready to receive the applications again and resume the operations in the local site, you prepare the remote site for the next step.

24.6.8 Prepare to return to local site

The local site is back and operational again. Assume that the local site did not lose the data at the time when the swap to the remote site occurred. It is then possible to just re-synchronize the changed data from B to A before returning the application to the local site. This is achieved with a FAILBACK from B to A (Figure 24-16).

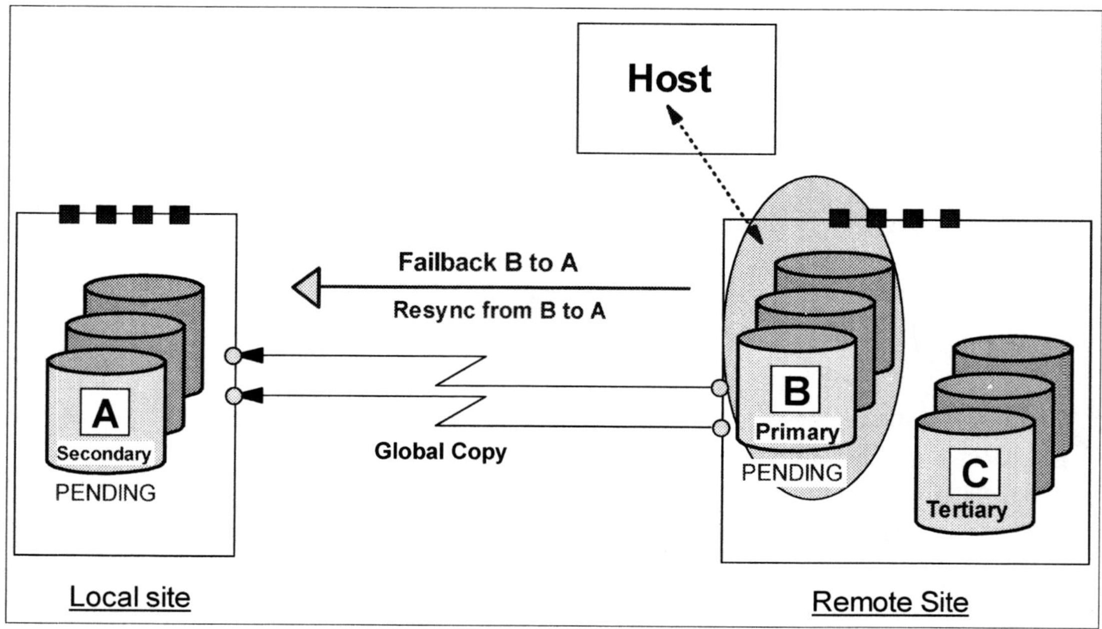

Figure 24-16 Failback from B to A to prepare for return to local site

Note the FAILBACK is issued to the B volume as the primary and the A volume as the secondary. This command changes the A volume from its previous state primary PENDING to secondary PENDING and starts to re-synchronize the changes from the B to A volume.

Before the FAILBACK, ensure that the PPRC paths are also established from the remote site LSS to its corresponding local site LSS. Note that PPRC over Fibre Channel allows you to define PPRC paths in either direction on the very same PPRC link. During this operation the application just continues at the remote site to minimize the application down for the site swap. Example 24-13 shows a TSO command example to FAILBACK from the B to A volume.

Example 24-13 FAILBACK from B to A volume before returning to the local site

```
//* ----------------------- PPRC FAILBACK B -> A  ---------------- ***
//EPAIRFB EXEC PGM=IKJEFT01
//SYSPRINT  DD SYSOUT=*
//SYSTSPRT  DD SYSOUT=*
//SYSTSIN   DD DDNAME=SYSIN

 CESTPAIR  DEVN (X'3C00')                      +
           PRIM (X'3C00' 73081 X'00' X'0C')    +
           SEC  (X'2C00' 27131 X'00' X'0C')    +
           ACTION(FAILBACK)                    +
           ONLINSEC(NO)  MSGREQ(NO)  CRIT(NO) +
           OPTION  (XD)              CASCADE(NO)
```

A remark on the ONLINSEC parameter here: With ONLINSEC(NO) it is checked whether any connected system has the concerned secondary volume, here device number 2C00, online. When it is detected in the corresponding path group information in the storage server that a system has this volume as ONLINE, the CESTPAIR will not be executed. This is a safety precaution and protects you from overwriting an active volume by accident. On the other side, there may be a z/VM system, for example, which has this volume also defined and is IPLed with this device as ONLINE during startup. The TSO commands are executed in another z/OS system and will fail the CESTPAIR.

24.6.9 Return to local site

Once the local site is ready for the swap from remote to local, quiesce the application in the remote site. Then a FAILOVER - FAILBACK sequence from the A to B volumes will turn Global Copy back to what it used to be before the local site failure (Figure 24-17).

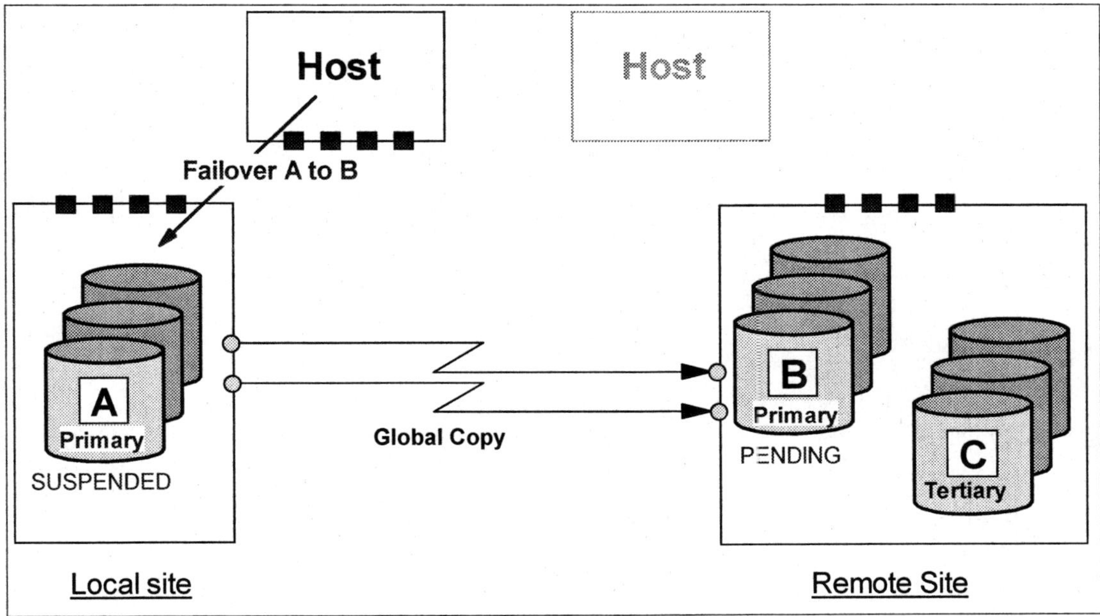

Figure 24-17 Failover from A to B

Figure 24-17 above indicates the action from the local host to FAILOVER from A to B volume. Again the FAILOVER just changes the volume state from secondary PENDING to primary SUSPENDED and starts to record potential track changes in bitmaps in the local storage servers.

Once the FAILOVER has completed, the host issues a FAILBACK command from A to B (Figure 24-18).

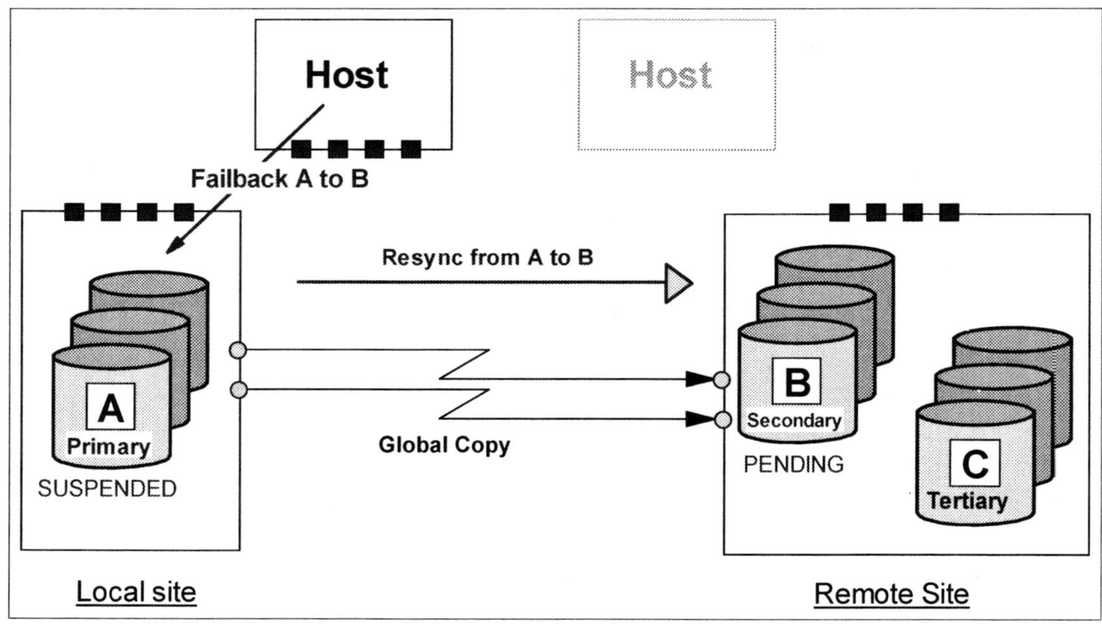

Figure 24-18 Failback from A to B and resync Global Copy volumes

Figure 24-18 shows the FAILBACK command issued from the local host to the local storage server. Note that the FAILBACK changes the state of the device at the remote site from primary PENDING to secondary PENDING and then starts to replicate updates from A to B.

In this case the application did not start yet, so there is no update at the local site. This will quickly change the state of the local volume A from primary SUSPENDED to primary PENDING, which is the normal state for Global Copy volume pairs (Figure 24-19).

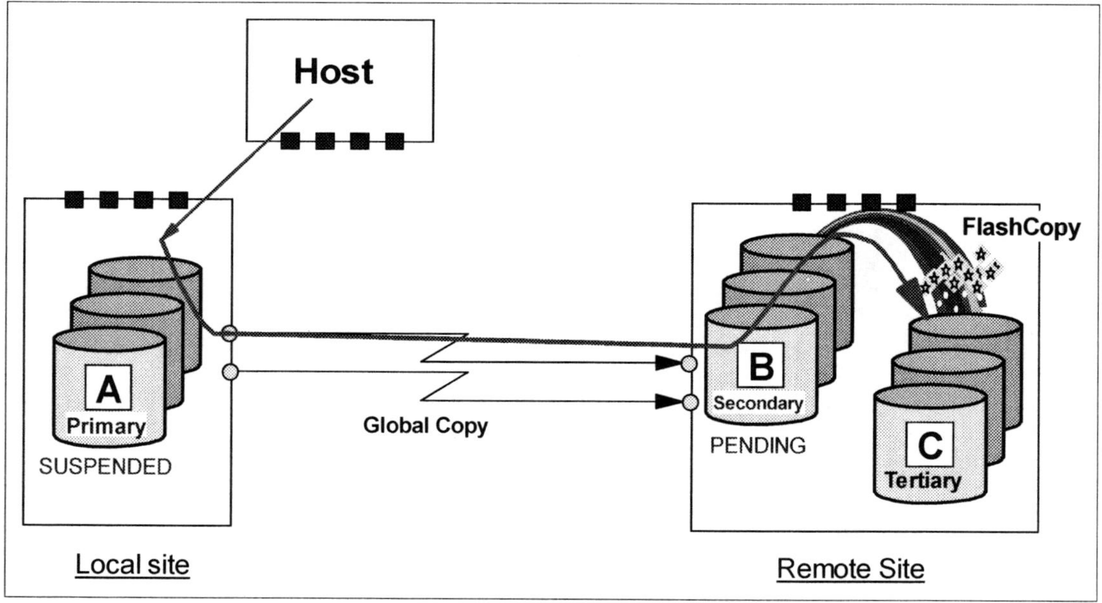

Figure 24-19 Establish Global Mirror FlashCopy relationship between B and C

Last but not least, if you did not already establish the FlashCopy relationship from B to C volumes during the FAILOVER / FAILBACK sequence at the remote site, then you have to do it now. This may be an inband FlashCopy as shown in Figure 24-19.

A TSO command example is provided in Example 24-14.

Example 24-14 Establish FlashCopy from B to C via inband TSO command

```
//* ---------------------------- TSO ------------ CREATE (3) ----- ***
//* FLASHCOPY B -> C START CHANGE RECORDING NOCOPY ETC. THROUGH    ***
//*                 MODE(ASYNC) OPTION (GET READY FOR GM)          ***
//* -------------------------------------------------------------- ***
//* Inband Command 2C00 is Global Copy primary                     ***
//*                LSS OC CAA 00 is  Global Copy secondary         ***
//*                              and FlashCopy source              ***
//*                LSS OD CAA 00 is  FlashCopy target              ***
//* -------------------------------------------------------------- ***
//FCESTBL EXEC PGM=IKJEFT01
//SYSPRINT  DD SYSOUT=*
//SYSTSPRT  DD SYSOUT=*
//SYSTSIN   DD DDNAME=SYSIN

 FCESTABL  DEVN(X'2C00') SOURCE(73081 00 OC)              +
                         TARGET(73081 00 OD)              +
                         REMOTE(YES) SSID(3C00) MODE(ASYNC)
```

The last step is to start the Global Mirror session again, as shown in Figure 24-20. Then the application may resume at the local site.

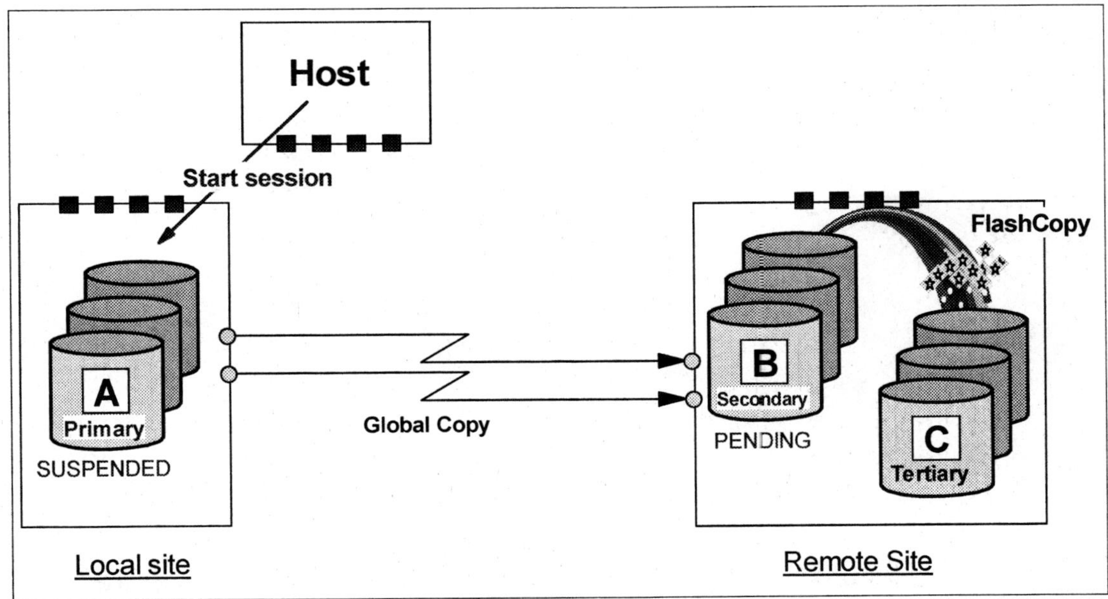

Figure 24-20 Start Global Mirror session and resume application I/O at local site

24.6.10 Conclusions on failover/failback example

This concludes the sequence of steps you have to go through for a swap to the remote site and coming back to the local site after service is restored at the local site.

In particular, the check on a valid Consistency Group after a primary site failure is a challenge when you consider a large configuration with thousands of remote copy volume pairs. The scope of managing Global Mirror as well as for Metro Mirror and Global Copy is on a volume pair. Each command usually addresses a single pair of volumes. With thousands of volume pairs, this requires automation, for example, to check all the FlashCopy relationships after a primary site failure. Note that for a planned site swap, you may have not to check for a valid Consistency Group because through a proper command sequence and verifying their successful completion, the exposure for an inconsistent group of C volumes is very minimal if at all.

Global Mirror is a 2-site solution with the freedom to bridge any distance between both sites. There are ready-to-use solutions and services available to implement a disaster recovery solution based on a 2-site remote copy configuration. This applies for many years for GDPS and eRCMF in the context with Metro Mirror. eRCMF supports not only Global Copy and Metro Mirror based configurations, but also Global Mirror configurations. GDPS is also going to support a 2-site disaster recovery based on Global Mirror. Another automated approach provides the Global Mirror Utility, GMU. See Part 9, “Solutions” on page 527 for more information on these solutions, which utilize Global Mirror in an automated fashion.

25

Global Mirror interfaces

In this chapter we provide an overview of what features are available to manage and control Global Mirror configurations. Especially, we detail the recently available TSO command support to manage Global Mirror configurations through new TSO commands.

We also include a brief discussion of DS CLI for managing a Global Mirror configuration in a z/OS environment and provide some basic DS CLI examples.

Then we describe the ICKDSF device facility utility and ANTRQST macro support to manage Global Mirror.

Last but not least, we also discuss the DS Storage Manager or Web-based user interface, GUI, which may be used for Global Mirror management.

For command details and syntax, refer to the corresponding manuals:

- *z/OS DFSMS Advanced Copy Services*, SC35-0428
- *IBM TotalStorage DS8000 Command-Line Interface User's Guide*, SC26-7625
- *Device Support Facility User's Guide and Reference Release 17*, SC35-0033

25.1 Interfaces to manage Global Mirror environments

Global Mirror is comprised of Global Copy and FlashCopy, which are both combined and utilized in an autonomic fashion by the microcode. There are commands intended for Global Copy and FlashCopy, as well as commands that address a Global Mirror session construct. All these components can be managed through one of the following interfaces or a combination of the following interfaces:

- TSO commands
- DS CLI
- ICKDSF
- GUI
- ANTRQST macro

There are differences not only in the look and feel between the different interfaces to manage Global Mirror, but also on the number of options, parameters, and attributes to achieve the same results.

For example, FlashCopy within Global Mirror needs the attribute NOCOPY besides the INHIBIT TARGET WRITE and START CHANGE RECORDING attributes when it is set up for a Global Mirror environment. Note that these particular attributes are not explicitly available through all interfaces. For example, the TSO command to create such a particular FlashCopy relationship for Global Mirror combines these three attributes into a single parameter, in the MODE(ASYNC) option.

25.2 Utilize different interfaces for the same function

An example up front is to establish this FlashCopy relationship between the B volume and the C volume within a Global Mirror session, as Figure 25-1 shows.

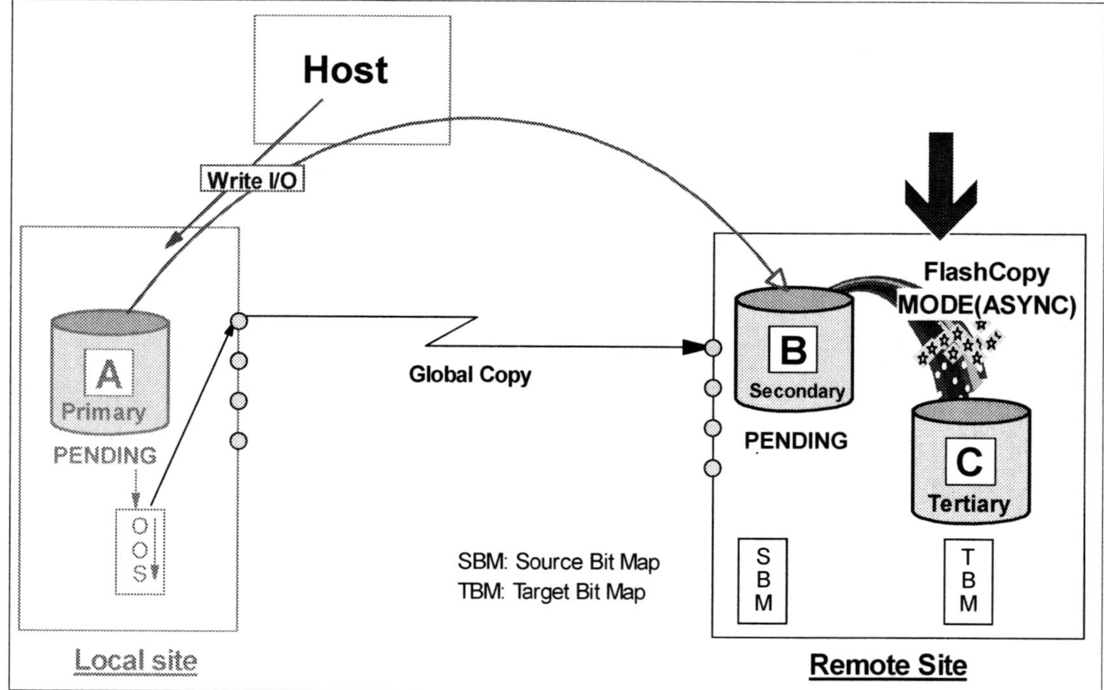

Figure 25-1 Establish FlashCopy relationship within Global Mirror

The following examples provide a first impression of the various interfaces and should give you an idea of the usability and how these different interfaces look and feel. Note that this is only a step out of the 5-6 steps for when you establish a Global Mirror environment. It just creates the FlashCopy relationship, when you set up a Global Mirror session.

25.2.1 TSO example to establish FlashCopy between volume B and volume C

Example 25-1 shows a TSO command that creates this FlashCopy relationship between the B volume and the C volume.

Example 25-1 Establish FlashCopy between B volume and C volume with TSO command

```
FCESTABL  SDEVN(X'3C00') TDEVN(X'3E00')  MODE(ASYNC)
```

Example 25-1 shows the TSO command `FCESTABL`. The source volume and the target volume are identified by their z/OS device number. This does not require any further information such as serial numbers or WWNNs to identify the involved volumes, nor does it need to identify an HMC or SMC to address the function. `MODE(ASYNC)` implicitly combines all necessary attributes for this FlashCopy relationship, such as START CHANGE RECORDING, INHIBIT TARGET WRITE, and NOCOPY.

Example 25-2 shows the inband version of this FlashCopy command when the FlashCopy creation is triggered from the local site. Here the FlashCopy command is issued to the Global Copy primary volume at the local site and then propagated inband over the PPRC paths to the remote site. Note that this example assumes that the Global Copy paths and pairs have already been established.

Example 25-2 inband TSO command to create a FlashCopy between B volume and C volume

```
FCESTABL  DEVN(X'2C00') SOURCE(73081 00 0C)  +
                        TARGET(73081 00 0E)  +
                        REMOTE(YES) SSID(3C00) MODE(ASYNC)
```

There is no change for the FlashCopy attributes. The only related addition is to address the corresponding Global Copy primary volume by the DEVN z/OS device address and to identify the FlashCopy source and target volumes at the remote site by corresponding SOURCE and TARGET parameters. You use a command, as in Example 25-2, when there is no host channel connection from the local server to the remote storage server. Example 25-2 assumes that there is a Fibre Channel connection from the local storage server to the remote storage server. It assumes further that the remote devices are also defined and configured in the system from where you issue the command.

25.2.2 DS CLI example to establish FlashCopy between volumes B and C

Example 25-3 does the same step, but uses the DS CLI command **mkflash**.

Example 25-3 Create FlashCopy between B volume and C volume with DS CLI

```
dscli mkflash -record -persist -nocp -seqnum 0000 6500:6502 -cfg
$DSCLI/profile/DS8300-box2.profile
```

The **mklfash** DS CLI command identifies the B volume and the C volume through additional information in a configuration file. Example 25-4 shows an example of what this configuration file looks like. Usually it contains the serial number of the involved disk storage servers. It also reveals that this command has to go through the DS8000 HMC, which is identified by its corresponding IP address. In case of a DS6000 it would identify the external SMC with the necessary software stack to handle the Copy Services commands. Note the fake IP number to protect the environment used.

For simplicity, a required user id and password is specified in plain text. Administrators of the disk storage server have to set up a user ID and password for users who want to work through the HMC. This information is usually hidden in an encrypted password file.

Example 25-4 Content of -cfg file $DSCLI/profile/DS8300-box2.profile

```
hmc1:         192.168.93.14
username:     Jack
password:     Stor123agE
devid:        IBM.2107-7573731
remotedevid: IBM.2107-7506551
```

Example 25-5 shows the creation of a FlashCopy relationship. The source volume and target volume are indicated by the LSS and device number pair 6500:6502. It also indicates the start change recording attribute, which actually implies the persistent attribute. It also indicates the NOCOPY option. An optional FlashCopy sequence number makes it simpler to refer to this FlashCopy relationship in further commands.

Note that you may put the configuration information in the DS CLI command as Example 25-4 shows.

Example 25-5 Create FlashCopy between B and C with DSCLI and explicit device specifications

```
dscli mkflash -record -persist -nocp -seqnum 0000 6500:6502 -dev ibm.2107-7573731-remotedev
ibm.2107-7506551
```

An inband triggered FlashCopy as shown in Example 25-2 on page 289 would require a different DS CLI command **mkremoteflash**, as shown here in Example 25-6.

Example 25-6 Create FlashCopy between B and C with DS CLI over inband process

```
dscli mkremoteflash -dev ibm.2107-7506551 -conduit ibm.2107-7573731/00 -tgtinhibit -record
-nocp -seqnum 0000 6500:6502
```

The parameter **-conduit** is equivalent to the DEVN parameter in the TSO Example 25-2 on page 289 to select the PPRC primary volume at the local site that receives the command. Note that the DS CLI has to go through the HMC or an external HMC, whereas the TSO commands are directly targeted to the storage servers through the host channel connection.

25.2.3 ICKDSF example to establish FlashCopy between volumes B and C

ICKDSF is usually the interface that is used to manage PPRC configurations in z/VM and z/VSE™ environments. It is a batch oriented approach and requires the JCL to invoke ICKDSF (Example 25-7).

Example 25-7 Create FlashCopy between B volume and C volume with ICKDSF for Global Mirror

```
//* ------------------------------------------------------------ ***
//FCBTOC  EXEC PGM=ICKDSF
//SYSPRINT  DD SYSOUT=*
//SYSIN     DD *

  FC   UNIT(3C00)   ESTABLISH              -
       TARGETVOL    (X'0E',X'00',3E00) -
       CHRCD        (YES)                  -
       NOTGTWT      (YES)                  -
```

```
         MODE          (NOCOPY)
```

Example 25-7 shows the actual FlashCopy command to create the Global Mirror FlashCopy relationship. ICKDSF also lists the individual attributes that are required to create a FlashCopy relationship for Global Mirror.

The equivalent to Example 25-2 on page 289 or to Example 25-6 on page 290 to create an inband FlashCopy command and issue the FlashCopy at the local site to the remote site is given here in Example 25-8, which shows the ICKDSF version.

Example 25-8 Create FlashCopy between B and C with ICKDSF over inband management

```
//* ------------------------------------------------------------- ***
//FCBTOCIN EXEC PGM=ICKDSF
//DD01      DD UNIT=3390,VOL=SER=AA6000,DISP=SHR
//SYSPRINT  DD SYSOUT=*
//SYSIN     DD *

 FC     DDNAME(DD01)     ESTABLISH                                -
        SRCVOL           (X'00',X'00',X'0002' AAVCA)              -
        TGTVOL           (X'00',X'00',6500)                       -
        CHRCD            (YES)      /* CHANGE RECORDING       */ -
        NOTGTWR          (YES)      /* INHIBIT TARGET WRITES  */ -
        MODE             (NOCOPY)   /* NO BACKGROUND COPY     */ -
        TGTCANCOMEONLINE (NO)
```

Note the syntax variation for the SRCVOL and TGTVOL parameter when hex notation is used and when it is not used. In the SRCVOL parameter, the serial number of the storage server is not in hex notation, but all the other parameters are. The TGTVOL parameters are also in hex notation, except for the z/OS device number of the FlashCopy target volume.

25.2.4 Which interface to choose

Which interface you may choose depends on your preferences and experience you gathered in the past. In our examples above, we left out the DS Storage Manager or GUI, which is also an alternative. A fully automated solution like GDPS relieves you of the decision of which interface to use to manage a Global Mirror environment. GDPS/Global Mirror support was announced in October 2005. The interface decision is also decided if you select solutions based on eRCMF or GMU. eRCMF and GMU provide support to manage a Global Mirror environment.

When you decide to construct your own Global Mirror management package, you have the choice of which interface to use.

TSO commands

TSO commands seem to have some advantage over DS CLI and DS Storage Manager, because they do not involve the DS Storage Manager. As ICKDSF does too, TSO commands are submitted via an inband approach over the host channel directly to the storage server. No active HMC or DS SM is required to trigger Copy Services functions.

You can issue the TSO commands from procedures that are similar to the scripting approach in open systems environments.

Note that TSO requires a z/OS system at the recovery site when you recover a Global Mirror environment at the remote site.

DS CLI

DS CLI has its strength through its scripting capability. You can easily create and modify corresponding script files. From a syntax level the DS CLI looks a bit more complicated and it tends to extend single lines for single commands, which makes it harder to read when you have to maintain such script files. Again this may be a matter of experience.

ICKDSF

ICKDSF is the only direct interface for z/VM and z/VSE environments. It is also very quick, just as the TSO commands are, because it does not need other components and networks in-between to trigger Copy Services functions.

DS Storage Manager

DS Storage Manager or GUI is suited best when you need to perform ad hoc actions and there is no time left to either create a script or there are difficulties with the DS CLI. It is not the best choice when you have to create a big and complex Global Mirror environment.

ANTRQST Macro

We do not cover the ANTRQST macro here. This macro is used by software that provides a full function management of a Global Mirror configuration of any size rather than by a conventional implementation. GDPS is such an example.

Again, at the end it is your choice depending on personal preferences. When you have no bias, generally speaking we consider the TSO commands as the best interface to manage a Global Mirror configuration in a z/OS environment. Through the inband approach over host channels and without other agents in-between, TSO commands execute very quickly. The TSO command syntax is also rather simple. TSO as an integral part of z/OS standard software, which stands for reliability, availability, and serviceability. For a first try with a rather small test environment, the DS Storage Manager or GUI is a possibility.

25.3 TSO commands to manage Global Mirror

TSO commands are commonly used in z/OS environments to manage all kinds of PPRC configurations. TSO commands may be generated by REXX or CLIST procedures. They may also be generated out of other software tools.

TSO commands have the advantage that these commands do not need a DS8000 HMC or a DS6000 SMC or any other storage management server. They are directly and via an inband approach forwarded to the related storage server function. This happens over the host based channel connectivity, which is usually a FICON channel. In the case of the DS8000 it may still be also over an ESCON channel. This allows a very quick command transfer. It does not depend on additional software stacks utilized in between the issuing of the command and the advanced function itself in the storage server microcode.

Generally a TSO PPRC command uses a z/OS device number to aim for the device, LSS, or storage server to trigger a PPRC function. Note this approach is not - yet - implemented for the new Global Mirror TSO command support. The new Global Mirror TSO commands require an online VOLSER as a parameter.

25.3.1 Establish a Global Mirror environment with TSO commands

The following sections exercise in a step-by-step approach how to build up a Global Mirror environment with the new TSO command support for Global Mirror. The sequence of the following steps is recommended, although it is not required, to succeed to establish a Global

Mirror environment. But the following sequence guarantees a clean and straight forward creation of a Global Mirror environment.

25.3.2 Define PPRC paths through TSO commands

Before you create a Global Copy volume pair relationship, you have to establish Global Copy paths first. A Global Copy path, or a Metro Mirror path, or generically a PPRC path is a logical construct and defines a remote copy connectivity between two LSSs, the primary LSS and the secondary LSS, over a physical Fibre Channel connection. Such a physical Fibre Channel connection is also called a PPRC link in the context when defining PPRC paths. These links are either directly connected for PPRC paths and use dedicated FCP ports, or you may define PPRC paths over a SAN based connectivity and share FCP ports between multiple PPRC paths. You may also share FCP ports between PPRC paths and use the same port also for a host based connectivity through the SAN. You may consider dedicated PPRC ports though to separate host I/O from PPRC based I/O, which is recommended for Metro Mirror. For Global Copy and Global Mirror it is feasible to consider an FCP port sharing with the storage servers.

Many paths can be mapped onto a PPRC link. You can also define PPRC paths in either direction on the very same PPRC link.

There is no change in how to define a PPRC path on the DS6000 or DS8000 as compared to the ESS 800 with TSO commands.

Figure 25-2 shows two LSSs. Usually each LSS is in a different storage server and both storage servers are connected either directly or over a SAN. The figure shows four physical PPRC links and each link connects to a FCP port. Because both storage servers may be apart from each other over a big distance these links are either going through a SAN network or over an IP based network. There is no distance limit for a Global Mirror configuration and Global Mirror pairs may even span across continents.

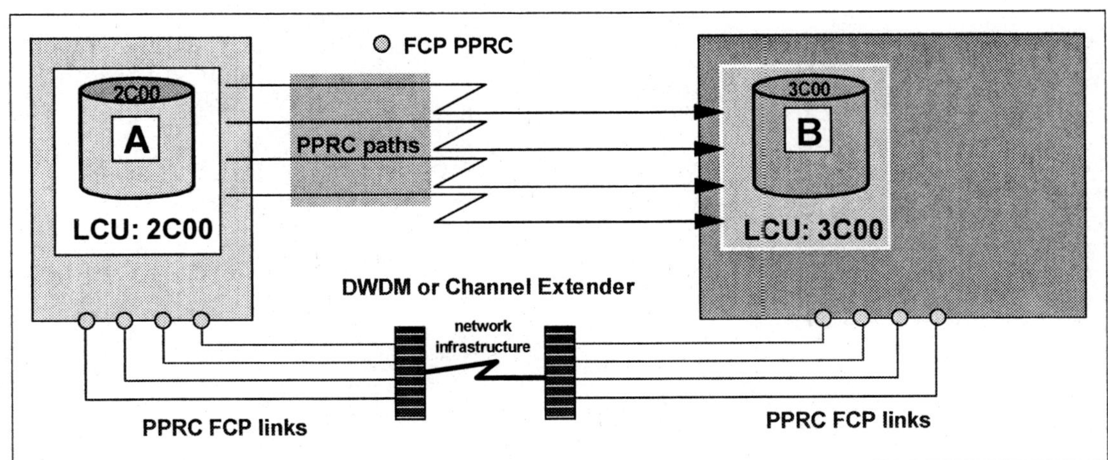

Figure 25-2 Define PPRC paths between two LSS

Example 25-9 shows the corresponding TSO command to create four PPRC paths at once between a primary LSS and its corresponding secondary LSS.

Example 25-9 Define PPRC paths

```
//* ---------------------------- TSO ------------ CREATE (1) ----- ***
//* ESTABLISH PPRC PATH(S)                                          ***
//* --------------------------------------------------------------- ***
//EPATHS  EXEC PGM=IKJEFT01
```

```
//SYSPRINT  DD SYSOUT=*
//SYSTSPRT  DD SYSOUT=*
//SYSTSIN   DD DDNAME=SYSIN

   CESTPATH  DEVN (X'2C00')                           +
             PRIM (X'2C00' 5005076303FFC228  X'0C') +
             SEC  (X'3C00' 5005076303FFC422  X'0C') +
             LINK (X'00300030' X'01300130'           +
                   X'02300230' X'03310330') CGROUP(NO)
   CQUERY    DEVN (X'2C00') PATHS
```

Primary and secondary LSSs are identified by their respective subsystems IDs (SSID), the WWNN of the storage servers involved, and by the LSS number. The LINK parameters contain the System Adapter IDs (SAID) in pairs with the source port ID and the target port ID. Note that for Global Copy it does not make sense to establish the CGROUP attribute for extended long busy (ELB). You can check that all paths you intended to be defined are actually established.

Note: A PPRC path has the scope of an LSS pair. For each LSS pair you repeat the command and adapt the SSID and LSS numbers accordingly.

25.3.3 Define PPRC paths for multiple primary storage servers

Once you intend to use Global Copy primary volumes from multiple storage servers and put them into a Global Mirror session, you need to define also PPRC paths between the primary storage servers (Figure 25-3).

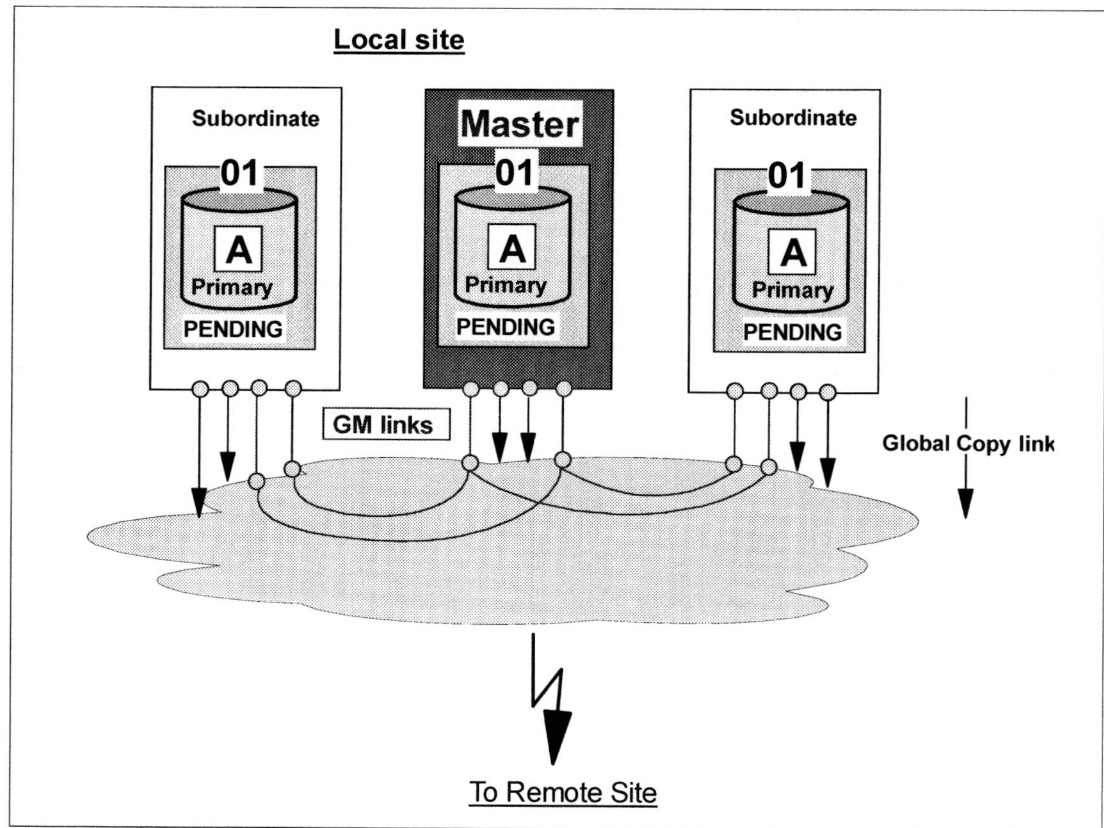

Figure 25-3 Establish PPRC links between local primary storage servers; decide on a Master

This is a conventional CESTPATH command with the Master storage server as the primary and the corresponding Subordinates as the secondary storage servers. You need to decide now which storage server is becoming the Master. You can use any LSS in the Subordinate storage servers to receive management orders from the Master.

For redundancy it is recommended to define two paths between these primary storage servers. Note that the FCP ports may be shared through a SAN fabric, as Figure 25-3 suggests.

25.3.4 Create Global Copy volume pairs through TSO commands

After the PPRC paths are established, you create Global Copy pairs (Figure 25-4).

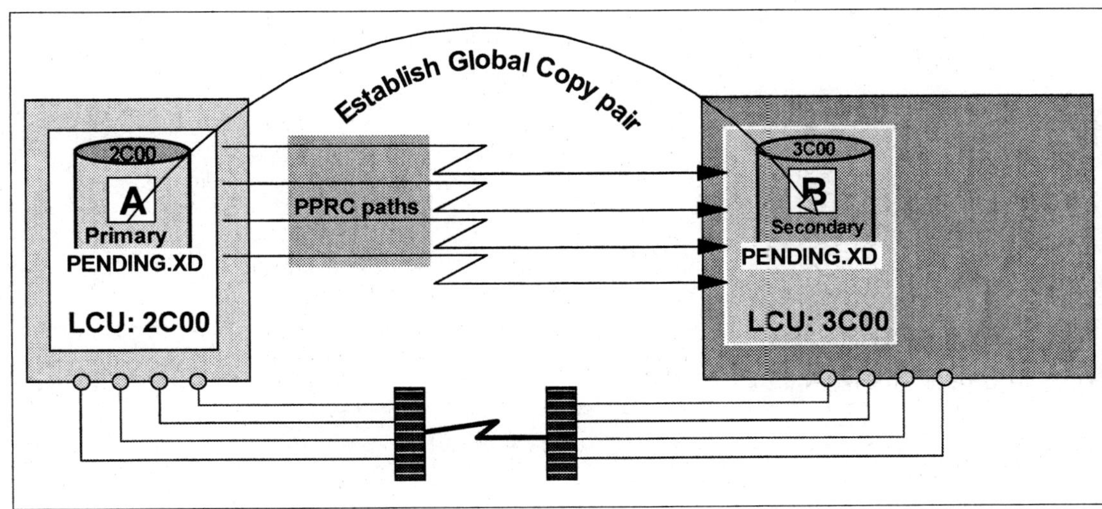

Figure 25-4 Establish Global Copy pair

Figure 25-4 indicates a Global Copy pair relationship that is maintained over four PPRC paths. Example 25-10 shows the corresponding TSO command.

Example 25-10 Define Global Copy pair through TSO command

```
//* ---------------------------- TSO ------------ CREATE (2) ----- ***
//* ESTABLISH PPRC-XD PAIR(S)                                       ***
//* -------------------------------------------------------------- ***
//EPAIR    EXEC PGM=IKJEFT01
//SYSPRINT  DD SYSOUT=*
//SYSTSPRT  DD SYSOUT=*
//SYSTSIN   DD DDNAME=SYSIN

 CESTPAIR  DEVN (X'2C01')                       +
           PRIM (X'2C00' 27131 X'01' X'00')     +
           SEC  (X'3C00' 73081 X'01' X'01')     +
           ONLINSEC(NO)  MSGREQ(NO)    CRIT(NO) +
           OPTION  (XD)  MODE   (COPY) CASCADE(NO)
```

OPTION(XD) indicates a Global Copy relationship. Once the command successfully ends, Global Copy immediately starts a first complete pass through the primary volumes, and replicates all concerned tracks to the secondary volumes (Example 25-11).

Example 25-11 Query Global Copy pair immediately after establish

```
CQUERY    DEVN(X'2C00')
 CQUERY FORMATTED LVL 3
 VOLUME REPORT
 ************** PPRC REMOTE COPY CQUERY - VOLUME ********************
 *                                          (PRIMARY)   (SECONDARY) *
 *                                        SSID CCA LSS SSID CCA LSS*
 *DEVICE   LEVEL      STATE     PATH STATUS  SERIAL#     SERIAL#    *
 *------ --------- ---------- ----------- ---------    ---------  *
 * 2C00  PRIMARY..  PENDING.XD   ACTIVE..   2C00 00 0C   3C00 00 0C *
 *       CRIT(NO).......       CGRPLB(NO). 000000027131 000000073081*
 * PATHS PFCA SFCA STATUS: DESCRIPTION                              *
 * ----- --------- ------  -------------------                      *
 *   4   0030 0030   13    PATH ESTABLISHED...                      *
 *       0130 0130   13    PATH ESTABLISHED...                      *
 *       0230 0230   13    PATH ESTABLISHED...                      *
 *       0331 0330   14    (UNDETERMINED).....                      *
 * IF STATE = PENDING/SUSPEND:    TRACKS OUT OF SYNC =   49599      *
 *                                TRACKS ON VOLUME   =   50085      *
 *                              PERCENT OF COPY COMPLETE =   1%     *
 *  SUBSYSTEM         WWNN                      LIC LEVEL           *
 * -----------  ----------------             -----------           *
 * PRIMARY....  5005076303FFC228             5.0.03.0097            *
 * SECONDARY.1  5005076303FFC422                                    *
 ********************************************************************
 CQUERY COMMAND COMPLETED FOR DEVICE 2C00. COMPLETION CODE: 00
```

Example 25-11 shows the very first starting phase of replicating the primary volume to the secondary volume. This is indicated by the output section that reports the number of tracks out of sync. Example 25-12 provides the same information as Example 25-11, but in a space-saving unformatted format. The details for these commands can be found in *z/OS DFSMS Advanced Copy Services,* SC35-0428.

Example 25-12 Unformatted query output

```
CQUERY    DEVN (X'2C00') UNFORMAT
 CQUERY UNFORMATTED LVL 3
 VOLUME REPORT
 2C00,PRIMARY,PENDING XD,ACTIVE,
 2C000C,00,000000027131,3C000C,00,000000073081,N,N,
 1,00300030,13,01300130,13,02300230,13,03310330,14,
 0047599,0050085,005,
 5005076303FFC228,5005076303FFC422,
```

Once the first replication phase is completed the CQUERY output report will be changed by the removal of the TRACKS OUT OF SYNC section of the report, as Example 25-13 shows.

Example 25-13 Global Copy first replication phase completed

```
CQUERY    DEVN(X'2C00')
 CQUERY FORMATTED LVL 3
 VOLUME REPORT
 ************** PPRC REMOTE COPY CQUERY - VOLUME ********************
 *                                          (PRIMARY)   (SECONDARY) *
 *                                        SSID CCA LSS SSID CCA LSS*
 *DEVICE   LEVEL      STATE     PATH STATUS  SERIAL#     SERIAL#    *
 *------ --------- ---------- ----------- ---------    ---------  *
 * 2C00  PRIMARY..  PENDING.XD   ACTIVE..   2C00 00 0C   3C00 00 0C *
 *       CRIT(NO).......       CGRPLB(NO). 000000027131 000000073081*
```

```
* PATHS PFCA SFCA STATUS: DESCRIPTION                                    *
* ----- --------- ------ -------------------                            *
*   4   0030 0030   13    PATH ESTABLISHED...                           *
*       0130 0130   13    PATH ESTABLISHED...                           *
*       0230 0230   13    PATH ESTABLISHED...                           *
*       0331 0330   14    (UNDETERMINED).....                           *
*  SUBSYSTEM          WWNN                    LIC LEVEL                 *
* -----------  ----------------            -----------                  *
* PRIMARY....  5005076303FFC228            5.0.03.0097                  *
* SECONDARY.1  5005076303FFC422                                         *
*************************************************************************
CQUERY COMMAND COMPLETED FOR DEVICE 2C00. COMPLETION CODE: 00
```

It is recommended to wait until this first replication phase is finished before you continue to establish the Global Mirror FlashCopy relationship between the B volume and the C volume.

Note that at a later point-in-time, you may again observe the TRACKS OUT OF SYNC portion of the report, as Example 25-11 shows, but then it is not related to the first replication phase.

25.3.5 Define FlashCopy relationship for Global Mirror through TSO command

Once the first replication phase is completed for the Global Copy pairs, create the FlashCopy relationship between volume B and volume C (Figure 25-5).

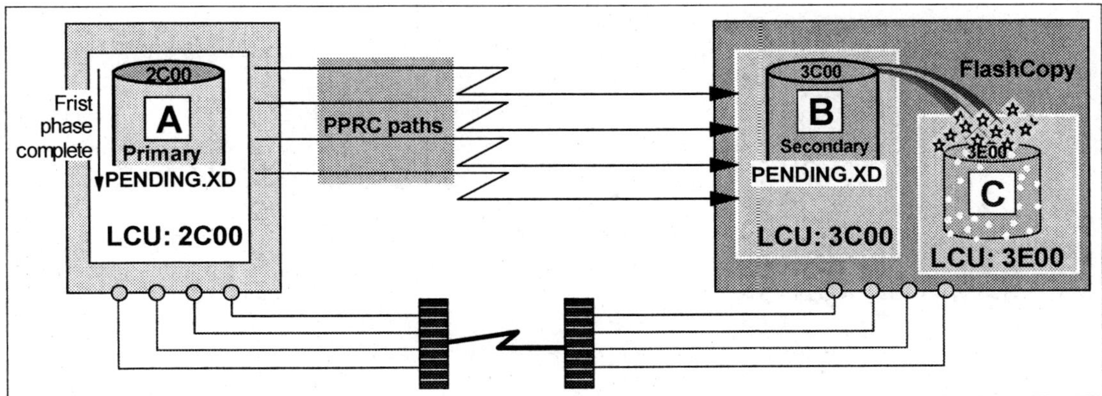

Figure 25-5 Establish Global Mirror FlashCopy relationship between B and C

Although Figure 25-5 only indicates FlashCopy between volume B and volume C, it is a very specific FlashCopy relationship with particular FlashCopy attributes set. Refer to Chapter 6., "FlashCopy overview" on page 45.

Example 25-14 shows a TSO command that creates this FlashCopy relationship through the Global Copy primary volume, volume A, and propagates the command via inband to the secondary storage server.

Example 25-14 TSO command to create a FlashCopy pair between B volume and C volume

```
FCESTABL  DEVN(X'2C00') SOURCE(73081 00 0C)            +
                        TARGET(73081 00 0E)            +
                        REMOTE(YES) SSID(3C00) MODE(ASYNC)
```

This is most likely required when the remote site is not connected to the local site. DEVN points to the concerning local primary volume and SOURCE and TARGET contain the information for the target storage server. MODE(ASYNC) implicitly includes the specific FlashCopy attributes that are required for Global Mirror and Consistency Group processing.

25.3.6 Define a Global Mirror session through TSO commands

Before a Global Mirror session can receive volumes to form Consistency Groups it requires a token under which this session is represented and addressed.

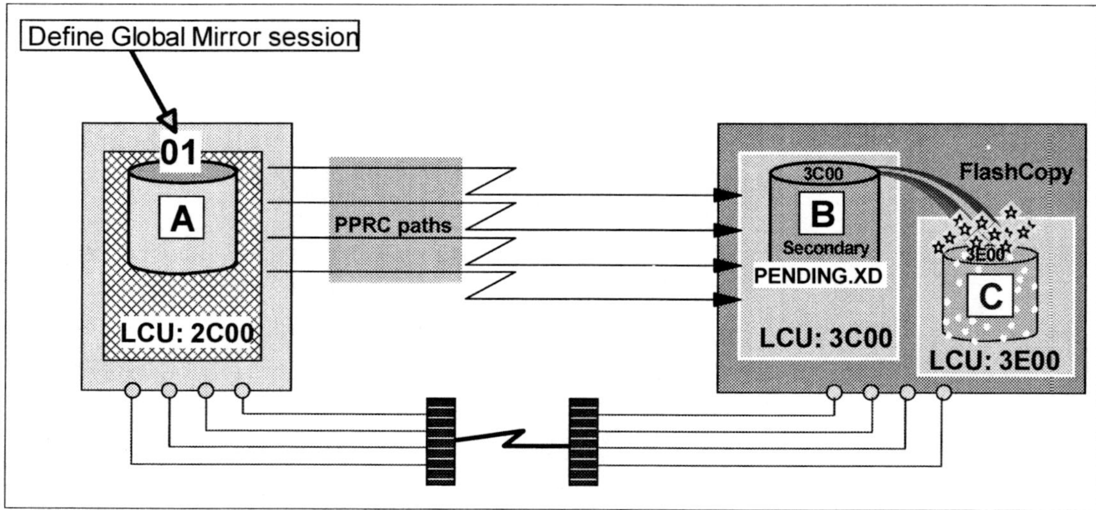

Figure 25-6 Define a Global Mirror session number

Figure 25-6 shows a volume within an LSS that will later contain Global Copy primary volumes that are going to be part of the Global Mirror session. At the moment it is recommended to use a kind of utility device within each LSS. This utility device needs to be online to the z/OS system from where you issue Global Mirror commands. You may consider using a volume that is not part of the Global Mirror session but within the same LSS as the Global Copy primary volumes that are going to belong to the Global Mirror session. As soon as the Global Mirror TSO commands will allow you to specify just any device number within the concerned LSS, whether the device is online or not, then this recommendation can be dropped.

Example 25-15 TSO command example to define a Global Mirror session

```
//* ---------------------------- TSO ------------ CREATE (4) ----- ***
//* DEFINE GM SESSION NUMBER X'01' TO LSS X'0C' AND LSS X'0D'      ***
//* ---------------------------------------------------------------- ***
//DEFSESS EXEC PGM=IKJEFT01
//SYSPRINT  DD SYSOUT=*
//SYSTSPRT  DD SYSOUT=*
//SYSTSIN   DD DDNAME=SYSIN

  RSESSION   SNBR(01) VOLSER(XX2C00)         +
             ACTION(DEFINE)                  +
             LSSTYPE(CKD) LSSNBR(0C)         +
             ESSSERIAL(27131)                +
             MSSERIAL (27131)

  RSESSION   SNBR(01) VOLSER(XX2D00)         +
             ACTION(DEFINE)                  +
             LSSTYPE(CKD) LSSNBR(0D)         +
             ESSSERIAL(27131)                +
             MSSERIAL (27131)
```

The new TSO command RSESSION is used to control and manage a Global Mirror session. This includes the ability to DEFINE a Global Mirror session as Example 25-15 shows. Other options are to START and STOP a Global Mirror session, as well as PAUSE and RESUME a session, or to delete (UNDEFINE) the session. This is indicated through the ACTION parameter.

This example also indicates that you have to define this Global Mirror session number to all LSSs at the primary site with the potential for Global Copy primary volumes, which are going to become part of this session.

As with all TSO commands, you can issue this command interactively through ISPF menu 6 or from the TSO READY status. In the z/OS SYSLOG this RSESSION command is only logged as the command itself but not the response to this command. It is, therefore, recommended to always use TSO in batch for documentation purpose and to be able to track all commands and their outcomes.

25.3.7 Populate a Global Mirror session with volumes through TSO commands

After you successfully created a Global Mirror session, you populate the session with corresponding Global Copy primary volumes. These are all the primary or A volumes that are going to comprise the Global Mirror session at the local site (Example 25-16).

Example 25-16 Add Global Copy primary volumes to Global Mirror session

```
//* ---------------------------- TSO ------------ CREATE (5) ----- ***
//* POPULATE SESSION X'01' WITH PRIMARY VOLUMES                    ***
//*                                                                ***
//*         VOLUME LIST CONTAINS CCA NUMBERS                       ***
//* ------------------------------------------------------------- ***
//JOIN    EXEC PGM=IKJEFT01
//SYSPRINT  DD SYSOUT=*
//SYSTSPRT  DD SYSOUT=*
//SYSTSIN   DD DDNAME=SYSIN

  RVOLUME    SNBR(01) VOLSER(XX2C00)         +
             ACTION   (JOIN)                 +
             LSSTYPE  (CKD) LSSNBR(0C)       +
             ESSSERIAL(27131)                +
             VOLLIST  (00)

  RVOLUME    SNBR(01) VOLSER(XX2D00)         +
             ACTION   (JOIN)                 +
             LSSTYPE  (CKD) LSSNBR(0D)       +
             ESSSERIAL(27131)                +
             VOLRANGE (00:01)
```

Example 25-16 shows the new TSO command RVOLUME. This command is utilized when you populate the Global Mirror session with A volumes via the ACTION(JOIN) parameter.

Through this command you also remove Global Copy primary or A volumes from the session. The corresponding parameter is ACTION(REMOVE).

Through VOLLIST or VOLRANGE, you define those volumes that are added to the session or removed from the session. VOLLIST is a list of channel connection addresses (CCA) that identify the concerned A volumes. VOLRANGE allows you to specify a range of CCAs. In Example 25-16, a volume with CCA x'00' from LSS x'0C' is added to the session number x'01'. Two more volumes are added to the session from LSS x'0D' with the VOLRANGE parameter. 00:01 reads from CCA x'00' to CCA x'01'.

25.3.8 Start a Global Mirror session with TSO commands

The new RSESSION command is used to start the Global Mirror session (Example 25-17). Through the ACTION(START) parameter, you indicate the start to form Consistency Groups.

Example 25-17 Start Global Mirror session

```
//* ---------------------------- TSO ------------ CREATE (6) ----- ***
//* START    SESSION X'01' THROUGH LSS X'0C'                         ***
//*                                                                  ***
//*          THEN LSS X'0C' BECOMES THE MASTER LSS (DS)              ***
//*          NOTE: LSS SYNTAX IS WITHOUT X AND QUOTES ...            ***
//*                                                                  ***
//*          CGINTERVAL - BUILD CG WITHOUT A BREAK                   ***
//*          CGDRAIN    - ALLOW 10 MINUTES FOR DRAINING              ***
//*          COORDINTERVAL - ALLOW 5 MS MAX FOR COORDINATION         ***
//* ---------------------------------------------------------------- ***
//START    EXEC PGM=IKJEFT01
//SYSPRINT  DD SYSOUT=*
//SYSTSPRT  DD SYSOUT=*
//SYSTSIN   DD DDNAME=SYSIN

  RSESSION   SNBR(01)      VOLSER(XX2C00)    +
             ACTION        (START)           +
             LSSTYPE       (CKD) LSSNBR(0C)  +
             ESSSERIAL     (27131)           +
             MSSERIAL      (27131)           +
             CGINTERVAL    (00)              +
             CGDRAIN       (600)             +
             COORDINTERVAL(05)
```

Example 25-17 shows the START command to form Consistency Groups for session number x'01'. Besides the ACTION parameter, you address the LSS number that receives this command. This also decides the Master LSS, which is LSS number x'0C' in Example 25-17. You may override the default values of the Global Mirror session parameters.

In Example 25-17 we keep the default value for CGINTERVAL. But we change the defaults for CGDRAIN to 10 minutes as the maximum Consistency Group Drain time. We also change the maximum coordination time COORDINTERVAL to 5 ms.

25.3.9 Query a Global Mirror session with TSO commands

A new TSO query command provides information with regard to a Global Mirror session. This new command is RQUERY. Several types or ACTIONS provide information on the status of a Global Mirror session and which volumes are involved and the status of these volumes. For examples, see 27.2.1, "Query a Global Mirror session" on page 343.

Example 25-18 shows the basic structure of the new RQUERY command.

Example 25-18 New TSO RQUERY command

```
RQUERY SNBR(01) VOLSER(volser) ACTION(action) LSSNBR(lss) LSSTYPE(type) DVCNBR(###)
```

RQUERY is the TSO command processor name.

- SNBR is the Global Mirror session number from which a query report is requested. This parameter is optional. When omitted RQUERY will report all session numbers that are available in the concerned primary storage server.

- VOLSER is currently required as an ONLINE z/OS volume with *volser* as its six character label or volume serial number. This volume points the RQUERY command to the LSS from which a query report is requested.
- ACTION is required and specifies which kind of query report is requested. Currently there are three different query reports indicated by its action parameter:
  - GMLSTAT provides summary information pertaining to the Global Mirror session. This includes information about the Master storage server and potential Subordinate storage servers as well as the number of successfully created Consistency Groups and how often Consistency Group creation failed. It also includes the parameter values for the session.
  - GMPSTAT provides a summary of the status of an LSS that the VOLSER points to concerning Global Mirror information. A key number may be the number of tracks that are still in the out-of-sync bitmap at the primary LSS and are waiting to be replicated to the corresponding secondary LSS. It also details the total number of Global Mirror volumes within this LSS and how many volumes out of this total number contain out-of-sync tracks.
  - DVCSTAT provides an overview of all involved devices in a Global Mirror session from the LSS that the VOLSER points to.
- LSSNBR specifies the LSS number for which a query report is requested. This parameter is required when LSSTYPE(FB) is specified. It is not required when LSSTYPE defaults to CKD or specifies CKD.
- LSSTYPE identifies whether this is an LSS with fixed blocked (FB) devices for open systems or count-key-data (CKD) devices for zSeries. CKD is the default.
- DVCNBR is required when LSSTYPE(FB) is specified and contains the LUN for which the query report is requested.

Example 25-19 shows an RQUERY command with ACTION(GMLSTAT) and the formatted line output concerning the LSS to which the VOLSER(XX2C00) points to.

Example 25-19 RQUERY TSO command example with ACTION(GMLSTAT)

```
  RQUERY     SNBR(01) VOLSER(XX2C00) ACTION(GMLSTAT)
RQUERY Output Volser(XX2C00) Action(GMLSTAT) Version(001)
SNbr GMLStat    GoodCg   Pct CrnBadCG TotBadCG LastGoodCGSCnt Clock
--   ---------- -------- --- -------- -------- --------------------
01   Running    00000001 100                   19 May 2005 22:02:35
.
Master: Serial       SSID LSS   CGInt CGDrn CrdInt
        ------------ ---- --    ----- ----- -----
        000107527131 2C00 0C        0   600     5
READY

  RQUERY     SNBR(01) VOLSER(XX2D00) ACTION(GMLSTAT)
RQUERY Output Volser(XX2D00) Action(GMLSTAT) Version(001)
SNbr GMLStat    GoodCg   Pct CrnBadCG TotBadCG LastGoodCGSCntlClock
--   ---------- -------- --- -------- -------- --------------------
01   NoConfig
READY
```

Example 25-19 shows a second RQUERY command. The first command is issued to the Global Mirror Master LSS. The second command is issued to another LSS that is not a Master LSS. This documents that this ACTION parameter with GMLSTAT is only useful for the Master LSS to query Global Mirror session information.

Besides the section about the Master LSS, there is also information about the number of Consistency Groups created, the number of failed attempts, and also, the last successfully created Consistency Group with the internal timestamp from the concerned storage server.

The status of the Global Mirror session is also important. Example 25-19 on page 301 shows for this status *Running*. Refer to *z/OS DFSMS Advanced Copy Services*, SC35-0428, for a description of different status indications.

Example 25-20 shows the status of Global Mirror from the view of an LSS and its concerned Global Copy primary or A volumes.

Example 25-20 RQUERY TSO command example with ACTION(GMPSTAT)

```
READY
   RQUERY     SNBR(01) VOLSER(XX2D00) ACTION(GMPSTAT)
 RQUERY Output Volser(XX2D00) Action(GMPSTAT) Version(001)
 SNbr LSS GMPStatus  RvrtStatus FCSeqNbr TotVol OOSVol OOSTrks
 --   --  ---------- ---------- -------- ------ ------ --------
 01   0D  CGInPrgrs  AllNRv&Eq  42937FE2      2      2 00003E02
 READY
 END
```

The formatted output in Example 25-20 provides the following columns and their meaning:

- LSS number 0D contains 2 volumes in the session number 01 (*SNbr*, *LSS*, and *TotVol*).
- Both volumes contain tracks that are not yet replicated by Global Copy to their corresponding secondary volumes (*OOSVol*).
- The number of out-of-sync tracks is indicated in hexa decimal (*OOSTrks*).
- The Global Mirror status as it pertains to this LSS 0D indicates the process of currently forming a Consistency Group (*GMPStatus*).
- The FlashCopy status of the corresponding FlashCopy pairs that belong to these Global Copy volumes is *AllNRvEq*, which indicates that all FlashCopy relationships are non-revertible with the same FlashCopy sequence number (*RvrtStatus*). A potential recovery action is not required.

Note that the RQUERY output format as shown in Example 25-20 may change after this book is published. Refer to the most recent suffix of the standard manual *z/OS DFSMS Advanced Copy Services*, SC35-0428 for the current RQUERY output format.

Example 25-21 documents a potentially unbalanced Global Mirror configuration (unbalanced in the sense that LSS x'0C' receives many fewer write I/Os than LSS x'0D').

Example 25-21 Workload in concerned LSS within Global Mirror session is unbalanced

```
READY
   RQUERY     SNBR(01) VOLSER(XX2C00) ACTION(GMPSTAT)
 RQUERY Output Volser(XX2C00) Action(GMPSTAT) Version(001)
 SNbr LSS GMPStatus  RvrtStatus FCSeqNbr TotVol OOSVol OOSTrks
 --   --  ---------- ---------- -------- ------ ------ --------
 01   0C  CGInPrgrs  AllNRv&Eq  42937FE2      1      0 00000000
 READY
   RQUERY     SNBR(01) VOLSER(XX2D00) ACTION(GMPSTAT)
 RQUERY Output Volser(XX2D00) Action(GMPSTAT) Version(001)
 SNbr LSS GMPStatus  RvrtStatus FCSeqNbr TotVol OOSVol OOSTrks
 --   --  ---------- ---------- -------- ------ ------ --------
 01   0D  CGInPrgrs  AllNRv&Eq  42937FE2      2      2 00003E02
 READY
```

Also, Example 25-21 documents a test with only a few write I/Os to the A volume in LSS x'0C' but significantly more write I/Os to the two volumes in LSS x'0D'.

Both LSSs replicate their data over the very same PPRC links and are also configured with the same number of PPRC paths. Note the identical FlashCopy sequence numbers for both LSSs. Both LSSs provide a healthy set of consistent C volumes at the remote site. This is indicated by the same FlashCopy sequence number and by *AllNRv&Eq* in the column *RvrtStatus*. See also 24.6.4, "Verify for valid Consistency Group state" on page 274.

Example 25-22 shows two TSO RQUERY commands with ACTION(DVCSTAT). These commands detail each individual A volume within the LSS that belongs to the corresponding Global Mirror session.

Example 25-22 RQUERY Global Copy primary volumes in premature status, Global Mirror session

```
READY
   RQUERY     SNBR(01) VOLSER(XX2C00) ACTION(DVCSTAT)
 RQUERY Output Volser(XX2C00) Action(DVCSTAT) Version(001)
 SNbr LSS Dvc VolStat              PriPPRCStat SecCascStat
 --   --  --  -------------------- ----------  ----------
 01   0C  00  NIn+JoinP+1st        DplxPendng  Simplex
 READY
   RQUERY     SNBR(01) VOLSER(XX2D00) ACTION(DVCSTAT)
 RQUERY Output Volser(XX2D00) Action(DVCSTAT) Version(001)
 SNbr LSS Dvc VolStat              PriPPRCStat SecCascStat
 --   --  --  -------------------- ----------  ----------
 01   0D  00  NIn+JoinP+1st        DplxPendng  Simplex
      0D  01  NIn+JoinP+1st        DplxPendng  Simplex
 READY
```

Example 25-22 indicates that the volumes in both referenced LSS are still not in session and are running through their initial copy phase and have not completed their first pass. This is the device with CCA x'00' in LSS x'0C' and the device with CCA x'00' and x'01' in LSS x'0D'.

Example 25-23 shows the very same RQUERY TSO commands as in Example 25-22, but this time the initial copy phase is complete and all volumes are in session, which means they contribute when forming Consistency Groups at the remote site.

Example 25-23 Global Copy primary volumes in Global Mirror session

```
READY
   RQUERY     SNBR(01) VOLSER(XX2C00) ACTION(DVCSTAT)
 RQUERY Output Volser(XX2C00) Action(DVCSTAT) Version(001)
 SNbr LSS Dvc VolStat              PriPPRCStat SecCascStat
 --   --  --  -------------------- ----------  ----------
 01   0C  00  InSession            DplxPendng  Simplex
 READY
   RQUERY     SNBR(01) VOLSER(XX2D00) ACTION(DVCSTAT)
 RQUERY Output Volser(XX2D00) Action(DVCSTAT) Version(001)
 SNbr LSS Dvc VolStat              PriPPRCStat SecCascStat
 --   --  --  -------------------- ----------  ----------
 01   0D  00  InSession            DplxPendng  Simplex
      0D  01  InSession            DplxPendng  Simplex
 READY
```

For more details and different *VolStat* indications, refer to *z/OS DFSMS Advanced Copy Services*, SC35-0428.

25.4 DS CLI to manage Global Mirror volumes in z/OS

The DS CLI introduces a new set of commands, which are common between the DS6000, DS8000, and the ESS 800 from LIC level 2.4.3 on, to manage a Copy Services environment. Although PPRC over Fibre Channel links is supported since ESS 800 LIC level 2.3.0+ the newer LIC level is required for the ESS 800 to support the new DS CLI.

We briefly present a DS CLI example of how to remove a Global Mirror environment with the DS CLI.

Refer to Chapter 27., "Global Mirror examples" on page 341 for further examples to use DS CLI for Global Mirror management in a zSeries environment. Also refer to Chapter 4., "DS Command-Line Interface" on page 29.

25.4.1 Remove a Global Mirror environment with DS CLI commands

The following sections present exercises in a step-by-step approach showing how to completely remove a Global Mirror environment through DS CLI commands.

This sequence of steps worked fine with TSO and ICKDSF:

1. Stop the Global Mirror session.
2. Remove the A volumes or Global Copy primary volumes from the Global Mirror session.
3. Un-define or remove the session from all concerned primary LSSs.
4. Withdraw the FlashCopy relationship from B volumes to C volumes.
5. Delete the Global Copy volume pairs.
6. Remove all PPRC paths between local and remote LSSs as well as potentially between the Master LSS and Subordinate LSSs.

We use a different sequence of steps with the DS CLI. The following sequence guarantees also a clean removal of a Global Mirror environment.

Figure 25-7 shows the sample configuration to which the DS CLI commands refer to in the following sections. LSS numbers, device numbers and serial numbers are used in the DS CLI examples, so you can refer to Figure 25-7 to find out what is source and target for the different DS CLI commands and relate certain parameters to the corresponding storage servers.

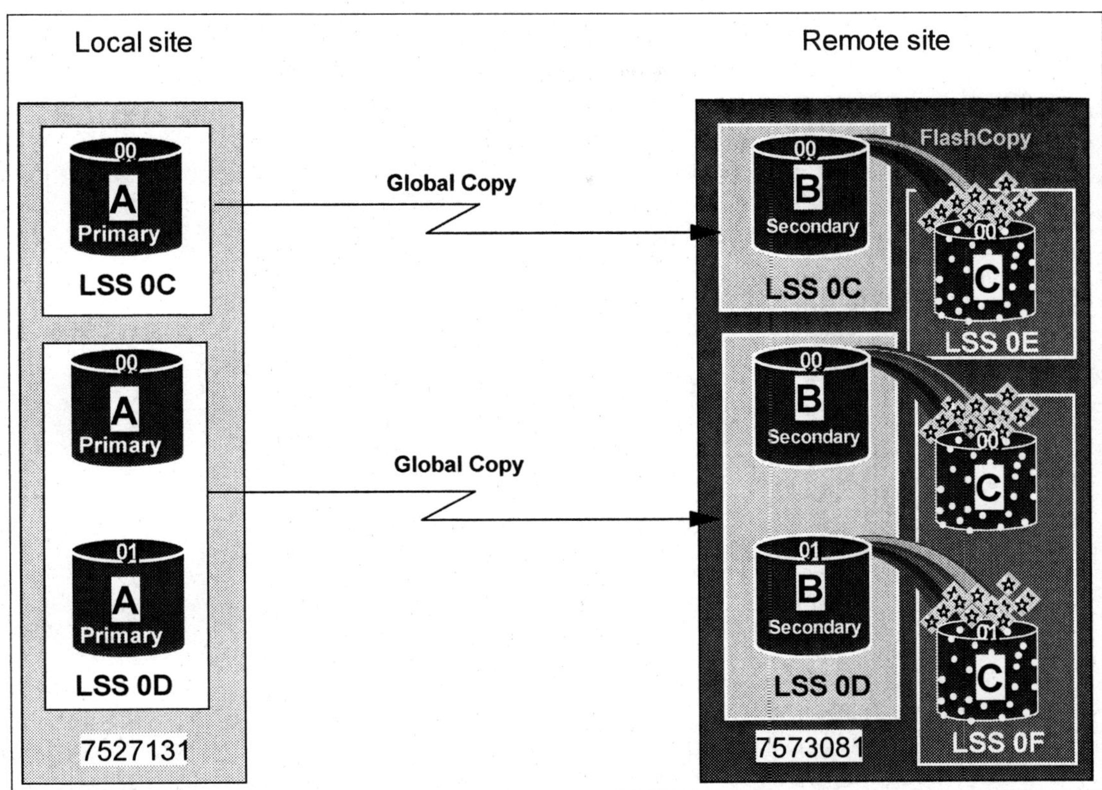

Figure 25-7 Global Mirror sample environment for DS CLI commands example

25.4.2 Stop a Global Mirror session with DS CLI command

The command in Example 25-24 tries to remove a Global Mirror session.

Example 25-24 Attempt to stop Global Mirror session number 01 with DS CLI

```
dscli> rmsession -lss 0c          01

Date/Time: 30. Mai 2005 04:38:30 CEST IBM DSCLI Version: 5.0.3.75 DS: IBM.2107-7527131
CMUC00148W rmsession: Are you sure you want to close session 01? [y/n]:y
CMUN03107E rmsession: Copy Services operation failure: volumes in session
```

The command fails because there are still volumes defined to the session.

In the following sections, the sequence of DS CLI commands to remove a Global Mirror environment is a little bit different here as compared to TSO or ICKDSF. The following sequence was successful to remove a Global Mirror environment:

1. Stop the Global Mirror session.
2. Withdraw the FlashCopy relationship from B volumes to C volumes.
3. Delete the Global Copy volume pairs.
4. Remove the A volumes or Global Copy primary volumes from the Global Mirror session.
5. Remove the Global Mirror session.
6. Remove all PPRC paths between local and remote LSSs as well as potentially between the Master LSS and Subordinate LSSs.

The first thing is still to stop forming Consistency Groups. This keeps Global Copy still active and all volumes are still in the Global Mirror session.

It is not very logical to remove the FlashCopy relationship as the next step. But you may remove the FlashCopy relationship between the B and C volumes at this stage. You may also delete the Global Copy volume pairs as a next step. But as the fourth step implies, these volumes would still remain in the Global Copy session structure. After removing the A volumes from the session, you may finally remove the Global Mirror session and the session number from the local storage servers. As the last step you may remove all PPRC paths.

Example 25-25 shows a DS CLI command example and the response of the system. The command is a Global Mirror command and is, therefore, aimed to the Master LSS.

Example 25-25 Stop Global Mirror with DS CLI command

```
dscli> rmgmir -lss 0c -session 01

Date/Time: 30. Mai 2005 04:53:45 CEST IBM DSCLI Version: 5.0.3.75 DS: IBM.2107-7527131
CMUC00166W rmgmir: Are you sure you want to stop the Global Mirror session 01:? [y/n]:y
CMUC00165I rmgmir: Global Mirror for session 01 successfully stopped.
```

Now the session is stopped. Global Mirror does not form Consistency Groups any longer.

Note that the Global Copy replication process still continues. But there are no FlashCopy operations any longer because they are part of the process to form Consistency Groups. But from now on Consistency Groups are no longer created. Note also that an ongoing process to form a Consistency Group may not come to a successful end and may be terminated. In contrast, to TERMINATE a PAUSE would finish an ongoing process to form a Consistency Group, which may be in the middle when the PAUSE was issued. This Consistency Group creation process completes before the PAUSE stops the creation of further Consistency Group formations.

Example 25-26 shows a DS CLI **showgmir** command and the response to this command.

Example 25-26 Global Mirror session no longer active

```
dscli> showgmir -fullid 0c

Date/Time: 30. Mai 2005 04:55:55 CEST IBM DSCLI Version: 5.0.3.75 DS: IBM.2107-7527131
ID                           IBM.2107-7527131/0C
Master Count                 0
Master Session ID            -
Copy State                   -
Fatal Reason                 -
CG Interval (seconds)        -
XDC Interval(milliseconds)   -
CG Drain Time (seconds)      -
Current Time                 -
CG Time                      -
Successful CG Percentage     -
FlashCopy Sequence Number    -
Master ID                    -
Subordinate Count            -
Master SSID                  -
Subordinate SSID             -
```

Although the session still exits, the **showgmir** reflects only the fact that the session is stopped.

Example 25-27 is an example to show Global Mirror session metrics.

Example 25-27 No Global Mirror session numbers after stopping the session

```
dscli> showgmir -metrics 0c

Date/Time: 30. Mai 2005 04:56:01 CEST IBM DSCLI Version: 5.0.3.75 DS: IBM.2107-7527131
ID                            IBM.2107-7527131/0C
Total Failed CG Count         -
Total Successful CG Count     -
Successful CG Percentage      -
Failed CG after Last Success  -
Last Successful CG Form Time  -
Coord. Time (seconds)         -
Interval Time (seconds)       -
Max Drain Time (seconds)      -
First Failure Control Unit    -
First Failure LSS             -
First Failure Reason          -
First Failure Master State    -
Last Failure Control Unit     -
Last Failure LSS              -
Last Failure Reason           -
Last Failure Master State     -
Previous Failure Control Unit -
Previous Failure LSS          -
Previous Failure Reason       -
Previous Failure Master State -
```

The command response in Example 25-27 no longer shows any session metrics. This makes sense because the session is stopped. A stop or terminate session removes all management structures except the session number itself. In contrast to stop or terminate, a pause would have kept the session structures and counters.

Example 25-28 shows a pause example. Both session query commands still show the session state and session metrics, because the session is only paused and not terminated as was done in Example 25-25 on page 306. This illustrates the difference between stop and pause of a Global Mirror session.

Example 25-28 Pausing a Global Mirror Session keeps the internal management structures

```
dscli> pausegmir -lss 0c -session 01

Date/Time: 29. Mai 2005 23:39:03 CEST IBM DSCLI Version: 5.0.3.75 DS: IBM.2107-7527131
CMUC00163I pausegmir: Global Mirror for session 01 successfully paused.

dscli> showgmir  -fullid 0c

Date/Time: 29. Mai 2005 23:40:00 CEST IBM DSCLI Version: 5.0.3.75 DS: IBM.2107-7527131
ID                           IBM.2107-7527131/0C
Master Count                 1
Master Session ID            0x01
Copy State                   Paused
Fatal Reason                 Not Fatal
CG Interval (seconds)        0
XDC Interval(milliseconds)   2
CG Drain Time (seconds)      10
Current Time                 05/29/2005 23:39:33 CEST
CG Time                      05/29/2005 23:38:38 CEST
Successful CG Percentage     100
FlashCopy Sequence Number    0x429A365E
```

```
Master ID                IBM.2107-7527131
Subordinate Count        0
Master SSID              -
Subordinate SSID         -

dscli> showgmir -metrics 0c

Date/Time: 29. Mai 2005 23:40:38 CEST IBM DSCLI Version: 5.0.3.75 DS: IBM.2107-7527131
ID                             IBM.2107-7527131/0C
Total Failed CG Count          0
Total Successful CG Count      155094
Successful CG Percentage       100
Failed CG after Last Success   0
Last Successful CG Form Time   05/29/2005 23:38:38 CEST
Coord. Time (seconds)          2
Interval Time (seconds)        0
Max Drain Time (seconds)       10
First Failure Control Unit     IBM.Unknown-UnknownUnknown
First Failure LSS              0x00
First Failure Reason           No Error
First Failure Master State     -
Last Failure Control Unit      IBM.Unknown-UnknownUnknown
Last Failure LSS               0x00
Last Failure Reason            No Error
Last Failure Master State      -
Previous Failure Control Unit IBM.Unknown-UnknownUnknown
Previous Failure LSS           0x00
Previous Failure Reason        No Error
Previous Failure Master State -
```

25.4.3 Withdraw FlashCopy relationships with DS CLI commands

Example 25-29 shows DS CLI commands that remove the FlashCopy relationship between the B and C volumes.

Example 25-29 Remove FlashCopy relationships, B to C volumes, with DS CLI inband commands

```
dscli> rmremoteflash -dev ibm.2107-7573081 -conduit ibm.2107-7527131/0c 0c00:0e00

Date/Time: 30. Mai 2005 04:43:59 CEST IBM DSCLI Version: 5.0.3.75 DS: IBM.2107-7573081
CMUC00179I rmremoteflash: Are you sure you want to remove the remote FlashCopy pair {0}?
[y/n]:y
CMUC00180I rmremoteflash: Removal of the remote FlashCopy volume pair 0C00:0E00 has been
initiated successfully. Us
e the lsremoteflash command to determine when the relationship is deleted.

dscli> rmremoteflash -dev ibm.2107-7573081 -conduit ibm.2107-7527131/0d 0d00:0f00 0d01:0f01

Date/Time: 30. Mai 2005 04:44:32 CEST IBM DSCLI Version: 5.0.3.75 DS: IBM.2107-7573081
CMUC00179I rmremoteflash: Are you sure you want to remove the remote FlashCopy pair {0}?
[y/n]:y
CMUC00180I rmremoteflash: Removal of the remote FlashCopy volume pair 0D00:0F00 has been
initiated successfully. Us
e the lsremoteflash command to determine when the relationship is deleted.
CMUC00179I rmremoteflash: Are you sure you want to remove the remote FlashCopy pair {0}?
[y/n]:y
CMUC00180I rmremoteflash: Removal of the remote FlashCopy volume pair 0D01:0F01 has been
initiated successfully. Us
e the lsremoteflash command to determine when the relationship is deleted.
```

Note that Example 25-29 on page 308 addresses two LSS pairs. Each FlashCopy withdraw or remove remote FlashCopy command addresses a LSS pair. This example addresses only a few volumes. The number of involved volumes is not limited per command and can be any number as long as the command timeout is not reached.

For example, you may address 256 volumes pairs with the command shown here in Example 25-30.

Example 25-30 Address 256 volume pairs within a single DS CLI command

```
dscli> rmremoteflash -dev ibm.2107-7573081 -conduit ibm.2107-7527131/0d 0d00-0dff:0f00-0fff
```

Because we use inband commands in Example 25-29 on page 308 we address actually the Global Copy primary volume through the **-conduit** parameter that contains the corresponding LSS number after the slash. Through inband communication, this command is propagated over the PPRC link to the remote storage server that is identified by the **-dev** parameter. The FlashCopy source and target pairs are specified at the end of the command line. The second **rmremoteflash** to the other LSS, LSS 0d, withdraws two FlashCopy relationships (Example 25-31).

Example 25-31 Verify FlashCopy relationship between B and C volume with DS CLI command

```
dscli> lsremoteflash -dev ibm.2107-7573081 -conduit ibm.2107-7527131/0c -l 0c00:0e00

Date/Time: 30. Mai 2005 04:45:31 CEST IBM DSCLI Version: 5.0.3.75 DS: IBM.2107-7573081
CMUC00052E lsremoteflash: Storage image IBM.2107-7573081 does not exist.

dscli> lsremoteflash -dev ibm.2107-7573081 -conduit ibm.2107-7527131/0d -l 0d00:0f00
0d01:0f01

Date/Time: 30. Mai 2005 04:44:59 CEST IBM DSCLI Version: 5.0.3.75 DS: IBM.2107-7573081
CMUC00052E lsremoteflash: Storage image IBM.2107-7573081 does not exist.
```

Example 25-31 again shows inband commands. FlashCopy query or list commands verify that there are no longer any FlashCopy relationships. Each query addresses an LSS that was previously involved with FlashCopy relationships within the Global Mirror configuration. The line output of this list command proves that the FlashCopy relationships no longer exist.

25.4.4 Delete Global Copy pairs with DS CLI commands

Although the Global Copy primary volumes are still defined to the Global Mirror session we now delete the Global Copy volume pairs. This will change the volume state from PRIMARY - PENDING.XD and SECONDARY - PENDING.XD to SIMPLEX for both volumes, the Global Copy primary and secondary volume.

Example 25-32 Delete Global Copy volume pairs with DS CLI command

```
dscli> rmpprc -remotedev ibm.2107-7573081  0d00:0d00  0d01:0d01

Date/Time: 30. Mai 2005 04:49:58 CEST IBM DSCLI Version: 5.0.3.75 DS: IBM.2107-7527131
CMUC00160W rmpprc: Are you sure you want to delete the Remote Mirror and Copy volume pair
relationship 0d00:0d00:?
[y/n]:y
CMUC00155I rmpprc: Remote Mirror and Copy volume pair 0D00:0D00 relationship successfully
withdrawn.
CMUC00160W rmpprc: Are you sure you want to delete the Remote Mirror and Copy volume pair
relationship 0d01:0d01:?
[y/n]:y
```

```
CMUC00155I rmpprc: Remote Mirror and Copy volume pair 0D01:0D01 relationship successfully
withdrawn.

dscli> rmpprc -remotedev ibm.2107-7573081  0c00:0c00

Date/Time: 30. Mai 2005 04:50:19 CEST IBM DSCLI Version: 5.0.3.75 DS: IBM.2107-7527131
CMUC00160W rmpprc: Are you sure you want to delete the Remote Mirror and Copy volume pair
relationship 0c00:0c00:?
[y/n]:y
CMUC00155I rmpprc: Remote Mirror and Copy volume pair 0C00:0C00 relationship successfully
withdrawn.
```

Example 25-32 shows two **rmpprc** commands. Each command addresses the volumes within a LSS pair. It is going to be possible to specify volume pairs within the same **rmpprc** command from different LSS pairs. This allows you to combine both commands in Example 25-32 into a single **rmpprc** command.

25.4.5 Remove Global Copy primary volumes from session with DS CLI

Although we deleted the Global Copy volume pairs in both concerned LSSs, LSS 0c and LSS 0d, the A volumes are still defined to the Global Mirror session as Example 25-33 shows.

Example 25-33 Session number 01 is still active in all concerned LSS

```
dscli> lssession -l   0c

Date/Time: 30. Mai 2005 04:54:18 CEST IBM DSCLI Version: 5.0.3.75 DS: IBM.2107-7527131
LSS ID Session Status Volume VolumeStatus PrimaryStatus   SecondaryStatus
FirstPassComplete AllowCascading
===========================================================================================
=================
0C     01      Normal 0C00   Active       Primary Simplex Secondary Simplex True
Disable


dscli> lssession -l   0d

Date/Time: 30. Mai 2005 04:55:00 CEST IBM DSCLI Version: 5.0.3.75 DS: IBM.2107-7527131
LSS ID Session Status Volume VolumeStatus PrimaryStatus   SecondaryStatus
FirstPassComplete AllowCascading
===========================================================================================
=================
0D     01      Normal 0D00   Active       Primary Simplex Secondary Simplex True
Disable
0D     01      Normal 0D01   Active       Primary Simplex Secondary Simplex True
Disable
```

An attempt to remove the Global Mirror session at this stage still fails, as Example 25-34 shows.

Example 25-34 Remove session still fails

```
dscli> rmsession -dev ibm.2107-7527131  -lss 0c  01

Date/Time: 30. Mai 2005 04:59:02 CEST IBM DSCLI Version: 5.0.3.75 DS: IBM.2107-7527131
CMUC00148W rmsession: Are you sure you want to close session 01? [y/n]:y
CMUN03107E rmsession: Copy Services operation failure: volumes in session
```

Lastly, you have to remove now the A volumes from the Global Mirror session before you finally may remove the session itself.

Example 25-35 is a DS CLI command example that removes the A volumes from the Global Mirror session with the session number 01. The session number is a positional parameter at the end of the **chsession** command.

Example 25-35 Remove Global Copy primary volumes from Global Mirror session

```
dscli> chsession                         -lss 0c  -action remove -volume 0c00  01

Date/Time: 30. Mai 2005 05:01:14 CEST IBM DSCLI Version: 5.0.3.75 DS: IBM.2107-7527131
CMUC00147I chsession: Session 01 successfully modified.


dscli> chsession                         -lss 0d  -action remove -volume 0d00-0d01  01

Date/Time: 30. Mai 2005 05:01:43 CEST IBM DSCLI Version: 5.0.3.75 DS: IBM.2107-7527131
CMUC00147I chsession: Session 01 successfully modified.
```

Each LSS requires a corresponding **chsession** command to remove the A volumes from the session within the concerned LSS.

Note that the second DS CLI command in Example 25-35 removes two A volumes. The **-volume** parameter specifies a range of volumes in LSS 0d with device number 00 to 01.

25.4.6 Remove Global Mirror session with DS CLI command

In Example 25-36 you may remove the Global Mirror session from all involved LSSs at the local site.

Example 25-36 Remove session through DS CLI command

```
dscli> rmsession -dev ibm.2107-7527131  -lss 0c  01

Date/Time: 30. Mai 2005 05:02:12 CEST IBM DSCLI Version: 5.0.3.75 DS: IBM.2107-7527131
CMUC00148W rmsession: Are you sure you want to close session 01? [y/n]:y
CMUC00146I rmsession: Session 01 closed successfully.
```

Example 25-36 shows a command example to remove or close a Global Mirror session. The session number is again a positional parameter at the end of the **rmsession** command.

Example 25-37 verifies that the session is removed from the concerned LSS.

Example 25-37 Verify Global Mirror session

```
dscli> lssession -l   0c

Date/Time: 30. Mai 2005 05:02:25 CEST IBM DSCLI Version: 5.0.3.75 DS: IBM.2107-7527131
CMMCI9003W No Sessions instances found in the system.
```

The PPRC paths are still active and may be removed now as well.

25.5 ICKDSF support for Global Mirror

ICKDSF used to be a disk management tool to initialize and diagnose disk volumes. Over time it evolved and today ICKDSF contains functional support to manage all available Copy Services functions.

ICKDSF supports all zSeries based operating systems including z/OS, z/VM, and VSE/ESA™. Therefore ICKDSF is a common platform for all zSeries operating systems to provide an interface to the DS8000, DS6000, and ESS 800 Copy Services functions. This includes all functional flavors of Metro Mirror, Global Copy, Global Mirror, and FlashCopy.

ICKDSF covers Global Mirror management since the introduction of Global Mirror was announced in April 20, 2004 for the ESS 800. This includes now also the DS8000 and DS6000.

25.5.1 Establish a Global Mirror environment with ICKDSF

The following sections exercise in a step-by-step approach how to build up a Global Mirror environment with ICKDSF. The sequence of the following steps is recommended, although it is not required, to succeed to establish a Global Mirror environment. But the following sequence guarantees a clean and straight forward creation of a Global Mirror environment (Figure 25-8).

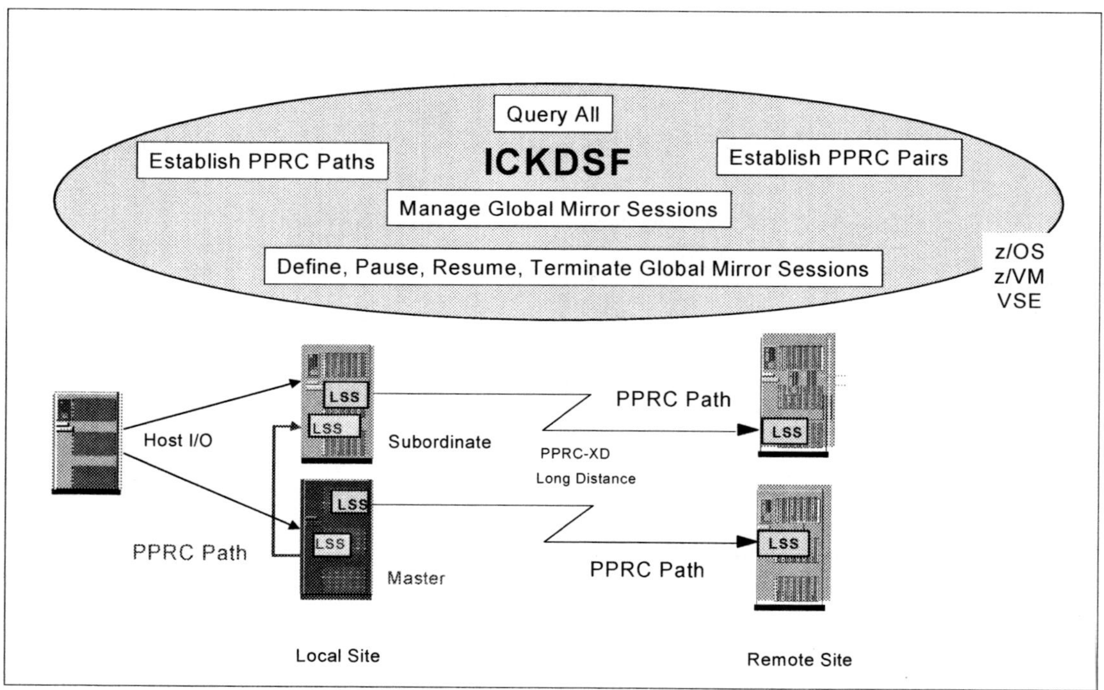

Figure 25-8 ICKDSF support for Global Mirror

Figure 25-8 provides the complete picture of a Global Mirror session. ICKDSF is used to:

- Establish PPRC paths
- Establish PPRC pairs
- Create FlashCopy relationships
- Manage Global Mirror session in adding or removing primary volumes to or from the Global Mirror session.

- Commands to address the entire Global Mirror session that may be pausing or resuming a Global Mirror session. Also start and terminate are commands that address a Global Mirror session.

The following sections go through the creation of a Global Mirror session using ICKDSF.

25.5.2 Define PPRC paths with ICKDSF

There is no change on how to define a PPRC paths on the DS6000 or DS8000 as compared to the ESS 800 when you use ICKDSF. See Figure 25-9.

> **Note:** Only PPRC links over Fibre Channel are supported on the DS6000 and the DS8000.

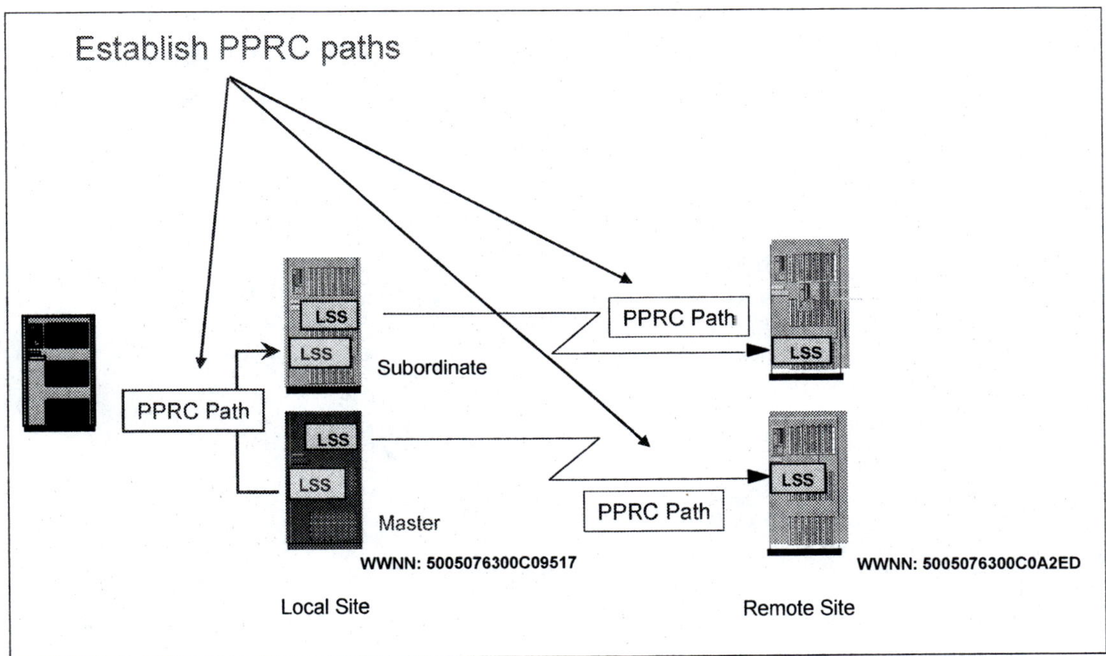

Figure 25-9 Establish all Global Mirror paths through ICKDSF

Also note that you need to define PPRC paths between the involved primary storage servers, when you utilize more than a single storage server at the local site.

Example 25-38 shows the JCL and command lines to define PPRC paths between two storage servers. Note that an online volume cannot be referred to via the ICKDSF UNIT parameter. ICKDSF implies the volume to be offline when you use the UNIT parameter with a corresponding z/OS device number. On the other side it is most likely that a Global Copy primary volume is online to the system from where you issue the ICKDSF jobs. This requires for each device you address through an ICKDSF PPRC command to provide a JCL DD statement for this device.

Example 25-38 ICKDSF example to define PPRC paths

```
//* -------------------------------------------------------------- ***
//STEP01  EXEC PGM=ICKDSF
//SYSPRINT  DD SYSOUT=*
//DD01      DD UNIT=3390,VOL=SER=RS7000,DISP=SHR
//SYSIN     DD *
```

```
PPRCOPY DDNAME(DD01) ESTPATH     -
        PRI(X'7000' 22399)       -
        SEC(X'7800' 25941)       -
        LSS(X'00' X'00')         -
        FCPPATHS(X'000C000C'     -
                 X'008C008C')    -
        WWNN(5005076300C09517    -
             5005076300C0A2ED)

PPRCOPY DDNAME(DD01)  QUERY  PATHS
/*
```

Note the extra parameter to identify the concerned LSS; primary and secondary parameters contain the SSID besides the serial number. FCPPATHS contain the sending system adapter ID (SAID) and the receiving SAID. A WWNN is also required to identify the source and target storage server.

Issue a corresponding query command to verify whether the path establish was successful. It may happen that not all paths may be successfully established and you want to find out immediately.

25.5.3 Establish Global Copy pairs with ICKDSF

There is no new syntax to establish Global Copy pairs with ICKDSF. This was always possible with ICKDSF. Figure 25-10 shows that Global Copy pairs are established as usual. There is nothing particular concerning Global copy for this step.

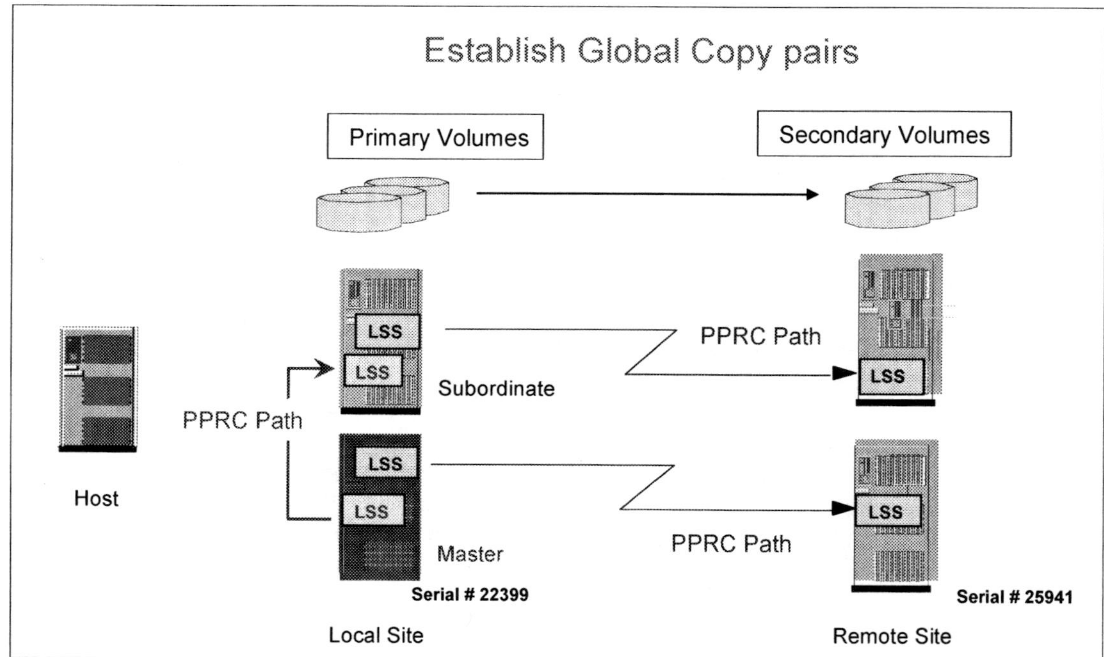

Figure 25-10 Establish Global Copy pairs

Example 25-39 shows the JCL and command lines to create a Global Copy pair.

Example 25-39 Establish Global Copy pair through ICKDSF

```
//* ------------------------------------------------------------- ***
//STEP01  EXEC PGM=ICKDSF
//SYSPRINT  DD SYSOUT=*
```

```
//DD01      DD UNIT=3390,VOL=SER=RS7000,DISP=SHR
//SYSIN     DD *

 PPRCOPY DDNAME(DD01) ESTPAIR           -
         PRI(X'7000' 22399 X'00')       -
         SEC(X'7800' 25941 X'00')       -
         LSS(X'00' X'00')               -
         MODE(COPY) OPTION(XD)

 PPRCOPY DDNAME(DD01)  QUERY
/*
```

Note again the requirement for a JCL DD statement for the involved Global Copy primary volume. This may become a bit cumbersome when you intend to establish hundreds or even thousand of Global Copy pairs. You then would need to add the same number of JCL DD statements and refer to each DD statement through the DDNAME parameter. Note also that the volume has to be online when you used the DDNAME approach. With the UNIT parameter the volume must be offline to the system, from where you execute the ESTPAIR command.

Again the LSS parameter identifies the involved LSS. The primary and secondary parameters require positional parameters with SSID in the first specification. The second parameter is the serial number of the corresponding storage server, not in hex notation. In hex notation the third parameter refers to the channel connection address (CCA) of the concerned device.

25.5.4 Establish FlashCopy relationship through ICKDSF

The next step creates this particular FlashCopy relationship between the B volume and the C volume at the remote site. Figure 25-11 visualizes how this step addresses the storage servers at the remote site.

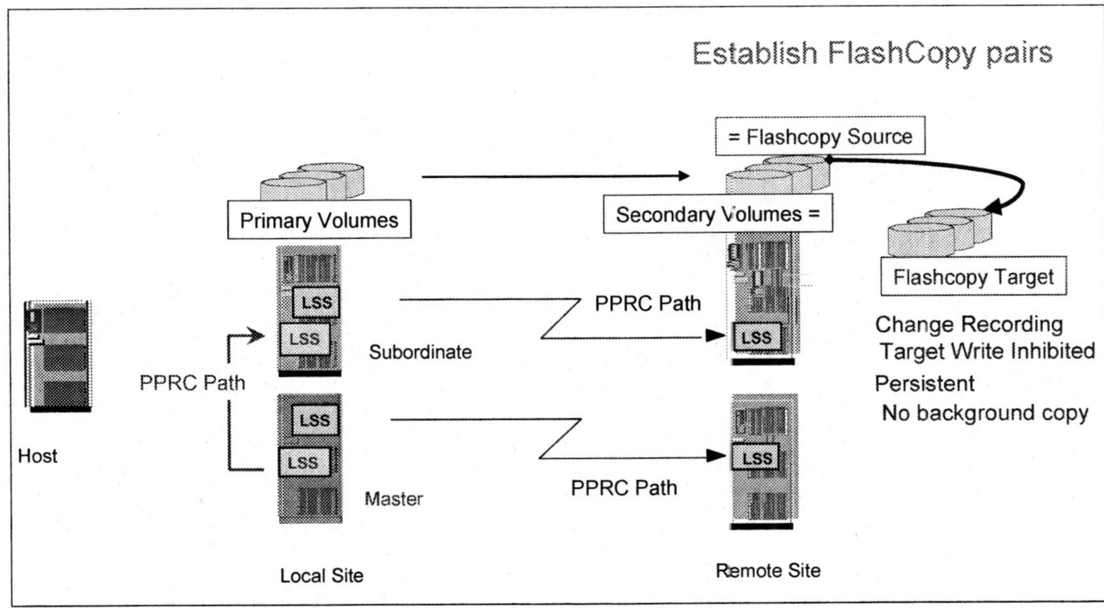

Figure 25-11 ICKDSF - create FlashCopy relationship for Global Mirror

Depending whether you connect to the remote site or to the local site, the FlashCopy command is either directly issued to the remote storage server or via inband command. The inband command is targeted to the local primary volume and provides addressing information for the FlashCopy source and FlashCopy target volume at the remote site.

Example 25-40 shows an inband ICKDSF job example under the assumption that usually there is no host connection from the local site to the remote storage server, which may reside on another continent.

Example 25-40 ICKDSF FlashCopy establish via inband command

```
//* ------------------------------------------------------------ ***
//STEP01  EXEC PGM=ICKDSF
//SYSPRINT  DD SYSOUT=*
//SYSIN     DD *

 FLASHCPY   UNIT(7000) ESTABLISH                       -
            SOURCEVOL(X'00' X'00' X'7800' 25941)       -
            TARGETVOL(X'01' X'00' 7900)                -
            CHANGERCD(YES)                             -
            INHIBWRTS(YES)                             -
            MODE(NOCOPY)                               -
            TARGETCANCOMEONLINE(NO)

 FC         UNIT(7000) QUERY    -
            SRCVOL(X'00' X'00' X'7800' 25941
/*
```

The ESTABLISH inband command has some complexity. UNIT points to the local primary Global Mirror volume. SOURCEVOL identifies the FlashCopy source volume at the remote site. Note this volume is also the Global Mirror secondary volume. TARGETVOL identifies the FlashCopy target volume. Both parameters require certain positional parameters. All parameters are in hex notation except the serial number in SOURCEVOL as the last positional parameter. In TARGETVOL, the last positional parameter is the z/OS device number of the FlashCopy target volume, which is also not specified in hex notation. For details refer to *Device Support Facility User's Guide and Reference Release 17*, SC35-0033.

The second FlashCopy command is a query of the FlashCopy pair that just has been established in the previous command. Note that FLASHCOPY can be abbreviated as well as SOURCEVOL can. This FlashCopy command is also an inband command and is targeted to the FlashCopy source volume by the SRCVOL parameter, which is the same as in the previous FlashCopy command.

The job shown in Example 25-40 refers to the A volume or Global Copy primary volume via the UNIT parameter. This requires the device on address 7000 to be offline. When the device is online to the system and when this job executes, ICKDSF will return with an error message and fail the command.

Example 25-41 shows how to structure your commands and use abbreviated parameters.

Example 25-41 ICKDSF inband FlashCopy with abbreviated parameters

```
//* ------------------------------------------------------------ ***
//FCBTOC  EXEC PGM=ICKDSF
//SYSPRINT  DD SYSOUT=*
//DD01      DD UNIT=3390,VOL=SER=XX2C00,DISP=SHR  local PPRC device
//SYSIN     DD *

  FC   DDNAME(DD01) ESTAB                        -
       SRCVOL       (X'0C',X'00',X'2C00' 03461)  -
       TGTVOL       (X'0E',X'00',3E00)           -
       CHRCD        (YES)                        -
       NOTGTWT      (YES)                        -
       MODE         (NOCOPY)
```

```
 FC    DDNAME(DD01) QUERY                            -
       SRCVOL        (X'0C',X'00',X'2C00' 03461)
/*
```

Example 25-41 again shows the commands that are targeted to the online volume and, therefore, require a corresponding JCL DD statement for the concerned primary Global Copy volume.

25.5.5 Define a Global Mirror session through ICKDSF

This step creates a session for all concerned LSSs. Each LSS that potentially contributes Global Copy primary volumes to the Global Mirror session requires this define session before adding volumes to the session.

Figure 25-12 indicates that the session number applies only to the concerned LSS at the local site.

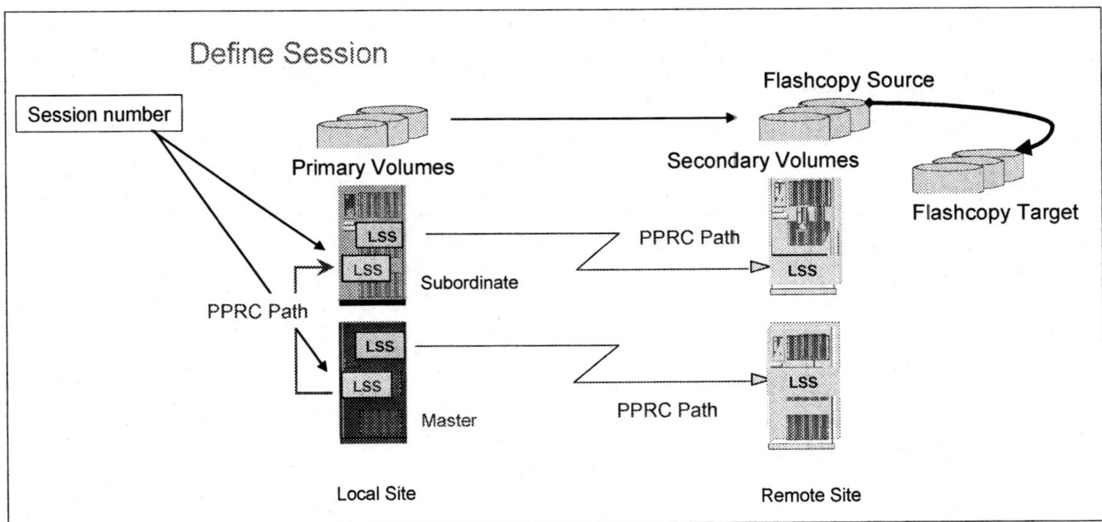

Figure 25-12 ICKDSF - define Global Mirror session

Example 25-42 shows an ICKDSF job that defines a Global Mirror session to the LSS where the volume RS7000 belongs to. Note that with this Global Mirror command, you do not need to define an LSS number, nor a CCA, nor SSID.

Example 25-42 ICKDSF job to define a Global Mirror session to an LSS

```
//* -------------------------------------------------------------- ***
//STEP01  EXEC PGM=ICKDSF
//SYSPRINT  DD SYSOUT=*
//DD01      DD UNIT=3390,VOL=SER=RS7000,DISP=SHR
//SYSIN     DD *

 PPRC DDNAME(DD01) DEFINESESSION   -
                   OPEN            -
                   SESSIONNO(001)

/*
```

Example 25-42 points again to an online volume by the DDNAME parameter. A session is created in the corresponding LSS and is 001 in this example.

25.5.6 Add volumes to session through ICKDSF

This step adds Global Copy primary volumes to the Global Mirror session. Figure 25-13 indicates that this addresses only the Global Copy primary volumes.

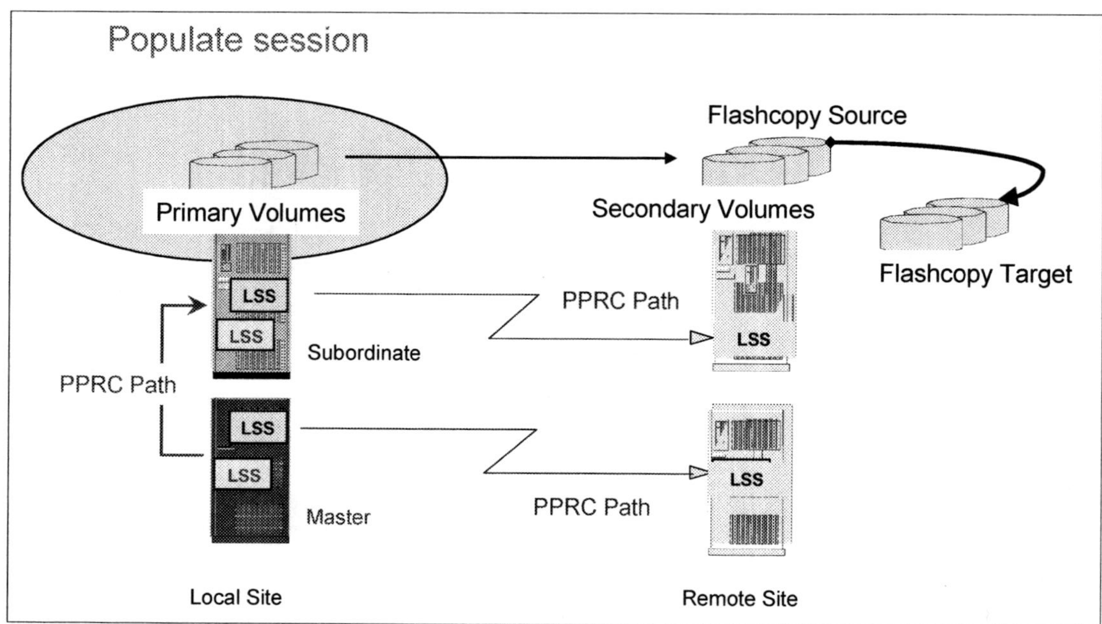

Figure 25-13 ICKDSF - populate Global Mirror session with primary volumes

Example 25-43 shows JCL and a command example of how to add volumes to a Global Mirror session.

Example 25-43 Add volumes to session through ICKDSF

```
//* ------------------------------------------------------------ ***
//STEP01  EXEC PGM=ICKDSF
//SYSPRINT  DD SYSOUT=*
//SYSIN     DD *

 PPRC  UNIT(7000)       POPULATESESSION         -
                        JOIN SESSIONNO(001)     -
                        RANGE(NO) VOLCOUNT(1)   -
                        IVOLLIST((X'00'))

 PPRC  UNIT(7100)       POPULATESESSION         -
                        JOIN SESSIONNO(001)     -
                        RANGE(YES) VOLCOUNT(1)  -
                        RVOLLIST(X'00',X'0F')


 PPRC  UNIT(7000)       QUERY                   -
                        SESSIONSDEVICES
/*
```

Through a list parameter you identify the Global Copy primary volumes that ought to become a member of the Global Mirror session. This is either a list of CCA addresses, IVOLLIST, or a range of CCA addresses in the RVOLLIST parameter.

You need to understand the VOLCOUNT parameter in Example 25-44. It shows an example of multiple ranges of volumes with the populate command. Note that this command applies only to the LSS that is addressed by the UNIT parameter.

Example 25-44 Multiple volume ranges in ICKDSF Global Mirror command with RVOLLIST

```
RVOLLIST ((X'00',X'1F'),(X'30',X'3F')) VOLCNT(2)
```

Note that the VOLCNT parameter counts the number of ranges you specify in the RVOLLIST parameter. In Example 25-44 on page 319 the VOLCNT is 2 because RVOLLIST contains two ranges.

Instead of RVOLLIST, you can select dedicated volumes that are going to become a part of Global Mirror session through the IVOLLIST. Volume count VOLCNT has a similar meaning with IVOLLIST as with RVOLLIST, as Example 25-45 shows.

Example 25-45 Multiple volumes in ICKDSF Global Mirror command with IVOLLIST

```
IVOLLIST((X'00'),(X'02')) VOLCNT(2)
```

Note that each POPULATESESSION command addresses an LSS, and you need at least as many POPULATESESSION commands as LSSs that are involved in a Global Mirror session.

25.5.7 Start Global Mirror through ICKDSF

Once all Global Mirror components are defined and ready to be used, you start the Global Mirror session (Figure 25-14).

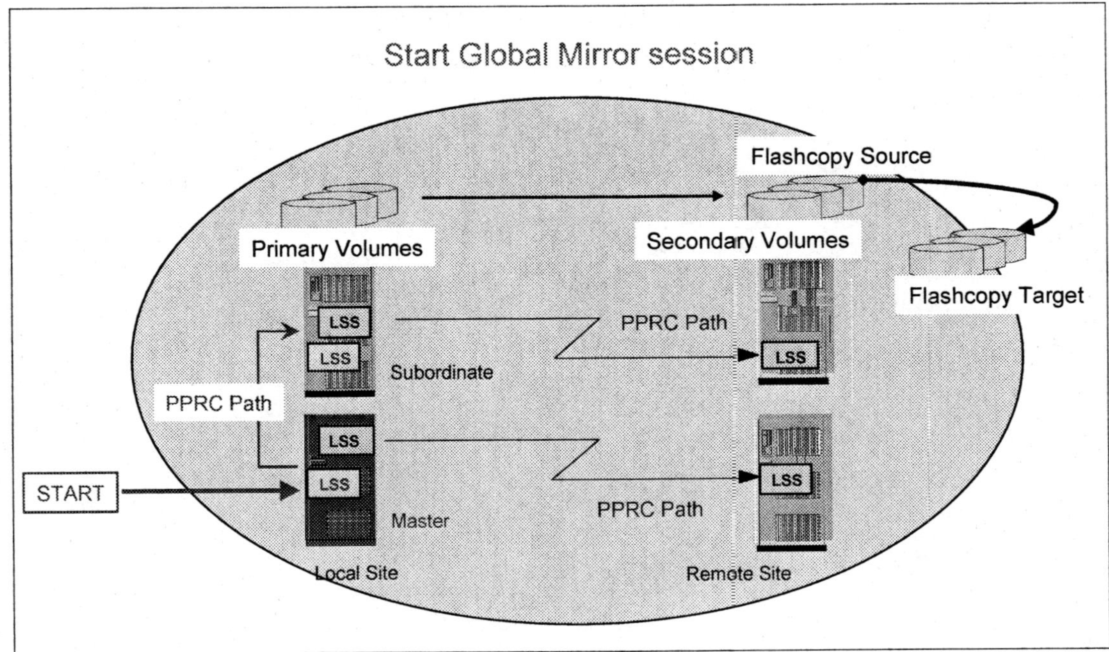

Figure 25-14 ICKDSF - start Global Mirror session

With the very first Global Mirror start command, you decide which LSS becomes the Master LSS. All further Global Mirror session commands have to go through the Master LSS.

Note that the Master LSS may also contain Global Copy primary volumes that are part of the Global Mirror session. Note also that you need only Global Mirror control paths, PPRC paths, between a LSS in the Master and a LSS in the corresponding Subordinate storage server. Global Mirror communication within a storage server is happening over internal communication paths (Example 25-46).

Example 25-46 ICKDSF example to start a Global Mirror session

```
//* ------------------------------------------------------------ ***
//STEP01  EXEC PGM=ICKDSF
//SYSPRINT  DD SYSOUT=*
//SYSIN     DD *

 PPRC  UNIT(7000) STARTASYNCCOPY START                 -
                  SESSIONNO(001)    -
                  MAXCOORDTIME(05)  -
                  MAXDRAINTIME(60)  -
                  CGINTERVALTIME(0)

 PPRC  UNIT(7000) QUERY ASYNCCOPY
/*
```

Example 25-46 shows an example of how to start a Global Mirror session through ICKDSF. From now on Global Mirror builds Consistency Groups, CG. See 23.3, “Form Consistency Group” on page 251 for more on how to form Consistency Groups.

25.5.8 Query active Global Mirror session through ICKDSF

Figure 25-15 shows an ICKDSF command to query the devices and their session status. At the very moment when the query session executed, a Consistency Group formation process was going on.

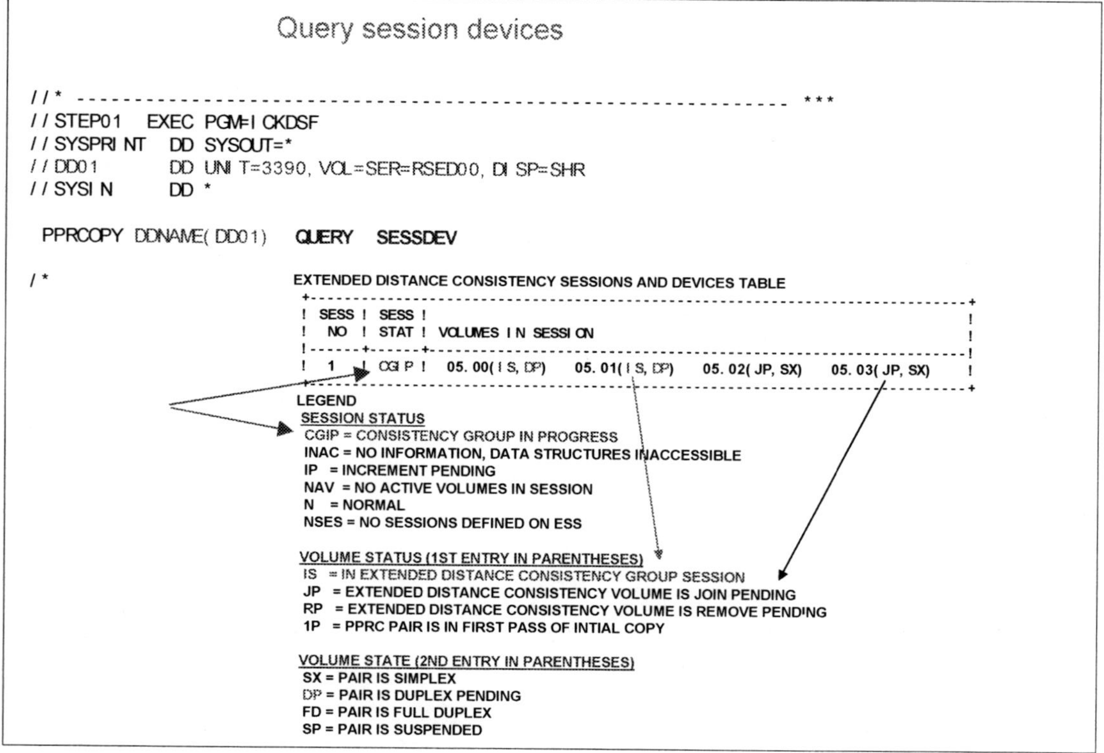

Figure 25-15 ICKDSF - query devices in Global Mirror session

Figure 25-15 also shows that there are four volumes in the Global Mirror session within the LSS where the DDNAME volume points to. The first two volumes are in session (IS). The next two volumes are defined to the session but they are in a JOIN PENDING state and they are not Global Copy primary volumes (SIMPLEX). This means the volumes are added to the session with the POPULATESESSION command although these volume are not Global Copy primary volumes. This is indicated by the SX code.

Figure 25-16 provides an ICKDSF query command of a Global Mirror session and its edited output.

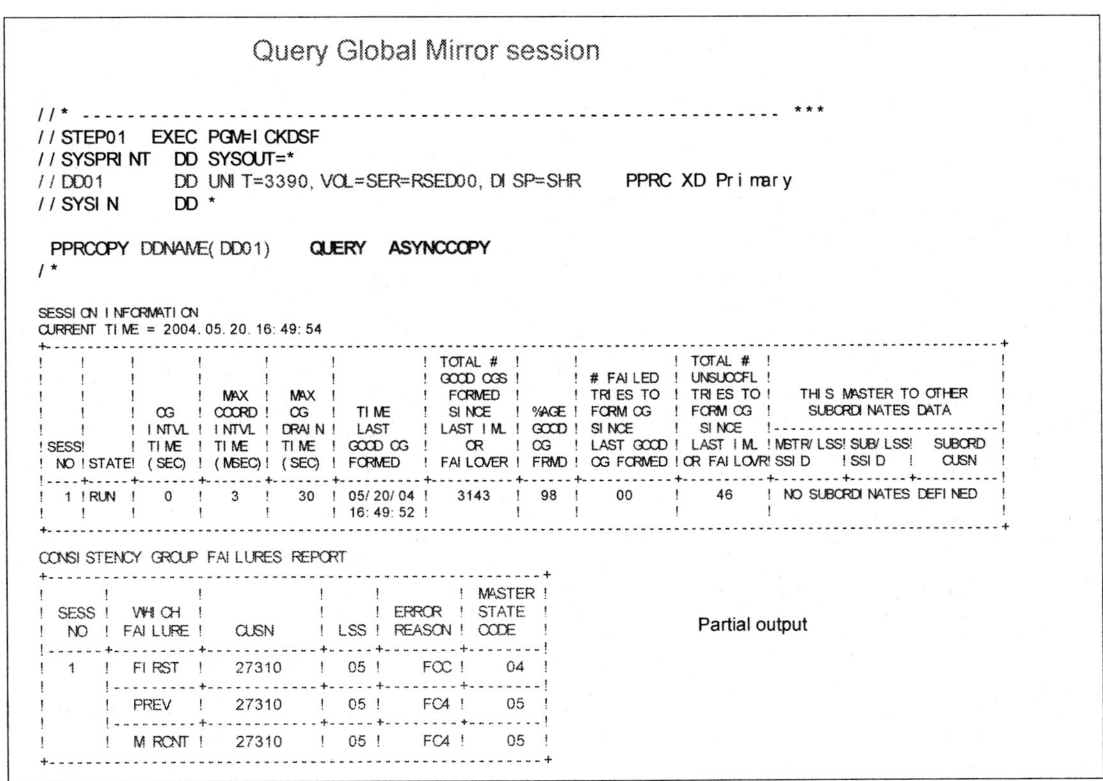

Query Global Mirror session

```
//* ------------------------------------------------------------ ***
//STEP01   EXEC PGM=ICKDSF
//SYSPRINT   DD SYSOUT=*
//DD01       DD UNIT=3390,VOL=SER=RSED00,DISP=SHR     PPRC XD Primary
//SYSIN      DD *

 PPRCOPY DDNAME(DD01)    QUERY   ASYNCCOPY
/*

SESSION INFORMATION
CURRENT TIME = 2004.05.20.16:49:54
+-------------------------------------------------------------------------------------------------------------+
!    !     !       !       !       !         ! TOTAL #  !     !            ! TOTAL #   !                          !
!    !     !       !       !       !         ! GOOD CGS !     ! # FAILED   ! UNSUCCFL  !                          !
!    !     !       ! MAX   ! MAX   !         ! FORMED   !     ! TRIES TO   ! TRIES TO  ! THIS MASTER TO OTHER     !
!    !     ! CG    ! COORD ! CG    ! TIME    ! SINCE    !%AGE ! FORM CG    ! FORM CG   !  SUBORDINATES DATA       !
!    !     ! INTVL ! INTVL ! DRAIN ! LAST    ! LAST IML !GOOD ! SINCE      ! SINCE     !--------------------------!
!SESS!     ! TIME  ! TIME  ! TIME  ! GOOD CG !   OR     ! CG  ! LAST GOOD  ! LAST IML  !MSTR/LSS!SUB/LSS! SUBORD  !
! NO !STATE! (SEC) ! (MSEC)! (SEC) ! FORMED  ! FAILOVER !FRMD ! CG FORMED  !OR FAILOVR!SSID    !SSID   ! CUSN    !
!----+-----+-------+-------+-------+---------+----------+-----+------------+----------+--------+-------+---------!
!  1 !RUN  !   0   !   3   !  30   !05/20/04 !  3143    ! 98  !    00      !   46     ! NO SUBORDINATES DEFINED  !
!    !     !       !       !       !16:49:52 !          !     !            !          !                          !
+-------------------------------------------------------------------------------------------------------------+

CONSISTENCY GROUP FAILURES REPORT
+----------------------------------------------------------+
!      !         !             !     !        ! MASTER !
! SESS ! WHICH   !             !     ! ERROR  ! STATE  !
!  NO  ! FAILURE !    CUSN     ! LSS ! REASON ! CODE   !
!------+---------+-------------+-----+--------+--------!
!  1   ! FIRST   !   27310     ! 05  !   FCC  !   04   !
!      !---------+-------------+-----+--------+--------!
!      ! PREV    !   27310     ! 05  !   FC4  !   05   !
!      !---------+-------------+-----+--------+--------!
!      ! M RCNT  !   27310     ! 05  !   FC4  !   05   !
+----------------------------------------------------------+
```

Partial output

Figure 25-16 ICKDSF - query session information and CG failure report

You point with the DDNAME and its corresponding volume to the Master LSS. This query command provides two reports. Under session information you find details on forming Consistency Groups. The table also shows the Global Mirror session tunable variables that are active.

The Consistency Group failure report is the second report and provides codes about why forming Consistency Groups failed. Example 25-47 provides the corresponding legend to understand the codes that are shown in this report.

Example 25-47 Legend to address ICKDSF Consistency Group FAILURE REPORT

```
LEGEND
   SESS NO
     UA   : UNABLE TO RETRIEVE INFORMATION, DATA STRUCTURES UNAVAILABLE. WAIT A FEW MINUTES
AND RETRY.

   WHICH FAILURE
     FIRST : FIRST Consistency Group FAILURE
     PREV  : PREVIOUS Consistency Group FAILURE
     M RCNT: MOST RECENT Consistency Group FAILURE
```

```
LSS, ERROR REASON, OR MASTER STATE CODE
  FO/IM: INFORMATION UNAVAILABLE DUE TO FAILOVER OR IML
  N/A  : NOT AVAILABLE, PERHAPS DUE TO FAILOVER OR IML, OR NOT APPLICABLE

ERROR REASON
  01  : ASYNCHRONOUS PPRC STRUCTURES CANNNOT BE ACCESSED
  02  : ASYNCHRONOUS PPRC COMMUNICATION PATH FAILURE
  03  : EXTENDED DISTANCE CONSISTENCY SESSION MEMBERS NOT IN CORRECT STATE
  04  : MAXIMUM Consistency Group DRAIN TIME EXCEEDED
  400 : INVALID PARAMETER
  FYY : FORMAT OXOF ERROR, WHERE YY IS THE REASON CODE
  7ZZZ: MICROCODE LOGIC ERROR - ZZZ DESCRIBES ERROR
  F005: TEMPORARILY UNAVAILABLE
  F01D: LONG BUSY

MASTER STATE
  01: PAUSE/TERMINATE ASYNCHRONOUS PPRC IN PROGRESS
  02: START/RESUME ASYNCHRONOUS PPRC IN PROGRESS
  03: ASYNCHRONOUS PPRC IS BETWEEN Consistency Group FORMATIONS
  04: XDC START INCREMENT IN PROGRESS
  05: XDC RUN IN PROGRESS
  06: DRAIN IN PROGRESS
  07: FLASHCOPY ESTABLISH WITH REVERTIBLE IN PROGRESS
  08: FLASHCOPY WITHDRAW WITH COMMIT IN PROGRESS
  09: XDC INCREMENT COMPLETE IN PROGRESS
  0A: FLASHCOPY WITHDRAW WITH REVERT IN PROGRESS
  0B: ASYNCHRONOUS PPRC IS PAUSED
  0C: ASYNCHRONOUS PPRC IS PERFORMING POST-Consistency Group TASKS
  0D: ASYNCHRONOUS PPRC IS FATAL
  0E: ASYNCHRONOUS PPRC IS COMPLETING ERROR RECOVERY
```

For more details, refer to *Device Support Facility User's Guide and Reference Release 17*, SC35-0033.

25.5.9 Remove a Global Mirror environment with ICKDSF

The following sections exercises in a step-by-step approach how to completely remove a Global Mirror environment with ICKDSF. The sequence of the following steps is recommended, although it is not required, to succeed to remove a Global Mirror environment. But the following sequence guarantees a clean and straightforward removal of a Global Mirror environment.

This is the recommended sequence to remove a Global Mirror environment:

1. Stop the Global Mirror session.
2. Remove the A volumes or Global Copy primary volumes from the Global Mirror session.
3. Un-define or remove the session from all concerned primary LSSs.
4. Withdraw the FlashCopy relationship from B volumes to C volumes.
5. Delete the Global Copy volume pairs.
6. Remove all PPRC paths between local and remote LSSs as well as potentially between the Master LSS and Subordinate LSSs.

25.5.10 Stop a Global Mirror session with ICKDSF

First you stop the Global Mirror session (Example 25-48). Note that this is a session command you target to the Master LSS. The command that was used in Example 25-24 on page 305 just stops the Consistency Group formation process.

Example 25-48 Stop Global Mirror session with ICKDSF

```
//* ------------------------------------------------------------- ***
//TERMSESS EXEC PGM=ICKDSF
//SYSPRINT  DD SYSOUT=*
//DD01      DD UNIT=3390,VOL=SER=AA6000,DISP=SHR
//SYSIN     DD *

 PPRCOPY DDNAME(DD01) TMASYNC     -
         SESSNO(001)              -
         TERMINATE                -
         MASTER
/*
```

Note that the Global Copy replication process still continues, but there are no longer any FlashCopy operations, because they are part of the process to form Consistency Groups. But from now on Consistency Groups are not created any longer. Note also that an ongoing process to form a Consistency Group may not come to a successful end and may be terminated. In contrast to TERMINATE, a PAUSE would finish an ongoing process to form a Consistency Group that may be in the middle when the PAUSE was issued. This Consistency Group creation process completes, before the PAUSE stops the creation of further Consistency Group formations.

25.5.11 Remove volumes from Global Mirror session with ICKDSF

The next step is to remove the A volumes or Global Copy primary volumes from the Global Mirror session. Note this session still exists. The previous command just stopped the formation of Consistency Groups (Example 25-49).

Example 25-49 Remove the A volumes from the Global Mirror session through ICKDSF

```
//* ------------------------------------------------------------- ***
//REMOVE  EXEC PGM=ICKDSF
//SYSPRINT  DD SYSOUT=*
//DD01      DD UNIT=3390,VOL=SER=AA6000,DISP=SHR
//SYSIN     DD *

 PPRCOPY DDNAME(DD01) POPSESS           -
         REMOVE                         -
         SESSNO   (001)                 -
         VOLCOUNT (1)                   -
         RANGE    (YES)                 -
         RVOLLIST ((X'00',X'03'))
```

Example 25-49 is an ICKDSF example that removes four Global Copy primary volumes from session number 001. DDNAME points to the concerned LSS. Note that this does not stop Global Copy from replicating newly arrived data at the local site to the remote site.

This command is required for each LSS at the local site that contains volumes that belong to the Global Mirror session number 001.

25.5.12 Un-define or remove the Global Mirror session with ICKDSF

Now we remove or delete or un-define the session and its session number from all involved LSSs at the local site (Example 25-50).

Example 25-50 Remove session from LSS with ICKDSF

```
//* ------------------------------------------------------------ ***
//CLOSESS EXEC PGM=ICKDSF
//SYSPRINT  DD SYSOUT=*
//DD01      DD UNIT=3390,VOL=SER=AA6000,DISP=SHR
//SYSIN     DD *

 PPRCOPY DDNAME(DD01) DEFSESS     -
         SESSNO(001)              -
         CLOSE
/*
```

Although the ICKDSF command in Example 25-50 says DEFINESESSION or DEFSESS the parameter CLOSE will remove the Global Mirror session and the concerned session number from the LSS where the DDNAME parameter points to. This command is repeated for all LSSs that were involved in the Global Mirror session number 001.

Now we remove in the next steps the FlashCopy relationships and delete the Global Copy pairs that belonged to the session we just deleted.

25.5.13 Withdraw FlashCopy relationships with ICKDSF

Example 25-51 shows an ICKDSF job/step that removes the FlashCopy relationships between the B and C volumes.

Example 25-51 Withdraw FlashCopy relationship between B and C volume with ICKDSF

```
//* ------------------------------------------------------------ ***
//* FLASHCOPY WITHDRAW (B -> C VOLUME RELATIONSHIP) inband      ***
//* ------------------------------------------------------------ ***
//*   SRCVOL (X'LSS' X'CCA' X'SSID' SERIAL#)                     ***
//*   TGTVOL (X'LSS' X'CCA' DEVICE#)                             ***
//* ------------------------------------------------------------ ***
//WITHDRW EXEC PGM=ICKDSF
//SYSPRINT  DD SYSOUT=*
//DD01      DD UNIT=3390,VOL=SER=AA6000,DISP=SHR
//DD02      DD UNIT=3390,VOL=SER=AA6001,DISP=SHR
//DD03      DD UNIT=3390,VOL=SER=AA6002,DISP=SHR
//DD04      DD UNIT=3390,VOL=SER=AA6003,DISP=SHR
//SYSIN     DD *

 FC  DDNAME(DD01)   WD                        /* WITHDRAW     */ -
     SRCVOL         (X'00',X'00',0002,AAVCA)  /* B VOLUME     */ -
     TGTVOL         (X'01',X'00',0003)        /* C VOLUME     */

 FC  DDNAME(DD02)   WD                        /* WITHDRAW     */ -
     SRCVOL         (X'00',X'01',0002,AAVCA)  /* B VOLUME     */ -
     TGTVOL         (X'01',X'01',0003)        /* C VOLUME     */

 FC  DDNAME(DD03)   WD                        /* WITHDRAW     */ -
     SRCVOL         (X'00',X'02',0002,AAVCA)  /* B VOLUME     */ -
     TGTVOL         (X'01',X'02',0003)        /* C VOLUME     */

 FC  DDNAME(DD04)   WD                        /* WITHDRAW     */ -
```

```
    SRCVOL          (X'00',X'03',0002,AAVCA)    /* B VOLUME      */ -
    TGTVOL          (X'01',X'03',0003)          /* C VOLUME      */
```

Note that we issue this FlashCopy WITHDRAW or WD command at the local site to the Global Copy primary volume. The primary volume is identified by a JCL DD statement to which the ICKDSF FC command via the DDNAME parameter points to. This is an inband FLASHCOPY or FC command. Through the SRCVOL and the TGTVOL we identify the FlashCopy source and target volume pair at the remote site. This command will end the FlashCopy relationship between the B and C volumes.

25.5.14 Delete Global Copy pairs with ICKDSF

Example 25-52 is an example to delete the Global Copy volume pairs.

Example 25-52 Delete Global Copy pairs with ICKDSF commands

```
//* -------------------------------------------------------------- ***
//DELPAIR EXEC PGM=ICKDSF
//SYSPRINT  DD SYSOUT=*
//DD01      DD UNIT=3390,VOL=SER=AA6000,DISP=SHR
//DD02      DD UNIT=3390,VOL=SER=AA6001,DISP=SHR
//DD03      DD UNIT=3390,VOL=SER=AA6002,DISP=SHR
//DD04      DD UNIT=3390,VOL=SER=AA6003,DISP=SHR
//SYSIN     DD *

 PPRCOPY DDNAME(DD01) DELPAIR      -
         LSS(X'00' X'00')          -
         PRI(X'2060' AAGXA X'00') -
         SEC(X'0002' AAVCA X'00')

 PPRCOPY DDNAME(DD02) DELPAIR      -
         LSS(X'00' X'00')          -
         PRI(X'2060' AAGXA X'01') -
         SEC(X'0002' AAVCA X'01')

 PPRCOPY DDNAME(DD03) DELPAIR      -
         LSS(X'00' X'00')          -
         PRI(X'2060' AAGXA X'02') -
         SEC(X'0002' AAVCA X'02')

 PPRCOPY DDNAME(DD04) DELPAIR      -
         LSS(X'00' X'00')          -
         PRI(X'2060' AAGXA X'03') -
         SEC(X'0002' AAVCA X'03')
```

Note that ICKDSF explicitly refers to the source and target LSS. The PRI and SEC parameter identify the concerned SSID, serial number, and CCA of the concerned volumes.

25.5.15 Remove all PPRC paths with ICKDSF

Finally, you may remove all PPRC paths between the local and remote LSSs, as well as between the Master LSS and potential Subordinates.

25.6 ANTRQST macro enhanced to manage Global Mirror

The ANTRQST macro is part of the System Data Mover (SDM) component in DFSMSdfp™ and is enhanced to support Global Mirror.

This includes the following new request types to manage Global Mirror sessions:

- RSESSION

  This request type allows you to control Global Mirror sessions and includes DEFINE, UNDEFINE, START, STOP, PAUSE, and RESUME. These actions address a Global Mirror session.

- RVOLUME

  This request type is used to add Global Copy primary volumes to a session or remove Global Copy primary volumes from a session. The corresponding action is either JOIN or REMOVE.

- RQUERY

  This is also a new request type to support Global Mirror. There are several action parameters that determine what information to obtain from a Global Mirror session. The API allows you to get more information out of a Global Mirror session than through respective TSO commands or ICKDSF commands.

The ANTRQST macro allows you to direct the query output to a pre-allocated data set with a logical record length or 120 byte fixed length.

The ANTRQST macro is not detailed here.

If you need more information about the Copy Services functions and how they are triggered through the macro then refer to *z/OS DFSMS Advanced Copy Services*, SC35-0428. This manual contains also an Assembler sample program that starts a Global Mirror session.This session is comprised of a Master and three Subordinate storage servers.

25.7 DS Storage Manager or GUI for Global Mirror management

At the writing of this book and the staged availability of the enhanced functions and their management through the GUI, we were in the transition to the GUI as well.

Here is an example of the new GUI for the DS6000 and the DS8000 to give you an impression on the look and feel of this new GUI. It is very different compared to the ESS 800 based GUI to manage Copy Services functions.

Figure 25-17 shows the entry point into the Global Mirror real-time application.

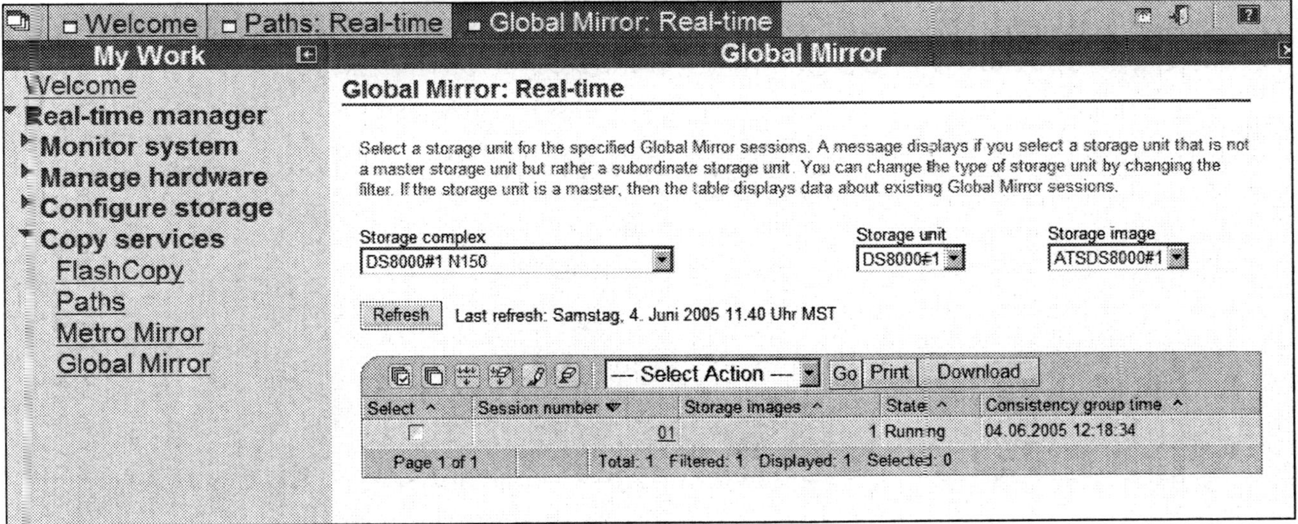

Figure 25-17 Select Global Mirror real-time application

From here on you select session number 01 with the check box. From the action pull down list you select an action and then click **Go**.

In the following sections we are going to find out about the volumes that are in the Global Mirror session number 01. A pause and resume of the session number 01 follows in the next section.

25.7.1 View Global Mirror volumes in session through the GUI

After starting with the panel in Figure 25-17, we select the View session volumes from the pull-down list and then click **Go** as shown in Figure 25-18.

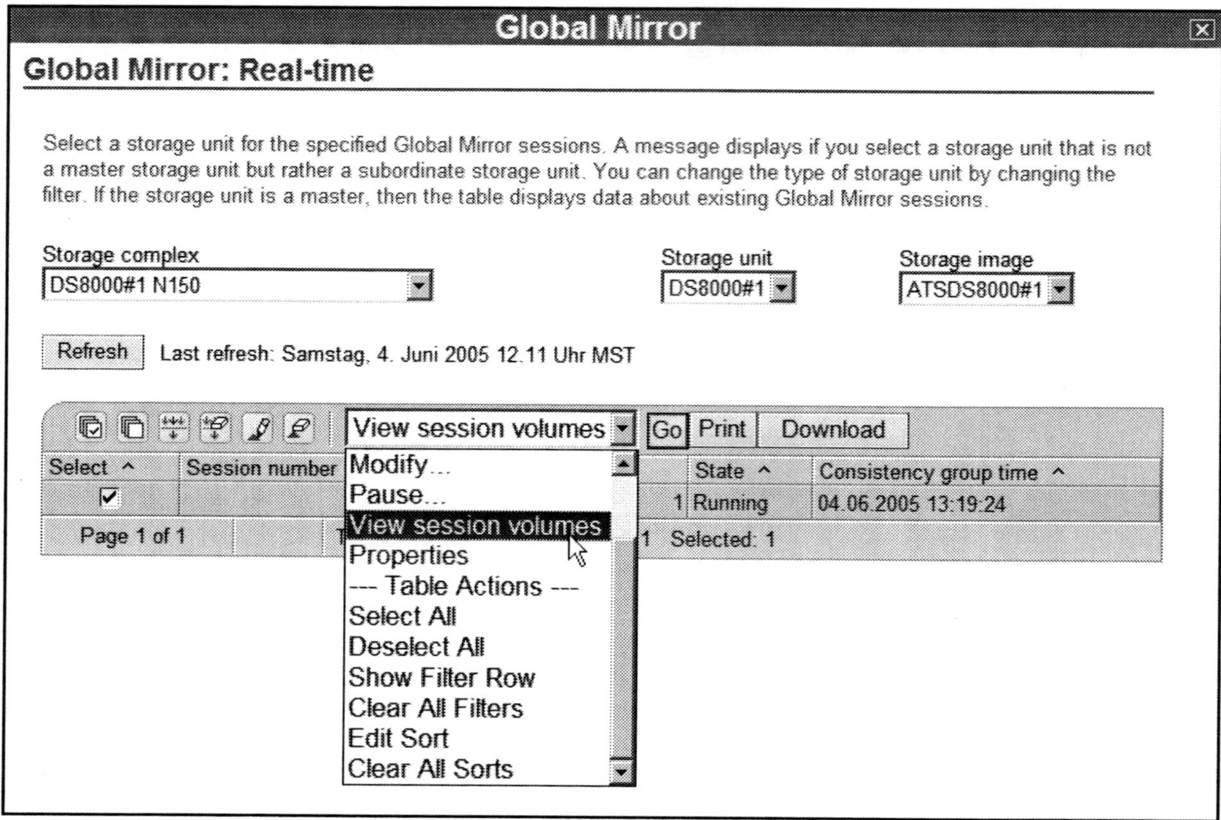

Figure 25-18 View Global Mirror volumes in session1 - select action

The next panel, shown in Figure 25-19, provides the requested list of Global Copy primary volumes that are defined to session number 01.

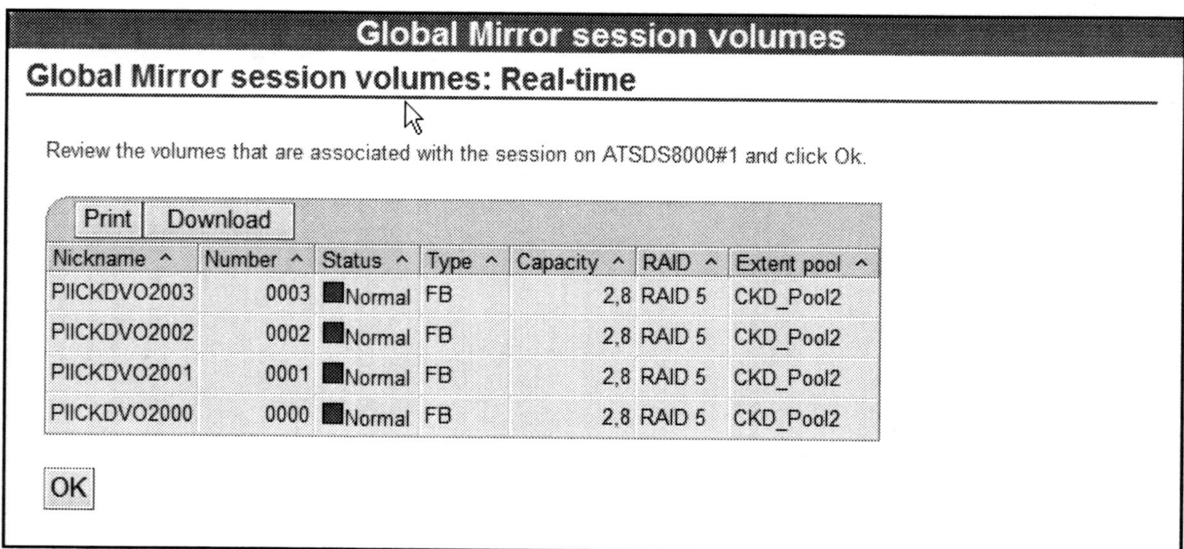

Figure 25-19 View Global Mirror volumes in session1 - volume list

Note the minor mistake in the Type column that indicates FB although it is really CKD. This issue has been fixed in a later GUI release. Figure 25-19 also suggests to choose meaningful nicknames for the volumes, when you define the volume to the DS8000 or to the DS6000. These nicknames indicate that the volumes belong to Extent Pool2, which is a CKD pool and the corresponding z/OS device numbers are 2000+. The syntax of the nicknames is a bit limited and does, for example, not allow you to use numerics in the prefix part of the nickname when defined through the GUI.

25.7.2 Pause and resume Global Mirror session through the GUI

The following sequence of GUI panels provides some insight on what to expect with the GUI.

The goal of this little exercise is to pause the Global Mirror session number 01 and then resume the session number 01 again (Figure 25-20).

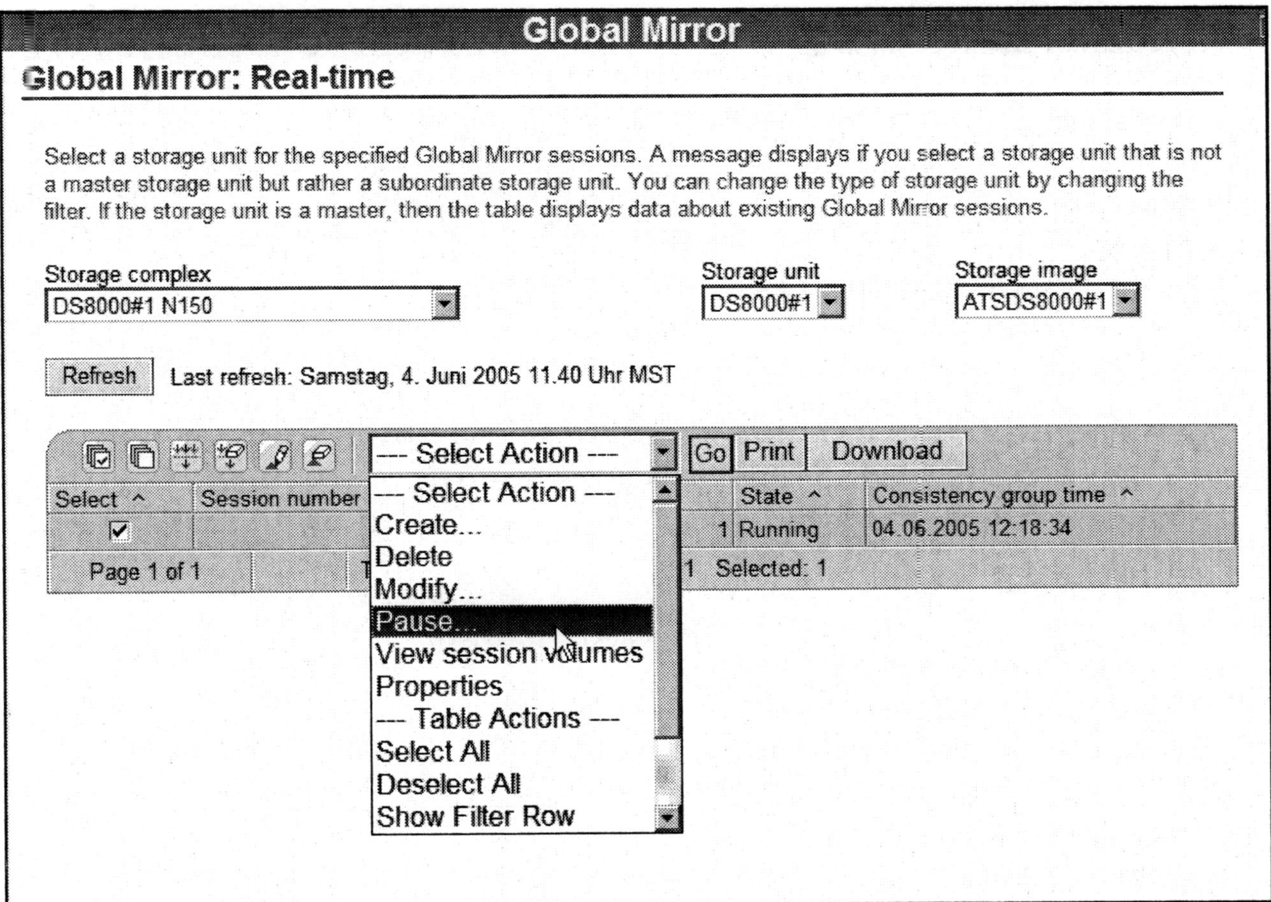

Figure 25-20 Start to pause selected session number 1 through the GUI - select action

As Figure 25-20 shows, you start again with the pull-down action list. Select **Pause** and then click **Go**.

Next you receive a confirmation panel as shown in Figure 25-21.

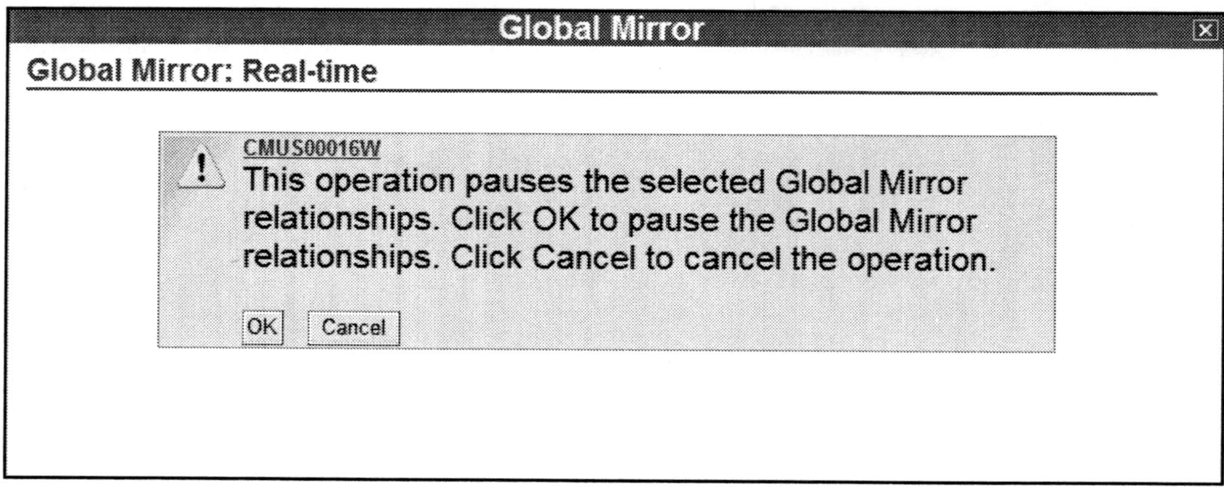

Figure 25-21 Start to pause selected session number 1 through the GUI - confirmation panel

Click **Go** and you receive the next panel (Figure 25-22).

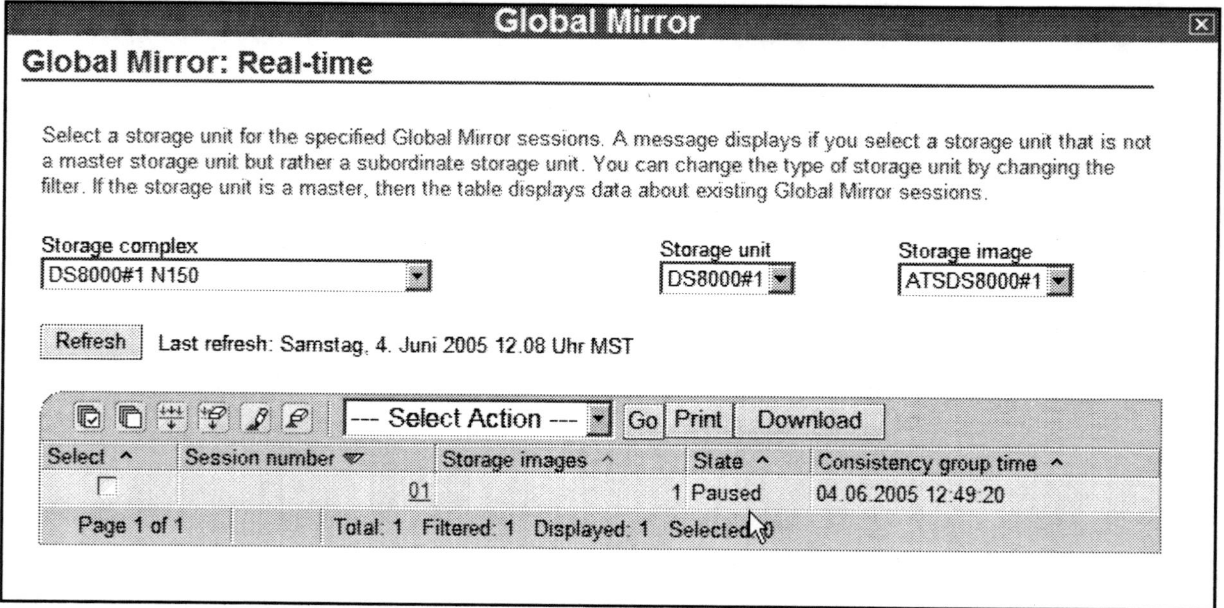

Figure 25-22 Session is paused

Figure 25-22 shows the result as well as the session number 01 as paused.

We immediately resume the session. Again, this suggests to select the corresponding action parameter in the pull-down list and click **Go** as shown in Figure 25-23.

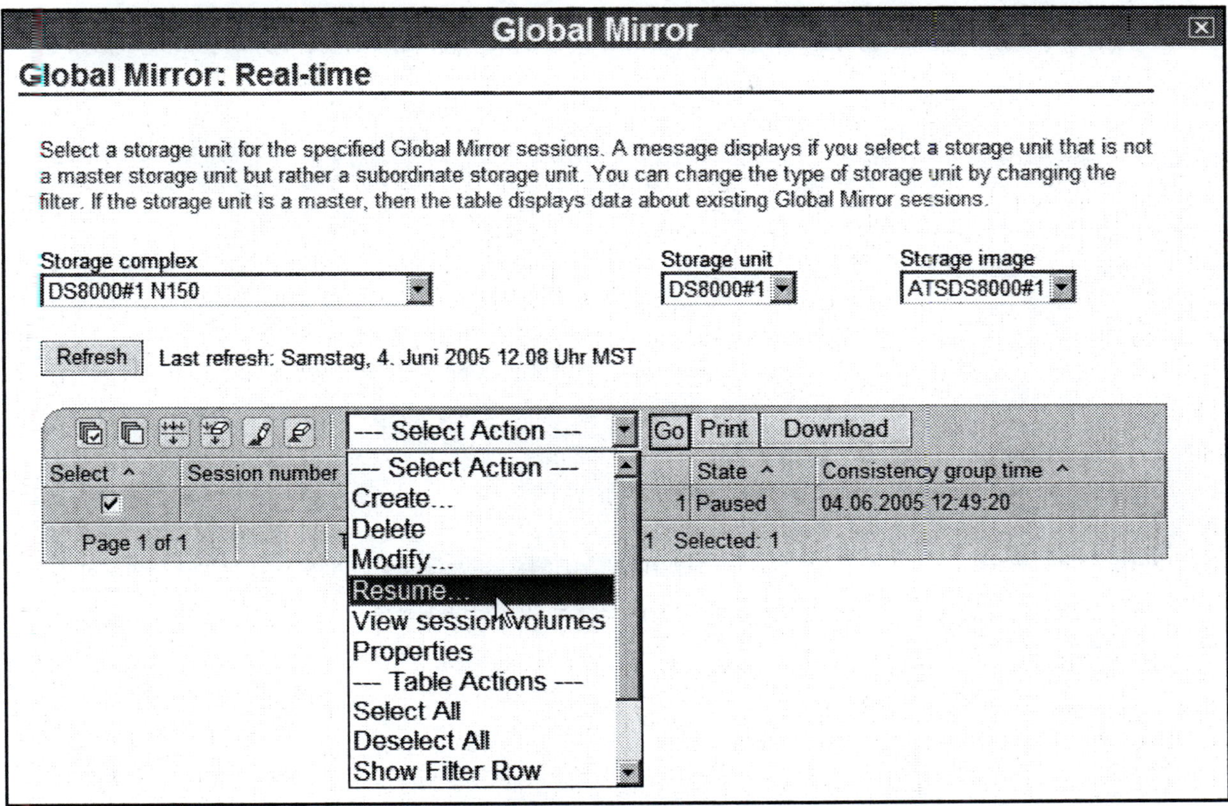

Figure 25-23 Start to resume paused session number 1 through the GUI - select action

You receive another confirmation panel asking whether to continue with the resume operation, see Figure 25-24.

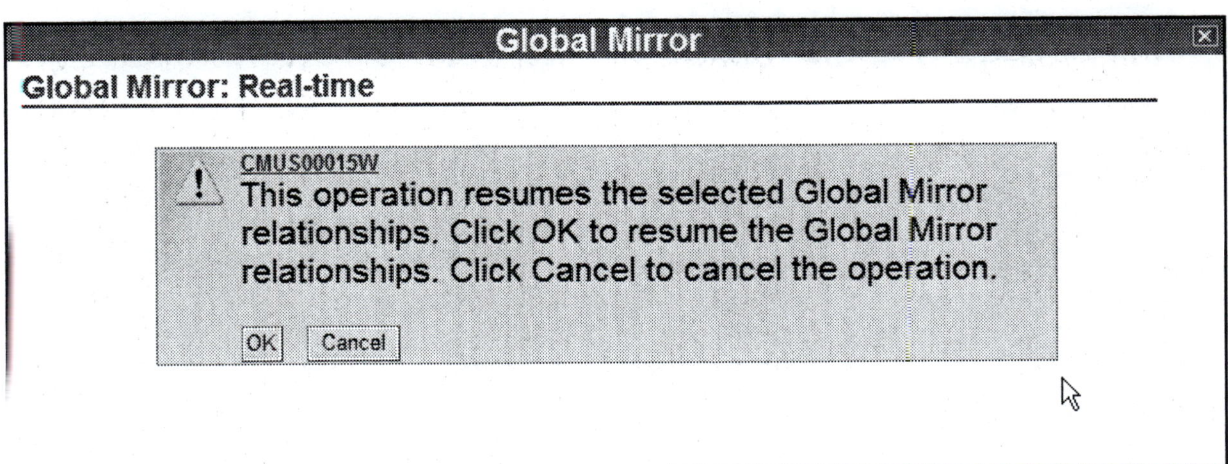

Figure 25-24 Start to resume paused session number 1 through the GUI - select action

We click **OK** and receive the next panel shown in Figure 25-25.

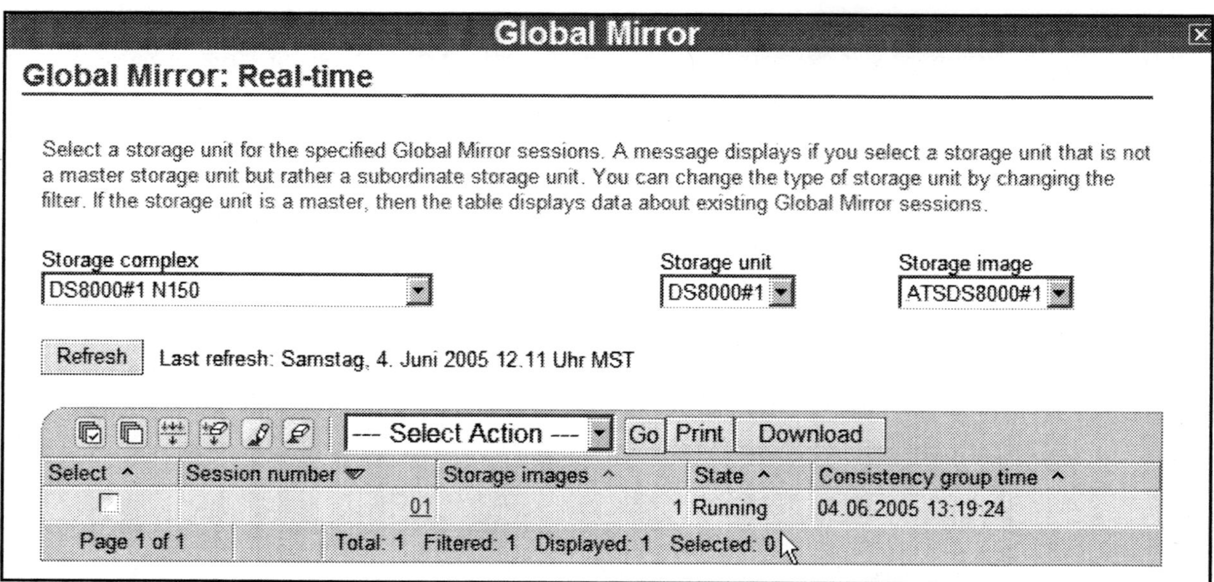

Figure 25-25 Start to resume paused session number 1 through the GUI - session is running

The session is back and running.

There is a more extensive exercise based on the GUI in Chapter 27., "Global Mirror examples" on page 341.

26

Global Mirror performance and scalability

In this chapter we discuss the performance aspects you need to consider when planning and configuring for Global Mirror.

We also explain a potential impact that the three phases to form a Consistency Group may impose to application write I/Os, when Global Mirror creates a Consistency Group.

Distributing the B volumes and the C volumes across different Ranks and to provide extra care for very busy volumes is also covered.

26.1 Performance aspects for Global Mirror

Global Mirror is basically comprised of Global Copy and FlashCopy and combines both functions to create a solution that provides consistent data at a distant site.

Global Copy has at most only a minimal impact to the response time of an application's write I/O to a Global Copy primary volume.

FlashCopy NOCOPY implies additional internally triggered I/Os within the storage server for any write I/O to the FlashCopy source volume. This I/O preserves the track from the FlashCopy source volume and copies this track to the FlashCopy target volume before the source track gets updated. This happens within two FlashCopy establish operations.

Note that NOCOPY does not start a background copy operation from the source volume to target volume. It only maintains a set of FlashCopy bitmaps for the source volume and the target volume. These bitmaps are established at the first time when a FlashCopy relationship is created with NOCOPY. Before a source track is modified between the creation of two Consistency Groups the track is copied to the target volume to preserve the previous point-in-time copy. This includes updates to corresponding bitmaps to reflect the new location of the track that belongs to the point-in-time copy. Note that each Global Copy write to its secondary volume within the window of two adjacent Consistency Groups triggers such a FlashCopy I/O operation (Figure 26-1).

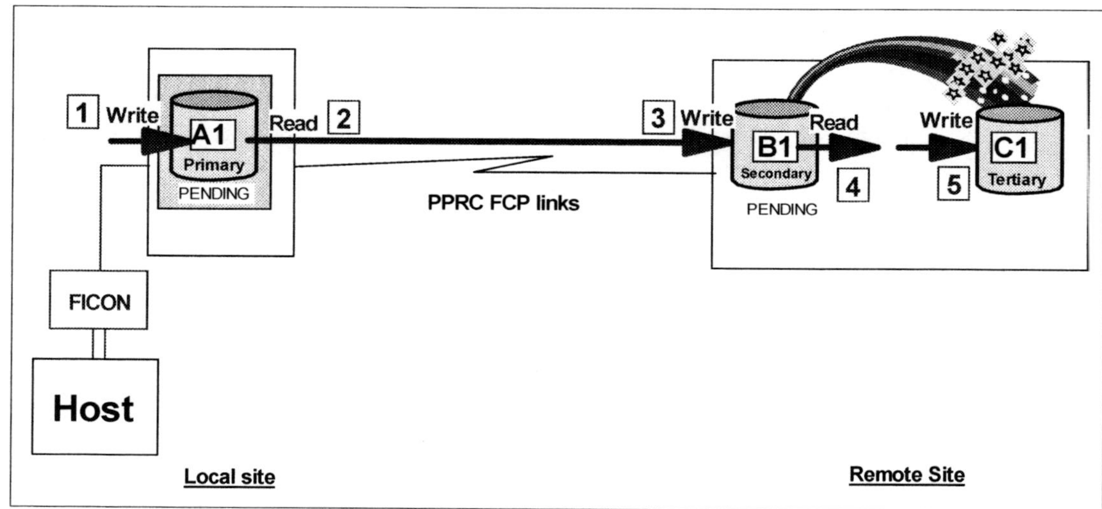

Figure 26-1 Global Copy with write hit at the remote site

An I/O in this context is also a Global Copy I/O when Global Copy replicates a track from a primary volume to a Global Copy secondary volume. This implies an additional read I/O in the primary storage server and a corresponding write I/O to the secondary storage server. In a Global Mirror environment the Global Copy secondary volume is also the FlashCopy source volume. This may have some effect in a very busy disk subsystem.

Figure 26-1 summarizes roughly what happens between two Consistency Group creation points when application writes come in. The application write I/O completes immediately at the local site (1). Eventually Global Copy replicates the application I/O and reads the data at the local site (2). Before the track gets updated on the B volume the FlashCopy source track is preserved on the C volume due to the NOCOPY attribute. Note that this is not necessarily the exact sequence of internal I/O events but some approximation. There are optimization and consolidation effects that make the entire process at the end more efficient.

Figure 26-1 shows the normal sequence of I/Os within a Global Mirror configuration. The critical path is between (2) and (3). Usually (3) is a write hit in the persistent memory or NVS in B1 and some time later and after (3) the original FlashCopy source track is copied from B1 to C1 before the modified sectors or track is applied from server storage to the B1 volume.

There is some potential impact on the Global Copy data replication operation depending on whether persistent memory or non-volatile cache is over committed in the secondary storage server. This may cause that the FlashCopy source tracks have to be preserved first to the FlashCopy target volume, before the Global Copy write completes for its secondary volume (Figure 26-2).

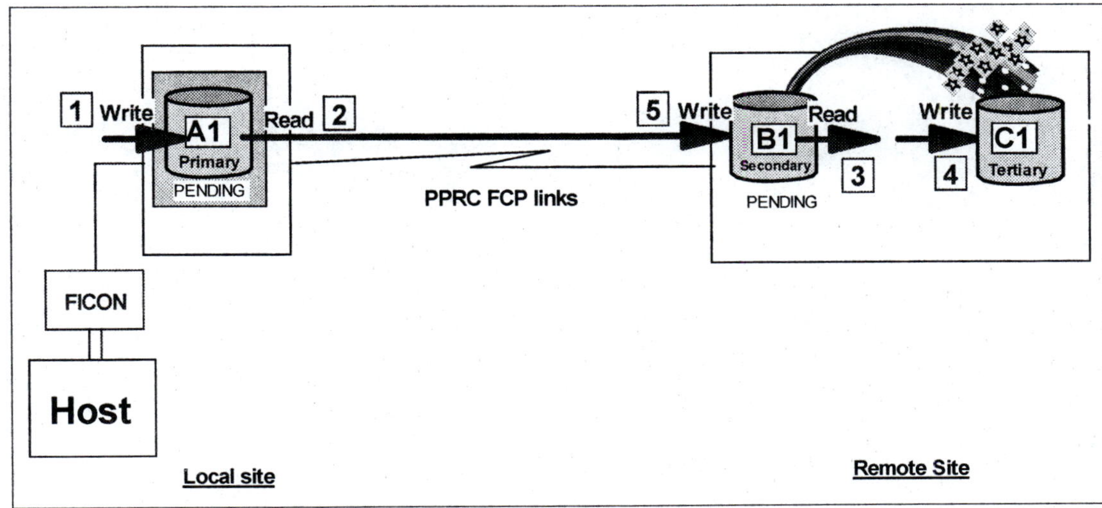

Figure 26-2 Application write I/O within two Consistency Group points

Figure 26-2 summarizes roughly what happens when persistent memory or NVS in the remote storage server is over committed. A read (3) and a write (4) to preserve the source track and write it to the C volume is required first before the write (5) can complete. Eventually the track gets updated on the B1 volume to complete write (5). But usually all writes are quick writes to cache and persistent memory and happen in the order as outlined in Figure 26-1 on page 334.

A write I/O to the FlashCopy source volume also triggers the maintenance of a bit map for the source volume that is created when the FlashCopy volume pair is established with the *start change recording* attribute. This allows you to only replicate the changed recording bitmap to the corresponding bitmap for the target volume in the course of forming a Consistency Group. See 23.3, "Form Consistency Group" on page 251.

Note that this all applies only to write I/Os to Global Mirror primary volumes.

26.2 Performance considerations at coordination time

When looking at the three phases when Global Mirror goes through the process to create a set of data consistent volumes at the secondary site, the first question that comes to mind is whether the coordination window imposes an impact to the application write I/O (Figure 26-3).

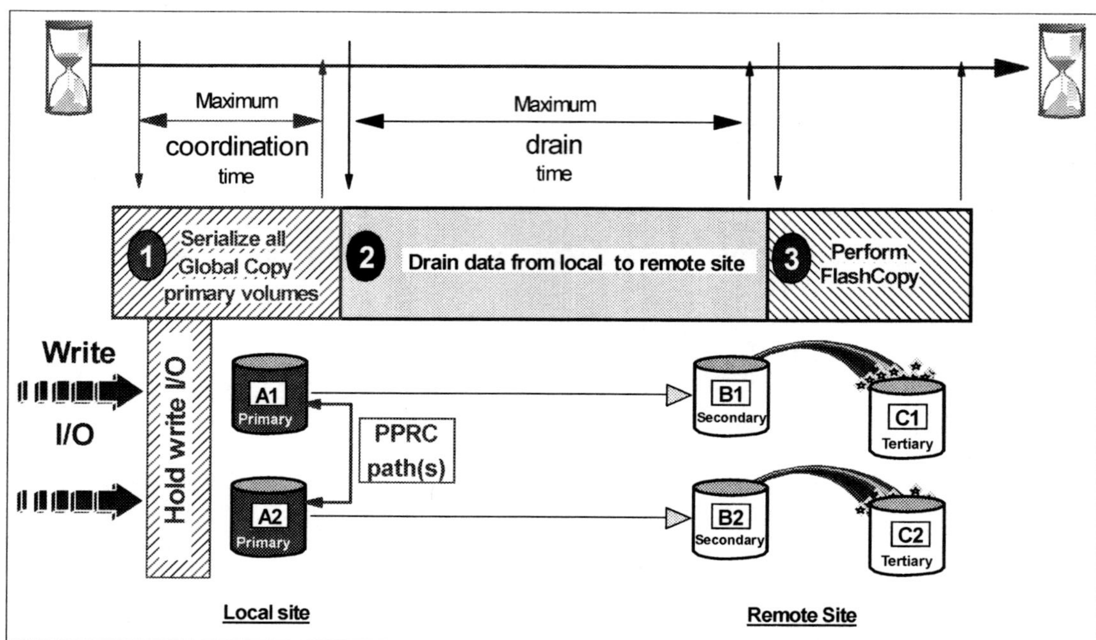

Figure 26-3 Coordination time - how does it impact application write I/Os?

The coordination time that you can limit by specifying a number of ms is the maximum impact to application write I/Os you will allow when forming a Consistency Group. The intention is to keep this time window as small as possible. The default of 50 ms may be a bit high in a transaction processing environment. A valid number may be also a very low number in the single digit range. The required communication between the Master storage server and potential Subordinate storage servers is inband over PPRC paths between the Master and Subordinates. This communication is highly optimized and allows you to minimize the potential application write I/O impact to 3 ms, for example. Note that this communication is performed over PPRC FCP links. There is at least one PPRC FCP link required between a Master storage server and any potential Subordinate storage servers. For redundancy we suggest to use two PPRC FCP links.

The following example addresses the impact of the coordination time when Consistency Group formation starts and whether this impact has the potential to be significant or not.

Assume a total aggregated number of 5,000 write I/Os over two primary storage servers with 2,500 write I/Os per second to each storage server. Each write I/O takes 0.5 ms. You specified 3 ms maximum to coordinate between the Master storage server and its Subordinate storage server. Assume further that a Consistency Group is created every 3 seconds, which is a goal with the Consistency Group interval time of zero.

- 5,000 write I/Os
- 0.5 ms response time for each write I/O
- Maximum coordination time is 3 ms
- Every 3 seconds a Consistency Group is created

This is 5 I/Os for every millisecond or 15 I/Os within 3 ms. So each of these 15 write I/Os experience a 3 ms delay. This happens every 3 seconds. Then we observe an average response time delay of approximately:

(15 IOs * 0.003 sec) / 3*5000 IO/sec) = 0.000003 sec or 0.003 ms.

The response time increases in average from 0.5 ms to 0.503 ms. RMF is currently not capable to even show such a small difference.

26.3 Consistency Group transmission

Once the Consistency Group is established at the primary storage servers by establishing corresponding bitmaps within the coordination time window, all remaining data that is still in the out-of-sync bitmap is sent to the secondary storage server using Global Copy.

This drain period may be also limited to replicate all remaining data from primary to secondary storage server within a time limit set by maximum drain time. The default is 30 seconds and is considered to be too small in a potentially write intensive workload. A number in the range of 300 seconds to 600 seconds may be considered.

This replication process usually does not impact the application write I/O. There is a very slight chance that the same track within a Consistency Group is updated before this track is replicated to the secondary site within this drain time period. When this unlikely event happens, the concerned track is immediately replicated to the secondary storage server before the application write I/O does modify the original track. The concerned application write I/O is going to experience a similar response time as if the I/O would have been written to a Metro Mirror primary volume. Note that further subsequent writes to this same track do not experience any delay because the tracks has been already replicated to the remote site.

26.4 Avoid unbalanced configurations

Example 26-1 shows a formatted RQUERY output of two LSSs that are part of a Global Mirror session. LSS 0C contains one volume that is very current regarding data replication through Global Copy. This is indicated by zero tracks out-of-sync. This means there are currently no tracks remaining at the local site for LSS 0C that are not yet transferred to the remote site.

This is different with LSS 0D. This LSS contains two volumes within the same session, session number 01. Both volumes still contain data that is not yet transferred to the remote site. The number of tracks that are still waiting to be replicated from the local to the remote site is x'3E02' or 15,874 tracks or 1,058 cylinders or roughly 890 MB. This indicates that there seems to be a significant write I/O skew between LSS 0C and LSS 0D.

This particular configuration has source and target FlashCopy volumes within the very same Rank. Either you may consider putting one of the two busy volumes in LSS 0D into LSS 0C and distribute the load over both LSSs. Another approach might be to configure the FlashCopy source volume and its corresponding target volume into different Ranks or LSS. See "Remote storage server configuration" on page 338

Example 26-1 Unbalanced load on Global Mirror configuration

```
READY
  RQUERY     SNBR(01) VOLSER(XX2C00) ACTION(GMPSTAT)
 RQUERY Output Volser(XX2C00) Action(GMPSTAT) Version(001)
 SNbr LSS GMPStatus  RvrtStatus FCSeqNbr TotVol OOSVol OOSTrks
 --   --  ---------- ---------- -------- ------ ------ --------
 01   0C  CGInPrgrs  AllNRv&Eq  42937FE2      1      0 00000000
 READY
  RQUERY     SNBR(01) VOLSER(XX2D00) ACTION(GMPSTAT)
 RQUERY Output Volser(XX2D00) Action(GMPSTAT) Version(001)
 SNbr LSS GMPStatus  RvrtStatus FCSeqNbr TotVol OOSVol OOSTrks
 --   --  ---------- ---------- -------- ------ ------ --------
 01   0D  CGInPrgrs  AllNRv&Eq  42937FE2      2      2 00003E02
 READY
```

When the load distribution is unknown in your configuration, you may consider developing some rudimentary code — based on REXX, for example — which regularly issues RQUERY commands as shown in Example 26-1 on page 337. You may then process the output of the RQUERY command to better understand the write load distribution over the Global Mirror volumes or better: over the Global Copy primary volumes.

Note that the numbers in Example 26-1 on page 337 may be just a brief peak period. It is still feasible to use the conventional approach with RMF post processor reports to investigate into the write workload. The focus may be on the amount of data to be written to the Global Copy primary volumes.

26.5 Remote storage server configuration

There will be I/O skews and hot spots in storage servers. This is true for the local and remote storage servers. In local storage servers you may consider a horizontal pooling approach and spread each volume type across all Ranks. Volume types are in this context, for example, DB2® database volumes, logging volumes, batch volumes, temporary volumes, etc. Your goal may be to have the same number of each volume type within each Rank.

Through a one-to-one mapping from local to remote storage server you achieve the same configuration at the remote site for the B volumes and the C volumes. Figure 26-4 proposes to spread the B and C volumes across different Ranks at the remote storage server.

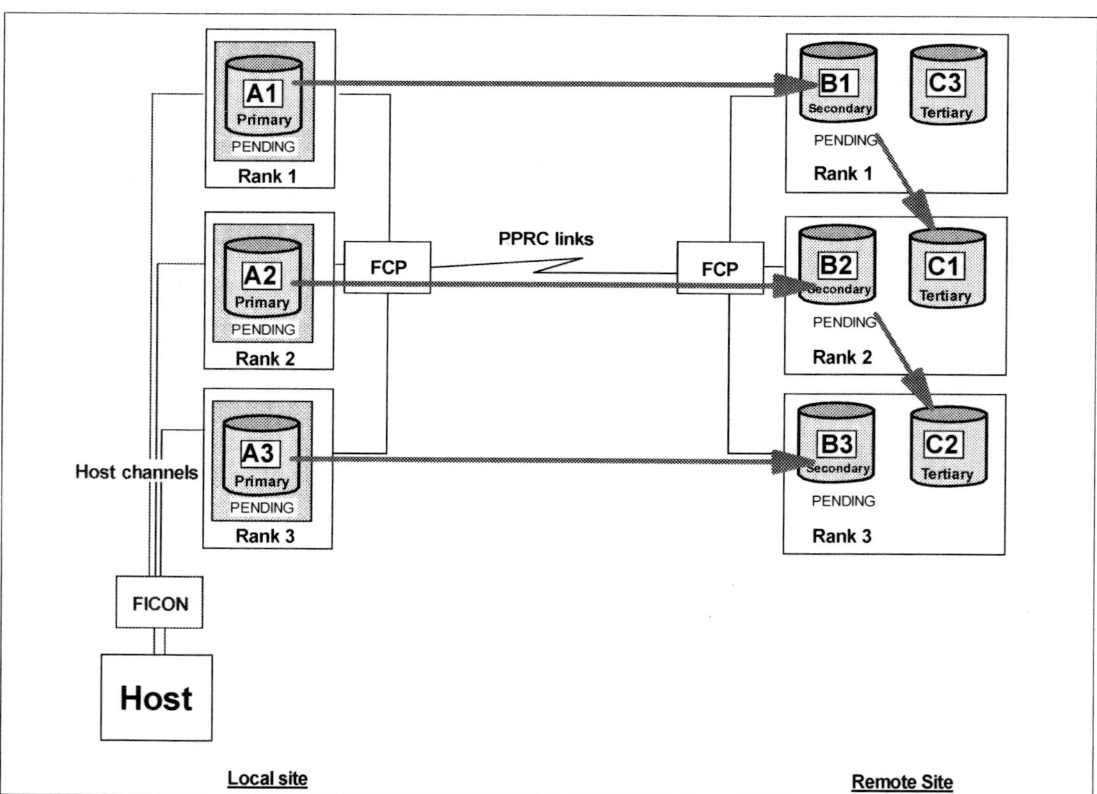

Figure 26-4 Remote storage server configuration - all Ranks contain equal numbers of volumes

The goal is to put the same number of each volume type into each Rank. As volume type here we refer to B volumes and C volumes within a Global Mirror configuration. In order to avoid the situation shown in Example 26-1 on page 337, you can spread busy volumes over multiple Ranks. Otherwise, hot spots will be concentrated on single Ranks when you put the B and C volume on the very same Rank. We recommend spreading B and C volumes as suggested in Figure 26-4.

Another aspect may be to focus on very busy volumes and keep those volumes on separate Ranks than all the other volumes.

With mixed Disk Drive Module (DDM) capacities and different speeds at the remote storage server you may consider spreading the B volumes not only over the fast DDMs but over all Ranks. Basically, follow a similar approach as recommended in Figure 26-4 on page 338. You may keep particular busy B volumes and C volumes on the faster DDMs.

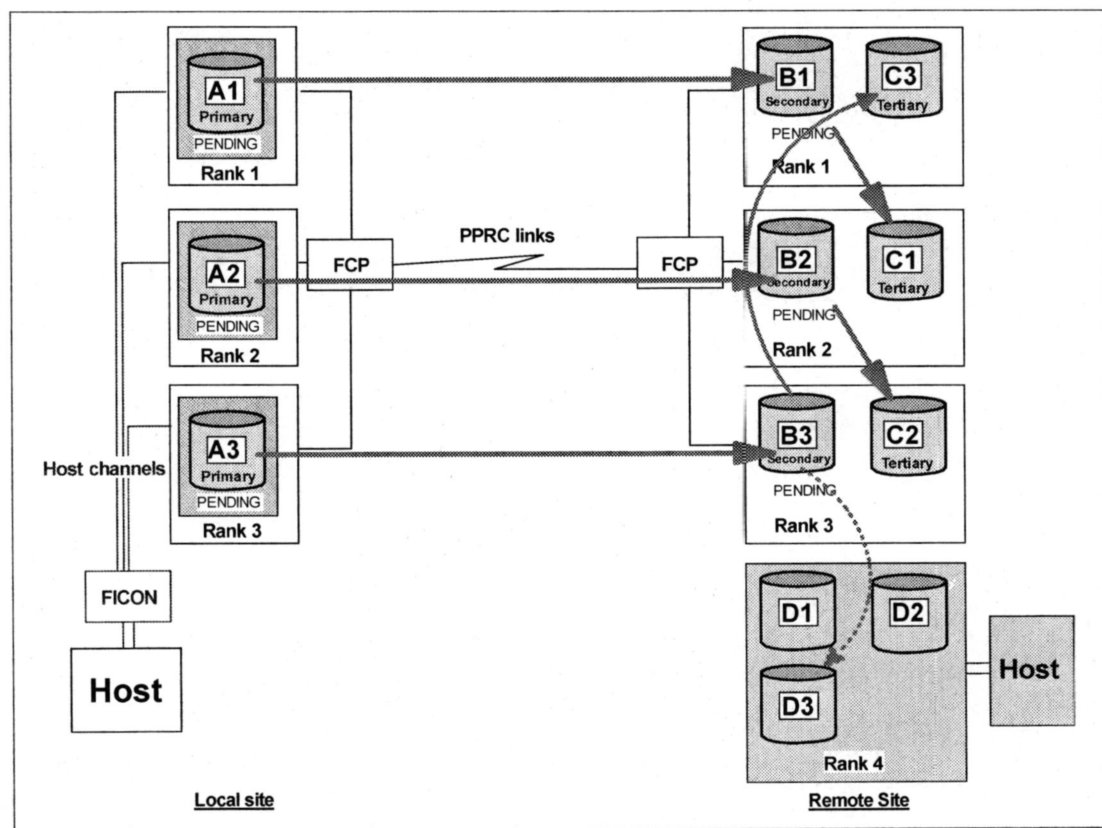

Figure 26-5 Remote Storage Server with D volumes

Figure 26-5 on page 339 shows besides the three Global Mirror volumes, also the D volumes that may be created once in a while for test or other purposes. Here we suggest as an alternative, a Rank with larger and perhaps slower DDMs. The D volumes may be read from another host and any other I/O to the D volumes does not impact the Global Mirror volumes in the other Ranks. Note that a NOCOPY relationship between B and D volume will read the data from B when coming through the D volume. So you may consider a COPY when you create D volumes on a different Rank to fence additional I/O off from the Ranks with the B volumes when accessing the D volumes.

An option here may be to spread all B volumes across all Ranks again and also configure the same number of volumes in each Rank.

Still put the B and C volumes in different Ranks. It is further recommended to configure corresponding B and C volumes in such a way that these volumes have an affinity to the same server. Ideal would be to also have the B volumes connected to a different DA pair than the C volumes.

26.6 Growth within Global Mirror configurations

When you add a rather large number of volumes at once to an existing Global Mirror session then the available resources for Global Copy within the affected Ranks may be over-utilized or even monopolized by the initial copy pass. To avoid too much impact, you may consider adding many new volumes to an existing Global Mirror session in stages. If possible and as a rough rule of thumb (ROT) add only a few volumes within a Rank during application peak I/O periods. Once the first initial copy completes, add the next volume. Again as a ROT, plan for one or two volumes within a Rank during peak I/O load on the concerned Ranks for the first initial copy pass.

If possible then plan a massive add of new Global Copy volumes into an existing session during off-peak periods.

Global Mirror examples

In this chapter we provide a set of examples that have been exercised during the residency project.

This includes the following examples, based on TSO commands:

- Query a Global Mirror session.
- Establish a Global Mirror environment using TSO commands.
- Deal with a primary site failure and recovery at the backup site. This example outlines the steps that are necessary to take in case of a primary site failure and recovery at the secondary site.
- Clean up a Global Mirror session.

In conclusion, we establish a Global Mirror session through the DS SM and CLI.

Note that the examples chosen do not reflect the wide variety of Global Mirror configurations.

For command details and syntax, refer to the corresponding manuals:

- *z/OS DFSMS Advanced Copy Services*, SC35-0428
- *IBM TotalStorage DS8000 Command-Line Interface User's Guide*, SC26-7625
- *Device Support Facility User's Guide and Reference Release 17*, SC35-0033

27.1 Global Mirror examples setup

In order to provide the principal use of commands to manage a Global Mirror environment, the following examples are limited to a few volumes only to keep these examples as simple as possible and avoid confusing complexity.

Figure 27-1 shows the volumes with their device numbers and their SSIDs, which are used throughout most of the examples within this chapter. Some other configuration data may be used for DS CLI examples or examples based on ICKDSF.

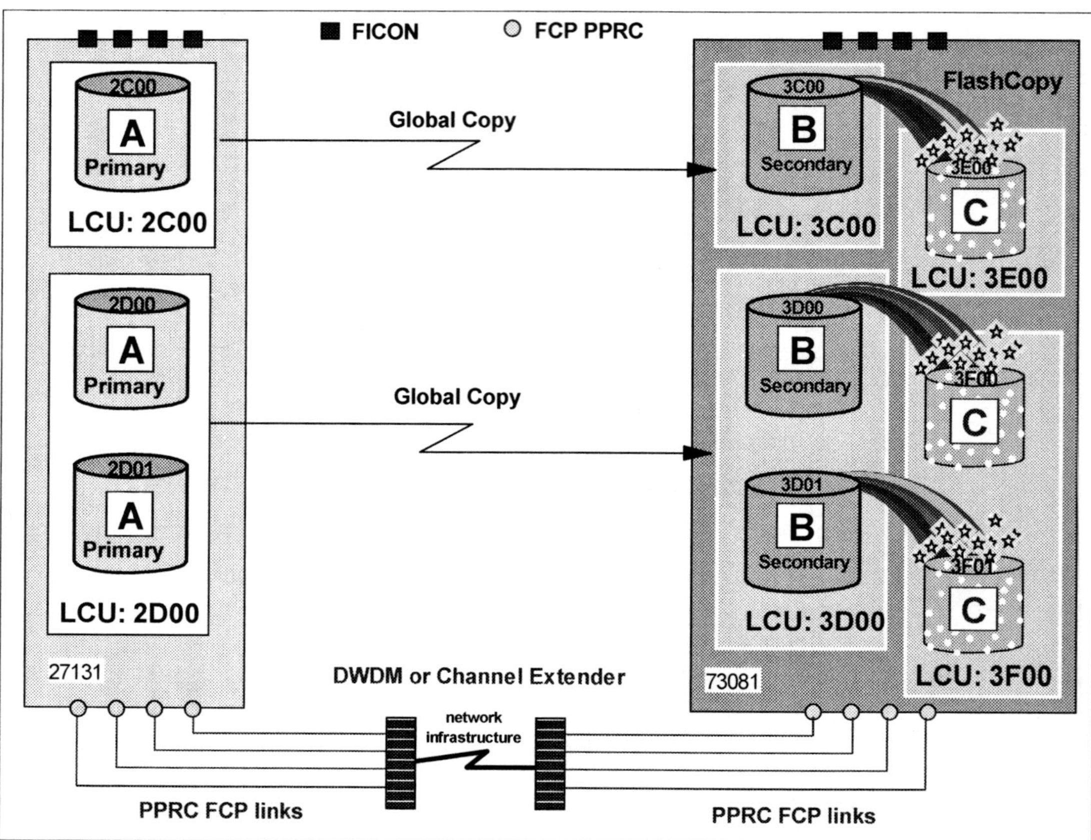

Figure 27-1 Global Mirror base configuration for the following examples

Note that a primary volume resides in SSID 2C00 and two primary volumes belong to SSID 2D00 in a DS8000. These primary volumes are also referred to as A volumes.

The corresponding secondary volumes are in respective SSIDs in the second DS8000; so are the FlashCopy target volumes.

When a Global Mirror configuration is in normal operation the Global Copy secondary volume is identical with the FlashCopy source volume. These volumes are referred to as B volumes.

The FlashCopy target volumes are referred to as C volumes.

27.2 Global Mirror examples

The following examples describe how to create a Global Mirror configuration. The first examples focus on the new query capabilities, which have been enhanced for Global Mirror when you use TSO commands.

27.2.1 Query a Global Mirror session

The RQUERY command provides information about a Global Mirror session. RQUERY has the following options:

- DVCSTAT
- GMLSTAT
- GMPSTAT

The following sections contain examples that refer to the configuration shown in Figure 27-1 on page 342.

Query Global Mirror volume status in concerned LSS

The DVCSTAT option returns information pertaining to the volumes in the LSS where the VOLSER points to. Note that the specified VOLSER itself does not have to be a Global Mirror volume. You direct this command to an LSS that contains a Global Mirror session.

Example 27-1 RQUERY TSO command with DVCSTAT option and formatted output

```
RQUERY     SNBR(01) VOLSER(XX2C00) ACTION(DVCSTAT)

RQUERY Output Volser(XX2C00) Action(DVCSTAT) Version(001)
SNbr LSS Dvc VolStat              PriPPRCStat SecCascStat
--   --  --  -------------------- ----------  ----------
01   0C  00  InSession            DplxPendng  Simplex
```

In Example 27-1 the query is targeted to the first LSS with a Global Copy volume in session number 01. This is the device 2C00 in Figure 27-1.

Through the VOLSER parameter, the next RQUERY points to the other LSS that is involved in this Global Mirror session. See Example 27-2.

Example 27-2 RQUERY with DVCSTAT of the second LSS with Global Mirror volumes

```
RQUERY     SNBR(01) VOLSER(XX2D00) ACTION(DVCSTAT)

RQUERY Output Volser(XX2D00) Action(DVCSTAT) Version(001)
SNbr LSS Dvc VolStat              PriPPRCStat SecCascStat
--   --  --  -------------------- ----------  ----------
01   0D  00  InSession            DplxPendng  Simplex
     0D  01  InSession            DplxPendng  Simplex
```

All three volumes are in Global Mirror session number 01. You may consider omitting the session number parameter SNBR, then RQUERY returns whatever session is currently active in the concerned LSS and its Global Mirror volumes.

Query Global Mirror session summary

RQUERY points through the VOLSER parameter to the Global Mirror Master LSS and summarizes its involved volumes in the session.

When you address an LSS that is not the Global Mirror Master LSS, the GMLSTAT option does not return Global Mirror session information, as Example 27-3 illustrates.

Example 27-3 RQUERY GMLSTAT output when not addressing an LSS with an active session

```
RQUERY      SNBR(01) VOLSER(XX2D00) ACTION(GMLSTAT)

RQUERY Output Volser(XX2D00) Action(GMLSTAT) Version(001)
SNbr GMLStat    GoodCg   Pct CrnBadCG TotBadCG LastGoodCGSCntlClock
--   ---------- -------- --- -------- -------- --------------------
01   NoConfig
```

LSS 2D00 has an active Global Mirror volume but it is not the Master LSS. Therefore, RQUERY in Example 27-3 does not provide session summary information although both LSSs reside in the very same primary storage server. Note that the decision of which LSS is the Master LSS, is made when the Global Mirror session is started.

Example 27-4 shows the formatted output of the RQUERY command with the ACTION(GMLSTAT) parameter specified.

Example 27-4 Session summary as the Master LSS reports

```
RQUERY      SNBR(01) VOLSER(XX2C00) ACTION(GMLSTAT)

RQUERY Output Volser(XX2C00) Action(GMLSTAT) Version(001)
SNbr GMLStat    GoodCg   Pct CrnBadCG TotBadCG LastGoodCGSCntlClock
--   ---------- -------- --- -------- -------- --------------------
01   Running    0000D0C1 99           00000005 19 May 2005 19:08:00
.
Master: Serial       SSID LSS   CGInt CGDrn CrdInt
        ------------ ---- --    ----- ----- -----
        000107527131 2C00 0C        0   600     5
.
BadCGrpFormation: When  Serial       SSID LSS Reason     Activity
                  ----- ------------ ---- --- ---------- ----------
                  Last  000107527131 2C00 0C  CmdRej FCC StrtIncr
                  Prev  000107527131 2C00 0C  CmdRej FCC StrtIncr
                  First 000107527131 2C00 0C  CmdRej FCC StrtIncr
```

This is the active Global Mirror session as was shown in Figure 27-1 on page 342. During these queries, a write workload was running on all three Global Mirror primary volumes.

Global Mirror session status for each LSS

The ACTION(GMPSTAT) option returns information from the Global Mirror session with volume counts, Consistency Group revertible status, and out-of-sync tracks information that relate to the LSS in question.

Example 27-5 RQUERY session status for LCU 2C00, LSS 0C

```
RQUERY      SNBR(01) VOLSER(XX2C00) ACTION(GMPSTAT)

RQUERY Output Volser(XX2C00) Action(GMPSTAT) Version(001)
SNbr LSS GMPStatus  RvrtStatus FCSeqNbr TotVol OOSVol OOSTrks
--   --  ---------- ---------- -------- ------ ------ --------
01   0C  CGInPrgrs  AllNRv&Eq  428E26CC      1      0 00000000
```

Example 27-5 shows the formatted output with the session status details for LCU 2C00.

Example 27-6 shows the output for LCU 2D00 on the same session. Both RQUERY commands are executed one after another in less than a second. Both examples show the same FlashCopy sequence number (FCSeqNbr) and they are equal. The revertible status (RvrtStatus) is *all non-revertible and equal* (AllNRv&Eq). This indicates that the C volumes are all in a consistent state and no action to the Consistency Group is necessary if the primary site would fail right now.

Example 27-6 RQUERY session status for LCU 2D00, LSS 0D

```
RQUERY     SNBR(01) VOLSER(XX2D00) ACTION(GMPSTAT)

RQUERY Output Volser(XX2D00) Action(GMPSTAT) Version(001)
SNbr LSS GMPStatus  RvrtStatus FCSeqNbr TotVol OOSVol OOSTrks
--   --  ---------- ---------- -------- ------ ------ --------
01   0D  CGInPrgrs  AllNRv&Eq  428E26CC      2      2 00000BDA
```

Note that you currently have to use an online volume to address the LSS from which to fetch the Global Mirror related information. It is the plan to change this eventually to the same standard of what other TSO PPRC commands can do and use a z/OS device number. It would not check whether the volume is ONLINE or OFFLINE except if there are particular parameters that instruct the command to do so.

Timing information

Creating consistency groups relies also on internal timing information. You need to understand that the internal timer in the DS6000 and DS8000 is not synchronized with an external clock.

Example 27-7 shows an RQUERY example and a TIME command just before the RQUERY command. The TSO TIME command displays the CPU based timer, which displays 10:09:32. Consistency Group drain time limit is 60 seconds or one minute. RQUERY displays the internal disk subsystem clock time with 14:37:59 as the time of the last good Consistency Group. Both timers are about 4 1/2 hours apart of each other. Even with a few failed attempts to form Consistency Groups the disk subsystem clock time would be just a few minutes behind the CPU based clock.

Example 27-7 Internal timer is not synchronized with external timer

```
TIME-10:09:32 AM. CPU-00:00:00 SERVICE-255 SESSION-00:00:00 JUNE 17,2005
READY
  RQUERY              VOLSER(AA601F) ACTION(GMLSTAT)
RQUERY Output Volser(AA601F) Action(GMLSTAT) Version(001)
SNbr GMLStat    GoodCg   Pct CrnBadCG TotBadCG LastGoodCGSCntlClock
--   ---------- -------- --- -------- -------- --------------------
01   Running    00000125  98 00000003 00000005 17 Jun 2005 14:37:59
.                                                                    .
Master: Serial       SSID LSS   CGInt CGDrn CrdInt
        ------------ ---- --    ----- ----- -----
        0002013AAGXA 2060 00       15    60     5
.                                                                    .
BadCGrpFormation: When  Serial       SSID LSS Reason     Activity
                  ----- ------------ ---- --- ---------- ----------
                  Last  0002013AAGXA ???? FF  DrTimeExcd DrnInPrg
                  Prev  0002013AAGXA ???? FF  DrTimeExcd DrnInPrg
                  First 0002013AAGXA 2060 00  CmdRej FC4 RunInPrg
READY
```

Note that you cannot rely on the internal disk subsystem clock time information as an absolute wall clock timing type. You may set the internal disk subsystem clock time with the help of an IBM customer engineer as close to the actual wall clock as possible.

27.2.2 Establish a Global Mirror environment utilizing TSO commands

The following sequence of examples establishes a Global Mirror environment through the new TSO command support. Most steps to create a Global Mirror environment can be done in any order. But we recommend the following order to create a Global Mirror environment:

1. Establish all necessary PPRC paths between Global Copy primary LSS and its corresponding Global Copy secondary LSS. You may establish PPRC paths here also between the Master and any Subordinate storage servers that will participate in the Global Mirror session at the local site. When there is only a primary storage server involved, you do not need any PPRC paths between the primary LSSs. The communication between LSSs in a single primary storage server is done internally.
2. Establish the Global Copy (PPRC-XD) pairs with the MODE(COPY). You may wait till the first initial copy is complete before continuing to the next step.
3. Establish FlashCopy relationships between the B and C volumes. See Figure 27-1 on page 342. Use MODE(ASYNC) with the corresponding TSO FCESTABL command.
4. If you didn't define the PPRC paths between the Master LSS and any potential Subordinate storage servers then this is the time to do that before you continue on.
5. Define the Global Mirror session and create a session ID between 1 and 255. Note 0 (zero) is not a valid session number and may be used in, for example, RQUERY to query any active session in the concerned LSS. Define this session number to the Master storage server and its LSS that will participate in the session.
6. Define the same session number to all LSSs in Subordinate storage servers that are going to participate in the session.
7. Populate the session with the Global Copy primary volumes. Note that it is recommended to put these Global Copy primary volumes first into the session, once they have completed their first pass for initial copy.
8. Start the session. This command actually defines the Master LSS. All further session commands have to go through this LSS. You may specify with the start command these Global Mirror tuning parameters like maximum drain time, maximum coordination time, and Consistency Group interval time.

Volumes can be added to the session at any time after the session number is defined to the LSS where the volumes resides. Once the session is started, volumes can be added to the session or can be removed from the session at any time.

Note: You only add Global Copy primary volumes to a Global Mirror session.

Volumes may be added to a session in any state like SIMPLEX, PENDING, DUPLEX, or SUSPENDED. Volumes that have not completed their initial copy phase stay in a *join pending* state until the first initial copy is complete. If a newly added volume to a session is a primary SUSPENDED the first attempt to form a Consistency Group will fail. It is recommended to add only Global Copy primary volumes that completed their initial copy or first pass.

When you plan to add a new Subordinate storage server to an active session, you have to stop the session first. Then add the new Subordinate storage server and start the session again with the updated RSESSION command, which then contains also the new Subordinate storage server.

When you add a new LSS to an active session and this LSS belongs to a storage server that already has another LSS, which belongs to the Global Mirror session, you may just add the new LSS to the session without stop and start of the session. This is true for either the Master storage server or for a Subordinate storage server.

Establish PPRC paths

First you define PPRC paths from A to B; see Example 27-8.

Example 27-8 Define paths for Global Copy from A to B

```
//* ---------------------------- TSO ---------------------------- ***
//* ESTABLISH PPRC PATH(S)                                          ***
//* ------------------------------------------------------------- ***
//EPATHS   EXEC PGM=IKJEFT01
//SYSPRINT  DD SYSOUT=*
//SYSTSPRT  DD SYSOUT=*
//SYSTSIN   DD DDNAME=SYSIN

   CQUERY    DEVN (X'2C00') PATHS
   CESTPATH  DEVN (X'2C00')                          +
             PRIM (X'2C00' 5005076303FFC228  X'0C') +
             SEC  (X'3C00' 5005076303FFC422  X'0C') +
             LINK (X'00300030' X'01300130'          +
                   X'02300230' X'03310330') CGROUP(NO)
   CQUERY    DEVN (X'2C00') PATHS

   CQUERY    DEVN (X'2D00') PATHS
   CESTPATH  DEVN (X'2D00')                          +
             PRIM (X'2D00' 5005076303FFC228  X'0D') +
             SEC  (X'3D00' 5005076303FFC422  X'0D') +
             LINK (X'00300030' X'01300130'          +
                   X'02300230' X'03310330') CGROUP(NO)
   CQUERY    DEVN (X'2D00') PATHS
```

Verify through query commands after the path is established that all paths are defined and operational.

Despite the fact that the above commands complete successfully, a subsequent CQUERY reveals that there is a problem with one of the PPRC paths, as Example 27-9 shows.

Example 27-9 Verify successful path creation

```
*************** PPRC REMOTE COPY CQUERY - PATHS ********************
* PRIMARY UNIT: SERIAL#= 000000027131 SSID= 2C00 SS= 2107 LSS= 0C  *
*              FIRST         SECOND          THIRD          FOURTH   *
*            SECONDARY     SECONDARY      SECONDARY      SECONDARY   *
*SERIAL NO: 000000073081  ............  ............  ............ *
* SSID LSS:   3C00 0C        .......       .......       .......    *
*    PATHS:      4             0              0              0      *
*           PFCA SFCA S*  SAID DEST S*  SAID DEST S*  SAID DEST S* *
*           --------- --  --------- --  --------- --  --------- -- *
*        1: 0030 0030 13  ---- ---- 00  ---- ---- 00  ---- ---- 00 *
*        2: 0130 0130 13  ---- ---- 00  ---- ---- 00  ---- ---- 00 *
*        3: 0230 0230 13  ---- ---- 00  ---- ---- 00  ---- ---- 00 *
*        4: 0331 0330 14  ---- ---- 00  ---- ---- 00  ---- ---- 00 *
*  SUBSYSTEM         WWNN                    LIC LEVEL              *
* -----------   ----------------            -----------             *
* PRIMARY....   5005076303FFC228            5.0.03.0097             *
* SECONDARY.1   5005076303FFC422                                    *
```

```
*                                                             *
* S* = PATH STATUS:                                           *
* 00=NO PATH          01=ESTABLISHED ESCON   02=INIT FAILED        *
* 03=TIME OUT         04=NO RESOURCES AT PRI 05=NO RESOURCES AT SEC*
* 06=SERIAL# MISMATCH 07=SEC SSID MISMATCH   08=ESCON LINK OFFLINE *
* 09=ESTABLISH RETRY  0A=PATH ACTIVE TO HOST 0B=PATH TO SAME CLUSTR*
* 10=CONFIG ERROR     FF=UNABLE TO DETERMINE                       *
* 13=ESTABL FIBRE PTH 14=FIBRE PATH DOWN     15=FIBRE RETRY EXCEED *
* 16=SEC ADPTR INCPBL 17=SEC ADPTR UNAVAIL   18=FIBRE LOGIN EXCEED *
*******************************************************************
```

You may also consider establishing PPRC paths in the reverse direction. After a site failover and before you return to the local site it may be required to re synchronize the volumes from the remote site to the local site. This requires PPRC paths from the remote site to the local site. In contrast to PPRC over ESCON, PPRC over FCP links allows you to establish PPRC paths in either direction over the very same link.

Establish Global Copy volume relationships

Create Global Copy pairs as the next step. TSO requires a dedicated PPRC CESTPAIR command for each single Global Copy pair, see Example 27-10.

Example 27-10 Establish Global Copy volume pairs

```
//* ---------------------------- TSO ---------------------------- ***
//* ESTABLISH PPRC-XD PAIR(S)                                       ***
//* ------------------------------------------------------------- ***
//EPAIR   EXEC PGM=IKJEFT01
//SYSPRINT  DD SYSOUT=*
//SYSTSPRT  DD SYSOUT=*
//SYSTSIN   DD DDNAME=SYSIN

 CESTPAIR  DEVN (X'2C00')                         +
           PRIM (X'2C00' 27131 X'00' X'0C')       +
           SEC  (X'3C00' 73081 X'00' X'0C')       +
           ONLINSEC(YES) MSGREQ(NO)  CRIT(NO)     +
           OPTION(XD)    MODE(COPY)

 CESTPAIR  DEVN (X'2D00')                         +
           PRIM (X'2D00' 27131 X'00' X'0D')       +
           SEC  (X'3D00' 73081 X'00' X'0D')       +
           ONLINSEC(YES) MSGREQ(NO)  CRIT(NO)     +
           OPTION(XD)    MODE(COPY)
 CESTPAIR  DEVN (X'2D01')                         +
           PRIM (X'2D00' 27131 X'01' X'0D')       +
           SEC  (X'3D00' 73081 X'01' X'0D')       +
           ONLINSEC(YES) MSGREQ(NO)  CRIT(NO)     +
           OPTION(XD)    MODE(COPY)

 CQUERY    DEVN (X'2C00')
 CQUERY    DEVN (X'2D00')
 CQUERY    DEVN (X'2D01')
```

Note that the ONLINSEC parameter is YES here. It is recommended to leave this parameter at its default of NO to avoid that an active volume is overridden by accident. When the potential Global Copy secondary volume is online to any system, the establish pair command will fail. When you specify YES, the establish will happen independently of whether the potential secondary volume is online or offline.

Make sure the establish commands complete successfully and the initial copy starts. See Example 27-11.

Example 27-11 Verify that the establish Global Copy succeeded

```
************** PPRC REMOTE COPY CQUERY - VOLUME ********************
*                                         (PRIMARY)    (SECONDARY) *
*                                         SSID CCA LSS SSID CCA LSS*
*DEVICE   LEVEL      STATE      PATH STATUS  SERIAL#      SERIAL#    *
*------ --------- ---------- ----------- ---------    ---------  *
* 2D00  PRIMARY..  PENDING.XD   ACTIVE..   2D00 00 0D   3D00 00 0D *
*       CRIT(NO).......       CGRPLB(NO). 000000027131 000000073081*
* PATHS PFCA SFCA STATUS: DESCRIPTION                              *
* ----- --------- ------ -------------------                       *
*   4   0030 0030   13    PATH ESTABLISHED...                      *
*       0130 0130   13    PATH ESTABLISHED...                      *
*       0230 0230   13    PATH ESTABLISHED...                      *
*       0331 0330   13    PATH ESTABLISHED...                      *
* IF STATE = PENDING/SUSPEND:    TRACKS OUT OF SYNC =   49812      *
*                                TRACKS ON VOLUME   =   50085      *
*                              PERCENT OF COPY COMPLETE =    1%     *
*  SUBSYSTEM          WWNN                    LIC LEVEL            *
* -----------  ----------------            -----------             *
* PRIMARY....  5005076303FFC228            5.0.03.0097             *
* SECONDARY.1  5005076303FFC422                                    *
********************************************************************
CQUERY COMMAND COMPLETED FOR DEVICE 2D00. COMPLETION CODE: 00
```

Note that the PPRC CQUERY commands and their output is also written to SYSLOG. This may flood the SYSLOG when you issue many CQUERY commands. An alternative may be to query the Global Copy volume pairs and their status with ICKDSF-based PPRC query commands.

Establish Global Mirror FlashCopy relationship

Once the first pass is completed for Global Copy, establish the FlashCopy relationship between the B volumes and the C volumes. Example 27-12 shows three FCESTABL TSO commands to establish FlashCopy pairs. One FlashCopy pair in the first LSS pair and two FlashCopy pairs in the second LSS pair. Note that Example 27-12 implies that there is a host connectivity to the remote storage server, because the FlashCopy commands are directed to the source and target FlashCopy volumes via their z/OS device numbers. No inband FlashCopy TSO command is used here.

Example 27-12 Establish FlashCopy relationship between B and C volume with TSO command

```
//* ---------------------------- TSO ---------------------------- ***
//* FLASHCOPY B -> C START CHANGE RECORDING NOCOPY ETC. THROUGH    ***
//*                  MODE(ASYNC)                                  ***
//* ------------------------------------------------------------- ***
//* SOURCE AND TARGET REQUIRED / ONLINTGT(YES) - JUST IN CASE     ***
//* ------------------------------------------------------------- ***
//FCESTBL EXEC PGM=IKJEFT01
//SYSPRINT  DD SYSOUT=*
//SYSTSPRT  DD SYSOUT=*
//SYSTSIN   DD DDNAME=SYSIN

   FCQUERY    DEVN (X'3C00')
   FCESTABL   SDEVN(X'3C00')  TDEVN(X'3E00') +
              MODE (ASYNC)    ONLINTGT(YES)
   FCQUERY    DEVN (X'3C00')
```

```
FCQUERY   DEVN (X'3D00')
FCESTABL  SDEVN(X'3D00')  TDEVN(X'3F00')   +
          MODE (ASYNC)    ONLINTGT(YES)
FCQUERY   DEVN (X'3D00')

FCQUERY   DEVN (X'3D01')
FCESTABL  SDEVN(X'3D01')  TDEVN(X'3F01')   +
          MODE (ASYNC)    ONLINTGT(YES)
FCQUERY   DEVN (X'3D01')
```

Note the ONLINTGT parameter. Although we used here YES to make sure that the FlashCopy command completes successfully independent of whether the target volume is online or offline, we still recommend to use the default of NO. This ensures that the FlashCopy command is only successful when the target volume is offline.

You may query the FlashCopy status of the source volumes before and after the FlashCopy establish command to verify that a FlashCopy relationship is successfully established. See Example 27-13.

Example 27-13 FlashCopy status before and after FCESTABL

```
FCQUERY   DEVN (X'3C00')
FCQUERY Formatted -2
DEVN SSID LSS CCA  CU     SERIAL       ACT    MAX XC PC CC RV  SEQNUM
3C00 3C00  0C  00 2107 000000073081      0  50099  N  S  N  N 00000000
FCQUERY COMMAND COMPLETED FOR DEVICE 3C00. COMPLETION CODE: 00
READY
   FCESTABL  SDEVN(X'3C00')  TDEVN(X'3E00')        MODE (ASYNC)    ONLINTGT(YES)
FCESTABL COMMAND COMPLETED FOR DEVICE 3C00. COMPLETION CODE: 00
READY
   FCQUERY   DEVN (X'3C00')
FCQUERY Formatted -2
DEVN SSID LSS CCA  CU     SERIAL       ACT    MAX XC PC CC RV  SEQNUM
3C00 3C00  0C  00 2107 000000073081      1  50099  N  S  N  N 00000000
FCQUERY COMMAND COMPLETED FOR DEVICE 3C00. COMPLETION CODE: 00
```

This concludes the setup for Global Copy and FlashCopy. Global Copy replicates the data from the local to the remote volumes.

Establish Global Mirror session

Example 27-14 shows the new TSO command RSESSION with the ACTION parameter of DEFINE. This establishes a Global Mirror session in the concerned LSS or LCU at the local site. You define the same session number to all LSSs that potentially contribute to the Global Mirror session.

Example 27-14 Define Global Mirror session to all involved LSS

```
//* ---------------------------- TSO ------------ CREATE (4) ----- ***
//* DEFINE GM SESSION NUMBER X'01' TO LSS X'0C' AND LSS X'0D'      ***
//* ------------------------------------------------------------- ***
//DEFSESS EXEC PGM=IKJEFT01
//SYSPRINT  DD SYSOUT=*
//SYSTSPRT  DD SYSOUT=*
//SYSTSIN   DD DDNAME=SYSIN

  RSESSION   SNBR(01) VOLSER(XX2C00)          +
             ACTION(DEFINE)                   +
             LSSTYPE(CKD) LSSNBR(0C)          +
```

```
          ESSSERIAL(27131)              +
          MSSERIAL (27131)

RSESSION  SNBR(01) VOLSER(XX2D00)       +
          ACTION(DEFINE)                +
          LSSTYPE(CKD) LSSNBR(0D)       +
          ESSSERIAL(27131)              +
          MSSERIAL (27131)
```

Note that the VOLSER parameter is used to point to the LSS that contains the potential Global Copy volumes for Global Mirror. These volumes have to be online to the system on which this job executes. This asks for a kind of utility volume within each LSS that potentially contains Global Mirror primary volumes. This command creates only a session number, which is 01, here, for each LSS. It does not affect the Global Copy, which is still replicating the write data from the local site to the remote site.

Populate the session with Global Copy primary volumes

Once the session is defined to both primary LSSs, we add Global Copy primary volumes to the session. Example 27-15 shows the new RVOLUME TSO command.

Example 27-15 Populate Global Mirror session with volumes from two LSS

```
//* ---------------------------- TSO ------------ CREATE (5) ----- ***
//* POPULATE SESSION X'01' WITH PRIMARY VOLUMES                     ***
//*                                                                 ***
//*          VOLUME LIST CONTAINS CCA NUMBERS                       ***
//* ------------------------------------------------------------- ***
//JOIN    EXEC PGM=IKJEFT01
//SYSPRINT  DD SYSOUT=*
//SYSTSPRT  DD SYSOUT=*
//SYSTSIN   DD DDNAME=SYSIN

  RVOLUME    SNBR(01) VOLSER(XX2C00)        +
             ACTION   (JOIN)                +
             LSSTYPE  (CKD) LSSNBR(0C)      +
             ESSSERIAL(27131)               +
             VOLLIST  (00)

  RVOLUME    SNBR(01) VOLSER(XX2D00)        +
             ACTION   (JOIN)                +
             LSSTYPE  (CKD) LSSNBR(0D)      +
             ESSSERIAL(27131)               +
             VOLRANGE (00:01)
/*
```

Again we need an online volume to aim into the concerned LSS. The first RVOLUME command adds a volume from LSS 0C into session 01. Here we use the VOLLIST parameter that contains the channel connection address (CCA) of the Global Copy primary volume.

The second RVOLUME command adds two volumes from LSS 0D into session 01. Here, we use the VOLRANGE parameter, which contains also CCAs of the concerned Global Copy primary volumes. VOLRANGE reads here CCA from 00 to 01, which is just two volumes in this case.

Note that this does still not perform any Consistency Group creation. The only activity that is constantly going on is Global Copy between the Global Copy primary and secondary volumes.

Start Global Copy session

The last step is to finally start the Global Mirror session and create Consistency Groups at the remote site (Example 27-16).

Example 27-16 Start Global Mirror session

```
//* ---------------------------- TSO ------------ CREATE (6) ----- ***
//* START     SESSION X'01' THROUGH LSS X'0C'                       ***
//*                                                                 ***
//*           THEN LSS X'0C' BECOMES THE MASTER LSS (DS)            ***
//*           NOTE: LSS SYNTAX IS WITHOUT X AND QUOTES ...          ***
//*                                                                 ***
//*           CGINTERVAL - BUILD CG WITHOUT A BREAK                 ***
//*           CGDRAIN    - ALLOW 10 MINUTES FOR DRAINING THE STUFF  ***
//*           COORDINTERVAL - ALLOW 5 MS MAX FOR COORDINATION       ***
//* ------------------------------------------------------------- ***
//START    EXEC PGM=IKJEFT01
//SYSPRINT  DD SYSOUT=*
//SYSTSPRT  DD SYSOUT=*
//SYSTSIN   DD DDNAME=SYSIN

  RSESSION  SNBR(01)       VOLSER(XX2C00)    +
            ACTION        (START)            +
            LSSTYPE       (CKD) LSSNBR(0C)   +
            ESSSERIAL     (27131)            +
            MSSERIAL      (27131)            +
            CGINTERVAL    (00)               +
            CGDRAIN       (600)              +
            COORDINTERVAL(05)
/*
```

Example 27-16 shows the new TSO command RSESSION, but this time with the ACTION(START) parameter. As the parameter implies, the microcode now starts to create Consistency Groups at the secondary storage server. Again, an online volume in VOLSER is required on the system where this job executes. START allows you to provide the session tuneables when you decide to use different values than the default values. Here we decided to continuously create Consistency Groups. The maximum drain time window is set to 10 minutes. The maximum application impact time is set to 5 milliseconds at the beginning of the process to form a new Consistency Group.

This step concludes the step by step process to build a Global Mirror environment with three Global Copy primary volumes spread over two LSSs.

27.2.3 Primary site failure scenario and recovery utilizing TSO commands

This example goes through the required steps to recover from a primary site failure using TSO commands. The example continues with the configuration established in the previous example in 27.2.2, "Establish a Global Mirror environment utilizing TSO commands" on page 346. The very same volumes and LSSs are shown in all corresponding TSO command examples.

Figure 27-2 shows the configuration during normal operations.

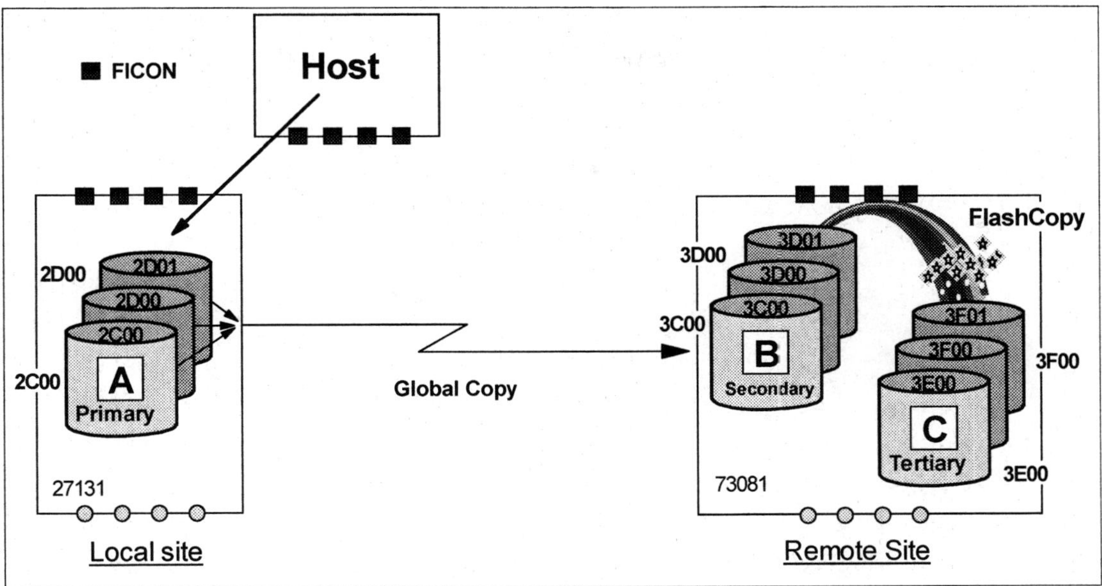

Figure 27-2 Global Mirror example before unplanned primary failure

An application writes to three primary volumes. These volumes are part of a Global Mirror session as created in "Establish a Global Mirror environment utilizing TSO commands" on page 346.

Primary site failure

We simulate a primary site failure that may not be fatal to the storage server.

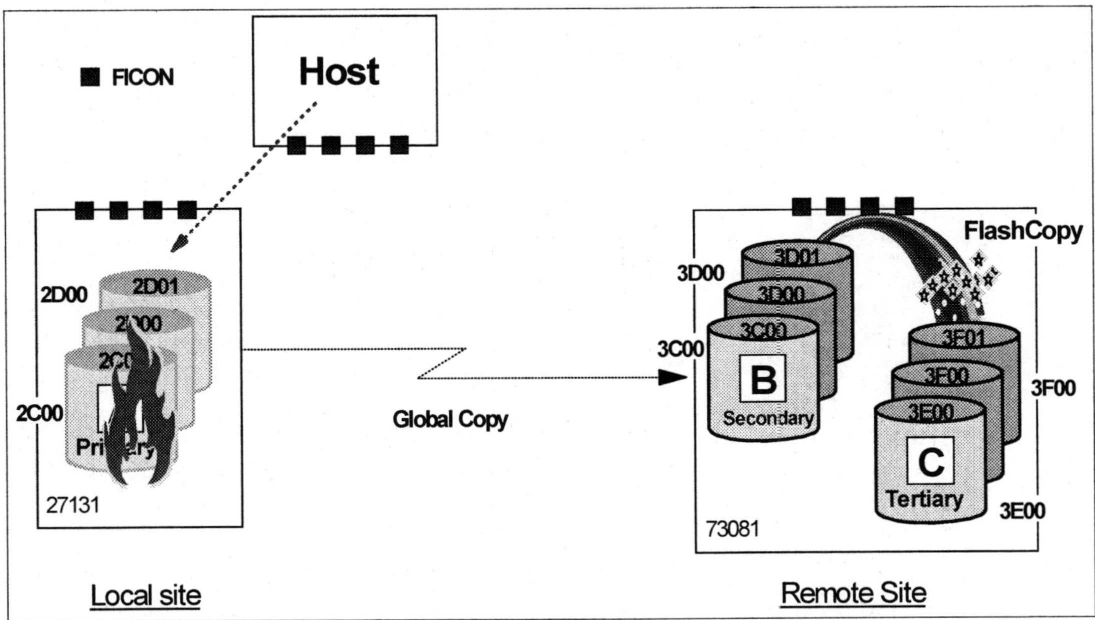

Figure 27-3 Global Mirror unplanned primary site failure

We simulated a primary failure with a CGROUP FREEZE command to both involved LSSs. See Figure 27-3 and Example 27-17.

A more strict primary volume failure may be simulated through a V OFFLINE,FORCE to the Global Copy primary volumes. This will also fail the application I/Os to the concerned volumes. Do not forget to reply to the corresponding WTOR for each V OFFLINE,FORCE.

Example 27-17 Simulate primary site failure through CGROUP FREEZE

```
//* ---------------------------- TSO ------------ FAILO  (2) ----- ***
//* SIMULATE PRIMARY FAILURE WITH CGROUP FREEZE/RUN               ***
//* HARDER PRIMARY FAILURE THROUGH VARY OFFLINE,FORCE             ***
//* ------------------------------------------------------------- ***
//FREEZE  EXEC PGM=IKJEFT01
//SYSPRINT  DD SYSOUT=*
//SYSTSPRT  DD SYSOUT=*
//SYSTSIN   DD DDNAME=SYSIN

 CGROUP    DEVN (X'2C00')                  +
           PRIM (X'2C00' 27131 X'0C')      +
           SEC  (X'3C00' 73081 X'0C')      +
           FREEZE

 CGROUP    DEVN (X'2D00')                  +
           PRIM (X'2D00' 27131 X'0D')      +
           SEC  (X'3D00' 73081 X'0D')      +
           FREEZE

//* ------------------------------------------------------------- ***
//RUN     EXEC PGM=IKJEFT01
//SYSPRINT  DD SYSOUT=*
//SYSTSPRT  DD SYSOUT=*
//SYSTSIN   DD DDNAME=SYSIN

 CGROUP    DEVN (X'2C00')                  +
           PRIM (X'2C00' 27131 X'0C')      +
           SEC  (X'3C00' 73081 X'0C')      +
           RUN

 CGROUP    DEVN (X'2D00')                  +
           PRIM (X'2D00' 27131 X'0D')      +
           SEC  (X'3D00' 73081 X'0D')      +
           RUN
```

CGROUP FREEZE immediately removes the PPRC paths between the primary and corresponding secondary LSS. An immediate CGROUP RUN would end a potential extended long busy (ELB) timer. Note that ELB is not possible and not useful for Global Copy.

Stop Global Mirror session

When the local storage server is still operational, you may explicitly stop the Global Mirror session; see Example 27-18.

Example 27-18 Stop Global Mirror session when local site is still accessible

```
//* ------------------ TSO --------------------------------------- ***
//* Terminate GM session number X'01'                             ***
//* ------------------------------------------------------------- ***
//TERM    EXEC PGM=IKJEFT01
//SYSPRINT  DD SYSOUT=*
//SYSTSPRT  DD SYSOUT=*
//SYSTSIN   DD DDNAME=SYSIN

 RSESSION   SNBR(01) VOLSER(XX2C00)          +
```

```
ACTION(STOP)                    +
LSSTYPE(CKD) LSSNBR(0C)         +
ESSSERIAL(27131)                +
MSSERIAL (27131)
```

Note: Perform all Global Mirror session commands to the Master LSS. This is the LSS that received the Global Mirror START command

Failover from B to A volumes

Once the primary volumes fail and the application I/O stops at the primary site, the PPRC status of the secondary volumes or B volumes changes from SECONDARY PENDING to PRIMARY SUSPENDED. See Example 27-19.

Example 27-19 Failover from B volume to A volume

```
//* ---------------------------- TSO --------- FAILOVER (3) ------ ***
//* ESTABLISH PPRC-XD PAIR(S) FAILOVER B -> A                     ***
//*                                                               ***
//*   NOTE: ACTION IS NOT VALID WITH MODE(COPY)                   ***
//* ------------------------------------------------------------- ***
//EPAIRFO EXEC PGM=IKJEFT01
//SYSPRINT  DD SYSOUT=*
//SYSTSPRT  DD SYSOUT=*
//SYSTSIN   DD DDNAME=SYSIN

 CESTPAIR  DEVN (X'3C00')                      +
           PRIM (X'3C00' 73081 X'00' X'0C')    +
           SEC  (X'2C00' 27131 X'00' X'0C')    +
           ACTION(FAILOVER)                    +
           ONLINSEC(NO)  MSGREQ(NO)  CRIT(NO)  +
           OPTION(XD)                CASCADE(NO)

 CESTPAIR  DEVN (X'3D00')                      +
           PRIM (X'3D00' 73081 X'00' X'0D')    +
           SEC  (X'2D00' 27131 X'00' X'0D')    +
           ACTION(FAILOVER)                    +
           ONLINSEC(NO)  MSGREQ(NO)  CRIT(NO)  +
           OPTION(XD)                CASCADE(NO)
 CESTPAIR  DEVN (X'3D01')                      +
           PRIM (X'3D00' 73081 X'01' X'0D')    +
           SEC  (X'2D00' 27131 X'01' X'0D')    +
           ACTION(FAILOVER)                    +
           ONLINSEC(NO)  MSGREQ(NO)  CRIT(NO)  +
           OPTION(XD)                CASCADE(NO)
```

The FAILOVER parameter does not need to communicate to the local or primary volumes. This parameter just changes the PPRC status of the secondary volume to PRIMARY SUSPEND. This includes the creation of a change recording bit map for the B volumes, which allows you to re-synchronize at a later point-in-time when returning to the local site.

Check Global Mirror FlashCopy status between B and C volumes

At this stage you have to verify the FlashCopy status of each FlashCopy pair. For details refer to 24.6.4, "Verify for valid Consistency Group state" on page 274. We assume that all FlashCopy pairs are in a good state with the same FlashCopy sequence number and all FlashCopy pairs are in non-revertible state.

Create a data consistent set of B volumes

The next step is to create a set of consistent volumes. This requires a new FlashCopy operation, which is fast reverse restore, FRR. See Figure 27-4.

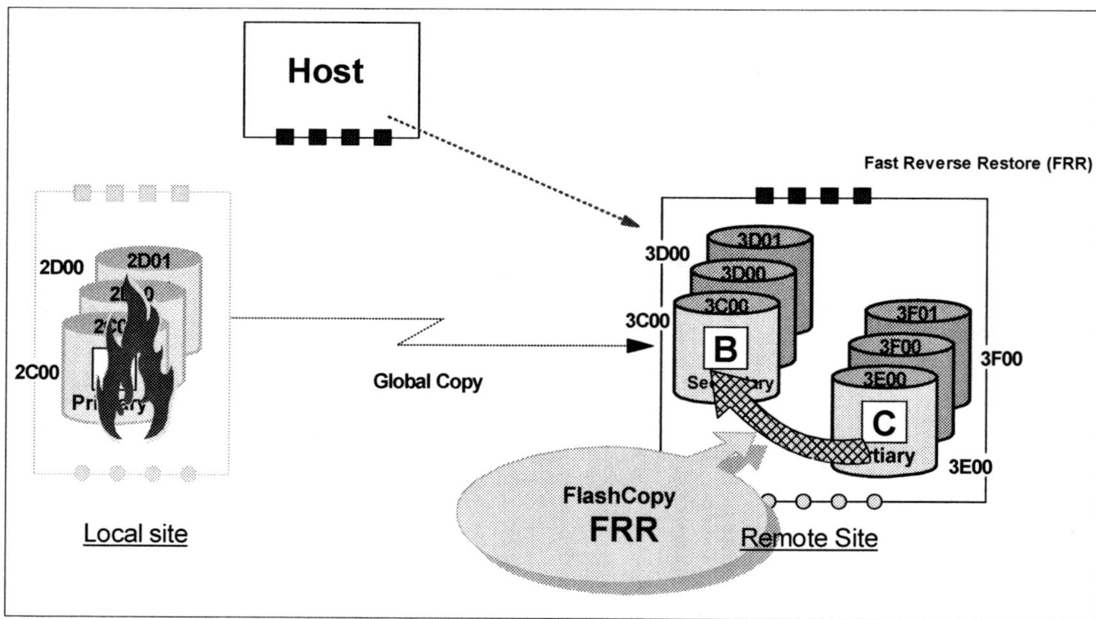

Figure 27-4 Global Mirror establish FlashCopy to B from last consistent FlashCopy on C

This FlashCopy command uses the C volume as source volume and the B volume as the target volume. Example 27-20 implies host connectivity to the remote or secondary storage server because we use source and target z/OS device numbers.

Example 27-20 Create a set of consistent volumes on B volumes

```
//* ------------------------------------------------------------ ***
//FCFRR    EXEC PGM=IKJEFT01
//SYSPRINT  DD SYSOUT=*
//SYSTSPRT  DD SYSOUT=*
//SYSTSIN   DD DDNAME=SYSIN

 FCESTABL  SDEVN(X'3E00')  TDEVN(X'3C00') ACTION(FRR)
 FCESTABL  SDEVN(X'3F00')  TDEVN(X'3D00') ACTION(FRR)
 FCESTABL  SDEVN(X'3F01')  TDEVN(X'3D01') ACTION(FRR)
```

This is a background copy operation that copies only the changed tracks from the C volumes to the B volumes, those which changed since the last Consistency Group formation. Once the background copy completes, the FlashCopy relationship between the C volume and the B volumes is withdrawn and ends. After that the C volume is not usable and only the B volume is now a set of data consistent volumes.

Create an optional extra copy of data consistent volumes

To create a second copy of valid data you may create a copy of the B volumes on the D volumes. See Example 27-21.

Example 27-21 Create optional second copy of data consistent D volumes

```
//* ---------------------------- TSO ------------ CREATE (5) ----- ***
//* FLASHCOPY B -> D TO CREATE COPY TO WORK (TEST) WITH             ***
//* ------------------------------------------------------------ ***
```

```
//FCESTBL EXEC PGM=IKJEFT01
//SYSPRINT  DD SYSOUT=*
//SYSTSPRT  DD SYSOUT=*
//SYSTSIN   DD DDNAME=SYSIN

   FCESTABL  SDEVN(X'3C00')  TDEVN(X'3E02')
   FCQUERY   DEVN (X'3C00')

   FCESTABL  SDEVN(X'3D00')  TDEVN(X'3F02')
   FCQUERY   DEVN (X'3D00')

   FCESTABL  SDEVN(X'3D01')  TDEVN(X'3F03')
   FCQUERY   DEVN (X'3D01')
```

Again, Example 27-21 is optional. You may use these D volumes for further tests.

Create data consistent volume set on C volumes

We recommend to create at least a second set of consistent volumes on the C volumes after you have created the B volumes as described in "Create a data consistent set of B volumes" on page 356.

Example 27-22 Setup Global Mirror FlashCopy between B and C volume again

```
//* ---------------------------- TSO ---------------------------- ***
//* FLASHCOPY B -> C START CHANGE RECORDING NOCOPY ETC. THROUGH     ***
//*                  MODE(ASYNC) OPTION (GET READY FOR GM)          ***
//* ------------------------------------------------------------- ***
//FCESTBL EXEC PGM=IKJEFT01
//SYSPRINT  DD SYSOUT=*
//SYSTSPRT  DD SYSOUT=*
//SYSTSIN   DD DDNAME=SYSIN

 FCESTABL  SDEVN(X'3C00') TDEVN(X'3E00')  MODE(ASYNC)
 FCQUERY   DEVN (X'3C00')

 FCESTABL  SDEVN(X'3D00') TDEVN(X'3F00')  MODE(ASYNC)
 FCQUERY   DEVN (X'3D00')

 FCESTABL  SDEVN(X'3D01') TDEVN(X'3F01')  MODE(ASYNC)
 FCQUERY   DEVN (X'3D01')
```

Example 27-22 does a reestablish of the previous Global Mirror FlashCopy relationship between the B volumes and the C volumes. This prepares the configuration when returning to the local site and resuming Global Mirror as used before. It also provides at the same time another copy of data consistent volumes on the C volumes. At this stage B volumes and C volumes are identical.

When you have to restart again because a previous restart to the B volumes was faulty or the restart was not setup correctly, you may flash again from C to B to recreate a data consistent set of volumes again on the B volumes.

Prepare to return to the local site

Eventually you may plan to return to the local site. The intention here is to apply the changes from the B volumes to the A volumes before resuming operations at the local site. Before you may apply these changes from the B to A volumes, you have to establish PPRC paths from B to A volumes.

Replicate the changes from B to A volumes

When the PPRC paths are active between the B and A volumes, you may still keep the application running at the remote site and updating the B volumes. See Figure 27-5.

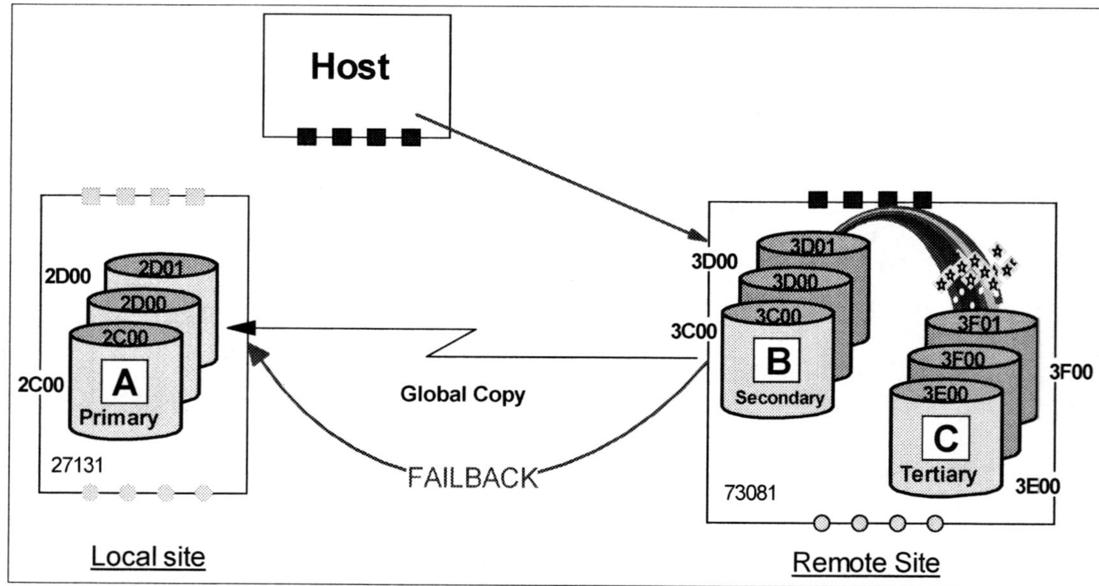

Figure 27-5 FAILBACK from B to A to prepare for site failback to local site

Through the FAILBACK parameter we apply the changes from the B volumes to the A volumes (Example 27-23).

Example 27-23 FAILBACK from B to A volumes before returning to local site

```
//* ---------------------------- TSO ----------------------------- ***
//* ESTABLISH PPRC-XD PAIR(S) FAILBACK B -> A  ONCE A IS BACK      ***
//* ------------------------------------------------------------ ***
//EPAIRFB EXEC PGM=IKJEFT01
//SYSPRINT  DD SYSOUT=*
//SYSTSPRT  DD SYSOUT=*
//SYSTSIN   DD DDNAME=SYSIN

 CESTPAIR  DEVN (X'3C00')                         +
           PRIM (X'3C00' 73081 X'00' X'0C')    +
           SEC  (X'2C00' 27131 X'00' X'0C')    +
           ACTION(FAILBACK)                       +
                          MSGREQ(NO)  CRIT(NO) +
           OPTION(XD)                 CASCADE(NO)

 CESTPAIR  DEVN (X'3D00')                         +
           PRIM (X'3D00' 73081 X'00' X'0D')    +
           SEC  (X'2D00' 27131 X'00' X'0D')    +
           ACTION(FAILBACK)                       +
                          MSGREQ(NO)  CRIT(NO) +
           OPTION(XD)                 CASCADE(NO)
 CESTPAIR  DEVN (X'3D01')                         +
           PRIM (X'3D00' 73081 X'01' X'0D')    +
           SEC  (X'2D00' 27131 X'01' X'0D')    +
           ACTION(FAILBACK)                       +
                          MSGREQ(NO)  CRIT(NO) +
           OPTION(XD)                 CASCADE(NO)
```

Return to the local site and resume Global Mirror

Eventually you may want to return the application to the local site. This requires you to quiesce the application at the remote site. Then you issue a FAILOVER / FAILBACK command sequence to the A volumes, which will change the Global Copy direction as Example 27-24 shows. These commands are very quick because there is no data to replicate.

Example 27-24 FAILOVER and FAILBACK from A to B volumes

```
//* ---------------------------- TSO --------- FAILOVER ---------- ***
//* ESTABLISH PPRC-XD PAIR(S) FAILOVER A -> B                     ***
//* ------------------------------------------------------------- ***
//EPAIRFO EXEC PGM=IKJEFT01
//SYSPRINT  DD SYSOUT=*
//SYSTSPRT  DD SYSOUT=*
//SYSTSIN   DD DDNAME=SYSIN

 CESTPAIR  DEVN (X'2C00')                    +
           PRIM (X'2C00' 27131 X'00' X'0C')  +
           SEC  (X'3C00' 73081 X'00' X'0C')  +
           ACTION(FAILOVER)                  +
                          MSGREQ(NO)  CRIT(NO) +
           OPTION(XD)                 CASCADE(NO)

 CESTPAIR  DEVN (X'2D00')                    +
           PRIM (X'2D00' 27131 X'00' X'0D')  +
           SEC  (X'3D00' 73081 X'00' X'0D')  +
           ACTION(FAILOVER)                  +
                          MSGREQ(NO)  CRIT(NO) +
           OPTION(XD)                 CASCADE(NO)
 CESTPAIR  DEVN (X'2D01')                    +
           PRIM (X'2D00' 27131 X'01' X'0D')  +
           SEC  (X'3D00' 73081 X'01' X'0D')  +
           ACTION(FAILOVER)                  +
                          MSGREQ(NO)  CRIT(NO) +
           OPTION(XD)                 CASCADE(NO)


//* ---------------------------- TSO ---------------------------- ***
//* ESTABLISH PPRC-XD PAIR(S) FAILBACK A -> B                     ***
//* ------------------------------------------------------------- ***
//EPAIRFB EXEC PGM=IKJEFT01
//SYSPRINT  DD SYSOUT=*
//SYSTSPRT  DD SYSOUT=*
//SYSTSIN   DD DDNAME=SYSIN

 CESTPAIR  DEVN (X'2C00')                    +
           PRIM (X'2C00' 27131 X'00' X'0C')  +
           SEC  (X'3C00' 73081 X'00' X'0C')  +
           ACTION(FAILBACK)                  +
                          MSGREQ(NO)  CRIT(NO) +
           OPTION(XD)                 CASCADE(NO)

 CESTPAIR  DEVN (X'2D00')                    +
           SEC  (X'3D00' 73081 X'00' X'0D')  +
           PRIM (X'2D00' 27131 X'00' X'0D')  +
           ACTION(FAILBACK)                  +
                          MSGREQ(NO)  CRIT(NO) +
           OPTION(XD)                 CASCADE(NO)
 CESTPAIR  DEVN (X'2D01')                    +
```

```
SEC  (X'3D00' 73081 X'01' X'0D')   +
PRIM (X'2D00' 27131 X'01' X'0D')   +
ACTION(FAILBACK)                   +
               MSGREQ(NO)  CRIT(NO) +
OPTION(XD)                 CASCADE(NO)
```

Global Copy then replicates the data from the local site to the remote site as before, when the application resumes I/O at the local site as illustrated in Figure 27-2 on page 353.

Then you need to restart Global Mirror to resume the Consistency Group formation process. Note that you have to stop the Global Mirror session during the failover processing from the local site to the remote site.

27.2.4 Clean up a Global Mirror session with TSO commands

To remove a Global Mirror environment, follow these steps in this order:

1. Stop the session.
2. Remove volumes from session.
3. Delete the session.
4. Withdraw the FlashCopy relationships.
5. Delete the Global Copy pairs.
6. Remove the PPRC paths.

The following paragraphs provide this process step by step and use TSO commands to cleanup a Global Mirror session.

Cleanup session: Session stop

The first thing to do is to stop the Global Mirror session. Example 27-25 shows the TSO command to stop the session, which is used throughout the examples in this chapter.

Example 27-25 Cleanup session: step 1 - stop session

```
//* ------------------ TSO -------------------- CLEANUP (1) ------ ***
//* Terminate GM session number X'01'          first thing to do  ***
//* ---------------------------------------------------------------- ***
//TERM     EXEC PGM=IKJEFT01
//SYSPRINT  DD SYSOUT=*
//SYSTSPRT  DD SYSOUT=*
//SYSTSIN   DD DDNAME=SYSIN

  RSESSION   SNBR(01) VOLSER(XX2C00)          +
             ACTION(STOP)                     +
             LSSTYPE(CKD) LSSNBR(0C)          +
             ESSSERIAL(27131)                 +
             MSSERIAL (27131)

  RQUERY     SNBR(01) VOLSER(XX2C00) ACTION(DVCSTAT)
  RQUERY     SNBR(01) VOLSER(XX2C00) ACTION(GMLSTAT)
  RQUERY     SNBR(01) VOLSER(XX2C00) ACTION(GMPSTAT)
```

The GMPSTAT query shows that session 01 is not active any longer. Numbers are reset to zeros (Example 27-26).

Example 27-26 Session query after session stop

```
RQUERY     SNBR(01) VOLSER(XX2C00) ACTION(GMPSTAT)

RQUERY Output Volser(XX2C00) Action(GMPSTAT) Version(001)
SNbr LSS GMPStatus  RvrtStatus FCSeqNbr TotVol OOSVol OOSTrks
--   --  ---------- ---------- -------- ------ ------ --------
01   0C  NotStarted            00000000      1      0 00000000
```

Cleanup session: Remove volumes from session

After the session has been stopped, remove the Global Mirror primary volumes from the session.

Example 27-27 Cleanup session - step 2 - remove volumes from session

```
//* ------------------ TSO ----------------- CLEANUP (2) --------- ***
//* REMOVE VOLUMES FROM SESSION NUMBER 01  AFTER SESSION STOPPED   ***
//*                                                                ***
//*          VOLUME LIST CONTAINS CCA NUMBERS                      ***
//* -------------------------------------------------------------- ***
//REMOVE  EXEC PGM=IKJEFT01
//SYSPRINT  DD SYSOUT=*
//SYSTSPRT  DD SYSOUT=*
//SYSTSIN   DD DDNAME=SYSIN

  RVOLUME    SNBR(01) VOLSER(XX2C00)          +
             ACTION(REMOVE)                   +
             LSSTYPE(CKD) LSSNBR(0C)          +
             ESSSERIAL(27131)                 +
             VOLLIST  (00)

  RVOLUME    SNBR(01) VOLSER(XX2D00)          +
             ACTION(REMOVE)                   +
             LSSTYPE(CKD) LSSNBR(0D)          +
             ESSSERIAL(27131)                 +
             VOLLIST  (00,01)

  RQUERY     SNBR(01) VOLSER(XX2C00) ACTION(DVCSTAT)
  RQUERY     SNBR(01) VOLSER(XX2D00) ACTION(DVCSTAT)
```

The subsequent RQUERY commands, after removing the Global Copy primary volumes, still display the session number 01, but no longer any volumes. This is shown in Example 27-28.

Example 27-28 Query Global Mirror volumes after removal

```
RQUERY     SNBR(01) VOLSER(XX2C00) ACTION(DVCSTAT)

RQUERY Output Volser(XX2C00) Action(DVCSTAT) Version(001)
SNbr LSS Dvc VolStat              PriPPRCStat SecCascStat
--   --  --  -------------------- ----------  ----------
01           NoVolumes
READY

RQUERY     SNBR(01) VOLSER(XX2D00) ACTION(DVCSTAT)

RQUERY Output Volser(XX2D00) Action(DVCSTAT) Version(001)
SNbr LSS Dvc VolStat              PriPPRCStat SecCascStat
--   --  --  -------------------- ----------  ----------
01           NoVolumes
```

Cleanup session: Un-define session

The next step is to remove the Global Mirror session from all concerned LSSs. See Example 27-29.

Example 27-29 Cleanup session - step 3 - remove Global Mirror session

```
//* ------------------ TSO ----------------- CLEANUP (3) --------- ***
//* UNdefine GM session number X'01' through both involved LSS #s  ***
//* ==                                                             ***
//* ------------------------------------------------------------- ***
//UNDEFINE EXEC PGM=IKJEFT01
//SYSPRINT  DD SYSOUT=*
//SYSTSPRT  DD SYSOUT=*
//SYSTSIN   DD DDNAME=SYSIN

  RSESSION   SNBR(01) VOLSER(XX2C00)          +
             ACTION(UNDEFINE)                 +
             LSSTYPE(CKD) LSSNBR(0C)          +
             ESSSERIAL(27131)                 +
             MSSERIAL (27131)

  RSESSION   SNBR(01) VOLSER(XX2D00)          +
             ACTION(UNDEFINE)                 +
             LSSTYPE(CKD) LSSNBR(0D)          +
             ESSSERIAL(27131)                 +
             MSSERIAL (27131)

  RQUERY     SNBR(01) VOLSER(XX2C00) ACTION(DVCSTAT)
  RQUERY     SNBR(01) VOLSER(XX2C00) ACTION(GMLSTAT)
  RQUERY     SNBR(01) VOLSER(XX2C00) ACTION(GMPSTAT)
```

Cleanup session: Remove FlashCopy relationship

After the Global Mirror session is cleaned up, you may start to remove the FlashCopy relationships between the B and C volumes. See Example 27-30.

Example 27-30 Cleanup session - step 4 - remove FlashCopy relationship

```
//* ------------------ TSO ----------------- CLEANUP (4) --------- ***
//* Remove FlashCopy relationship from B -> C                      ***
//* ------------------------------------------------------------- ***
//FCWDRW  EXEC PGM=IKJEFT01
//SYSPRINT  DD SYSOUT=*
//SYSTSPRT  DD SYSOUT=*
//SYSTSIN   DD DDNAME=SYSIN

   FCQUERY   DEVN (X'3C00')
   FCWITHDR  SDEVN(X'3C00')  TDEVN(X'3E00')
   FCQUERY   DEVN (X'3C00')

   FCQUERY   DEVN (X'3D00')
   FCWITHDR  SDEVN(X'3D00')  TDEVN(X'3F00')
   FCQUERY   DEVN (X'3D00')

   FCQUERY   DEVN (X'3D01')
   FCWITHDR  SDEVN(X'3D01')  TDEVN(X'3F01')
   FCQUERY   DEVN (X'3D01')
```

You may verify, with a last FlashCopy query, that the FlashCopy relationship is removed. Example 27-31 shows an example.

Example 27-31 FlashCopy commands and their response

```
READY
   FCQUERY   DEVN (X'3C00')
FCQUERY Formatted -2
DEVN SSID LSS CCA  CU      SERIAL        ACT    MAX XC PC CC RV  SEQNUM
3C00 3C00  0C  00 2107 000000073081        1  50099  N  S  N  N 429334DE
FCQUERY COMMAND COMPLETED FOR DEVICE 3C00. COMPLETION CODE: 00
READY
   FCWITHDR  SDEVN(X'3C00')  TDEVN(X'3E00')
FCWITHDR COMMAND COMPLETED FOR DEVICE 3C00. COMPLETION CODE: 00
READY
   FCQUERY   DEVN (X'3C00')
FCQUERY Formatted -2
DEVN SSID LSS CCA  CU      SERIAL        ACT    MAX XC PC CC RV  SEQNUM
3C00 3C00  0C  00 2107 000000073081        0  50099  N  S  N  N 00000000
FCQUERY COMMAND COMPLETED FOR DEVICE 3C00. COMPLETION CODE: 00
READY
```

The ACT column with the number 1 indicates an active FlashCopy relationship. The 0 (zero) in the FlashCopy query, after the FlashCopy withdraw command, indicates that the FlashCopy relationship is removed.

Cleanup session: Delete Global Copy volume pairs

Remove all Global Mirror volume pairs. Example 27-32 shows the TSO commands that are involved.

Example 27-32 Cleanup session - step 5 - delete Global Copy volume pairs

```
//* ------------------ TSO ---------------- CLEANUP (5) ---------- ***
//* Delete PPRC-XD (Global Copy) volumes                             ***
//*                                                                  ***
//*         DELETE PRIMARY X'2C00'                                   ***
//*                        X'2D00'                                   ***
//*                        X'2D01'                                   ***
//*                                                                  ***
//*       PRIM(X'2C00' 27131 X'00' X'0C')                            ***
//*              SSID  #####  CCA   LSS                              ***
//* ---------------------------------------------------------------- ***
//DPAIR   EXEC PGM=IKJEFT01
//SYSPRINT  DD SYSOUT=*
//SYSTSPRT  DD SYSOUT=*
//SYSTSIN   DD DDNAME=SYSIN
//SYSTSIN   DD DDNAME=SYSIN

 CQUERY    DEVN(X'2C00')
 CQUERY    DEVN(X'2D00')
 CQUERY    DEVN(X'2D01')

 CDELPAIR  DEVN(X'2C00')                             +
           PRIM(X'2C00' 27131 X'00' X'0C')           +
           SEC (X'3C00' 73081 X'00' X'0C')
 CDELPAIR  DEVN(X'2D00')                             +
           PRIM(X'2D00' 27131 X'00' X'0D')           +
           SEC (X'3D00' 73081 X'00' X'0D')
 CDELPAIR  DEVN(X'2D01')                             +
           PRIM(X'2D00' 27131 X'01' X'0D')           +
```

```
            SEC (X'3D00' 73081 X'01' X'0D')

 CQUERY     DEVN(X'2C00')
 CQUERY     DEVN(X'2D00')
 CQUERY     DEVN(X'2D01')
```

You may check the Global Copy primary volume status before and after the CDELPAIR command sequence. Example 27-33 and Example 27-34 show examples with corresponding CQUERY TSO commands with their formatted output.

Example 27-33 CQUERY before deleting the Global Copy pair

```
READY
 CQUERY     DEVN(X'2C00')
CQUERY FORMATTED LVL 3
VOLUME REPORT
************** PPRC REMOTE COPY CQUERY - VOLUME ********************
*                                           (PRIMARY)   (SECONDARY) *
*                                          SSID CCA LSS SSID CCA LSS*
*DEVICE   LEVEL      STATE     PATH STATUS  SERIAL#      SERIAL#    *
*------ --------- ---------- ----------- ---------    ---------     *
* 2C00  PRIMARY.. PENDING.XD   ACTIVE..   2C00 00 0C   3C00 00 0C   *
*       CRIT(NO).......      CGRPLB(NO). 000000027131 000000073081*
* PATHS PFCA SFCA STATUS: DESCRIPTION                               *
* ----- --------- ------  -------------------                       *
*   4   0030 0030   13    PATH ESTABLISHED...                       *
*       0130 0130   13    PATH ESTABLISHED...                       *
*       0230 0230   13    PATH ESTABLISHED...                       *
*       0331 0330   14    (UNDETERMINED).....                       *
*  SUBSYSTEM         WWNN                     LIC LEVEL             *
* -----------  ----------------            -----------              *
* PRIMARY....  5005076303FFC228            5.0.03.0097              *
* SECONDARY.1  5005076303FFC422                                     *
*******************************************************************
```

Example 27-34 CQUERY after deleting the Global Copy pair

```
READY
 CQUERY     DEVN(X'2C00')
CQUERY FORMATTED LVL 3
VOLUME REPORT
************** PPRC REMOTE COPY CQUERY - VOLUME ********************
*                                           (PRIMARY)   (SECONDARY) *
*                                          SSID CCA LSS SSID CCA LSS*
*DEVICE   LEVEL      STATE     PATH STATUS  SERIAL#      SERIAL#    *
*------ --------- ---------- ----------- ---------    ---------     *
* 2C00  ......... SIMPLEX...   INACTIVE   2C00 00 0C   ..........   *
*       ...............      ........... 000000027131 ............*
* PATHS SAID DEST STATUS: DESCRIPTION                               *
* ----- --------- ------  -------------------                       *
*   0   ---- ----   00    NO PATH...........                        *
*       ---- ----   00    NO PATH...........                        *
*       ---- ----   00    NO PATH...........                        *
*       ---- ----   00    NO PATH...........                        *
*  SUBSYSTEM         WWNN                     LIC LEVEL             *
* -----------  ----------------            -----------              *
* PRIMARY....  5005076303FFC228            5.0.03.0097              *
* SECONDARY.1  5005076303FFC422                                     *
*******************************************************************
CQUERY COMMAND COMPLETED FOR DEVICE 2C00. COMPLETION CODE: 00
```

Note that this bulky formatted output is also written to SYSLOG. When you issue many CQUERY commands at once, this is going to flood your SYSLOG, it is going to quickly exhaust WTO buffers, and it will lead to corresponding buffer shortage messages. There is also an un-formatted output of the CQUERY command that provides the same information as the formatted output, but in fewer output lines (Example 27-35).

Example 27-35 CQUERY and its un-formatted output

```
READY
   CQUERY    DEVN (X'2C00')        UNFORMAT
CQUERY UNFORMATTED LVL 3
VOLUME REPORT
2C00,,SIMPLEX,INACTIVE,
2C000C,00,000000027131,,,,,,
,,,,,,,,,
,,,
5005076303FFC228,5005076303FFC422,
,,
CQUERY COMMAND COMPLETED FOR DEVICE 2C00. COMPLETION CODE: 00
```

This format is harder to read and requires knowledge about the positional output information. Refer to *z/OS DFSMS Advanced Copy Services*, SC35-0428 for details.

Cleanup session: Remove Global Mirror paths

Last but not least, remove the Global Copy paths from the local LSS to the remote LSSs (Example 27-36).

Example 27-36 Cleanup session - step 6 - remove Global Mirror paths

```
//* ------------------ TSO ----------------- CLEANUP (6) --------- ***
//* Delete PPRC path(s)          this completes the GM cleanup     ***
//* -------------------------------------------------------------- ***
//DPATH    EXEC PGM=IKJEFT01
//SYSPRINT  DD SYSOUT=*
//SYSTSPRT  DD SYSOUT=*
//SYSTSIN   DD DDNAME=SYSIN

    CQUERY     DEVN(X'2C00') PATHS
    CDELPATH   DEVN(X'2C00')                        +
               PRIM(X'2C00'  5005076303FFC228  X'0C') +
               SEC (X'3C00'  5005076303FFC422  X'0C')
    CQUERY     DEVN(X'2C00') PATHS

    CQUERY     DEVN(X'2D00') PATHS
    CDELPATH   DEVN(X'2D00')                        +
               PRIM(X'2D00'  5005076303FFC228  X'0D') +
               SEC (X'3D00'  5005076303FFC422  X'0D')
    CQUERY     DEVN(X'2D00') PATHS
```

This concludes the example on how to remove the Global Mirror session that was built up in 27.2.2, “Establish a Global Mirror environment utilizing TSO commands” on page 346.

27.3 Planned outage example managed through ICKDSF

This section briefly outlines a planned outage example and its corresponding ICKDSF commands (Figure 27-6).

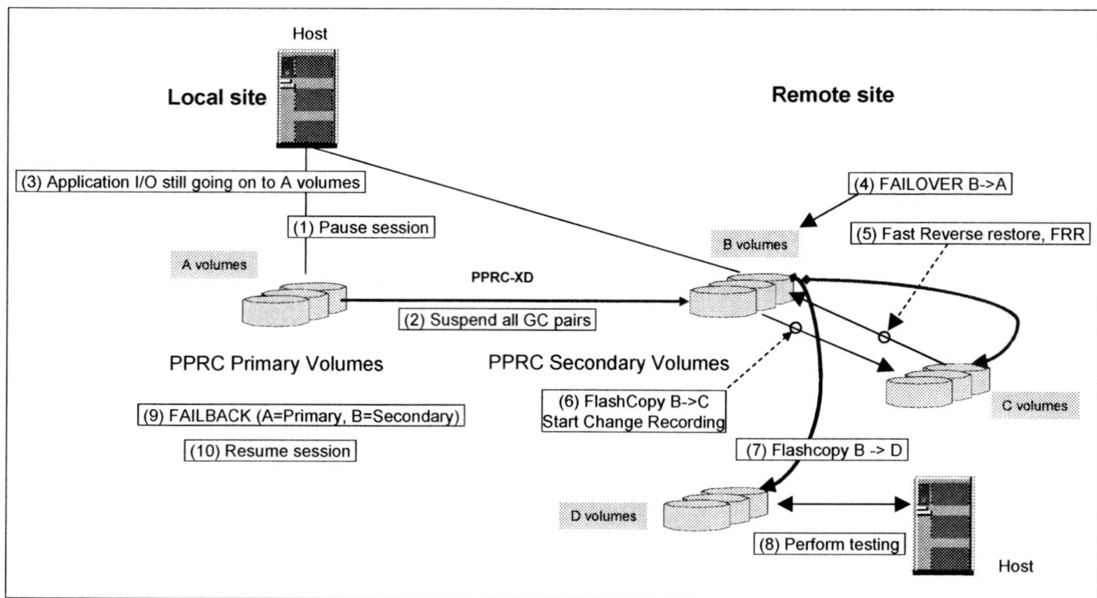

Figure 27-6 Global Mirror planned outage scenario

Figure 27-6 summarizes the scenario. The numbers indicate the sequence of events and relate also to Figure 27-7 and the corresponding ICKDSF commands:

1. Pause the Global Mirror session.
2. Suspend Global Copy pairs.
3. Application I/O continues all the time.
4. Failover from B to A, which turns the B volumes into a PRIMARY SUSPENDED GC volume.
5. Create a data consistent set of B volumes with Fast Reverse Restore (FRR) from C to B volumes
6. Reestablish Global Mirror FlashCopy relationship from B to C. Both volumes afterwards are identical.
7. Create another optional data consistent set of D volumes.
8. Use D volumes for test or other purposes.
9. In order to prepare and continue with Global Mirror, apply the changes that were accumulated at the local site from the A volumes to the B volumes. This does FAILBACK with A volumes as primary and B volumes as secondary volumes.
10. Resume Global Mirror.

```
(1) Pause session

PPRCOPY DDNAME(DD01) TMASYNC -
        SESSNO(001)          -
        PAUSE                -
        MASTER

(2) Suspend all XD pairs

PPRCOPY DDNAME(DD01) SUSPEND         -
        LSS(X'05'  X'00')            -
        PRI(X'E500'  27310  X'00')   -
        SEC(X'7000'  22399  X'00')

(4) FAILOVER B->A

PPRCOPY UNIT  (7000)  ESTPAIR        -
        FAILOVER                     -
        PRI(X'7000'  22399  X'00')   -
        SEC(X'E500'  27310  X'00')   -
        LSS(X'00',X'05')             -
        OPTION(XD)

(5) Fast Reverse restore, FRR

FC      UNIT(7100)     ESTABLISH          /* C VOLUME                */ -
        TARGETVOL(X'00',X'00',7000)       /* B VOLUME                */ -
        FASTREVERSERESTORE                /* REVERSE DIRECTION       */ -
        MODE              (COPY)          /* START BACKGROUNDCOPY    */ -
        ONLINTGT          (YES)                                         -
        TGTOKPRIM         (YES)                                         -
        TGTCANCOMEONLINE  (NO)

(6) FlashCopy B->C  Start Change Recording

FC      UNIT(7000)        ESTABLISH                                      -
        TARGETVOL         (X'01',X'00',7100)                             -
        CHRCD             (YES)      /* CHANGE RECORDING          */    -
        NOTGTWR           (YES)      /* INHIBIT TARGET WRITES     */    -
        MODE              (NOCOPY)   /* NO BACKGROUND COPY        */    -
        ONLINTGT          (YES)                                          -
        TGTCANCOMEONLINE  (NO)

(7) Flashcopy B -> D

FC      UNIT(7000)        ESTABLISH             /* B VOLUME     */ -
        TARGETVOL         (X'01',X'10',7110)    /* D VOLUME     */ -
        ONLINTGT          (YES)                                    -
        TGTCANCOMEONLINE  (NO)

(9) FAILBACK (A=Primary, B=Secondary)

PPRCOPY DDNAME(DD01)  ESTPAIR                     /* A VOLUME     */ -
        FAILBACK                                                     -
        PRI           (X'E500'  27310  X'00')     /* A VOLUME     */ -
        SEC           (X'7000'  22399  X'00')     /* B VOLUME     */ -
        LSS           (X'05',X'00')                                  -
        OPTION        (XD)

(10) Resume session

PPRCOPY DDNAME(DD01)  STASYNC   -
        MODIFY                  -
        SESSNO(001)             -
        CGIT(0)                 -
        MXCT(3)                 -
        MXDT(030)
```

Figure 27-7 ICKDSF command sequence for planned outage example

Figure 27-7 shows all related ICKDSF commands to step through the process of a planned outage to create a data consistent set of D volumes. Note that in most command examples ICKDSF refers through the DDNAME parameter to a corresponding JCL DD statement. This DD statement points to the concerned LSS or volume.

For command details, refer to *Device Support Facility User's Guide and Reference Release 17*, SC35-0033.

27.4 Establish a Global Mirror environment through the DS SM

You may establish a Global Mirror environment with the DS Storage Manager (SM) or GUI. A Global Mirror session relies on the following components, which are independent of the interface used, but are repeated here in case you are only reading this section:

- PPRC paths to define communication links between primary LSS and secondary LSSs. Paths are also required for a potential topology between Master and Subordinate storage images.
- Global Copy pairs, which are also referred to as A volumes and B volumes for the PPRC primary volume and its corresponding PPRC secondary volumes.
- FlashCopy pairs, which are part of Global Mirror. You establish these FlashCopies in the secondary or remote storage server between the B volumes and the C volumes. Note that the B volumes are not only the FlashCopy source but also the Global Copy secondary at the same time. C volumes are the FlashCopy target volumes.

Note that up to eight storage images can contribute their volumes to a Global Mirror session at the primary site. The same number applies for the secondary site.

To create a Global Mirror session requires you to go through a series of consecutive steps:

1. Create PPRC paths:
   a. Between the source LSSs on the source Storage Images on site 1 and the target LSSs on the target Storage Images on site 2.
   b. Within site 1 between the Master Storage Image LSS, or for short Master, and to potential Subordinate Storage Image LSSs. This task is not required if you have only one source Storage Image. All communication between Master and Subordinate LSSs is managed internally and does not need your attention.
2. Create Global Copy pairs with primary or source volumes on site 1 and secondary or target volumes on site 2.
3. Create FlashCopy pairs in site 2 between the Global Copy secondary volumes being the FlashCopy source volumes and their corresponding target volumes, which also may be called journal volumes.
4. Create a common Global Mirror session for each LSS on the primary or source Storage Images. This session has to be defined to all involved LSS at the primary or source Storage Images.
5. Create a Global Mirror session relationship between the Global Mirror Master and its Subordinates. Note that all Global Mirror sessions with the same session number are interconnected through PPRC control paths.

Now you can start the session to form Consistency Groups.

The following sections show how to create a Global Mirror session, whether using the DS Storage Manager or using the DS Command-Line Interface.

27.4.1 Establish PPRC paths for Global Copy with DS Storage Manager

To create new PPRC paths between two LSSs on two different Storage Images, it is necessary to pass through a six-step process with the DS Storage Manager.

> **Note:** You need to repeat this wizard for each data path between the primary or source LSS on the source Storage Images on site 1 and the secondary or target LSSs on the target Storage Images on site 2. You need to do this also for each control path between the Master Storage Image LSS and the Subordinates Storage Image LSSs.

> **Terminology:** The GUI and DS CLI usually use *source* for the local or primary PPRC volume and *target* for the remote or secondary PPRC volume. The same terms are used for FlashCopy, FlashCopy source, and FlashCopy target. This requires you to be specific, when using source and target, regarding just which Copy Services function you are referring to.
>
> In zSeries environments, you may find a differentiation between PPRC and FlashCopy volumes. Here it may be a PPRC primary for the PPRC source volume and a PPRC secondary for the PPRC target volume. For FlashCopy, it is source and target.
>
> So a primary volume is a PPRC primary or PPRC source volume. A secondary volume corresponds to the primary volume. A FlashCopy source volume is, just for short, a source volume. Similar conventions apply for a target volume.

To launch this wizard, first you need to go to the **Paths** panel under the **Copy Services** menu of the DS Storage Manager GUI. In the **Select Action** pull-down list, choose **Create** and click **Go** to proceed with the first step of the wizard. See Figure 27-8.

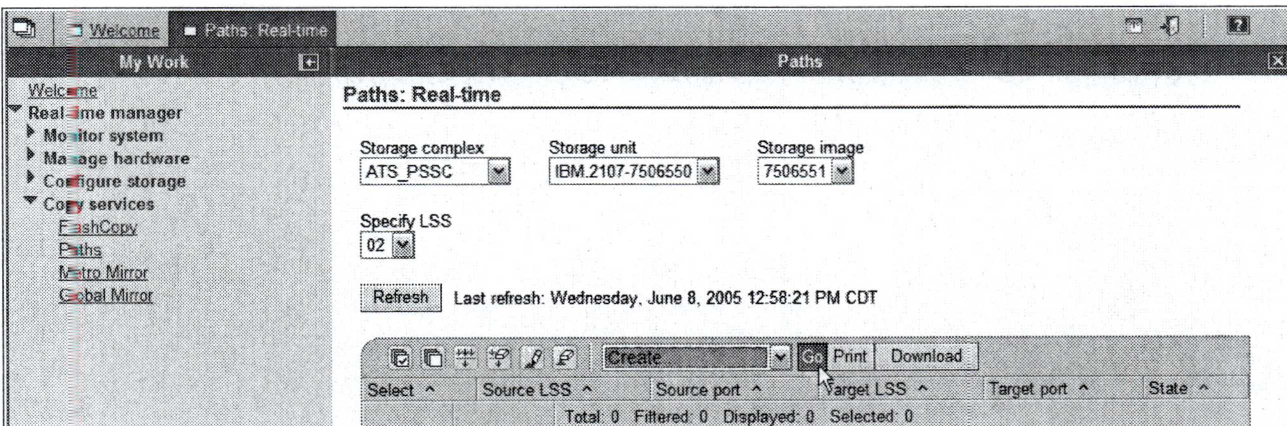

Figure 27-8 Global Copy paths creation - launch the creation process

When the creation wizard displays the **Select source LSS** panel (see Figure 27-9), select from the pull-down lists the **Storage complex**, then the **Storage unit**, then the **Storage Image** and finally the **LSS**, which contains the source volumes of the Global Copy pairs. These are the volumes that are going to become a member of the Global Mirror sessions. Click **Next** to proceed with the second step of this wizard.

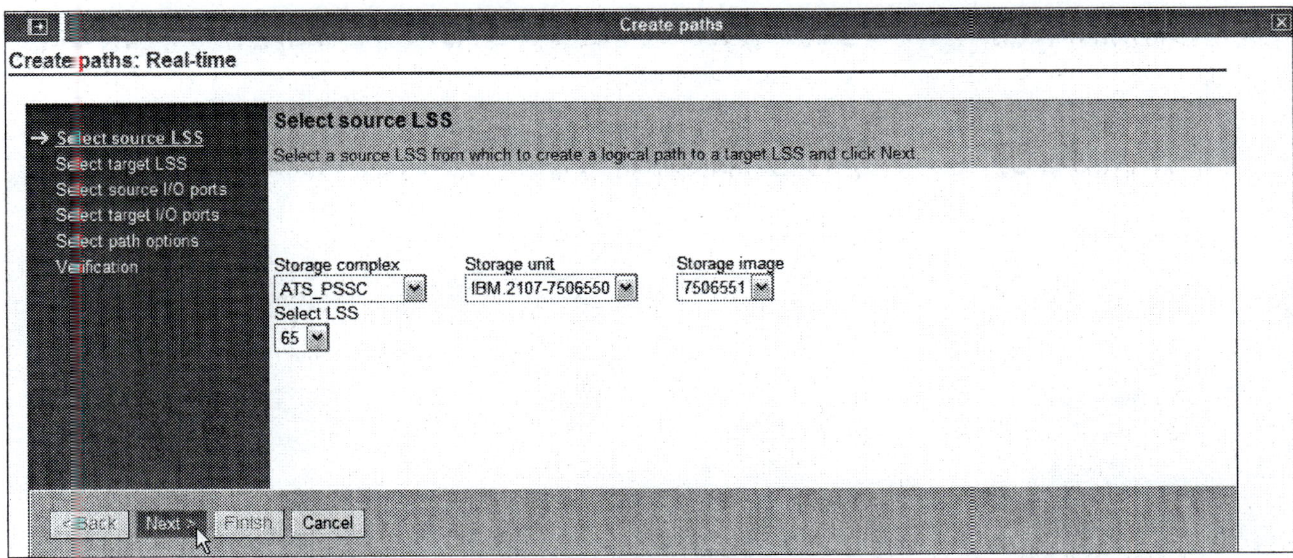

Figure 27-9 Global Copy paths creation - step 1 - select the source LSS

When the creation wizard is displaying the **Select target LSS** panel (see Figure 27-10), select from the pull-down lists the **Storage complex**, then the **Storage unit**, then the **Storage Image** and finally the **LSS**, which contains the corresponding target volumes of the Global Copy pairs. Click **Next** to proceed with the third step of this wizard.

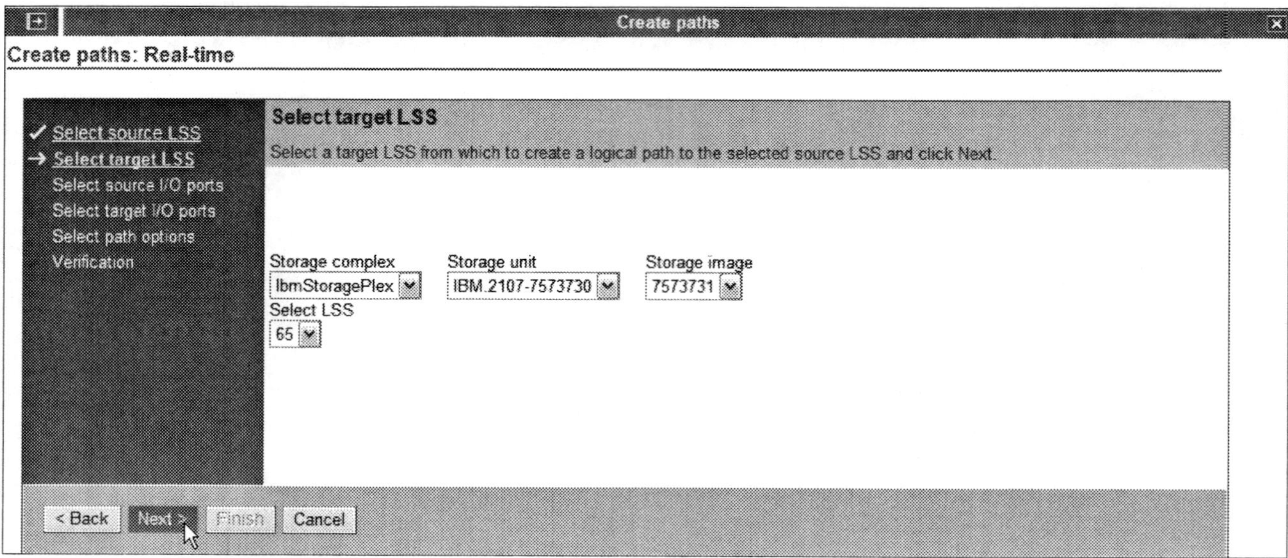

Figure 27-10 Global Copy paths creation - step 2 - select the target LSS

When the creation wizard displays the **Select source I/Os ports** panel (see Figure 27-11), select with the check boxes the I/O ports through which we intend to connect the source LSS to the target LSS. In the location column, four digits indicate the location of a port:

- The first digit - **R** - is to locate the frame.
- The second digit - **E** - is for the I/O enclosure.
- The third digit - **C** - is for the adapter.
- The fourth digit - **P** - is for the adapter port.

Click **Next** to proceed with the fourth step of this wizard.

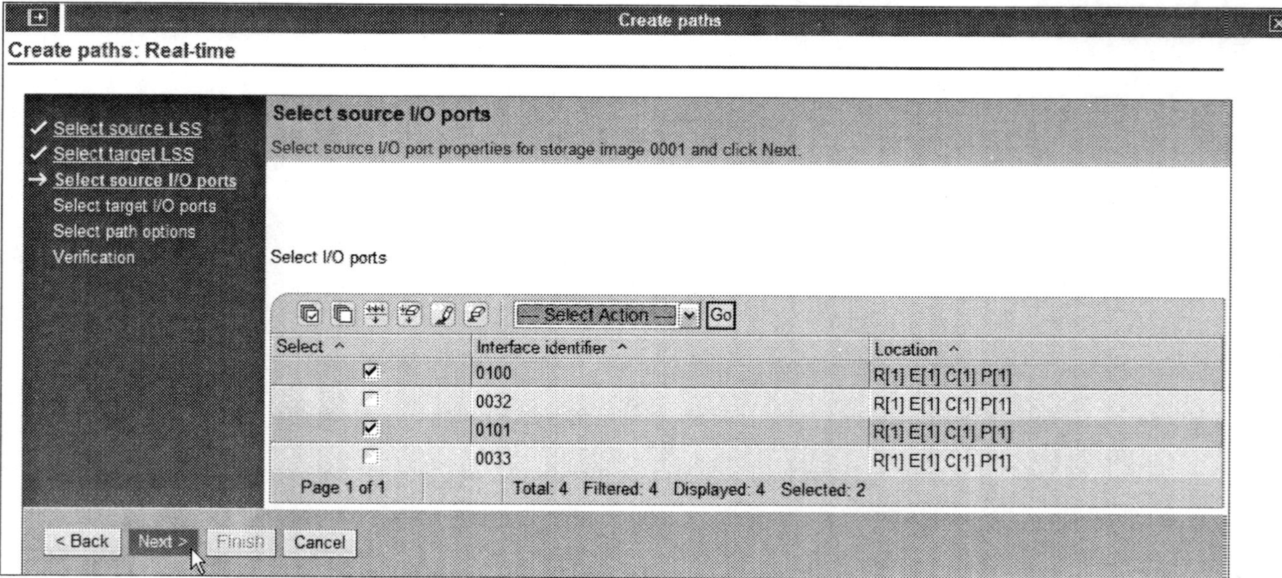

Figure 27-11 Global Copy paths creation - step 3 - select the source I/O ports

When the creation wizard displays the **Select target I/Os ports** panel (see Figure 27-12), select from the pull-down list the target I/O ports that you intend to connect with the source I/O ports. Click **Next** to proceed with the next step of this wizard.

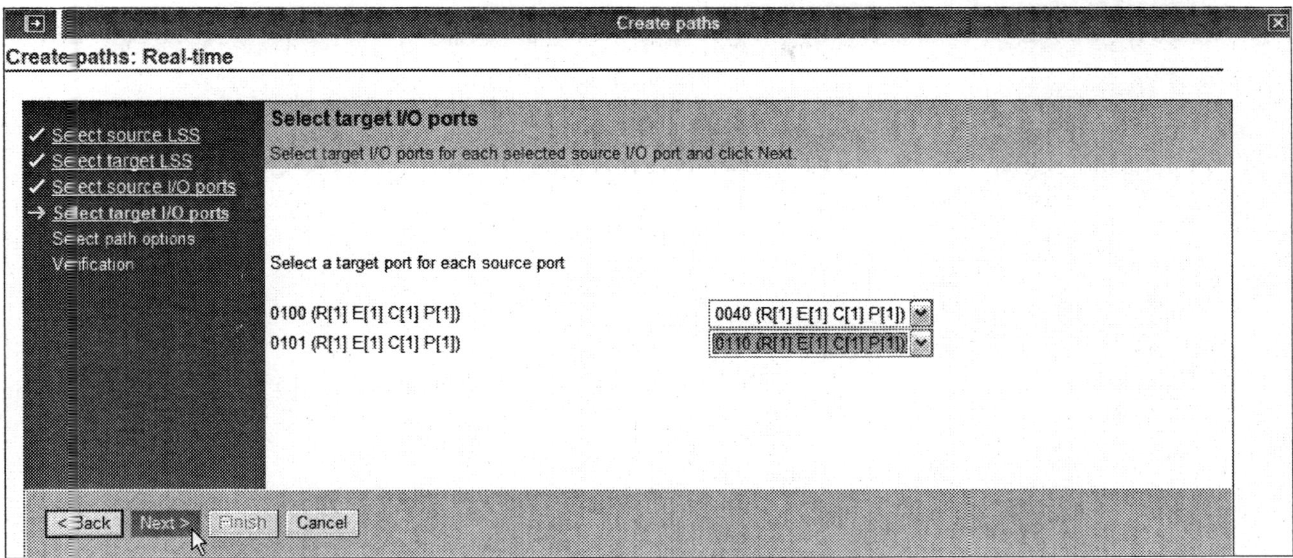

Figure 27-12 Global Copy paths creation - step 4 - select the target I/O ports

When the creation wizard displays the **Select path options** panel (see Figure 27-13), you can select with the check box the option **Define as Consistency Group**.

> **Note:** This option is used in the context with Metro Mirror. Global Mirror will manage consistency by its own design and provides a consistent set of volumes at the remote site without relying on this option. So this option, *Define as Consistency Group*, applies to Metro Mirror or Synchronous PPRC. The scope of this Consistency Group is all Metro Mirror volumes within this LSS pair.
>
> Normally when an error occurs to a primary volume of a Metro Mirror pair, the Storage Unit places the concerned volume in a suspended state and all other volumes in this LSS are not affected. If the volume is participating in a Consistency Group, however, a timer starts and holds back all write I/Os to all other volumes within this LSS based Consistency Group. The timer default is 120 seconds and may be altered to a shorter time window. This time window is also called extended long busy (ELB).

Click **Next** to proceed with the sixth and last step of this wizard (Figure 27-13).

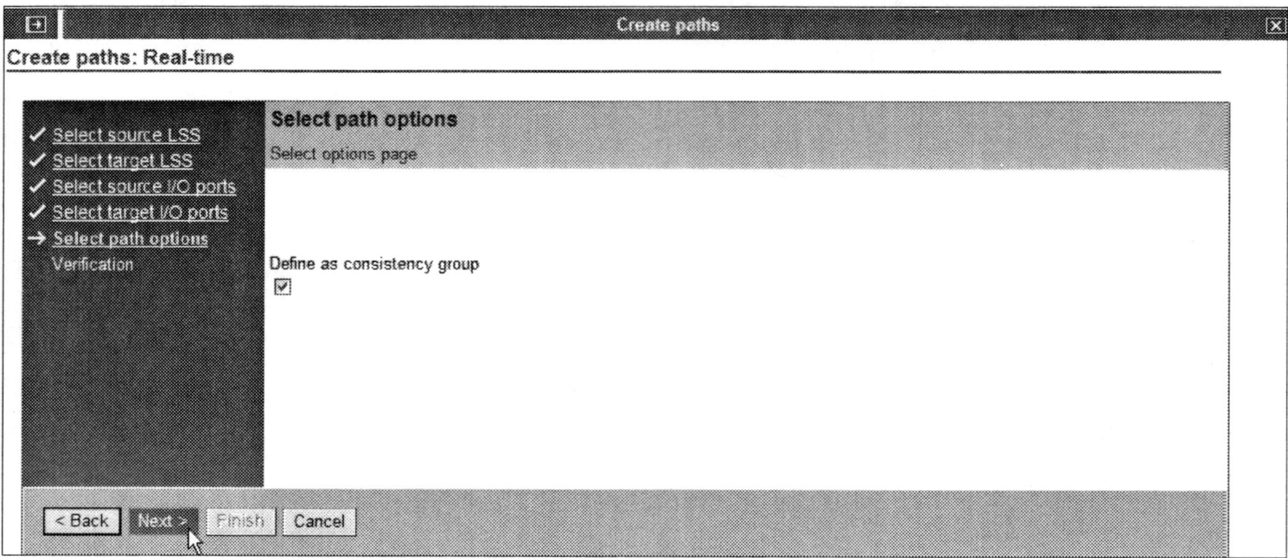

Figure 27-13 Global Copy paths creation - step 5 - select the paths options

In the **Verification** panel, check all the components of your PPRC path configurations and if necessary click **Back** to correct any of them or click **Finish** to validate the configuration and end the wizard. See Figure 27-14.

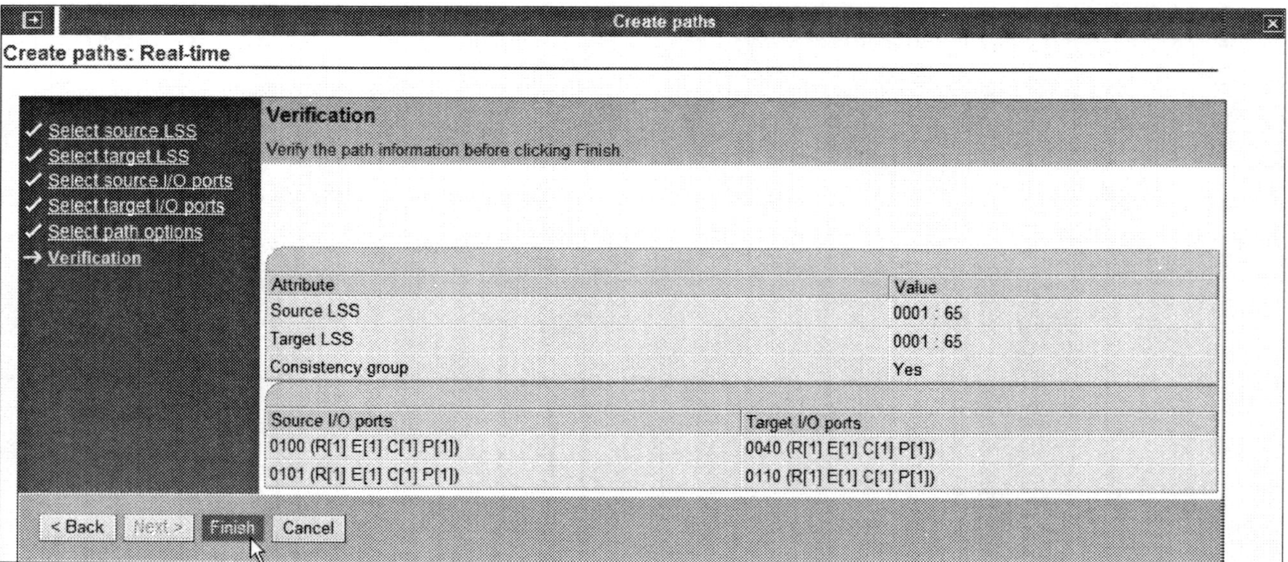

Figure 27-14 Global Copy paths creation - step 6 - verification

27.4.2 Create Global Copy volume pairs with DS Storage Manager

To create Global Copy volume pairs with DS Storage Manager for a new Global Mirror session, you have to go through another staged process with corresponding panels. This procedure is exercised in this section.

> **Note:** If Global Copy pairs are in several LSSs, do not forget to select all of them during this wizard or run the wizard again on each LSS. If Global Copy pairs are spread over several Storage Images, run this wizard again on each of them.

To launch this wizard you need first to go to the **Metro Mirror** panel under the **Copy Services** menu of DS Storage Manager GUI. In the **Select Action** pull-down list choose **Create** and click **Go** to proceed with the first step of the wizard. See Figure 27-15.

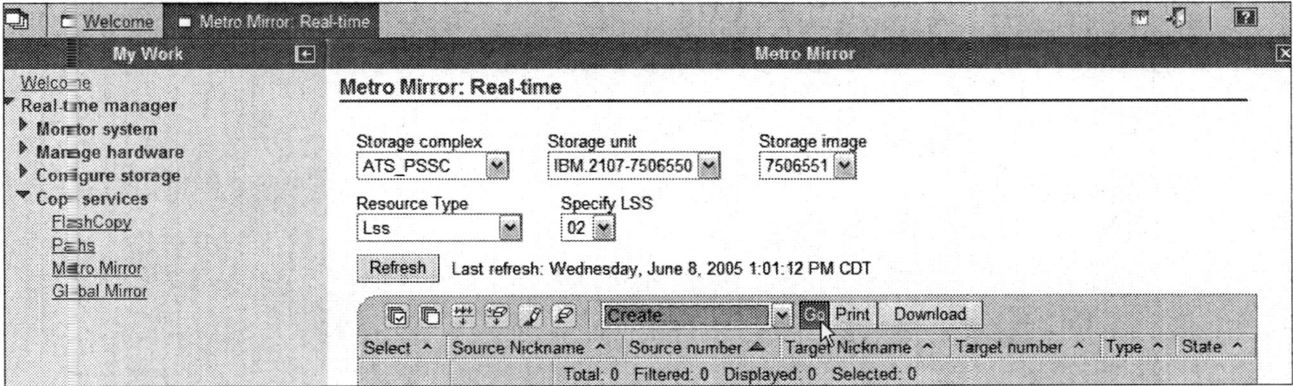

Figure 27-15 Global Copy creation - launch the creation process

When the creation wizard is displaying the **Volume Pairing Method**, select the radio button **Manual volume pair assignment** and click **Next** to proceed with the second step of this wizard. See Figure 27-16.

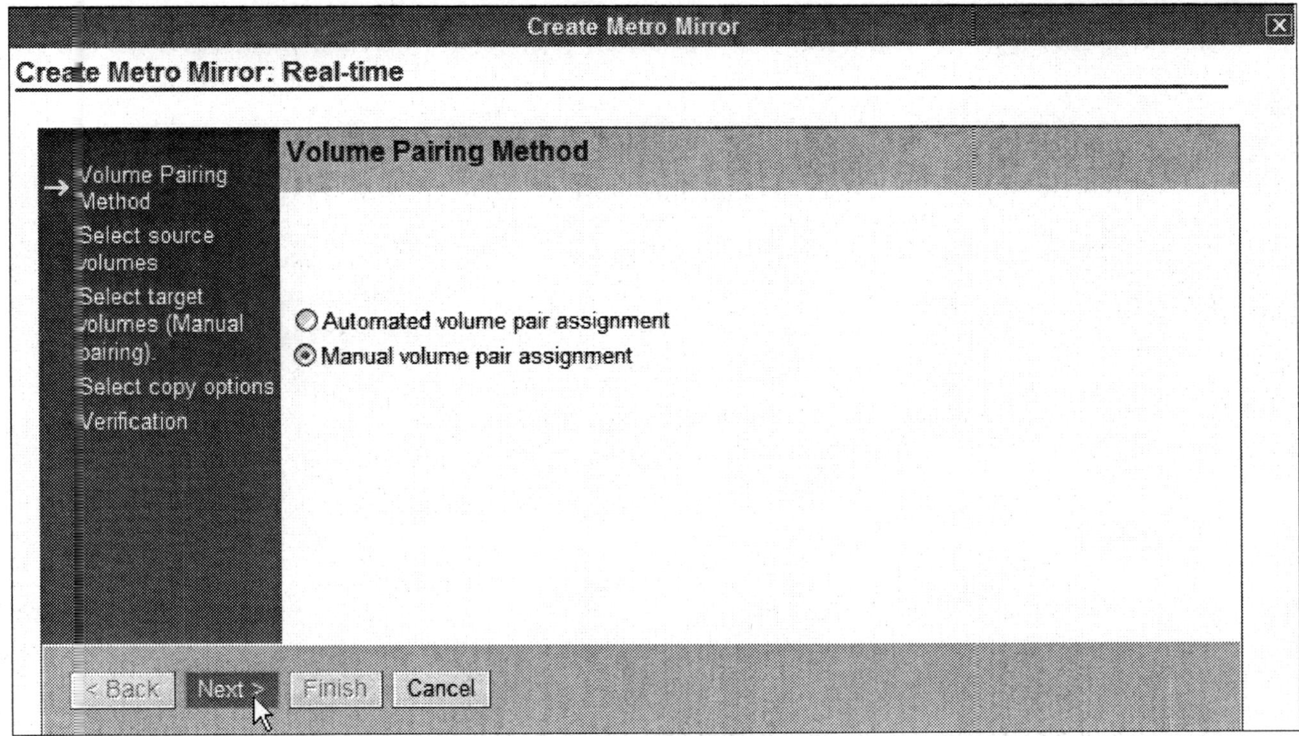

Figure 27-16 Global Copy creation - step 1 - choose volume pairing method

When the creation wizard is displaying the **Select source volumes** panel, select from the pull-down lists the **Storage complex**, then the **Storage unit**, then the **Storage Image**, then the **Resource type** and, if necessary, its appropriate parameter to display the list of volumes. If you have chosen the **Resource type** *LSS*, select from the pull-down lists the LSS number that contains the source volumes you intend to use. Select with the check boxes the source volumes you plan to use as Global Copy pairs in the Global Mirror session. Click **Next** to proceed with the third step of this wizard. See Figure 27-17.

Note: If PPRC paths are not yet created at this step, you can click **Create Paths** to launch the wizard to create PPRC paths as described in the previous section.

Note: Although the following panels refer not to CKD volumes but to open systems volumes, it applies in the very same fashion to CKD volumes.

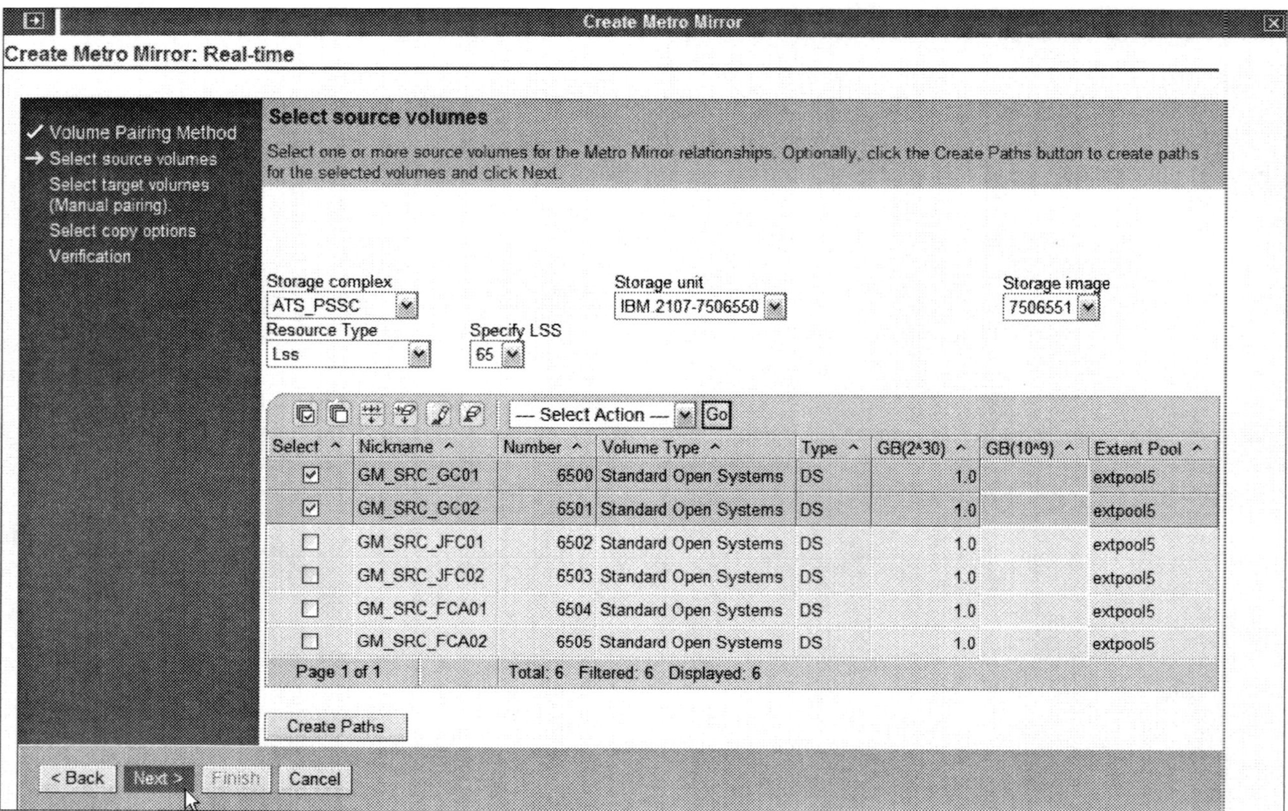

Figure 27-17 Global Copy creation - step 2 - select the source volumes

When the creation wizard displays the **Select target volumes** panel (see Figure 27-18), we notice that only one source volume is indicated on the top of the panel. It means that we need to repeat the third step for each volume we have selected during the second step.

Select from the pull-down lists the **Storage complex**, then the **Storage unit**, then the **Storage Image**, then the **Resource type** and, if necessary, its appropriate parameter to display the list of volumes. Click the required Storage Unit, then on the required LSS select the check box for the target volume we wish to use with this first Global Copy. Click **Next** to proceed with the selection of the second target volume.

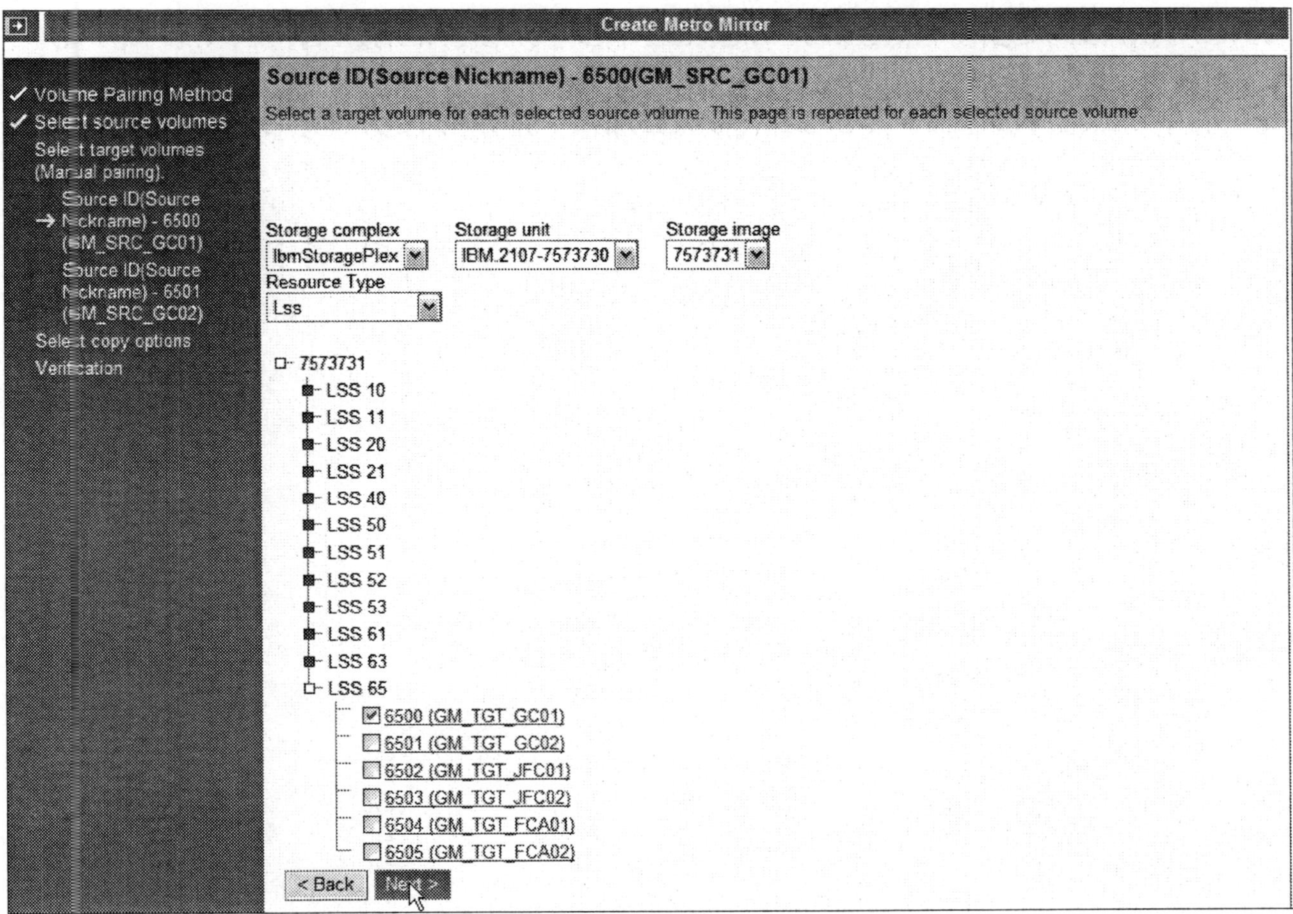

Figure 27-18 Global Copy creation - step 3 - select the target volume 1

When the creation wizard displays the **Select target volumes** panel as before, you may notice that only the indicated source volume on the top of the panel is different. Once again, select from the pull-down lists the **Storage complex**, then the **Storage unit**, then the **Storage Image**, then the **Resource type** and, if necessary, its appropriate parameter to display the list of volumes.

Click the required Storage Unit, then click the required LSS, and select the check box for the target volume you plan to use with this second Global Copy pair. If you had selected more source volumes, you would once again proceed to the next target volume selection panel. Since it is the second and last volume in our selection, click **Next** to proceed with the fourth step of this wizard. See Figure 27-19.

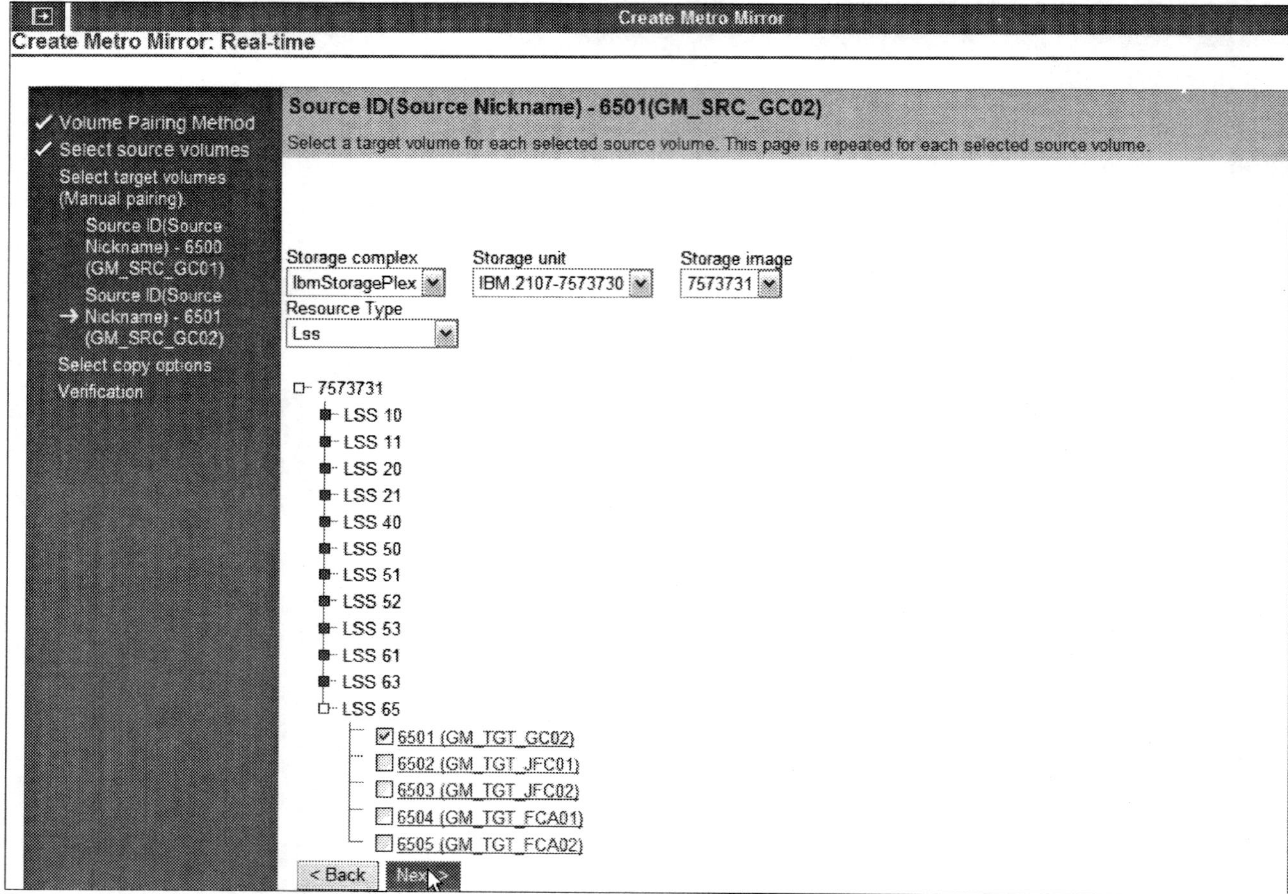

Figure 27-19 Global Copy creation - step 3 - select the target volume 2

When the creation wizard displays the **Select copy options** panel (see Figure 27-20), select the radio button **Global Copy** to define the relationship type of replication. If this is the first synchronization between source and target volumes of these pairs, select the check box for **Perform initial copy**. Click **Next** to proceed with the last step of this wizard.

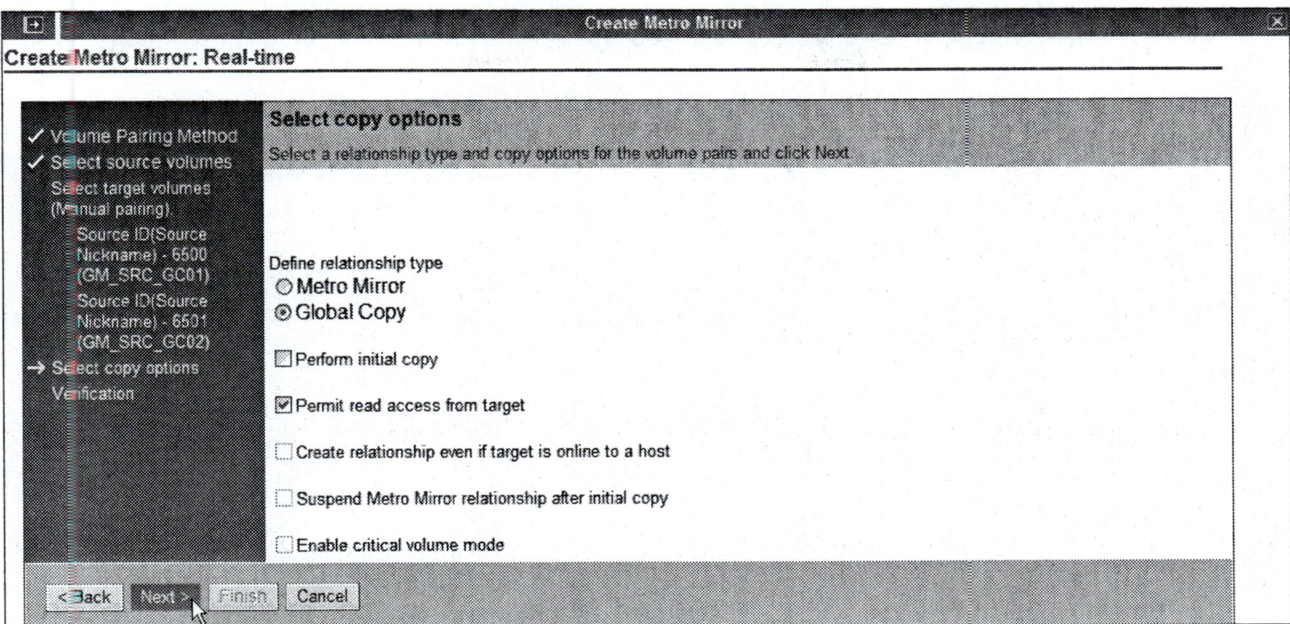

Figure 27-20 Global Copy creation - step 4 - select the copy options

In the **Verification** panel (see Figure 27-21) check all the components of your Global Copy session configurations, and, if necessary, click **Back** to correct any of them or click **Finish** to validate. In Figure 27-20 you may move back to correct the **Permit read access from target**.

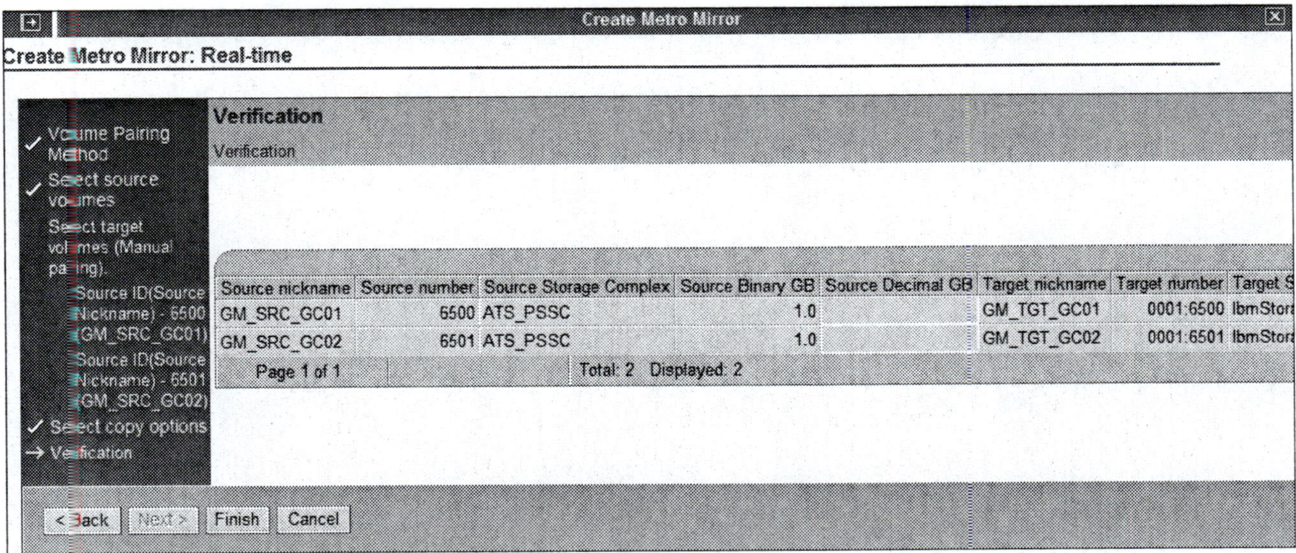

Figure 27-21 Global Copy creation - step 5 - verification

27.4.3 Establish FlashCopy relationships with the DS Storage Manager

To create FlashCopy pairs with DS Storage Manager, you have to work through another series of steps and GUI panels.

> **Note:** If FlashCopy pairs are in several LSSs, do not forget to select all of them during this wizard or run the wizard again on each LSS. If FlashCopy pairs are spread over several Storage Images, run this wizard again on each of them.

To launch this wizard, you need to first go to the **FlashCopy** panel (see Figure 27-22) under the **Copy Services** menu of DS Storage Manager GUI. In the **Select Action** pull-down list choose **Create** and click **Go** to proceed with the first step of the wizard.

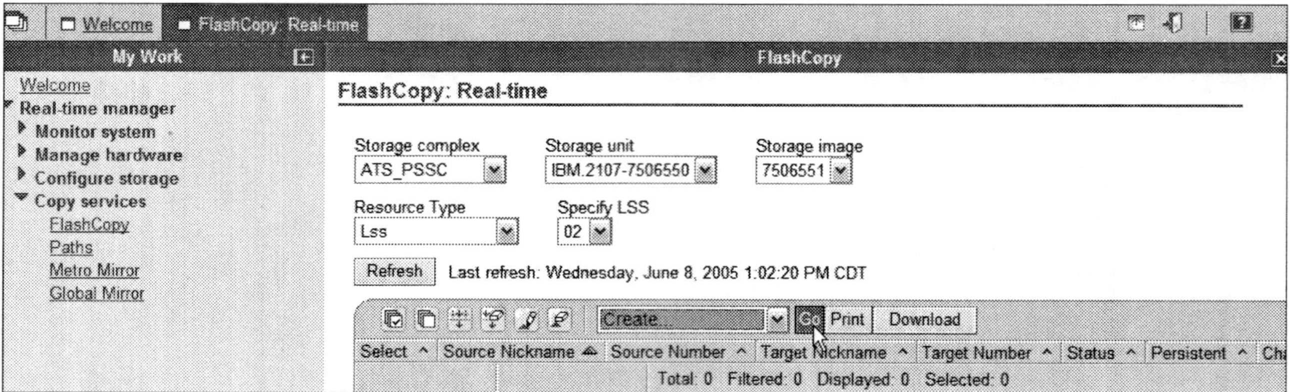

Figure 27-22 FlashCopy creation - launch the creation process

When the creation wizard is displaying the **Define relationship type** panel (Figure 27-23), select the radio button **A single source with a single target** because we must activate the *record* option on the fourth step of this wizard and click **Next** to proceed to the second step of this wizard.

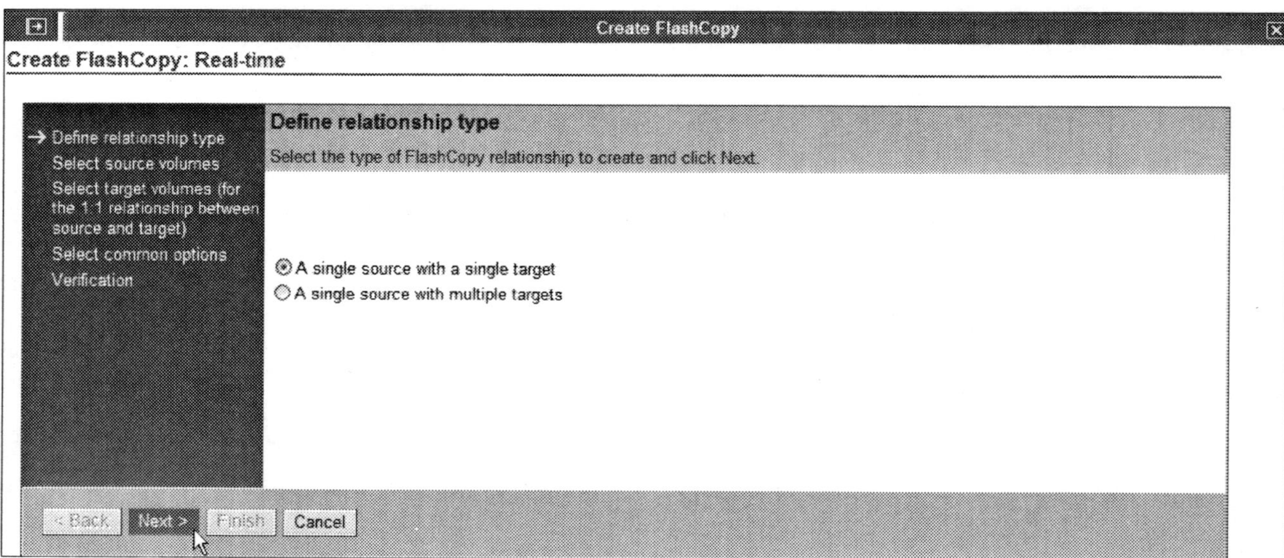

Figure 27-23 FlashCopy creation - step 1 - select the relationship type

When the creation wizard displays the **Select source volumes** panel (see Figure 27-24), select from the pull-down lists the **Storage complex**, then the **Storage unit**, then the **Storage Image**, then the **Resource type** and, if necessary, its appropriate parameter to display the list of volumes. If you have chosen the **Resource type** *LSS*, then select from the pull-down lists the LSS number that contains the source volumes you want to use. Select with the check boxes the source **volumes** you plan to use for FlashCopy within the Global Mirror session.

Note: Although the following panels show open systems volumes, the panels and their order apply also to CKD volumes.

Click **Next** to proceed with the third step of this wizard (Figure 27-24).

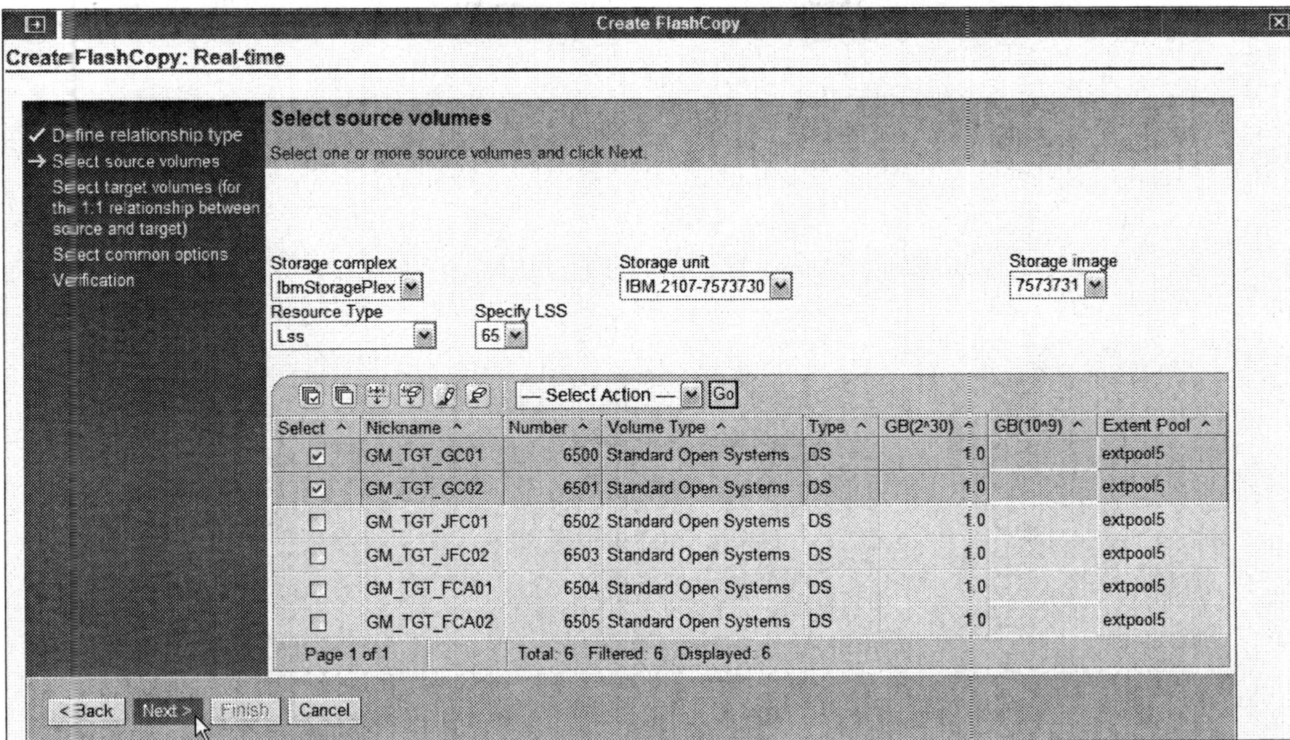

Figure 27-24 FlashCopy creation - step 2 - select the source volumes

When the creation wizard displays the **Select target volumes** panel (see Figure 27-25), select from the pull-down lists the **Resource type** and if it is necessary its appropriate parameter to display the list of volumes. If you have chosen the **Resource type** *LSS* select from the pull-down lists the LSS number that contains the target volumes you plan to use. Select with the check boxes the target **volumes** you want to use for the FlashCopy pairs within the Global Mirror session. Click **Next** to proceed with the fourth step of this wizard.

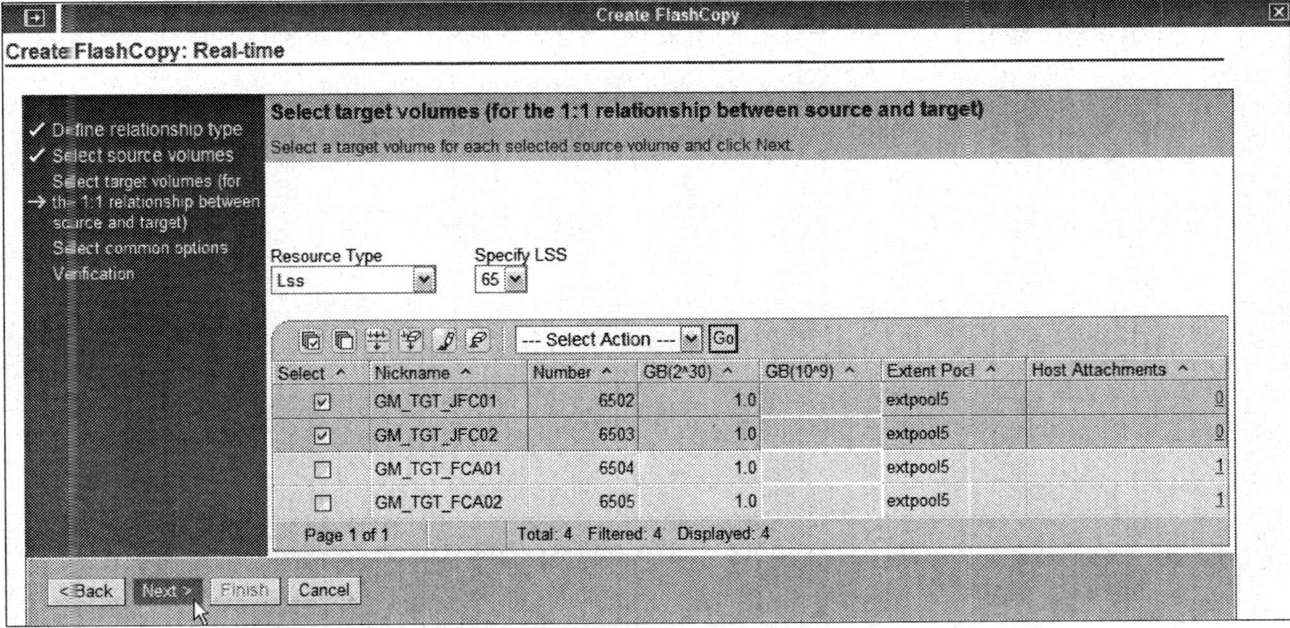

Figure 27-25 FlashCopy creation - step 3 - select the target volumes

When the creation wizard displays the **Select common options** panel (see Figure 27-20 on page 377), select the check box for **Enable change recording**. It should automatically also select the check box for **Make relationship(s) persistent**. You can leave the ***Sequence number for these relationships** field with its default value since Global Mirror will take care of it automatically. Click **Next** to proceed with last step of this wizard (Figure 27-26).

Note: Do *not* select the check box for **Initiate background copy**.

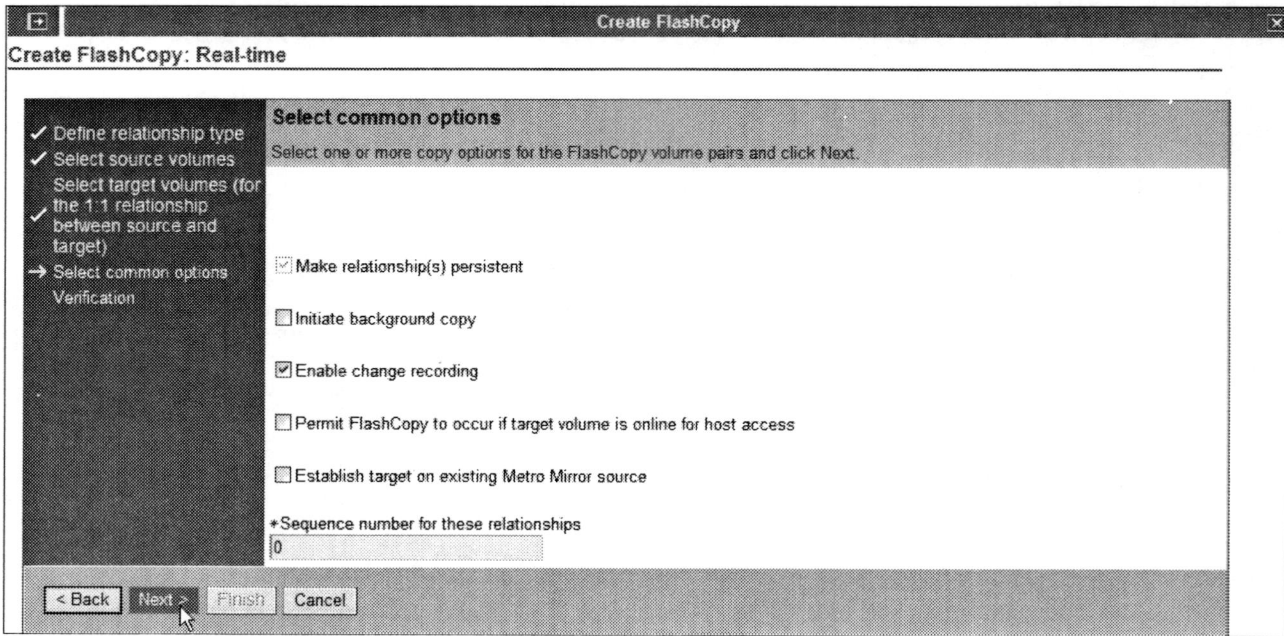

Figure 27-26 FlashCopy creation - step 4 - select the common option

In the **Verification** panel (see Figure 27-27) check all the components of your FlashCopy session configurations and if necessary click **Back** to correct any of them, or click **Finish** to validate.

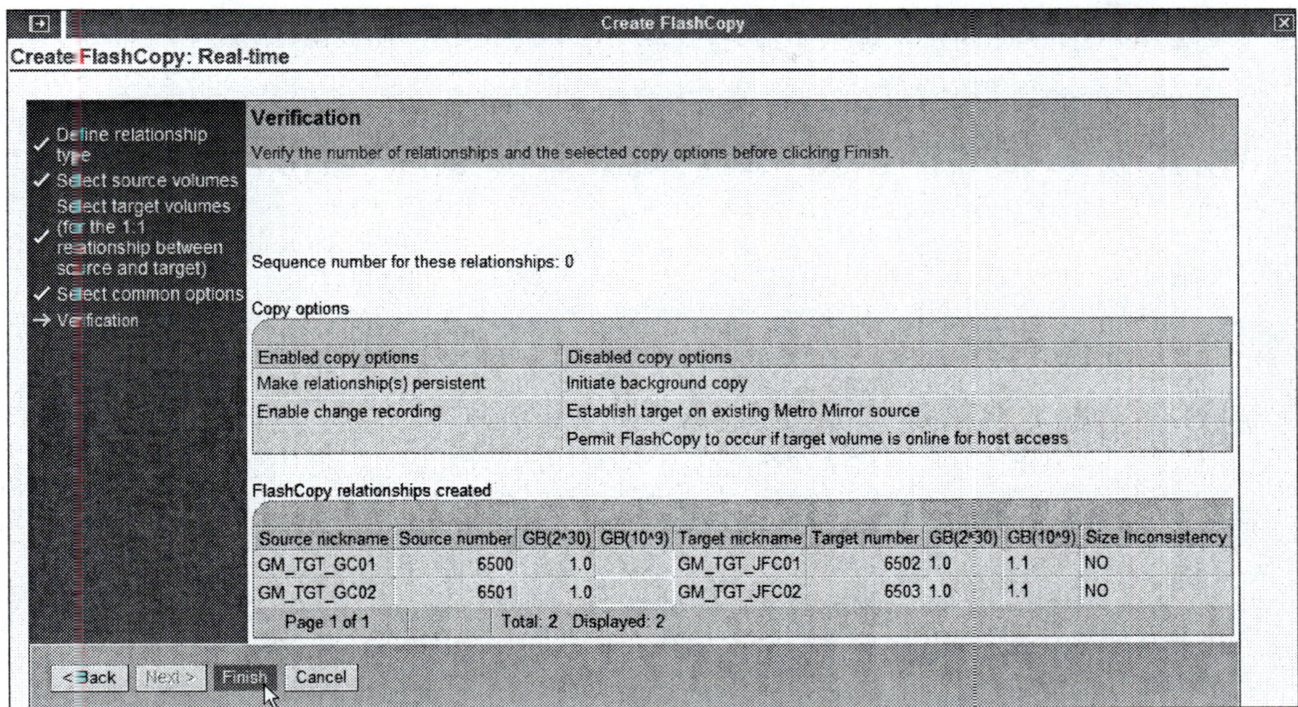

Figure 27-27 FlashCopy creation - step 5 - verification

27.4.4 Create Global Mirror session with DS Storage Manager

To define a Global Mirror session with DS Storage Manager, you go through another staged panel process.

To launch this wizard you first need to go to the **Global Mirror** panel under the **Copy Services** menu of DS Storage Manager GUI. In the **Select Action** pull-down list choose **Create** and click **Go** to proceed with the first step of the wizard. See Figure 27-28.

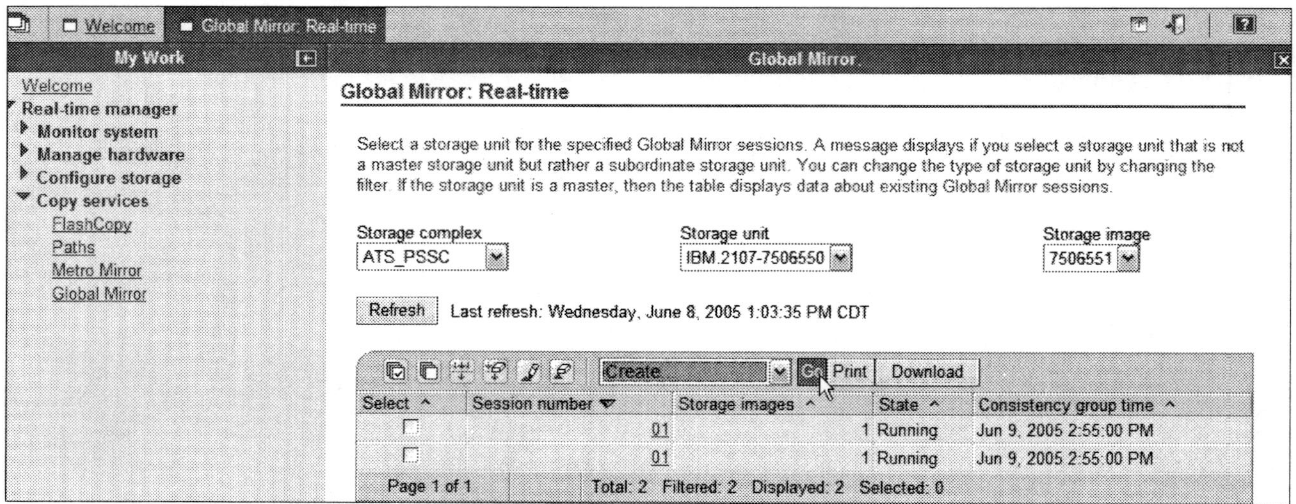

Figure 27-28 Global Mirror creation - launch the creation process

When the creation wizard displays the **Select volumes** panel (see Figure 27-29), click the required Storage Unit, then on the required LSS, and select the check box for the source volumes that we wish to include in the Global Mirror session. Click **Next** to proceed with the second step of this wizard.

> **Note:** At this step, if Global Copy pairs and FlashCopy pairs are not yet created, you may click **Create Metro Mirror** to launch the wizard as described in "Create Global Copy volume pairs with DS Storage Manager" on page 372. You may also click **Create FlashCopy** to launch the wizard described in 27.4.3, "Establish FlashCopy relationships with the DS Storage Manager" on page 377.

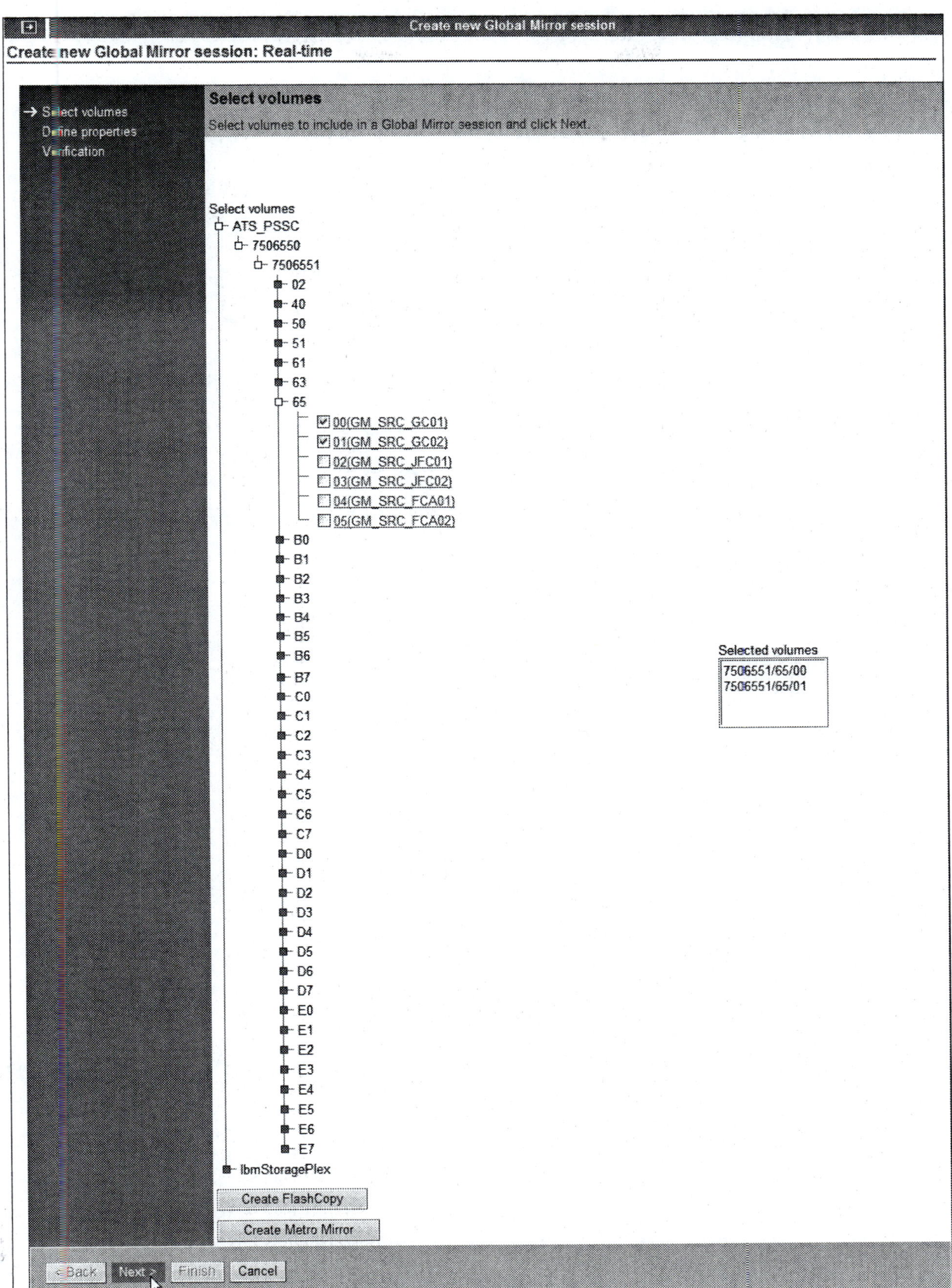

Figure 27-29 Global Mirror creation - step 1 - select volumes

When the creation wizard displays the **Define properties** panel (see Figure 27-30), the **Enter session number** field with the appropriate session number. We can click **Get Available Session Numbers** if we have forgotten the one we want to use. There are also these three Global Mirror tuning parameters:

- **Consistency Group interval time:** Specifies in seconds on how long to wait between the formation of Consistency Groups. If this number is not specified or is set to zero, Consistency Groups are formed continuously. The maximum is 18 hours.
- **Maximum coordination interval:** Indicates in milliseconds (ms) the maximum time that Global Mirror holds back on host I/Os to start forming a Consistency Group.
- **Maximum time writes inhibited to remote site:** Specifies in seconds the maximum Consistency Group drain time to replicate the remaining data from the primary site to the secondary site. This is the data that is still in the out-of-sync bitmap in the primary storage server and waiting to be replicated to the secondary storage server.

  When it cannot complete replicating all outstanding data within this time window, then the process to form a new Consistency Group will fail. After five contiguous failures due to this condition Global Mirror will force the formation of a new Consistency Group independent of how long it takes to replicate all remaining data from the primary to secondary volumes.

See also 23.3, “Form Consistency Group” on page 251.

Click **Next** to proceed with the third and last step of this wizard (Figure 27-30).

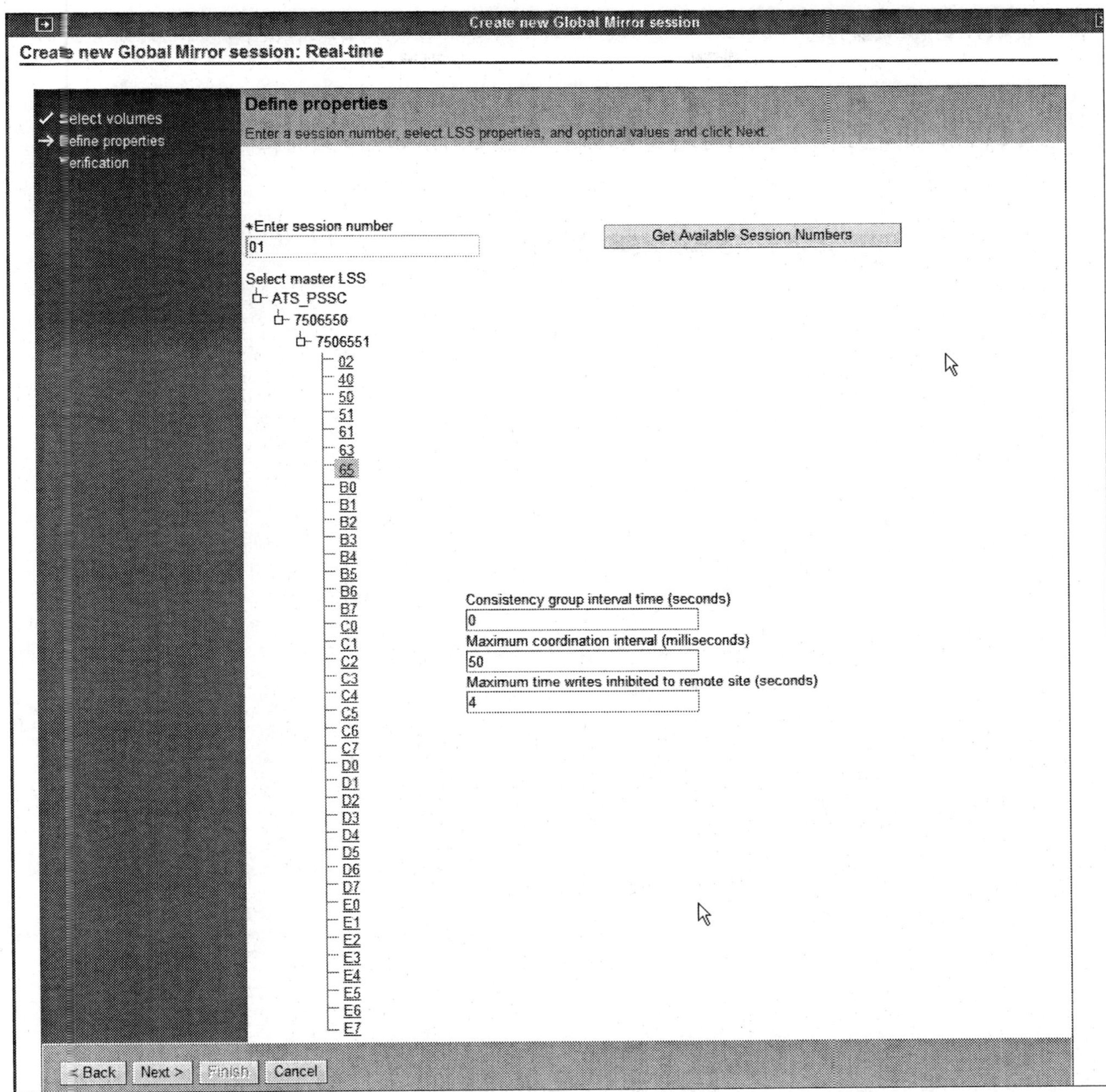

Figure 27-30 Global Mirror creation - step 2 - define properties

In the **Verification** panel (see Figure 27-31), check all the components of your Global Mirror session configuration and, if necessary, click **Back** to correct any of them or click **Finish** to validate.

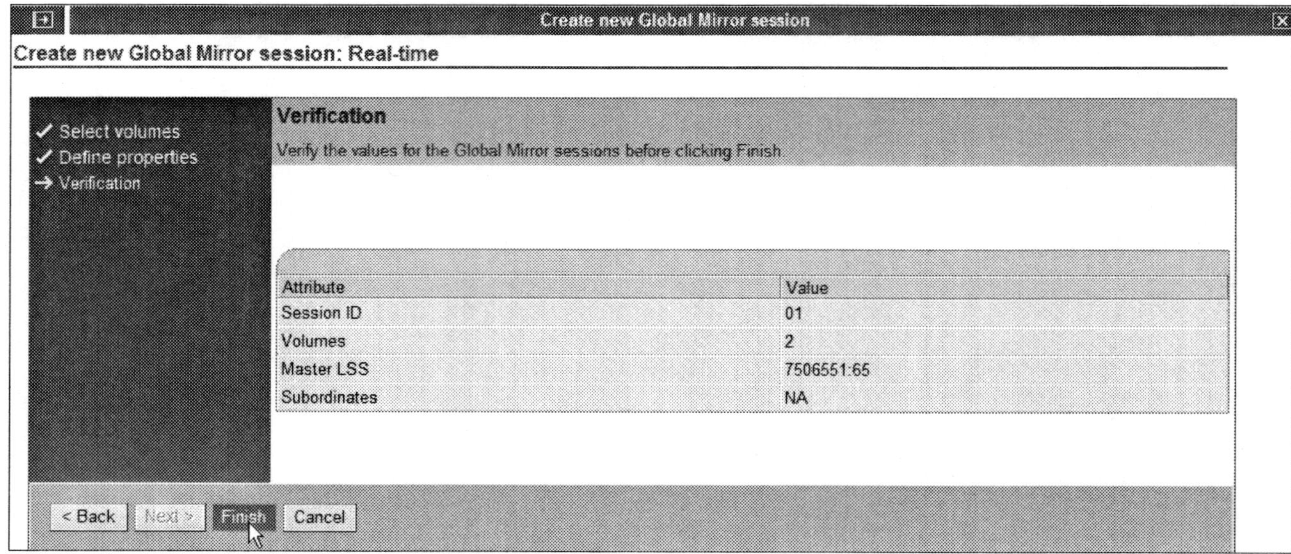

Figure 27-31 Global Mirror creation - step 3 - verification

To visualize the state of the Global Mirror session go to the **Global Mirror** panel under the **Copy Services** menu of DS Storage Manager GUI. Select from the pull-down lists the **Storage complex**, then the **Storage unit**, then the **Storage Image**, which is the Master Global Mirror session, and wait until the screen is refreshed. If it is necessary, click **Refresh** to refresh the panel. See Figure 27-32.

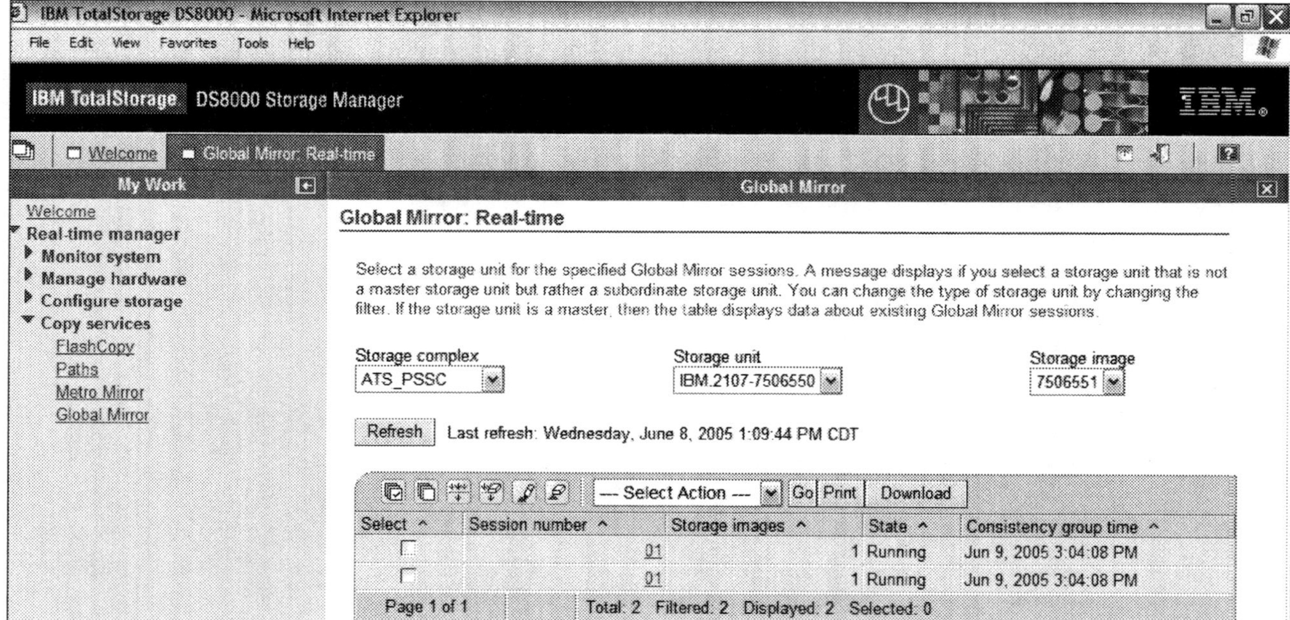

Figure 27-32 Global Mirror - visualize the session status

27.5 Establish a Global Mirror session with the DS CLI

You may consider implementing a standard task like creating a Global Mirror session through a more automated process than the DS SM or GUI approach. The DS CLI provides a good approach that is similar to what you may do with REXX procedures or other software based tools in zSeries environments to assist when managing Remote Copy configurations.

The GUI has its value in a situation when you have to react somehow, ad hoc. The GUI also has some advantage over the DS CLI when you need to retrieve information from certain storage images, which may be not so easy to understand through the DS CLI if you are not accustomed to working with the DS CLI. Try a DS CLI **lsflash** and see if you can understand all the headings compared to a profile panel in the GUI of a FlashCopy relationship.

27.5.1 DS CLI profile files

To simplify DS CLI commands, we use configuration files. See Example 27-37 and Example 27-38. These profiles are stored in the default directory *c:\Program Files\IBM\dscli\Profile* for Windows systems.

Because we are using two storage servers and there is a local entry and a remote entry in these files indicated by **devid** and **remotedevid**, we created two profile files. Each file has a local and a remote device ID with the corresponding storage server serial numbers.

Example 27-37 Sample DS CLI Configuration file DS-01.profile

```
hmcl: xxx.yyy.zzz.xxx
username: admin
password: passw0rd
devid:IBM.2107-7506551
remotedevid:IBM.2107-7573731
fullid: off
banner: on
verbose: off
paging: off
olc: off
```

Example 27-38 Sample DS CLI Configuration file DS-02.profile

```
hmcl: xxx.yyy.zzz.yyy
username: admin
password: passw0rd
devid:IBM.2107-7573731
remotedevid:IBM.2107-7506551
fullid: off
banner: on
verbose: off
paging: off
olc:off
```

27.5.2 Create PPRC paths with the DS CLI

To create new PPRC paths with the DS CLI from a source LSS to a target LSS, you go through the following processing steps. Note that you need PPRC paths from the primary to secondary and also Global Mirror PPRC paths or Global Mirror control paths between Master and Subordinate storage servers, when you use more than a storage server with Global Mirror volumes at the primary site.

Note: You need to repeat this process for each data path between LSSs on the source Storage Images on site 1 or local site and the target LSSs on the target Storage Images on site 2 or remote site. You need to repeat this also for each control path between the Master LSS and a LSS in each corresponding Subordinate storage server.

The first step in this process is to see which I/O ports are available for PPRC paths between the source and the target LSSs:

dscli lsavailpprcport -remotewwnn <WWN of your remote Storage Image> <Source_LSS_ID>:<Target_LSS_ID> -cfg <Source device configuration file>

Example 27-39 provides a list of available PPRC paths from the source LSS 65 on a DS8000 on site 1 to a target LSS 65 on a DS8000 on site 2.

Example 27-39 lsavailpprcport

```
dscli lsavailpprcpport -remotewwnn 5005076303FFC426 65:65 -cfg $DSCLI/profile/DS-01.profile
Date/Time: June 14, 2005 6:18:16 PM EDT IBM DSCLI Version: 5.0.3.134 DS: IBM.2107-7506551
Local Port Attached Port Type
=============================
I0100      I0040         FCP
I0101      I0040         FCP
I0100      I0110         FCP
I0101      I0110         FCP
I0032      I0240         FCP
I0033      I0240         FCP
I0032      I0310         FCP
I0033      I0310         FCP
```

Note: An I/O port number has four digits to indicate its location:

- The first digit locates the frame - R.
- The second digit indicates the I/O enclosure - E.
- The third digit is for the adapter - C.
- The fourth digit is for the Adapter port - P.

The second step in this process is to choose at least a pair from the list of available I/O ports and create the PPRC path. Note for availability reasons, choose at least two PPRC links and paths.

dscli mkpprcpath -remotewwnn <WWN of your remote Storage Image> -consistgrp -srclss <Source_LSS_ID> -tgtlss <Target_LSS_ID> -cfg <Source device configuration file> <Source_IO_Port>:<Target_IO_PORT> <Source_IO_Port>:<Target_IO_PORT> ...

Note: The *consistgrp* option is intended for Metro Mirror.

Example 27-40 provides an example of how to create a PPRC path from the source LSS 65 on a DS8000 on site 1 to a target LSS 65 on a DS8000 on site 2.

Example 27-40 mkpprcpath

```
dscli mkpprcpath -remotewwnn 5005076303FFC426 -consistgrp -srclss 65 -tgtlss 65 -cfg
$DSCLI/profile/DS-01.profile I0100:I0040 I0101:I0110
Date/Time: June 14, 2005 3:26:06 PM EDT IBM DSCLI Version: 5.0.3.134 DS: IBM.2107-7506551
CMUC00149I mkpprcpath: Remote Mirror and Copy path 65:65 successfully established.
```

To list the newly created PPRC paths, use the command **lspprc**, which is described in "Query PPRC paths" on page 392.

27.5.3 Create Global Copy pairs with the DS CLI

To create Global Copy pairs, you may first list the potential volumes that may become Global Copy pairs. Once you identify the potential volume pairs, you establish — or make — these pairs with the corresponding DS CLI commands.

Note: The following examples cover FB volumes. This is very similar for CKD volumes. The command sequence and structure is identical for both volume types. The focus here is rather on which DS CLI commands to use and on the sequence of these commands.

The first step is to see which Fixed Block volumes are available for Global Copy on the source and the target LSS:

dscli lsfbvol -lss <Source_LSS_ID> -cfg <Source device configuration file>

dscli lsfbvol -lss <Target_LSS_ID> -cfg <Target device configuration file>

Example 27-41 shows which volumes are available for the source LSS 65 on a DS8000 and the potential target volumes at the secondary DS8000.

Example 27-41 lsfbvol

```
dscli lsfbvol -lss 65 -cfg $DSCLI/profile/DS-01.profile
Date/Time: June 14, 2005 7:11:56 PM EDT IBM DSCLI Version: 5.0.3.134 DS: IBM.2107-7506551
Name         ID   accstate datastate configstate deviceMTM datatype extpool cap (2^30B) cap
(10^9B) cap (blocks)
==========================================================================================
=====================
GM_SRC_GC01  6500 Online   Normal    Normal      2107-900  FB 512   P5              1.0
-       2097152
GM_SRC_GC02  6501 Online   Normal    Normal      2107-900  FB 512   P5              1.0
-       2097152

dscli lsfbvol -lss 65 -cfg $DSCLI/profile/DS-02.profile
Date/Time: June 14, 2005 7:12:30 PM EDT IBM DSCLI Version: 5.0.3.134 DS: IBM.2107-7573731
Name         ID   accstate datastate configstate deviceMTM datatype extpool cap (2^30B) cap
(10^9B) cap (blocks)
==========================================================================================
=====================
GM_TGT_GC01  6500 Online   Normal    Normal      2107-900  FB 512   P5              1.0
-       2097152
GM_TGT_GC02  6501 Online   Normal    Normal      2107-900  FB 512   P5              1.0
-       2097152
GM_TGT_JFC01 6502 Online   Normal    Normal      2107-900  FB 512   P5              1.0
-       2097152
GM_TGT_JFC02 6503 Online   Normal    Normal      2107-900  FB 512   P5              1.0
-       2097152
```

Once you identify your Global Copy pairs, use the following DS CLI command to create these pairs:

dscli mkpprc -type gcp -tgtread -mode full -cfg <Source device configuration file> <Source_Volume>:<Target_Volume> <Source_Volume>:<Target_Volume> ...

Note: The *type gcp* option is required to create Global Copy pairs. Use the option *mode full* to force a first full replication of the Global Copy pair.

Example 27-42 shows an example to create two Global Copy pairs with the source volumes 6500 and 6501 on a DS8000 on site 1and with the target volumes 6500 and 6501 on a DS8000 on site 2.

Example 27-42 mkpprc with two Global Copy pairs

```
dscli mkpprc -type gcp -tgtread -mode full -cfg $DSCLI/profile/DS-01.profile 6500:6500
6501:6501
Date/Time: June 14, 2005 3:27:45 PM EDT IBM DSCLI Version: 5.0.3.134 DS: IBM.2107-7506551
CMUC00153I mkpprc: Remote Mirror and Copy volume pair relationship 6500:6500 successfully
created.
CMUC00153I mkpprc: Remote Mirror and Copy volume pair relationship 6501:6501 successfully
created.
```

To list the Global Copy pairs use the command **lspprc** as described in "Query PPRC paths" on page 392.

27.5.4 Create FlashCopy relationships for Global Mirror with the DS CLI

The next step is to create new FlashCopy pairs between the B volumes and the C volumes.

> **Note:** If FlashCopy pairs are in several LSSs, do not forget to select all of them during this process, or run the process again on each LSS. If FlashCopy pairs are spread over several Storage Images, run this process again on each of them.

You may first identify which volumes are available for FlashCopy pairs on the target or remote Storage Image:

```
dscli lsfbvol -lss <LSS_ID> -cfg <Device configuration file>
```

Example 27-43 shows a list command to list potential volumes for FlashCopy relationships.

Example 27-43 lsfbvol to identify FlashCopy volume pairs

```
dscli lsfbvol -lss 65 -cfg $DSCLI/profile/DS-02.profile
Date/Time: June 14, 2005 7:12:30 PM EDT IBM DSCLI Version: 5.0.3.134 DS: IBM.2107-7573731
Name        ID   accstate datastate configstate deviceMTM datatype extpool cap (2^30B) cap
(10^9B) cap (blocks)
===========================================================================================
=====================
GM_TGT_GC01  6500 Online   Normal    Normal      2107-900  FB 512   P5           1.0
-      2097152
GM_TGT_GC02  6501 Online   Normal    Normal      2107-900  FB 512   P5           1.0
-      2097152
GM_TGT_JFC01 6502 Online   Normal    Normal      2107-900  FB 512   P5           1.0
-      2097152
GM_TGT_JFC02 6503 Online   Normal    Normal      2107-900  FB 512   P5           1.0
-      2097152
```

This is the actual command to establish FlashCopy relationships:

```
dscli mkflash -record -persist -nocp -cfg <Device configuration file>
<Source_Volume>:<Target_Volume> <Source_Volume>:<Target_Volume> ...
```

> **Note:** The *record* option is required to record the changed tracks on both volumes. Using *record* implies the *persist* option to keep the relationship. This FlashCopy relationship for Global Mirror is also built on the *nocp* option to inhibit a background copy between source and target volumes.

Example 27-44 shows an example that creates two FlashCopy relationships in this example sequence.

Example 27-44 mkflash

```
dscli mkflash -record -nocp -cfg $DSCLI/profile/DS-02.profile 6500:6502 6501:6503
Date/Time: June 14, 2005 3:28:58 PM EDT IBM DSCLI Version: 5.0.3.134 DS: IBM.2107-7573731
CMUC00137I mkflash: FlashCopy pair 6500:6502 successfully created.
CMUC00137I mkflash: FlashCopy pair 6501:6503 successfully created.
```

To list the new FlashCopy pairs, use the command **lsflash** as described in “Query FlashCopy session” on page 393.

27.5.5 Create Global Mirror session with the DS CLI

To create a new Global Mirror session, the DS CLI command **mksession** includes both of the capabilities to define a session number and to populate the Global Mirror session with Global Copy primary volumes from the corresponding LSS.

You perform the following command to each LSS which has potential Global Mirror volumes:

dscli mksession -lss <LSS_ID> -cfg <Device configuration file> -volume <Volume> <Volume> ... <Session_Number>

Example 27-45 shows an example to create a Global Mirror session number 01 for LSS 65 and add two Global Copy primary volumes to this session.

Example 27-45 mksession

```
dsscli mksession -lss 65 -volume 6500-6501 -cfg $DSCLI/profile/DS-01.profile 01
Date/Time: June 14, 2005 3:29:46 PM EDT IBM DSCLI Version: 5.0.3.134 DS: IBM.2107-7506551
CMUC00145I mksession: Session 01 opened successfully.
```

Note that this only adds volumes to the newly defined session number 01.

To list the new session, use the **lssession** command, which is described in “Query a LSS session” on page 394.

When more than one storage server participates with its primary volumes in a common Global Mirror session you have to specify topology information in the command that starts the Global Mirror session. The **mkmir** command has the following syntax:

dscli mkgmir -lss <Master LSS ID> -cginterval <Number of seconds> -coordinate <Number of milliseconds> -drain <Number of seconds> -session <Session_ID> -cfg <Master device configuration file> <Master_Control_Path_LSS_ID>:<Subordinate_Control_Path_LSS_ID> ...

- **cginterval**: Specifies how long to wait between the formation of Consistency Groups. If this number is not specified or is set to zero, then Consistency Groups are formed continuously.

- **coordinate**: Indicates the maximum time that Global Mirror processing queues host I/Os when Global Mirror starts to form a new Consistency Group. The default is 50 ms.
- **drain**: Specifies the maximum Consistency Group drain time in seconds and the maximum amount of time that the consistent set of data is allowed to drain to the remote site before failing the current build of a new Consistency Group. The default is 30 seconds.

See 23.3, "Form Consistency Group" on page 251.

Example 27-46 shows an example that contains the small Global Mirror environment that we built up in this example section. It starts the session and the actual Consistency Group creation process. It uses the default session parameters.

Example 27-46 mkgmir

```
dscli mkgmir -lss 65 -session 01 -cfg $DSCLI/profile/DS-01.profile
Date/Time: June 14, 2005 3:30:33 PM EDT IBM DSCLI Version: 5.0.3.134 DS: IBM.2107-7506551
CMUC00162I mkgmir: Global Mirror for session 01 successfully started.
```

To list a Global Mirror session, use the command **showgmir as** described in "Show a Global Mirror session" on page 394.

27.5.6 Query a Global Mirror environment

This section lists several useful commands to query the Global Mirror Environment.

Query PPRC paths

Query a PPRC path with the DS CLI command **lspprcpath**:

dscli lspprcpath <Source_LSS_ID> -cfg <Source device configuration file>

If we want to list PPRC paths of the source LSS 65 in a DS8000 on site 1, we have the following result in Example 27-47.

Example 27-47 lspprcpath

```
dscli lspprcpath 65 -cfg $DSCLI/profile/DS-01.profile
Date/Time: June 14, 2005 3:26:29 PM EDT IBM DSCLI Version: 5.0.3.134 DS: IBM.2107-7506551
Src Tgt State   SS   Port  Attached Port
=========================================
65  65  Success FF65 I0100 I0040
65  65  Success FF65 I0101 I0110
```

Query Global Copy session

Query a Global Mirror session with the DS CLI command **lspprc**:

dscli lspprc -cfg <Source device configuration file>
<Source_Volume>:<Target_Volume> <Source_Volume>:<Target_Volume> ...

or

dscli lspprc -l -cfg <Source device configuration file> <Source_Volume>
<Source_Volume> ...

dscli lspprc -l -cfg <target device configuration file> <Target_Volume>
<Target_Volume> ...

If we want to list Global Copy sessions of the volume pairs with the source volumes 6500 and 6501 in a DS8000 on site 1 with the target volumes 6500 and 6501 in a DS8000 on site 2, we see the following result in Example 27-48.

Example 27-48 lspprc

```
dscli lspprc -l -cfg $DSCLI/profile/DS-01.profile 6500-6501
Date/Time: June 14, 2005 3:28:08 PM EDT IBM DSCLI Version: 5.0.3.134 DS: IBM.2107-7506551
ID        State        Reason Type        Out Of Sync Tracks Tgt Read Src Cascade Tgt
Cascade Date Suspended SourceLSS Timeout (secs) Critical Mode First Pass Status
==========================================================================================
========================================================================================
6500:6500 Copy Pending -      Global Copy 0                  Enabled Disabled    Disabled
Wed Dec 31 18:59:59 EST 1969 65         300           Disabled      True
6501:6501 Copy Pending -      Global Copy 0                  Enabled Disabled    Disabled
Wed Dec 31 18:59:59 EST 1969 65         300           Disabled      True

dscli lspprc -l 6500-6501 -cfg $DSCLI/profile/DS-02.profile
Date/Time: June 14, 2005 3:28:33 PM EDT IBM DSCLI Version: 5.0.3.134 DS: IBM.2107-7573731
ID        State               Reason Type        Out Of Sync Tracks Tgt Read Src Cascade
Tgt Cascade Date Suspended              SourceLSS Timeout (secs) Critical Mode First Pass
Status
==========================================================================================
==========================================================================================
====
6500:6500 Target Copy Pending -      Global Copy 0                 Enabled  Disabled
Disabled    Wed Dec 31 18:59:59 EST 1969 65         unknown       Disabled      Invalid
6501:6501 Target Copy Pending -      Global Copy 0                 Enabled  Disabled
Disabled    Wed Dec 31 18:59:59 EST 1969 65         unknown       Disabled      Invalid
```

Query FlashCopy session

Query a FlashCopy session with the DS CLI **lsflash**:

dscli lsflash -cfg <Device configuration file> <Source_Volume>:<Target_Volume> <Source_Volume>:<Target_Volume> ...

If we want to list FlashCopy sessions for the volume pairs with the source volumes 6500 and 6501 and the target volumes 6502 and 6503 on a DS8000 on site 2, we see the following result in Example 27-49.

Example 27-49 lsflash

```
dscli lsflash -l -cfg $DSCLI/profile/DS-02.profile 6500:6502 6501:6503
Date/Time: June 14, 2005 3:29:22 PM EDT IBM DSCLI Version: 5.0.3.134 DS: IBM.2107-7573731
ID        SrcLSS SequenceNum Timeout ActiveCopy Recording Persistent Revertible
SourceWriteEnabled TargetWriteEnabled BackgroundCopy OutOfSyncTracks DateCreated
DateSynced
==========================================================================================
==========================================================================================
========================
6500:6502 65     0         300    Disabled  Enabled  Enabled   Disabled  Disabled
Disabled Disabled       16384          Tue Jun 14 15:32:41 EDT 2005 Tue Jun 14 15:32:41
EDT 2005
6501:6503 65     0         300    Disabled  Enabled  Enabled   Disabled  Disabled
Disabled Disabled       16384          Tue Jun 14 15:32:41 EDT 2005 Tue Jun 14 15:32:41
EDT 2005
```

Query a LSS session

Query a LSS session with the DS CLI **lssession**:

dscli lssession <LSS_ID> -cfg <Device configuration file>

If we want to list the volumes assigned to a session, we can do this as in Example 27-50.

Example 27-50 lssession (session not assigned)

```
dscli lssession 65 -cfg $DSCLI/profile/DS-01.profile
Date/Time: June 14, 2005 3:30:10 PM EDT IBM DSCLI Version: 5.0.3.134 DS: IBM.2107-7506551
LSS ID Session Status Volume VolumeStatus PrimaryStatus       SecondaryStatus
FirstPassComplete AllowCascading
==============================================================================================
=====================
65     01      Normal 6501   Join Pending Primary Copy Pending Secondary Simplex True
Disable
65     01      Normal 6500   Join Pending Primary Copy Pending Secondary Simplex True
Disable
```

If we want to list the volumes of a Global Mirror session, we see the following result in Example 27-51. Note that the status of the volumes is now *Active* and no longer *Join Pending*.

Example 27-51 lssession (session assigned)

```
dscli lssession 65 -cfg $DSCLI/profile/DS-01.profile
Date/Time: June 14, 2005 4:47:50 PM EDT IBM DSCLI Version: 5.0.3.134 DS: IBM.2107-7506551
LSS ID Session Status         Volume VolumeStatus PrimaryStatus       SecondaryStatus
FirstPassComplete AllowCascading
==============================================================================================
==============================
67     01      CG In Progress 6701   Active       Primary Copy Pending Secondary Simplex
True              Disable
67     01      CG In Progress 6700   Active       Primary Copy Pending Secondary Simplex
True              Disable
```

Show a Global Mirror session

Query a Global Mirror session with the DS CLI **showsession**:

dscli showgmir -metrics <Master_LSS_ID> -cfg <Master device configuration file>

> **Note:** The option metrics is used to display performance statistics.

If we want to show the Global Mirror session of the Master Storage Image and not the Subordinates, we see the following result in Example 27-52.

Example 27-52 showgmir (running session, Master only)

```
dscli showgmir 65 -cfg $DSCLI/profile/DS-01.profile
Date/Time: June 14, 2005 3:30:57 PM EDT IBM DSCLI Version: 5.0.3.134 DS: IBM.2107-7506551
ID                          IBM.2107-7506551/65
Master Count                1
Master Session ID           0x01
Copy State                  Running
Fatal Reason                Not Fatal
CG Interval (seconds)       0
XDC Interval(milliseconds) 50
```

```
CG Drain Time (seconds)     30
Current Time                06/14/2005 15:34:17 EDT
CG Time                     06/14/2005 15:34:17 EDT
Successful CG Percentage    100
FlashCopy Sequence Number   0x42AF3139
Master ID                   IBM.2107-7506551
Subordinate Count           0
Master SSID                 -
Subordinate SSID            -
```

We would have the following result if there was the Master and one Subordinate in a running Global Mirror session as Example 27-53 shows.

Example 27-53 showgmir of running session

```
dscli showgmir 65 -cfg $DSCLI/profile/DS-01.profile
Date/Time: June 14, 2005 5:00:35 PM EDT IBM DSCLI Version: 5.0.3.134 DS: IBM.2107-7506551
ID                          IBM.2107-7506551/65
Master Count                1
Master Session ID           0x01
Copy State                  Running
Fatal Reason                Not Fatal
CG Interval (seconds)       0
XDC Interval(milliseconds) 50
CG Drain Time (seconds)     30
Current Time                06/14/2005 17:03:55 EDT
CG Time                     06/14/2005 17:03:55 EDT
Successful CG Percentage    93
FlashCopy Sequence Number   0x42AF463B
Master ID                   IBM.2107-7506551
Subordinate Count           1
Master SSID                 0xFF65
Subordinate SSID            0xFF67
```

If we want to show the Global Mirror session on the LSS 65 of the Master Storage Image but no Subordinates, Example 27-54 shows the shows the **showgmir** command and its output.

Example 27-54 showgmir (paused session, Master only)

```
dscli showgmir 65 -cfg $DSCLI/profile/DS-01.profile
Date/Time: June 15, 2005 10:23:07 AM EDT IBM DSCLI Version: 5.0.3.134 DS: IBM.2107-7506551
ID                          IBM.2107-7506551/65
Master Count                1
Master Session ID           0x01
Copy State                  Paused
Fatal Reason                Not Fatal
CG Interval (seconds)       0
XDC Interval(milliseconds) 50
CG Drain Time (seconds)     30
Current Time                06/15/2005 10:26:25 EDT
CG Time                     06/15/2005 10:25:57 EDT
Successful CG Percentage    100
FlashCopy Sequence Number   0x42B03A75
Master ID                   IBM.2107-7506551
Subordinate Count           0
Master SSID                 -
Subordinate SSID            -
```

And we would have the following result if there were the Master and one Subordinate in a paused Global Mirror session. See Example 27-55.

Example 27-55 showgmir of a paused session with Master and Subordinate

```
dscli showgmir 65 -cfg $DSCLI/profile/DS-01.profile
Date/Time: June 15, 2005 11:33:07 AM EDT IBM DSCLI Version: 5.0.3.134 DS: IBM.2107-7506551
ID                           IBM.2107-7506551/65
Master Count                 1
Master Session ID            0x01
Copy State                   Paused
Fatal Reason                 Not Fatal
CG Interval (seconds)        0
XDC Interval(milliseconds)   50
CG Drain Time (seconds)      30
Current Time                 06/15/2005 11:37:46 EDT
CG Time                      06/15/2005 11:36:01 EDT
Successful CG Percentage     100
Successful CG Percentage     94
FlashCopy Sequence Number    0x42AF463B
Master ID                    IBM.2107-7506551
Subordinate Count            1
Master SSID                  0xFF65
Subordinate SSID             0xFF67
```

27.5.7 Pause a Global Mirror session

We can pause a Global Mirror session for a set of volumes between the Master Storage Image and all its Subordinates LSSs with the DS CLI command **pausegmir**:

dscli pausegmir -lss <Master LSS ID> -session <session_ID> -cfg <Master device configuration file> <Master_Control_Path_LSS_ID>:<Subordinate_Control_Path_LSS_ID> ...

If we want to pause a Global Mirror session with only one Storage Image on the site 1, we have the following result in Example 27-56.

Example 27-56 pausegmir with Master only

```
dscli pausegmir -lss 65 -session 01 -cfg $DSCLI/profile/DS-01.profile
Date/Time: June 15, 2005 10:22:39 AM EDT IBM DSCLI Version: 5.0.3.134 DS: IBM.2107-7506551
CMUC00163I pausegmir: Global Mirror for session 01 successfully paused.
```

If we want to pause a Global Mirror session with 2 Storage Images in site 1 and control paths from the LSS 65 of the Master to the LSS 67 of its Subordinate, Example 27-57 shows the **pausegmir** command and its output.

Example 27-57 pausegmir with Master and Subordinate

```
dscli pausegmir -lss 65 -session 01 -cfg $DSCLI/profile/DS-01.profile
IBM.2107-7506551/65:IBM.2107-7505801/67
Date/Time: June 15, 2005 11:32:46 AM EDT IBM DSCLI Version: 5.0.3.134 DS: IBM.2107-7506551
CMUC00163I pausegmir: Global Mirror for session 01 successfully paused.
```

To visualize a paused Global Mirror session, use the command **showgmir** as described in "Show a Global Mirror session" on page 394 and especially Example 27-54 on page 395 and Example 27-55 on page 396.

27.5.8 Resume a Global Mirror session

Resume a Global Mirror session for a set of volumes between the Master and its Subordinate LSSs with the DS CLI command **resumegmir**:

dscli resumegmir -lss <Master LSS ID> -cginterval <Number of seconds> -coordinate <Number of milliseconds> -drain <Number of seconds> -session <session_ID> -cfg <Master device configuration file> <Master_Control_Path_LSS_ID>:<Subordinate_Control_Path_LSS_ID> ...

- **cginterval**: Specifies how long to wait between the formation of Consistency Groups. If this number is not specified or is set to zero, Consistency Groups are formed continuously.
- **coordinate**: Indicates the maximum time that Global Mirror processing queues Primary/Host/IO to start forming a Consistency Group.
- **drain**: Specifies the maximum Consistency Group drain time in seconds and the maximum amount of time that the consistent set of data is allowed to drain to the remote site before failing the current Consistency Group.

Note: For a better understanding of these options and how to use them, see Chapter 24., "Global Mirror options and configuration" on page 255.

If we want to resume a Global Mirror session with only one Storage Image on the site 1, Example 27-58 shows the following results.

Example 27-58 resumegmir with Master only

```
dscli resumegmir -lss 65 -session 01 -cfg $DSCLI/profile/DS-01.profile
Date/Time: June 15, 2005 10:56:51 AM EDT IBM DSCLI Version: 5.0.3.134 DS: IBM.2107-7506551
CMUC00164I resumegmir: Global Mirror for session 01 successfully resumed.
```

To visualize your resumed Global Mirror session use the command **showgmir** as described in "Show a Global Mirror session" on page 394 and especially Example 27-52 on page 394 and Example 27-53 on page 395.

27.5.9 Change an LSS session participating in a Global Mirror session

Change an LSS session participating in a Global Mirror session by adding or removing a volume from the session with the DS CLI command **chsession**:

dscli chsession -lss <LSS ID> -action <add or remove> -volume <volume_ID> <Session_ID> -cfg <Device configuration file>

If we want to remove the volume 6500 from the session 01 on LSS 65, Example 27-59 shows the following results.

Example 27-59 chsession

```
dscli chsession -lss 65 -action remove -volume 6500 01 -cfg $DSCLI/profile/DS-01.profile
Date/Time: June 15, 2005 2:19:19 PM EDT IBM DSCLI Version: 5.0.3.134 DS: IBM.2107-7506551
CMUC00147I chsession: Session 01 successfully modified.
```

To visualize your changed LSS session, use the command **lssession** as described in "Query a LSS session" on page 394.

27.5.10 Perform Global Copy failover

Perform Global Copy failover with the DS CLI command **failoverpprc**:

```
dscli failoverpprc -type gcp -cfg <Target device configuration file>
<Source_Volume>:<Target_Volume> <Source_Volume>:<Target_Volume> ...
```

Note: A failover from site 1 to site 2 means that site 2 will be active in a *suspended* state, but the replication process will not be active anymore, neither from site 1 to site 2, nor from site 2 to site 1.

- If there was no outage on the primary site, at the end of a failover on the recovery site, the primary and the recovery volumes will still be available and accessible.
- If there was an outage on the primary site, at the end of a failover on the recovery site, only the recovery volumes will still be available and accessible.

If we want to failover two Global Copy pairs at the secondary site, Example 27-60 shows the following results.

Example 27-60 failover

```
dscli failoverpprc -type gcp 6500:6500 6501:6501 -cfg $DSCLI/profile/DS-02.profile
Date/Time: June 15, 2005 14:56:32 PM EDT IBM DSCLI Version: 5.0.3.134 DS: IBM.2107-7573731
CMUC00196I failoverpprc: Remote Mirror and Copy pair 6500:6500 successfully reversed.
CMUC00196I failoverpprc: Remote Mirror and Copy pair 6501:6501 successfully reversed.
```

To visualize your changed Global Copy sessions use the command **lspprc** as described in "Query Global Copy session" on page 392.

27.5.11 Perform Global Copy failback

Perform Global Copy failback with the DS CLI command **failbackpprc**:

```
dscli failback -type gcp -cfg <Target device configuration file>
<Source_Volume>:<Target_Volume> <Source_Volume>:<Target_Volume> ...
```

Note: A failback on site 2 means that site 2 will be active as the source volume of a Global Copy replication process from site 2 volumes to site 1 target volumes and therefore will erase data on site 1 target volumes.

Example 27-61 shows a failback of two former Global Copy pairs.

Example 27-61 failback - erasing data on site 1 with data from site 2

```
dscli failbackpprc -type gcp -tgtread 6500:6500 6501:6501 -cfg $DSCLI/profile/DS-02.profile
Date/Time: June 15, 2005 12:32:27 PM EDT IBM DSCLI Version: 5.0.3.134 DS: IBM.2107-7573731
CMUC00197I failbackpprc: Remote Mirror and Copy pair 6500:6500 successfully failed back.
CMUC00197I failbackpprc: Remote Mirror and Copy pair 6501:6501 successfully failed back.
```

To visualize the changed Global Copy sessions use the command **lspprc** as described in "Query Global Copy session" on page 392.

27.5.12 Create a FlashCopy for Backup or Disaster Recovery practice

To create a new FlashCopy relationship with the DS CLI for one or several pairs of volumes, it is necessary to pass through a two step process.

> **Note:** If FlashCopy pairs are in several LSSs, do not forget to select all of them during this process or run the process again on each LSS. If FlashCopy pairs are spread over several Storage Images, run this process again on each of them.

The first step in this process is to see which Fixed Block volumes are available for FlashCopy pairs on the Global Mirror target Storage Image:

dscli lsfbvol -lss <LSS_ID> -cfg <Device configuration file>

For CKD volumes use the command:

dscli lsckdvol -lss <LSS_ID> -cfg <Device configuration file>

Example 27-62 shows the following results from a **lsfbvol** command.

Example 27-62 lsfbvol

```
dscli lsfbvol -lss 65 -cfg $DSCLI/profile/DS-02.profile
Date/Time: June 14, 2005 7:15:47 PM EDT IBM DSCLI Version: 5.0.3.134 DS: IBM.2107-7573731
Name         ID   accstate datastate configstate deviceMTM datatype extpool cap (2^30B) cap
(10^9B) cap (blocks)
==========================================================================================
=====================
GM_TGT_GC01  6500 Online   Normal    Normal      2107-900  FB 512   P5              1.0
-       2097152
GM_TGT_GC02  6501 Online   Normal    Normal      2107-900  FB 512   P5              1.0
-       2097152
GM_TGT_JFC01 6502 Online   Normal    Normal      2107-900  FB 512   P5              1.0
-       2097152
GM_TGT_JFC02 6503 Online   Normal    Normal      2107-900  FB 512   P5              1.0
-       2097152
GM_TGT_FCA01 6504 Online   Normal    Normal      2107-900  FB 512   P5              1.0
-       2097152
GM_TGT_FCA02 6505 Online   Normal    Normal      2107-900  FB 512   P5              1.0
-       2097152
```

The second step is to create FlashCopy pairs with the command **mkflash**:

dscli mkflash -wait -tgtinhibit -cfg <Device configuration file>
<Source_Volume>:<Target_Volume> <Source_Volume>:<Target_Volume> ...

> **Note:** The *wait* option is not required, but can help in knowing when the process is finished, and the *tgtinhibit* option is also not required, but can prevent any misuse of the target volumes during the FlashCopy process.

If we want to create two FlashCopy pairs with the source volumes 6500 and 6501 and the target volumes 6504 and 6504 on a DS8000 on site 2, Example 27-63 shows the following results.

Example 27-63 mkflash

```
dscli mkflash -record -nocp -cfg $DSCLI/profile/DS-02.profile 6500:6504 6501:6505
Date/Time: June 14, 2005 3:35:09 PM EDT IBM DSCLI Version: 5.0.3.134 DS: IBM.2107-7573731
CMUC00137I mkflash: FlashCopy pair 6500:6504 successfully created.
CMUC00137I mkflash: FlashCopy pair 6501:6505 successfully created.
```

To visualize your newly created FlashCopy session use the command **lsflash** as described in "Query FlashCopy session" on page 393.

27.5.13 Investigate the FlashCopy status between B and C volumes

After a primary or local site failure, you have to check the last FlashCopy status of all FlashCopy pairs within the Global Mirror session.

To visualize the *sequence number* and *revertible* state of your FlashCopy sessions, first use the command **lsflash** as described in "Query FlashCopy session" on page 393.

> **Note:** At this level, we do not use the command **setflashrevertible** because Global Mirror has already issued this command internally.

Secondly, and depending on whether or not the FlashCopy pairs were successfully set to a revertible state and depending on whether or not their sequence numbers are equal or not, we issue either the **commitflash** or the **revertflash** commands.

Note: We need to remember that Global Mirror is a distributed solution:

- When a Consistency Group is processed, the Master acts as a session manager and issues an Incremental Revertible FlashCopy on its own recovery site and at the same time is asking its Subordinates to also perform such a task at their recovery sites.
- When a Consistency Group is in progress, several Incremental Revertible FlashCopies may be running. The FlashCopy process is looking at the *Change Recording Bit Map* on B volumes and is comparing it with the *Target Bit Map* on the C volumes. When the Incremental FlashCopy is finished, the *Change Recording Bit Map* is cleared and, therefore, all the changes are committed on the C volumes. The corresponding FlashCopy pairs are set to a *Non-Revertible* state by the Master.

This is the reason why one of these five situations could occur:

1. If all FlashCopy pairs are Non-Revertible and their sequence numbers are equal, it means that the Consistency Group process is finished.

   There is no action required because the Consistency Group is intact on the C volumes.
2. If some FlashCopy pairs are revertible and their sequence numbers are equal and others are not revertible and their sequence numbers are equal, but do not match the revertible FlashCopies sequence number, means that some FlashCopy pairs are running in a Consistency Group process and some have not started yet their Incremental process.

   To preserve the consistency we need to overwrite new data with data saved at the last consistency formation for the FlashCopy pairs already in the new Consistency Group process. It is like using the **revertflash** command of the DS CLI.
3. If all FlashCopy pairs are Revertible and their sequence numbers are equal, it means that all the FlashCopy pairs are running in a Consistency Group process and none have finished there Incremental process.

   We need to overwrite new data with data saved at the last consistency formation for all the FlashCopy pairs. It is like using the **revertflash** command of the DS CLI.
4. If some FlashCopy pairs are revertible and at least one is not revertible, but all their sequence numbers are equal, it means that some FlashCopy pairs are running in a Consistency Group process and some have already finished their Incremental process.

   We need to commit data to a target volume to form a consistency between the source and target. Only the FlashCopy pairs that have not already finished their Incremental process will have to commit the changes since Non-Revertible pairs have already committed theirs. It is like using the **commitflash** command of the DS CLI. Using this command on FlashCopy pairs that are not revertible will only display error messages.
5. If none of the 4 above situations are possible, then the Consistency Group is corrupted.

```
dscli revertflash -seqnum <FlashCopy_Sequence_NB> -cfg <Device configuration file>
<Source_Volume> <Source_Volume> ...
```

```
dscli commitflash -seqnum <FlashCopy_Sequence_NB> -cfg <Device configuration file>
<Source_Volume> <Source_Volume> ...
```

If we want to use the **revertflash** command on the FlashCopy pairs with the source volumes 6500 and 6501 on a DS8000 on site 2 and the **lsflash** command displays the sequence number 9D9B as the actual sequence number for both pairs, Example 27-64 shows the **revertflash** command and the following command results:

Example 27-64 revertflash

```
dscli revertflash -seqnum 9D9B 6500 6501 -cfg $DSCLI/profile/DS-02.profile
Date/Time: June 15, 2005 5:31:34 PM EDT IBM DSCLI Version: 5.0.3.134 DS: IBM.2107-7573731
CMUC00171I revertflash: FlashCopy volume pair 6500:6500 successfully reverted.
CMUC00171I revertflash: FlashCopy volume pair 6501:6501 successfully reverted.
```

When we need to reverse the FlashCopy relation and copy the data from the target volume to the source volume, also called the Fast Reverse Restore process, we use this command:

dscli reverseflash -fast -tgtpprc -seqnum <FlashCopy_Sequence_NB> -cfg <Device configuration file> <Source_Volume> <Source_Volume> ...

If we want to use the **revertflash** command on the FlashCopy pairs with the source volumes 6500 and 6501 on a DS8000 on site 2, Example 27-65 shows the results of the corresponding **revertflash** command.

Example 27-65 revertflash

```
dscli reverseflash -fast -tgtpprc 6500:6502 6501:6503 -cfg $DSCLI/profile/DS-02.profile
Date/Time: June 15, 2005 6:23:50 PM EDT IBM DSCLI Version: 5.0.3.134 DS: IBM.2107-7573731
CMUC00169I reverseflash: FlashCopy pair 6500:6502 successfully reverse.
CMUC00169I reverseflash: FlashCopy pair 6501:6503 successfully reverse.
```

To visualize your FlashCopy session status, use the command **lsflash** as described in "Query FlashCopy session" on page 393.

27.6 Clean up a Global Mirror environment with DS CLI

In this section we provide the details on how to clean up a Global Mirror environment with the DS Command-Line Interface.

The Global Mirror environment cleanup process can be separated into five consecutive parts:

1. Remove a Global Mirror session relationship between Master and its Subordinates. This is all the Global Mirror sessions with the same session number interconnected through PPRC control paths.
2. Remove the common Global Mirror session from each LSS on the source Storage Images.
3. Remove FlashCopy for each FlashCopy pair.
4. Remove Global Copy for each pair of source volumes on site 1 and the target volumes on site 2.
5. Remove PPRC paths:
   a. Between the LSSs on the source Storage Images on site 1 and the target LSSs on the target Storage Images on site 2.
   b. Within site 1 between the Master and the Subordinate LSSs. This task is not required if you only have one source Storage Image.

27.6.1 Remove Global Mirror session relationship

Before you remove a Global Mirror session for a set of volumes using the DS CLI, you should first display your Global Mirror sessions with the command **showgmir** as described in "Show a Global Mirror session" on page 394. Then remove the Global Mirror session with the command **rmgmir**:

```
dscli rmgmir -quiet -lss <Master LSS ID> -cfg <Master device configuration file>
<Master_Control_Path_LSS_ID>:<Subordinate_Control_Path_LSS_ID> ...
```

> **Note:** The *quiet* option turns off the confirmation prompt for this command.

If we want to remove a Global Mirror session with only one Storage Image on the site 1, we use the command as shown in Example 27-66.

Example 27-66 rmgmir (Master only)

```
dscli rmgmir -quiet -lss 65 -session 01 -cfg $DSCLI/profile/DS-01.profile 01
Date/Time: June 15, 2005 2:18:17 PM EDT IBM DSCLI Version: 5.0.3.134 DS: IBM.2107-7506551
CMUC00165I rmgmir: Global Mirror for session 01 successfully stopped.
```

27.6.2 Remove common Global Mirror session for each LSS

Before you remove the common Global Mirror session for each LSS, first display the LSS sessions with the command **lssession** as described in "Query a LSS session" on page 394. Then remove from each session the associated volumes with the command **chsession** as described in "Change an LSS session participating in a Global Mirror session" on page 397. And finally, remove the sessions with the command **rmsession**:

```
dscli rmgmir -quiet -lss <LSS_ID> -cfg <Device configuration file> <Session_Number>
```

> **Note:** The *quiet* option turns off the confirmation prompt for this command.

Remove session number 01 for the LSS 65 on the Master with the command as shown in Example 27-67.

Example 27-67 rmsession

```
dscli rmsession -quiet -lss 65 01 -cfg $DSCLI/profile/DS-01.profile
Date/Time: June 15, 2005 2:20:05 PM EDT IBM DSCLI Version: 5.0.3.134 DS: IBM.2107-7506551
CMUC00146I rmsession: Session 01 closed successfully.
```

27.6.3 Remove FlashCopy session

Remove FlashCopy pairs with the **rmflash** command.

> **Note:** If FlashCopy pairs are in several LSSs do not forget to select all of them during this process or run the process again on each LSS. If FlashCopy pairs are spread over several Storage Images run this process again on each of them.

```
dscli rmflash -quiet -seqnum <FlashCopy_Sequence_NB> -cfg <Device configuration
file> <Source_Volume>:<Target_Volume> <Source_Volume>:<Target_Volume> ...
```

Note: The *quiet* option turns off the confirmation prompt for this command.

In Example 27-68 we remove two FlashCopy pairs with the source volumes 6500 and 6501 and the corresponding target volumes 6502 and 6503.

Example 27-68 rmflash

```
dscli rmflash -quiet -seqnum 0000 6500:6502 6501:6503 -cfg $DSCLI/profile/DS-02.profile
Date/Time: June 15, 2005 2:21:21 PM EDT IBM DSCLI Version: 5.0.3.134 DS: IBM.2107-7573731
CMUC00140I rmflash: FlashCopy pair 6500:6502 successfully removed.
CMUC00140I rmflash: FlashCopy pair 6501:6503 successfully removed.
```

27.6.4 Remove Global Copy session

Remove Global Copy pairs with the command **rmpprc**:

```
dscli mkpprc -type gcp -tgtread -mode full -cfg <Source device configuration file>
<Source_Volume>:<Target_Volume> <Source_Volume>:<Target_Volume> ...
```

Note: If Global Copy pairs are in several LSSs do not forget to select all of them during this process or run the process again on each LSS. If Global Copy pairs are spread over several Storage Images run this process again on each of them.

In Example 27-69 we remove two Global Copy pairs with the source volumes 6500 and 6501 in a DS8000 in the local site and the same volume numbers in a DS8000 at the remote site.

Example 27-69 rmpprc

```
dscli rmpprc -quiet 6500:6500 6501:6501 -cfg $DSCLI/profile/DS-01.profile
Date/Time: June 15, 2005 2:23:19 PM EDT IBM DSCLI Version: 5.0.3.134 DS: IBM.2107-7506551
CMUC00155I rmpprc: Remote Mirror and Copy volume pair 6500:6500 relationship successfully
withdrawn.
CMUC00155I rmpprc: Remote Mirror and Copy volume pair 6501:6501 relationship successfully
withdrawn.
```

27.6.5 Remove PPRC paths

Finally we remove the PPRC paths from a source LSS to a target LSS with the command **rmpprcpath**.

Note: You need to repeat this process for each data path between LSSs on the source Storage Images on site 1 and the target LSSs on the target Storage Images on site 2. Also do this for each control path between Master LSS and potential Subordinate Storage Image LSSs.

```
dscli mkpprcpath -remotewwnn <WWN of your remote Storage Image> -consistgrp -srclss
<Source_LSS_ID> -tgtlss <Target_LSS_ID> -cfg <Source device configuration file>
<Source_IO_Port>:<Target_IO_PORT> <Source_IO_Port>:<Target_IO_PORT> ...
```

In Example 27-70 we remove a PPRC path from the source LSS 65 on a DS8000 on site 1 to a target LSS 65 on a DS8000 on site 2.

Example 27-70 rmpprcpath

```
dscli rmpprcpath -quiet 65:65 -cfg $DSCLI/profile/DS-01.profile
Date/Time: June 15, 2005 2:24:05 PM EDT IBM DSCLI Version: 5.0.3.134 DS: IBM.2107-7506551
CMUC00150I rmpprcpath: Remote Mirror and Copy path 65:65 successfully removed.
```

Part 7

z/OS Global Mirror

In this part of the book, we describe the characteristics and operation of DS8000 z/OS Global Mirror. We also discuss considerations that you may find useful when planning the implementation of z/OS Global Mirror.

z/OS Global Mirror overview

In this chapter we describe the characteristics and operation of IBM TotalStorage z/OS Global Mirror, previously known as Extended Remote Copy (XRC). Also discussed are the considerations for its implementation on the IBM TotalStorage DS8000.

28.1 Overview

z/OS Global Mirror is a copy function available for the z/OS and OS/390 operating systems. It involves a System Data Mover (SDM) that is found only in OS/390 and z/OS. z/OS Global Mirror maintains a copy of the data asynchronously at a remote location, and can be implemented over unlimited distances. It is a combined hardware and software solution offering data integrity and data availability that can be used as part of business continuance solutions, for workload movement, and for data migration. The z/OS Global Mirror function is an optional function. To use it, you must purchase the Remote Mirror for z/OS function authorization model (RMZ).

28.2 z/OS Global Mirror processes

z/OS Global Mirror is a software centric remote copy implementation. A DFSMSdfp component called System Data Mover (SDM) will copy the writes issued to primary volumes to the secondary devices. Although the main z/OS Global Mirror implementation consists of host resident software, special z/OS Global Mirror support is required in the DS8000 that attaches the z/OS Global Mirror primary volumes.

28.2.1 z/OS Global Mirror components

Some definitions of the components include the following terms.

Primary storage subsystem

The primary storage subsystem is a collection of volumes that is designated to be copied to a secondary site. This collection of volumes may be all the volumes at the primary site, or a subset of them. A z/OS Global Mirror primary volume must be part of a primary storage subsystem that is z/OS Global Mirror capable — like the DS8000 with the optional z/OS Global Mirror feature enabled. Attaching the primary volumes are one or more host applications running on one or more z/OS (or OS/390) system images.

Secondary storage subsystem

The secondary site storage subsystem is a collection of volumes that holds copies of the primary volumes. Each z/OS Global Mirror primary volume has a corresponding secondary volume. The z/OS Global Mirror secondary volumes can be part of any storage subsystem supported by the secondary system, and by the z/OS system where the SDM is running.

Tip: You may wish to make the secondary subsystem a z/OS Global Mirror capable subsystem, in the interests of being able to mirror your environment back to the original site (or elsewhere) after a disaster.

Attention: It is highly recommended that your secondary storage subsystem be of similar performance to the primary storage subsystem. If it is not, you may experience production impact due to z/OS Global Mirror not being able to keep up with production data updates.

System Data Mover (SDM)

The System Data Mover (SDM) is part of the DFSMSdfp software, and must have connectivity to the primary volumes and to the secondary volumes. When primary systems write to the primary volumes, the SDM manages the process of copying those updates to the secondary volumes.

Multiple z/OS Global Mirror sessions can be in effect per z/OS (or OS/390) system (up to 5 with or without coupling them). Multiple instances of the SDM on separate z/OS images are also possible. Each SDM will have one z/OS Global Mirror session that is responsible for a group of volumes. The SDM maintains the updates' sequence consistency for the volumes participating in the z/OS Global Mirror session, across LCUs in the DS8000 and across DS8000s (as well as with other primary storage subsystems which support z/OS Global Mirror). In a coupled z/OS Global Mirror environment (also known as CXRC), the update sequence integrity is managed across the coupled SDM sessions.

Journal, Control, and State data sets

The *Journal data set*, *Control data set*, and *State data set* are used by the SDM to harden — on disk — consistent time groups of updated records received from the primary volumes, and to control the process of applying them to the secondary volumes thus maintaining sequence consistency. The SDM creates Consistency Groups and writes them to the journal data sets.

The Control data set has pointers into the Journal data sets indicating the last set of Consistency Groups written to the secondary volumes and the amount of data written to the journal.

The State data set maintains a list of z/OS Global Mirror primary and secondary volumes, and is updated whenever a volume pair status for that session is changed.

Master data set

The Master data set is only required for a coupled z/OS Global Mirror (CXRC) environment. It ensures recoverable consistency among all z/OS Global Mirror subsystems contained within the CXRC system. At regular intervals the SDM writes data to the Master data set. This data includes the last Consistency Group written to the secondary volumes, and the last Consistency Group written to the journal data sets. In the same I/O operation, the SDM reads the status of the last Consistency Group written to the secondary volumes, and the last Consistency Group written to the journal data set by all other SDMs in the coupled sessions. It also writes information about its own journal and write consistency time.

28.2.2 z/OS Global Mirror operation: Data flow

For an overview of the z/OS Global Mirror components, see Figure 28-1.

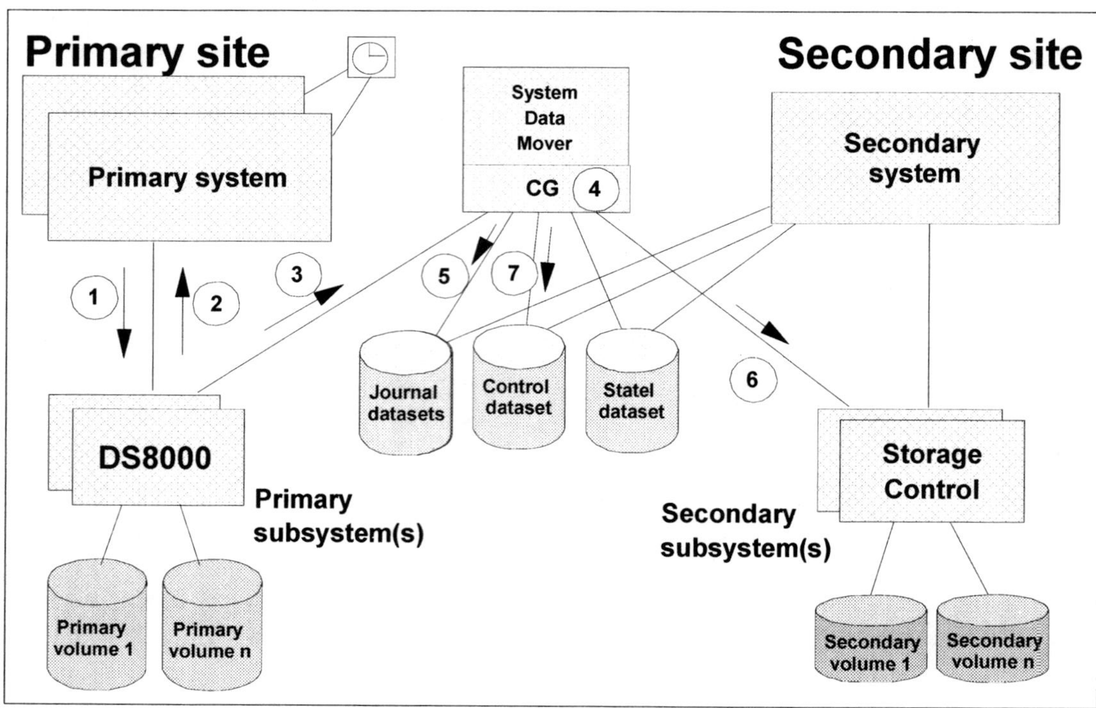

Figure 28-1 z/OS Global Mirror data flow

Figure 28-1 illustrates a simplified view of the z/OS Global Mirror components and the data flow logic. But before discussing the logic, let us understand a key issue for the characteristic consistency of this process: timestamping.

28.2.3 Common time reference

When a z/OS Global Mirror pair is established, this is signalled to the primary system, and the host system DFSMSdfp software starts to time stamp all write I/Os to the primary volumes. This is necessary to provide data consistency across multiple LCUs. If those primary volumes are shared by systems running on different CECs, an IBM Sysplex Timer® is required to provide a common time reference. If all the primary systems are running in different LPARs on the same CEC, the system time-of-day clock can be used.

You should be aware that the primary systems use Universal Time Coordinated (UTC) time.

z/OS Global Mirror is implemented in a cooperative way between the DS8000s on the primary site and the DFSMSdfp host system software component System Data Mover (SDM). The logic for the data flow is as follows (refer to Figure 28-1):

1. The primary system writes to the primary volumes.
2. The application I/O operation is signalled completed when the data is written to primary DS8000 cache and NVS; this is when channel end and device end are returned to the primary system. Thus, the application write I/O operation has completed, and now the updated data will be mirrored asynchronously as per the following steps.
3. The DS8000 groups the updates into record sets which are asynchronously off-loaded from the cache to the SDM system. As z/OS Global Mirror uses this asynchronous copy technique, there is no performance impact on the primary applications' I/O operations.

4. The record sets, perhaps from multiple primary storage subsystems, are processed into Consistency Groups (CGs) by the SDM. The CG contains records that have their order of update preserved across multiple LCUs within an DS8000, across multiple DS8000s and across other storage subsystems participating in the same z/OS Global Mirror session. This preservation of order is absolutely vital for dependent write I/Os such as databases and their logs. The creation of CGs guarantees that z/OS Global Mirror will copy data to the secondary site with update sequence integrity.
5. When a CG is formed, it is written from the SDM real storage buffers to the Journal data sets.
6. Immediately after the CG has been hardened on the Journal data sets, the records are written to their corresponding secondary volumes. Those records are also written from SDM's real storage buffers. Because of the data in transit between the primary and secondary sites, the currency of the data on secondary volumes lags slightly behind the currency of the data at the primary site.
7. The control data set is updated to reflect that the records in the CG have been written to the secondary volumes.

28.3 z/OS Global Mirror storage control sessions

When you start a z/OS Global Mirror session (using the TSO command XSTART) and establish the first volume pair (using the TSO command XADDPAIR), a *z/OS Global Mirror storage control session* (z/OS Global Mirror SC session) is created within the DS8000 LCU where the primary volume belongs. This z/OS Global Mirror storage control session in the LCU has a counterpart in the SDM. It is possible to have multiple z/OS Global Mirror storage control sessions within an LCU per SDM. The SDM will use a separate utility device and run a separate subtask per z/OS Global Mirror storage control session, making it possible to transfer data in parallel between one LCU and one SDM. This functionality is also referred to as *multiple reader support*.

You can use the SCSESSION parameter in the XADDPAIR command to route a primary volume to a specific storage control session within an LCU. The primary volume will be part of the default z/OS Global Mirror storage control session when no SCSESSION parameter is specified.

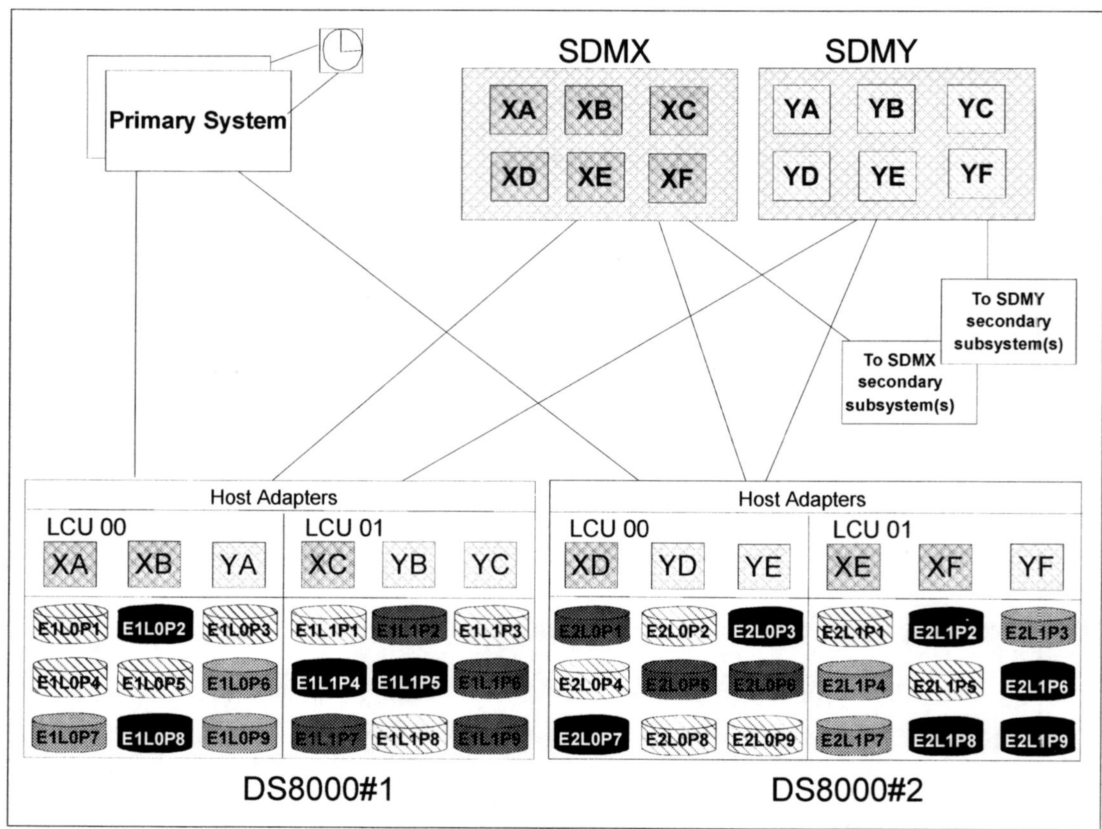

Figure 28-2 z/OS Global Mirror sessions and z/OS Global Mirror storage control sessions

Figure 28-2 illustrates an example with multiple *z/OS Global Mirror sessions* per LCU and multiple *z/OS Global Mirror storage control sessions* per z/OS Global Mirror session per LCU. Each z/OS Global Mirror storage control session is responsible for a group of volumes and uses a separate *utility device.*

> **Note:** Remember that with the DS8000 the LCU (or LSS) is no longer tied to a particular physical disk array, giving added flexibility when designing your z/OS Global Mirror environment.

In the example illustrated in Figure 28-2 we have two SDMs (SDMX and SDMY) and two DS8000 primary subsystems (DS8000#1 and DS8000#2) each with two LCUs (LCU 00 and LCU 01):

- DS8000#1/LCU 00 has three z/OS Global Mirror storage control sessions: XA and XB in the SDMX session and YA in the SDMY session.
- DS8000#1/LCU 01 has three z/OS Global Mirror storage control sessions: XC in SDMX session and YB and YC in SDMY session.
- DS8000#2/LCU 00 has three z/OS Global Mirror storage control sessions: XD in SDMX session and YD and YE in SDMY session.
- DS8000#2/LCU 01 has three z/OS Global Mirror storage control sessions: XE and XF in the SDMX session and YF in the SDMY session.

28.4 Utility devices

For any host system to read data from a disk storage control unit in z/OS (or S/390), that storage control unit must provide a device address. This is a requirement of the zSeries I/O architecture and applies also when reading from the DS8000.

So, when the SDM issues channel commands to read updates from the primary storage control unit cache, it has to specify a device address even though the data in the cache in reality *belongs to* several different devices. This device address used by the SDM to offload updates from primary subsystem cache is referred to as the *utility device*.

If the SDM has multiple z/OS Global Mirror storage control sessions in one LCU, the SDM will need one utility device per storage control session.

It is important that the utility device is not heavily used by the primary system because this could prevent the SDM from getting access to the device, and the offload process would slow down.

28.4.1 Utility device selection method

You can specify the method of selection of the utility devices using the XSET command with the UTILITY parameter. You can choose that a specific (*fixed*) device be used, or you can allow the DS8000 to determine which utility device (*floating*) to use.

You can also select fixed or floating utility devices in the z/OS Global Mirror PARMLIB dataset.

Fixed utility device

For *fixed utility devices* z/OS Global Mirror always reads data from the storage control using this device, thus eliminating application contention for devices. The following recommendations apply to these devices:

- Select dedicated fixed utility devices that are not used for any other purpose.
- Ensure that the device is not reserved by other applications.
- Ensure that the first device added to a session for a particular storage control be a fixed utility device.
- Define the fixed utility device as a single cylinder device if the storage control is a DS8000. Specify a single fixed utility device per storage control session.

Floating utility devices

z/OS Global Mirror can use a *floating utility device* with the DS8000. This means that the microcode in the DS8000 will continuously monitor the usage of utility device candidates, select the least used device, and pass this address to the SDM. The SDM will then use this device address on the next offload operation.

When using floating utility devices, all primary devices in the z/OS Global Mirror storage control session are eligible to be used as a utility device, plus all devices added to the storage control session with the XRCUTL parameter in the XADDPAIR command.

XRCUTL devices are not really part of the session because they are not copied to secondary volumes, but they can be used to extend the range of eligible utility devices.

Tip: In a channel-extender configuration, it is highly recommended that you define fixed rather than floating utility devices. In these configurations, the telecommunication links tend to be the most vulnerable. If they fail, it is essential that you do not leave a production volume in the status of a z/OS Global Mirror utility device. If an application attempts to reserve a primary volume that is currently being used as a utility device, message `IEA482I WAITING FOR CONTROL UNITS` is written to the system log. The application program will not be able to proceed until the storage control session is suspended. Also, you can define utility devices on additional paths to improve resilience and performance.

28.5 Consistency Groups

This section discusses in more detail the characteristics of timestamping and the Consistency Groups.

28.5.1 Timestamping process

Maintaining the update sequence for applications whose data is being copied in real time is a critical requirement for applications that execute dependent write I/Os. If data is copied out of sequence, serious integrity exposures could render the recovery procedures useless. z/OS Global Mirror uses special algorithms to provide update sequence consistency for all data. The starting point for maintaining update sequence integrity is when a record is first written by an application system to a primary volume of a z/OS Global Mirror managed pair. When the record is written, the LCU maintains the data (including the time-stamp information) and transfers it to the SDM along with other updated records. This process is shown in Figure 28-3.

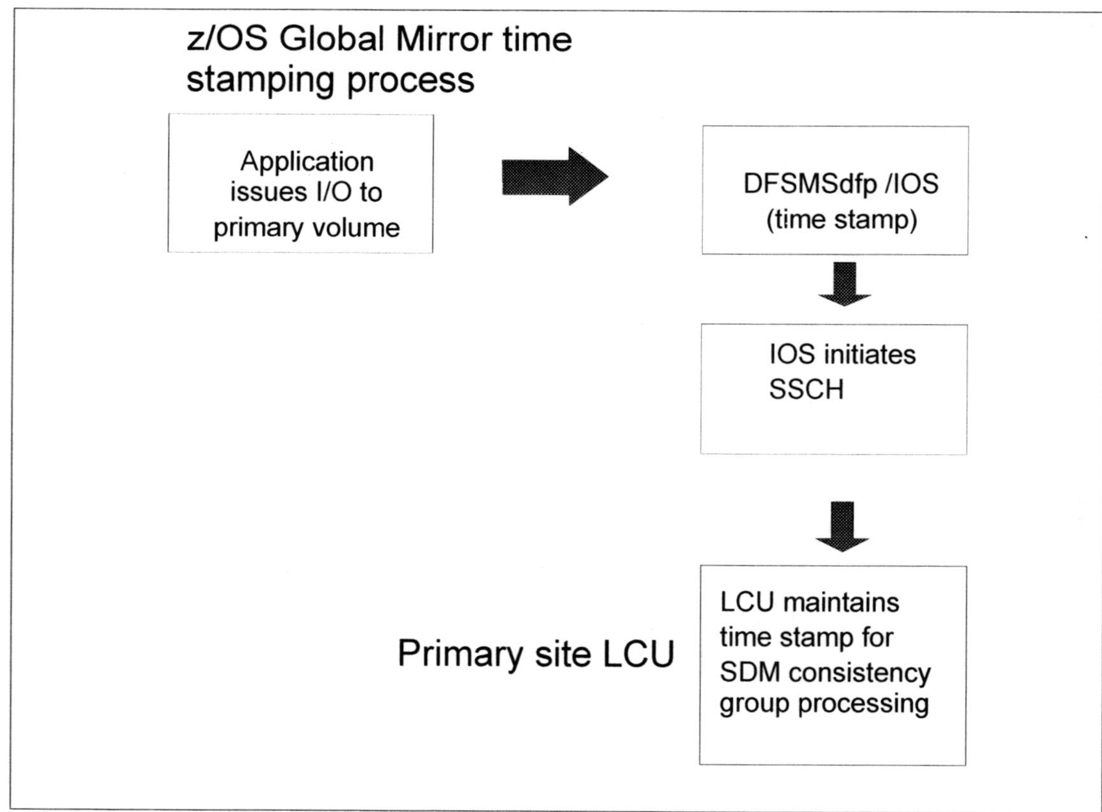

Figure 28-3 z/OS Global Mirror timestamping process

Whenever a z/OS Global Mirror-managed pair of volumes is established by the **XADDPAIR** command, all attached primary systems are informed of their duplex status. Thus, DFSMSdfp can be selective when performing the timestamping process. Only those records that are being written to z/OS Global Mirror primary volumes are timestamped for future analysis by the SDM.

Identification of records that require this special treatment is a result of the pack change interrupt, which is issued when the volumes come under z/OS Global Mirror control after the XADDPAIR command is executed. The pack change interrupt allows all attached hosts to update their internal control blocks to reflect the z/OS Global Mirror status of the volumes, and thus provides an efficient way for DFSMSdfp to identify which records should be timestamped, and which should not.

The timestamping code is an extension of the IOS SSCH code, so it applies to all data. Deferred writes held in main storage buffers for database applications are processed in SSCH order. This ensures that the timestamping process delivers update sequence integrity support accurately and efficiently.

28.5.2 z/OS Global Mirror update sequence consistency example

The example shown in Figure 28-4 illustrates how the Consistency Groups are created.

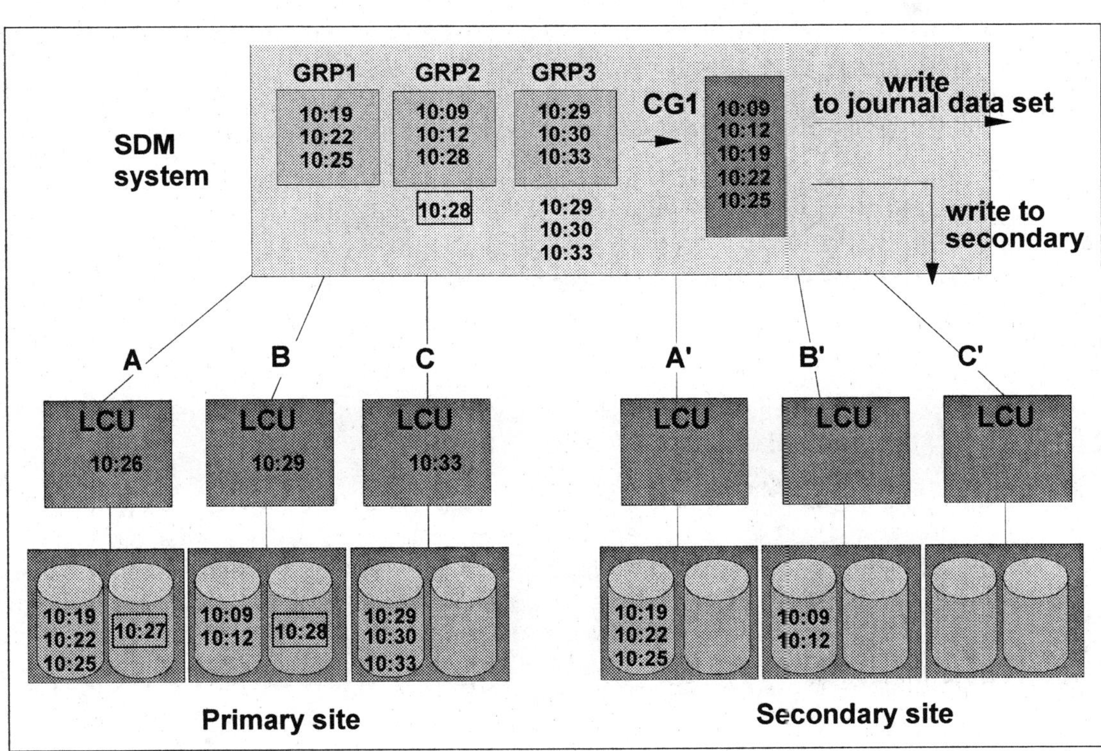

Figure 28-4 Creation of Consistency Group - CG1

In Figure 28-4 we see a configuration with six primary volumes attached to three LCUs at the primary site, and six secondary volumes attached to three LCUs at the secondary site. The SDM system has connectivity to the three LCUs at the primary site and the three LCUs at the secondary site. We assume a one-for-one relationship between the LCUs and the primary volumes at the primary site, and the LCUs and secondary volumes at the secondary site (A, B, C, copied to A', B', C', respectively).

The applications running on the primary system update records on the primary volumes at certain times. In our example, the first volume attached to LCU(A) at the application site has three records updated at 10:19, 10:22, and 10:25. Similarly, the times recorded for the other five volumes are the times when their records are updated (ignore the secondary site disk for the time being).

Two record updates are highlighted on two volumes at the primary; we use these two records as our dependent writes. The first record is the log update on the second volume attached to LCU(A), which takes place at 10:27. The second record is the database update on the second volume attached to LCU(B), which takes place at 10:28.

Now, we define a point-in-time when the SDM reads the updated records from each primary LCU. Notice the time in each of the three LCUs at the primary site. We assume that this is the time that the SDM will read the records that have been updated from that LCU.

So, at 10:26, the SDM will read updates from LCU(A); at 10:29, from LCU(B); and at 10:33, from LCU(C). We look at each LCU individually and describe the record transfer to the SDM and the CG processing that takes place when all LCUs have sent their updates to the SDM.

- The SDM reads from LCU(A) at 10:26:

  At 10:26, the SDM will read three records from the LCU(A) — the records written at 10:19, 10:22, and 10:25. The SDM will not read the highlighted log record because it has not been written at this point-in-time (the log will be written at 10:27). We deliberately stress test the SDM by creating a scenario that could easily result in copying data out of sequence. This group of records will be stored in the SDM's real storage buffers and is designated as GRP1 on the diagram. The SDM will not write this data yet, because it must determine whether the other LCUs have dependent record updates that are included in the session.

- The SDM reads from LCU(B) at 10:29:

  At 10:29, the SDM will read three records from LCU(B) — the records written at 10:09, 10:12, and 10:28. Note that the highlighted database update (10:28) is included in this group of records, which is described as GRP2 in the diagram. This poses a potential problem because the SDM has read the database update, but not the log update. If the SDM simply writes data as it receives it, the serious data integrity exposure described before would prevail. The SDM's ability to avoid these exposures becomes clear as we proceed with this example.

- The SDM reads from LCU(C) at 10:33:

  At 10:33, the SDM will read three records from LCU(C) — the records written at 10:29, 10:30, and 10:33. This group of updated records is called GRP3. At this stage, the SDM has received responses from all three LCUs that have volumes in the z/OS Global Mirror session. The next phase of providing the remote copy function is to perform the update sequence integrity check for all of the updated records read from all of the primary storage subsystems in the z/OS Global Mirror session.

- The SDM creates CG:

  The SDM now has three groups of records that it uses to create a CG. The CG is the unit of data transfer to the journal data sets at the secondary site. It contains records that the SDM has determined can be safely written to the secondary site without risk of out-of-sequence updates. To compile the CG, the SDM uses all of the record groups read from the LCUs as input. In our case, we have three record groups that the SDM uses as input to produce a single CG output.

The SDM compares the maximum timestamp for each individual record group (GRP1 = 10:25, GRP2 = 10:28, GRP3 = 10:33) and selects the smallest value (10:25) to calculate which records should be included in the CG. The SDM calculates that all records written at or before this smallest value time can be written together to the remote site journals as a CG.

In our example, five records (10:09, 10:12, 10:19, 10:22, and 10:25) qualify for inclusion in the first Consistency Group of CG1. Using this calculation, the SDM ensures that dependent write records are not written *ahead* of time as demonstrated by the fact that the database update at 10:28 has not been included in the CG. This is vital because the log update (10:27) is located behind a different LCU(A) and has not yet been read into the SDM's real storage buffers for inclusion in the *Consistency Group creation algorithm.*

Now, we see the importance of using the maximum timestamp in each individual record group, and selecting the minimum of all of the maximums across record groups as the CG *upper limit* timestamp.

The SDM has *retained* the database update along with other possibly dependent write sensitive records in its real storage, until it calculates that it is safe to include them in a future CG. In the diagram, these four records are listed beneath their respective original record groups (10:28 in GRP2 and 10:29, 10:30, and 10:33 in GRP3).

- The SDM writes CG to journal data sets:

  Having created a group of records that can be safely written together, the SDM then writes this group to the journal data sets at the secondary site. Thus the SDM can harden the updates as quickly as possible in one I/O to a single data set.

- The SDM writes the updates to the secondary volumes:

  After the CG has been written to the journal data set, the SDM immediately writes out the individual records to their appropriate secondary volumes. This transfer takes place from the SDM's real storage buffers (the journal data sets are only read during recovery using the XRECOVER command). Updating the secondary volumes could involve several I/Os, because the record updates could be directed to several volumes located behind several LCUs. In this example, the CG comprises five records directed to two volumes attached to two LCUs. The figure illustrates that the five records have been successfully copied to their corresponding secondary volumes — 10:19, 10:22, and 10:25 written to the first volume of LCU(A'), and 10:09 and 10:12 written to the first volume of LCU(B').

Figure 28-5 concludes the example on update sequence consistency by stepping forward in time and describing how the dependent write updates are copied to the secondary site.

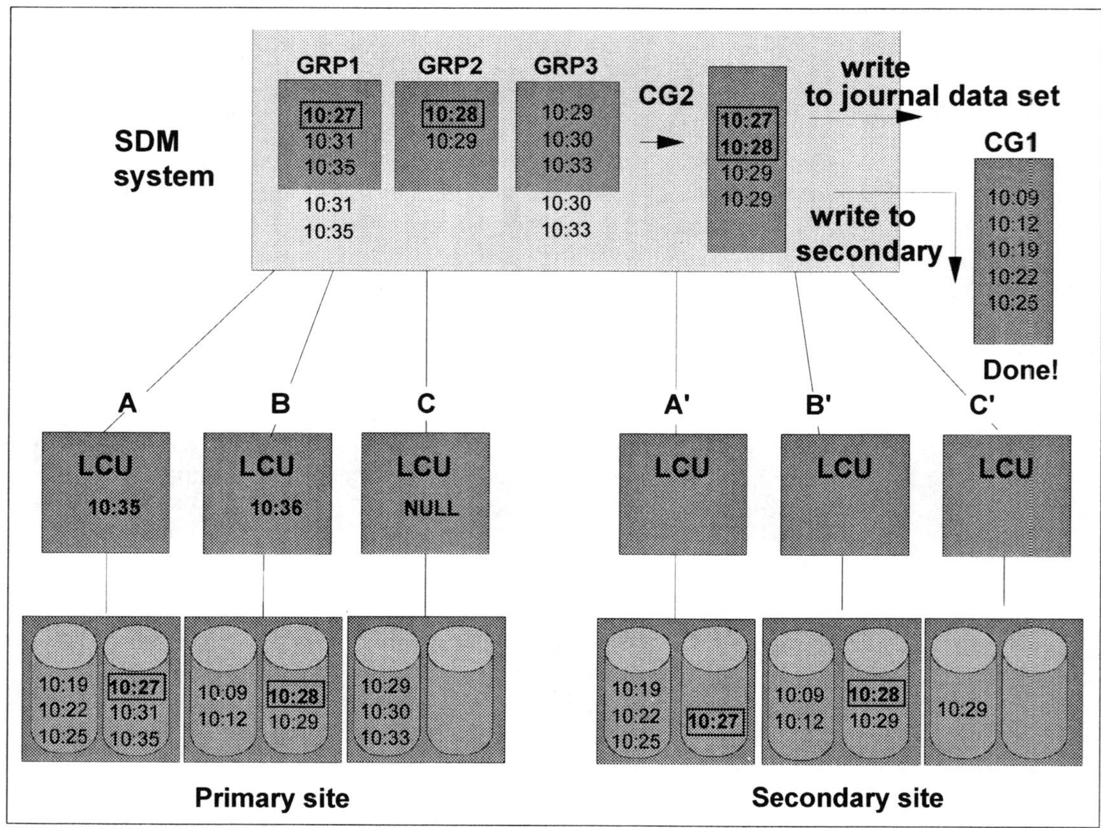

Figure 28-5 Creation of Consistency Group - CG2

The SDM copies data in real time, so it constantly transfers updated records from perhaps multiple LCUs in a z/OS Global Mirror session. In our example, we simulate moving the *clock forward* in time and tracing the steps taken by the SDM in the production of its second CG.

Notice that LCU(A) and LCU(B) at the primary site now have different times indicating when the SDM reads the updated records. We proceed as before:

- The SDM reads from LCU(A) at 10:35:

  At 10:35, the SDM reads three records from LCU(A) (10:27, 10:31, and 10:35). Note that the log update (10:27) has now been read. This group of three records has been designated GRP1 in the diagram.

- The SDM reads from LCU(B) at 10:36:

  At 10:36, the SDM reads one record from LCU B (10:29). This record can now keep the database update record (10:28) company in SDM real storage (these two records are in GRP2 in the diagram). Remember that the database update record (10:28) was not included in the previous CG and was kept in real storage by the SDM along with other *residual* records.

- The SDM detects NULL response from LCU(C):

  Finally, the SDM completes its cycle of updated records collection by establishing that the third LCU(C), which also connects volumes in this z/OS Global Mirror session, has *nothing to report*. The NULL response must be sent even if the LCU has no updates, because it indicates that the LCU has not suffered an outage, thus the record groups retrieved to date from other LCUs can be used to build a valid CG.

- The SDM creates CG:

  The SDM creates the second CG using the same algorithm as before. We can see that the two dependent writes (the log update at 10:27 and the database update at 10:28) have been *captured* in this CG.

  Notice that the record group transferred from LCU(B) produced a maximum timestamp, which also turns out to be the smallest of the three GRP maximums. Notice also that this value (10:29) enabled all records written before or at this time to be included in the CG — thus allowing the log update and the database update to accompany each other on the journey to the secondary site when written to the journal data sets.

The diagram shows that when the SDM writes the records to the secondary volumes, the relationship between the contents of the log and the database, which is vital for recovery, has been protected. The record residue (10:31 and 10:35 from GRP1, and 10:30 and 10:33 from GRP3) will be processed during the next SDM record group collection cycle.

28.6 Single command for recovery

One of the most valuable features of z/OS Global Mirror is its ability to do a single command recovery. After a disaster that effects the primary site, the secondary site must be made ready for takeover. This involves getting the secondary volumes to a state where their contents are usable in anticipation of application restart. z/OS Global Mirror has a single command that performs this task, the XRECOVER command.

XRECOVER commits the last available Consistency Groups to the secondary volumes, reports the consistency time for the secondary volumes, and then clips the volume serial number of each secondary device to that of its matching primary device.

z/OS Global Mirror options and configuration considerations

There are various options available to you when you are planning your z/OS Global Mirror system. Some are related to placement of the SDM (at the primary, an intermediate, or the secondary site), others relate to performance and tuning options.

When planning for a successful z/OS Global Mirror implementation, it is also important to consider the hardware and software requirements.

In this chapter we cover some of these options and configuration considerations.

29.1 z/OS Global Mirror operating mode

A z/OS Global Mirror session can operate in one of two modes:

- **XRC:** z/OS Global Mirror is operating in recovery mode, using State, Journal, and Control datasets. Secondary volume consistency is guaranteed. This mode should be used for z/OS Global Mirror sessions intended for use for disaster recovery purposes.
- **Migration:** z/OS Global Mirror will maintain data consistency within the session, but it is not using the Journal or Control datasets and so cannot be used for recovery after a disaster. This mode is mainly intended for data migration or workload movement purposes.

29.2 Utility device usage

The DS8000 can use either fixed or floating utility devices, as described in 28.4, "Utility devices" on page 415. Our recommendation is to use fixed utility devices.

If you are using floating utility devices and there are many primary volumes in a z/OS Global Mirror Storage Control session, there should be a good chance for DS8000 to find volumes with low utilization to use as a utility device.

Normally, there will be a relation between the number of z/OS Global Mirror primary volumes and the amount of data to be offloaded by the SDM. Consequently, there will be a relation between the number of primary volumes in a DS8000 LCU and the number of utility devices to be used.

If you are running performance monitors like RMF on the SDM system, you could check the device utilization of the primary volumes during peak offloading periods.

29.3 XADDPAIR processing

The XADDPAIR command will, unless you specify the NOCOPY parameter, instruct SDM to make the initial copy of the primary volumes to the secondary volumes. XADDPAIR is also used to resynchronize suspended volumes.

z/OS Global Mirror allows updates to the primary volumes during this synchronization or resynchronization process, and copies the updates to the secondary volumes.

> **Note:** You can use the QUICKCOPY option on the XADDPAIR command to copy only allocated tracks from the primary volume to the secondary. However, as a reserve is issued against the primary volume during initial processing, this option should not be used in a channel extender environment, as if the links fail, the reserve may not be released, thus impacting the applications.

Here are some comments on XADDPAIR elapsed times:

- Concurrent active applications will elongate the elapsed time for XADDPAIR operation.
- Concurrent active applications can be negatively impacted (residual counts can grow as well as response times) by the XADDPAIR operation.

The SDM does monitor the update and XADDPAIR activity, and attempts to throttle the XADDPAIR activity such that the update activity is minimally impacted. Even though this control is present, it is important to monitor the system activity during XADDPAIR times, and reducing the SCSYNCH and SYNCH parameters may be required. See Chapter 31., "z/OS Global Mirror performance and scalability" on page 457.

29.4 Write Pacing and Device Blocking

Write Pacing is a recent enhancement to z/OS Global Mirror. It works by injecting a small delay as each z/OS Global Mirror record set is created in cache for a given volume. As the device residual count increases, so does the magnitude of the pacing, eventually reaching a maximum value at a target residual count. Both this maximum value, and the target residual count at which it is effective, can be specified for each volume through z/OS Global Mirror commands. This provides a greater level of flexibility than Device Blocking, whose threshold could only be specified at a session level. The device also remains ready to process I/O requests, allowing application read activity to continue while the device is being paced.

Device Blocking is the mechanism previously used to allow z/OS Global Mirror to catch up to application I/O if it is having difficulty keeping pace with the volume of writes. Device Blocking allows pacing of application writes to occur for brief intervals, and only on the specific volumes that have accumulated a large number of updates in cache. The z/OS Global Mirror PARMLIB is used to set the level of updates that trigger pacing.

For more information on how to specify values for Write Pacing or Device Blocking, refer to *z/OS DFSMS Advanced Copy Services*, SC35-0428.

29.5 Database recovery with z/OS Global Mirror

The recovery of data is probably the most complex and vital component of a disaster recovery plan. The most crucial aspect of recovering databases is to ensure consistency of the recovered data. With z/OS Global Mirror, data consistency can be guaranteed to an identified point-in-time across all volumes in the z/OS Global Mirror session. This is done by the creation of a Consistency Group, and this is independent of applications and databases.

29.5.1 Today's backup recovery process

To achieve database consistency today, the backup and recovery steps may be similar to these:

1. Back up the database according to business needs. Different backup philosophies can be implemented, such as periodic backup from a time when all files are:
   - Closed with no forward recovery
   - Closed with forward recovery
   - Open with forward recovery
2. Ship to the secondary site:

   Periodically ship image copies to the recovery site.
3. Transfer log data sets:

   Use communication lines or manual transport to transfer the log after the log data set has been closed.

The recovery process includes the following activities:

1. Restore the latest image copies:

   If the latest image copies are not available, the recovery process will take longer because of additional forward recovery tasks.

2. Forward recovery with logs:

   Restore the databases to a known point-in-time. Apply the log data to make the database as current as possible.

3. Take image copies:

   Take image copies of the recovered database to have a consistent restart point.

4. Reprocess orphan data:

   Orphan data can consist of non-transferable log data and/or transferable log data sets at the primary site, and log data sets that have not yet arrived at the secondary site.

5. Check consistency of databases:

   Before you restart the applications, we highly recommend that you check the consistency of the databases.

29.5.2 Backup recovery process with z/OS Global Mirror

Your normal operational requirements will already include procedures for restarting online applications in case of a short term outage (a power failure or CEC failure for instance).

For z/OS Global Mirror disaster recovery, the same procedure should be used at the secondary site. The same checks for guaranteeing data consistency and restarting your applications must be done at your secondary site, just as they are done today at your application site.

z/OS Global Mirror provides data currency across all volumes in the z/OS Global Mirror session. In the event of a disaster at the primary site, updates in flight are lost. Nevertheless, recovery can be achieved to an identified consistent point-in-time. The recovery technique does not require database restore followed by forward recovery. Recovery can follow the procedure used at the primary site for a system outage, consistent to the point-in-time given. Any transaction that has been completed after this point-in-time might require investigation and be recreated against the secondary disks after recovery (using XRECOVER) or accounted for in your business process.

29.6 z/OS Global Mirror requirements

This section provides references about the software and hardware requirements when using z/OS Global Mirror with the DS8000.

29.6.1 Hardware requirements

z/OS Global Mirror hardware requirements are as follows:

- zSeries hardware must be used.
- For the primary DS8000s, the z/OS Global Mirror optional feature must be enabled.
- Primary systems must have a common time reference. z/OS Global Mirror uses timestamped record information to ensure that updates are not copied out of sequence at the secondary site:

- In environments where the primary systems are on different CECs, an IBM Sysplex Timer is required.
- When you have only one primary system, or the primary systems are running on different LPARs on the same CEC, the system time-of-day clock is used.

- A compatible secondary volume must be available for each primary volume you want to copy. The secondary volume must have the identical track capacity and number of tracks per cylinder as the primary volume. The capacity of the secondary volume can be the same or larger than that of the primary volume.

29.6.2 Software requirements

The data mover function requires current OS/390 and z/OS releases with the latest maintenance applied. For the latest maintenance information, refer to the Web site:

```
http://www.storage.ibm.com/software/sms/sdm/index.html
```

Then click the **Technical Updates** link.

29.6.3 VM considerations

When z/OS Global Mirror manages volumes that are also attached to a VM system, you can define z/OS Global Mirror volumes to VM either as unsupported disks or as minidisks.

Note that for a disk device that is defined as unsupported under VM, the SET PATH GROUP command is unable to reestablish the path group once a path has been removed.

The data mover can run either on a separate z/OS LPAR, or on a z/OS guest running on the same or different VM system. If a z/OS guest system is used, the volumes must be defined as unsupported to the host VM system.

If applications run on a native VM system, writes will not be timestamped. z/OS and Linux operating systems do timestamp writes, even when run as guests under VM.

29.7 Initial z/OS Global Mirror planning

Before you do further planning, you have to decide which volumes are going to be included in the z/OS Global Mirror solution, because this will determine the sizing of your z/OS Global Mirror resources. You also have to evaluate your data consistency requirements. This section discusses the considerations when addressing these two topics for the initial planning for z/OS Global Mirror.

29.7.1 Selecting volumes for remote copy

In this section, we discuss some considerations regarding which volumes to include in the remote copy solution.

Volume level copying

z/OS Global Mirror copies the entire contents of a volume. As a result, all data sets on a primary volume are copied to the secondary volume. This support is for all data types, independent of the applications.

29.7.2 What data should be copied?

Before you start up your z/OS Global Mirror environment, you have to identify the data you will want to mirror onto the secondary site. This may differ depending on whether you use z/OS Global Mirror for data or workload migration, or for a disaster recovery solution.

In the remainder of this section, we are assuming that z/OS Global Mirror is used for Disaster Recovery.

You should identify the type of data required for a successful recovery. Many installations with an existing secondary site may have completed this task already.

The SYSRES, Master catalog, SPOOL volumes, as well as other data sets required to initialize the secondary system (including those used to start up JES, TSO, and RACF®) can be copied by z/OS Global Mirror. The idea is that even if we do not need the data on some of these volumes, we do need either the data sets correctly allocated and the space formatted (pages, spool, SMF man data sets) available for the production jobs to use (temporary storage groups). Some of these volumes can be initially synchronized and then suspended, so z/OS Global Mirror stops copying their updates.

However, the focus for remote copy is on your application data sets that are updated regularly, and are essential for your company. If a disaster occurs, critical application volumes must be made available to your primary application as quickly as possible, depending on the speed of recovery required. z/OS Global Mirror offers a single command recovery strategy, which makes it the fastest method for recovering data at the secondary site. A single XRECOVER command recovers all the volumes in a z/OS Global Mirror session at once, and all of the volumes are consistent to a single point-in-time.

29.7.3 Application volumes

Different applications at the primary site may have different priorities. Some of these applications may not warrant the investment required for remote copy. If only a subset of applications is to be copied, the volumes belonging to those applications must be identified and included in the z/OS Global Mirror configuration. Even if all applications are required at the recovery site, there still may be volumes that need not be copied.

Because applications deal with data sets and not volumes, multi-volume data sets require special attention. Multi-volume data set types include data sets that reside on multiple volumes, striped data sets, and VSAM spheres. If you want a copy of a multi-volumes data set at the secondary location, you therefore have to copy all volumes on which this data set resides.

29.7.4 System volumes

The data sets described in the following sections should be given special consideration, as they might be eliminated from a particular installation's z/OS Global Mirror configuration.

Page

Page data sets are of no use during recovery at the recovery site. They are owned by the host application site. However, if we do not have the page data sets, then we will not be able to IPL the production system at the recovery site until we create and catalog new ones. What can be done is to initially synchronize and then suspend the page data sets. You do not want to have the page data sets in duplex due to the type of I/O that they use.

Spool

The spool data sets should be copied to the recovery site if they are necessary for recovery. Copying the spool increases the amount of copy activity to the secondary. If the contents of the spool are easily re-created, consider excluding spool volumes from the z/OS Global Mirror configuration. Alternatively, you can initially synchronize the spool volumes and then suspend them as with the page data sets.

Temporary data sets

Volumes containing temporary data sets (that is, those that exist for the duration of a job or step) can be re-created at the secondary by resubmitting jobs. These volumes should be excluded.

SYSRES volume

The change activity against data sets residing on the SYSRES often does not affect the applications. However, some installations share the SYSRES volume with active data, so the decision on whether to copy the SYSRES volume can depend on the data stored there. Because z/OS Global Mirror copies data at the volume level, all data residing on that volume is copied.

If the SYSRES volume is not copied by z/OS Global Mirror operations, another method must be used to ensure that a copy is available at the secondary site. Nevertheless, commonly the SYSRES as well as other system volumes will be copied.

Master catalog and user catalogs

Catalog changes are limited, but they are essential for recovery, and therefore they must be considered for z/OS Global Mirror copying.

Program libraries

All program libraries that contain modules for z/OS Global Mirror applications are essential for recovery and should be considered for z/OS Global Mirror copying.

Control data sets

Control data sets, such as RACF, SMS, HSM, and RMM are essential for recovery and should be considered for z/OS Global Mirror copying.

HSM migration level 1 volumes

Consider whether migrated data is required at the secondary site. If not, exclude HSM migration level 1 volumes. If migrated data is required but is not critical, these volumes could be copied daily by other means to reduce the amount of copying z/OS Global Mirror has to do as migrations and recalls occur.

29.7.5 The ERRORLEVEL parameter

As part of the planning process, you should evaluate your data consistency requirements in the event of a failure. To specify how z/OS Global Mirror should process certain error conditions, use one of the following ERRORLEVEL subparameters:

- `VOLUME`
- `SESSION`
- `group_name`

You specify the default error level for the entire session with the ERRORLEVEL parameter on the XSTART command, but you can change the error level for specific volume pairs with the XADDPAIR ERRORLEVEL parameter.

- The VOLUME option suspends a z/OS Global Mirror volume pair that encounters a device error.
  z/OS Global Mirror continues to process all other volumes in the session. You must correct the error condition and then resynchronize the volume so it is consistent with the other volumes in the session.

  If a volume that is suspended due to an error contains data that is dependent on data on other volumes, data consistency cannot be assured in the event of a disaster. In those cases you should use group_name or SESSION (see below) as the error level specification.

- The SESSION option suspends all volume pairs in a z/OS Global Mirror session. You must correct the error and resynchronize all the suspended pairs.

  If a volume with error level SESSION encounters an error, all volumes in the z/OS Global Mirror session will be suspended. If a failure occurs on a single LCU, and that LCU attaches to any duplex volume pair with error level SESSION specified, then all volume pairs in the z/OS Global Mirror session are put into the suspended state.

  z/OS Global Mirror also suspends volume pairs that are in pending state, and the pairs remain where they are in the synchronization process.

- The group_name option allows you to associate any valid TSO name with one or more volume pairs. If a volume with error level group_name encounters an error, z/OS Global Mirror will suspend all volume pairs which have the same group name specified.

  An error that occurs on a single LCU that attaches to any duplex volume pair that has group_name specified causes z/OS Global Mirror to suspend all volume pairs with the same group name specified.

  Use group_name to associate volumes belonging to an application to ensure consistency in the application.

Table 29-1 summarizes what we have discussed so far on how ERRORLEVEL options determine volume pair suspension in the event of different types of failures.

Table 29-1 ERRORLEVEL and suspension of volume pairs

ERRORLEVEL options	Single volume failures	Primary LCU failures	SDM failures
VOLUME	One duplex volume pair is suspended.	All active volumes on the LCU are suspended.	All duplex volume pairs in the z/OS Global Mirror session are suspended.
SESSION	All duplex volume pairs in the session are suspended.	All active volumes in the session are suspended.	All duplex volume pairs in the z/OS Global Mirror session are suspended.
group name	All duplex volume pairs in the group are suspended.	All active volumes on the LCU are suspended, and all active volumes in this group on any LCU are suspended.	All duplex volume pairs in the z/OS Global Mirror session are suspended.

29.8 Capacity and performance

Planning the resources required in a z/OS Global Mirror environment is essential for a successful z/OS Global Mirror implementation. A smooth data flow is crucial, and in this section we provide some guidance in the capacity and performance planning process.

29.8.1 SDM requirements

The SDM manages the z/OS Global Mirror activity for all volume pairs in a z/OS Global Mirror session.

Volumes

Up to five z/OS Global Mirror sessions are allowed in each z/OS (or OS/390) system image. If you have more then 1500 to 1800 volumes in a single z/OS Global Mirror session, you may need to split these into two or more z/OS Global Mirror sessions. In addition to the workload balancing split, also note that unless you use CXRC there is no write sequence consistency between z/OS Global Mirror sessions, so you must consider splitting the volumes between z/OS Global Mirror sessions on an application basis also.

Virtual storage

z/OS Global Mirror operates in up to six address spaces on a single LPAR. ANTAS000 is always active and processes z/OS Global Mirror commands. Up to five z/OS Global Mirror sessions may be started at a time. Each z/OS Global Mirror session that is started on a system occupies its own address space, ANTAS001 through ANTAS005.

The ANTAS000 address space uses 65 MB of virtual storage, which includes a 20 MB trace data space. An ANTASnnn (started when the XSTART command is issued) has the following virtual storage requirements:

- Approximately 20 MB is needed for base code.
- Approximately 30 MB is needed for trace data spaces.
- Volume initialization requires 360 KB for each concurrent volume initialization task.
- About 35 MB for each active z/OS Global Mirror storage control session, up to a maximum of 1.7 GB. The SDM uses this space for buffers to hold data read from the primary LCU. These data buffers are required from the time when the data is first read from the DS8000 cache, through the Consistency Group formation process, the journaling process, and the writes to the cache and NVS of the secondary subsystem.

z/OS Global Mirror needs a minimal amount of space (0.2 KB) in the extended common service area (ECSA). All other storage used is within the z/OS Global Mirror address spaces.

Real storage

The main real storage requirements for SDM will be for storage buffers used during I/O operations. Those pages will be fixed for the duration of the input or output operation.

The actual real storage required at a given point depends on how much concurrent activity is occurring. You should provide enough real storage on the SDM system to support the projected peak I/O load.

For example, as SDM requires up to 35 MB data buffers from the time the data is read from the DS8000 cache until the data is written to the secondary volumes, you should plan for a real storage requirement equal to 35 MB times the number of z/OS Global Mirror storage control sessions. Part or all of this can be permanently fixed real storage, using the PAGEFIX parameter of the XSET command. All storage beyond the PAGEFIX limit is fixed and freed as required. Specifying a high PAGEFIX value will reduce the MIPS required for fixing and freeing pages for those data buffers.

Tip: It is highly recommended that all storage used by the SDM be pagefixed.

Paging space

The SDM requires paging space to support the address spaces, and you should plan for up to 2 GB for this space, depending on your virtual storage requirements (see "Virtual storage" on page 431). We recommend that you use expanded storage for paging.

Processor (MIPS) requirements

The processor consumption is usually expressed as the number of MIPS required per 100 writes/sec to primary volumes from primary systems (z/OS Global Mirror writes).

This number varies mainly depending on the blocksize and the write I/O rate. With a larger blocksize, the SDM has to move more data, and consequently uses more resources. At a high I/O rate, SDM tends to be more efficient than at a low write rate. There may be some increase in the MIPS requirement when using channel extenders.

SMS

If the journal data sets are striped (which we recommend), they must be on SMS managed volumes. The state data set is a PDSE. Journal data set allocation is discussed in the manual *z/OS DFSMS Advanced Copy Services*, SC35-0428.

29.8.2 Primary DS8000

You have to assess the capacity of the primary DS8000. In addition to reads and writes issued from the primary systems, the DS8000 must also be able to handle the reads associated with the SDM offloading process. The data written to primary volumes by primary systems will be grouped into record sets in cache, and those record sets will be offloaded by the SDM system with the read record set channel command.

The cache requirement should also be evaluated. If there is no separate copy in the cache of the data to be offloaded, the DS8000 merely builds a logical queue using a directory structure.

When the SDM operation is balanced (meaning that the SDM does not get delayed when retrieving data from the primary DS8000s and committing those updates to the journal data sets and secondary volumes) the primary DS8000 needs little more cache than what is normally required to satisfy primary application performance requirements.

As long as the SDM manages to retrieve the updates before the DS8000 caching algorithms would have removed them out of cache, minimal additional cache is required.

However, if the primary systems write rate is (temporarily) more than the SDM can absorb, or if there is a (temporary) disruption in the SDM data flow, the cache will be used as a buffer (see 29.15, "Unplanned outage support" on page 439).

Our recommendation is that you evaluate the cache size required to satisfy your primary application needs, and then plan for z/OS Global Mirror buffers. This may mean you should install more cache (if possible), or increase your cache-to-backstore ratio by spreading the volumes across multiple DS8000s. Your IBM Field Technical Sales Specialist can help you determine the cache needed for z/OS Global Mirror by running the Disk Magic modeling tool.

29.8.3 Secondary storage subsystem

The secondary storage subsystem can be any subsystem supported by the SDM system, as long as it provides volumes with the same track capacity, the same number of tracks per cylinder, and at least the same capacity as its corresponding primary volume.

If a secondary volume has more capacity than a primary volume, it has to be carefully considered if a copy-back procedure is implemented. This is because z/OS Global Mirror cannot copy from a large primary volume to a smaller secondary volume. If a disaster recovery has been invoked and you are operating off the secondary volume, you would need to ensure the volume did not expand to use cylinders beyond the capacity of the primary volume. The easiest solution is to have primary and secondary volumes of the same size.

The secondary site needs the same number of z/OS Global Mirror volumes as the primary site. Although there is no requirement to use DS8000s as secondary storage subsystems, doing so will give you all the benefits of DS8000's performance characteristics. In addition, it also makes it possible to use z/OS Global Mirror in a copy-back implementation. With DS8000s at the secondary, you can also combine z/OS Global Mirror and FlashCopy functions as described in 32.6, "Using z/OS Global Mirror with FlashCopy and tertiary volumes" on page 475.

Ideally, the number of LCUs at the secondary site should match the number of LCUs at the primary site, in order to provide configuration symmetry.

The secondary site storage controls must be configured to handle all of the primary volume writes plus the I/Os to the Journal, Control and State data sets as a minimum. In addition they must also be capable of supporting the I/O activity related to the primary application's requirements in a disaster recovery situation.

29.8.4 SDM to primary site bandwidth

One of the key elements in the sizing of a z/OS Global Mirror configuration is to determine the required bandwidth between the SDM and the primary DS8000s.

You could use ESCON or FICON channels to connect the sites if the distance allows it; otherwise, you have to use channel extenders and telecommunication lines.

Regardless of connection technology used, you have to analyze the workload to determine the peak requirements. The peak period should cover a short duration, so that lower workload levels do not lower the average peak workload. Typically, you should analyze online requirements during the 5 minutes peak period, and batch requirements during the 15 minutes peak. Taking this approach, you can still benefit from the dynamic workload balancing function in z/OS Global Mirror, without really compromising application throughput or response time.

The challenge can be to find the peak intervals, because the period with the highest write activity is not necessarily the period with the highest bandwidth requirement. Typically, the write activity during daytime processing can be high, but this processing uses short write blocksizes. The required bandwidth can therefore be higher during batch processing, even if the write rate is lower, because of the larger blocksizes.

You could use report generator products to identify peaks of write I/Os and data transfer based on information in SMF record type 74. Subtype 1 (device activity) contains information about I/O rates and connect times, and subtype 5 (cache activity) contains information about the number of reads and number of writes per device. Make sure that the known peak days, like the end of month processing, are included in the analysis.

29.9 SDM placement

See Figure 29-1 for an overview of SDM placement in regard to the connections involved.

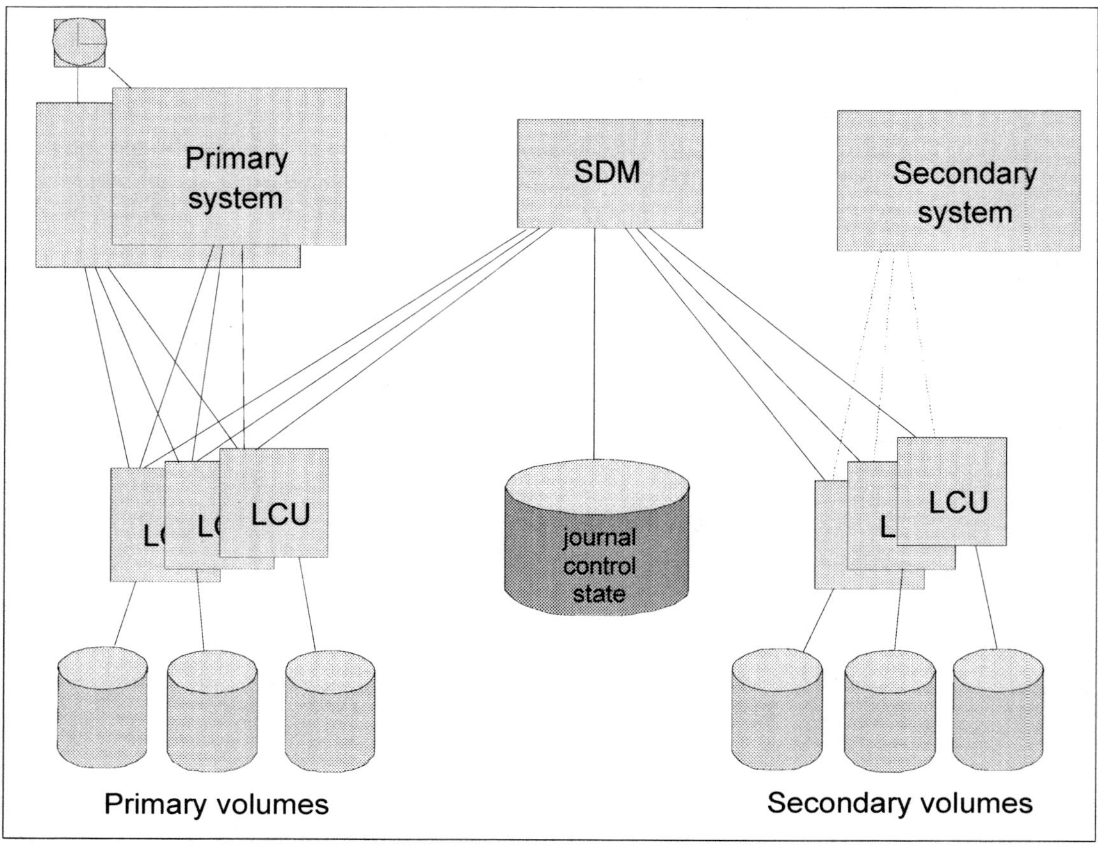

Figure 29-1 z/OS Global Mirror connections

The SDM can be located at the secondary site, the primary site, or an independent site. Figure 29-1 illustrates the connections required between the components involved in a z/OS Global Mirror solution, *independent* of where the SDM is located.

Connectivity requirements may differ between normal z/OS Global Mirror operation and recovery operation.

29.9.1 Normal operation

The connectivity requirements while in normal operation are as follows:

- **Primary systems:** The primary z/OS systems reside on single or multiple CECs, in one or more LPARs, and need only connectivity to primary volumes.

  If the primary systems are running on different CECs, they also need connection to a Sysplex timer.
- **Secondary system:** The secondary system does not need to be connected to any other z/OS Global Mirror components during normal operation.
- **SDM:** The SDM needs to be connected to all primary volumes, to all secondary volumes and to the Journal, Control, and State data sets. The Journal, Control, and State data sets will generally reside at the secondary site.

29.9.2 Recovery operation

During the recovery operation, that is, when executing the XRECOVER command, the SDM only needs access to the secondary volumes and the Journal, Control, and State data sets. Primary volumes, if connected, should be varied offline.

After the recovery operation has finished, the secondary system needs connection to the secondary volumes.

29.10 SDM at a secondary site

Connectivity requirements when SDM is located at a secondary site are shown in Figure 29-2. The SDM and the secondary system could run in separate CECs, in separate LPARs on the same CEC, or in the same z/OS image.

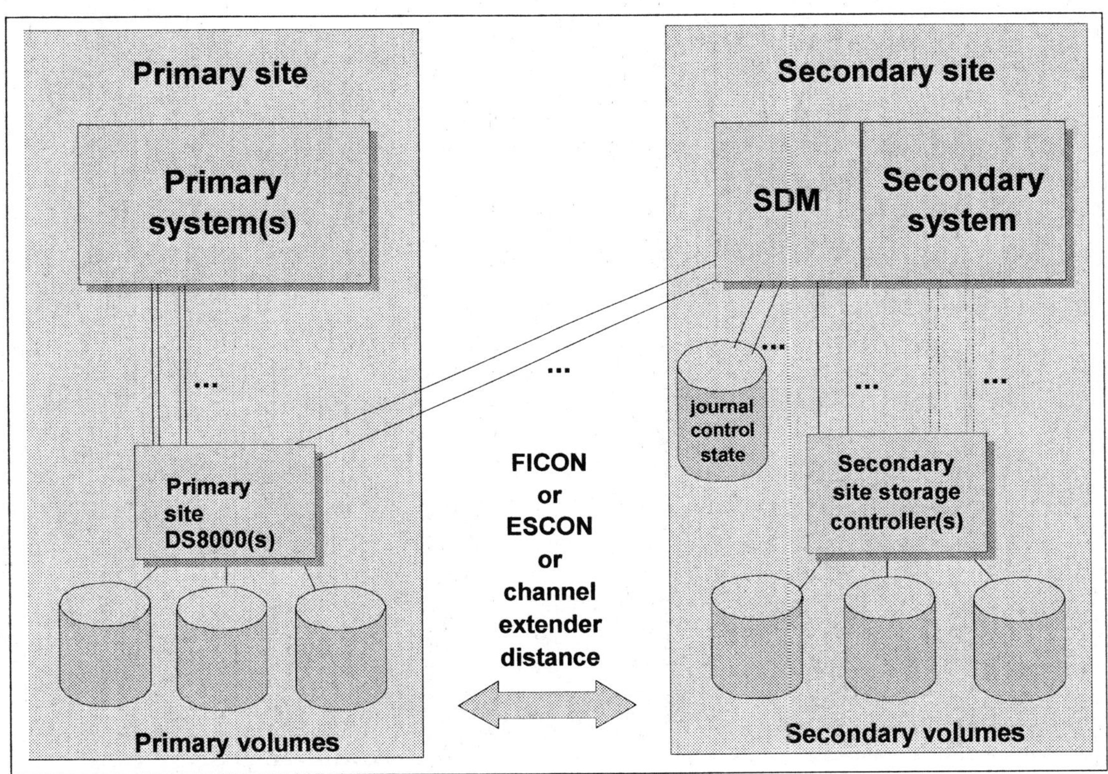

Figure 29-2 SDM at secondary site

The advantages we see when locating the SDM at a secondary site are as follows:

- Data availability:

  Updated records will undergo three transfers during z/OS Global Mirror copying. First, the records are read from the primary site DS8000 cache and stored in SDM processor storage. Second, they are written from SDM processor storage to the journal data sets. Third, they are written from SDM processor storage to the secondary volumes. The data is considered safe from a primary site outage when it has been journaled at the secondary site.

However, if the SDM is located at the secondary site, data that has been read from the primary site DS8000 cache and stored in SDM buffers is not lost if the primary site subsequently suffers an outage. Although the data has not been hardened on disk, a copy of it still exists in SDM storage, and thus can be journaled from there. If the primary site suffers an outage, only the records that were updated in DS8000 cache and not read into SDM storage would be lost.

- Performance:

  The primary site DS8000 and SDM use special communications to transfer data so that multiple records can be read from the DS8000 to SDM in a single transfer command. However, when writing data to the secondary volumes, normal write chains are used, and this could result in multiple I/Os to multiple volumes.

  It is much more efficient to perform a single data transfer over an extended distance followed by multiple data transfers over shorter distances than it is to perform a single data transfer over a shorter distance followed by multiple data transfers over an extended distance. Thus, performance will be improved if SDM is located at the secondary site because the DS8000 and SDM special communications eliminate multiple writes over extended distances.

29.11 SDM at an independent site

SDM can run at a site that is independent of both primary and secondary sites. Locating SDM at an independent site can extend the maximum distance between the primary and recovery sites. This configuration is shown in Figure 29-3.

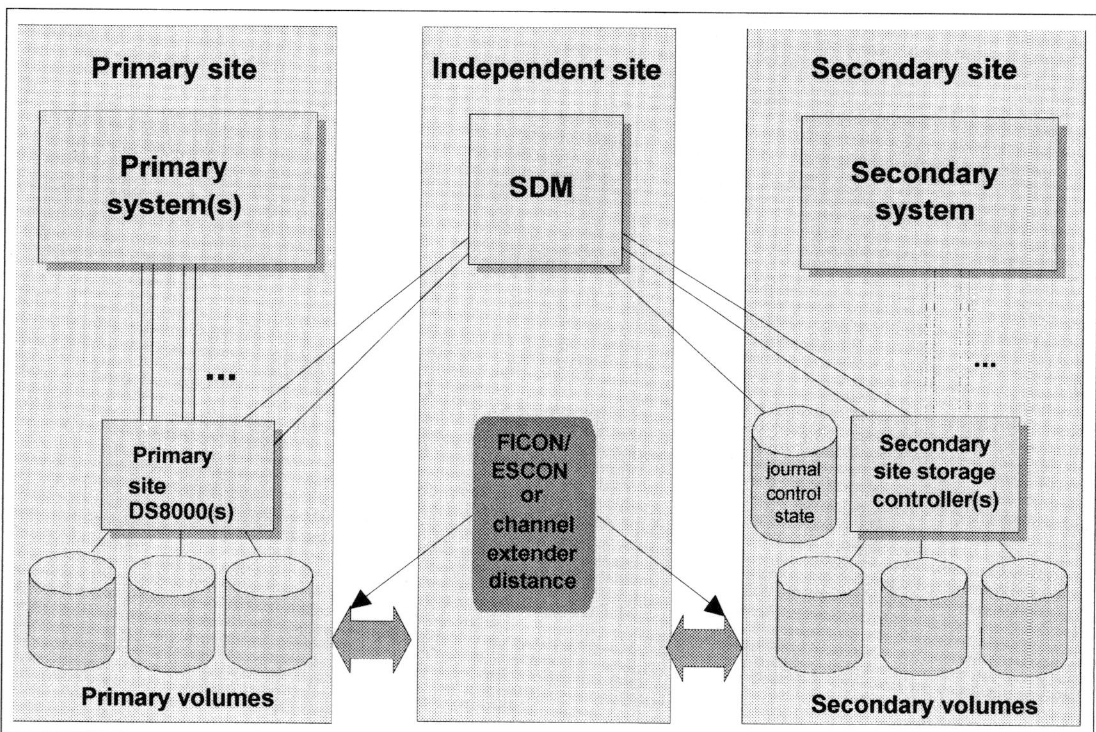

Figure 29-3 SDM at an independent site

The following considerations apply when the SDM is located at an independent site:

- Data availability:

  When SDM is physically remote from the application site, records read into SDM storage buffers are not lost if the primary site suffers an outage.

- Performance:

  In this case we may assume that SDM has the dedicated use of processor resources. Thus SDM tasks will always execute with priority, the maximum number of real storage buffers can be defined for SDM operations, and SDM can optimize channel path selection both for reading from the primary site and writing to the secondary site, because there is no contention for channel resource.

  However, an extended distance between the independent site and the secondary site will impact performance for journaling and copying to secondary volumes.

29.12 SDM at the primary site

The SDM can run in the same z/OS image as the primary system or in a separate image. The separate image could be in a different LPAR on the same CEC, or on a different CEC.

During a recovery operation, a SDM must be established at the secondary site. This SDM must connect to Journal, Control, and State data sets, and to all z/OS Global Mirror participating secondary volumes in order to do z/OS Global Mirror recovery processing.

Connectivity requirements when SDM is located at the primary site are shown in Figure 29-4.

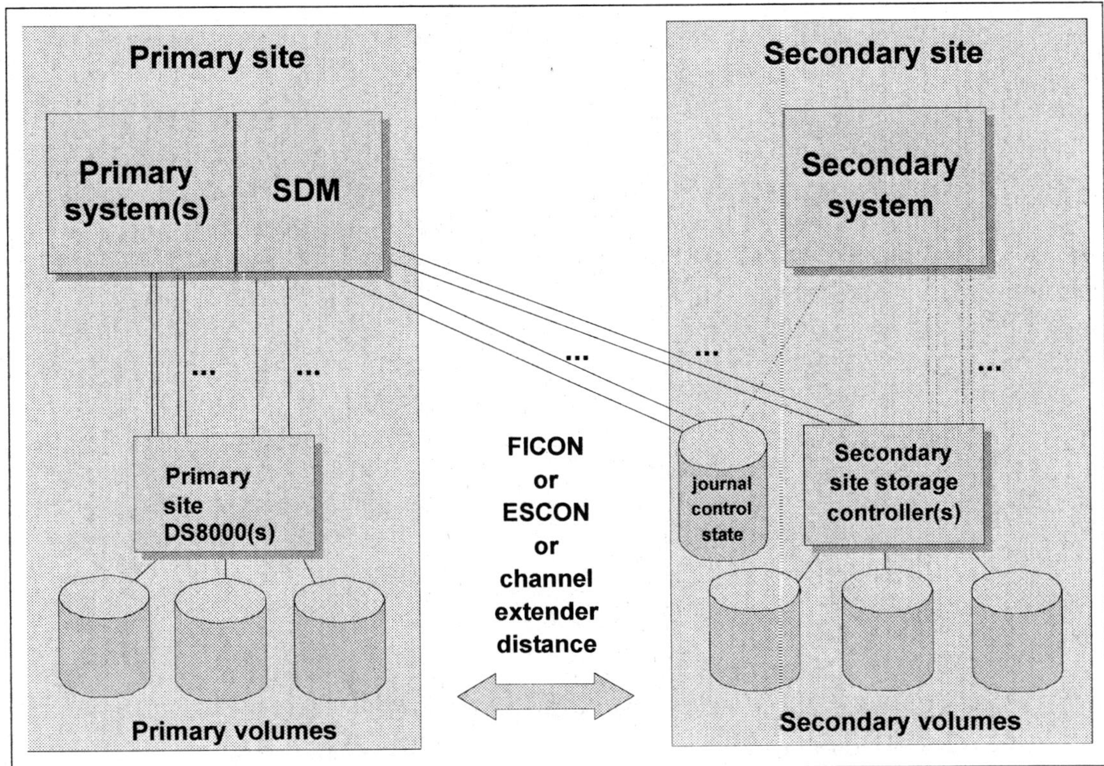

Figure 29-4 SDM at primary site

The following considerations apply when the SDM is located at the primary site:

- Data availability:

  When the SDM is located at the primary site, updated records read from the primary site DS8000 are not safe until written to the Journal data set at the remote site location. Thus, if the primary site suffers a disaster, record updates in the DS8000 cache and in SDM storage will be lost.

- Performance:

  The updates read from the primary site DS8000 will use the special protocol defined for DS8000 and SDM data transfer, but the journaling and copying to the secondary volumes will incur delays associated with writing over extended distances. And in this case, the updated records have to be transmitted between the primary and secondary sites twice: once to the Journal data sets and another time to the secondary volumes.

- Other considerations:

  To enable recovery, SDM must have access to the Journal, State, and Control data sets as well as the secondary volumes. If the SDM is located at the primary site, which has been rendered inoperative because of the disaster, a second SDM must be started at the recovery site. This is to allow the XRECOVER command to apply any outstanding journal updates to the secondary volumes, and to change the volsers of those volumes.

There may be reasons why you choose to configure the SDM at the application site, but the above points should be considered.

29.13 Concurrent Copy sessions

Concurrent Copy (CC) also uses a data mover when creating a point-in-time copy. This data mover runs in an address space, ANTMAIN, which is automatically started at IPL. Whenever we use the term system data mover or SDM in this chapter, we are referring to z/OS Global Mirrors SDM. Concurrent Copy is discussed inAppendix B., “Concurrent Copy” on page 631.

The CC data mover communicates with a *CC storage control session* in the DS8000 LCU, so in fact we can have two types of storage control sessions in the DS8000 LCU: *z/OS Global Mirror storage control sessions* and *CC storage control sessions*. When we refer to a storage control session in this chapter, we are referring to z/OS Global Mirror storage control sessions.

29.14 Planned outage support

As the DS8000 provides z/OS Global Mirror *hardware bit map* support, suspension of a z/OS Global Mirror session has no primary system impact since the DS8000 maintains a *hardware bit map* of updates, thus not consuming cache resources while sessions are suspended.

29.14.1 Suspending a z/OS Global Mirror session

The SDM supports two types of suspension. One is an XSUSPEND VOLUME(ALL) suspension. With this, the SDM address space is not terminated. The ANTASnnn address space continues to run and with primary disk subsystems not supporting hardware bit maps the SDM continues to read updates. With the DS8000 as the primary disk subsystem the hardware bit map is used to track updated tracks. No updates are applied to the journals or secondary volumes.

The second type of suspension is a *session suspension*. This is accomplished by using the XSUSPEND TIMEOUT command. This command is issued when you want to terminate the SDM for a planned activity such as a maintenance update, or moving the SDM to a different site or a different LPAR.

The XSUSPEND TIMEOUT command will end the ANTASnnn address space and inform the involved LCUs that the z/OS Global Mirror session is suspended. The DS8000 will then use the hardware bit map to record changed tracks, and will free the write updates from the cache.

When the z/OS Global Mirror session is restarted with the XSTART command and volumes are added back to the session with the XADDPAIR command, the hardware bit map maintained by the DS8000 while the session was suspended will be used to resynchronize the volumes, and thus full volume resynchronization is avoided.

29.14.2 Suspending volumes

The XSUSPEND VOLUME command will accept a list of volumes (up to 100 volume pairs can be specified) or ALL (meaning all volumes in the session). If ALL is specified, z/OS Global Mirror will suspend all volumes in the z/OS Global Mirror session at the same consistency time. If a volume list is specified, then z/OS Global Mirror will suspend all the volumes in the list at the same consistency time. If it is necessary to suspend more than 100 pairs, but not all the volumes in the session, then multiple XSUSPEND VOLUME(volser,volser,...) ATTIME() commands with the same ATTIME will cause the volumes to suspend with the same consistency time. Be sure to pick an ATTIME far enough in the future to allow all commands to be processed.

When volumes are suspended with the XSUSPEND VOLUME command, the ANTASnnn address space remains active; for the suspended volumes, the hardware bit map maintained by the DS8000 will be used later during the resynchronization process.

29.15 Unplanned outage support

The DS8000, with its capability of maintaining hardware bit maps, supports *unplanned outages*. This is the capability of avoiding full resynchronization of volumes after an unexpected failure on one or more of the components in the SDM data path.

When data starts to accumulate in cache, there can be several reasons:

- A temporary write peak from the primary systems
- A temporary lack of resource for the SDM
- An outage in one or more of the components necessary for the SDM data moving process (for example, a failure in channel extender links, or failure of the SDM address space itself)

The dynamic workload balancing algorithm (described in 31.1.3, "Dynamic workload balancing" on page 464) is designed to reduce the effects for situations described in 1 and 2 above, but if this is an outage of a vital SDM component, this mechanism does not help.

When the data in the cache exceeds a predefined level, a time interval starts to decrease. This time interval value is set by the TIMEOUT parameter in the XSET command (not to be confused with the TIMEOUT parameter in the XSUSPEND command!), and can be set individually for each LCU.

The TIMEOUT interval is reset every time the SDM reads from the storage control session. If there is no draining of the cache, the data will continue to accumulate, and will eventually reach a predefined high threshold.

A *long busy* condition will then be presented to the primary systems, and I/Os will be queued in the primary hosts. The duration of the *long busy* condition is the remaining part of the TIMEOUT interval.

When the interval expires, this is what will happen: The Storage Control session is suspended. The hardware bit map will be used to reflect the changed tracks, and the cache resources will be freed. The outage can be of any duration, the primary systems continue to run without any impact from the z/OS Global Mirror environment, and the DS8000 keeps track of the write updates in the hardware bit map. This bit map is used at the later time when the problem is fixed and the volume pairs are eventually added back to the z/OS Global Mirror session with the XADDPAIR command.

29.16 z/OS Global Mirror session and z/OS Global Mirror Storage Control session: Configuration rules

The following configuration rules apply when defining z/OS Global Mirror and z/OS Global Mirror Storage Control sessions:

- A maximum of 64 combined z/OS Global Mirror Storage Control sessions and Concurrent Copy sessions for each primary site DS8000 LCU.
- A maximum of 80 z/OS Global Mirror Storage Control sessions in total (across multiple DS8000 LCUs) for each SDM.

29.17 z/OS Global Mirror testing

In this section we provide a summary of the recommended testing to go through before z/OS Global Mirror is put into production.

29.17.1 Functional testing

This is to test that all z/OS Global Mirror commands execute as expected and with correct return codes.

When performing these tests you should use XQUERY to produce various reports, both to get familiar with the content, but also to verify that the status of volumes, volume pairs and session is as expected.

29.17.2 Operational testing

This is to ensure that all required procedures are in place for operating the z/OS Global Mirror environment. You should test scenarios that may be used in a production environment, like suspending sessions, adding utility devices, changing error recovery levels, suspending and resynchronizing volume pairs, and so on.

Some suggested operational scenarios are documented in the publication *z/OS DFSMS Advanced Copy Services,* SC35-0428.

29.17.3 Error injection testing

You may want to simulate various failure situations to verify that your operating procedures work.

When simulating a disaster, the most likely scenario is that one or more DS8000s, or the links to these, are lost. These potential failure situations are best simulated, for example, through the ESCON director. Individual links may be removed, breaking the connection between the SDM and the primary DS8000s. The recovery scenario can then be tested on the secondary site. A *rolling disaster* may be simulated by breaking the connections between the SDM and the primary DS8000s at different times.

29.17.4 Automation testing

If you follow our automation recommendations, you need to test the automation code to ensure that it operates correctly, generates complete and useful reports, intercepts error messages, and initiates the required actions.

29.17.5 Walk-through

If you are planning to use z/OS Global Mirror for Disaster Recovery or workload migration, you may not have the facilities to test in a *production equivalent* environment. In these cases it can be a useful option to do a walk-through of the critical procedures. This can identify problems such as ownership of responsibilities, and access to critical data. If you rely on manual intervention for *go* or *no-go* on Disaster Recovery, then the process must be clearly documented at both the primary and recovery sites.

29.17.6 Dress rehearsal

The proof of a disaster recovery test is a full-scale dress rehearsal, preferably one that can be initiated without warning. Because z/OS Global Mirror supports SUSPEND/RESUME processing, you can test recovery at a secondary site without disruption to your production environment. Once the test is complete, changes that have been accumulated at the primary site can be propagated to the secondary site, restoring disaster protection.

If it is essential to maintain disaster protection during a disaster recovery test; FlashCopy provides an ideal tool to take a quick backup of data at the secondary site. The disaster test can proceed against the FlashCopy of the secondary devices, while z/OS Global Mirror between the primary and secondary devices is resumed.

Once a disaster recovery plan has been successfully validated by a full-scale test, it is important to make sure that documentation is maintained, and that the test is repeated at regular intervals.

29.17.7 ICKDSF and z/OS Global Mirror volumes

Recent developments in z/OS Global Mirror and ICKDSF have eliminated the need to XDELPAIR z/OS Global Mirror volumes prior to relabeling DASD volumes. These developments allow for concurrent management and operations, as well as increasing z/OS Global Mirror's readiness as a disaster recovery solution.

> **Note:** You must be running on recent ICKDSF and z/OS Global Mirror maintenance to use this feature.

When ICKDSF is used to initialize a volume, the updates will be captured by z/OS Global Mirror and not written to the secondary DASD. z/OS Global Mirror will update its control blocks so that a subsequent recovery will reflect the new volser of the primary volume. The V<volsername> member of the State dataset is not updated until the next time the volume is suspended and XADDPAIR SUSPENDED.

The volser in the z/OS UCB control block is not updated until the next VARY OFFLINE/ONLINE is performed. It is also recommended that an XRC CONFIG be performed to resync GDPS. We no longer have to do an XDELPAIR/XADDPAIR full volume copy, but we do still have some operations to *sync up* z/OS Global Mirror, z/OS, and GDPS.

Here is a procedure to update the VOLSER while z/OS Global Mirror is running:

1. Vary the primary volume offline during ICKDSF operation.
2. ICKDSF to relabel the VOLSER (z/OS Global Mirror control blocks are now correct).
3. Vary primary volume online after ICKDSF operation (UCB is now correct).
4. z/OS Global Mirror SUSPEND VOLUME followed by an immediate z/OS Global Mirror XADDPAIR SUSPENDED to update the State dataset's member name (can be done anytime).
5. *GDPS only*: GDPS CONFIG to update GDPS's policy (again, this can be done anytime).

29.17.8 SMF

For an active z/OS Global Mirror session, SDM writes an SMF record type 42 subtype 11 whenever the SMF time interval expires. This record contains data about the LCUs participating in the z/OS Global Mirror session and z/OS Global Mirror statistics that can be used for further reporting to monitor z/OS Global Mirror activity. See the *z/OS V1R3.0 MVS System Management Facilities (SMF),* SA22-7630 for a complete layout of SMF type 42 records.

30

z/OS Global Mirror interfaces

z/OS Global Mirror can be managed either through the set of z/OS TSO commands, the application programming interface (API), or through the Remote Copy Management Facility (RCMF) offering. In this chapter we consider the z/OS Global Mirror interfaces.

30.1 TSO commands

Like most TSO commands, z/OS Global Mirror commands are deferred requests. The initial message that you receive reports on the validity of the command syntax and that the system has accepted the command for processing. When you specify a userid (MSGROUTEID) in the command, only that ID receives the command processing messages. If this user ID is not logged on, the messages are saved in the TSO BRODCAST data set.

For a more detailed description of the z/OS Global Mirror TSO commands, and the required and optional parameters, see *z/OS DFSMS Advanced Copy Services,* SC35-0428.

30.1.1 Including z/OS Global Mirror TSO commands in procedures

You can include z/OS Global Mirror TSO commands in procedures such as REXX CLISTs. Within the procedure, use the MSGROUTID parameter to specify the TSO user ID to which you want z/OS Global Mirror to send messages.

z/OS Global Mirror routes operational messages to the user ID that issued the command. In order to have these messages appear in the syslog, ensure that the SYS1.PARMLIB CONSOLxx member *permits write to programmer* on the ROUTCODE parameter.

After you issue the XEND, XDELPAIR, and XSUSPEND commands, z/OS Global Mirror prompts you (unless you have specified NOVERIFY) to confirm the requests. If those commands are invoked through a CLIST written in REXX, you should either specify NOVERIFY, or place your response to the prompt in the data stack prior to issuing the command. In a batch environment, you can stack the response.

30.1.2 Issuing z/OS Global Mirror TSO commands

The mode of SDM (see 29.1, "z/OS Global Mirror operating mode" on page 424) determines which commands you can issue. Refer to *z/OS DFSMS Advanced Copy Services*, SC35-0428 for more information on commands available and their syntax.

Table 30-1 lists the z/OS Global Mirror TSO commands and indicates for which sessions you can issue them.

Table 30-1 z/OS Global Mirror TSO commands

TSO command	This command can be issued when z/OS Global Mirror session is:						
	Active	**Inactive**	**Suspended**	**Recovery**	**Coupled Active**	**Coupled Inactive**	**Master**
XADDPAIR	Yes	No	No	No	Yes	No	No
XADVANCE	Yes	Yes	Yes	No	Yes	Yes	No
XCOUPLE ADD	Yes	No	No	No	No	No	No
XCOUPLE DELETE	No	No	No	No	Yes	No	No
XCOUPLE PURGE	No	No	No	No	No	Yes	No
XCOUPLE RELEASE	No	No	No	No	No	No	Yes
XDELPAIR	Yes	No	No	No	Yes	No	No

TSO command	This command can be issued when z/OS Global Mirror session is:						
	Active	**Inactive**	**Suspended**	**Recovery**	**Coupled Active**	**Coupled Inactive**	**Master**
XEND	Yes	No	No	No	Yes (1)	No	Yes (2)
XQUERY	Yes	No	No	Yes	Yes	No	Yes
XQUERY MASTER	No	No	No	No	No	No	Yes
XRECOVER	No	Yes	Yes	Yes	No	Yes	No
XSET	Yes	No	No	No	Yes	No	No
XSTART	No	Yes	Yes	No	No	Yes	No
XSUSPEND (Volume)	Yes	No	No	No	Yes	No	Yes (2)
XSUSPEND (Session)	Yes	No	No	No	Yes (1)	No	Yes (2)

Notes:
1. You may issue the XEND and the XSUSPEND commands to a coupled, active session after all volumes have been suspended (AVS) or there are no volumes in the session (NOV).
2. The XEND, XSUSPEND (VOLUME) and XSUSPEND (SESSION) commands issued to a Master session will cause the specified command to be coordinated on the member coupled sessions.

30.2 XSTART command

The XSTART command (Example 30-1) starts a z/OS Global Mirror session by creating the ANTASnnn address space. Volume pairs can now be established. The XSTART command also assigns a name to the session.

The XSTART command is also used to restart a suspended session. When the suspended session becomes active, the suspended volumes are not automatically resynchronized. You have to use the XADDPAIR command to resynchronize the volume pairs within the session. The XSTART command also validates and opens the state, control, and journal data sets with names that match the session ID when you specify SESSIONTYPE(XRC). When SESSIONTYPE(MIGRATE) is specified, the control and journal data sets are not required.

Example 30-1 shows a sample XSTART command, where a z/OS Global Mirror session is started with the name SBSESS.

Example 30-1 XSTART command

```
XSTART SBSESS SESSIONTYPE(XRC) ERRORLEVEL(SESSION)
```

The SESSIONTYPE parameter can either be XRC or MIGRATE:

- XRC specifies that z/OS Global Mirror operate in recovery mode. In this mode z/OS Global Mirror makes use of the journal and control data sets to guarantee secondary volume consistency. You must use this mode for disaster recovery solutions.
- In MIGRATE mode, the journal and control data sets are not used. This means that the Consistency Groups are not written to the journal data, and if an error occurs during the write to secondary volumes, z/OS Global Mirror cannot guarantee data consistency across the secondary volumes.

However, the SDM applies updates to the secondary volumes on a Consistency Group basis, and data consistency is maintained on secondary volumes in a controlled environment. In this mode you do not need to allocate the journal and control data sets, but the state data set is required. This mode can be used for migrating data and workload to avoid the I/O activity to journal and control data sets. XRECOVER can be used after ending the session to clip secondary volume serial numbers.

ERRORLEVEL is an important parameter because it specifies how the z/OS Global Mirror session responds when an error occurs that causes the session to become unable to process a volume. This may impact the data consistency on secondary volumes. The ERRORLEVEL specified with the XSTART is the default for all volumes in the session, but can be overridden by specifications on the XADDPAIR command.

30.2.1 XADDPAIR command

The XADDPAIR command (Example 30-2) can be used for:

- Defining new volume pairs to a z/OS Global Mirror session. z/OS Global Mirror makes an initial copy of the primary volume to the secondary volume unless you specify NOCOPY.
- Adding volume pairs that were previously suspended. z/OS Global Mirror automatically resynchronizes suspended pairs and processes them ahead of new volume pairs. z/OS Global Mirror will use the hardware bit map in the DS8000 during the resynchronization process (or the software bit map in the state data set if the primary storage control does not support hardware bit mapping). Instead of specifying the volume pairs by volser, the SUSPENDED parameter can be used to instruct z/OS Global Mirror to add all suspended volumes into the session and schedule them for resynchronization.
- Adding a utility device to a storage control session. You specify a utility volume by using XRCUTL instead of secondary volser. z/OS Global Mirror does not copy data from a utility volume, and z/OS Global Mirror ignores NOCOPY and ERRORLEVEL options.

A maximum of 50 pairs can be specified on a single XADDPAIR command.

z/OS Global Mirror allows the primary systems to update the primary volumes while the XADDPAIR copy operation is processing.

Example 30-2 XADDPAIR examples

```
1. XADDPAIR SBSESS VOLUME(PVOL01,SVOL01) DONOTBLOCK
2. XADDPAIR SBSESS VOLUME(PVOL03,SVOL03) ERRORLEVEL(VOLUME)
3. XADDPAIR SBSESS VOLUME(PMIN01,XRCUTL) SCSESSION(AA)
4. XADDPAIR SBSESS SUSPENDED
5. XADDPAIR SBSESS VOLUME(PVOL03,SVOL03) NOCOPY
6. XADDPAIR SBSESS VOLUME(PVOL04,SVOL04) QUICKCOPY
```

Example 30-2 shows various examples of XADDPAIR commands:

- **Example 1:** DONOTBLOCK

  If the SDM is unable to drain updates from the DS8000 cache rapidly enough, then the DS8000 microcode will by default slow down write activity from the primary systems to the primary volumes with high write I/O activity. The DONOTBLOCK parameter specifies that z/OS Global Mirror should not block write I/Os issued by the primary systems to the PVOL01 primary volume.
- **Example 2:** ERRORLEVEL

  This parameter, specified in this case with the XADDPAIR command, overrides the default value specified in the XSTART command.

- **Example 3:** XRCUTL

  This specifies that PMIN01 is a utility device, and PMIN01 is not copied to a secondary volume.

- **Example 4:** SCSESSION

  This instructs z/OS Global Mirror to assign the volumes (in this case a utility volume) to the storage control session specified (AA). You can assign one or two alphabetic characters for the storage control session value.The SCSESSION designation cannot be changed for suspended volumes.

- **Example 5:** SUSPENDED

  This specifies that z/OS Global Mirror should add all suspended volumes back into the session (SBSESS) and schedule them for resynchronization. Suspended volumes keep the same characteristics that existed when the suspension occurred, and you should therefore not use this option to add volumes back into a session if you want to change any of the volume pair characteristics (such as error level, storage control session assignment, or device blocking).

  The SUSPENDED keyword is mutually exclusive with the VOLUME, DONOTBLOCK, NOCOPY, SCSESSION, FULLCOPY, QUICKCOPY, and ERRORLEVEL keywords.

- **Example 6:** NOCOPY

  The NOCOPY option bypasses the initial primary to secondary volume copy; z/OS Global Mirror only starts mirroring updates to the primary volume after the volume is added.

  Because of potential data integrity exposures, the NOCOPY option should be used selectively, and only when installation procedures can guarantee that the primary and secondary volumes are exact copies (excluding volsers) at the time the command is issued.

- **Example 7:** QUICKCOPY

  The QUICKCOPY option specifies that only *allocated* tracks will be copied onto the secondary volume when the pair is being established.

  z/OS Global Mirror ignores QUICKCOPY when establishing utility volumes and when resynchronizing volumes.

  To ensure data integrity, the initial processing for QUICKCOPY must issue a reserve and then a release for the primary volume during the initial phase of the synchronization process. If access to the primary volume is through a channel extender, and the connection fails while z/OS Global Mirror has the volume reserved, applications at the primary site will not be able to access the primary volume.

30.2.2 XQUERY command

The XQUERY command (Example 30-3) is the primary tool to request information about the z/OS Global Mirror environment. XQUERY provides status at the session and volume level for all primary and secondary volume pairs.

Parameters are available to customize the reports, both regarding the type of information and the level of detail. The following are examples of reports available by selecting XQUERY command parameter options:

- z/OS Global Mirror session statistics report
- z/OS Global Mirror volume pair reporting
- z/OS Global Mirror session default setting report
- z/OS Global Mirror related storage control statistics report
- z/OS Global Mirror related configuration report

The data consistent time in the XQUERY report is the consistency time for volumes in the session at the time the report is given. The timestamp variable specifies the UTC time from the application system. z/OS Global Mirror generates this time from the updates received from the application system. Data on the secondary volumes was last consistent up to this timestamp.

XQUERY also reports a delay time. This is the current delay between the last application I/O to a primary LCU, and the update made by the data mover to a secondary volume. This field provides an approximation of the time delay between the primary and secondary volumes.

Output from XQUERY directed to the system log has `ANTQxxxx` message identifiers, and *z/OS MVS System Messages, Volume 1 (ABA-AOM),* SA22-7631 contains more explanations about XQUERY output.

XQUERY output can be directed to a sequential data set, and our recommendation is that you have the command automated, and that you direct the output to a data set for further processing.

The sample command shown in Example 30-3 will direct the XQUERY output to data set XQUERY.OUT, and this output will be appended to this existing data set. Only the volumes from session SBSESS, which match the serial number prefix PVOL will be reported.

Example 30-3 XQUERY example

```
XQUERY SBSESS VOLUME(PVOL*) dataset(XQUERY.OUT) DISP(MOD)
```

XQUERY MASTER in a coupled environment

You can issue the XQUERY MASTER command (Example 30-4) to a Master session to display information about coupled z/OS Global Mirror sessions associated with the Master session, including the z/OS Global Mirror session name, session status, command pending status, journal delta time, RCV/ADV delta time, Master session status, Master session recoverable time, and Master pending command.

Example 30-4 shows an example of a command where the Master session name is **`HOSPITAL`**, and the high level qualifier of the Master session control data set is **`SYS2`**.

Example 30-4 XQUERY MASTER example

```
XQUERY HOSPITAL MASTER MHLQ(SYS2) dataset(XQUERY.OUTPUT2) DISP(OLD)
```

30.2.3 XDELPAIR command

The XDELPAIR command (Example 30-5) directs the z/OS Global Mirror session to stop processing a primary volume and its secondary volume. For each volume, the XDELPAIR command returns a timestamp indicating that the data on the secondary volume is consistent with the data that was on the primary at that time.

You can delete any z/OS Global Mirror volume pair with the XDELPAIR command, regardless of the status of the pair. Volume pairs in pending, duplex, copy, seqcheck, and suspend status all become inactive when deleted, and are no longer eligible for recovery.

You may delete up to 100 volume pairs in a single XDELPAIR command. Note that z/OS Global Mirror does not process any volumes if there is a command syntax error, or if any of the volumes in the list are not part of the z/OS Global Mirror session.

Example 30-5 XDELPAIR examples

```
1. XDELPAIR SBSESS VOLUME(PVOL01 PVOL02 PVOL03) DRAIN
2. XDELPAIR SBSESS VOLUME(PVOL02) CANCEL
3. XDELPAIR SBSESS VOLUME(ALL)
```

Example 30-5 shows various examples of XDELPAIR commands:

- **Example 1:** As an optional parameter you can specify when the pairs are going to be deleted, by specifying IMMEDIATE, DRAIN, or ATTIME:

  IMMEDIATE: This is the default. IMMEDIATE specifies that z/OS Global Mirror immediately process the delete request. z/OS Global Mirror deletes the volume pair or pairs when the current Consistency Group has been applied. The secondary volumes are consistent up to the UTC timestamp that is reported on the successful completion of the command. This is the only option that can be used for suspended volumes.

  DRAIN: The DRAIN function ensures that all timestamped record updates that the SDM has not yet written to the secondary storage control are drained from the primary storage control, and applied to the secondary volume or volumes. All secondary volumes are consistent up to the UTC timestamp that is reported by successful completion of the command.

  This option could be used whenever you have quiesced the application activity on the primary volumes and to ensure that z/OS Global Mirror has applied all the updates to the secondary volumes before the volume pairs are deleted.

  ATTIME: This option specifies that the z/OS Global Mirror will delete the specified volume pairs after applying all updates, up to the specified time, to the secondary volumes. z/OS Global Mirror will not apply any updates beyond the specified UTC timestamp to the secondary volumes. All affected secondary volumes are consistent up to the UTC timestamp that is reported on successful completion of the command.

  You could use this option in environments where applications continue to update the primary volumes even after the time specified on the ATTIME keyword has expired.

- **Example 2:** CANCEL

  Specifies that z/OS Global Mirror cancel the previous XDELPAIR command with an ATTIME or DRAIN request. The cancel option is only valid when there is a pending XDELPAIR command.

- **Example 3:** VOLUME(ALL)

  Specifies that z/OS Global Mirror should delete all eligible volumes in the session, including utility volumes. The z/OS Global Mirror session will still be active.

30.2.4 XEND command

Use the XEND command (Example 30-6) to stop all z/OS Global Mirror activity to active volumes and to end the z/OS Global Mirror session. Issuing the XEND command stops all updates to the secondary volumes at the specified time.

The XEND command returns a timestamp indicating that the data on the secondary volumes of all active pairs is consistent with the corresponding data that was on the primary volumes at the specified time.

In a coupled environment you can issue the XEND command to a Master session to have all sessions end with their volumes consistent to the same time.

With XEND you have the same optional parameters as XDELPAIR to specify when the session should end and how the updates should be applied to secondary volumes (ATTIME, DRAIN, IMMEDIATE and CANCEL). See 30.2.3, "XDELPAIR command" on page 448 for further description of those parameters.

Example 30-6 XEND example

```
XEND SBSESS
```

The example in Example 30-6 ends session **SBSESS** and all its associated volumes. IMMEDIATE is the default.

30.2.5 XSUSPEND command

Use the XSUSPEND command (Example 30-7) to suspend either:

- A z/OS Global Mirror session
- One or more volume pairs from the z/OS Global Mirror session

When a z/OS Global Mirror session is suspended, the ANTASnnn address space is ended. The system data mover is no longer active and the volume pairs are in suspended state. You should use the XSUSPEND command to suspend a session as part of a planned outage when you stop applications or intend the outage to be brief.

In a coupled environment, you may either suspend all z/OS Global Mirror sessions coupled to the Master session, or suspend all volume pairs from sessions that are coupled to the Master session.

The SDM remains active when volume pairs are suspended. The SDM continues to read record updates from the primary LCUs, and z/OS Global Mirror will use the DS8000 hardware bit map during resynchronization.

As the DS8000 supports hardware bit maps, the DS8000 will continue to record changed tracks, and there will be no impact to the primary systems. z/OS Global Mirror will use this bit map to resynchronize the volumes when the session is restarted, and volumes added back to the session with XADDPAIR command.

Example 30-7 XSUSPEND examples

```
1. XSUSPEND SBSESS VOLUME(PVOL03) DRAIN
2. XSUSPEND SBSESS VOLUME(ALL)
3. XSUSPEND SBSESS TIMEOUT(01:15:00)
```

Example 30-7 shows various examples of XSUSPEND commands:

- **Example 1:**

  The VOLUME parameter indicates that this is a volume suspension. The VOLUME parameter is mutually exclusive with the TIMEOUT parameter.

  The IMMEDIATE, ATTIME, and DRAIN keywords allow you to control when the suspension occurs. For more information about those parameters; see 30.2.3, "XDELPAIR command" on page 448.

- **Example 2:**

  When VOLUME(ALL) is specified, z/OS Global Mirror suspends all volumes in the session, but does not suspend utility devices.

- **Example 3:**

  TIMEOUT indicates that the entire z/OS Global Mirror session should be suspended, and the ANTASnnn address space ended. The value specified in the TIMEOUT parameter specifies the maximum time that the storage control can wait for the z/OS Global Mirror session to restart.

  The TIMEOUT parameter is mutually exclusive with the VOLUME parameter.

30.2.6 XSET command

You can use the XSET command (Example 30-8) to change the characteristics of an active session without requiring that you quiesce or restart the session. The XSET command enhances serviceability and availability by allowing the storage administrator to dynamically change the z/OS Global Mirror session tuning values. z/OS Global Mirror saves the values in the state data set and uses them to suspend or restart a z/OS Global Mirror session.

The XSET command changes the characteristics of the z/OS Global Mirror session. The changes made with the XSET command remain in effect for the duration of the session, even through session suspension and restart, unless changed with another XSET command.

Example 30-8 XSET examples

```
1. XSET SBSESS PAGEFIX(140) PRIORITY(LOAD)
2. XSET SBSESS SCSYNCH(2,2) SYNCH(4)
3. XSET SBSESS RTRACKS(8000)
4. XSET SBSESS TIMEOUT(00:00:45) SSID(ALL)
5. XSET SBSESS UTILITY(FIX)
```

Example 30-8 shows various examples of XSET commands:

- **Example 1:** PAGEFIX and PRIORITY

  PAGEFIX specifies the number of megabytes that are assigned to the SDM as permanently fixed real storage. The value specified here may impact SDM's performance.

  The PRIORITY parameter specifies the priority algorithm used by z/OS Global Mirror when volumes are synchronized or resynchronized with the XADDPAIR command.

- **Example 2:** SCSYNCH and SYNCH

  The SCSYNCH and SYNCH parameters control the synchronization and resynchronization process in z/OS Global Mirror. SCSYNCH specifies the maximum number of volume pairs processed concurrently per LCU, while SYNCH specifies the maximum number of pairs processed concurrently in the z/OS Global Mirror session.

- **Example 3:** RTRACKS

  The RTRACKS or RFREQUENCY parameters can be used to control when the DS8000 or SDM should reset resynchronization bit maps.

- **Example 4:** TIMEOUT

  This TIMEOUT parameter can be used to specify the acceptable primary application impact for *unplanned outage* SDM processing. For comparison, the TIMEOUT parameter in the XSUSPEND command can be used to specify acceptable application impact for a planned outage.

- **Example 5:** UTILITY

  The UTILITY parameter can be used to specify how the utility device is selected for reading data from the primary storage control - either FIX or FLOAT.

30.2.7 XRECOVER command

The XRECOVER command (Example 30-9) will bring data on the secondary volumes to a consistent, recoverable state where they are equivalent to the primary volumes, as of the given timestamp.

If the session was started with SESSIONTYPE(XRC), the z/OS Global Mirror recovery function must continue to have access to the appropriate Journal, Control, and State data sets that were in use at the time of the failure, or when the z/OS Global Mirror session ended. In this case XRECOVER will add valid, non-applied journal data to the secondary volumes. For SESSIONTYPE(MIGRATE), only the State data set is required. In both cases will XRECOVER label the secondary volumes with the volume serial numbers of the primary volumes.

If the z/OS Global Mirror session has either been suspended or ended normally by a command, the XRECOVER command reports the timestamp that all data is consistent up to. The XRECOVER command will also automatically generate an XQUERY storage control report. The report includes the last applied timestamp that defines the recovered, consistent state for all volumes.

You should not issue the XRECOVER command to an active z/OS Global Mirror session. If a session is active when you issue the XRECOVER command, z/OS Global Mirror rejects the command. You must first issue an XSUSPEND or XEND command for the session, and then make all primary volumes offline to the SDM system.

You can also issue the XRECOVER command to recover a group of interlocked coupled sessions to the same consistency time. In order to provide Master session consistency, CXRC applies updates to volumes on the sessions that are behind to allow them to advance to the forward session. CXRC will forward-recover volumes that are suspended because of an error, and that have the necessary journal data available. It will not forward-recover volumes that are suspended because of an XSUSPEND command.

Example 30-9 XRECOVER example

```
XRECOVER SBSESS
```

Example 30-9 shows an example of a XRECOVER command for bringing the data of session SBSESS to a consistent and recoverable state. You have to specify the session_name that was previously specified on the XSTART command.

30.2.8 XADVANCE command

You can issue the XADVANCE TSO command (Example 30-10) to both coupled and noncoupled sessions.

The XADVANCE command differs from the XRECOVER command in that it obtains a consistent set of secondary volumes without updating the secondary volume VOLSERs. This makes it easier for you to create a time-consistent backup of the secondary volumes before restarting z/OS Global Mirror and resynchronizing volumes.

The XADVANCE command requires all volumes in the session to be suspended. It may be used with an active or an inactive session. You cannot use this command when the session is active on another system, or if the session has any non-suspended volumes. The XADVANCE command does not apply any data to volumes that were suspended because of a command, or that were suspended because of errors that occurred before the last Consistency Group.

If an error occurs while writing to a secondary volume that results in all volumes being suspended, that volume will be suspended at a different consistency time than the other volumes in the session. To resolve the time discrepancy, correct the error on the secondary volume, and issue the XADVANCE command to update that volume to the same consistency time as other volumes in the session.

Use the XADVANCE TSO command to update secondary volumes of a session to a time that is consistent with the volumes of other sessions that are coupled to the Master session. The XADVANCE command applies secondary volume updates to the minimum Master journal time or the pending Master command time. This is the same time to which an XRECOVER command would recover the session.

The XADVANCE command produces an XQUERY report that displays YES in the ADV column to indicate if each volume in the session was eligible to have updates applied. A NO in the column indicates that the volume was not eligible to have updates applied. The report also displays NO for volumes that have not reached duplex, that were suspended through a command, or that were suspended at a time before the consistency time that exists as of the beginning of the XADVANCE operation.

Issuing an XADVANCE command to a Master session automatically generates an XQUERY MASTER report for the coupled sessions.

Example 30-10 XADVANCE example

```
XADVANCE UMC HLQ(SYS1) MSGROUTEID(OPER3)
```

Example 30-10 shows an example of an XADVANCE command for session UMC. SYS1 is the high level qualifier of the Journal, State, and Control data sets that were used with this session.

30.2.9 XCOUPLE command

Use the XCOUPLE TSO command (Example 30-11) to add z/OS Global Mirror sessions to, or delete z/OS Global Mirror sessions from, a Master session. You can also use this command to manage the status of the Master session. Specifically:

- The XCOUPLE(ADD) command couples the specified z/OS Global Mirror session into a Master session, which is then used to coordinate the consistency time and data recovery of multiple z/OS Global Mirror sessions. When two or more z/OS Global Mirror sessions are coupled, the journal and consistency times of the sessions are maintained such that the entire group of sessions can always be processed by the XRECOVER or XADVANCE commands to a consistent point-in-time. The XCOUPLE(ADD) command is not allowed for sessions where you specified SESSIONTYPE(MIGRATE) on the XSTART command.
- The XCOUPLE(DELETE) command uncouples the specified active z/OS Global Mirror session from the Master session. In a coupled environment, when the last volume is deleted, the system will automatically perform the XCOUPLE DELETE command to remove the session from the Master session.
- The XCOUPLE(PURGE) command is issued to an inactive coupled session. If the Master session is active, this command clears information about the coupled z/OS Global Mirror session from the Master data set.
- The XCOUPLE(RELEASE) command removes the HOLD status of the Master session. Use the RELEASE option only if you no longer need to protect the recoverable state of the coupled z/OS Global Mirror sessions in the Master session and are ready to resume normal remote copy operations.

Example 30-11 XCOUPLE examples

```
1. XCOUPLE STJOSEPH ADD MSESSION(HOSPITAL) MHLQ(MSTRHOSP)
2. XCOUPLE GENERAL DELETE MSGROUTEID(OPER2)
3. XCOUPLE STJOSEPH PURGE MSESSION(HOSPITAL) MHLQ(MSTRHOSP) HLQ(STJOS1)
4. XCOUPLE HOSPITAL RELEASE MHLQ(MSTRHOSP)
```

Example 30-11 shows various examples of XCOUPLE commands:

- **Example 1:** Couple z/OS Global Mirror session STJOSEPH to Master session HOSPITAL, whose Master session control data set has the high level qualifier MSTRHOSP.
- **Example 2:** Delete z/OS Global Mirror session GENERAL from the Master session to which it is coupled.
- **Example 3:** Remove information about the inactive z/OS Global Mirror session STJOSEPH from the Master session.
- **Example 4:** Indicates that all manual, operator-initiated actions have been performed to protect the recoverable status of the coupled z/OS Global Mirror sessions associated with Master session HOSPITAL. The HOLD status of the Master session is to be removed.

30.3 ANTRQST application programming interface (API)

The ANTRQST macro provides an application program call to the z/OS system data mover's application programming interface (API). This macro allows you to call z/OS Global Mirror, Metro Mirror, Global Mirror, FlashCopy, and SnapShot copy functions. You may need to ensure that necessary address spaces such as ANTAS000, ANTASnnn, or ANTMAIN are active when you execute the macro.

The ANTRQST macro is described in detail in *z/OS DFSMS Advanced Copy Services*, SC35-0428.

30.4 Managing a z/OS Global Mirror environment

In this section we provide some recommendations, tools, and procedures to help you manage the z/OS Global Mirror environment.

30.4.1 Automation

A z/OS Global Mirror environment may involve hundreds if not thousands of volumes. We recommend that you keep the configuration as simple and symmetric as possible, for example, a one-to-one correspondence between primary and secondary LCUs.

Nevertheless, you should implement some form of automation. Automation for z/OS Global Mirror may range from simple JCL or REXX code, to fully automated monitoring and recovery actions.

JCL or REXX generation

JCL or REXX generation is recommended to minimize errors when performing z/OS Global Mirror operations. Code can be automatically generated to XADDPAIRs, to XSUSPEND, and so on. This will ensure that all eligible volumes are included in all lists. Even if major operations such as migration and recovery are going to be under manual control, errors can be minimized by automatic generation of jobs to be executed.

Error recovery

Many systems management software packages allow error messages to be intercepted, filtered, and directed to an automation package. For example, if a volume drops out of duplex status, an operator could be notified, or an automatic XADDPAIR may be initiated.

Automation code may also be built to automate the full z/OS Global Mirror recovery process in the event of a disaster. For disaster recovery it is important not to rely on personnel who may not be available to perform the recovery actions.

30.5 z/OS Global Mirror and GDPS

GDPS, an industry leading e-business availability solution available through IBM Global Services, is a multi-site solution that is designed to provide the capability to manage the remote copy configuration and storage subsystems, automate Parallel Sysplex operational tasks, and perform failure recovery from a single point of control, thereby helping to improve application availability. GDPS supports both the Synchronous Metro Mirror, as well as the asynchronous z/OS Global Mirror forms of remote copy.

Geographically Dispersed Parallel Sysplex (GDPS) is an integrated solution offering that manages all aspects of switching computer operations from one site to another, planned or unplanned. The SDM is placed outside the production sysplex. This support of z/OS Global Mirror as a remote copy technology should accommodate two types of installations:

- Installations that cannot tolerate the performance impact of the synchronous remote copy technology.
- Installations that need more distance between their primary and secondary sites than what can be handled with ESCON/FICON and dark fiber.

One subset of the GDPS solution is the Remote Copy Management Facility (RCMF) offering. RCMF is an automated disk subsystem and remote copy management facility, with a high-level user interface. This interface is implemented in the form of ISPF like displays, and virtually eliminates the tedious and time consuming work with TSO commands.

Managing z/OS Global Mirror with RCMF could be the first step of a full GDPS implementation. GDPS is discussed in Chapter 37., "GDPS overview and positioning" on page 529.

31

z/OS Global Mirror performance and scalability

In this chapter we discuss some of the issues relating to z/OS Global Mirror performance and scalability.

31.1 z/OS Global Mirror performance

In this section we discuss some of the performance and tuning options available with z/OS Global Mirror.

31.1.1 z/OS Global Mirror control dataset placement

The z/OS Global Mirror control datasets (the Journal, Control, and State datasets) are critical to the performance of your z/OS Global Mirror environment. The Journals are particularly important, and you need to consider how to allocate them for best performance.

You have two options, depending on your available space and your configuration:

- Dedicate an LSS to the Journals. This will avoid any interference from other workload with the Journal's I/O. This option is more attractive now than it may have been on previous generations of hardware, as you do not necessarily have to dedicate a Rank to the LSS.
- Distribute the Journals across all available disk. This can assist to balance out the workload and avoid any potential hot-spots.

In most environments, where the Control datasets are allocated on the secondary disk subsystem, you will also need to consider the I/O from the mirrored volumes when making this decision.

31.1.2 z/OS Global Mirror tuning parameters

This section discusses the tuning parameters available for z/OS Global Mirror. For additional information on the topics discussed in the present section, the following IBM publication can be referred to: *z/OS DFSMS Advanced Copy Services,* SC35-0428.

z/OS Global Mirror offers the flexibility of allowing SDM operations to be tailored to installation requirements. z/OS Global Mirror supports the modification of key parameters, either from a PARMLIB data set or through the XSET command.

Creating a PARMLIB data set

The main purpose of creating a z/OS Global Mirror PARMLIB data set is to provide a single method to specify parameters for each system in a multisystem environment, without modifying the ANTXIN00 member of SYS1.PARMLIB. z/OS Global Mirror uses a PARMLIB data set name in one of the following forms: `hlq.XCOPY.PARMLIB` or `SYS1.XCOPY.PARMLIB`.

PARMLIB members

When z/OS Global Mirror first starts up using the XSTART command, it searches for member ANTXIN00 in SYS1.PARMLIB. When the value in the ANTXIN00 member differs from the value specified in the XSTART command, the value in the XSTART command always overrides the value found in ANTXIN00.

After processing the ANTXIN00 member, z/OS Global Mirror then looks for member ALL in the data set called *hlq*.XCOPY.PARMLIB, where hlq is the value found for the hlq parameter in the ANTXIN00 member, or the value entered in the XSTART command. The ALL member can contain values that you want to be common across all logical sessions on a system. hlq.XCOPY.PARMLIB must be allocated as RECFM fixed, with LRECL=80 and DSORG=PO. Finally, z/OS Global Mirror reads *hlq*.XCOPY.PARMLIB for a member whose name matches the session ID of the session.

XSET PARMLIB

To invoke PARMLIB support at times other than z/OS Global Mirror start up, you can issue the XSET PARMLIB command. You can use the XSET PARMLIB both before and after you issue an XSTART command. If XSET PARMLIB is invoked before an XSTART command, you can check the validity of the parameter syntax without applying any of the parameters.

PARMLIB parameters

PARMLIB parameters use syntax similar to that of TSO commands. Parameters consist of a category name, parameter names, and values. Refer to the IBM publication *z/OS DFSMS Advanced Copy Services,* SC35-0428 for the table describing possible PARMLIB parameters, and their associated XSET parameter, if applicable.

To determine the current settings for the PARMLIB parameter values, issue the XQUERY ENVIRONMENT(PARM) command. To find the default values for the parameters, issue the XQUERY ENVIRONMENT(PARM) command to an inactive session.

Description and use of flags

Flags are diagnostic tools that perform a specific action if the triggering event occurs. Users turn these flags on and off according to their preferred response to the triggering event. You can determine the current settings for each indicated flag by giving the MODIFY command without specifying ON or OFF. To determine the default values for all flag names at once, issue the XQUERY ENVIRONMENT(FLAG) command to an inactive session. This displays the values in the control address space (ANTAS000).

PARMLIB example

Figure 31-1 shows an example of member ZOWIE, which was created in PARMLIB *hlq*.XCOPY.PARMLIB for use when starting z/OS Global Mirror session ZOWIE.

```
/* */
/*ZOWIE */
/* */
/*This is an initialization parmlib member for z/OS Global Mirror logical session */
/*ZOWIE.*/
/* */
/*Change Activity:*/
/**/
/*$L0=OW52938,HDZ11E0,010630,TUCRNC:XRC parmlib support */
/**/
VOLINIT -
MaxNumberInitializations(3)-
InitializationsPerPrimary(1)-
InitializationsPerSecondary(1)-
TracksPerRead(2)-
TracksPerWrite(2)
SHADOW -
StorageControlTimeout(00.04.05)-
MaxBytesTransferred(750001)-
MaxTracksUpdated(2)-
MaxTracksFormated(2)
BITMAP -
DelayTime(00.02.05)-
ChangedTracks(800)
FLAG -
Name(Abend_Lic)-
Action(On)
FLAG -
Name(SCTRAP)-
Action(On)
```

Figure 31-1 PARMLIB example

Refer to *z/OS DFSMS Advanced Copy Services,* SC35-0428 for a complete description of the parameters contained in this example.

PAGEFIX parameter in XSET command

This parameter specifies the number of megabytes that are assigned to the SDM as permanent page-fixed real storage. This is the maximum amount of storage that remains page-fixed for the duration of the z/OS Global Mirror session. The default PAGEFIX value is 8 MB.

Each SC session requires up to 35 MB for its data buffers. If you have *n* SC sessions running concurrently in the SDM address space, up to *n* x 35 MB data buffers will be required. For example, with 6 primary LCUs and 2 SC sessions for each LCU, up to 420 MB data buffers will be required. If you can page-fix most or all of those data buffers, this will minimize the required MIPS and maximize the potential throughput. The SDM will fix and free any amount of additional real storage required.

Changes specified with the PAGEFIX parameter take place when the next SC buffers are processed.

Note: PARMLIB option STORAGE PermanentFixedPages parameter has the equivalent function.

TIMEOUT parameter in XSET command

This parameter specifies the maximum primary system impact that the z/OS Global Mirror session will allow. In 29.14, "Planned outage support" on page 438 there is a detailed description of how this parameter is used. You should set this parameter to a value that is acceptable to your application production environment.

We recommend that you do not set this value lower than the MIH value for the primary volumes.

If you are using channel extenders between the primary site and the SDM location, you should not set the TIMEOUT value lower than the channel extender value.

You can specify the subsystem id (SSID) to which the TIMEOUT value will apply. Each LCU in an DS8000 has a unique SSID, which is set during the installation and configuration process. If you do not specify any SSID, the TIMEOUT value applies to all LCUs in the z/OS Global Mirror session.

You should not confuse this TIMEOUT parameter with the TIMEOUT parameter in the XSUSPEND command. These parameters are used for different purposes.

Note: PARMLIB parameter SHADOW StorageControlTimeout has the equivalent function.

TIMEOUT parameter in XSUSPEND command

When you suspend a session with the XSUSPEND command, you must specify a TIMEOUT value (or you can specify that the LCU's default value set in the LCU is to be used, which is normally set to 5 minutes). The SDM communicates this value to all primary LCUs.

This value specifies the maximum time that an LCU can wait for the z/OS Global Mirror session to be restarted with an XSTART command. How this parameter is used is discussed in 29.14, "Planned outage support" on page 438.

RFREQUENCY/RTRACKS parameters in XSET command

For DS8000s with hardware bit map support, a hardware bit map in the DS8000 will continuously be updated to reflect changed tracks on primary volumes. This bit map will be used to add suspended volumes back to a session, and by this avoid a full volume synchronization.

SDM will also continuously maintain a software bit map as long as the ANTASnnn address space is active. This bit map is kept in the State data set and, with XRC Version 2, was used during resynchronization of a suspended volume. If the ANTASnnn address space is not active, or the data path between the SDM and the primary LCU is broken, SDM is unable to update this bit map. Unplanned outages were therefore not supported in XRC version 2.

You can use the RFREQUENCY and/or the RTRACKS parameters in the XSET command to tell the DS8000 (for hardware bit maps) and the SDM (for software bit maps) when those bitmaps should be reset. DS8000 and SDM will reset bit maps according to those parameters for all active volumes, bit maps for suspended volumes will not be reset.

In the RFREQUENCY parameter you can specify how often, in hours, minutes, and seconds, the bit maps should be reset. With the RTRACKS parameter, you specify the number of tracks that must change before the bitmaps are reset.

The default for RFREQUENCY is 30 minutes. If you specify a value of 0, z/OS Global Mirror will not reset the bit maps as a result of elapsed time.

The default for RTRACKS is 7500 tracks. If you specify a value of 0 (or a value greater than the number of tracks on a volume), z/OS Global Mirror will not reset the bit maps as a result of the number of tracks that have changed.

z/OS Global Mirror uses whatever happens first of the RFREQUENCY or RTRACKS specifications.

Specifying high values in the RTRACKS and RFREQUENCY (for RFREQUENCY it depends on the update rate on primary volumes) means that the resynchronization time can take longer. For example, if you have specified RTRACKS 7500 (and let us assume that RFREQUENCY is 0) and a volume is suspended when 4000 tracks have been changed since the bit map was reset last time, 4000 tracks have to be resynchronized.

Specifying a low value in the RTRACKS and RFREQUENCY can put a greater demand on DS8000 and SDM processing resources.

We recommend that you keep the defaults unless you have specific needs.

Note: PARMLIB parameters BITMAP ChangedTracks and DelayTime have an equivalent function.

DONOTBLOCK parameter in the XADDPAIR command

In 31.1.3, "Dynamic workload balancing" on page 464 we explained how z/OS Global Mirror will try to balance the needs of the primary system and z/OS Global Mirror when data starts to accumulate in the cache. Data paths to primary volumes with high write activity will progressively be blocked. That is, writes from the primary host will be inhibited until SDM can catch up. If there are volumes in your z/OS Global Mirror configuration which you do not want to have device blocking active for, you can specify those volumes with the DONOTBLOCK parameter.

Example 31-1 shows an example of the use of the DONOTBLOCK parameter on an XADDPAIR command.

Example 31-1 DONOTBLOCK parameter

```
XADDPAIR MAIN1 VOLUME(PRIM01 SECD01) DONOTBLOCK
```

You should specify this option only for high performance, sensitive volumes that generate very short updates, like the IMS™ WADS volumes and spool data sets.

DVCBLOCK parameter in the XADDPAIR command

The DVCBLOCK parameter of the XADDPAIR command can be used to control whether write pacing is enabled, disabled, or has a different value to the default for the session for the volumes it is specified for. It is mutually exclusive with the DONOTBLOCK parameter described in "DONOTBLOCK parameter in the XADDPAIR command" on page 462.

Example 31-2 shows examples of the use of the DVCBLOCK parameter on the XADDPAIR command. The first example has switched off write pacing for the specified volume pair. The second example has defined write pacing level 1 for the specified volume pair.

Example 31-2 DVCBLOCK parameter

```
XADDPAIR MAIN1 VOLUME(PRIM01 SECD01) DVCBLOCK(OFF)
XADDPAIR MAIN1 VOLUME(PRIM02 SECD02) DVCBLOCK(WP1)
```

WP1-WP7 results in pacing maximums ranging from 0.02 to 2 ms per recordset, and are useful for volumes with high rates of small blocksize writes, such as data base logs, where minimal response time impact is essential.

PRIORITY parameter in the XSET command

The PRIORITY parameter in the XSET command specifies the priority that the XADDPAIR command uses for selecting the next volume to synchronize or resynchronize.

The first priority is to resynchronize existing volume pairs, then to add new volume pairs to the z/OS Global Mirror session.

If you specify PRIORITY(FIFO), z/OS Global Mirror processes the volumes that were listed by an XADDPAIR command in the order that they are listed. First, z/OS Global Mirror processes all volumes that are eligible for resynchronization. Next, z/OS Global Mirror processes all volumes that are eligible for synchronization. z/OS Global Mirror processes the volumes within the limits that you specified in the SYNCH and SCSYNCH parameters of the XSET command.

If you specify PRIORITY(LOAD), z/OS Global Mirror processes the volumes that were listed by an XADDPAIR command based on the primary and secondary storage control load. First, z/OS Global Mirror processes all volumes that are eligible for resynchronization. z/OS Global Mirror can defer the initialization if the associated storage control has too much activity at the time that the volume is eligible.

The volume continues to be eligible for processing when the activity level has decreased. That is, it processes in the order you specify, but will skip volumes if they are busy, and come back and try again later. Next, z/OS Global Mirror processes all volumes that are eligible for synchronization. Again, z/OS Global Mirror can defer the initialization if the primary storage control activity is too high. z/OS Global Mirror performs both resynchronization and synchronization processing within the limits that the SYNCH and SCSYNCH parameters of the XSET command specify.

Changes specified with the PRIORITY parameter take place when the next volume is processed. The default value is PRIORITY(LOAD).

Note: PARMLIB parameter VOLINIT SelectionAlgorithm has the equivalent function.

SCSYNCH and SYNCH parameters in XSET command

The SDM monitors the update activity and the XADDPAIR activity by subsystem, and attempts to throttle the XADDPAIR activity such that the update activity is minimally impacted.

The SCSYNCH/SYNCH parameters can be set up to allow multiple concurrent `XADDPAIRs` across multiple primary LCUs.

SCSYNCH: This parameter specifies the maximum number of volume pairs that the SDM can synchronize or resynchronize concurrently per LCU. You can specify the SCSYNCH keyword as SCSYNCH(p,s) or as SCSYNCH(n), where:

- **p** is the maximum number per primary LCU
- **s** is the maximum number per secondary storage control
- **n** applies to both primary and secondary storage control

The parameter value applies to an LCU, regardless of the number of SC sessions that are active on the storage subsystem.

Set the SCSYNCH value in conjunction with the SYNCH parameter, which specifies the session limits for concurrent volume synchronization tasks.

Changes specified with the SCSYNCH parameter take place when the next volume initialization is processed. The default is SCSYNCH(2,2)

SYNCH: This parameter specifies the maximum number of volume synchronization or resynchronization tasks that z/OS Global Mirror can concurrently start in the z/OS Global Mirror session. The range is from zero to 45 tasks; the default value is four. Specify a value of zero to ensure that z/OS Global Mirror does not start any new volume initialization.

Changes specified with the SYNCH parameter take place when z/OS Global Mirror process the next volume.

Note: PARMLIB parameters VOLINIT MaxNumberInitializations, InitializationsPerPrimary and InitializationsPerSecondary have the equivalent function.

31.1.3 Dynamic workload balancing

With z/OS Global Mirror (XRC) Version 2, a dynamic workload balancing algorithm was introduced. The objective of this mechanism is to balance the write activity from primary systems, and SDM's capability to offload cache during write peaks or temporary lack of resources to SDM, and with minimal impact to the primary systems.

In situations where the SDM offload rate falls behind the primary systems write activity, data starts to accumulate in cache. This is dynamically detected by the primary DS8000 microcode, and it responds by slowly but progressively reducing available write bandwidth for the primary systems, thus giving the SDM a chance to catch up.

The DS8000 implements device level blocking. The update rate for a volume continues unrestricted unless a volume reaches a residual count threshold waiting to be collected by the SDM. Whenever that threshold is exceeded, application updates to the single volume are paused to allow the SDM to read them from the cache of the subsystem.

By using the DONOTBLOCK parameter of the XADDPAIR command, you can request z/OS Global Mirror not to block specific devices. This option can be used for IMS WADs, DB2 logs, CICS® logs, or spool data sets which use small blocksizes, do numerous updates, and are critical to application response time.

Refer to *z/OS DFSMS Advanced Copy Services*, SC35-0428 for more information on device blocking, and the new Write Pacing option available.

31.1.4 z/OS Global Mirror secondary PAV exploitation

APAR OA09238 introduced new function for z/OS Global Mirror to enable use of multiple tasks when writing to z/OS Global Mirror secondary volumes - this enables exploitation of the PAV feature of DS8000 disk subsystems. The degree of parallelism is controlled by two new z/OS Global Mirror parmlib parameters: `PavByteThreshold` and `PavVolumes`. Refer to *z/OS DFSMS Advanced Copy Services*, SC35-0428 for further information on these parameters and their values.

31.2 IBM TotalStorage XRC Performance Monitor

The IBM TotalStorage XRC Performance Monitor is a licensed IBM program product which can be used to monitor and evaluate a z/OS Global Mirror system, in terms of tuning, system constraint determination, evaluation of system growth, and for capacity planning. For more details refer to *IBM TotalStorage XRC Performance Monitor Installation and User's Guide,* GC26-7479.

31.3 Scalability

z/OS Global Mirror scales up from a small environment, which may only have one session, to large environments with thousands of volumes involved, which may have multiple sessions running as coupled sessions.

31.3.1 Multiple z/OS Global Mirror sessions

It is possible to have a maximum of five z/OS Global Mirror sessions active on one z/OS LPAR. If you find you need more than this you will need to set up another SDM LPAR. A single session will typically be able to manage 1500 to 1800 volume pairs. Note that unless you use coupled z/OS Global Mirror sessions (also known as CXRC) there is no write sequence consistency between z/OS Global Mirror sessions, so you must consider splitting the volumes between sessions on an application basis.

31.3.2 Coupled z/OS Global Mirror sessions

If you have a large z/OS Global Mirror environment, you may have a need for multiple z/OS Global Mirror sessions. If you need to have data consistency across sessions, you will need to couple the sessions together. You will do this with the creation of a z/OS Global Mirror Master dataset, then use z/OS Global Mirror commands to couple the sessions together. You can couple up to 14 sessions together.

Figure 31-2 shows a graphical representation of this concept. Refer to *z/OS DFSMS Advanced Copy Services*, SC35-0428 for more information on this subject.

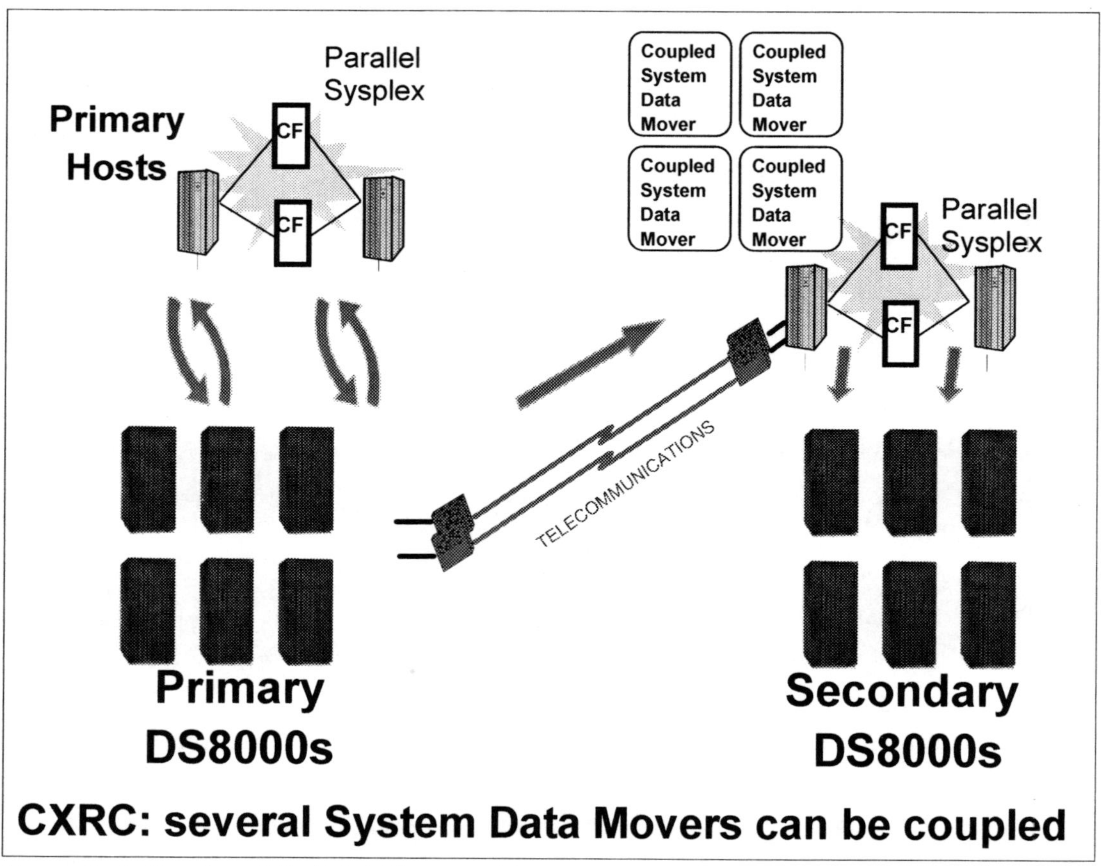

Figure 31-2 Coupled z/OS Global Mirror sessions

31.3.3 Multiple z/OS Global Mirror Storage Control sessions

For a high activity environment it is possible that the z/OS Global Mirror utility volume may become a bottleneck. To resolve this you could move workload around to reduce load on this utility device, or you could set up additional z/OS Global Mirror Storage Control sessions (also known as *SC sessions* or *readers*).

Adding another SC session to an LSS allows you to split the workload for the SDM to another utility device. To do this, you need to:

1. Add another utility device for the LSS using the XADDPAIR command, and specifying the SCSESSION parameter to identify the SC session name this utility volume is for.
2. XDELPAIR and then XADDPAIR primary volumes with the SCSESSION parameter to move them to the new SC session.

The SDM workload which previously would have been directed to one utility volume will now be split over two based on the primary volumes you have removed and then redefined to the new SC session. Figure 31-3 shows a logical view of before and after an example of this change. Note that the secondary disk subsystem is omitted from this picture for simplicity.

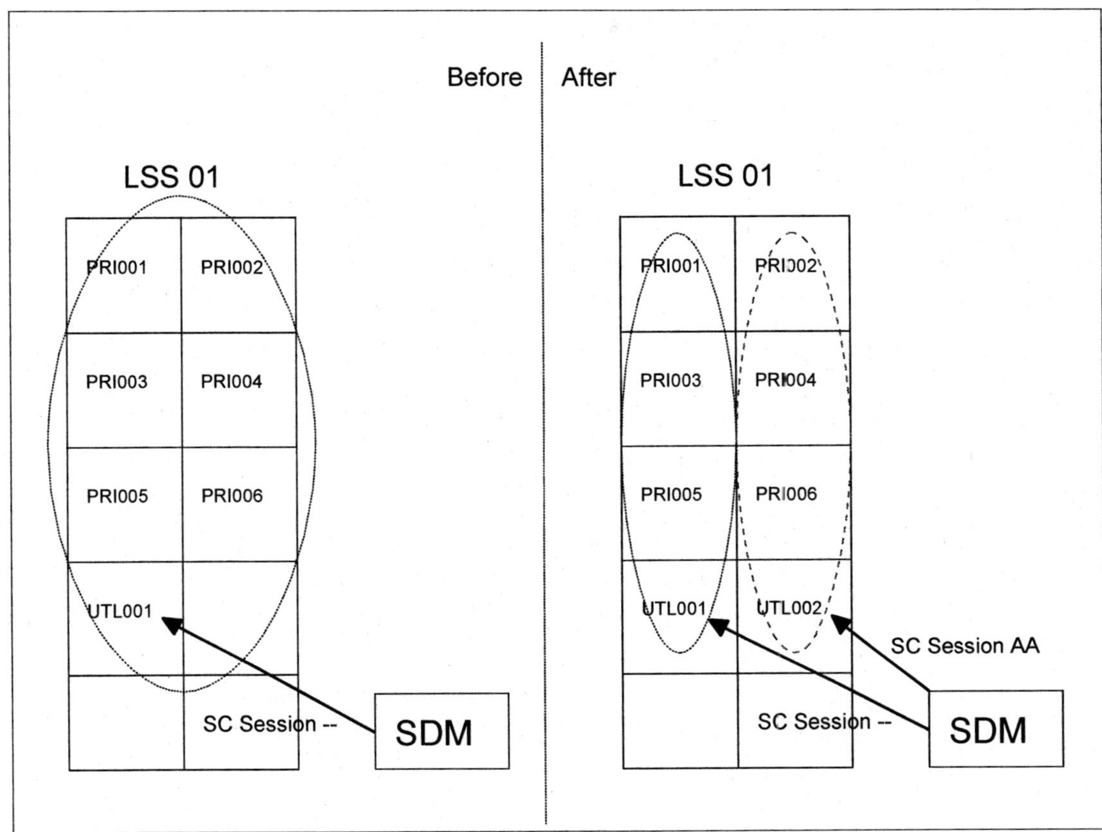

Figure 31-3 Multiple SC sessions

At the start there are six primary volumes which are being mirrored from LSS 01 using z/OS Global Mirror session XRCTEST. There is one utility volume for this LSS, and it has taken the default SC session identifier of --. The commands which could set up this z/OS Global Mirror session are shown in Example 31-3.

Example 31-3 z/OS Global Mirror command example - one SC session

```
XSTART XRCTEST ERRLVL(SESSION) SESSIONTYPE(XRC) HLQ(SYS1)
/* ADD UTILITY VOLUMES */
XADDPAIR XRCTEST VOLUME(UTL001 XRCUTL)
/* ADD VOLUME PAIRS */
XADDPAIR XRCTEST VOLUME(PRI001 SEC001)
XADDPAIR XRCTEST VOLUME(PRI002 SEC002)
XADDPAIR XRCTEST VOLUME(PRI003 SEC003)
XADDPAIR XRCTEST VOLUME(PRI004 SEC004)
XADDPAIR XRCTEST VOLUME(PRI005 SEC005)
XADDPAIR XRCTEST VOLUME(PRI006 SEC006)
```

We have now determined that the workload is too great for one SC session, so we decide to add another SC session (session identifier *AA*) to this LSS for this z/OS Global Mirror session. The commands to do this could be as shown in Example 31-4.

Example 31-4 z/OS Global Mirror commands - split into two SC sessions

```
/* ADD UTILITY VOLUMES */
XADDPAIR XRCTEST VOLUME(UTL002 XRCUTL) SCSESSION(AA)
/* DELETE VOLUME PAIRS */
XDELPAIR XRCTEST VOLUME(PRI004 SEC004)
XDELPAIR XRCTEST VOLUME(PRI005 SEC005)
XDELPAIR XRCTEST VOLUME(PRI006 SEC006)
/* ADD VOLUME PAIRS TO NEW SCSESSION */
XADDPAIR XRCTEST VOLUME(PRI004 SEC004) SCSESSION(AA)
XADDPAIR XRCTEST VOLUME(PRI005 SEC005) SCSESSION(AA)
XADDPAIR XRCTEST VOLUME(PRI006 SEC006) SCSESSION(AA)
```

Primary volumes PRI001 to PRI003 continue to use the default SC session, and primary volumes PRI004 to PRI006 are now using the new SC session *AA*. The SDM will now access utility volume UTL001 for SC session --, and volume UTL002 for SC session *AA*.

32

z/OS Global Mirror examples

In this chapter we present some examples of z/OS Global Mirror usage.

32.1 Sample PARMLIB

Example 32-1 shows a sample PARMLIB member for a session. Note that only values for which we wish to set non-default values have to be specified.

Example 32-1 Sample z/OS Global Mirror PARMLIB member

```
MONITOR -
     MONITOROUTPUT(ON)
SHADOW -
     MAXTRACKSREAD(112)               -
     UTILITYDEVICE(FIX)               -
     STORAGECONTROLTIMEOUT(00.00.30)  -
     DEVICEBLOCKINGTHRESHOLD(192)     -
     CONSISTENCYGROUPCOMB(5)          -
     READRECORDSPRIORITY(252)         -
     RESIDUALLEFTTOREAD(112)          -
     LOWATTENTION(112)                -
     WRITERECORDSPRIORITY(253)
```

32.2 Sample session start

Example 32-2 shows the commands to start a z/OS Global Mirror session called XRCTEST and the associated messages issued on the system console.

Example 32-2 z/OS Global Mirror session start commands

```
PROC 0
/* ------------------------------------------------------------------ */
/* MEMBER XRCTEST                                                      */
/*                                                                     */
/* THIS IS THE PRIMARY XADDPAIR MEMBER FOR THE XRCTEST XRC SESSION.    */
/* IT CONTAINS ALL XADDPAIR STATEMENTS FOR VOLUMES THAT ARE            */
/*                                                                     */
/* THIS MEMBER NEEDS TO BE RUN EVERYTIME A FULL SYNCH IS REQUIRED.     */
/*                                                                     */
/* ------------------------------------------------------------------ */
XSTART XRCTEST ERRLVL(SESSION) SESSIONTYPE(XRC) HLQ(SYS1)
/* ADD UTILITY VOLUMES */
XADDPAIR XRCTEST VOLUME(PR202E XRCUTL)
XADDPAIR XRCTEST VOLUME(PR202F XRCUTL) SCSESSION(AA)
/* ADD VOLUME PAIRS */
XADDPAIR XRCTEST VOLUME(PR2028 SE2128)
XADDPAIR XRCTEST VOLUME(PR2029 SE2129)
XADDPAIR XRCTEST VOLUME(PR202A SE212A)
XADDPAIR XRCTEST VOLUME(PR202B SE212B) SCSESSION(AA)
XADDPAIR XRCTEST VOLUME(PR202C SE212C) SCSESSION(AA)
XADDPAIR XRCTEST VOLUME(PR202D SE212D) SCSESSION(AA)
```

Example 32-3 shows the system messages that were issued after the XSTART command and associated XADDPAIR commands were issued.

Example 32-3 System messages issued after XSTART

```
ANTL8800I XSTART XRCTEST ERRLVL(SESSION) SESSIONTYPE(XRC) HLQ(SYS1)
ANTL8800I XADDPAIR XRCTEST VOLUME(PR202E XRCUTL)
ANTL8800I XADDPAIR XRCTEST VOLUME(PR202F XRCUTL) SCSESSION(AA)
```

```
ANTL8800I XADDPAIR XRCTEST VOLUME(PR2028 SE2128)
ANTL8800I XADDPAIR XRCTEST VOLUME(PR2029 SE2129)
ANTL8800I XADDPAIR XRCTEST VOLUME(PR202A SE212A)
ANTL8800I XADDPAIR XRCTEST VOLUME(PR202B SE212B) SCSESSION(AA)
ANTL8800I XADDPAIR XRCTEST VOLUME(PR202C SE212C) SCSESSION(AA)
ANTL8800I XADDPAIR XRCTEST VOLUME(PR202D SE212D) SCSESSION(AA)
IRR813I NO PROFILE WAS FOUND IN THE STARTED CLASS FOR 359
       ANTAS001 WITH JOBNAME ANTAS001. RACF WILL USE ICHRIN03.
IEF196I         1 //IEESYSAS JOB TIME=1440,
IEF196I           // MSGLEVEL=1
IEF196I         2 //ANTAS001 EXEC IEESYSAS,PROG=ANTXAINI
IEF196I  STMT NO. MESSAGE
IEF196I         2 IEFC001I PROCEDURE IEESYSAS WAS EXPANDED USING SYSTEM
IEF196I LIBRARY SYS1.PROCLIB.IBM
IEF196I         3 XXIEESYSAS PROC PROG=IEFBR14
IEF196I                   00050000
IEF196I         4 XXIEFPROC  EXEC PGM=&PROG
IEF196I                   00100000
IEF196I           XX* THE IEESYSAS PROCEDURE IS SPECIFIED IN THE
IEF196I                   00150000
IEF196I           XX* PARAMETER LIST TO IEEMB881 BY MVS COMPONENTS
IEF196I                   00200000
IEF196I           XX* STARTING FULL FUNCTION SYSTEM ADDRESS SPACES.
IEF196I                   00250000
IEF196I           IEFC653I SUBSTITUTION JCL - PGM=ANTXAINI
IEF403I IEESYSAS - STARTED - TIME=12.14.20
IEE252I MEMBER ANTXIN00 FOUND IN SYS1.PARMLIB.IBM
IEF196I IEF237I DMY  ALLOCATED TO SYSTSIN
IEF196I IEF237I DMY  ALLOCATED TO SYSTSPRT
IEF196I IEF285I   SYS1.PARMLIB                                KEPT
IEF196I IEF285I   VOL SER NOS= GK5CAT.
IEF196I IEF285I   SYS1.PARMLIB.IBM                            KEPT
IEF196I IEF285I   VOL SER NOS= GK5RS1.
ANTI1020I PARAMETERS FOUND IN MEMBER ANTXIN00 OF DATA SET SYS1.FARMLIB+
HAVE BEEN APPLIED
IGD103I SMS ALLOCATED TO DDNAME ANTJSTAT
IEF196I IGD103I SMS ALLOCATED TO DDNAME ANTJSTAT
IKJ56228I DATA SET SYS1.XCOPY.XRCTEST.JRNL05 NOT IN CATALOG OR CATALOG
CAN NOT BE ACCESSED
IEF196I IKJ56228I DATA SET SYS1.XCOPY.XRCTEST.JRNL05 NOT IN CATALOG OR
IEF196I CATALOG CAN NOT BE ACCESSED
IEE252I MEMBER ANTXIN00 FOUND IN SYS1.PARMLIB.IBM
IEF196I IEF285I   SYS1.PARMLIB                                KEPT
IEF196I IEF285I   VOL SER NOS= GK5CAT.
IEF196I IEF285I   SYS1.PARMLIB.IBM                            KEPT
IEF196I IEF285I   VOL SER NOS= GK5RS1.
ANTI1020I PARAMETERS FOUND IN MEMBER ANTXIN00 OF DATA SET SYS1.PARMLIB+
HAVE BEEN APPLIED
IEF196I IEF285I   SYS1.XCOPY.PARMLIB                          KEPT
IEF196I IEF285I   VOL SER NOS= GK5USR.
IEF196I IEF285I   SYS1.XCOPY.PARMLIB                          KEPT
IEF196I IEF285I   VOL SER NOS= GK5USR.
ANTI1020I PARAMETERS FOUND IN MEMBER XRCTEST OF DATA SET SYS1.XCOPY.PARM
LIB HAVE BEEN APPLIED
ANTS8100I XSTART COMPLETE FOR XRC SESSION(XRCTEST) WITH SESSIONTYPE(XRC)
, ERRORLEVEL(SESSION), HLQ(SYS1).  SESSION NOW ACTIVE
ANTA8005I XADDPAIR UTILITY VOLUME PR202E IS FIXED FOR SESSION(XRCTEST),
SCSESSION(--)
ANTA8005I XADDPAIR UTILITY VOLUME PR202F IS FIXED FOR SESSION(XRCTEST),
SCSESSION(AA)
```

```
ANTA8101I XADDPAIR COMPLETE FOR VOLUME PAIR(PR2028,SE2128) FOR
SESSION(XRCTEST) WITH ERRORLEVEL(SESSION), SCSESSION(--)
ANTA8101I XADDPAIR COMPLETE FOR VOLUME PAIR(PR2029,SE2129) FOR
SESSION(XRCTEST) WITH ERRORLEVEL(SESSION), SCSESSION(--)
ANTA8101I XADDPAIR COMPLETE FOR VOLUME PAIR(PR202A,SE212A) FOR
SESSION(XRCTEST) WITH ERRORLEVEL(SESSION), SCSESSION(--)
ANTA8101I XADDPAIR COMPLETE FOR VOLUME PAIR(PR202B,SE212B) FOR
SESSION(XRCTEST) WITH ERRORLEVEL(SESSION), SCSESSION(AA)
ANTA8101I XADDPAIR COMPLETE FOR VOLUME PAIR(PR202C,SE212C) FOR
SESSION(XRCTEST) WITH ERRORLEVEL(SESSION), SCSESSION(AA)
ANTA8101I XADDPAIR COMPLETE FOR VOLUME PAIR(PR202D,SE212D) FOR
SESSION(XRCTEST) WITH ERRORLEVEL(SESSION), SCSESSION(AA)
VARY 2128,OFFLINE
VARY 2129,OFFLINE
IEF281I 2128 NOW OFFLINE
IEF281I 2129 NOW OFFLINE
ANTI8023I FULL INITIALIZATION STARTED FOR XRC VOLUME PAIR(PR2029,SE2129)
ANTI8023I FULL INITIALIZATION STARTED FOR XRC VOLUME PAIR(PR2028,SE2128)
```

32.3 Sample session suspend

Example 32-4 shows the commands and messages issued for a suspension of all volumes in a z/OS Global Mirror session. Since the DS8000 supports hardware bit maps the started task for the session ends, and the volumes can have out-of-sync tracks resynchronized at a later time. You may choose to do this when hardware maintenance is required at your secondary site.

Example 32-4 z/OS Global Mirror session suspend

```
XSUSPEND XRCTEST VOLUME(ALL) IMMEDIATE NOVERIFY
ANTL8800I XSUSPEND XRCTEST VOLUME(ALL) IMMEDIATE NOVERIFY
```

A subsequent XQUERY XRCTEST VOL(ALL) command was issued, and the output as shown in Example 32-5 was displayed. This display indicates the session is still active, however, the volumes are suspended.

Example 32-5 XQUERY after XSUSPEND command

```
XQUERY XRCTEST VOL(*)
XQUERY STARTED FOR SESSION(XRCTEST) ASNAME(ANTAS001) 802
XQUERY VOLUME REPORT - 003
PRIM   SEC     ERROR  SYNCH
VOL    VOL     LEVEL     % STA CMD OP -------TIMESTAMP--------
----------------------------------------------------------
PR202A SE212A SESSION  86 SUS         2005.153 16:19:38.509704
PR202B SE212B SESSION  86 SUS         2005.153 16:19:38.509704
PR202C SE212C SESSION  86 SUS         2005.153 16:19:38.509704
PR202D SE212D SESSION  86 SUS         2005.153 16:19:38.509704
PR202E XRCUTL          -- UTL
PR202F XRCUTL          -- UTL
PR2028 SE2128 SESSION  99 SUS         2005.153 16:19:38.509704
PR2029 SE2129 SESSION  86 SUS         2005.153 16:19:38.509704
TOTAL=8  DUP=0  CPY=0  PND=0  SUS=6  SEQ=0  UTL=2
DATA CONSISTENT(2005.153 16:19:38.509704)    IDLE(00:13:39.0)
SESSIONTYPE(XRC)  ERRORLEVEL(SESSION)  HLQ(SYS1)
DEFAULT TIMEOUT(STORAGE_CONTROL_DEFAULT)
XQUERY VOLUME REPORT COMPLETE FOR SESSION(XRCTEST)
```

32.4 Sample XADDPAIR SUSPENDED

Example 32-6 shows the execution of an XADDPAIR SUSPENDED command for the XRCTEST session. This can be used to resume mirroring of previously suspended z/OS Global Mirror volumes.

Example 32-6 XADDPAIR SUSPENDED command

```
XADDPAIR XRCTEST SUSPENDED
ANTL8800I XADDPAIR XRCTEST SUSPENDED
ANTA8101I XADDPAIR COMPLETE FOR VOLUME PAIR(PR2028,SE2128) FOR
SESSION(XRCTEST) WITH ERRORLEVEL(SESSION), SCSESSION(--)
ANTA8101I XADDPAIR COMPLETE FOR VOLUME PAIR(PR2029,SE2129) FOR
SESSION(XRCTEST) WITH ERRORLEVEL(SESSION), SCSESSION(--)
ANTA8101I XADDPAIR COMPLETE FOR VOLUME PAIR(PR202A,SE212A) FOR
SESSION(XRCTEST) WITH ERRORLEVEL(SESSION), SCSESSION(--)
ANTA8101I XADDPAIR COMPLETE FOR VOLUME PAIR(PR202B,SE212B) FOR
SESSION(XRCTEST) WITH ERRORLEVEL(SESSION), SCSESSION(AA)
ANTA8101I XADDPAIR COMPLETE FOR VOLUME PAIR(PR202C,SE212C) FOR
SESSION(XRCTEST) WITH ERRORLEVEL(SESSION), SCSESSION(AA)
ANTA8101I XADDPAIR COMPLETE FOR VOLUME PAIR(PR202D,SE212D) FOR
SESSION(XRCTEST) WITH ERRORLEVEL(SESSION), SCSESSION(AA)
ANTA8124I XADDPAIR SUSPENDED COMPLETED FOR SESSION(XRCTEST)
ANTI8023I RESYNC INITIALIZATION STARTED FOR XRC VOLUME PAIR(PR2029,
SE2129)
ANTI8023I RESYNC INITIALIZATION STARTED FOR XRC VOLUME PAIR(PR2028,
SE2128)
ANTI8024I XRC VOLUME PAIR(PR2028,SE2128) IN DUPLEX STATUS AT TIME OF
2005.153 16:39:00.936157
ANTI8023I RESYNC INITIALIZATION STARTED FOR XRC VOLUME PAIR(PR2C2A,
SE212A)
ANTI8024I XRC VOLUME PAIR(PR2029,SE2129) IN DUPLEX STATUS AT TIME OF
2005.153 16:39:23.013906
ANTI8023I RESYNC INITIALIZATION STARTED FOR XRC VOLUME PAIR(PR202B,
SE212B)
ANTI8024I XRC VOLUME PAIR(PR202A,SE212A) IN DUPLEX STATUS AT TIME OF
2005.153 16:39:28.819489
ANTI8023I RESYNC INITIALIZATION STARTED FOR XRC VOLUME PAIR(PR202C,
SE212C)
ANTI8024I XRC VOLUME PAIR(PR202C,SE212C) IN DUPLEX STATUS AT TIME OF
2005.153 16:39:56.601708
ANTI8024I XRC VOLUME PAIR(PR202D,SE212D) IN DUPLEX STATUS AT TIME OF
2005.153 16:40:16.495676
ANTX8120I 6 VOLUMES IN SESSION(XRCTEST) ARE NOW DUPLEX
```

32.5 Sample session recovery

Example 32-7 shows the execution of an XRECOVER command to make the secondary volumes available. This is usually done from the secondary site. The secondary volumes are clipped with the primary volsers and are then available for use. In this example the primary volumes were still online so the duplicate volsers on the secondaries could not be brought online.

Example 32-7 z/OS Global Mirror session recovery

```
ANTL8800I XRECOVER XRCTEST HLQ(SYS1)
IRR813I NO PROFILE WAS FOUND IN THE STARTED CLASS FOR 940
        ANTAS001 WITH JOBNAME ANTAS001. RACF WILL USE ICHRIN03.
IEF196I         1 //IEESYSAS JOB TIME=1440,
IEF196I           // MSGLEVEL=1
IEF196I         2 //ANTAS001 EXEC IEESYSAS,PROG=ANTXAINI
IEF196I  STMT NO. MESSAGE
IEF196I         2 IEFC001I PROCEDURE IEESYSAS WAS EXPANDED USING SYSTEM
IEF196I LIBRARY SYS1.PROCLIB.IBM
IEF196I         3 XXIEESYSAS PROC PROG=IEFBR14
IEF196I                   00050000
IEF196I         4 XXIEFPROC  EXEC PGM=&PROG
IEF196I                   00100000
IEF196I           XX* THE IEESYSAS PROCEDURE IS SPECIFIED IN THE
IEF196I                   00150000
IEF196I           XX* PARAMETER LIST TO IEEMB881 BY MVS COMPONENTS
IEF196I                   00200000
IEF196I           XX* STARTING FULL FUNCTION SYSTEM ADDRESS SPACES.
IEF196I                   00250000
IEF196I           IEFC653I SUBSTITUTION JCL - PGM=ANTXAINI
IEF403I IEESYSAS - STARTED - TIME=12.42.21
IEF196I IEF237I 1100 ALLOCATED TO SYS00083
IEF196I IEF285I   SYS1.TCPIP.SEZALOAD                          KEPT
IEF196I IEF285I   VOL SER NOS= GK5RS1.
IEE252I MEMBER ANTXIN00 FOUND IN SYS1.PARMLIB.IBM
IEF196I IEF237I DMY  ALLOCATED TO SYSTSIN
IEF196I IEF237I DMY  ALLOCATED TO SYSTSPRT
IEF196I IEF285I   SYS1.PARMLIB                                 KEPT
IEF196I IEF285I   VOL SER NOS= GK5CAT.
IEF196I IEF285I   SYS1.PARMLIB.IBM                             KEPT
IEF196I IEF285I   VOL SER NOS= GK5RS1.
ANTI1020I PARAMETERS FOUND IN MEMBER ANTXIN00 OF DATA SET SYS1.PARMLIB+
HAVE BEEN APPLIED
IGD103I SMS ALLOCATED TO DDNAME ANTJSTAT
IEF196I IGD103I SMS ALLOCATED TO DDNAME ANTJSTAT
IKJ56228I DATA SET SYS1.XCOPY.XRCTEST.JRNL05 NOT IN CATALOG OR CATALOG
CAN NOT BE ACCESSED
IEF196I IKJ56228I DATA SET SYS1.XCOPY.XRCTEST.JRNL05 NOT IN CATALOG OR
IEF196I CATALOG CAN NOT BE ACCESSED
ANTR8108I XRECOVER STARTED FOR SESSION(XRCTEST) AT STARTING CONSISTENCY_
GROUP TIME(2005.153 16:41:38.763300), HLQ(SYS1)
ANTQ8200I XQUERY STARTED FOR SESSION(XRCTEST) ASNAME(ANTAS001) 976
ANTQ8202I XQUERY RECOVER REPORT - 002
ANTQ8271I ------ORIGINAL-------
ANTQ8274I PRIMARY  SECONDARY STA CON CLP  ------TIMESTAMP---------
ANTQ8203I -------------------------------------------------------------
ANTQ8275I PR2028   SE2128    DUP YES YES
ANTQ8275I PR2029   SE2129    DUP YES YES
ANTQ8275I PR202A   SE212A    DUP YES YES
ANTQ8275I PR202B   SE212B    DUP YES YES
ANTQ8275I PR202C   SE212C    DUP YES YES
ANTQ8275I PR202D   SE212D    DUP YES YES
ANTQ8237I TOTAL=6   DUP=6   PND=0   SUS=0
ANTQ8231I DATA CONSISTENT(2005.153 16:41:38.763300)
ANTQ8232I SESSIONTYPE(XRC)  ERRORLEVEL(SESSION)  HLQ(SYS1)
ANTQ8201I XQUERY RECOVER REPORT COMPLETE FOR SESSION(XRCTEST)
IGD104I SYS1.XCOPY.XRCTEST.STATE                     RETAINED,
DDNAME=ANTJSTAT
IEF196I IGD104I SYS1.XCOPY.XRCTEST.STATE                     RETAINED,
```

```
IEF196I DDNAME=ANTJSTAT
IEF196I IEF285I   SYS1.XCOPY.XRCTEST.JRNL01                    KEPT
IEF196I IEF285I   VOL SER NOS= DS6401.
IEF196I IEF285I   SYS1.XCOPY.XRCTEST.JRNL02                    KEPT
IEF196I IEF285I   VOL SER NOS= DS6402.
IEF196I IEF285I   SYS1.XCOPY.XRCTEST.JRNL03                    KEPT
IEF196I IEF285I   VOL SER NOS= DS6403.
IEF196I IEF285I   SYS1.XCOPY.XRCTEST.JRNL04                    KEPT
IEF196I IEF285I   VOL SER NOS= DS6404.
ANTR8102I XRECOVER COMPLETE FOR SESSION(XRCTEST) AT RECOVERED CONSISTENC
Y_GROUP TIME(2005.153 16:41:38.763300)
JOBNAME  PROCSTEP STEPNAME  CPU TIME      EXCPS     RC
ANTAS001 ANTAS001 IEFPROC   00:00:00        352     00
IEF404I IEESYSAS - ENDED - TIME=12.42.22
IEF196I IEF142I IEESYSAS ANTAS001 - STEP WAS EXECUTED - COND CODE 0000
V 2128-212D,ONLINE
IEF502I UNIT 2128 NOT VARIED. DUPLICATE VOLUME PR2028 IS ON UNIT 2028
IEF502I UNIT 2129 NOT VARIED. DUPLICATE VOLUME PR2029 IS ON UNIT 2029
IEF502I UNIT 212A NOT VARIED. DUPLICATE VOLUME PR202A IS ON UNIT 202A
IEF502I UNIT 212B NOT VARIED. DUPLICATE VOLUME PR202B IS ON UNIT 202B
IEF502I UNIT 212C NOT VARIED. DUPLICATE VOLUME PR202C IS ON UNIT 202C
IEF502I UNIT 212D NOT VARIED. DUPLICATE VOLUME PR202D IS ON UNIT 202D
D U,,,2128,00006 VARY RANGE DISPLAY
IEE457I 12.44.12 UNIT STATUS 070
UNIT TYPE STATUS        VOLSER     VOLSTATE
2128 3390 OFFLINE                      /RSDNT
2129 3390 OFFLINE                      /RSDNT
212A 3390 OFFLINE                      /RSDNT
212B 3390 OFFLINE                      /RSDNT
212C 3390 OFFLINE                      /RSDNT
212D 3390 OFFLINE                      /RSDNT
```

32.6 Using z/OS Global Mirror with FlashCopy and tertiary volumes

The use of DS8000s at the recovery site provides the opportunity to combine FlashCopy functions with z/OS Global Mirror functions.

For example, you can use this combination to create data for disaster recovery testing or consistent data for point-in-time backup purposes. This technique also allows you to keep the existing data mover session active while you perform the recovery test.

> **Note:** During a real Disaster Recovery (DR), z/OS Global Mirror will verify that the secondary VOLSERs and device numbers match those used in the last active z/OS Global Mirror session, and will fail the recovery if they do not. This is done to ensure that z/OS Global Mirror is recovering the correct information. When FLASHCOPY is used to create another set of secondary volumes for DR testing, all data, including the VOLSER, is copied to a new device number. At this point the VOLSER and device number do not match. The ONLINE parameter indicates that recovery is using tertiary DASD and z/OS Global Mirror is to verify only the VOLSER, allowing any device online with a VOLSER that matches a valid secondary VOLSER to be used for recovery.

The following scenario describes one method of creating data for disaster recovery testing by using FlashCopy and z/OS Global Mirror commands. The following text is taken from the APAR OA06955, PTF UA10897, which applies to z/OS V1.1 and DFSMS V1.3 onward.

1. Suspend all volume pairs in the z/OS Global Mirror session using the XSUSPEND VOLUME(ALL) command.
2. Issue FlashCopy commands to copy secondary volumes to tertiary volumes. Do not include volumes that contain the Journal, State, Control, and Master data sets.
3. Use the DFSMDdss COPY DATASET command with the RENAMEUNCONDITIONAL option specifying a different high level qualifier, and the TOLERATE(ENQFAILURE) option, copy Journal, State, Control, and Master data sets to tertiary volumes. If the session has been suspended, the TOLERATE(ENQFAILURE) option is not required. The high level qualifier used must not be the same as that used for the active session HLQ and MHLQ, and the high level qualifier used must be the same for all these data sets, including the Master data set.
4. Issue the XADDPAIR command with the SUSPENDED parameter specified, to add suspended volumes back into the session. Wait until all suspended pairs are in duplex state.
5. Vary the secondary volumes (FlashCopy source volumes) offline to the system on which the XRECOVER or XADVANCE commands will be issued.
6. Vary the tertiary volumes online to the system on which the XRECOVER or XADVANCE commands will be issued.
7. Issue the XRECOVER or XADVANCE command with the ONLINE parameter and the HLQ parameter with the new high level qualifier specified in step 3. Specifying the ONLINE parameter with the HLQ parameter will indicate to z/OS Global Mirror that the HLQ will be used for all of the z/OS Global Mirror data sets, including the Master data set. Remember that the XRECOVER command will clip (match) the volsers to secondary volsers, but the XADVANCE command will not.

Note: The XRECOVER command must not be issued on the same system as an active session with the same z/OS Global Mirror logical session name. Otherwise, the command will fail with a return code RC416. The command may be issued on a different system running in the same Sysplex.

Part 8

Interoperability

In this part of the book, we discuss the interoperability of the various Copy Services functions (Metro Mirror, FlashCopy, and z/OS Global Mirror). We also describe the interoperability of the DS8000 with other IBM TotalStorage disk subsystems in Copy Services implementations.

33

Metro Mirror and FlashCopy

In this chapter we discuss the interoperability of Metro Mirror and FlashCopy. We also give some examples and suggestions for this interoperability.

33.1 Metro Mirror and FlashCopy

There are various ways in which Metro Mirror and FlashCopy can interact. We discuss these possibilities in this section.

33.1.1 FlashCopy to Metro Mirror primary

You are able to establish a FlashCopy relationship where the target is also a remote mirror primary volume. This enables you to create full or incremental point-in-time copies at a local site and then use remote mirroring commands to copy the data to the remote site. Figure 33-1 shows this interaction.

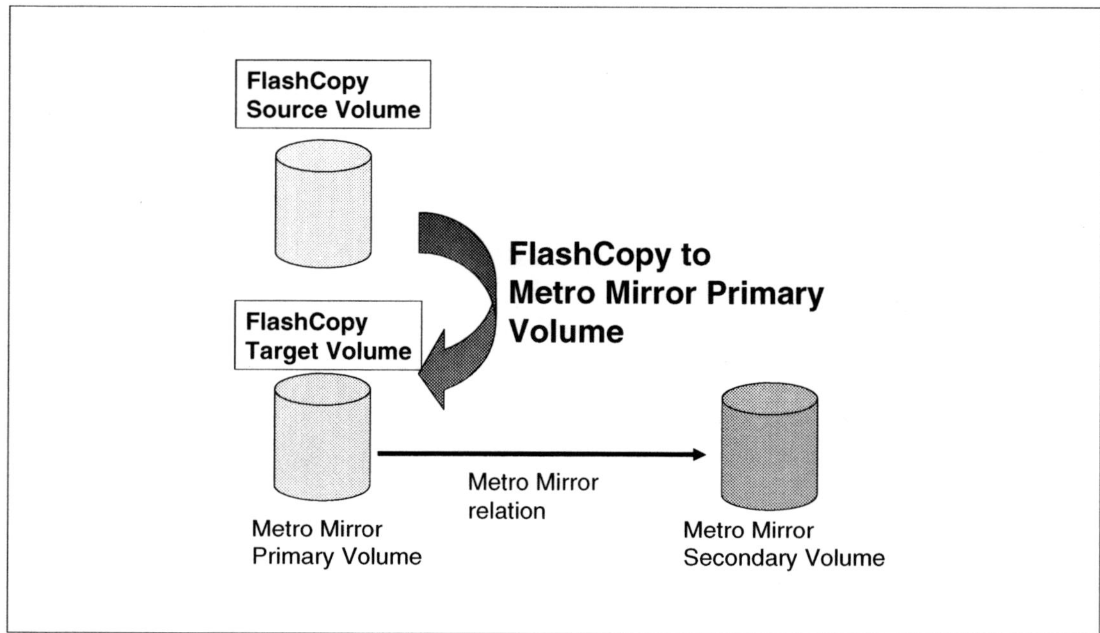

Figure 33-1 FlashCopy to Metro Mirror primary volume

This is done through one of the FlashCopy interfaces:

- Through TSO command, use the TGTPPRIM parameter of the FCESTABL command.
- Through DS CLI, use the **mkflash** command with the **tgtpprc** parameter.
- Through ICKDSF, use the FLASHCPY ESTABLISH command with the TGTOKASPPRCPRIM(YES) parameter.
- Through DFSMSdss, use the FCTOPPRCPrimary parameter of the COPY command.

33.1.2 FlashCopy of Metro Mirror secondary

You are able to establish a FlashCopy relationship where the source is a Metro Mirror secondary volume. This enables you to create a copy of a secondary volume at the remote site. You can use this copy for various purposes - for backups, for refresh of a testing environment, for disaster recovery testing, and so on.

Note that if you need consistent data from the FlashCopy, you will need a way of ensuring this. There are a several ways of doing this:

- Quiescing the host application at the primary site so that no updates are happening at the time of the FlashCopy.

- Suspending the Metro Mirror pairs at a consistent point using CGROUP FREEZE (or equivalent command in the other interfaces), performing the FlashCopy, then resuming Metro Mirror pairs.
- Using the FlashCopy Consistency Group function to Freeze and subsequently Thaw the I/O to the FlashCopy source volume.

Depending on your requirements, one of these options will suit best.

33.1.3 Remote FlashCopy commands

In a remote mirror environment, commands to manage FlashCopy at the remote site can be issued from the local or intermediate site and transmitted over the remote mirror Fibre Channel links. This eliminates the need for a network connection to the remote site solely for the management of FlashCopy.

This is done through one of the FlashCopy interfaces:

- Through TSO, use the FCESTABL command with the REMOTE parameter. There are restrictions on the use of this parameter; refer to *z/OS DFSMS Advanced Copy Services*, SC35-0428 for more information.
- Through ICKDSF, use the FLASHCPY ESTABLISH command with the SOURCEVOL parameter. Refer to *Device Support Facilities User's Guide and Reference*, GC35-0033 for more information.
- Through DS CLI, use the **mkremoteflash** command. Refer to *IBM TotalStorage DS8000 Command-Line Interface User's Guide*, SC26-7625 for more information on this command and its parameters.

34

Metro Mirror and z/OS Global Mirror

In this chapter we discuss the interoperability of the Metro Mirror and z/OS Global Mirror Copy Services functions. We also give some examples and suggestions for this interoperability.

34.1 IBM TotalStorage z/OS Metro/Global Mirror

z/OS Metro/Global Mirror uses z/OS Global Mirror to mirror primary site data to a remote location, and also uses Metro Mirror for primary site data to a location within Metro Mirror distance limits. This gives you a three-site high-availability and disaster recovery solution. Figure 34-1 shows an example of a three-site z/OS Metro/Global Mirror solution.

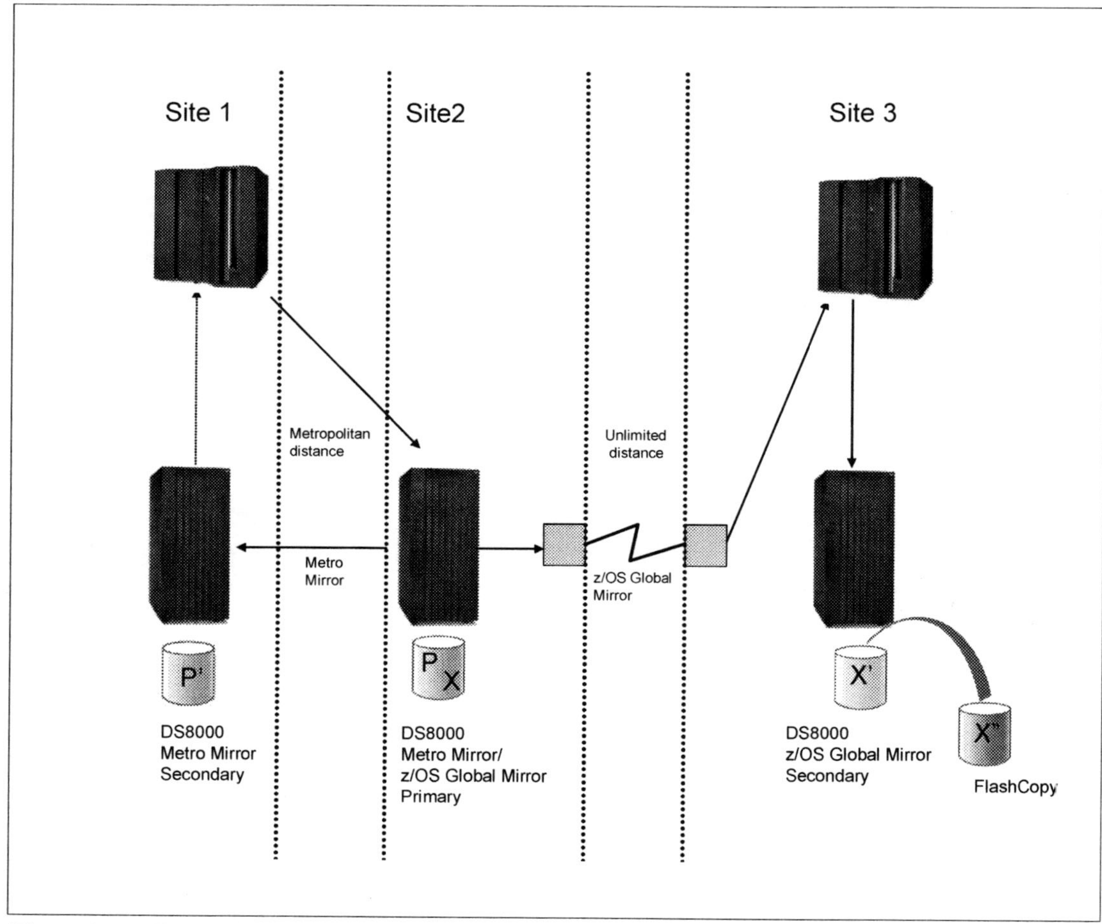

Figure 34-1 Example three site configuration with z/OS Metro/Global Mirror

In the example shown in Figure 34-1, we see that the zSeries server in Site 1 is normally accessing the DS8000 disk in Site 2. These disks are mirrored back to Site 1 via Metro Mirror to another DS8000. At the same time, the Site 2 disk has z/OS Global Mirror pairs established to Site 3, which can be at continental distances from Site 2. We have covered for the following scenarios:

- **Site 1 disaster:** Site 3 can be brought up after a short wait, by which time the Site 2 updates will have mirrored across to Site 3. Site 3 FlashCopy disk can be used to preserve a copy of the original recovery point.
- **Site 2 disaster:** Site 1 can switch to using Site 1 disk. Mirroring to Site 3 will be suspended.
- **Site 1 and Site 2 disaster:** Site 3 can be brought up on Site 3 FlashCopy disk to preserve original recovery point. Inflight updates may be lost.
- **Site 3 disaster:** Sites 1 and 2 continue to operate normally.

35

Interoperability between DS6000 and DS8000

In this chapter we show the interoperability between the Copy Services functions in the DS6000 and the DS8000. We cover the following topics:

- DS8000 and DS6000 Copy Services interoperability
- Preparing the environment
- PPRC: Establishing paths between DS6000 and DS8000
- Managing Metro Mirror or Global Copy pairs
- Managing DS6000 to DS8000 Global Mirror
- Managing DS6000 and DS8000 FlashCopy

35.1 DS8000 and DS6000 Copy Services interoperability

Copy Services operations are supported between the DS8000 and the DS6000. This means you can have a mixed Copy Services environment that contains both devices.

35.2 Preparing the environment

Before starting Copy Services operations in a mixed DS6000, DS8000 environment, you need to ensure that this environment is set up correctly.

35.2.1 Minimum microcode levels

To manage Copy Services in a mixed environment, you need to have licensed internal code bundle 6.0.600.9 or higher on your DS6000. You also need to have your IBM Service Representative install the code bundle 6.0.500.52 or higher on your DS8000.

35.2.2 Hardware and licensing requirements

To establish PPRC pairs between a DS6000 and a DS8000, the DS6000 and the DS8000 must both have Remote Mirror and Copy (RMC) licenses.

The DS6000 and DS8000 must also have Fibre Channel adapters that have connectivity to each other, either directly or via Fibre Channel switches. ESCON adapters cannot be used to mirror a DS6000 with a DS8000.

z/OS Global Mirror RMZ (formerly XRC)

The DS6000 cannot be used as a z/OS Global Mirror primary Storage Unit. There is consequently no feature code for z/OS Global Mirror (RMZ) for DS6000. The DS6000 can be used as a secondary Storage Unit.

35.2.3 Network connectivity

Network connectivity requirements depend on how you want to manage the environment. If you plan to use zSeries interfaces like TSO or ICKDSF, there are no network connectivity requirements. The commands are sent inband via FICON or ESCON. If however, you plan to use the DS CLI or the DS GUI, your requirements will be as follows:

For FlashCopy management:

- If you want to use the DS8000 DS GUI to manage FlashCopy on the DS6000, then you need network connectivity between the DS8000 HMCs and the DS6000 SMCs.
- If you want to use the DS6000 DS GUI to manage FlashCopy on the DS8000, then you need network connectivity between the DS8000 HMCs and the DS6000 SMCs.
- If you want to use the DS CLI to manage FlashCopy on either the DS6000 or the DS8000 then the DS8000 HMCs and the DS6000 SMCs do not need to be connected via a network. However, the machine on which the DS CLI is installed, needs to have network connectivity to both the SMC and the HMC.
- If you have PPRC links between the DS6000 and DS8000, you can also use remote FlashCopy to establish FlashCopies of the Remote Mirror target volumes.

For creating Remote Mirror and Copy (RMC), also known as Peer-to-Peer Remote Copy (PPRC) paths and pairs:

- In a mixed environment, one machine will be the source machine (local) and one will be the target machine (remote). If you want the ability to manage the PPRC paths and pairs from either machine, then you will need network connectivity between the DS6000 SMC and the DS8000 HMC. If you use DS CLI, the SMC and HMC do not need to be able to communicate with each other, but the DS CLI machine needs to be able to communicate with both the HMC and the SMC.
- If, however, you do not plan to ever use the remote machine as a source machine and you also do not intend to use the DS GUI to manage the pairs and paths, then you do not need to have network connectivity to the remote machine (assuming the remote machine is at a remote site). This is because when using the DS CLI, all path and pair establishment is done by connecting to the source machine (the local machine). However, this means that in a disaster recovery scenario, you will need to travel to the remote site to perform management tasks on the remote machine. This setup is not recommended because it is less flexible.

35.2.4 Create matching user ids and passwords

When you want to use the DS CLI or DS GUI to perform Copy Services operations, you need to authenticate with a valid user ID and password. When you use the DS6000 DS GUI to perform an operation that will require it to issue a command to an DS8000, it needs to authenticate with the DS8000. The DS user ID and password that you used to log on to the DS6000 DS GUI with, is used to authenticate with the DS8000 HMC. The same applies if you use the DS8000 DS GUI to manage a DS6000. This means that the same user ID and password needs to be defined in both the SMC and the HMC. This task needs to be manually performed. If instead of the DS GUI, you only use the DS CLI, then this requirement does not exist, but in this case it is still of benefit to use a matching user ID and password to manage machines in either Storage Complex.

Note: A DS8000 Storage Complex is made of up of either one or two HMCs that together manage one or two DS8000 Storage Units. A DS6000 Storage Complex consists of either one or two SMCs that together manage one or two DS6000 Storage Units.

35.2.5 Updating the DS CLI profile

If you plan to use the DS CLI to manage your mixed environment, you can create a profile to simplify: connection to the DS CLI, commands, and script operations. To achieve this, add extra lines as shown in Example 35-1. In this example, the DS6000 is considered the local machine, while the DS8000 is considered the remote machine.

Example 35-1 Possible modification to a DS CLI profile

```
# DS6000
# hmc1 is the DS6000 SMC
hmc1: 10.0.0.100
# devid is the serial number of the DS6000
devid: IBM.1750-1300247
# remotedevid is the serial number of the DS8000
remotedevid: IBM.2107-7503461
# Username is a user created on the ESS Specialist that matches the userid on the DS6000
 username:admin
# The password for the admin user id. Placing it here is not very secure.
password:passw0rd
# The password file is created using the managepwfile and is a better way to manage this.
# pwfile:security.dat
```

Placing the password in the profile is not very secure (because it is stored in a plain text file), but may prove more convenient. A password file can be created using the **managepwfile** and is a better way to manage this. After creating the password file (which by default is called *security.dat*), you can remove the password from the profile and instead specify the pwfile file.

The command to create a passwd file in this example is:

```
managepwfile -action add -name admin -pw passw0rd
```

A simple method when you have multiple machines to manage is to create multiple profile files. Then when starting DS CLI, you can specify the profile file you wish to use with the **-cfg** parameter. In a Windows environment you could have multiple Windows batch files (BAT files), one for each machine you wish to manage. The profile shown in Example 35-1 could be saved in the C:\program files\ibm\dscli\profile directory as 1750source.profile. Then you could create a simple Windows BAT file with three lines as shown in Example 35-2.

Example 35-2 Windows BAT file to start a specific profile

```
title DS CLI Local DS6800 1300247 Remote IBM.2107-7503461
cd C:\Program Files\ibm\dscli\profile
dscli -cfg 1750source.profile
```

We save the BAT file onto the Windows desktop and start it by double clicking on the icon. The DS CLI will open and will start the specified profile. By creating a BAT file and profile for each machine, we can simplify the process of starting the DS CLI. We can also specify the profile when starting DS CLI from inside a script, or when running the DS CLI in script mode.

35.2.6 Adding the Storage Complex

If you wish to use a single DS GUI to manage both FlashCopy and Remote Mirror and Copy pairs on your DS6000 and DS8000, you have to add the Storage Complex of one Storage Unit (such as a DS6000) to the Storage Complex of the other Storage Unit (such as a DS8000). Note that we have to do this operation once in each direction. In other words you have to add the DS6000 to the DS8000 and then add the DS8000 to the DS6000.

Adding the DS6000 Storage Complex to a DS8000 Storage Complex

You add a DS6000 Storage Complex to a DS8000 Storage Complex as follows.

> **Important:** Make sure the user ID you use to log on to the DS8000 DS GUI also exists on the DS6000 SMC and that it has the same password. If not, the operation to add the Storage Complex will fail. You will need to always use this same user ID for multi-complex management.

1. Connect to the DS8000 HMC using the DS GUI.
2. Click **Real-time manager**.
3. Click **Manage hardware**.
4. Click **Storage complexes**.
5. Select **Add** and click **Go**.

Figure 35-1 shows the Add Storage Complex panel.

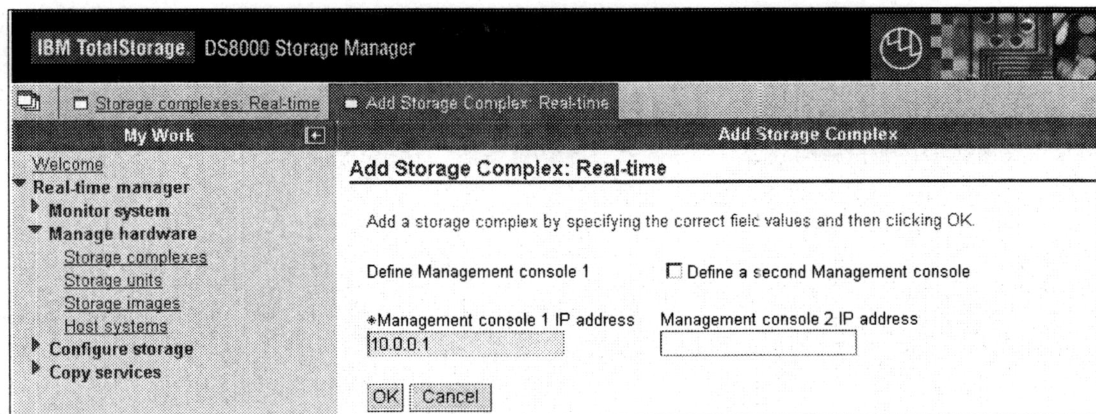

Figure 35-1 Add DS6000 complex to DS8000

6. Enter the IP address of the DS6000 SMC into the Management console 1 IP address box. If you have a second SMC, select the **Define a second Management console** box and enter the second SMC address into the Management console 2 IP address box. Now select **OK**.
7. When the add Storage Complex operation completes, the Storage Complex screen will now show the DS6000 SMC as an additional Storage Complex.
8. Having added the DS6000 Storage Complex to the DS8000 Storage Complex, you are now able to use the DS8000 DS GUI to create paths and Remote Mirror and Copy pairs, where the DS6000 is the source device. You can also use the DS8000 DS GUI to manage FlashCopy pairs on the DS6000.

Note: The steps to add the DS6000 Storage Complex to the DS8000 Storage Complex cannot be performed using the DS CLI. This is by design. However, if you don't plan to use the DS GUI, this will not be an issue.

Adding the DS8000 Storage Complex to a DS6000 Storage Complex

You add a DS8000 Storage Complex to a DS6000 Storage Complex as follows:

Important: Make sure the user ID you use to log on to the DS6000 DS GUI also exists on the DS8000 HMC and that it has the same password. If not, the operation to add the Storage Complex will fail. You will need to always use this same user ID for multi-complex management.

1. Connect to the DS6000 SMC using the DS GUI.
2. Click **Real-time manager**.
3. Click **Manage hardware**.
4. Click **Storage complexes**.
5. Select **Add Storage Complex** and click **Go**.

Figure 35-2 shows the Add Storage Complex panel.

Figure 35-2 Add DS8000 complex to DS6000

6. Enter the IP address of the DS8000 HMC into the Management console 1 IP address box. If you have a second DS8000 HMC, select the **Define a second Management console** box and enter the second HMC address in the Management console 2 IP address box. Now select **OK**.
7. When the add Storage Complex operation completes, the Storage Complex screen will now show the DS8000 HMC as an additional Storage Complex. In Figure 35-3 we have a DS6000 SMC, an ESS 800 Copy Services Server and a DS8000 HMC all defined on the one DS6000 DS GUI.

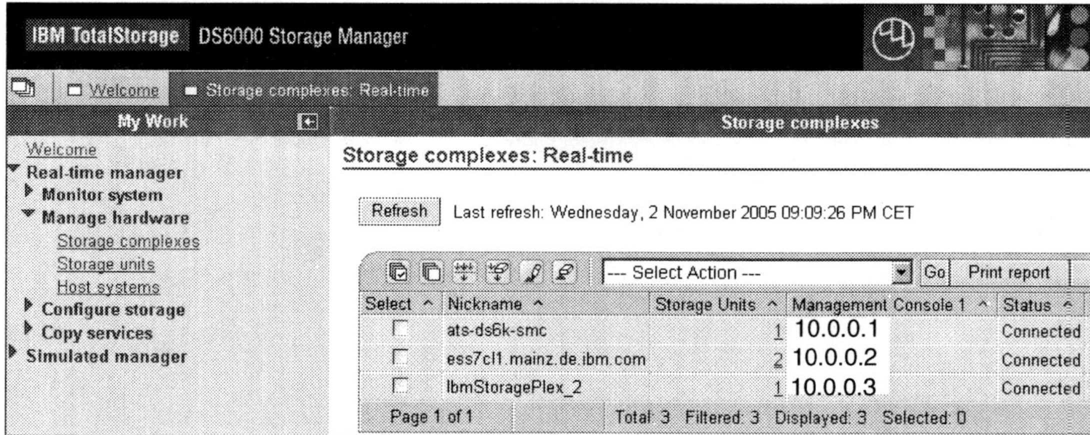

Figure 35-3 DS6000 GUI showing multiple complexes

8. Having added the DS8000 Storage Complex to the DS6000 Storage Complex, you are now able to use the DS6000 DS GUI to create paths and Remote Mirror and Copy pairs, where the DS8000 is the source device. You can also use the DS6000 DS GUI to manage FlashCopy pairs on the DS8000.

Note: The steps to add the DS8000 Storage Complex to the DS6000 Storage Complex cannot be performed using the DS CLI.

User ID management

There are two important considerations when managing multiple Storage Complexes from a single DS GUI:

1. The user ID you use to add the alternative complex must exist on both complexes. You must continue to use this user ID for all multi complex operations. If you logon to either DS GUI with a user ID that does not exist on the other Complex, the remote Complex will not appear in the Storage Complex screen.
2. Even when you have successfully added one complex to another, new user IDs created in one complex will not mirror to the other complex. They have to be manually created and managed in each complex.

Storage management

You cannot use the DS8000 DS GUI to perform storage configuration on a DS6000. Likewise you cannot use the DS6000 DS GUI to perform storage configuration on a DS8000. You can only perform Copy Services management tasks on the alternative device. If you are logged onto the DS6000 DS GUI and wish to configure some storage on the DS8000, you will need to log off and then log on to the DS8000 DS GUI. The same applies if you are logged onto the DS8000 DS GUI and wish to configure storage on the DS6000. You must log on to the DS6000 DS GUI to do this.

35.2.7 Volume size considerations for PPRC

When using PPRC to copy the contents of a CKD volume from one storage device to another, it is possible for the PPRC target volume to be larger than the PPRC source volume. However, if an attempt is made to reverse the relationship so that the source becomes the target, then this attempt will fail because the source is now larger than the target. For this reason it is always recommended that the source and target volumes be the same size. Prior to creating a PPRC relationship, check the volumes sizes to ensure they are the same on each storage device.

Determining DS6000 and DS8000 CKD volume size

When CKD volumes are created on a DS6000 or DS8000, the size must be specified in cylinders. In Example 35-3, two CKD volumes of 3339 cylinders are created. This means that if we use these volumes in a PPRC relationship, their partner volumes should also be 3339 cylinders.

Example 35-3 CKD volume size in DS CLI

```
dsc i> mkckdvol -extpool P2 -cap 3339 -name av_6K_CKD_#h 0600-0601
Date/Time: 8 November 2005 22:58:31 IBM DSCLI Version: 5.1.0.204 DS: IBM.1750-1300247
CMUC00021I mkckdvol: CKD Volume 0600 successfully created.
CMUC00021I mkckdvol: CKD Volume 0601 successfully created.
dsc i> lsckdvol -lcu 06
Date/Time: 9 November 2005 3:58:42 IBM DSCLI Version: 5.1.0.204 DS: IBM.1750-1300247
Name            ID   accstate datastate configstate deviceMTM voltype  orgbvols extpool cap (cyl)
=================================================================================================
av_6K_CKD_0600 0600 Online   Normal    Normal      3390-3    CKD Base -        P2           3339
av_6K_CKD_0601 0601 Online   Normal    Normal      3390-3    CKD Base -        P2           3339
```

35.3 PPRC: Establishing paths between DS6000 and DS8000

To create a PPRC relationship between a DS8000 and an DS6000 we first need to create logical paths (over the physical Fibre Channel connections). If we are using the DS GUI, then provided we added the other machines Storage Complex, we can establish paths in either direction (DS6000 to DS8000 or DS8000 to DS6000).

35.3.1 Decoding port IDs

When viewing port IDs in the DS GUI or DS CLI, the port IDs can be decoded to show which physical port on the DS8000 or DS6000 is in use.

For DS8000, port IDs look like I0000 or I0123, which actually breaks out as IEECP. The EE is the enclosure number (minus 1), C is the card slot number (minus 1) and P is the port number on the card. So I0123 is enclosure 2 (1+1), slot 3 (2+1), port 3.

For DS6000, port IDs range from I0000 to I0001 and I0100 to I0103, which actually breaks out as IEECP. The EE is the controller number(00 or 01), C is the card slot number (always zero) and P is the port number on the card (0 to 3). So I0103 is controller 1, card slot 0, port 3.

35.3.2 Path creation using the DS GUI

Path creation between a DS6000 and a DS8000 is no different to the process used to create paths between two DS8000s or two DS6000. See 13.5, "Metro Mirror links" on page 125.

Paths in the reverse direction

The example above showed how to create a path from the DS8000 to the DS6000. In many cases it may be likely that you will need paths from DS6000 to the DS8000. Regardless, having established paths in one direction you can then establish paths in the opposite direction. Fibre Channel allows for bi-directional mirroring over the same physical path.

Adding or deleting paths

You can add additional paths to an LSS pair by simply creating more paths. To remove a path, just display the Paths screen, select the relevant source machine and LSS, select the path you wish to delete and use the delete option from the Select Action pull-down.

35.3.3 Establish logical paths between DS8000 and DS6000 using DS CLI

You can also use the DS CLI to establish logical paths. One additional step is that you need to know the WWNN of the target Storage Image. The three commands we will use to establish a path are: `lssi`, `lsavailpprcport` and `mkpprcpath`.

Determining the remote device WWNN

First we need to determine the WWNN of the remote storage device. If you started DS CLI by connecting to the DS8000 HMC, then the remote storage device is the DS6000. If you started DS CLI by connecting to the DS6000, then the remote Storage Image is the DS8000.

How to determine the DS6000 WWNN using DS GUI

1. Click **Real-time manager**.
2. Click **Manage hardware**.
3. Click **Storage units**.
4. Click in the **Select** column for the DS6000 Storage Unit, and from the **Select Action** pull-down, choose **Properties** and click **Go**.
5. The DS6000 Storage Unit WWNN will be displayed on the subsequent properties screen.

How to determine DS6000 WWNN using DS CLI

In Example 35-5 we show how to display the WWNN of a Storage Image using the `lssi` command.

Example 35-4 Determine the WWNN of a DS6000

```
dscli> lssi
Date/Time: 3 November 2005 1:05:50 IBM DSCLI Version: 5.1.0.204
Name ID               Storage Unit      Model WWNN             State  ESSNet
============================================================================
-    IBM.1750-1300247 IBM.1750-1300247 511   500507630EFFFE16 Online Enabled
```

How to determine the DS8000 WWNN using DS GUI

1. Click **Real-time manager**.
2. Click **Manage hardware**.
3. Click **Storage images** (not the Storage Unit).
4. Click in the **Select** column for the DS8000 Storage Image, and from the **Select Action** pull-down, choose **Properties** and click **Go**.
5. The DS8000 Storage Image WWNN will be displayed on the subsequent properties screen.

How to determine DS8000 WWNN using DS CLI

In Example 35-5 we show how to display the WWNN of a DS8000 Storage Image using the **lssi** command.

Example 35-5 Determine the WWNN of a DS8000

```
dscli> lssi IBM.2107-7503461
Date/Time: 1 November 2005 3:08:52 IBM DSCLI Version: 5.1.0.204
Name ID               Storage Unit      Model WWNN             State  ESSNet
============================================================================
-    IBM.2107-7503461 IBM.2107-7503460 922   5005076303FFC08F Online Enabled
```

Listing the available ports using DS CLI

Having determined the remote devices WWNN, we can now display the ports that are available to establish PPRC paths. In Example 35-6 we are logged onto the DS8000 using DS CLI, so the remote device is the DS6000. We display ports available to establish paths between LSS 14 on the DS8000 and LSS 18 on the DS6000.

> **Note:** When using the **lsavailpprcport** command you must specify LSSs that actually exist.

Example 35-6 Displaying available ports for PPRC path establishment

```
dscli> lsavailpprcport -remotedev IBM.1750-1300247 -remotewwnn 500507630EFFFE16 08:06
Date/Time: 8 November 2005 23:07:38 IBM DSCLI Version: 5.1.0.204 DS: IBM.2107-7503461
Local Port Attached Port Type
=============================
I0001      I0103         FCP
I0131      I0003         FCP
```

Establishing the logical paths using DS CLI

Having determined which ports are available, for each LSS pair that we wish to copy and mirror between, we now establish a one-way path using the **mkpprcpath** command. We can then display established paths using the **lspprcpath** command.

In Example 35-7, we first establish a single path between LSS 14 on the DS8000 and LSS 18 on the DS6000. We then display the paths available for LSS 14 on the DS8000.

Example 35-7 Using DS CLI to establish PPRC paths

```
dscli> mkpprcpath -remotedev IBM.1750-1300247 -remotewwnn 500507630EFFFE16 -srclss 14
-tgtlss 18 I0001:I0103
Date/Time: 3 November 2005 20:37:09 IBM DSCLI Version: 5.1.0.204 DS: IBM.2107-7503461
CMUC00149I mkpprcpath: Remote Mirror and Copy path 14:18 successfully established.
dscli> lspprcpath 14
Date/Time: 3 November 2005 20:37:14 IBM DSCLI Version: 5.1.0.204 DS: IBM.2107-7503461
Src Tgt State   SS   Port  Attached Port Tgt WWNN
=========================================================
14  18  Success FF18 I0001 I0103         500507630EFFFE16
```

In Example 35-8 we add an additional path between LSS 14 on the DS8000 and LSS 18 on the DS6000. Take careful note though, we include the existing path when creating a new path. Otherwise the existing path is removed and only the new path will be available for use.

Example 35-8 Establishing additional paths using DS CLI

```
dscli> mkpprcpath -remotedev IBM.1750-1300247 -remotewwnn 500507630EFFFE16 -srclss 14
-tgtlss 18 I0001:I0103 I0131:I10003
Date/Time: 3 November 2005 20:37:49 IBM DSCLI Version: 5.1.0.204 DS: IBM.2107-7503461
CMUC00149I mkpprcpath: Remote Mirror and Copy path 14:18 successfully established.
dscli> lspprcpath 14
Date/Time: 3 November 2005 20:37:53 IBM DSCLI Version: 5.1.0.204 DS: IBM.2107-7503461
Src Tgt State   SS   Port  Attached Port Tgt WWNN
=========================================================
14  18  Success FF18 I0001 I0103         500507630EFFFE16
14  18  Success FF18 I0131 I0003         500507630EFFFE16
```

To establish paths where the DS6000 is the source, we should connect to the DS6000 using DS CLI and follow the same process, but specify the DS8000 as the remote device.

Important: When you connect using DS CLI to the DS8000 HMC, the DS8000 is the local device and the DS6000 is the remove device. If you connect using DS CLI to the DS6000, then the DS6000 is now the local device and the DS8000 is the remote device.

Attention: The **rmpprcpath** command will remove all paths between the source and target LSSs. To just reduce the path count, use the **mkpprcpath** command specifying only the paths you wish to continue using.

35.3.4 Path creation using TSO

In Example 35-9 we establish Metro Mirror paths from a DS6000 to an DS8000 using a TSO command. The command breaks out as follows:

```
Device that command is issued to:E200
Primary LCU SSID:6000
Primary DS6000 WWNN:500507630EFFFE16
Primary DS6000 LSS ID:06
Secondary DS8000 LCU SSID:2105
Secondary DS8000 WWNN:5005076303FFC08F
Secondary DS8000 LSS ID:05
First path established:I0003 to I0003
Second path established:I0103 to I0103
```

Example 35-9 CESTPATH commands

```
/* ----------------------------------------------------------------- */
/*                                                                   */
/* ISSUE PPRC CESTPATH TO ESTABLISH PPRC PATHS                       */
/*                                                                   */
/* ----------------------------------------------------------------- */
 CESTPATH DEVN(X'E200') PRIM(X'6000' 500507630EFFFE16 X'06') -
          SEC(X'2105' 5005076303FFC08F X'05') -
          LINK(X'00030003' X'01030103') -
          CGROUP(NO)
/* ----------------------------------------------------------------- */
```

35.4 Managing Metro Mirror or Global Copy pairs

Having established paths, we can now establish volume pairs.

35.4.1 Managing Metro Mirror or Global Copy pairs using the DS GUI

Establishing and managing Metro Mirror and Global Copy pairs between a DS6000 and a DS8000 using the DS GUI is no different than using the DS GUI to establish pairs between two DS8000s or DS6000s. See Part 4, "Metro Mirror" on page 115 and Part 6, "Global Mirror" on page 233.

35.4.2 Managing Metro Mirror pairs using the DS CLI

Having established paths, we can now establish volume pairs. In this example we show how you can establish Metro Mirror volume pairs between a DS8000 and a DS6000 with the DS CLI. In this example we create two Metro Mirror pairs. Volumes 0801 and 0802 from the DS8000 are the source volumes, and the target volumes on the DS6000 are 0601 and 0602.

In Example 35-10 we create two pairs using the **mkpprc** command. We then list them using the **lspprc** command. We then remove one pair using the **rmpprc** command.

Example 35-10 Creating Metro Mirror pairs using DS CLI

```
dscli> mkpprc -remotedev IBM.1750-1300247 -type mmir -mode full 0801:0601 0802:0602
Date/Time: 9 November 2005 2:40:32 IBM DSCLI Version: 5.1.0.204 DS: IBM.2107-7503461
CMUC00153I mkpprc: Remote Mirror and Copy volume pair relationship 0801:0601 successfully
created.
CMUC00153I mkpprc: Remote Mirror and Copy volume pair relationship 0802:0602 successfully
created.
dscli> lspprc 0801-0802
Date/Time: 9 November 2005 2:40:38 IBM DSCLI Version: 5.1.0.204 DS: IBM.2107-7503461
ID        State        Reason Type         SourceLSS Timeout (secs) Critical Mode First
==================================================================================
0801:0601 Copy Pending -      Metro Mirror 08        unknown        Disabled     Invalid
0802:0602 Copy Pending -      Metro Mirror 08        unknown        Disabled     Invalid
dscli> rmpprc -remotedev IBM.1750-1300247 0801:0601
Date/Time: 9 November 2005 2:41:18 IBM DSCLI Version: 5.1.0.204 DS: IBM.2107-7503461
CMUC00160W rmpprc: Are you sure you want to delete the Remote Mirror and Copy volume pair
relationship 0801:0601:? [y/n] y
CMUC00155I rmpprc: Remote Mirror and Copy volume pair 0801:0601 relationship successfully
withdrawn.
dscli>
```

In Example 35-10 we connected to the DS8000 HMC using DS CLI, so the DS6000 is the remote device. If we wish to establish pairs where the DS6000 is the source device, we need to connect to the DS6000 using DS CLI. This will make the DS8000 the remote device.

> **Important:** If you specify the wrong **-remotedev** or you are using a profile where a different remote device to the one you intended to work on is specified, you may get an error message, CMUN03057 saying you are specifying an invalid subsystem ID. This may be because you are specifying the wrong remote device serial number. If you have multiple possible remote devices, do not place a **remotedev** entry in your DS CLI profile.

35.4.3 Managing Global Copy pairs using DS CLI

Having established paths, we can now establish volume pairs. In this example we show how you can establish Global Copy volume pairs between a DS8000 and an DS6000 with the DS CLI. In this example we create two Global Copy pairs. Volumes 0801 and 0802 from the DS8000 are the source volumes, and the target volumes on the DS6000 are 0600 and 0601.

In Example 35-10 we create two pairs using the **mkpprc** command. We then list them using the **lspprc** command. We then pause one pair using the **pausepprc** command.

Example 35-11 Using DS CLI to manage Global Copy

```
dscli> mkpprc -remotedev IBM.1750-1300247 -type gcp 0801:0601 0802:0602
Date/Time: 9 November 2005 2:43:39 IBM DSCLI Version: 5.1.0.204 DS: IBM.2107-7503461
CMUC00153I mkpprc: Remote Mirror and Copy volume pair relationship 0801:0601 successfully
created.
CMUC00153I mkpprc: Remote Mirror and Copy volume pair relationship 0802:0602 successfully
created.
dscli> lspprc 0801-0802
Date/Time: 9 November 2005 2:43:46 IBM DSCLI Version: 5.1.0.204 DS: IBM.2107-7503461
ID        State        Reason Type        SourceLSS Timeout (secs) Critical Mode First Pass
==========================================================================================
0801:0601 Copy Pending -      Global Copy 08        unknown        Disabled      False
0802:0602 Copy Pending -      Global Copy 08        unknown        Disabled      False
dscli> pausepprc -remotedev IBM.1750-1300247 0801:0601
Date/Time: 9 November 2005 2:44:04 IBM DSCLI Version: 5.1.0.204 DS: IBM.2107-7503461
CMUC00157I pausepprc: Remote Mirror and Copy volume pair 0801:0601 relationship
successfully paused.
dscli> lspprc 0801
Date/Time: 9 November 2005 2:44:08 IBM DSCLI Version: 5.1.0.204 DS: IBM.2107-7503461
ID        State     Reason      Type        SourceLSS Timeout (secs) Critical Mode First
==========================================================================================
0801:0601 Suspended Host Source Global Copy 08        unknown        Disabled      False
```

35.5 Managing DS6000 to DS8000 Global Mirror

The establishment of Global Mirror between a DS8000 and an DS6000 is achieved using the same methods as explained in Chapter 27., "Global Mirror examples" on page 341.

35.5.1 Managing Global Mirror pairs using DS CLI

In Example 35-12 we establish a Global Copy pair between volume 0601 on the DS6000 and volume 0801 on the DS8000. We then create session 90 for LSS 08. We then create a Global Mirror using session 90 and LSS 08.

Example 35-12 Establishing Global Mirror using DS CLI

```
dscli> mkpprc -remotedev IBM.1750-1300247 -type gcp -tgtread -mode full 0801:0601
Date/Time: 9 November 2005 2:45:53 IBM DSCLI Version: 5.1.0.204 DS: IBM.2107-7503461
CMUC00153I mkpprc: Remote Mirror and Copy volume pair relationship 0801:0601 successfully created.
dscli> lspprc 0801
Date/Time: 9 November 2005 2:46:04 IBM DSCLI Version: 5.1.0.204 DS: IBM.2107-7503461
ID        State        Reason Type        SourceLSS Timeout (secs) Critical Mode First Pass Status
===================================================================================================
0801:0601 Copy Pending -      Global Copy 08        unknown        Disabled      False
dscli> mkremoteflash -dev IBM.1750-1300247 -conduit IBM.2107-7503461 -record -nocp 0601:0602
Date/Time: 2 November 2005 21:49:00 IBM DSCLI Version: 5.1.0.204 DS: IBM.1750-1300247
CMUC00173I mkremoteflash: Remote FlashCopy volume pair 0601:0602 successfully created. Use the
lsremoteflash command to determine copy completion.
dscli> mksession -lss 08 -volume 0801 90
Date/Time: 9 November 2005 2:57:18 IBM DSCLI Version: 5.1.0.204 DS: IBM.2107-7503461
CMUC00145I mksession: Session 90 opened successfully.
ddscli> lssession 08
Date/Time: 9 November 2005 2:57:55 IBM DSCLI Version: 5.1.0.204 DS: IBM.2107-7503461
LSS ID Session Status Volume VolumeStatus PrimaryStatus        SecondaryStatus   FirstPassComplete
===========================================================================================================
08     90      Normal 0801   Join Pending Primary Copy Pending Secondary Simplex True
dscli> mkgmir -lss 08 -session 90
Date/Time: 9 November 2005 2:58:19 IBM DSCLI Version: 5.1.0.204 DS: IBM.2107-7503461
CMUC00162I mkgmir: Global Mirror for session 90 successfully started.
ddscli> showgmir 08
Date/Time: 9 November 2005 2:58:42 IBM DSCLI Version: 5.1.0.204 DS: IBM.2107-7503461
ID                           IBM.2107-7503461/08
Master Count                 1
Master Session ID            0x90
Copy State                   Running
Fatal Reason                 Not Fatal
CG Interval (seconds)        0
XDC Interval(milliseconds)   50
CG Drain Time (seconds)      30
Current Time                 11/09/2005 02:59:58 EST
CG Time                      11/09/2005 02:59:58 EST
Successful CG Percentage     100
FlashCopy Sequence Number    0x4370CB7E
Master ID                    IBM.2107-7503461
Subordinate Count            0
Master/Subordinate Assoc     -
```

35.6 Managing DS6000 and DS8000 FlashCopy

Provided that a FlashCopy license is present on the device, it is possible to manage FlashCopy using the DS GUI. The establishment of a FlashCopy pair on a DS6000, using the DS8000 DS GUI, is no different than establishing a DS8000 FlashCopy pair, see Part 3, "FlashCopy" on page 43. The establishment of a FlashCopy pair on an DS8000, using the DS6000 DS GUI, is again no different than establishing a DS6000 FlashCopy pair. For DS CLI, you connect directly to the relevant SMC or HMC, so it is also not different.

35.6.1 Creating a remote FlashCopy on a DS6000 using DS CLI

It is also possible to use DS CLI to create a remote FlashCopy on an DS6000 where the source PPRC device is a DS8000 or vice versa. In Example 35-13, we connect using the DS CLI to a DS8000. We determine there are established paths from LSS 08 on the DS8000 to LSS 06 on the DS6000. We create a Metro Mirror pair from volume 0801 on the DS8000 to volume 0601 on the DS6000. We then create a remote FlashCopy on the DS6000 between DS6000 volumes 0601 and 0602. We then remove the remote FlashCopy.

Example 35-13 Creating a remote FlashCopy where the DS6000 is the remote target

```
dscli> lspprcpath 08
Date/Time: 9 November 2005 3:01:10 IBM DSCLI Version: 5.1.0.204 DS: IBM.2107-7503461
Src Tgt State   SS   Port  Attached Port Tgt WWNN
=======================================================
08  06  Success 6000 I0001 I0103         500507630EFFFE16
ddscli> mkpprc -remotedev IBM.1750-1300247 -type mmir 0801:0601
Date/Time: 9 November 2005 3:02:36 IBM DSCLI Version: 5.1.0.204 DS: IBM.2107-7503461
CMUC00153I mkpprc: Remote Mirror and Copy volume pair relationship 0801:0601 successfully created.
dscli> mkremoteflash -dev IBM.1750-1300247 -conduit IBM.2107-7503461/08 -persist -nocp 0601:0602
Date/Time: 3 November 2005 22:35:45 IBM DSCLI Version: 5.1.0.204 DS: IBM.1750-1300247
CMUC00173I mkremoteflash: Remote FlashCopy volume pair 0601:0602 successfully created. Use the
lsremoteflash command to determine copy completion.
dscli> lsremoteflash -dev IBM.1750-1300247 -conduit IBM.2107-7503461/08 0601:0602
Date/Time: 9 November 2005 3:04:07 IBM DSCLI Version: 5.1.0.204 DS: IBM.1750-1300247
ID        SrcLSS SequenceNum ActiveCopy Recording Persistent Revertible SourceWriteEnabled
====================================================================================================
0601:0602 06     0           Disabled   Enabled   Enabled    Disabled   Enabled
dscli> rmremoteflash -dev IBM.1750-1300247 -conduit IBM.2107-7503461/08 0601:0602
Date/Time: 3 November 2005 22:36:19 IBM DSCLI Version: 5.1.0.204 DS: IBM.1750-1300247
CMUC00179I rmremoteflash: Are you sure you want to remove the remote FlashCopy pair {0}? [y/n]:y
CMUC00180I rmremoteflash: Removal of the remote FlashCopy volume pair 0601:0602 has been initiated
successfully. Use the lsremoteflash command to determine when the relationship is deleted.
```

You could also reverse the scenario and use the DS6000 as the source machine in a PPRC pair and then create the remote FlashCopy on the DS8000.

> **Note:** Commands that work with remote FlashCopies use the **-dev** parameter to define the machine on which the FlashCopy is to be performed. Other commands, such as **mkpprc** commands, will refer to this same device as the remote device, using **-remotedev**. However, since a FlashCopy has to be sent to the remote site and then performed locally on that site, the use of the **-dev** parameter to refer to the remote machine is correct.

35.7 z/OS Global Mirror

It is a supported configuration to use a DS8000 as the primary Storage Unit and a DS6000 as a secondary Storage Unit, for the purposes of z/OS Global Mirror. However, we did not test this as part of the IBM Redbooks. More importantly, if you plan to use z/OS® Global Mirror (previously known as Extended Remote Copy or XRC), be aware that a z/OS Global Mirror environment that includes a DS8000 as a primary Storage Unit and a DS6000 as a secondary Storage Unit is not recommended for failover and failback operations because of the following limitations.

Performance mismatch (mirroring)

If the secondary Storage Unit, the DS6000, and its connectivity to the System Data Mover (SDM) that runs on z/OS Global Mirror, is significantly less capable (lower performing) than the primary Storage Unit and its connectivity to the application systems, the overall z/OS Global Mirror performance may suffer degraded performance. That is, if applications can write faster to primary Storage Units than the SDM can write to the secondary Storage Units, then implementation problems will result. (The SDM is the function that copies data from the primary Storage Unit to the secondary Storage Unit in a z/OS Global Mirror environment.)

Performance mismatch (running applications)

Suppose that a disaster or failure occurs and that applications failover to the secondary (or recovery) site and are running using the secondary Storage Units. If the secondary Storage Unit, the DS6000, is less capable (performance wise) than the primary Storage Unit, it is likely that you will not be able to complete primary business applications in the required or expected time frame.

z/OS Global Mirror-capable local (or primary) Storage Units

Suppose that a disaster or failure occurs in a z/OS Global Mirror environment and applications failover to the secondary site and are running at the secondary site on the secondary Storage Units. Later, after the primary site has been repaired and is ready to resume as the primary site, the secondary Storage Unit can then use z/OS Global Mirror to failback to the primary site. However, for the failover and failback operations to work successfully, the secondary Storage Unit must be a z/OS Global Mirror-capable primary Storage Unit, which means it must be capable of being an z/OS Global Mirror primary Storage Unit. The DS6000 does not have the appropriate microcode functionality to be a z/OS Global Mirror-capable primary Storage Unit; and therefore, cannot be used to failback to the primary site.

36

Interoperability between DS8000 and ESS 800

In this chapter we show the interoperability between the Copy Services functions in the DS8000 and the ESS 800. We cover the following topics:

- PPRC: Establishing paths between DS8000 and ESS 800
- Managing Metro Mirror or Global Copy pairs
- Managing ESS 800 Global Mirror
- Managing ESS 800 FlashCopy

36.1 DS8000 and ESS 800 Copy Services interoperability

Copy Services operations are supported between the DS8000 and the IBM Enterprise Storage Server Model 800 (ESS 800) and Model 750. For the rest of this chapter, all references to the ESS 800 also apply to the ESS 750. On the ESS 800, Remote Mirror and Copy (RMC) is called Peer-to-Peer Remote Copy (PPRC). All references to PPRC are interchangeable with RMC.

36.2 Preparing the environment

Before starting Copy Services operations in a mixed DS8000, ESS 800 environment, you need to ensure that this environment is set up correctly.

36.2.1 Minimum microcode levels

To manage the ESS 800 Copy Services from the DS8000, you need to have your IBM Service Representative install licensed internal code Version 2.4.3.65 or higher on the ESS 800, and DS8000 code bundle 6.0.500.52 or higher on the DS8000.

36.2.2 Hardware and licensing requirements

To establish PPRC pairs between an ESS 800 and a DS8000, the ESS 800 must have a PPRC license and the DS8000 must have a Remote Mirror Copy (RMC) license.

The ESS 800 must also have Fibre Channel adapters that have connectivity to the DS8000. ESCON adapters cannot be used to mirror a ESS 800 to a DS8000. You cannot have a Copy Services relationship between a 2105 E20 or F20 and a DS8000. You could, however, have a cascaded installation where an ESS F20 was mirrored to an ESS 800 that was then mirrored to a DS8000. The ESS F20 to ESS 800 relationship would have to be managed with ESS management tools such as the ESS CLI or the ESS Web Copy Services GUI.

36.2.3 Network connectivity

Network connectivity requirements depend on how you want to manage the environment. If you plan to use zSeries interfaces like TSO or ICKDSF, there are no network connectivity requirements. The commands are sent inband via FICON or ESCON. If, however, you plan to use the DS CLI or the DS GUI, your requirements will be as follows:

For FlashCopy management:

- If you want to use the DS8000 DS GUI to manage FlashCopy on the ESS 800, then you need network connectivity between the DS8000 HMCs and the ESS 800 Copy Services servers.
- If you want to be able to use the DS CLI to manage FlashCopy on the ESS 800 then you need network connectivity between the machine on which you are running the DS CLI and at least one of the ESS 800 Copy Services servers.

For creating Remote Mirror and Copy (RMC), also known as Peer-to-Peer Remote Copy (PPRC) paths and pairs:

- If you wish to use the ESS 800 as a PPRC source machine, then you will need network connectivity to the ESS 800 Copy Services servers, either from a machine running DS CLI, or from the DS8000 HMC.

- If, however, the ESS 800 will purely be a remote target for PPRC, and you do not plan to ever use it as a source machine and you do not intend to use DS GUI to manage the pairs and paths, then you do not need to have network connectivity to the ESS 800 Copy Services servers. This is because all path and pair establishment is done by connecting to the source machine (which would be the DS8000). This setup is not recommended because it is less flexible.

36.2.4 Create matching user IDs and passwords

When you want to use the DS CLI or DS GUI to perform Copy Services operations, you need to authenticate with a valid user ID and password. When you use the DS GUI to perform an operation that will require it to issue a command to an ESS 800, it needs to authenticate with the ESS 800. To do this it uses the DS user ID and password that you used to log on to the GUI with. This means that this user ID and password needs to be defined in the ESS Specialist. This task needs to be manually performed. If instead of the DS GUI, you only use the DS CLI, then you will be logging onto the ESS 800 Copy Services server directly, so the requirement will not be there. For simplified management you may still want to create a matching user ID and password.

Create a user ID on the DS8000

The first step is to log on to the DS8000 HMC using the DS GUI and create a user ID that is in either the *admin*, *op_storage* or *op_copy_services* groups. Log off and then log on with that user ID and change the initial password.

Creating a userid on the ESS 800

Once you have created a DS user ID, you need to create a matching user ID using the ESS 800 Web Specialist:

1. Start a Web Browser and connect to the IP address of either ESS 800 cluster.
2. Click **ESS Specialist**.
3. Log with a ESS Specialist user ID that has admin privileges.
4. Click **Users** tab.
5. Click **Modify Users**. Enter the user ID name and password you created in the DS CLI or GUI. It must be given the *Administration* access level.
6. Click **Add** to move the user ID to the right hand box.
7. Click **Perform Configuration Update** and wait for the completion message.

Important: The ESS Web Copy Services user IDs are not used by the DS CLI or DS GUI. You only need to create a matching ESS Specialist user ID.

36.2.5 Updating the DS CLI profile

If you plan to use the DS CLI to manage your ESS 800, you can create a profile to simplify connection, commands, and scripted operations. Add extra lines as shown in Example 36-1.

Example 36-1 Possible modification to a DS CLI profile

```
# ESS 800
# hmc1 is the Copy Services server A
hmc1: 10.0.0.100
# devid is the serial number of the ESS 800 - note there are only 5 digits after the 2105
devid: IBM.2105-22399
# remotedevid is the serial number of the DS8000
```

```
remotedevid: IBM.2107-7503461
# Username is a user created on the ESS Specialist that matches the userid on the DS8000
 username: admin
# The password for the admin user id. Placing it here is not very secure.
password: passw0rd
# The password file is created using the managepwfile and is a better way to manage this.
# pwfile: security.dat
```

Placing the password in the profile is not very secure (because it is stored in plain text), but may prove more convenient. A password file can be created using **managepwfile** and is a better way to manage this. After creating the password file (which by default is called *security.dat*), you can remove the password from the profile and instead specify the pwfile file.

The command to create a passwd file in this example is:

managepwfile -action add -name admin -pw passw0rd

A simple method when you have multiple machines to manage is to create multiple profile files. Then when starting the DS CLI, you can specify the profile file you wish to use with the **-cfg** parameter. In a Windows environment you could have multiple Windows batch files (BAT files), one for each machine you wish to manage. The profile shown in Example 36-1 could be saved in the C:\program files\ibm\dscli\profile directory as 2105source.profile.Then you create a simple Windows BAT file with three lines, as shown in Example 36-2.

Example 36-2 Windows BAT file to start a specific profile

```
title DS CLI Local 2105 22399 Remote IBM.2107-7503461
cd C:\Program Files\ibm\dscli\profile
dscli -cfg 2105source.profile
```

We save the BAT file onto the Windows desktop and start it by double clicking on the icon. The DS CLI will open and will start the specified profile. By creating a BAT file and profile for each machine, we can simplify the process of starting the DS CLI. We can also specify the profile when starting DS CLI from inside a script, or when running the DS CLI in script mode.

36.2.6 Adding the Copy Services Domain

If you wish to use the DS GUI to manage FlashCopy on an ESS 800, or Remote Mirror and Copy paths and pairs between an ESS 800 and a DS8000, you have to add the ESS Copy Services domain to the DS HMC. You need the IP address of the ESS 800 Copy Services servers (server A and if desired, server B). You can get these by connecting with a Web Browser to either cluster of the ESS, and clicking on the Copy Services tab. They will be displayed on the first window you see.

You add an ESS Copy Services domain with the DS Storage Manager to the DS8000 as follows:

1. Click **Real-time manager**.
2. Click **Manage hardware**.
3. Click **Storage complexes**.
4. Select **Add 2105 Copy Services Domain** and click **Go**.

Figure 36-1 shows the Add 2105 Copy Services Domain panel.

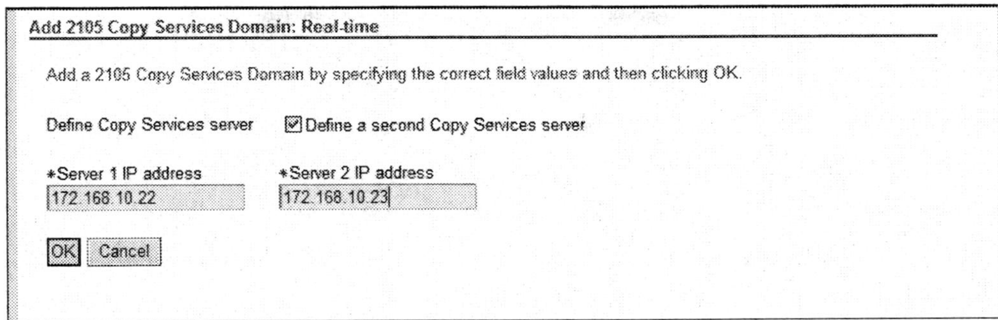

Figure 36-1 Add 2105 Copy Services Domain

5. Enter the IP address of the ESS Copy Services server A in the Server 1 IP address box. If you have a Server B, select the **Define a second Copy Services server** box and enter the Server B IP address in the Server 2 IP address box. However, if Server B is running on a 2105-F20, you should not define it.

Having added the ESS 800 Copy Services domain to the DS GUI, you are now able to use the DS GUI to create paths and Remote Mirror and Copy pairs, where the ESS 800 is the source device. You can also use the DS GUI to manager FlashCopy pairs on the ESS 800.

Note: The steps to add the ESS 800 Copy Services Domain to a DS8000 cannot be performed using the DS CLI. However, if you don't plan to use the GUI, this will not be an issue.

Restriction: You cannot use the ESS Copy Services Server Web GUI to manage Copy Services relationships between an ESS 800 and a DS8000. The Volumes tab will only show ESS 800 volumes, not DS8000 volumes. The Paths tab will not shows paths between an ESS 800 and a DS8000. It will only show paths between ESS 800s. If you are using PPRC between a DS8000 and an ESS 800, all management of that PPRC relationship must be done with DS CLI or via the DS GUI.

Storage management

You cannot use the DS8000 DS GUI to perform storage configuration on an ESS 800. Likewise you cannot use the ESS 800 Web Specialist to perform storage configuration on a DS8000. You can only perform Copy Services management tasks on the alternative device. If you are logged onto the DS8000 DS GUI and wish to configure some storage on the ESS 800, you will need to log on to the ESS 800 Web Specialist.

36.2.7 Volume size considerations for PPRC

When using PPRC to copy the contents of a CKD volume from one storage device to another, it is possible for the PPRC target volume to be larger than the PPRC source volume. However, if an attempt is made to reverse the relationship so that the source becomes the target, then this attempt will fail because the source is now larger than the target. For this reason it is always recommended that the source and target volumes be the same size. Prior to creating a PPRC relationship, check the volumes sizes to ensure they are the same on each storage device.

Determining DS6000 and DS8000 CKD volume size

When CKD volumes are created on a DS6000 or DS8000, the size must be specified in cylinders. In Example 36-3, two CKD volumes of 3339 cylinders are created. This means that if we use these volumes in a PPRC relationship, their partner volumes should also be 3339 cylinders.

Example 36-3 CKD volume size in DS CLI

```
dscli> mkckdvol -extpool P2 -cap 3339 -name av_6K_CKD_#h 0600-0601
Date/Time: 8 November 2005 22:58:31 IBM DSCLI Version: 5.1.0.204 DS: IBM.1750-1300247
CMUC00021I mkckdvol: CKD Volume 0600 successfully created.
CMUC00021I mkckdvol: CKD Volume 0601 successfully created.
dscli> lsckdvol -lcu 06
Date/Time: 9 November 2005 3:58:42 IBM DSCLI Version: 5.1.0.204 DS: IBM.1750-1300247
Name             ID   accstate datastate configstate deviceMTM voltype  orgbvols extpool cap (cyl)
==================================================================================================
av_6K_CKD_0600 0600 Online   Normal    Normal      3390-3    CKD Base -        P2           3339
av_6K_CKD_0601 0601 Online   Normal    Normal      3390-3    CKD Base -        P2           3339
```

Determining ESS volume size

To view the ESS volume sizes, you can use the ESS Specialist.

1. Start a Web Browser and connect to the IP address of either ESS 800 cluster.
2. Click on **ESS Specialist**.
3. Log on with a ESS Specialist user ID.
4. Click on the **Storage Allocation** tab.
5. Click on the **S/390 Storage** tab.
6. Highlight the LCU that contains the volumes you wish to check.
7. Take note of the value in the cylinders column for the volumes you are interested in, as shown in Figure 36-2. In this example the volumes are all 3339 cylinders in size.

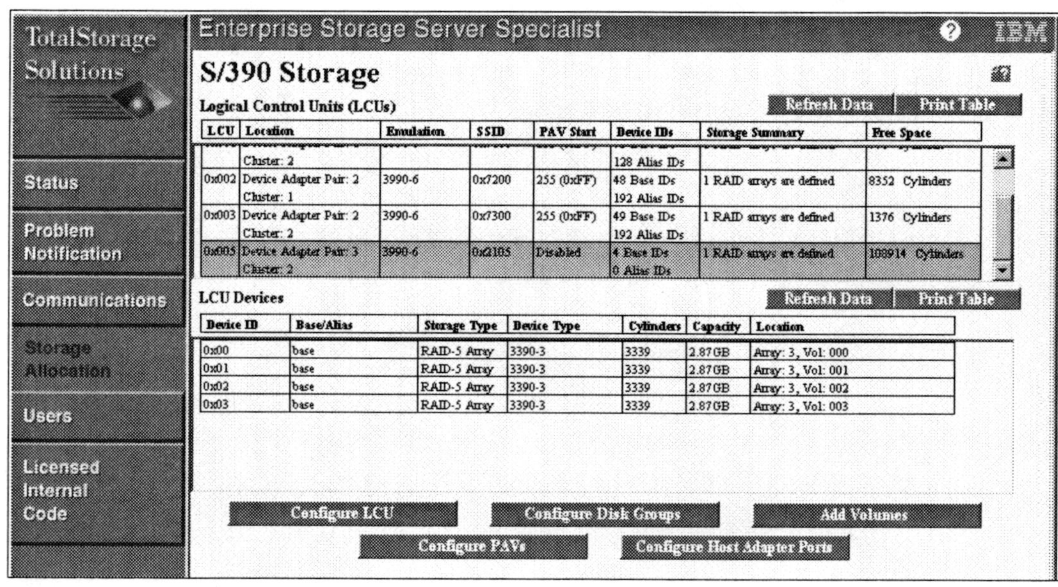

Figure 36-2 Viewing ESS 800 volume size using ESS Specialist GUI

You can also use the ESS CLI to view the volume size, as shown inExample 36-4.

Example 36-4 Using ESS CLI to list CKD volumes

```
C:\Program Files\ibm\ESScli>esscli -u copy -p servlces -s 9.155.51.237 list volume
Wed Nov 09 04:07:52 EST 2005 IBM ESSCLI 2.4.0
Volume    Cap  Units  VolType  LSS  VS    Serial    Label
------  -----  -----  -------  ---  ----  --------  -----
0500    3339  Cyls    3390     05   vs6   ***       ***
0501    3339  Cyls    3390     05   vs6   ***       ***
0502    3339  Cyls    3390     05   vs6   ***       ***
0503    3339  Cyls    3390     05   vs6   ***       ***
```

Note: You cannot use the DS CLI to check volume sizes on a ESS 800. You must either use the ESS Specialist or the ESS CLI.

36.2.8 Volume address considerations on the ESS 800

On the ESS 800, open systems volume IDs are given in an 8 digit format, xxx-sssss where xxx is the LUN ID and sssss is the serial number of the ESS 800. When referring to them in the DS CLI, you must add 1000 to the volume ID, so volume 000-22399 is volume ID 1000 and volume 001-22399 is volume ID 1001. This is very important because on the ESS 800, the following address ranges are actually used:

0000 to 0FFF	CKD zSeries volumes (4096 possible addresses)
1000 to 1FFF	Open systems fixed block LUNs (4096 possible addresses)

If we intend to use FlashCopy to copy ESS open systems LUN 000-22399 onto 001-22399 using the DS CLI, we must specify 1000 and 1001. If instead we specify 0000 and 0001, we will actually run the FlashCopy against CKD volumes. This may result in an unplanned outage on the zSeries system that was using CKD volume 0001.

36.3 PPRC: Establishing paths between DS8000 and ESS 800

To create a PPRC relationship between a DS8000 and an ESS 800, we first need to create logical paths (over the physical Fibre Channel connections). If we are using the DS GUI, then provided we added the ESS Copy Services Domain to the DS8000, we can establish paths in either direction (ESS 800 to DS8000 or DS8000 to ESS 800). If the ESS Copy Services domain was not added, then paths can only be established where the DS8000 is the source.

36.3.1 Decoding port IDs

When viewing port IDs in the DS GUI or DS CLI, the port IDs can be decoded to show which physical port on the DS8000 or ESS 800 is in use. For DS6000 or DS8000, port IDs look like I0000 or I0123, which actually breaks out as IEECP. The EE is the enclosure number (minus 1), C is the card slot number (minus 1) and P is the port number on the card. So I0123 is enclosure 2 (1+1), slot 3 (2+1), port 3.

However, the ESS 800 port IDs, do not follow the same rule. To decode them, take the last two digits in the port ID and then use Figure 36-3. So port ID I0020 is the adapter in host bay 2, slot 1 and port ID I00AC is the adapter in host bay 4, slot 4.

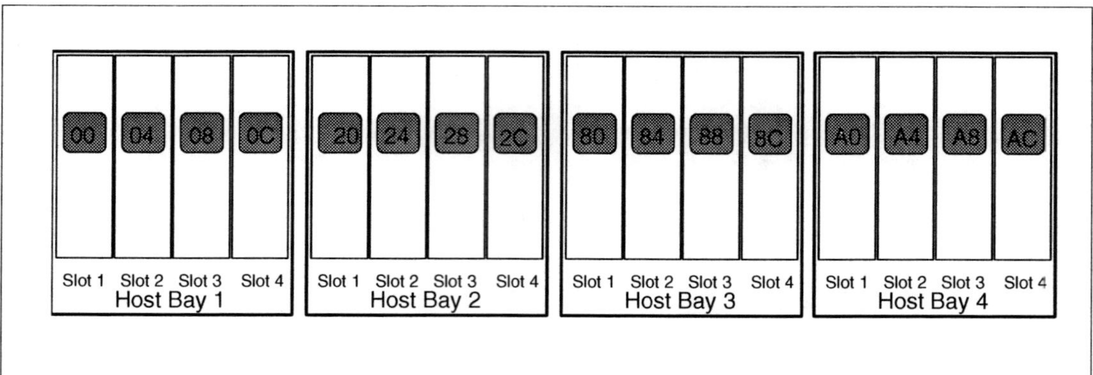

Figure 36-3 ESS 800 Port IDs decoded

36.3.2 Path creation using the DS GUI

In this example we show how to establish two PPRC paths with the DS Storage Manager from DS8000 LSS 04 to ESS LSS 05.

> **Tip:** CKD LCUs on an ESS 800 are always LSS 00 to LSS 0F. If you select ESS 800 LSS 10 to ESS 800 LSS 1F, you are working with open systems LSSs on the ESS 800.

1. Click **Real-time manager**.
2. Click **Copy Services**.
3. Click **Paths**.
4. Select the Storage Complex, Storage Unit, and Storage Image from which you want to create PPRC paths. For this path, this machine will be providing the source LSS.
5. Click **Create** and **Go**; see Figure 36-4.

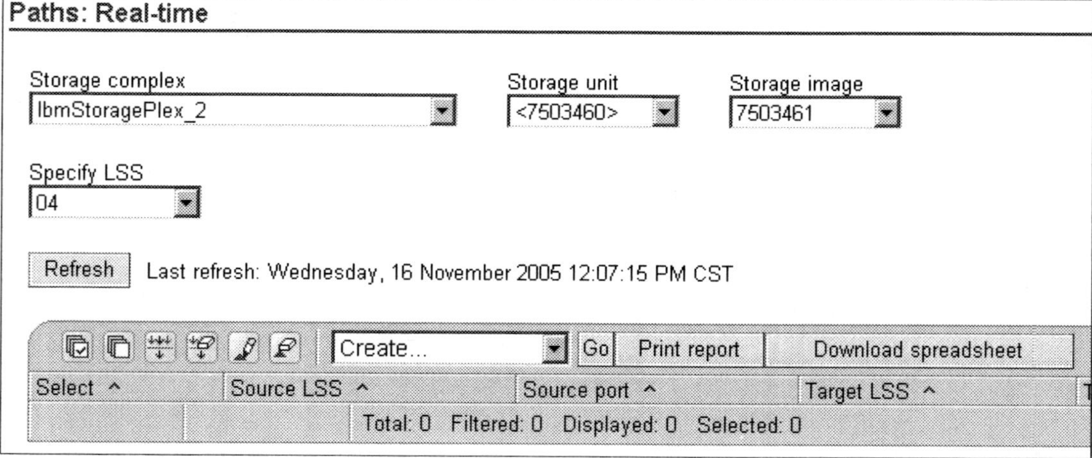

Figure 36-4 Path panel

6. You will now be prompted to select the source LSS of the DS8000 from which you want to establish the PPRC paths. You then click **Next**. In this example we want to establish PPRC paths from LSS 04.See Figure 36-5.

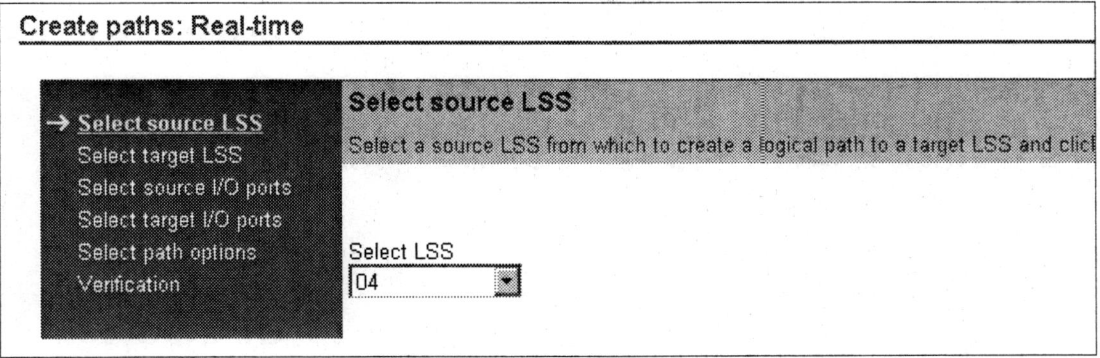

Figure 36-5 Select source LSS

7. Now you have to select the target LSS. First select in the Storage Complex pull-down menu the Storage Complex for the ESS. Then select from the Storage Unit pull-down menu the appropriate Storage Unit and the LSS from the Storage Unit. When you are finished, click **Next** to continue. In Figure 36-6 the target LSS on the ESS is LSS 05.

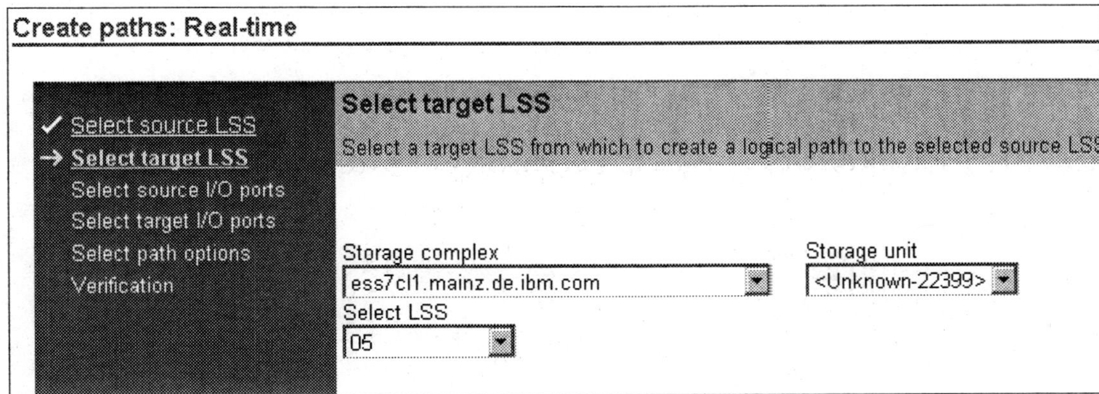

Figure 36-6 Select target LSS

8. The next panel shows you which Fibre Channel ports are available to establish Metro Mirror and Copy paths; see Figure 36-7. Select the ports and click **Next**. Since we want to establish two paths from the DS8000 to the ESS we have to select two I/O ports from the DS8000 that are available for PPRC. You will only see physical connections that actually exist. To get connections listed, the HBAs in the DS8000 and ESS 800 have to either be zoned together or directly connected.

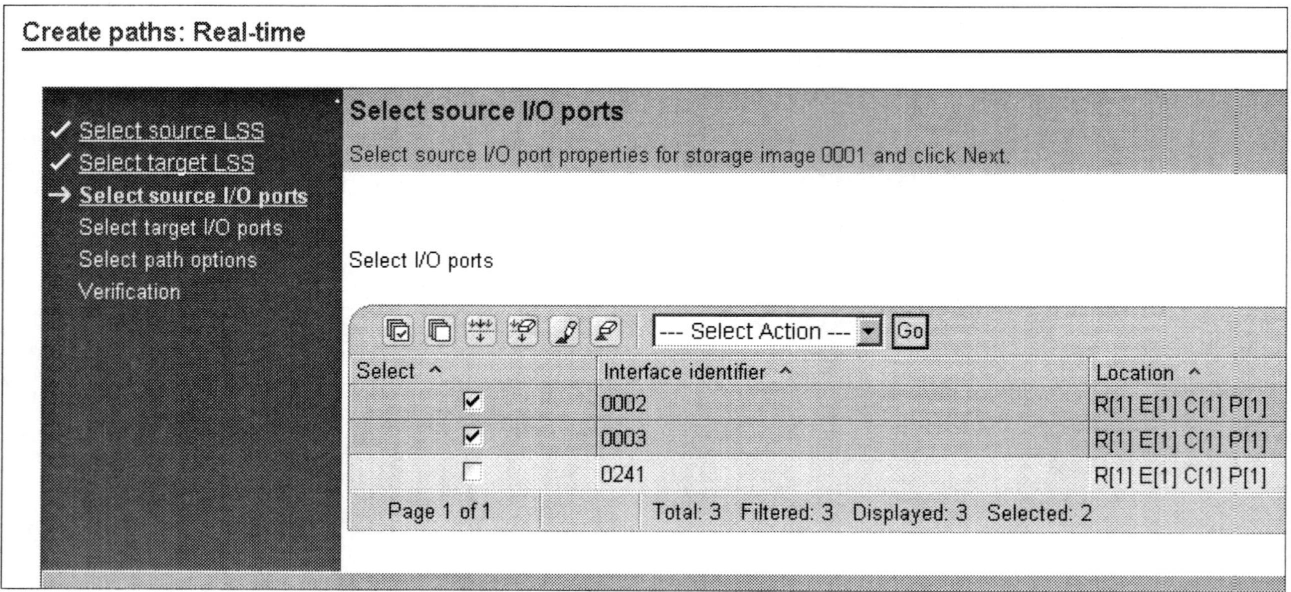

Figure 36-7 Select source I/O ports

9. In the next panel (see Figure 36-8) you have to select for each source I/O port from the DS8000 a target I/O port on the ESS. When done click **Next**.

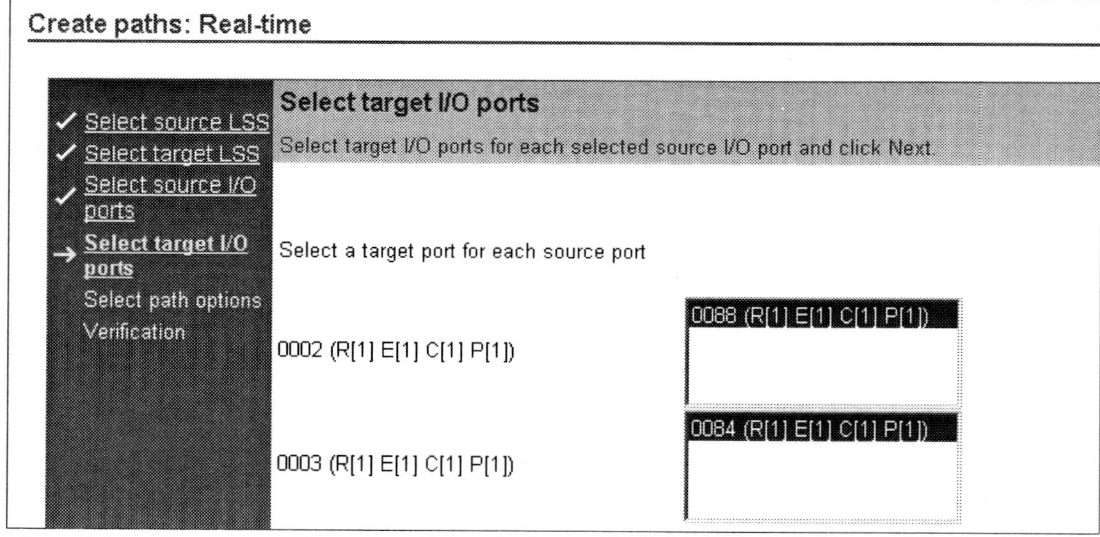

Figure 36-8 Select target I/O ports

10. On the next two panels you will be asked whether you want built a Consistency Group and to verify the information you entered during the process. After you verify the information you entered, click **Finish** to establish the PPRC paths.

11. Figure 36-9 shows the two PPRC paths we have established for LSS 04. To manage the established paths (for example, delete path) you can select the path you want to manage and then select from the pull-down menu the appropriate action you want to perform.

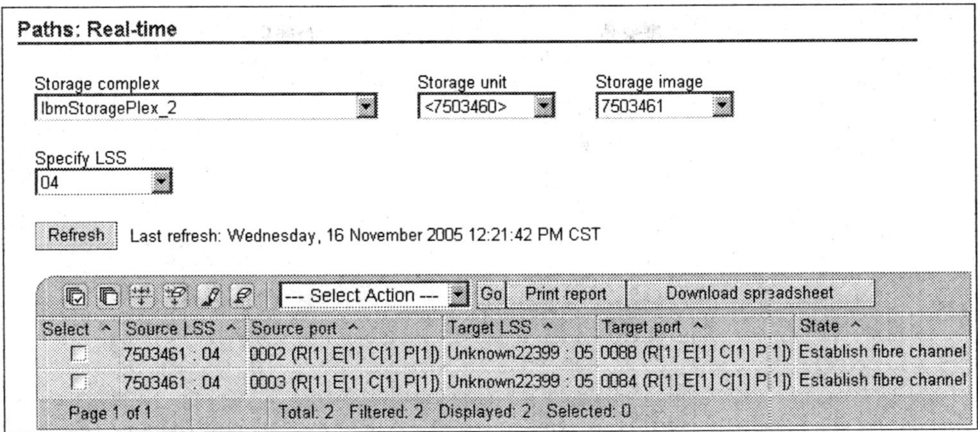

Figure 36-9 Path panel

Paths in the reverse direction

The example above showed how to create a path from the DS8000 to the ESS 800. In many cases it may be likely that you will need paths from ESS 800 to the DS8000. Regardless, having established paths in one direction you can then establish paths in the opposite direction. Fibre Channel allows for bi-directional mirroring over the same physical path.

Adding or deleting paths

You can add additional paths to an LSS pair by simply creating more paths. To remove a path, just display the Paths screen, select the relevant source machine and LSS, select the path you wish to delete and use the delete option from the Select Action pull-down.

36.3.3 Establish logical paths between DS8000 and ESS 800 using DS CLI

You can also use the DS CLI to establish logical paths. One additional step is that you need to know the WWNN of the target Storage Image. The three commands we will use to establish a path are: `lssi`, `lsavailpprcport`, and `mkpprcpath`.

Determining the remote device WWNN

First we need to determine the WWNN of the remote storage device. If you started DS CLI by connecting to the DS8000 HMC, then the remote storage device is the ESS 800. If you started DS CLI by connecting to the ESS 800, then the remote Storage Image is the DS8000.

How to determine the DS8000 WWNN using DS GUI

1. Click **Real-time manager**.
2. Click **Manage hardware**.
3. Click **Storage images** (not the Storage Unit).
4. Click in the **Select** column for the DS8000 Storage Image, and from the **Select Action** pull-down, choose **Properties** and click **Go**.
5. The DS8000 Storage Image WWNN will be displayed on the subsequent properties screen.

How to determine DS8000 WWNN using DS CLI

In Example 36-5 we show how to display the WWNN of a Storage Image using the **lssi** command.

Example 36-5 Determine the WWNN of a DS8000

```
dscli> lssi IBM.2107-7503461
Date/Time: 1 November 2005 3:08:52 IBM DSCLI Version: 5.1.0.204
Name ID               Storage Unit     Model WWNN             State  ESSNet
============================================================================
-    IBM.2107-7503461 IBM.2107-7503460 922   5005076303FFC08F Online Enabled
```

How to determine the WWNN of the ESS 800 using the ESS Specialist

1. Point your browser at the IP address of either cluster of the ESS 800.
2. On the opening screen, click on the **ESS Specialist** button.
3. You will receive a log on prompt. Log on to the ESS Specialist using a ESS Specialist user ID and password.
4. On the welcome screen, you will see the WWNN as shown in Figure 36-10. You will need to write it down.

Figure 36-10 Using ESS 800 Specialist GUI to display the ESS 800 WWNN

How to determine the WWNN of the ESS 800 using the ESS CLI

If you have the ESS CLI installed on a PC, then you can use the **list server** command to display the ESS 800 WWNN.

> **Note:** This is not the DS CLI. ESS CLI is a separate software package that you can get from your IBM Service Representative if you don't already have it.

An example of the command syntax is shown in Example 36-6. This technique has the advantage that you can copy and paste the output.

Example 36-6 Using ESS CLI to display the ESS 800 WWNN

```
C:\Program Files\ibm\ESScli>esscli -u storwatch -p specialist -s 10.0.0.1 list server
Tue Nov 01 03:28:59 EST 2005 IBM ESSCLI 2.4.0

  Server    Model Mfg         WWN          CodeEC    Cache   NVS  Racks
----------  ----- ---  ----------------  --------  -----  -----  -----
2105.22399   800  013  5005076300C09517  2.4.3.79   32GB    2GB    1
```

Listing the available ports using DS CLI

Having determined the remote devices WWNN, we can now display the ports that are available to establish PPRC paths. In Example 36-7 we are logged onto the 2107 using DS CLI, so the remote device is the ESS 800.

Note: When using the `lsavailpprcport` command you must specify LSSs that actually exist.

Example 36-7 Displaying available ports for PPRC path establishment

```
dscli> lsavailpprcport -remotedev IBM.2105-22399 -remotewwnn 5005076300C09517 08:05
Date/Time: 8 November 2005 23:12:56 IBM DSCLI Version: 5.1.0.204 DS: IBM.2107-7503461
Local Port Attached Port Type
=============================
I0002      I0088         FCP
I0003      I0084         FCP
I0241      I00A4         FCP
I0311      I0024         FCP
```

Note: When issuing commands that refer to an ESS 800, the ESS 800 serial number is only five digits, not seven as the DS6000 or DS8000 are. So in our examples, the serial number syntax we use is IBM.2105-22399, not IBM.2105-1322399.

Establishing the logical paths using DS CLI

Having determined which ports are available, for each LSS pair that we wish to copy and mirror between, we now establish a one-way path using the **mkpprcpath** command. We can then display established paths using the **lspprcpath** command.

In Example 36-8, we first establish a single path between LSS 08 on the DS8000 and LSS 05 on the ESS 800. We then display the paths available for LSS 08 on the DS8000.

Example 36-8 Using DS CLI to establish PPRC paths

```
dscli> mkpprcpath  -remotedev IBM.2105-22399 -remotewwnn 5005076300C09517 -srclss 08
-tgtlss 05 I0002:I0088
Date/Time: 8 November 2005 23:23:40 IBM DSCLI Version: 5.1.0.204 DS: IBM.2107-7503461
CMUC00149I mkpprcpath: Remote Mirror and Copy path 08:05 successfully established.
ddscli> lspprcpath 08
Date/Time: 8 November 2005 23:24:17 IBM DSCLI Version: 5.1.0.204 DS: IBM.2107-7503461
Src Tgt State   SS   Port  Attached Port Tgt WWNN
=========================================================
08  05  Success 2105 I0002 I0088         5005076300C09517
```

In Example 36-9 we add an additional path between LSS 08 on the DS8000 and LSS 05 on the ESS 800. Take careful note though, we include the existing path when creating a new path. Otherwise the existing path is removed and only the new path will be available for use.

Example 36-9 Establishing additional paths using DS CLI

```
dscli> mkpprcpath  -remotedev IBM.2105-22399 -remotewwnn 5005076300C09517 -srclss 08
-tgtlss 05 I0002:I0088 I0003:I0084
Date/Time: 8 November 2005 23:25:34 IBM DSCLI Version: 5.1.0.204 DS: IBM.2107-7503461
CMUC00149I mkpprcpath: Remote Mirror and Copy path 08:05 successfully established.
dscli> lspprcpath 08
Date/Time: 8 November 2005 23:25:51 IBM DSCLI Version: 5.1.0.204 DS: IBM.2107-7503461
Src Tgt State   SS   Port  Attached Port Tgt WWNN
=========================================================
```

```
08  05  Success 2105 I0002 I0088          5005076300C09517
08  05  Success 2105 I0003 I0084          5005076300C09517
```

To establish paths where the ESS 800 is the source, we should connect to the ESS 800 using DS CLI and follow the same process, but specify the DS8000 as the remote device.

> **Important:** When you connect using DS CLI to the DS8000 HMC, the DS8000 is the local device and the ESS 800 is the remove device. If you connect using DS CLI to the ESS 800, then ESS 800 is now the local device and the DS8000 is the remote device.

> **Attention:** The **rmpprcpath** command will remove all paths between the source and target LSSs. To just reduce the path count, use the **mkpprcpath** command specifying only the paths you wish to continue using.

36.3.4 Path creation using TSO

In Example 36-10 we give the TSO command to establish Metro Mirror paths from a DS8000 to an ESS 800. The command breaks out as follows:

Device that command is issued to: 202B
Primary LCU SSID: 1710
Primary DS8000 WWNN: 5005076303FFC08F
Primary DS8000 LSS ID: 00
Secondary ESS 800 LCU SSID: 1070
Secondary ESS 800 WWNN: 5005076300C09517
Secondary ESS 800 LSS ID: 00
First path established: I0002 to I0088
Second path established: I0311 to I0024

Example 36-10 CESTPATH command

```
/* ----------------------------------------------------------------- */
/*                                                                   */
/* ISSUE PPRC CESTPATH TO ESTABLISH PPRC PATHS                       */
/*                                                                   */
/* ----------------------------------------------------------------- */
 CESTPATH DEVN(X'202B') PRIM(X'1710' 5005076303FFC08F X'00') -
          SEC(X'1070' 5005076300C09517 X'00') -
          LINK(X'00020088' X'03110024') -
          CGROUP(NO)
/* ----------------------------------------------------------------- */
```

36.4 Managing Metro Mirror or Global Copy pairs

Having established paths, we can now establish volume pairs.

36.4.1 Managing Metro Mirror or Global Copy pairs using the DS GUI

In this example we show how you can establish Metro Mirror volume pairs between a DS8000 and an ESS 800 with the DS Storage Manager. In this example we create two Metro Mirror pairs. Volumes 0800 and 0801 from the DS8000 are the source volumes, and the target volumes are 0500 and 0501 from the ESS. We would follow the same method to setup a Global Copy pair, except that Global Copy would be selected in Figure 36-16.

1. Click **Real-time manager**.
2. Click **Copy services**.
3. Click **Metro Mirror**.
4. Select the Storage Complex, Storage Unit, and Storage Image on which the Metro Mirror source volumes are.
5. Click **Create** and **Go**; see Figure 36-11.

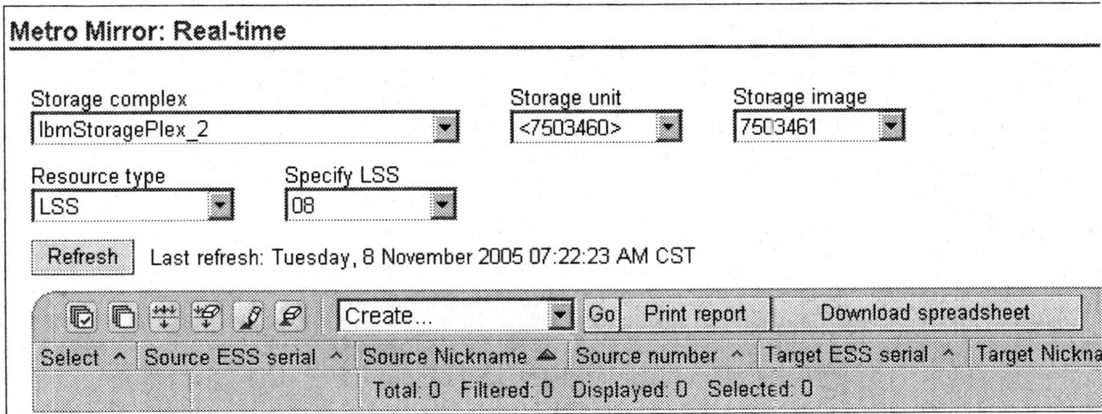

Figure 36-11 Metro Mirror

In the next panels you will be guided through the process of creating Metro Mirror volume pairs. At the last panel you have the possibility to review the information you entered before you establish the Metro Mirror pairs. During the process you have at any time the possibility to go back to modify specifications you have already done or you can cancel the process.

6. You have the option to choose between **Automated volume assignment** and **Manual volume pair assignment**; see Figure 36-12. If you click the **Automated volume pair assignment**, the first selected source volume is paired automatically with the first selected target volume. If you click **Manual volume pair assignment**, you must select each specific target volume for each selected source volume. In this example we assign the volume pairs manually.

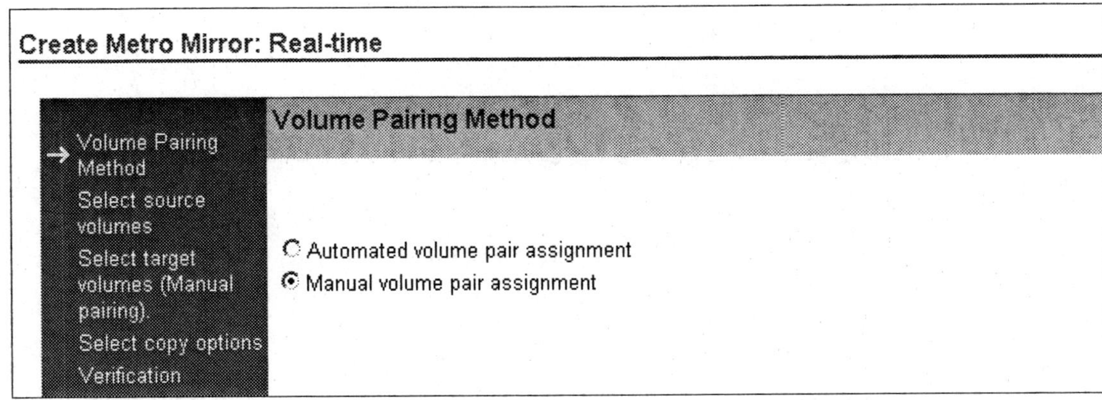

Figure 36-12 Pairing method

7. The source volumes we want to use are on the DS8000 in LSS 08. We select two volumes and click **Next**; see Figure 36-13. Note you also have the option from this panel to create paths.

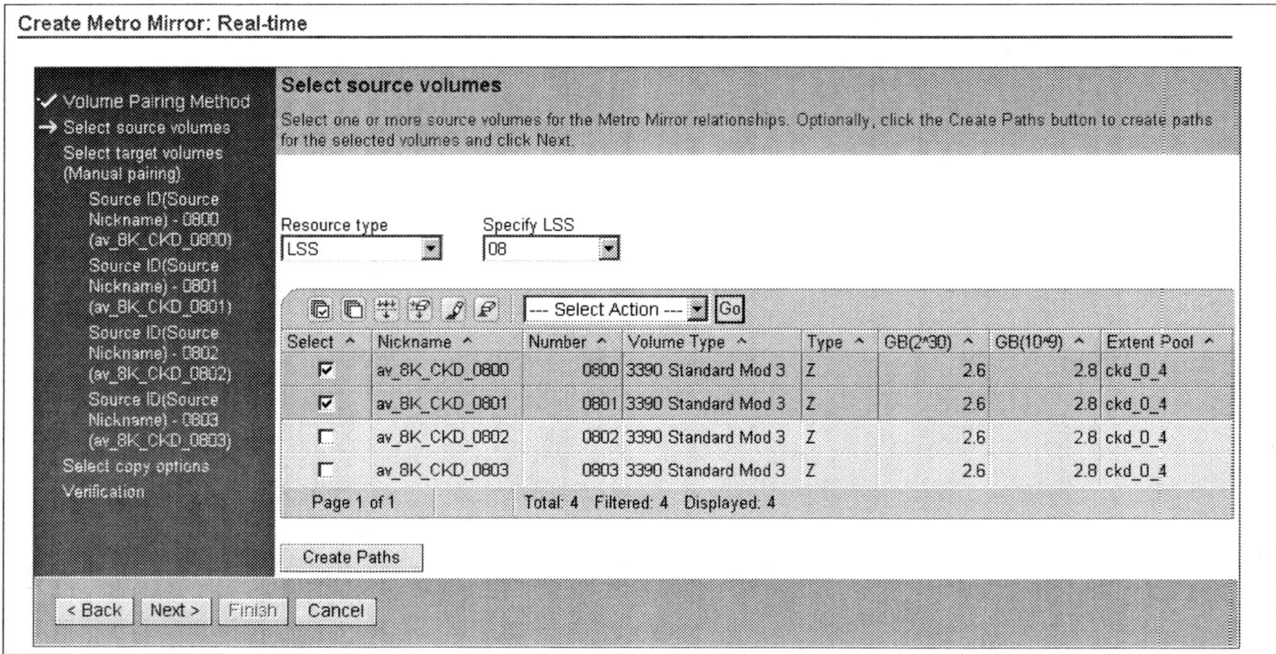

Figure 36-13 Select source volume

8. First we have to select the Storage Complex and Storage Unit of the LSS with the target volumes. Then we can select the target volume for the first source volume. To expand the choices you must select the small blue boxes. When done we click **Next**; see Figure 36-14.

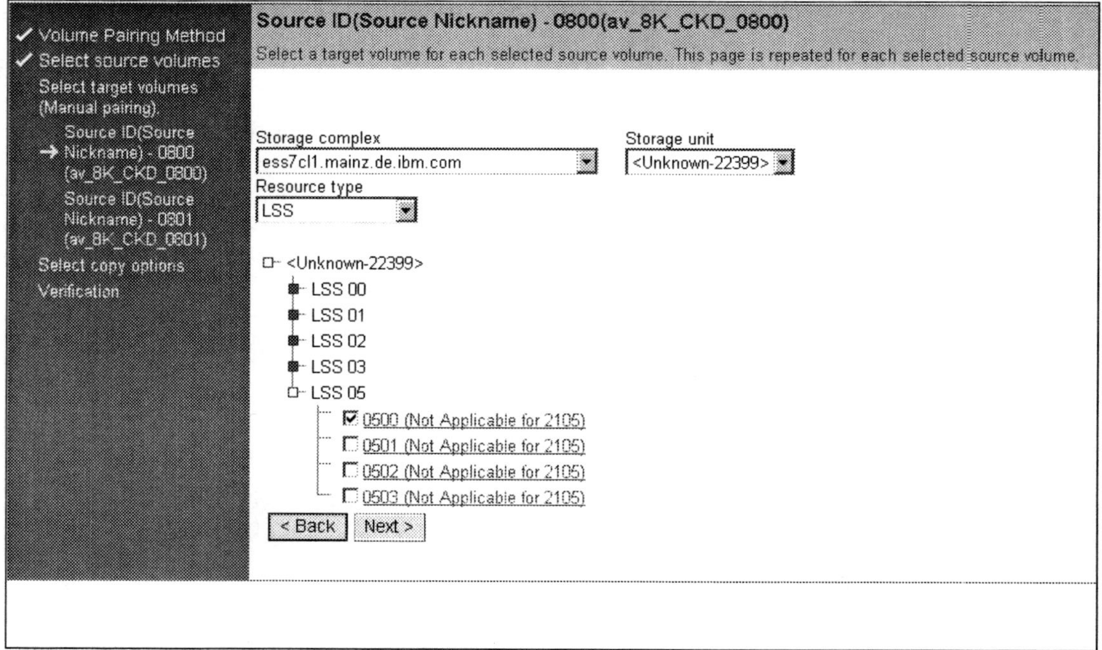

Figure 36-14 First Metro Mirror target volume

9. Next we have to select the target volume for the second source volume; see Figure 36-15. To expand the choices you must select the small blue boxes.

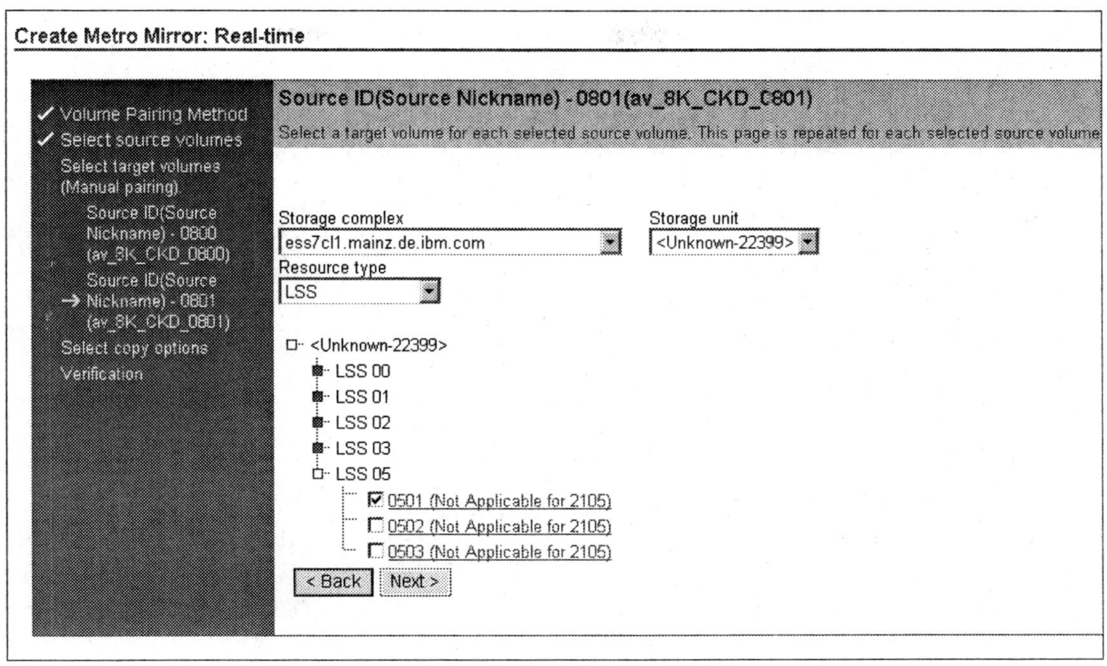

Figure 36-15 Second Metro Mirror target volume

10. We now have the choice to specify various copy options as shown in Figure 36-16. In this example we choose **Define relationship type** Metro Mirror and check **Perform initial copy**. If you wished to instead use Global Copy, this is where you would select it.

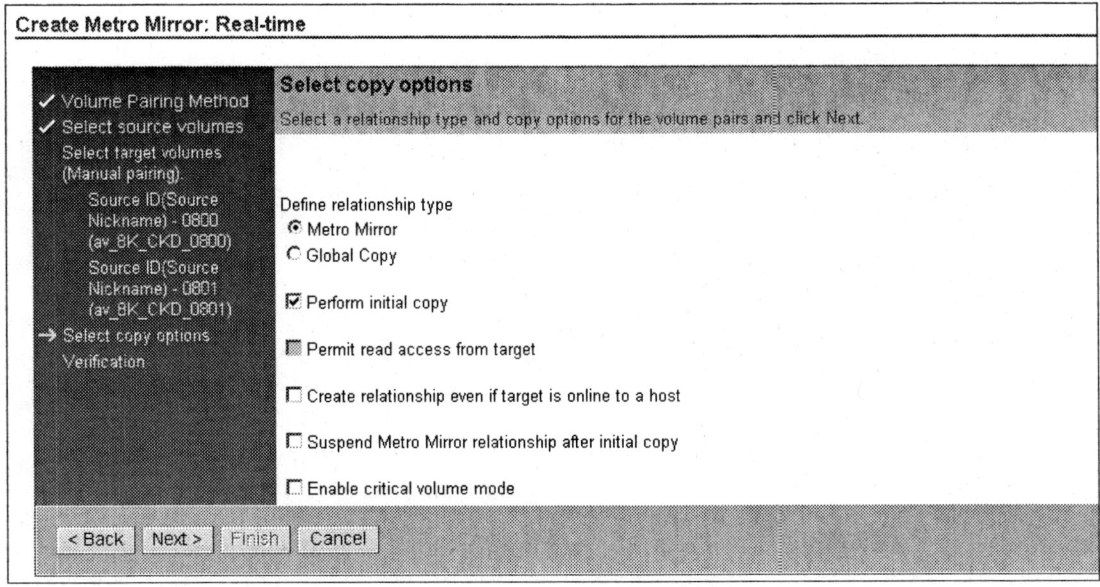

Figure 36-16 Copy options

11. Once you reach the Verify panel you have the possibility to verify the information you entered. If everything is correct, click **Finish** to establish the Metro Mirror volume pairs. Figure 36-17 shows the Metro Mirror pairs for LSS 08 that we have established. To manage the established pairs (for example, suspend pair) you can select the volume pair you want to manage and then select from the pull-down menu the appropriate action you want to perform.

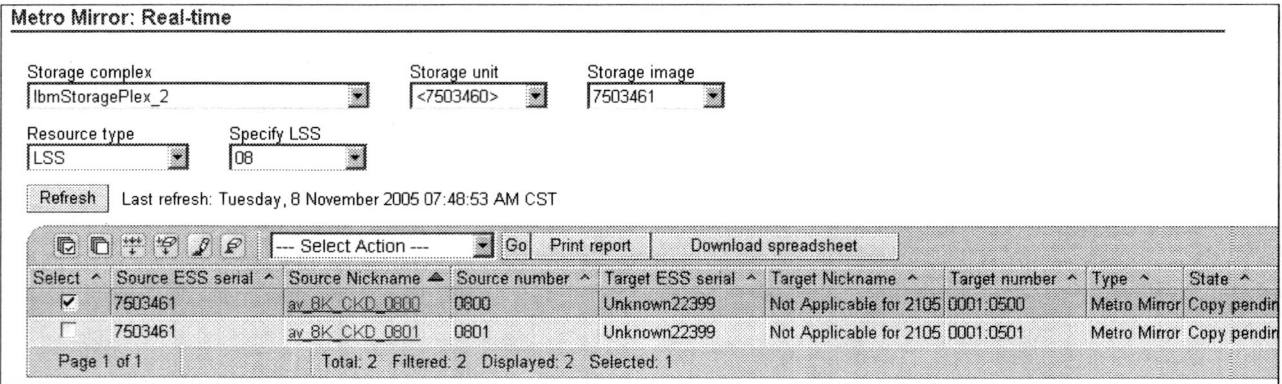

Figure 36-17 Managing Metro Mirror pairs

36.4.2 Managing Metro Mirror pairs using the DS CLI

Having established paths, we can now establish volume pairs. In this example we show how you can establish Metro Mirror volume pairs between a DS8000 and an ESS 800 with the DS CLI. In this example we create two Metro Mirror pairs. Volumes 0800 and 0801 from the DS8000 are the source volumes, and the target volumes on the ESS are 0500 and 0501.

In Example 36-11 we create two pairs using the **mkpprc** command. We then list them using the **lspprc** command. We then remove one pair using the **rmpprc** command.

Example 36-11 Creating Metro Mirror pairs using DS CLI

```
dscli> mkpprc -remotedev IBM.2105-22399 -type mmir -mode full 0800:0500 0801:0501
Date/Time: 9 November 2005 0:44:57 IBM DSCLI Version: 5.1.0.204 DS: IBM.2107-7503461
CMUC00153I mkpprc: Remote Mirror and Copy volume pair relationship 0800:0500 successfully
created.
CMUC00153I mkpprc: Remote Mirror and Copy volume pair relationship 0801:0501 successfully
created.
dscli> lspprc 0800-0801
Date/Time: 9 November 2005 0:45:26 IBM DSCLI Version: 5.1.0.204 DS: IBM.2107-7503461
ID        State        Reason Type         SourceLSS Timeout (secs) Critical Mode First
=========================================================================================
0800:0500 Copy Pending -      Metro Mirror 08        unknown        Disabled      Invalid
0801:0501 Copy Pending -      Metro Mirror 08        unknown        Disabled      Invalid
dscli> rmpprc -remotedev IBM.2105-22399 0800:0500
Date/Time: 9 November 2005 0:46:21 IBM DSCLI Version: 5.1.0.204 DS: IBM.2107-7503461
CMUC00160W rmpprc: Are you sure you want to delete the Remote Mirror and Copy volume pair
relationship 0800:0500:? [y/n]:
y
CMUC00155I rmpprc: Remote Mirror and Copy volume pair 0800:0500 relationship successfully
withdrawn.
dscli>
```

In Example 36-11 we connected to the DS8000 HMC using DS CLI, so the ESS 800 is the remote device. If we wish to establish pairs where the ESS 800 is the source device, we need to connect to the ESS 800 using DS CLI. This will make the DS8000 the remote device.

Important: If you specify the wrong **-remotedev** or you are using a profile where a different remote device to the one you intended to work on is specified, you may get an error message, CMUN03057 saying you are specifying an invalid subsystem ID. This may be because you are specifying the wrong remote device serial number. If you have multiple potential remote devices, do not specify a **remotedev** in your DS CLI profile.

36.4.3 Creating Metro Mirror pairs using TSO

In Example 36-12 we use the same paths that were created in "Path creation using TSO" on page 514. We establish a volume pair with Metro Mirror from the DS8000 to the ESS 800.

Example 36-12 CESTPAIR command

```
//* ---------------------------------------------------------------- */
/*                                                                   */
/* ISSUE PPRC CESTPAIR TO ESTABLISH VOLUME PAIRS                     */
/*                                                                   */
/* ---------------------------------------------------------------- */
 CESTPAIR DEVN(X'202B') PRIM(X'1710' 03461 X'2B' X'00') -
          SEC(X'1070' 22399 X'2B' X'00') -
          OPTION(SYNC) MODE(COPY)
```

36.4.4 Managing Global Copy pairs using DS CLI

Having established paths, we can now establish volume pairs. In this example we show how you can establish Global Copy volume pairs between a DS8000 and an ESS 800 with the DS CLI. In this example we create two Global Copy pairs. Volumes 0800 and 0801 from the DS8000 are the target volumes, and the source volumes on the ESS are 0500 and 0501.

In Example 36-11 we create two pairs using the **mkpprc** command. We then list them using the **lspprc** command. We then pause one pair using the **pausepprc** command.

Example 36-13 Using DS CLI to manage Global Copy

```
dscli> mkpprc -remotedev IBM.2107-7503461 -type gcp 0500:0800 0501:0801
Date/Time: 9 November 2005 2:14:08 IBM DSCLI Version: 5.1.0.204 DS: IBM.2105-22399
CMUC00153I mkpprc: Remote Mirror and Copy volume pair relationship 0500:0800 successfully
created.
CMUC00153I mkpprc: Remote Mirror and Copy volume pair relationship 0501:0801 successfully
created.
dscli> lspprc 0500-0501
Date/Time: 9 November 2005 2:14:16 IBM DSCLI Version: 5.1.0.204 DS: IBM.2105-22399
ID        State        Reason Type        SourceLSS Timeout (secs) Critical Mode First Pass
=========================================================================================
0500:0800 Copy Pending -      Global Copy 05        unknown        Disabled      False
0501:0801 Copy Pending -      Global Copy 05        unknown        Disabled      False
dscli> pausepprc -remotedev IBM.2107-7503461 0500:0800
Date/Time: 9 November 2005 2:14:38 IBM DSCLI Version: 5.1.0.204 DS: IBM.2105-22399
CMUC00157I pausepprc: Remote Mirror and Copy volume pair 0500:0800 relationship
successfully paused.
dscli> lspprc 0500
Date/Time: 9 November 2005 2:14:47 IBM DSCLI Version: 5.1.0.204 DS: IBM.2105-22399
ID        State     Reason      Type        SourceLSS Timeout (secs) Critical Mode First
=========================================================================================
0500:0800 Suspended Host Source Global Copy 05        unknown        Disabled      True
```

36.4.5 Establishing Global Copy pairs using TSO

In Example 36-14 we use the same paths that were created in "Path creation using TSO" on page 514. We establish a volume pair with Global Copy from the DS8000 to the ESS 800.

Example 36-14 Syslog messages from Global Copy TSO commands

```
ANTP8802I CESTPAIR DEVN(X'202B') PRIM(X'1710' 03461 X'2B' X'00')
   SEC(X'1070' 22399 X'2B' X'00')          OPTION(XD)
ANTP8802I (CONT)  MODE(COPY)
ANTP0001I CESTPAIR COMMAND COMPLETED FOR DEVICE 202B. COMPLETION CODE:
00
IEA494I 202B,PR202B,PPRC PAIR PENDING,SSID=1710,CCA=2B
ANTP8802I CQUERY DEVN(X'202B')
ANTP0090I CQUERY FORMATTED LVL 3 590
VOLUME REPORT
************** PPRC REMOTE COPY CQUERY - VOLUME ********************
*                                        (PRIMARY)   (SECONDARY) *
*                                       SSID CCA LSS SSID CCA LSS*
*DEVICE   LEVEL      STATE     PATH STATUS  SERIAL#     SERIAL#    *
*------ --------- ----------  ----------- ---------    --------- *
* 202B  PRIMARY..  PENDING.XD   ACTIVE..   1710 2B 00   1070 2B 00 *
*       CRIT(NO).......       CGRPLB(NO). 000000003461 000000022399*
* PATHS PFCA SFCA STATUS: DESCRIPTION                              *
* ----- --------- ------  -------------------                      *
*   2   0002 0088   13    PATH ESTABLISHED...                      *
*       0311 0024   13    PATH ESTABLISHED...                      *
*       ---- ----   00    NO PATH...........                       *
*       ---- ----   00    NO PATH...........                       *
*  SUBSYSTEM         WWNN                    LIC LEVEL             *
* -----------   ----------------           -----------             *
* PRIMARY....   5005076303FFC08F           5.0.03.0196             *
* SECONDARY.1   5005076300C09517                                   *
* SECONDARY.2   5005076300C09517                                   *
* SECONDARY.3   5005076300C09517                                   *
********************************************************************
ANTP0001I CQUERY COMMAND COMPLETED FOR DEVICE 202B. COMPLETION CODE: 00
```

36.5 Managing ESS 800 Global Mirror

The establishment of Global Mirror between a DS8000 and an ESS 800 is achieved using the same methods as explained in Chapter 27., "Global Mirror examples" on page 341.

36.5.1 Managing Global Mirror pairs using DS CLI

In Example 36-15 we establish a Global Copy pair between volume 0800 on the ESS 800 and volume 0500 on the DS8000 and a remote FlashCopy to support it. We then create session 70 for LSS 05. We then create a Global Mirror using session 70 and LSS 05.

Example 36-15 Establishing Global Mirror using DS CLI

```
dscli> mkpprc -remotedev IBM.2107-7503461 -type gcp 0500:0800
Date/Time: 9 November 2005 2:14:08 IBM DSCLI Version: 5.1.0.204 DS: IBM.2105-22399
CMUC00153I mkpprc: Remote Mirror and Copy volume pair relationship 0500:0800 successfully created.
dscli> mkremoteflash -dev IBM.2107-7503461 -conduit IBM.2105-22399/05 -nocp -record 0800:0801
Date/Time: 9 November 2005 2:18:19 IBM DSCLI Version: 5.1.0.204 DS: IBM.2107-7503461
CMUC00173I mkremoteflash: Remote FlashCopy volume pair 0800:0801 successfully created. Use the
lsremoteflash command to determine copy completion.
dscli> mksession -lss 05 -volume 0500 70
Date/Time: 9 November 2005 2:21:28 IBM DSCLI Version: 5.1.0.204 DS: IBM.2105-22399
CMUC00145I mksession: Session 70 opened successfully.
dscli> lssession 05
Date/Time: 9 November 2005 2:23:16 IBM DSCLI Version: 5.1.0.204 DS: IBM.2105-22399
LSS ID Session Status Volume VolumeStatus PrimaryStatus        SecondaryStatus   FirstPassComplete
==================================================================================================
05     70      Normal 0500   Join Pending Primary Copy Pending Secondary Simplex True
dscli> mkgmir -lss 05 -session 70
Date/Time: 9 November 2005 2:23:30 IBM DSCLI Version: 5.1.0.204 DS: IBM.2105-22399
CMUC00162I mkgmir: Global Mirror for session 70 successfully started.
dscli> showgmir 05
Date/Time: 9 November 2005 2:23:37 IBM DSCLI Version: 5.1.0.204 DS: IBM.2105-22399
ID                           IBM.2105-22399/05
Master Count                 1
Master Session ID            0x70
Copy State                   Running
Fatal Reason                 Not Fatal
CG Interval (seconds)        0
XDC Interval(milliseconds)   50
CG Drain Time (seconds)      30
Current Time                 11/09/2005 02:12:55 EST
CG Time                      11/09/2005 02:12:54 EST
Successful CG Percentage     50
FlashCopy Sequence Number    -
Master ID                    IBM.2105-22399
Subordinate Count            0
Master/Subordinate Assoc     -
Master/Subordinate Assoc     -
```

36.6 Managing ESS 800 FlashCopy

Provided a FlashCopy license is present on the ESS 800 it is possible to manage ESS FlashCopy using the DS CLI or SM GUI. The establishment of a FlashCopy pair on an ESS 800, using the DS GUI, is no different than establishing a DS8000 FlashCopy pair, see Part 3, “FlashCopy” on page 43. The establishment of a FlashCopy pair on an ESS 800 using the DS CLI is also no different. In a situation where the ESS 800 is the target device in a PPRC relationship, it is also possible to create remote FlashCopies on the ESS 800 using the **mkremoteflash** command. In each case, creating, changing and removing the FlashCopy is done using the same commands.

36.6.1 Creating an ESS 800 FlashCopy using DS GUI

The steps to create a FlashCopy on the ESS 800 using the DS GUI include these:

1. Click **Real-time manager**.
2. Click **Copy Services**.
3. Click **FlashCopy**.
4. From the **Storage Complex** pull-down choose the ESS 800 Copy Services Domain
5. From the **Storage Units** pull-down select the ESS you wish to perform the FlashCopy on.
6. Make selections from the **Resource type** and **Specify LSS** pull-downs.
7. From the **Select Action** pull-down, choose **Create**, as shown in Figure 36-18. Now click **Go**.

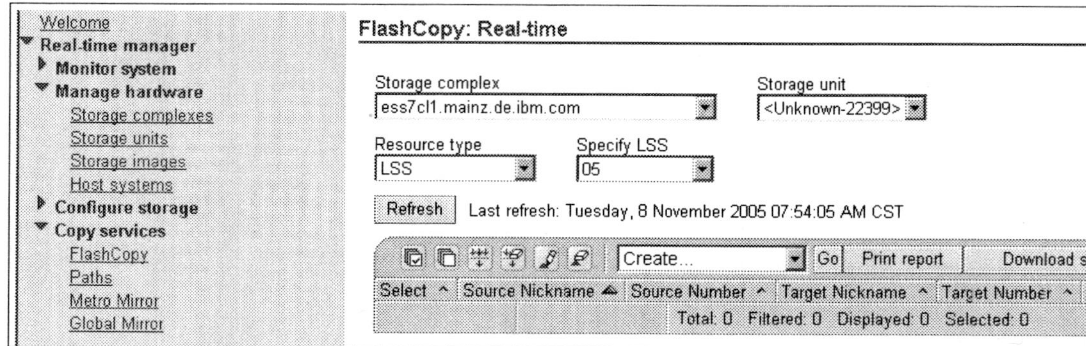

Figure 36-18 Creating ESS 800 FlashCopy using DS GUI

8. Choose between **A single source with a single target** or **A single source with multiple targets** and click **Next**.
9. You will now need to select the source volumes, as shown in Figure 36-19. Note that some of the columns have *Not Applicable for 2105* in them. This is normal.

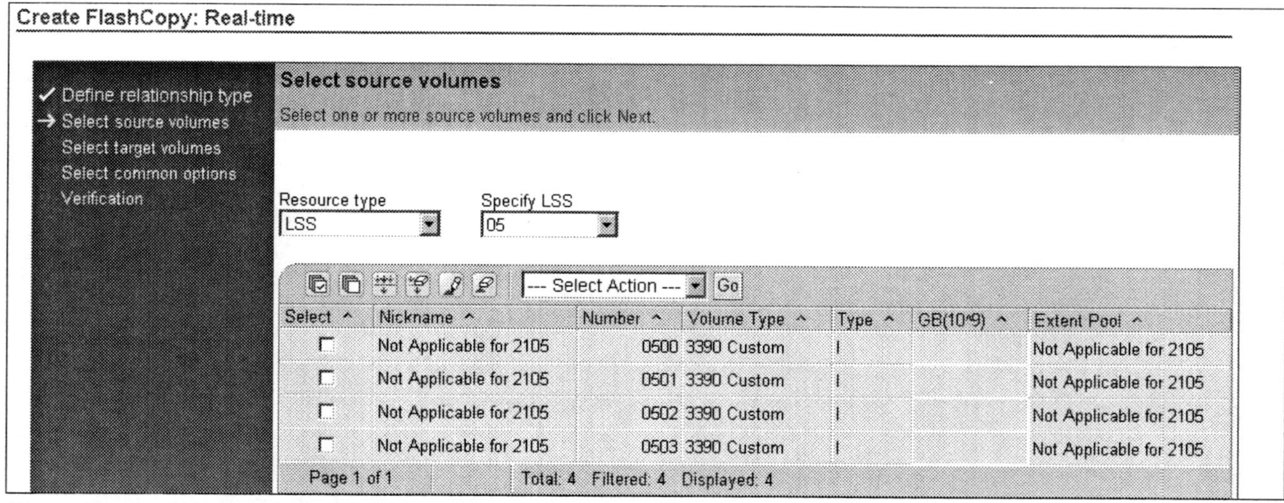

Figure 36-19 Selecting ESS 800 source volumes for FlashCopy

10. You will now need to select the target volumes and click **Next**.
11. You will now need to select what options you plan to use and click **Next**.
12. You will now get a verification screen, review your selections and click **Finish**.

36.6.2 Creating an ESS 800 FlashCopy using DS CLI

You will need to start the DS CLI and connect to the ESS 800. Then issue DS CLI commands as per normal. An example is shown in Example 36-16.

Example 36-16 Using DS CLI to create an ESS 800 FlashCopy

```
dscli> mkflash -nocp -record -persist 0800:0801
Date/Time: 2 November 2005 20:04:33 IBM DSCLI Version: 5.1.0.204 DS: IBM.2105-22399
CMUC00137I mkflash: FlashCopy pair 0800:0801 successfully created.
dscli> lsflash 1001
Date/Time: 2 November 2005 20:04:37 IBM DSCLI Version: 5.1.0.204 DS: IBM.2105-22399
ID        SrcLSS SequenceNum Timeout ActiveCopy Recording Persistent Revertible SourceWrite TargetWrite
=======================================================================================================
0800:0801 10     0           45      Disabled   Enabled   Enabled    Disabled   Enabled     Enabled
dscli> rmflash 0800:0801
Date/Time: 2 November 2005 20:04:54 IBM DSCLI Version: 5.1.0.204 DS: IBM.2105-22399
CMUC00144W rmflash: Are you sure you want to remove the FlashCopy pair 0800:0801:? [y/n]:y
CMUC00140I rmflash: FlashCopy pair 0800:0801 successfully removed.
```

36.6.3 Creating a remote FlashCopy on an ESS 800 using DS CLI

It is also possible to use DS CLI to create a remote FlashCopy on a DS8000 where the source PPRC device is an ESS 800. In Example 36-17, we connect using the DS CLI to a ESS 800. We create a Global Copy pair from volume 0500 on the ESS 800 to volume 0800 on the DS8000. We then create a remote FlashCopy on the DS8000 between volumes 0800 and 0801. We then remove the remote FlashCopy.

Example 36-17 Creating a remote FlashCopy where the ESS 800 is the remote target

```
dscli> mkpprc -remotedev IBM.2107-7503461 -type gcp 0500:0800
Date/Time: 9 November 2005 2:14:08 IBM DSCLI Version: 5.1.0.204 DS: IBM.2105-22399
CMUC00153I mkpprc: Remote Mirror and Copy volume pair relationship 0500:0800 successfully created.
dscli> mkremoteflash -dev IBM.2107-7503461 -conduit IBM.2105-22399/05 -nocp -record 0800:0801
Date/Time: 9 November 2005 2:18:19 IBM DSCLI Version: 5.1.0.204 DS: IBM.2107-7503461
CMUC00173I mkremoteflash: Remote FlashCopy volume pair 0800:0801 successfully created. Use the
lsremoteflash command to determine copy completion.
dscli> rmremoteflash -dev IBM.2107-7503461 -conduit IBM.2105-22399/05 0800:0801
Date/Time: 9 November 2005 2:27:37 IBM DSCLI Version: 5.1.0.204 DS: IBM.2107-7503461
CMUC00179I rmremoteflash: Are you sure you want to remove the remote FlashCopy pair {0}? [y/n]:y
CMUC00180I rmremoteflash: Removal of the remote FlashCopy volume pair 0800:0801 has been initiated
successfully. Use the lsremoteflash command to determine when the relationship is deleted.
dscli>
```

You could also reverse the scenario and use the DS8000 as the source machine in a PPRC pair and then create the remote FlashCopy on the ESS 800.

> **Note:** Commands that work with remote FlashCopies, use the **-dev** parameter to define the machine on which the FlashCopy is to be performed. Other commands, such as **mkpprc** commands will refer to this same device as the remote device, using **-remotedev**. However, since a FlashCopy has to be sent to the remote site and then performed locally on that site, the use of the **-dev** parameter to refer to the remote machine is correct.

36.6.4 z/OS Global Mirror

The DS8000 can operate in a z/OS Global Mirror pair with the ESS. This is accomplished using normal z/OS Global Mirror commands, as seen in the examples in this section.

The XADDPAIR command is no different when using an ESS as the secondary device than it would be when using another DS8000. Example 36-18 shows the sample XADDPAIR commands we are using to establish the pairs between the DS8000 and ESS devices.

Example 36-18 Sample XADDPAIR command

```
XADDPAIR XRCTEST VOLUME(PR2028 SCB128)
XADDPAIR XRCTEST VOLUME(PR2029 SCB129)
XADDPAIR XRCTEST VOLUME(PR202A SCB12A)
XADDPAIR XRCTEST VOLUME(PR202B SCB12B) SCSESSION(AA)
XADDPAIR XRCTEST VOLUME(PR202C SCB12C) SCSESSION(AA)
XADDPAIR XRCTEST VOLUME(PR202D SCB12D) SCSESSION(AA)
```

Example 36-19 shows the DEVSERV command output for the primary and secondary devices, showing the device types (2107 and 2105).

Example 36-19 Sample DS command output

```
IEE459I 15.40.14 DEVSERV PATHS 458
UNIT DTYPE  M CNT VOLSER  CHPID=PATH STATUS
     RTYPE   SSID CFW TC   DFW   PIN  DC-STATE CCA  DDC   ALT  CU-TYPE
2028,33903 ,O,000,PR2028,3A=< 3B=+ 4A=< 4B=+
     2107    1710  Y  YY.  YY.    N   SIMPLEX   28   28        2107
2029,33903 ,O,000,PR2029,3A=< 3B=+ 4A=< 4B=+
     2107    1710  Y  YY.  YY.    N   SIMPLEX   29   29        2107
202A,33903 ,O,000,PR202A,3A=< 3B=+ 4A=< 4B=+
     2107    1710  Y  YY.  YY.    N   SIMPLEX   2A   2A        2107
202B,33903 ,O,000,PR202B,3A=< 3B=+ 4A=< 4B=+
     2107    1710  Y  YY.  YY.    N   SIMPLEX   2B   2B        2107
202C,33903 ,O,000,PR202C,3A=< 3B=+ 4A=< 4B=+
     2107    1710  Y  YY.  YY.    N   SIMPLEX   2C   2C        2107
202D,33903 ,O,000,PR202D,3A=< 3B=+ 4A=< 4B=+
     2107    1710  Y  YY.  YY.    N   SIMPLEX   2D   2D        2107
************************ SYMBOL DEFINITIONS ************************
O = ONLINE                           + = PATH AVAILABLE
< = PHYSICALLY UNAVAILABLE
IEE459I 15.40.51 DEVSERV PATHS 472
UNIT DTYPE  M CNT VOLSER  CHPID=PATH STATUS
     RTYPE   SSID CFW TC   DFW   PIN  DC-STATE CCA  DDC   ALT  CU-TYPE
E128,33903 ,O,000,SCB128,3A=+ 3B=< 4A=< 4B=+
     2105    1071  Y  YY.  YY.    N   SIMPLEX   28   28        2105
E129,33903 ,O,000,SCB129,3A=+ 3B=< 4A=< 4B=+
     2105    1071  Y  YY.  YY.    N   SIMPLEX   29   29        2105
E12A,33903 ,F,000,      ,3A=+ 3B=< 4A=< 4B=+
     2105    1071  Y  YY.  YY.    N   SIMPLEX   2A   2A        2105
E12B,33903 ,F,000,      ,3A=+ 3B=< 4A=< 4B=+
     2105    1071  Y  YY.  YY.    N   SIMPLEX   2B   2B        2105
E12C,33903 ,O,000,SCB12C,3A=+ 3B=< 4A=< 4B=+
     2105    1071  Y  YY.  YY.    N   SIMPLEX   2C   2C        2105
E12D,33903 ,O,000,SCB12D,3A=+ 3B=< 4A=< 4B=+
     2105    1071  Y  YY.  YY.    N   SIMPLEX   2D   2D        2105
************************ SYMBOL DEFINITIONS ************************
F = OFFLINE                          O = ONLINE
+ = PATH AVAILABLE                   < = PHYSICALLY UNAVAILABLE
```

Example 36-20 shows the system messages from the XSTART and XADDPAIR commands for this example session.

Example 36-20 Sample system messages for XSTART session

```
ANTL8800I XSTART XRCTEST ERRLVL(SESSION) SESSIONTYPE(XRC) HLQ(SYS1)
ANTL8800I XADDPAIR XRCTEST VOLUME(PR202E XRCUTL)
ANTL8800I XADDPAIR XRCTEST VOLUME(PR202F XRCUTL) SCSESSION(AA)
ANTL8800I XADDPAIR XRCTEST VOLUME(PR2028 SCB128)
ANTL8800I XADDPAIR XRCTEST VOLUME(PR2029 SCB129)
ANTL8800I XADDPAIR XRCTEST VOLUME(PR202A SCB12A)
ANTL8800I XADDPAIR XRCTEST VOLUME(PR202B SCB12B) SCSESSION(AA)
ANTL8800I XADDPAIR XRCTEST VOLUME(PR202C SCB12C) SCSESSION(AA)
ANTL8800I XADDPAIR XRCTEST VOLUME(PR202D SCB12D) SCSESSION(AA)
ANTI1020I PARAMETERS FOUND IN MEMBER XRCTEST OF DATA SET SYS1.XCOPY.PARM
LIB HAVE BEEN APPLIED
ANTS8100I XSTART COMPLETE FOR XRC SESSION(XRCTEST) WITH SESSIONTYPE(XRC)
, ERRORLEVEL(SESSION), HLQ(SYS1).  SESSION NOW ACTIVE
ANTA8005I XADDPAIR UTILITY VOLUME PR202E IS FIXED FOR SESSION(XRCTEST),
SCSESSION(--)
ANTA8005I XADDPAIR UTILITY VOLUME PR202F IS FIXED FOR SESSION(XRCTEST),
SCSESSION(AA)
ANTA8101I XADDPAIR COMPLETE FOR VOLUME PAIR(PR2028,SCB128) FOR
SESSION(XRCTEST) WITH ERRORLEVEL(SESSION), SCSESSION(--)
ANTA8101I XADDPAIR COMPLETE FOR VOLUME PAIR(PR2029,SCB129) FOR
SESSION(XRCTEST) WITH ERRORLEVEL(SESSION), SCSESSION(--)
ANTA8101I XADDPAIR COMPLETE FOR VOLUME PAIR(PR202A,SCB12A) FOR
SESSION(XRCTEST) WITH ERRORLEVEL(SESSION), SCSESSION(--)
ANTA8101I XADDPAIR COMPLETE FOR VOLUME PAIR(PR202B,SCB12B) FOR
SESSION(XRCTEST) WITH ERRORLEVEL(SESSION), SCSESSION(AA)
ANTA8101I XADDPAIR COMPLETE FOR VOLUME PAIR(PR202C,SCB12C) FOR
SESSION(XRCTEST) WITH ERRORLEVEL(SESSION), SCSESSION(AA)
ANTA8101I XADDPAIR COMPLETE FOR VOLUME PAIR(PR202D,SCB12D) FOR
SESSION(XRCTEST) WITH ERRORLEVEL(SESSION), SCSESSION(AA)
```

Part 9

Solutions

In this part of the book we discuss solutions offered by IBM to assist you in the management, automation, and control of your Copy Service implementation on the DS8000. After presenting an overview of the solutions, we discuss the options available and give you some examples of the use of the solutions.

37

GDPS overview and positioning

Today's on demand data centers must be resilient enough to handle planned and unplanned system outages without impacting the business of the enterprise.

Most solutions that help to provide continuous IT services availability are based on cluster server software, mirrored storage, and redundant networks. When a failure occurs, an integrated disaster recovery solution will execute, in a pre-determined fashion, a set of tasks to restart the operating system, recover storage servers and networks, and restart applications on a different set of servers and storage in another location. This level of functionality is also defined as IT continuous availability.

GDPS or Geographically Dispersed Parallel Sysplex is such a full function solution and provides various levels of IT continuous availability through different implementation levels. GDPS as a continuous availability and near-transparent disaster recovery solution is based on Parallel Sysplex server functionality and disk mirroring utilizing Metro Mirror and Global Mirror.

This chapter provides an overview of the various features that GDPS offers. Most of this chapter is a slightly modified version of the information from Chapter 8 of the redbook, *IBM TotalStorage Business Continuity Solutions Guide*, SG24-6547.

Note that GDPS is a continuous availability solution for zSeries and is an IBM implementation service and not a product.

Also see the following URLs:

```
http://www.ibm.com/servers/eserver/zseries/gdps/
http://www.ibm.com/services/storage
```

37.1 GDPS introduction

The zSeries Geographically Dispersed Parallel Sysplex (GDPS) offerings are a family of zSeries-based Business Continuity solutions that include Tier 7 and Tier 6 solutions.

Our discussion of GDPS is organized in the following way:

- A review of the base zSeries Parallel Sysplex technology, which provides key system services for GDPS from the server side.
- A GDPS overview of the different solution offerings.
- A technical and detailed overview of the GDPS components.

> **Note:** The GDPS naming convention still uses the original IBM Advanced Copy Services names for disk mirroring:
>
> - GDPS/PPRC refers to the use of IBM Metro Mirror disk mirroring, which was formerly known as Peer to Peer Remote Copy (PPRC).
> - GDPS/XRC refers to the use of z/OS Global Mirror disk mirroring, which was formerly known as XRC.

37.2 zSeries Parallel Sysplex overview

IBM clients of every size, and across every industry, are looking for ways to make their businesses more productive and more resilient in the face of change and uncertainty. They need the ability to react to rapidly changing market conditions, manage risk, outpace their competitors with new capabilities, and deliver clear returns on investment. The zSeries server family was introduced in 2000 to deliver the mainframe expectations in terms of security, reliability, availability, manageability and recoverability. In a zSeries Central Electronic Complex (CEC), you can run single or multiple z/OS images. With IBM Parallel Sysplex technology, you can harness the power of up to 32 z/OS systems making them behave like a single system. You can have a Parallel Sysplex either in multi-image single CEC or in a multi-image multi-CEC environment.

The IBM Parallel Sysplex technology is a highly advanced z/OS clustered system that aggregates the capacity of multiple z/OS systems to execute common workloads.

Parallel Sysplex is not required for the GDPS/XRC environment, but is supported in a GDPS/XRC installation. Parallel Sysplex is required for full GDPS/PPRC, and for current GDPS/PPRC HyperSwap™ Manager.

37.2.1 Different clustering types

There are three main types of clustering environments.

The first type is a high-availability or *failover* type, where in case of a failure of the primary server, the processing is transferred to the backup server. See Figure 37-1.

The second type uses parallel clusters, where the clusters share the workload and provide availability and scalability. The major drawback of this clustering technique is that the workload should be carefully distributed between clusters or you could incur under or over utilization. Other drawbacks include database re-partitioning and distributing paths to data that could require a lot of work during the initial configuration and after, when your workload grows or your business needs change. See Figure 37-1.

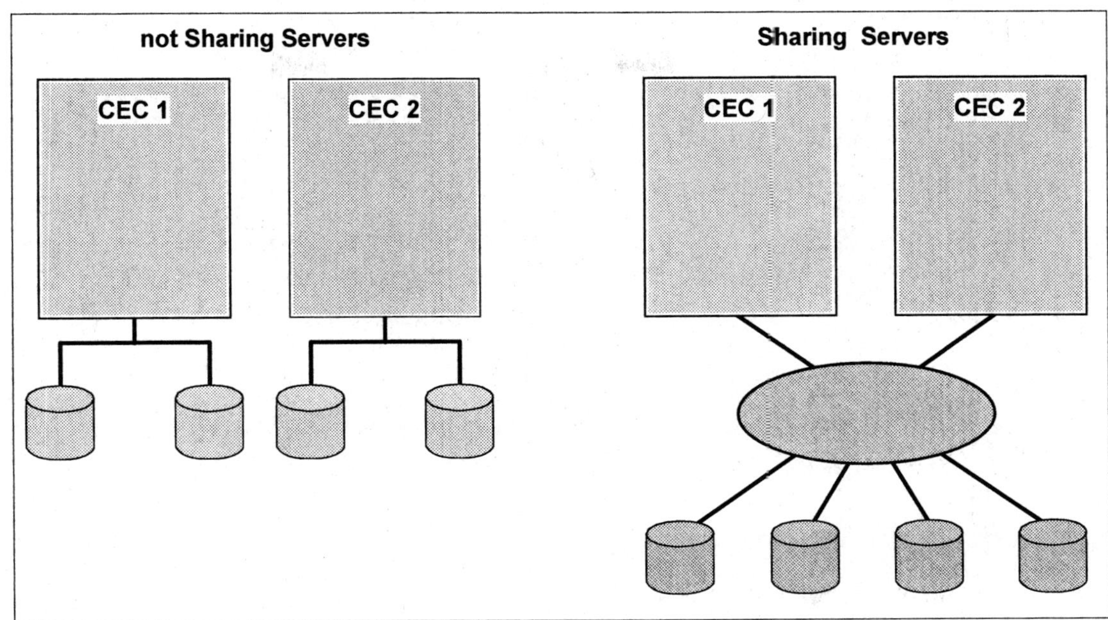

Figure 37-1 Dedicated servers and shared storage at different server scope

The third type offers the most efficient form of clustering, where the clustered servers appear as a single system to the applications. See Figure 37-2. This is a *shared data, shared access* approach where every cluster node has access to all of the data and could run any part of your business transactions or batch jobs in parallel on the available processor capacity. Other benefits include automatic workload balancing for continuous availability, continuous operation and scalability, and a single point of control.

The IBM Parallel Sysplex technology is the zSeries implementation of the single system image type of clustering.

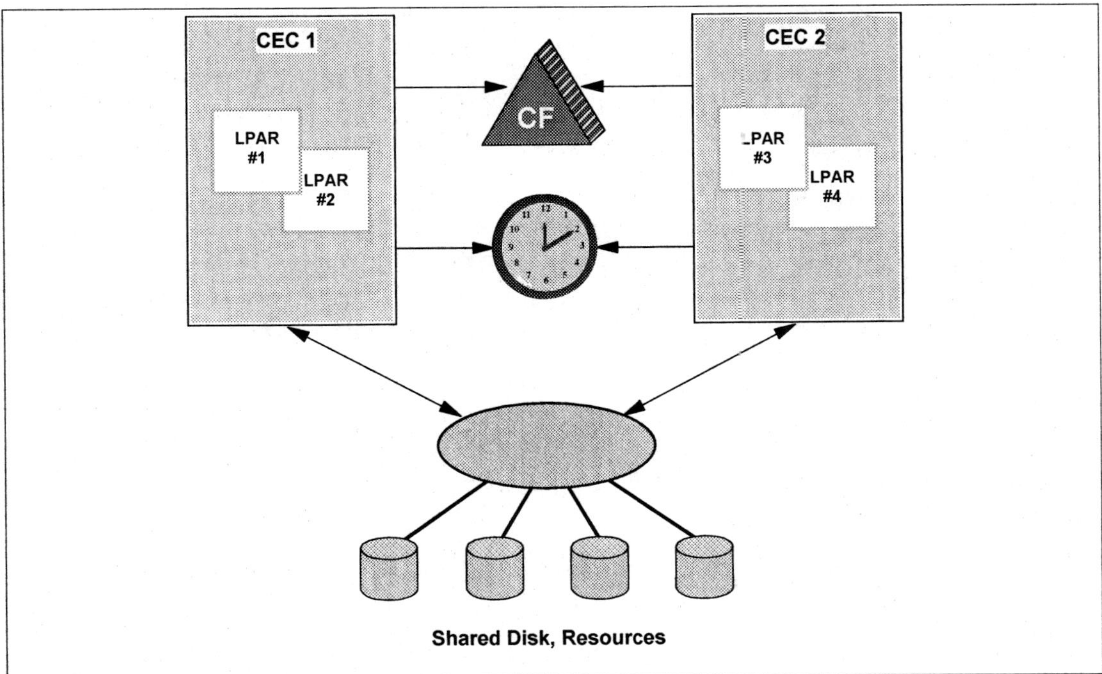

Figure 37-2 Shared storage servers, shared access, and shared resources

37.2.2 Parallel Sysplex components

In this section, we briefly describe the components of a Parallel Sysplex:

- zSeries server or CEC (Central Electronic Complex)
- Single/multiple z/OS images
- ICF/CF (Internal Coupling Facility/Coupling Facility)
- Sysplex timer

The coupling facility is the repository of all the data structures used to allow the z/OS images to share resources and data. It can be redundant and duplexed for maximum availability. It consists of special microcode running on a general purpose or dedicated processor. It can reside on standalone CF hardware, a CF LPAR on a CEC or defined as an internal CF using dedicated processors.

The sysplex timer is a dedicated hardware component used to give time consistency to the entire Parallel Sysplex complex.

37.2.3 Benefits of a Parallel Sysplex

The Parallel Sysplex is a way of managing this multisystem environment, providing benefits that include:

- Continuous availability
- Capacity
- Dynamic workload balancing
- Ease of use
- Single system image
- Non-disruptive growth
- Application compatibility

Within a Parallel Sysplex cluster, it is possible to construct a parallel processing environment, and by providing redundancy in the hardware configuration, a significant reduction in the total single points of failure is possible. See Figure 37-3.

Even though they work together and present a single image, the nodes in a Parallel Sysplex cluster remain individual systems, making installation, operation, and maintenance non-disruptive. The Parallel Sysplex environment can scale nearly linearly from two to 32 systems. This can be a mix of any servers that support the Parallel Sysplex environment. Just as work can be dynamically distributed across the individual processors within a single SMP server, so, too, can work be directed to any node in a Parallel Sysplex cluster having the available capacity.

The Parallel Sysplex solution satisfies a major client requirement for continuous 24x7x365 availability (24-hours-a-day, 7-days-a-week, 365-days-a-year).

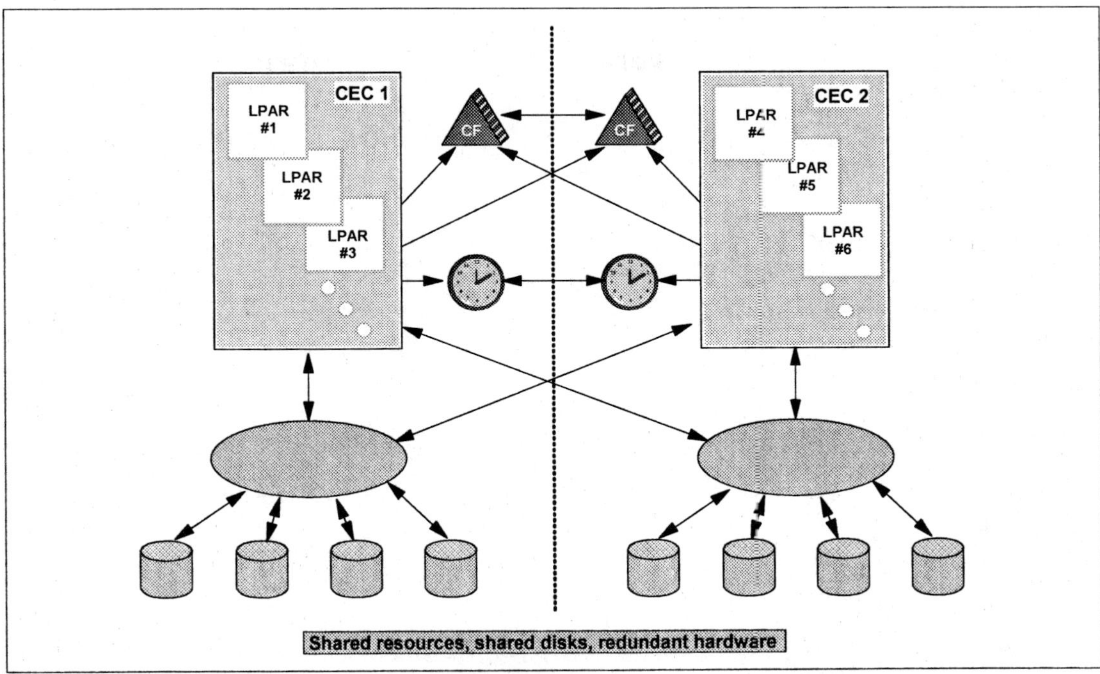

Figure 37-3 Shared data, shared access, shared resources, and redundant hardware

In summary, the zSeries Parallel Sysplex is a key Business Continuity technology in its own right. Parallel Sysplex is also a key technology for support of various GDPS family solution offerings.

37.3 GDPS solution offerings

GDPS is a family of offerings, for single site or a multi-site application availability solution, with the capability to manage the remote copy configuration and storage subsystems, automate zSeries operational tasks, manage and automate planned reconfigurations, and do failure recovery from a single point of control.

GDPS is a integrated end to end solution composed of software automation, software, servers and storage, networking, and IBM Global Services to configure and deploy the solution, as shown in Figure 37-4. The GDPS solution has components in the areas denoted by dark shading.

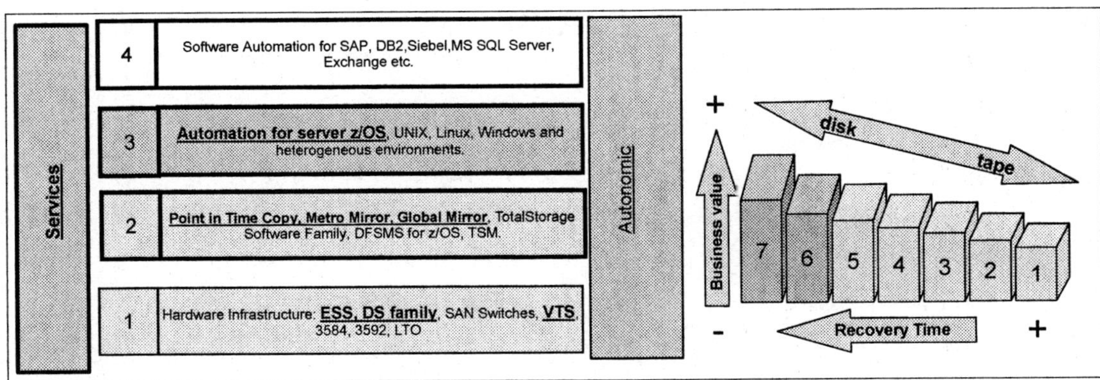

Figure 37-4 Positioning of GDPS solution offerings

The benefits of GDPS are: a highly reliable, highly automated IT infrastructure solution with a zSeries-based control point, which can provide very robust application availability.

GDPS is independent of the transaction manager like CICS Transaction Server, IMS Transaction Server, WebSphere® Server or database manager like DB2, IMS Database Server, and VSAM being used, and is enabled by means of key IBM technologies and architectures, including:

- zSeries processor technology and zSeries Parallel Sysplex
- Tivoli NetView® for z/OS
- System Automation for z/OS
- IBM TotalStorage DS6000 and DS8000 series and Enterprise Storage Server (ESS)
- Peer-to-Peer Virtual Tape Server (PtP VTS)
- Optical Dense or Coarse Wavelength Division Multiplexer (DWDM or CWDM)
- Metro Mirror architecture for GDPS/PPRC
- z/OS Global Mirror architecture for GDPS/XRC
- Virtual Tape Server remote Copy architecture

Depending on the client requirements, only the required components from the above list are selected.

GDPS supports both the synchronous (Metro Mirror) as well as the asynchronous (z/OS Global Mirror or Global Mirror) forms of remote copy. GDPS also supports Peer-to-Peer Virtual Tape Server (PtP VTS) for remote copying tape data. The GDPS solution is a non proprietary solution, working with IBM as well as Other Equipment Manufacturer (OEM) disk vendors, as long as the vendor meets the specific functions of the Metro Mirror, Global Mirror, and z/OS Global Mirror architectures required to support GDPS functions.

GDPS automation manages and protects IT services by handling planned and unplanned exception conditions. Depending on the GDPS configuration selected, availability can be storage resiliency only, or can provide near-continuous application and data availability. Regardless of the specific configuration variation, GDPS provides a zSeries-based Business Continuity automation and integration solution to manage both planned and unplanned exception conditions.

To attain high levels of continuous availability and near-transparent DR, the GDPS solution is based on geographical clusters and disk mirroring.

Figure 37-5 is a diagram of some of the many possible components supported in a GDPS configuration. GDPS is configured to meet the specific client requirements. Not all of the components shown in Figure 37-5 are necessary in all GDPS offerings or GDPS solutions.

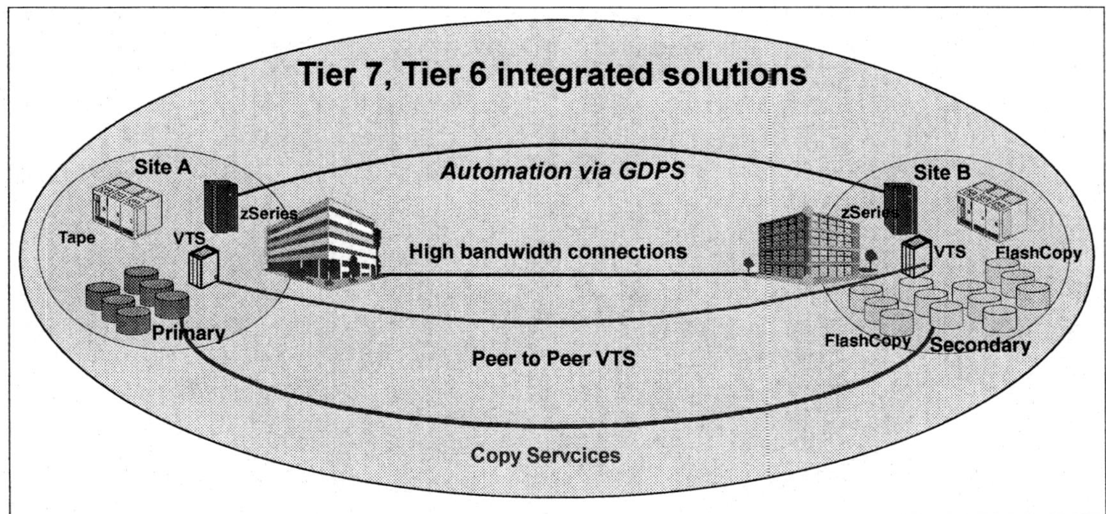

Figure 37-5 GDPS integrates many components

The GDPS family of zSeries Business Continuity solutions consists of two major offering categories, and each category has several sub-offerings. Each GDPS solution is delivered through IBM Global Services, specifically tailored to fit a specific set of client recovery needs, budgetary requirements, physical distance and infrastructure, and other factors.

The two major categories of GDPS solutions are:

- GDPS/PPRC solutions, based on IBM TotalStorage Metro Mirror. Metro Mirror was formerly known as Peer-to-Peer Remote Copy (PPRC).
- GDPS/XRC solutions, based on TotalStorage z/OS Global Mirror. z/OS Global Mirror was formerly known as Extended Remote Copy (XRC).

The sub-offerings within these two GDPS major categories include the following offerings:

GDPS/PPRC:

- GDPS/PPRC, a Tier 7 solution
- GDPS/PPRC HyperSwap Manager, a Tier 6 solution
- RCMF/PPRC, a remote copy management solution for PPRC

GDPS/XRC:

- GDPS/XRC, a Tier 7 solution
- RCMF/XRC, a remote copy management solution for XRC

Certain of the above GDPS offerings can also be combined into three site GDPS solutions, providing Tier 7 recoverability in a multi-site environment.

37.3.1 GDPS/PPRC introduction

GDPS/PPRC is designed with the attributes of a *continuous availability and disaster recovery solution*. Metro Mirror (PPRC) is a hardware solution that synchronously mirrors data residing on a set of disk volumes, called the primary volumes, to secondary disk volumes in a second system. Only when the primary storage subsystem receives "write complete" from the secondary storage subsystem is the application I/O signaled to be completed.

In GDPS/PPRC, since IBM Parallel Sysplex clustering technology is designed to enable resource sharing and dynamic workload balancing, enterprises can now dynamically manage workloads across multiple sites, which can enable them to achieve high levels of availability.

GDPS/PPRC has a major sub-offering named GDPS/PPRC HyperSwap Manager, described later in this book. With this sub-offering, Parallel Sysplex availability can now be extended to disk subsystems, even if multiple sites are not available and the Parallel Sysplex is configured in one site.

GDPS/PPRC complements a multisite Parallel Sysplex implementation by providing a single, automated solution to dynamically manage storage subsystem mirroring, disk and tape, processors, and network resources designed to help a business to attain *continuous availability* and *near transparent business continuity (disaster recovery)* with no or minimal data loss. GDPS/PPRC is designed to minimize and potentially eliminate the impact of any failure including disasters, or a planned outage.

GDPS/PPRC is designed to provide the ability to perform a controlled site switch for both planned and unplanned site outages, with no or minimal data loss, maintaining full data integrity across multiple volumes and storage subsystems and the ability to perform a normal Data Base Management System (DBMS) restart – not DBMS recovery – in the second site. GDPS/PPRC is application independent and therefore can cover the customer's complete application environment.

37.3.2 GDPS/PPRC overview

GDPS/PPRC is designed to manage and protect IT services by handling planned and unplanned exception conditions, and maintain data integrity across multiple volumes and storage subsystems. By managing both planned and unplanned exception conditions, GDPS/PPRC can help to maximize application availability and provide business continuity.

GDPS/PPRC is capable of the following attributes:

- Near continuous Availability solution
- Near transparent D/R solution
- Recovery Time Objective (RTO) less than an hour
- Recovery Point Objective (RPO) of zero (optional)
- Protects against localized area disasters with a typical distance between sites limited of up to 100 km fiber distance

The GDPS/PPRC solution offering combines zSeries Parallel Sysplex capability and ESS, DS6000, and/or DS8000 Metro Mirror disk mirroring technology to provide a Business Continuity solution for IT infrastructures that have zSeries at the core. GDPS/PPRC offers efficient workload management, system resource management, Business Continuity or Disaster Recovery for z/OS servers and open system data and provides data consistency across all platforms using the Metro Mirror Consistency Group function.

The GDPS solution uses automation technology to provide end-to-end management of z/Servers, disk mirroring, tape mirroring, and workload shutdown and startup. GDPS will manage the infrastructure to minimize or eliminate the outage during a planned or unplanned site failure. Critical data is disk mirrored, and processing is automatically restarted at an alternate site in the event of a primary planned site shutdown or site failure.

GDPS/PPRC automation provides scalability to insure data integrity at a very large number of volumes, across hundreds or thousands of Metro Mirror pairs.

37.3.3 GDPS/PPRC topology

The physical topology of a GDPS/PPRC consists of a base or Parallel Sysplex cluster spread across two sites known as site 1 and site 2 and separated by up to 100 kilometers (km) of fiber, which is approximately 62 miles with one or more z/OS systems at each site. See Figure 37-6.

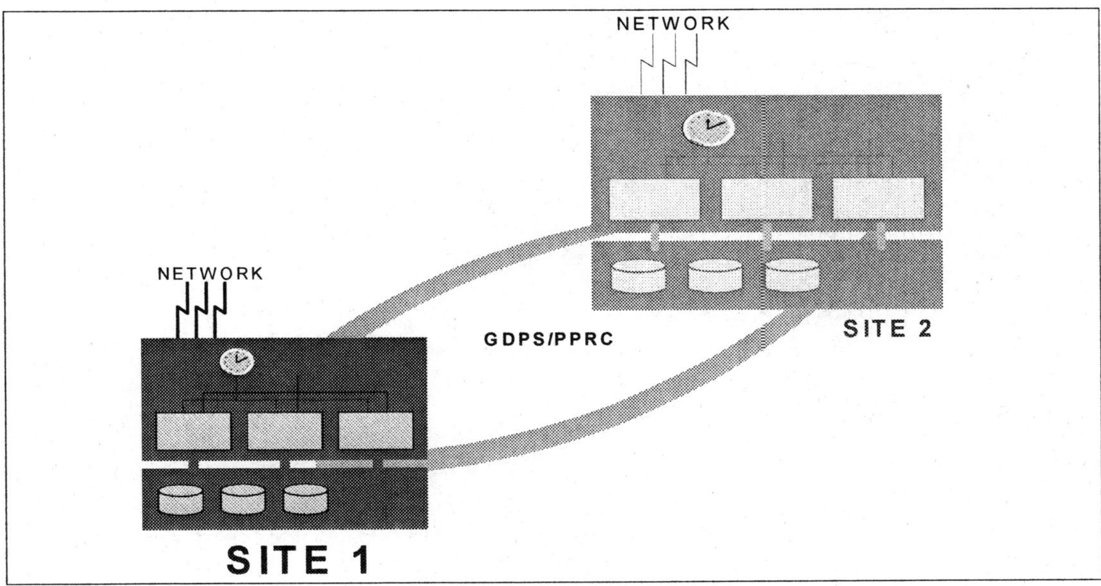

Figure 37-6 GDPS/PPRC topology

The multisite sysplex cluster must be configured with redundant hardware. For example, a Coupling Facility and a Sysplex Timer in each site and the cross-site connections must be redundant. All critical data resides on storage subsystem(s) in site 1, the primary copy of data, and is mirrored to the storage subsystem(s) in site 2, the secondary copy of data via PPRC synchronous remote copy or Metro Mirror.

Customers have the capability to configure GDPS/PPRC with up to 100 km of fiber between two sites. An immediate advantage of this extended distance is to potentially decrease the risk that the same disaster will affect both sites, thus permitting customers to recover their production applications at another site.

GDPS/PPRC supports IBM Metro Mirror over Fiber Channel Protocol (FCP) on the DS6000, DS8000, and ESS 800 disk subsystems. IBM Metro Mirror over FCP requires only one protocol exchange compared to two or three exchanges when using Metro Mirror over ESCON. The resulting performance and throughput allows GDPS solutions to extend the distance between sites while maintaining acceptable application performance. The efficiency of the IBM disk mirroring FCP protocol is also expected to lower the total cost of ownership as IBM recommends that for almost all workloads two Metro Mirror FCP disk mirroring links between each pair of ESS, DS6000, and/or DS8000 disk subsystems are considered sufficient for most workloads. This allows a reduction in cross-site SAN port infrastructure and HBA requirements.

37.3.4 PPRC and HyperSwap

Exclusive to GDPS in the PPRC environment is HyperSwap. This function is designed to broaden the near continuous availability attributes of GDPS/PPRC by extending the Parallel Sysplex redundancy to disk subsystems. The HyperSwap function can help significantly reduce the time needed to switch to the secondary set of disks while keeping the z/OS systems active together with their applications.

With the recent release of GDPS/PPRC V3.2 the HyperSwap function has been enhanced to exploit the Metro Mirror Failover/Failback (FO/FB) function. For planned reconfigurations FO/FB may reduce the overall elapsed time to switch the disk subsystems, thereby reducing the time that applications may be unavailable to users.

For unplanned reconfigurations FO/FB allows the secondary disks to be configured in the suspended state after the switch and record any updates made to the data. When the failure condition has been repaired, resynchronizing back to the original primary disks requires only the changed data to be copied, thus eliminating the need to perform a full copy of the data. The window during which critical data is left without Metro Mirror protection following an unplanned reconfiguration is thereby minimized.

GDPS/PPRC HyperSwap Manager overview

The GDPS/PPRC HyperSwap Manager solution is a subset of the full GDPS/PPRC solution, designed to provide a very affordable entry point to the full family of GDPS/PPRC offerings.

GDPS/PPRC HyperSwap Manager (GDPS/PPRC HM) expands zSeries Business Resiliency to customers by providing a single-site near continuous availability solution as well as a multi-site entry-level disaster recovery solution.

Within a single site GDPS/PPRC HyperSwap Manager extends Parallel Sysplex availability to disk subsystems by masking planned and unplanned disk outages caused by disk maintenance and disk failures. It also provides management of the data replication environment and automates switching between the two copies of the data without causing an application outage, therefore providing near-continuous access to data. Figure 37-7 shows an example of a GDPS/PPRC HM configuration.

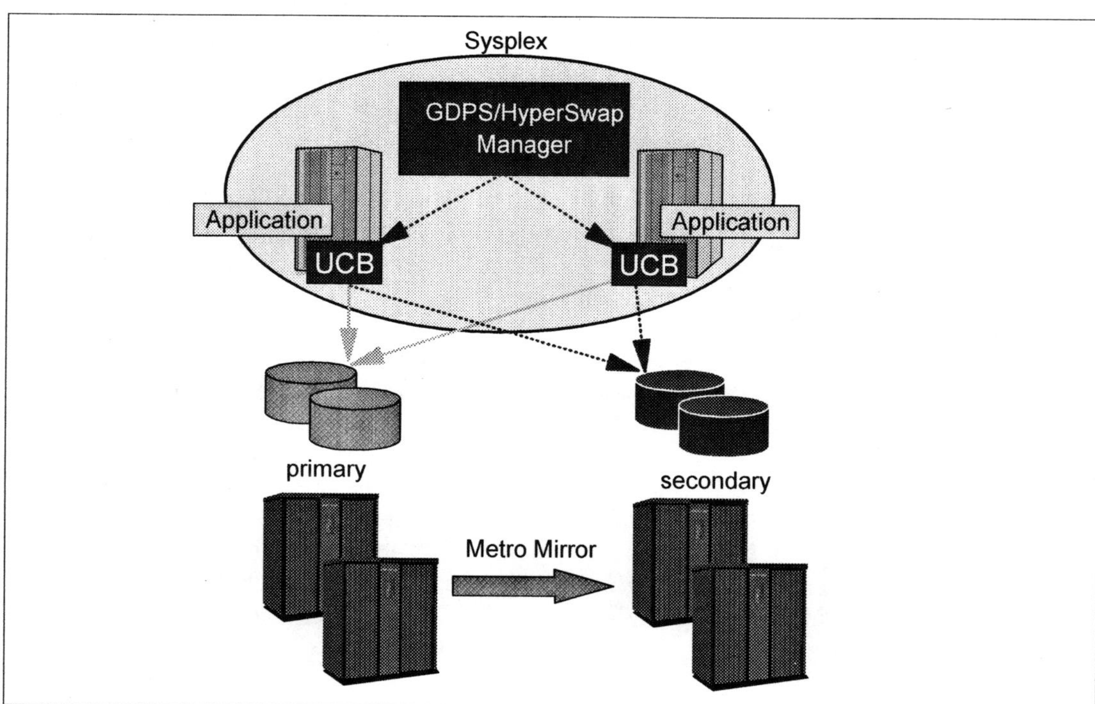

Figure 37-7 GDPS/PPRC HyperSwap Manager

In the multisite environment GDPS/PPRC HyperSwap Manager provides an effective entry-level disaster recovery offering for those zSeries customers that have the need for very high levels of data availability.

Note: The GDPS HyperSwap Manager offering features specially priced limited function Tivoli System Automation and NetView software products, thus satisfying the GDPS software automation prerequisites with a lower initial price and a cost-effective initial entry point to the GDPS family of GDPS offerings.

Users who already have the full function Tivoli System Automation and NetView software products may continue to use them as the pre-requisites for GDPS HyperSwap Manager.

In addition a customer can migrate to the full function GDPS/PPRC capability across multiple sites as business requirements demand shorter Recovery Time Objectives provided by a second site. The initial investment in GDPS/PPRC HM is protected when customers choose to move to full-function GDPS/PPRC by leveraging the existing GDPS/PPRC HM implementation and skills.

Note: The limited function Tivoli System Automation and NetView software will require upgrade to the full function versions upon migration from an entry-level GDPS HyperSwap Manager to full GDPS/PPRC.

GDPS/PPRC HyperSwap Manager simplifies the control and management of the Metro Mirror environment for both z/OS and open systems data. This reduces storage management costs while reducing the time required for remote copy implementation.

GDPS/PPRC HyperSwap Manager provides support for FlashCopy. GDPS/PPRC HyperSwap Manager can be set up to automatically take a FlashCopy of the secondary disks before resynchronizing the primary and secondary disks following a Metro Mirror suspension event, ensuring a consistent set of disks are preserved should there be a disaster during the re-synch operation.

37.3.5 Planned reconfiguration support with GDPS/PPRC

GDPS/PPRC planned reconfiguration support automates procedures performed by an operations center. These include standard actions to:

- Quiesce a system's workload and remove the system from the Parallel Sysplex cluster — for example, to stop the system prior to a hardware change window.
- IPL a system — for example, to start the system after a hardware change window.
- Quiesce a system's workload, remove the system from the Parallel Sysplex cluster, and re-IPL the system — for example, to recycle a system to pick up software maintenance.

Standard actions can be initiated against a single system or a group of systems. With the introduction of HyperSwap, you now have the ability to perform disk maintenance and planned site maintenance without requiring applications to be quiesced. Additionally, GDPS/PPRC provides customizable scripting capability for user defined actions. For example, a planned disk maintenance or planned site switch in which the workload is switched from processors in site 1 to processors in site 2.

All GDPS functions can be performed from a single point of control, which can help simplify system resource management. Panels are used to manage the entire remote copy configuration rather than individual remote copy pairs. This includes the initialization and monitoring of the remote copy volume pairs based upon policy and performing routine operations on installed storage subsystems – disk and tape. GDPS can also perform standard operational tasks and monitor systems in the event of unplanned outages.

The Planned HyperSwap function is designed to provide the ability to transparently switch all primary disk subsystems with the secondary disk subsystems for planned reconfigurations. During a planned reconfiguration HyperSwap can provide the ability to perform disk configuration maintenance and planned site maintenance without requiring any applications to be quiesced. Large configurations can be supported as HyperSwap is designed to provide capacity and capability to swap large number of disk devices very quickly. The important ability to re-synchronize incremental disk data changes in both directions between primary and secondary disks is provided as part of this function.

37.3.6 Unplanned reconfiguration support with GDPS/PPRC

GDPS/PPRC unplanned reconfiguration support not only can automate procedures to handle site failures but can also help minimize the impact and potentially mask a z/OS system, processor, Coupling Facility, disk or tape failure, based upon GDPS/PPRC policy. If a z/OS system fails the failed system and workload can be automatically restarted. If a processor fails the failed system(s) and their workload can be restarted on other processors.

The Unplanned HyperSwap function is designed to transparently switch to use secondary disk subsystems that contain mirrored data consistent with the primary data in the event of unplanned outages of the primary disk subsystems or a failure of the site containing the primary disk subsystems.

With Unplanned HyperSwap support:

- Production systems can remain active during a disk subsystem failure. Disk subsystem failures will no longer constitute a single point of failure for an entire sysplex.
- Production systems can remain active during a failure of the site containing the primary disk subsystems (site 1), if applications are cloned and exploiting data sharing across the two sites. Even though the workload in site 2 will need to be restarted an improvement in the Recovery Time Objective (RTO) is accomplished.

37.3.7 Support for heterogeneous environment with GDPS/PPRC

GDPS/PPRC has been extended to support heterogeneous operating systems platforms, including other zSeries operating systems, and open systems operating systems.

zSeries based environments

In addition to managing images within the base or Parallel Sysplex cluster GDPS can now also manage other zSeries production operating systems. These systems include z/OS, Linux for zSeries, z/VM, and VSE/ESA. The operating systems have to run on servers that are connected to the same Hardware Management Console (HMC) Local Area Network (LAN) as the Parallel Sysplex cluster images. For example, if the volumes associated with the Linux images are mirrored using PPRC, GDPS can restart these images as part of a planned or unplanned site reconfiguration. The Linux for zSeries images can either run as a logical partition (LPAR) or as a guest under z/VM.

Open systems environments

GDPS/PPRC technology has been extended to manage a heterogeneous environment of z/OS and open systems data. If installations share their disk subsystems between the z/OS and open systems platforms, GDPS/PPRC can manage the Metro Mirror and Metro Mirror FREEZE for open systems storage, thus providing a common Consistency Group and data consistency across both z/OS and open systems data. This allows GDPS to be a single point of control to manage business resiliency across multiple tiers in the infrastructure, improving cross-platform system management and business processes.

Multi-platform resiliency for zSeries

GDPS/PPRC has been enhanced to provide a new function called *GDPS/PPRC Multi-Platform Resiliency for zSeries*. This function is especially valuable for customers who share data and storage subsystems between z/OS and z/VM Linux guests on zSeries. For example, an application server running on Linux on zSeries and a database server running on z/OS.

Within a multi-tiered, multi-operating system environment, there is a need to provide a coordinated, near Continuous Availability/Disaster Recovery solution for both z/OS and zLinux. GDPS/PPRC can now provide that. z/VM 5.1 has been enhanced to provide support of the HyperSwap function so that the virtual device, for example, associated with zSeries LINUX guests running under z/VM, associated with one real disk, can be swapped transparently to another disk. HyperSwap can be used to switch to secondary disk storage subsystems mirrored by Peer-to-Peer Remote Copy (PPRC, or Metro Mirror). If there is a hard failure of a storage device GDPS coordinates the HyperSwap with z/OS for continuous availability spanning the multi-tiered application. For site failures GDPS invokes the FREEZE function for data consistency and rapid application restart without the need for data recovery. HyperSwap can also be helpful in data migration scenarios to allow applications to migrate to new disk volumes without requiring them to be quiesced.

GDPS/PPRC will provide the reconfiguration capabilities for the Linux on zSeries servers and data in the same manner as for z/OS systems and data. To support planned and unplanned outages GDPS provides the recovery actions such as the following examples:

- Re-IPL in place of failing operating system images
- Site takeover/failover of a complete production site
- Coordinated planned and unplanned HyperSwap of disk subsystems, transparent to the operating system images and applications using the disks.
- Linux node or cluster failures
- Transparent disk maintenance or failure recovery with HyperSwap across z/OS and Linux applications
- Data consistency with FREEZE functions across z/OS and Linux

37.3.8 RCMF/PPRC overview

Remote Copy Management Facility/PPRC (RCMF/PPRC) is the name given to a subset of the GDPS/PPRC offerings. RCMF/PPRC includes the storage interface management functions only.

RCMF/PPRC provides panels and code that execute under NetView and provides an operator interface for easier management of a remote copy configuration in setup, initialization, and any planned outage operational mode. This provides benefits for businesses looking to improve their management of PPRC for normal running circumstances.

Note that RCMF/PPRC does not provide any monitoring capability and is not designed to notify the operator of an error in the remote copy configuration. Thus RCMF does not support the Freeze function for GDPS/PPRC, FlashCopy automation, or the unplanned outage functions available through the other versions of GDPS.

RCMF/PPRC is positioned as a remote copy management control tool, designed to make much easier the task for operators to stop and start remote copy sessions.

The highlights of RCMF/PPRC include:

- Central point of control - full screen
- Global PPRC configuration awareness
- Functional, tree-structured interface
- TSO commands not needed
- Initialize and maintain Remote Copy configuration
- Single keystroke function invocation
- Initiate functions per pair, subsystem, or all
- Automatically establish target configuration at system startup
- Supports adding, moving, removing pairs, subsystems and links
- RCMF does not manage unplanned outage secondary data consistency
- Drive Peer-to-Peer/Dynamic Address Switching (P/DAS)
- User-initiated status and exception reporting
- Can run as a NetView application - System Automation not required

37.3.9 GDPS/XRC introduction

GDPS/XRC has the attributes of a *disaster recovery* solution. z/OS Global Mirror (XRC) is a combined hardware and software asynchronous remote copy solution. The application I/O is signaled completed when the data update to the primary storage is completed. Subsequently a DFSMSdfp component called System Data Mover (SDM), typically running in the recovery site (site 2), asynchronously off loads data from the primary storage subsystem's cache and updates the secondary disk volumes. Refer to <ref> refer to XRC chapter <ref> for details on how the SDM provides data update sequence consistency for all volumes participating in the XRC session.

In GDPS/XRC, the production system(s) located in site 1 can be a single system, multiple systems sharing disk, or a base or Parallel Sysplex cluster. GDPS/XRC provides a single, automated solution, designed to dynamically manage storage subsystem mirroring (disk and tape) to allow a business to attain *near transparent* disaster recovery with minimal data loss. GDPS/XRC is designed to provide the ability to perform a controlled site switch for an unplanned site outage, maintaining data integrity across multiple volumes and storage subsystems and the ability to perform a normal Data Base Management System (DBMS) restart – not DBMS recovery – in the recovery site. GDPS/XRC is application independent and therefore can cover the customer's complete application environment.

GDPS/XRC overview

IBM TotalStorage z/OS Global Mirror, formerly known as Extended Remote Copy (XRC), is a combined hardware and z/OS software asynchronous remote copy solution for zSeries data. z/OS Global Mirror is designed to provide premium levels of scalability, reaching into the tens of thousands of zSeries volumes. Consistency of the data is maintained via the Consistency Group function within the System Data Mover.

GDPS/XRC includes automation to manage z/OS Global Mirror remote copy pairs and automates the process of recovering the production environment with limited manual intervention, including invocation of CBU, thus providing significant value in reducing the duration of the recovery window and requiring less operator interaction.

GDPS/XRC provides the following attributes:

- Disaster recovery solution
- RTO between an hour to two hours
- RPO less than two minutes, typically 3-5 seconds
- Protects against localized as well as regional disasters; unlimited distance between sites
- Minimal remote copy performance impact

GDPS/XRC topology

The physical topology of a GDPS/XRC, as illustrated in Figure 37-8, consists of production system(s) in site 1. The production systems could be a single system, multiple systems sharing disks, or a base or Parallel Sysplex cluster. Site 2, the recovery site, can be located at a virtually unlimited distance from site 1, the production site.

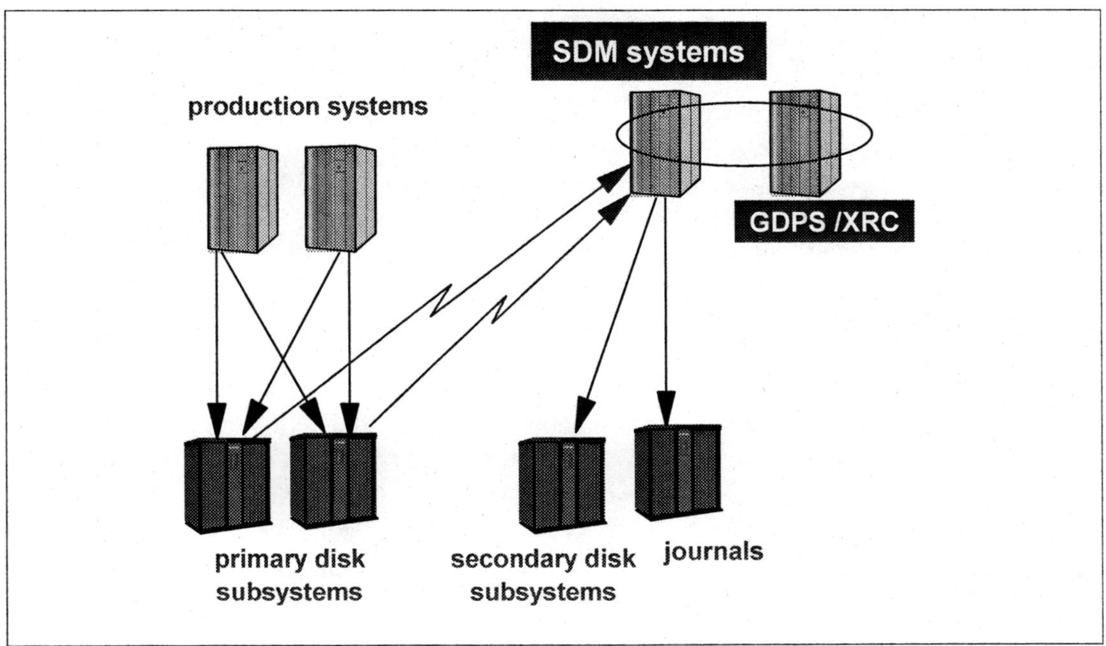

Figure 37-8 GDPS/XRC topology

During normal operations one or more XRC System Data Mover(s) execute in site 2 and are in a Base Sysplex with the GDPS controlling system. All critical data resides on storage subsystem(s) in site 1 and is mirrored to the storage subsystem(s) in site 2 via z/OS Global Mirror (XRC) asynchronous remote copy.

Planned and unplanned reconfiguration support with GDPS/XRC

Planned and unplanned reconfiguration actions include:

- Quiesce a system's workload and remove the system from the Parallel Sysplex cluster. For example, to stop the system prior to a site switch
- Reconfigure and IPL system(s)
- Quiesce a system's workload, remove the system from the Parallel Sysplex cluster, and re-IPL the system(s)

These actions are provided by GDPS/XRC for the System Data Mover (SDM) Sysplex in site 2. If need GDPS/XRC can manage the temporary relocation of the SDM.

GDPS/XRC provides a highly automated solution to minimize the dependency on key human skills being available at the remote site to recover from a disaster. GDPS/XRC is designed to automate the process of recovering the production environment with minimal manual intervention, which can provide significant value in minimizing the duration of the recovery window.

Coupled SDM support

GDPS/XRC supports the z/OS Global Mirror support for Coupled Extended Remote Copy (CXRC). CXRC expands the capability of z/OS Global Mirror so that customers who have configurations consisting of thousands of primary volumes can recover all their volumes to a consistent point-in-time. A single SDM can typically manage approximately 1000 to 2000 volume pairs based on the write I/O rate. CXRC can provide the scalability that is required to support larger z/OS Global Mirror configurations. CXRC allows customers the capability of coupling of multiple XRC sessions together into a master session. CXRC coordinates the consistency of data for coupled sessions in a master session, which allows you to recover all the volumes in the coupled sessions to a consistent point-in-time.

Commands are now capable of being executed in parallel across multiple SDMs in a GDPS/XRC configuration, which provides improved scalability. The parallelism is across multiple SDMs provided there is only one SDM per z/OS image. If there are multiple SDMs per z/OS image then processing is sequential by SDM within the z/OS image.

37.3.10 RCMF/XRC overview

Remote Copy Management Facility/XRC (RCMF/XRC) is a subset of GDPS/XRC that provide the capability to manage the z/OS Global Mirror configuration for planned and unplanned outages. RCMF/XRC is not intended to manage the system and workload environment. RCMF/XRC provides a central point of control of z/OS Global Mirror disk mirroring configurations where the environment does not require more than one SDM. Those environments that require multiple SDMs and/or coupled SDMs will require the full GDPS/XRC.

RCMF/XRC solution highlights include:

- Functional full screen interface
- Initialize and maintain z/OS Global Mirror Remote Copy configuration
- User initiated status collection and exception monitoring
- NetView application, does not require System Automation for z/OS

RCMF/XRC provides panels and code that execute under NetView and provides an operator interface for easier management of a remote copy z/OS Global Mirror configuration in setup, initialization, and any planned outage operational mode. This provides benefits for businesses looking to improve their management of XRC for normal running circumstances.

RCMF/XRC is positioned as a remote copy management control tool, designed to make it easier for operators to stop and start a single SDM z/OS Global Mirror remote copy session.

37.3.11 GDPS three site solution overview

GPDS also supports three site configuration solutions by using a combination of the previous GDPS solutions. A three site solution can combine the advantages of metropolitan distance Business Continuity and regional or long distance Disaster Recovery.

The currently available configuration for the three site requirements is GDPS/PPRC and GDPS/XRC off of the same primary volumes as shown in Figure 37-9.

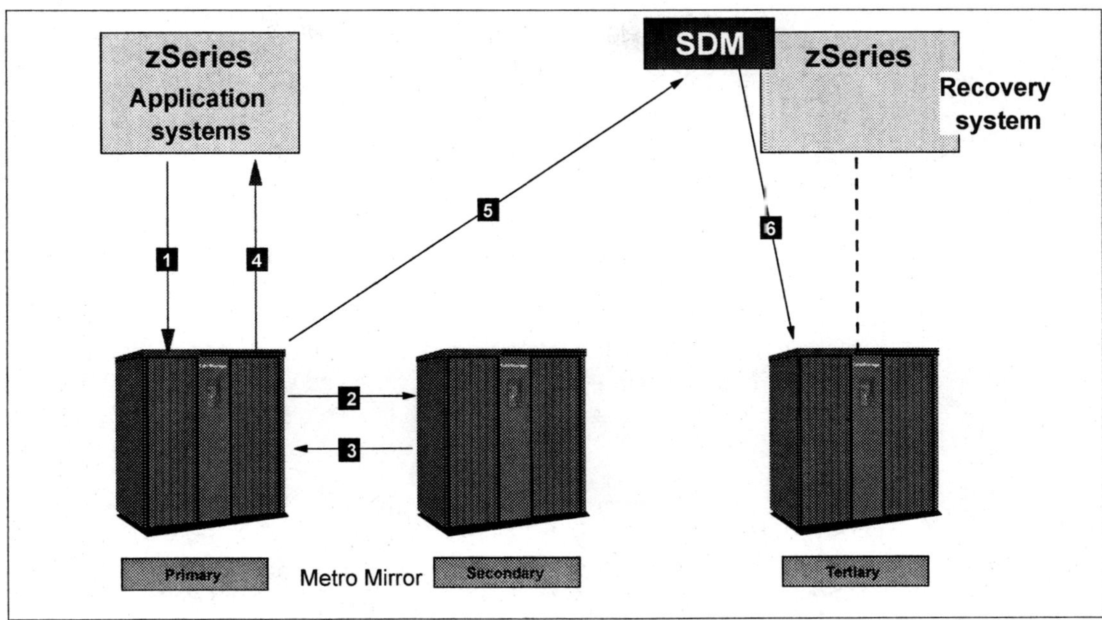

Figure 37-9 GDPS three site configuration with GDPS/PPRC and GDPS/XRC

The same primary volume for PPRC and XRC can be supported by two different GDPSs, a GDPS/PPRC for metropolitan distance and Business Continuity, and a GDPS/XRC for regional distance and Disaster Recovery.

The two mirroring technologies and GDPS implementations work independently of each other, yet provide the synergy of a common management scheme and common skills.

More details on GDPS three site configurations can be obtained from your IBM GDPS representative.

> **Note:** GDPS/XRC supports zSeries data for z/OS, LINUX on z/VM, z/VM, and z/VSE. GDPS/XRC and GDPS/PPRC off of the same volume is a zSeries solution only.

37.3.12 Common functions for GDPS/PPRC and GDPS/XRC

The following functions are supported by both GDPS/PPRC and GDPS/XRC.

Peer-to-Peer Virtual tape Server support

GDPS also supports Peer-to-Peer Virtual Tape Server (PtP VTS). By extending GDPS support to data resident on tape, the GDPS solution is intended to provide continuous availability and near transparent business continuity benefit for both disk and tape resident data. Enterprises may no longer be forced to develop and utilize processes that create duplex tapes and maintain the tape copies in alternate sites. For example, previous techniques created two copies of each DBMS image copy and archived log as part of the batch process and manual transportation of each set of tapes to different locations.

Operational data or data that is used directly by applications supporting end users is normally found on disk. However, there is another category of data that *supports* the operational data, which is typically found on tape subsystems. Support data typically covers migrated data, point-in-time backups, archive data, etc. For sustained operation at the recovery site, the support data is indispensable. Furthermore, several enterprises have mission critical data that only resides on tape.

The PtP VTS provides a hardware-based duplex tape solution and GDPS can automatically manage the duplexed tapes in the event of a planned site switch or a site failure. Control capability has been added to allow GDPS to *freeze* copy operations so that tape data consistency can be maintained across GDPS managed sites during a switch between the primary and secondary VTSs.

FlashCopy support

FlashCopy, which is available on the IBM TotalStorage DS Family and IBM TotalStorage Enterprise Storage Server (ESS) is designed to provide an instant point-in-time copy of the data for application usage such as backup and recovery operations. FlashCopy can enable you to copy or dump data while applications are updating the data. Prior to the release of FlashCopy V2 in 2003 both source and target volumes had to reside on the same logical subsystem. Since this constraint has been removed with FlashCopy V2 GDPS will now allow a FlashCopy from a source in one LSS to a target in a different LSS within the same disk subsystem.

FlashCopy before resynchronization is automatically invoked based upon GDPS policy whenever a resynchronization request is received. This function provides a consistent data image to fall back to, in the rare event that a disaster should occur while resynchronization is taking place. FlashCopy can also be user-initiated at any time. Customers can then use the tertiary copy of data to conduct D/R testing while maintaining D/R readiness, perform either test/development work, shorten batch windows, etc.

FlashCopy can operate in either of two modes: the COPY mode, which runs a background copy process, and the NOCOPY mode, which suppresses the background copy. Previously GDPS/PPRC and GDPS/XRC have provided support for both COPY and NOCOPY.

With the release of GDPS/PPRC V3.2 and GDPS/XRC V3.2 two FlashCopy enhancements are now available. The first enhancement is to support NOCOPY2COPY, which allows changing an existing FlashCopy relationship from NOCOPY to COPY. This gives you the option of always selecting the NOCOPY option of FlashCopy and then converting it to the COPY option when you want to create a full copy of the data in the background at a non-peak time. Another FlashCopy enhancement is available with GDPS V3.2. It supports now also Incremental FlashCopy. This provides the capability to refresh a volume in a FlashCopy relationship and reduce background copy time when only a subset of the data has changed. With Incremental FlashCopy the initial relationship between a source and target is maintained after the background copy is complete. When a subsequent FlashCopy establish is initiated only the data updated on the source since the last FlashCopy is copied to the target. This reduces the time needed to create a third copy thus giving you the option to perform a FlashCopy on a more frequent basis.

37.3.13 IBM Global Services offerings for GDPS

The various GDPS offerings are not products. They are delivered as IBM Global Service offerings. GDPS is a end to end solution in which IBM Global Services tailors and installs the specific combination of components, integrated within the client's environment. GDPS integration work, including education, is done using IBM Global Services, in addition to the planning and installation of the code. This assures that the GDPS solution provides the intended value to all parts of the business and IT processes.

The following GDPS services and offerings are provided by IBM Global Services (IGS).

GDPS technical consulting workshop (TCW)

TCW is a two day workshop where IGS specialists work with your representatives to understand your business objectives, service requirements, technological directions, business applications, recovery processes, cross-site and I/O requirements. High-level education on GDPS is provided along with the service and implementation process. Various remote and local data protection options are evaluated.

IGS specialists present a number of planned and unplanned GDPS reconfiguration scenarios with recommendations on how GDPS can assist you in achieving your objectives. At the conclusion of the workshop the following items are developed: acceptance criteria for both the test and production phases, a high level task list, a services list, and project summary.

Remote Copy Management Facility (RCMF)

With this service, the RCMF/PPRC or RCMF/XRC automation to manage the remote copy infrastructure will be installed, the automation policy customized, and the automation verified along with providing operational education for the enterprise.

GDPS/PPRC HyperSwap Manager

IBM Implementation Services for GDPS/PPRC HyperSwap Manager helps simplify implementation by working with you to get GDPS/PPRC HyperSwap Manager and its prerequisites up and running with limited disruption to your business. On-site planning, configuration, implementation, testing, and education will help make your new IBM Implementation Services for GDPS/PPRC HyperSwap Manager solution accessible in the most efficient manner.

GDPS/PPRC and GDPS/XRC

IBM Implementation Services for GDPS/PPRC or GDPS/XRC will assist you with planning, configuration, automation code customization, testing, onsite implementation assistance, and training in IBM's GDPS solution. Either option supports Peer-to-Peer Virtual Tape Server (PtP VTS) form of tape data mirroring.

37.3.14 GDPS value summary

Some of the many values of the GDPS Business Continuity automation offerings are as follows.

Repeatability, reliability of recovery: Successful, reliable, repeatable business continuity and recovery necessitates a dependency upon automation rather than people. Automation can help reduce risks that critical skilled personnel will not be fully available to recover the business, in the event of a site outage.

GDPS automation supports fast, reliable switching all resources from one site to another from a single trigger point, from a single point of control, with minimal operator interaction required.

Control of Metro Mirror Data Consistency: GDPS/PPRC and GDPS/PPRC HyperSwap Manager automation assures that the secondary copy of the data at the Metro Mirror secondary site is *data consistent.* Data consistency means that from an application's perspective the secondary disk's data is time and data consistent. Data consistency in the secondary copy of the data means that databases can be restarted in the secondary location without having to go through a lengthy and time consuming data recovery process, avoiding a time-consuming process of restoring database tape backups and applying logs.

Support of data consistency for tape and disk storage: It is important to note that GDPS also supports and manages data consistency in the IBM Peer-to-Peer Virtual Tape Server (PtP VTS), a hardware-based tape mirroring solution. This helps clients maintain consistency between disks and tapes, and therefore provides a total business continuity solution for the entire storage.

Integration: GDPS automation integrates many technologies, including, but not limited to, zSeries Parallel Sysplex, z/OS System Automation, Tivoli NetView, and the storage subsystem's advanced mirroring features to form an integrated, automated business continuity and disaster recovery solution.

Exploitation of zSeries Capacity Backup: GDPS automation exploits the zSeries Capacity BackUp (CBU) feature, which can provide additional processing power at the alternate site and help lower costs.The CBU feature increments capacity temporarily at the time it is needed, in the event of a disaster or outage.

CBU adds Central Processors (CP) to the available pool of processors and can be activated only in an emergency. GDPS CBU management can also automate the process of dynamically returning reserved CPs after the emergency period has expired.

38

Enterprise Remote Copy Management Facility

TotalStorage Rapid Data Recovery is a service offering solution from IBM Global Services based on enterprise Remote Copy Management Facility (eRCMF).

The enterprise Remote Copy Management Facility (eRCMF) is a standalone tool to provide a management layer for ESS Model 750 and 800, DS8000 and DS6000 Copy Services in 2-site or 3-site topologies. It is a common management tool for both z/OS and open system environments. The Copy Services functions Managed by eRCMF are Metro Mirror, Global Copy, Global Mirror, and Metro/Global Mirror. At each site, a FlashCopy of the local volumes can also be managed.

This solution simplifies the process of repairing inconsistent Remote Copy pairs after an error with the copy process. eRCMF assists the user in automating the Remote Copy and FlashCopy processes.

eRCMF is a scalable and flexible solution that protects business data and maintains consistent data. It can be used to manage copy relationships for both:

- Planned outages such as hardware and software upgrades, or disaster practice
- Unplanned outages such as an actual disaster

The solution provides basic commands through the FO/FB Session Manager Proxy, which utilizes the ESS Open API functions to accomplish either a planned or unplanned FO/FB sequence. eRCMF commands can be incorporated in any user scripts or utilities that may further link user's overall datacenter operations. However, it is the user's responsibility for creation, maintenance and any liabilities associated with such scripts or utilities. Therefore, eRCMF offers a simple way to implement Remote Copy disaster recovery procedures via command line. eRCMF applies the commands to a set of configuration files that describe the disk subsystem configuration (paths and sets of volumes).

The solution does not depend on the operating system as no client installation is required.

Solution highlights

The main solution highlights and benefits are summarized in the following list:

- Provides automation capability
- Simplifies disaster recovery operations
- Improves protection of critical business data guarantying data consistency and ensuring restart capabilities
- Avoids human errors
- Reduces risk of downtime
- Lets you stay competitive, maintaining market readiness by managing risk more efficiently
- Enables test and practice of disaster recovery setup regularly
- Reduces testing risk
- Provides a central, scalable, flexible, enterprise class solution that protects your business
- Simplifies the configuration:
  - Simple configuration description
  - Provides tools to verify configuration
- Simplifies the utilization with simple commands to fix problems
- Needs no predefined Copy Services tasks

38.1 Overview

In a Business Continuity solution based on disk remote mirroring, we want to restart a database application following an outage without having to restore the database. This process has to be consistent, repeatable, and fast, measurable in minutes.

A Database Recovery where you have to restore the last set of Image Copy tapes and apply the log changes to bring the database up to the point of failure is a process that can be measured in hours or even days. And this is what you want to avoid in a Tier 4 or higher solution. However, in a real disaster (fire, explosion, earthquake) you can never expect the components of your complex to fail all at the same moment. Failures will be intermittent and gradual, and the disaster will occur over many seconds or even minutes. This is known as a *Rolling Disaster*. The architecture of a viable disk mirroring disaster recovery solution must avoid data corruption caused during a Rolling Disaster.

In any operating system, the sequence in which updates are being made is what maintains the integrity of the data. If that sequence is changed, data corruption will occur. The correct sequence must be maintained within a volume, across volumes, and across multiple storage devices. For instance, in Figure 38-1, we show the relationship between a database and its log, which demonstrates the requirement for maintaining I/O integrity. Data consistency across the storage enterprise must be maintained to insure data integrity.

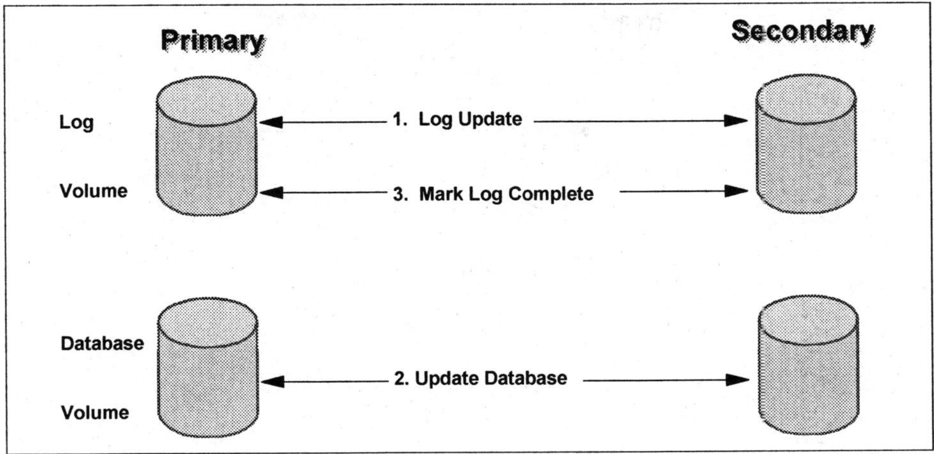

Figure 38-1 Sample update sequence in a database

The order of Dependent Writes across volumes must be maintained at remote locations. Failure to do so results in data corruption. The data consistency is lost.

In Figure 38-2 we illustrate this concept with an example. The intention to update the database is logged in the database log files at both the primary and secondary volumes (step 1). The database datafile is updated at the primary volume, but the update does not reach the remote volume which contains the mirrored datafile. The primary location is not aware of the write failure to the secondary volume (step 2). The database update is marked complete in the log files at both the primary and remote locations (step 3). The result is that the secondary site log files say the update was done, but the updated data is not in the database at the secondary location. There is no way to know that the data was corrupted.

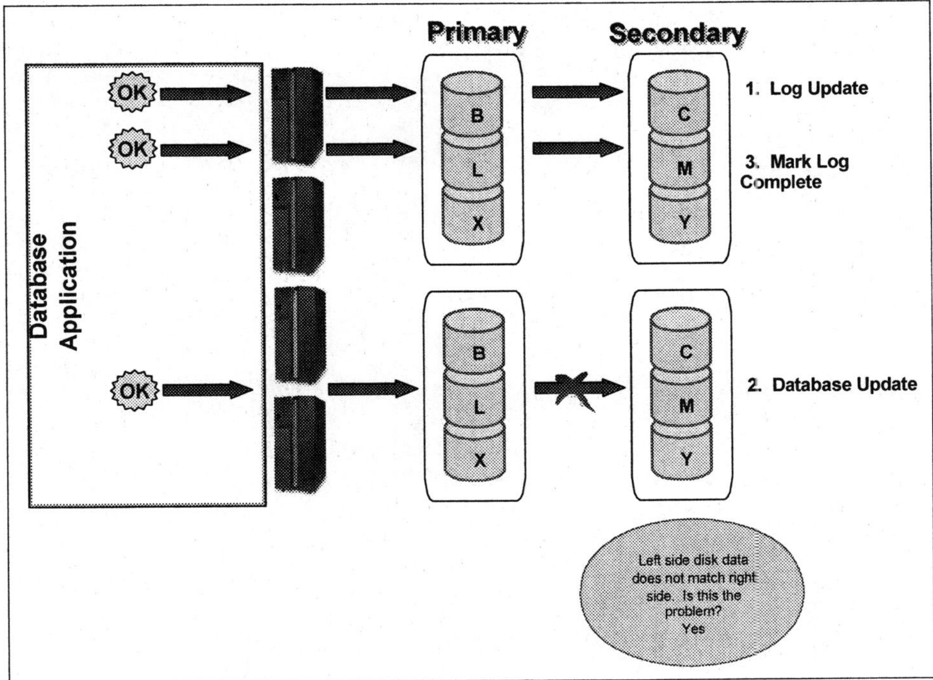

Figure 38-2 Sample Rolling Disaster

So, the issue is that the disk subsystem can't do it all and we must avoid this Rolling Disaster system problem.

For this reason, it is strongly recommended that, at a minimum, Consistency Groups be put in place for any mirroring solution. Consistency Groups are an implementation of technology which assists with the consistency of application data capable of dependent writes. To guarantee a fully consistent remote copy, multiple volumes require a Consistency Group functionality. ESS and DS6000 / DS8000 Remote Copy microcode already has the Consistency Group function for both z/OS and open systems. SAN Volume Controller Metro Mirror's and DS4000 Remote Mirror's microcode has a Consistency Group function for open systems.

If any volume within a Consistency Group is unable to complete a write to its counterpart in the Remote Copy relationship, an Extended Long Busy (ELB) for mainframe environments or a SCSI Queue Full condition for open systems will be issued, preventing further writes to any of the volumes within the Consistency Group. This wait period is the perfect time to issue a freeze to all volumes involved to maintain consistency. Figure 38-3 illustrates this mechanism. If a write is unable to complete, the storage subsystem will not back out incomplete transactions on its own. Instead the application will need to recognize that the transaction was incomplete and take the appropriate actions. Once the storage subsystem holds application I/O to the affected primary volumes, the write dependent mechanism of the application prevents the Remote Copy secondaries from becoming inconsistent.

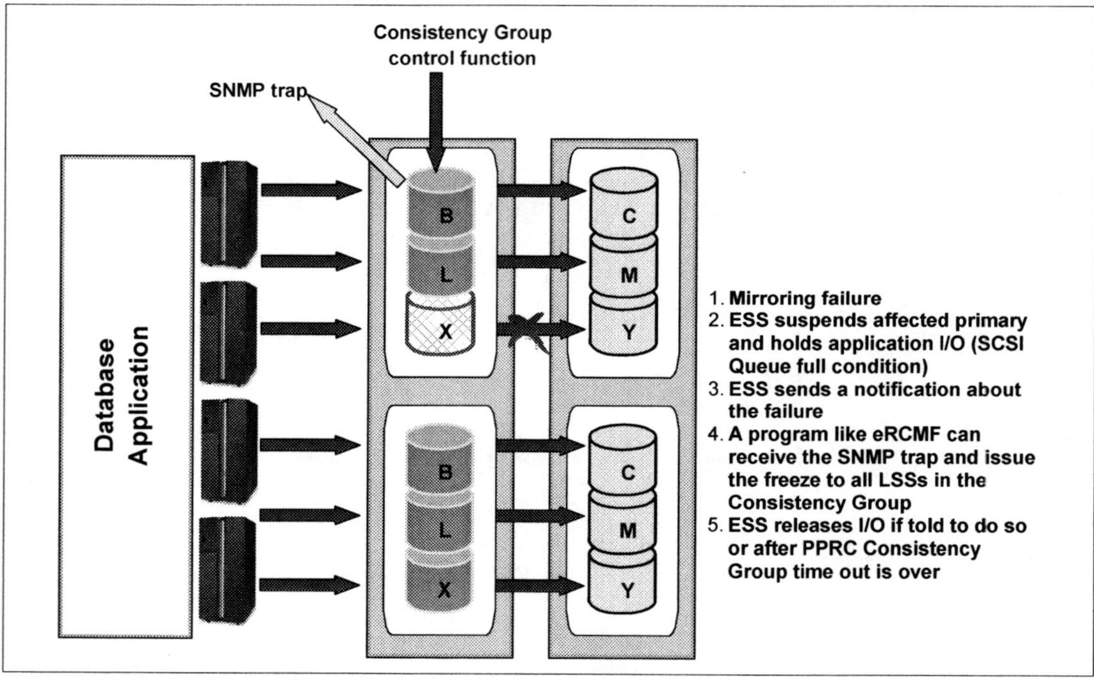

Figure 38-3 Dependent write protection of database integrity

`Freeze` is a command available through DS Command-Line Interface, DS Storage Manager (Graphical User Interface), the ESS API, ICKDSF or TSO, that stops the write activity on all of the active Remote Copy primary and secondary volumes of a given source and target Logical Subsystem (LSS) pair. This function ensures consistency between the primary and secondary volumes and can affect any LSS volumes that are in an active Remote Copy state between the frozen LSS pair: duplex, duplex pending SYNC or duplex pending XD states. It does not affect the suspended and simplex volumes that may be in the LSS.

The freeze operation has three effects:

1. The paths that connect the pair of LSSs being frozen are terminated.

2. The active volumes under the frozen LSS pair are suspended. This state transition, to suspended, is then communicated to the host with alert messages. These alert messages can be used by automation routines to trigger other recovery operations.
3. If the consistency group option was enabled at path definition time, then the ELB or SCSI Queue Full condition is instigated, so that the write activity to the primary LSS is temporarily queued. During this interval, other automated operations can be triggered; such as, freezing other application-related LSS pairs.

When using freeze through DS Storage Manager (Graphical User Interface) or ICKDSF, it will take effect on each LSS individually. This is useful for creating a point-in-time copy of the data, but because of slight delays between the issuing of each iteration of the freeze command it is unsuitable for preventing rolling disasters and should be done at periods of low utilization to ensure the of the secondary data can be used.

When Remote Copy is used in conjunction with automation, such as the Geographically Dispersed Parallel Sysplex (GDPS) or enterprise Remote Copy Management Facility (eRCMF) service offerings from IBM Global Services, a freeze command can be simultaneously issued to all LSSs within the configuration. This ensures globally consistent data across all LSSs in the secondary copy of data during a disaster.

The goal of the TotalStorage Rapid Data Recovery for UNIX and Windows solution, based on the combination of ESS or DS6000 or DS8000 Copy Services with enterprise Remote Copy Management Facility (eRCMF), is to protect your data from being a mirror of a dying scenario.

Using Remote Copy Consistency Group, this solution freezes your environment at a known point instead of mirroring literally hundreds of time-offset failures in a short amount of time.

TotalStorage Rapid Data Recovery is based on enterprise Remote Copy Facility (eRCMF), an IBM Global Services offering. The current eRCMF version 4 is designed as a two- or three-site Disaster Recovery solution which runs on dedicated Productivity Center Machines (PCMs) running WebSphere on AIX 5L™ (pSeries, RS/6000®, LPAR) which will be used as eRCMF servers.

Note: It is strongly recommended that the PCMs be installed and run from different physical sites to ensure their backup capability.

eRCMF is a multi site disaster recovery solution which manages data on volumes for Fixed Block (open systems hosts) and CKD (z/OS). The solution does not depend on the operating system as no client installation is required.

This solution simplifies the process of repairing inconsistent Remote Copy pairs after an error with the copy process. eRCMF assists the user in automating the Remote Copy and FlashCopy processes.

eRCMF is a scalable and flexible solution that protects business data and maintains consistent data. It can be used to manage copy relationships for both:

- Planned outages such as hardware and software upgrades, or disaster practice
- Unplanned outages such as an actual disaster

eRCMF is a Tier 4 and 6 solution, as shown in Figure 38-4.

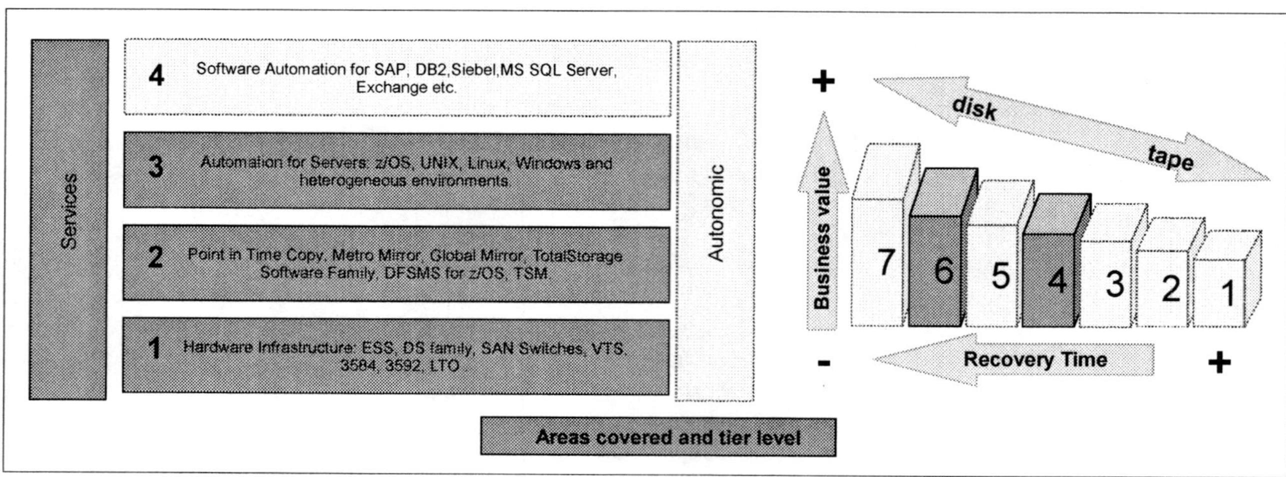

Figure 38-4 eRCMF protection tier

eRCMF is build on the technologies of Remote Copy, Java, WebSphere, and ESS Network Interface. This is because ESS800, DS6000 and DS8000 share the same Copy Services functions that you can mix these Storage Servers in this solution. With DS8000 and DS6000, no Copy Services Server is required since each Storage Server can handle the Copy Services. The eRCMF version 2 code required the Copy Services Server (CSS) to be hosted on the PCM dedicated servers. Since Version 3, eRCMF supports the existing ESS Copy Services Infrastructure and it no longer requires the Copy Services Server to be run on the PCMs.

38.2 Architecture

eRCMF is a 2-site or 3-site solution. According to the diagrams Figure 38-5 and Figure 38-6, one PCM is placed in each data center. The PCM in the primary data center runs the Master Process. This process is the interface into eRCMF. It handles all queries and commands for local processes through either a command-line or socket interface. It also manages commands and queries from the Backup Process.

A second PCM can be placed in the secondary (or backup) data center or, in a three site strategy, in the tertiary (or remote) data center. This PCM runs the Backup Process which maintains the state information of the configuration. This information is transferred to the second PCM in the form of logs from the Master Process. These logs are then used to update state information in case the Backup Process must take control of the configuration as well as for documentation purposes if there is an alternate site failure.

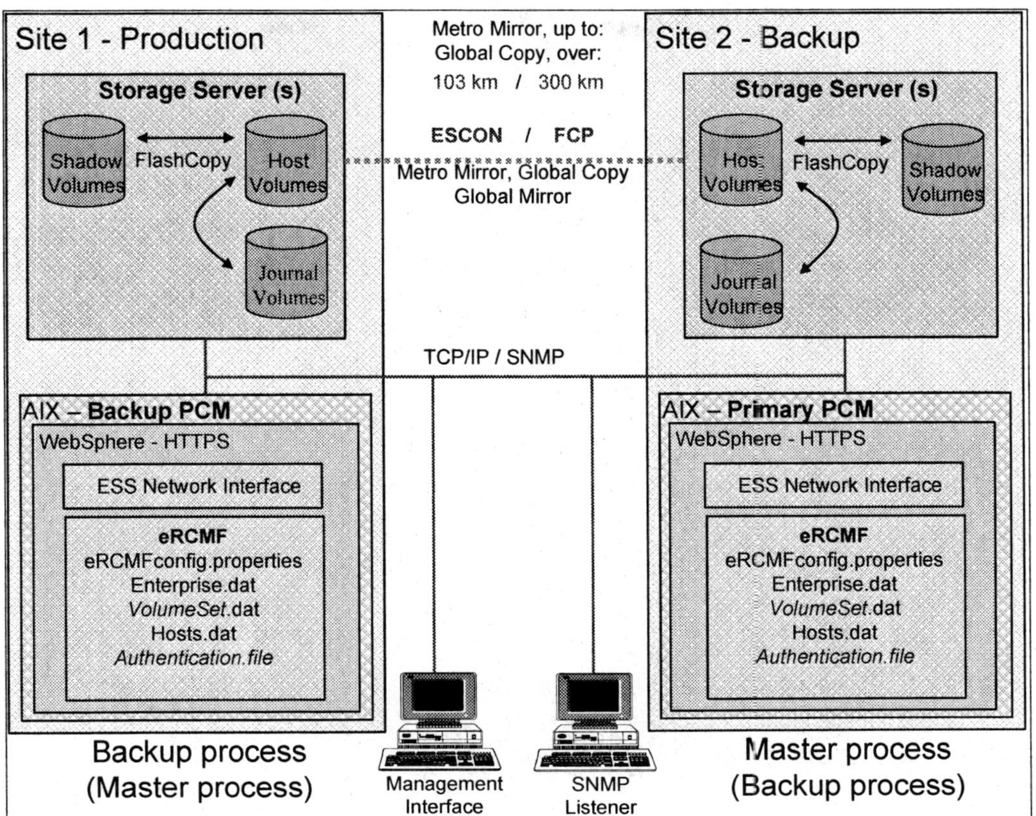

Figure 38-5 eRCMF Architecture: 2 site configuration

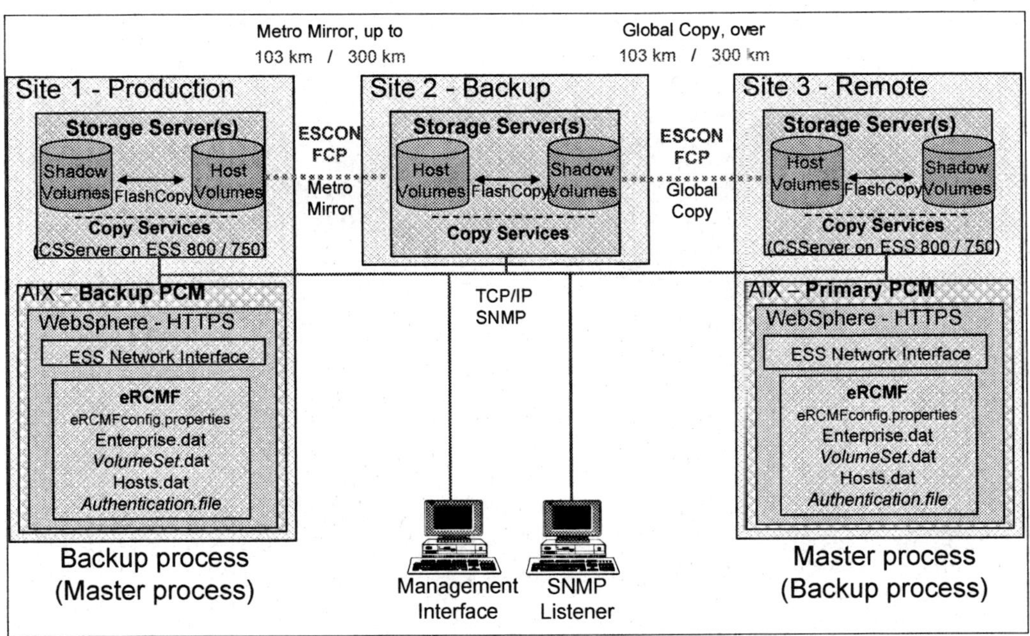

Figure 38-6 eRCMF Architecture: 3 site configuration

The Master Process continuously monitors and manages the entire environment at two levels:

- Enterprise level
- VolumeSet level

The distinction between these levels is primarily the scope of actions performed at each level. The Enterprise level represents the entire monitored environment, which consists of two or three data processing locations containing storage managed by eRCMF. The VolumeSet level corresponds to a set of Storage Servers volumes which must be maintained in a consistent state and managed using the same type of copy operations. Some examples of a VolumeSet are the volumes used by a set of applications, the volumes allocated to a set of servers, or the members of a volume group.

Management at the Enterprise level affects the entire monitored environment. These actions typically affect every volume of every VolumeSet being managed by eRCMF. For example, the **freeze** command will cause suspension of Remote Copy pairs between the storage subsystems on multiple sites as you can see in Figure 38-7.

eRCMF adds a central control function to coordinate the Remote Copy Freeze function and stops transmission of data to the remote site consistently across single/multiple frames. When this function is centrally coordinated, data is consistent. Data consistency allows a very fast, very consistent restart time at the secondary site.

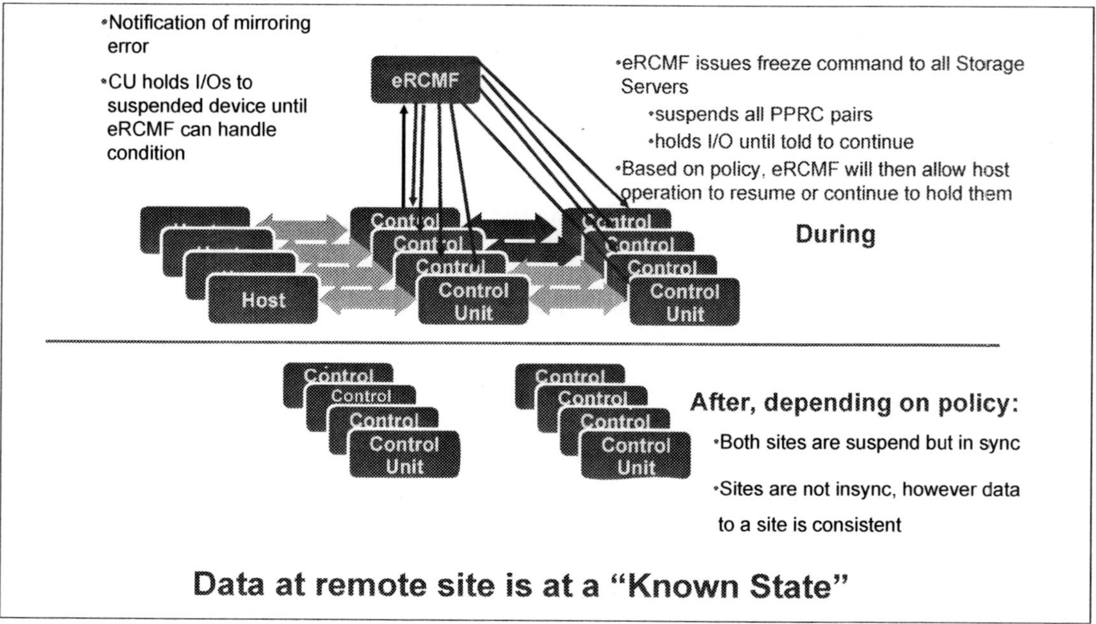

Figure 38-7 eRCMF issues freeze command in a disaster recovery scenario

There are two methods of maintaining consistent data:

- Metro Mirror:
  - Use Synchronous Remote Copy to ensure that data is secure at the remote site before signaling the host that the write is complete.
  - During a disaster, you can combine the Consistency Group and Freeze functions in the Storage Server with software, such as eRCMF, to insure that all Remote Copy pairs of the Consistency Group are split in a manner that assures data consistency at the remote site.
- Global Mirror:
  - Storage Server periodically forms Consistency Groups. Testing has shown, that given enough bandwidth, Storage Servers can form these groups on an average of every 3 to 5 seconds.

– When recovering to the recovery copy, software such as eRCMF, examines the states of the Global Mirror relationships and directs the Storage Server through the steps necessary to recover that data to the last committed consistent copy.

It should be noted that eRCMF neither performs an automated recovery nor an automated restart of systems in the remote site. Instead, eRCMF's **freeze** performs a controlled site **split** only. If a higher level of automation is required, eRCMF provides interfaces such as execution scripts or a command line interface, which can be utilized and customized. When this occurs, mirroring between Site 1 and Site 2 stops, ensuring the consistency of data. Further response by the automation is determined by policies which are selected based on individual business requirements:

- *Freeze and Go* quickly executes the **freeze** to ensure data consistency, but then immediately allows I/Os to continue. This allows processing to continue in the production data center while maintaining a consistent copy of the data in either the backup or remote data center. Meanwhile, the business is able to determine the cause of the event and whether it is a disaster. If a disaster has not occurred, production has not been impacted by an unnecessary site switch. If a disaster has occurred, then the data since the time of the site split may need to be recreated if recovering to a backup or a remote data center.
- *Freeze and Stop* quickly executes the **freeze** to ensure consistency but, rather than immediately allowing the I/Os to continue, causes the ESS to block all further I/Os until told otherwise. This ensures that no transactions, other than those in-flight at the time of the event, need to be recreated following a disaster. If the event turns out not to be a disaster, however, the production will be halted until the I/Os are freed.

38.3 Concept

Once eRCMF is configured and the Remote Copy state of all specified volumes is known, it automatically handles many error conditions that may occur. eRCMF Version 3 or later assists in the overall disaster recovery solution by providing:

- Support for Metro Mirror, Global Copy, and Global Mirror between two sites.
- Support for three sites for Metro/Global Copy (Asynchronous Cascading PPRC).
- Monitoring for the states of mirrored pairs, links, and Consistency Groups.
- Easy-to-use commands to manage the consistency of volumes and their Remote Copy and Flash Copy relationships. For example, if the data is out-of-synchronization, the **resync** command causes eRCMF to scan the specified volumes and issue commands necessary to bring the volumes back into synchronization.
- Consistency on an application (VolumeSet) level across LSSs and storage subsystems. Consistency Groups can span multiple Storage Servers.
- Automatic site split capabilities for planned and unplanned conditions.
- Support for Remote Copy over Fibre with a configuration restriction of physical links between an ESS pair must be either ESCON or FCP. Mixed physical links between the same ESS pair are not supported by eRCMF, as this is unlikely to exist between same sites in customer environments.
- Support for Remote Copy Failover / Failback to minimize re synchronization time.
- Notification capability. When failures occur it can notify Operations and other automation processes via SNMP messages.
- Tools for configuration checks. These checks verify that the eRCMF configuration correctly matches the physical setup of the customer environment. This insures that the data eRCMF is managing is the data the customer needs to successfully recover from a site disaster.

- Flexibility and simplification with Remote Copy as there is no need to create and maintain a scripting solution or CSS Tasks.
- A Command-Line Interface (CLI) for external application usage of the eRCMF Remote Copy management functionality (such as clustering software or other automation). For instance HACMP/XD uses this feature and so it is possible to create an integrated Disaster Recovery Tier 7 solution based on these two products.
- Support for FlashCopy configurations on either site.
- Support for Incremental FlashCopy to minimize the physical background copy on various FlashCopy tasks.

This solution manages Copy Services dynamically and does not require pre-defined Copy Services tasks on the Copy Services Server. ESS Copy Services tasks are a set of actions to be executed on an ESS. They let you automate a series of steps that otherwise would be performed through the ESS Copy Services Web User Interface. For instance, Remote Copy tasks are used to manage the Remote Copy volume pairs and the associated PPRC paths. Currently PPRC tasks must be created and modified by the ESS Copy Services Web User Interface for the Enterprise Storage Server Model 800.

When you enter the Multiple Selection Mode, you can select multiple volume pairs owned by one LSS for each Storage Server, when you create tasks for both FlashCopy and Remote Copy. This mode is very useful to save time when creating the tasks. When there are many volumes this is a GUI activity that can become very time-consuming.

A new service called ESS Copy Services Task Creator provides an interface to the Copy Services Server of the ESS to create tasks in the repository. This interface will read either a text file with the ESSCLI Show Task format or a text file with its utility own format. The content of these files gets then converted into the Copy Services task that will be saved in the repository of the ESS.

IBM personnel can get additional information about this service on the IBM internal Web site at:

```
http://web.mainz.de.ibm.com/ATSservices
```

The new DS Command-Line Interface, which replaces the Copy Services Command-Line Interface and ESS Command-Line Interface, also provides new functions to dynamically create and manage FlashCopy and Remote Copy relationships without any use of a GUI. DS CLI commands can be saved as scripts which significantly reduces the time to create, edit and verify their content.

eRCMF specifically does not refer to PPRC Primary or Secondary volumes nor does it refer to FlashCopy Source or Target volumes, it manages these kinds of volumes:

- **Host Volumes:** LUNs that servers connect to.
  - Whether a host can actually access the data depends on the state (which site is production active on, what type of VolumeSet, what state is the VolumeSet in (for example, InSync, SplitSite, RecoverySiteActive)
- **Shadow Volumes:** LUNs used in FlashCopy configurations. Servers do not normally attach to them. They add further redundancy and additional data protection
- **Journal Volumes:** LUNs used to build automatic consistent data sets by Global Mirror configurations

Figure 38-5 on page 555 and Figure 38-6 on page 555 provide an overview of the architectures. The illustrations also show the relationship of ESSs and the PCMs with the Copy Services Servers and Copy Services Clients. The Management Interface is either a graphical console attached to the PCMs or any host that has TCP/IP access to the PCMs for remote connection. It is used to control the eRCMF processes and interact with eRCMF.

38.4 Requirements

We discuss the requirements for eRCMF in this section, including the required hardware and software modules.

38.4.1 Hardware requirements

The hardware requirements for using eRCMF include:

- Two dedicated Productivity Machines (PCMs) running on AIX 5L (pSeries, RS/6000, LPAR), which will be used as the eRCMF servers. For a real disaster recovery setup which can also handle a site disaster, each PCM needs to be in a different physical site (one in site 1 and one optional server in site 2). They are used as the primary and backup eRCMF servers. The PCMs should be scaled depending on the quantity of managed Storage Servers and tuples. A *tuple* contains from one to three volumes per site that are used for data mirroring (Remote Copy and Flash Copy). All volumes in a tuple need to be of the same size to guarantee copy functionality in each direction. A tuple usually contains just a part of an application data set (for example, DB log files, part of DB files). The most important criteria to consider is memory for future expansion and required PCM upgrades.
- A TCP/IP connection from each PCM to each Storage Server that will be managed by eRCMF. A connection between both PCMs is also required. The PCMs should be in the Storage Servers' sub network in order to reduce response times between PCMs and the Storage Servers.
- Minimum two storage subsystems:
  - DS8000 and DS6000
  - ESS750 or ESS800 with microcode 2.4.1.56 or higher, located in different physical sites to build a redundant, eRCMF supported Copy Services Server domain (server A and server B).
  - Further ESS800, ESS750 or ESSF20 with previous microcode releases are supported as Copy Services Clients in a supported Copy Services Server domain.
  - Two supported storage subsystems linked by a minimum of two Peer-to-Peer Remote Copy links (to enable logical PPRC paths in both directions).

You should also check supported microcode versions for your storage subsystems.

If you need channel extenders you can find a list of supported devices in the interoperability matrixes located on the Web:

- IBM TotalStorage ESS Model 800

  `http://www-1.ibm.com/servers/storage/disk/ess/ess800/interop-matrix.html`
- IBM TotalStorage DS8000

  `http://www-1.ibm.com/servers/storage/disk/ds8000/interop.html`
- IBM TotalStorage DS6000

  `http://www-1.ibm.com/servers/storage/disk/ds6000/interop.html`

38.4.2 Software requirements

The software requirements for using eRCMF include:

- AIX 5L (5.1 ML4 or higher, 5.2 ML1 or higher) installed on the PCM
- Netscape 4.79 installed on the PCM (to be installed with AIX)
- Installation image of IBM WebSphere Application Server V5.0.x (includes Java 1.3.1 and IBM HTTP Server 1.3.26) with Fix Pack 2. One WebSphere license per machine.
- Installation and configuration of IBM WebSphere Application Server V5.0.x and IBM HTTP Server is part of the eRCMF Installation.
- Installation image of IBM 2105 ESS Command-Line Interface for AIX V2.2.0 or higher.
- Installation image of IBM 2107 or 1742 DS Command-Line Interface for AIX.

38.4.3 Other requirements

Other requirements include:

- eRCMF uses SNMP messages for external notification. An SNMP listener application (For example, Tivoli NetView) is highly recommended in a production environment to trap eRCMF SNMP messages and trigger customer operations as appropriate.
- A graphical console or remote X-Window connection to the PCMs is required for eRCMF installation as there are GUI driven applications that need to be executed.
- On hosts which want to use the optional eRCMF Command-Line Interface, a Java Runtime Environment (JRE) V1.3.0 or higher must be installed.

To verify the latest hardware and software pre-requirements we suggest you refer to the enterprise Remote Copy Management Facility eRCMF V3 Implementation Guide, found at:

`http://www-1.ibm.com/servers/storage/support/software/opensystems.html`

38.4.4 eRCMF limitations

eRCMF Version 4 currently has the following limitations, which need to be considered for the environment and configuration planning of the eRCMF Disaster Recovery solution:

- There is only one active eRCMF PCM that manages the environment. eRCMF commands need to be issued against this active PCM. The backup eRCMF PCM is just monitoring for environment changes and reacts to ESS Trap 200s to initiate the site split.
- There is no automatic takeover by the backup eRCMF PCM if the active eRCMF PCM goes down. The takeover must be invoked manually.
- Any Shadow, Journal or Practice volume defined with eRCMF must be on the same LSS as the Host volume. eRCMF establishes FlashCopy relationships between Host, Shadow, Journal and Practice volumes in either direction. The CSS functionality for FlashCopy across multiple LSS, is not exploited due to the configuration complexity of the logical PPRC paths.
- The ESS Copy Services Servers must be configured to run an ESS Model 750 or 800 at the required firmware level. eRCMF Version 4 will not operate if the Copy Services Server is operating on an ESS Model Fxx, as eRCMF Version 4 does not support the previous Copy Services Interface. However, ESS Models Fxx may be attached as Copy Services Clients to supported CSSs in order to have their PPRC managed by eRCMF.
- Global Mirror VolumeSets only support an optional FlashCopy configuration using Practice Volumes on either site. As the VolumeSet consistency will be managed by the Master ESS, it is recommended to define Global Mirror VolumeSets between Site 1 and Site 3 or Site 2 and Site 3 in order to avoid unnecessary impact by eRCMF consistency group management between Site 1 and Site 2.

38.5 Installation

TotalStorage Rapid Data Recovery (eRCMF) is a solution based on a combination of software and hardware products together with a service engagement. Because of its complex implementation, IBM Global Services (IGS) will work with your IT department to install and configure the solution to match your unique business environment. The storage servers, servers, and WebSphere software have to be ordered through the normal process. IGS provides eRCMF software and experts which support the implementation, education and skill transfer for this solution. The setup is tailored to the clients' needs. For more information, contact your IBM sales representative.

38.6 Configuration

Since this is an IBM services installation only, in this section we show how each of these components were configured during our testing and explain why it is IBM services only.

38.6.1 Copy Services functions

Again, eRCMF can manage any ESS or DS6000 or DS8000 Remote Copy functions:

- Metro Mirror (formerly Synchronous PPRC)
- Global Copy (formerly Extended PPRC)
- Global Mirror (formerly Asynchronous PPRC)
- Metro Global Copy (formerly Cascaded PPRC)

Establishing Metro Mirror pairs

Under eRCMF's management Remote Copy pairs are automatically established in the most efficient method possible.

- First the data will be copied through Global Copy (even if the relationship will ultimately be Metro Mirror, synchronous mode). This has the advantage of being a more effective way to migrate data to the secondary volumes than Metro Mirror and avoids any application I/O impact.
- When enough data has been passed to the secondary site, it will be considered *near sync* at which point eRCMF will attempt to *go to sync*.
- The data will briefly become *out of sync* and then will be considered *Insync*.

Support for Global Copy

Although the majority of Global Copy transactions are fuzzy and unusable for disaster recovery purposes until being synchronized, eRCMF is still a valuable tool for Global Copy environments. eRCMF is capable of managing the Global Copy and FlashCopy commands for such environments. Its interface provides an improved interface for managing commands to synchronize volumes as well as to create Flash Copies in production and recovery data centers. This is in addition to its management of commands to freeze Global Copy and swap the location of production data.

Support for FlashCopy

In a disaster recovery environment the FlashCopy feature is something to consider.

You can use it to make a copy at the backup site for disaster recovery tests and new application tests. While doing such tests on the production copy, Remote Copy can be re-established by eRCMF to protect real production data during the testing period.

In a real Disaster Recovery, you should do the FlashCopy of your source volumes and run from the target. It allows you to practice operations execution in a disaster recovery environment. In this way the source volumes containing the original data are not at risk to change when we are trying to recover the applications. If something else goes wrong and the data get corrupted, you still have the original secondary. You can shut down your servers, repeat FlashCopy, and try again. Moreover you can (should) immediately start a backup on the original secondary.

In a real site disaster, you need to consider a temporary disaster recovery solution on the backup site while repairing the primary site. FlashCopy can be used for creating regular point-in-time copies of your data.

Finally, taking a FlashCopy of consistent secondaries before re-synchronizing sites is a good rule because the secondary is out of sync during resync.

eRCMF enables businesses to create and maintain FlashCopies in any or all data centers. Use of eRCMF without FlashCopy is possible, but not recommended, because of the exposures that it creates.

38.6.2 Remote Copy configurations

It is important to note that Remote Copy architectures are defined at the VolumeSet level. In this section, we give details on how to configure eRCMF sets of volumes depending or which Remote Copy function architecture we use.

A variation to these configurations allows the FlashCopy volumes to be used only for practice and they are not directly involved in Remote Copy relationships.

Metro Mirror, Global Copy, and Global Mirror implementation

There are four different ways that eRCMF can be implemented in a Disaster Recovery environment. As a result it is possible to use NOFCPY on some less critical VolumeSets and ALLFCPY on critical VolumeSets.

Note: The prefix for Global Mirror VolumeSet Tuple Type is GLOBAL. The prefix for Global Copy (eXtended Distance) VolumeSet Tuple Type is XD.

Attention: In all implementations the tuples of the Global Mirror VolumeSet consist of four volumes: a host volume on both sites and a journal volume on each site.

(GLOBAL)(XD)NOFCPY

In a configuration using *NOFCPY*, no FlashCopies are created at either the production site or the recovery site; see Figure 38-8.

This is a lower cost, but higher risk solution. Because there are no point-in-time backups, there is no environment in which to test and there is no data to fail back on if something happens to the recovery copy during or after a disaster. Even so, this might be acceptable for data which is less critical and should be copied, but is not absolutely necessary.

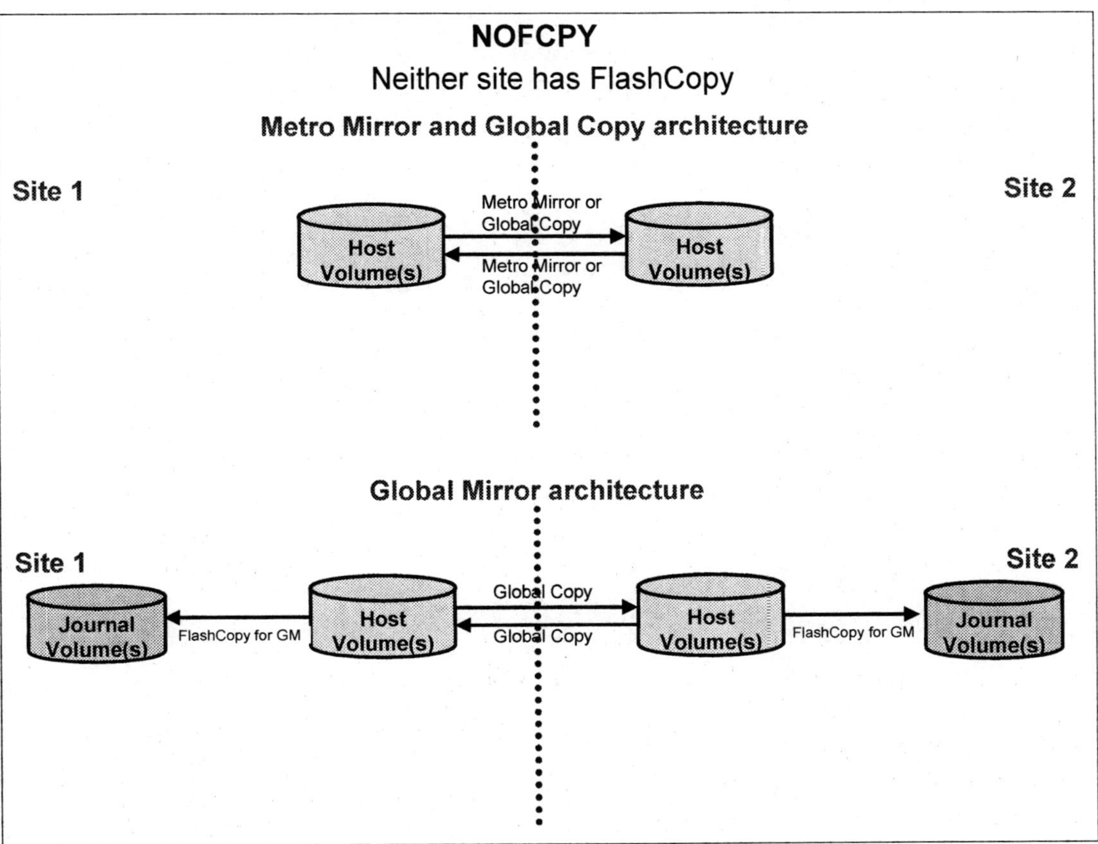

Figure 38-8 NOFCPY

(GLOBAL)(XD)SITE1FCPY

In a configuration using *SITE1FCPY*, FlashCopies are created at the production site 1; see Figure 38-9.

This allows data to be created for backups in the production location. No FlashCopies are created in the recovery site 2, so the ability to test with this implementation is limited.

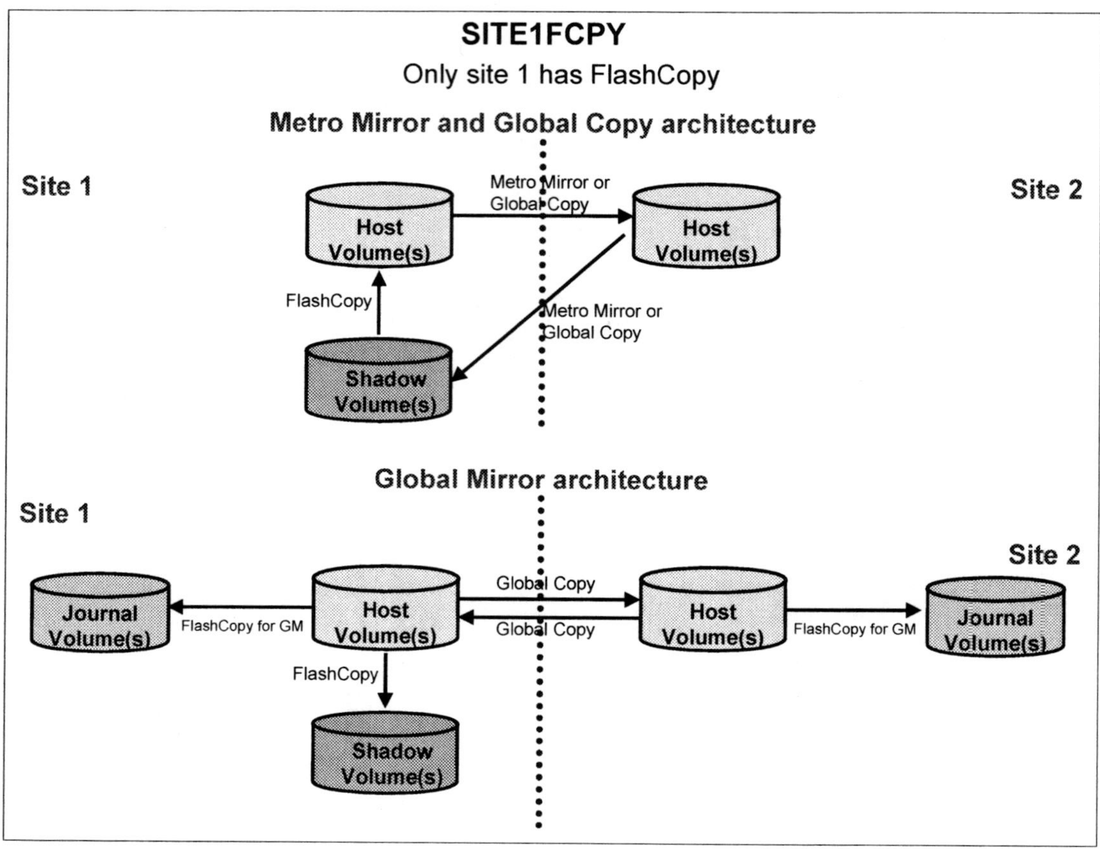

Figure 38-9 SITE1FCPY

(GLOBAL)(XD)SITE2FCPY

In a configuration using *SITE2FCPY*, FlashCopies are created at the recovery site 2; see Figure 38-10.

This is useful from the perspective that it provides a copy of data which can be used for testing. This copy of data is also the only one in the recovery site that can normally be accessed. The target volumes of the Remote Copy relationship are not used for either recovery or testing. Only the FlashCopy target volumes are ever used. As a result, one copy of data in the backup site is always safe. Additionally, when a new copy of data is created in the production site after a disaster, the copy is only made from the FlashCopy. Because of this, if a problem occurs which compromises the data, a new FlashCopy can quickly be made and the PPRC Establish can be attempted again.

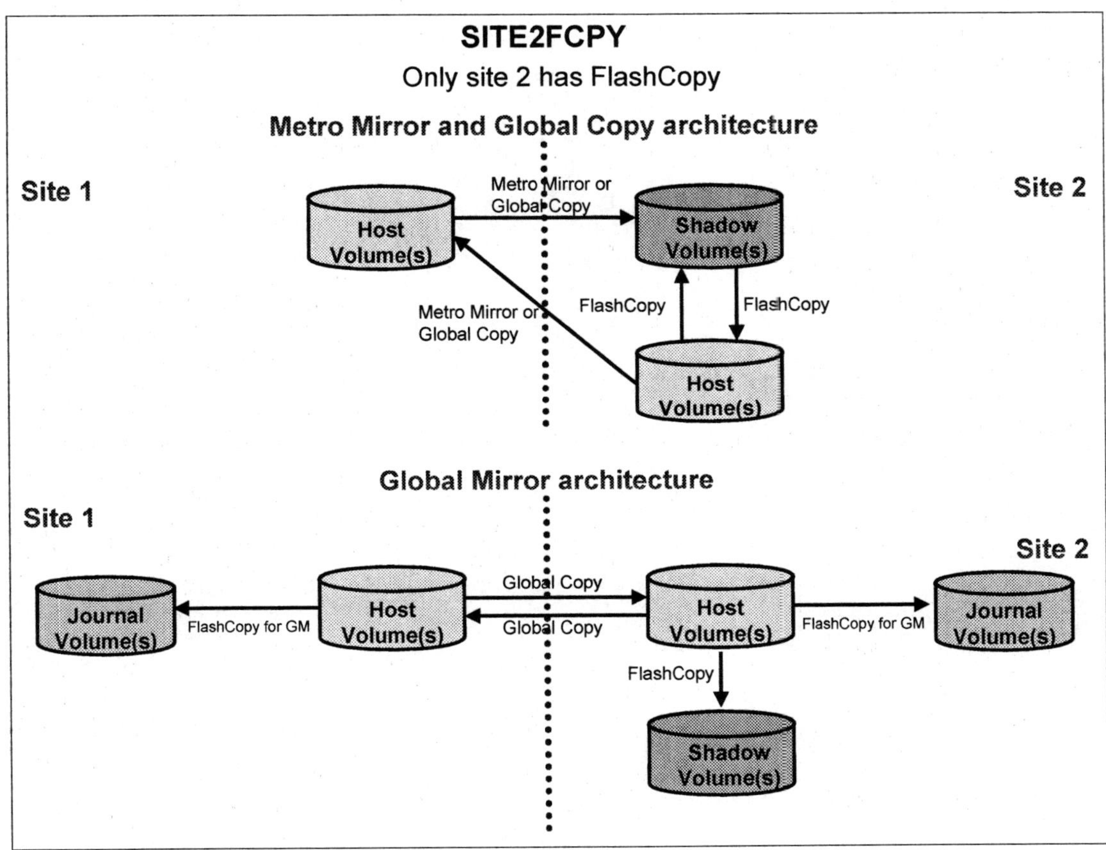

Figure 38-10 SITE2FCPY

(GLOBAL)(XD)ALLFCPY

In a configuration using *ALLFCPY,* FlashCopies are made at either the production site or the recovery site; see Figure 38-11.

While being the most expensive implementation, this provides the strongest protection of data and the best environment for testing.

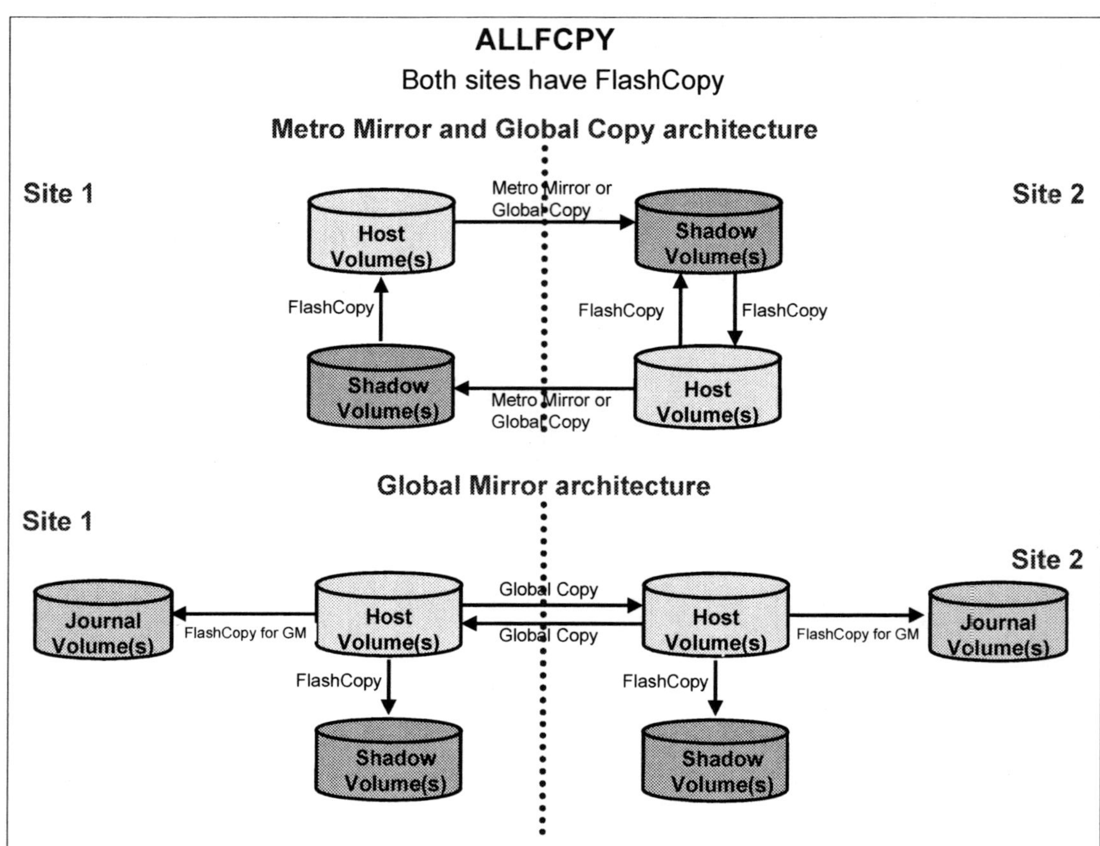

Figure 38-11 ALLFCPY

Metro Global Copy Asynchronous Cascading PPRC

Under Asynchronous Cascading PPRC similar options are possible. It is possible to configure FlashCopy to occur at any or all locations.

CASNOFCPY

Under this implementation there is no FlashCopy in any of the ESSs in the configuration. This is less expensive but creates exposures for testing and recovery.

CAS(1,2,3)FCPY

This implementation sets the configuration to have FlashCopies at one or multiple sites in the configuration. The sites are listed as 1,2, and 3 and are listed in the CASxxxFCPY command. This allows for flexibility when creating testing and recovery environments. It also allows FlashCopies to be created in site 3 periodically to maintain the ability to recover if the first two ESSs are destroyed.

38.6.3 Configuration files

eRCMF's configuration is defined and managed by five types of configuration files:

- The eRCMF Properties File (eRCMFconfig.properties)
- The Enterprise Definition File (Enterprise.dat)
- One or more VolumeSet definition File(s)
- The Host Access Configuration File (Hosts.dat)
- Storage Subsystem authentication files

There is one Enterprise Definition File and one Host Configuration File for the entire installation. There is also at least one VolumeSet Definition File, but there could be many depending on the requirements of the Disaster Recovery solution.

Another type of file that is required is an encrypted file containing authentication information for each storage subsystem managed by eRCMF. This authentication information is required during background storage subsystem CLI calls. The configuration check utility verifies the physical configuration of the installation. Additionally, the authentication file is used for Copy Services Server (CSS) authentication required by eRCMF management and the issuance of Copy Services reset commands to all storage subsystem clusters.

eRCMF's configuration files must be created using an ASCII-compatible text editor. The files have the extension *.dat except for the authentication file which is maintained by a special tool. This file may have any, or no, extension.

In order to support creation of the eRCMF configuration files (*.dat files), the eRCMF software package contains some template files with the required structure and keywords. These templates are located in the */templates* subdirectory in the eRCMF home directory; see the section, "Creating Configuration Files" in the *IBM eRCMF V4 Implementation Guide* for more details.

Note: RCMF automatically synchronizes the configuration files between the primary and backup PCMs.

Enterprise file

The *Enterprise.dat* file is a structured configuration file that describes eRCMF's operational characteristics through required and optional keywords and parameters.Keywords followed by zero or more parameters are referred to below as elements.

Elements must be included in the order presented below unless otherwise noted. Each contains one or more tokens per line and must begin on a separate line. Keywords and parameters (sometimes collectively referred to as "tokens"), are separated by white space (blank spaces and tabs). Anything beyond the last required token on a line or beyond the // or # characters is considered a comment. Indentation is not required but helps readability.

The *Enterprise.dat* file's section layout is:

1. Global declarations:
   a. Optional Execution script definitions
2. SNMP definitions
3. Copy Services domain definitions:
   a. ESS Copy Services Server domain definitions with managed ESS declarations
   b. DS6000/DS8000 Management Console definitions with managed DS declarations
4. Storage system pair definitions
5. VolumeSet definitions

Example 38-1 is a sample 2-site Enterprise.dat file used in a DS6000 environment.

Example 38-1 Sample Enterprise.dat file

```
Freeze&Go
TwoWay
enableSync
enableTrace
CopyServicesV2

SITES SITE1 SITE2

BEGIN_SNMP
END_SNMP

BEGIN_MC # MOP-DS8300-01
   CONSOLE HMC1
   SITE SITE1
   DS 2107-75:06551 5005076303ffc0B7
END_MC

BEGIN_MC # MOP-DS8300-02
   CONSOLE HMC2
   SITE SITE2
   DS 2107-75:73731 5005076303ffc426
END_MC

BEGIN_ESS_PAIR
   ## Definition of the DS8300 on SITE1 of MOP
   DS 2107-75:06551 5005076303ffc0b7
   NUM_LINKS 2
   PPRC_LINK 64 28 00
   PPRC_LINK 65 6e 00

   ## Definition of the DS8300 on SITE2 of MOP
   DS 2107-75:73731 5005076303ffc426
   NUM_LINKS 2
   PPRC_LINK f0 20 00
   PPRC_LINK 136 21 00

   LSS_PAIRS
   61 * 61 *
   63 * 63 *
   65 * 65 *
END_ESS_PAIR

VOLUME_SETS
DS8K_MM
DS8K_GC
DS8K_GM
```

Under eRCMF there are two options for configuring Remote Copy. The proper configuration for a given business will, as always, vary depending on its particular business requirements. The options available are as follows:

- *OneWay* configurations require all Remote Copy traffic to go in the same direction. This means that all data flows in the same direction. All production work is based in one site. This option is valid if there is only a single VolumeSet defined and ESCON links are used for Remote Copy.

- *TwoWay* configurations permit traffic to go in both directions across PPRC paths. As a result it is possible to define production VolumeSets and make use of production servers in two separate data centers. The Storage Servers in each location will then host mirrored data from the other. If more than one VolumeSet is to be used then this option must be taken, even if all production work is based in one data center.

For more information on each element of the *Enterprise.dat* file, refer to the following guides:

- *enterprise Remote Copy Management Facility eRCMF V4 Implementation Guide*
- *enterprise Remote Copy Management Facility eRCMF V4 User's Guide.*

Hosts file

This file defines a list of hostnames (as known to the storage servers) that have access to one or more host volumes managed by eRCMF. This validates that all storage servers' volumes attached to these hosts are known to eRCMF.

The *Hosts.dat* file's section layout is:

1. Global declarations: The global declaration keywords may be specified in any order prior the definition of the host groups.
2. Host groups: The host or server group definition contains information about hosts that have common access to certain VolumeSets; The host groups may be defined in any order; The definition starts with the *BEGIN_groupname* and ends with the *END_groupname* keywords, where *groupname* is a user-defined name for this host group; The host group block is repeated for each group of hosts to be defined.

Example 38-2 is a sample 2-site *Hosts.dat* file used in a DS6000 environment.

Example 38-2 Sample Hosts.dat file

```
OnlyDefinedHostAccess# Only the specified hosts may access host volumes and each VolumeSet
host is assigned to all Host Volumes in the VolumeSet
#SharedDefinedHostAccess # Only the specified hosts may access host volumes and at least
one VolumeSet host is assigned to the Host Volumes in the VolumeSet
#AnyHostAccess        # Any host is allowed to access host volumes but unassigned Host
Volumes are still not allowed.

#NoShadowAccess# This is the default setting if nothing specified. No host is allowed to
access shadow volumes
AnyShadowAccess# Any host is allowed to access shadow volumes
#OtherShadowAccess# hosts other than those specified in this configuration file are allowed
to access Shadow Volumes

NoJournalAccess# No host is allowed to access journal volumes
#AnyJournalAccess# Any host is allowed to access journal volumes
#OtherJournalAccess# hosts other than those specified in this configuration file are
allowed to access journal volumes

#AutFile path/filename# This specifies the full path and filename for the encrypted
authentication file (case sensitive)

#CliFile path/filename# This specifies the full path and filename for the installed IBM
ESSCLI software (case sensitive)

DsCliFile /opt/ibm/dscli/dscli  # This specifies the full path and filename for the
installed IBM DSCLI software (case sensitive)

#ESSCLIDELAY 4000# 4 seconds delay between the parallel CLI requests
```

```
#DummyHost name# name specifies the dummy host name as known to storage system

ShowVolumeInfo


BEGIN_WIN

  VolumeSet DS8K_MM# name = Name of a volume set (Case sensitive)

    Site SITE1# sitename = Name of the accessing site for following hosts

      Host wintesta# hostname = Define a host to this volumeset on this site.

    Site SITE2# sitename = Name of the accessing site for following hosts

      Host wintestb# hostname = Define a host to this volumeset on this site.

END_WIN


BEGIN_AIX

  VolumeSet DS8K_GC# name = Name of a volume set (Case sensitive)
  VolumeSet DS8K_GM# name = Name of a volume set (Case sensitive)

    Site SITE1# sitename = Name of the accessing site for following hosts

      Host aixtesta# hostname = Define a host to this volumeset on this site.

    Site SITE2# sitename = Name of the accessing site for following hosts

      Host aixtestb# hostname = Define a host to this volumeset on this site.

END_AIX


#BEGIN_ZOS

#    VolumeSet
#    Site SITE1# sitename = Name of the accessing site for following hosts

#      Host GDP5# hostname = Define a host to this volumeset on this site.

#    Site SITE2# sitename = Name of the accessing site for following hosts

#      Host SDM1# hostname = Define a host to this volumeset on this site.

#END_ZOS
```

For more information on each element of the *Enterprise.dat* file, refer to the following guides:

- *enterprise Remote Copy Management Facility eRCMF V4 Implementation Guide*
- *enterprise Remote Copy Management Facility eRCMF V4 User's Guide*

VolumeSet

A VolumeSet is a set of volumes managed in a monolithic manner.

This contains the following attributes:

- *Name* of the VolumeSet

- *Type* of the VolumeSet:
  - Governs how data is moved between locations using a combination of Remote Copy and / or FlashCopy technologies
  - Is a Metro Mirror, Global Mirror, Global Copy or Cascaded VolumeSet (Metro Mirror/Global Copy).
- *State*: Are the Remote Copy pairs all insync? Is there a recovery action underway? Which site is currently the production site.
- Volumes being managed as a part of this VolumeSet:
  - All volumes required by an application must be part of the same VolumeSet.
  - All applications with dependencies must share the same VolumeSet.
  - All volumes are in production on the same site.

VolumeSet Level management establishes a child process for each VolumeSet defined to the CSS. These processes then continually monitor the state of PPRC and report back to the CSS, enabling the system to quickly detect events on any of the VolumeSets in the environment and take action appropriately.

This level of management also provides a simplified interface for viewing and changing the states of both Remote Copy and FlashCopy for each individual VolumeSet. For instance it makes it possible to set and modify the copy mode for Metro Mirror, Global Copy or Global Mirror relationships. Then the managers of heterogeneous open systems and z/OS environments can quickly identify whether data is consistent. This also allows for the state to be changed as appropriate. If, for example, data is found to be out of sync, the operator can issue a simple **resync** command. This will cause eRCMF to scan the volumes within the VolumeSet and automatically issue the commands necessary to bring the volumes back into sync.

Additionally, this level of management allows users to change or **swap** the location of production data. As a result, a user who has been running production of a given application in site 1 and mirroring to site 2 may change the state of the data in both sites so that site 2 mirrors to site 1.

VolumeSet Level also manages the creation of extra copies of data using FlashCopy.

Management of site splits is handled at the Enterprise level. Since the Freeze function works on LSS pairs, and multiple VolumeSets may share the same LSS pair, the LSSs must be managed at the overall, or Enterprise level. By allowing consistency management at the VolumeSet level, eRCMF allows customers to run different applications with different types of VolumeSets (for instance, FlashCopy usage, Global Mirror or Metro Mirror and so on) and allows different applications to be running on different sites (for instance, it allows failover of one application for a server error). See Example 38-3, Example 38-4, and Example 38-5.

Example 38-3 Metro Mirror VolumeSet without FlashCopy

```
# VolumeSet for the 2 DS8300 at Montpellier (France)

NAME DS8K_MM

TYPE NOFCPY# No flashcopy is used for this volumeset

PRODUCTION SITE1

2107-75:06551:61:000 * 2107-75:73731:61:000 *  # Metro Mirror
2107-75:06551:61:001 * 2107-75:73731:61:001 *  # Metro Mirror
```

Example 38-4 Global Copy VolumeSet with FlashCopy at the Recovery site

```
# VolumeSet for the 2 DS8300 at Montpellier (France)

NAME DS8K_GC

TYPE XDNOFCPY# Extended distance volumeset: No flashcopy is used for this volumeset

PRODUCTION SITE1

2107-75:06551:63:000 * 2107-75:73731:63:000 *  # Global Copy
2107-75:06551:63:001 * 2107-75:73731:63:001 *  # Global Copy
```

Example 38-5 Global Mirror VolumeSet with FlashCopy at the Recovery site

```
# VolumeSet for the 2 DS8300 at Montpellier (France)

NAME DS8K_GM

TYPE GLOBALALLFCPY# Global Mirror volumeset: Site 2 in this volumeset uses flashcopy
PRACTICESITE12FCPY

# Master on site 1
BEGIN_MASTER 2107-75:06551 65 * 1
END_MASTER

# Master on site 2
BEGIN_MASTER 2107-75:73731 65 * 1
END_MASTER

PRODUCTION SITE1

2107-75:06551:65:000 2107-75:06551:65:004 2107-75:06551:65:002 2107-75:73731:65:000
2107-75:73731:65:004 2107-75:73731:65:002 # Global Mirror
2107-75:06551:65:001 2107-75:06551:65:005 2107-75:06551:65:003 2107-75:73731:65:001
2107-75:73731:65:005 2107-75:73731:65:003 # Global Mirror
```

38.6.4 Configuration check

eRCMF needs to be configured to match the customer environment and Disaster Recovery configuration. To ensure that the eRCMF configuration actually matches how storage server's LUNs are configured, a configuration check can be performed periodically. The resulting notification can be done via e-mail or SNMP messages, but e-mail contains detailed check results.

The following major items are verified:

- eRCMF Host Volume access depending on policy.
- eRCMF Shadow Volume access depending on policy.
- eRCMF Journal Volume access depending on policy.
- The defined Hosts access the defined Volumes on the correct site.
- All volumes in a tuple have the same capacity (for Remote Copy, FC).
- All volumes accessed by eRCMF Hosts are defined to eRCMF.
- The defined storage servers exist and the defined network address is correct.
- All defined volumes exist on storage servers.

38.7 Commands

eRCMF commands are internally composed of one or several Advanced Copy Services commands in the right sequence to execute Remote Copy and FlashCopy tasks. It also has built in macro commands to test and practice your Disaster Recovery environment.

The commands are executed manually under the PCM management Command-Line Interface or can be scripted alone or integrated in the already existing client's scripts using eRCMF CLI client.

38.7.1 Enterprise level commands

Enterprise level commands control the entire environment and the following are commands that operate at this level:

- **arm** - The default is that automatic site split is not armed. This command enables an automatic site split. In this state, either a Storage Server SNMP Trap200 or the discovery of a suspended Remote Copy pair in an InSync VolumeSet causes a freeze action to be invoked. This command is a prerequisite for the **freeze** command.
- **autocheck** - This command manually invokes **check** on all VolumeSets. This verifies the complete environment has been initialized by the master process.
- **disarm** - This is the default. This command disables an automatic site split and prevents the **freeze** command from being successfully issued.
- **exit** - This command causes the current management process to quit and be terminated. If eRCMF was installed as a standalone application, and not as a daemon under WebSphere Application Server, and the command is issued by the master console, the master process will shut down completely. Otherwise, only the socket connection to the master process will be closed and the master process will continue to run.
- **fenceESS** or **fenceSite** - These commands fence the ESS or all the ESSs in a site. eRCMF will not issue I/O of any kind to a fenced ESS, nor request status from it.
- **freeze** - This command simulates a suspending event. If eRCMF is armed, it will cause an automatic site split by issuing a freeze command to all defined LSS pairs. eRCMF will block I/Os if the Freeze and Stop option is configured, otherwise, it will release I/Os after a successful site split.
- **release** - This command unblocks held I/Os from a previous **freeze**. This is used when the Freeze and Stop option is configured.
- **resetCSServers** - This command resets the Copy Services clients on the ESSs. All Copy Services agents on the ESS clusters that are controlled by eRCMF will be reset. This command is similar to the domain wide reset function of the CSS running on an ESS. An authentication file with the proper ESS access is required to issue resets.
- **shutdown** - This command operates the same way as the Exit command, but with the addition that if eRCMF was installed as a standalone application and the command was issued from a client, it will shut down the master process.
- **states** - This command displays the eRCMF memory state of each VolumeSet. The VolumeSet level commands **check** or **display** must be used to query the actual status from CSS.
- **unfenceESS** or **unfenceSite** - These commands unfence the Storage Server or all the Storage Servers in a site.

38.7.2 VolumeSet commands

The form of the VolumeSet level commands is one of the following:

- **<command>** <VolumeSetName> parameters: This executes the command on the specified VolumeSet.
- **<command>** SITE <SiteName> parameters: This executes the command on any VolumeSet which has sitename as its current production site.

The following are commands that operate at the VolumeSet level:

- **async** - This command re-synchronizes or switches PPRC pairs to the appropriate asynchronous mode - for XD VolumeSets, this will be *XDMode*; for Global Mirror VolumeSets, this will be *GlobalMirrorOutOfSync*. This command can only be issued to XD or Global Mirror VolumeSets.
- **check** - Check the consistency of the VolumeSet. This is automatically invoked when eRCMF is started and whenever a Storage Server event changes the state of a volume or PPRC link.
- **display** - Displays the current status and volumes of the VolumeSet, lists the volumes in the VolumeSet and then executes **check**. The output of **display** can be directed to an output file rather than the display screen.
- **flash** - A utility for running FlashCopy on an ESS. You need to specify one of the following forms along with a VolumeSet name and parameter:
  - **flash** <VolumeSetName> **Production**: This will cause a FlashCopy from the host to the shadow volumes on the current production site. For Global Mirror without FlashCopy, eRCMF will FlashCopy to the journal volume instead.
  - **flash** <VolumeSetName> **Backup**: This will cause a FlashCopy from the shadow to the host volumes on the current backup site.
  - **flash** <VolumeSetName> **Recover**: This is a recovery action that assumes the host copy on the production site is corrupt and the shadow copy can be used to recover. It further assumes that hosts accessing the data have all been shut down.
- **freeshadow** - This command frees shadow volumes after a recovery action completes.
- **forceswap** - This command swaps sites after a cluster failure. It is only valid with VolumeSets of type GLOBALNOFCPY, XDNOFCPY, XDALLFCPY, ALLFCPY, or NOFCPY; or if all shadow volumes specified are in fact practice volumes.
- **load** - This command loads a new VolumeSet or dynamically reloads an existing VolumeSet for eRCMF management. A new VolumeSet can be loaded without restarting the eRCMF master process, however, the VolumeSet name needs to be added to the Enterprise.dat configuration file to ensure that the new VolumeSet will be managed after a restart of the master process.
- **practice** - This command allows for a practice disaster by setting up the backup site as if it was production, but leaving production on the original production site.
- **recover** - This command causes a recover at the backup site putting the related VolumeSets in recovery mode and switching production data to the backup site.
- **split** - This command is only valid for asynchronous VolumeSets (Global Mirror and Global Copy types). If this command is invoked, eRCMF will attempt to synchronize the sites before suspending pairs.
- **resync** - This command will cause the sites to re-synchronize. In doing so it will reestablish PPRC links, establish or reestablish Remote Copy pairs, where appropriate it may initiate FlashCopy. For Global Mirror type VolumeSets it may also start, restart, or repair the Global Mirror session.

- **swap** - This command swaps the production and backup sites. It is valid only in the InSync state. It assumes that all of the application servers are currently down and will swap the production and backup sites. It uses FlashCopy to synchronize the host volumes with the shadow volumes on each site, terminates existing PPRC pairs, and establishes PPRC with the no-copy option in the opposite direction.
- **sync** - This command operates just like the **resync** command above except that it will force the PPRC pairs to Synchronous PPRC (terminating Global Mirror sessions if necessary).
- **unload** - This command will remove a VolumeSet from eRCMF management.

Further relevant commands available on the PCM where the Backup Process is running are:

- **recover** - Instruct the Backup Process to become the Master Process. It performs a site split and then become the Master Process. The **recover** command can be aborted if necessary.

> **Note:** The **recover** command assumes that the Master Process on the other PCM is down.

- **takeover**: Causes a takeover of eRCMF management by becoming the Master Process, but without issuing the **freeze** command first (that is without a site split).

38.8 Some eRCMF Disaster Recovery scenarios

We have seen an overview of eRCMF. Let us discuss how it works in some possible scenarios. Failover/Failback procedures are handled by eRCMF based on the FlashCopy option of the VolumeSet in a disaster recovery situation.

- Failover is the process of moving operations from a failed resource (the current production site) to a backup resource (the current recovery site).
- Failback is the process of resuming operations at the original production site after the situation which caused the failover has been repaired.

This section gives detailed examples of Failover/Failback cycles with the various Metro Mirror and Global Copy architectures possible with eRCMF.

38.8.1 NOFCPY and XDNOFCPY

In the following diagrams, we show the Failover/Failback cycle for an NOFCPY or XDNOFCPY VolumeSet Type.

> **Note:** Since Global Copy without FlashCopy at the recovery site does not guarantee the integrity of the data at the recovery site, this scenario might not be relevant.

Figure 38-12 shows the normal operation mode when Metro Mirror or Global Copy is copying from Site 1 Host Volume to the Site 2 Host Volume and the state is *InSync* (for Metro Mirror) or *XDMode* (for Global Copy).

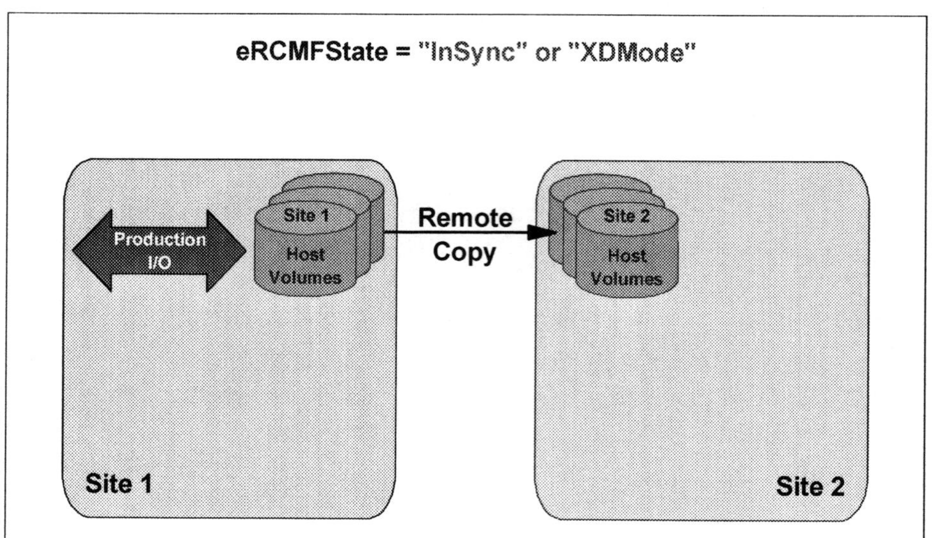

Figure 38-12 Normal operation for an NOFCPY or XDNOFCPY VolumeSet

When a disaster strikes, as in Figure 38-13, eRCMF automatically splits the sites by freezing I/O for the defined LSS pairs and suspending the defined Remote Copy pairs. Depending on the policy specified in the *Enterprise.dat* configuration file, I/O will be held or released after the site split.

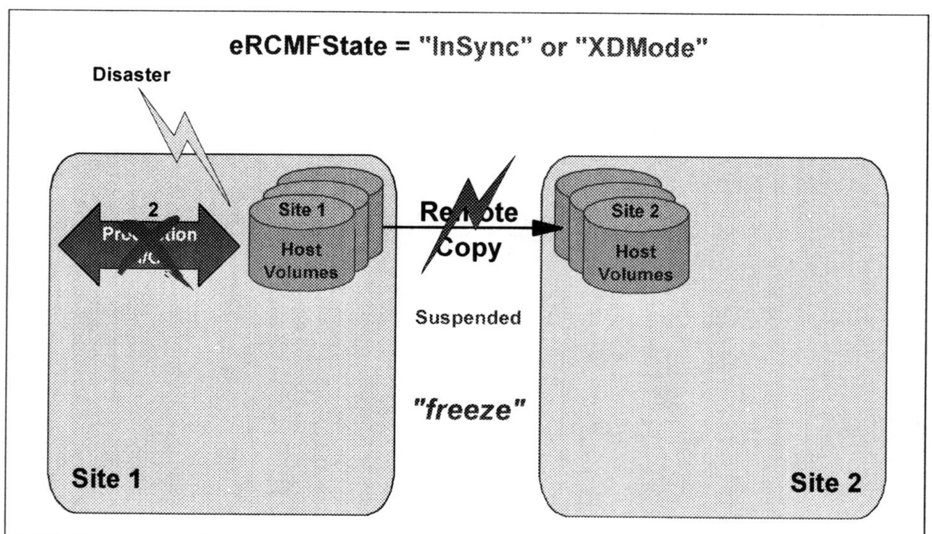

Figure 38-13 Disaster and freeze for an NOFCPY or XDNOFCPY VolumeSet

The **recover** command starts recovery at the backup site by restarting operations on the Site 2 host volumes. Figure 38-14 illustrates this phase.

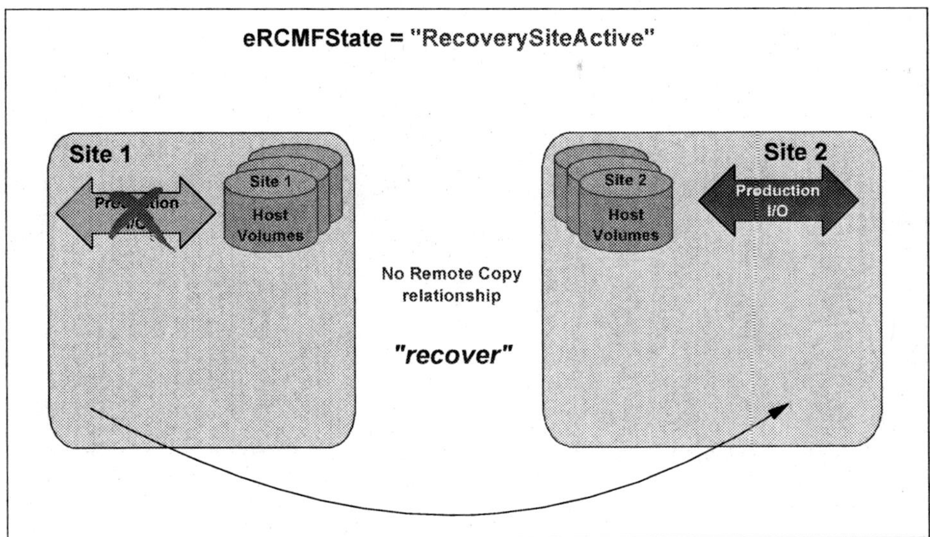

Figure 38-14 Recovery at the backup site for an NOFCPY or XDNOFCPY VolumeSet

To resynchronize back to the original site, the **resync** command will:

1. Terminate existing Remote Copy relationships.
2. Establish Logical Paths from Site 2 to Site 1.
3. Do a Remote Copy full-copy from the Host Volumes on Site 2 to the Host Volumes on Site 1.

Figure 38-15 shows the re-synchronization phase.

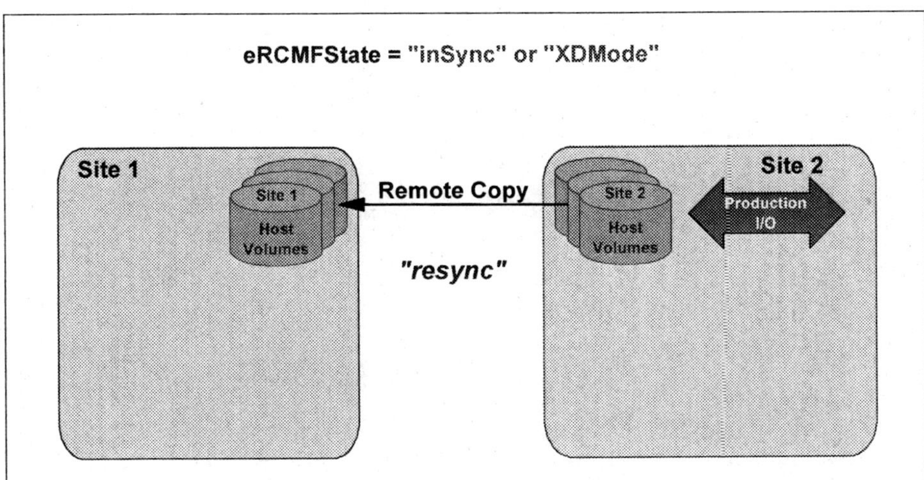

Figure 38-15 Resynchronize back to original site for an NOFCPY or XDNOFCPY VolumeSet

As shown in Figure 38-15, once the state is InSync again, the **swap** command will move production back to the original site and do the following:

1. Make sure servers on the recovery site are unassigned or shut down.
2. Terminate Remote Copy pairs.
3. Reverse paths if OneWay is specified.

4. Reestablish Remote Copy pairs in the original direction - the Host Volumes on Site 1 to the Host Volumes on Site 2 with the NOCOPY option (Figure 38-16).

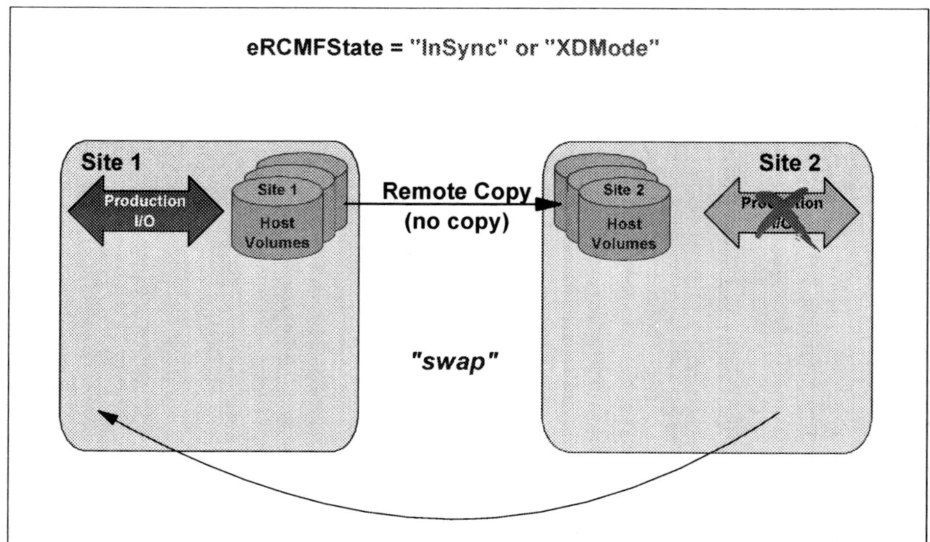

Figure 38-16 Move production back to original site for an NOFCPY or XDNOFCPY VolumeSet

Finally, applications can be restarted on the original production servers.

38.8.2 SITE1FCPY and XDSITE1FCPY

In the following diagrams, we show the Failover/Failback cycle for an SITE1FCPY or XDSITE1FCPY VolumeSet Type.

> **Note:** Since Global Copy without FlashCopy at the recovery site does not guarantee the integrity of the data at the recovery site, this scenario might not be relevant.

Figure 38-17 shows the normal operation mode when Metro Mirror or Global Copy is copying from Site 1 Host Volume to the Site 2 Host Volume and the state is *InSync* (for Metro Mirror) or *XDMode* (for Global Copy).

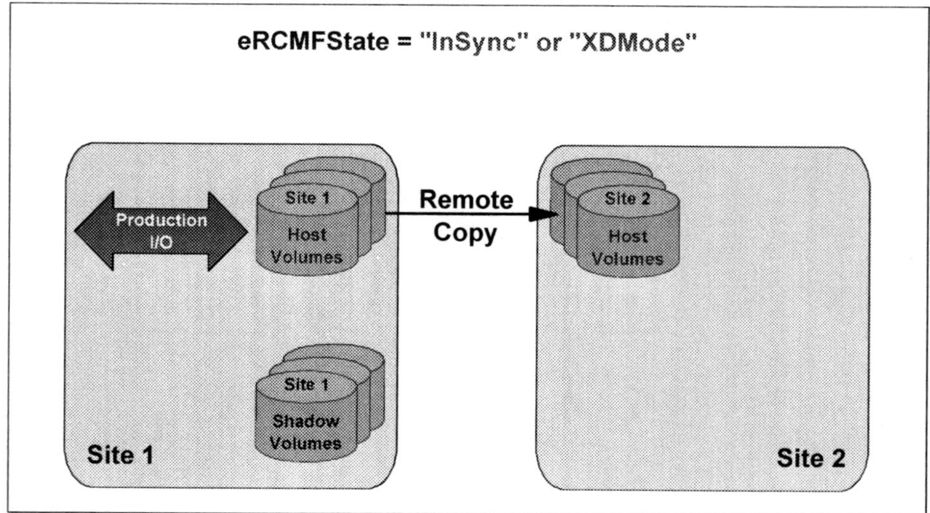

Figure 38-17 Normal operation for an SITE1FCPY or XDSITE1FCPY VolumeSet

When a disaster strikes, as in Figure 38-18, eRCMF automatically splits the sites by freezing I/O for the defined LSS pairs and suspending the defined Remote Copy pairs. Depending on the policy specified in the *Enterprise.dat* configuration file, I/O will be held or released after the site split.

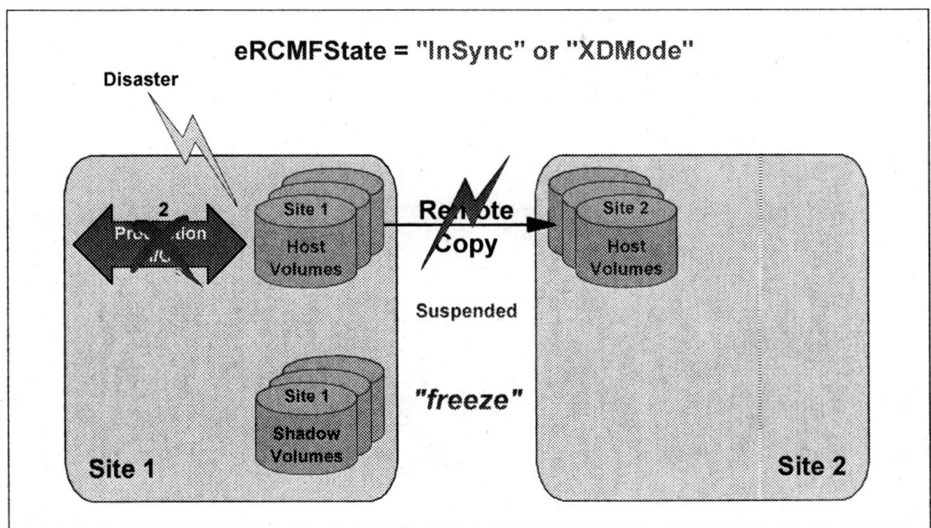

Figure 38-18 Disaster and freeze for an SITE1FCPY or XDSITE1FCPY VolumeSet

The **recover** command starts recovery at the backup site by restarting operations on the Site 2 host volumes. Figure 38-19 illustrates this phase.

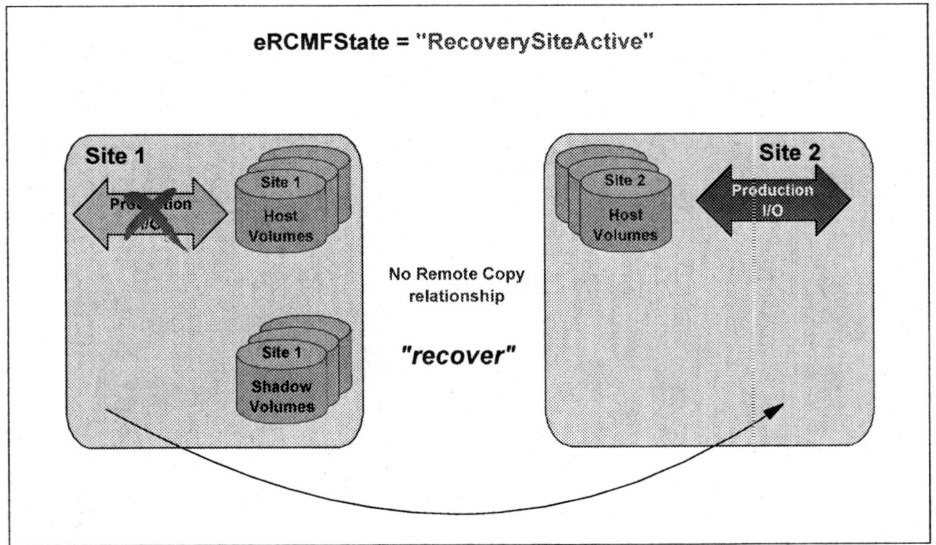

Figure 38-19 Recovery at the backup site for an SITE1FCPY or XDSITE1FCPY VolumeSet

To resynchronize back to the original site, the **resync** command will:

1. Terminate existing Remote Copy relationships.
2. Establish Logical Paths from Site 2 to Site 1.
3. Do a Remote Copy full-copy from the Host Volumes on Site 2 to the Shadow Volumes on Site 1.

Figure 38-20 shows the re-synchronization phase.

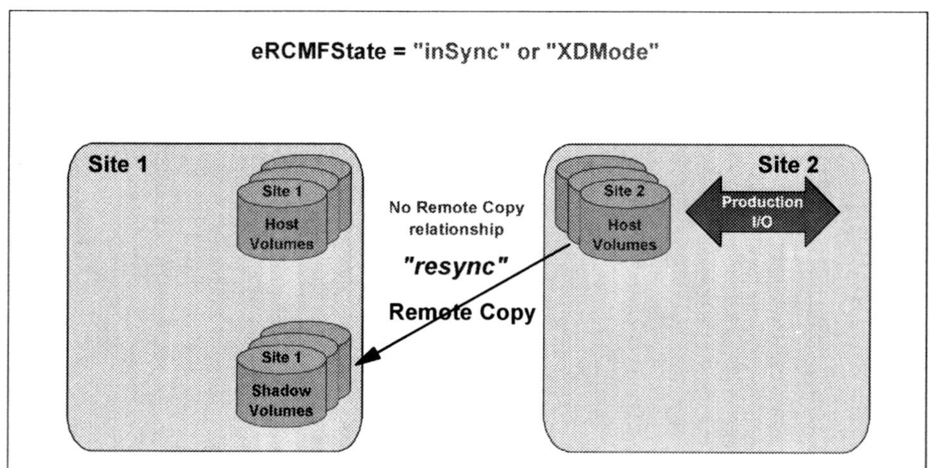

Figure 38-20 Resynchronize back to original site for SITE1FCPY or XDSITE1FCPY VolumeSet

As shown in Figure 38-21, once the state is InSync again, the **swap** command will move production back to the original site and do the following:

1. Make sure servers on the recovery site are unassigned or shut down.
2. Terminate Remote Copy pairs.
3. Reverse paths if OneWay is specified.
4. Do a FlashCopy from the Shadow Volumes on Site 1 to the Host volumes on Site 1.
5. Reestablish Remote Copy pairs in the original direction - the Host Volumes on Site 1 to the Host Volumes on Site 2 with the NOCOPY option.

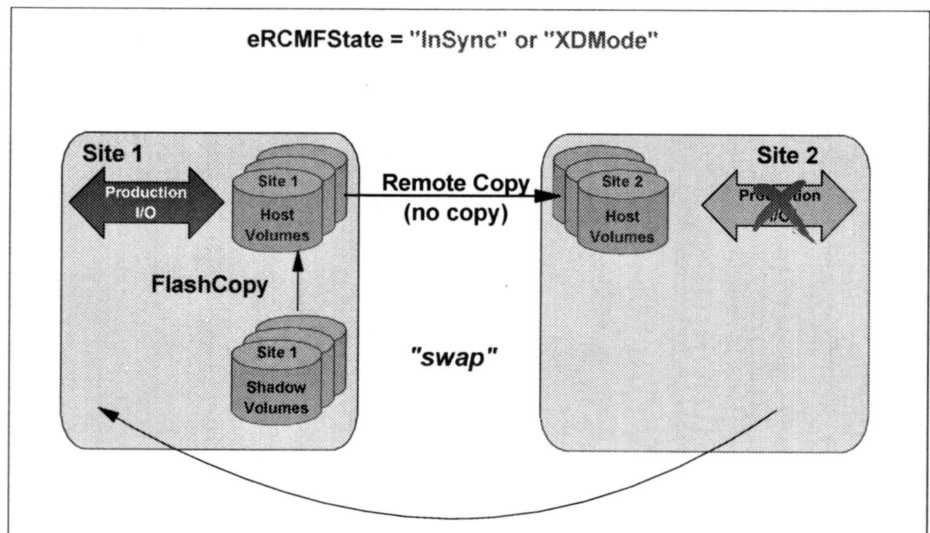

Figure 38-21 Move production to original site for SITE1FCPY or XDSITE1FCPY VolumeSet

Finally applications can be restarted on the original production servers.

38.3.3 SITE2FCPY and XDSITE2FCPY

In the following diagrams, we show the Failover/Failback cycle for an SITE2FCPY or SITE2ALLFCPY VolumeSet Type.

Figure 38-22 shows the normal operation mode when Metro Mirror or Global Copy is copying from Site 1 Host Volume to the Site 2 Shadow Volume and the state is *InSync* (for Metro Mirror) or *XDMode* (for Global Copy).

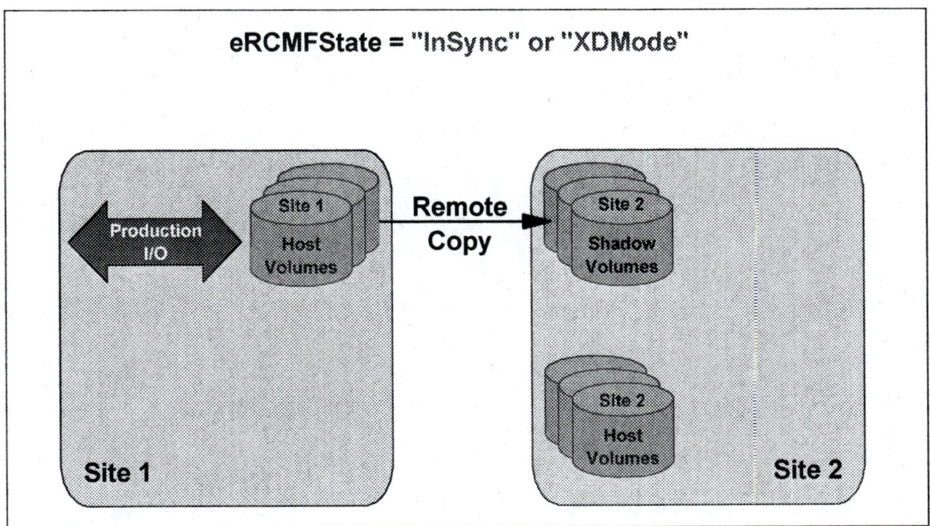

Figure 38-22 Normal operation for an SITE2FCPY or XDSITE2FCPY VolumeSet

When a disaster strikes, as in Figure 38-23, eRCMF automatically splits the sites by freezing I/O for the defined LSS pairs and suspending the defined Remote Copy pairs. Depending on the policy specified in the *Enterprise.dat* configuration file, I/O will be held or released after the site split.

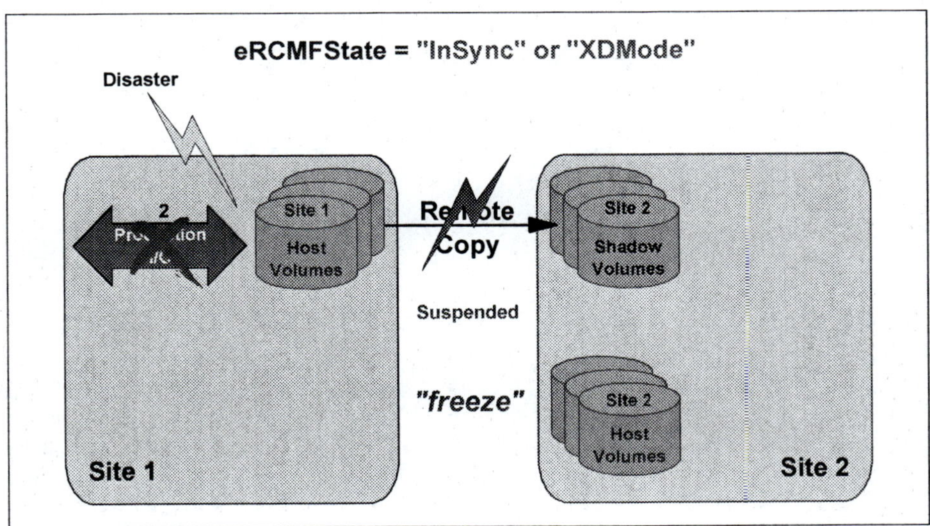

Figure 38-23 Disaster and freeze for an SITE2FCPY or XDSITE2FCPY VolumeSet

The **recover** command starts recovery at the backup site by issuing a FlashCopy from the Site 2 shadow volume to the Site 2 host volume and restarting operations on the Site 2 host volume. Figure 38-24 illustrates this phase.

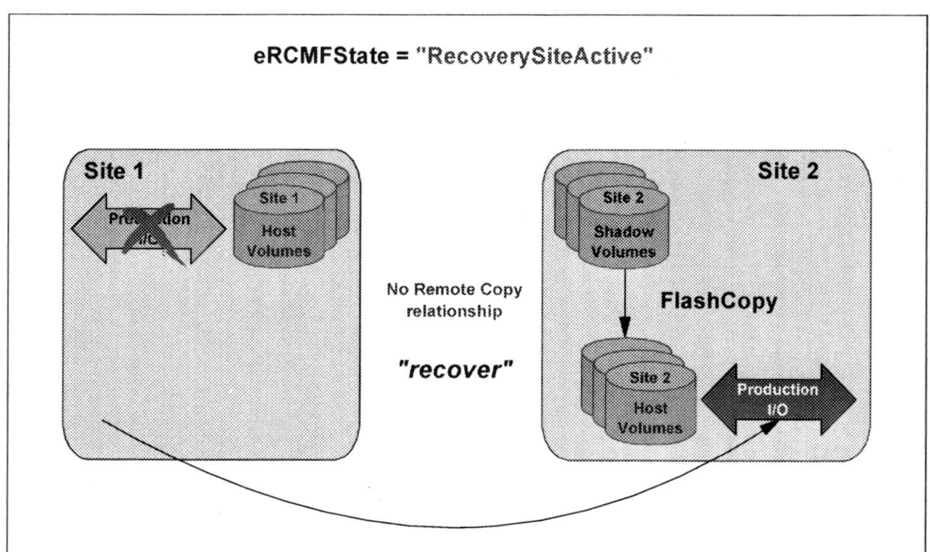

Figure 38-24 Recovery at the backup site for SITE2FCPY or XDSITE2FCPY VolumeSet

To resynchronize back to the original site, the **resync** command will:

1. Terminate existing Remote Copy relationships.
2. Establish Logical Paths from Site 2 to Site 1.
3. Do a Remote Copy full-copy from the Host Volumes on Site 2 to the Host Volumes on Site 1.

Figure 38-25 shows the re-synchronization phase.

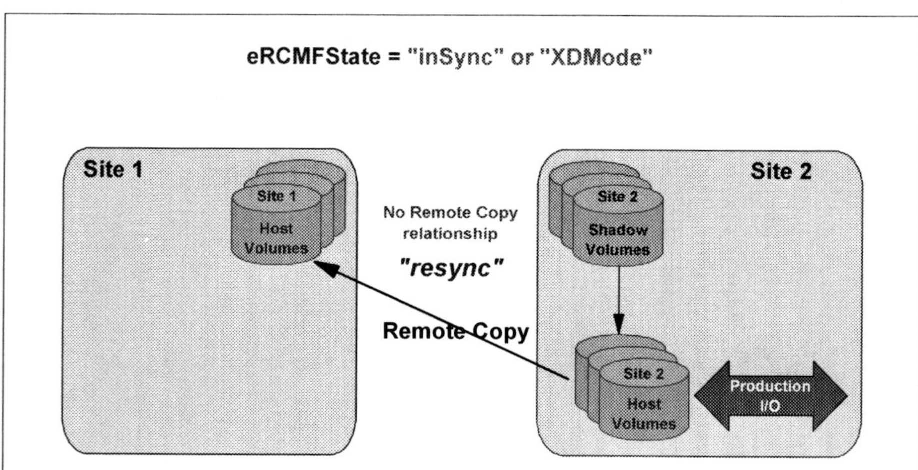

Figure 38-25 Resynchronize back to original site for SITE2FCPY or XDSTE2FCPY VolumeSet

As shown in Figure 38-26, once the state is *InSync* again, the **swap** command will move production back to the original site and do the following:

1. Make sure servers on the recovery site are unassigned or shut down.
2. Terminate Remote Copy pairs.
3. Reverse paths if OneWay is specified.
4. Do a FlashCopy from the Host Volumes on Site 2 to the Shadow Volumes on Site 2.

5. Reestablish Remote Copy pairs in the original direction — the Host Volumes on Site 1 to the Shadow Volumes on Site 2 with the NOCOPY option (Figure 38-26).

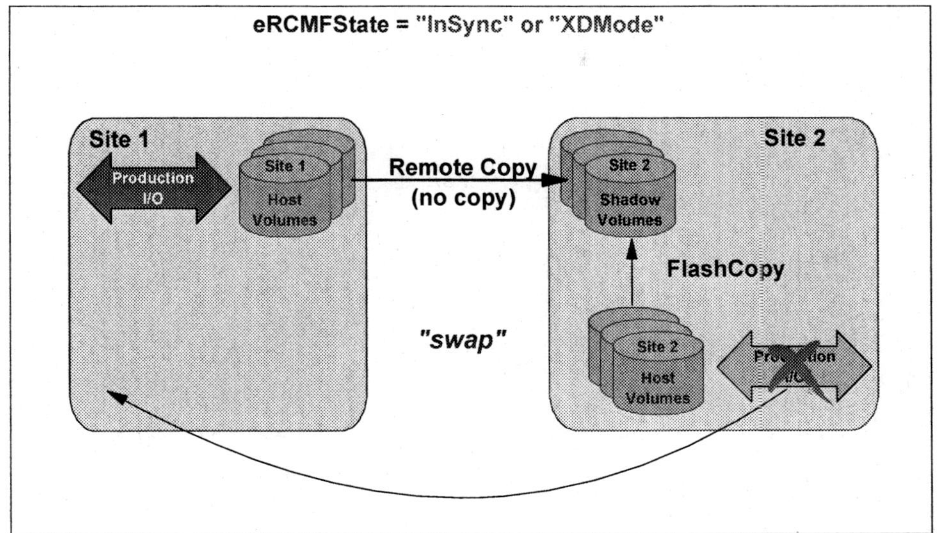

Figure 38-26 Move production to original site for SITE2FCPY or XDSITE2FCPY VolumeSet

Finally applications can be restarted on the original production servers.

38.8.4 ALLFCPY and XDALLFCPY

In the following diagrams, we show the Failover/Failback cycle for an ALLFCPY or XDALLFCPY VolumeSet Type.

Figure 38-27 shows the normal operation mode when Metro Mirror or Global Copy is copying from Site 1 Host Volume to the Site 2 Shadow Volume and the state is *InSync* (for Metro Mirror) or *XDMode* (for Global Copy).

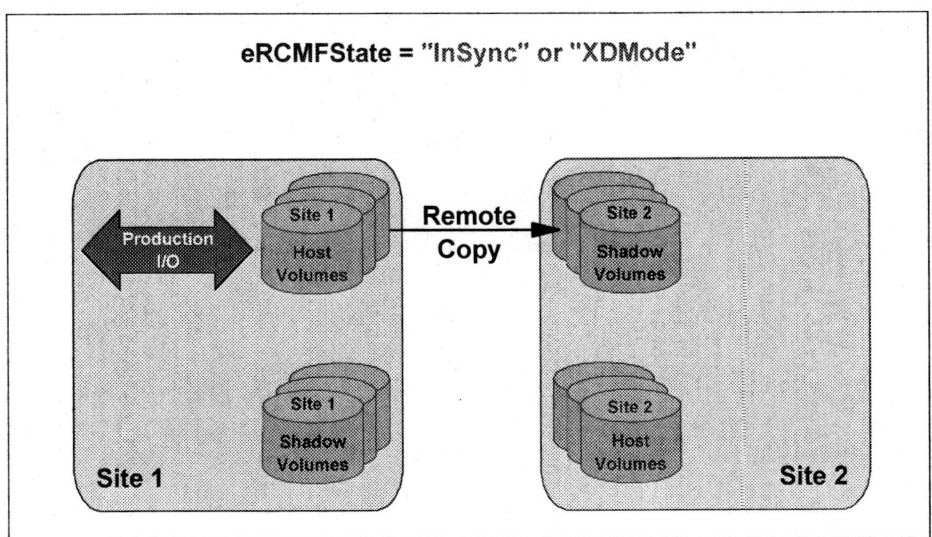

Figure 38-27 Normal operation for an ALLFCPY or XDALLFCPY VolumeSet

When a disaster strikes, as in Figure 38-28, eRCMF automatically splits the sites by freezing I/O for the defined LSS pairs and suspending the defined Remote Copy pairs. Depending on the policy specified in the *Enterprise.dat* configuration file, I/O will be held or released after the site split (Figure 38-28).

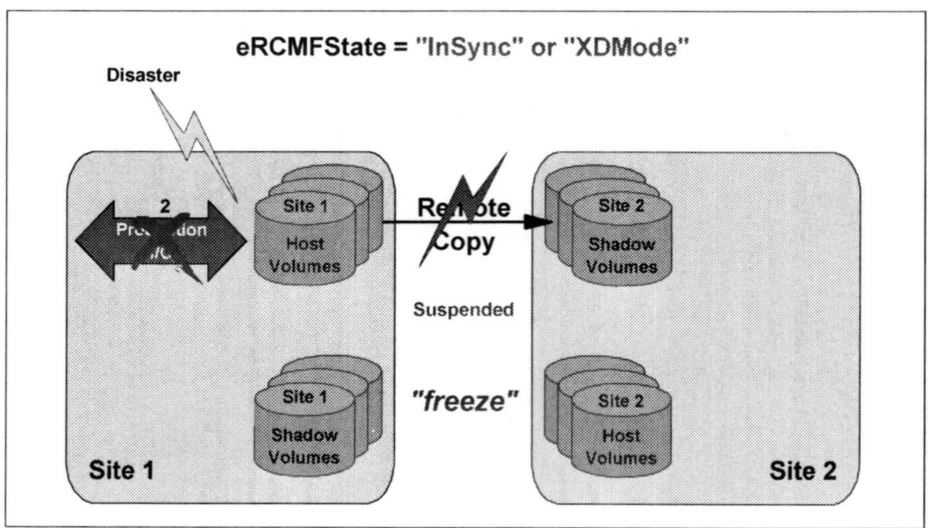

Figure 38-28 Disaster and freeze for an ALLFCPY or XDALLFCPY VolumeSet

The **recover** command starts recovery at the backup site by issuing a FlashCopy from the Site 2 shadow volume to the Site 2 host volume and restarting operations on the Site 2 host volume. Figure 38-29 illustrates this phase.

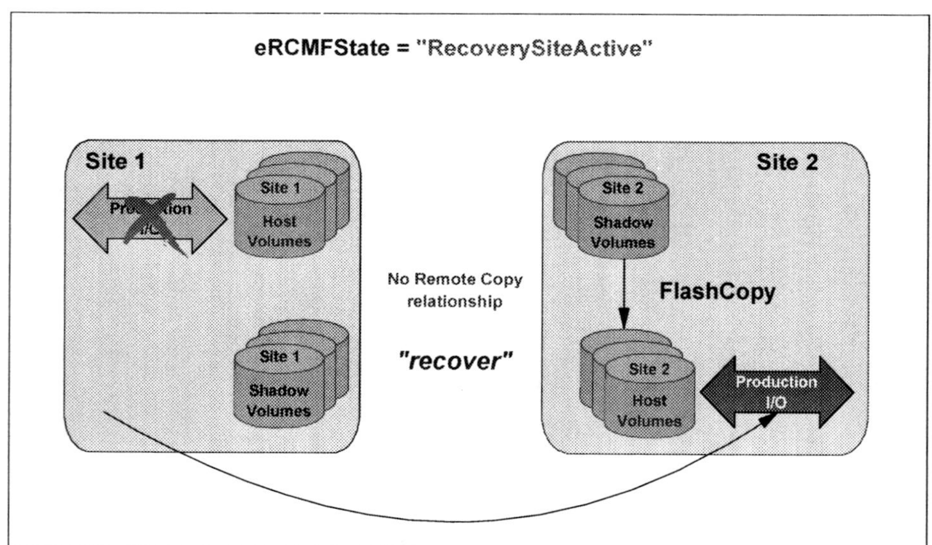

Figure 38-29 Recovery at the backup site for an ALLFCPY or XDALLFCPY VolumeSet

To resynchronize back to the original site, the **resync** command will:

1. Terminate existing Remote Copy relationships.
2. Establish Logical Paths from Site 2 to Site 1.
3. Do a Remote Copy full-copy from the Host Volumes on Site 2 to the Shadow Volumes on Site 1.

Figure 38-30 shows the re-synchronization phase.

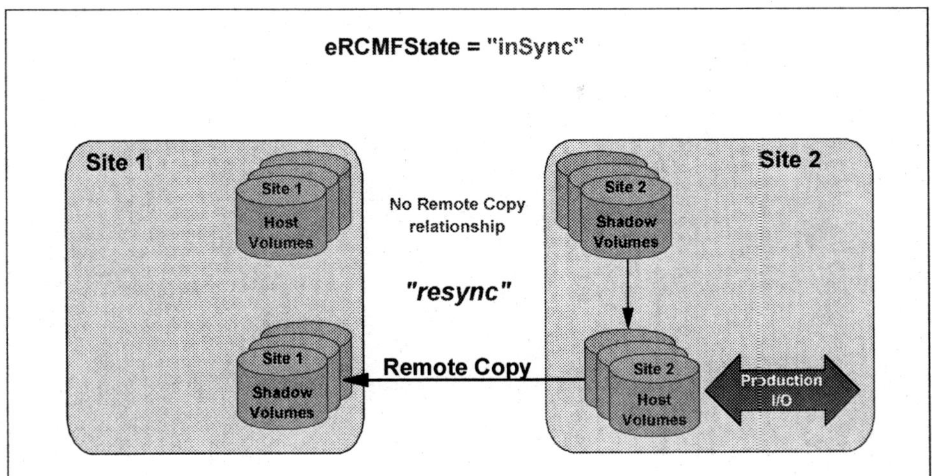

Figure 38-30 Resynchronize back to original site for ALLFCPY or XDALLFCPY VolumeSet

As shown in Figure 38-31, once the state is InSync again, the **swap** command will move production back to the original site and do the following operations:

1. Make sure servers on the recovery site are unassigned or shut down.
2. Terminate Remote Copy pairs.
3. Reverse paths if OneWay is specified.
4. Do a FlashCopy from the Host Volumes on Site 2 to the Shadow Volumes on Site 2 and from the Shadow Volumes on Site 1 to the Host volumes on Site 1.
5. Reestablish Remote Copy pairs in the original direction — the Host Volumes on Site 1 to the Shadow Volumes on Site 2 with the NOCOPY option.

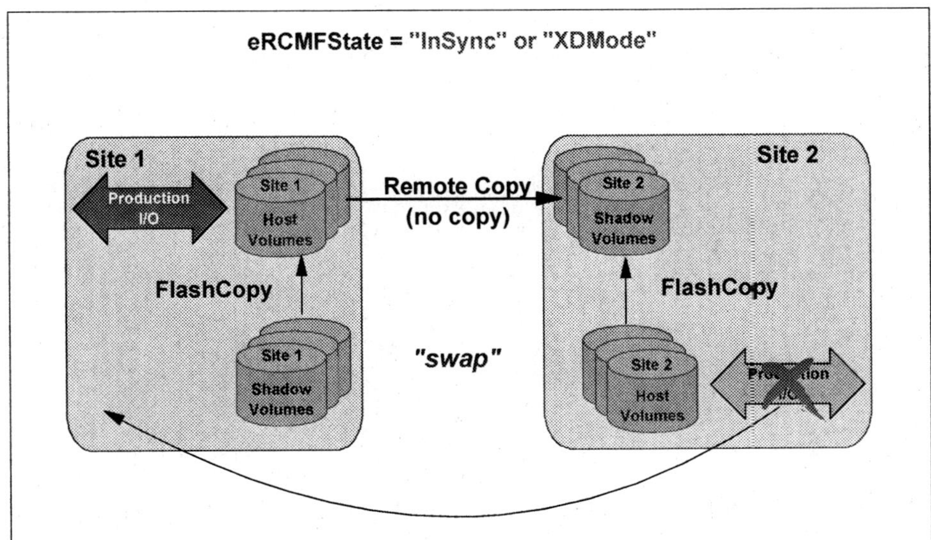

Figure 38-31 Move production back to original site for ALLFCPY or XDALLFCPY VolumeSet

Finally, applications can be restarted on the original production servers.

38.9 Additional information

Further information can be found on the IBM Web site at:

```
http://www-1.ibm.com/services/us/index.wss/so/its/a1000110
```

IBM personnel can also access the following IBM internal Web site to get additional information about this offering:

```
http://web.mainz.de.ibm.com/ATSservices
```

For further information, you can refer to the following papers:

- *enterprise Remote Copy Management Facility eRCMF V4 Implementation Guide*
- *enterprise Remote Copy Management Facility eRCMF V4 User Guide*

You can find these papers at:

```
http://www-1.ibm.com/support/docview.wss?uid=ssg1S7001074
```

For more information, contact your IBM sales representative.

39

IBM TotalStorage Global Mirror Utility

The Global Mirror Utility (GMU) is a standalone tool to provide a management layer for ESS Model 800, DS8000 and DS6000 Global Mirror (formerly Asynchronous PPRC) 2-site or 3-site Failover/Failback (FO/FB) support. It is a common management tool for both z/OS and open system environments and requires a small hardware investment.

The solution provides basic commands through FO/FB Session Manager Proxy that utilizes the ESS Open API functions to accomplish either a planned or unplanned FO/FB sequence. GMU commands can be incorporated in any user scripts or utilities that may further link the user's overall datacenter operations. However, it is the user's responsibility for creation, maintenance and any liabilities associated with such scripts or utilities. Therefore, GMU only offers a simple way to implement Failover/Failback and Global Mirror disaster recovery procedures via command line. GMU applies the commands to a set of XML files that describe the disk subsystem configuration (paths and sets of volumes).

GMU is a Tier 6 solution, as you can see in Figure 39-1.

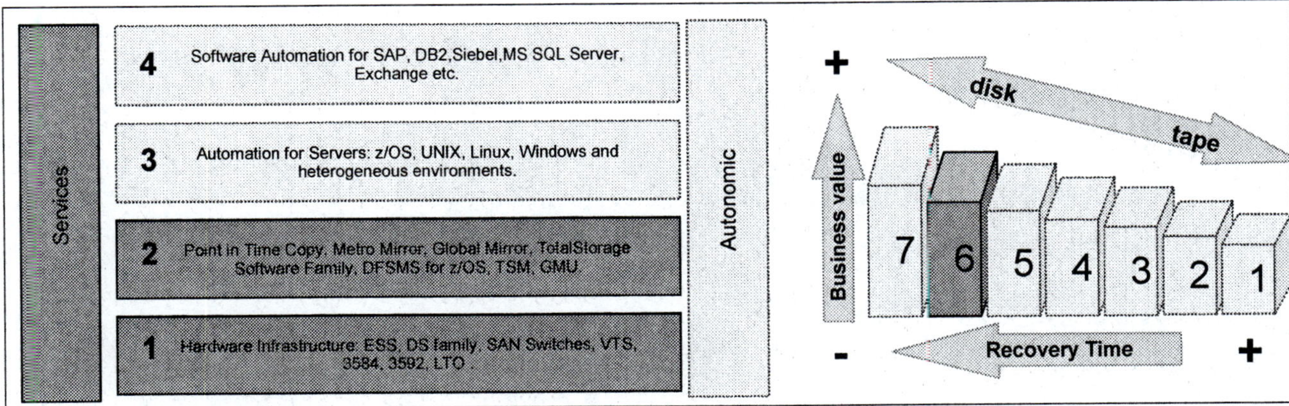

Figure 39-1 IBM TotalStorage Global Mirror Utility protection Tier

39.1 Product overview

GMU is a client/server application where the server is a Global Mirror Session Manager and the clients run command scripts. This client can be on the same machine as the server or on a standalone machine.

On the event of a planned or unplanned FO/FB, the system administrator will issue the GMU commands and orchestrate the FO/FB recovery of consistent data on the remote site and direct host I/O activities on the remote site. Upon local site recovery or when remote host practice test runs are complete, the system administrator will resume host activity on the local site, but not before copying a consistent set of data to all backup volumes at the remote site.

This solution relies on ESS and DS Open Asynchronous API support (ESSNI). However, the solution is managed separately on an outboard WebSphere Application Server. The IBM ESS or DS API provide connection and service conduit between this solution and Copy Services Servers functions. See Figure 39-2.

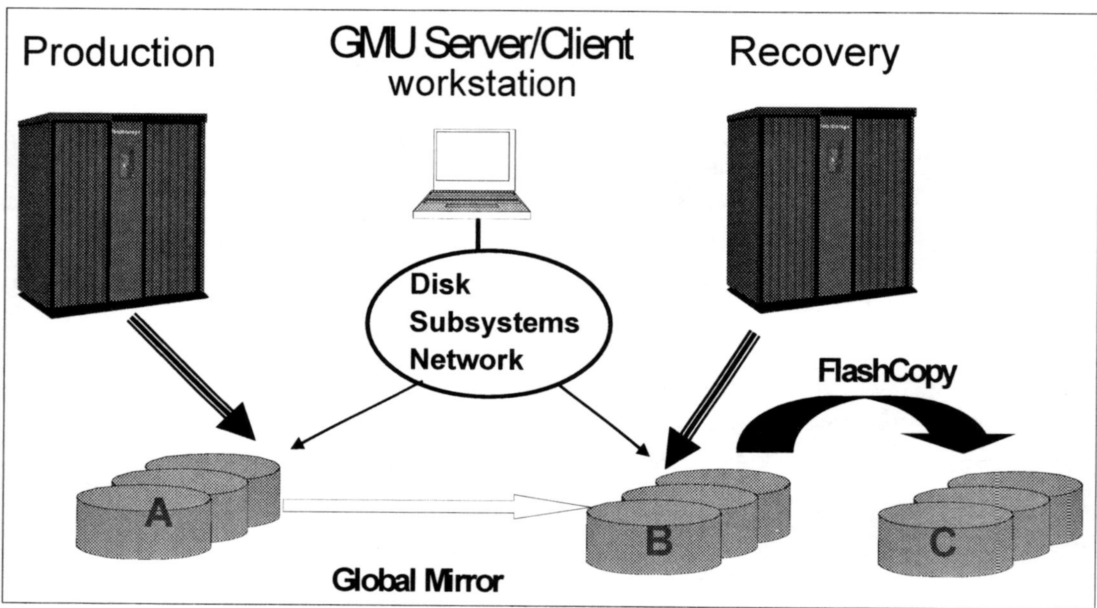

Figure 39-2 GMU server and client connected to the same disk subsystems network

39.2 Product requirements

In this section we detail the hardware and software requirements to build a solution with GMU server, its clients, and managed disks subsystems.

Server requirements:

- Intel® P4 or compatible host server
- Microsoft® Windows 2000 Standard Edition (SP3 minimum) or Microsoft Windows 2000 Advanced Server (SP3 minimum) or Windows 2003 Standard Edition or Windows 2003 Enterprise Edition or Windows XP Professional
- Minimum memory requirement is 1 GB
- Minimum disk space is 10 GB
- WebSphere Application Server 5.1

Client requirements:

- MS Windows 2000 or XP
- Java2 Runtime Environment, Standard Edition Build 1.3.1
- The client should be included in the same TCP/IP network as the disk subsystems in order for the user to be able to access the ESS HMC, DS HMC (DS8000), DS SMC (DS6000).

Disk subsystem Requirements:

- ESS VRMF level 2.4.0 or higher LIC
- Any DS8000,DS6000, ESS800 or combination of the three

39.3 Objectives, limitations, and optional features

The GMU tool can be used for free in a single Global Mirror copy services domain (up to eight storage subsystems), it is a service for bigger configurations, or if clients need specific customizing.

39.3.1 The primary objectives of GMU

GMU, with DS and ESS API driver, performs Global Mirror session creation, modification, and management of FO/FB operations. Since the creation of a Global Mirror session is performed automatically, users can save time and are prevented from making any errors associated in such a creation process.

Besides the Global Mirror session creation commands, GMU also provides commands to perform FO/FB operations, practice operations, and query operation status. It also has commands to add new members to the session and perform the session FO/FB management on the new members.

GMU provides the flexibility to let users incorporate part or all of its commands with its own data center management scripts (or software utilities). However, IBM does not support such scripts or utilities without a specific service arrangement. IBM specific service arrangements are highly recommended for large configurations and Disaster Recovery testing with GMU before putting it into production. Any special customizing of GMU commands and functions is also available through IBM service offerings.

39.3.2 The primary limitations of GMU

GMU only queries and reports Global Mirror FO/FB operations status. It is not providing volume status and Global Mirror session status information. For that, users have to either use ESS StorWatch Specialist/CopyServices GUI or DS Storage Manager or DS Command-Line Interface (CLI).

39.3.3 GMU additional features through IBM Service Offerings

GMU will not perform other Copy Services tasks, such as Metro Mirror, FlashCopy, and Global Copy. However, GMU will be able to externalize such commands through IBM Service Offerings.

GMU does not provide volume mapping and discovery services. This is the reason why users need to create their own configuration files. If users desire to automatically create the configuration files from external tools such as an MS Excel® Spread Sheet, a macro can be provided as part of the IBM service offerings.

It is highly recommended to get IBM Service Offerings to setup more complex Global Mirror Configuration with GMU. Such configuration may include mix of DS8000, DS6000 and ESS 800 boxes, configuration with more than 8 ESS, or with multiple CopyServices Domains.

Note: For large Global Mirror configurations, IBM offers services to install GMU, create configuration files and test disaster recovery readiness with GMU.

39.4 GMU utilization and CD content

Besides the license agreement files and the readme file, there are two folders on the CD:

- Service folder content:
  - fofbservice.ear
  - install.jacl
  - serverinstall.properties
  - serverinstall.xml
  - ant – folder containing ant libraries and other dependencies
  - serversetup.cmd
  - uninstall.jacl
- Client folder content:
  - clientsetup.bat
  - client.jar

39.5 Server installation procedure

In this section we detail how to install GMU either using the command line method or using the WebSphere Application Server Administration Console.

Prerequisites

These are the prerequisites:

- IBM WebSphere Application Server base version 5.1 is installed and running.
- WAS_HOME\java\bin is in the PATH environment variable of your Windows Server.

39.5.1 Uninstallation from WebSphere Application Server administration console

Before the uninstall, make sure to save the configuration XML files, security files, and the *fofbserver.properties* file.

1. Log into the WebSphere Application Server administration console using your browser at the URL *http://<WAS IP address>:9090:admin*. Your WebSphere Application Server administrator may have secured the server. If it is the case, you might need to type `https` instead of `http`, and the default port `9090` might be changed to another one. Type only the login name if the WebSphere Application Server is not secured, or ask your administrator for a login name and password if it is necessary.

2. Click the **Applications** menu then the **Enterprise Application** menu. *DO NOT CLICK* **Install new Application** because we need to be sure the application is not already installed (see Figure 39-3).

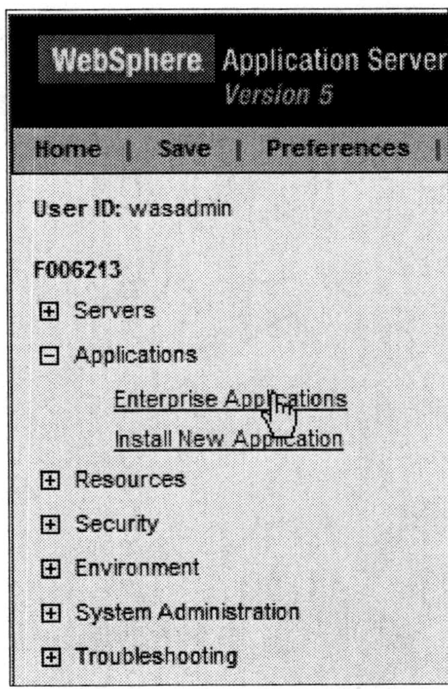

Figure 39-3 WebSphere Application Server administration console menu

3. When the window *Enterprise Applications* is displayed, select **FoFbServiceEAR** and click the button **Stop** (see Figure 39-4).

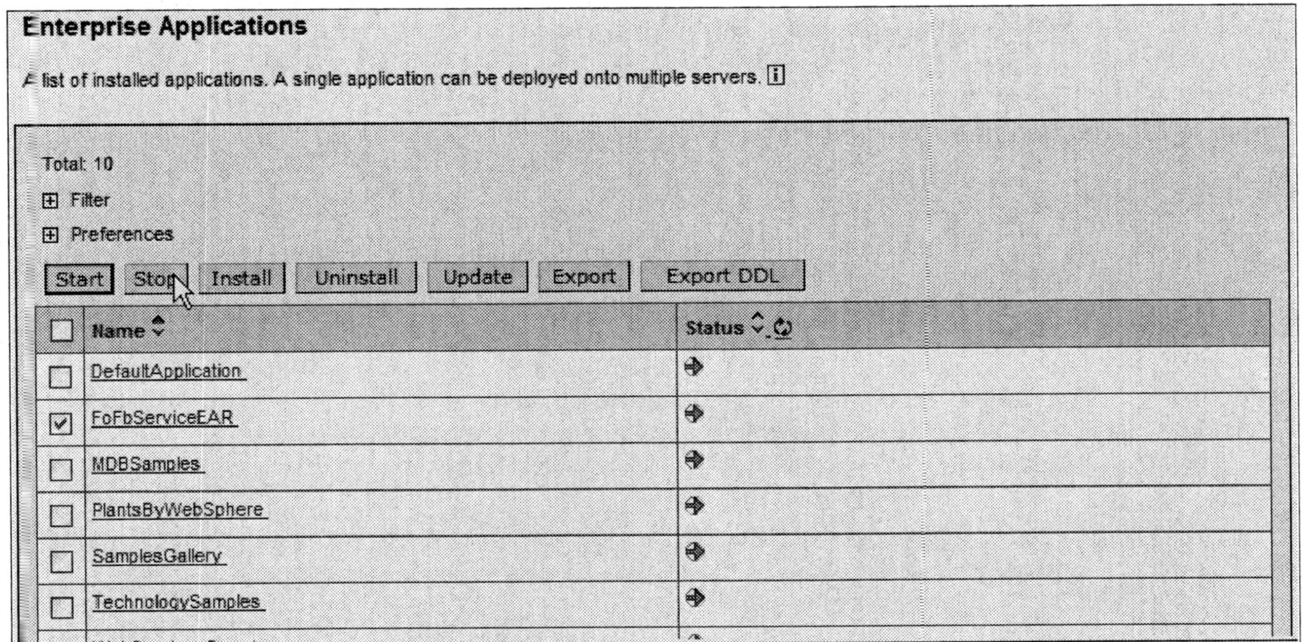

Figure 39-4 GMU server uninstallation - stop application

4. When the window **Enterprise Application** is displayed again, select **FoFbServiceEAR** and click **Uninstall** (see Figure 39-5).

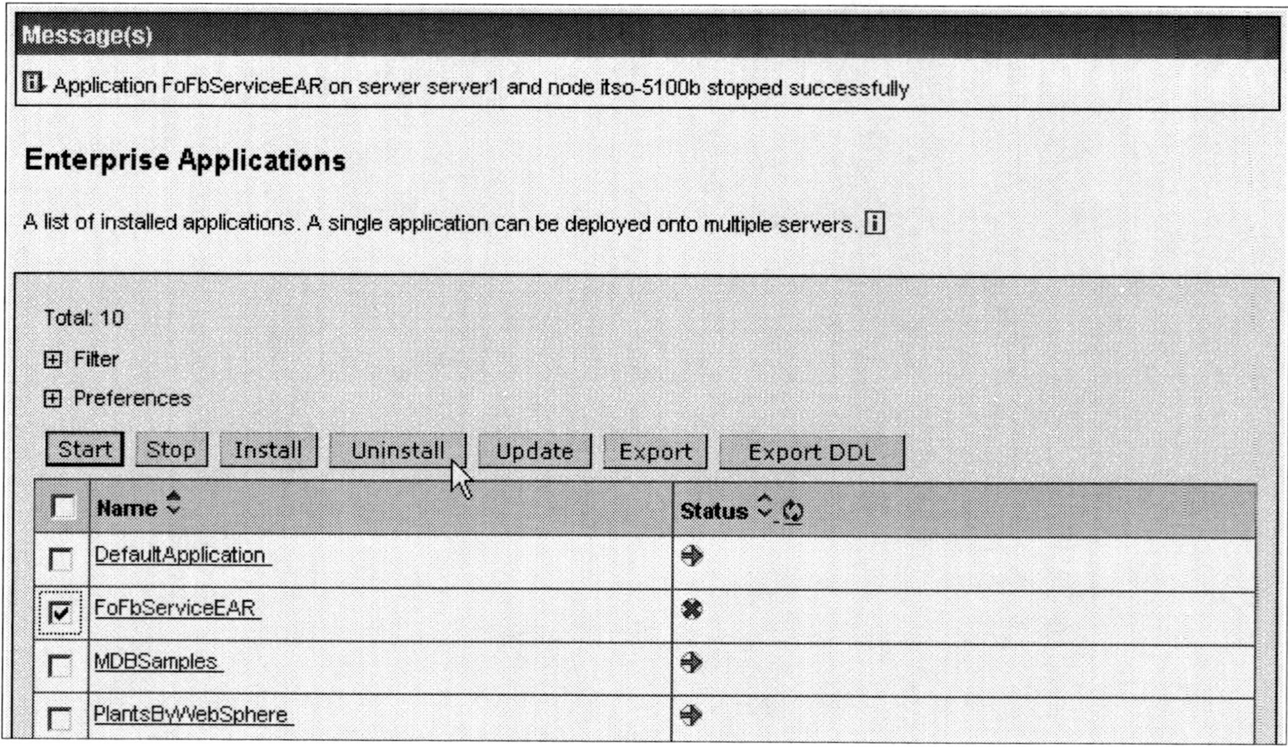

Figure 39-5 GMU server uninstallation - uninstall the application

5. Save the WebSphere Application server configuration as indicated on the console. (see Figure 39-6).

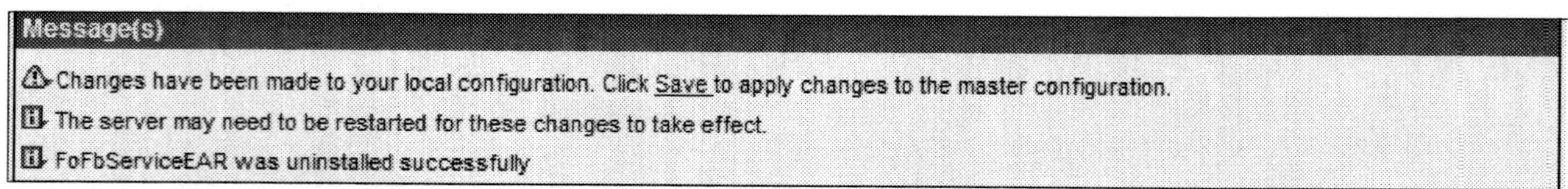

Figure 39-6 GMU Server uninstallation - Confirmation

6. Restart WebSphere Application Server service after the uninstallation is completed.

39.5.2 Installation from WebSphere Application Server administration console

1. Log into the WebSphere Application Server administration console using your browser at the URL *http://<WAS IP address>:9090:admin*. Your WebSphere Application Server administrator may have secured the server. If it is the case, you might need to type **https** instead of **http**, and the default port **9090** might be changed to another one. Type only the login name if the WebSphere Application Server is not secured or ask your administrator a login name and password if it is necessary.
2. Click the **Applications** menu then the **Enterprise Application** menu. *DO NOT CLICK* **Install new Application** because we need to be sure the application is not already installed (see Example 39-3 on page 591).
3. When the window **Enterprise Application** is displayed, click **Install** (see Figure 39-7).

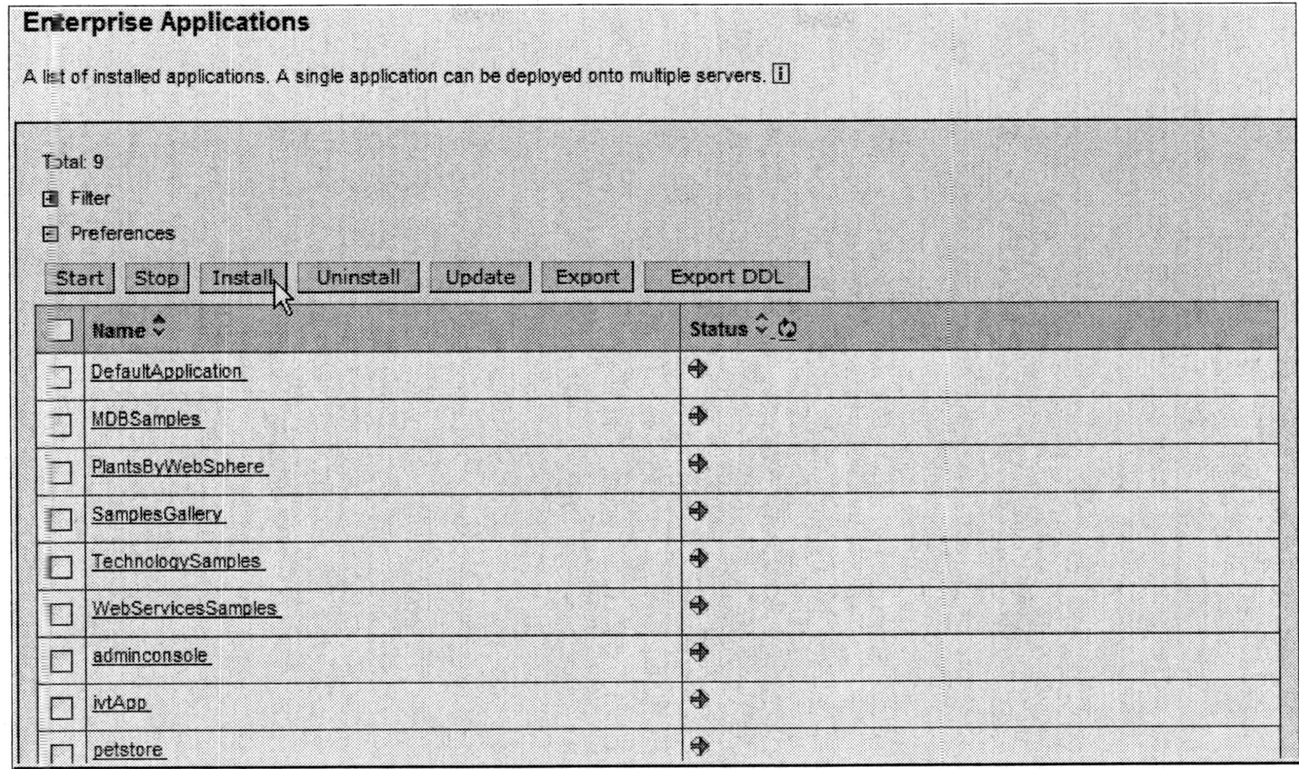

Figure 39-7 GMU server installation - Enterprise Applications panel

4. Select **Local path** and browse to the service directory where the CD image is copied to choose the file *fofbservice.ear* (see Figure 39-8) and click **Next**.

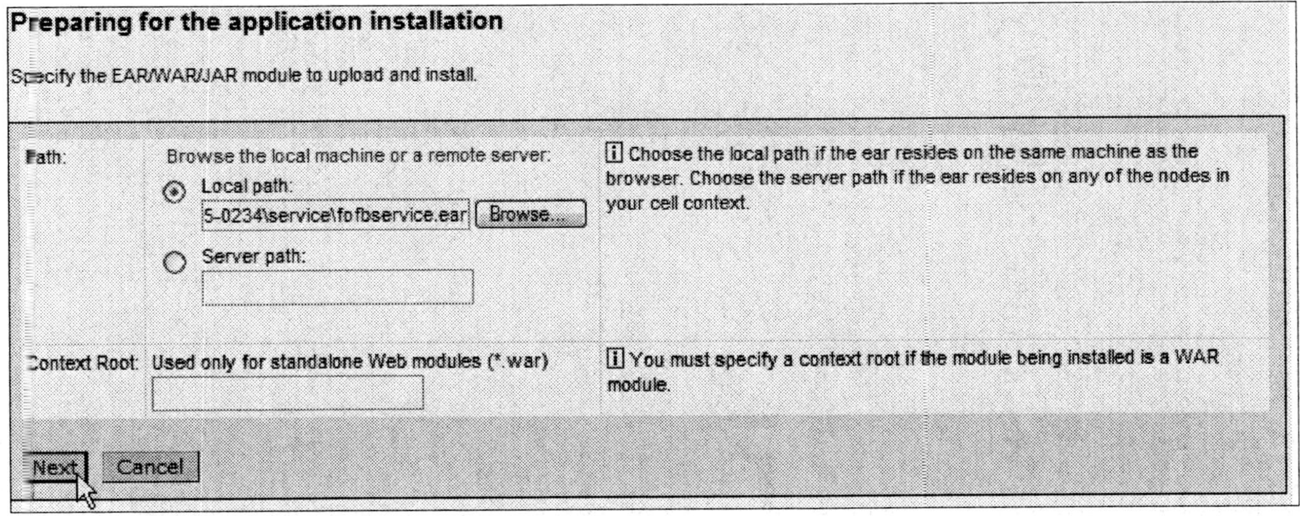

Figure 39-8 GMU server installation - selecting the installation file

5. For the next few panels displayed, click **Next** (see Figure 39-9 on page 594 through Figure 39-12 on page 595).

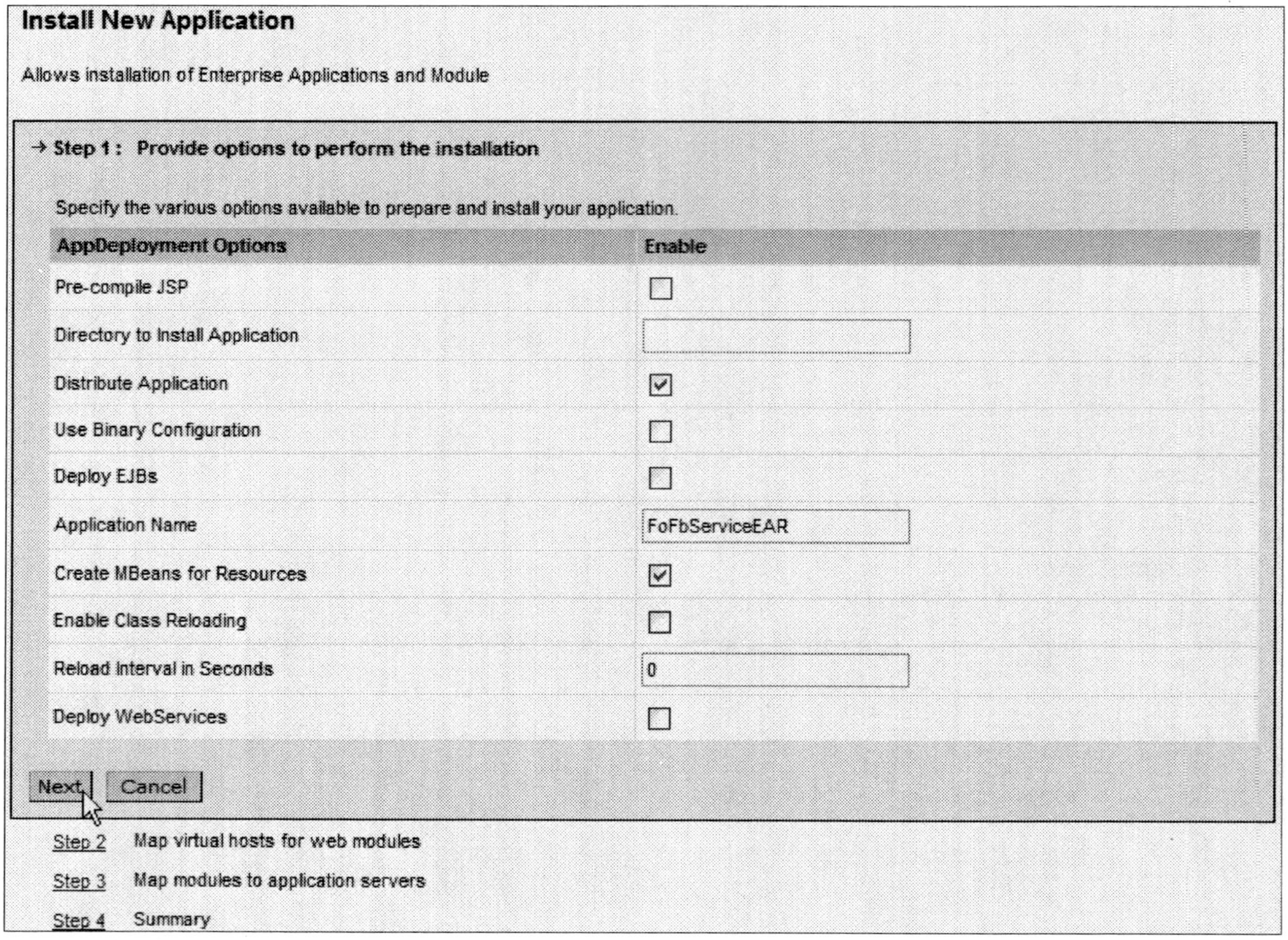

Install New Application

Allows installation of Enterprise Applications and Module

→ **Step 1 : Provide options to perform the installation**

Specify the various options available to prepare and install your application.

AppDeployment Options	Enable
Pre-compile JSP	☐
Directory to Install Application	
Distribute Application	☑
Use Binary Configuration	☐
Deploy EJBs	☐
Application Name	FoFbServiceEAR
Create MBeans for Resources	☑
Enable Class Reloading	☐
Reload Interval in Seconds	0
Deploy WebServices	☐

Next | Cancel

Step 2 Map virtual hosts for web modules

Step 3 Map modules to application servers

Step 4 Summary

Figure 39-9 GMU server installation -step 1-A

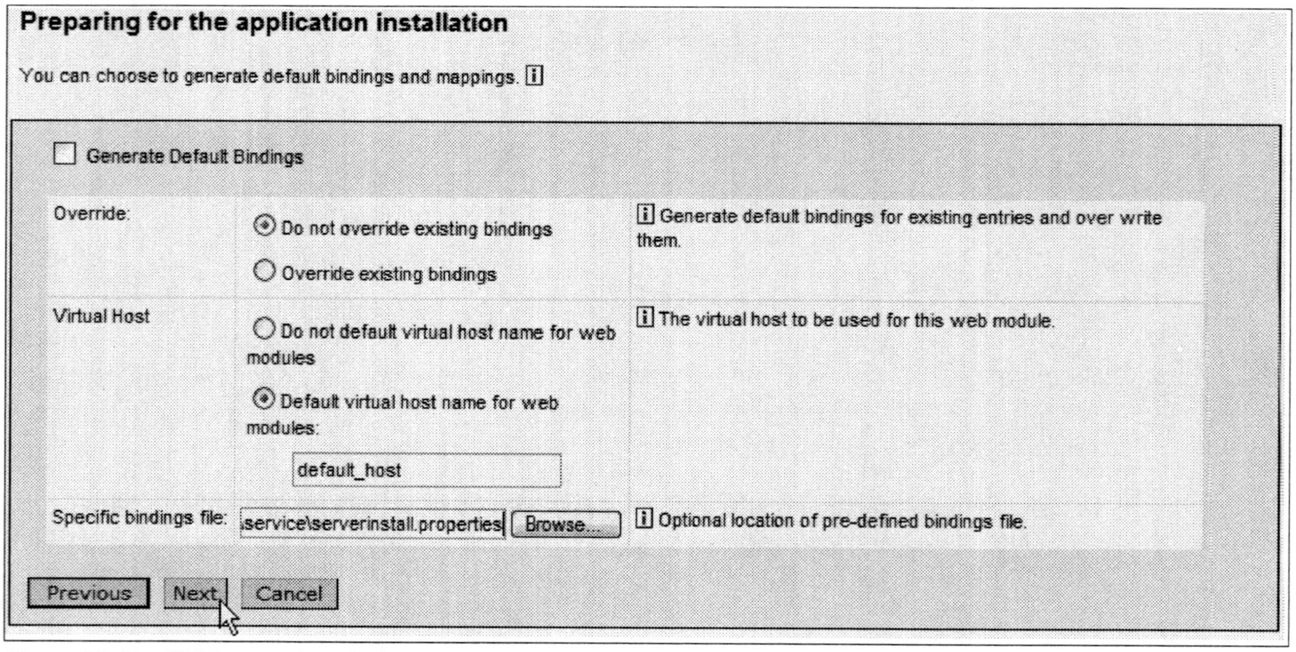

Preparing for the application installation

You can choose to generate default bindings and mappings.

☐ Generate Default Bindings

Override:	◉ Do not override existing bindings ○ Override existing bindings	Generate default bindings for existing entries and over write them.
Virtual Host	○ Do not default virtual host name for web modules ◉ Default virtual host name for web modules: default_host	The virtual host to be used for this web module.
Specific bindings file:	service\serverinstall.properties Browse...	Optional location of pre-defined bindings file.

Previous | Next | Cancel

Figure 39-10 GMU server installation - step 1-B

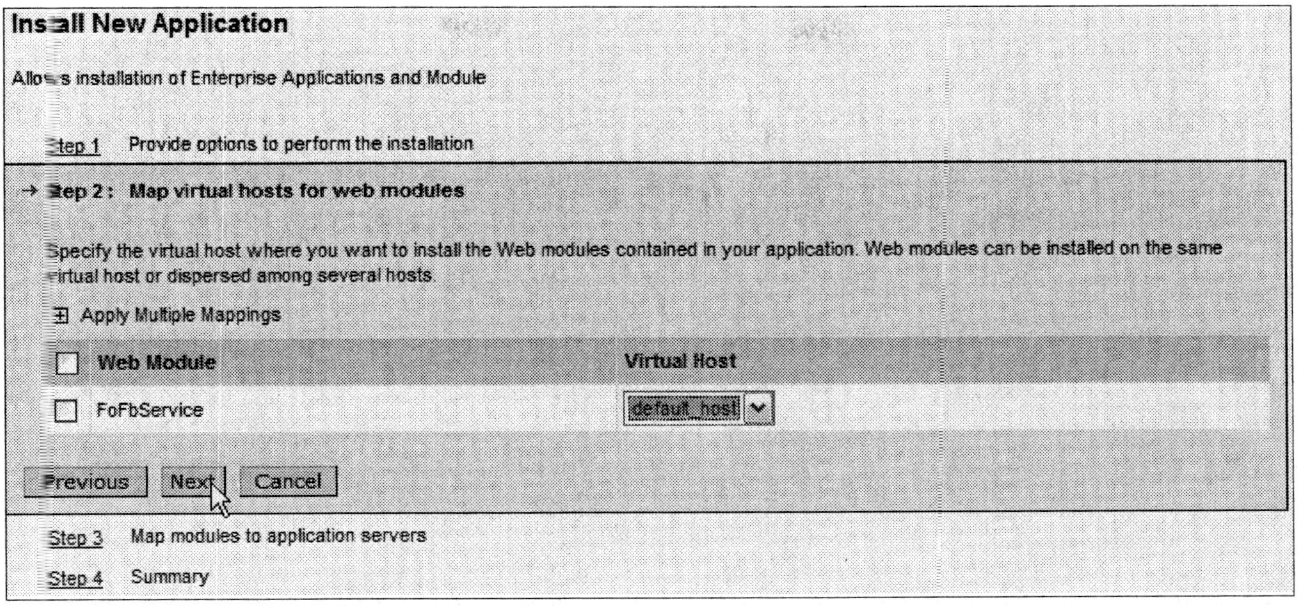

Install New Application

Allows installation of Enterprise Applications and Module

Step 1 Provide options to perform the installation

→ Step 2 : Map virtual hosts for web modules

Specify the virtual host where you want to install the Web modules contained in your application. Web modules can be installed on the same virtual host or dispersed among several hosts.

⊞ Apply Multiple Mappings

☐ Web Module	Virtual Host
☐ FoFbService	default_host

Previous Next Cancel

Step 3 Map modules to application servers

Step 4 Summary

Figure 39-11 GMU server installation - step 2

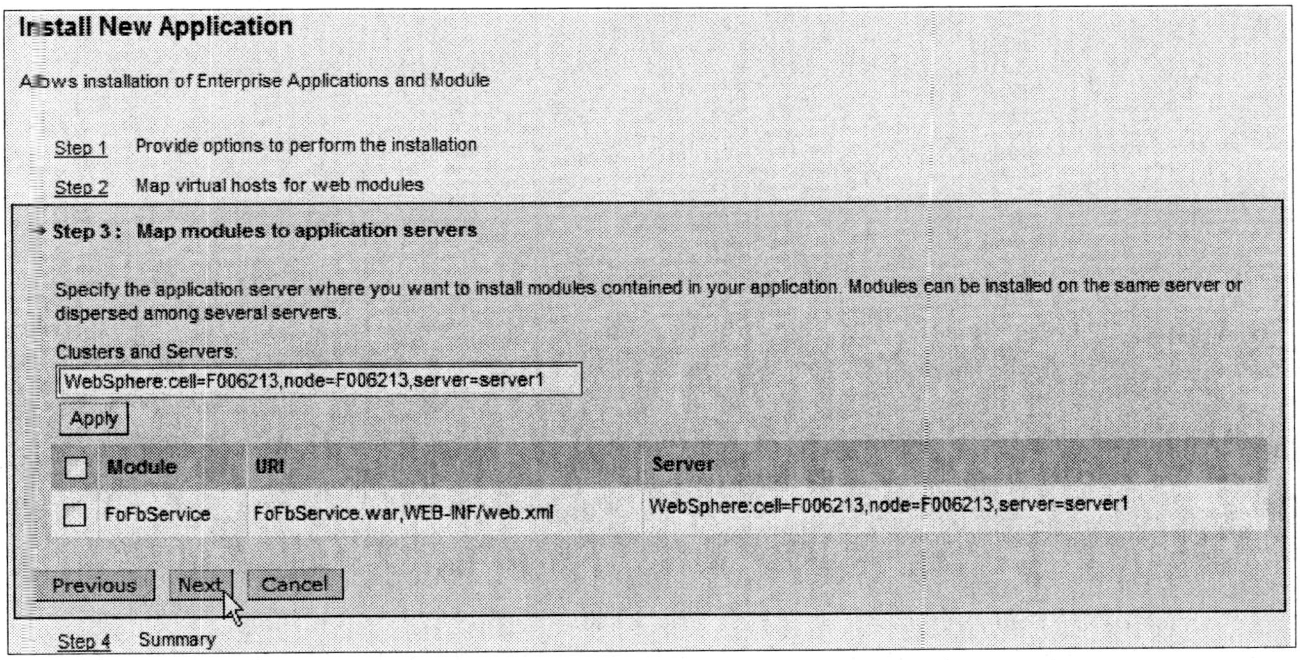

Install New Application

Allows installation of Enterprise Applications and Module

Step 1 Provide options to perform the installation

Step 2 Map virtual hosts for web modules

→ Step 3 : Map modules to application servers

Specify the application server where you want to install modules contained in your application. Modules can be installed on the same server or dispersed among several servers.

Clusters and Servers:

WebSphere:cell=F006213,node=F006213,server=server1

Apply

☐ Module	URI	Server
☐ FoFbService	FoFbService.war,WEB-INF/web.xml	WebSphere:cell=F006213,node=F006213,server=server1

Previous Next Cancel

Step 4 Summary

Figure 39-12 GMU server installation - step 3

6. For the last panel of the installation wizard, click **Finish** (see Figure 39-13).

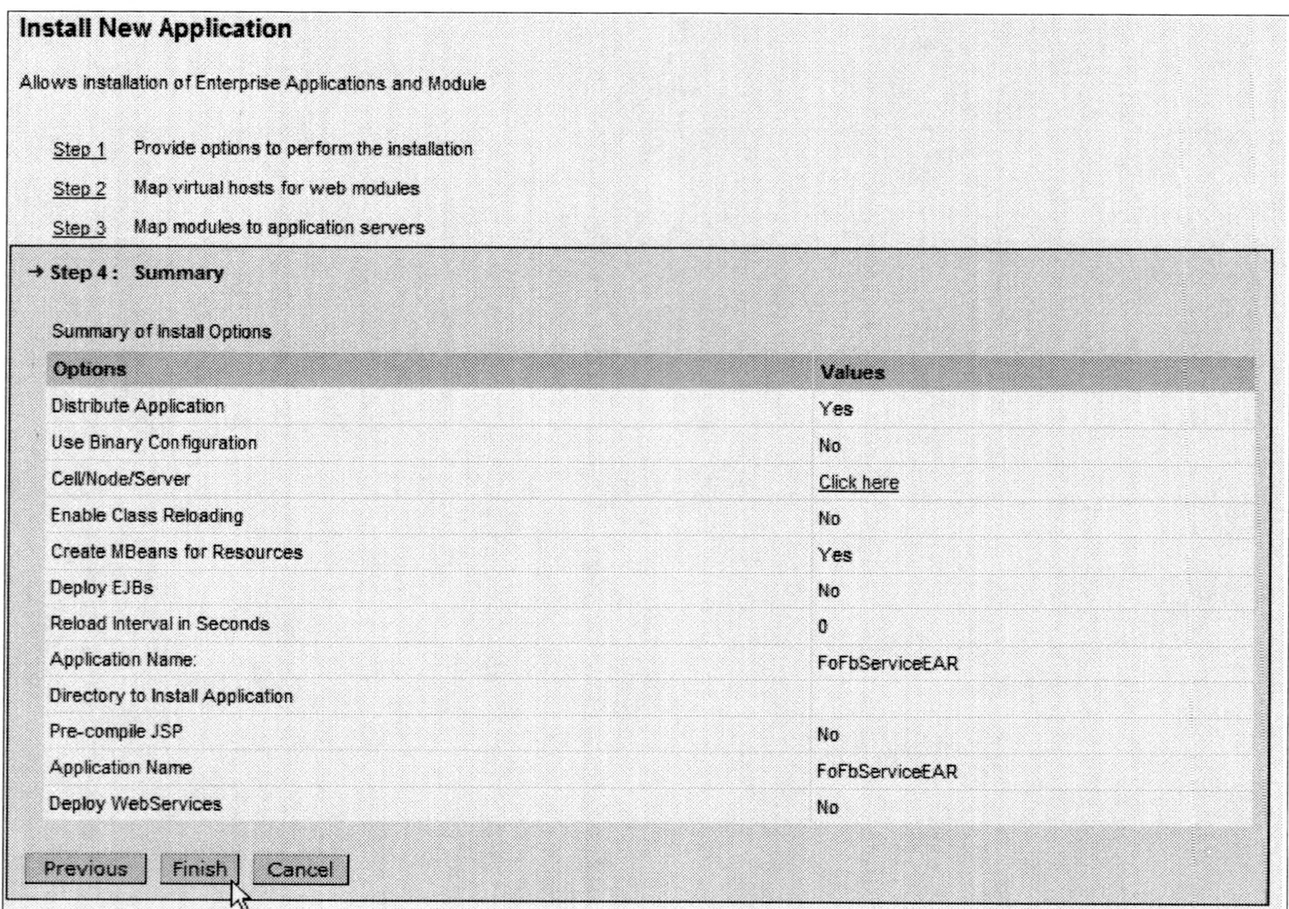

Figure 39-13 GMU server installation - step 4

7. If the installation process was successful, you should have the following panel: Figure 39-14. Click the link **Save to Master Configuration**.

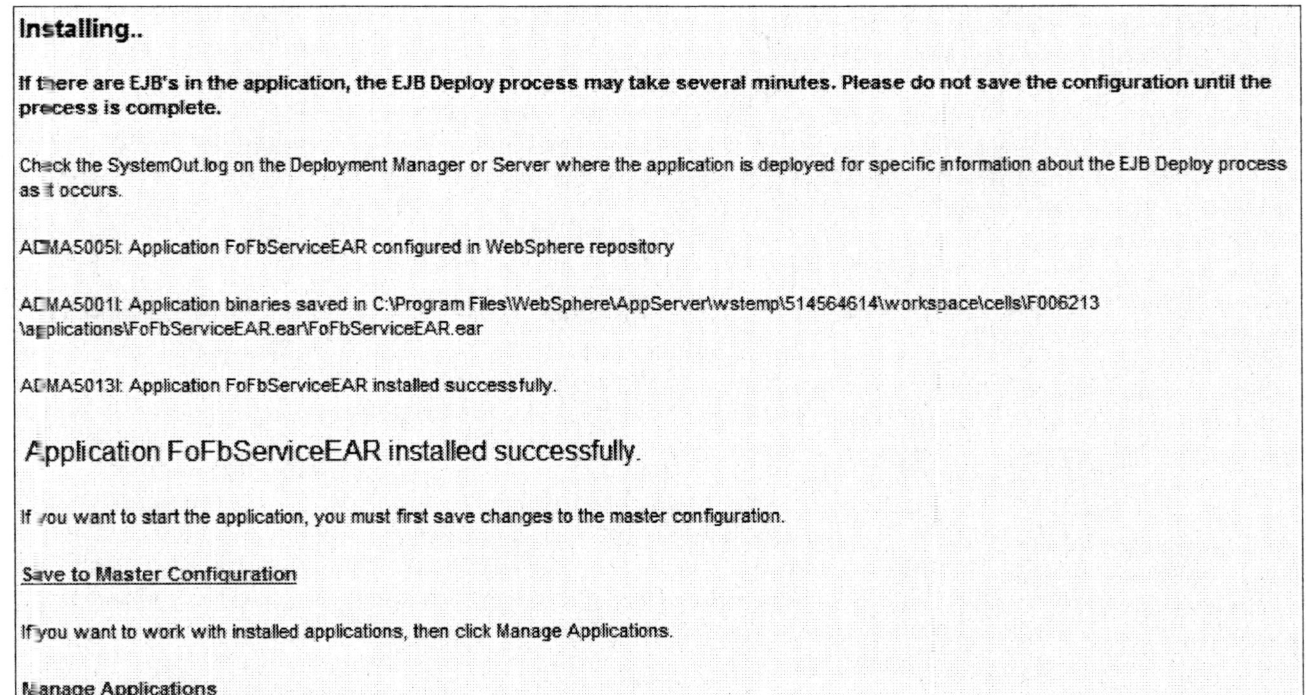

Figure 39-14 GMU server installation - wizard result

8. Click **Save**. See Figure 39-15.

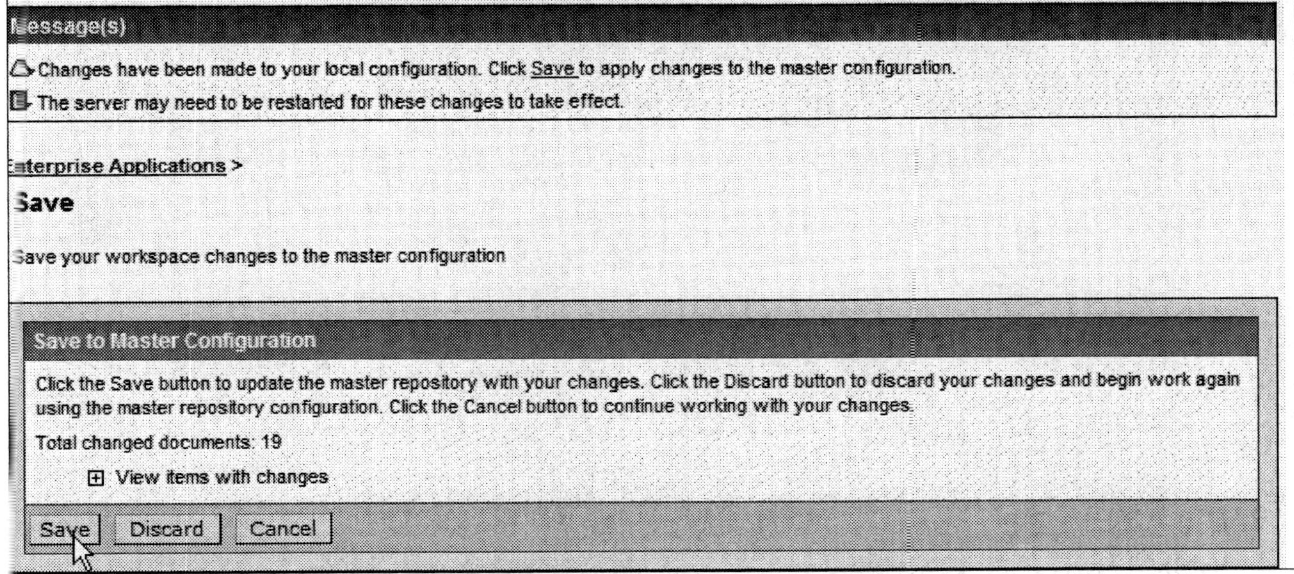

Figure 39-15 GMU server installation - save WebSphere Application Server configuration

9. Restart WebSphere Application Server service after the installation is completed.

39.6 Server configuration procedure

In this section we describe the various configuration components of this solution.

39.6.1 Global Mirror session configuration file

Create your configuration files (or restore them if it is an update of GMU and your configuration files were backed up). A name other than *config* may be used for this file based on the user's preference. All configuration files must reside on the WebSphere Application Server in the directory:

```
WAS_HOME\installedApps\NODE_NAME\FoFbServiceEAR.ear\FoFbService.war\WEB-INF\niconf
```

The base version of GMU can support up to 8 disks subsystems. GMU is able to support for disks subsystems with a special service offering contract. As far as ESS is concerned, the base version of GMU will support one CopyServices domain. GMU is able to support more than one Copy Services domain with a special service offering contract.

For ESSs, a primary and a backup Copy Services server is required with its notion of domain. In order to support multiple ESS domain applications, there is a need to create one *config.xml* file for each domain. The name of the config file for each domain needs to be unique. There are some domain configurations that may contain only the source ESSs, and other domains may contain only PPRC target ESSs, and some may contain both, so the naming convention for the configuration XML file for multiple ESS domains implementation may be as follows:

- XML file used for source domain should be named with "_S". (i.e. config_S.xml).
- XML file used for target domain should be named with "_T". (i.e. config_T.xml).
- XML file used for both source and target domains, there is no need to add any S or T indications.

For DS6000 and DS8000 the notion of Copy Services servers and domains does not exist because each DS Storage Manager SMC for DS6000 and HMC for DS8000 can handle Copy Services. In order to configure GMU we need to create one configuration file for the DS boxes on site A and another identical configuration file on site B.

- XML file used for source DS boxes should be named with "_S". (See Example 39-1).
- XML file used for target DS boxes should be named with "_T". (See Example 39-2).

Note: The two configuration files in Example 39-1 and Example 39-2 happen to look identical because the A site to B site relationship is symmetrical. However, note that in other cases, if the relationship is not symmetrical, where there are multiple A site boxes with PPRC control path relationships and multiple B site boxes, then the configurations files won't be identical.

Example 39-1 Sample DS8000 source configuration file configA2B_S.xml (2 site solution)

```
<!--
This file is the async configuration file that satisfy sections 5.a and 5.c of
"Thresher Shark Asynchronous PPRC FO/FB Session Manager Design Specifications"
-->
<asyncpprc>
<!--
This section of the file defines the sharks that will be used in this AsyncPPRC
session.  The only _REQUIRED_ attributes are the wwnn and sequence attributes.
Possible Attributes:
wwnn     - #REQUIRED  - the World Wide Node Name
sequence - #REQUIRED  - the sequence number of the shark
type     - (Optional) - the machine type of the shark.  Default = Unknown
```

```
model     - (Optional) - the model of the shark. Default = Unknown
pom       - (Optional) - the place of manufacture of the shark. Default = Unknown
-->
<boxes>
<ess wwnn="5005076303FFC0B7" sequence="06551">
<lss num="0x065" ssid="0000"/>
</ess>
<ess wwnn="5005076303FFC426" sequence="73731">
<lss num="0x065" ssid="0000"/>
</ess>
</boxes>
<pprcpaths>
<path source="06551:0x065" target="73731:0x065">
<said source="0032" target="0240" />
<said source="0101" target="0110" />
</path>
</pprcpaths>
<!--
This section is designed to satisfy section 5.c of the previously mentioned doc.
All interval units are seconds.
-->
<session id="01" cginterval="30" maxdraintime="240" maxcoordinterval="75">
<master lss="06551:0x065"/>
</session>
<!--
This section is designed to satisfy section 5.a of the previously mentioned doc.
Ugly as it is, to avoid a large, tedious datafile, each volume identifier in the
relationship
tags below is formatted as follows:
"ess_alias:lss_num(hex):vol_num" (Single Volume)
"ess_alias:lss_num(hex):vol_numS-vol_numE" (Range of Volumes)
"ess_alias:lss_num(hex):**" (Entire LSS)
Where ess_alias is defined above in the ess definition, lss_num is the number of the lss,
and
vol_num is the number of volume within the LSS
-->
<volumes>
<!--
****
**** Test this approach of volume range which will be most adopted by users ****
****
-->
<relationship avol="06551:0x065:000-001" bvol="73731:0x065:000-001"
cvol="73731:0x065:002-003" />
</volumes>
</asyncpprc>
```

Example 39-2 Sample DS8000 target configuration file configA2B_T.xml (2 site solution)

```
<!--
This file is the async configuration file that satisfy sections 5.a and 5.c of
"Thresher Shark Asynchronous PPRC FO/FB Session Manager Design Specifications"
-->
<asyncpprc>
<!--
This section of the file defines the sharks that will be used in this AsyncPPRC
session.  The only _REQUIRED_ attributes are the wwnn and sequence attributes.
Possible Attributes:
wwnn     - #REQUIRED  - the World Wide Node Name
sequence - #REQUIRED  - the sequence number of the shark
```

```
type      - (Optional) - the machine type of the shark.  Default = Unknown
model     - (Optional) - the model of the shark. Default = Unknown
pom       - (Optional) - the place of manufacture of the shark. Default = Unknown
-->
<boxes>
<ess wwnn="5005076303FFC0B7" sequence="06551">
<lss num="0x065" ssid="0000"/>
</ess>
<ess wwnn="5005076303FFC426" sequence="73731">
<lss num="0x065" ssid="0000"/>
</ess>
</boxes>
<pprcpaths>
<path source="06551:0x065" target="73731:0x065">
<said source="0032" target="0240" />
<said source="0101" target="0110" />
</path>
</pprcpaths>
<!--
This section is designed to satisfy section 5.c of the previously mentioned doc.
All interval units are seconds.
-->
<session id="01" cginterval="30" maxdraintime="240" maxcoordinterval="75">
<master lss="06551:0x065"/>
</session>
<!--
This section is designed to satisfy section 5.a of the previously mentioned doc.
Ugly as it is, to avoid a large, tedious datafile, each volume identifier in the
relationship
tags below is formatted as follows:
"ess_alias:lss_num(hex):vol_num" (Single Volume)
"ess_alias:lss_num(hex):vol_numS-vol_numE" (Range of Volumes)
"ess_alias:lss_num(hex):**" (Entire LSS)
Where ess_alias is defined above in the ess definition, lss_num is the number of the lss,
and
vol_num is the number of volume within the LSS
-->
<volumes>
<!--
****
**** Test this approach of volume range which will be most adopted by users ****
****
-->
<relationship avol="06551:0x065:000-001" bvol="73731:0x065:000-001"
cvol="73731:0x065:002-003" />
</volumes>
</asyncpprc>
```

Sample files are also provided in the CD with multi-disk subsystem topologies.

39.6.2 Global Mirror session security file

Create your security files (or restore them if it is an update of GMU and your security files were backed up). All configuration files must reside on the WebSphere Application Server in the directory:

```
WAS_HOME\installedApps\NODE_NAME\FoFbServiceEAR.ear\FoFbService.war\WEB-INF\niconf
```

This file contains the access information of the CopyServices Server (ESS800) or the DS Storage Manager Servers for DS6000 (SMC) and DS8000 (HMC).

For DS6000 and DS8000, two security files need to be created, one configured for the site A (see Example 39-3) and one configured for the site B (see Example 39-4).

For ESS800, put in the security file both the Primary and Backup Copy Services Servers' user ID and password and the server name to match the configuration (see Example 39-5).

The security file name needs to be the same as the configuration file name in the multiple domain implementations because there are multiple security files. So if the config.xml file name happens to be *config.xml,* then the corresponding security file is *config.txt*.

Example 39-3 Sample DS8000 source security file configA2B_S.txt

```
servera.username=admin
servera.password=passw0rd
servera.server=xxx.yyy.zzz.xxx
```

Example 39-4 Sample DS8000 source security file configA2B_T.txt

```
servera.username=admin
servera.password=passw0rd
servera.server=xxx.yyy.zzz.yyy
```

Example 39-5 Sample ESS source security file configA2B.txt

```
ervera.username=admin
servera.password=passw0rd
servera.server=xxx.yyy.zzz.xxx
erverb.username=admin
serverb.password=passw0rd
serverb.server=xxx.yyy.zzz.xxx
```

Sample files are also provided in the CD.

39.6.3 GMU logs

The GMU server log file *FoFbService.log* resides in the directory:

```
WAS_HOME\installedApps\NODE_NAME\FoFbServiceEAR.ear\FoFbService.war\WEB-INF\logs\
```

Edit the properties file *fofbServer.properties* (see Example 39-6) in the directory:

```
\WAS_HOME\installedApps\NODE_NAME\FoFbServiceEAR.ear\FoFbService.war\WEB-INF\conf\
```

Also make sure the path for *FoFbService.log* is correct for the variable: log4j.appender.dest2.File.

Example 39-6 fofbServer.properties sample file

```
########## This is FOFB Server project properties file##################
#######################################################
#WebService Authenticaiton
#######################################################
fofbservice.username=admin
fofbservice.password=passw0rd
########################################################
# log4j properties
########################################################
log4j.rootCategory=DEBUG, dest1, dest2
#First Appender writes to the Console
log4j.appender.dest1=org.apache.log4j.ConsoleAppender
log4j.appender.dest1.layout=org.apache.log4j.PatternLayout
log4j.appender.dest1.layout.ConversionPattern=%-5p:  %m%n
#Second Appender writes to the file
log4j.appender.dest2=org.apache.log4j.DailyRollingFileAppender
log4j.appender.dest2.File=D:/IBM/WebSphere/logs/FoFbService.log
#log4j.appender.dest2.MaxFileSize=100KB
#log4j.appender.dest2.MaxBackupIndex=1
log4j.appender.dest2.layout=org.apache.log4j.PatternLayout
log4j.appender.dest2.layout.ConversionPattern=%d{date} %-5p: %r  %m%n
```

The WebSphere Application Server *systemout.log* also includes all the entries in the *FoFbService.log*. The *systemout.log* setting is default and user does not need to do anything. This log is in the directory *WAS_HOME\logs\server1*.

39.7 Client installation procedure

In this section we describe how to install GMU using the command line method.

Prerequisites

- Java2 Runtime Environment, Standard Edition (version 1.3.1).
- Set JAVA_HOME to Java 1.3.1:
  a. On the Desktop, right click **My Computer** and select **Properties**.
  b. Click **Advanced Tab** and click **Environment Variables**.
  c. Scroll down the **System Variables** to check if there already is a variable named *JAVA_HOME*. Edit it and make sure it points to the correct *JAVA_HOME*.
  d. *JAVA_HOME* can also be set up through the command line.
  e. Run **set JAVA_HOME=c:\<your jdk1.3.1 folder>**, and then verify that the correct variable is set by issuing **echo %JAVA_HOME**.

To download the Java2 Runtime Environment, Standard Edition (version 1.3.1), go the URL:

http://java.sun.com/j2se/1.3/download.html

During the installation process, click **Yes** to agree to the license agreement. Choose your destination folder for the installation.

Note: To avoid muddling your already installed Java 2 Runtime Environments from newer versions, do *not* select any browser as indicated in Figure 39-16.

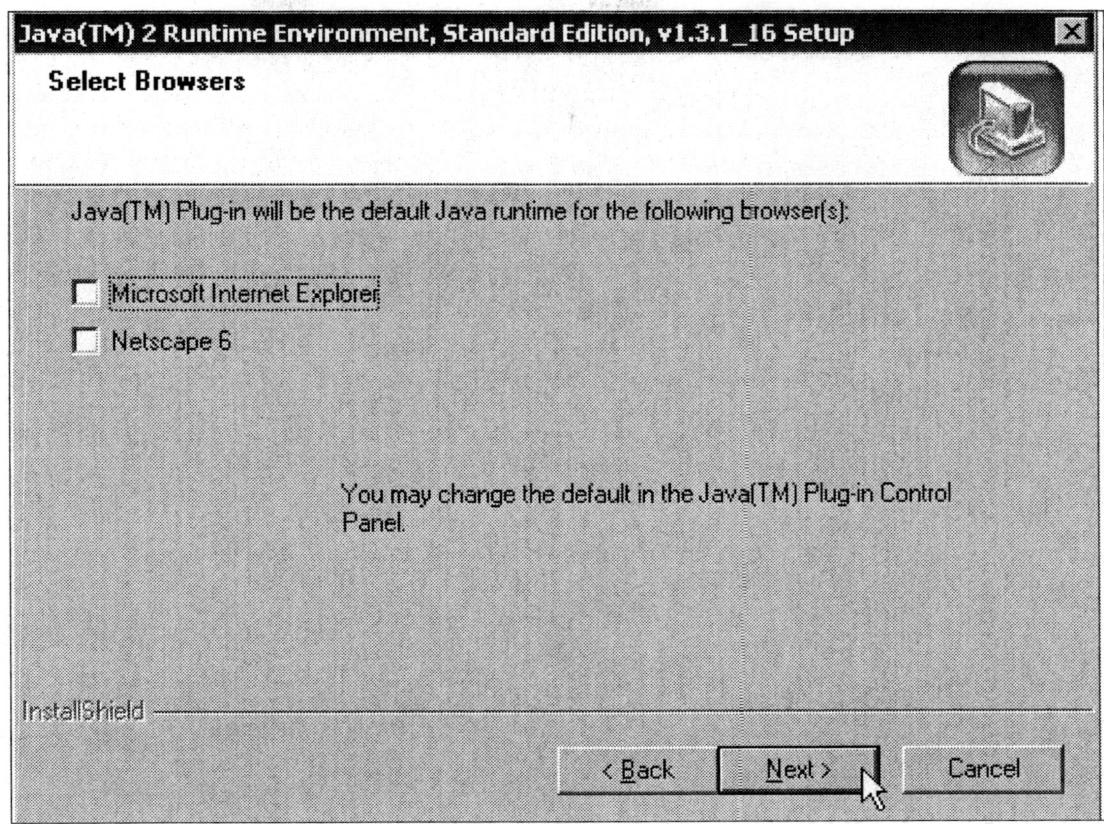

Figure 39-16 Java2 Runtime Environment Select Browsers

Installation

Here are the steps:

1. Copy the client folder to a local folder.
2. Open a command window and navigate to the client folder.
3. Open the file *clientsetup.bat* and make sure that the drive is the same as the local drive (see Example 39-7).

Example 39-7 clientsetup.bat

```
@echo off
REM ############################################
REM #File for setting up the client environment
REM ############################################
REM #Making the client directory
mkdir c:\FoFbClient
REM #copying the jarfile to the client directory
copy client.jar c:\FoFbClient
REM go to the client directory
cd c:\FoFbClient
REM #unjar the jar file for client setup
jar -xvf client.jar
REM #delete the jar file as it is no longer needed
del client.jar
```

4. Run **clientsetup** from the command window. This will extract the contents from *client.jar* and put them into the *<localdrive>:\FoFbClient* folder. If it does not work, you can use any application capable of opening a ZIP or TAR file to extract the content of the *client.jar* file.
5. Navigate to the *<localdrive>:\FoFbClient* folder where the following sub folders were extracted: *bin*, *lib*, *conf*, and *logs*.
6. Navigate to the *bin* sub-directory and open the file *runfofb.bat*.(see Example 39-8).Change the settings of the local drive and add a line to set the JAVA_HOME to the directory where you installed the Java2 Runtime 1.3.1 (by default it is in the directory *c:\Program Files\javasoft\jre\...)*, then save the file.

Example 39-8 Sample fofbclient.bat

```
@echo off
set JAVA_HOME=c:\progra~1\javasoft\jre\1.3.1_16
if "%JAVA_HOME%" == "" goto NoHome
set FOFB_HOME=..
set OLD_CLASSPATH=%classpath%
echo ========================================================================
echo Using JAVA_HOME:       %JAVA_HOME%
echo Using FOFB_HOME:       .
echo ========================================================================
rem if not exist "%FOFB_HOME%\lib" goto NoLib
set FOFB_CLASSPATH=%FOFB_HOME%/lib/commons-discovery.jar;
set FOFB_CLASSPATH=%FOFB_CLASSPATH%;%FOFB_HOME%/lib/commons-logging.jar
set FOFB_CLASSPATH=%FOFB_CLASSPATH%;%FOFB_HOME%/lib/fofbclient.jar
set FOFB_CLASSPATH=%FOFB_CLASSPATH%;%FOFB_HOME%/lib/j2ee.jar
set FOFB_CLASSPATH=%FOFB_CLASSPATH%;%FOFB_HOME%/lib/log4j-1.2.8.jar
set FOFB_CLASSPATH=%FOFB_CLASSPATH%;%FOFB_HOME%/lib/mailapi.jar
set FOFB_CLASSPATH=%FOFB_CLASSPATH%;%FOFB_HOME%/lib/qname.jar
set FOFB_CLASSPATH=%FOFB_CLASSPATH%;%FOFB_HOME%/lib/ras.jar
set FOFB_CLASSPATH=%FOFB_CLASSPATH%;%FOFB_HOME%/lib/soap.jar
set FOFB_CLASSPATH=%FOFB_CLASSPATH%;%FOFB_HOME%/lib/webservices.jar
set FOFB_CLASSPATH=%FOFB_CLASSPATH%;%FOFB_HOME%/lib/wsdl4j.jar
set FOFB_CLASSPATH=%FOFB_CLASSPATH%;%FOFB_HOME%/lib/wsexception.jar
set FOFB_CLASSPATH=%FOFB_CLASSPATH%;%FOFB_HOME%/lib/xercesImpl.jar
set classpath=%FOFB_CLASSPATH%;
"%JAVA_HOME%\bin\Java" com.ibm.storage.ess.fofb.client.FoFbClient %*
@echo off
goto END
:NoLib
ECHO ""
#ECHO "%FOFB_HOME%\lib" directory required with all necessary libraries (fofb) in it.
goto END
:NoHome
ECHO ""
ECHO Please set the JAVA_HOME environment variable to the root java installation folder
this command.
:END
set classpath=%OLD_CLASSPATH%
```

7. In the *conf* sub-folder, change the following variables in the *fofbclient.properties* file (see Example 39-9):
   a. For the URL of the Web service in the variable *fofbservice.URL*, replace the *localhost* with the IP address of the WebSphere Application Server. Also change the port number if the application is listening at a different port.
   b. Indicate the location of the log file for the variable *log4j.appender.dest2.File*.

c. Specify the fully qualified domain name (For example, MCS6.sanjose.ibm.com) of the client workstation for the variable *client_logger_ip*.

d. For Web services authentication, make sure the *fofbservice.username* and *fofbservice.password* in the *fofbclient.properties* file is the same as those in the *fofbserver.properties* which resides on the server host (Example 39-6 on page 602).

e. The client log resides in FOFB_HOME\logs\fofbclient.log.

Example 39-9 Sample fofbclient.properties file

```
####################################################
#WebService Location
####################################################
fofbservice.URL=http://localhost:9080/FoFbService/services/FoFbService
####################################################
#WebService Authenticaiton
####################################################
fofbservice.username=admin
fofbservice.password=admin
####################################################
#Status Listener
####################################################
client_logger_ip=localhost
client_logger_port=9901
#####################################################
# log4j properties
#####################################################
log4j.rootCategory=INFO, dest1, dest2
#First Appender writes to the Console
log4j.appender.dest1=org.apache.log4j.ConsoleAppender
log4j.appender.dest1.layout=org.apache.log4j.PatternLayout
log4j.appender.dest1.layout.ConversionPattern=%d{DATE} %-5p:  %m%n
#Second Appender writes to the file
log4j.appender.dest2=org.apache.log4j.DailyRollingFileAppender
log4j.appender.dest2.File=c:/FoFbClient/logs/FoFbClient.log
#log4j.appender.dest2.MaxFileSize=100KB
#log4j.appender.dest2.MaxBackupIndex=1
log4j.appender.dest2.layout=org.apache.log4j.PatternLayout
log4j.appender.dest2.layout.ConversionPattern=%d{DATE} %-5p: %r %d %m%n
```

39.7.1 Commands

Every GMU command is internally composed of several Advanced Copy Services commands in the right sequence to execute Global Mirror tasks. It also has built in macro commands to test and practice your disaster recovery environment.

The commands are executed on the client as simple commands or they can be scripted alone or integrated in the already existing client's scripts. Use the **runfofb -help** command if you need any help.

The GMU tool queries and reports about Global Mirror operations status, but it does not provide volume status or Global Mirror session status information. You can use the ESS Web Copy Services GUI, or DS Storage Manager or DS CLI.

Syntax: runfofb.bat -c <command> -f <configuration files separated with a comma and no space>

The XML configuration file is required with all commands:

```
runfofb –c createsession –f config.xml
```

Or if there are multiple domains:

```
runfofb –c createsession –f config1.xml,config2.xml,config3.xml
```

There is no space before or after the comma. Remember, the config file for only PPRC source or target domains should have _S or _T as indicators:

```
runfofb –c createsession –f config1_S.xml,config2_S.xml,config3_T.xml,config5.xml
```

(This is a sample of a mix of source, target ESS domain, and an ESS domain which contains both.)

> **Note:** Also make sure you have the proper credentials setup in the file *FoFbClient.properties* and do not input the user ID and password, because the GMU client and server are taking care of the authentication.

The configuration file is required with all commands (but not with the command **help**). Depending on whether the source or the target or both source and target configuration files are required, you may have different combination of configuration files.

This is the list and a description of the currently available GMU commands:

- **runfofb.bat -c validate -f config_S.xml or config_T.xml**

  This is the first command to issue for any new Global Mirror session configuration file, to allow the user to verify the syntax and logical configuration of the XML file. This command reports status strings if any configuration error is found, and success or failure as a result of validation of the given configuration file.

- **runfofb.bat -c initialize -f config_S.xml,config_T.xml**

  This is the first command to issue before creating or starting a new Global Mirror session. All other commands, which are detailed below, should be issued after the successful completion of this command. This command should also be issued if the WebSphere Application Server or if the Copy Services Server is re-started. Before initializing a new Global Mirror session, use the validate command to validate the content of its configuration file. This command returns success/ failure.

- **runfofb.bat -c createsession -f config_S.xml,config_T.xml**

  This command creates a Global Mirror session with all its necessary components. The **createsession** command will perform the following steps automatically:

  a. Create PPRC paths between source A to target B.
  b. Create PPRC paths used for the control path.
  c. Create Global Copy pairs from A to B.
  d. Create FlashCopy pairs from B to C with the *record, persist* and *nocp* options.
  e. Create Global Mirror session.

  This command stops at any steps above which fail and lets the user fix the problem. When the command is re-issued, it will execute from the failed step until all the steps have been successfully completed. This command returns success/ failure of each step.

- **runfofb.bat -c startsession -f config_S.xml**

  This command starts a Global Mirror session. This command returns success/ failure.

- **runfofb.bat -c pausesession -f config_S.xml**

  This command pauses a Global Mirror session. This command returns success/ failure.

- **runfofb.bat -c terminatesession -f config_S.xml**

  This command removes a Global Mirror session. To force terminate a Global Mirror session. This command must be run before the **withdrawrelations** command or orphaned subordinates will remain. If it occurs, use ESS StorWatch Copy Services GUI or DS Storage Manager or Command-Line Interface (CLI) to remove the orphaned subordinates. This command returns success/ failure.

- **runfofb.bat -c resumesession -f config_S.xml**

  This command resumes a Global Mirror session. Make sure the session is paused before issuing the command. This command returns success/ failure.

- **runfofb.bat -c failover -f config_T.xml**

  This command provides the failover function for a Global Mirror session when the primary production site is down and it is necessary to switch production to the secondary site. The **failover** command performs the following steps automatically:

  a. Failover Global Copy to B volumes (B volumes are available in a suspended state and A volumes are still available for production, but there is no more replication between A and B).

  b. Recover to make B volumes consistent. It will query all B and C volumes to get a status of their FlashCopy relation and may or may not issue an additional command depending on the following statements. This is like using the **setflashrevertible** command of the DS CLI and then doing one of the scenarios developed above:

     i. If all FlashCopy pairs are Non-Revertible and their sequence numbers are equal, it means that the Consistency Group process is finished.

        There is no action required because the Consistency Group is intact on the C volumes.

     ii. If some FlashCopy pairs are revertible (and their sequence numbers are equal) and others are not revertible (and their sequence numbers are equal), it means that some FlashCopy pairs are running in a Consistency Group process and some have not started yet their Incremental process.

        To preserve the consistency, we need to overwrite new data with data saved at the last consistency formation for the FlashCopy pairs already in the new Consistency Group process. It is like using the **revertflash** command of the DS CLI.

     iii. If all FlashCopy pairs are Revertible and their sequence numbers are equal, it means that all the FlashCopy pairs are running in a Consistency Group process and none have finished there Incremental process.

        We need to overwrite new data with data saved at the last consistency formation for all the FlashCopy pairs. It is like using the **revertflash** command of the DS CLI.

     iv. If some FlashCopy pairs are revertible and at least one is not revertible, but all their sequence numbers are equal, it means that some FlashCopy pairs are running in a Consistency Group process and some have already finished their Incremental process.

        We need to commit data to a target volume to form a consistency between the source and target. Only the FlashCopy pairs which have not already finished their INcremental process will have to commit the changes since Non-Revertible pairs have already committed theirs. It is like using the **commitflash** command of the DS CLI. Using this command on FlashCopy pairs that are not revertible will only display error messages.

v. If none of the 4 above situations are possible, then the Consistency Group is corrupted.

> **Note:** When a Consistency Group is in progress, several Incremental FlashCopy process may be running. The Incremental FlashCopy process is looking at the the *Change Recording Bit Map* on B volumes and is comparing it with the *Target Bit Map* on the C volumes. When the Incremental Flash Copy is finished, the *Change Recording Bit Map* is cleared and therefore all the changes are committed on the C volumes. The corresponding FlashCopy pairs are now in a *Non-Revertible* state.

c. Create FlashCopy pairs from B to C volumes with Fast Reverse Restore, this step waits until the FlashCopy is complete and withdrawn and notify the user to mount the recovery B volumes and start I/O back the recovery hosts.

> **Note:** If this step is too long, GMU maybe hang because no event has reported back from ESSNI, you can use **Ctrl+C** to terminate this step and move to the next step.

d. Create FlashCopy pairs from B to C with the *record*, *persist*, and *nocp* options.

This command stops at any steps above which fail and lets the user fix the problem. When the command is re-issued, it will execute from the failed step until all the steps have been successfully completed. This command returns success/ failure of each step.

- **runfofb.bat -c failback -f config_S.xml,config_T.xml**

This command provides the failback functions for the Global Mirror session when the primary production site is up and the user needs to switch I/O back to the primary site from the recovery site. It will perform the following steps automatically:

a. Create PPRC paths from B to A.

b. Failback Global Copy from B to A (B is available in production and A is its read-only replication target).

> **Note:** This step will first query for the 1st pass OOS bitmap completion and then notify users to quiesce I/O on the recovery host, finally it will wait until the OOS bitmap is drained. If this step is too long, you can use the command **Ctrl+C** to terminate this step and move to the next step.

c. Create PPRC paths from A to B (if necessary).

d. Failover Global Copy pairs to A (A is available in a suspended state and B is still available in production, but there is no more replication between B and A).

e. Failback Global Copy pairs from A to B (A is available in production and B is its read-only replication target).

f. Create PPRC paths used for control path if (necessary).

This command stops at any steps above which fail and lets the user fix the problem. When the command is re-issued, it will execute from the failed step until all the steps have been successfully completed. This command returns success/ failure of each step.

After the **failback** is complete, issue **startsession** or **resumesesson** commands.

- **runfofb.bat -c practicefailover -f config_S.xml,config_T.xml**

  This command provides a Disaster Recovery readiness test. Before you issue the practicefailover command, issue the **pausesession** command and wait until the session is successfully paused. The **practicefailover** command will perform the following steps automatically:

  a. Remove FlashCopy pairs from B to D (if necessary).

  b. Failover Global Copy to B (B is available in a suspended state and A is still available for production, but there is no more replication between A and B).

  c. Create FlashCopy pairs from B to C with Fast Reverse Restore, this step waits until the FlashCopy completes and is withdrawn.

  d. Create FlashCopy pairs from B to C with the *record*, *persist*, and *nocp* options.

  e. Create FlashCopy pairs from B to D.

  This command will also stop at any steps above which fail and lets the user fix the problem. When the command is re-issued, it will execute from the failed step until all the steps have been successfully completed. This command returns success/ failure of each step.

  After the **practicefailover** is complete, wait for B->D FlashCopy to complete before issuing any other commands. Make the D copy available immediately for Disaster Recovery testing use.

- **runfofb.bat -c practicefailback -f config_S.xml,config_T.xml**

  After the successful completion of the command **practicefailover** and the end of the Disaster Recovery testing on the D volumes, issue this command to failback to A volumes.

  a. Failback Global Copy from A to B (A is available in production and B is its read-only replication target)

  After the **practicefailback** is complete, issue **startsession** or **resumesession** commands to restart the Global Mirror session and therefore form the next Consistency Group. This command returns success/ failure.

- **runfofb.bat -c withdrawrelations -f config_S.xml,config_T.xml**

  This command removes a Global Mirror session with all its related components. Issue the **terminatesession** command first before issuing this command so to not leave any orphan subordinates. If it occurs, use ESS StorWatch Copy Services GUI or DS Storage Manager or Command-Line Interface (CLI) to remove the orphaned subordinates. The **createsession** command will perform the following steps automatically:

  a. Remove Global Copy pairs from A to B.
  b. Remove Global Copy pairs from B to A.
  c. Remove FlashCopy pairs from B to C.
  d. Remove PPRC Paths from A to B.
  e. Remove PPRC Paths used for control path.
  f. Remove Global Mirror sessions.

  This command returns success/ failure of each step.

> **Note:** GMU is also taking an internal checkpoint on command execution, so in case of error, it can start the execution from the point of failure, taking care of the consistency of the process. The user can bypass all the internal error handling by issuing the **initialize** command, and the utility command will start from the beginning on every device.

Some command outputs are shown in Example 39-10.

Example 39-10 Samples GMU commands outputs

```
C:\FoFbClient\bin>runfofb.bat -c terminatesession -f configA2B_S.xml
=======================================================================
Using JAVA_HOME:       C:\Progra~1\JavaSoft\JRE\1.3.1_16
Using FOFB_HOME:       .
=======================================================================
08 Jul 2005 18:04:25,334 INFO :  Executing  : terminatesession
08 Jul 2005 18:04:27,638 INFO :  Domain[configA2B_S.xml]: Terminate(stop) AsyncPPRC Session
PASSED!
08 Jul 2005 18:04:27,878 INFO :  Execution Complete. Terminate session completed
successfuly!

C:\FoFbClient\bin>runfofb.bat -c withdrawrelations -f configA2B_S.xml,configA2B_T.xml
=======================================================================
Using JAVA_HOME:       C:\Progra~1\JavaSoft\JRE\1.3.1_16
Using FOFB_HOME:       .
=======================================================================
08 Jul 2005 18:04:58,372 INFO :  Executing  : withdrawrelations
08 Jul 2005 18:05:00,796 INFO :  Domain[configA2B_S.xml]: Remove PPRCXD Pairs A->B PASSED!
08 Jul 2005 18:05:02,378 INFO :  Domain[configA2B_T.xml]: Remove PPRCXD Pairs B->A PASSED!
08 Jul 2005 18:05:06,514 INFO :  Domain[configA2B_T.xml]: Remove FC Pairs B->C PASSED!
08 Jul 2005 18:05:07,846 INFO :  Domain[configA2B_S.xml]: Remove PPRC DATA Paths A->B
PASSED!
08 Jul 2005 18:05:08,116 INFO :  Domain[configA2B_S.xml]: Remove PPRC CONTROL Paths A->B
PASSED!
08 Jul 2005 18:05:12,332 INFO :  Domain[configA2B_S.xml]: Remove AsyncSession PASSED!
08 Jul 2005 18:05:12,602 INFO :  Execution Complete. Withdraw relations completed
successfuly!
```

39.7.2 Some GMU scenarios

These are some examples of scenarios that can be managed by the GMU tool.

Create a Global Mirror session

To set up a Global Mirror session with the topology presented in Figure 39-17, use the following commands; see Example 39-11:

```
runfofb.bat -c validate -f configA2B_S.xml
runfofb.bat -c validate -f configA2B_T.xml
runfofb.bat -c initialize -f configA2B_S.xml,configA2B_T.xml
runfofb.bat -c createsession -f configA2B_S.xml
runfofb.bat -c startsession -f configA2B_S.xml
```

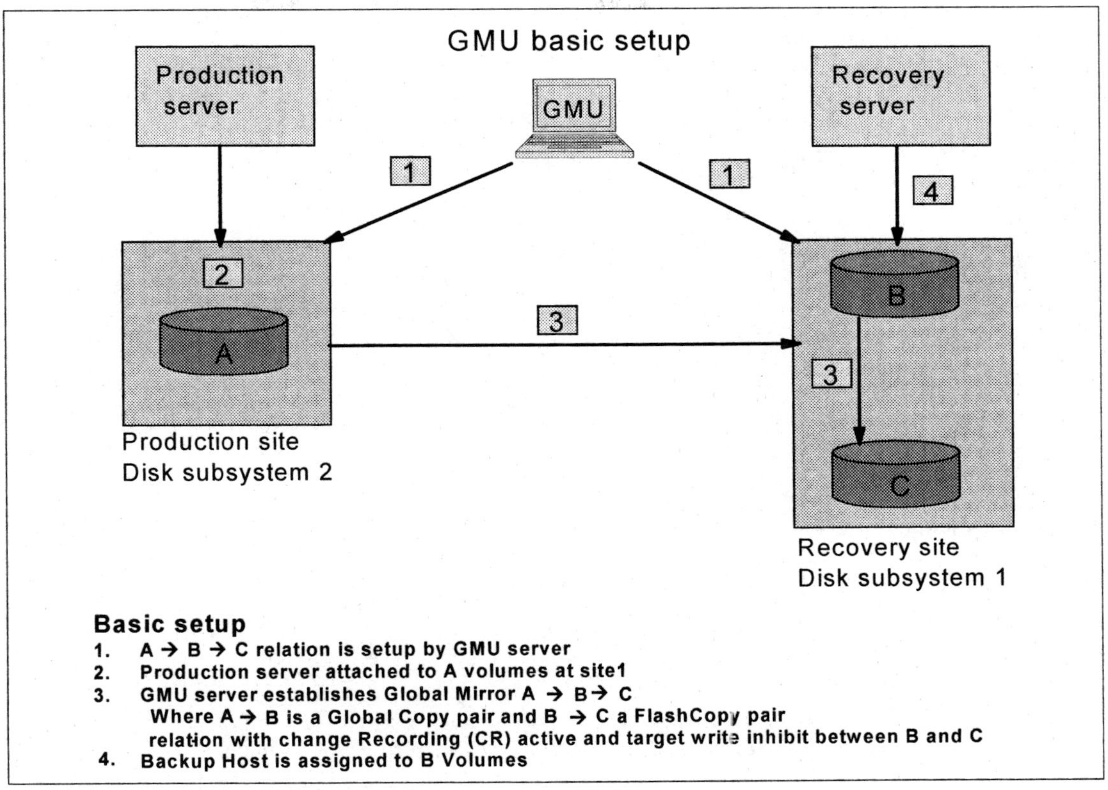

Figure 39-17 GMU Global Mirror setup

Example 39-11 Samples GMU commands outputs to create a Global Mirror session

```
C:\FoFbClient\bin>runfofb.bat -c initialize -f configA2B_S.xml,configA2B_T.xml
=====================================================================
Using JAVA_HOME:       C:\Program Files\JavaSoft\JRE\1.3.1_16
Using FOFB_HOME:       .
=====================================================================
14 Jun 2005 16:20:22,830 INFO :  Executing  : initialize
14 Jun 2005 16:20:23,111 INFO :  This command may take several minutes to complete. Please
wait...
14 Jun 2005 16:20:28,159 INFO :  A Username: admin
14 Jun 2005 16:20:28,159 INFO :  A Username: admin
14 Jun 2005 16:20:28,159 INFO :  A Password: passw0rd
14 Jun 2005 16:20:28,159 INFO :  Loading the library...
14 Jun 2005 16:20:28,174 INFO :        Loading library with information from Domain
served by server /xxx.yyy.zzz.xxx
14 Jun 2005 16:20:34,737 INFO :        Now running discover on Domain  served by server
/xxx.yyy.zzz.xxx
14 Jun 2005 16:21:02,408 INFO :        Finished running discover on Domain  served by
server /xxx.yyy.zzz.xxx
14 Jun 2005 16:21:02,408 INFO :        --- The library contains the following ESSes ---
14 Jun 2005 16:21:02,424 INFO :  IBM.2107-7506551
14 Jun 2005 16:21:02,424 INFO :        ---------------------------------------------
14 Jun 2005 16:21:02,939 INFO :  Done loading library.
14 Jun 2005 16:21:02,955 INFO :  A Username: admin
14 Jun 2005 16:21:02,971 INFO :  A Username: admin
14 Jun 2005 16:21:02,971 INFO :  A Password: passw0rd
14 Jun 2005 16:21:02,971 INFO :  Loading the library...
14 Jun 2005 16:21:02,971 INFO :        Loading library with information from Domain
served by server /xxx.yyy.zzz.yyy
```

```
14 Jun 2005 16:21:06,377 INFO :        Now running discover on Domain  served by server
/xxx.yyy.zzz.yyy
14 Jun 2005 16:21:21,486 INFO :        Finished running discover on Domain  served by
server /xxx.yyy.zzz.yyy
14 Jun 2005 16:21:21,486 INFO :        --- The library contains the following ESSes ---
14 Jun 2005 16:21:21,486 INFO :  IBM.2107-7506551
14 Jun 2005 16:21:21,486 INFO :  IBM.2107-7573731
14 Jun 2005 16:21:21,486 INFO :        ---------------------------------------------
14 Jun 2005 16:21:21,986 INFO :  Done loading library.
14 Jun 2005 16:21:22,002 INFO :  Intialize ANILibary completed!
14 Jun 2005 16:21:58,892 INFO :  Service Initialization was successful!
14 Jun 2005 16:21:58,892 INFO :  Intialize completed!
14 Jun 2005 16:21:59,938 INFO :  Execution Complete.

C:\FoFbClient\bin>runfofb.bat -c createsession -f configA2B_S.xml,configA2B_T.xml
=====================================================================
Using JAVA_HOME:       C:\Program Files\JavaSoft\JRE\1.3.1_16
Using FOFB_HOME:       .
=====================================================================
14 Jun 2005 16:45:00,483 INFO : Executing  : createsession
14 Jun 2005 16:45:26,345 INFO : Domain[configA2B_S.xml]: Create PPRC DATA paths A->B
PASSED!
14 Jun 2005 16:45:34,126 INFO : Domain[configA2B_S.xml]: Create PPRC CONTROL Paths
Master->Subordinate PASSED!
14 Jun 2005 16:45:42,407 INFO : Domain[configA2B_S.xml]: Create PPRCXD Pairs A->B PASSED!
14 Jun 2005 16:46:03,905 INFO : Domain[configA2B_T.xml]: Create FC Pairs B->C PASSED!
14 Jun 2005 16:46:15,216 INFO : Domain[configA2B_S.xml]: Create AsyncSession PASSED!
14 Jun 2005 16:46:16,397 INFO : Execution Complete. Create session completed successfuly!

C:\FoFbClient\bin>runfofb.bat -c startsession -f configA2B_S.xml
=====================================================================
Using JAVA_HOME:       C:\Program Files\JavaSoft\JRE\1.3.1_16
Using FOFB_HOME:       .
=====================================================================
14 Jun 2005 16:52:45,336 INFO : Executing  : startsession
14 Jun 2005 16:52:51,225 INFO : Domain[configA2B_S.xml]: Start Async PPRC Session PASSED!
14 Jun 2005 16:53:54,397 INFO : Execution Complete. Start session completed successfuly!

C:\FoFbClient\bin>runfofb.bat -c terminatesession -f configA2B_S.xml
=====================================================================
Using JAVA_HOME:       C:\Program Files\JavaSoft\JRE\1.3.1_16
Using FOFB_HOME:       .
=====================================================================
14 Jun 2005 17:01:09,697 INFO : Executing  : terminatesession
14 Jun 2005 17:01:16,077 INFO : Domain[configA2B_S.xml]: Terminate(stop) AsyncPPRC Session
PASSED!
14 Jun 2005 17:01:16,397 INFO : Execution Complete. Terminate session completed
successfuly!
```

Simulate a Disaster Recovery

To practice a Disaster Recovery Plan with GMU as presented in Figure 39-18, use the following commands, see Example 39-12:

```
runfofb.bat -c pausesession -f configA2B_S.xml
runfofb.bat -c practicefailover -f configA2B_S.xml,configA2B_T.xml
runfofb.bat -c practicefailback -f configA2B_S.xml,configA2B_T.xml
runfofb.bat -c startsession -f configA2B_S.xml
```

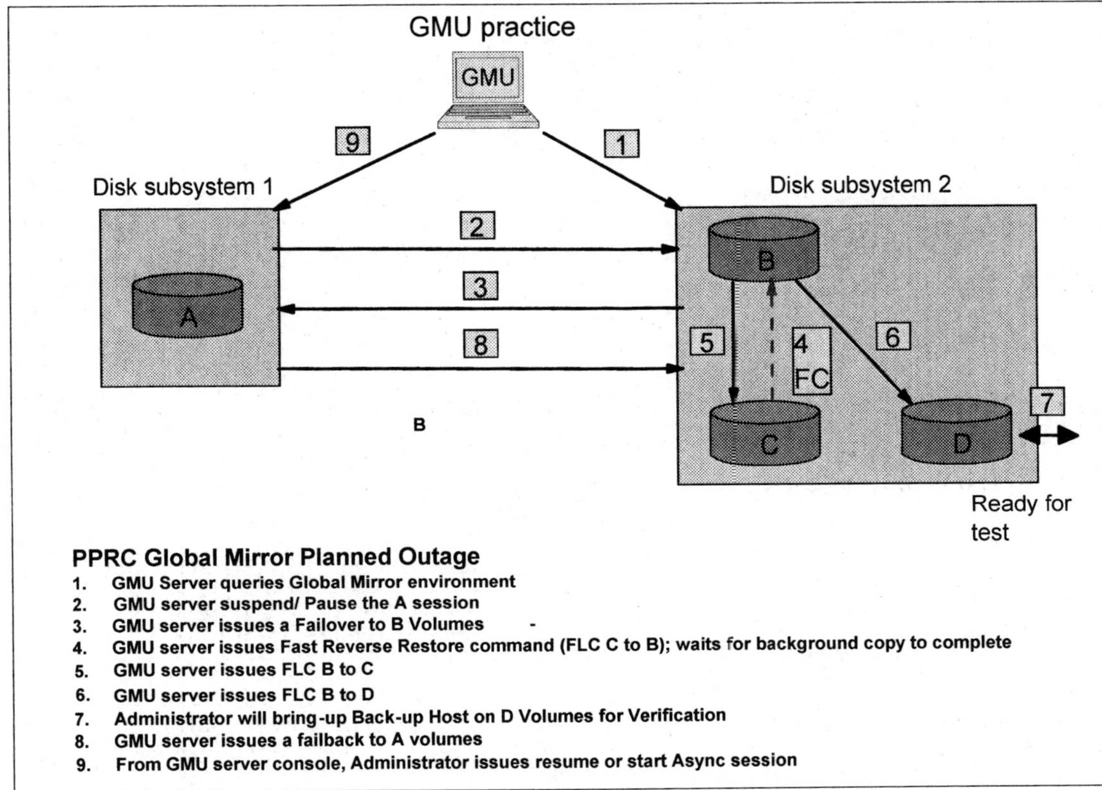

Figure 39-18 GMU Global Mirror test

Example 39-12 Samples GMU commands outputs to simulate a Disaster Recovery

```
C:\FoFbClient\bin>runfofb.bat -c pausesession -f configA2B_S.xml
=====================================================================
Using JAVA_HOME:       C:\Progra~1\JavaSoft\JRE\1.3.1_16
Using FOFB_HOME:       .
=====================================================================
08 Jul 2005 16:54:13,768 INFO :  Executing  : pausesession
08 Jul 2005 16:54:16,733 INFO :  Domain[configA2B_S.xml]: Pause Async PPRC Session command
issued
08 Jul 2005 16:54:16,733 INFO :  Domain[configA2B_S.xml]: Waiting For Pause event to
Complete...
08 Jul 2005 16:54:16,733 INFO :  Domain[configA2B_S.xml]: Pause COMPLETED!
08 Jul 2005 16:54:16,953 INFO :  Execution Complete. Pause session completed successfuly!

C:\FoFbClient\bin>runfofb.bat -c practicefailover -f configA2B_S.xml,configA2B_T.xml
=====================================================================
Using JAVA_HOME:       C:\Progra~1\JavaSoft\JRE\1.3.1_16
Using FOFB_HOME:       .
=====================================================================
08 Jul 2005 16:56:05,509 INFO :  Executing  : practicefailover
08 Jul 2005 16:56:08,203 INFO :  Domain[configA2B_T.xml]: Remove FC Pairs B->D PASSED!
08 Jul 2005 16:56:32,578 INFO :  Domain[configA2B_S.xml]: Suspend PPRC XD Pairs A->B Passed
08 Jul 2005 16:57:54,666 INFO :  Domain[configA2B_T.xml]: Create PPRCXD Pairs B->A Failover
PASSED!
08 Jul 2005 17:00:58,861 INFO :  Domain[configA2B_T.xml]: Create FC Pairs B->C FRR PASSED!
08 Jul 2005 17:00:58,861 INFO :  Domain[configA2B_T.xml]: Waiting for Background copy to
Complete...
08 Jul 2005 17:01:04,980 INFO :  Domain[configA2B_T.xml]: Background copy Completed!
08 Jul 2005 17:02:19,217 INFO :  Domain[configA2B_T.xml]: Create FC Pairs B->C PASSED!
08 Jul 2005 17:04:59,077 INFO :  Domain[configA2B_T.xml]: Create FC Pairs B->D PASSED!
08 Jul 2005 17:04:59,296 INFO :  Execution Complete. Practice Failover completed
successfuly!

C:\FoFbClient\bin>runfofb.bat -c practicefailback -f configA2B_S.xml,configA2B_T.xml
=====================================================================
Using JAVA_HOME:       C:\Progra~1\JavaSoft\JRE\1.3.1_16
Using FOFB_HOME:       .
=====================================================================
08 Jul 2005 17:08:01,549 INFO :  Executing  : practicefailback
08 Jul 2005 17:08:04,573 INFO :  Domain[configA2B_S.xml]: Create PPRCXD Pairs A->B Failback
PASSED!
08 Jul 2005 17:08:04,803 INFO :  Execution Complete. Practice Failback completed
successfuly!

C:\FoFbClient\bin>runfofb.bat -c resumesession -f configA2B_S.xml
=====================================================================
Using JAVA_HOME:       C:\Progra~1\JavaSoft\JRE\1.3.1_16
Using FOFB_HOME:       .
=====================================================================
08 Jul 2005 17:09:13,272 INFO :  Executing  : resumesession
08 Jul 2005 17:09:16,116 INFO :  Domain[configA2B_S.xml]: Resume AsyncPPRC Session Pairs
PASSED!
08 Jul 2005 17:09:16,376 INFO :  Execution Complete. Resume session completed successfuly!
```

Disaster Recovery Plan

To launch a real Disaster Recovery Plan with GMU where the production site is destroyed as presented in Figure 39-19, use the command:

```
runfofb.bat -c failover -f configA2B_S.xml,configA2B_T.xml
```

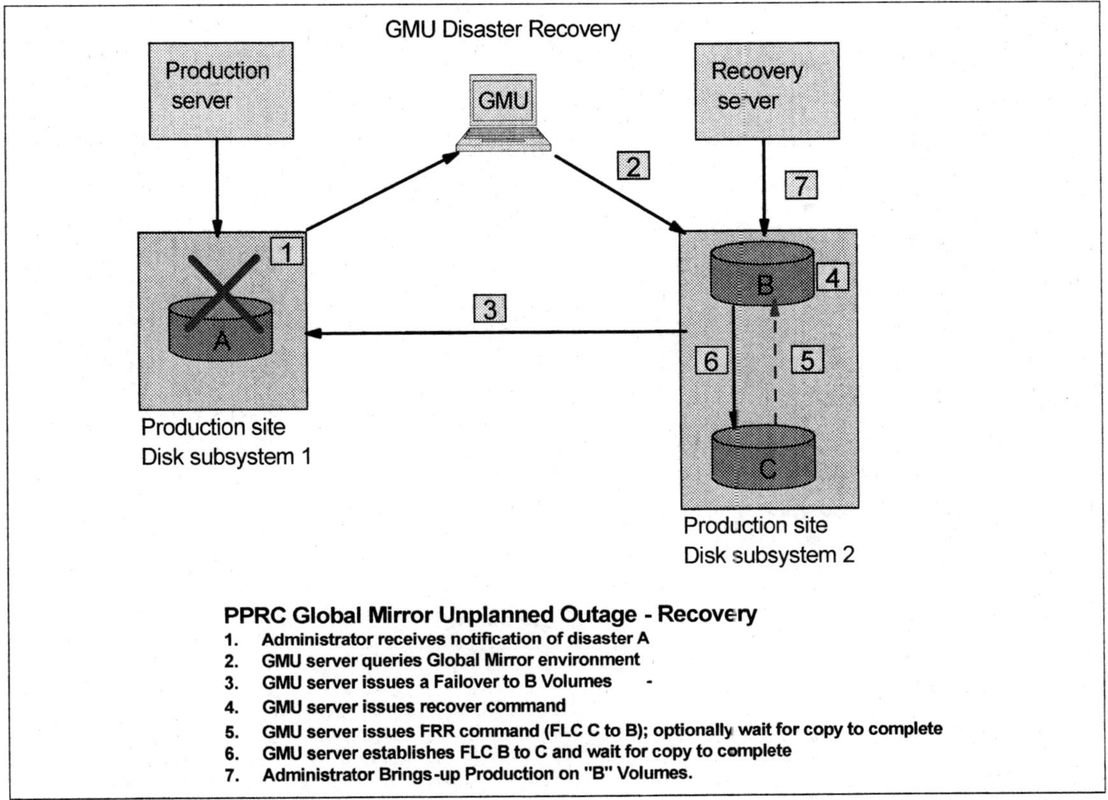

Figure 39-19 GMU Global Mirror disaster scenario

Then, when the production site is available again as presented in Figure 39-20, use the following commands in sequence:

```
runfofb.bat -c failback -f configA2B_S.xml,configA2B_T.xml
runfofb.bat -c startsession -f configA2B_S.xml
```

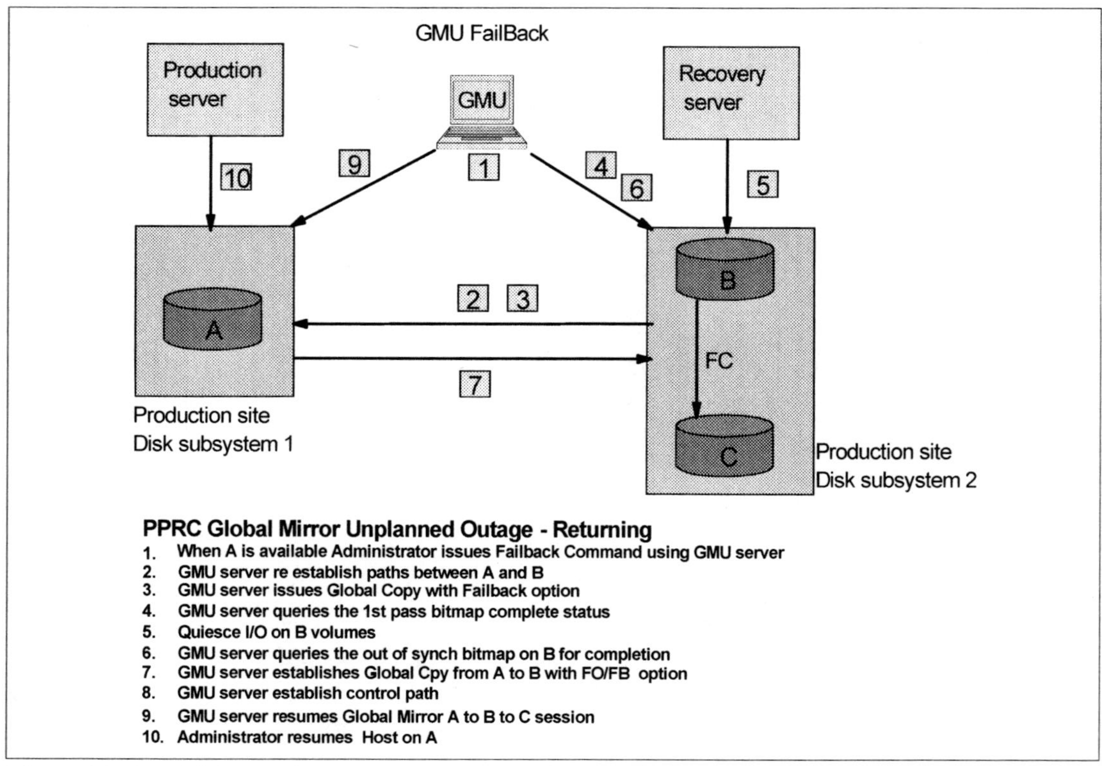

Figure 39-20 GMU in a failback scenario

39.7.3 GMU troubleshooting

The Global Mirror task status information is displayed on the client console when executing any of the commands. The execution will terminate at the step which failed. You can then do troubleshooting on the failed devices and re-execute the previously failed command. The execution will continue from the failed step until all steps are completed successfully. You can also issue an **initialize** command to clear the internal execution operation pointer and execute the command from the very beginning.

If the communication problem persists between Copy Services Server or HMC (DS8000) or SMC (DS6000) and the application, reset the Copy Services Server or HMC (DS8000) or SMC (DS6000) and then issue the **initialize** command again.

You can find more execution status and session devices status from the *FoFbService.log*, or WebSphere *SystemOut.log*. The *FoFbService.log* contains detailed information on each device, each event notification, and each status querying call. The client log stores the same information that is shown on the user's console.

You can also find more execution status and session devices status directly from the Copy Services Server or HMC (DS8000) or SMC (DS6000).

In the event of a command hanging during any execution step, you can issue **`Ctrl+C`** from the client console to get out of the command session. The execution operation pointer index will stop at the hanging step. You can perform debugging to fix the root cause of the hanging problem, then issue the command again. The session execution will continue from the hanging step onwards. If the hanging occurs at an event waiting step, such as a FlashCopy Background Copy Completion event or a Global Mirror Out of Sync Bitmap Drain event, the session execution will continue from the next step after the event.

For more information on error messages, you can refer to the *User's Guide* provided with the installation CD, or you can download it at the following Web site:

`http://www-1.ibm.com/servers/storage/support/index.html`

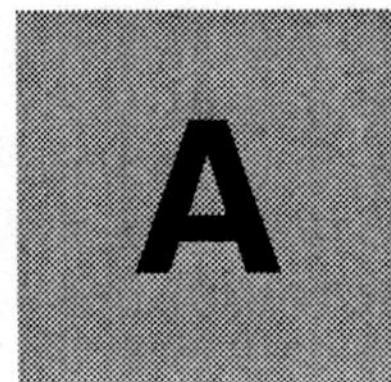

OS specific (z/OS)

In this appendix we provide some z/OS specific information that may help the user in installing the DS8000:

- Planning considerations
- Planning for Copy Services

Planning considerations

The DS8000 supports three basic types of host connection features; Short Wave FCP/FICON(#31x1), Long Wave FCP/FICON(#32x1), and ESCON(#33x1). The FCP/FICON host attachment features come packaged as a four 2Gb Lucent Connector (LC) port card adapter. Each port of the FCP/FICON Host Adapter can be configured as FCP or FICON as needed (but a single port cannot operate as both FCP and FICON simultaneously). The 64-bit ESCON host attachment feature supports a two MT-RJ port card adapter.The DS8000 attaches to a variety of hosts. Complete and current information on all supported servers (including supported models and Host Adapters) is available on the Internet at the following Web site:

http://www-1.ibm.com/servers/storage/disk/ds8000/pdf/ds8000-matrix.pdf

Additional servers may be supported on a Request for Price Quotation (RPQ) basis. If a server on this site is described as having RPQ support, the installation support information can be found on the IBM Technical Documents Web site at:

http://www-1.ibm.com/support/techdocs/atsmastr.nsf/Web/Techdocs

The DS8000 is capable of all advanced functions of its predecessor product the ESS 800. The available PPRC and FlashCopy functions are Version 2. This means, for example, that only FCP PPRC links are supported (PPRC Version 2 capability). The DS8000 Licensed Function features are based on the physical capacity of the DS8000. Licensed Function features are ordered against the base model, but the licensed capacity is calculated across the base and all attached expansion frames. The purchased capacity license for Licensed Functions can range from the entire installed capacity to the FB or CKD formatted capacity of a Storage Image. The installed capacity of the DS8000 is the required size of the Operating Environment License. Customers are allowed further granularity when they obtain authorization keys for input to the online configurator. The size of each purchased license needs to cover all instances of planned use of each licensed function in the DS8000.

Removal of a Licensed Feature is performed by adding a feature with zero capacity. This will translate to a disruptive configuration change because the feature to be removed cannot be disabled without a machine Initial Microcode Load (IML). There is no way to deactivate the feature without withdrawing it from use.

DS8000 server attachment

There are three options available for attaching the DS8000 to a server. Fibre Channel Protocol (FCP) attachments are possible for open environments. For the zSeries user, ESCON, FICON, or FCP can be used. The maximum number of host adapters cannot exceed 32. Plant installation of pairs of Host Adapter features within a frame alternates between the bottom and top IO Drawers (starting with the bottom IO drawers).

From zero to 64 ESCON channels are supported per DS8000 Storage Image; there are two per ESCON host adapter. ESCON addressing for the DS8000 is limited to the first 16 LSSs (0-F), this will limit the configurable capacity of ESCON attachment to the DS8000. This also requires that the first 16 LSSs defined are CKD (and not FB) when the logical configuration is performed. PPRC V2 requires FCP connections between the primary and secondary storage images. ESCON is not supported for PPRC links to/from DS8000.

The 64 bit ESCON host adapter (#33x1) is used for DS8000 attachment to ESCON channels. The adapter has been enhanced with a faster microprocessor and offers up to a 45% improvement in sequential bandwidth and up to 10% increase in channel throughput for random operation workloads as compared to the Enhanced ESCON host adapter. This adapter has the same features as the 2105 feature code (3013).

The 64-bit adapter features an LED-type interface and supports two ESCON links with each link supporting up to 64 logical paths, and supports use of 62.5 micron multimode fiber optic cable terminated with small form factor, industry standard MT-RJ connector.

An ESCON link consists of two fibers, one for each direction, connected at each end by an ESCON connector to an ESCON port. Each ESCON adapter card supports two ESCON ports or links; and each port supports 64 logical paths. With the maximum of 64 ESCON ports, the maximum number of n-port logins is 2000 per Storage Image.

With the DS8000, four Fibre Channel/FICON Ports supporting Fibre Channel speeds up to 2 gigabits are available as the following features:

- 2 Gb Fibre Channel/FICON (long wave) Host Adapter (32x1)
- 2 Gb Fibre Channel/FICON (short wave) Host Adapter (31x1)

These adapters have auto-sensing to allow attachment to a server or SAN whose adapter is running at 1gigabit speeds. FCP is used for PPRC communication between primary and secondary DS8000 Models, DS6000 models, and ESS models 800 and 750. Specific characteristics include:

- Each 2 Gb adapter provides four ports with an LC Duplex connector type and provides an interface that supports full duplex data transfer.
- The adapter ports support FICON and FCP, but not simultaneously; the protocol to be used is configurable by customers on a port by port basis.
- Fibre Channel is supported on point-to-point, fabric, and arbitrated loop (private loop) topologies.
- FICON is supported on point-to-point and fabric topologies.
- Fabric components from IBM, McDATA and Brocade are supported in both the FCP and FICON environments.
- The DS8000 supports up to 32 host adapters which allows for a maximum of 128 Fibre Channel/FICON ports per machine. Both long wave and short wave adapters can be used in a single DS8000.
- 31 meter, plenum-rated cables can be ordered with each Fibre Channel adapter. The cables can have either LC connectors on both ends, or an LC connector on one end and an SC connector on the other.

The Fibre Channel/FICON (long wave) Host Adapter, when used with 9 micron single-mode fibre cable, extends the point-to-point distance to 10 km. The Fibre Channel/FICON (short wave) Host Adapter, when used with 50 micron multi-mode fibre cable, supports point-to-point distances of up to 300 meters. Additional distance can be achieved with the use of appropriate SAN fabric components.

The Fibre Channel/FICON Host Adapters have the LC connector type. Fibre cable couplers can be used to attach a cable with SC Duplex connector type to a server or fabric component port with a LC connector type. A FICON link consists of two fibers, one for each direction, connected at each end by a FICON connector to a FICON port. Each FICON adapter card supports four FICON ports or links. A FICON port supports 2000 logical paths. With the maximum of 64 FICON ports, the maximum number of channel connections per fiber port is 509 and 2048 n-port logins.

FICON considerations

When migrating from ESCON paths to FICON, the following rules of thumb may be useful:

- For lightly utilized ESCON channels (around 20 percent or less), a good rule of thumb is one FICON channel for every four ESCON. This is dependent on the current ESCON channel peak, aggregate utilization.
- In general, tape and disk should not be daisy chained in a FICON environment.

The following is a rule of thumb for assessing the aggregation of ESCON channels into FICON. It may not apply to all situations.

Current ESCON channel utilization patterns are an important input to the FICON channel consolidation analysis process. On a G5 or G6 processor, up to 200% ESCON channel utilization can be consolidated onto a single FICON channel. This means that as long as the peak of the sum of all the utilizations of the ESCON channel consolidation candidates stays below the 200% limit, these channels can be consolidated onto a single G5 or G6 FICON channel. There is no requirement on the peak of any individual ESCON channel. For example, during the time interval that represents the peak of the sum of all the utilizations, the individual ESCON channel utilizations could be as follows: (100%, 50%, 30%, 15%, 5%, 0%) or (100%, 100%) or (25%,25%, 25%, 25%, 25%, 25%, 25%, 25%) or (30%, 40%, 50%, 60%) or any other combination that adds up to less than or equal to 200%. This 200% limit grows to 300% on the zSeries if two or more DS8000 ports are connected to the same FICON channel (perhaps using a FICON director). It approaches 400% with the FICON Express adapters for the zSeries.

The Fibre Channel/FICON Host Adapter must match that on the zSeries and/or 9672 G5/G6 FICON. When you are using a long wave adapter on one end, there must be a long wave adapter at the other end. If you have a short wave adapter, the same is true.

Planning for Copy Services

For the purposes of data exchange with PPRC, the DS8000, the DS6000, and the functions available with PPRC Version 2 (on the ESS models 750 and 800) are interoperable. The exceptions to the available 2105 functions are:

- PPRC Metro/Global Copy is not available on DS6000 or DS8000.
- The commands used in the Copy Services Command-Line Interface are different (invalidating existing 2105 CLI scripts for use on the DS8000).
- PPRC links are required to be FCP (ESCON PPRC links are not supported on DS8000 or DS6000).

PPRC primary or secondary volumes can reside on any of these Storage Images and exchange data. If the secondary Storage Image for PPRC usage is located in another building on the campus, fiber optic cables need to be provided for FCP connection between the two locations. If a Metro Mirror PPRC connection travels off the campus, the two storage images may be up to 300 kilometers apart. (Longer distance support may be requested using the RPQ process.) These distances may influence disk response time and will require some form of distance extension. Distance extension of PPRC FCP links can be accomplished with channel extension or some form of Fibre Channel to WAN topology. Channel extension could require at least one pair of Dense Wavelength Division Multiplexers (DWDM) to transport multiple protocols over the same fiber optic cable. Each pair can be separated by up to 50 km (31 miles) of fiber. This fiber can be dark fiber (such as leased from a common carrier like a telephone company or cable TV operator) as long as it meets the vendor's attachment criteria.

IBM supports the use of the following channel extenders products for PPRC. The product vendors should be consulted regarding hardware and software prerequisites when using their products in an DS8000 PPRC configuration. IBM supports the use of PPRC over all the network technologies that are currently supported by the channel extender products. Support of PPRC configurations using channel extender products are the sole responsibility of the channel extender vendor.

- ADVA FSP 2000
- CIENA CN 2000 Storage Extension Platform
- CIENA IP Storage Service Modules
- Cisco CWDM Distance Solution
- Cisco ONS 15530/15540
- CNT Edge Storage Router
- Nortel Networks OPTera Metro 5200/5300

Global Copy

Global Copy for DS8000 brings new flexibility to the DS8000 and PPRC with the introduction of a non-synchronous long distance copy option suitable for data migration, transmission of database logs, and periodic offsite backup. With Global Copy, updates are continually transferred to the secondary DS8000 at the remote site in a non synchronous mode. This means updates to the DS8000 primary at the local site are considered complete (that is, ending status is returned to the application) before they are transmitted to the secondary DS8000 at the remote site. With a non-synchronous operation, the distance between the primary and secondary DS8000 will have only a minimal effect on the application response time. Therefore, Global Copy can operate at very long distances. Distances well beyond the 300 km supported with Metro Mirror (Synchronous PPRC) for DS8000 - with the distance limited only by the capabilities of the network and channel extension technologies.

When operating in Global Copy (PPRC-XD) mode, the DS8000 primary and secondary do not transition to full synchronous mode. This can result in a "*fuzzy copy*" at the remote site since application dependent writes are not assured to be applied on the secondary Storage Image in the same sequence as they were written to the primary Storage Image. To obtain a consistent copy, PPRC-XD mode can simply be changed to PPRC-SYNC (synchronous mode). Upon reaching full duplex mode (consistency), the PPRC pairs can be temporarily suspended, followed by a FlashCopy on the secondary Storage Image, and then a resumption of PPRC-XD mode.

This operation, which may take tens of seconds or less depending upon the level of I/O activity on the primary, provides a point-in-time consistent copy at the remote site which is suitable for data migration, backup, and disaster recovery purposes. Global Copy (PPRC-XD) is provided with the Remote Mirror and Copy (RMC) optional feature on the DS8000 (#0740). The RMC optional feature on the DS8000 requires that the DS8000 Licensed Feature Authorization (2244-RMC) be ordered for the primary and secondary Storage Images. It is supported in the same environments as PPRC and is managed via a Web interface provided through the IBM DS Storage Manager. It is also supported by the DS Command-Line Interface (CLI) in selected open systems environments, by TSO commands in z/OS, and by ICKDSF R17 for z/OS zVM and VSE/ESA.

Global Mirror (Asynchronous PPRC)

Global Mirror is designed to enable a two-site disaster recovery and backup solution for both the zSeries and open systems environments using IBM Storage Images (ESS Model 800/750, DS8000, and DS6000). Global Mirror operates over high-speed, Fibre Channel communication links and is designed to provide the following benefits:

- A high-performance, long-distance remote copy solution using asynchronous technology.
- Support for virtually unlimited distance between the local and remote sites, with the distance typically limited only by the capabilities of the network and channel extension technologies. This can better enable you to choose your remote site location based on business needs and enables site separation to add protection from localized disasters.
- A consistent and restartable copy of the data at the remote site, created with minimal impact to applications at the local site.
- Data currency where, for many environments, the remote site lags behind the local site an average of 3 to 5 seconds, minimizing the amount of data exposure in the event of an unplanned outage. Data currency is also known as the recovery point objective (RPO). The actual lag in data currency experienced will depend upon a number of factors, including specific workload characteristics and bandwidth between the local and remote sites.
- Dynamic selection of the desired RPO based upon business requirements and optimization of available bandwidth.
- Session support whereby data consistency at the remote site is internally managed across up to eight IBM Storage Images located among the local and remote sites.
- Efficient synchronization of the local and remote sites with support for PPRC failover and failback modes, helping to reduce the time required to switch back to the local site after a planned or unplanned outage.

Asynchronous PPRC Bandwidth Sizing Spreadsheet for Global Mirror is a spreadsheet which enables you to estimate the effect on bandwidth of different Consistency Group formation times. This can be obtained from:

`http://w3-1.ibm.com/sales/systems`

select tools, then select disk from the pull-down menu. This is only available to IBMers so contact your IBM representative for assistance.

Licensed functions

The Licensed functions on the DS8000 operate on a tiered pricing structure based on the configured capacity of the subsystem. For every storage unit system, you must order an operating environment licensing (OEL). OEL licenses the operating environment and is based on the total physical capacity of the model configuration (base model plus any expansion models). It authorizes you to use the model configuration at a given capacity level.

Once your OEL licensing has been activated, you can configure the Storage Unit. Activating the OEL license means that you have obtained the activation key and entered it into the DS8000 DS Storage Manager. The feature number that you select for the OEL must reflect the total configured capacity of the model configuration. The model configuration includes the base model (921, 922, or 9A2), plus any expansion models (92E or 9AE) connected to that base model.

The Licensed functions include:

- Point-in-time Copy (PTC) — also known as FlashCopy
- Remote Mirror and Copy (RMC) — also known as PPRC, RMC includes the functions of:
  - Metro Mirror (Synchronous PPRC)
  - Global Mirror (Asynchronous PPRC)
  - Global Copy (PPRC-XD)

- Remote Mirror and Copy for z/OS (RMZ) - also known as z/OS Global Mirror (Extended Remote Copy (XRC))
- Parallel Access Volumes (PAV)

When you order the Licensed functions, you specify the feature code that represents the physical capacity allowed for the function.

You can combine feature codes to order the exact capacity that you need. Remote Mirror and Copy for z/OS (RMZ) and Parallel Access Volumes (PAV) are supported only on zSeries servers, so a license is only required for that capacity which is configured as CKD. For an LPAR configuration, you can license each LPAR independently or the DS8000 subsystem as a whole.

General items

For z/OS Copy Services considerations, be sure to check the Copy Services Web site at:

`http://www-1.ibm.com/servers/storage/support/solutions/bc.html`

for technical topics, recent maintenance, and publication updates. System/390® customers who will use ICKDSF to support PPRC need to review APAR PQ43495. Remember that the documentation for PPRC enhancements is contained in the this APAR and PQ26800. APAR AQ84968 is needed to add FlashCopy and Global Mirror command support to ICKDSF.

Metro Mirror was previously known as Synchronous PPRC. Metro Mirror is supported at PPRC V2 function only. Only FCP links are supported. Metro Mirror is interoperable between DS8000, DS6000, ESS 800 and ESS 750.

Global Copy was previously known as PPRC-XD. Global Copy is interoperable between DS8000, DS6000, ESS 800 and ESS 750. PPRC Global Copy is supported with the use of SAN fabric products, DWDM, and channel extenders. A complete and current list of supported environments is available at:

`http://www-1.ibm.com/servers/storage/disk/ds8000/interop.html`

IBM recommends that you use different logical and physical paths for Metro Mirror pairs and Global Copy pairs during normal PPRC operations. By keeping the logical and physical paths separate, the synchronous writes to a secondary DS8000 do not adversely affect the I/O performance of the Global Copy pairs. This recommendation applies only to environments where the distance between primary and secondary servers does not exceed 300 kilometers.

Metro/Global Copy was previously known as Asynchronous Cascading PPRC. Metro/Global Copy is not supported on the DS8000.

FlashCopy function on the DS8000 is FlashCopy Version 2 function. The source and target volumes or LUNs must be in the same DS8000 image (LPAR). The size of the target volume must be as large as the source (unless data set /extent copy is requested) and multiple copy relationships can exist between a source and targets volumes. For persistent FlashCopy relationships, an incremental FlashCopy capability exists. FlashCopy commands can now be also sent across PPRC Links. There is support for the use of a PPRC primary volume as a FlashCopy target. This support is also provided in DFSMSdss with APAR OA06196. FlashCopy supports source volumes in a Consistency Group.

Remote Mirror for z/OS was previously known as XRC. If the customer wants to move data from the secondary site using XRC (for recovery or data migration) then remember that the secondary DS8000 must also be licensed for Remote Mirror for z/OS.

Minimum software for IBM System/390 and zSeries platforms

The minimum software levels required to support the DS8000 are:

- z/OS 1.4+
- z/VM 4.4 or z/VM 5.1
- VSE/ESA 2.7
- TPF 4.1 is the minimum level and requires a PTF.
- The minimum supported level of Linux is the SuSE SLES 8 for zSeries

FlashCopy is available for all zSeries platforms, but not all versions/releases. Operating system initiated FlashCopy is available natively or using the DS8000 Web Copy Services. Under z/OS FlashCopy can also be controlled using DFSMSdss or TSO commands. FlashCopy support is provided as part of z/VM and VSE/ESA. Peer-to-Peer Remote Copy support is also supported through the Copy Services part of the DS8000 Hardware Management Console. PPRC continues to be supported by ICKDSF R17 on zSeries platforms and by TSO commands in z/OS.

The DS8000 should be defined as a 2107. There is very little additional effort to install the IODF/HCD Support beyond the device support (that is in any circumstance, the DS8000 responds that it is a 2107). Once the appropriate software support for full 2107 support is available you can exploit the extended addressibility of the DS8000 by defining it as a 2107.For sample HCD definitions refer to System/390 and zSeries IOCP and IODF Examples, 2107 in 2105 Mode, TR014402. The Techdocs database is accessible on the following IBM internal Web site:

```
http://w3-03.ibm.com/support/techdocs/atsmastr.nsf/Web/TechDocs
```

IBM Business Partners can access this document at:

```
http://partners.boulder.ibm.com/src/atsmastr.nsf/WebIndex/TD1008
```

Contact your IBM representative to obtain more information on this.

Check the PSP bucket for latest software information.

Each PAV address must have an associated address in the HCD/IOCP. Issue the D M=CHP(xx) MVS command shortly after installation to verify that the aliases are bound where they are expected to be. The MVS option LOCANY=NO/YES for the device addresses applies only to base addresses. (Alias addresses are ESQA). Additional PAV alias addresses can be dynamically added (or removed) using the DS8000 logical configurator. Any change in alias assignment using the configurator generates a device change interrupt to z/OS. z/OS initiates a process to add/remove the alias address to/from the specified base address without requiring an IML of the DS8000, a shutdown and re-IPL of z/OS, or the base address' being varied offline/online. Only base addresses may be designated as a member of a PPRC pair. Do not set Missing Interrupt times for PAV alias addresses.

Alias recommendations: PAV aliases can be shared among base addresses within the same LSS. Wherever possible use dynamic PAV with the Workload Manager to maximize the benefit of your available aliases. The correct number of aliases for your workload can be determined from an analysis of RMF. If you are currently using PAV on an ESS you can use the same base:alias ratio as you do currently. The DS8000 logical configurator allows you to specify a fractional ratio of aliases to base addresses. You can apply a ratio to all LSSs or to specific LSSs as part of the configuration process.

In the absence of workload data, a rule of thumb may be applied:

- Define as many aliases as the number of FICON channels to the LSS multiplied by six times.

When adding large numbers of logical devices to a zSeries server, remember that the high storage area (HSA) may increase in size as it adjusts to the new devices. This may impact the amount of storage being dedicated to an LPAR. It will also require that a power on reset (POR) be done to redefine the HSA. z/OS users should also check the channel management blocks (CMB) to make sure that there are enough CMBs available to reflect the new logical devices that will be dynamically added.

This is controlled by the IEASYS parameter CMB=. CMBs are 32-byte control blocks in the ESQA. CMBs are used to store the number of non-DASD and tape devices defined to the system. Additionally, they contain any dynamically activated devices. If there are insufficient CMBs, those dynamically added devices, that overflow the space, will not be reflected in the SMF data that is being collected. Those that fit within the CMBs will be reflected on the performance data. Changing the CMB value will require a re-IPL since there is no SET command for IEASYS.

RMF considerations

RMF will report all I/O activity against the Base PAV address not by the Base and associated Aliases. The performance information for the Base includes all Base and Alias activity. New reports have been designed for reporting FICON channel utilization. RMF also provides support for PPRC link utilization statistics and a new SMF 74.8 record for DS8000 statistics. This support is delivered by APAR OA04877. PTFs are available for z/OS V1R4 and above.

Cache and NVS reporting

RMF's cache reporting and the results of a LISTDATA STATUS command report a cache size that is half the actual size. This is because the information returned represents only the cluster to which the logical control unit is attached. Each LSS on the cluster reflects the cache and NVS size of that cluster. z/OS users will find that only the SETCACHE CFW ON | OFF command is supported while other SETCACHE command options (for example. DEVICE, SUBSYSTEM, DFW, NVS) are not accepted.

Dynamic Parallel Access Volumes

Remember that Workload Manager (WLM) must be in goal mode to cause PAVs to be shifted from one device to another (dynamic PAVs). Information regarding the dynamic PAVs can be found on the Internet at

```
http://www.ibm.com/s390/wlm/
```

Remember that the WLM can theoretically assign up to 255 addresses as aliases for a base. Changing or reassigning PAVs dynamically can be accomplished but care needs to be taken. In general, it is not recommended. (Review APAR OW54096 before deleting PAVs dynamically.)

JES2 and Coupling data sets

It is well documented in z/OS publications that primary and secondary copies of data sets critical to z/OS operation should be placed on volumes selected to avoid any single points of failure. For example, the manual *z/OS V1R6.0 MVS Setting up a Sysplex* (SA22-7625-09) states "To avoid a single point of failure in a sysplex, IBM recommends that, for all couple data sets, you create an alternate couple dataset on a different device, control unit, and channel from the primary". In the case of a storage subsystem like the DS8000 which emulates multiple logical control units, this should be interpreted to mean separate physical control units (if possible) not just separate logical control units normally controlled by different clusters internal to the physical storage control.

In normal operation, the DS8000 operates as two independent clusters each controlling half of the storage capacity. A catastrophic failure in one cluster will cause the failover of the operations of that cluster to the surviving cluster. During failover, the surviving cluster will send a state change pending (that is. long busy) to all the system images, take ownership of resources formerly controlled by the failed cluster, reestablish fault-tolerant operation using the cache and non-volatile storage in the surviving cluster, and then resume operation of all LCUs and logical disk devices. If the primary and secondary copies of a z/OS critical dataset both reside in the same physical storage subsystem, the temporary pause caused by the state change pending can be interpreted as a failure of both copies — even though both copies will be accessible when the failover operation completes.

For best availability, primary and secondary copies of z/OS critical data sets should be placed on separate physical storage subsystems accessed through separate path groups whenever possible.

TDMF considerations

Softek Transparent Data Migration Facility (TDMF) for z/OS and Replicator Version 3.6 have been tested by IGS with DS8000 and DS6000. TDMF and Replicator also support large capacity volumes.

Check with Softek for any outstanding maintenance for TDMF or Replicator.

FDRPAS considerations

Innovation Data Processing's FDRPAS Supported release is 5.4/30. Check with Innovation Data Processing for any outstanding maintenance for using FDRPAS with DS8000 or DS6000. FDRPAS supports very large disks in V5.4/42 or higher. FDRPAS may identify these disks in messages such as *3390-54*.

MIH considerations

The DS8000 will supply a recommended interval of 30 seconds as part of the Read Configuration Data. z/OS will use this information to set its MIH value. For SyncSort MIH is recommended to be set at 2 minutes due to the long CCW chains typically used by SyncSort.

IBM zSeries z/VM

The minimum software levels required to support the DS8000 are:

- z/VM 4.4 or z/VM 5.1

PAV considerations

When running an z/OS guest under VM/ESA®, PAV support can be used with a release of z/OS that supports PAVs. (VM APAR VM62295 allows z/OS guests to issue the commands enabling PAVs.) To verify that PAV aliases are bound to the correct bases, use the command F QUERY CHPID xx combined with QUERY PAV rdev-rdev. (xx is the CHPID whose device addresses should be displayed showing the addresses and any aliases. rdev is the real device address.)

Remember that VM/ESA does not have any support for PAV other than allowing a z/OS guest to use it. LCUs which are not attached to an exploitation-capable z/OS guest will remain as a 3990-3/6 LCU and, as such, are capable of storing any other information not associated with this guest — including VM system disks, CMS mini-disks and data belonging to other non-exploitation guests. Additional VM/ESA technical information describing the support for PAV can be found on the VM/ESA Technical Web site at

```
http://www.ibm.com/vm/techinfo/pav.html
```

MIH considerations

The DS8000 will supply a recommended interval of 30 seconds as part of the Read Configuration Data. VM/ESA and z/VM take the 30 second value, add 25% rounded to the next increment of 5 (10 seconds) and use the resulting 40 seconds as its MIH value so that any guest will receive the 30 second MIH before it does.

VM/ESA Peer-to-Peer Remote Copy considerations

Peer-to-Peer Remote Copy support for guests will require that the guest have the following options specified as noted in the *Device Support Facility User's Guide and Reference*:

- MAINTCCW
- DEVMAINT

FlashCopy considerations for z/VM

z/VM's support permits making an image from a source volume. It also allows a minidisk to be copied from the source volume to a target volume with the restriction that the physical extents must be the same for both the source and the target. Native support for VM is incorporated into z/VM using the FLASHCOPY command for Class B users. With z/VM, FlashCopy support requires VM APAR VM62416 before a z/OS guest can utilize FlashCopy.

IBM zSeries VSE/ESA

The minimum software levels required to support the DS8000 is:

- VSE/ESA 2.7

32,760 Cylinder volume considerations

APAR DY46113 is required for exploitation of large DASD support in VSE 2.7 to correct a potential data integrity exposure with legacy file definitions.

MIH considerations for VSE/ESA

The DS8000 will supply a recommended interval of 30 seconds as part of the Read Configuration Data. VSE supports the missing interrupt handler (MIH) and sets its timer value to a default of 180 seconds. This can be changed to the suggested DS8000 value of 30 seconds by using the SIR MIH command which is documented in the Hints and Tips for VSE/ESA document which is downloadable from the VSE/ESA Web page at:

```
http://www-1.ibm.com/servers/eserver/zseries/os/vse/library/library.htm
```

PPRC considerations VSE/ESA

Peer-to-Peer Remote Copy support is provided using the ICKDSF utility. This support is documented in the *Device Support Facility User's Guide and Reference.*

FlashCopy considerations for VSE/ESA

VSE Support for FlashCopy is equivalent to the FlashCopy support on ESS 800. There is no support for FlashCopy V2 functions, and therefore no support for Global Mirror.

Concurrent Copy

In this appendix we describe the Concurrent Copy function on the DS8000 series.

Concurrent Copy

This appendix describes the characteristics and operation of Concurrent Copy. We also discuss the considerations involved when planning to use Concurrent Copy.

The information presented in this chapter can be complemented with the following publications:

- *z/OS DFSMS Advanced Copy Services*, SC35-0428
- *z/OS DFSMSdss Storage Administration Reference*, SC35-0424
- *z/OS V1R3.0 DFSMS Installation Exits*, SC26-7396
- *DFSMS: Implementing System Managed Storage*, SC26-7407
- *DFSMShsm Storage Administration Guide*, SC35-0388
- *DFSMS/MVS Managing Catalogs*, SC26-4914

Overview

Concurrent Copy is a copy function that helps you keep your high data availability objectives by allowing point-in-time copies of your data *concurrent* with normal application processing. Concurrent Copy works with the IBM TotalStorage DS8000 and the DFSMS System Data Mover (SDM). Concurrent Copy is available for the z/OS and OS/390 operating systems, and requires software support provided in DFSMS/MVS.

Concurrent Copy works not only on a full-volume basis, but also at a data set level. Also, the target is not restricted only to DASD volumes in the same DS8000, but the target can also be a tape cartridge or a DASD volume on another DS8000 (see Figure B-1).

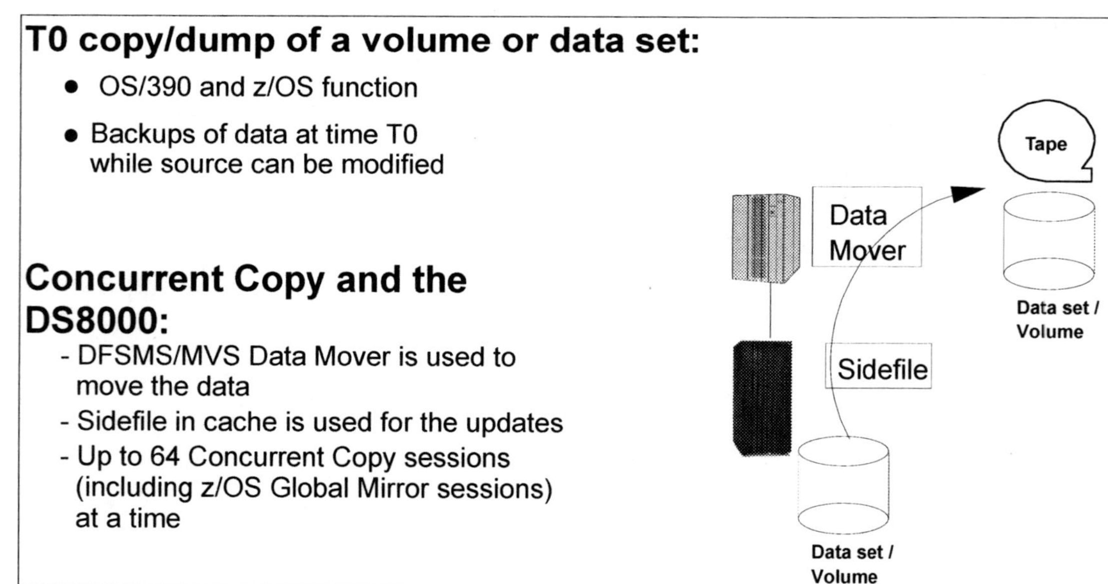

Figure B-1 Concurrent Copy characteristics

Concurrent Copy terminology

This section lists the definitions of the terms used with Concurrent Copy. These terms will be discussed in detail in the following sections.

Session

A session is a logical concept representing a single invocation of Concurrent Copy (a single DFSMSdss DUMP/COPY command). A session can include one or more data sets or volumes, on the same DS8000 or across different DS8000s. An individual DS8000 can support up to 16 simultaneous Concurrent Copy sessions per volume, with a maximum of 64 simultaneous sessions per LSS.

Session ID

The system assigns a unique session ID to each Concurrent Copy session. The system uses the session ID to identify and coordinate all host and DS8000 resources associated with a particular Concurrent Copy session.

Concurrent Copy domain

The set of devices and tracks identified during the initialization of a Concurrent Copy session is called the Concurrent Copy domain. It represents the set of data that Concurrent Copy copies.

Intercepted writes

When an application tries to update information that is included in a Concurrent Copy domain, the DS8000 intercepts those writes, thus maintaining a copy of the data as it was at the time when the Concurrent Copy was requested.

Sidefile

A sidefile is a temporary repository for Concurrent Copy domain tracks that still have not been copied by the SDM and are about to receive an update. During the processing of an intercepted write, the DS8000 copies a before-image of the track being updated into a sidefile for later processing. Together, the DS8000 and the SDM maintain two sidefiles, one in the DS8000 cache and another in processor storage.

Terminate

The Concurrent Copy terminates when DFSMSdss has copied the Concurrent Copy domain and both the sidefiles are empty. In error situations, either the DS8000 or the SDM can terminate the Concurrent Copy session before the entire domain has been copied.

Fuzzy copy

Without a tool like Concurrent Copy, if you make a copy of the data while the data is being updated then the copy will not reflect a point-in-time version of the original data. In this case, the copy will be fuzzy, because it does not represent any particular point-in-time status. A fuzzy copy is a set of data with no logical consistency from the application perspective.

Consistent copy

A consistent copy is a set of data with logical consistency from the application perspective. The logical consistency of the source data is guaranteed by the application itself. The logical consistency of the copied data must be ensured by a mechanism like Concurrent Copy. With the application taking care at all times that the original data is consistent, you are then able with Concurrent Copy to produce a point-in-time copy of the complete set of data. The copy will hold the same logical consistency status as the original data at that certain point-in-time.

Benefits of using Concurrent Copy

Concurrent Copy can dramatically reduce the amount of time that is required to back up your application data, hence increasing the application's availability time. When you use Concurrent Copy, application processing is interrupted for only a minimum time while the system initializes the Concurrent Copy session. Once Concurrent Copy is active, your applications continue to process the data while it is being backed up using Concurrent Copy.

Concurrent Copy provides point-in-time data consistency. The system serializes access to the data being dumped or copied just long enough for the Concurrent Copy session to be initialized. This serialization takes a very short time to complete, and this process ensures the point-in-time copy will be consistent while the copy is being done with your applications running.

Note: Many of the benefits of using Concurrent Copy also apply to using FlashCopy, with the added benefits of not using host resources (channel bandwidth, memory). However, you will need to allow for FlashCopy space in your disk subsystems. You will need to decide which technique offers the best return for your business requirements.

Concurrent Copy operation

For details on the operation of Concurrent Copy, refer to the manual *z/OS DFSMS Advanced Copy Services*, SC35-0428.

Invoking Concurrent Copy

Concurrent Copy (CC) can be invoked by either the DFSMSdss or the DFSMShsm™ functions. IMS, CICS, DFSMSrmm™, and DB2 can use CC for their backups.

DFSMSdss has the option of using Concurrent Copy when data sets are copied or dumped. To invoke Concurrent Copy, the CONCURRENT keyword must be specified on a DFSMSdss COPY or DUMP commands.

With DFSMShsm, system-managed data may be backed up automatically with Concurrent Copy by use of management class parameters. DFSMShsm also allows Concurrent Copy to be used when copying data using Aggregate Backup and Recovery Support (ABARS).

Using the CONCURRENT control statement of the DB2 COPY utility, you can invoke Concurrent Copy to make a full image copy. During recovery, DB2 can automatically use the most recent image copy and then apply records from the log.

Concurrent Copy requires the software support provided in DFSMS/MVS. For details on using Concurrent Copy with these products, refer to the appropriate product manual.

Concurrent Copy on the DS8000

Concurrent Copy is initiated using the CONCURRENT keyword in DFSMSdss or in applications that internally call DFSMSdss as the copy program, for example, the DB2 COPY utility.

The System Data Mover establishes a Concurrent Copy session with the DS8000. There can be up to 64 sessions active at a time (including sessions for z/OS Global Mirror)) per DS8000 logical subsystem (LSS).

Concurrent Copy and FlashCopy

Concurrent Copy and FlashCopy can coexist in the same DS8000.

If DFSMSdss is instructed to do a Concurrent Copy by specifying the CONCurrent (CC) keyword, and the copy is for a full volume (DFSMSdss COPY FULL command) the following will be honored based on whether FlashCopy is installed:

- With the target within the same logical subsystem or DS8000 as the source and FlashCopy installed, DFSMSdss will start a FlashCopy copy process instead of Concurrent Copy.

So, you get a FlashCopy invocation with a DFSMSdss COPY FULL command even if the CONCurrent (or CC) parameter is coded in the command.

The FASTREPLICATION parameter of the COPY command does not affect Concurrent Copy, it only applies for FlashCopy and SnapShot invocation. FASTREPLICATION(REQuired) and CONCURRENT cannot be used together in the same COPY command.

Sizing and requirements

Concurrent Copy requirements and information on sizing the storage requirements can be found in the manual *z/OS DFSMS Advanced Copy Services*, SC35-0428.

Central and expanded storage

Running many Concurrent Copy jobs simultaneously can cause auxiliary (AUX) storage shortages. PTF OW50284 introduced methods to limit the amount of auxiliary storage used and will appropriately either terminate existing CC jobs, or will fail to copy data sets using Concurrent Copy. The SDM provides the ability to modify the Concurrent Copy AUX values that are used in evaluating the AUX storage that is used by Concurrent Copy.

Example B-1 shows the system command to modify the Concurrent Copy AUX delta to determine at what percentage value new Concurrent Copy data sets will not be copied using Concurrent Copy. The SDM subtracts this delta value from the lower MVS percentage. The newly computed SDM percentage is then compared to the total current system AUX storage percentage being used. The default value is -1, indicating that SDM will not perform a percentage check for AUX storage usage by Concurrent Copy. The nnnn value may be any non-negative value (including zero).

Example: B-1 Modifying auxiliary storage delta for new Concurrent Copy data set

```
F ANTMAIN,P .CMTUN+3A X'FFFF' X'nnnn'
```

Example B-2 shows the system command to modify the Concurrent Copy AUX delta to determine at what percentage value existing Concurrent Copy data sets will be terminated. The SDM subtracts this delta value from the upper MVS percentage. The newly computed SDM percentage is then compared to the total current system AUX storage percentage being used. The default value is -1, indicating that SDM will not perform a percentage check for AUX storage usage by Concurrent Copy. The nnnn value can be any non-negative value (including zero).

Example: B-2 Modifying auxiliary storage delta for existing Concurrent Copy data set

```
F ANTMAIN,P .CMTUN+3C X'FFFF' X'nnnn'
```

Production and performance considerations

When planning to use Concurrent Copy, you will be paying attention to system performance considerations such as:

- Application response time
- Storage subsystem utilization
- System throughput
- Concurrent Copy throughput

Your workload flow and your hardware configuration will determine how these factors affect your ability to use Concurrent Copy.

Also when planning for the production use of Concurrent Copy, some other things you will want to address are:

- When to schedule Concurrent Copy operations
- Where to use Concurrent Copy
- Number of simultaneous sessions (z/OS Global Mirror and Concurrent Copy) that you can run

Let us look at these latter considerations in more detail.

When to schedule Concurrent Copy

Many factors influence when you can schedule Concurrent Copy operations. For example, the structure of your overnight batch processing determines at what stages in the processing you can use Concurrent Copy. Similarly, factors like availability of tape drives could restrict the intervals during which running a Concurrent Copy operation is feasible.

If other considerations are not a factor, you can use Concurrent Copy at times of lowest activity, especially lowest update activity. It may, however, be beneficial to use Concurrent Copy to back up data even during periods of higher I/O activity. In some cases, ensuring data availability may be more important than preserving levels of application performance.

Where to use Concurrent Copy

You can use Concurrent Copy to back up any data that can be backed up using DFSMSdss because DFSMSdss is the external interface to Concurrent Copy. The general-purpose design of Concurrent Copy simplifies the use of Concurrent Copy because it builds on existing experience with DFSMSdss.

For example, IMS databases can be backed up using DFSMSdss. During the recovery process, IMS database recovery control (DBRC) coordinates recovery of the DFSMSdss dump and the application of updates from the IMS log. The same is available also for DB2. Data sets that are consistently in use, such as DFSMShsm control data sets, databases, and libraries, require specialized facilities to ensure that data set backups are non-disruptive and preserve data set integrity.

Management class attributes let you choose how DFSMShsm and DFSMSdss should process data sets that are in use during availability management. Point-in-time capabilities using Concurrent Copy on the ESS allow you to:

- Use DFSMSdss to create a point of consistency backup of CICS, IMS, or DB2 databases without needing to quiesce them during the entire backup process.
- Use DFSMSdss to create backups of data sets without requiring serialization during the entire backup process. DFSMSdss serializes the data during the Concurrent Copy initialization period (the time between the start of DFSMSdss and the issuing of the ADR734I message).

- Create and maintain multiple backup versions of DFSMShsm control data sets, while increasing the availability of DFSMShsm functions, such as recall.
- Use the backup-while-open capability for CICS VSAM data sets with DFSMSdss in batch mode or with automated DFSMShsm, to provide backups with data integrity even when the data sets are being updated. Data integrity is assured for VSAM KSDSs even when CICS access results in control interval or control area splits or data set obtaining another extent.

Concurrent Copy coexistence with z/OS Global Mirror

z/OS Global Mirror is designed to work together with the DS8000, thus efficiently managing the available resources. The SDM issues I/Os to efficiently drain from the cache records that are designated to be copied by z/OS Global Mirror. Also with the z/OS Global Mirror system data mover sessions, separate storage control sessions (SC sessions) can be defined to more effectively manage the remote copy environment.

Concurrent Copy and z/OS Global Mirror both use DS8000 cache. If you run z/OS Global Mirror and start up heavy Concurrent Copy activity, the cache may become rapidly consumed. In this case, Concurrent Copy activity may become canceled, and z/OS Global Mirror may start to pace primary updates. You may instead want to run Concurrent Copy during low z/OS Global Mirror update activity periods, or else run Concurrent Copy against the secondary volumes of the z/OS Global Mirror pair.

Equip all the storage subsystems with adequate cache and channel connections to handle the work associated with the z/OS Global Mirror sessions and the coexisting Concurrent Copy sessions. If adequate resources are not provided, the data mover may not be able to empty cache rapidly enough, and the cache could become overcommitted.

Simultaneous Concurrent Copy sessions

As said before, each Concurrent Copy session generates additional channel load and increases utilization of the storage paths within the DS8000. If you are running multiple simultaneous Concurrent Copy sessions it is possible you may generate contention for these resources, resulting in greater than normal queueing and extended response times.

Number of data mover-allowed sessions

In addition to the server and storage resources needed for running multiple SDM sessions, you must consider the following design maximums:

- 16 data mover sessions per device (combined total of Concurrent Copy and/or z/OS Global Mirror)
- 64 data mover sessions per DS8000 logical subsystem (combined total of Concurrent Copy and/or z/OS Global Mirror)
- 16384 data mover sessions per DS8000 (16 Address Groups times16 LSSs times 64)

If you attempt to use more than 16 data mover sessions per device, or more than 16384 data mover sessions per DS8000 at the same time, you will receive an error message, and the copy will continue using the traditional DFSMSdss copy.

Sessions for aggregate group

If you relate Concurrent Copy processing to the ABACKUP command for an aggregate group that includes numerous data sets that are on multiple devices and LSS, a separate Concurrent Copy session is created for each LSS that has volumes containing data defined by the aggregate.

SMF information

The SDM writes a system management facility (SMF) type 42 subtype 4 record that contains session statistics for each Concurrent Copy session when the session ends. Concurrent Copy records contain the identifier CC. Among other things, you can use the information in this record to determine the following statistics:

- Session initialization time
- Maximum size of host cached storage subsystem sidefiles
- Number of intercepted writes

The SMF type 42 subtype 4 record is described in detail in the publication *z/OS DFSMS Advanced Copy Services*, SC35-0428.

Examples of Concurrent Copy invocation

This section illustrates some examples of how Concurrent Copy can be invoked for either:

- Full volume dump
- Logical data set dump
- Logical data set copy
- Full volume copy invoking FlashCopy

Also discussed in this section is the invocation of Concurrent Copy from an application program.

DFSMSdss: Dump and copy examples

Example B-3 shows a DFSMSdss full volume dump using Concurrent Copy. No special action is required to perform a restore operation afterwards.

Example: B-3 DFSMSdss full volume dump with Concurrent Copy

```
//DSSJOB JOB ...
//DUMPSTEP EXEC PGM=ADRDSSU
//SYSPRINT DD    SYSOUT=*
//DASD     DD    UNIT=SYSDA,VOL=SER=(SSDASD),DISP=OLD
//TAPE     DD    UNIT=TAPE,VOL=SER=(TAPE01,TAPE02,TAPE03),LABEL=(1,SL),
//  DISP=(NEW,KEEP),DSN=USER.BACKUP
//SYSIN    DD    *
       DUMP FULL INDDNAME(DASD) OUTDDNAME(TAPE) -
                 COMPRESS CONCURRENT
/*
```

Example B-4 shows a DFSMSdss logical data set dump of three fully qualified data sets using Concurrent Copy. No special action is required to perform a restore operation after a Concurrent Copy dump operation.

Example: B-4 Logical data set dump operation with CONCURRENT

```
//JOB6      JOB ...
//DUMPSTEP EXEC PGM=ADRDSSU
//SYSPRINT DD    SYSOUT=*
//TAPE     DD    UNIT=TAPE,VOL=SER=(TAPE01,TAPE02,TAPE03),LABEL=(1,SL),
//  DISP=(NEW,KEEP),DSN=USER.BACKUP
//SYSIN    DD    *
       DUMP DATASET(INCLUDE(USER.LOG,USER.TABLE,USER.XREF)) -
            OUTDDNAME(TAPE) OPTIMIZE(4) CONCURRENT
/*
```

Example B-5 shows a DFSMSdss logical data set copy using Concurrent Copy.

Example: B-5 Data set Copy with CONCURRENT

```
//DSSJOB JOB ...
//COPYSTEP EXEC PGM=ADRDSSU
//SYSPRINT DD   SYSOUT=*
//SYSIN    DD   *
       COPY DATASET(INCLUDE(USER.LOG,USER.TABLE,USER.XREF)) -
            OUTDYNAM(OVOL01,OVOL02,OVOL03,OVOL08) -
            ALLDATA(*) ALLEXCP CONCURRENT -
            STORCLAS(BACKUP) RENAMEUNCONDITIONAL(USERX)
/*
```

DFSMSdss: FlashCopy example

Example B-6 shows an example of the use of FlashCopy and Concurrent Copy together. It is a full volume copy between two volumes in the same LSS. As such, they were eligible for FlashCopy, and FlashCopy was used as shown by the message ADR806I. At the same time, the CC keyword is specified so you get both ADR806I and ADR734I Concurrent Copy initialization successful messages.

Example: B-6 Using FlashCopy and Concurrent Copy together

```
//STEPT40 EXEC PGM=ADRDSSU
//SYSPRINT DD SYSOUT=*
//SYSUDUMP DD SYSOUT=V,OUTLIM=3000
//SYSIN   DD *
//*
COPY FULL -
   INDYNAM ((CP11S3)) -
     OUTDYNAM ((TP11S3)) -
    COPYVOLID -
      CC
ADR101I (R/I)-RI01 (01), TASKID 001 HAS BEEN ASSIGNED TO COMMAND 'COPY '
ADR109I (R/I)-RI01 (01), 2000.107 16:09:59 INITIAL SCAN OF USER CONTROL STATEMENTS
COMPLETED.
ADR016I (001)-RI01 (01), RACF LOGGING OPTION IN EFFECT FOR THIS TASK
ADR006I (001)-STEND(01), 2000.107 16:10:00 EXECUTION BEGINS
ADR241I (001)-DDTFP(01), TARGET VTOC BEGINNING AT 000550:0000 AND ENDING AT 000550:0014 IS
OVERLAID
ADR806I (001)-TOMI (02), VOLUME COPIED USING A FAST REPLICATION FUNCTION.
ADR734I (001)-TOMI (03), 2000.107 16:10:12 CONCURRENT COPY INITIALIZATION SUCCESSFUL FOR
VOLUME CP11S3. SERIALIZATION FOR THIS DATA
                         IS RELEASED IF DFSMSDSS HELD IT. THE INTERMEDIATE RETURN CODE IS
0000.
ADR320I (001)-SBRTN(01), VOLUME SERIAL TP11S3 ON UNIT D70C IS CHANGED TO CP11S3
ADR344I (001)-SBRTN(01), VOLSER ON UCB D70C IS A DUPLICATE. VOLUME MADE UNAVAILABLE.
ADR006I (001)-STEND(02), 2000.107 16:10:35 EXECUTION ENDS
ADR013I (001)-CLTSK(01), 2000.107 16:10:35 TASK COMPLETED WITH RETURN CODE 0000
ADR012I (SCH)-DSSU (01), 2000.107 16:10:35 DFSMSDSS PROCESSING COMPLETE. HIGHEST RETURN
CODE IS 0000
```

Invocation from an application program

When DFSMSdss is invoked from an application program, you can use the user interaction module (UIM) to interact with DFSMSdss. For user interactions to take place, the application must invoke DFSMSdss and must provide a pointer to a user interaction module (UIM) list. DFSMSdss can be invoked by any of the following system macros:

```
ATTACH EP=ADRDSSU,PARAM=(OPTPTR,DDPTR,PAGEPTR,UIMPTR,UAPTR),VL=1

LINK EP=ADRDSSU,PARAM=(OPTPTR,DDPTR,PAGEPTR,UIMPTR,UAPTR),VL=1

CALL (15),(OPTPTR,DDPTR,PAGEPTR,UIMPTR,UAPTR),VL
```

When a UIM exit routine is specified, DFSMSdss processes normally, then at each point in the process (DFSMSdss exit points), the UIM exit routine is called conditionally to allow some types of user operations. The exit identification block is passed to the UIM every time DFSMSdss gives control to it.

Among the exit points available with DFSMSdss (EIOPTION 1 to 26), DFSMSdss calls the UIM with option code 24 (EIOPTION 24) to inform it that the initialization of the Concurrent Copy session for a given data set or volume has completed. For full volume or tracks operation, there is only one call (because there is only one input volume). For a physical data set operation, there is one call for each input volume. For a logical data set operation, there is one call for every data set.

DFSMSdss does not call the UIM with this option code if the CONCURRENT keyword is not specified. DFSMSdss provides the UIM with information through the EIREC24 structure within the exit identification block, ADREIB (in the ADREIDO macro).

For a detailed description of the DFSMSdss interaction with the user interface module (UIM) when invoking from an application program, refer to the publication *z/OS DFSMSdss Storage Administration Reference*, SC35-0424.

Installation options exit

Usage of the Concurrent Copy function can also be controlled through the installation options exit, a product-sensitive programming interface intended for users. Refer to Options Installation Exit Routine (ADRUIXIT) described in *z/OS DFSMS Installation Exits*, SC26-7396, for more information.

Simple Network Management Protocol (SNMP) notification for remote copy environments

In this appendix we describe SNMP traps that are sent out in a remote copy environment.

SNMP overview

The DS8000 will send out SNMP traps when a state change in a remote copy services environment occurs. Therefore 13 traps are implemented. The traps 1xx are sent out for a state change of a physical link connection, the 2xx traps are sent out for state changes in the logical copy services setup.

The DS HMC can be set up to send SNMP traps to up to 2 defined IP addresses. The Tools *eRCMF* (see Chapter 38., "Enterprise Remote Copy Management Facility" on page 549) and *GMU* (see Chapter 39., "IBM TotalStorage Global Mirror Utility" on page 587) are listening to SNMP traps of the DS8000. Also a Network Management program, like Tivoli Netview, can be used to catch and process the SNMP traps.

Physical connection events

With the trap 1xx range, a state change of the physical links will be reported. The trap will be sent out, if the physical remote copy link is interrupted. The link traps will be sent from both DS8000s, the primary and the secondary system. The *PLink* and *SLink* columns are in use for the 2105.

If one or several links of multiple links are interrupted, a trap 100, as shown in Example C-1, is posted and will indicate that the redundancy is degraded. The *RC* column in the trap will represent the reason code for the interruption of the link. The reason codes are listed in Table 39-1.

Example: C-1 Trap 100: PPRC links degraded

```
PPRC Links Degraded
UNIT: Mnf Type-Mod SerialNm LS
PRI:  IBM 2107-922 75-20781 12
SEC:  IBM 2107-9A2 75-ABTV1 24
Path: Type  PP   PLink  SP   SLink  RC
1:    FIBRE 0143 XXXXXX 0010 XXXXXX 15
2:    FIBRE 0213 XXXXXX 0140 XXXXXX OK
```

If all links are interrupted, a trap 101, as shown in Example C-2, is posted. This event is indicating that no communication between primary and secondary system is possible any more.

Example: C-2 Trap 101: PPRC links down

```
PPRC Links Down
UNIT: Mnf Type-Mod SerialNm LS
PRI:  IBM 2107-922 75-20781 10
SEC:  IBM 2107-9A2 75-ABTV1 20
Path: Type  PP   PLink  SP   SLink  RC
1:    FIBRE 0143 XXXXXX 0010 XXXXXX 17
2:    FIBRE 0213 XXXXXX 0140 XXXXXX 17
```

Once the DS8000 can communicate again via any of the links, trap 102, as shown in Example C-3, is sent once the interrupted links are available again.

Example: C-3 Trap 102:PPRC links up

```
PPRC Links Up
UNIT: Mnf Type-Mod SerialNm LS
PRI:  IBM 2107-9A2 75-ABTV1 21
```

```
SEC:  IBM 2107-000 75-20781 11
Path: Type  PP   PLink  SP   SLink  RC
1:    FIBRE 0010 XXXXXX 0143 XXXXXX OK
2:    FIBRE 0140 XXXXXX 0213 XXXXXX OK
```

Table 39-1 PPRC path reason codes

Reason code	Description
00	No path.
01	ESCON path established.
02	Initialization failed. ESCON link reject threshold exceeded when attempting to send ELP or RID frames.
03	Time out. No reason available.
04	No resources available at primary for the logical path establishment.
05	No resources available at secondary for the logical path establishment.
06	Secondary CU Sequence Number or Logical Sub- system number mismatch.
07	Secondary CU SS ID mismatch or failure of the I/O that collects secondary information for validation.
08	ESCON link is offline. This is caused the lack of light detection coming from a host, peer or switch.
09	Establish failed but will retry when conditions change.
0A	The primary control unit port or link cannot be converted to channel mode since a logical path is already established on the port or link. The establish paths operation will not be retried within the control unit automatically.
0B	Reserved for use by StorageTek.
10	Configuration Error. The source of the error is one of the following: 1. The specification of the SA ID does not match the installed ESCON adapter cards in the primary controller. 2. For ESCON paths, the secondary control unit destination address is zero and an ESCON Director (switch) was found in the path. 3. For ESCON paths, the secondary control unit destination address is non-zero and an ESCON Director does not exist in the path. That is, the path is a direct connection.
11	Reserved.
12	Reserved.
13 / OK	Fibre path established.
14	Fibre Channel Path Link Down.
15	Fibre Channel Path Retry Exceeded.
16	Fibre Channel Path Secondary Adapter not PPRC capable. This could be due to 1. Secondary Adapter not configured properly, or does not have the correct microcode loaded. 2. The secondary adapter is already a target of 32 different ESS, DS8000 and DS6000.
17	Fibre Channel Path Secondary Adapter not available.
18	Fibre Channel Path Primary Login Exceeded.
19	Fibre Channel Path Secondary Login Exceeded.

Remote copy events

If you have configured Consistency Groups and a volume within this *Consistency Group* is suspended due to a write error to the secondary device, trap 200 as shown in Example C-4, will be sent out. One trap per LSS, that is configured with the consistency group option. This trap could be handled by automation software like *eRCMF* to freeze this Consistency Group.

Example: C-4 Trap 200: LSS-pair Consistency Group PPRC-pair error

```
LSS-Pair Consistency Group PPRC-Pair Error
UNIT: Mnf Type-Mod SerialNm LS LD SR
PRI:  IBM 2107-922 75-03461 56 84 08
SEC:  IBM 2107-9A2 75-ABTV1 54 84
```

Trap 202, as shown in Example C-5, will be sent out if a remote Copy Pair goes into a suspend State. The trap does contain the serial number (*SerialNm) of* the primary and secondary machine, the LSS (*LS*) and the logical device (*LD*). To avoid SNMP trap flooding, the number of SNMP traps for the LSS will be throttled. The complete suspended pair information is represented in the summary. The last row of the trap represents the suspend state for all pairs in the reporting LSS. The suspended pair information contains a hexadecimal string of a length of 64 characters. By converting this hex string into binary, each bit will represent a single device. If the bit is 1, then the device is suspended, otherwise the device is still in full duplex mode.

Example: C-5 Trap 202: Primary PPRC devices on LSS suspended due to error

```
Primary PPRC Devices on LSS Suspended Due to Error
UNIT: Mnf Type-Mod SerialNm LS LD SR
PRI:  IBM 2107-922 75-20781 11 00 03
SEC:  IBM 2107-9A2 75-ABTV1 21 00
Start: 2005/11/14 09:48:05 CST
PRI Dev Flags (1 bit/Dev, 1=Suspended):
C000000000000000000000000000000000000000000000000000000000000000
```

Global Mirror related SNMP traps

Trap 210, as shown in Example C-6, is sent out when a Consistency Group in a Global Mirror enviroment is successfully formed.

Example: C-6 Trap210: `Asynchronous PPRC initial Consistency Group successfully formed`

```
2005/11/14 15:30:55 CET
Asynchronous PPRC Initial Consistency Group Successfully Formed
UNIT: Mnf Type-Mod SerialNm
      IBM 2107-922 75-20781
Session ID: 4002
```

Trap 211, as shown in Example C-7, will be sent out if the Global Mirror setup got into a severe error state, where no attempts will be done to form a Consistency Group.

Example: C-7 Trap 211: Asynchronous PPRC Session is in a fatal state

```
Asynchronous PPRC Session is in a Fatal State
UNIT: Mnf Type-Mod SerialNm
      IBM 2107-922 75-20781
Session ID: 4002
```

Trap 212, as shown in Example C-8, is sent out when a Consistency Group could not be created in a Global Mirror Copy relation. Some of the reasons could be:

- Volumes have been taken out of a copy session.
- The remote copy link bandwidth might not be sufficient.
- The FC link between the PPRC primary and secondary system is not available.

Example: C-8 Trap 212: `Asynchronous PPRC Consistency Group failure - retry will be attempted`

```
Asynchronous PPRC Consistency Group Failure - Retry will be attempted
UNIT: Mnf Type-Mod SerialNm
      IBM 2107-922 75-20781
Session ID: 4002
```

Trap 213, as shown in Example 39-13, will be sent out when a Consistency Group in a Global Mirror enviroment could be formed after a previous consistency group formation failure.

Example 39-13 Trap 213: `Asynchronous PPRC Consistency Group successful recovery`

```
Asynchronous PPRC Consistency Group Successful Recovery
UNIT: Mnf Type-Mod SerialNm
      IBM 2107-9A2 75-ABTV1
Session ID: 4002
```

Trap 214, as shown in Example C-9, will be sent out if a Global Mirror Copy Session is terminated using the DS CLI command **rmgmir** or the corresponding GUI function.

Example: C-9 Trap 214: `Asynchronous PPRC Master terminated`

```
2005/11/14 15:30:14 CET
Asynchronous PPRC Master Terminated
UNIT: Mnf Type-Mod SerialNm
IBM 2107-922 75-20781
Session ID: 4002
```

Trap 215, as shown in Example C-10, will be sent out if, in the Global Mirror environment, the Master has detected a failure to complete the FlashCopy commit. The trap will be sent out after a number of commit retries have failed.

Example: C-10 Trap 215: `Asynchronous PPRC FlashCopy at remote site unsuccessful`

```
Asynchronous PPRC FlashCopy at Remote Site Unsuccessful
A UNIT: Mnf Type-Mod SerialNm
        IBM 2107-9A2 75-ABTV1
Session ID: 4002
```

Trap 216, as shown in Example C-11, will be sent out if a Global Mirror *Master*, cannot terminate the Global Copy relationship at one of its *Subordinates* (*slave*). This might occur if the Master is terminated with **rmgmir** but the Master cannot terminate the copy relationship on the Subordinate. The user may need to run a **rmgmir** against the Subordinate to prevent any interference with other Global Mirror sessions.

Example: C-11 Trap 216: Asynchronous PPRC slave termination unsuccessful

```
Asynchronous PPRC Slave Termination Unsuccessful
UNIT:   Mnf Type-Mod SerialNm
Master: IBM 2107-922 75-20781
Slave:  IBM 2107-921 75-03641
Session ID: 4002
```

Trap 217, as shown in Example C-12, will be sent out if a Global Mirror Copy environment was suspended by the DS CLI command **pausegmir** or the corresponding GUI function.

Example: C-12 Trap 217: Asynchronous PPRC paused

```
Asynchronous PPRC Paused
UNIT: Mnf Type-Mod SerialNm
      IBM 2107-9A2 75-ABTV1
Session ID: 4002
```

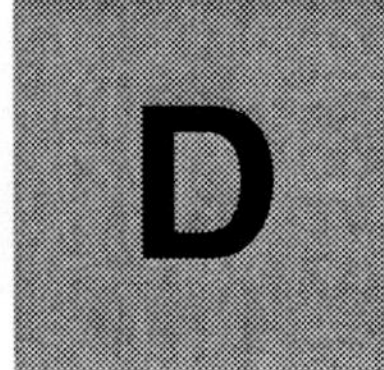

Licensing

In this appendix we describe how the licensing functions for Copy Services for the DS8000 Series are arranged. This appendix contains descriptions and examples to illustrate the basic operation of these functions. The charging process is also described.

Licenses

All DS8000 Series machines must have an Operating Environment License or OEL for the total storage installed, as defined in decimal TB. The application of licenses to Copy Services functions is defined as the *Scope*, which refers to the type of operating environment. The options are CKD for z/OS environments, FB for open or heterogeneous environments, and ALL where Copy Services are required in both environments. There are six types of licenses possible for a DS8000:

- **OEL:** Operating Environment License; mandatory for capacity of all installed storage.
- **FICON:** z/OS attachment. Count/Key/Data (CKD) configuration for z/OS, at any level, with one time charge for activation.
- **PAV:** Parallel Access Volumes. CKD FICON attachment only, which is a prerequisite.

The following licenses apply to Copy Services:

- **PTC:** Point-in-Time Copy also known as FlashCopy. Either CKD, FB or ALL installed storage.
- **RMC:** Remote Mirror and Copy, also know as PPRC. Either CKD, FB or ALL. An RMC license is required on the remote machine as well.
- **RMZ:** Remote Mirror and Copy for z/OS, also known as z/OS Global Mirror (or XRC). CKD environment only.

It should be noted that the RMC License provides the functions of Metro Mirror, Global Copy, and Global Mirror, depending on how it is configured during installation. These functions were previously known as PPRC and its variants. z/OS Global Mirror (previously called XRC) is now known as RMZ.

Authorized level

All Copy Services functions require licensing to be activated. This means that the customer must purchase a license for the appropriate level of storage for each Copy Service function that is required. They then have to install the License Key generated using the Disk Storage Feature Activation application (*DSFA)*. Another consideration relates to the authorized level required. In most cases the total capacity installed must be licensed; this is the total capacity in decimal TB equal to or greater than the actual capacity installed, including all RAID parity disks and hot spares.

An exception may be where a mix of both zSeries and open systems hosts are using the same storage server. In this case it is possible to acquire Copy Services licenses for just the capacity formatted for CKD, or just the capacity formatted for FB storage. This would imply that licensed Copy Services function is needed only for open systems hosts, or only for zSeries hosts. If, however, a Copy Services function is required for both CKD and FB, then that Copy Services license needs to match the total configured capacity of the machine. Authorization level is maintained by the licensed code in the controller and the DSFA application.

Example: The actual capacity is 15 TB, used for both CKD and FB, the scope for the OEL is therefore a type of ALL and the installed OEL must be at least 15 TB. If the client has split storage allocation, with 8 TB for CKD, and only CKD storage is using FlashCopy, then the scope type for the PTC license can be set to CKD. Now the PTC license can be purchased at the CKD level of 8 TB. However, this means that no open systems hosts can use the FlashCopy function.

The actual ordered level of any Copy Service license can be any level above that required or installed. Licenses can be added and have their capacities increased, non-disruptively to an installed system.

Important: A decrease in the scope or the capacity of a license requires a disruptive IML of the DS8000 Storage Facility Image.

Charging example

A client can choose to purchase any or all DS8000 licenses at an authorization level at or above the installed raw disk capacity. It may be more cost effective to pre-install authorization to use greater than the currently installed storage capacity.

A simple rule for charges is remembering that the required authorization level depends upon the license scope:

- If the license scope is FB, the authorization level must be equal to or greater than the total amount of physical capacity within the system that will be logically configured as FB.
- If the license scope is CKD, the authorization level must be equal to or greater than the total amount of physical capacity within the system that will be logically configured as CKD.
- If the license scope is ALL, the authorization level must be equal to or greater than the total system physical capacity.

The dual Storage Facility Image (SFI) version of DS8300 (the model 9A2) uses the same logic, in this case added between the two SFIs. So all of the above applies to each SFI separately. It is possible to license Copy Services for a single *scope* in one SFI.

Here is an explanation of this scenario:

- If you activate a licensed function on only SFI 1 with a license scope of FB:
  - The authorization level must be equal to or greater than the total amount of physical capacity within SFI 1 that will be logically configured as FB.
- If you activate a licensed function on SFI 1 and SFI 2, both with a license scope of CKD:
  - The authorization level must be equal to or greater than the total amount of physical capacity within both SFI 1 and SFI 2 that will be logically configured as CKD.
- If you activate a licensed function on SFI 1 with a license scope of FB and on SFI 2 with a license scope of ALL:
  - The authorization level must be equal to or greater than the total amount of physical capacity within SFI 1 that will be logically configured as FB and the total physical capacity within SFI 2.

Terms comparison

Table D-1 shows the nomenclature linking the various Copy Services functions and ordering codes associated with them.

Table D-1 Copy Services nomenclature comparison to ESS

DS8000 Term	DS8000 term for ordering	ESS Copy Services Version Term	ESS term for ordering
Point-in-time copy	Point-in-time copy or PTC	FlashCopy	FLC
Metro Mirror	Remote Mirror and Copy or RMC	Synchronous PPRC	PRC
Global Mirror	Remote Mirror and Copy or RMC	Asynchronous PPRC	PRC
Global Copy	Remote Mirror and Copy or RMC	PPRC-XD	PRC
Parallel Access Volume	PAV	PAV	PAV
z/OS Global Mirror	Remote Mirror for z/OS or RMZ	Extended Remote Copy	XRC

CLI migration

In this appendix we describe the way you can migrate Copy Services tasks on the ESS environment to the DS Copy Services environment. The Copy Services interfaces described here cover the Graphical User Interface (GUI) and the Command-Line Interface (CLI). Excluded are the Copy Services interfaces, which are executed directly by the z/OS.

Migrating ESS CLI to DS CLI

With the introduction of the new IBM DS8000 Storage Unit, a new Copy Services application is also introduced. The Copy Services functions can be issued via the DS Graphical User Interface (GUI) or via the DS CLI.

The Advanced Copy Services functions that are available on the ESS 800 are also available on the DS8000 (except for IBM TotalStorage Metro/Global Copy). Although the functions are still available, there are also some differences that need to be considered in replacing your ESS CLI with a DS CLI. These are:

- Point-in-Time Copy (FlashCopy) does not support Consistency Groups on the GUI.
- Fibre Channel is used for Metro Mirror, Global Mirror, Global Copy.
- The GUI runs real time only (tasks cannot be saved) while the CLI can be invoked using a saved script.
- The DS CLI supports both the ESS 800/750 and the DS8000.
- ESS 800 must be at Licensed Internal Code (LIC) level 2.4.3.15 or higher.

Review the ESS tasks to migrate

Review what Copy Services tasks you wish to migrate. You may check these tasks from your ESS GUI or ESS CLI. Example E-1 shows the **esscli list** command to display the tasks.

Example: E-1 esscli list task

```
esscli list task -s copy_services-server -u csadmin -p passw0rd

Wed Nov 24 10:29:31 EST 2004 IBM ESSCLI 2.4.0
Task Name                        Type                            Status
-------------------------------------------------------------------------
H_Epath_test16                   PPRCEstablishPaths              NotRunning
H_Epath_test17                   PPRCEstablishPaths              NotRunning
Brocade_pr_lss10                 PPRCEstablishPair               NotRunning
Brocade_pr_lss11                 PPRCEstablishPair               NotRunning
Flash10041005                    FCEstablish                     NotRunning
```

You can use the ESS CLI to display the contents of each saved task and write the contents to a file. See Example E-2.

Example: E-2 esscli show task

```
esscli show task -s copy_services_server -u csadmin -p passw0rd -d "name=Flash10041005"

Wed Nov 24 10:37:17 EST 2004 IBM ESSCLI 2.4.0
Taskname=Flash10041005
Tasktype=FCEstablish
Options=NoBackgroundCopy
SourceServer=2105.23953
TargetServer=2105.23953
SourceVol                TargetVol
-------------------------------------------------------------------------
1004                     1005
```

You can also check your saved tasks via the ESS GUI. See Figure E-1.

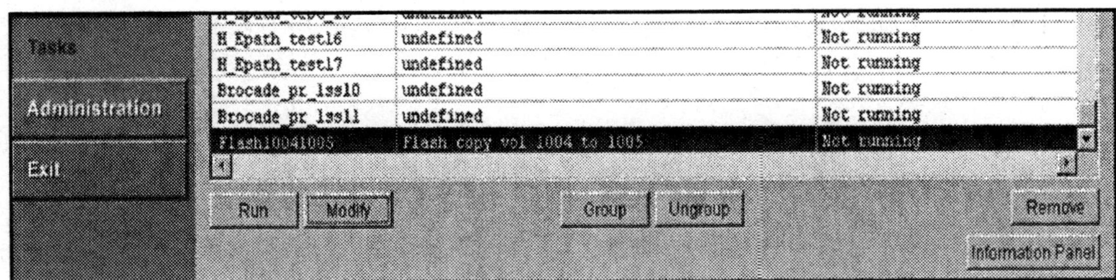

Figure E-1 ESS Copy Services GUI tasks panel

Highlight the task and click the information panel. See Figure E-2.

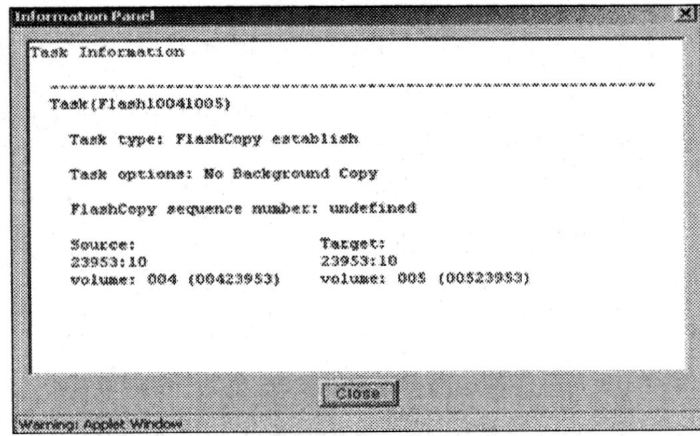

Figure E-2 ESS task information

Review also the specific server scripts (depending on the OS) that perform tasks which set up and execute saved ESS CLI saved tasks. You may need to edit or translate these scripts in order to run your DS CLI tasks.

Important: On the ESS 800, open systems volume IDs are given in an 8-digit format, xxx-sssss, where xxx is the LUN ID and sssss is the serial number of the ESS 800. In the example used in this appendix, the volumes shown are 004-23953 to 005-23953. These volumes are open systems, or fixed block volumes. When referring to them in the DS CLI, you must add 1000 to the volume ID, so volume 004-23953 is volume ID 1004 and volume 005-23953 is volume ID 1005. This is very important because on the ESS 800, the following address ranges are actually used:

0000 to 0FFF CKD zSeries volumes (4096 possible addresses)
1000 to 1FFF Open systems fixed block LUNs (4096 possible addresses)

If we intend to use FlashCopy to copy ESS LUN 004-23953 onto 005-23953 using the DS CLI, we must specify 1004 and 1005. If instead we specify 0004 and 0005, we will actually run the FlashCopy against CKD volumes. This may result in an unplanned outage on the zSeries system that was using CKD volume 0005.

The ESS CLI command, **show task**, will show the correct value for the volume ID.

Convert the individual tasks

Choose the ESS CLI tasks which you need to translate to DS CLI. Refer to the *IBM TotalStorage DS8000 Command-Line Interface User's Guide* book, SC26-7625. You can then save each translated task and be able to run it in the DS8000 CLI environment.

> **Note:** The 2107 GUI (via DS HMC) does not save Copy Services tasks unlike the ESS GUI. You can only use the DS GUI for Copy Services in real time mode.

Translate also (if needed) and edit the individual server scripts that will set up and execute the saved DS CLI scripts. See Table E-1 for an example of command translation.

Table E-1 Converting ESS CLI to DS CLI

Task parameter	ESS CLI parameter	DS CLI conversion	Description
Tasktype	FCEstablish	mkflash	establish FlashCopy
Options	NoBackgroundCopy	-nocp	No background copy upon FlashCopy
SourceServer	2105.23953	-dev IBM.2105-23953	device ID
TargetServer	2105.23953	N/A	used only once in DS CLI
Source and Target vols.	1004 1005	1004:1005	separated by a colon in DS CLI

DS CLI commands

Example E-3 is the translation to DS CLI commands.

Example: E-3 DS CLI command

```
dscli> mkflash -nocp -dev IBM.2105-23953 1004:1005
CMUC00137I mkflash: FlashCopy pair 1004:1005 successfully created.
dscli> lsflash -dev IBM.2105-23953 1004:1005
ID        SrcLSS SequenceNum Timeout ActiveCopy Recoding Persistent Revertible
==============================================================================
1004:1005 10     0           120     Disabled   Disabled Disabled   Disabled
```

See Figure E-3 for the GUI output.

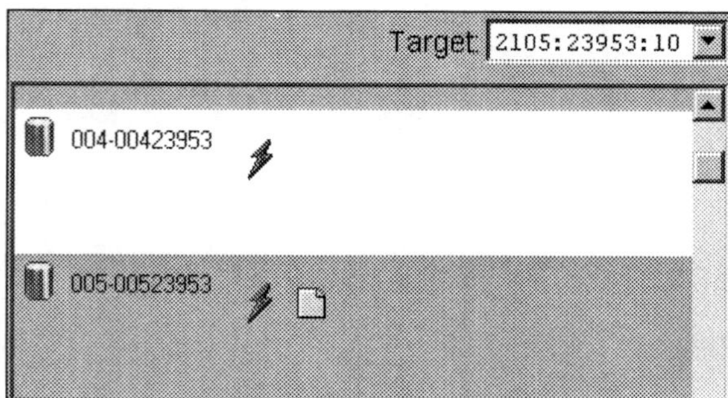

Figure E-3 ESS GUI FlashCopy window

ESS / DS CLI comparison

Table E-2 shows a brief comparison of the major components between the ESS CLI and the DS CLI.

Table E-2 ESS and DS CLI commands and parameters comparison

ESS CLI	DS CLI	Comments
list server	lsserver	Like the 2105, the 2107 storage facility image contains one pair of servers.
list volumespace	lsextpool, showextpool, lsRank, showRank, lsarray, showarray, lsarraysite	See Note 1
create volumespace	Mkextpool, mkarray, mkRank	
delete volumespace	rmRank, rmarray, rmextpool	
list diskgroup	lsarraysite	a 2107 Array Site consists of eight disk drives (DDMs) that are made into a RAID array. The 2107 does not support the JBOD Array configuration.
list port	lsioport, showioport	The 2107 CLI lsioport and showioport commands include the –metrics parameter that returns the performance counter values for the respective I/O port IDs. The –metrics parameter provides the means to monitor I/O port performance statistics.
set port	setioport	See Note 2
list volume	lsfbvol, lsckdvol	See Note 3
create volume	mkfbvol, mkckdvol	
set volume	chfbvol, chckdvol	
list pav	lsckdvol, showckdvol	
create pav	mkckdvol	
delete pav	rmckdvol	
list volumeaccess	lsvolgrp, showvolgrp	See Note 4
create volumeaccess	mkvolgrp, chvolgrp	
delete volumeaccess	rmvolgrp	
list hostconnection	lshostconnect, showhostconnect	The 2107 CLI commands include the volume group ID parameter. For 2107, the hostconnect commands concern SCSI-FCP host port connections to ESS I/O ports that are configured for SCSI-FCP and "identified" access mode.
create hostconnection	mkhostconnect	
delete hostconnection	rmhostconnect	
set hostconnection	chhostconnect	

ESS CLI	DS CLI	Comments
list log	N/A	
list featurecode	lsda, lshba, lsioencl, lsuser, mkuser, rmuser, chuser, lsstgencl	The 2107 CLI commands can display feature codes when the appropriate parameters are used with the commands.
list task	NA	
show task	NA	
list pprcpaths	lspprcpath	Unlike the 2105, the 2107 CLI Copy Services functions are not task oriented. The 2107 CLI provides a complete set of FlashCopy and PPRC make, change, remove, list, and show commands.
rsExecuteTask	mkflash, rmflash, mkpprc, rmpprc, mkpprcpath, rmpprcpath, mksession, chsession, rmsession	The 2107 CLI provides a complete set of FlashCopy and PPRC commands that may be used in the coding of scripts that emulate 2105 Copy Services tasks.
rsList2105s	lssu	The 2107 CLI lssu command returns both 2105 and 2107 objects that are contained by the ESS Network Interface domain
rsQuery, rsQueryComplete, rsFlashCopyQuery	lsflash, lspprc	These 2107 Copy Services CLI commands are equivalent to the respective 2105 CLI commands. The 2107 mkflashcopy and mkpprc commands provide a wait flag that delays command response until copy complete status is achieved.
rsTestConnection	lsaavailpprcport	

Note1: Volume space configuration is a primary difference between 2105 and 2107. Like the 2105, a 2107 storage facility image volume space contains a Raid-5 or Raid-10 Array and Rank that are configured from an Array Site. For 2105, one command configures an Array Site into a RAID Array and Rank. For 2107, one command configures an Array Site into an Array, and a second command configures an Array into a Rank. For 2105, a Rank is configured as fixed block or CKD, and a CKD Rank can contain "interleave" CKD volumes. For 2107, a Rank is assigned to a user-defined Extent Pool object, which the user defines as either the fixed block or CKD storage type. The "interleave" volume construct does not exist for 2107. For 2105, a volume is configured from a specific Rank, and cannot span Rank boundaries. For 2107, a volume is configured from an Extent Pool. An Extent Pool can contain multiple Ranks. A 2107 volume consists of one or more extents that can be allocated from one or more Ranks. A CKD extent is 0.94 GB or 1113 CKD cylinders.

For 2105, a Rank is either assigned to server 0 or server 1, dependent on Array Site location. A 2105 Rank is assigned to one of 32 possible LSS IDs, dependent on device adapter pair location and storage type configuration.

For 2107, an Extent Pool is assigned to server 0 or server 1. A Rank that is configured from any Array Site can be assigned to a server 0 or 1 Extent Pool. Array site position and device adapter pairs are not factors for the Rank to Extent Pool assignment. A volume that is created from a server 0 Extent Pool is assigned to an even numbered LSS ID. A volume created from a server 1 Extent Pool is assigned to odd numbered LSS IDs. A user must define at least two Extent Pools (0 and 1) but can define as many Extent Pools as there are Ranks. For 2105, a user can delete a Rank but cannot delete a volume. For 2107, a user can delete a single volume, Rank, or Extent Pool. The 2107 CLI **showrank** and **showextpool** commands include a metrics parameter that returns the performance counter values for a specified Rank or Extent Pool ID. The metrics parameter provides the means to monitor Rank and Extent Pool performance statistics.

Note2: A 2107 ESCON I/O port is used for zSeries host attachment but cannot be configured as a PPRC path. Each ESCON I/O port must be assigned to one and only one address group. An address group is a set of 16 LSS IDs that are configured as CKD LCUs, For example, 0x00 to 0x0F. ESCON I/O port access to 2107 CKD volumes is constrained to the first address group volumes, 0000 to 0FFF, which is up to 4096 volumes.

A 2107 Fibre Channel port is configured for either SCSI-FCP or FICON protocol. Like 2105, a FICON port is restricted to the point-to-point/switched fabric topology setting. A FICON I/O port is used for zSeries host attachment, but cannot be configured as a PPRC path. A FICON port must be configured for *anonymous* access mode, meaning that any zSeries host system port (WWNN/WWPN) has unrestricted access to all CKD volumes, up to 65,280 volumes.

Like 2105, a 2107 Fibre Channel SCSI-FCP I/O port can be configured for either the point-to-point/switched fabric or FC-AL connection topologies. A port that uses the point-to-point/switched fabric topology can be simultaneously used for OS host system I/O and for PPRC path configurations. The Fibre Channel SCSI-FCP IO port only allows "identified" host system ports to access volumes. A host system port WWPN must be is identified (registered) to each ESS IO port through which volume access is intended. Host system port WWPN identification is accomplished by the CLI mkhostconnect command

Note3: A 2107 storage facility image can contain up to 65,280 volumes. A 2105 Storage Unit can contain up to 4096 FB volumes and 4096 CKD volumes. Otherwise, the 2105 and 2107 volume definitions and characteristics are essentially identical.

For 2107 CKD PAV volumes, the CLI list and show commands identify both the original base and current base volume assignments. The original and current base concept exists for 2105, but specific relationships are not identified in the output.

The 2107 CLI provides a specific set of volume commands for each storage type, fixed block or CKD, as a means to clarify input parameter and output device adapter definitions.

The 2107 CLI showfbvol and showckdvol commands include a metrics parameter that returns the performance counter values for a specified volume ID. The metrics parameter provides the means to monitor volume performance statistics.

Note4: The 2105 volumeaccess commands concern volume ID assignment to a SCSI-FCP host port initiator, or WWPN. For 2107, volume IDs are assigned to a user defined volume group ID (mkvolgrp and chvolgrp). A volume group ID is then assigned to one or more host system ports (mkhostconnect and chhostconnect) as a means to complete the volume access configuration.

The volume group construct also exists in the 2105 internal code, but the construct is not externalized by the 2105 Specialist or CLI commands.

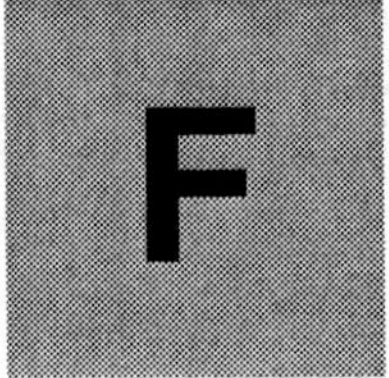

Service offerings

In this appendix we provide information about the service offerings that are available for the DS6000 and DS8000 series at the time of publication. It should be noted that services detailed here are not necessarily available in all geographies or countries. The following service offerings are described:

- IBM Implementation Services for TotalStorage disk systems
- IBM Implementation Services for TotalStorage Copy Functions
- IBM Implementation Services for TotalStorage Command-Line Interface
- IBM Migration Services for eServer™ zSeries data
- IBM Migration Services for open systems attached to TotalStorage disk systems
- IBM Geographically Dispersed Parallel Sysplex (GDPS)
- Enterprise Remote Copy Management Facility (eRCMF)
- IBM TotalStorage Continuous Availability for Windows
- IBM eServer iSeries Copy Services
- IBM Operational Support Services - Support Line

The following sections include a brief description of each offering as well as where you can find more information on the Web.

IBM Web sites for service offerings

IBM Global Services (IGS) and the IBM Systems Group can offer comprehensive assistance, including planning and design as well as implementation and migration support services. For more information on all of the following service offerings, contact your IBM representative or visit the following Web sites:

The IBM Global Service Web site can be found at:

http://www.ibm.com/services/us/index.wss/home

The IBM System Group Web site can be found at:

http://www.ibm.com/servers/storage/services/

IBM service offerings

This section describes the service offerings available from IBM Global Services and IBM Systems Group.

IBM Implementation Services for TotalStorage disk systems

This service includes planning for a new IBM TotalStorage disk system followed by implementation, configuration, and basic skills transfer instruction. For more information, visit the following Web site:

http://www.ibm.com/services/us/index.wss/so/its/a1005008

IBM Implementation Services for TotalStorage Copy Functions

This service is designed to assist in the planning, implementation, and testing of the IBM TotalStorage advanced copy functions, point-in-time copy and remote mirroring solutions. For more information, visit the following Web site:

http://www.ibm.com/services/us/index.wss/so/its/a1005009

IBM Implementation Services for TotalStorage Command-Line Interface

IBM provides a service through Global Services to help you with using the Command-Line Interface (CLI) in your system environment. It is designed to provide you with the ability to create and apply configurations online. For more information, visit the following Web site:

http://www.ibm.com/services/us/index.wss/so/its/a1005334

IBM Migration Services for eServer zSeries data

IBM provides a technical specialist at your site to help plan and assist in the implementation of non-disruptive DASD migration to a new or existing IBM TotalStorage disk systems. The migration is accomplished using the following software and hardware that allows DASD volumes to be copied to the new storage devices without interruption to service.

- Innovation Fast Dump Restore Plug and Swap (FDRPAS)
- Peer-to-Peer Remote Copy Extended Distance (PPRC-XD)
- Softek Replicator (TDMF)
- IBM Piper hardware assisted migration

Additional information about this offering is on the following Web site:

http://www.ibm.com/servers/storage/services/featured/hardware_assist.html

For more information about IBM Migration Services for eServer zSeries data, visit the following Web site:

http://www.ibm.com/services/us/index.wss/so/its/a1005010

IBM Migration Services for open systems attached to disk systems

IBM Migration Services for open systems attached to TotalStorage disk systems include planning for and implementation of data migration from an existing UNIX or Windows server™ to new or existing larger capacity IBM storage with minimal disruption. This service uses the following hardware and software tools:

- Remote Mirror and Copy (RMC), and Remote Mirror and Copy for z/OS (RMZ)
- Softek Replicator (TDMF) for Open
- Native operating system mirroring
- IBM Piper hardware assisted migration

The IBM hardware-assisted data migration services (IBM Piper), which we already mentioned in regard to the zSeries environment, can also be used in an open systems environment. For the latest information about this service, visit the following Web site:

http://www.ibm.com/servers/storage/services/featured/hardware_assist.html

For more information about IBM Migration Services for open systems attached to TotalStorage disk systems, visit the following Web site:

http://www.ibm.com/services/us/index.wss/so/its/a1005012

IBM Geographically Dispersed Parallel Sysplex (GDPS)

A Geographically Dispersed Parallel Sysplex (GDPS) is the ultimate disaster recovery and continuous availability solution for a zSeries multi-site enterprise. This solution automatically mirrors critical data and efficiently balances workload between the sites. The GDPS solution also uses automation and Parallel Sysplex technology to help manage multi-site databases, processors, network resources and storage subsystem mirroring. For the latest information on this service, visit the following Web site:

http://www-1.ibm.com/services/us/index.wss/offering/its/a1000189

Enterprise Remote Copy Management Facility (eRCMF)

IBM Implementation Services for enterprise Remote Copy Management Facility (eRCMF) is intended as a multisite Disaster Recovery solution for open systems and provides automation for repairing inconsistent RMC pairs. This is the software that communicates with the DS8000, DS6000 or ESS Copy Services server.

It is a scalable, flexible open systems solution that protects the business (data) and can be used for both:

- Planned outages (hardware and software upgrades)
- Unplanned outages (Disaster Recovery, testing a disaster)

It simplifies the disaster recovery implementation and concept. Once eRCMF is configured in the customer environment, it will monitor the RMC states of all specified LUNs/volumes. Visit the following Web site for the latest information:

http://www.ibm.com/services/us/index.wss/so/its/a1000110

Geographically Dispersed Sites for Microsoft Cluster Services

IBM TotalStorage Support for Geographically Dispersed Sites for Microsoft Cluster Service (MSCS) is designed to allow Microsoft Cluster installations to span geographically dispersed sites. It helps to protect clients from site disasters or storage subsystem failures. This service is designed to enable a tier 7 disaster recovery solution. It also provides high availability for applications and data running in Windows clustered server environments, by extending the distance that cluster nodes and storage can be separated, mirroring data between two IBM TotalStorage disk subsystems, and providing improved failure detection. You can find the latest information on this service on the following Web site:

```
http://www.ibm.com/servers/storage/services/featured/microsoft_application_environment.h
tml#GDSSolution
```

IBM eServer iSeries Copy Services

For the iSeries environment IBM offers a special toolkit, which allows you to use the advanced Copy Services functions with the iSeries. For more information on this, and the availability of iSeries services, refer to the following Web site:

```
http://www-1.ibm.com/servers/eserver/iseries/service/itc
```

IBM Operational Support Services - Support Line

IBM offers telephone or electronic access to highly-trained technical support specialists, who can serve as your one source for remote software support services.

Highlights of the offering are as follows:

- High-quality technical support for IBM and select multivendor software including the Linux operating system and Linux clusters
- A supplement to your internal staff with IBM's skilled services specialists
- Fast, accurate problem resolution to help keep your IT staff productive
- Options for enhanced coverage and a single interface for remote support
- Support for your international environment

For more information on the IBM Support Line, visit the following Web site:

```
http://www.ibm.com/services/us/index.wss/so/its/a1000030
```

In Figure 39-21 you can see an example for the Support Product List (SPL) of the IBM Support Line with the DS6800 support and the DS8100 support highlighted. You can get the complete SPL on the following Web site:

```
http://www.ibm.com/services/sl/products/java3.html
```

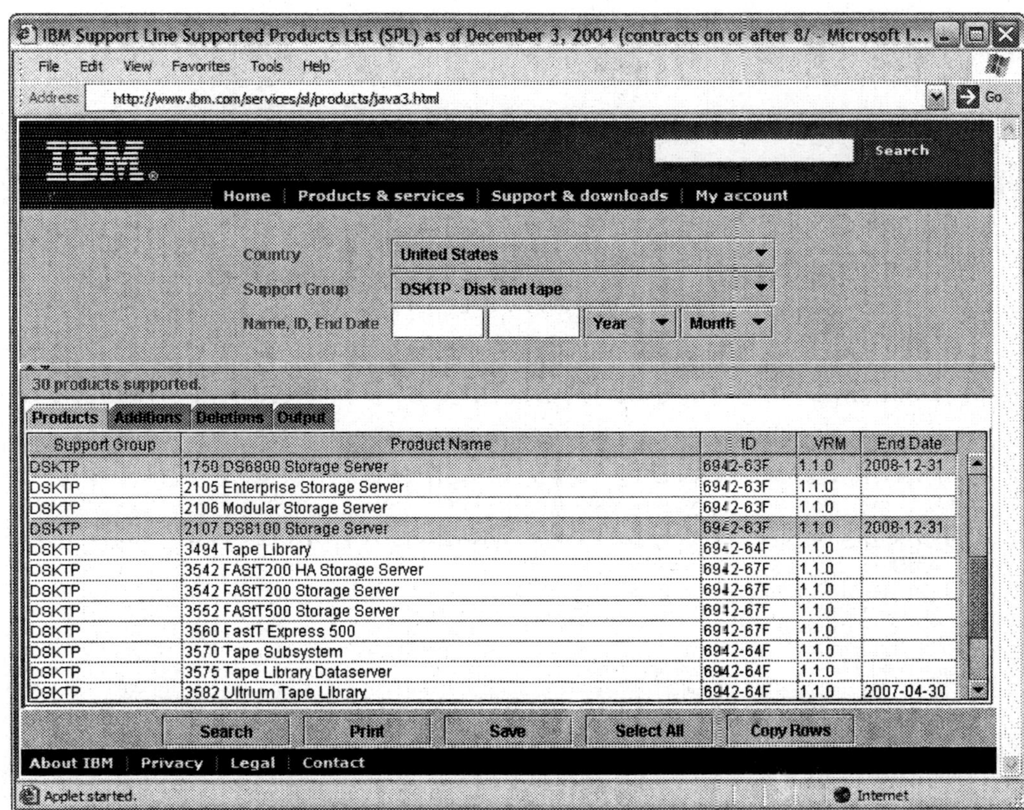

Figure 39-21 Example of the Supported Product List (SPL) from the IBM Support Line

Related publications

The publications listed in this section are considered particularly suitable for a more detailed discussion of the topics covered in this redbook.

IBM Redbooks

For information on ordering these publications, see "How to get IBM Redbooks" on page 667. Note that some of the documents referenced here may be available in softcopy only.

- *IBM TotalStorage DS8000 Series: Implementation,* SG24-6786
- *IBM TotalStorage DS8000 Series: Concepts and Architecture,* SG24-6452
- *IBM TotalStorage Solutions for Disaster Recovery,* SG24-6547
- *The IBM TotalStorage Solutions Handbook,* SG24-5250
- *IBM TotalStorage DS8000 Series: Copy Services in Open Environments,* SG24-6788

If you are implementing Copy Services in a mixed technology environment you may be interested in referring to the following manuals on the ESS and DS6000.

- *IBM TotalStorage Enterprise Storage Server: Implementing ESS Copy Services in Open Environments,* SG24-5757
- *IBM TotalStorage Enterprise Storage Server: Implementing ESS Copy Services with IBM eServer zSeries*, SG24-5680
- *IBM TotalStorage DS6000 Series: Copy Services with IBM eServer zSeries,* SG24-6782
- *BM TotalStorage DS6000 Series: Copy Services in Open Environments,* SG24-6783
- *DFSMShsm ABARS and Mainstar Solutions,* SG24-5089
- *Practical Guide for SAN with pSeries,* SG24-6050
- *Fault Tolerant Storage - Multipathing and Clustering Solutions for Open Systems for the IBM ESS*, SG24-6295
- *Implementing Linux with IBM Disk Storage*, SG24-6261
- *Linux with zSeries and ESS: Essentials*, SG24-7025

Other publications

These publications are also relevant as further information sources. Note that some of the documents referenced here may be available in softcopy only.

- *IBM TotalStorage DS8000 Command-Line Interface User's Guide,* SC26-7625
- *IBM TotalStorage DS8000: Host Systems Attachment Guide,* SC26-7628
- *IBM TotalStorage DS8000: Introduction and Planning Guide,* GC35-0495
- *IBM TotalStorage Multipath Subsystem Device Driver User's Guide*, SC30-4096
- *IBM TotalStorage DS8000: User's Guide*, SC26-7623
- *IBM TotalStorage DS Open Application Programming Interface Reference*, GC35-0493
- *IBM TotalStorage DS8000 Messages Reference*, GC26-7659

- *z/OS DFSMS Advanced Copy Services*, SC35-0248
- *Device Support Facilities: User's Guide and Reference*, GC35-0033

Online resources

These Web sites and URLs are also relevant as further information sources:

- IBM Disk Storage Feature Activation (DSFA) Web site at

  `http://www.ibm.com/storage/dsfa`
- The PSP information can be found at:

  `http://www-1.ibm.com/servers/resourcelink/svc03100.nsf?OpenDatabase`
- Documentation for the DS8000:

  `http://www.ibm.com/servers/storage/support/disk/2107.html`
- The interoperability matrix:

  `http://www.ibm.com/servers/storage/disk/ds8000/interop.html`
- Fibre Channel host bus adapter firmware and driver level matrix:

  `http://knowledge.storage.ibm.com/servers/storage/support/hbasearch/interop/hbaSearch.do`
- ATTO:

  `http://www.attotech.com/`
- Emulex:

  `http://www.emulex.com/ts/dds.html`
- JNI:

  `http://www.jni.com/OEM/oem.cfm?ID=4`
- QLogic:

  `http://www.qlogic.com/support/ibm_page.html`
- IBM:

  `http://www.ibm.com/storage/ibmsan/products/sanfabric.html`
- McDATA:

  `http://www.mcdata.com/ibm/`
- Cisco:

  `http://www.cisco.com/go/ibm/storage`
- CIENA:

  `http://www.ciena.com/products/transport/shorthaul/cn2000/index.asp`
- CNT:

  `http://www.cnt.com/ibm/`
- Nortel:

  `http://www.nortelnetworks.com/`
- ADVA:

  `http://www.advaoptical.com/`

How to get IBM Redbooks

You can search for, view, or download Redbooks, Redpapers, Hints and Tips, draft publications and Additional materials, as well as order hardcopy Redbooks or CD-ROMs, at this Web site:

ibm.com/redbooks

Help from IBM

IBM Support and downloads

ibm.com/support

IBM Global Services

ibm.com/services

Index

Numerics

A

B

C

D

E

F

G

H

I

T

U

V

W